THE HISTORY OF MODERN CULTURE

MAURICE PARMELEE, Ph.D.

THE
HISTORY
OF
MODERN
CULTURE

PHILOSOPHICAL LIBRARY
New York

Copyright, 1960, by
Philosophical Library, Inc.
15 East 40th Street, New York, N. Y.

All rights reserved

Library of Congress Catalog Card Number: 60-13655

CONTENTS

Part I

Origins and Early Evolution

Part II

Emergence of Modern Culture

Part III

Geographical and Functional Factors

PREFACE

The present treatise was conceived in 1907, inspired by Herbert Spencer's *Autobiography*, which outlined his *Synthetic Philosophy*. In 1909 I began an Introduction describing its organic background. This grew into a book of 443 pages published in 1913, entitled *The Science of Human Behavior, Biological and Psychological Foundations*. This was the first book on Behaviorism in the English language. In the Preface I said: "This book is the first of a series in which I propose to deal with the evolution of culture and of human nature."

During the more than half a century since its inception, I have written many books which contributed to it. The substance of some of these books is incorporated in the present treatise. Among them are my *Oriental and Occidental Culture, An Interpretation*, based on my travels in the Far East; *Personality and Conduct; Criminology; Farewell to Poverty; Bolshevism, Fascism, and the Liberal-Democratic State*, founded on long residence in Europe; *Geo-Economic Regionalism and World Federation*; etc.

This treatise traces the main course of cultural evolution, so far as is feasible, thus eliminating the non-essential. Culture includes everything made or changed by mankind, such as tools, houses, cultivated soil, boats, domesticated animals, and also mental products, such as language, institutions, social organizations, religion, art, and science. Cultural evolution therefore comprises both human and cultural phenomena.

The point of view and method are strictly scientific, uninfluenced by ethical, magical, political, economic, racial, national, patriotic, or esthetic considerations, in so far as I am able to avoid these biases. Human and cultural phenomena are studied and analyzed like other natural phenomena, in order to determine where and when the decisive steps have taken place and how they have been disseminated. Among them are tool-making, agriculture, mining, and metallurgy, which have set human and cultural activities in new directions. The history of modern culture requires a description of its origins and early evolution, its emergence in modern times, and a portrayal of its geographical and functional factors.

Among the important topics often ignored in similar treatises, are the predatory exploitation of the masses by the upper classes, which has permeated history to the present; the powerful influence of sex and its play function in human and social behavior; and the features of a genuine social economy as distinguished from the illusive world postulated by the so-called "science" of economics.

Technological change and geo-economic factors are more adequately treated than by most philosophers of history and cultural historians. Religion and magic are depicted in their animistic and anthropocentric attributes, instead of ignoring these fallacious traits. Science as the substitute for magic and religion, its far-reaching effect on human ideas and beliefs, and its role in transforming technology, are emphasized. Science and technology emerge in their practical application in the industrial and the fine arts.

The relations between the Oriental and the Occidental cultural zones are defined. The contrast between them, and their gradual amalgamation are suggested. A cautious glance is taken at future forces for change, within the limits of scientific prevision, but with no messianic or utopian prophecies.

The contrast between Nationalism, with its proclivity to war, and a World Federation of geo-economic regions which would enable mankind to survive in the atomic age, is emphasized. The conflict between Capitalism and Collectivism is depicted. Among the functional factors which are described are Invention and Diffusion, Radicalism and Conservatism, Institutional Selection and Survival, Revolution and Permanence. Of special importance for the United States is the rise of American imperialism in the Twentieth Century. All these phenomena have been observed during extensive travels around the world.

My treatise terminates with a brief discussion of Theories of Cultural Evolution, and of Fallacies Concerning Culture. The most important theories are the Unilinear, the Diffusionist, the Cyclical, and the Configurationist or Pattern. The major fallacies are *fideism,* or faith, in the place of knowledge, often resulting in mysticism; *accident,* or chance, instead of causation; *particularism,* or emphasis on an exceptional factor; the *group fallacy,* that the whole is greater and superior to the sum of its parts; the *teleological* interpretation, that function precedes structure; and the *super-organic fallacy,* that assumes a fundamental duality in the universe. These fallacies involve animistic and anthropomorphic beliefs which pervade human thinking.

MAURICE PARMELEE

September, 1960.

PART I

ORIGINS AND EARLY EVOLUTION

Part I

ORIGINS AND EARLY EVOLUTION

Chapter I

The Universe and Mankind

THE sky on a clear, moonless night is one of the most beautiful as well as impressive spectacles in human experience. A little knowledge of physics and of astronomy enhances greatly the significance of what is seen therein. It enables the human mind to realize at least dimly the vastness if not the infinitude of space and the eternity of time.

The velocity of light is 299,796±1 kilometers or about 186,284 miles per second of time. The distance light travels in one year is about 5,878,713,000,000 or nearly six trillions of miles. This is 63,257 times the mean distance of the earth from the sun. The nearest star, Alpha Centauri, is 4.3 light-years away. Compared with the 92,870,000 miles which separate the earth from the sun, this distance seems enormous because it is 272,000 times as far away as the sun. It is insignificant compared with many sidereal distances which have been measured. The closest to the sun is a very small star, Proxima Centauri, which is 4.27 light-years away.

The Milky Way is the galaxy of stars to which the sun belongs. It is estimated to be at least 100,000 light-years in diameter and 10,000 light-years in thickness. Outside of our stellar system are innumerable spiral nebulae the nearest of which is estimated to be about 85,000 light-years away.[1] How much greater distances exist in the universe depends upon whether space is finite or infinite, or relative in extent, according to Einstein's special theory of relativity.

Many other measurements are of a corresponding degree of vastness. The sun is estimated to be at least 2,000,000,000 years of age.[2] The planets including the earth receive only about one out of every twenty million parts of the energy radiated from the sun. And yet the sun has been radiating at least as much energy as at present for many

---

[1] George Gamow, *The Birth and Death of the Sun, Stellar Evolution and Sub-atomic Energy*, with a Foreword by Albert Einstein, New York, 1945; *One, Two, Three . . . Infinity, Facts and Speculations of Science*, New York, 1953.

[2] J. H. Jeans, *The Stars in Their Courses*, New York, 1931.

millions of years without any perceptible loss of energy. While the surface temperature of the sun is 6000° Absolute Centigrade, the surface temperature of the relatively hot star Rigel is 16,000°. The internal temperatures of the stars attain many millions of degrees.

The mean diameter of the earth is 7918 and of the sun 864,000 miles. The diameter of the giant star Betelgeuse is about 270,000,000 miles or over 300 times the diameter of the sun, though its mass may be no more than five times the solar mass. The sun is traveling through space at the rate of about twelve miles a second. The velocities of many of the stars are much greater. The tail of a certain comet swinging around the sun with the head as its axis is estimated to have traveled at the rate of 100,000 miles a second or more than half as fast as light.

In like fashion, the exceedingly small objects furnish as amazing figures as the enormously great. All the physical elements are composed of atoms which are so minute that they cannot be seen even through the most powerful microscope. The atom is composed of a nucleus or proton and a varying number of electrons. An electron is estimated to weigh 1/1840 of the lightest atom. It would take about 50,000,000,000 electrons in a line to stretch across the period at the close of this sentence. A proton is even smaller in volume though about 1800 times heavier than an electron. These sub-atomic entities are so infinitesimally small that their distances from each other are relatively great within the area of an atom. And yet these minute atoms contain energies which when released can be horribly destructive as well as eminently useful to mankind.

Beyond the distances and masses which we can measure are the immeasurably great and small which our instruments cannot compass. With instruments which are more powerful or more delicate, we may be able to see much farther and measure with much greater refinement. The 200-inch reflector installed on Mount Palomar in California doubled the distance at which the astronomers can observe stars. But even if the universe is finite, we can never discern its external limits nor probe into its innermost complexity.

These facts are impressive and significant enough in themselves. But do they have much significance for mankind? Helium was discovered in the sun by means of the spectroscope, recognized later in other stars, and then found on the earth where it is now used for various purposes. No elements have been detected in the stars which have not been found on the earth. While most of the subject matter of astronomy may seem too remote to have any mundane significance, astrophysics has made many important contributions to physics. The nature of organic matter can be understood only through physical and chemical analysis. On the other hand, no other planetary systems have been discovered. Even if any exist, the possibility that organic evolu-

4

tion has taken place outside of the solar system is too remote to be seriously considered.[3]

Apart from their contributions to science which have a mundane applicability, the physical sciences dealing with the universe have great significance in their influence upon human thinking. The immeasurably small as well as the incalculably great indicate the limitations upon human ability to observe and study the universe. The immeasurably great in particular has rendered untenable the anthropocentric tendency to regard man as of any importance in the universe. The expansion of scientific knowledge has destroyed the myths of the supernatural which have influenced mankind greatly down to the present day.

It is not with regard to measurement alone that the physical sciences encounter ultimate problems. What is the ultimate nature of the electron, of electricity, of light, and of any other radiations which may exist in the universe? What is gravitation? Is space finite or infinite? That it is finite seems incredible, because the question at once arises as to what is beyond space. On the other hand, infinity is beyond human comprehension. The same dilemma exists with regard to time. A limited time seems incredible, because the question immediately arises as to what happened before time began and what will happen after it terminates. Timelessness as much as spacelessness implies a void of nothingness which is inconceivable to a mind accustomed to a space populated with things and a time which is a flow of events. And yet an eternity of time is as far beyond human comprehension as an infinity of space. The mind staggers and is impaled upon the horns of this dilemma which seems insoluble in logic as well as by any means of measurement. Whether or not a theory of relativity will solve this dilemma remains to be seen.

Baffled by the apparent insolubility of these ultimate problems, many have sought consolation in a solipsistic philosophy. Knowledge of the universe can reach us only through our senses. Hence this knowledge may be wholly illusory. There is no guarantee that the senses represent to us the universe as it really is. It may even be that there is no universe outside of ourselves. Its representation may be no more than a fantasmagoria of our imaginations. Or it may be one phase of

---

[3] The Astronomer Royal of England reached the following cautious conclusion: "The conditions needed for birth to be given to a planetary system may be so exceptional that amongst the vast number of stars in any one stellar universe we may expect to find only a very limited number that have a family of planets; and amongst these families of planets there cannot be more than a small proportion where the conditions are suitable for life to exist. Life elsewhere in the universe is therefore the exception and not the rule." H. Spencer Jones, *Life on Other Worlds*, New York, 1949, p. 155.

5

the life or consciousness of this self which comprehends the universe. Such a belief professes to solve these ultimate problems, or at any rate render them of negligible importance. Furthermore, it is very gratifying to the ego. What could be more egocentric than solipsism? In its less extreme forms it postulates a universal consciousness or soul into which are merged individual souls. In this mystical conception of the universe time, space, matter and energy cease to have meaning and perturb its devotees no longer. These mystics envelop themselves in their self-aggrandizement and in their alleged omniscience which is a negation of knowledge.

A solipsistic conception of the universe cannot suffice for science in its unending analysis of things as they are. It must assume an objective reality even though our knowledge of it is subjective. That the impressions of many different individuals, as well as the impressions of the same individual at different times, in the main coincide is *a priori* evidence of its existence. Hence we are justified in postulating a universe outside of ourselves and of devoting effort to its study.[4] Whether it is finite or infinite in extent, eternal or limited in duration, and what is the nature of its ultimate components, we can never ascertain with our inadequate means of perception. While resigning ourselves to the insolubility of these ultimate problems, we can devote ourselves with still greater zeal to the study of mankind. This is the field of science which is of the greatest interest as well as of utmost utility.

Science arose in a measure out of magical and religious beliefs, but in large part out of the development of technology. Man's first attempts to acquire knowledge may have been due to his desire to apply it. At what point an interest in the nature of the universe and a desire for knowledge for its own sake began to exercise an influence, it is impossible to ascertain. It is highly probable that it was preceded by the pragmatic interest in knowledge.

The utilitarian origin of science has given to it an anthropocentric tendency which is not easily overcome. In its earliest attempts to picture the universe it placed man at the center. Increasing knowledge showed the absurdity of this notion. The physical sciences have largely freed themselves from this tendency. The physicist dealing with an hypothetical curvature of space, the astronomer measuring the distances of celestial bodies many light-years away, and the

---

4 As I have said elsewhere: "All our knowledge comes to us through our senses in the form of sensations, and we cannot be absolutely certain that these sensations represent to us truly the nature of the world which is exterior to us. For scientific purposes, however, we need to practice what is sometimes called 'naive realism' and assume that things in the exterior world are actually as our senses represent them to be." (Maurice Parmelee, *The Science of Human Behavior*, New York 1913, p. 4.)

mathematician unraveling the intricacies of the nth dimension need not concern themselves with man.

It is much more difficult to avoid anthropocentrism in the biological, psychological and social sciences, because these sciences deal with man himself. The social scientist is subjected not only to the inward urge to solve problems which interest him vitally, but also to external pressure from numerous persons who demand a speedy solution of problems of human importance. Many sociologists succumb to this pressure, and some of them consider hopeless the attempt to develop social science like the physical and biological sciences. For this reason meliorist and propagandist tendencies have been prevalent and influential among social scientists.

Hence it is that the scientist is placed in somewhat of a dilemma. As a man, he is deeply concerned with the effects of science upon himself and his congeners. But he must recognize that the universe was not created for man. As a scientist, he should not be influenced by the human significance of his work, whatever he may think, say and do in other capacities. Temporarily he must ignore the practical applications of his researches, whatever their utilitarian value may be. Scientific research should be carried on regardless and in part independent of its effects upon mankind. Pure science is a necessary phase of scientific development.

A good deal of science has arisen out of the pragmatic impulse, and has eventually been applied. Between the initial impulse and the ultimate application there should be a period of unbiased and objective study and research during which what may be termed pure science can prevail. Otherwise the end sought is likely to influence the conclusions reached, which will in turn vitiate their application. Scientists should always guard themselves against being influenced unduly by whatever social system they happen to live and work under and the ethics and mores which pervade it.

Science is the same everywhere and for all human beings in so far as it it genuine, namely, an accurate description of observable phenomena. The ideology of individual scientists varies according to their inherent traits and social environment. These factors may enhance or diminish the value of their scientific work, as the case may be. Science as an organon of verified data, interpreted and explained so far as is feasible, goes on from generation to generation independent of, or, at any rate, superior to, the vagaries of the individual scientists who contribute to it.

In the physical sciences it is comparatively easy to maintain an objective and impersonal attitude. Physics, astronomy and mathematics have no obvious and little direct bearing upon the fortunes of mankind. It is much more difficult to retain an impersonal attitude in the social sciences. The anthropocentric and egocentric point of view is likely to intrude and to bias the attitude of the social scientist. The ideology of the dominant system is almost certain to color his thinking in some degree.

The demarcations between the sciences are arbitrary and only for purposes of convenience. So far as we can discern, natural phenomena form one infinite and eternal continuum. Both from an inductive and from a theoretical as well as from a practical point of view, the study and solution of problems and not the development of any one science as such are of importance. In the study of any problem it may be necessary to traverse the field of several sciences.

The present treatise is an attempt to trace the main course of cultural evolution. By culture I mean all that has been created by mankind. This includes not only tools, buildings, clothing and other material goods, but also language, forms of social organization, religion, science, art, ethical ideas, political and economic institutions, and the whole structure and framework of society. While all phenomena are in the broad sense natural, cultural phenomena are artificial in that they are the artifacts of man. Land, animals and plants are natural phenomena. Domesticated animals, plowed and fertilized land, and cultivated plants are artificial to the extent that they have been modified by mankind. A distinction between the natural and and the artificial can be made only in relation to man and from a human point of view.

In this work cultural evolution will be studied and analyzed like any other natural phenomena in order to determine, in so far as the limited data render it possible, where and when the decisive steps have taken place and how they have been disseminated. No attempt will be made to describe cultural manifestations at all places and times, even when and where the data are available. In accordance with my aim to delineate the main course of cultural evolution, all that is non-essential for this purpose will be eliminated.

Culture is a peculiarly and almost exclusively human phenomenon because only rudimentary traces of it are found among a few of the higher animals. It has, however, evolved in the course of mental and social evolution. It is both a mental and a social phenomenon. As mankind shares many of its mental and social traits with the animals, some knowledge of animal psychology and sociology is essential to an understanding of the background of cultural evolution. Hence the next few chapters will be devoted to the non-human antecedents and correlatives of the mental and social traits which have rendered culture possible. The material basis will be described only in so far as is necessary to explain and illustrate these mental and social traits.

Throughout this treatise it is assumed that there is nothing super-

8

natural or miraculous, nothing mystical or divine, in the universe. Much has seemed to be mysterious and wonderful owing to human ignorance. Science tries to explain the phenomena of the universe, but assumes a cautious and watchful reticence toward what is not yet explained, instead of the blundering and erroneous interpretations of magic and religion.

Chapter II

The Threshold of Social Evolution

THE living cell is the primordial and basic unit in the organic world. Among the protozoa a single cell constitutes an organism. Metazoan animals consist of aggregations of cells. Certain of the protozoan species and some of the lower metazoa form so-called colonies in which the individual members are organically connected with each other. These connections aid nutrition. In some of the colonial species, as, for example, the infusoria which form colonies, there is no vascular connection, that is to say, ducts through which nutritive fluid passes from one organism to another. In other colonial species, such as certain of the polyps, mollusks and worms, there is vascular connection which increases considerably the degree of interdependence in the nutritive processes.

Physiological division of labor develops in some of these colonial species. In several of them the relations between the individual members become so close as to make each colony almost a distinct organism. These colonies are called associations, and even societies, by some writers. They cannot be regarded as such, even though a high degree of interdependence may exist between them, because there is no mental interaction. Nevertheless, the study of these aggregations has significance for social evolution, for this inborn tendency to unite may persist throughout the remainder of organic evolution and furnish the basis or occasion for the mental interaction which develops later.

Several factors give rise to aggregations of the simplest organisms apart from any innate disposition to associate together. These factors arise out of the characteristic nature of living matter. Its constituent elements are found in the air and in the sea. Air contains nitrogen, oxygen and carbonic acid. Sea water contains hydrogen, sodium, magnesium, potassium, calcium, etc., which are some of the necessary constituents of living matter.[1] Out of these constituents was

---

[1] *Cf.* H. Spencer Jones, *Life on Other Worlds*, New, York, 1949.

formed protoplasm which is an emulsion of colloids and crystalloids in an aqueous medium. A colloid has gluelike consistency, lacks crystalline structure and cannot go into ordinary solution in certain solvents. Out of protoplasm evolved the organic cell which is colloidal rather than crystalline in structure.

At first sight it appears as if life must have originated in the sea. Here in solution are found the essential constituents of living matter. Here also the lowest organisms come into immediate contact with their food. However, the organic elements may be too diluted and too widely diffused in water to permit of the origin of life. If that be so, protoplasm must have formed in the muddy bottom of shores of the sea, where land and sea meet. When the necessary elements were deposited in a sufficiently concentrated form and near enough to each other to permit of interaction, the conditions were favorable for the formation of protoplasm and then of the organic cell.[2]

In such an environment in water or in a porous or muddy soil, not one but many organisms come into being. Thus there was an aggregation soon after the commencement of life which continued within the favorable environment because the individuals that drifted away into an unfavorable environment perished. Density of population also is in some cases essential for survival. This is because the organisms themselves excrete substances which render the environment habitable and thus condition their own surroundings. Studies of certain kinds of organisms have determined the optimal degree of crowding for them.[3] Densities above and below the optimum are not so favorable for survival.

These factors for the concentration of organisms in a limited area imply no reactions on the part of the organisms. But protoplasm and the organisms composed of it possess characteristics which result in the formation of aggregations. These traits are metabolism, growth, reproduction, rhythmicity, irritability and conductivity, and adaptability. Metabolism is basically a phenomenon of chemical affinity. The chemical constituents of the organisms have an affinity for the chemical constituents of the food which leads to its absorption. In the more complex organisms metabolism becomes something more

[2] "The ocean, once supposed to be the scene of life's start on this globe, no longer appears to be the most likely place for the beginning of life, for the essential constituents which must be brought together were there diluted and widely diffused and, furthermore, were in a more stable condition. But in the porous soils along the shores and on land, the requisite materials in unstable state were brought into closest interaction, attended by the most favorable conditions for organization into living matter." (R. T. Chamberlin, in *The Nature of the World and of Man*, edited by H. H. Newman, Chicago, 1927, p. 53.)

[3] *Cf.* W. C. Allee, *Animal Aggregations, A study in general sociology*, Chicago, 1931.

than a phenomenon of chemical affinity because special organs within the organism are devoted to the assimilative process. Other organs, such as those of vision, hearing and smell, locate the food at a distance and locomotor organs bring the organism to it. The simpler organisms are able to absorb through chemical affinity only the food with which they come into bodily contact so that they congregate in close proximity to the food supply.

Metabolism leads to growth of the unicellular organism. But the assimilative capacity of the living cell is limited. When it attains a certain size its surface cannot adequately supply it with food because its bulk increases more rapidly than its surface. Furthermore, it becomes too bulky for the strength of the cell walls and breaks into two parts. Thus commences reproduction through fission, because these parts grow and become full-sized cells which are more or less exact copies of the parent cell. Two other modes of reproduction which characterize certain unicellular and some of the lower multicellular species and which are comparatively rare in occurrence are reproduction by budding and by sporulation. In budding new cells grow out of the parent organism and form temporarily a multicellular organism which later breaks up into independent unicellular organisms. In sporulation the parent cell breaks up into several parts each of which becomes a new cell. Whatever the method of reproduction, it leads to a greater aggregation within a given area.

All the activities of living organisms are due to the sensitiveness or irritability of protoplasm. This trait arises out of the unstable and mobile nature of organic matter. The organic compounds are often called carbon compounds because all of them contain carbon. The three types of carbon compounds especially characteristic of protoplasm are carbohydrates, fats and proteids. The fats are derived from the carbohydrates. Protein, derived from the proteids, has a high degree of molecular complexity. Carbon is allotropic; it assumes several forms such as diamond, graphite and amorphous carbon owing apparently to different arrangements of the atoms within the molecules of the elements. Many organic compounds are isomeric, that is to say, they assume different forms apparently as a result of varying arrangements of the molecules of the elements within the molecules of the compounds. These two peculiarities and the fact that it is composed of unlike elements render organic matter less stable and more liable to change than most forms of inorganic matter, and also make it relatively mobile. Instability and mobility render possible the capacity to differentiate and integrate which make adaptation and organic evolution possible.

Owing to its irritability, organic matter is more sensitive to the external forces which act upon it than inorganic matter. The direct reactions of organisms to these forces are tropisms. Heliotropism or phototropism is the direct reaction to light, chemotropism to chemical substances, geotropism to the force of gravity and electrotropism or galvanotropism to electricity. These forces acting upon the sensitive matter of the organism tend to orient it with respect to the source of stimulation. If an organism is symmetrical so that corresponding points on the two sides of the body are equally sensitive to light, the muscles or locomotor organs on the light side will be stimulated to greater activity, so that the organism will be pulled around into a position parallel with the rays of light.

In similar fashion organisms are oriented by reactions to chemical substances. By chemical substance is meant a chemical compound diffused in the surrounding medium, namely, the water or the air. Chemotropic reactions often have great functional value, especially for coming into contact with food and in the higher organisms for mating. In fact, this so-called chemical sense is the rudimentary form out of which have differentiated the senses of smell and of taste just as the sense of vision developed out of photopathic sensitiveness to light.

Any one of these tropisms may bring organisms together by attracting them toward the source of light or of a chemical substance or whatever the attractive force may be. If the reaction is negative, it may serve to disperse organisms. In either case it is not a social or anti-social trait inherent in the organisms themselves which is giving rise to an aggregation or is causing its dispersal. In the more complex organisms are numerous specialized organs which determine in considerable part their behavior, so that often they do not respond directly to external forces. Tropisms persist, however, in the behavior of many of the cells in multicellular organisms. The reactions of the cells in the blood are often chemotropic. Certain animals and plants display tropisms of the whole or a large part of the organism. The earthworm is negatively phototropic which causes it to burrow in the ground during the day and to come out at night to feed and to have sexual intercourse. Certain winged ants become positively phototropic at sexual maturity which causes them to take the nuptial flight during which they pair in the air. Many plants are heliotropic and turn their flowers toward the sun. Gravity influences the growth of sessile organisms so that in plants the roots grow downward because they are positively geotropic while the stems grow upward because they are negatively geotropic.

Some writers have been so impressed by the fact that aggregations of organisms often take place that they assume that an innate ten-

13

dency toward association, mutualism, cooperation and social relations exists even in the lowest organisms.[4] The preceding description indicates that these aggregations of the lower organisms can be explained as reactions to external forces. No such innate tendency need be postulated. To attribute cooperation and gregariousness to the lowest animals and to plants is to interpret their behavior in a very anthropomorphic manner.

Even among the higher animals aggregations are not necessarily due to an associative tendency. External forces often bring them together. Marine animals will gravitate toward the area where the temperature is most favorable for their life processes. If this area happens to be small, a large number of the same species may be found in close proximity to each other and yet have come together independently and through no mutual interaction. The pressure of the water may also influence this orientation. Large shoals of fish are to be found in certain strata of water which is to be explained in part by the temperature and the pressure. The location of food determines the orientation of the members of all species to a large extent. If the food of a species is distributed over a small area, its members come together in the course of their food quest.

Many though by no means all animals live intermittently or permanently in association with other animals usually of their own species, and their behavior is more or less affected by such association. Association may mean simply that animals are in close proximity to each other, in other words, that they form an aggregation. This would not necessarily involve their affecting each other's behavior. By association, therefore, is usually meant the sort of proximity which results in affecting behavior. The meaning of the term is often limited still further so as to apply only to proximity which affects behavior through mental interaction. By a society is usually meant a group characterized by more or less permanent association.

Social phenomena form a minute and transient portion of universal phenomena and social evolution is a part of the organic evolutionary process in general on this planet. It is, however, not justifiable to postulate an associative tendency in order to explain these phenomena. The same is true of the so-called gregarious instinct which

---

[4] The following are illustrations from two such writers:

"The phenomena of mutualism and cooperation are, indeed, so prevalent among plants and animals and affect their structure and behavior so profoundly that there has arisen within very recent years a new school of biologists, who might be called 'symbiotists'." (W. M. Wheeler, *Social Life Among the Insects*, New York, 1923, p. 4.)

"Many of the so-called 'altruistic' drives in man apparently are the development of these innate tendencies toward co-operation, which find their early physiological expression in many simpler animals." (W. C. Allee, *op. cit.*, p. 361.)

14

is often cited in attempting to explain the later stages of social evolution. Without assuming that an associative tendency has been at work throughout organic evolution I shall briefly survey the probable causes of social evolution.

The phenomena of association have displayed themselves at many points in organic evolution and among many species. Is it possible to arrange these phenomena in their evolutionary order so that each group will have evolved directly from the group which precedes it? This can be so for social phenomena no more than it is for other organic phenomena. There have been many divergent lines of social evolution as well as of organic evolution. Along some of these lines social evolution has proceeded independent of other lines. In so far as social evolution has been due to hereditary causes, the divergence must always have been as great as the divergence in the organic series. So far as social evolution has been due to forces other than hereditary, the degree of divergence has depended upon conditions which will be discussed later. This does not mean necessarily that each divergent line if traced back far enough does not reach a common source with every other line. It is also possible to grade social phenomena in series according to their degree of complexity or according to any other standard, even though evolution has not actually taken place according to that series.

If, therefore, we are to assume that human social phenomena are of the highest type, it does not follow that all lower types have been in the same evolutionary series. In order to determine the series for man, it is necessary to determine to what organic series he belongs, and the series for social phenomena will correspond in large part to the organic series.

Human society is not entirely in the same evolutionary series with any other animal society now in existence because the humanoid stock diverged some time ago from the line of descent of the other primates of today. Nevertheless the study of these other societies throws light upon the evolution of human society. This is true, in the first place, because these species, including the human species, have inherited in common certain structural forms and other traits which have determined in part and have conditioned the social phenomena displayed by all of these species. Second, all of these species have been subjected to a certain extent to the same conditions, so that their social traits are in part due to similar environmental conditions. Similar structural forms and functions, such as those of nutrition and reproduction, on the one hand, and similar environmental conditions, such as topography, climate and the distribution of food, on the other hand, have produced along divergent lines of organic evolution social phenomena which are to a certain extent similar. The same is true of mental phenomena. To study either the mental or the social phenomena of any species is to throw light upon the corresponding phenomena of other species. Social evolution, like mental evolution, has had many beginnings along widely divergent lines of organic evolution, and yet there have been many analogies and likenesses between these different lines of social evolution.

I have already spoken of the way in which the food quest brings together members of the same species when their food is distributed over a small area. As organic evolution progresses, reproduction plays a more and more important part as a cause of association. At the beginning of organic evolution organisms were independent in their power to reproduce. That is to say, reproduction could take place simply by fission. But comparatively early in time conjugation became necessary between individuals. In other words, it became necessary for independent lines of descent to cross occasionally or else they would lose reproductive power. Conjugation in these low species probably takes place usually as the result of chemotropic attraction. Here was a force bringing members of the same species into contact with each other. Then gradually among the lower metazoan species began to arise the anatomical and physiological differentiation between the two sexes. When the physiological division of labor in reproduction based upon this differentiation became established, cooperation between the two sexes became almost invariably necessary for the perpetuation of the species. In the higher species there developed a combination of reflexes called the sexual instinct which has ever since been a cause for association along many divergent lines of evolution. This instinct is a common heritage of all species that have become characterized by social traits.

As organic evolution continued, more than the sexual instinct became necessary for reproduction to be effected successfully. As animal forms developed and became more complex, more time was needed for the development of the individual animal from the beginning of its life to its full development. During part of the time necessary for attaining maturity the animal was helpless and in need of care. Thus there evolved the parental instincts leading one or both parents to care for the young during this period of helplessness. Where the care is given by one parent, usually it is the female, though sometimes it is the male as in the case of certain fishes and birds. From parental care there results association between parents and their offspring which, when it becomes more or less permanent and stable, constitutes the family. In these instincts is another common heritage of many of the species that have embarked on a course of social evolution.

As the nervous system, and especially the central nervous system,

16

evolved, the anatomical basis for the development of intelligence was furnished. The differentiation of the nerve cells from the other somatic cells began very early among metazoan species, but the development of the nervous system has taken place along many divergent lines of evolution. Whenever the nervous system has developed in such a fashion as to make association feasible, intelligence has become possible and has appeared along many lines. Wherever it has made its appearance and has developed to any degree, it has become a powerful force for association in various ways. It has made members of a species susceptible to suggestion from their congeners and has led them to imitate. It has enabled members of the same species to communicate with each other and has led to the conservation of ideas by transmitting from one generation to another in the form of tradition. In the anatomical basis of intelligence is still another common heritage of most or all of the species that have started on a line of social evolution.

I have now indicated the conditions and factors which give rise to association. They are *environmental conditions,* such as the distribution of food, topography, temperature and climate; *inborn traits,* such as the sexual and parental instincts; and the *acquired characteristics* comprised under the name of intelligence, which is made possible by an inherited anatomical structure. There are numerous data with respect to the beginnings and early stages of social evolution along various divergent lines of evolution, though they are still very limited in comparison with the number and complexity of the problems involved. Some of these facts are paleontological and furnish evidence, in the form of fossils distributed in small areas, of association on the part of extinct species. Most of them are concerning living species representing many lines of descent.

Chapter III

The Emergence of Mankind

MAN'S ancestry is to be sought along with that of his nearest relatives —the great apes. The earliest anthropoid ape whose remains have been found was *Propliopithecus* in the Lower Oligocene of the Fayum in Northwest Egypt. In the same region and of the same geological period was found *Parapithecus,* the earliest known monkey of the *Cercopithecidae* family. The Old-World monkeys and the apes were apparently being differentiated from a tarsioid ancestry at about the same time.

Propliopithecus resembled the gibbon but was somewhat smaller. *Pliopithecus,* which may have descended from the former, was larger and more like the gibbon. It existed in the Miocene in Africa and Asia and is found in the lower Pliocene of Europe. These two fossil apes probably belong to the line of descent of the smallest of the extant apes.

In the Miocene of India was found *Palaeosimia,* a larger ape which may have been an ancestor of the orang-utan. It is probable that the orang diverged in the lower Miocene from the large anthropoid stock earlier than the gorilla, chimpanzee and man. The orangs inhabiting Borneo and Sumatra are the last remnants of this line of descent.

In the Siwalik Hills of northern India was found *Dryopithecus,* a large ape of the middle and later Miocene. Six or more species of this fossil genus have been found in Africa and Europe as well as in Asia. In 1932 were reported at least two additional species of *Dryopithecus* from a lower Miocene deposit in Uganda.[1] These species varied considerably in size but some of them were as large as a chimpanzee.

---

[1] *Man*, September, 1932, Vol. XXXII, p. 208
In 1934 the Yale North Expedition reported the discovery of three extinct apelike genera—*Ramapithecus, Sugrivapithecus,* and *Brampithecus,* the latter having been related to *Dryopithecus. (New York Times,* April 1, 1934.)

In the upper Miocene of India was found *Sivapithecus indicus* which resembled *Palaeosimia* in some respects and *Dryopithecus* in other respects. The chimpanzee and the gorilla probably are descended from an ancestry similar to the *Dryopithecus* or *Sivapithecus*. Both of the latter possessed some resemblance to man, and man's ancestry was in all likelihood in the *Sivapithecus-Dryopithecus* group.

In the Pliocene or early Pleistocene of South Africa was found *Australopithecus*, a fossil ape as large as a chimpanzee, which according to some anthropologists is more closely related to man than *Dryopithecus*.[2] This was an upright-walking anthropoid about four feet high which apparently inhabited the grasslands of the Vaal River area. Its teeth were similar to those of man. Its brain was from 450 to 650 cubic centimeters in size, or larger than the brain of a chimpanzee or gorilla. In 1949 Professor Raymond Dart, who had discovered this genus in 1924, found in central Transvaal remains of fire and bone tools in the same deposit with *Australopithecus prometheus*. This was apparently a fire using and tool making ape. It probably existed from 500,000 to 1,000,000 years ago and may have been contemporary with primitive men.[3]

The paleontological record is far from complete. Enough has been discovered to show that during the Miocene and Pliocene in the tropical and subtropical regions of the Eastern Hemisphere were evolving the three great apes and mankind of today. Further discoveries may render more clear the relationships between the simians and humanoids and their common ancestors.

As the primates increased in size an arboreal life became less suitable for them. A small animal can run along the smaller branches and larger twigs and leap from its hind legs from branch to branch. A large animal must restrict itself to the larger branches and stay near the trunk of the tree where its weight receives adequate support. Its movements are predominantly vertical as it moves up and down parallel with the trunk of the tree, whereas the small animal moves horizontally in a pronograde position much of the time. The large primates which remained in the trees were reaching upward constantly and swinging with their arms. These movements doubtless prepared the way for the evolution of the semi-erect and eventually the erect attitude. In the animals which are habitually pronograde the viscera of the abdominal region swing more or less loosely as if in a bag. In the upright position such viscera would sag greatly. In the erect primates these viscera are fastened more or less firmly to the backbone.

[2] See, for example, G. Elliot Smith, *Human History*, New York, 1929.
[3] See Loren C. Eiseley, "The Fire Apes," *Harper's Magazine*, September 1949, pages 47-55.

In the trees large primates can with difficulty secure an adequate food supply. On the ground it is more plentiful, or at any rate large animals can procure it more readily. The large primates adopted a terrestrial life at least in part. The baboons reverted almost entirely to a pronograde position. The anthropoid apes assumed a semi-erect posture. The humanoid group attained an erect posture rendered possible by the human foot and abandoned the trees entirely. At what point in time and space this took place we do not know. The human foot displays a complete adaptation to walking. The big toe is non-opposable so that the foot is not prehensile. The toes are shorter than those of the anthropoids. The sole is placed firmly upon the ground. In fact, the foot is the anatomical feature which distinguishes the humanoid group most decisively from the other primates.

The earliest type of fully erect primate known was *Pithecanthropus erectus* discovered at Trinil in Java in 1891 or 1892 in a late Pliocene or early Pleistocene deposit. This primate was of about the same size as man and in its posture and gait was essentially human. Its dentition strongly resembled that of mankind. Its skull was more or less apelike. Its cranial capacity of about 940 cubic centimeters was about midway between that of the great apes and that of man. While it belonged to the family of the *Hominidae* it was of a different genus from man. The endocranial cast indicates that the areas of the brain related to speech were in process of development.

Pithecanthropus could hardly have been a direct ancestor of mankind. There is reason to believe that more nearly human types were already in existence as early as the time at which the specimen found in Java lived. So that it represented one of the lines of descent from a common ancestor which had acquired an erect posture and adopted a terrestrial life. No implements were found with it.

In 1929 and 1930 were found near Peking in China two skulls of a primitive humanoid type of which several teeth and portions of the lower jaw had been found in 1922, 1927 and 1928. This type has been named *Sinanthropus pekinensis* and apparently belonged to a genus hitherto unknown. Its location and the fauna with which it was associated seem to indicate an early Pleistocene age. Carbonized material and crudely chipped stones of a different character from the adjacent rock suggest the use of fire and tools. Its cranial capacity was somewhat larger than that of *Pithecanthropus*. Endocranial casts show a brain capacity of about 1,100 cubic centimeters. Its teeth were primitive but essentially human. In other respects the skull was very primitive. The forehead receded. There were prominent brow ridges. There was little or no chin. *Sinanthropus* was apparently a very early type of man or of humanoid intermediate between *Pithecanthropus* and man.

In 1907 was discovered near Heidelberg in Germany a lower jaw with all the teeth in place. The jaw is very large and heavy and without a chin. But the teeth are human in form though larger than human teeth of today. This feature renders it possible that it belonged to the same genus as man. It has been named *Homo heidelbergensis* and also *Palaeanthropus*. Its resemblance to the Neanderthal type described below renders its human character all the more probable. So that while no other fragments have been found and no cultural remains accompanied it, it is reasonable to suppose that it walked erect and had a fairly large brain, perhaps as much as 1,300 cubic centimeters. It was found eighty-two feet below the surface of an ancient river valley where a sandpit had been dug. The geological formation and the faunal remains indicate that it belonged to the first or second interglacial period, probably the first. In any case it must have been early Pleistocene.

In northern Rhodesia in Africa fourteen degrees south of the equator is a cave in Broken Hill which contains many fossil bones. Mining operations have penetrated deep into this cave 110 feet below the summit of the hill and sixty feet below the ground level. Here in 1921 near the bottom of the cave were found an almost complete human skull, bones of the lower limbs and various other parts of the skeletons of two or more individuals. The geological evidence is very uncertain. These bones may have been deposited only a few thousands of years ago or they may be Pleistocene. No cultural remains were associated with them, but near the mouth of the cave were signs of human occupation. Stone implements were found such as are made by the small yellow-skinned Bushmen. But the Bushmen left this region a long time ago. The modern inhabitants have been the tall, black Bantus.

The Rhodesian type has been named *Homo rhodesiensis* and may have constituted a distinct human species. It presents a remarkable combination of primitive and modern traits. The lower limbs indicate an erect posture but were very large and massive. The height was probably about five feet ten inches (1.8 meters), and the weight about 200 pounds. The skull bones were large and massive. The supra-orbital ridges were larger than in any humanoid type so far discovered, including *Pithecanthropus*, and resembled those of a gorilla. The forehead was very low. The lower jaw is missing. The upper teeth were of the modern human type, but were very large. The cranial capacity was probably about 1,300 cubic centimeters which was small for so large a skull. Most of the convolutions of the frontal lobes were not highly developed. But the inferior frontal convolution, which is the region of speech, was well developed. The parietal, occipital and temporal lobes also were very primitive. The sensory and kinesthetic regions were not well developed. On the whole, Rhodesian man had a brain which was inferior not only in size but in quality. With such a brain it is doubtful if he could have developed handicraft. While the speech area was well developed the auditory area was small so that his language must at best have been very rudimentary. However, the visuo-psychic area in the occipital lobe was well developed.

The heavy brow-ridges, low frontal region, and large face and jaws of Rhodesian man were simian traits which point to a Pliocene origin. On the other hand, his brain though inferior was of a human pattern, his posture entirely erect, his palate and teeth human. Whether he was an early type which survived until a recent time, or a modern type in which persisted certain primitive traits, it is impossible to determine at present.[4]

In 1889 and 1890 were found at Wadjak in Java parts of two skulls in a Pleistocene deposit. Wadjak is about sixty miles southeast of Trinil where *Pithecanthropus* was discovered in 1891. These skulls were associated with fossilized fauna which are still extant in Java, so that they were probably late Pleistocene. They had a very large cranial capacity. One of them, probably a female, had a capacity of about 1,550 cubic centimeters, which is two hundred more than the average cranial capacity of modern European woman. The other, probably a male, had a capacity of about 1,650 cubic centimeters, or one hundred and fifty more than the average cranial capacity of modern European man.

In other respects the Wadjak skulls were primitive. The brow ridges were highly developed, the forehead somewhat receding, the palatal area exceptionally great, the jaws massive, the teeth large but entirely human. Keith suggested that the Wadjak type seems to bridge the gap between Rhodesian man and the Australian aborigine of to-day.[5] But the male Australian has an average cranial capacity of about 1,300 cubic centimeters which is about three hundred less than the Wadjak capacity.

About the year 1885 at Talgai in Queensland, northern Australia, was found a skull in a deposit said to be Pleistocene. Its cranial capacity was about 1,300 cubic centimeters. As it belonged to a boy of four-teen or fifteen the adult capacity would be somewhat larger. The forehead was somewhat receding and the face very prognathous. The palate was very large like those of the Rhodesian and Wadjak skulls.

[4] Stibbe expressed the opinion that the Heidelberg and Rhodesian types were of the same species. (E. P. Stibbe, *An Introduction to Physical Anthropology*, London, 1930.) I know of no other anthropologist who is of the same opinion. Likenesses between the Rhodesian and Neanderthal types have been noted by several anthropologists.

[5] Arthur Keith, *The Antiquity of Man*, Philadelphia, 1925, revised edition, Vol. II.

The teeth were large but human. In most respects the skull resembled that of an Australian aborigine of today, though like the Wadjak skulls it was of a larger cranial capacity. Keith asserted that it was the earliest form of true *Homo sapiens* so far discovered, that it represented the ancient Australoid type, and that the Australian aborigine is the best living representative of Pleistocene time.[6] Later will be discussed to what extent Pleistocene man in Europe has persisted to the present day.[7]

The preceding brief survey indicates how fragmentary is our record of humanoid evolution. Of *Pithecanthropus, Sinanthropus, Homo Heidelbergensis* and *Homo Rhodesiensis* only one or two specimens each have so far been found. More finds may modify somewhat our conception of these types. Other types will probably be discovered with which we are not at present acquainted. What we now have is nevertheless of great significance. It not only furnishes a partial picture of the evolutionary series. It also indicates that there have been various combinations of what we choose to call primitive and of modern traits. These terms do not necessarily imply inferiority and superiority. In every line of organic descent certain traits persist for a long time unchanged or relatively unchanged while other traits vary rapidly. Varying environmental conditions cause a series of changes in certain parts of the organism while other parts remain relatively stable. Thus one group will vary in a certain direction while another group belonging to the same species, genus, family, or order will under somewhat different conditions vary in another direction.

On the other hand, convergence with respect to certain traits may take place along lines of descent which have already diverged from each other. This may be due to a latent evolutionary bias which manifests itself along two or more divergent lines.[8] The five unfused digits characteristic of the primates constitute a primitive trait found among the amphibia which has been inherited by all of the primates. The human foot is a highly specialized and comparatively recent development which characterized *Pithecanthropus* and all of the other humanoid types.

Similar combinations of traits are found in all other organic groups. The family of the horse (*Equidae*) has been more fully described in its evolutionary aspect than most animal groups. It presents great variation as to size, degree of specialization of the digits into a hoof, etc. Owing to breeding and selection by man during the past few centuries or millennia, the dog displays within the narrow limits of a

[6] A. Keith, *op. cit.*, Vol. II. See also his *Recent Discoveries Relating to the Antiquity of Man*, London, 1931.

[7] *Cf.* G. G. MacCurdy, *Early Man*, New Haven, 1937.

[8] See, for example, A. Keith, *op. cit.*, Vol. II.

single species a great variety as to size, hair, shape of the limbs, structure of the muzzle, etc., and to a lesser degree as to its mental traits.

It is not surprising that there is considerable variation not only in the primate but also in the anthropoid and even in the humanoid group. In comparison with many organic groups the number of varieties is not great. The primate order is small and insignificant in the animal world. In view of the gaps it is not easy to work out the relationships between the known types. Various hypotheses have been proposed, some of them rather far-fetched. According to one such hypothesis, Pleistocene man already possessed modern dentition and fossil types with human dentition must have been humanoid, so that the anthropoid apes must have branched off from a humanoid stem, the chimpanzee being the latest to do so.[9] While the dentition of the apes strongly resembles that of mankind, the *Simiidae* lack the specialized human foot and have not attained a completely erect posture. These and many other differences make it extremely doubtful that the ancestry of the apes was humanoid, just as it is somewhat less doubtful that the ancestry of the *Hominidae* was simian.

The white, yellow and black races interbreed, which is a sign of a very close relationship, indeed, of belonging to the same species. So far as is known, man cannot interbreed with any of the simians.

Fertility is the best criterion of a species. So long as interbreeding can go on within any organic group the members of the group will remain more or less similar. As soon as infertility arises, the group will break up into two or more groups which are or will soon become new species. From that time on these groups are certain to drift apart, even though convergence may take place with regard to a few traits. Thus arise in course of time the distinctions not only between species but also between genera, families, orders, classes, and phyla.

No higher primates, living or fossil, have been found in the Western Hemisphere. The only American primates are the *Hapalidae* and *Cebidae* both of which are small monkeys with tails. So far as we can ascertain, the whole of humanoid evolution took place in the Eastern Hemisphere. *Pithecanthropus* was found in southeastern and *Sinanthropus* in northeastern Asia, the Heidelberg type in Europe, and the Rhodesian man in Africa. The simian types, fossil and extant, have been found scattered over a similar area most of which is tropical or sub-tropical. The only primate which inhabits a temperate or relatively cold climate is the Tibetan monkey.

Persons in charge of the Central Asiatic expeditions of the American Museum of Natural History have advanced the hypothesis that mankind originated in central Asia. These expeditions have not

9 Adloff, *The Significance of the Dentition*, International Congress of Prehistoric Sciences, reported in *Man*, 1932, Vol. XXXII.

yielded a shred of evidence in support of this hypothesis. The most elaborate presentation of it and of its general zoological setting has been made by Matthew. According to him the principal lines of migration of land vertebrates in the later geological epochs have been radial from holarctic (northern) centers of dispersal, the primates including mankind having been dispersed from central Asia. Matthew has asserted that man is not primarily adapted to a tropical climate partly because he is too thin-skinned for tropical forests. He alleged that the loss of hair is due to wearing clothes, and argued that hairlessness is most complete on the back and abdomen because pelts were worn on the back and tied around the waist.[10]

Matthew's hypothesis implies the transmission of acquired characters which is, to say the least, highly improbable. Even if it were possible, it is difficult to understand how the wearing of skins or of other forms of clothing would lead to hairlessness by such a process. Neither disuse nor shortening nor extraction of the hairs is involved. Experiments have shown that cutting and shaving the hair in various parts of the body have no effect upon the growth of the hair. The same seems to be true with respect to the influence of light, X-rays, applications of cold cream, and other alleged agencies for promoting or inhibiting its growth.

The only way in which clothing might lead to hairlessness would be through a process of selection. If clothes superimposed upon fur were harmful, the individuals with less hair would be more likely to survive. It is highly improbable that a covering would be adopted until the hair had already begun to decrease or had disappeared in considerable part, thus giving rise to the need for protection against cold. In fact, all hypotheses which attribute the loss of hair to clothing put the effect before the cause. The use of clothes would naturally follow hairlessness and not precede it. Having lost his hair man covered his body when venturing into cold regions. Cultural factors also played a part in the adoption of dress which will be discussed in a later chapter. This did not necessarily intensify the degree of hairlessness. The white race which has inhabited cold climates and worn clothing more than any other race is much more hairy than the black or the yellow races. The pubic region has the most luxuriant covering of hair in spite of the fact that it is most often covered.

The causes of hairlessness are probably to be found apart from the factor of clothing. Hair is characteristic of mammals in the same way that feathers characterize birds. Many of the mammals have lost much of their hair. This is true among others of some of the cetaceans, sirenians, and ungulates. Where the hair is scanty there is likely to be

[10] W. D. Matthew, *Climate and Evolution*, in the *Annals of the New York Academy of Sciences*, Vol. XXIV, pp. 171-318, 1915.

a subcutaneous layer of fat. In the case of mankind there seems to be a correlation between the decrease of hair and the evolution of the brain. The more bare the skin the greater the number of stimuli which can go from it to the brain. Whether this establishes a causal relationship between hairlessness and the growth of the brain, it is difficult to say. The human infant has perhaps as many hair follicles as the simian infant. But it has much more subcutaneous fat, and the hairs fail to grow. The endocrine secretions also seem to have a bearing upon the development of hair. Hooton has summed up the situation in the following words: "The most plausible theory accounting for the denudation of the human body is that of Elliot Smith and Keith which connects it with increased sensitiveness of the skin, deposition of a layer of subcutaneous fat, and an altered functioning of the glands of internal secretion. Possibly the nutritional factor is also important. But man's relative hairlessness cannot be brought into any causal relationship with the erect posture, the free prehensile function of the fore limbs, nor with the extremes of cold or heat encountered in different latitudes." [11]

Taylor has propounded a hypothesis of human dispersal, similar to that of Matthew. He divided the terrestrial world into three great peninsulas, namely, Eur-Africa, Australasia and America. He alleged that peoples are more and more primitive as we move away from Asia, most primitive in Tasmania, Cape Colony, Greenland, and Brazil. According to Taylor the last evolved races are found at the center where the stimuli leading to evolution are the greatest. Hence he believed that primitive races are found where they did not originate. His conclusion is that man probably developed in a moist, warm climate in central Asia where the climate later became cooler and more arid driving him to the tropics where he has stagnated.[12]

Even if it were true that central Asia was at one time moist and warm, there is not the slightest evidence that mankind originated there rather than in any other region which has been or is moist and warm. It is not necessarily true that animals and species are never or are rarely ever found where they originated. Climatic as well as other changes have often caused animal migrations. They have not always been in the directions postulated by the hypotheses of Matthew and Taylor. It is better to have no hypothesis whatsoever than to give vent to baseless and fantastic hypotheses.

With regard to chronology we have seen that *Pithecanthropus*

11 E. A. Hooton, *Up From the Ape,* New York, 1931, p. 205. See G. Elliot Smith, *Essays on the Evolution of Man, the Brain,* London, 1924; A. Keith, *The Human Body,* London, 1912.

12 Griffith Taylor, *Environment and Race,* London, 1927; *Environment, Race and Migration,* Chicago, 1937.

was in existence in the early Pleistocene and perhaps much earlier. *Sinanthropus* was apparently in existence in the early Pleistocene. Heidelberg man was probably somewhat later in the Pleistocene. Rhodesian man may have survived until comparatively recently, but there is no evidence as to how early it came into existence. In other words, humanoid types were already evolved by Pliocene and more or less human types by Pleistocene time.

Estimates of geological time vary greatly. Wells summarized the estimates of several geologists and said that Cenozoic time, or the so-called "age of mammals," may have ranged anywhere from four to forty millions of years in length. The beginning of the Pleistocene he placed 550,000 years ago.[13] Kroeber thought that Cenozoic time lasted five million years and asserted that according to the prevailing opinion Quaternary or Pleistocene time commenced about one million years ago.[14] Keith displayed a tendency to shorten the time considerably. He allowed only about two million years for Cenozoic time which he divided as follows: Eocene, 600,000; Oligocene, 600,000; Miocene, 450,000; Pliocene 250,000; Pleistocene and recent, 200,000.[15] However, he dated the Guenz or first glacial period 300,000 years ago. This would place the commencement of the Pleistocene at least as long ago, because it is usually understood to cover all of the era of the glaciations. Romer assigned 55,000,000 years to Cenozoic time of which only 1,000,000 is given to the Quaternary.[16]

Some of the chronological estimates in geological textbooks follow. Schuchert said that according to the "radioactive clock" the age of the earth is at least 500,000,000 years. He assigned four per cent or 20,000,000 years to the Cenozoic era of which one half is allotted to the Eocene and Oligocene periods and one half to the Miocene, Pliocene and Pleistocene periods. He said that the commencement of the Pleistocene is "estimated by geologists to be somewhere between 400,000 and 1,400,000 years ago." [17] Chamberlin and Salisbury allotted "more than a million years at least for the Quaternary period, and probably a multiple of this figure." [18] Miller estimated that according to radioactive transformations the Cenozoic era lasted 50,000,000 years.[19]

These estimates make it probable that the Pleistocene lasted

[13] H. G. Wells, *The Outline of History*, New York, 1920.

[14] A. L. Kroeber, *Anthropology*, New York, 1923.

[15] A. Keith, *The Antiquity* of Man, revised edition, Philadelphia, 1925.

[16] A. S. Romer, *Man and the Vertebrates*, Chicago, 1933, p. 8.

[17] L. V. Pirsson and Charles Schuchert, *A Textbook of Geology*, New York, revised edition, 2 vols. Vol. 2, *Historical Geology*, by C. Schuchert, p. 688.

[18] T. C. Chamberlin and R. D. Salisbury, *College Textbook of Geology*, New York, 1930, revised edition, 2 vols. Vol. 2, p. 820.

[19] William J. Miller, *Elements of Geology*, New York, 1931,

from five hundred thousand to one million or considerably more years. Many books on geology make no attempt to measure the length of geological periods.[20] The geologists are justified in being very cautious. But the question of time is important both in organic and in cultural evolution. At twenty years to the generation 25,000 generations could take place in 500,000 years, and 50,000 generations in one million years. This affords ample opportunity for many variations and for a long selective process. Hence it is not surprising that several human or humanoid types have existed during the Quaternary or age of man. It also furnishes a vast amount of time for cultural evolution.

We have seen that the humanoid *Sinanthropus,* as well as the fossil ape *Australopithecus,* are the only ones of these early types which were accompanied by cultural remains. As only one or two or a very few specimens of each type has so far been found, this does not necessarily mean that some or all of the other types were not characterized by culture. In the following chapter it will be shown that cultural objects not associated with skeletal remains have been discovered which are as old as some if not all of these types. In fact, it is probable that all of the humanoid and early human types were characterized by at least a small amount of culture.

We now turn to types which are distinctly human and which are accompanied by an abundance of cultural remains. The first of these is the so-called Neanderthal type or *Homo primigenius* or *antiquus.* More than twenty specimens of this type have been found so that its skeletal features are well known. Furthermore, many of these specimens were associated with remains of a distinct type of culture known as the Mousterian. Consequently, Neanderthal man is sometimes called *Homo mousteriensis.*

The Neanderthal type has been found in western and central Europe and a variant of it as far east as Palestine. Many of the finds were burials in caves which seem to have taken place during a glacial period.[21] It is almost certain that it inhabited Europe as late as the last glacial advance and during the preceding interglacial period. How much earlier it was in existence is uncertain.

The Neanderthaloid skull was large and heavily built. The forehead was low and receding. The supra-orbital or brow ridges were very large. The nose was broad. The upper jaw was prognathous,

20 The *Columbia University Encyclopedia,* 1953, estimates that the Cenozoic Era lasted 75 Million years; and its epochs in Million years—Eocene, 36; Oligocene, 11; Miocene, 16; Pliocene, 11; Pleistocene, 1.

21 Radioactive Carbon—14 determined the age of organic remains at 43,000± 2000 years in a Syrian cave once occupied by humans of the Middle Paleolithic flake culture. (C. S. Coon, *The Seven Caves,* New York, 1957.)

the lower jaw heavy and with almost no chin. The latter resembled the lower jaw of the Heidelberg type but was not so massive. In all of these traits Neanderthal man resembled somewhat the anthropoid apes but he was far more closely related to man of today than he was to the apes. His cranial capacity was probably as great as that of modern man. Endocranial casts, however, indicate differences between the Neanderthaloid and the modern human brain. The pattern of the convolutions was more crude and simple. Conformably with the low and receding forehead the frontal lobes were smaller. In the apes these lobes include about 32 per cent of the cerebral surface, in man of today about 43 per cent, and in the best preserved Neanderthal specimen, the man of La Chapelle-aux-Saints in southern France, about 36 per cent. The frontal lobes were more developed than in *Pithecanthropus,* especially the inferior frontal convolution where is the speech area. The temporal lobe was well developed, especially the auditory eminence which plays an important part in speech. The parietal lobes were comparatively large indicating a good sensory development and excellent control over manual movement. The visual areas in the occipital lobes were well developed.

The Neanderthal type resembled some of the primitive peoples of modern times such as the Australians. It is not certain that any living race has descended directly from Neanderthaloid ancestors, though Neanderthaloid blood may persist among modern men as a result of hybridization. There was probably a close relationship between the Heidelberg and Neanderthal types. Boule attached the Heidelberg lower jaw to the skull of the Neanderthal man of La Chapelle-aux-Saints and found that they fitted together very well.[22] This resemblance indicates that the Neanderthal type probably survived from early Pleistocene into comparatively recent times. The thigh bones were somewhat curved as in the anthropoid apes suggesting a somewhat shuffling gait. The feet retained some of the traits of a prehensile organ.

The Neanderthal type was succeeded in Europe by a man of the modern type called *Homo sapiens.* This type seems to have come into Europe from elsewhere and to have destroyed or driven out Neanderthal man with possibly a small amount of assimilation. Where the modern type came into being and how long it had been in existence is as yet unknown. There are a few rather uncertain and questionable indications that *Homo sapiens* had already been in Europe and is of great antiquity, perhaps as old as Neanderthal man. Among these indications are the finds at Galley Hill in England; at Abbeville (pit of Moulin Quignon), Clichy and Grenelle near Paris, in France; and

[22] Marcellin Boule, *Les Hommes fossiles,* 2nd edition, Paris, 1923; English translation, *Fossil Man,* London, 1923.

Olmo and Castenedolo in Italy. In each of these cases the reputed geological horizon was at least as old as early Pleistocene. But all of these discoveries were prior to 1870 with the exception of Galley Hill which was in 1888, and there was no very competent geological control present in any of these cases. More weighty evidence is needed before it is certain or even likely that *Homo sapiens* existed at so early a date.

About the year 1930 on the shore of Lake Victoria Nyanza in East Africa Leakey excavated a human mandible which he believed to be the oldest fragment of true *Homo* thus far found. The geological and archeological evidence seems to indicate that it dated from the early Pleistocene. Leakey has asserted that *"Homo kanamensis* must be regarded as standing much nearer to *Homo sapiens* than do any known other human genera or species, and that in all probability *Homo kanamensis* is the direct ancestor of *Homo sapiens,"* and that "it was found with a culture which is older than the Chellean but which is probably directly ancestral to this culture." [23] In the same region he found remains of a primitive race of large-headed men with certain infantile characters. He has asserted that "the Kanjara human remains demonstrate that the true *Homo sapiens* was already in existence long before the time of the great spread of the Neanderthal people in Europe." [24]

Partly owing to the latter conclusion Leakey has asserted that the main human stem, which had diverged from the common stem of the anthropoids and hominoids during the Oligocene, split during the Miocene into the main stems of the *Palaeoanthropidae* and the *Neoanthropidae*. To the former he assigned *Pithecanthropus, Sinanthropus, Palaeoanthropus heidelbergensis, P. rhodesiensis, P. europeus (neanderthalensis)*, and *P. palestinus* (a variant of *neanderthalensis*). To the latter he assigned *Homo kanamensis* and all extinct and extant types of *Homo sapiens*.[25] However, there is difference of opinion among anthropologists as to the morphological classification of human types. For example, Zuckerman has assigned *Sinanthropus, Pithecanthropus, Homo neanderthalensis* and *Homo rhodesiensis* to the *Palaeanthropidae,* and upper paleolithic and modern man to the *Neanthropidae*. These two divisions he had characterized as subfamilies of the Hominidae.[26]

Among the specimens found in the late Pleistocene are the

[23] L. S. B. Leakey, *The Stone Age Races of Kenya,* London, 1935, pp. 23, 136.
[24] *Op. cit.*, p. 36.
[25] L. S. B. Leakey, *Adam's Ancestors,* London, 1934, See also his *Stone Age in Africa,* London, 1936.
[26] S. Zuckerman, *Sinanthropus and Other Fossil Men,* in the *Eugenics Review,* London, January 1933, Vol. XXIV, No. 4, pp. 273-284.

Aurignacian, Cro-Magnon, Grimaldi and Brunn types. They are in their essential anatomical traits of the modern type, so that all of them probably are varieties of *Homo sapiens*. As this is not a treatise on physical anthropology, they need not be described in detail. They will be mentioned in connection with the cultural record in later chapters. The antiquity of the modern human type is of significance for cultural evolution. Whether or not the early stages of cultural evolution were created by the modern type or by other types depends in part upon the antiquity of the modern type which cannot at present be determined.

The preceding discussion gives some indication how the human type emerged from the primates in particular and the mammals in general. First to be noted is the ability to manipulate. The marine mammals, namely, the cetaceans, the sirenians, and the pinnipedians or aquatic carnivores, developed flippers which are not suitable for manipulation. The wings of the bats are equally unsuitable for this purpose. In the hoofs of the ungulates the five digits are almost entirely fused together and are covered with a horny substance which renders them wholly unable to manipulate. The paws and claws of the terrestrial carnivores are much more flexible, but are able to grasp and to hold to a very limited degree. The paws of the rodents are still more flexible and are somewhat prehensile. The prehensile hand appeared in the early arboreal primates or their arboreal insectivorous ancestors. The digits lengthened, and the thumb became opposable thus enabling the hand to grasp.

Arboreal life developed four hands in the primates. It was not until man's ancestors came down to the earth that the foot could develop which distinguishes man from the other primates. The foot rendered an erect posture and bipedal gait possible. This in turn released the hand from locomotor uses and made it an exclusively manipulative organ. An expansion of sight and hearing took place. Binocular vision was perfected. The change from arboreal to a terrestrial mode of life resulted in visual, auditory and equilibratory readjustments. The volitional control of the arms and legs increased. An adjustment took place of the simultaneous movements of eyes, head and hands necessary for skilled acts.[27]

This postural regulation of the body and its extremities gave rise to modifications in automatic associated movements rendering some of them more volitional and less automatic in their character. This was probably due in part at least to the fact that the ground furnishes a more stable basis for locomotion than the trees. Hence movements which would have to be automatic to preserve life and

[27] *Cf.* Frederick Tilney, *The Brain from Ape to Man*, New York, 1928, 2 vols.

31

limb in arboreal life could with safety become volitional in terrestrial life. At the same time the brain was increasing in size. Especially significant was the growth of the frontal lobes and the increase in the number and depth of the frontal convolutions. Most significant of all was the development of the third inferior convolution utilized in speaking. Endocranial casts indicate this speech area sufficiently prominent in *Pithecanthropus* to render language conceivable, almost as well developed in Neanderthal as in modern man, but somewhat less developed in Rhodesian man.

The causal relationships between these changes are difficult to trace. Anatomical transformations and the changes in behavior resulting therefrom apparently had their effect in increasing the size and complexity of the brain. These cerebral changes reacted in turn upon the anatomical structure. The environment acted as a selective force in favoring the survival of the large-brained humanoid type with an erect posture. Other traits not conserved by selection tended to disappear. It is by a similar process of variation and selection that every organic species comes into being. The first step toward an explanation as to how and why a species has originated is a description of the changes from one type to another and of the environmental conditions under which these changes have taken place. With an increase in the mass of pertinent data and their correlation in time and space an ever closer approximation can be made to a causal analysis. The proximate hypotheses of today may in due course of time lead to more or less satisfactory theories of human origin.

Certain it is that man did not originate through conscious volition on his own part, nor is there any evidence that he is a special creation of a designing creator. It would be superfluous to make such an assertion if some of the scientists did not make misleading statements which imply that man is an exception in the organic world. For example, a neurologist has spoken as follows of the men of the Cro-Magnon type: "They signalize that new spirit which had been breathed into mankind, that devotion to the beautiful in life which created an abiding enthusiasm in all of our race for the highest ideals and loftiest purposes." [28] A student of dental evolution has expressed himself in the following teleological fashion: "Man's ascent from the lower primates has been a struggle towards better brains, better intelligence and better morals. Through the improvement of the frontal lobes and other parts of the brain, in the latter stages of his history, Man is slowly overcoming his selfish impulses and awakening to the

[28] Frederick Tilney, *The Master of Destiny, A Biography of the Brain*, New York, 1930.

32

vast possibilities of advance through the spirit of mutual tolerance and helpfulness." [29] A physical anthropologist and somatologist has alleged that "man is a miracle. whether he is a miracle of chance, of nature, or of God." [30] Why man is more miraculous than any other object in the universe, he did not explain. Even scientists are at times all too human.[31]

The manipulative, locomotor and cerebral specializations characteristic of man were possible because his primate ancestors did not acquire certain specializations which characterize other mammalian orders. The hand is a very primitive organ inherited from the amphibia. Inasmuch as it did not become specialized through a fusion of the digits or other transformations, it remained plastic and flexible and could be adapted to any use directed by the brain. The posterior limbs and hands became specialized into the humanoid legs and feet and liberated the anterior limbs and hands from locomotion. The expansion of sight and hearing and perfecting of binocular vision furnished an exceptional degree of contact with the external world and increased the range of sensory stimuli received by the brain.[32] The two forward-looking eyes gave a more acute appreciation of the third dimension and a special power of focussing the attention which in turn stimulated the development of manual skill. The disappearance

[29] William K. Gregory, 1924, quoted in the Hall of Man of the American Museum of Natural History, New York City.

[30] E. A. Hooton, *Up From the Ape*, New York, 1931, p. 604.

[31] The most misleading statements emanate from religious and sacerdotal sources as illustrated by the following quotation from an article entitled "Man, Christian Anthropology" by an apologist for Roman Catholicism: "The argument from design in the world for the existence of a creator is now actually stronger than ever in scientific minds, and a review of all the purposes that exist among living things makes it quite impossible to believe that they were developed without a Designer." (*Encyclopedia Americana*, 1948 edition.)

Such statements often appear in the course of attacks upon the theory of organic evolution by priests, parsons and theologians. They are gratifying to the egocentric and anthropocentric prejudices which have been instilled into mankind and fostered by the religions of the world.

The argument from design, that creation occurs, and that a Creator exists is conclusively refuted by posing the single question: "Who created the Creator!"

[32] Elliot Smith has expressed the peculiarly human traits resulting from this combination of factors in the following words: "The seeing eye guiding the adaptable right hand conferred upon Man his intellectual supremacy because the brain developed in such a way as to make learning and understanding attainable through the practice of skilled manipulation." (G. Elliot Smith, *The Evolution of Man*, London, 1927, 2nd edition, p. 189.)

"The anatomical features which distinguish men from apes are comparatively few. Bone for bone, muscle for muscle, organ for organ, almost every feature of the ape is repeated in the human body. . . . The differences are related mainly to locomotor habits and brain growth." (A. S. Romer, *op. cit.*, p. 230.)

of the hairy covering increased also the range of tactile stimuli received from the outside. Several of these factors played their part in increasing the size and complexity of the brain. This paragraph perhaps furnishes as close an approximation as can for the present be attained to an explanation as to how and why mankind emerged from its primate and mammalian ancestors.

Chapter IV

The Dynamics of Behavior

ALL knowledge is in the first instance subjective. It is acquired through the sense organs in the form of sensations from which images, percepts, ideas and concepts are derived. We cannot be certain that our sensations represent accurately the world which is exterior to us. According to the solipsist philosophies only knowledge of the self is possible, or, stated in a more extreme form, the self alone exists. If that were the case, the ego would include the whole universe, so that there would be nothing external to the self. The panorama of universal change would be no more than a reflection of the ego, or a fantasmagoria created by its imagination. But the fact that many other selves appear to exist and to be passing through similar experiences renders solipsism dubious. It is an extreme form of subjective idealism which leads immediately to an impasse of negation. For the advancement of science as well as for pragmatic reasons a more realistic attitude toward the universe is inevitable. Hence we are compelled to assume that there is an external world and that the things in it are actually or approximately as our senses represent them to be.[1]

We can introspect ourselves from immediate experience and by means of self-examination, and describe our own subjective processes. Those of others we can infer only through observation of their behavior. The study of behavior is, therefore, essential in order to understand the subjective as well as the objective aspects of social and cultural phenomena. The authenticity and accuracy of one's own perception of the world and validity of one's own concepts can be tested by comparing them with those of others as revealed by their non-

[1] Solipsism is etymologically derived from the Latin words *solus* and *ipse*, namely, alone and himself.

Bradley stated the solipsist hypothesis as follows: "I cannot transcend experience, and experience must be my experience. From this it follows that nothing beyond myself exists; for what is experience is its states." (F. H. Bradley, *Appearance and Reality*, 1893.) He criticized solipsism, though he thought that he found three partial truths in it.

verbal and verbal, their overt and covert behavior, in so far as the latter can be inferred and surmised.

The plasticity of animal behavior is due to certain peculiarities of organic matter which have been mentioned in the chapter on the threshold of social evolution. These traits are the instability and mobility of organic matter which give rise to protoplasm's irritability and sensibility to stimui. This responsiveness is fundamentally nothing more than the facility with which organic matter changes as a result of the molecular and molar forces which act upon it. In this regard organic matter differs not in kind but only in degree from inorganic matter, because all matter changes as a result of the action of forces upon it.

The analysis of behavior is always and fundamentally biological, because it involves the study of anatomical structure and physiological process. It is psychological when mental factors are involved in determining behavior. Sometimes it is also sociological because a certain amount of behavior is influenced by association. In bringing together the pertinent data from these three sciences, a small part of biology and most or all of psychology and sociology are included, because mental and social phenomena can be reduced to terms of behavior. While not a primary science, it is a systematic study of certain organic phenomena, and may, therefore, be called the science of behavior.[2]

The genetic method is of value for several reasons. The modes of behavior of various species are compared and contrasted. The complex forms of behavior are resolved into their simpler elements, thus rendering them easier to understand. By so doing many experiments are rendered unnecessary. At the same time what experiments should be made is indicated. The function of behavior in the scheme of organic evolution is thereby demonstrated.

The three fundamental types of overt behavior are the tropism, the reflex action, and the instinctive act. Each of these is a movement or action of an animal or part of an animal which is perceptible from the outside. There are certain internal movements which are physiological processes like these forms of behavior, and which influence some kinds of behavior. These internal processes, consisting of numerous minute and refined movements, most of which are within the nervous system, are usually called psycho-physical processes, and collectively they determine what are called mental phenomena.

The analysis of mental phenomena is not easy. Inasmuch as the

[2] So far as I am aware, my book entitled *The Science of Human Behavior, Biological and Psychological Foundations*, New York, 1913 was the first book on behaviorism ever published. Professor John B. Watson, the founder of the behaviorist school of psychology, had already published articles and monographs, but his first comprehensive book, entitled *Behavior*, was not published until 1914.

movements involved are internal and very minute and refined, they are more or less intangible and difficult to observe. Hitherto the method utilized in studying mental phenomena has ordinarily been subjective and introspective rather than objective. Introspection will continue to be a source of information concerning mental phenomena. But the study of these phenomena cannot become thoroughly scientific until the method used is in the main objective.

The direct motor reaction of a whole organism to an external stimulus is usually called a tropism. The unicellular and the lowest multicellular organisms can react as a whole organism to an external stimulus. In the more complex organisms only a part of an organism can respond directly to such a stimulus. The reactions of these organisms are more or less indirect and much more complicated.

The actions of organisms are determined in the long run by external forces. That is to say, the forms of these organisms have been determined in the past by these external forces. Their past experience has been determined by their forms and by external forces. Inasmuch as the behavior of an organism at any moment is not determined entirely by the immediate stimulus, but in part by its form and by its past experience, its behavior as a whole can in the last analysis be traced back to external forces.

The structure of a given organism limits the number and kinds of actions which that organism can perform. Each organism is capable of a number of simple movements and a larger number of combinations of these simple movements. The whole set of these actions taken together may be called its action system. Among the higher animals an animal without wings does not fly nor does an animal without feet walk. Among the lower organisms behavior is limited and determined to a large extent by structure. For example, the protozoan class *Infusoria* can be divided according to its behavior, which is determined in this respect by structure, into the infusorians that are sessile, those that creep over surfaces, and those that swim freely.

By reflex action is often meant the contraction of a muscle when a nerve is stimulated. It is called reflex because the stimulation is transmitted along the sensory nerve to the central nervous system and is then reflected along a motor nerve to a muscle. For this sort of reflex action a nervous system is necessary. The term is sometimes applied to any instance of an invariable reaction to a given stimulus. In this sense it is merely a type of reaction without regard to the existence of a nervous system. It is sometimes asserted that all of the reactions of the lower organisms are reflex in the sense that they are invariable. But the same stimulus does not necessarily produce the same reaction invariably, because changes in the physiological state of the organism may cause variations in the reaction.

The tendency to characterize the behavior of the lower organisms as purely reflex arises out of the desire to explain their behavior on mechanical grounds without assuming the presence of consciousness. Even when this behavior is not invariable, we do not have to assume that consciousness is present and that the behavior is not wholly mechanical. The physiological state of the organism may be regarded as a part of its mechanical structure, so that when variations in its behavior are explained by changes in its physiological state, the explanation is on mechanical grounds. The behavior of higher organisms can be explained in similar fashion, so that no distinction in this regard can be made between the behavior of the higher and of the lower organisms. If by reflex action is meant an invariable reaction to a given stimulus, no species is characterized by it. If it means that all organic behavior is determined by physical and chemical forces, the behavior of every organism is reflex and no distinction can be made between the higher and the lower species in this regard.

The physiological state of an organism may be changed by progressive internal processes, especially those of metabolism. Or it may be changed by the action of external forces. The resolution of one physiological state into another takes place more readily the more often it is repeated. When a number of states follow each other in a series, the resolution of one into the other may take place so rapidly as to be instantaneous, so that only the last state determines what the form of behavior is to be. This process furnishes a basis for memory, association, habit formation, and learning in the higher organisms. It applies to the lower organisms as well, and the only differences between organisms in this regard lie in the readiness with which the speedy resolution of one physiological state into another becomes established and the extent to which such a habit is permanent.

Self-determination of behavior increases with a rise in the organic scale. This is due in large part to the evolution of the nervous system to which the characteristic features of the behavior of the higher animals are to be attributed. This system consists of nerve cells and fibers which extend throughout the body and influence organic behavior by determining the actions of the muscles and glands with which they are connected. The functions performed by the nervous system are so peculiar to itself that a sharp line of distinction has sometimes been drawn between it and the rest of the organism. On the other hand, it must be recognized that nervous substance is no more than a somewhat specialized form of protoplasm.

There is no absolute distinction between the nervous system and the rest of the organism, because all parts of the organism have a common origin and have differentiated from the primordial protoplasm. In the higher animals the nervous system, because of its well developed conductibility, integrates a complex organism in a way which would be impossible without it. While nervous matter is in the same evolutionary order with other organic matter, and while most if not all of the features of behavior in animals with a nervous system are to be found in a rudimentary form in the species without it, such behavior becomes far more complex in the higher animals. Most of the mental phenomena which characterize the higher species would have been impossible without a nervous system.

By reflex action I mean the reaction of a muscle or gland or other effector caused by a nervous stimulus. The conductibility possessed by nervous matter is not peculiar to it, because it characterizes in varying degrees protoplasm in general. Stimuli are carried through protoplasm either by mechanical or by chemical means. In a multicellular organism, if the intercellular material is solid, stimuli are likely to be carried by mechanical means; if the intercellular material is fluid, they are usually carried by chemical means. In both cases the conduction of the stimulus is delayed by the passage from one cell to another. Where rapidity of conduction is needed, a special class of cells began to develop whose characteristic function it is to carry these stimuli and connect the organic parts. These cells are usually elongated and stretch out protoplasmic threads in the direction in which the stimuli are to travel.

The nerve cells, like all organic matter, evolved through the forces of variation and selection. The individuals which responded most readily and advantageously to the stimuli of life-or-death importance were selected out for survival, so that there evolved this system of cells which are exceptionally sensitive to stimuli. This sensitiveness would be of no value if there were no effectors in the form of muscles which could take organisms away from harmful stimuli and propel them toward those which are beneficial, such as food. It seems probable that the effectors began to evolve before the nervous system, but later they evolved together.

The receptors or sense organs vary greatly among themselves. In each case is represented a protoplasmic trait which has become highly specialized in the cells of the sense organ. The essential part of the eye consists of cells which have become very sensitive to photic stimuli. A rudimentary eye is found even in the lowest organisms, such as some of the protozoa, in the form of a spot which is unusually sensitive to light. The sense organs of taste and of smell consist of cells which are highly sensitive to chemical stimuli. The sense organs of touch and of hearing consist of cells which are very sensitive to mechanical stimuli. Some of these organs have become very complex mechanisms, such as the eye with its lens, cornea, retina, etc., and the ear with its otoliths, cochlea, circular canals, etc.

39

The sense organs are not necessarily nerve cells just as the effectors are not nerve cells. In fact, most of these organs are not nerve cells. They are peripheral; that is to say, they are on a surface which is exposed to stimuli. But they are not necessarily on the outside of the body. Many of them are on the surface of the intestines and the other internal organs. All of the sense organs are connected with effectors, in the higher animals at any rate, by means of nerves.

There are few if any reflexes in the vertebrates which do not pass through the central nervous system. Three levels of reflex arcs are usually distinguished. The first is an arc on the spinal level in which the stimulus passes by means of the processes of a neurone from the receptor organ to the cell body of a sensory neurone in the central nervous system. From this neurone it is transferred to a neurone connected with the effector organ and by means of whose processes it is conducted to the effector. The second level of arcs is where loops are formed on the arcs of the spinal level by their neurones becoming connected with each other so that these reflexes influence each other. The third level is attained when the brain develops so that the reflexes become interconnected in a much more complex fashion. The cerebrum is made up largely of association centers; that is to say, of neurones which are not directly connected with receptor or effector organs, but whose neural processes are devoted entirely to connecting other neurones with each other.

The connections established between neurones by the central nervous system result in two important phenomena. The first is *facilitation;* namely, the reinforcement of the excitation of a motor system by the stimulation of other sensory neurones connected with the same motor system. The second is *inhibition,* or the partial or complete prevention of the spread of excitement from a sensory neurone to a motor system, caused apparently by the simultaneous excitation of some other motor system. A sensory neurone can receive stimuli only from the sense organ with which it is connected. But an effector may receive stimuli from several sensory neurones. These facts have been stated in the principle of the common path which may be used by like reflexes at the same time, but not by unlike reflexes, because an effector cannot be made to do two things at the same time. These characteristics of the common path make it a coordinating mechanism which prevents confusion by restricting the use of the effector to one action at a time.

The coordination effected by the common path illustrates the main function of the nervous system in general, namely, its integrative function. Indeed, in a sense this function includes all the other functions of the nervous system. In its integrative action it sends physico-

40

chemical stimuli along its lines of stationary cells which release energy in distant organs. Nervous integration is usually more rapid than other forms of integration in which the means of communication is intercellular material, such as connective tissue, or where material in mass has to be transferred, as in the circulation of blood. The unit mechanism in nervous integration, as in the nervous system as a whole, is the reflex arc. Nervous integration is accomplished entirely by means of reflexes, of which two kinds may be distinguished, namely, the simple reflex, of which there are probably none in the higher animals, and the compound reflex. All or most of the behavior of the higher animals is reflex, because all or most of it is integrated by the nervous system.

The functional divisions of the nervous system are the somatic sensory, the somatic motor, the visceral sensory, and the visceral motor. The visceral nerves, sometimes called the sympathetic system, are not under voluntary control, but are connected with other parts of the nervous system. The central nervous system of vertebrates is divided into segments called neuromeres, which correspond with the segments or metameres of the spinal column. The leading segments develop much more than the other segments, because they are subjected to a rigorous process of selection. Those individuals tend to survive whose receptors in the leading segments adapt them to their environment. This results in the refinement of the ability of these receptors to discriminate between benign and malign stimuli until they are highly adaptive.

Especially significant is the evolution of the distance-receptors. In one sense no receptor can be a distance-receptor, because every receptor reacts directly to mechanical forces which act upon it. Thus visual receptors react directly to the vibrations of light. Auditory receptors react directly to vibrations in air or water or whatever fluid or solid matter the conducting medium may be. In this respect they are similar to tango-receptors, which react directly to massive, material objects which come into contact with them as well as to vibrations of heat and of electricity. They are distance-receptors in the sense that they determine reactions which adapt the individual to objects which are at a distance, but from which are emanating forces which directly affect the receptors. The organs of vision, hearing, and smell are the principal distance-receptors. The olfactory sense organ is acted upon by minute particles, so that it may appear not to be a distance-receptor. But the particles acting upon the organ cause the organism to adapt itself to the object at a distance from which these particles are emanating, so that this sense organ may also be called a distance-receptor. The gustatory sense organ is a distance-receptor to the least degree

41

because material objects must come into direct contact with the taste-buds in the mouth to stimulate this sense. These two chemical senses guide the organism to its appropriate food.

The nervous equipment of the head consists of the neuromeres or sections of the spinal cord which correspond to the segments of the spinal column from which evolve the skull or bony enclosure of the head. These neuromeres have become large and complex as compared with their original state. This development is due to the same causes as the enlargement of the sections of the spinal cord where the fibers from the limbs enter. The neuromeres of the leading segments receive stimuli from many more receptors than do most of the neuromeres of the spinal cord. Some of these are distance-receptors from which are received sensations for which many association paths are established.

The neuromeres of the head constitute the brain, which consists of four parts—the cerebrum, the cerebellum, the pons Varolii, and the medulla oblongata. The latter connects the spinal cord wth the pons. The pons connects all four parts of the brain with each other. The most important parts of the brain are the cerebrum and the cerebellum.

As the brain is highly differentiated, it possesses considerable differentiation of function. The anatomical method furnishes certain presumptions as to how these functions are distributed. Anatomical study cannot be carried on to a great extent in the living subject, so that most of these researches are made when the brain is not functioning. The method of extirpation is valuable but not always certain, because surgical shock may cause changes greater than the effect of the extirpation alone. Furthermore, other parts of the brain sometimes compensate for the parts which have been extirpated.

The cerebellum is behind and somewhat below the cerebrum, and is an enlargement of certain segments of the spinal cord back of the segments from which the cerebrum has developed. The cerebellum receives stmuli from the spinal cord before they reach the cerebrum, and makes simpler reactions such as involve coordination with respect to space. The cerebrum is reached later and makes more complex coordinations of sequence, such as are involved with respect to time. There has been difference of opinion as to the functions of the cerebellum. Its importance has been both overestimated and underestimated. It probably has a direct control over the movements initiated in the cerebrum and serves to coordinate these movements.

The cerebrum is the largest and most important neural organ. Of particular interest is the pallium or cerebral cortex in which the highest functions of the brain are performed. The study of this part of the cerebrum is mainly a study of cerebral localization.

42

The three principal methods of studying the cerebral functions are the anatomical, the physiological, and the clinico-pathological. The anatomists dissect the nervous system and ascertain the distribution of the nerve cells and the paths of the nerve fibers. From such study many inferences may be drawn as to the functions of the different parts of the nervous system. If an effector is not neurally connected with a central organ, it is reasonable to suppose that it is not governed by that organ. The nervous system is so complex and so thoroughly integrated that it is doubtful that any effector is wholly unconnected with a central nervous organ. When the connection is indirect and slight, it may be assumed that the degree of control is slight. In similar fashion when the connection is direct and by many fibers, it may be assumed that the central organ has a high degree of control over the effector.

Physiological research includes the methods of stimulation and extirpation. By stimulating parts of the nervous system and observing the motor and vascular reactions obtained, functional relations between different parts of the nervous system and effectors may be determined. By extirpating part of the nervous system and then observing the effect upon the behavior of the organism, inferences may be drawn as to the functions of the parts extirpated. The extirpation method is of value particularly for the study of the parts of the cerebrum which are not excited by direct stimuli. The study of pathological conditions in the brain may throw light upon cerebral localization. If a lesion of a part of the brain is followed by a derangement in the behavior of certain effectors, it may be assumed that there is a functional relation between that part of the brain and those effectors.

The cerebrum, like the rest of the cerebro-spinal system, is composed of white and gray matter. The white matter is made up chiefly of bundles of medullated axones. The gray matter is composed chiefly of cell bodies and dendrites. Stimuli from receptor sense organs terminate in the gray matter, and impulses to effector organs start from the gray matter. These stimuli and impulses are carried in large part by the white matter. The cerebral gray substance may be divided into three groups, namely, the cortical, the ganglionar, and the central or ventricular. The cortical gray substance is of special interest, because in it are determined in the main behavior characterized by mental traits. The part of the cerebral cortex devoted to receiving stimuli from receptor organs and sending impulses to effector organs is divided up into several areas called the sensori-motor areas. Another and larger part of the cortex is devoted to establishing associations between the sensory and motor centers. This part is divided into what are called the association centers.

In the physiological study of cerebral localization two methods of research are used, namely, stimulation and extirpation. Electricity is often used in stimulating the cerebrum. Clinico-pathological investigations have also thrown light upon cerebral localization. Where there has been derangement of behavior it has sometimes been possible by trephining in the living and autopsies in the dead to locate the lesion which was the cause of the derangement. Thus conclusions can be reached as to the localization of the deranged functions. This method has exceptional value for the study of human cerebral localization. The patient can often give detailed information as to the nature of the derangement, which aids especially in the study of localization in the association areas.

The clinico-pathological and the physiological methods are closely related. A pathological lesion and an experimental extirpation may have the same effect, because in each case a certain part of the cerebrum has been destroyed or has been cut off from the rest of the nervous system so that it can no longer perform its function. In other words, the experimenter does intentionally what disease or accident may do unintentionally. Many data have been gathered with regard to the relations between pathological mental conditions and forms of behavior and abnormal conditions of the brain.

While many brain diseases can be localized in the cerebrum, other diseases are caused by a general abnormal or pathological cerebral condition. A distinction is often made between the so-called functional and the organic diseases of the brain. The functional diseases are believed to occur without any anatomical changes, and are supposed to be cured by methods which have no anatomical effect. The functional as well as the organic diseases have an anatomical basis. They differ only in that the changes are not so great, are more numerous and more widely distributed in the functional diseases. It would perhaps be better if the distinction between functional and organic diseases were abandoned entirely, because in the last analysis all diseases are both functional and organic.

Instincts may be defined as congenital tendencies to more or less definite modes of action. But this definition includes tropisms and reflex actions as well. If instinct is to be identified with reflex action, the term would be superfluous. As practically all the actions of the higher animals are determined by the nervous system, almost all of their behavior is reflex. Hence it is impossible to apply the term instinct to behavior which is not reflex. The only way of utilizing the term is to apply it to a special group of reflex actions. They are acts which have an outward manifestation. Furthermore, there are more than one of these acts, and they are so combined and related to each other that they work toward a unified end. That is to say, each is adapted not only by itself, but also in relation to all the others. In-

44

stincts appear in the course of the integration of the behavior of the organism which is effected by the nervous system. When instinct is regarded in this fashion, the mystery and obscurity in which it has often been shrouded disappears, and its nature becomes clear.

Instincts are based upon structure, and the relation between instinct and structure is the same as the relation between structure and physiological activities. The origin and evolution of instincts is correlated with that of structure. Structural forms evolve either as the result of the accumulation of slight variations which are preserved because they have utility, or as the result of mutations of more or less extent which appear independent of utility and which may or may not prove to be useful. In the first case, an instinct would probably make its appearance slowly and would be useful from the outset. In the second case, an instinct would probably appear suddenly and would not necessarily be useful at its inception. No such sudden appearance of an instinct as the result of a mutation has been observed. As instinct is based upon structure, and as structural forms may result from mutations, it is conceivable that instincts may appear in this sudden fashion. It may be alleged that such new forms of behavior are not instincts if they are not useful. While in the long run instincts are certain to be useful, for otherwise they would be eliminated, an instinct which has been useful may lose its utility.

Instincts are hereditary just as the structures upon which they are based are hereditary. An instinct tends to become a specific trait because if it proves to have sufficient utility the individuals possessing it will be preserved, while those which do not possess it will be eliminated. But at its inception an instinct cannot belong to a whole species unless it in itself, or rather the structural form upon which it is based, marks what turns out to be the beginning of a new species. If an instinct is the result of a mutation, it will at first belong to but one individual. Then it will be transmitted to the immediate descendants of this individual, and if it proves to have great utility, it may become a specific trait in the manner indicated above.

Instincts can be no more permanent than the structural forms upon which they are based. Variations and mutations cause new instincts to come into existence. In similar fashion, variations and mutations cause changes in instincts already in existence because they change the structural basis of these instincts. These changes in instincts are hereditary. Any changes in the instinctive tendencies of the individual which are not hereditary must be due to structural modifications which cannot be inherited, such as castration which weakens or destroys the sexual tendencies, or cerebral lesions which injure any of the nerve centers connected with instincts.

A simple reflex action is not likely to be changed, because its structural basis is simple, and changes in it are not likely to take place. The structural basis for the unified behavior of the whole organism which arises out of a group of reflexes which have been integrated together by the nervous system and which is called instinctive is much more complex, and the possibility of changes taking place in this structural basis is correspondingly greater. It is in the nervous system that these structural changes usually take place. This system is so delicate and so complex that changes in it which are slight in extent may have great effect upon the behavior of the organism. These changes may, however, take place in other parts of the organism. For example, one of the most important and permanent of the instincts is that of sex. Its structural basis is in part in the sexual organs and partly in the nervous system. If the sexual organs are removed in part or entirely, the instinctive sexual tendency will disappear in part or entirely. If such a change in an instinct is not detected, it is because a habit has become established on the instinctive foundation which persists in full strength even though its structural basis has been partly removed.

An instinctive act is performed without any previous training or experience the first time that the appropriate stimuli act upon the organism. There can be no knowledge or foresight of the consequences of the act before it is performed. It may be adaptive and therefore useful, but owing to lack of foresight it cannot be purposive. When the act is repeated, however, the factor of experience enters in. If the consequences have been pleasant, the tendency to perform this act are strengthened. If the consequences have been unpleasant, the tendency to perform the act is weakened and may in course of time be inhibited entirely. Thus it is that through associations established in the central nervous system instincts are reinforced or inhibited.

An instinctive action is stimulated by any one of a group of objects which starts off the series of reflexes which constitute the instinct. If it is stimulated in an organism several times by the same one of this group, the habit of responding to this one object may become established, so that when the organism is subjected to stimulus from other objects of this group, it will be prevented from responding because of this habit. Thus the tendency to respond to the first object will be reinforced, while the tendency to respond to the other objects will be inhibited. Such reinforcement and inhibition arise out of paths of association established in the central nervous system.

An instinctive reaction may be stimulated by the image of one of the group of objects which ordinarily arouse it. The image of an object arises out of an association center or group of association centers which is connected with the sensory center which that object stimulates. If this center or group of centers is also connected with the

46

motor center which governs the instinctive reaction, stimulation of this center or group of centers may be sufficient to arouse the motor center. Thus an instinctive reaction may be aroused by the image of an object, even though the organism has not been subjected to the stimulus of the object itself. In similar fashion, an instinctive reaction may be stimulated by another object or the image of another object which is connected by paths of association with the object which ordinarily arouses the instinctive reaction, and also with the motor center which governs the instinctive reaction. The neural basis for the fact that the same instinctive action can be stimulated from several sensory and association centers is indicated in the principle of the common path mentioned above.

Variations in instinctive reactions due to habit based upon experience are especially characteristic of man, whose behavior is controlled to a certain extent by intelligence and is influenced by imitation. Such variations are most likely to take place in instincts which ripen slowly, because intelligence has time to influence the form the instinctive reaction is to take. Different instincts may be stimulated at the same time and then inhibit each other in part or entirely, or they may be combined in forms of behavior in which each reaction becomes somewhat modified. Transient instincts which appear temporarily at a certain point in the lifetime are characteristic of a whole group, usually a species.

In the organic world utility in the struggle for existence is the criterion of excellence. Instincts are perfect to the extent to which they are useful in this struggle. Selection is always at work preserving the useful instinctive reactions and eliminating the injurious ones, and, to a certain extent those which are no longer useful. But selection has never succeeded in making an organ or organic trait entirely adaptive and useful. This is true even of so highly developed an organ as the human eye. No instinct was ever perfect in the sense that it was completely adapted to the needs of the organism. It would be more difficult for an instinct to attain such perfection than for most organic traits, because of the complexity of the series of reflexes which constitute an instinctive reaction. Even if an instinct did become approximately perfect, it could not remain so always, because the needs of the organism would change in course of time and require changes in the instinctive reaction.

The preceding discussion indicates that an instinct is distinct from a tropism because it is based upon and conditioned by a nervous system, it is distinguished from a reflex because it is made up of an integrated series of reflexes, and it differs from an internal physiological process because it is an external activity of an organism. *An instinct may, therefore, be defined as an inherited combination of reflexes which have been integrated by the central nervous system so as to cause an external activity of the organism which usually characterizes a whole species and is usually adaptive.*[3]

The cerebrum does not have as much to do with instinct as other parts of the central nervous system, but is more particularly the organ of intelligence. The instincts are localized mainly in the spinal cord, the medulla, and the cerebellum. Some of them are simple and are manifested in a single external action. They are sometimes called impulsive instincts, and most of them are localized in the spinal cord. Other instincts are more complex and involve a series of acts. Most, if not all, of these are localized in the brain. They may be complex because a single external stimulus arouses a reflex connected with a number of reflexes each of which determines an external act, so that a series of such acts take place. Or they are complex because the first act brings the organism under the influence of a new stimulus which causes the second act, and so forth. Such a series of instinctive actions is sometimes called a chain instinct.

Every chain instinct starts with a reflex stimulated from outside. The action which results brings the organism under the influence of an external force which stimulates a new reaction. Or the first reflex causes a physiological change which stimulates a new reaction. Thus a series of acts may become causally connected with each other. Such a series would not necessarily have utility. External selective forces are constantly at work eliminating the harmful and sometimes also those which are merely useless, and preserving the useful. In the case of the more complex of these chain instincts it seems almost incredible that so high a degree of adaptation could have been attained. In most of these cases the instincts have existed through thousands of generations, so that the selective forces have had sufficient time to accomplish their work of adaptation.

Instincts are often not at all obvious in human behavior, thus giving rise to the notion that man has few instincts. We have seen how an instinctive tendency is inhibited by becoming concentrated upon one object which thereafter serves as the only stimulus for it. Where instincts are numerous they may be inhibited and become apparently nonexistent by neutralizing each other because they are contradictory. The principal reason why instincts seem to disappear in the higher animals and especially in man is because the instinctive tendencies are being guided and influenced more and more by past experience and therefore by intelligence. While the instincts are still at work furnishing the primary motive power, they become more

[3] See my *Science of Human Behavior*, Chapter XI entitled "The Nature of Instinct."

or less hidden from observation.

There are certain general, inborn modes of behavior which are often regarded as distinct instincts, but which cannot be regarded as such because at different times they involve different parts of the nervous system. Inasmuch as an instinct has a specific neural mechanism which is utilized every time the instinctive action takes place, a mode of behavior which involves at different times entirely different parts of the nervous system cannot be regarded as an instinct. Among these general innate or partly innate tendencies which are often mistaken for instincts are imitation, suggestion, sympathy, play, emulation, workmanship, gregariousness and habit.

Imitation cannot be regarded as an instinct, because it involves very different modes of behavior. Furthermore, there are certain kinds of imitation which are not caused by an inborn tendency, such as rational imitation which results from experience and intelligence. Suggestion is sometimes called a general innate tendency. If it is meant to imply that it is an external form of behavior, it is an erroneous definition. Suggestion is an internal process, but leads to an external mode of behavior in the form of imitation. Sympathy also is an internal process which leads to the stimulation in one person of an emotion already experienced by another. Like suggestion it has been mistakenly called a general innate tendency in the sense of being an external mode of action. Sympathetic action is no more than imitative behavior which is accompanied by sympathetically induced emotion.

Playful activities are widespread among animals. Play may be defined as the expenditure of energy for pleasure without being directed toward any useful purpose. At any rate, no useful purpose is the immediate object of play, though it may serve a useful end in the long run. Playful activities are most common among the young, who spend most or all of their time in play. Different kinds of activity are involved in play, so that play is not a distinct instinct. Inborn physiological traits require that surplus energy be expended. The instincts furnish well-worn grooves into which the expenditure of this energy may fall, so that playful activities often are instinctive activities as well.

Emulation or rivalry, which is sometimes regarded as an instinct, stands in much the same relationship to instinct as imitation or play. It does not involve a single integrated series of reflexes. In the course of emulation many kinds of behavior may be used. In fact, emulation is to a larger extent imitation.

The tendency to work involves many kinds of activity. Work may be defined as effort devoted to the production of things of value for the preservation and welfare of the organism. Like play, it is due in part to the physiological need of the organism to expend energy. It is also in large part due to the needs of subsistence. In human society this takes the form of economic pressure in the struggle for existence. The so-called instinct of workmanship is very complex in its character and cause, and is far from being a distinct instinct.

Some of the higher species are gregarious even when there is no occasion for association other than an innate tendency toward gregariousness. It is often assumed that there is a gregarious instinct. If instinct is conceived as an integrated series of reflexes, it is hardly conceivable that there is a specific series of reflexes which causes association. However, the primary causes of association are instincts in so far as association comes about through subjective or internal causes, especially the sexual and parental instincts. Habit also has much to do with gregariousness.

It is a universal organic tendency to perform an act more readily upon repetition. After ease has been attained and the same sort of invariable response to given stimuli manifested by instincts, it is called a habit. Before the habit is formed it was a reflex action and may have been instinctive. A habit may arise directly out of an instinct. It may be an instinctive mode of action which has become reinforced through repetition. Or it may be a combination of instinctive modes of action. The tendency to form habits is inborn, while the modes of action which are to become habitual are at first inborn, though they may vary in the course of habitual use. So that habits are always based upon reflexes and sometimes upon instincts, but habits are not merely reflexes or instincts.

Chapter V

The Directives of Behavior

THE phrase "intelligent behavior" is often used as if intelligence is a form of behavior, or an organ which determines that type of behavior. Intelligence is not an organ, but has the same relation to intelligent behavior as instinct has to instinctive behavior. Such behavior always arises out of experience. No organism lacking experience can display intelligent behavior. Intelligence is not inherited, but is acquired by the individual. Intelligent behavior is not an inherited form of reaction, though it is based upon and consists largely of inherited modes of behavior. It is a modification of an inherited mode of behavior due to experience, and is usually more varied than inherited modes of behavior.

Intelligent behavior consists of tropismatic, reflex, and instinctive actions which have been combined as a result of experience so as to constitute new forms of behavior. An organism must be amenable to the effects of its experience in order to develop these new forms of behavior. In other words, it must possess a good deal of plasticity, and in this plasticity is the structural basis for intelligent behavior. Organs are required which are sensitive to the effects of experience, and which are specially devoted to combining and rearranging the inherited modes of behavior. The principal organ devoted to this function is the unspecialized correlation tissue or gray matter of the nervous system, which is mainly in the association areas of the cerebral cortex of the brain.

The demarcation between intelligent and unintelligent behavior, between conscious and unconscious behavior, between psychic or mental and non-psychic behavior is at least as high in the organic scale as the line between the animals without and those with a central nervous system. An animal without a central nervous system is incapable of intelligent and conscious behavior and cannot manifest psychic phenomena. Such behavior and phenomena may appear as the central nervous system develops. This demarcation may be still higher in the organic scale.

The inherited reactions are more or less fixed. The parts of the nervous system which determine these reactions are already specialized for these purposes at birth. Intelligence is in a more or less direct ratio to the amount of gray matter in proportion to the total size of the body. The extent of the gray matter is determined mainly by the size of the cerebrum and by the number of convolutions in the cerebral cortex. In this unspecialized nerve tissue association paths become established which correlate the inherited modes of action into new combinations which constitute new forms of behavior which may be called intelligent.

Every animal begins its life with an equipment of inherited reactions. The forces of the environment are continually acting upon it, causing these reactions to vary by reinforcing some of them and by inhibiting others. These variations are not necessarily intelligent. The cumulative effect of some of these forces may cause changes in structure which will give rise to permanent changes in behavior. The lower animals do not possess a special mechanism for recording the effects of past stimuli in such a fashion that these effects will be more or less accurately reproduced by future stimuli which may or may not be similar to the original stimuli. Such a mechanism appears in the form of the central nervous system. As soon as this system begins to develop, intelligent behavior becomes a possibility.

The central nervous system is specially adapted for recording the effects of stimuli. The association areas of the cerebrum serve as an organ of memory. A rudimentary form of memory exists without this organ because of the plasticity of all organic matter. This organ retains a more clear-cut and well-defined record of these effects. If it could accomplish no more, intelligence would not be possible because these effects would be reproduced under the same circumstances as when first produced. However, within the central nervous system these effects are connected with sense organs other than those from which they originated and with motor organs other than those through which they were originally discharged. The kind of memory based upon the central nervous system is called associative memory. These memories do not stand alone but become intimately interrelated in a complex fashion. *In an animal with a well-developed central nervous system which has acquired a large and varied store of memories, the behavior which results from a certain stimulus may be vastly different from the purely inherited reaction which would respond to that stimulus if these memories were not present to vary and complicate the behavior. Such behavior is intelligent, and the capacity for such variations in behavior constitutes intelligence.*

52

The inherited modes of reaction must be relatively modifiable before intelligence can make its appearance. Simple reflexes or compound reflexes which are not instincts cannot furnish a basis for intelligent behavior. A sufficient number of readily modifiable instincts must be present before there can be intelligent variations in behavior. As indicated in the preceding chapter, an instinct is an integration and correlation of reflexes by the central nervous system. This kind of integration and correlation is inherited and is performed by the sensory and motor parts of the central nervous system which are specialized for these purposes. When a certain number of these instincts which are relatively modifiable have evolved, and when the central nervous system has developed parts which are not specialized at birth so that they can serve as association areas, intelligence may make its appearance.

Intelligence has appeared along several divergent lines of evolution whenever the requisite conditions have been fulfilled. In one sense all organisms are capable of learning. Owing to the plasticity of organic matter the behavior of all organisms may be modified by external forces. In order to give the term utility in distinguishing between different types of behavior, I shall limit learning to the modifications in the behavior of an animal capable of forming images when it retains a memory of the experiences through which it passes. It is sometimes contended that all organisms have memory because of the plasticity of organic matter. It is preferable to restrict this term to the ability to reproduce or reconstruct in some fashion an experience through which the animal has passed. This does not result from the undifferentiated plasticity of protoplasm which cannot reproduce the experience through which it has passed, though it may be modified by it. A special organ of memory is needed and this organ is in the association areas of the cerebrum. Impressions received through the senses are recorded upon these areas. When these areas are stimulated, the sensations will be revived partially or fully without the original causes of the sensation being present.

The process of learning consists in part in forming images of sensations experienced. These images influence behavior. If an image is of a sensation which gave rise to an act, it will be connected with the motor impulse which went to the motor organ. When this image is stimulated in the future, it may in turn stimulate the motor center, which will send an impulse to the motor organ and thus give rise to the same act. This is ideo-motor action, which follows upon an image and not upon a stimulus from without, as in the case of sensori-motor action. Only animals that can form images are capable of ideo-motor action.

The act connected with an image will not necessarily follow when that image is aroused. That will depend in part upon what has been the result of that act in the past. If the effect has been pleasing, the path from the motor center to the end organ will be reinforced, so that the act is more likely to be repeated. If the effect has been unpleasant, the pathway to the end organ will be weakened or blocked. Painful and pleasurable phenomena are peculiar to nervous matter, and are apparently never experienced apart from such matter. Presumably they arise out of the states of the neurones involved. If the effect of an act upon the neurones is harmful, the pathway to the end organ which caused that act will probably be weakened so that the act is not so likely to take place again. This weakening probably results from a weakening of the synapses or junctures between the neurones along the pathway to the end organ.

The process of learning therefore includes the formation of images and the strengthening and weakening of associations. These two factors introduce much uncertainty into the behavior of an animal. An observer cannot know what images are recorded in its brain. Nor can he know all the pleasurable and painful feelings it has experienced and the associations which have been established by them.

The formation of images and variation in the strength of associations are probably the only factors which play a part in the intelligent behavior of all but a few of the higher animals. In these few animals these processes become more complex, thus making the behavior all the less predictable. As the association areas increase in extent and the radiation of association fibers becomes more refined, these images become related to each other in a complicated fashion. Thus arise the higher forms of intelligence. The first is the idea which is little if anything more than an image, though sometimes an idea may be formed by the association of several images together. Ideas may be held by animals which have not yet attained a high grade of intelligence.

An idea stimulates another idea and that one still another, and so on, by means of the connections between their nerve centers in the associative tracts of the cerebrum. Thinking is the name for the mental process which is the result from or the concomitant of this cerebral process. In order to have thought, a large supply of ideas which are interrelated is necessary. A more complex form is conceptual thought in which concepts constitute the flow of thinking. A concept is a generalized image of a trait common to a number of images. Introspection on the part of most persons reveals images as the basis of all ideas and of all thinking. These images may be visual, auditory, tactile, kinesthetic, olfactory, or gustatory, according to the nature of the sensations they reproduce. The introspective method

54

is helpful at this point because it throws light upon the origin and nature of these phenomena.

A large store of ideas is necessary for the appearance of reason. In the flow of thought from one idea to another, similarities and differences between them are recognized or other relations established which constitute reasoning. It is often asserted that reason is peculiar to man. If this means that there is no continuity in mental development from the lower animals to mankind, reason cannot be regarded as a human peculiarity. If it means that no other animal has a sufficiently large store of ideas to furnish material for reason, it is conceivable that reason is to that extent peculiar to mankind.

Man's intelligence is due in part to the superiority of certain of his senses in acquainting him with his environment, inasmuch as they are the functions of distance-receptors. It is due in part to his action-system, which enables him to perform an unusually varied number of movements. It is due also to his extended association areas, which furnish the basis for an unusually extensive and complicated system of connections between sensations, images, and movements. The monkeys and anthropoid apes mark the development and the transition along all of these lines from the lower mammals to mankind.[1]

Sensations are the impressions made upon the nervous system by stimuli received through the sense organs. If these sense impressions do not reach the higher nerve centers so that the acts which result from them are sensori-motor, they cannot be conscious in the meaning that the receptive organism is aware of them. If they reach the higher nerve centers, they may become conscious, provided they are connected in the association areas with the images of the same or of other sensations. However, this alone may not be sufficient to render sensations conscious. If other sensations are being received at the same time, it may be necessary for attention to be centered upon these sensations in order to make them conscious. By attention I mean that the nervous system responds to certain sensations to the total or partial exclusion of other sensations which are being received at the same time. This may be due to the fact that certain sensations are more powerful than the others being received simultaneously. Or it may be due to the fact that these sensations, though weak as compared with the other sensations being received at the same time, are connected with images which are sufficiently numerous or sufficiently vivid as to monopolize wholly or in part the capacity of the nervous system for responding.

Feeling is an important constituent of that sort of awareness which is ordinarily called consciousness. It is probable that all feelings are either pleasurable or painful. Feelings which seem to belong to

[1] See my *Science of Human Behavior*, New York, 1913, Chapter XIV entitled "The Nature of Intelligence."

neither of these classes appear so because they are close to the border-line between the two. Feeling therefore consists of or arises in large part if not entirely out of pleasurable or painful sensations.

As pleasure and pain are never experienced apart from the nervous system, there is reason to believe that their mechanism is neural. In the higher animals which display these affective traits they can never be stimulated in those parts of the organism which do not contain nerve fibers, such as the hair, the nails, and the bony parts of the body. Furthermore, there is evidence that the species without a well developed central nervous system do not display pain and pleasure, or display them only to a slight extent if we are to assume that the avoidance of harmful objects and experiences is due to painful sensations.

Pleasure and pain can be observed directly only by means of introspection, in which respect they are like all other mental and psychic phenomena. Such phenomena in others can be predicated only by inference. Behavior in others which is in us the accompaniment of certain mental and psychic phenomena suggests that these others are experiencing the same mental and psychic phenomena. In this fashion can be judged the manifestation of pain and pleasure by other species. If when injured they do not manifest any reactions at all, or do not manifest the sort of reactions given by us when pained, there is reason to believe that they are incapable of experiencing painful feelings. The same applies *pari passu* to pleasurable feelings. The reactions in other species may be very different from those in man. In many cases which have been studied among the lower animals and even among the lower vertebrates, either no reactions were given when injury was inflicted, or else the reactions were of such a nature as could be explained on other grounds than as manifestations of painful feelings. The warm-blooded vertebrates, and especially the mammals, give unmistakable indications of painful and pleasurable feelings. These are movements of drawing away from painful stimuli and approaching pleasurable stimuli, the utterance of cries and other sounds, the expression of the face in some of the higher animals, etc.

Feeling is apparently limited to animals with a well developed central nervous system. Feelings are certain kinds of sensations, or, at any rate, aspects of them. Sensations constitute the basis for feelings just as they furnish the raw material for consciousness, and as, indeed, they are the basis for all psychic phenomena.

Painful feelings tend to inhibit the acts which give rise to them or to draw the animal away from the stimuli which cause them, while pleasurable feelings tend to reinforce the acts which give rise to them and to draw the animal toward the stimuli which cause them. Feelings are therefore significant both as factors in the determination of behavior and as forming a part of the contents of consciousness.

The emotions accompany certain tendencies to action, and are the by-products, so to speak, of these tendencies. A simple reflex action could not be accompanied by an emotion because the organic processes involved are not sufficiently complex. The instincts are these tendencies to action which are accompanied by emotions.

The part played by the viscera in the emotions is illustrated in the heightened beating of the heart in anger and other emotions, the contraction of the blood vessels causing a blanching of the skin in fear, the expansion of the blood vessels causing a flushing in shame, the stimulation of the bowels in fear, etc. The vascular system also plays a part. An illustration may be the secretion of the lachrymal gland in grief. In both cases the process is somewhat as follows. Almost all the stimuli to action in the higher animals come through the nervous system. If action takes place, there is involved the cooperation of the muscles, viscera, vascular system, etc. The movements of these parts of the organism react upon the nervous system to a certain extent, and the emotions appear to be some, if not all, of the results from this reaction. The reaction is principally upon the sympathetic system, which furnishes most of the nerves for the visceral and vascular systems. The emotions are the feelings which are aroused in the nervous system by these internal processes, and the visceral, vascular including vasomotor, and muscular movements which accompany the emotions are their causes.

The stimuli for the sensations out of which emotions arise may not come from outside. They are none the less sensations. Many of them are kinesthetic sensations which are caused by movements of the muscles. Moreover, they are sensations with a distinctly affective character. That is to say, all of them are either pleasurable or painful. They are usually more powerful than ordinary feelings and accompany and reinforce definite types of behavior, so that they play a larger part than ordinary feelings in the determination of behavior. They seem to impart an unusually rich "feeling-tone" to consciousness. They may have a longer history than any other element in consciousness, because they are to a large extent contemporaneous with the instincts. If so, they form the earliest group of feelings. They do not constitute consciousness when they stand alone, but when consciousness has made its appearance they add a good deal to its character. In fact, the emotional quality of a state of consciousness colors to a considerable degree and sometimes greatly awareness both of self and of the external world, so that it influences not only behavior but also the intellectual elements in consciousness, such as ideas and concepts.

Watson, the founder of the behaviorist school of psychology, has denied the validity of the concepts of instinct and emotion. In his book on behaviorism he said of instinct that "even from the earliest movement we find habit factors present—present even in many acts so apparently simple that we used to call them physiological reflexes." Concerning emotion he asserted that "there is just as little evidence for a wholesale inheritance of those complicated patterns of response commonly called instinctive." And yet he recognized that in the youngest human infants, loud sounds and removal of support cause fear; holding or restraint causes rage; and stroking of the skin, especially in the erogenous zones, causes love.[2]

As I have already indicated, the experience of the individual influences his instinctive tendencies and emotional states. The formation of habits results in the strengthening, weakening and combining of instinctive tendencies. However much the original instincts and emotions may become overlaid by cerebral associations and habitual tendencies, they remain as the innate basis for the acquired traits. It is often not easy and sometimes impossible to disentangle the inherited from the acquired traits in impulsive tendencies and affective states. But no amount of conditioning in the course of the lifetime of the individual can obliterate the innate basis, so that its presence must always be assumed. While consciousness conceived as an awareness of the self and of the external world is acquired, its range and limits are determined in the first instance by the inborn instinctive tendencies, affective states, and inherited mechanism for the awakening of intelligence by means of memory and learning.

The highest plane of consciousness is attained in self-consciousness or the awareness of personality. Consciousness of the self is based upon the more or less permanent psychic element. There are sensations and feelings which often recur and ideas which are more or less persistent. Self-consciousness could not arise in an animal whose feelings and ideas were constantly changing so that its psychic equipment is almost entirely transformed within a short interval of time. With a more or less permanent equipment of psychic elements, self-consciousness appears as a result of a process of integration which gives unity to these diverse elements. This integration takes place by means of the same mechanism which performs the other types of integration which have been described, namely, the central nervous system and in particular the association areas of the brain. The kind of integration involved in personality is, however, different from that

[2] J. B. Watson, *Behaviorism*, New York, 1925, pp. 104, 129. See also his *Psychology from the Standpoint of a Behaviorist*, Philadelphia, 1919, 3rd edit., 1929; *The Psychological Care of Infant and Child*, New York, 1928.

involved in instinct in that it is not inherited but is acquired in the course of the lifetime of the individual.

Self-consciousness cannot develop very far until it becomes an idea. Its evolution as an idea has been principally if not entirely among men. To trace fully the development of the idea of personality would be to trace the whole course of human, mental and social evolution. Personality could hardly be conceived by an individual living in isolation. This idea grows out of the observation of the similarities and differences between the observer and other individuals. It is in large part a social product. Language played an important part because it gave to the idea of personality definiteness and clearness just as it has done so to all ideas.

Self-consciousness is not a distinct entity, as is indicated by the phenomenon of so-called "multiple" personality. Every personality is to a certain extent multiple. Each individual possesses several sets of feelings and ideas, each of which is stimulated by an appropriate environment or by suitable physiological conditions. Ordinarily these sets are not separated from each other to such a degree that the individual fails to recognize them as belonging to himself. Under pathological conditions, however, the separation between them may become so great that the individual does not recognize them as his own, so that the phenomena of multiple personality and of mental alienation arise. In the idiot and imbecile prenatal cerebral defects render him incapable of becoming more than faintly aware of himself as a personality.

The effect of drugs and narcotics in disintegrating the consciousness of self temporarily and sometimes permanently is another indication that it is not a distinct and permanent entity. The way in which the awareness of personal identity is decreased and sometimes changed in dreams is also an indication of this fact. These phenomena cannot be explained on the ground of a subconscious self. To do so would be to assume the existence of two distinct, permanent entities, whereas there is no reason to believe in the existence of even one permanent entity such as an immortal soul. Awareness of personal identity is at most an ephemeral phenomenon which can be readily weakened or destroyed even short of death. Such phenomena can be explained only on the assumption of a unification of the contents of consciousness by the integrative mechanism of the central nervous system. This unification can, however, be destroyed in varying degrees or can be disintegrated into several smaller unities.

The will or volition is usually regarded as an expression of the self. Volition manifests itself when the idea of an act, which arises out of its memory images and other contents of the memory influence

59

behavior. A stimulus to a certain action is received and the act is performed unless the contents of the memory consciously inhibit it, in which case volition has been exercised. If the inhibition is unconscious as the result of habit, it is not volitional. Or the idea of a certain act may be aroused and serve as a stimulus to its performance, in which case a volitional act has been performed. In each case of a volitional act the stimuli to action are either inhibited or reinforced by the contents of the memory and other traits of the individual, and the process is accompanied by consciousness, so that there often arises the illusion that the act is determined entirely by the self, independent of external forces.

Consciousness cannot develop very far without the ideas which intelligence furnishes and which constitute an important part of its contents. But consciousness includes the feelings as well. It has sometimes been suggested that consciousness originated in the form of feeling. This may be putting its temporal origin too far back. It is possible that it did not appear until after the origin of intelligence. It may even be more accurate not to recognize consciousness until after the idea of the self has made its appearance. At whichever point of time is placed the origin of consciousness, it contains more than the ideas which belong to intelligence, so that the two are not entirely identical.

Some psychologists have considered the ability to learn as the criterion of consciousness. This depends upon the answer to the question as to when consciousness originated. If consciousness appeared before intelligence, the ability to learn would not always be a test of consciousness. If the two appeared at the same time, it would always serve as a test. If consciousness appeared after intelligence, a very slight ability to learn would not necessarily indicate the presence of consciousness. However, in most cases and for all practical purposes the ability to learn serves as a criterion of consciousness, because intelligence and consciousness accompany each other all the time, with the possible exception of the earliest stages of the one or the other. The same is true of mutable behavior as a criterion of consciousness.

Even in complex nervous systems there are many responses which are unconscious, because the pathway from stimulus to response is so firmly fixed that there is little likelihood of variation. It is doubtful if even in man the number of conscious actions ever exceeds the number of unconscious ones. In the first place, there are many inherited modes of reaction which never become varied in the course of individual experience. This is especially true of the reactions controlled by the lower nerve centers. In the second place, there are numerous acts which were at first conscious because they involved individual adjustment to the environment, but which have become habitual, that is to say, the pathway has become so firmly fixed that variation is not likely to take place, so that the acts have become unconscious. This transition from conscious to unconscious behavior has led some psychologists to think that all behavior was at first conscious, which is obviously fallacious. Consciousness fluctuates as if in accordance with the law of parsimony. It appears when needed but disappears when no longer necessary.

Consciousness exists whenever behavior is influenced by ideas or by feelings. This statement still leaves the conception of consciousness rather vague. It could be made more precise by limiting consciousness to self-consciousness, and there are several reasons for doing so. While it is impossible to determine just when the sense of personality first made its appearance, we can probably come nearer to it than we can to determining when consciousness in general first made its appearance. Furthermore, the awareness of personality marks off a stage in mental evolution more definitely than does consciousness in general.

The meaning of words is determined in the long run by usage. At present consciousness has the wider and vaguer meaning. For scientific reasons it would be preferable to limit it to the awareness of personality. Consciousness may be defined as a complex process made up of feelings and ideas which are unified by awareness of self or sense of personality. This awareness may begin as a vague feeling but becomes in course of time a clear-cut idea.[3]

Mind is usually regarded as including all of intelligence, feeling and consciousness. There have been many theories as to its nature. The most prevalent have been the theories of psycho-physical parallelism and of psycho-physical interactionism. The first theory regards mind as something super-phenomenal, if not supernatural, which for an unaccountable reason always accompanies certain material processes without, however, influencing these processes. The second regards mind as capable of causal interaction with the body. It assumes, like the parallelist theory, that mind accompanies certain bodily processes, but differs from it in assuming that mind influences these bodily processes and is influenced by them. Both of these theories regard mind as a distinct entity of a super-phenomenal if not supernatural sort. To assume the existence of such an entity is not a scientific theory, but the most speculative and improbable of hypotheses.

Mental processes are determined by minute and refined physiological processes which take place in certain parts of the central nervous system. While mind in its most general meaning is an inclu-

[3] See my *Science of Human Behavior*, Chapter XV entitled "Consciousness."

sive term for the phenomena subsumed under feeling, intelligence and consciousness, in its essential nature it is a stage in the determination of certain kinds of behavior. It is the step between the reception of a stimulus through a sense organ or otherwise and the discharge of an impulse to a motor organ which causes an external form of behavior. It manifests itself to the person experiencing it in the form of images, ideas, feelings, emotions, etc., while its presence is made known to an observer by means of certain kinds of variations in behavior. It may influence behavior so greatly as to change it almost completely from what the behavior would have been if the mental stage had not intervened.

The preceding discussion explains satisfactorily the so-called "power of mind over matter" and disposes of the alleged superiority of the psychic over the physical which are often regarded as mysterious characteristics of mind. These notions are widespread and hard to extirpate because they flatter the egocentric and anthropocentric prejudices of mankind. The quantitative disproportion between the presumptive cause and the apparent result in these cases of "the power of mind over matter" has led to the belief that mind is immensely superior in quality to matter and entirely different from it. Hence it is believed that a causo-mechanical explanation of mental and social phenomena is impossible. The preceding discussion has demonstrated that there is nothing exceptionally mysterious about this power, but that similar phenomena take place constantly in nature whenever a small amount of molecular or molar force releases a large amount of energy. This happens whenever a small amount of force in the form of heat is applied to a combustible such as dynamite and results in the dissipation of a large amount of energy. It has even been suggested that a process of radio-active change started in the elements might result in the disintegration of the earth. Fission of the atomic elements illustrates such a process.

The mind, therefore, works like the trigger of a gun or a button which releases an electric current which explodes a mass of nitroglycerin. The amount of energy involved in the mental process is wholly disproportionate to the amount displayed in the behavior which it influences and may even control. This does not prove that it is absolutely different qualitatively from other material processes.

It may be questioned as to whether knowledge of mind is purely subjective or partly objective. Many psychologists believe it is purely subjective, thus placing psychology upon an entirely introspective basis. Looked at from one point of view, this may seem to be true. Sensations, ideas, feelings, etc., as such, are experienced only by the subject. But the behavior which results from them may be observed by another, and the character of these psychic phenomena has to be described in large part in terms of behavior. Furthermore, scientific research has shown that these phenomena are determined by neural processes which may be observed. While the aspects which mental phenomena present to the subject are sensational and ideational, to the outside observer they are manifestations of potential and kinetic energy. The fact that some observers have been able to introspect their mental processes more effectively because of their knowledge of these neural processes indicates that there is an objective as well as a subjective source of knowledge concerning mind.

Chapter VI

The Integration of Behavior

HEREDITY and environment determine mental phenomena and behavior as they do all other organic phenomena. In the protozoa the environment may cause hereditary changes directly. In the metazoa this becomes less feasible as organs specialized for reproduction evolve. In all of the more complex organisms each generation is derived from the germ cells of its immediate ancestors. These germ cells apparently originate as ordinary somatic cells. In the genital organs they develop into cells which differ greatly from somatic cells and contain the bearers and determinants of the characteristic traits of the species. Thus a hereditary factor comes into existence which is in part independent of the environment.

The germ cell consists of a jelly-like substance called cytoplasm in which is the nucleus containing the chromosomes. In the chromosomes are the chromomeres which are microscopically visible as strings of minute particles. These chromomeres probably are the genes or ultimate determinants of the traits of the organism which develops from the fertilized egg cell. Genes usually are in pairs in which both members of the pair have the same function. The genes compose the genetic system of an individual or of a species. There is constant interaction between the genes and the cytoplasm.

The ground plan of an organism is laid down in the cytoplasm of an egg cell. The nucleus of the ovum pours its fluid into the cytoplasm and the ground plan appears. The genes are reduced by half. Then the egg cell is fertilized by the sperm cell which replaces the eliminated genes, thus restoring the full complement of genes for a given species. The genes derive their sustenance from the cytoplasm which constitutes their cellular environment. The outside environment influences the germ cell as a whole and the cytoplasm mainly through the kind of food which it supplies. Thus the outside environment has an indirect effect upon the genes and chromosomes. But the traits of the growing organism are primarily and predominantly

64

decided by these determinants which transmit the traits of its ancestors.

The hormones are secretions of the genital glands, adrenal, thyroid and parathyroid glands, the adrenal or suprarenal bodies, the pituitary body or hypophysis, the thymus gland, the pineal gland, and other ductless glands. From these glands they are absorbed into the blood and circulate throughout parts or all of the organism. As their name implies, these hormones have a stimulating or exciting effect upon physiological processes, some of them upon growth in particular. For example, the thymus gland situated in the lower part of the neck furnishes a secretion necessary for growth. It controls the development of the sex organs until puberty is attained and then has a tendency to atrophy. These secretions are, as it were, intermediate steps between the genes and the fully developed traits. That is to say, they carry on the work begun by the genes. Some of these hormones have been synthesized, such as adrenalin, thyroidin, and insulin or the pancreatic hormone. These synthetic products have been experimentally introduced into the circulation of the blood and their effects upon metabolism, growth, behavior, etc., observed and studied.

The number of chromosomes in the germ cells of certain species have been counted. In the human species there are forty-eight chromosomes forming twenty-four pairs. There is one pair which apparently determines the sex of the offspring. One-half of all human males have only one chromosome of this pair which is known as the X-chromosome. This chromosome goes to a female offspring whereas a male offspring always derives his X-chromosome from his mother. It contains many genes determining various traits. Owing to the fact that the X-chromosome is transferred back and forth from one sex to the other, the traits which it bears are in like fashion transferred from one sex to the other in succeeding generations.

In addition to the X-chromosome there is a rudimentary Y-chromosome whose functions are little known. The autosomes are the chromosomes other than the X- and the Y-chromosomes. The traits of the germinating organism in general are distributed according to the distribution of all of these chromosomes.

Another important factor in the mechanism of heredity is in the phenomena of dominance and recessiveness. Many traits are dominant as contrasted with other traits which are recessive. This may be true as to size, color, or shape. In each case of a contrasted pair the dominant trait recurs much more often than the recessive trait. In many lines of descent the recessive trait becomes eliminated while in relatively fewer lines of descent the dominant trait becomes eliminated. Whenever the dominant and the recessive traits of a given contrasted pair of traits are crossed, the recurrence and the elimination of these traits take place in these disproportionate ratios in the descendants, though in some cases a blending of traits may occur where such blending is feasible. Hence it is that the genes and chromosomes bearing the dominant traits are more potent for reproduction and recurrence than the genes and chromosomes bearing the recessive traits.

The rates of recurrence and elimination of certain contrasted pairs of traits have been calculated for various plant and animal species. They have been stated in the Mendelian laws of inheritance. Organic conditions and traits which are defective for a healthy and fully developed individual representing the more or less normal type of a given species are usually recessive.

It has been estimated that in mankind feeblemindedness exists to the extent of one-third of one per cent of the human population, and that 11 per cent of the feebleminded come from matings among the feebleminded themselves and 89 per cent from matings in the carrier group.[1] Exclusion of the feebleminded from mating would reduce feeblemindedness only 11 per cent and very little thereafter. It is difficult and usually impossible to recognize the normal carriers of the determinants of defects, that is to say, the normal individuals who carry latent in their germ cells the genes which determine these defects. If these defective genes latent in normal parents happen to come together, a feebleminded offspring will result from the mating. These defective genes cannot be detected so as to control the matings of their carriers.

The same holds true in varying degrees of other traits and of other types. The members of a family have more genes in common than individuals taken at random. But superior parents may produce inferior offspring by a recombination of genes and especially by a coincidence of the latent determinants of defective traits. Or by a similar combination of genes and coincidence of latent determinants of normal and superior traits, inferior parents may produce superior offspring. In no given mating can the traits of the offspring be foretold. This is illustrated by the many differences between the children of the same parents. Even in the case of dissimilar twins there may be and usually are great differences between the twins. Identical twins manifest most strikingly the power of heredity. Such twins probably germinate from the splitting of a fertilized egg cell. This accounts for the high degree of similarity which exists between them, because they have commenced their individual existences with the hereditary back-

---

[1] R. A. Fisher, *Elimination of Mental Defect, Journal of Heredity,* Vol. XVIII, 1927, pp. 529-31. See H. S. Jennings, *The Biological Basis of Human Nature,* New York, 1930.

ground of the same germ cell. Variations in development introduce some dissimilarity even during the intra-uterine period of growth.

The laws of inheritance are, therefore, the rules of the distribution of chromosomes and genes with the facts of the dominance and recessiveness of traits. Through the processes described by these laws of inheritance come into being not only individuals but also families, races, species, and wider organic groups characterized by hereditary likenesses. But heredity is not the sole factor. The environment is an ever present force and condition which existed long before the commencement of organic evolution brought the hereditary factor into play. Nor are these factors to be conceived as mutually exclusive, and therefore antagonistic to each other. On the contrary, heredity and environment are constantly acting upon each other. The origin, growth and traits of organisms are the joint product of this interaction of hereditary and environmental factors.

Race mixture may give rise to incompatibility of chromosomes which may result in a comparable incompatibility of structures and functions. Miscegenation may result in hybrid vigor or in sterility. It may give rise to harmonious combinations or to disharmonious combinations or lack of harmony in details.

New types may result from changes in organization or in materials. The number or structure of the chromosomes may change. Mutations in the genes have apparently been caused by exposure to the short wave-length radiations from radioactive substances in the earth's crust or from space, to heat or cold, to metallic salts, and to various other forces. Most of the mutated genes are recessive, thus restricting somewhat the power of mutation for permanent and widespread change. Numerous small mutations are, however, constantly occurring rather than a smaller number of large mutations or saltations. Upon these hybrid mixtures of older types as well as upon the new types the environment is constantly acting as a selective agent. Many of these are eliminated because unfitted to survive under the existing environmental conditions. A much smaller number survive because fitted for survival.

The alimentation secured from the environment is a powerful factor for strengthening or weakening the germ cells, and for stimulating or checking mutations. The genes are, on the whole, well protected against injurious substances. But poisons, such as alcohol, introduced into the organism act in many species as a selective factor. The poisons generated within an organism by a zymotic disease play a similar role.

In numerous ways the environment stimulates or inhibits mutations and hybridizations, and acts as a selective agent upon those

67

which come into existence. There is, however, no reason to believe that traits acquired by an organism can be transmitted by heredity. No well-authenticated case of such transmission has been observed. Furthermore, no mechanism has been discovered by means of which such transmission could take place. As we have seen, the only traits which can be transmitted by heredity are those determined and carried by the genes and chromosomes in the germ cells. Traits acquired by the organisms are in the form of changes in the somatic cells of the body, such as increased size of muscles, establishment of associations between nerve cells, and the like. They are not represented in the germ cells by determinants which can transmit them to the offspring. Acquired traits can affect the germ cells only indirectly in so far as they influence the environment of the germ cells and determine the survival or elimination of potential parents.

Habits and all cultural traits cannot be transmitted by heredity because they are acquired by the individual. The mechanisms which render mental traits possible are transmitted by heredity. Tropisms, reflex actions and instincts are certain to manifest themselves whenever the appropriate stimuli are applied and no inhibiting factors are present. And the same is true of the feelings and emotions. While the mechanism of intelligence is inherited, its manifestation in the individual is due to the acquisition of a large number of habits, such as the establishment of many neural associations, the accumulation of a large store of memories, and the like. The intelligence may be said to be in part inherited and in part acquired.

The two preceding chapters have discussed the dynamics and directives of behavior. Tropisms, reflex actions and instincts are dynamic factors directed by inherited mechanisms. Intelligence is a directive factor acquired by the organism by means of certain inherited organs. Feelings and emotions are more difficult to characterize. There has been much controversy as to whether they are dynamic or directive factors, or both or neither. There has been question as to whether the emotions constitute a distinct type of mental phenomena or are to be regarded as subsidiary or even integral parts of instincts.

In the preceding chapter we have seen that feelings are sensations of a pleasurable or painful character. It is possible that all sensations are of such a character, however slight the painful or pleasurable content may be in many sensations. We are not conscious of most of our sensations, so that we cannot be conscious of their pleasurable or painful character as individual sensations. The great mass of sensations may, however, become fused into a general state of consciousness which is predominantly pleasurable or painful.

In the first instance there is a consciousness of well-being and of happiness, in the second instance, of ill-being and of depression even when there are no acute pains. What pleasure and pain are in the last analysis it is difficult to say, because they are the most subjective of mental phenomena. We can only surmise that they have adaptive value because they indicate in the long run which sensations are beneficial or harmful to the organism. In their more pronounced forms they give objective indications of their presence through facial expressions, movements of the body, and certain physiological processes which can be observed.

Feelings are experienced when the organism is relatively quiescent. They then appear to have no relation with behavior. Even during the most quiescent state they are preparing the way for behavior by gradually accumulating or reinforcing an impulse to act and also determining in part the direction which that action is to take. Probably it is justifiable to assume that they are both dynamic and directive factors for behavior. Pleasurable feelings induce attempts to perpetuate them, while painful feelings arouse efforts to remove their causes.

Emotions are complicated states of feelings which are more or less directly connected with definite modes of behavior. Their neural basis and mechanism are in large part in the autonomic nervous system. This system is presumably so named because it controls the involuntary physiological processes, that is to say, those not directed and controlled by conscious volition. It includes the nerves which control the vascular or circulatory system, namely, the conveyance of fluids such as blood and lymph throughout the body. It also includes the nerves which control the vasomotor system of muscles which contract and dilate the walls of vessels such as the blood vessels. The most extensive portion of the autonomic system is the sympathetic nervous system which controls the viscera, in particular those of the abdominal region. The central neurons of the autonomic system are in the spinal cord and are, therefore, in the cerebro-spinal nervous system, thus connecting the two systems closely together.

The receptors of the autonomic system are mainly in the muscular and mucous lining of the viscera. Its efferent fibers give rise to contractions in the smooth or unstriped visceral muscles. There are twelve pairs of cranial nerves of which five constitute the cranial section of the autonomic system. These nerves serve the eyes, the salivary glands, the heart, the bronchial tubes, and the digestive system. The emotional responses involved are related to the satisfaction of hunger and thirst and are correlated with a general bodily tone which is pleasant.

The sympathetic section of the autonomic system includes eight cervical pairs of nerves, twelve thoracic pairs, and five lumbar pairs.[2] These nerves serve the sweat glands, the hair of the body, and the peripheral blood vessels, and many of them are connected with the internal organs, such as the heart, lungs, digestive, sexual and excretory organs. The functions which they perform which are of particular significance with reference to the emotions are to increase the action of the heart, to constrict the blood vessels, to inhibit the digestive processes by contracting the smooth muscles, and to check the flow of the digestive glands. The sympathetic nerves play an important part in the emotions of anger and of fear, and are likely to be associated with an unpleasant or painful organic tone.

The sacral section of the autonomic system includes five pairs of sacral nerves and the coccygeal pair. These nerves are connected with the sexual and excretory organs whose activities usually give rise to pleasant sensations. In this regard the sacral is similar to the cranial section and contrasted with the sympathetic section. The first two sections are to a certain extent opposed to the last one, because when the sympathetic nerves are in operation the cranial or sacral nerves are inhibited and *vice versa*. As already suggested, the cranial nerves set in operation the digestive organs while the sympathetic nerves check their activities. The cranial and sacral nerves function in a positive and pleasant fashion, while the sympathetic nerves function in a protective and unpleasant fashion.

There is, however, reason to believe that certain parts of the cerebro-spinal system also play an important part in the functioning of the emotions. On either side of the third ventricle and near the center of the brain is one of a pair of oblong masses of gray matter covered on their free surfaces with a layer of white matter. It is known as the optic thalamus because it receives stimuli from the retina of the eye. The two thalami receive stimuli from all parts of the body. In fact, all sensory stimuli pass through this organ on their

---

[2] There is difference of opinion among neurologists as to how many pairs of spinal nerves should be included in the sympathetic system. Sherrington limits it as follows: "The sympathetic is that part of the autonomic system which is connected with the spinal roots from the second thoracic to the second lumbar inclusive (man)." (C. S. Sherrington, *Encyclopaedia Britannica*, 14th edition, 1942, Vol. 21, p. 703.)

Hunter described the sympathetic system as follows: "The sympathetic system, which is intimately connected with the cerebro-spinal system, is composed of the following parts: (1) a chain of ganglia lying ventral to and on either side of the spinal cord; (2) three or four large masses of nerve tissue called plexuses lying in the body cavity and in close connection with the organs controlled; and (3) smaller ganglia scattered throughout the organism, in the eye-socket, in the thoracic cavity, on the walls of the heart, and elsewhere." (W. S. Hunter, *Human Behavior*, Chicago, 1928, pp. 159-62.)

way to the cerebral cortex with the exception of some of the olfactory stimuli. The thalamus correlates stimuli passing from the lower to the cerebral centers. Afferent stimuli from various parts of the body are thereby somewhat integrated before they reach the cortex. Between the thalamus and the cerebral cortex is the corpus striatum which also correlates and integrates afferent impulses. If a sensory impulse stimulates a motor center in or through one of the correlating organs, a reflex action takes place without involving the cortex.

Affective and emotional disturbances result from thalamic disease. Painful sensations are among the reactions of the thalamus. Unilateral thalamic lesions indicate that the expression of the emotions and the accompanying behavior are controlled in part by neural processes in the thalamus.[3] In fact, Cannon goes so far as to say that "the peculiar quality of the emotion is added to simple sensation when the thalamic processes are aroused."[4]

These facts as well as other facts to be adduced presently seem to contradict the James-Lange theory of the emotions.[5] According to this theory internal such as visceral behavior is the cause and the characteristic feature of emotion. These internal responses result from the stimuli for reflex and instinctive reactions and accompany or immediately follow those reactions. As James has said, "an emotion is a tendency to feel, and an instinct is a tendency to act characteristically when in the presence of a certain object in the environment." Both James and Lange were of the opinion that emotions are incidental results of these organic reactions. But James thought that they result from the effects of the organic reaction upon the viscera, while Lange thought that they result from the effects of the organic reaction upon the vascular and the vasomotor systems.

Cannon and his associates have carried on many experiments which indicate that during emotional excitement, as in fear or rage, and while pain caused by injury is being experienced, the adrenal glands are stimulated through the neural fibers of the sympathetic nervous system and secrete more adrenalin which is thrown into the blood. Among the results are that blood is driven from the viscera to the skeletal muscles thus increasing muscular efficiency, there is an increase of red corpuscles in the blood, more glycogen from the liver is converted into blood sugar, and the blood coagulates more rapidly. These bodily changes are useful because adrenalin is an antidote to

[3] See for example H. Head and G. Holmes "Sensory Disturbances from Cerebral Lesions," *Brain*, XXXIV, 1911, pp. 109 ff.

[4] W. B. Cannon, *Bodily Changes in Pain, Hunger, Fear and Rage* 2nd edition, New York, 1929, p. 369.

[5] C. Lange and W. James, *The Emotions*, reprinted from their original works in "Psychological Classics," Baltimore, 1922.

fatigue, sugar is a source of energy, rapid coagulation checks the loss of blood, etc. Thus pain immediately resulting from wounds inflicted upon the body and great emotional excitement have an energizing influence upon the organism.

Cannon believed that total separation of the viscera from the central nervous system does not alter emotional behavior, and that the same visceral changes occur in emotional and non-emotional states. He asserted that the viscera are relatively insensitive, and that visceral changes are too slow to cause emotional feeling. Some of his experiments seem to indicate that artificially induced visceral changes do not produce emotions. His general conclusion was that emotional expression results from the action of subcortical centers. As he stated in the above quotation, thalamic processes are a source of affective experiences.

Cannon's experiments demonstrate, however, that fear, rage, and injurious stimulation inhibit the normal contractions of the stomach and intestines, and check the salivary and gastric secretions. His experiments were concerned in particular with the combative emotions and painful stimulation, and not with the more pacific and pleasurable emotions, such as those relating to sex and those arising out of the gratification of various of the senses.

Crile propounded the theory that civilization restrains mankind from acting upon many natural impulses which express themselves in strong emotions. As he expressed it, "a phylogenetic fight is anger; a phylogenetic flight is fear; a phylogenetic copulation is sexual love." [6] It is often true that action relieves emotional states for reasons which will be discussed presently. Cannon's work indicates that these states are due in part to visceral and glandular preparations for vigorous acts by intensifying the appropriate organic processes. Restraint from action renders these preparations abortive and dams up, so to speak, these physiological processes. Some action is necessary in most cases to give rise to the initial emotional state. Furthermore, many emotional states are intense even when there is no restraint upon action. Crile's theory is far from being a comprehensive explanation of the emotions.

Emotions sometimes arise when no external action takes place. Darwin and Spencer attempted to explain these cases by the hypothesis that they are reminiscences of ancestral modes of behavior in response to certain stimuli where these modes of behavior have in the main disappeared. This hypothesis implies the transmission by heredity of acquired habits which is not tenable. Part of an instinctive tendency to a certain mode of action may disappear as a result of

[6] G. W. Crile, *The Origin and Nature of the Emotions*, Philadelphia, 1915, p. 76.

changes in the nervous system, so that the organic reaction to the appropriate stimulus would be only sufficient to give rise to the emotion but not to the external action. It is more likely that when an emotion is aroused without any outward act taking place it is due to an inhibitory force which checks the act but not the emotion. An acquired habit of self-control may restrain an individual from striking when a combative impulse is aroused, but cannot inhibit the rise of the emotion of anger which is accompanied by increased heart action, tense muscles, etc. Self-control may check an individual from fleeing from an object of danger, but cannot prevent the emotion of fear accompanied by a contraction of some of the blood vessels, trembling of the knees, etc. It sometimes happens that the emotion is strongest when the external act is inhibited, because action usually relieves the organic conditions which give rise to the emotion. This fact indicates how an emotion may reinforce and strengthen a tendency to an act in order to secure the relief which comes through action. It explains in part why emotions become powerful factors in the determination of behavior.

Experiments have been made which seem to contradict the theory that the emotions are aroused by the reaction of the viscera and other internal organs to external stimuli. Sherrington, by means of appropriate spinal and vagal transection in dogs, removed the sensations of the viscera and of all of the skin and muscles behind the shoulder, and destroyed the connection between the organs of consciousness and the whole of the circulatory apparatus of the body.[7] Such animals displayed the emotions of anger, joy, disgust, fear, etc., as much as before the operation, thereby indicating that these emotions can be aroused in the brain independently of the viscera, etc.

Certain psychologists denied that these experiments disproved the theory that emotions are caused by the reaction of the viscera and other organs on the ground that the mechanism for these emotions had already been developed in these animals so that the emotions could be aroused independently of the viscera, etc.[8] Sherrington replied by stating that one of the dogs was only nine weeks old when the operation took place, and yet this animal displayed disgust when offered dog's flesh to eat. He was of the opinion that it had not lived long enough for this emotion to become fixed in the brain so that it could

[7] C. S. Sherrington, *The Integrative Action of the Nervous System*, New Haven, 1906, pp. 255-68.

[8] See, for example, C. Lloyd Morgan, *Animal Behaviour*, 2nd edition, London, 1908, p. 92; J. R. Angell, *Psychology*, New York, 1908, p. 371, and *A Reconsideration of James's Theory of Emotion in the Light of Recent Criticisms*, in the *Psychological Review*, XXIII, 1916, pp. 251-61.

be aroused independently of visceral stimulation. As a result of these experiments, he was inclined to believe that emotions originate in the brain and not in the viscera.[9]

Sherrington cited as further evidence of his theory the decerebration experiments of Goltz who kept alive for many months a dog from whom the hemispheres of the brain had been removed.[10] During this time it gave no sign of fear, joy, affection, or sexual emotion, but it repeatedly expressed anger and displeasure both by gesture and by voice. This experiment seemed to indicate that a higher nervous organization is needed for the former emotions than for anger and displeasure. Sherrington thought that it furnished evidence "that emotion is primarily a cerebral reaction." This is not necessarily the case, because the brain is as necessary for emotion as a psychic phenomenon if the stimulus which gives rise to it comes from the viscera as it is if the emotion originates in the brain independent of the viscera. Probably no one who believes in the visceral or vascular origin of the emotions thinks that they are felt in these organs, but that all emotions are felt in the nervous system, and that as psychic phenomena most, if not all, emotions manifest themselves in the brain, *e.g.*, in the optic thalami.

More experiments must be made before we can know with certainty where emotions originate. It is probably safe to say that the viscera and other internal organs and the vascular including the vasomotor system are involved in emotional states as well as the nervous system. Sherrington recognized and accepted this point of view in the following words: "In view of these general considerations and of the above experiments, we may with James accept visceral and organic sensations and the memories and associations of them as reinforcing rather than initiating the psychosis. Organic and vascular reaction, though not the actual excitant of emotion, strengthen it." [11]

In their conception of emotion psychologists tend to regard it

---

[9] "We are forced back toward the likelihood that the visceral expression of emotion is *secondary* to the cerebral action occurring with the psychical state. There is a strong bond of union between emotion and muscular action. Emotion 'moves' us, hence the word itself. If developed in intensity, it impels toward vigorous movement. Every vigorous movement of the body, though its more obvious instrument be the skeletal musculature of the limbs and trunk, involves also the less noticeable cooperation of the viscera, especially of the circulatory and respiratory. The extra demand made upon the muscles that move the frame involves a heightened action of the nutrient organs which supply to the muscles the material for their energy. This increased action of the viscera is colligate with this activity of muscles. We should expect visceral action to occur along with the muscular expression of emotion. The close tie between visceral action and states of emotion need not therefore surprise us." (C. S. Sherrington, *op. cit.*).

[10] F. Goltz, "Der Hund ohne Grosshirn," in *Pflueger's Archiv*, Band LI, 1892.

[11] C. S. Sherrington, *op. cit.*, p. 305.

74

either as a passive mental state or as an impulse to action. In the first case emotion is not a dynamic but may be a directive factor. In the second case it is a dynamic but may or may not be a directive factor. The first attitude is represented by Bernard who said that emotion belongs to consciousness rather than to overt action or expression and is in the same category as feeling and thinking. He regarded feeling as the psychic correlate of neural dispositions in action, and thinking as the neuro-psychic counterpart or substitute for interrupted or inhibited overt action.[12]

The second attitude is stated in the following characterization of emotion which could be applied as well to many instinctive responses. "An emotional response, like any other, serves to adjust the individual to some stimulating condition; but it differs from other types of responses in that it involves a massive unpremeditated reaction of the entire body."[13] There is also a tendency, especially among the behaviorist psychologists, to merge emotions with instincts. As Hunter has expressed it: "There is little scientific justification for distinguishing emotional and instinctive behavior."[14] Watson has advocated that the term "activity stream" be substituted for James' "stream of consciousness," thus eliminating the concept of consciousness and of passive mental states.[15] Dunlap related emotions closely to habits. "An emotional state is a response. All responses, including emotional responses, are capable of becoming habitual."[16]

As I have already indicated, feeling is the most subjective of mental phenomena. While it is readily discernible through introspection, it is difficult to observe by objective methods. Painful sensations are the most easily localized. The nerve endings or receptors through which painful sensations can be received, sometimes called noci-ceptors, vary greatly in number and distribution in different parts of the body.[17] Pleasurable sensations are not so readily localized, and seem to be due more often to generalized and massive organic conditions. The

[12] L. L. Bernard, *Instinct*, New York, 1924, p. 455.

[13] M. and I. C. Sherman, *The Process of Human Behavior*, New York, 1929, p. 144. "What we call the emotions, therefore, are not present in the infant at birth, but develop, as a result of experience, as specific patterns of response." (p. 145.)

[14] W. S. Hunter, *op. cit.*, p. 203. "Instincts and emotions are forms of behavior controlled by co-ordinations of synapses in the nervous system." p. 215.

[15] J. B. Watson, *Behaviorism*, New York, 1925.

[16] Knight Dunlap, *Habits Their Making and Unmaking*, New York, 1932, p. 237.

[17] "Experimenters have estimated that the verbal response 'pain,' which by training has been conditioned to the stimulus of the pin-prick, can be aroused from some 2,000,000-4,000,000 spots on the body. About 500,000 spots can be stimulated by light contacts. An equal number are sensitive to a decrease in temperature; and some 30,000 call forth responses when stimulated by an increase of temperature." (W. S. Hunter, *op. cit.*, p. 233.)

emotions whether painful or pleasurable, are more or less generalized organic states.[18]

While it is not yet possible to formulate a definitive theory of pain and pleasure, of feeling and emotion, it is nevertheless possible to detect to a considerable extent the influence of these mental states upon behavior. This is all the more feasible to the degree in which it is legitimate to assimilate the emotions with the instincts.

The infant performs automatically from birth the acts involved in respiration, circulation, digestion, metabolism, and excretion. The mechanisms and processes are innate and unlearned with respect to hunger, thirst, sensitive zone reactions, withdrawal from painful stimuli, fear, rage, and to a certain extent sexual activity.[19] As I have stated in the preceding chapter, experiments made by Watson indicate that in the new-born child loud sounds and removal of support arouse fear, holding or restraint causes rage, and stroking of the skin, especially in the erogenous zones, gives rise to sexual feelings. He believed that all other expressions of emotion are due to associations which become established between these innate emotional responses and other stimuli, in other words, that they are conditioned emotional responses.

The main function of the nervous system is its integrative function, which in a sense includes all of its functions. I have defined instinct as an inherited combination of reflexes which have been integrated by the central nervous system. A few writers question the utility of the term "instinct" because it is made up of reflexes, as, for example, Pavlov. "Instincts and reflexes are alike the inevitable responses of the organism to internal and external stimuli, and therefore we have no need to call them by two different terms." [20] But reflexes are localized responses while instincts are usually responses of the organism as a whole. While there is no difference in kind, there is variation in degree of generality of response which justifies a distinction in terms.[21]

It must, however, always be remembered that reflexes shade al-

18 "We restrict the term 'feeling' to the apparently simpler 'some things felt,' such as pleasure, pain, excitement and strain; and we apply the term 'emotion' to the more complex things felt, such as anger, fear and sorrow. The distinction is obviously of a tentative sort, but it is worth while to observe it." (K. Dunlap, *op. cit.*, p. 238.)

19 Allport enumerates "six important classes of human prepotent reflexes," namely, (1) Starting and withdrawal, (2) Rejecting, (3) Struggling, (4) Hunger reactions, (5) Sensitive zone reactions, and (6) Sex reactions. (F H. Allport, *Social Psychology*, Boston, 1924, p. 50.) According to Allport these "prepotent reflexes" give rise to " prepotent habits." (p. 80.)

20 I. P. Pavlov, *Conditioned Reflexes*, Oxford, 1927, translated from the Russian, p. 11.

21 See, for example, L. L. Bernard, *Social Psychology and Adjustment Behavior,*

most imperceptibly into instincts and that no sharp line of division can be drawn between them. All the reflexes which we are able to differentiate are compound, and it is doubtful if there are any simple reflexes in the higher organisms. With regard to many compound reflexes it is difficult to decide whether or not they involve the whole organism to a sufficient degree to call them instincts. However, this is a question of terminology which arises constantly throughout scientific research and thinking, because there are, so far as we can discern, no absolute distinctions in the universe.

The principal danger involved in the use of the term "instinct" is that it is often applied to responses which are only in part inherited and which are mingled with conditioned reflexes or habits and influenced by intelligence. This is particularly true of the delayed instincts which are almost certain to be combined with habits which have already been acquired. Practically all of the instincts relating to sex and reproduction are of this nature, because they do not appear in the earliest infancy but later in life. This is true also of the earliest instincts, such as those relating to eating, which soon become conditioned and therefore modified in their mode of expression.[22] It is difficult and often impossible to segregate instinctive responses in their pristine innate purity, because they are likely to be mingled with acquired traits. Nevertheless we are justified in assuming that the innate reflex and instinctive tendencies are at the basis of organic behavior, if for no other reason because broad likenesses appear between individuals and groups of the same or allied species where no limitation or learning could have taken place. In every species the sexes come together and indulge in characteristic acts. The offspring arouse characteristic reactions in the parent organisms. Characteristic hunting and fighting responses manifest themselves without previous experience. Hence there is some justification for speaking of sexual, parental, hunting, fighting, etc., instincts. It must be remembered that in any particular instance acquired factors are likely to be involved.[23]

in the *American Journal of Sociology*, July, 1932, Vol. XXXVIII, No. 1. "The behaviorist classifies response or behavior patterns as 'random movements,' 'reflexes,' 'instincts,' 'habits,' and 'tropisms,' The first two of these are primarily local responses; the third and fourth may be either local or general, but tend to be general; and the fifth is necessarily a response of the organism entire." (p. 3.)

See also W. S. Hunter, *op. cit.*, "An instinct is an inherited co-ordination of reflexes, i.e., a co-ordination which is predominantly unlearned." (p. 182.)

[22] Dunlap at first insisted that instincts are habits, but later admitted that there must be "a certain initial equipment of unlearned responses." (K. Dunlap, *op. cit.*, p. 38.)

[23] Pavlov criticized the broad use of the term instinct, but apparently primarily because he preferred to use the term reflex: "Their classification under such headings as 'alimentary,' 'defensive,' 'sexual,' 'parental,' and 'social' instincts is thoroughly

The integration attained through compound reflexes and instincts is not sufficient because of the variability of the environment. Owing to this variability no two situations are exactly alike and often very different. The organism learns to adjust itself to the situations in which it finds itself and the inherited responses are modified accordingly. Through repeated adjustments there arise habits, and the ability to make these adjustments which are modifications of inherited modes of response constitutes intelligence.

Feelings and emotions are the internal correlates and concomitants of external modes of behavior. After being experienced they condition future behavior because of their pleasurable or painful character. In other words, stimuli which have caused painful affective states are almost certain to be avoided, while stimuli which have given rise to pleasurable affective states are likely to be sought or at least not avoided. In this fashion feelings and emotions serve as selective factors and thus become directives of behavior.

The question is often raised as to whether human behavior, social phenomena and culture are predominantly instinctive, emotional or intelligent in their character. All three theories have been advocated. For example, a book by a clergyman entitled "Emotion as the Basis of Civilization" gives no indication whatsoever as to the nature of emotion. Such books are misleading and worse than useless. In a book on social psychology the author stated that he formerly adhered to an intellectualistic theory of cultural phenomena, but then concluded that they are primarily emotional in their character. Unilateral theories are to be found in scientific as well as unscientific works.

The preceding discussion has demonstrated that the original factors in all animal behavior are the compound reflexes, instincts, prepotent reflexes, or whatever we choose to call the inherited drives or impulses to action. Closely interwoven with these inherited impulses are the feelings and emotions. Inasmuch as the autonomic system is one of the oldest divisions of the nervous system, some writers have thought that the feelings and emotions are coeval with if indeed they do not antedate the instincts. It is possible that the autonomic system was the original seat of the instincts before the cerebrospinal system developed. This consideration alone would not lend support to the notion that these affective traits are older than the instincts. Whether or not they are as old is a question of academic importance for our purpose. In all probability their evolution was in the main contemporaneous. The emotions at times apparently reinforce inherited impulses to action, they often condition them and

inadequate. Under each of these heads is assembled often a large number of individual reflexes." (I. P. Pavlov, *op. cit.*, p. 11.)

78

by serving as selective agents they play an important part in the building up of habits.

While the instincts and emotions continue with unabated force to furnish the fundamental drives for human behavior, the intelligence plays an ever increasing role in directing it. As the following chapters will show, the manufacture and use of tools, the evolution of language, and every other phase of culture are due immediately and directly to the application of intelligence. A vast number of ideas influence human behavior which play no part whatsoever in the behavior of other animals. In so far as culture can be attributed to any one aspect of the mind, it is the characteristic product of the intellect.[24]

[24] See my *Science of Human Behavior*, New York, 1913; Chapter XVI entitled "The Nature of Mind."

Chapter VII

The Threshold of Cultural Evolution

WHILE the vast majority of animal species are not gregarious, social phenomena are widely though sparsely distributed in the organic world. Apart from mankind, however, there is scarcely a rudimentary trace of culture throughout the animal world. With only minor exceptions no animal other than man makes or even uses tools, wears clothing and ornaments, constructs buildings, ships, roads, etc., invents methods of exploiting and slaughtering its congeners, and communicates by means of language. No other animal organizes political and economic institutions, designs works of art, holds religious beliefs, formulates and is influenced by ethical ideas, carries on warfare, and devises scientific or any other kind of explanations of things. Hence it is that while social behavior and life in association are widespread though rather infrequent organic traits, culture is an almost exclusively human phenomenon.

Several writers on the differences between social and cultural phenomena have asserted that the former are organic, hereditary and precultural, and the latter super-organic, traditionally accumulative and independent of organic changes.[1] The distinction postulated between the organic and the super-organic is so tenuous that its utility is questionable. All so-called super-organic phenomena have an organic basis and are organically determined in the last analysis. Culture cannot, therefore, be entirely independent of organic changes. Slight organic changes may have no effect upon culture. It was a long series of organic changes which produced the humanoid animal cap-

---

[1] See, for example, B. J. Stern, *Concerning the Distinction between the Social and the Cultural*, in *Social Forces*, Vol. VIII, No. 2, December, 1929, pp. 264-71.

Among the writers who have emphasized the alleged distinction between the organic and the "super-organic" are A. L. Kroeber, *The Superorganic*, in the *American Anthropologist*, Vol. XIX, No. 2, April-June, 1917, revised and published as a monograph at Hanover, N. H., 1927; and W. F. Ogburn, *Social Change*, New York, 1922; revised edition 1951.

able of creating, acquiring and transmitting culture. It is conceivable that organic changes in the future may deprive man of this capacity, or may change greatly the character of his culture. Mankind may, indeed, destroy this culture by nuclear warfare without any extensive human organic changes taking place.

Social traits are to a large extent hereditary. The most striking example is among the social insects whose life span is annual or seasonal. Each year all of the individuals perish. A new generation appears the following year from the eggs. Or only a queen female survives from each group to reconstitute a new group. Each group reproduces the social phenomena of its ancestors with whom it had had no relations other than that of biological descent. Social traits may also vary independently of hereditary factors. Environmental and climatic factors increase or decrease social phenomena. Among men cultural factors have had a marked effect upon social traits without corresponding organic variations.

The unquestionable distinction between social and cultural phenomena is that culture is always traditionally accumulative and socially transmissible, whereas social traits are in part and sometimes entirely transmissible by heredity. Inasmuch as culture is only socially transmissible, social life is essential for its survival. In other words, culture is imbedded in and conditioned by social life. A culture could not be developed and transmitted by an isolated individual independent of his congeners. But the social is not dependent upon the cultural. Most of the social phenomena of the organic world exist independent of and apart from culture. Only one species, *Homo sapiens,* of the many social species has given a cultural character to its social life.

This distinction is useful in determining to what extent rudimentary traces of culture exist among animals other than men. Many birds construct nests. Many mammals burrow in the ground to make lairs. The beaver fells trees with its teeth and constructs a dam to form a pond and then builds a hut of sticks and mud in the water. All these structures bear some resemblance to the works of mankind. They are, however, built usually by individuals or pairs or groups which have learned nothing from their congeners. In other words, they are due to hereditary tendencies toward such forms of behavior. The structures erected by the human species, on the contrary, many of which are very complicated, are due to knowledge gradually accumulated and transmitted by example and by language from individuals to individuals, from groups to groups, and from generation to generation. An individual or group of individuals cut off early in life from these sources of information could not reproduce these structures.

81

Culture can, therefore, arise among animals as among men only when there are individual variations from hereditary modes of behavior which are transmitted by example and imitation or by some means of communication to other individuals and to groups. There are many of these individual variations in behavior. Some of them are socially transmitted and become cultural traits. The plasticity of animal behavior is due to the instability and mobility of organic matter which give rise to the irritability and sensitiveness to stimuli of protoplasm. The latter traits cause the facility with which organic matter changes as a result of the molecular and molar forces which act upon it. In this regard organic matter differs not in kind but only in degree from inorganic matter. All matter changes as a result of the action of forces upon it.

The environment is constantly influencing the plastic organism and giving rise to variations from inherited tendencies. While the innate drives or impulses to action are always in operation, the precise manner in which they express themselves depends to a certain extent upon the surroundings. This environment is in part social when other organisms are present. Through imitation or learning uniformities of behavior may be acquired which are not only social in their origin but may become a form of culture.[2]

Among some of the avian species the mother bird teaches her young to fly or at least sets an example. This may be witnessed on almost any lawn in early summer when the young robins leave their nests. In similar fashion in some of the mammalian species the female parent teaches her young to hunt or fish or at least sets an example. These acts on the part of the parents may be entirely instinctive. It is impossible to determine to what extent if at all they are prompted by a conscious desire or intention on the part of the parents to teach or induce the young to fly or to hunt or to fish. In similar fashion the responses of the young may be entirely instinctive. The parental behavior may furnish the appropriate stimulus for the ripened innate impulse to express itself. In all probability most of this behavior, both parental and filial, is largely if not entirely instinctive, because it is in accord with the characteristic behavior of the given species.

Individual differences are perhaps as common among animals as among men. They give rise to some degree of variation in responses to stimuli and in the expression of innate tendencies. Marked variations from ancestral modes of behavior are rare. Imitations of such variations are still more rare. Marked variations are artificially induced in animals domesticated by mankind. This is due in part to

---

[2] "Imitation is a term referring to behavior uniformities which have as a partial stimulus the equivalent behavior of other individuals." (W. S. Hunter, *Human Behavior*, Chicago, 1928, p. 137.)

the fact that the animal has to adjust itself in a measure to the human mode of living. It is due still more to the fact that certain forms of behavior are imposed upon these domesticated animals by their human masters. Men train and teach their chattel beasts to serve them by means of labor or by furnishing food or as pets. This training sometimes exercises to a higher degree the learning capacity of the animal than is usually required in a state of nature. Under domestication the animal may, therefore, acquire traces of the culture of mankind. But it is readily comprehensible why there can be very little of a sub-human culture.

Some of the human traits which have rendered culture possible have been described in the preceding chapter. Among them are a relatively large brain with a deeply convoluted cerebral cortex, an erect posture, the prehensile hand with opposable thumb, bi-focal and stereoscopic eyes, vocal organs suitable for speech, etc. Each of these traits is possessed in some degree by other animals. It was the fortuitous combination of them in the human species which furnished the basis for the emergence of culture for the first and probably the last time upon this planet and perhaps in the universe. Solar and mundane changes will eventually extinguish the existence of human and all other organic life.

The question as to which were the initial steps in the evolution of culture is beset with many difficulties which are in large part insuperable because of the impossibility of securing adequate data. Among these steps were the use of tools, the manufacture of artifacts, the discovery and use of fire, language, and the formation of concepts which arose largely out of the use of language.

No data can be secured as to the earliest use of sticks and stones as tools. We can only conjecture from the very limited use made of them by the primates. Artifacts made of stone are the earliest tangible evidences of culture. Traces of the use of fire have been found in some of the earlier stages of culture. The earliest indubitable evidence of language is furnished by the earliest traces of writing. The origin of language probably long antedated its written form. In similar fashion the earliest indubitable evidence of human concepts is furnished through the medium of written language. The existence of many of these concepts long before the invention of writing can be inferred from art objects, burial customs, and various other traces of early mankind. Furthermore, many of these concepts have been found among numerous pre-literate peoples.

A survey of the early stages of cultural evolution must commence with artifacts because of their tangible nature. Practically all of the artifacts of the distant past made from perishable materials have disintegrated and disappeared. Almost all of the ancient artifacts which have survived are made of stone. The kinds of stone ordinarily used were flint, quartzite, siliceous sandstone or quartz, jade and obsidian. Flint is a stone which flakes readily and was used more than any other mineral. It is found in large nodules in the chalk of the upper Cretaceous.

The classification of the early stages of cultural evolution is based, in the main, upon those stone implements. Tools may be classified as primary, secondary, and tertiary in their character. Primary tools are taken directly from nature and are not artifacts. A stone used as a hammer, a flint chip with a sharp edge or a point used to cut or to bore, a stick used to knock fruit off a tree is a primary tool. Secondary tools are made with the aid of primary tools. A chip knocked off a flint nodule by a hammer stone is a secondary tool. Tertiary tools are made with the aid of primary and secondary tools and their ultimate use is not the shaping of implements. A stick which has been sharpened with a knife and then used as a spear is a tertiary tool.

The anthropoid apes have been observed to make occasional use of primary tools. There is no well authenticated case of their using secondary and tertiary tools. This leads us to believe that the earliest and most primitive implements were not made by the apes or their precursors. Their manufacture probably required a degree of intelligence possessed only by man or his immediate precursors.

Flint is readily fractured by heat, cold, percussion and pressure. It can be worked and shaped relatively easily and accurately. When fractured it has hard, keen edges, which can be resharpened when they become dull. Owing to its great utility it has been used whenever available and when metals could not be substituted for it.

The patination of stone caused by exposure to air and various soil conditions sometimes aids in determining the approximate or relative age of artifacts. The color sequence is from blue to white to cream to buff and then to dark brown or black. This test can be applied only to objects taken from the same site or from sites under the same conditions of soil.

The cultural stages have been distinguished and their sequence determined almost exclusively in Europe. This has been due mainly to the fact that there has been more anthropological research in Europe than elsewhere. There has been much digging in search of cultural remains. The relatively dense population has caused a great deal of excavation for houses, railroads, etc., which has brought to light many accidental finds. In some of these cases the anthropologists have been at hand to study these finds.

The earliest cultural stage which has been distinguished was the eolithic or dawn stone age. It may have been preceded by an alithic

84

culture of wood and perhaps of bone. In the eolithic age natural objects of stone, and probably of wood and bone, were adapted to human uses with little or no concept of form. Natural fragments were crudely shaped, flint nodules and river pebbles were broken open, and flakes were slightly retouched. The principal identifying marks of eoliths are abrasions from use, bulbs of percussion caused by blows upon nodules and nuclei, and regular chipping consistent in direction as distinguished from the irregular chipping sometimes caused by natural forces. Many so-called eoliths can hardly be distinguished from natural objects, so that their authenticity as artifacts has often been questioned. The eoliths consisted largely of primary tools found in nature, such as hammerstones and flint chips with a sharp edge or point, and of a few types of simple secondary tools, such as artificial chips. Among the eolith artifacts were cleavers, picks, scrapers and spokeshaves. The two latter implements suggest the use of wood and bone, and perhaps also of horn and ivory.

Eoliths are found mainly in the pliocene horizon. The European fauna of this period, which was relatively warm, included the straight-tusked elephant, the southern elephant, the mastodon, and Steno's horse. The eolithic cultural stage may, however, have extended into the cool phase of the early pleistocene, leading up to the Guenz glaciation. Artifacts with eolithic facies are common in the paleolithic and even in the neolithic horizons. This is in accordance with the continuity of culture and the persistence of archaic forms. The paleolithic and neolithic stages consisted not so much in driving out the eolithic entirely as in adding new types and forms which became predominant.

The known distribution of the eolithic culture was England, from the Iberian peninsula to the Baltic Sea and Italy in Europe, South Africa, India, and Burma. This wide range suggests that further discoveries will indicate a much more extensive distribution of this primordial culture. It may also have extended much farther back in time. Objects believed to be eoliths have been found prior to the pliocene, in the miocene and even in the oligocene horizon. This extension suggests that the culture originated with the humanoid precursors of man at some time in the tertiary age. The eolithic may therefore be characterized as the earliest known industry when man or his precursors used stones as tools and sometimes chipped flint in pliocene time and perhaps earlier. There is no reason to believe that the eolithic culture ever existed in the western hemisphere. Mankind apparently entered the Americas at a much later date and with a higher culture.

The vast majority of eolithic finds have not been accompanied by humanoid or human remains. Of the earliest remains described in Chapter III, with Sinanthropus, which seems to have belonged to the early pleistocene, were found crudely chipped stones and carbonized material which suggested the use of fire. These few uncertain data seem to indicate that the eolithic culture characterized widely divergent human types. If this culture extended far back into tertiary time, it must have been originated by humanoid precursors of mankind, or by closely related anthropoid primates. Inasmuch as it was characterized by no distinct type forms, it is possible that it came into existence independently at many times and in many places. The eolithic culture may be regarded as comprising the first crude attempts to create a material culture. These attempts may have been oft repeated and many of them doubtless came to nought. They were wiped out by wild beasts and other forces of nature which often exterminated the creators of the culture. But here and there the eolithic proved to be the starting point for a higher form of culture.

The quaternary was an age of glaciations which lasted probably from 500,000 to one million years and terminated about 12,000 to 17,000 years ago. The glaciation may not have been as extensive or as intense as in several earlier ages. It was, however, of peculiar significance for mankind because of its influence upon the concurrent cultural evolution. There were four main glaciations which have been named after four small rivers in Switzerland, where intensive studies of the glacial period have been made by Penck and other geologists and which are listed in the accompanying table.

Pleistocene or Quaternary Glacial and Interglacial Periods in Europe

Period	Estimated length in years	Began *circa*
Guenz glaciation	70,000	B.C. 950,000
Guenz-Mindel interglacial	180,000	B.C. 880,000
Mindel glaciation	150,000	B.C. 700,000
Mindel-Riss interglacial	250,000	B.C. 550,000
Riss glaciation	120,000	B.C. 300,000
Riss-Wuerm interglacial	100,000	B.C. 180,000
Wuerm glaciation (until B.C. 15,000-10,000)	70,000	B.C. 80,000
	940,000	

The geological sequence of the quaternary in Europe was somewhat as follows. The figures given are estimates and therefore only roughly approximate and subject to extensive revision. They at least give some indication of the relative length of the glacial and interglacial periods. The Guenz glaciation lasted about 70,000 years and came down to the region of the Baltic Sea. It was followed by the Guenz-Mindel interglacial period which lasted about 180,000 years. The temperature rose to a point somewhat above the present level. Then came the Mindel glaciation which lasted about 150,000 years and was the principal glaciation of the quaternary. The glaciers came down to southern Germany close to Switzerland. It was followed by the Mindel-Riss interglacial period which lasted about 250,000 years. The temperature rose above the present temperate level. The Riss glaciation lasted about 120,000 years. The glaciers came down to southern Germany but not as far down as the Mindel glaciation. The Riss-Wuerm interglacial period lasted about 100,000 years and was somewhat warmer than the present temperate period.

The Wuerm glaciation lasted about 70,000 years and came down to northern Germany. It terminated with the close of the pleistocene at about 15,000 to 10,000 B.C. According to the above estimates the Guenz, Mindel, Riss and Wuerm glaciations, and their three interglacial periods lasted 940,000 years. This can probably be regarded as the upper limit of the length of the quaternary or pleistocene age.

As in all the glaciations, the latter part of the quaternary was characterized by a series of small advances and retreats of the glaciers which formed a part of the general retreat from the Wuerm glaciation. After Wuerm I, the major phase of the last glaciation, came the Laufen retreat of about 6,000 years, followed by Wuerm II, the minor phase, which lasted about 3,000 years. After an interval of unknown length came the Achen retreat of about 3,000 years. Then came the Buehl stadium or moderate advance of about 6,000 years followed by the Buehl-Gschnitz inter-stadium or retreat of unknown length. The Gschnitz stadium or advance of about 1,500 years was followed by the Gschnitz-Daun inter-stadium or retreat of unknown length. The Daun stadium or advance lasted about 1,000 years and probably terminated at approximately 10,000 B.C. We are still in the period of the general retreat from the Wuerm glaciation. Whether or not this retreat will lead to a climate as warm as in the antecedent interglacial periods cannot now be determined. Nor can we know whether or not another glaciation is to follow.

The ice ages were due to a lower temperature or an increased snowfall or both. Penck, who has made extensive studies of the glaciations in the Alps and in Germany, has asserted that the temperature fell about 4° centigrade (7.2° Fahrenheit) during the last glaciation known as the Wuerm in the Alps, the Weichsel in northern Germany, and the Wisconsin in North America. According to him, the ice ages were colder and dryer, and the interglacial periods warmer and wetter, than the present climate of the world.[3]

The accompanying table shows the sequence of the paleolithic culture periods in Europe with their estimated length in years and probable geological horizons. It was long believed that the earliest culture was the Chellean during the major or Mindel-Riss interglacial period. Then came the discovery of the eolithic culture described above. Since that time much evidence has accumulated which indicates an intermediate culture usually called the Pre-Chellean. This culture was characterized by the production of more or less well defined types of implements designed for specific uses. In other words, secondary tools were more prevalent than in the eolithic culture. Among these stone implements were the cleaver, knife, perforator, point, and the scraper of various forms, such as keeled, side, end and disc scrapers. The Pre-Chellean forms foreshadowed the Chellean types but were sufficiently characteristic to designate a distinct cultural stage.

Paleolithic Culture Periods in Europe

Period	Estimated Length in Years	Probable Geological Horizons in Glacial and Interglacial Periods
Pre-Chellean	400,000	Guenz, Guenz-Mindel, Mindel
Chellean	200,000	Mindel-Riss
Acheulian	150,000	Mindel-Riss,Riss
Micoquian	50,000	Riss, Riss-Wuerm
Mousterian	100,000	Riss-Wuerm, Wuerm I, Laufen Retreat
Aurignacian	13,000	Wuerm II, Achen Retreat
Solutrean	3,000	Achen Retreat
Magdalenian (until B.C. 10,000?)	12,000	Buehl, Buehl-Gschnitz, Gschnitz
	928,000	

[3] Albrecht Penck, "Die Ursachen der Eiszeit," in the *Sitzungsberichte der Preussischen Akademie der Wissenschaften*, Berlin, 1928, pp. 76-85.

"Unser Ergebnis, dass die Eiszeit nicht eine besonders niederschlagsreiche, sondern eine nicht unwesentlich kühlere Periode als heute gewesen ist, steht im Einklang mit dem Ergebnis unserer Untersuchungen in den Alpen." (p. 82.)

In Berlin in 1937 the late Professor Albrecht Penck gave me his latest estimates of the length of these glacial and interglacial periods, and I heard him lecture at the Prussian Academy of Sciences.

The Pre-Chellean culture developed during the Guenz glaciation with its cold fauna including the mammoth, musk-ox and reindeer. It continued through the Guenz-Mindel interglacial period, and may have persisted into the Mindel glaciation. The outstanding warm interglacial fauna were the straight-tusked and the southern elephants, the Etruscan rhinoceros, the hippopotamus and the saber-toothed tiger. The earliest Pre-Chellean industry may have been the Foxhallian, followed by the Cromerian, named after sites in eastern England. The Mesvinian industry was named after a site in Belgium. There were several concurrent or subsequent industries in various parts of the eastern hemisphere. The known distribution of the Pre-Chellean culture in Europe was the same as the eolithic, and also in Asia Minor, western and northern Africa including Egypt, and in China. This cultural period probably lasted about 400,000 years in Europe.

Leakey has asserted that in Kenya Colony and Tanganyika Territory in eastern Africa, "there has been a long sequence of successively progressive culture stages from the dawn of the Pleistocene to the beginning of the present era." In the lower Pleistocene was the Oldowan culture, named from the Oldoway site in Tanganyika whose principal tool was "a water-worn pebble, or a nodule of chert, or any lump of rock, with very simple trimming along one side to give a jagged cutting edge, in fact a rough chopper." From this culture evolved the Chellean hand-ax culture of which there were five stages, followed by the Acheulian of which there were six stages. At the close of the Middle Pleistocene, "the sixth and last stage of the Acheulean is found to be contemporary with three other cultures, namely, the Nanyukian (a form of Micoque), Early Aurignacian, and an early Mousterian. At the close of the Kamasian pluvial, which is also regarded as the close of the Middle Pleistocene, there are thus four distinct contemporary cultures." [4]

After the close of the Pre-Chellean period in Europe there appears to have been a long cultural break. The great Mindel glaciation had spread over much of Europe and had lowered considerably the temperature of the remainder of the continent. It is possible that man was exterminated in or driven from Europe by the encroaching cold. However, this does not mean that culture was obliterated. Mankind survived elsewhere. It is probable that there was cultural continuity in western Asia, Egypt, elsewhere in Africa and possibly also farther east in Asia. Most of these regions were not affected by the glaciation. It is possible that the eolithic culture was obliterated more than once by the catastrophes of nature. By the time the Pre-Chellean

<hr>

[4] L. S. B. Leakey, *The Stone Age Races of Kenya*, London, 1935, pp. 1, 4-5. See also his *The Stone Age Cultures of Kenya Colony*, London, 1931.

culture was attained it is hardly likely that human culture could have been completely wiped out at any one time.

The Chellean culture, named after a site in northern France, and its related industries, was contemporary with the early and middle portions of the Mindel-Riss or second inter-glacial period. Among the warm fauna of this long period of perhaps 250,000 years were the straight-tusked elephant, Merck's rhinoceros, the hippopotamus, cave bear and cave hyena. The Chellean implements were more symmetrical than the Pre-Chellean. The most common tool was the amygdaloid or almond-shaped cleaver. This hand-ax had a thick butt and wavy edges due to the alternate chipping characteristic of this industry. The known distribution of this culture was the same as the eolithic in Europe and also in western Asia and in northern, western, eastern and southern Africa. The Chellean culture probably lasted about 200,000 years in Europe.

The Chellean was followed by the Acheulian culture named after a site in northern France. The cleaver continued to be the predominant tool. It was smaller, finer in execution and somewhat different in form. Improved methods of chipping rendered relatively straight edges possible. Flake implements were more common. In the later part of the Acheulian period appeared the so-called "Levallois" flake which was made from a tortoise-shaped nucleus and whose surfaces were completely worked.

The Acheulian culture was co-extensive with the later part of the Mindel-Riss interglacial period and with most or all of the Riss glaciation. The interglacial warm fauna included the straight-tusked elephant, trogontherium mammoth, rhinoceros, hippopotamus, horse, ox and bison. The cold fauna included the mammoth, woolly rhinoceros and reindeer. The known distribution of the Acheulian and related industries was the same as the Chellean with central Africa added. The Acheulian cultural stage probably lasted about 150,000 years in Europe.

The Pre-Chellean, Chellean and Acheulian periods constituted the lower part of the paleolithic age which in Europe commenced relatively soon after the beginning of the pleistocene. It may have commenced earlier in other parts of the world. It lasted in Europe about 750,000 years or three-quarters of the pleistocene. It was, therefore, three times as long as all the succeeding cultural periods put together. This illustrated the increase in the tempo of cultural evolution which was to be greatly accentuated as recent time was approached.

There has been no certain or even probable identification of race with lower paleolithic culture. Pithecanthropus, Sinanthropus and the Heidelberg man, each or all of them may have possessed the eolithic or the Pre-Chellean culture. Lower paleolithic man dwelt in the open and rarely ever resorted to caves and rock shelters. His remains rapidly disintegrated and disappeared. They were not left in close and unquestionable association with his cultural products. His culture has sometimes been called a river-drift culture because he usually lived beside a river. This was because he had no vessels of wood, stone, pottery, skin or metal in which to conserve water. Many of the lower paleolithic artifacts have been found in gravel deposited in river beds. His mortal remains, exposed to the elements, disintegrated and were swept away.

Future discoveries may reveal the racial identity of some of the lower paleolithic men. At some of the paleolithic sites the geological stratification reveals the succession of cultural stages. For example, at St. Acheul, the type station for the Acheulian period, the stratification ranges from the lower to the upper paleolithic as follows: (1) limestone; (2) gravel, early Chellean; (3) sand, late Chellean; (4) loam, early Acheulian; (5) flood sand; (6) loess; (7) late Acheulian; (8) pebbles, Mousterian; (9) loess; (10) upper paleolithic. At this station 20,000 Chellean cleavers were found. It was probably at one time a lower paleolithic workshop.

The nature of these paleolithic implements gives some indication of their uses. The hammerstone was a primary tool used principally to flake flint and make secondary tools. The cleaver was the most common and typical of the lower paleolithic implements. It could be used to hack branches from trees, to split wood, to kill large game, and to cut and dress hides. Hence it could serve roughly and crudely as an ax, saw, knife, and scraper. A large cleaver could serve as a pick to excavate holes. The scrapers of various shapes were used to scrape wood, bone and hides. The spokeshave was used to smooth and round sticks of wood. The utility of the knife does not require description. The perforator was used to make holes in wood, bone and hides. The point was probably inserted in the tip of a dart, javelin or spear.

The most important use for many of these implements probably was hunting. Through the chase paleolithic man secured much of his food because he did not practice agriculture. Darts and spears may have been used to catch fish. To what extent these implements were used in fighting there is nothing to indicate. There is no evidence of building in stone by paleolithic man. He may have put up wind shields and rude structures of wood. He may have used hides as a crude form of clothing. The temperature of many of the regions inhabited by lower paleolithic man necessitated some protection against the cold.

There is no conclusive evidence that lower paleolithic man possessed and used fire as a protection against the cold and for cooking. Fire exists in nature in volcanoes, lightning, and as a result of friction, such as branches rubbing together. Man may have procured fire from natural sources before he discovered how to produce it. Burnt flints have been found in the lower paleolithic and even earlier. The first well-defined hearths appeared in the middle paleolithic. The first artificial means of producing fire have been found in the upper paleolithic. These included pyrites and strike-a-lights. The uses of fire extended greatly during neolithic time. As soon as fuel was used freely and extensively a vast supply of power extraneous to the human body was made available to man.

There is no evidence of the so-called "higher" culture in lower paleolithic time. No objects of art have been found. To what extent language had developed it is impossible to determine. Whether or not animistic ideas and beliefs were yet in existence cannot be ascertained. Presumably mankind lived in small family groups or possibly in somewhat larger hordes. The number of implements and rejecta found at the important workshops gives a slight indication of the aggregation of population. The nature of the social organization cannot even be surmised.

The Micoquian culture, named after the site at la Micoque in southern France, was transitional from the lower to the middle paleolithic. At about this period Neanderthal man apparently entered Europe, probably from the southeast. A conflict may have taken place between Neanderthal and lower paleolithic man in which the latter was exterminated or driven out. At any rate the nature and ultimate fate of lower paleolithic man are as yet unknown. The Micoquian industry contained features of both the preceding Acheulian and the succeeding Mousterian cultures. It was characterized by small cleavers, perforators and thin flake implements. The latter were Mousterian in form and chipping. The Micoquian culture was contemporaneous with the late Riss glaciation and the early Riss-Wuerm interglacial period. It probably lasted about 50,000 years in Europe to which continent it may have been limited.

The Mousterian or middle paleolithic culture was dominated by Neanderthal man. In a considerable number of sites this human type has been found in unquestionable association with this culture. The Mousterian culture was apparently developed outside of Europe though it was named after a site in southern France. The region of its origin is unknown. It differed considerably from the lower paleolithic culture of Europe. Its industry improved technique by retouching stone implements but did not go beyond secondary tools. Acheulian flaking was developed further so that the chipping was finer and often was stepped. The cleaver appeared occasionally but was supplanted early as the typical implement by the Mousterian point. The cleaver became smaller and degenerated in other respects. Among the other Mousterian implements were the hammerstone, bola (sling stone), disc graver, drill, spokeshave, saw, knife, and Levallois flake. The lower portion of the Mousterian period coincided with the latter part of the Riss-Wuerm interglacial period.

Very few of the Mousterian sites are in the open. Most of them are in rock shelters and caves which were commonly used as dwelling places. In many of these shelters and caves are well-defined hearths which indicate that fire was used for warmth and perhaps also for cooking. The earliest known burials appeared during the Mousterian period. This indicated not only care of the dead but probably animistic beliefs as well.[5]

The middle portion of the Mousterian period was characterized by a preponderance of knives and scrapers over points. End, disc and beaked scrapers, spokeshaves and ribbon flakes were more fully developed than hitherto. The implements in general showed more refinement of form and workmanship than those of the lower Mousterian. The middle Mousterian was coextensive with the first or major phase of the Wuerm glaciation, sometimes known as Wuerm I.

The last part of the Mousterian was characterized by a continued preponderance of knives over points. The specialized implements of the middle Mousterian continued to appear though usually made from thinner and less regular flakes. The ribbon flakes became much more common. There was a recrudescence of the cleaver. The outstanding feature of this cultural substage was the efflorescence of the industrial use of bone in many implements, among them being skinning tools and the compressor to retouch flint. The upper Mousterian was contemporaneous with the so-called Laufen retreat of the glaciers which took place between the major and the minor phases of the Wuerm glaciation. This retreat was taking place approximately B.C. 35,000 and lasted about 6,000 years. It was followed by the minor phase of the Wuerm glaciation sometimes called Wuerm II.

The known distribution of the Mousterian and related cultures in the eastern hemisphere was Europe (where it covered a larger area than the lower paleolithic), western Asia, north, east and south Africa, India, north and central China (in the valleys of the Yellow and upper Yangtze rivers), and Siberia (on both sides of Lake Baikal). The Riss-Wuerm interglacial fauna included the straight-tusked elephant, Merck's rhinoceros and the hippopotamus. The Wuerm I glacial

---

[5] "Why were the dead given such careful burial and supplied with the necessary tools and weapons? Did Paleolithic man desire to save his dead from total destruction? Did he believe in life after death? Or was he safeguarding the living from ghostly visitations?" (H. E. Barnes, *History of Western Civilization*, New York, 1935, Vol. I, p. 17.)

fauna included the mammoth, woolly rhinoceros and reindeer. The cold steppe fauna of the Laufen retreat included the lemming and musk ox. The Mousterian period probably lasted about 100,000 years in Europe.

The Aurignacian culture, named after a site in southern France, was the first stage of the upper paleolithic. The change in Europe from the middle to the upper paleolithic was apparently due to ethnic replacement. Man of the modern type, namely, *Homo sapiens,* came from Africa or Asia and exterminated or drove out Neanderthal man. A comparatively new cultural complex appeared in Europe and the Neanderthal racial type has apparently disappeared entirely. This cultural pattern must have developed elsewhere and then have been imported into Europe by *Homo sapiens.*

The Aurignacian paleoliths were with few exceptions made from narrow flint flakes. The cleaver disappeared almost entirely. The lamp, and highly developed bone implements and objects of art appeared for the first time in the culture pattern. The Aurignacian industry included many tools well adapted for woodworking made from narrow bladelike flakes and from small cores. Bone came into prominence as a material for the manufacture of implements and as a medium of artistic expression. The fine arts of engraving, painting and sculpture developed. This probably indicated that animistic beliefs and ideas were now playing a cultural role.

The lower Aurignacian stone industry was based on bladelike flakes from which various tools were fashioned. The most typical of these, apart from numerous unspecialized blades, were the end scraper, graver and Chatelperron knife which had one straight edge and one curved, retouched edge. A distinct bone industry developed which included spatulas and bodkins. There were outline drawings and engravings of various faunal types, shown in profile, associated with these industries.

The most typical implements of the middle Aurignacian were the carinate or keeled scraper, notched blade and beaked scraper. The side and end scrapers, knife and simple blade also were present. There were bone implements of several types. The most common were the awl, javelin head and shaft-straightener. Profile engravings and outline drawings similar to those of the lower Aurignacian were present.

The upper Aurignacian stone artifacts included the gravette blade, lateral and medial graver, and small flake implements. Its bone work included pedunculate or stalk-like javelin points in addition to those typical of the middle Aurignacian. The upper Aurignacian art was finer in execution and more lifelike in treatment than the

94

earlier art. For the first time shading appeared in the drawings. There were many fine examples of sculpture.

The Aurignacian culture was contemporary with the second brief phase of the Wuerm glaciation, known as Wuerm II, and the Achen retreat of the glaciers. Each of these probably lasted about 3,000 years with an unknown interval between during which there was no marked advance or retreat of the glaciers. The glacial fauna associated with Wuerm II included the mammoth and reindeer. The cold steppe fauna associated with the Achen retreat included the horse, stag and saiga antelope. The African phase of the Aurignacian is called the Caspian culture. The known distribution of the Aurignacian culture in the eastern hemisphere was Europe, western Asia, north, east and south Africa, India, China and Siberia. It was apparently not quite so widespread as the Mousterian culture.

The Aurignacian period probably lasted about 13,000 years. This indicated a great acceleration of cultural changes. It was little more than one-tenth as long as the Mousterian period. And yet it included changes and improvements which were probably as great as or greater than those which took place during the Mousterian period.

The Solutrean, named after a site in eastern France, was an east European development of the upper paleolithic culture. It spread westward as far as England thus intruding into the Aurignacian culture of western Europe. In several west European sites the Solutrean deposit is stratigraphically between the Aurignacian and Magdalenian deposits. At other sites the two latter cultures merge into each other without a Solutrean intrusion. The autochthonous west European paleolithic culture continued without a break in certain localities during the Solutrean incursions. Pressure flaking was highly developed by the Solutrean culture. The laurel-leaf, willow-leaf and shouldered (tanged) points were made by this technique. Objects of bone were relatively common. There were occasional drawings on bone and murals in bas-relief.

The Solutrean culture was contemporaneous with the Achen retreat. The horse and reindeer were the common faunal types. The presence of the woolly elephant and the woolly rhinoceros indicated the coming of the tundra conditions of the early Magdalenian. As the Solutrean culture has not been found outside of Europe, it was apparently much more restricted than the Aurignacian and Magdalenian cultures. The Solutrean period probably lasted about 3,000 years.

The Magdalenian culture, named after a site in southern France, developed directly out of the Aurignacian. The Solutrean intrusion from the east did not break the cultural continuity of the upper paleolithic in western Europe. During the Magdalenian period there was perhaps a regression in the stone industry but progress in the bone and reindeer horn industry. The Magdalenian flint work, while typologically similar to the Aurignacian, displayed a greater prevalence of small flake implements. The secondary chipping, though finer, became less frequent. The stone industry was characterized by a simplification of the secondary chipping, and by a multiplicity of combination tools such as side-end scrapers and end scraper-gravers. The prevalence of the small flake implements foreshadowed the microliths of the following mesolithic or epi-paleolithic period which preceded the neolithic. Toward the end of the Magdalenian there appeared a stone industry which was almost identical with the upper Aurignacian. It included carinate or keeled scrapers, beaked gravers, curved blades with worked backs, perforators, and blades strongly resembling the gravette type.

The Magdalenian stone industry was exceptionally uniform. It would be difficult to distinguish sub-stages on the basis of its products. This can be done on the basis of the industry in bone, horn and ivory. In contrast to the typological continuity of the stone artifacts, the bone artifacts displayed many changes as the culture developed. This was strikingly manifested in the javelin and harpoon points. There were also dart throwers and perforated *"batons de commandement"* which may have been arrow straighteners. The presence of bone needles, buttons and toggles almost certainly indicated the use of sewn and buttoned garments. There were many and varied utilitarian and esthetic uses of bone, horn and ivory. Paleolithic art reached its peak during the Magdalenian period.

The Magdalenian culture was contemporary with the Buehl stadium, a minor advance of the glaciers, the Beuhl-Gschnitz interstadium, or brief retreat of the glaciers, and the Gschnitz stadium which was a still smaller advance of the glaciers. The Buehl glaciation was accompanied by a cold tundra fauna which included the mammoth, woolly rhinoceros and reindeer. The Buehl-Gschnitz interglacial period was accompanied by a steppe fauna which included the saiga antelope, bison and horse. The Gschnitz glaciation was accompanied by a cool forest fauna which included the red deer and stag. The known distribution of the Magdalenian culture in the eastern hemisphere was Europe, western Asia, north, east, central and south Africa, India, China and Siberia. It probably lasted about 12,000 years and terminated in Europe from 10,000 to 12,000 years ago.

The Magdalenian marked the close of the paleolithic culture. Paleolithic man was predominantly if not exclusively a food-gatherer and not a food-producer. He procured his food mainly by hunting and fishing and gathering edible plants growing in a state of nature. The domestication of animals probably commenced near the close of the paleolithic. The domestication of plants and agriculture did not commence until the neolithic period. In hunting paleolithic man used the flint knife, bola (sling-stone), wooden club, throwing stick, dart thrower, javelin and harpoon. According to de Mortillet, 66 species of mammals were hunted by paleolithic man in Europe. Only about half as many mammalian species were hunted during the neolithic and bronze ages. The most primitive fishhooks of bone and reindeer horn date from the paleolithic.

If the geological chronology which has been used is approximately correct, the lower paleolithic was seven times as long as the middle paleolithic, and the latter four times as long as the upper paleolithic. During this lengthy period of one million years, or about 50,000 generations, mankind had only the crudest of implements to attain its ends. But this was more than was possessed by any other animals. The human animal is much weaker than a considerable number of animals. Man is no better fitted for survival than many animal types. It is possible that mankind will perish long before the ants and other insect types. Under certain environmental conditions its artificial equipment has furnished mankind an advantage for survival. It has rendered it possible for man to live in cold climates for which mankind is not fitted by nature. It has enabled men to survive in regions where they could not procure adequate food except by slaughtering animals by means of artifacts designed for the chase.

The principal anatomical differences between man and the higher apes are due to human adjustment to an erect posture. The equilibrium on a vertical spinal column in man was restored by an increased brain case and a decreased face. The great increase of the brain case rendered possible a relatively greater expansion of the frontal lobes with their undifferentiated association areas. The ratio of the superficies of the frontal lobes to the total surface of the cerebral hemispheres is 32 per cent in the anthropoids, 36 per cent in the Neanderthal type, and 46 per cent in *Homo sapiens* or modern man. The brain, well balanced on an erect spinal column, the stereoscopic vision, and the hands formed a physical complex which rendered the human mental type possible. This complex probably arose during the late tertiary period and rendered possible the cultural beginnings of the quaternary period.

The potential human mental ability manifested its effects very slowly. For more than three-quarters of a million years the lower paleolithic culture produced little more than crude stone implements. The wide distribution of these relics suggests that various measures may have been used against the cold. Fire procured from nature may have been utilized at times but was probably not produced. Rude shelters against wind, rain and snow may have been constructed of which no traces remain. Pelts may have been worn to protect the furless human body. It is certain that artifacts were used to hunt animal food made necessary by the frugality of nature in many human habitats. As we have seen, there is no evidence whatsoever of the so-called "higher" culture in the lower paleolithic. To what extent language began to develop it is impossible to determine. This problem will be discussed in Chapters IX and X.

Fire was extensively used and may also have been produced during the middle paleolithic culture. The practice of burial of the dead suggests that Neanderthal man possessed certain animistic ideas. This in turn suggests a considerable development of language. Neanderthal man was therefore the earliest human type to whom some of the elements of the higher culture can be attributed with assurance.

The upper paleolithic culture in Europe marked the first known appearance of modern man. But *Homo sapiens* had probably long been in existence in Africa or Asia or in both continents. The upper paleolithic stone industry manufactured long slender blades, gravers, small knives, awls and microliths which rendered possible an extensive use of bone, ivory and reindeer horn. With the secondary shaping tools derived from the bladelike flint flakes were fashioned the bone needle, the javelin point and shaft, the dart thrower and the harpoon. Some of the polished stone implements characteristic of the neolithic culture were also produced during the latter part of the upper paleolithic. Two of the principal results from the upper paleolithic stone industry were production in abundance of tertiary tools, and the rise of the fine arts.

Most if not all of the pleistocene fine art was the product of the upper paleolithic culture. The larger part of it was Magdalenian. Paleolithic art was in the main realistic in its character. Sculpture came first, probably because it is a simpler art. Then came engraving. There was almost no paleolithic pottery and little modeling in clay. Painting apparently followed after engraving. Except for a few deer in stone at Solutré, all representations of animals were Magdalenian.

Animal profiles constituted the majority of paleolithic engravings and paintings. Composition in these works of art was rare. Many of these animal figures probably were votive offerings to the mysterious powers which were supposed to govern the animal world. These figures often were hidden from view in caves for magical purposes. Some of these animal figures were mutilated, probably for magical reasons, *i.e.*, in order to aid in killing these animals in the chase. Female animal figures were in the majority, probably because they were symbolic of fecundity. There were few figures of birds, probably because paleolithic man had not the bow and arrow or any other effective means of hunting them. In similar fashion, there were few representations of invertebrate animals and of plants.

Human figures were not so numerous or so well portrayed as animal figures in the upper paleolithic art. As in the case of the animals portrayed, female human figures were more abundant than the male, probably because they were associated with fecundity. Much attention was paid to the primary and secondary sex characteristics. The frequent recurrence of the female figure was suggestive of the Hottentot and Bushman art of modern times.

Before the close of the Magdalenian period symbolic and conventionalized art appeared. Alphabetiform signs, chevrons, frets, spirals, volutes, wave ornaments, claviform (club-shaped) signs, and tectiform (roof-shaped) signs were used. Some of this conventionalized art was in the form of geometric ornamentation. With the close of the Magdalenian much of this art disappeared. In the portable paleolithic art were used stone, bone, ivory, reindeer and stag horn. Bone and stone were the principal materials utilized. Wood also was probably used, but the ornaments of wood have not been preserved. Ochre and oxide of manganese were applied as coloring matter in painting and for other ornamental purposes. Skins for clothing probably were decorated. The human body itself may have been painted.[6]

[6] A comprehensive survey of the eolithic and paleolithic cultures is furnished in G. G. MacCurdy, *Human Origins*, 2 vols., New York, 1924. See also J. de Morgan, *Prehistoric Man*, 1925, translated from the French; and Oswald Menghin, *Weltgeschichte der Steinzeit*, Vienna, 1931.

Chapter VIII

The Pre-Literate Accumulation of Material Culture

THE mesolithic or epi-paleolithic culture was intermediate between the paleolithic and the neolithic. It was a period of cultural
diversification and intermixture. Local cultural phases had developed
in the upper paleolithic of Europe. It was not until the mesolithic
that several divergent European cultures occurred contemporaneously.
The most important of these were the Azilian and Tardenoisian,
named after sites in southern and northern France respectively, the
final Capsian phase in Spain and northern Africa, and the Maglemosean
named after a site in Denmark.

In Europe the mesolithic period was contemporaneous with the
Gschnitz-Daun interstadium, or retreat of the glaciers, and the Daun
stadium or minor glaciation. Both of these geological periods had a
cool, moist climate with modern fauna. The mesolithic probably
lasted about 3,500 years in Europe and terminated *circa* 5,000 B.C.
Its known distribution in the eastern hemisphere was Europe, western
Asia, north, west, east, central and south Africa, India and Siberia.

The mesolithic culture was characterized by an extensive use of
microliths. Many of these small stone implements, such as points,
knives and lunettes, were inserted in rows in hafts of wood, bone or
horn, and thus used as saws, hatchets, etc. Implements of bone, horn
and ivory were not so plentiful as in the upper paleolithic. The mammoth and the elephant, which had furnished ivory, disappeared from
Europe. The reindeer retreated to the north. Bone-work and the fine
arts fell considerably below the high level attained in the Magdalenian
culture.

The Azilian phase of the mesolithic culture was characterized by
numerous small, round and bullet-shaped scrapers, spatulate scrapers,
small flakes with blunted backs, crude gravers, flat bone and stag-horn
harpoon points, and stag-horn wedges, chisels and picks. Its character-

istic art was delineated on pebbles with geometric designs painted in red. A French anthropologist, Piette, thought that these designs represented a system of cursive writing, but this is purely hypothetical. The Azilian culture apparently was a degeneration of the Magdalenian culture and probably originated in the northern Pyrenees. It spread from western Europe to Switzerland. Associated with the Tardenoisian it was widely distributed in Europe, Africa and Asia.

The Tardenoisian phase of the mesolithic culture commenced perhaps a little later than the Azilian but was in the main contemporaneous with it. It was characterized by numerous minute microliths whose purpose is often unknown. Some of them which were very thin and brittle flint chips may have been used for tattooing. The Tardenoisian culture has been found in coastal regions in Africa and Asia as far east as India.

The Maglemosean was a Scandinavian phase of the mesolithic culture. It merged into the kitchen midden culture revealed by the excavation of shell heaps and mounds of refuse. In these kitchen middens have been found remains of the dog and of primitive pottery. The latter belonged to the dawn of the neolithic rather than to the mesolithic culture.

The neolithic culture arose in Europe following the final minor advance of the last or Wuerm glacial period. The climate changed from cold and dry to relatively warm and humid. The rise of temperature may have encouraged the advent of the higher culture. The warmer climate increased the security of life and thereby the population. Hunting was no longer sufficient to support the population. The domestication of animals and of plants ensued. The division of labor became more complicated.

It cannot, however, be assumed that the cultural progress was due entirely or even in large part to the enhanced temperature and humidity. The temperature was even higher during the preceding Riss-Wuerm, Mindel-Riss and Guenz-Mindel interglacial periods. And yet no culture corresponding to the neolithic arose. The neolithic culture in Europe as elsewhere was in large part the spontaneous and normal development of the mesolithic. The European neolithic was also stimulated by influences emanating from an earlier and more highly evolved neolithic culture in Egypt, western Asia, the Mediterranean, and possibly also in central Asia. As we have seen, the Mousterian and Aurignacian cultures apparently entered Europe from elsewhere. The European cultural evolution was doubtless influenced from outside on other occasions. In fact, it is highly probable that the larger part of cultural evolution took place outside of Europe. The area comprised by northern Africa and western Asia, with its more temperate and stable climate, undisturbed by glacial incursions, was better suited for cultural evolution. Europe probably was in the main a cultural offshoot and peninsula of the dominant and most fruitful cultural area.

The neolithic culture was characterized by (1) stone tool-making by grinding and polishing, (2) domestication of animals and pastoral life, (3) pottery, (4) domestication of plants and agriculture. These cultural traits were not necessarily developed in the same order in all areas. Nor were they all present at the same time and place except in the highest neolithic stage. Their development and presence were determined in large part by local conditions of climate and topography.

The early neolithic, sometimes called the proto-neolithic, industries in Europe included the kitchen-midden of northern Europe, the Campignian, named after a site in northern France, and the Asturian in Spain. These industries represented local phases of the same culture. The typical implements of this early neolithic culture were crudely chipped but effective picks, tranchets or chisel-shaped flints, transverse arrow-heads, flint axes, knives and saws. Art at first continued at the low mesolithic level. The local cultural variations resulted from additions to the fundamental set of traits, and from minor differences in the form and technique of specialized implements.

The kitchen-midden culture of Scandinavia and the Baltic region was revealed by excavating shell heaps and mounds of refuse. As mentioned above, in some of them were found remains of the dog and primitive pottery. At Campignian sites in France were found remains of crude huts. Many Campignian tools were found in association with house pits. Pottery and crude querns or stones for grinding grain were found at some of the Campignian sites. In the early neolithic period mankind began to master its environment, principally by controlling its food supply. The domestication of animals, the rise of agriculture, furnishing a regularly recurring supply of food, the manufacture of pottery and of baskets to store liquids and solids, and the invention of the textile art to furnish clothing, all played their part in the development of this control. The construction of temporary or permanent dwellings furnished protection against the often inclement European weather.

The proto-neolithic period in Europe lasted from approximately 5,000 to 3,000 B.C., or about 2,000 years. Its known distribution in the eastern hemisphere was Europe, western Asia, north, east, central and south Africa, India, the Malay Peninsula, Sumatra, Indo-China and Siberia. The proto-neolithic culture of India resembled the Campignian of Europe.

The polishing of stone implements has usually been regarded as the most characteristic feature of the neolithic culture. A few polished tools have also been found in paleolithic sites. On the other

102

hand, polished implements did not always accompany traits of the neolithic cultural complex. However, in Europe the efflorescence of the neolithic culture was marked by the invention or adoption of the polished stone ax. Stone implements are polished by grinding with granite, sandstone or loose damp sand. While their manufacture does not necessarily involve more skill than the manufacture of the more highly developed paleoliths, it requires much patient and persistent effort.

The polished stone ax increased human efficiency considerably, especially in woodworking. The neolithic period witnessed a relatively rapid increase of the material culture. Permanent houses, boat building and local navigation, loom weaving, and many other important inventions were among the accomplishments of this period. The rise of the ceramic and textile arts stimulated the fine arts because they furnished opportunities for design and coloration. Partly for this reason there was a renascence of the fine arts during the neolithic after their decline during the mesolithic.

The expansion of the industrial arts led to a good deal of local specialization, stimulating in turn the exchange of commodities in trade. Diverse ethnic and cultural groups were brought into contact with each other by trade and also by migration. This contact accelerated the diffusion and assimilation of culture. It caused racial intermixture probably to a greater degree than at any previous period. Miscegenation resulted also from warfare and the capture of prisoners who were enslaved because they could be used profitably in agriculture. Thus a foreign ethnic element was gradually absorbed into the community. The control of the food supply due to the domestication of live stock and agriculture, and permanent dwellings due to the rise of the art of architecture, rendered possible village and settled communal life on a wider scale than at any earlier period. This in turn resulted in a rapid development of social organization and of the basic social institutions which will be discussed in later chapters.

The known distribution of the higher neolithic culture in the eastern hemisphere was all of Europe, most of Africa, and Asia with the exception of northern Asia. The duration of this latter part of the neolithic period in Europe was approximately from 3,000 to 1,900 B.C., or about 1,100 years. Outside of Europe the neolithic culture was of greater antiquity. The domestication of animals originated in part independently in Europe, Asia Minor, Africa, Indo-China and America, and possibly elsewhere. The dog was domesticated as early as the neolithic and apparently in the mesolithic or later paleolithic. The ox, ass, horse, pig, sheep and goat were domesticated not later than the neolithic. The cat was domesticated in Egypt perhaps in the neolithic or soon after, apparently in order to combat the pest of

103

rodents. In fact, by the end of the neolithic period most of the animals and plants now used by mankind had been domesticated.

In many grassland regions the domestication of live stock resulted in the pastoral life by nomadic tribes. This manner of life prevented settled communities and discouraged agriculture. It limited the industrial development of the neolithic culture and permitted only a part of this cultural complex. The nomadic and unsettled character of the pastoral life renders it difficult to determine its chronology. In the settled agricultural communities most of the important metals began to be used, thus stimulating the rise of industry. Urban centers began to grow. All of the known languages were already in existence, but literacy had hardly commenced.

The cultivation of the cereals probably resulted at first from the accidental and then from the intentional scattering of grains, which had been gathered while growing in a state of nature. The tilling of the soil and planting of the seeds which followed were much more efficient methods of cultivation. No wild species can be assigned as the origin of any widely cultivated plant or domesticated animals. All of the domesticated varieties are hybrids. With the exception of maize and barley, all cultivated plants are polyploids. The number of chromosomes in each of them is a multiple of the diploid or haploid number which characterizes the wild or normal species. Polyploidy provides material susceptible of variations on which selection can work.

In Egypt the paleolithic merged into the neolithic period considerably earlier than in Europe. The Egyptian neolithic preceded the European by about 2,000 years. Until the fifth millennium B.C., flint, chert, and rarely obsidian, were used to make implements. At that time the Egyptians were pastoralists and to some extent agriculturists. The first dynasty probably began about 3100 B.C. Wheat of a comparatively advanced type has been found in Egyptian predynastic tombs. Similar wheat was found in an early Sumerian house in Mesopotamia which dated back to about 3500 B.C. Wheat was also found in a neolithic site at Anau in the Turkmenistan S. S. R. (Socialist Soviet Republic) near the Caspian Sea. The original excavators (Raphael Pumpelly and Ellsworth Huntington) dated this site back to about 8000 B.C., but its true date probably was about 3900-3300 B.C. Wheat has been found in most or all of the pile-dwellings over water in Switzerland and elsewhere in Europe. At many of these sites the refuse which had fallen into the mud of the lake or river bottom has been exposed by natural means or by excavation after the water has receded. Barley and flax also were grown at an early date in many of the neolithic sites. The flax and hair and wool from the domesticated animals furnished the raw material for the newly invented

104

neolithic textile industry. Weaving may have first appeared in the wattlework roofs or walls of pile-dwellings and then in basketry and matting.

The first agricultural tool was the digging stick, followed by the spade, hoe, sickle, and plow. The most primitive form of agriculture probably arose spontaneously at many places both in the eastern and in the western hemisphere. It may have commenced as a system of irrigation of plants growing in nature. Whether agriculture first developed fully in a fertile river valley such as that of the Nile, or in a prairie or plateau region, it is impossible at present to determine conclusively. There is some evidence that a round-headed race living south and east of the Caspian Sea developed to a high degree the culture of cereals. This helped these plants to spread slowly over Europe from Egypt and Asia Minor as well as from central Asia. The neolithic commerce in flint, obsidian, jade, salt, amber, shells, and probably also in furs and cattle, may have aided the spread of these practices by providing means of communication.

The earliest known phase of the Egyptian neolithic was the Tasian in upper Egypt about 5500 B.C. This was prior to the appearance of agriculture which was introduced later, probably from the near east if it was not invented in Egypt. The Tasian phase was followed by the Delta-Fayum-Badarian group of cultures which were both pastoral and agricultural. The Sahara neolithic culture was a fusion of the final Capsian or late paleolithic or mesolithic in northern Africa with elements of the Fayum culture. Prehistoric querns for grinding grain have been found at many places in the Sahara region. The desert was much better watered at that time than now. The process of desiccation is still in progress. The Guinea neolithic culture along the Gold Coast of western Africa, especially in Ashanti and Togo, differed considerably from the neolithic culture of northern Africa.

The Badarian Nilotic culture followed the Tasian, Fayum and Merimde neolithic cultures. Its relation to the predynastic period has been stated as follows: "By 'Predynastic' is meant the age which is now so well known from the work of Professor Petrie and others, and which has been subdivided into the three divisions of Early (or Amratian), Middle (or Gerzean), and late (or Semaimian); by Badarian is meant a new period of the Predynastic age which precedes that known as Early. . . . There can be no question that the Badarian culture in very many of its manifestations is akin to the Amratian or Early Predynastic."[1] Petrie has applied his method of sequence dating according to ceramic styles and has divided the Badarian pottery which

[1] Guy Brunton and Gertrude Caton-Thompson, *The Badarian Civilisation*, London, 1928, pp. 1, 39.

105

has been excavated into nine sections dating from S.D. (Sequence Date) 21 to S.D. 29. Petrie also studied 60 Badarian crania and concluded that they were not like any Mediterranean or negro type. "The length and narrowness of the skull is like the primitive Indian, and that is the only type at all similar to the Badarian. . . . The Badarians were a fellow-branch with the Indians, both radiating from some Asiatic centre. . . . It is to Palestine and Syria that we must look for any traces of the earlier history of the Badarians."[2]

As Petrie's S.D. 80 was the commencement of the dynastic period at about 3100 B.C., and his S.D. 50 was probably about 4000 B.C., the Badarian culture may have existed considerably prior to the latter date. The Badarians had herds of oxen, sheep and goats, and cultivated cereals. Copper was used to a small extent, so that this culture may be regarded as upon the threshold of the chalcolithic age. The copper was imported from the north. Other imported materials were porphyry, stealite, basalt, ivory, shells and turquoise, indicating a considerable amount of trade. Their ceramic, tanning and weaving industries were highly developed. The Nile encouraged navigation. The Badarians and the Amratians, who succeeded them, had boats which were forerunners of sea-going ships.

The Somrong Sen neolithic culture of southeastern China, named after a site in Cambodia, extended over the Yunnan region of southern China, Indo-China, and as far west as the Ganges delta in India. It has usually been found in caves and kitchen middens. Only the dog and the pig were domesticated in this culture. It was based upon hunting and fishing more than upon agriculture.

The Japanese neolithic culture was complex in certain of its aspects. Its pottery was highly developed. So far as is now known, it had no agriculture nor animal husbandry. The Siberian neolithic culture also had no agriculture. It was a low form of the neolithic based upon hunting and fishing. Only the dog was domesticated. It was constituted apparently of a few elements of the neolithic culture which reached Siberia from Europe and central Asia.

The European neolithic culture was derived mainly from the southeast through the basin of the Danube River, and from the eastern Mediterranean through Spain. The neolithic of western Europe was divided into the pre-megalithic and megalithic major phases. The neolithic of northern Europe comprised the Ertebølle, Wohnplatz-Arctic, megalithic, and single grave (barrow) or battle-ax stages. These four phases overlapped and existed contemporaneously to a certain extent. In each region of Europe the neolithic culture was constituted

---

[2] Flinders Petrie, in Brunton and Caton-Thompson, pp. 26, 68. See also W. M. F. Petrie, *Social Life in Ancient Egypt*, 1923.

of indigenous and imported elements influenced and modified by local climatic and topographical conditions.

In the earliest stages of architectural evolution dwellings probably consisted of interlaced branches of wattlework sometimes daubed with mud and clay. Huts or houses elevated on piles as protection against animal or human enemies have existed in various parts of the world. In northern Italy in the valley of the river Po and elsewhere pile dwellings on mounds of marl are known as terremare after the Italian words for land and marl. In Switzerland the lake dwellings are known as palafittes after the Italian words for pile works. In Ireland the pile dwellings on island refuges in lakes or bogs are known as crannogs. The location over water or surrounded by it was doubtless chosen for safety. These dwellings were often grouped in villages for mutual protection. Some of the first cities in river valleys arose from these villages of pile dwellings. At a later stage acropolises on heights were constructed for similar reasons of protection, after massive stone fortifications had become possible.

Neolithic lacustrine dwellings and villages have been found on both sides of the Alps from eastern France to Yugoslavia. The horn-hafted tools, ornaments of bone and teeth, and flint objects found in them were of mesolithic origin. The pile dwellings themselves may also have been of the same origin. Their pottery, agriculture and animal husbandry were probably of Danubian provenance, whence they had come from the southeast or east. The Swiss lake-dwellers possessed basketry, netting and linen cloth. They practised spinning, twining, plaiting, knitting and weaving of flax. They used looms which indicated a high development of the textile art. In fact, the basic principles of this art were already mastered at the neolithic level and the industry progressed only by minor improvements thereafter, until power was applied within the last century or two by the invention of the power loom by Edmund Cartwright in 1785, which was made practical for weaving patterns by the invention of the Jacquard loom in 1801-04. These neolithic lacustrine dwellers cultivated flax and several varieties of barley, wheat and millet. For vegetables they had carrots, parsnips, beans, peas and lentils. As additional sources of food they procured game, fish, wild berries and fruits. Their debris which dropped into the lakes and was preserved in the mud until exposed in recent times has furnished us a detailed record of the higher stages of neolithic culture. The lake-dwelling period in Europe is sometimes called the Robenhausian after the site at Robenhausen on Lake Pfaeffikon in the Swiss canton of Zurich.

During the neolithic period were constructed many tombs and megalithic monuments. They included dolmens or stone tombs, passage graves, tumuli or mounds for burial purposes, single graves or barrows, menhirs or upright stones standing alone, cromlechs or circles, ovals and rectangles, and alignments of stones. They were constructed, probably in all cases, for magical or religious reasons. Many of them were intended for the worship of the sun. Such tombs and monuments have been found in Europe, Africa, Asia Minor, and Asia as far east as India. In the case of many of them, the custom originated in the east and traveled westward. They can be traced along the north coast of Africa and then the west coast of Europe where they arrived during the latter part of the neolithic period. Many megalithic monuments are to be found in Brittany and a considerable number in England. The megalithic period in Europe is sometimes called the Carnacian after the site at Carnac in Brittany.

The first means of transportation on water perhaps were the log, later the pointed log, and logs or bundles of reeds gathered in the raft. These were probably used during the paleolithic period. In the neolithic period and perhaps earlier the pointed log was hollowed into a dugout. Later its sides were built up with strakes which were pegged or sewn on so that the dugout became in effect the keel or bottom of the plank boat or ship. Rafts of inflated skins were used on the Euphrates and reed floats on the Nile and elsewhere. The raft may have been the precursor of the flatboat. It is not certain that the boat and ship dated back to the neolithic. According to Elliot Smith, the first seagoing ships were constructed in Egypt about 3000 B.C., which was after the close of the Egyptian neolithic.[3] According to Gilfillan, the first sails were hoisted in Egypt in about B.C. 6000, and the first Egyptian ships sailed the sea in the third dynasty, between the beginning and middle of the third millennium B.C.[4]

On land, the drag, the sled, and rolling pins or poles under sled runners were used at an early date, as means of transportation. The megaliths used during the neolithic period and later could not have been transported without such means. The first wheels may have been sections of tree trunks. But these would require a heavy and sharp saw and would be likely to split along the grain as the result of a side blow. Perhaps the first wheels were made from planks. It is not known when and where it was invented. Later the wheel was made light by the use of spokes. In course of time a metal tire was attached to strengthen it. In order to be fully developed the cultural complex of the wheel required motive power, metal, and a roadway which could not be fulfilled until after the neolithic. Among these requirements were draft animals, a harness, horseshoes, a wagon which could be steered, rather inexpensive iron, hard roads, bridges, and more or less stable political organization over rather extensive areas.

3 G. Elliot Smith, *Human History,* London, 1924.
4 S. C. Gilfillan, *Inventing the Ship,* 1935.

Agriculture and house-building made neolithic life more sedentary than the hunting, fishing and food-gathering paleolithic life. The coming of the copper age, namely, the period when tools and weapons were usually made of copper, caused a great change. In Egypt and Greece it marked the beginning of the historical period though this was merely coincidental. It characterized the earliest settlements at Anau, Hissarlik (Troy), and Susa, the latter being before the earliest Sumerians of whom we know. In Egypt there was a great increase of copper implements in the late predynastic period at about S.D. (Sequence Date) 60-63. This was apparently due to importation of copper from Asia. The Egyptian copper age attained its height during the first dynasty which commenced about 3100 B.C., namely about S.D. 79. In Greece the copper age came much later but was also due to Asiatic contacts. Throughout south-eastern Europe copper was found wherever contact with Asia was easy. The Caucasus has a great deal of copper but no tin, while Bohemia has much tin but no copper. Speaking of the development of early civilization, Frankfort said: "The invention of metallurgy appears to be a most momentous event, which gave a sudden impetus to that development and brings it within the sphere of our knowledge." "Our earlier researches on the relative chronology of the Southern Mesopotamian civilizations have enabled us to state that the Copper Age started earlier in Susa than either in Egypt, the Aegean or Anatolia. . . . In the hardly explored regions of Armenia or Transcaucasia may well be found the centre from which the knowledge of metal-working spread."[5]

Speiser commented in similar fashion upon the significance of the copper age: "Neolithic man may have lived in Egypt, Crete, or in Elam, in comparative isolation from other cultural provinces. But with the introduction of copper the tempo of life was powerfully accelerated. . . . Migrations due to climatic conditions, wars, trade connections, all of these contributed to a more or less intimate interrelationship between the various members of the ancient world at the beginning of the Copper Age." "In Susa I as well as in the related cultures, there was found evidence of the first known application of metallurgy, as distinct from a casual utilization of metals. At the same time the use of neolithic implements continued for a long time: hence the name 'aeneolithic.' "[6]

The industries of mining and of metallurgy created a new cultural era. Even before the end of the neolithic period a little native metal had been mined and used and there had been crude attempts to refine ore. A few metal implements have been found in the later neolithic

[5] H. Frankfort, *Studies in Early Pottery of the Near East, II,* London, 1927, pp. 119, 147.

[6] E. A. Speiser, *Mesopotamian Origins,* Philadelphia, 1930, pp. 2, 60.

109

sites. The general substitution of metallic for stone tools, and to a large extent for wood and bone, revolutionized the material basis of culture.

The world's principal deposits of copper are in Cornwall in England, at Burra Burra in Australia, Katanga in Africa, the Lake Superior distict in North America, and in Chile and Bolivia in South America. Copper is relatively soft and malleable and therefore easily worked in its pure native state. It was worked at an early date in the Lake Superior region. This had no influence upon the culture of the eastern hemisphere, and little in the western hemisphere except in Middle and Andean America where was developed the hardening of copper with an alloy of tin, and other metallurgical arts. Copper was used in Egypt as early as 5000 B.C., and perhaps still earler in Elam. It was produced from ore at an early date in Cyprus, and for many centuries was the most plentiful and useful metal in industry.

The accidental softening of copper by heat probably led to heating it in a furnace and to the rise of metallurgy. The occasional native copper having been picked up, copper ores had to be mined, heated and hammer finished. By itself copper is too soft for most industrial uses; but alloyed with any of several other metals it is much harder. In ancient time it was mixed with antimony, arsenic, zinc, or nickel; but most often with tin, making bronze. Copper was relatively plentiful but tin was scarce in the ancient world, hardly being found in Europe except in Cornwall, Bohemia, Spain and Portugal. Good bronze is an alloy in which tin constitutes about 10 percent and copper 90 percent of the mixture, but a smaller proportion of tin was often necessary. According to de Morgan, the bronze industry probably commenced in Egypt, Chaldea and Elam about 4000 B.C., in northern Persia and the Caucasus about 3000 B.C., in the eastern Mediterranean and Mycenae in Greece about 2500 B.C., and in Gaul about 2000 B.C. According to Elliot Smith, it appeared in western Asia about 2000 B.C.,[7] in western Europe about 1500 B.C., and in Britain and Scandinavia about 1000 B.C. The oldest known piece of bronze is a rod discovered in the pyramid of Medum in Egypt dating from about 3700 B.C. A bronze statuette of Gudea found in Babylonia dated from about 2500 B.C.

Bronze was probably introduced into Europe by the round-headed invaders who had earlier brought agriculture. It is possible that no bronze was manufactured in Europe during prehistoric times but that all of it was brought from Asia or elsewhere. It was used many times over by heating and reshaping. Bronze tools were manufactured by hammering or by casting when softened by heat. In

[7] J. de Morgan, *Prehistoric Man*, translated from the French, 1924.

110

France alone 57 prehistoric bronze foundries have been discovered and many in other European countries. Iron began to replace bronze in France from 900 to 600 B.C., and in Britain from 400 to 300 B.C. Roughly speaking, the bronze age lasted in Europe from 1900 to 900 B.C., or approximately 1,000 years.

The wheel also was introduced into Europe during the bronze age and stimulated transportation and mechanics. Sea-going vessels were built for the first time in Europe during this period. As one result of the improvement of transportation, commerce expanded greatly. The villages of the bronze like those of the neolithic age were terrestrial, lacustrine, crannogs or terremare. The introduction of bronze helped the development of various fundamental elements already present in the neolithic culture, such as industrial production.

Iron beads and an iron blade in a pyramid have been found in Egypt which were used during the fourth dynasty or about 2600 B.C. Iron was found in the second city of Troy in Asia Minor dating from 2000 B.C. The Assyrians probably used iron as early as from 2000 to 1500 B.C. Iron ores are comparatively easily reduced by heat. Iron smelting requires a temperature of about 1,525° Centigrade, and pure copper of about 1,080° Centigrade. The neolithic peoples did not succeed in reaching this melting point. They heated the iron ore or crude iron as high as they could and then hammered the spongy, red-hot bloom into whatever shapes and pieces they could fashion after knocking out the slag. Iron softens at red heat and can be welded at white heat.

The discovery at an unknown date prior to B.C. 1300 by the Hittites in Asia Minor of an effective method of reducing iron ore, and the diffusion of this invention, rendered possible the ready and widespread use of this metal. Its capacity to take and keep an edge and a point and the variable qualities available through its carbon alloys in steel give iron its unique value. On the other hand, iron rusts, could not be cast until it could be smelted, and is less attractive in appearance than some other metals. With relatively abundant ore available it became possible to use this metal for almost every kind of tool. Iron is estimated to constitute four to five percent of the earth's crust and is the fourth most abundant metal, though much of it is not in a sufficiently rich ore to be worth mining. "It has been estimated that the iron ore reserves of the world in millions of tons are: actual, 57,812; possible, 167,663; total, 225,475. This total is distributed among the continents in percentages as follows: North and Central America, 61.5; Europe, 17.5; Asia, 11.2; Africa, 5.0; South America, 3.6."[8] To render iron usable probably was the most valuable

[8] Maurice Parmelee, *Geo-Economic Regionalism and World Federation*, New York, 1949, pages 73 to 74.

single invention since fire-making. Iron may have overtaken the slowly spreading bronze because it was easier to work, was so much more useful, and in many places was locally available, as in western Asia, Europe, and in the northern half of the western hemisphere. The iron age which ensued stimulated a great expansion and refinement of the bronze age culture.

The iron age commenced in Egypt and Mesopotamia about 1300 to 1200 B.C., and in Crete about 1200 B.C. In Africa south of the Sahara Desert the iron age apparently followed the neolithic period without an intervening bronze age. This may have been because Africa has moderately large iron deposits, especially west of the upper Nile. Iron was carried to India with the army of Alexander and to America after Columbus. In Europe the iron age commenced about 900 B.C., and possibly as early as 1100 B.C. in Greece and Italy. North of the Alps its first epoch, known as the Hallstatt stage after a station in Austria, lasted from about 900 to 500 B.C. Its second epoch, known as the La Tene stage after a station in Switzerland lasted from about 500 to 1 B.C. By this time most of the cultures of the eastern hemisphere had entered the literate period. The written record began to furnish information about cultural evolution. As this historical information became more abundant, the archeological record became relatively less important, but will always be valuable as a record of the past.

So far in this description no account has been given of cultural or of ethnic evolution in the western hemisphere. The only primates indigenous to the western world are the *Hapalidae* or marmosets and *Cebidae* or cebus monkeys of Central and South America. Other primates whose remains have been found in the Americas became extinct probably before the beginning of the pleistocene. No authentic remains of early man or of his precursors have as yet been discovered, so that mankind apparently evolved in the eastern hemisphere.

The native American population is of the mongoloid type. As an American anthropologist has expressed it: "The affinities of New World man are with Mongolians and, to a less marked degree, with Polynesians. With the former we have close parallels in hair, form of eye, breadth of face, and bodily proportions. With the Polynesians, the agreements are chiefly in pigmentation and to some extent, in the hair."[9] It is reasonable to suppose that man first entered the western hemisphere by way of Behring Strait and thence spread over the two American continents. None of the early immigrants could have come from Polynesia because Polynesia was populated at a relatively late date and is separated by thousands of miles of water from the Ameri-

[9] C. Wissler, *The American Indian,* 2nd edition, New York, 1922, p. 339.

can coast. If any Polynesians reached America in pre-Columbian time, it could have been only a few navigators carried there in their frail boats by chance winds and currents and within the last 2,000 years. Such immigrants could have had little influence upon American culture, and even less on race.

No conclusive evidence has been found of interglacial man in America. There is little evidence of a paleolithic stage of cultural evolution in the western hemisphere. The few paleoliths which have been found bear some resemblance to Solutrean and Magdalenian artifacts. The earliest immigrants arrived from the north bringing with them a late paleolithic or early neolithic culture. This event probably took place during or soon after the close of the last glacial period. They brought with them the low neolithic Siberian culture mentioned earlier in this chapter. This culture furnished the basis and starting point for American cultural evolution. Wissler has enumerated these cultural traits as follows: "The New World received a detachment of early mongoloid people at a time when the main body had barely developed stone polishing. That this was contemporaneous with the appearance of stone polishing in Europe does not necessarily follow, for future research in Asia may show it to have been much earlier. . . . Some of the probable traits brought from the mother-land are the firedrill, stone chipping, twisting of string, the bow, throwing stick, the harpoon, simple basketry and nets, hunting complexes, cooking with stones in vessels of wood, bark or skin, body-painting, and perhaps tattooing, and the domestication of the dog. . . . Independently, the New World developed agriculture, pottery, the higher types of basketry and cloth weaving, the working of the softer metals and the manufacture of bronze."[10] Another American anthropologist has enumerated the assumed early elements of American culture as the following: The dog, bow, harpoon, firedrill, woven and twined basketry, family groups, men's house, shamanism, crisis ceremonies, especially for girls at puberty and whipping of boys.[11] These lists are compiled by noting the traits possessed by all groups in America and then assuming that these traits were contained in the common inheritance from Asia. There were probably later migrations from Asia.

From the point of entry in the extreme north mankind spread over the two American continents to the extreme south in Patagonia. Within this wide range there developed a great diversity and disparity of culture. A notable example is the large number of linguistic stocks. There have been identified 56 languages in the United States and Canada, 29 in Mexico and Central America, and 84 in South America, making a total of 169 in the western hemisphere. Contrasted with this

[10] C. Wissler, op. cit., pp. 398-9.
[11] A. L. Kroeber, Anthropology, New York, 1923, p. 340.

large number there are 21 linguistic stocks or families in Asia and Europe and only six in Africa. Upon further study the number of American families is being reduced. Even after such reduction the number of families recognized will probably be greater than the number in the eastern hemisphere. Furthermore, no resemblances indicating a common origin have been detected between an American linguistic stock and any stock in any other part of the world. This does not mean that man did not have speech when he came to America and that the whole course of linguistic evolution took place independently in the western hemisphere. Complete isolation over a long period of time could cause divergence so wide that resemblances indicating a common origin can no longer be detected.

With two or three notable exceptions, there were no large political units in the western hemisphere. Much of the population was scattered in small independent groups. This may have encouraged the linguistic diversity. All of the American linguistic families, however, belonged to the same morphological class, namely, that of the agglutinative languages. In this regard they displayed greater morphological unity than the languages of the eastern hemisphere which are divided between the inflective, isolating and agglutinative linguistic classes.

The linguistic diversity suggests that mankind may have arrived in America earlier than is generally supposed. Other features of the cultural situation suggest the same thing. There was a great disparity between the lowest and highest cultural levels. If we assume that all of the immigrants or, at any rate, all of the earlier immigrants were of the same low level, it must have taken a relatively long time to develop the much higher culture of the most advanced groups. These groups were located in the middle American region. The two leading groups were the Mayan in Mexico and Central America, and the Andean in Peru. Their cultures included all features of the American substratum and much besides. Kroeber has suggested the following reasons for the high middle American culture: "Possibly the environmental feature of greatest value to cultural progress in Middle America was its diversity. Mountain and coast, temperate highland and hot lowland, humid and arid tracts, tropical jungle and open country, were only a few hours apart. In each locality the population worked out its necessary adaptations, and yet it was near enough others of a different adaptation for them to trade, to depend on one another, to learn. Custom therefore came in contact with custom, invention with invention. The discrepancies, the very competitions would lead to reconciliations, readaptations, new combinations. Cultural movement and stimulus would normally be greater than in a culturally uniform area." [12]

[12] A. L. Kroeber, op. cit., p. 353.

114

At the time of the discovery of America its highest cultures did not possess the horse, cattle, plow, wheel, iron nor any of the cereals of the eastern hemisphere. The absence of these fundamental traits suggests an entirely independent evolution of the higher American culture. On the other hand, it possessed a highly developed and varied horticulture of its own. More than forty plants were cultivated whose wild ancestors were peculiar to America. Several of these, such as maize, potatoes and tobacco, have been borrowed and have attained great importance elsewhere in the world.

Among the features of the middle American culture were pottery, sculpture, stone buildings, the smelting, casting, alloying, plating and joining of metals, suspended warp or simple weaving frames, cotton growing and loom weaving, textile clothing and sandals, town life, markets, confederacy, priesthood, temples, human sacrifice, the solstitial calendar, and empires. The Mayans developed astronomy, mathematics including the zero, a highly accurate cycle calendar, and a form of writing which was a mixture of pictographic and ideographic signs. So far as can now be determined, all of these cultural traits were developed in America independent of the cultural evolution of the eastern hemisphere.

This relatively high middle American culture has suggested to some students of the subject that man has been longer in America than has usually been assumed. However, in all probability no one of the above-mentioned cultural traits evolved in the eastern hemisphere prior to the early neolithic. The evolution of the middle American culture is no more remarkable and presupposes no longer a time than the parallel evolution in the old world.

There have been a few finds of stone implements, such as at Trenton, New Jersey, and in the Mammoth Cave district of Kentucky, which resemble the Solutrean and Magdalenian paleoliths. These finds suggest the possibility that man may have entered during the last glacial period 20,000 or more years ago.[13] Later investigations farther west have brought to light paleoliths which appear to be much older. Renaud has asserted that paleoliths ranging in type from Chellean to Magdalenian have been found in Colorado, Wyoming, Nebraska, New Mexico and Oklahoma.[14] There is not as yet sufficient stratigraphical evidence to determine whether these American paleoliths coincide in time as well as in type to the corresponding European

[13] Gladwin thinks that men arrived in America from Asia at least 25,000 years ago. (Harold S. Gladwin, *Men Out of Asia*, New York, 1947.)

[14] Etienne-B. Renaud, *L'antiquité de l'homme dans l'Amerique du Nord*, in *L'Anthropologie*, Vol. 38, 1928; *Stations Paleolithique du sudouest du Wyoming*, in *Revue Anthropologique*, Paris, July-Sept., 1936, pp. 216-38.

types. A few culturally backward tribes may have produced very primitive implements.

The pre-Columbian American culture was less extensive and did not attain so high a point as the contemporary culture in the eastern hemisphere. Its highest phases, namely, the Mayan and the Andean, were ruthlessly destroyed by the European invaders. Consequently, it has contributed little to the general fund of culture, except for its gathered and cultivated plants. As an isolated and largely independent evolution, it has however, some value for comparison with the corresponding cultural evolution in Asia and America.

Nordenskiöld has enumerated fifty-four of the most important American discoveries and inventions unknown to the eastern hemisphere when America was discovered. Among them were maize, manioc, potatoes, beans, tobacco, cacao, rubber, quinine, llamas, alpacas, guinea-pigs, turkeys, domesticated bees, platinum, reinforcing pottery clay with sponge spicules, the hammock, and the Maya calendar. All of these fifty-four were found among the cultivators but only two, namely, tobacco and tobacco pipes, among the gleaners. To the north of Mexico were found only nine, in Mexico and Central America, eighteen, in the Amazonas region, thirty-six, and in the Inca realm, twenty. Nordenskiöld has remarked that "it is mostly where the Indians have been prosperous that one meets with a large proportion of inventions and discoveries. I am afraid it is not always true that necessity is the mother of invention." With regard to the indigenous American culture he said that "a good many things have been discovered and invented by the Indians. . . . Are we not justified in supposing that the race that has achieved all the discoveries enumerated above, together with the inventions therewith connected that were not known in the Old World in pre-Columbian times, also might have been capable of inventing something or other which was also known there?" [15]

[15] Erland Nordenskiöld, *Modifications in Indian Culture through Inventions and Loans,* Gothenburg, 1930, pp. 22-3, 25.

Chapter IX

The Linguistic Pre-Requisite of Culture

AS has been demonstrated in an earlier chapter, culture can evolve only in a social setting. An individual isolated throughout his life from his congeners cannot acquire or create it. But the social environment alone does not insure the emergence of a culture. There have been and are many gregarious and social animal species which have failed to develop it even in its most rudimentary form. Communication which permits of the exchange of information and of ideas and their transmission from generation to generation is essential for the efflorescence of a culture. Comparatively few ideas can be evolved prior to the existence of at least a rudimentary form of communication. As we shall see later in this chapter, human thinking itself is largely if not entirely in terms of inarticulate speech. Mankind is the only species which has a mode of communication in the form of speech adequate for the development of culture.

While many animals utter emotional and other cries which in some species are quite varied, man is the only animal which speaks a language in which sounds have acquired conventional meanings. Animals which dwell in forests may need for communication the auditory more than the visual and olfactory senses. Hence arise the singing and "small talk" or chattering of birds, the grunting of pigs and lemurs, etc. Though they are forest dwellers most of the anthropoid apes are usually silent and not very gregarious. The principal exceptions are the gibbons and siamangs which are very gregarious and make a good deal of noise. Some of the comparative anatomists have been of the opinion that the human ancestry was closer to that of these small apes than it was to that of the great apes. Yerkes, who sought evidence of the rudiments of language among the apes, found no indication of speech among the gibbons and siamangs about whose means of communication little is known. He concluded that no speech is indicated also for the gorilla and that its means of intercommunication are little developed. For the orang-utan he thought he found a very rudimentary speech. With regard to the chimpanzee he arrived at the conclusion that it possesses the beginnings of speech in affective vocalization and intercommunication based upon visual rather than auditory stimuli, namely, gestures.[1]

The nervous and muscular traits which have rendered speech possible in man have been described by various writers. Johnston has said that "the middle association field (island of Reil), situated as it is between the auditory area and that part of the somaesthetic area which receives sensations from the lips, tongue, throat, etc., is chiefly the association center for speech."[2] Romer has declared that "speech reception is localized in the temporal region, not far across the way from the frontal area having to do with speech production."[3] Injuries to these portions of the brain cause disturbances in speech or destroy it completely. Tilney has expressed the opinion that the cerebral speech centers developed out of the hand-gesture centers.[4] This theory may furnish support to the hypothesis that language originated from gesture signs.

Among the organs of articulate speech outside of the nervous system is the larynx which contains the vocal cords. The larynx apparently has not been modified by the evolution of language. A muscle of great utility in articulate speech is the genio-glossus or genio-hypoglossus. It originates as a small tendon from a point inside the lower jawbone about midway between the roots of the incisor teeth and the point of the chin. This tendon divides and spreads over the tongue and then goes back to the hyoid bone. It is supplied by the ninth or hypoglossal pair of the cerebral nerves. It serves to protrude and withdraw the tongue. This muscle is very small in the lower animals and larger in the apes in which it seems to enable the tongue to sort food. "In man the genio-glossus springs from the top of a bony prominence. In all the lower *Primates* it comes out of a pit. Moreover, in the apes it is found not only to be much smaller than in man which is a sure sign that it meets certain specific human needs but it is also obviously much less versatile, in that the separate fasciculi of the muscle are bound closely together."[5] According to Robinson, the development of this muscle among men can be traced by the gradual disappearance of the pit and the growth of the tubercle through the Heidelberg and Naulette specimens, the Bushmen, central African

---

[1] Robert M. and Ada W. Yerkes, *The Great Apes*, New Haven, 1929.

[2] J. B. Johnston, *The Nervous System of Vertebrates*, Philadelphia, 1906, p. 354.

[3] A. S. Romer, *Man and the Vertebrates*, Chicago, 1933, p. 298.

[4] Frederick Tilney, *The Brain from Ape to Man*, New York, 1928.

[5] Louis Robinson, *The Relations of Speech to Human Progress*, in *Science Progress*, No. 31, January 1914, pp. 528-9.

118

pygmies, Andamanese, Veddahs, and Hottentots. The size of the tubercle has apparently been directly correlated with the complexity of speech. Robinson has also suggested that the prominence of the chin and the shape of the cheeks and nose have been affected by speech.

The cerebral mechanism of speech includes the frontal speech area adjacent to the motor centers for lips and tongue, which is utilized in the production of words, the temporal acoustic area which joins these sounds into sentences, the parietal cortex between the sensory, acoustic, and visual areas which associates the sensations from these areas, and the cortical parts bordering upon the occipital area which constitute the "nominal" centers because visual perception aids greatly in the recognition and naming of objects. "All of these areas are linked together and coordinated in the reception, understanding, and production of speech. They constitute the 'central exchange.'"[6]

The modifications of the jaws which have been associated with the rise of articulate speech are "(a) an opening out and broadening of the floor of the jaws to give more freedom of movement to the tongue; (b) a pushing forward of the chin for the same purpose and a transfer of the bony braces of the symphysis from the inside to the outside of the chin region; (c) a development of bony tubercles as the seat of origin of the tongue muscles, replacing the pit in the backward sloping ape symphysis."[7]

The inner cast of the brain case of Pithecanthropus revealed a great enlargement of the rear portion of the second temporal convolution. Elliot Smith thought that this indicated a rapid expansion of the acoustic area concerned with speech as contrasted with the other anthropoids.[8] In Homo neanderthalensis also the cortical areas connected with auditory and motor speech were fairly well developed. These facts suggest that not only early man but even some of his immediate precursors may have possessed the faculty for speech.

The acquisition of the anatomical and physiological equipment for a linguistic faculty did not necessarily mean the immediate or rapid evolution of speech. It is possible that for a long time communication was largely if not entirely by gestures and a sort of sign language. Mimicry of sounds as well as of movements may also have been used before language came into existence. It has been alleged that the pantomimic use of the organs of articulation comes readily to children and probably to primitive men who have little or no language. Paget

[6] E. A. Hooton, *Up From The Ape,* New York, 1931, p. 166.

[7] *Op. cit.,* p. 174.

[8] G. E. Smith, *Essays on the Evolution of Man, the Human Brain,* London, 1924.

has suggested that the different languages may have arisen because every idea or action can be pantomimed in different ways.[9] However the latter may be, mimicry and pantomime doubtless played their part in the origin of language.

Language may be divided into eye-language discerned by the visual sense and ear-language apprehended by the auditory sense. Gestures by the hands and facial muscles constitute eye-language. Speech constitutes ear-language. Writing arises out of ear-language because it is a record of speech. It is also eye-language because it can be discerned by the visual sense, and touch-language for the blind who read the Braille raised dots.

Gestures may be classified as graphic or descriptive and as emotional or demonstrative. In similar fashion, inarticulate cries which convey some sort of meaning may be classified as imitative, mimetic or onomatopoetic and as emotional, affective or interjectional. Many animals utter emotional cries. Some of them may be understood by their congeners, or, at any rate, stimulate similar affective states in them. Many animals also make movements occasioned by emotional states which may stimulate similar affective states in their congeners. In none of these animals, with the possible exception of a few of the higher primates, have these emotional cries and movements given rise to language. As we have seen, Yerkes thought that he found the rudiments of language in the affective vocalization and movements of chimpanzees.

A male human child aged seven and a half months and a female chimpanzee two months older were reared together for nine months. The ape learned to understand many verbal stimuli, mainly commands, but did not acquire true speech. She displayed differentiation in her vocalizations, directed mostly to emotional situations, as displayed by children before they begin to talk. The boy, on the contrary, displayed the usual human phases of learning to speak. He prattled a great deal while learning whereas the ape did not do so at all. This contrast is probably due to neurological differences between the human and the anthropoid anatomy. It is cortical inadequacy rather than a deficiency in the vocal apparatus which prevents the ape from acquiring language. In this experiment the ape was more dominated by her emotions, especially fear, than was the boy, perhaps because she was in an environment alien to her species. The boy displayed greater imitative capacity which is probably of greater significance for the evolution and learning of language than are the emotions.[10]

Many animals use sounds to stimulate their congeners or to respond to them. This apparently is true of some of the insects, as, for

9 Richard Paget, *Human Speech,* New York, 1930.
10 W. N. and L. A. Kellogg, *The Ape and the Child,* New York, 1933.

example, the crickets, which stridulate by rubbing the legs against the body. The birds create sounds by means of their syrinx which is a pair of organs like reeds at the top of the lungs. Some birds, such as the parrots, can make a great variety of sounds. There is no evidence that these sounds have acquired an artificial and conventional meaning for these birds. Even though a parrot can imitate human speech it cannot grasp its meaning.

Most of the higher mammals possess a larynx which is a box of cartilage at the top of the windpipe. This organ, called the Adam's-apple in man, has within it two muscles which when taut are set in vibration by the outgoing breath. The sounds produced by these muscles, known as the vocal chords, constitute the voice. Most of the vocal mammals can make only a few sounds. Cats, for example, can only mew, purr, growl, hiss, and moan or yowl. Dogs can only bark, howl, yelp, and whine or whimper. The human voice can make a great variety of sounds, thus rendering possible a very complicated and elaborate speech.

Many of the higher animals use facial expressions, mimicry, and gesture to influence their congeners. Gesture accompanies a great deal of human speech. It is used in varying degrees by different races and social classes. Gesture languages have been used by certain communities as supplementary to or sometimes in the place of speech. Such languages have existed among certain primitive peoples, such as some of the North American Indians, among Trappist monks and working-class Neapolitans, and especially among deafmutes who are almost entirely incapacitated for speech by their physical defects.[11]

It will never be possible to determine whether gesture or vocalization furnished the starting point of language. Some suggestions as to the early stages in its evolution may be derived from the observation of infantile modes of expression and communication and from the study of primitive languages. The history of language in general may also throw some light on this subject. The development of gesture may be illustrated by the head-shaking reaction of the infant. This originates from the movement of withdrawing the head from food or any other object which is not desired. This movement becomes a conditioned response of avoidance before the undesired object approaches the infantile head. In course of time this movement of the head becomes a habitual sign of refusal. After speech has been acquired

[11] "Gesture language, in fact, is constantly reacting on the pictographic method of expression, and may be said to supply it with moods and tenses even without the aid of words. . . . Simple pictography, whether or not aided by gesture language, is one thing. The evolution of a regular script is quite another matter." (A. J. Evans, "The European Diffusion of Primitive Pictography and its Bearings on the Origin of Script," in *Anthropology and the Classics*, edited by R. R. Marett, Oxford, 1908, p. 24.)

it is still used at times as a symbol not only of refusal of physical objects but of dissent and of denial of statements made and of opinions expressed. In similar fashion other conditioned responses become gestures which supplement speech.

During its pre-linguistic period the child is in its laryngeal or glottal stage of expression. The cry of the newborn infant is weak and tremulous and sometimes rhythmical. Its laryngeal stage is comparable with the vocal behavior of the lower animals. The primitive glottal reflexes and coordinations become a part of the general emotional response of the child. Laryngeal or glottal vocalization existed long before articulate speech arose. Pre-linguistic man doubtless possessed as raw materials for the elements of speech not only laryngeal but also random articulate sounds.

The human infant soon after birth mingles laryngeal vocalization with random articulation. Before long it develops fixation or circular responses. Sounds are repeated, as *da da da*. In this fashion ear-vocal reflexes become conditioned. In a linguistic society it begins to imitate the articulate elements of the speech of its associates. These articulate utterances evoked by the stimulation of the talk of others become conditioned by objects and situations. In this fashion they acquire a meaning for the infant and growing child who gradually passes into its linguistic period. In this transformation during the first few years of its existence the comprehension of language in the case of most of its elements precedes its use. In other words, while mere imitation without comprehension may constitute the starting point of articulate speech in the infant, the bulk of language is acquired by comprehension rather than imitation. The infant soon passes from parrot-like imitation to human understanding.[12]

The development of speech in the human child suggests that language may have originated from a random articulation uttered by chance in association with a specific object or affective state, such as a feeling, or with an impulse to action or an idea, if ideas already existed in the pre-linguistic stage. By means of this association a sound became conditioned for the speaker and his hearers. The next time it was uttered it became a word response to a given situation. As these conditioned sounds or words increased in number, combinations of words constituting sentences became possible.

The theory of the origin of language in the imitation of sounds in nature has been called the "bow-wow" theory. The theory of its origin in affective sounds, such as emotional cries, has been called the "pooh-pooh" theory. Subsidiary theories are the "ding-dong" and the "yo-he-ho" theories. The former assumes that language originated

[12] Allport has discussed at length the development of language in children. (F. H. Allport, *Social Psychology*, Boston, 1924.)

from a vocal response to sounds which is only in part or not at all imitative and which may be in part affective. The latter assumes that it originated from a vocal response to rhythmic occupational action which is at least in part affective.[13]

It will never be possible to determine whether imitation or affective vocal expression was the origin of the first word or words. Observation of the acquisition of language by children suggests that after the first few steps imitation probably played a much larger part than affective vocal expression. But the affective factor has always influenced vocal expression to a considerable extent. The meaning of a word may be modified or added to by the inflection with which it is spoken. The "tone" of words in the Chinese and certain other languages may be a vestige of this early phase of linguistic evolution.

Jespersen has asserted that "language originated as play, and the organs of speech were first trained in this singing sport of idle hours. . . . Men sang out their feelings long before they were able to speak their thoughts. . . . Language, then, began with half-musical unanalyzed expressions for individual beings and solitary events."[14] This hypothesis suggests that language arose out of affective vocal expression which may have been in part collective in its nature. It is, therefore, closely related to the "pooh-pooh" theory mentioned above. There can be no evidence in support of Jespersen's hypothesis, which is, therefore, wholly gratuitous. Language doubtless originated not only in play but also in many other activities, such as the gathering of food, hunting, fishing, the manufacture of tools, sex relations, the care of children, and the like, in each of which appropriate sounds began to acquire a symbolic meaning. Thus there developed a vocabulary of considerable extent and variety. While these habits of singing have been observed among many peoples, even the most primitive of them already have relatively complicated languages which may have come into being long before these singing habits.

The foregoing discussion indicates that it will never be possible to discover the origin of language in a single field of activity, which is, to say the least, very doubtful. Jespersen has defined language in its rudimentary stage as follows: "We get the first approach to language proper when communicativeness takes precedence of exclamativeness, when sounds are uttered in order to 'tell' fellow-creatures something, as when birds warn their young ones of some imminent danger."[15] However plausible this definition may be, it is based upon

[13] Kimball Young has described these theories in his *Social Psychology*, New York, 1930.

[14] Otto Jespersen, *Language, Its Nature, Development and Origin*, London, 1922, pp. 433, 436, 441.

[15] O. Jespersen, *op. cit.*, p. 437.

unverifiable hypotheses. No human group has been discovered speaking a rudimentary language. Every extant language which has been studied, even of the preliterate peoples, is highly developed and complicated. While every human being has to acquire language for itself, the human infant is born into a linguistic society where it can learn a language by imitation and does not have to develop one by itself. Infantile babbling is not speech, and the so-called "languages" of older children are improvisations on the speech of the linguistic groups to which they belong.

Vendryes has declared that "the most general definition of language that can be given is that it is a system of signs."[16] Sapir has defined language in its developed form as "a purely human and noninstinctive method of communicating ideas, emotions, and desires by means of a system of voluntarily produced symbols."[17] He has characterized it as a system of phonetic symbols and as the principal form of communicative symbolism. This definition raises the question as to whether language preceded ideas or *vice versa,* which resembles the problem as to whether the hen preceded the egg or *vice versa.* All of the higher animals probably retain images of certain objects which have significance for them because they are related to food, sex, offspring, etc. These images with their associations may be termed specific ideas. It is doubtful if any animal possesses general ideas derived from a generalizing of specific ideas. It is almost certain that no animal possesses any abstract ideas derived from abstracting a concept or deducing a principle from many specific ideas. "As Wundt has said, animals are silent because they have nothing to say and many of the ideas to be expressed come only after the expression has been fairly well developed."[18]

Inasmuch as a large part of thinking is in terms of verbal imagery, it is certain that very little if any thinking was possible before the commencement of language. Since that time thought and language have acted and reacted to develop each other. Language has rendered possible the formulation of ideas. The expression of these ideas has stimulated new ideas which have sought linguistic formulation. Thus have arisen many new words and other linguistic forms. Some of the behaviorist psychologists have assimilated thought and language with each other by asserting that both of them are forms of verbal behavior.

If the foregoing considerations are valid, language was not only

[16] J. Vendryes, *Language: A Linguistic Introduction to History,* New York, 1925, p. 7.
[17] Edward Sapir, *Language,* New York, 1921, p. 7.
[18] W. B. Pillsbury and C. L. Meader, *The Psychology of Language,* New York, 1928, p. 114.

a prerequisite of culture but also has been influential in several important respects in cultural evolution. Language has rendered possible the conservation of experience which can be transmitted from generation to generation, and has thereby increased greatly the volume of social inheritance. It has also expanded greatly the range of social action and of cooperation. As Pillsbury and Meader have said: "In all animals that cooperate in any way in defense or offense, a means of communication however primitive would have its value."[19]

Language has furnished the individual the opportunity of influencing others by means of persuasion rather than force. As de Laguna has said: "Speech is the great medium through which human cooperation is brought about. . . . Men do not speak simply to relieve their feelings or to air their views, but to awaken a response in their fellows and to influence their attitudes and acts."[20] It has enabled human beings to take counsel and confer together, and has put a premium upon intelligence as contrasted with brute force. Allport has gone so far as to assert that self-adaptation and the control of others by inarticulate laryngeal sounds evolved as the earliest language, and that it was control of others rather than the desire to communicate which furnished the original drive behind the acquisition of language.[21] De Laguna has declared that "it is to the great superiority of speech over animal cries as a means of *social control* that we must look for the chief cause of its evolutionary origin and development."[22] However this may be with respect to its origin, language has rendered possible a good deal of social control. On the other hand, it has also given the individual the means to express himself. In this manner and to this extent it has promoted individual freedom, and has been of immeasurable value in the development of human personality.

Speech is a form of behavior as well as a mode of expression. The earliest vocal expressions, whether they were emotional cries or imitative sounds, acquired a meaning for listeners because they became associated with situations which called for characteristic responses. Thus a cry of fear might stimulate the impulse to flight. The imitation of an animal sound might arouse the desire to hunt. In this fashion speech not only added greatly to the human fund of ideas, but also gave rise in large part to the possibility for the concatenation and flow of ideas which constitute the process of thinking.[23] Some of the

[19] W. B. Pillsbury and C. L. Meader, *op. cit.*, p. 119.

[20] Grace A. de Laguna, *Speech, Its Function and Development*, New Haven, 1927, p. 19.

[21] F. H. Allport, *op. cit.*

[22] *Op. cit.*, p. 41.

[23] See Maurice Parmelee, *The Science of Human Behavior*, New York, 1913. Chapter XIV entitled "The Nature of Intelligence."

behaviorist psychologists have gone so far as to assert that all thought is sub-vocal speech. This would exclude the possibility of thinking from all speechless animals, in other words, from all animals apart from mankind. It would also mean that language must have preceded thought. It is, however, possible that not all thought is sub-vocal speech. Many ideas are derived from visual images, facial gestures, and kinesthetic sensations caused by movements of the hands, feet and other parts of the body. A small amount of rudimentary thinking may have arisen among animals, and among men before the origin of language.

Watson has described the relation between thinking and speech from a behaviorist point of view: "Thinking activity at successive moments of time may be kinaesthetic, verbal or emotional. When kinaesthetic organization becomes blocked or is lacking, then the verbal processes function; if both are blocked, the emotional organization becomes dominant. By hypothesis, however, the final response or adjustment, if one is reached, must be verbal (sub-vocal). It is convenient to call this final verbal act a judgment."[24] Dashiell has said that man is a speaking, tool using, and laughing animal, but surpasses in learning and thinking. He has described the social aspect of language from a behaviorist point of view: "The vocal segments of man's reactive equipment, by virtue of their relative freedom from the demands of his occupations and activities, have come to be the leading mode of inter-individual signaling, and by virtue of their capacity for subtle refinements they have become the symbolizing reactions *par excellence*. . . . Once built up as social stimuli and responses they become modes of self-stimulation as well. . . . These self stimuli may become implicit and, as a result of serial integration meanwhile, they may become systematized so that they come to serve as intraorganic controls of behavior operating with some independence of environmental agencies."[25]

Though written before behaviorism became influential, Wundt's voluminous treatise on the psychology of language is largely behaviorist. His concluding characterization of language reads as follows: "Sie ist eine lebendige Betätigung des menschlichen Geistes, die sich, wie alle andern geistigen Funktionen, mit den äussern und innern Bedingungen verändert, denen der Mensch unterworfen ist. Eben deshalb aber weil sie nicht ein selbständiges Dasein ausser dem Menschen führt, ist sie um so mehr ein treuer Abdruck des menschlichen Geistes selbst, und trägt in jeder ihrer besonderen Formen die Spuren der Natur-und Kulturbedingungen an sich, denen der Mensch in seiner

24 J. B. Watson, *Behaviorism*, New York, 1925, p. 214.
25 J. F. Dashiell, *Fundamentals of Objective Psychology*, Boston, 1928, p. 486.

eigenen Lebensgeschichte und in der seiner Vorfahren unterworfen war."[26]

Introspection proves conclusively that much the larger part of human thinking takes place in terms of words and sentences, namely, in the form of sub-vocal speech. This is all the more apparent when it is accompanied by movements of lips and sometimes by a muttering sound when the thinking becomes almost vocal. Thought is, therefore, largely if not entirely anticipatory or covert behavior which often leads to consummatory or overt behavior. When it arises entirely or in large part out of feeling, it has sometimes been called autistic or dereistic thinking. When it arises mainly out of visual, kinesthetic and other sensual images received from outside, it is more likely to be objective and realistic and therefore intellectual in its nature. The two types of thought are never entirely distinct from each other because even the most intellectual thinking must perforce take place in an affective setting which colors it in varying degrees. Language is necessary for the development of conceptual thought. Up to a certain point the evolution of the two go hand in hand. After a relatively complex language has come into being, thought may advance more rapidly so that existing language becomes inadequate for its expression. This situation leads to enlargement of the vocabulary and sometimes also to changes in the structure of a language. It may give rise to semantic consideration and discussion of words and phrases. Language is necessary to coordinate the intelligent behavior manifested in the use of tools and in the control of the non-social environment, as well as in social relations.

The thinking of the isolated individual is to a large extent a process of discussing and of reasoning or even arguing with himself. In social intercourse conversation broadens greatly the scope of this discussion. Conversation serves not only to communicate information and ideas but also to influence and modify the ideas of the participants. Thus opinions and beliefs take form and become fixed, and are more or less generally accepted or not, as the case may be. The institutions upon which a social order is based are in one of their aspects systems of spoken or written language. These institutions are, however, due in the last analysis to basic material factors which will be described in later chapters, and are not merely verbal expressions.

As has already been indicated, all known languages, even of the most primitive peoples, are highly developed. It is almost impossible to trace the stages of linguistic evolution. On *a priori* grounds it may seem plausible to assume that language has evolved from the simple

[26] Wilhelm Wundt, *Volkerpsychologie*, Erster Band, Zweiter Teil, second revised edition, Leipzig, 1904.

to the complex, from the analytic to the synthetic stages. Some philologists are, nevertheless, of the opinion that language has developed from the synthetic to the analytic. Jespersen has stated this theory emphatically: "The old theory of the three stages through which human language was supposed always to proceed, isolation, agglutination and flexion, was built upon insufficient materials. . . . The evolution of language shows a progressive tendency from inseparable irregular conglomerations to freely and regularly combinable short elements."[27] Pillsbury and Meader reflected this theory when they said that it is "likely that sentences and larger units developed first and words came to be completely recognized only after language had been committed to writing for some time."[28] This theory may seem contradictory to the "bow-wow" and the "pooh-pooh" theories of the origin of language. Emotional cries and imitative sounds originate by themselves and not as parts of sentences and longer units of speech. The complex forms of language could not come into existence until a considerable number of words were already in use. These would have to include nouns—common and proper—and verbs before even the simplest sentences could be formulated. A mere list of nouns or of verbs does not constitute a sentence. Adjectives and adverbs follow as abstractions from nouns and verbs. The other parts of speech might not be originated until later.

The theory that primordial language developed from the synthetic to the analytic in the sense that sentences preceded words is inherently impossible in its literal and obvious meaning. It is, however, possible that agglutinative language preceded the type of isolating languages now in existence. The latter may, indeed, have been derived from the former through the disintegration of compound words. Grammar as the science of linguistic structure probably did not commence until writing came into being. Not until then could words be fully and clearly distinguished as units of speech, though grammatical forms and structure had been developing from the early stages of linguistic evolution.

The extant languages and the extinct languages of which written records have been found may be classified from at least two points of view.[29] No known language, however, has belonged entirely to one class. The first classification is with respect to the degree of synthesis which they display:

1. Isolating
2. Partially synthetic

27 O. Jespersen, *op. cit.*, pp. 428, 429.
28 Pillsbury and Meader, *op. cit.*, p. 115.
29 *Cf.* Edward Sapir, "Language," in the *Encyclopaedia of the Social Sciences*, Volume 9, New York, 1933.

128

3. Synthetic or inflective
4. Polysynthetic or incorporating

An isolating language, of which Chinese is an example, is a language in which each idea is expressed by a separate word. All relations and forms are indicated by isolated words or particles instead of by inflection. In Chinese different ideas are often expressed by a word written with the same characters but pronounced in different tones indicated by radicles. This makes, in effect, several words of the same written word. It is probable that Chinese, and possibly all of the extant isolating languages, are examples of the last or one of the latest stages of the development of a synthetic language. In that case a disintegration took place in their ancestral languages so that compound words were broken up into their integral parts, and the inflec tion of words ceased. To what extent this constituted a reversion to a linguistic stage precedent to the synthetic, it is difficult if not impossible to determine in the present state of philological knowledge.

In the synthetic languages the meaning of a word may be varied by adding prefixes or suffixes or by changing the internal structure of a word or of its stem, in other words, by inflecting them. In this fashion, many relations or grammatical forms are expressed without using separate words. Most of the European languages are partially synthetic. Sanskrit, Latin, Greek and Arabic are examples of highly synthetic languages. In a polysynthetic language several ideas are often expressed in one word by compounding words so as to form almost a sentence. Eskimo and Algonkin are examples of such a language. In an incorporating language an object noun or pronoun is embodied in a verb or verb stem. Many of the American languages are incorporating.

The second point of view from which languages may be classified is with respect to the mechanical cohesion which they display. The following classification is not arranged according to the degree of cohesion manifested:

1. Isolating
2. Agglutinative
3. Inflective
4. Symbolistic

The isolating languages, of which there are few, display almost no mechanical cohesion. In an agglutinative language there is a tendency to join words together in order to form new words. The great majority of known languages are agglutinative in widely varying degrees. In the inflective languages, of which Latin and Greek are examples, varying degrees of agglutination are combined with the addition of affixes and the inflection of nouns, verbs, adjectives, and sometimes of other parts of speech. The symbolistic language, of which Arabic is an example, is an offshoot of the inflective type in which words are welded together to a high degree in compound and complex forms.

A language which is spoken over a large area or in several different regions usually evolves into a group of related languages. Distance and separation give rise to variations of speech which, when sufficiently accumulated, constitute a comparatively new language, especially when there are no ready means of communication, and no written language to maintain a standard speech. The original parent or so-called "primitive" language can usually be detected at least in part through its descendants. For example, primitive Indo-European, from which most Occidental languages are derived, was not only a prehistoric but a preliterate language. It has been related by common origin with only one language not derived from it. This is the extinct Hittite language known from cuneiform inscriptions in Asia Minor that commenced about 1400 B.C. The primitive Indo-European and the Hittite languages were presumably derived from an earlier parent language.

The study of related languages is carried on largely by comparisons which reveal common features. Even where differences exist, it is sometimes possible to demonstrate an original identity. This is illustrated by Grimm's Law which describes the consonantal change from the Greek or Latin p to the Germanic f in many words.

Chapter X

Language and Writing

AT the dawn of the historical period there were already many hundreds of distinct languages and several scores of linguistic families. Many of the extant and some of the known extinct languages have been identified with the linguistic groups to which they belong. With regard to a considerable number, it is not yet possible to determine to which groups they belong. Some of the more important cultural languages will be mentioned with reference first to the area in which the literate and historical period commenced, namely, the western Asiatic and eastern Mediterranean region.

The Sumerian language has furnished the earliest inscriptions which have so far been found. The hieroglyphic writing, which developed in the course of centuries into cuneiform writing, was probably invented to write this language. The ancestors of the Sumerians apparently were tribes which came from the mountains to the northeast of lower Mesopotamia. Prior to the fifth millennium B.C. they settled in the fertile region between the Tigris and the Euphrates rivers just north of the Persian Gulf. The earliest Sumerian inscriptions known are dated about 4000 B.C. Later the Sumerian language was submerged by the Semitic language known as Akkadian which was probably brought to Mesopotamia by invaders and conquerors from the Arabian peninsula. Until about 2000 B.C. Sumerian continued to be used as the written, literary and liturgical language. For some time longer it was the official language but was gradually restricted to its religious and scholarly use until the time of the Parthian Arsacid dynasty (c. 250 B.C.-227 A.D.). Thus the Sumerian language followed much the same course as Latin about two millennia later, though over a much longer period of time. Up to the present it has not been possible to relate Sumerian to any other language, and to place it in a linguistic group. It was an agglutinative language which has been called "a prehistoric philological remnant." Slight similarities to Turkish, a Turanian language, and Finnish and Esthonian have been noted, but apparently are of no significance. Many languages of various linguistic families were agglutinative in varying degrees. No language cognate to Sumerian has yet been identified.

Akkadian was a Semitic language which was spoken in several dialects in Babylonia and Assyria for about two millennia. After this region was conquered by the Persians in 539 B.C. it decreased in importance. As a spoken language it was displaced in large part by Aramaic which was another Semitic language. The Assyro-Babylonian language derived from the Akkadian persisted as a liturgical and literary language until about the beginning of the Christian era. It was written in the Sumerian cuneiform script.

The language of ancient Egypt has a longer history in one region than any other known language. It was there as early as 4000 B.C., was a spoken language as late as the seventh century after Christ, and still survives in part in the Coptic liturgy. It belonged to the Hamitic linguistic family with Semitic affinities. In fact, the division between the Hamitic and Semitic families is not clear. Archaic Egyptian was highly evolved at an early date, and diverged considerably from other Hamitic languages, especially in the formation of the verb. The earliest inscriptions in pictographs and hieroglyphs, date from the centuries between 4000 B.C. and the commencement of the dynastic period at about 3100 B.C. In other words, these inscriptiions were nearly or quite as ancient as the earliest Sumerian inscriptions which have been found.

Many other languages were spoken in western Asia which were not related to Sumerian, or Egyptian, or probably to the Semitic languages. Among them were Mitannian, Kassite, Hittite, Elamite or Susian, Cilician, Lydian, Lycian, etc. To some of these languages may have been related the Etruscan in Italy, perhaps derived from the Lydian in Asia Minor, and the Cretan and Cypriote languages. In this area of the eastern Mediterranean there developed out of the neolithic the ancient civilization which passed through the copper and bronze ages and commenced but did not go far with the iron age. During this period was evolved writing and especially alphabetic writing.

The Persian conquest of Mesopotamia in 539 B.C. introduced an Indo-Iranian language into this region.[1] Indo-European languages were already beginning to enter Asia Minor from the northwest and pos-

1 "Après une periode d' expansion que l'on peut situer anterieurement au Ve millenaire pour le sumerien et, pour les autres idiomes, entre 4000 et 1500 av. J. C., ces parlers ont donc peu à peu reculé devant le semitique. Puis, vers la moitié du IIe millenaire, l'influence indo-iranienne se manifeste clairement par des emprunts theologiques, par des noms de princes, des contaminations lexicologiques. L'influence indo-européenne s'accentuera lors de la poussée armenophrygienne vers l'Est et vers le Sud." (C. Autran, "Les langues propres de l'Asie anterieure ancienne," in A. Meillet et M. Cohen, Les Langues du Monde, Paris, 1924, p. 310.

sibly also from the northeast. The rapid spread of Islam from the seventh century A.D. carried with it the Arabic language. This Semitic tongue is now spoken over much of the area of the ancient civilization.

The preceding brief description of the linguistic situation in the region of the eastern Mediterranean indicates that there were numerous highly developed and widely divergent languages at the commencement of the ancient civilization. The evolution of spoken language took place almost entirely during the paleolithic and neolithic periods, how far back we cannot determine. Since that time the Indo-European linguistic family has spread over a large part of the world. This linguistic success has sometimes been attributed to the superior genius of the original or early carriers of these languages, or to their aristocratic character. There is not the slightest reason to believe that these people possessed any superior genius or were aristocratic in any sense which implies superior mind and character. In all probability, they were largely pastoral, migratory and warlike, which led them to conquer many other peoples, and thus to spread their languages.

There is great uncertainty as to where and when the Indo-European linguistic family originated. A comparative study of Indo-European vocabularies has led to the opinion that its birthplace was an inland cold region where were growing the oak, beech, and birch trees, and where the bear and the wolf were living. Furthermore, this comparative study seems to indicate that its carriers were people who built houses, domesticated animals, raised cereals, wove textiles, and used wheeled vehicles. In other words, they were probably in the neolithic stage, but also had a word for copper so were close to the chalcolithic stage.

The Indo-European languages may be divided into two groups according to the Latin and Avestan forms of the word for hundred. The "centum" group includes the Greek, Latin, Celtic, and Germanic languages, and Tocharian, an extinct language in Chinese Turkestan. The "satem" group includes the Indo-Iranian or "Aryan," Balto-Slavic, Armenian and Albanian languages. With the minor exception of Tocharian, all of the "centum" languages are in western Europe, and with the minor exception of Albanian, all of the "satem" languages are in Asia or eastern Europe. This significant fact suggests that the parent language originated somewhere in between. According to some of the earlier theories, it originated in central Asia, India, or elsewhere in Asia. According to other theories, it originated in Scandinavia, Germany, or elsewhere in northern or western Europe. The above-mentioned facts render eastern central or south-eastern Europe more probable. This theory has been stated as follows: "We have left, finally, the great plain of central and southeastern Europe, which embraces, roughly, the present Poland, Lithuania, Ukraine,

133

and Russia south and west of the Volga. . . . Almost every condition is satisfied by the conception of the Indo-Europeans as inhabiting some part of this plain as late as 3000 or 2500 B.C., . . . early differentiated linguistically into distinct groups and covering a vast territory, a pastoral people partially gone over to primitive agriculture, but still nomadic enough to change their habitat freely under changing economic or political conditions." [2]

Peake has propounded the theory that the Indo-Europeans originated in the southern Russian steppes and may have descended from Solutreans of paleolithic time.[3] Childe has also adhered to the theory that the cradle of the Indo-Europeans was in the southern Russian steppes.[4] He has suggested that they may have migrated into the basin of the Danube about 3000 B.C., destroying on the way some centers of Tripolye culture, such as Erösd. This was a neolithic culture, named after a site on the Dnieper River 35 miles south of Kiev, which dated from about B.C. 2750. The pressure of these steppe-folk may have caused the great migration into Greece. The Danubian II culture was probably a continuation of Danubian I with an Indo-European admixture. The Illyrian-Thracian-Phrygian people evolved with an ever-increasing Indo-European element.

Whatever may have been their ancestral home, the spread of these languages can be traced, and, to a certain extent, dated. During the many centuries that they were spreading, the common parent language was developing into a large family of languages. Some of these worked their way down into the Balkan peninsula and greater Greece around the northeastern end of the Mediterranean. Prior to them were spoken several unknown languages in Greece. The principal one probably was Pelasgian which was still spoken apparently as late as the fifth century B.C. along the Thracian coast, south of the Propontis, and in some of the Egean islands such as Imbros and Lemnos. The oldest Greek inscriptions on Attic vases are probably from the eighth or seventh century B.C. The earliest dated Greek inscription was found at Abou-Simbel in Egypt and described an expedition of Psammeticus II against Ethiopia in 591 B.C. There were already before these inscriptions several Greek dialects, among them being the Eolian, Achaean, Dorian and Ionian-Attic.

In similar fashion, the Indo-European languages worked their way down the Italian peninsula, eventually submerging the Etruscan

---

[2] H. H. Bender, *The Home of the Indo-Europeans*, Princeton, 1922.

[3] Harold Peake, "Racial Elements concerned in the First Siege of Troy," in the *Journal of the Royal Anthropological Institute*, 1916; *The Bronze Age and the Celtic World*, London, 1926.

[4] V. Gordon Childe, *The Aryans*, London, 1926.

and other earlier languages. In course of time Latin became predominant and was the progenitor of the romance languages of today. While the Hellenic and Italic languages were evolving, the Keltic languages were differentiating and traveling westward and the Germanic languages northward in Europe. Armenian seems to have become established in north-eastern Asia Minor about five or six centuries before Christ.

The Indo-Iranian or Aryan languages reached Persia, central Asia, and India at a comparatively early date. The Hindu Vedas or scriptures were composed in the Vedic Sanskrit, an Indo-European language. For many centuries they were transmitted orally. Later were composed the Brahmanas or commentaries on the Vedas, the Upanishads or philosophical treatises, and the Mahabharata and Ramayana or epic poems, in Vedic or classical Sanskrit. The earliest Sanskrit inscription known, found at Girnar, dates from 150 B.C. But the Vedas were probably being composed from 1500 to 1000 B.C., so that Indo-European languages may have reached Iran and India by 2000 B.C., or even earlier.[5] The earliest known Iranian inscriptions were written in cuneiform characters in ancient Persian at the behest of the Achemenid kings Darius (522-486 B.C.) and Xerxes (486-466 B.C.) who reigned at Babylon.

The present linguistic situation in the world is dominated by a limited number of standard languages. These are national common languages, in some cases shared by more than one nation, which have absorbed earlier languages and dialects. Where large political units, such as great states, are formed, the tendency is for a common language to emerge. Large migrations of populations may also play an important part in the establishment of standard languages. Writing has in some ways helped to standardize languages, though many written languages have also changed greatly during the historic period.

In Europe and Asia there are not more than twenty-five linguistic families. Of these not more than eight are important with regard to the number of speakers or the area covered. These are the Indo-European, Semitic, Dravidian, Sinitic, Ural-Altaic, Japanese, Korean and Malayo-Polynesian families. The Indo-European family possesses the largest number of speakers. It includes the Indic, Slavic, Teutonic (Germanic), and Romanic (Latin) branches, and many other languages such as Greek, Persian, Armenian and Keltic. The Sinitic family has almost as many speakers as the Indo-European. It includes the Chinese, Shan-Siamese, and Tibeto-Burman branches, and certain

---

[5] See Maurice Parmelee, *Oriental and Occidental Culture*, New York, 1928, pages 25-29, 33-37.

minor branches and languages. The Ural-Altaic family covers a vast area in northern and central Asia and in northern Europe, but has a proportionally small number of speakers. It includes the Turkish, Mongol, Tungus-Manchu, Samoyed, and Finno-Ugric branches. Arabic is the principal living member of the Semitic family to which have belonged the Babylonian, Assyrian, Phenician, Carthaginian, and Hebrew languages. Dravidian is spoken in southern India. The Japanese and Korean languages are restricted almost exclusively to Japan and Korea respectively. The Malayo-Polynesian languages extend eastward far out into the Pacific Ocean and as far west as Madagascar.

The largest speech-community is the Chinese of at least 475,000,-000 native speakers, which constitutes a family of mutually unintelligible languages. The principal Chinese languages are the Mandarin and Cantonese, each of which probably has from 100 to 200 million speakers. The Indic (Hindi, Bengali, etc.) speakers probably number 415,000,000. The English language has 265,000,000 native speakers, and is known in varying degrees to many millions of foreign speakers. It is by far the most widely spread spoken language in the world of the twentieth century. Russian has 120,000,000 or more native speakers, German about 100,000,000, Spanish about 150,000,000, and Japanese 90,000,000 or more. Other extant languages spoken by 50,000,000 or more native speakers are approximately in millions each: Indonesian 105, Dravidian 95, Sudanic 75, French 65, Arabic 65, Portuguese 63, Italian 50.

In Africa the Hamitic and Semitic linguistic families are dominant in the north. The latter is intrusive from western Asia, mainly owing to the spread of Islam. It has replaced in large part the Hamitic to which the ancient Egyptian language belonged. The Hamitic and Semitic families were probably derived from a common source in neolithic or earlier time. In central and west central Africa is a broad belt, including the Sudan, extending from the equator to Lat. 10° North, which is linguistically diversified, and includes several families whose classification has not yet been determined. South of the equator most of Africa is dominated by the Bantu linguistic family which covers a vast area. In the southwest are the Hottentot and Bushman linguistic families covering a considerable area, but with comparatively few speakers. Madagascar is linguistically Malayo-Polynesian.

In North America there are about seventy-five aboriginal linguistic families, and approximately the same number in South America. These one hundred and fifty linguistic stocks outnumber the twenty-five linguistic families of Europe and Asia. The most important with respect to area covered, number of speakers, or their cultural significance, are the Eskimo, Athabascan, Algonkin, Iroquois, Sioux, Muskogean, Uto-Aztec, and Maya, going generally from north to

136

south in North America; and the Chibcha, Arawak, Carib, Quechua or Inca, Tupi, Tapuya, and Araucanian, going in the main from north to south in South America. These fifteen families cover most of the two American continents.

The great multiplicity of American languages is a striking fact, even though further study may reduce somewhat the number of linguistic stocks. Many of these languages are or were spoken by a very small number of individuals, in some cases only a few hundred. Rivet has expressed the opinion that all of the American languages were derived from an extinct common language from which they have diverged widely. He has reduced the number of linguistic families to 123, of which 26 are in North America, 20 in Central America and 77 in South America.[6] The density of population was sparse over most of the western hemisphere. Many very small groups lived in comparative isolation. This encouraged the divergence from each other of the dialects of the common American language. The latter may have come originally or was derived from Asia. Furthermore, there were few languages of a high culture spoken by large populations which dominated large areas over a long period of time, thus wiping out many localized languages. In fact, there were probably only three such languages, namely, the Nahuatl language of the Aztec empire in Mexico, the Maya language of the Maya culture in Yucatan, and the Quechua language of the Inca empire in Peru.

A serious obstacle in the way of the study of the evolution and relationships of the American languages has been the lack of any written records of these languages prior to the sixteenth century A.D. These records were made by the incoming Europeans and no records exist from pre-Columbian times. This is because no American people developed a fully written language. The nearest approaches to writing were made by the Nahuatl and the Maya languages. The former utilized many pictographs representing objects, some of which were more or less conventionalized, and a few phonetic signs. The latter utilized certain signs for numbers, the days and the months of the Maya calendar. Other Maya signs which have not been deciphered probably are conventionalized pictographs, though a few of them may be phonetic.

The linguistic situation of the American aborigines probably is similar to an earlier situation in Europe and Asia when there was a larger number of languages. Small groups living in isolation, or with an attitude of hostility toward neighboring groups, may in the course of generations develop dialects, and then languages, and eventually

[6] P. Rivet, "Langues Americaines," in *Les Langues du Monde*, edited by A. Meillet and M. Cohen, Paris, 1924, pp. 597-712.

linguistic families. The forces making for nations in Europe and Asia have doubtless obliterated many languages. A somewhat similar process has probably taken place in Africa. The dominance of the Bantu languages in central and most of southern Africa may be due to extensive conquests and far-reaching political rule by Bantu peoples in a somewhat remote past. The areas of greatest linguistic diversity have been the Sudan in Africa, New Guinea, western North America, and the Amazon region in South America. The geographical and cultural reasons for this diversity are not easy to explain, especially in the case of a comparatively small area such as New Guinea.

Indo-European languages are now spoken by approximately one-third of mankind. Sinitic languages are spoken by about one-fourth of mankind. The Semitic, Ural-Altaic, Japanese, Malayo-Polynesian, Dravidian and Bantu linguistic families are spoken each by about fifty to one hundred million. These eight linguistic stocks include about nine-tenths of mankind. The babel of tongues is gradually being reduced. This may aid in harmonizing and unifying cultural and social relations.

There has been little relation between culture and language with respect to linguistic structure. Some of the languages of primitive peoples have had a complicated grammar, while some of the peoples of a highly developed culture have spoken comparatively simple languages. Vocabularies, however, are closely related to the complexity of culture. Even though a psychologist has said that "a language must be judged, not in terms of dictionaries, but in terms of its suitability to a particular environment,"[7] yet a culture which uses many things and includes many ideas requires a much larger vocabulary, and therefore dictionary, than a simple culture.

Bloomfield has classified the main types of speech in a complex speech-community as follows: (1) literary standard, (2) colloquial standard, (3) provincial standard, (4) sub-standard, (5) local dialect.[8] The ancient Greeks devoted some study to the structure of their language, and the Romans prepared Latin grammars after the Greek model. Hindu scholars had been preparing grammars and lexicons still earlier, the oldest of which that is known being Panini's grammar which was written between 350 and 250 B.C. Out of these grammatical and lexicographical studies arose the standard speech known as Sanskrit which became the official and literary language of Hindu India, and continued as the classical written language long after it was no longer spoken. Sanskrit, Greek, and Latin were derived from a prehistoric language which was the primitive or parent Indo-European

---

[7] W. S. Hunter, *Human Behavior*, Chicago, 1928, p. 144.

[8] L. Bloomfield, *Language*, London, 1935, p. 52.

speech. During the nineteenth and twentieth centuries A.D. an extensive comparative study of the Indo-European languages has been made.

Grammar is usually divided into syntax and morphology. The former deals with the structure of phrases and sentences, the latter with the structure of words and compound words. In many languages morphological structure is more elaborate than syntactical structure. Partly for this reason, languages vary more as to morphology than as to syntax. They range all the way from a highly analytic language like Chinese which consists mainly of one-syllable words to a very agglutinative language like Eskimo which synthesizes many words into long compound words. Consequently, it is impossible to determine precisely the number of words in any language. It has been estimated that every adult speaker of a fully developed language uses from 20,000 to 30,000 words, and, if well educated, many more. According to Bloomfield: "The power or wealth of a language consists of the morphemes and the tagmemes (sentence-types, constructions, and substitutions.) The number of morphemes and tagmemes in any language runs well into the thousands." [9]

Spoken or ear language was essential for the earlier stages of cultural evolution. Written or eye language as well was necessary for its later stages. The distinction between pre-literate and literate culture is usually accepted as the line of division between primitive and civilized mankind. However, no sharp dividing lines can be recognized in the evolution of culture. Many other factors played a part in the development of so-called "civilization," which is at best a vague and normative term with too much ethical and esthetic connotation to have scientific value. Writing has nevertheless been of enormous cultural significance in transmitting from generation to generation a much greater volume of knowledge, ideas, beliefs, and traditions than was formerly possible, in keeping permanent records, and in expanding the spatial transmission of information, news, instructions, and laws, which is almost absolutely essential for the administration of large enterprises and states.

Speech was developing during paleolithic time, and its rise may have taken place in an early cultural period. Writing can be traced back only to the neolithic or possibly to the late paleolithic period. Some of the paleolithic drawings may have been intended to communicate information or ideas. The alphabetiform and other symbolic signs of the Magdalenian and Azilian periods, mentioned in Chapters VII and VIII, were probably forms of conventionalized art and had nothing to do with writing. There is no conclusive evidence

---

[9] L. Bloomfield, *op. cit.*, p. 276.

of picture or pictographic writing before the neolithic, so that written language developed long after speech.[10]

Writing was graphic in its origin. Then it was gradually reduced to conventional symbols which represented sentences, words, or syllables. The earliest phonetic writing was the acrophonetic in which the initial syllable or sound of a word was indicated by a sign or character. Acrophony may have originated in the Egyptian hieroglyphic writing. The final development of phonetic writing was attained in an alphabet in which each sound used in a spoken language was given an arbitrary symbol. The evolution from pictographic through ideographic to alphabetic writing can be traced in part in the extant and other known written languages. The three stages of this evolution have been described as follows: "In the first place, the pictures had to become conventionalized, so that they always had the same appearance and designated the same object. Next, it was necessary that they should not only refer to a concrete object, but also become the symbols of abstract conceptions. Finally, it was essential that the conventionalized symbols should pass into that stage where they combined a representation of an abstract conception and the sound of the human voice." [11]

The earlier stages in the developmnt of writing probably took place from about 10,000 B.C. to 4,000 B.C. Pre-alphabetic writing was invented independently in several places. The Maya and Aztec pictographic writing arose independent of the eastern hemisphere, and perhaps also of each other. Chinese appears to have had no connection with the systems of the Mediterranean area, though certain philologists have noted similarities between the Sumerian and the Chinese scripts which have suggested a common origin, possibly in central Asia.[12]

Purely pictographic systems and mnemonic devices have been found among many primitive peoples. But writing had to pass beyond the pictographic, or even the purely ideographic stage, in order to express some of the parts of speech, such as pronouns, prepositions,

---

[10] "Pictographic writing going back to the neolithic and bronze ages has been found in many parts of Europe." (B. L. Ullman, *Ancient Writing and Its Influence*, New York, 1932.) See also William A. Mason, *A History of the Art of Writing*, New York, 1920.

[11] H. E. Barnes, *The History of Western Civilization*, New York, 1935, Vol. 1, p. 103.

[12] "That Chinese is related to the old Sumerian languages of Babylonia is a conclusion which appears inevitable, when we notice the great similarity of the two vocabularies." (C. J. Ball, *Chinese and Sumerian*, Oxford 1913.) This assertion probably exaggerates the similarities between Chinese and Sumerian. See also my *Oriental and Occidental Culture*, New York, 1928, pages 16-18.

conjunctions and adverbs, and many relational ideas and abstract concepts.

In the Mediterranean region the Sumerian, Babylonian, Egyptian, and possibly also the Cretan and Hittite scripts, may have arisen independently of each other.[13] However, there is a basic similarity between the first three, and also Chinese, which suggests the force of example, if not of direct copy and common origin or descent. This is a moot question which can be solved only by further evidence.

The Sumerians dominated lower Mesopotamia from about 4,000 B.C. to 2,600 B.C. As early as 3,000 B.C. they were using a phonetic system containing about 350 syllabic signs. The signs were written upon clay tablets with pointed reeds, which were wedge-shaped, and have since been known as cuneiform. A similar system was later used by the Babylonians, Assyrians, and various other peoples, such as the Hittites.

By 3,000 B.C. the Egyptians had developed a form of writing which is known as hieroglyphic because it was used mainly by the priests. This was a mixed system of ideographs originally pictographic; and rebus writing, *i.e.,* using an ideogram for its sound value for a syllable of different meaning, like using "2" for "to"; and also alphabetic letters. They continued to use this mixed system, with more easily written forms for the alphabetic characters, in its earlier hieratic and later demotic forms for three thousand years, even long after completely alphabetic systems had come into use in the neighboring Semitic and the Greek languages. The Egyptians wrote on the membrane of the papyrus reed pasted crosswise and dried, with ink manufactured from vegetable gum and soot, and pens made from sharpened pieces of reed. Papyrus was like the earliest form of paper and was much better adapted to writing than stone and clay. It was also more durable than the palm leaf available in India and other tropical countries which discouraged the keeping of permanent records.

Every language is always in process of change. Written records furnish direct information of linguistic changes as far back as these records exist. Beyond that point such changes can be surmised only by inference. In all probability words were the first spoken units to be

[13] The Cretan and Egyptian scripts display similarities which may have been due to a common neolithic source: "The Cretans and Egyptians both drew equally from the primitive source of the neolithic writings." (G. Glotz, *The Aegean Civilization*, New York, 1925, p. 373, translated from the French.)

Evans attributed more influence to the Cretan script than may be justified: "If we turn to Crete, the source of the developed pre-Phoenician scripts of Greece and the Aegean world, we find evidence of the same primitive stratum of linearized pictography." (A. J. Evans, "The European Diffusion of Primitive Pictography and its Bearings on the Origin of Script," in *Anthropology and the Classics*, edited by R. R. Marett. Oxford, 1908, pp. 41-2.)

symbolized in writing. Such writing has been called ideographic. As it represents primarily words of the spoken language and only indirectly ideas, it might be named logographic writing. It is very cumbersome because it must contain a vast number of symbols. As it develops into a phonographic system the first phonograms usually are syllabic symbols. These syllabaries come to represent the initial consonantal sounds of the words. From these symbols were derived the alphabetic symbols which denote single consonantal, and later vowel sounds, thus constituting a fully developed alphabet. So far as is known, this has happened only once in the history of writing. This was when an alphabet of twenty-four single consonants was derived from the Egyptian hieroglyphic and hieratic symbols, probably by 2000 B.C. or earlier. All of the alphabets of the Occident and of India have been derived from this Egyptian alphabet.[14]

The first exclusively alphabetic system of writing was originated in western Asia, perhaps by the Phenicians who spoke a Semitic language. It consisted of 21 or 22 consonantal signs derived largely from the Egyptian. It may have been invented by 1900 B.C. Early inscriptions in this alphabet have been found in southern Palestine and in the peninsula of Sinai. The earliest which can be approximately dated is that of Ahiram who was a contemporary of Rameses II, an Egyptian king of the Nineteenth Dynasty who ruled from 1298 to 1225 B.C. Because they were a commercial and sea-faring people, the Phenicians carried this alphabet far and wide, to Carthage, originally their own colony, to Greece, and elsewhere. It became the basis for all of the completely alphabetic scripts now extant.

The Phenician alphabet reached Greece probably by B.C. 1300. Later the Greeks added to it the vowel signs which were derived in part from Phenician letters whose original sounds were not in Greek. One form of the Greek alphabet spread to Italy where it developed into the Latin script, later used by all of the languages of central and western Europe. The Slavic alphabets of eastern Europe were derived directly from the Greek, with a few letters from Hebrew.

The Phenician alphabet also developed into the Aramaic, Hebrew, Syriac, and Arabic scripts. With the rapid spread of Islam the latter extended westward into Africa and eastward to Turkey. Persia, Afghanistan, India and Malaysia. From the Syriac were derived scripts in Persia, through central Asia, and in Manchuria. Influenced by the neighboring Chinese writing, the Manchu script is written vertically instead of horizontally.

Probably as early as the diffusion to Greece, the Phenician or early Semitic alphabet traveled to India where it was transformed into

[14] David Diringer, *The Alphabet, A Key to the History of Mankind*, New York, 1948.

142

the Brahmi alphabet. From the latter were derived the Sanskrit, Dravidian, Tibetan, and Pali (in Ceylon) alphabets. With the spread of Buddhism were derived from the latter the Burmese, Siamese, Cambodian, Javanese, and other Indonesian alphabets, and, most distant of all, the Korean. Like the adjacent Manchu, derived from the Semitic by an entirely different route, the Korean adopted the Chinese custom of writing vertically.

The principal rival system of writing is the Chinese which is still mostly ideographic, although some rebuses are used, and certain characters are phonetic in that they represent the pronunciation of words rather than objects or ideas. The standard dictionary, compiled during the Kang-h'si period (seventeenth century A.D.), contains nearly 45,000 distinct characters, of which about 4,000 are often used, each representing a word or phrase. There are 214 "radicals," or root-ideas, which are expressed by graphic signs, each of which is common to a group of characters. These signs are used as initial letters in arranging Chinese dictionaries. Until recently most Chinese writing was in the classical language and script comprehensible only to the literati. Only since the establishment of the republic in 1911 has an attempt been made to write in the Chinese vernacular, and with a somewhat simplified script and orthography.

About two thousand years after the evolution of alphabetic writing developed the art of printing. Seals had already been used in ancient Babylonia and Egypt, and in China as early as the third century B.C. Block-printing was invented in China, probably in the eighth century A.D.[15] Movable type was invented in the eleventh century A.D., and was first wooden and then metal. Paper had been manufactured in China as early as the second century A.D. Printing and paper traveled westward over the trade routes to Turkestan. For a time Islam prevented the introduction of printing into Europe because religious tradition prohibited the printing of the Koran. The Mongol invasions into eastern and central Europe overcame this obstacle. Printing reached Europe shortly before the Renaissance, which created a great need for it. Printing, and the paper which is essential for this art, rendered possible an enormous increase in the output of written language. They likewise stimulated a vastly greater diffusion of written literature.[16] The cultural significance of the invention of printing will be discussed in later chapters.

The spread and intermingling of languages constitute one of the principal forms of cultural diffusion. The most extensive kind of

[15] See T. F. Carter, *The Invention of Printing in China and its Spread Westward*, New York, 1925.

[16] See Maurice Parmelee, *Oriental and Occidental Culture*, New York, 1928, page 80.

linguistic diffusion is from one speech area to another. This takes place through the passage from one area to another not only of persons and material objects, technical methods, and the like. Their names travel with these objects, ideas, practices, etc., from one linguistic community to another.

Within each linguistic area takes place a narrower form of diffusion between dialects and between the manners of speech of lower and upper classes. In this form of diffusion the upper class has usually an advantage in the social prestige it enjoys. The most extreme case of a linguistic struggle within a given speech area is when a foreign language is introduced by conquerors. If the latter are sufficiently numerous, and have a superior culture, they may succeed in forcing their language upon the indigenous population. If, however, they are greatly in the minority, have an inferior culture, and especially if they have not brought their women with them, the intrusive language is likely to disappear after a few generations, having left more or less impress, as the case may be, upon the indigenous language.

The principal languages and linguistic groups comprising about 2,200 million of over 2,500 million of the world's population, are indicated in the following table: [17]

Linguistic and Linguistic Groups, Spoken Natively by
50 Million or More, Estimated in Millions, in 1955

Chinese (Mandarin, Cantonese, etc.)	475	Dravidian (Telegu, Tamil, etc.)	95
Indic (Hindi, Bengali, etc.)	415	Japanese	90
English	265	Sudanic (Hausa, etc.)	75
Russian	200	Arabic	65
Spanish	150	French	65
Indonesian (Javanese, Malay, etc.)	103	Portuguese	63
German	100	Italian	50

[17] *Information Please*, New York, 1955, p. 727.

Chapter XI

The Correlation of Material and Mental Culture

PRECEDING chapters have furnished a brief description of the material aspects of the prehistoric stages of cultural evolution. No direct evidence of the mental phases of these early cultural stages is available. We cannot know how paleolithic and neolithic men and women thought and felt, and we have only indirect evidence as to how they acted. Some of these mental phenomena can be inferred from the material aspects with varying degrees of assurance. Such inferences will be considered in their appropriate connections. They should always be regarded with utmost caution.

It is the almost incorrigible tendency of the human mind to jump from the insecure basis of inferences, however plausible or probable they may be, to the gratifying security of alleged certainty. In its avowedly illogical expression, the desire for certainty is exemplified in the dictum of certain churches: "Credo quia absurdum est." [1] This is the apex of the absurdity of faith in the unknown and the unknowable. This is fideism (faith in the place of knowledge) of the most extreme form. As an American sociologist has said: "Faced by the insecurities of a changing and frequently hostile world, we seek security by creating 'eternal verities' in our thoughts. The more inadequate we feel, the more we indulge in this type of wishful thinking. Conversely, as the clergy has always complained, in times of prosperity and security man tends to neglect his gods." [2]

The inadequacy of data for complete explanations, or the complexity which ofttimes characterizes the available data, leads to various nonsequiturs and other fallacies. There are, however, additional causes for these errors. Social pressure exists at times in favor of an hypothesis regardless of whether or not it is accurate. However fallacious such an hypothesis may be, it is required for the ideology of the

---

[1] "I believe because it is absurd."

[2] G. A. Lundberg, "The Thoughtways of Contemporary Sociology," in the *American Sociological Review*, Vol. 1, No. 5, October 1936, p. 703.

dominant social system. Thus a king is reputed to be divine, a pope is alleged to be infallible, one race is asserted to be inferior to another race, one class is presumed to be superior to another class, the prevailing system of exploitation is supposed to be based on eternal verities, and whatever upholds the authority of the exploiters, such as the sanction of a mythical god, is said to be right and just.

The desire for certainty and the unwillingness to undertake the onerous task of subjecting to careful scrutiny all of the available data induce many persons to jump to unwarranted assumptions. The mystical temperament arrogates to itself absolute knowledge independent of intellectual processes. A modern European mystic has alleged that "mysticism is the art of union with Reality. The mystic is a person who has attained that union in greater or less degree; or who aims at and believes in such attainment." [3] Religion in general must claim such knowledge of absolute truth or it cannot retain its hold upon the masses. Weariness or old age may encourage even the scientist, otherwise cautious, to adopt unjustifiable and unverifiable conclusions.

Errors are, however, inevitable in scientific research as in all other human activities. As soon as a considerable number of data concerning a given field of phenomena have accumulated, it becomes necessary to formulate tentative hypotheses with regard to their causation. In so far as possible, the hypotheses should be integrated so as to cover the phenomena under consideration. The question is as to the permissible range of such hypotheses. The criterion is the pragmatic test as to whether the hypothesis, or integration of hypotheses, in question explains satisfactorily or at least plausibly the given body of data. As soon as it fails to meet this test, a revision of it or an entirely new hypothesis is in order.

Apart from the temporary and tentative errors which are inevitable in hypotheses preliminary to the formulation of more or less reliable theories are certain fallacies which recur more or less often in the social and organic sciences in general as well as in the inorganic sciences. The commonest of these fallacies is the periodic reversion to animistic interpretations which takes place in every science on the part of some of its workers. When new data accumulate with overwhelming speed, the old hypotheses and theories are upset. Fundamental problems become more complicated than ever. The tendency then displays itself for some of the scientists to repudiate or at least to abandon causation and to attribute a series of events to "accident" which is a euphemism for chance. This opens the door to idealism and fideism, or faith in the place of knowledge, and to the cruder forms

3 Evelyn Underhill, *Practical Mysticism*, New York, 1915. p. 3.

146

of animism, such as a belief in a god. This situation has manifested itself recently in the physical sciences. The rapid accumulation of observations in physics, astronomy, astrophysics and chemistry has discouraged some of the workers in these sciences from attempting to rebuild their theories of the ultimate nature of physical phenomena and to fall back upon animistic concepts, such as a "mathematical" god!

In the case of individual scientists a tendency toward subjective interpretations may lead to a reaction against causal explanations. Such scientists display a hostile reaction against objective solutions of scientific problems. They prefer to seek such solutions in their inner consciousness, especially the solutions for ultimate problems. They are prone to depreciate the value of statistics, and of laboratory and experimental results. They deprecate behaviorist, determinist and mechanistic interpretations and minimize the significance of causal relations. But they approach no closer to satisfactory explanations by means of their subjective methods.[4]

A fallacy which crops up often is the hypothesis that the whole is greater than its parts. This error arises out of an inadequate analysis of the factors involved. Having failed to detect all of the factors at work, those who fall into this error assume that the result is greater than could be attained by the factors known to them. In other words, they are not acquainted with all of the parts.

A recent example of this fallacy is the hypothesis of emergent evolution. According to Wheeler, new relations arise out of the combination of elements, so that the whole is greater than its parts. For example, water has properties which are different from those of the hydrogen and oxygen of which it is composed.[5] Jennings asserts that according to emergent evolution the parts depend also upon the whole. The properties of the parts become altered by being merged in the emergent unit.[6]

Hypotheses similar to that of emergent evolution are various organicist theories, the theory of creative synthesis of Lester F. Ward, the philosophy of holism of Jan Smuts, the vague notions of the gestalt or configurationist psychologists, and the theistic vagaries of C. Lloyd Morgan and S. Alexander. The gestalt psychologists, for example, have presented a misty hypothesis of the organism acting as

---

[4] An example of the subjective point of view is R. M. MacIver, *Society Its Structure and Changes*, New York, 1931.

[5] W. M. Wheeler, *Emergent Evolution and the Development of Societies*, New York, 1928.

[6] H. S. Jennings, *The Biological Basis of Human Nature*, New York, 1930.

a whole as opposed to a mechanical theory of behavior. Their ideological point of view is, therefore, hostile to behaviorism.[7]

General Smuts' hypothesis of holism (from ὅλος=whole) is an exaggerated form of the fallacy that the whole is greater than the sum total of its parts. According to him, matter, life, and mind remain disparate; organized structure is the essential trait of the physical universe; and "the physical and chemical constitution of matter is almost entirely a matter of structure." The organic cell is "the second fundamental structure of the universe." Holism is a "marked power of regulation and co-ordination in respect of both the structure and the functioning of the parts." It is not only creative but self-creative, and gains on mechanism in the course of evolution. Mind is "the third great fundamental structure of holism" and is an organ of personality which is the latest and supreme whole built on the prior structures of matter, life, and mind.

Nowhere in his prolix exposition of his thesis does Smuts furnish the slightest inductive or concrete evidence of this hypothetical factor. It is assumed to be present apart from and in addition to the forces inherent in the phenomena observable by mankind. It is a purely gratuitous ideological assumption. The subjective factors in the author himself which have given rise to this assumption become more and more clear in the course of the book, especially in his discussion of personality. In the last paragraph he has asserted that his "holistic universe" is "at bottom a struggle for the Good, a wild striving towards human betterment. . . . The groaning and travailing of the universe is never aimless or resultless. Its profound labours mean new creation, the slow, painful birth of wholes, of new and higher wholes, and the slow but steady realisation of the Good which all the wholes of the universe in their various grades dimly yearn and strive for."[8]

The last passage indicates a teleological point of view, a reading of ends into the universe for which there is not the slightest justification. Furthermore, it is a narrowly anthropocentric teleology according to which this mighty universal process is being directed in the interest of mankind. Even if there were any evidence that nature is beneficent toward mankind, there is not the slightest evidence that the universe exists for a puny species passing an ephemeral life upon a small planet of an insignificant solar system in one of many galaxies of a universe which, so far as we know, is infinite and eternal and which can, therefore, be striving toward no end whatsoever.

---

[7] See the verbose treatise of W. Koehler, *Gestalt Psychology*, New York, 1929, translated from the German.

As used in this connection, the German words *Gestalt* and *Gestaltung* correspond most closely to the English word *Configuration*.

[8] J. C. Smuts, *Holism and Evolution*, London, 1926, p. 344.

148

However grotesque the hypothesis of holism may be, it is no more fallacious at bottom than the other theories mentioned above. All of these writers fail to realize that a certain amount of energy is expended in creating a whole out of its parts. This energy is one of the factors in the new situation created and is indeed a part which is overlooked. Furthermore, in the new whole the parts are juxtaposed to each other in a different manner from their previous relations and this is still another factor in the situation. The splitting of the atom has revealed that energy is continually being released which may form new combinations. These and other factors are involved which are ignored in these fallacious hypotheses. There is not the slightest evidence that the integral parts have changed in their essential nature by becoming synthesized. If the molecule of water is resolved into its component elements, the atoms of hydrogen and of oxygen will not differ from their erstwhile nature. This is true in spite of the fact that H_2O is radically different in its character and effects not only from H and O but also from any other possible combination of the two. A similar process occurs if hydrogen and oxygen are disintegrated.

An error similar to the preceding is the fallacy of the group or whole as superior to its individual members or parts. This fallacy often arises out of ethical beliefs with regard to the duty of the individual to subordinate and sometimes sacrifice himself for the benefit of his group. The welfare of the group is regarded as greater than the sum total of the welfare of its individual members. Class interests are often involved in such ethical ideas. The dominant class in a community induces the members of the community to sacrifice themselves, as in warfare, under the mistaken impression that they are helping the community as a whole when they are in reality aiding the dominant class. But apart from these moralistic considerations, with which we are not here concerned, the fallacy of the group gives rise to the notion that the group consists of more than the sum total of its individual members. This error leads to fantastic and quasi-mystical notions of the group apart from and in addition to its individual members. These notions render it difficult to arrive at realistic explanations of social phenomena in terms of causal relations.[9] The fallacy of the group is closely related to the organicist theories of

[9] Allport has rightly spoken of the error of "substituting the group as a whole as a principle of explanation in place of the individuals in the group."
F. H. Allport, "The Group Fallacy in Relation to Social Science," in the *Journal of Abnormal Psychology and Social Psychology*, Vol. XIX, No. 1, April-June 1924.

society and especially to the fallacy of the super-organic mentioned below.

Another fallacy is that of the temporal and evolutionary precedence of function over structure. This *ex post facto* interpretation of function is common among those who are prone to take a teleological view of natural phenomena. The apparent adaptation of means to ends exhibited by many of these phenomena leads many of these persons to jump to the conclusion that the ends existed prior to the means and that the latter were called into existence in order to serve the former. There is no evidence that any ends existed originally in the universe, or do now, for that matter, if the universe is indeed infinite in space and eternal in time. The apparent adaptation of means to ends is due to a process of selection. Swimming did not exist as a function and as an end before the animals which swim came into existence. Fishes became adapted to swim through a process of natural and unintentional selection because the ability to swim is essential or helpful for their survival. Hence it is not only superfluous but unwarranted to assume that the function existed *ab initio* and prior to the evolution of the adapted structure. Indeed, a function can exist only to the extent that there is a structure capable of performing it. The teleological interpretation is due in large part to ignorance of the long process of selection which has brought the adapted structure into being. It is also due to the irrepressible tendency on the part even of some scientists who should know better to see purpose and design in a universe which is, so far as we can perceive, undirected and unplanned.

Another animistic fallacy is the conception of mind implied in the hypotheses both of psycho-physical parallelism and of interactionism. The former hypothesis, as stated by one of its exponents, "regards the processes of the material universe (including those of the physical organism) as a closed chain of cause and effect, which is altogether removed from any psychical influence. Mental process is a concomitant of certain highly complex material processes, but not anything that affects these processes themselves."[10] The hypothesis of psychophysical interactionism not only assumes, like the parallelist hypothesis, that mental processes accompany certain physical processes, but also that the mental influence the physical processes and are influenced by the latter.[11]

Awareness of the universe is in the last analysis subjective. As I

[10] E. B. Titchener, "Were the Earliest Organic Movements Conscious or Unconscious." in the *Popular Science Monthly*, Vol. LX, March 1902, p. 458.

[11] For an avowedly animistic statement of psycho-physical interactionism see William McDougall, *Body and Mind, A History and Defense of Animism,* New York, 1911.

have said elsewhere: "All knowledge comes through our senses in the form of sensations, and we cannot be absolutely certain that these sensations represent to us truly the nature of the world which is exterior to us. For scientific purposes, however, we need to practise what is sometimes called 'naive realism', and assume that things in the exterior world are actually as our senses represent them to be." [12] In the face of the insolubility of the ultimate problems of being and of causation, such an assumption is pragmatically necessary. But the hypothesis of a super-physical, or any kind of a non-physical order, is not only superfluous but misleading and confusing. As has been demonstrated in Chapter V on the directives of behavior, behaviorist psychology has solved the so-called dilemma of psycho-physical parallelism and interactionism.

Ignorance of biology and psychology often leads to animistic and teleological interpretations of social phenomena. Biologists and psychologists also make such errors at times when venturing into the field of social science. Physicists and chemists are even more prone to make these errors. However scientific they may be in their own fields, they fall more or less readily into animistic errors with regard to the organic and social phenomena which they have never studied. Within the social sciences themselves the organicist theories of society approach the dangerline of animism. The theory of the super-organic, whose fallacious character has been demonstrated in the chapter on the threshold of cultural evolution, is an instructive illustration. Some of the organicist theories go hardly further than to suggest a close analogy between the organism and society. But the super-organic theory goes so far as to suggest an order of phenomena super-imposed upon the organic and radically different from them. It cannot be too strongly emphasized that organic factors render social and cultural phenomena possible and that the latter belong to the organic world. They can no more be divorced from the organic than the latter can be divorced from the inorganic phenomena out of which they arise.

Another fallacy which often arises out of an inadequate knowledge of causal factors is the particularist explanation of social and cultural phenomena. An "accidental" concatenation of events is regarded as a sufficient explanation. The "great" or "exceptional" man, or the so-called "superior" race, has often been used as the supposititious cause or explanation of a set of circumstances or train of events. Thus are "chance" and "accident", as if they were decisive factors of historical events and of social phenomena, elevated to the realm of the supernatural. These mystifying and obscurantist interpretations are facile attempts to supplant the arduous task of digging down to

[12] Maurice Parmelee, *The Science of Human Behavior*, New York, 1913, p. 4.

151

the roots of the economic and social processes which are the principal, if not, in the last analysis, the sole causal factors in history and social and cultural evolution, because survival of the individual and of the group is dependent upon them.

When adequate data are not available for the explanation of any given phenomena, it is preferable to formulate no theory whatsoever than to base an explanation solely upon a person, a race, or a climatic peculiarity. A causal evolutionary sequence can be established only when sufficient data have been interpreted by a harmonious application of inductive and deductive methods. Induction furnishes ample weight to all of the pertinent particulars. Deduction synthesizes these particulars into a unified whole in which each particular assumes its due importance in relation to all of the others. These methods insure that personal, racial, and national prejudices, and animistic superstitions, will not falsify these explanations and interpretations.

The naturalistic explanation of the emergence of mankind renders all anthropocentric hypotheses superfluous. As we have seen in Chapter III on the emergence of mankind, the manipulative, locomotor and cerebral specializations characteristic of man were possible because his primate ancestors did not acquire certain specializations which characterize other mammalian orders. The expansion of sight and hearing and perfecting of binocular vision furnished an exceptional degree of contact with the external world and increased the range of sensory stimuli received by the brain. Through a process of selection in the struggle for existence, several of these factors played their part in increasing the size and complexity of the brain.

As we have seen in Chapter VI on the integration of behavior, in so far as culture can be attributed to any one aspect of the mind, it is the characteristic product of the intellect. While the instincts and emotions continue with unabated force to furnish the fundamental drives for human behavior, the intelligence plays an ever increasing role in directing it. The manufacture and use of tools, the evolution of language, and every other phase of culture were due immediately and predominantly to the application of the intellect to the crucial problems of existence and of subsistence which confronted primitive men.

Molded by the forces of the environment, and the social and cultural processes of invention and of diffusion, many integrations of cultural traits have come into existence which we may call cultural patterns. Some of these patterns have survived to the present day, and faint traces of extinct patterns can be detected in the material remains of past cultures. To correlate the material and mental aspects of culture, past or present, is no easy task. Especially difficult is it to determine whether many relationships are causal or merely coincidental.

152

The mental factors of the past can only be inferred. Even since a portion of mankind has become literate, many of the attempts to describe mental traits and processes have been palpably misleading. From this mass of uncorrelated and undigested data, the cultural psychologist and historian must try to create an analysis and a description which are scientifically sound and logically consistent.

Chapter XII

The Origins of Social Organization

SO far as man, with his limited means of observation, can discern, the universe is continuous and unitary. Hence he must perforce assume that there are no rigid lines of division between the different groups of phenomena. Every science dealing with a specific phenomenal group borders upon and to a certain extent overlaps the sciences dealing with neighboring and similar groups of phenomena. Thus arise hybrid sciences or branches of sciences such as astrophysics, physical chemistry, biochemistry, physiological psychology, social psychology, and the like.

In similar fashion, social science has close relations with several other sciences. Biological sociology deals with the organic basis of culture and society. Psychological sociology is concerned with the mental aspect of all social and cultural phenomena. Ecological sociology deals with the effects of the natural environment upon society, and draws upon geology, geography, zoology, and botany for some of its data. These three branches of sociology include its principal relations with other sciences. However, like every other science, it may draw from time to time upon any other science, such as physics or chemistry, for pertinent data.

The scope of sociology may be indicated by a classification of its branches. While several classifications are possible, the following is useful for our purposes:

1. Biological Sociology
2. Psychological Sociology
3. Ecological Sociology
4. Cultural Evolution
5. Social Organization
6. Institutions
7. Social Control

154

In earlier chapters we have seen that association exists in many animal species, and that social phenomena of a rudimentary sort are not limited to mankind. But man is the only animal that has evolved a culture, because he has been able to modify his natural environment, to create artificial objects of utility, and to develop language. The whole range of cultural evolution is, therefore, almost identical, or at least closely correlated, with much of the range of human social evolution. Hence the study of the evolution of culture is not only the most extensive and one of the most important branches of sociology. It also furnishes the inductive basis for the analysis of human social phenomena, most of which may be subsumed under the terms organization, institution, and control.

The rudimentary social phenomena displayed by some of the mammalian orders include the horde among the gregarious mammals, and parental care among the mammals whose young are weak and helpless. The latter results in the uni-parental or bi-parental family, usually of temporary duration. In this connection the word family is used in a purely biological sense. The similar or corresponding phenomena among the arthropod, lower vertebrate, and avian classes and orders are of much less significance for our purpose. The mammalian diverged from the other vertebrate classes at an early stage in vertebrate evolution, and, like the birds, has followed an independent course of development which has rendered it unlike the other branches of the animal kingdom.

The main sources of information with regard to the origins and early stages of social organization are the material remains of extinct cultures, and the extant or recently extant primitive or preliterate cultures which have been observed and described. For the later or literate stages a vast mass of historical data is available which may be utilized in studying the origins of the more recent forms of social organization.

Several sociologists have distinguished between the material and the mental aspects of culture. Malinowski has characterized culture as "social heritage," and has said that it "is a well organized unity divided into two fundamental aspects—a body of artifacts and a system of customs."[1] Thurnwald has made the distinction more emphatic by characterizing the material aspect as "civilization."[2] MacIver has dis-

[1] B. Malinowski, in the *Encyclopedia of The Social Sciences*, article on "Culture," Vol. IV, New York, 1931.

[2] "Unter 'Zivilisation' wird ein Process der Vervollkommnung von Fertigkeiten und Kenntnissen verstanden. . . . Unter 'Kultur' versteht man die subjective Verarbeitung der Objekte der Zivilisation an einem Ort und zu einer Zeit Zusammenlebende Menschen." (Richard Thurnwald, "Das Gesellungsleben der Naturvolkern," in the *Lehrbuch der Volkerkunde*, edited by K. T. Preuss, Stuttgart, 1937, p. 241.)

tinguished in similar fashion by saying that "civilization includes the means and apparatus, culture the ends and expressions of living."[3]

As earlier indicated, civilization has so often been used as a normative term that it has become highly equivocal in meaning. The material and mental aspects of culture are too closely related to be segregated under two different terms. Neither could exist without the other, and their development takes place *pari passu*. Hence we shall regard them as correlated parts of mankind's equipment which are constantly acting and reacting upon each other, and are, therefore, wholly interdependent.

The extant primitive cultures have as long a history as the so-called higher cultures. Many of them are by no means simple, having a complexity of their own. In some cases they may be derived from earlier cultures whose material remains indicate that they are now extinct. In so far as they persist in the cultures of today, they are not extinct. In many cases it is impossible to determine whether the early cultures became wholly extinct. While many of them doubtless have been completely wiped out, in some cases certain of their inventions were transmitted by diffusion, and then preserved by surviving cultures. The relation between and relative importance of invention and diffusion constitute one of the cardinal problems of the study of cultural evolution to be studied later in this treatise.

The criterion of primitiveness is to a large extent unimportant and irrelevant. It is difficult to characterize primitiveness and to draw the line beyond which a culture ceases to be primitive. The term pre-literate is much more definite and significant. The invention of writing rendered it possible to keep records, transmit information, and to communicate ideas much more fully. The distinction between the prehistoric and the historic is perhaps the most important of all distinctions between cultural stages, at least for purposes of study.

The control over and comprehension of nature probably constitute the most significant criteria of cultural development. The majority of cultural phenomena are not only conditioned by but arise directly out of this control and comprehension, though there is a vast amount of miscomprehension of nature including human nature. The same holds true for a large part of social development. In certain regions of the earth, however, such as the tropics, where subsistence is readily gained, there may take place a considerable social development without much control over and comprehension of nature. On the other hand, certain forms of social organization and of institutions check or seriously hamper social or cultural development, even though the degree of control over and comprehension of nature already available would render possible a much higher development.

[3] R. M. MacIver, *Society Its Structure and Changes*, New York, 1931.

The latter situation now exists over a large portion of the earth. In another book I have described in detail the manifold ways in which science, invention, and technology are at present hampered and frustrated: "Capitalism sometimes aids in a haphazard fashion, but usually restrains scientists, inventors, engineers, and technicians in general. Bound hand and foot by the financial restrictions of a capitalist economy, they cannot carry out projects which are not only feasible but are most efficient and productive from a technical and social point of view. Capitalism utilizes scientific and technical progress only when profits are increased thereby. Many patented inventions are purchased and suppressed by capitalists because their utilization would decrease profits in the immediate or near future. Monopolies often smother patents in order to save the cost of new installations. Capitalists are interested primarily in cheap labor and not in educated and trained labor as such. In all these ways capitalism frustrates science, invention, and technology."[4] History reveals many instances in which the comprehension of and control over nature, represented by and exemplified in science and technology, have been limited by the exploitation of one group by another, and by various cultural survivals, such as magic and religion.

Social organization exists when a group of human beings live together more or less habitually, and are conscious of and recognize relationships which involve rights and duties and an authority which may be more or less collective in its origin and expression, or may arise out of the subjection of one portion of the group by another portion. In the earliest stages of social development the family, horde, and perhaps the tribe; during the earlier stages the clan, phratry, moiety, tribe, and village community constituted forms of social organization. In later stages arose the nation and the state.

An institution is a complex of beliefs, ideas or activities, shared by a considerable number of human beings who do not necessarily live together or within specific territorial limits, and may or may not be organized. Hence Malinowski's definition of institutions is much too inclusive: "The real component units of cultures which have a considerable degree of permanence, universality and independence are the organized systems of human activities called institutions. Every institution centers around a fundamental need, permanently unites a group of people in a cooperative task and has its particular body of doctrine and its technique of craft."[5] Such a definition includes most if not all of social organization as well as institutions. Religion, magic, science, art, language, writing, and many other institutions include a large part of human mental and physical activities. However, they are

[4] Maurice Parmelee, *Farewell to Poverty*, New York, 1935, p. 81.
[5] B. Malinowski, *op. cit.*

157

not necessarily organized and cooperative, and vary as to doctrine and technique. For example, specific religions vary greatly as to doctrine and technique. And yet all of them possess the distinctive traits of religion, namely, animistic beliefs in supernatural powers and beings, and attempts to influence these hypothetical powers and beings. Specific languages differ greatly in structure, vocabulary, and complexity. But all of them are forms of the distinctively human mode of communication.

Social control manifests itself through all forms of social organization, some institutions, as well as in ways which are neither organized nor institutional. Government, law, custom, public opinion, and religion constitute powerful means of control. Consequently, the study of social control cannot be divorced from the study of social organization and institution. This control is exercised through these forms of social structure which constitute the more or less stable and rigid framework of society. It is also expressed, probably to a smaller degree, through social relationships which are as yet too mobile and changeable to constitute either organization or institution.

It has long been a subject of discussion, if not of controversy, as to whether the horde or the family was the original human group which contained the germ of social organization. Owing to the weakness and prolonged infancy of the human child, maternal care is necessary. Under most circumstances more than maternal care was necessary. In other words, the mother needed protection and also assistance in procuring food. This protection and assistance would have to come either through a group with common interests habitually living together, or through the father of the children.

As we have seen in earlier chapters, the close association between the mammalian female and her offspring, required by suckling, usually terminates as soon as the young are able to take care of themselves. As the male parent rarely or never takes part in the care of the young, the mammalian family is maternal and temporary in duration. The manner of securing food and its distribution probably are the most influential factors in determing mammalian gregariousness. Predatory animals are usually solitary. Herbivorous animals often congregate for protection or because their food is geographically concentrated. These facts indicate that the mammals are not predominantly gregarious. The primates are less gregarious than the ungulata and more so than the carnivora. They are predominantly promiscuous in their sex relations. The great apes, which are not very gregarious display a tendency toward mating due to the long period of anthropoid infancy.

As has been shown earlier, among animals there is very little division of labor and cooperation which is genuinely social in origin. Animal division of labor and cooperation are due almost solely to the instincts aroused by the reproductive processes which give rise to care of the young. The so-called societies of the ants, termites, bees, wasps, and other insects, are purely reproductive groups. In many divisions of the animal world the female is superior to the male in size and strength, and dominates the family which is almost invariably maternal. While the maternal family comes into existence in the first instance through the operation of the sexual instinct which gives rise to the reproductive process, its existence is prolonged by the maternal instincts. Out of the relations between mother and offspring and amongst the offspring themselves may arise social habits. The low rate of increase of many primitive peoples, as of many other mammals, caused mainly by the very limited food supply, and also by accidents, disease, and predatory beasts, may have been due in part to prolonged suckling. Until lactiferous animals (goat, sheep, cow, mare, etc.) were domesticated, children had to depend for several years upon their mothers' milk for nourishment. All of these considerations from the animal world suggest that mankind was originally promiscuous in its sexual relations, and that the bi-parental and other complex forms of the family as well as of marriage came into existence later.[6]

The mammalian and primate background of mankind suggests that early men lived in groups which varied in size according to the distribution of food, nature of the climate, available shelter, and dangers encountered. Where food was plentiful, and abundant shelter in the way of caves, rock shelters, etc., was available, a considerable agglomeration of human beings might arise. Where food was scarce, the human population would have to scatter, perhaps in family groups consisting of one family or of a very few families. It is, however, not legitimate to assume that the bi-parental family existed from the outset, as some writers have asserted. It is much more plausible to postulate the horde as the original human group. The more highly organized groups, such as the tribe, and later the clan and phratry, could not have come into existence without the family and recognition of blood relationship. The experience of having been reared together in the same group was probably the first purely social bond as distinguished from the biological bonds arising out of the sexual and parental instincts.

Among the most primitive peoples which have been observed the men are hunters and fishers in addition to defending the group whenever necessary. The women are plant gatherers in addition to performing their reproductive functions. These groups often wander far and wide in search of food. Single families sometimes separate and

[6] For a lengthy argument in favor of original human promiscuity, see Robert Briffault, *The Mothers, The Matriarchal Theory of Social Origins,* London, 1927, 3 vols.; abridged edition in one volume, New York, 1931.

then come together again. While the family of parents and children forms a unity, families of brothers or sisters may form a larger family temporarily or permanently.

Marriage arose out of the family and is based on sexual attraction and biological division of labor between man and woman. It did not become an institution until it was recognized by the group and invested with rights and duties. Whether or not it came into existence as an institution before the biological fact of fatherhood was discovered, it is impossible to determine. Some primitive groups have been observed which were ignorant of this fact, though they practised marriage in some form. This was true of some of the Australian aborigines who thought that women are impregnated by spirits. Many forms of institutional marriage have existed, and acquired an economic significance extending far beyond its biological aspect, as will be discussed in later chapters.

Leaving aside for the moment the data accumulated from the observation of extant primitive peoples, let us turn again to the material remains of the extinct cultures of the more distant past, to consider how they may have determined or were correlated with the different forms of social organization. Menghin has made the most extensive and comprehensive survey of the stone age cultures.[7] He has attempted to classify these cultures as to type, place of origin, and distribution. The lithic cultures were probably preceded by an alithic wood culture of which no traces remain. He has distinguished three protolithic cultures, namely, (1) the blade (*Klingen*) culture which included the dagger and the lance, (2) the hand-ax (*Faustkeil*) culture, and (3) the bone (*Knochen*) culture. The probable place of origin of the bone culture was in northern Asia, of the blade culture in central Asia, and of the ax culture in India or possibly in central Africa. In India and Africa the bamboo and other tropical plants furnished material for knives and other cutting tools which may have been the prototypes of the stone cutting tools. The blade culture was the first of these three cultures to spread from Asia. This is indicated by the fact that the lowest lithic culture in Europe and Africa was a pure blade culture. The three principal stages of the European protolithic blade culture were (1) Pre-Chellean, (2) Levalloisian, (3) Mousterian. Much later the ax culture carried agriculture with it. The bone culture was the first to domesticate animals, namely, the dog and the reindeer.

The accuracy of Menghin's sweeping generalizations with regard to paleolithic culture will be severely tested by future discoveries, especially in Asia. They are not entirely in accord with the generali-

[7] Oswald Menghin, *Weltgeschichte der Steinzeit,* Vienna, 1931.

160

zations of other writers. For example, in a more recent but less comprehensive survey, Leakey has asserted that the Chellean and Acheulean cultures were created by the true ancestors of modern man. The Clactonian, Levalloisian, and Mousterian cultures were probably closely related. At least the two latter cultures were created by Neanderthal man, and all three of them were influenced by contact with Acheulean culture. The Levalloisian culture probably developed in Germany during the Mindel-Riss interglacial period, and was pushed southward into France by the glaciers. In France the true Mousterian was contemporaneous with the Combe Capelle stage of the Levalloisian, with the Micoquian, and with the Mousterian of Acheulean tradition. The Levalloisian in Europe lasted from the Mindel-Riss interglacial period to the Wuerm I-Wuerm II interglacial period.[8] In a later work Leakey has asserted that *Homo sapiens* was probably fully developed by the middle pleistocene, and has made the following generalization: "During the Middle Pleistocene there were two distinct major culture complexes. One of these was that which we have called the Chelleo-Acheulean hand-axe culture, and the other the Clactonian-Levalloisian complex, which subsequently gave rise to the Mousterian and developed Levalloisian. Now we know from discoveries in Europe and Palestine that the makers of the developed Levalloisian and Mousterian cultures—which were derived from the Clactonian-Levalloisian culture-complex were men of the Neanderthal species. In all probability men of the species *Homo sapiens* were responsible for the great hand-axe culture."[9]

Breuil has contended that the Chellean has been misnamed because no implements of this type are found in the site at Chelles. He has named this early paleolithic culture Abbevillian after the site at Abbeville in northern France. According to him, the Abbevillian was followed in succession by the Clactonian, Acheulean 1, 2, and 3, Levalloisian 1 and 2, Acheulean 4 and 5, Levalloisian 3 and 4, Acheulean 6 and 7, and Levalloisian 5, 6 and 7. Later cultures belong to the upper paleolithic period. The Mousterian corresponded to Levalloisian 5, 6 and 7, and perhaps extended back through Acheulean 6 and 7, and Levalloisian 3 and 4. The Tayacian, named after the site at Tayac in southern France, corresponded to Levalloisian 3 and 4, and Acheulean 6 and 7. The paleolithic commenced at least as far back as the Mindel-Riss interglacial period, and perhaps as far back as the Guenz-Mindel interglacial period.[10]

[8] L. S. B. Leakey, *Adam's Ancestors,* London, 1934.

[9] L. S. B. Leakey, *Stone Age Africa,* London, 1936, p. 164.

[10] Communicated verbally to the author in September 1937. Abbe Henri Breuil has published his findings and opinions in numerous articles and monographs in French anthropological literature.

The British Museum published in 1936 the following outline of the stone age in western Europe which differs somewhat from the continental versions:

Eolithic—Tertiary—climate uncertain.

Icenian—Darmsdenian (Suffolk)—Pre-Chellean—warm (preglacial?). No culture known in first glaciation (Guenz).

Cromerian—Early Chellean—warm (interglacial).

Clactonian, Stage I—cold, second glaciation (Mindel)—(Chellean apparently went southward).

Clactonian, Stage II—Late Chellean and Early Acheulian—warm (interglacial).

Clactonian, Evolved—Lower Middle Acheulian—warm (interglacial).

Early Levallois—Upper Middle Acheulian—cold, third glaciation (Riss).

Middle Levallois—Late Acheulean—warm (interglacial).

Late Levallois—Final Acheulean or La Micoque—Early Mousterian—colder.

Mousterian—cold, fourth glaciation (Wuerm).

Lower, Middle and Upper Aurignacian, then Solutrian—intermediate cool.

Magdalenian—cold, fourth glaciation (Wuerm).

The above citations from the British Museum, Breuil, Leakey, and Menghin indicate that the cultural situation in paleolithic time was more complicated than has heretofore been supposed. Instead of a continuous succession of cultures, there was a good deal of overlapping. Sometimes, and perhaps all of the time, there were two or more dissimilar cultures existing contemporaneously, not only in the world at large, but also in Europe, and even in western Europe. In some cases groups of members of the same race separated from each other, and under unlike environmental conditions created dissimilar cultures. Whatever the manner of origin, these cultures existed and co-existed, sometimes entirely isolated from each other, at other times coming into contact and influencing each other, sometimes annihilating each other, at other times transforming and assimilating each other.

Back of these processes were the powerful forces of nature, the mighty forward movement of the glaciers and their retreat, the changes in the relative distribution and area of land and sea, the progressive fertilizing or dessication of the soil owing to diverse pluvial or arid conditions, the variations of the temperature owing partly to the

162

shifting of the poles and the consequent changes in the degrees of latitude. In all of these respects the situation was not entirely unlike the situation in the later stages of cultural evolution, except that the period of time involved was vastly longer, and the environmental changes correspondingly greater, though the cultural situation may not have changed as greatly.

Turning now to the later stages, Menghin is on somewhat firmer ground in his description of neolithic culture, because there are many more data available than for paleolithic culture. He has distinguished three principal proto-neolithic cultures (6000-4000 B.C.) according to the animals domesticated and bred. These were (1) swine, (2) horned cattle, and (3) riding animals. The breeding of swine probably originated in southeastern Asia, perhaps in China or Indo-China. Cattle breeding originated in the region of western Turkestan, perhaps including the northern part of the Iranian plateau. The breeding of riding animals originated north of this region, and was closely associated with the mesolithic bone culture.

According to Menghin, the three principal cultures of the neolithic and of the early part of the metal ages (4000-2000 B.C.) were (1) the village, peasant and agriculture culture, (2) the city and rulers' (Herren) culture, and (3) the steppe, pastoral and warlike culture. The village culture evolved out of swine and cattle breeding. It arose spontaneously in many places where these two forms of animal breeding came together. This took place in the Orient in the fourth and in Europe in the third millennium B.C. The regional types of the neolithic village culture were as follows: (1) Tauric (Asia and the Balkans), (2) Nilotic (Egypt), (3) Eastern Mediterranean, (4) Syrian, (5) North African, (6) Danubian, (7) West European, (8) North European. The first four regional types became urban about 3000 B.C. or soon after. The second four types retained longer their village and peasant character. The Nilotic village culture in Upper Egypt south of the Fayum district included the Tasian, Badarian, Negade, Amrah, and Gerzeh stages or types of culture.

According to Menghin, the city culture evolved out of the village culture. But it was influenced, enriched, overlaid, and perhaps organized by the steppe culture of the breeders of riding animals. The conditions for the appearance of the urban culture were fulfilled first of all in western Turkestan at Anau from which the Mesopotamian-Sumerian city culture probably originated. The eastern Tauric village culture, namely, in northern Asia Minor, became urban about 2500 B.C. The Nilotic village culture developed into an urban culture in pre-dynastic times, namely, during the fourth millennium before Christ, and arose out of the Badarian or Amrah village cultures. The first territorial state came into existence in Egypt. Prior to Sargon of

Akkad (*ca.* 2500 B.C.), Mesopotamia had only city states of no great territorial extent. The regional types of the neolithic and early metal urban culture were as follows: (1) Central Asiatic in western Turkestan (Anau), (2) Tauric in northern and eastern Asia Minor, (3) Mesopotamian, (4) Nilotic, (5) Indian in the Indus valley (Mohenjodaro, etc.), (6) Eastern Mediterranean, (7) Syrian. The regional types of the neolithic steppe culture which influenced and perhaps took part in the organization of the early urban culture were as follows: (1) Pontic-Aral, (2) Syrian-Arabic, (3) East African.

I have cited Menghin's generalizations not because they are necessarily correct, but because they exemplify an attempt to describe the early cultures on the basis of their material remains. Owing to the paucity and one-sided character of these remains (only the more durable having survived), many anthropologists and sociologists have been tempted to assume that extant or recently extant preliterate cultures furnish fairly accurate examples of the early cultures. Sollas has compared the paleolithic cultures with the Eskimo and Tasmanian cultures. Concerning the Tasmanians he asserted that they "afford us an opportunity of interpreting the past by the present—a saving procedure in a subject where fantasy is only too likely to play a leading part." Later in his book he concluded that, isolated at an early date, they "had preserved almost unchanged the habits and industrial arts which existed in Europe during the later days of the Lower Mousterian age." [11] However great the likeness between the Tasmanians and the European Mousterians in their material equipment and industrial arts, Sollas did not, as, indeed, he could not, compare their social organization and institutions which determine a large part of the habits, customs, traditions, beliefs and ideas of every people.

With regard to certain implements which have been found among some primitive peoples and not among others, there is great uncertainty as to their antiquity. A case in point is the bow and arrow. In Chapter VII I said that paleolithic man probably did not have the bow and arrow because birds appear very little in paleolithic art and they could have been hunted most effectively with this implement of the chase. And yet many paleolithic tools could have been used in the manufacture of the bow and arrow. Among them were the point, perforator, scraper, spokeshave, and knife. As we have seen, the point was much used at least as far back as the Mousterian period. It was inserted in the dart, javelin, and spear. It may also have been inserted in the arrow. Aurignacian points have been found which look like arrowheads, and which were probably from 25,000 to 50,000 years old. There are also some paleolithic drawings in carvings which look

[11] W. J. Sollas, *Ancient Hunters and Their Modern Representatives*, London, 1924.

164

like archers, as for example, at Castellon in Spain, and elsewhere. It is also possible that the bow was used with an arrow with a wooden point long before a flint point was inserted. Such arrows as well as the bows would have disappeared long ago. In view of the usefulness of the bow and arrow during the neolithic period and later as an implement of the chase, as well as a weapon in warfare, it may well be questioned as to whether or not this implement had not been invented much earlier. Its invention would perhaps have been no more remarkable than that of the slingshot, bola, dart with throwing stick, javelin, and spear, all of which were apparently used by paleolithic man. The bow and arrow is an excellent illustration of the difficulties involved in dating the origin of many implements and other portions of the material culture. How much greater are the difficulties inherent in dating many aspects of the immaterial and intangible culture of which no tangible and material evidence of stone and bone can survive.

Another example of reading present or recent culture traits into the past, even as far back as the beginning of cultural evolution, was furnished by Benedict. She alleged that "there is only one means by which we may gain an approximate knowledge of these early beginnings. That is by a study of the distribution of those few traits that are universal or near-universal in human society." Of these traits she mentioned "animism," "exogamous restrictions upon mariage," and beliefs in "the human soul," and in "an after-life," which, she asserted, "have long since become automatic in human behavior."[12] None of these traits could have existed at the commencement of, or very early in, cultural evolution. It is quite conceivable that all four of these traits did not exist for hundreds of thousands of years after its commencement. Such concepts as those of the human soul and of an after-life require a good deal of abstract thinking, as Mrs. Benedict should have realized. It is also certain that none of these traits could become "automatic in human behavior," because then they would be reflex and instinctive, whereas all of them are conscious and ideational.

While the ancient and the more recent cultures concerned were similar in their limited and primitive equipment, there must have been great differences in other cultural phases. Early mankind had no language or only the most rudimentary linguistic equipment. Without language there could be no accumulation of traditions and of ideas, and only a very limited accumulation of customs. There could exist not even the beginnings of institutions, such as religion, magic, art, and so forth. There could be only the most elementary forms of social organization and structure in the horde and possibly

[12] Ruth Benedict, *Patterns of Culture*. New York, 1946, page 17.

in the family. All of the extant or recently extant primitive cultures which have been observed, have, on the contrary, possessed highly evolved languages, and have displayed a certain amount of institutional development. They have possessed a considerable accumulation of customs and of traditions, and have been characterized by more or less complicated forms of social organization and structure, such as the clan, moiety, tribe, exogamy, endogamy, various forms of the family and of marriage, and sometimes by germs of the state.[13]

Hence it is that any attempt to reconstitute the earlier stages of cultural evolution by analogy with present day primitive cultures should be made with constant recognition of these great differences. Not only have the so-called primitive cultures of today had as long a time for change and development as the so-called civilized cultures. They may not have been characteristic and representative even at an earlier stage of cultural evolution, as has been recognized in part by a German sociologist who has done much work in the field, and has made extensive use of data concerning extant primitive cultures in attempting to reconstruct the earlier stages.[14] An American anthropologist with a similar experience in the study of extant primitive cultures has also deprecated wholesale reasoning by analogy from the present to the past: "It is more than questionable whether it is justifiable to construct from a mere static examination of cultural forms the world over an historical sequence that would express laws of cultural development." He has, however, given far too much weight to the role of the "accident" which is only a misnomer for ignorance: "I am far from claiming that no general laws relating to the growth of culture exist. Whatever they may be, they are in every particular case overlaid by a mass of accidents that were probably much more potent in the actual happenings than the general laws."[15]

Numerous examples can be cited from contemporary anthropological and sociological literature of reasoning by analogy from present to past culture. Elliot Smith asserted that food-gatherers, past as well

13 An American anthropologist has asserted that "the germs of all possible political developments are latent but demonstrable in the ruder cultures and that a specific turn in communal experience—say, contact with a weaker or a stronger neighbor—may produce an efflorescence of novel institutions." (R. H. Lowie, *The Origin of the State*, New York, 1927.) This is a brief and fragmentary discussion of political origins in which are discussed associations for common ends, castes, the territorial tie, the size of the state, sovereignty, etc.

14 "Denn die heutigen Menschen, deren Kultur wir 'primitiv' nennen, entsprechen in ihrem koerperlichen Aussehen (und hoechstwahrscheinlich in ihrer psychischen Veranlagung) keineswegs dem koerperlichen Typ urgeschichtlicher Primitivitaet und sind daher auch psychisch anders zu werten." (R. Thurnwald, "Ein vorkapitalistisches Wirtschaftssystem in Buin," in the *Archiv fuer Rechts-und Sozialphilosophie*, Band XXXI, Heft 1, 1937.)

15 F. Boas, *Anthropology and Modern Life*, New York, 1928, pp. 209-10.

as present, have had no houses, clothing, pottery, metal, social classes and institutions, and that they lived in family groups, were almost always monogamous, and were peaceable and kindly.[16] While there is much evidence in support of these assertions concerning the material equipment, the generalizations concerning the social and institutional development are highly questionable. Perry, his leading disciple, has made many similar sweeping generalizations.[17] Frazer based his voluminous study of magic and religion almost entirely upon observations of extant primitive peoples and upon historical data, and made thereupon many dogmatic allegations with regard to the prehistoric past, most of which are nothing more than pure guesswork. For example, he alleged that magicians formed the earliest profession and attracted the ablest and most unscrupulous men. He asserted that this profession substituted monarchy for an oligarchy of old men and for democracy, and thereby increased liberty because in primitive democracy men were hidebound by custom.[18]

Largely on the basis of numerous citations of living primitive peoples, Westermarck concluded that mankind was originally monogamous and that "the family, not the tribe, formed the nucleus of every social group, and, in many cases, was itself perhaps the only social group.[19] Using a similar method, Morgan had already arrived at the opposite conclusion, to wit, that "low down in savagery community of husbands and wives, within prescribed limits, was the central principle of the social system," and that the Australian system "represents a striking phase of the ancient social history of our race."[20] The question may well be asked as to how either Morgan or Westermarck could arrive at the conclusion that the Australian aborigines or any other living people exemplify the family, marriage, and social organization as they existed in eolithic, early paleolithic, or even in late paleolithic time, if indeed all or any of these social and cultural phenomena existed at any or all of those periods of time. As an American anthropologist has said: "Australian culture is unusually meager on the industrial and economic side. . . . Social organization is much more complicated than the arts." After describing certain features peculiar to Australia, he asserted that "these variations must have originated among the Australians; and this raises the question whether many other traits may also be indigenous."[21] The same was true perhaps as much of the Tasmanians. Since they became extinct during

[16] G. Elliot Smith, *Human History*, New York, 1929.
[17] W. J. Perry, *The Growth of Civilization*, New York, 1923.
[18] J. G. Frazer, *The Golden Bough*, New York, 1922.
[19] E. Westermarck, *History of Human Marriage*, London, 1891.
[20] L. H. Morgan, *Ancient Society*, New York, 1877.
[21] A. L. Kroeber, *Anthropology*, New York, 1923. pp. 492, 493.

the nineteenth century, much less is known of their language, social organization, religion, magic, etc.

It is plausible to assume that the family and the horde existed at least as far back as late paleolithic time. But whether it was the maternal or the bi-parental family, and whether any of the more complex forms of the family, or of the extended or greater family, at that time existed, it is impossible to determine. In other words, we cannot know at what stage originated organization based upon kinship, which was the dominant form of social organization during several of the later stages of cultural evolution.

As to the horde, it must have varied greatly in size according to environmental conditions. Where the food was sparse and the shelter limited, hordes containing very few families may have been prevalent. Under more favorable conditions hordes containing several hundred individuals may have existed. Until agriculture was invented, furnishing an abundant and more or less regular food supply, and until a higher form of social organization was evolved, which could regulate the intercourse of a comparatively large population, the horde was probably limited in size to face-to-face relationship and acquaintance. The exceptionally large rock shelters of Laugerie Basse and Laugerie Haute in the valley of the Vezere in southern France probably accommodated hordes of two or three hundred persons each. At some of the paleolithic work shops have been found accumulations of many thousands of work flints. This suggests a considerable aggregation of population. However, these work shops may have been used simultaneously or at different times by many different hordes.

Chapter XIII

The Origins of Industrial Occupations

THE earliest industry of which we have evidence was stone chipping. Our knowledge of it is due to the durability of the materials which it used. It may well have been antedated by industries in wood, bone, and earth whose remains have long since disappeared. These industries, alithic and lithic, arose out of human activities which long preceded them, namely, hunting, fishing and plant gathering. At the outset these activities did not differ from those of animals. All of the herbivores gather plant food. Some of them store it for considerable periods of time. All of the carnivores are predaceous. Some of them fish as well as hunt. These activities became industries when mankind began to use secondary measures, not arising spontaneously out of innate traits which manifest themselves from generation to generation without previous experience and training.

The earliest industries, therefore, included the manufacture of implements to aid mankind to secure food, and the activities of hunting, fishing and plant gathering in which these artifacts were used. The distinction between production or capital goods industries, and consumption or consumers' goods industries had already appeared. At an early date also appeared the use of fire, which is indicated by hearths at Mousterian sites in Europe, and at Chou-kou-tien in China where the remains of *Sinanthropus* were found. Early paleolithic man may have discovered how to make fire with the aid of iron pyrites. Whether produced by artificial means or procured from natural sources, such as volcanoes, it was used at an early date for warmth, for cooking, and eventually in various industries. In fact, it was essential for all of the higher industrial evolution. Later were associated with it many magical and religious beliefs and practices and other cultural phenomena which rendered it of considerable institutional significance.

The industries constitute the useful arts because they produce objects which can be used. The fine arts are devoted to the orna-

169

mentation of the products of the useful arts, or to producing objects which cannot be used but which are pleasing to the senses. This distinction between the fine and the useful arts is, however, partly subjective. It is possible that primitive men considered the products of the fine arts as useful as those of the useful arts. In the present as well as in the past certain products of the fine arts are considered useful for magical and religious reasons. Much of modern art—architecture, sculpture, painting, music, and literature—adorns religious monuments, edifices, and ceremonies. The esthetic enjoyment derived from these arts may have arisen after primitive men had commenced to produce them for practical reasons. In later chapters this subject will be discussed in connection with the problem of their origins. Suffice it to say now that their products are found in Europe as far back as Aurignacian and probably Mousterian time.

With the development of the industries and of both the industrial and the fine arts, there came into being the social division of labor, and the consequent occupations and professions. The biological differences between the sexes caused a certain amount of sexual division of labor from the outset. The long period of human infancy and of lactation restricted somewhat the range of female activity. Among practically all of the food-gathering peoples which have been observed, the men have been the hunters and fishers, and also the warriors whenever warfare took place, while the women have been the plant-gatherers. In its early stages women played a prominent, if not preponderant, role in plant cultivation. As agricultural methods became more complicated and mechanized, and as household economy declined in the amount of labor entailed because of mechanization in the latest stages of cultural evolution, female labor has lost much of its distinctive significance and importance. Since the recent rise of industrial capitalism, it has been used a great deal outside of the home, but to a large extent in the same way as male labor, namely, for wage work in factory and office, so that the sexual division of labor has in considerable part disappeared.

Individual skill and personal preference may have influenced the distribution of labor to at least a slight extent from the outset. It is unlikely that anything in the nature of a genuine social division of labor came into existence until the earliest tool using industries began to develop. It may well be that at the outset each person made his own implements of wood, bone, and of stone. Individual skill varies greatly in the making of these tools. The persons possessing unusual aptitude would naturally specialize in tool making. They would then exchange their products for the food, shelter, protection, etc., provided by other members of their communities. Thus would arise exchange and barter—the rudimentary beginnings of commerce. Or the exchange

170

might be more socialized in that these craftsmen would be furnished their sustenance by their communities in return for their skilled labor which would be a primitive form of collectivism. Thus a paleolithic horde or tribe might in course of time become organized spontaneously and without forethought on an occupational basis. Each man within the community was a hunter, or fisher, or toolmaker, etc., while the gathering and preparation of plants for consumption was monopolized largely or entirely by the women, who, because of their child bearing and rearing functions, could not specialize so much as the men.

In course of time the division of labor passed beyond the horde or tribe and became intercommunal. A group located near a flint quarry produced a surplus of flint implements which it could exchange for the products of other groups. At some of the inland paleolithic sites in Europe have been found sea shells which had traveled a considerable distance. This may have been a result of intercommunal exchange and the first step toward international trade, which is a more plausible explanation than that whole groups traveled all the way from the seaside to these inland sites, and carried with them stores of sea shells.

It has often been alleged that the earliest occupations were those of magician and priest. An encyclopedia has asserted that "the oldest and earliest distinct occupations have everywhere been the 'spiritual' professions—those of magician, soothsayer, prophet, medicine man, singer."[1] There is no factual basis whatsoever for this wholly gratuitous assertion. All of the available evidence is against it. Such professions have not been found among all of the primitive peoples which have been observed. Even if such were the case, and even if in a few instances these professions were present where all of the industrial occupations were absent (an inconceivable situation), no evidence would exist for it. As I have amply demonstrated in the preceding chapter, the extant primitive cultures cannot be regarded as archetypes of the early cultures. All of them have as long a history back of them as the so-called civilized peoples of today. Total or partial regression has doubtless taken place in some of these extant cultures. It might conceivably happen in a few of these cases that the "spiritual" professions are highly developed while the industrial occupations are in a backward state.

The oft-repeated fallacy that female prostitution is the "oldest profession" is even more baseless and gratuitous, because this profession could arise only in a complicated society, which must include the

---

[1] Arthur Salz, article on "Occupation," *Encyclopedia of the Social Sciences,* Vol. XI, New York, 1933.

family as a form of social organization, highly developed property rights, the economic subordination of women, an elaborate system of exchange, and a conventionalized and sophisticated conception of sex relations far removed from the attitude of the more primitive peoples. Nothing that can be accurately described as professional prostitution existed until late in social evolution. The causal nexus between the above-mentioned social conditions and restraint upon, on the one hand, and license of sex, on the other hand, will be discussed in Chapter XVI and later.

The most significant facts available upon which to base an hypothesis as to the original occupations are those that demonstrate that mankind and its immediate ancestors were making tools as far back as the early pleistocene and perhaps even the pliocene. This implies the rise of industrial occupations at that early date. On the other hand, the earliest reliable evidence of animistic beliefs and practices dates back only as far as the middle paleolithic, which came very late, almost at the close of the pleistocene. Hence it is probable that the industrial occupations antedate the "spiritual" professions by several hundreds of thousands of years at the least.

Both of the above-mentioned widely believed fallacies with regard to which were the oldest occupations and professions indicate the presence, even in more or less scholarly circles, of widespread ignorance or misinterpretation of the descriptions of extant primitive peoples and of historical data. They denote failure to recognize the significance of a great deal of anthropological and archeological data; heedlessness of time relations, namely, chronology; lack of recognition of the scientific problems involved, especially with regard to the interweaving of social institutions; and, worst of all, the cardinal error of naively or blandly ignoring how great is our ignorance in comparison with the little that we know. Out of this mare's nest of blundering sins of commission and of omission arise the widespread practice of jumping at conclusions; far-reaching generalizations with inadequate inductive basis or no basis whatsoever; and, worst of all, dogmatic assertions which fly in the face of some or all of the available data. Description, explanation, and interpretation of the past are justified only to the extent that they have an inductive basis. A tentative and provisional uncertainty is far wiser than a fatuous and fallacious certainty. Some of these problems with regard to the past may still be soluble, but many of them can never be solved, because the evidence necessary for their solution has completely disappeared, so that we must accept our ineluctable ignorance with resignation.

One of the most pertinent if not crucial questions with regard to the origins of the occupations is the linguistic problem. Whether or not language, or speech of the most rudimentary sort, existed before the beginning of the manufacture of tools can never be determined. It is possible that industrial activities commenced before language. The anthropoid apes at times approach somewhat close to the making of tools, even though they cannot speak. It is also conceivable that there was a slight degree of specialization in industrial activities even before language, though this seems less likely. It is very unlikely that a systematic exchange of goods took place before language. It is almost certain that industries, occupations, and the exchange of commodities developed more or less *pari passu* with the evolution of language. Speech renders possible the description and discussion of methods of manufacture, and the transmission of these methods from person to person by means of teaching. It renders possible an overt understanding as to the differentiation and specialization of functions, in other words, a social division of labor. It permits of and greatly facilitates the haggling and bartering which are inevitable in the exchange of goods. It is reasonable to assume that these social phenomena were developing together during eolithic and early paleolithic time, which probably lasted for several hundred thousand years. That is perhaps as far as we are justified in going in characterizing the situation up to the middle paleolithic, and possibly even up to the neolithic.

The study of extant primitive and more or less primitive cultures has revealed several categories of exchange. Among them are a gift economy, a gift barter economy, pure barter, money barter, and money exchange. Whether or not this series of categories represents evolutionary stages, it is impossible to determine. As we shall see presently, money exchange came very late in social evolution. How far back exchange in the form of gifts originated, it is futile even to conjecture. The form and manner of the exchange in all probability depended mainly then as now upon the form of social organization which prevailed, namely, as to whether it was relatively individualistic upon the basis of the family, or communal upon the basis of the horde, clan, and tribe.

Much the same may be said with regard to occupations. In more or less primitive cultures have been observed corporate and caste organization of occupations. The latter is based upon heredity in that the same occupation is passed on from generation to generation in the same family. The former exists when an occupation is organized in the nature of a guild to which individuals are admitted only by means of prescribed formalities. Slavery also had its effect upon occupational organization. Certain occupations are usually relegated to the slaves. However, slavery appeared rather late in social evolution as a result of organized warfare, probably after agriculture had come into exist-

173

ence.[2] It is impossible to conjecture how far back caste and corporate organization of occupations appeared, but probably also rather late in social evolution.

With the advent of the neolithic period came a great industrial expansion and the rise of many new industries. One of the principal steps in cultural evolution now took place, namely, the transition from food-gathering to food-producing. Up to this time mankind had secured its food by killing or capturing wild animals and gathering uncultivated plants. The cultures of many food-gathering peoples have been observed. Among those extant or recently extinct are, in Africa, the Bushmen and the Negritos or Pygmies; in Asia, the Pre-Dravidian tribes of southern India, the Veddahs of Ceylon, the Andamanese, the Semang and Sakai of the Malay Peninsula, the Kubu of Sumatra, the Punan of Borneo, the Negritos of the Philippines, a tribe in the Aru or Aroe islands off the southwest coast of New Guinea, the Samoyedes and Ostiak of Siberia, who had, however, domesticated the reindeer. The food-gathering peoples which have been observed in North America are the Eskimo, the Déné of the Mackenzie River basin, the Beothuk of Newfoundland, the Paiute of Utah, and several tribes in California; in South America, various tribes of the upper Amazon and other river valleys, and several tribes in Tierra del Fuego; and in Australasia, the aboriginal Australians and Tasmanians. Probably some, and perhaps most, of these peoples were the first human inhabitants of the regions in which they have been found, inhabiting the world's left-over areas, which are least suited to agriculture or herding, because of climate and/or native plants. They have not invented any food-producing methods, and have had little or no contact with agricultural and animal breeding peoples. They exemplify in considerable part the pre-neolithic industrial status.

The two principal and fundamental food-producing industries are plant culture, *i.e.,* agriculture, and animal culture. It cannot be asserted with certainty which came first. There may have been a little animal culture during the latter part of the paleolithic before anything in the nature of agriculture had come into existence. It might have arisen through the capture when young of edible animals, their rearing and domestication, reproduction and selection. Primitive peoples the world over have raised many kinds of animals as pets. Some of these animals furnished not only food in the form of meat and milk, but also material for clothing, such as furs, and later the

[2] "The development of agriculture lays the foundation for systematic enslavement. Though made possible by agriculture, slavery is actually instituted by war. It appears with conquest as an alternative to slaughter or adoption." (M. R. Davie, *The Evolution of War*, New Haven, 1929, p. 174.)

animal fibers used in weaving textiles, *i.e.,* wool from various animals. Some of the larger and stronger animals became beasts of burden, certain of them being ridden by men. Animal and plant culture also act and react upon each other, because some agriculture is destined to produce food for domesticated animals, while certain animals have aided in agricultural activities. For example, cattle breeding rendered plow culture possible.

Mankind has at all times eaten the edible plants available in a state of nature. All primitive peoples which have been observed use plant food whenever available, whether wild or cultivated. How certain plants first came to be cultivated it will never be possible to ascertain. It may have been due to the observation that seeds accidentally dropped upon the ground soon sprouted. Nor can we determine when and where this discovery was first made. It probably happened several and perhaps many times in various parts of the world. In most of these cases it did not result in an extensive development of the art of agriculture.

It is not known whether agriculture first arose in tropical, temperate, pluvial, semi-arid, or arid regions. It could not arise in the cold regions or in the colder portions of the temperate zones. In much of the tropical region there is an abundance of wild plant food which discourages efforts at cultivation. Nevertheless, early attempts may have been made in the tropics where many kinds of edible plants can be produced with great ease. No evidence of such attempts has been found. It still remains an open question as to whether the germinal idea of plant cultivation originated in the tropical or the temperate zone. Of the two principal cereal crops, wheat is indigenous to a temperate, semi-arid climate, and rice to a tropical, pluvial climate. Whether either of these was the first cultivated plant is unknown.[3]

Some of the most important ancient agricultural peoples which have been observed or are to any extent known were mainly in the subtropical zone, some of them in semi-arid regions. Among the best known of these early cultures were those of Egypt watered periodically by the Nile, Babylonia irrigated from the Euphrates and Tigris, Syria, Crete formerly pluvial, and the Egean archipelago. Less known were those of India, China, Turkestan, and of various regions of Europe (Greece, Italy, the Danubian valley, and the Balkans).

Observation of extant primitive peoples has suggested that agriculture usually commenced with the cultivation of one plant. Later the cultivation of additional plants was learned from neighboring hordes or tribes. In some cases it commenced with replanting. Edible

[3] See Maurice Parmelee, *Geo-Economic Regionalism and World Federation,* New York, 1949, pages 71-72.

175

plants in a state of nature were dug up, sometimes with the aid of the digging stick, and replanted in a convenient place. Later came the discovery that crops can be raised from the planting of seeds, perhaps due to gathered wild seeds accidentally dropped near a settle ment where a crop would grow readily because fertilized by the human manure abundant in such a location. Another possible origin might be a magical ceremony such as the sacrifice of gathered wild grain to the earth spirit followed by a crop, as if in divine recompense. Gradually the consumption of cultivated and domesticated plants supplanted the use of wild species. In this fashion a people passed to an economy based upon agriculture. It was this transition from food-gathering to food-producing which marked the beginning of the neolithic period.

The two principal groups of cultivated plants are the grains or cereal crops, and the tubers or root crops. The most important grains have been wheat, rice, and maize. Most of the great cultures of neolithic and later times have been dependent in large part upon these three grains, usually upon one of them in each case. The less important grains have been rye, barley, oats, and millet. Several of these grains came from the western Asiatic region, namely, southern Turkestan, Persia, Turkey, and Transcaucasia. Wheat has been traced to wild species in this region, and was probably domesticated in Anatolia. Wheat and barley have been found in the neolithic sites of the western Mediterranean, while rye and oats came later to Europe. Rye was probably originally a weed under wheat in Asia, traveled with the wheat, and became independent in the colder European climate. It went from the Black Sea region to the area between the Alps and the Carpathians, and was found in southern France during the neolithic. Wheat and barley have been found in the oldest Egyptian and Babylonian graves. Maize was probably derived from teosinte, a wild grain in Mexico. It furnished the staple food of the great Pre-Columbian cultures in Mexico, Central America, and Peru, and had spread northward as far as climate permitted.

Grain may at first have been eaten raw. Then it was probably roasted over hot coals. This would not only make it more digestible and tasty but would loosen the shells of the kernels so that they could readily be rubbed off. The next stage in the preparation of grain probably was the cooking of groats or bruised grain. This would lead to the grinding of the grain, thus producing flour. From this flour mush could be prepared. Flat cakes made from mush and baked were the forerunner of bread. Wheat contains a large amount of gluten which makes bread light by causing the dough to rise. Rye contains less of this gluten, and barley and oats very little. Hence bread made from these three grains is not so light as wheaten bread. Yeast, which aids the rising of dough, came into existence with the brewing of beer which gave rise to malt. In Europe, however, yeast was not generally used in the making of bread until a few centuries ago.

The improvement of tools has been an important factor in the development of agriculture as of all industries. In all probability, as we have said, the earliest agricultural implement was the digging stick utilized by many primitive peoples, and developed with a notch for the foot. It has been used for planting, transplanting, weeding, and harvesting. In the course of time it developed into the hoe, a more efficient tool for the same purposes, although for a long time the blade was of stone, shell, or wood. Then came the plow, which is a sort of enlarged digging stick or hoe, dragged through the superficial soil. The domestication of draft animals made the plow more powerful, but many modern inventions have made it more efficient.

The various agricultural implements are adapted to the cultivation of different plants, the hoe for cereal maize or Indian corn, indigenous to America; the tuberous manioc or cassava, found in America and in Africa; and the tuberous taro, found in the Pacific islands. Largely for this reason hoe culture was prevalent in central and south Africa, America, and in the Pacific, the latter two areas also having no native draft animals suitable for domestication. The extensive cultivation of the grains other than maize requires plow culture. Hence the plow was of basic importance for all of the neolithic and later agricultural peoples of the eastern hemisphere.

Agriculture can support a relatively large population because it furnishes an abundant supply of food, and renders it more or less stable. As the population in fertile regions becomes too dense, it occasions the migration of the surplus population and its colonization elsewhere, usually in less fertile regions. Agriculture requires a considerable amount of cooperative action, in order to protect the crops day and night against wild animals. Sometimes such protection is needed also against hostile human groups. Cooperative action was also often involved in the selection of seed, and in the choice of the time for planting and harvesting. Like almost every other phase of primitive life, agriculture became interwoven with a network of magical and religious ceremonies, most of which were social in character, or at least had a social significance. The early "experts" for the ceremonies regulating the selection of seed and choice of time of planting and harvesting were magicians and priests rather than agronomists. All of these cooperative activities, especially the protective activities, led to the growth of villages and towns. Some of these towns, located at strategic points which could be fortified, grew into cities. The characteristic activities of these urban centers were military, political, and religious at first, then industrial and commercial.

The domestication of animals has accompanied the development of agriculture and has acted and reacted upon it. But the two have by no means been entirely dependent upon each other. An agricultural economy can be carried on without the aid and participation of animals, as in Mexico and Central America, where they had no animals better than the dog and the turkey, and perhaps the guinea pig which is a native of America. Pastoral peoples have devoted themselves exclusively to the breeding of animals, leading a migratory life in search of pasture for their flocks and herds. The cultures of migratory pastoral and of sedentary agricultural peoples have differed so greatly from each other that they have often clashed. Animal breeding encouraged father-right, while hoe culture, done by women, was often accompanied by mother-right. Warlike pastoral peoples have at times conquered more peaceful agricultural communities, and have exploited and enslaved them. Only in the later stages of cultural evolution, when political authority could spread wide over both the arable and the grazing land, have the pastoral and agricultural phases coalesced in harmonious fashion.

The domestication of animals commenced with the capture of wild animals, usually young ones, and raising and taming them. In their reproduction the selection of the individuals best adapted for human uses started animal breeding. Some of these animals have furnished meat, milk, and clothing, and others have served as beasts of burden and of traction, or for riding purposes. By furnishing high grade protein food, power for farm work, and manure to restore fertility to the soil, animal breeding has aided agriculture greatly. Cattle and grain together meant plow culture, much larger crops, a great increase and concentration of population, and encouraged the rise of cities and of urban civilization.

At Solutré in France was found a huge deposit of horses' bones. This indicates that late paleolithic man hunted and ate the horse, but domestication so early seems doubtful. The only animal which it is likely that paleolithic man domesticated was the dog, probably near the end of the epoch. The dog had little cultural significance, because it is only moderately useful for hunting and protection, still less for eating and traction, and was a drag on man from wanting the same food, and tending to tie him to hunting.

Cattle were probably first domesticated and bred in Asia, perhaps in eastern Asia, at an unknown date, but during the neolithic period. The horse was probably first tamed in central Asia before 5000 B.C., probably preceded by his gentler and more useful cousin the ass, as in Egypt. Horses may have been used at first as beasts of burden, and then later for riding purposes. During the neolithic in Asia were also domesticated the sheep, goat, hog, water buffalo, camel, reindeer, and chicken; in America the llama and its relative the alpaca, guinea pig, turkey, and possibly the bison. Each of the Asiatic animals, and in Peru the llama, has been of great value to the peoples possessing and utilizing it.

The principal factor for the domestication of animals has been their economic utility. A few writers have contended that animals were domesticated originally as pets, or because they were tribal totems. All sorts of pets from the wild have been found among primitive peoples. Certain animals have sometimes had a religious significance because they were regarded as sacred when they were tribal totems or for some other reason. Animals have also been used sometimes for purposes of divination. However, the factors of economic utility soon became the controlling consideration, except for the small dog, cat, and songbird, and the horse whose early value was largely military, but later became of great economic utility for agriculture and transportation.

Agriculture and animal breeding gave rise to a certain amount of division of labor between the sexes. The care and utilization of the larger domesticated animals were usually undertaken by the men, while the cultivation of plants during its earlier digging stick and hoe periods fell within the sphere of the women. Later on when plow culture with yoked draft animals was introduced, agriculture passed over in considerable part into the hands of the men. As already indicated, when animal breeding and agriculture have been more or less separated, the former has often been accompanied by father-right, and the latter by mother-right. In similar fashion, pottery was at first usually the task of the women. When the wheel was introduced, the ceramic art passed over in considerable part to the men, perhaps because the potter's wheel is associated with the draft animal, even when such an animal is not used. It has generally been true that occupations requiring extensive skills, and equipment larger than a needle or a small vessel, have been taken over by the men. The decline of hunting may have given neolithic man more time for craft labor.

Animal breeding has increased greatly the variability of domesticated species, by crossing different varieties and sub-species from thousands of miles apart. A comparatively rapid process of artificial selection directed toward conscious human ends has been substituted for the slow process of natural selection. The variability of the human species has also probably been somewhat accentuated. Cultural factors, such as social, hygienic, and esthetic considerations, have given rise to a certain amount of human selection for reproduction. These factors have played their part in originating racial and ethnic differences, so that culture and race act and react upon each other. Human breeding has, however, not been carried on in as conscious and intensive a manner as the breeding of animals by mankind. In societies where there is exploitation of the majority by a relatively small group, an almost universal situation so far, there is conscious selection of the best commodities by the dominant minority, and more or less unconscious as well as inevitable discrimination against the majority. Ill-fed slaves, serfs, and wage-earners cannot produce offspring on as high a biological plane as their well-fed masters and social and economic superiors. This subject will be discussed in later chapters on class dominance and social stratification.

The ceramic art arose long after the discovery of one of its necessary elements—fire. A French archeologist has asserted that crude pottery has been found among the Magdalenians of Belgium, and that pottery came into current use during the mesolithic or epipaleolithic period.[4] However that may be, it is doubtful if pottery was much used before the neolithic, when it usually accompanied agriculture. Its sporadic appearance in western Europe during the late paleolithic may have been due to the influence of the neolithic vanguard from Asia, or to its lack of utility. Pottery is of little use to a nomadic population, because it is heavy, bulky, and fragile, especially when of half baked clay, and cannot, therefore, be readily transported by food gathering peoples which have to move often. An encyclopedia has said that "it remains for future archaeological research to determine the time and place of origin of Old World pottery; the consensus of authoritative judgment places it in southwestern Asia not later than 6000 to 5000 B.C."[5] Pottery of the predynastic Badarian period has been found in Egypt. The ceramic art may have originated independently in the western hemisphere, the center of diffusion probably having been Central America. The potter's wheel, except in a very crude form, was not used in the western hemisphere, which suggests an independent line of development.

Several primitive peoples must have discovered that clay, which is found in most parts of the world, hardens upon coming in contact with fire. In some of these cases this observation may have led to the manufacture of crude vessels. It has been suggested that the ceramic art originated with the accidental burning of baskets plastered with clay. Baskets have, however, often been used as molds for pots. Primitive pottery developed at least four methods of manufacture, sometimes used in combination with each other. These four methods in their order of complexity are the direct shaping of a vessel from a

[4] J. de Morgan, *Prehistoric Man*, New York, 1925, trans. from the French.
[5] B. J. Stern, article on "Pottery" in the *Encyclopedia of the Social Sciences*, Vol. XII, New York, 1934.

lump of clay; the coiling method by which rolled strips of clay are built up into the prescribed form; the molding method by which the vessel is molded upon a form; and the turning method by which the matrix of clay is turned on a wheel, while being shaped by the hands or tools of the potter. The potter's wheel is said to have appeared in Egypt in the the Fourth Dynasty (*ca.* 2600-2500 B.C.), and somewhat earlier in Sumer where the wheeled cart had appeared shortly before 3000 B.C.[6]

With the rise of agriculture during the neolithic period the ceramic art attained a high level of technical skill and esthetic expression. Pottery became very useful because it furnished vessels in which to store various foods and seed to carry over from one harvest to the next. As an agricultural population is sedentary, it does not have to transport the heavy, bulky, and fragile pots from place to place. Pottery furnishes a ready medium for esthetic expression and decoration, both in the variability possible in its forms, and in the designs and depictions which can be put on its surface. Ceramic decoration became one of the leading fine arts during the neolithic. The ceramic art is of considerable archeological significance. Potsherds, or fragments of pottery, are imperishable, so that they are useful for stratigraphic chronology. The sherds accumulate rapidly in any permanent community. They are very reliable for sequence dating. As Frankfort has said: "Every object of pottery is a man's handiwork, *unalterable* when once fired, fragile and valueless when broken, and thus neither carried far from its place of origin nor long in use after it has been made."[7]

The shape of a pot is its most important feature, because dependent upon its use. It is instructive because it throws light upon the manner of life of its producers and users. Ceramic decoration is also instructive as to the manner of life of its producers. The naturalistic style depicts more or less faithfully and in detail animals, human beings, natural events, and many other things which aid in the reconstruction of the past. Style, however, tends to become conventionalized and abstract. The abstract style reproduces only what is characteristic and essential, at any rate, what is so according to the feelings and judgment of the artist. Naturalism elaborates in more or less photographic detail. It emphasizes the object depicted and is highly objective. The abstract style simplifies by elimination of many details, and conventionalizes the features selected and retained for reproduction. It thereby emphasizes the artist himself in relation to the object. It

[6] Stanley Casson, *Progress and Catastrophe*, London, 1937.
[7] H. Frankfort, *Studies in Early Pottery of the Near East*, Vol. I, "Mesopotamia, Syria and Egypt and their Earliest Interrelations," London, 1924.

181

is much more subjective than the naturalistic style, because it is the artist, or the whole school of artists, who perform this process of elimination and selection.

Each new art usually passes through a primitive stage of experimentation with the material it is trying to master. After various difficulties have been surmounted, and a good deal of technical skill acquired, it goes on to a period of intense life during which new ideas are introduced and are developed. After the climax has been reached, a period of degradation ensues which often is relatively long, and during which there is a dearth of new ideas and forms. Needless to say, this evolutionary cycle is conditioned by the culture and social organization in which it takes place and varies accordingly. It has been more or less clearly portrayed by the ceramic record of a good many regions and periods.

The development of the metallurgical industry followed and in some respects paralleled that of agriculture. Its rise characterized the termination of the neolithic period, just as the rise of agriculture heralded the commencement of the neolithic. It has furnished the material basis for the later stages of culture often called civilization.

Gold was probably the first metal used. It is widely distributed, and is often found in native purity as nuggets or grains. As it is relatively soft, it can be readily hammered into many shapes. Because it glitters brightly and does not tarnish, it has been much used for ornamentation since an early date. It has little practical utility, mainly because it is too soft to be given an edge, but long ago it became a means of displaying and storing wealth. In the more recent stages of cultural evolution, it has acquired an artificial and fictitious value as a medium of exchange, and as a standard of value for other kinds of metals used as money. The *reductio ad absurdum* of this fiction was attained at the middle of the twentieth century when the United States Government had stored $24,500,000,000 of gold at the rate of $35 per ounce avoirdupois. This sum corresponded to 43,750,000 pounds, or 21,875 short tons of 2,000 pounds each, of this metal lying idle and useless.

Copper also was used at an early date. It is sometimes found in a native state, but much less widely distributed than gold. It is rather soft and malleable. With hammering it hardens and can be brought to a sharp edge, though it does not retain this edge very long with use. It is superior to stone, and was the first metal used for the manufacture of sharp tools and weapons. Its significance has been stated, in somewhat exaggerated terms, as follows: "In the complexity of our modern society it is impossible to imagine how momentous a fact the coming of copper was to the ancient world. . . . We have to look to the beginning of the last century to find, in the revolution caused

182

by the utilization of steam, anything comparable with that older extension of man's power over nature."[8]

The supply of native metal is very limited. Until the art of reducing metallic ores by smelting was discovered, there could be no extensive use of metals. Smelting was probably discovered accidentally when pieces of ore fell into fire and melted, thus revealing the pure metal. It now became possible to utilize the vast supply of metallic ores, and so mining began. Flint had already been quarried by paleolithic men, and had even been sought underground. There had probably been sifting of alluvial gold in river gravels, and possibly also of tin. The first important stage in the mining of ores was outcrop mining. Copper, lead, silver, iron, etc., were secured from exposed veins in the rocks. Later came underground mining with shafts and galleries. These eventually went very deep and rendered available the great resources below the surface of the earth.

At some point in the early use of copper it was discovered, accidentally or otherwise, that a small admixture of tin, or of one or two other metals, produced a much harder and better metal. Bronze is an alloy of copper and tin, in proportions of about 9 to 1. Bronze soon replaced copper for almost all uses. Copper objects have been found in Mesopotamia and Egypt, dating probably from 4000 B.C. or earlier. Bronze was in all probability first made about 2500 B.C. in Asia Minor, but possibly in Mesopotamia or Persia. In Europe the bronze age began about 2000 B.C. But copper and bronze were still costly and rare. They replaced stone, bone, and horn only to a small extent, and were used largely for purposes of ornamentation by the wealthier classes.

The metal which has been the most used is iron. Partly because of its inherent traits, and partly owing to the large supply available, it has furnished more than any other one commodity the material basis for modern culture. A few specimens of iron, usually in the form of ornaments, have been found in Mesopotamia, Egypt, and Hissarlik (Troy), which probably date back as far as 3000 B.C. There is practically no iron in a native state. These early objects may have been of meteoric iron. Mining began is Asia Minor about 1500 B.C. In Boghazkeui has been found a letter from a Hittite king to Rameses II (1292-1225 B.C.) of the Nineteenth Dynasty about selling iron to Egypt. The iron age commenced about 1200 B.C. From 1000 B.C. onward the use of iron spread from Asia Minor over the Mediterranean area. Wrought iron and steel of a high quality were manufactured in India by 300 B.C. or earlier, although it is not certain that these processes were invented there. Smiths in Asia Minor had already discovered as early

[8] H. Frankfort, *Studies in Early Pottery of the Near East*, Vol. II, "Asia, Europe and the Aegean, and their Earliest Interrelations," London, 1927.

183

as the days of Homer that hot iron could be hardened by plunging it in cold water.

The demand for metals greatly stimulated early transportation and trade. From 2000 B.C. onward the Cretans were important transporters and traders in the Mediterranean. From 1200 B.C. onward the Phenicians began to play a similar role in the Mediterranean, and also to a less degree in the Atlantic. About 700 B.C. in Asia metallic coins began to be issued which facilitated commerce greatly.[9]

The development of these occupations, arts, and industries—agricultural, ceramic, mining, metallurgical, shipbuilding, etc.—centered largely around the sources of the raw materials. The mining and smelting of metals required much timber and fuel. The utilized amount of energy extraneous to man increased rapidly. The occupations arising out of these industries resulted in the concentration of population in the industrial areas. In the early stages, this took place mainly in the eastern Mediterranean region. The two principal centers were the valleys of the Tigris and of the Euphrates in Mesopotamia, and of the Nile in Egypt. These rivers furnished the water for irrigation which rendered possible large crops and an abundant food supply. The spring floods of the Tigris and of the Euphrates come in May. The water had to be stored in reservoirs and then distributed gradually during the summer. The Nile flood comes several months later, toward the end of the summer. It covered the valley for about six weeks, and deposited a fine silt well adapted for crops. After the water receded in October the crops could grow during the mild winter and be harvested in the spring or early summer. Wild barley as well as wheat or spelt grew in this region.

The early Mesopotamian and Egyptian cultures were based in the main upon a combination of irrigation, grain, the plow, the cart, the ox, and bronze. In Mesopotamia the Sumerian culture had been brought in part from its original home in the northeast. The Sumerians created the city state, and organized defense against nomadic tribes. They invented the first true form of writing, namely, cuneiform script, about 3000 B.C. or earlier. This marked the commencement of the historical stage of cultural evolution.[10] It has been much disputed as to whether Mesopotamia or Egypt made the most important contributions to this evolution. Egypt created great architectural mon-

[9] T. A. Rickard, *Man and Metals, A History of Mining in Relation to the Development of Civilization*, 2 vols., New York, 1932.

[10] Speaking of the contributions of the Sumerians, Casson says that "their great achievements were the moulding of agricultural life on a basis of urban centres, the complete development of metallurgy to a level not reached in Egypt until a much later date, and, possibly most important and far-reaching of all, the invention of writing." (S. Casson, *op. cit.*, p. 116.)

uments, many of which have survived to the present day. At least three such periods stand out. During the Fourth and Fifth Dynasties (*ca.* 2500 B.C.) were erected the great pyramids of Giza. During the Twelfth or Theban Dynasty (*ca.* 1800 B.C.) were built many splendid monuments. During the Eighteenth and Nineteenth Dynasties (*ca.* 1300 B.C.) an extensive but short-lived empire was established, and more monuments constructed. But the Egyptian culture early became dominated by, if not obsessed with, certain beliefs and practices of magic and of religion, and the alleged importance of a hypothetical after-life. A rigid social order came into being, governed by a hierarchy of priests, which was for a long time a serious obstacle to social change. Its favorable natural situation, however, maintained Egypt in a commanding position for more than two thousand years.

Chapter XIV

Environment and Institutional Evolution

WHILE the rudiments of social organization may be detected among some of the higher animals, nothing analogous to an institution has been found outside of mankind. As already defined in Chapter XII, an institution is a complex of beliefs, ideas, or activities, shared by a considerable number of human beings, who do not necessarily live together or within specific territorial limits, and which may or may not be organized. Institutions include not only the established forms or conditions of procedure characteristic of group activity, as they have been defined by MacIver.[1] This is the narrow and popular definition of the term, which is widely used. For example, religion is often called "institutionalized" when it is organized in the form of a church, although religion itself is an institution whether organized or not. Social organization in general has extensive repercussions upon institutions. It often stimulates, but may at times hinder, institutional development. As we shall see, there is more to institutions than their organized phase alone.

The ideas and beliefs necessary for the origin and growth of institutions could not have come into existence before language had evolved to a considerable degree. Language is itself the most important of institutions. Or it may be more accurate to say that it is the prerequisite for practically all of institutional development. Hence it is plausible to assume that language existed at least as far back as the earliest known traces of institutional phenomena. These traces are to be found as early as the middle paleolithic, as indicated by the Mousterian burials.

Words, grammar, and other linguistic elements last for thousands of years in traceable form, and afford clues to prehistoric culture and tribal movements. Yet the utterances spoken with words vanish immediately into thin air. They leave no permanent record, except in so

[1] R. M. MacIver, *Society Its Structure and Changes*, New York, 1931.

far as they impress the memories of hearers. Their immediate ranges in time and space are very limited. Their effects can be transmitted only in so far as the memories are repeated by word of mouth, and perpetuated by verbal tradition. These repetitions are subject to many variations, either unintentional through forgetfulness or misunderstanding, or willful through a desire to misrepresent, or to improve. The end product of speech is almost certain to be legendary as compared with the original.

Written language renders possible not only a permanent, but also an accurate record of what has been said and done, though written records are often as inaccurate as memories of spoken words. The available data indicate that written language began to develop about the end of the paleolithic or the beginning of the neolithic. Pictographs had been used still earlier. A few of them may already have become ideographs, that is to say, signs for words or ideas, rather than more or less direct representations of objects. At Mas d'Azil in southern France were found painted pebbles which may have been mnemonic aids. Hieroglyphic writing is composed of representative ideographic signs sometimes mingled with a few phonetic symbols. Systems of hieroglyphic writing have arisen in various parts of the world, such as Mesopotamia, Egypt, Crete, among the Hittites, in China, and in America (Mexico and Peru). From hieroglyphic writing was derived syllabic writing, and the cuneiform script of Sumer and elsewhere. The final development, described in Chapter X, was alphabetic writing, which has furnished the most ready and flexible means of written communication.

Writing, especially when combined with improved transport, and used under rulers able to issue orders, or to exercise cultural leadership over widespread kingdoms or empires, rendered possible the wider, if not the more rapid, dissemination of the beliefs, ideas or activities, which go to make up the cultural complexes which we have called institutions. Some institutions had become universal or widespread before the invention of writing. Among them were magic and religion; certain industrial processes, such as tool making and possibly agriculture; certain occupational and professional complexes arising out of the above-mentioned institutions; etc., etc. This was a very slow process prior to the invention of an institution at several different points, and then its diffusion from these centers. With the coming of writing, transport, and political agglomeration, this process was hastened, not only for institutions, but also for all other cultural phenomena.

Like most cultural phenomena, an institution is in large part a product of the social process of invention. An invention is usually a combination of already existing cultural elements into a new form. It

187

may be caused by the importation of foreign cultural elements. After coming into existence, it may be diffused to other culture areas and become a factor for new inventions. Thus the social processes of invention and of diffusion are constantly acting and reacting upon each other, or working in cooperation with each other. Among the important mechanisms of diffusion are the ethnic factors, namely, the migration of population and the establishment of colonies; conquest as a result of warfare; commerce, or the exchange of economic commodities; a technological, political, economic, or social revolution, which has repercussions outside of its own region; religious proselytizing, or missionary enterprise; and gradual infiltration of ideas and customs through the above or other agencies, which may be conscious and intentional, but which is largely if not mainly unconscious and unintended. The latter mechanism of diffusion is the most general. It depends more or less directly upon the extent of communication and of intercourse of all sorts between culture areas. The same is true in varying degrees of all of the means of diffusion.

It is difficult to generalize with regard to the relative importance of the roles played by duplicate invention and by diffusion. Whenever identical or similar institutions are observed in two or more culture areas, the question arises as to whether they have originated in each area by means of independent invention, or whether diffusion has taken place from one area to another. Needless to say, each case must be studied by itself. Certainty can be be attained only when sufficient data are available. There have, nevertheless, been at least two theories of the relative importance of invention and of diffusion. At one extreme is the diffusionist theory which asserts that invention is very rare, and that almost all inventions have taken place only once, and then have spread from their places of origin. Approaching the other extreme is the theory of culture strata which affirms that several cultures have arisen in different centers with varying degrees of likeness and dissimilarity between them. These cultures have spread from their respective centers. As a result of invasions or of migrations of peoples of different races, such cultures have in course of time overlapped each other. In this fashion, archeological layers of culture, so to speak, have come into being, which have formed cultural strata.[2]

[2] See, for example, F. Graebner, *Methode der Ethnologie,* Heidelberg, 1911; L. Frobenius, *Kulturgeschichte Afrikas,* Zuerich, 1933; and other writers who have set forth the theory of "Kulturkreise," "Kulturschichten," and "Kulturmorphologie."Frobenius has asserted that he first stated the "Kulturkreislehre" (theory of cultural regions) at the end of the nineteenth century. His theory of the "Kulturmorphologie" is vague, metaphysical, and mystical. His book on African cultural history is devoted almost exclusively to art and mythology. Through this narrow approach he attempted to describe cultural history. He characterized the paleolithic and neolithic stages as follows: "Freuhsteinzeit umfasst Chelleen, Acheuleen,

The most extreme example of the diffusionist theory is the "helio-lithic" theory of Elliot Smith and Perry.[3] They have asserted that practically all culture above that of the food-gatherers was diffused from Egypt, where the Nile floods furnished a favorable environment for the origin of agriculture. The Egyptian culture was based upon Solutrean techniques and Magdalenian industries. According to these writers, it included for the first time polished stone implements, copper implements, irrigation, megaliths, stone buildings, pottery and glaze, weaving, sea-going ships, work in ivory, mummification, the idea of immortality, the solar calendar, the sky-world, worship of the sun, images of the Great Mother, the myth of the divine origin of kings, the king as life-giver and creator and often identified with the sun, alchemy, the superstition of the State, etc. This culture was diffused by the "children of the sun," who went in search of gold, pearls, and other "life-giving" objects. According to Smith, the heliolithic culture left Egypt about 800 b.c., and spread along coast lines over much of the world, even reaching America and creating the higher cultures of Mexico, Central and South America.

Very few facts lend support to the heliolithic or Pan-Egyptian theory of cultural diffusion. Some of the assertions of Elliot Smith and of Perry are palpably wrong. Agriculture did not originate in Egypt alone, but at many different times and places the world over.[4] It is possible, but far from certain, that irrigation was first used in Egypt. Cultures have been started in irrigable lands along desert borders also in Mesopotamia, India, China, Mexico, Peru, and the Pueblo region in the southwestern United States. Irrigation in all probability originated independently in several of these regions, and the question of priority is moot. Dry farming did not necessarily always follow irrigation, but may in many cases have preceded it. Irrigation is, in any case, a rather highly developed form of agriculture. In the early neolithic period polished stone implements were manufactured in many regions. Copper implements were probably first manufactured in Asia Minor. Megaliths may have originated in India, or possibly in

Mousterien, in Afrika Aterien and das letzte Interglazial bis zur Mitte der letzten Eiszeit. Mittelsteinzeit umfasst Aurignacien, Solutreen, Magdalenien und endet im Campignien. In Afrika Capsien von der Mitte der letzten Eiszeit bis ueber die Vollendung der Abschmelze hinweg. Spaetsteinzeit vom Campignien ueber das Neolithikum bis zum Beginn des Metallzeitalters." (p. 49.)

[3] G. Elliott Smith, *The Migrations of Early Culture*, Manchester, 1915; *Human History*, New York, 1929. W. J. Perry, *The Children of the Sun*, London, 1923; *The Growth of Civilization*, London, 1926.

[4] Professor Merrill of Harvard University, who has studied domesticated plants in many parts of the world, has criticized the diffusionist theories of Elliot Smith and Perry. "Everywhere the spread of culture failed to keep pace with the spread of agriculture." (E. D. Merrill, "Domesticated Plants in Relation to the Diffusion of Culture," in *Early Man*, edited by G. G. MacCurdy, Philadelphia, 1937, p. 282.)

several different places. The belief in an after-life and idea of immortality probably dated back at least as far as the Mousterian period, if burial customs are any indication.

There is no evidence whatsoever that any of the higher American culture was derived from Egypt. Elliot Smith imagined that certain archeological remains in Mexico were decorated with the trunks and tusks of elephants, which are not natives of America. The animals depicted were probably indigenous birds with large beaks. Owing to this fanciful resemblance, Smith argued that knowledge of the elephant had been brought from Africa and Egypt in particular. The probability is that the first human migration into the western hemisphere took place during the neolithic period.[5] There is little evidence as yet that it took place any earlier. In a few regions where conditions were favorable, such as Mexico and Peru, a higher culture arose spontaneously upon the neolithic basis. This is no more remarkable than that such a development took place also in the eastern hemisphere.

However influential was the ancient Egyptian culture, the Mesopotamian culture, co-eval with the Egyptian, was at least as important. At the same time, significant developments were taking place elsewhere. The problem of diffusion is too complicated to be solved by the assumption that the prevalent culture at any given period has originated entirely or even in large part in any one region. Cultural diffusion takes place, as already indicated, either through the movement of population, or through contact and communication. The environmental conditions underlying either or both of these processes will now be stated.

Telluric and geophysical forces and processes have determined the conformation of land and of water, of continents and of oceans, of mountains and of lowlands, and the location of the poles in relation to which the isothermal zones are distributed. These conditions in turn, during every geological period, have influenced and in large part controlled topography, climate, and the distribution of raw materials and of power, such as water power. The environmental situation since mankind emerged, and cultural evolution commenced, can be understood only against this cosmic and geological background.

The basic geophysical process has been the slow cooling of this planet, and the gradual changes in the contour of the surface of the earth. The shrinkage due to this cooling gives rise to crumpling of the surface, over-thrusting and folding at many points, and thereby causes the uplift of mountain ranges. The cooling process has also

5 "Turning to America we find everywhere neolithic remains at the bottom of the cultural series." (H. J. Spinden, "First Peopling of America as a Chronological Problem," in *Early Man*, edited by G. G. MacCurdy, Philadelphia, 1937, p. 112.)

190

given rise to varying densities of the different strata of rock. The outer surface is the lighter and the more acid, while the underlying layers are the more dense the deeper they are. Suess has described three concentric layers of differential weight, the *sial* (silico [$S1O^2$]-aluminum), the *Sima* (silico-manganese), and the *Nife* (nickel iron).[6] The *Sial* or lighter external layer, was at first supposed to cover the whole of the globe, and to be thicker on the continents and thinner under the oceans. This layer of varying thickness rests upon the *Sima* of greater density, which in turn rests upon the *Nife* which has the greatest density of these three layers.

Wegener has contended that the *Sial* originally covered only about one-third of the surface of the globe, and formed one continuous sheet floating on the surface of the *Sima* which underlies the oceans. Since the close of the paleozoic era the *Sial* has split into several parts which have slowly drifted apart. Thus were formed the three major continental divisions, namely, the eastern hemisphere, the western hemisphere, and the Antarctic continent. Allowing for the effects of Tertiary folding, the edges of the continental shelves can be fitted together, thus reconstructing the original continuous sheet which covered about one-third of the earth. The geophysical evidence for this theory of continental drift is strongest and most plausible in relation to Africa and South America. Their coasts would fit fairly closely into each other if they were brought together, as a glance at a map of the world will indicate.[7]

Wegener's theory excludes the possibility of sunken continents, such as the mythical "Atlantis" in the Atlantic Ocean, and the equally mythical "Lemuria" in the Indian Ocean. Much is still written by credulous folk concerning these myths. At no time has there been the slightest shred of evidence of the former existence of these fabulous continents. This theory also excludes the possibility of former land bridges between South America and Africa, and between Africa and India. These hypothetical land bridges have been suggested as possible explanations of the paleontological similarities between these widely separated land areas. While this is a rather plausible hypothesis, the theory of continental drift would explain these similarities between Africa and South America by the former contiguity between the two continents.

Wegener has asserted that geodetic evidence in support of his theory of continental drift has been furnished by measurements during the past one hundred years which indicate a slight increase in the distance between the two hemispheres. In other words, they are ap-

[6] E. Suess, *Das Antlitz der Erde*, 1883 and 1909; English translation, 1904.

[7] Alfred Wegener, *Die Entstehung der Kontinente und Ozeane*, Braunschweig, 1936, fifth edition; English translation, 1924.

parently still drifting apart. Geological evidence is furnished by fitting together the mountain ranges, river valleys, etc., as they coincided before the drift began. The two hemispheres probably began to separate in the latter part of the Carboniferous epoch. Paleontological and biological evidence is furnished by animal and plant similarities and dissimilarities between the two hemispheres. There is also said to be paleoclimatic evidence which is probably due to climatic changes due to polar shift.

Gutenberg has somewhat modified Wegener's theory of continental drift by his own "Fliesstheorie," which postulates a plastic flowage both in the continental masses and also in the subcrust itself. He has estimated that the Atlantic, Indian, and southern Pacific water expanses are underlaid by the softer rock (*Sial?*) of the continental mass, which is about twenty kilometers deep; whereas the Arctic Ocean is underlaid by basalt which is forty to fifty kilometers deep. Land has been drifting northward, and the western hemisphere has been drifting away from the eastern hemisphere.[8] Whether or not this theory is true, most of the land area is at present in the northern hemisphere, and is concentrated around the contemporary north pole. If the land areas were originally continuous, they may have been located from the outset in what is now the northern hemisphere. In that case, Antarctica has drifted southward, and the bulk of the land mass has spread out in an east-west direction over the northern hemisphere.[9]

Assuming that continental drift has taken place, the question arises as to its cause or causes. The most plausible suggestion is that it is related in some way to polar shift. The poles have shifted greatly in the course of geological time. Regions at one time within the frigid zone are now within the torrid zone, and *vice versa*. These variations in temperature and climate have left their indelible marks upon the rocks, and in the paleontological record. The poles have shifted more than half of the distance between their present locations and the contemporary equator. Wegener has calculated the changes in north latitude in relation to Leipzig in Germany. This city now lies at Lat. 51° 20' N., and Long. 12° 23' E. of Greenwich. Its latitude since Carboniferous time has varied as follows: Carboniferous 0°, Permian 13°,

8 Beno Gutenberg, "Structure of the Earth's Crust and the Spreading of the Continents," in the *Bulletin of the Geological Society of America*, Vol. 47, 1936, pp. 1587-1610.

9 "The earth itself has a hard crystalline crust, made up in large parts of the silicates which tend to rise and of aluminum. (*Sial.*) The mantle is composed largely of silicates and magnesium and is vitreous. (*sima.*) " Ruth Moore, The Earth *We Live On*, New York, 1956, p. 361.

Over 90 percent of the earth is made up of four elements by weights, namely iron, 35%; oxygen, 28%; Magnesium, 17%; silicon, 13%.

Triassic 20°, Jurassic 19°, Cretaceous 18°, Eocene 15°, Miocene 39°, Early Quaternary 53°. In other words, in Carboniferous time the latitude of the present site of Leipzig was approximately at the equator. Since then it has fluctuated over a range of 53 degrees of latitude.

In connection with the theories of continental drift and polar shift, the positions of the north pole with reference to the present system of coordinates, namely, of latitude and of longitude, have been calculated as far back as Devonian time. It is assumed that the land mass or continent now known as Africa remained stationary so far as continental drift is concerned throughout this long period. In the accompanying table, the corresponding positions of Germany are given for purposes of comparison. They indicate that the latitude of this area has shifted over a range of 72 degrees. The latitude of Germany was determined by the changes in the longitude as well as in the latitude of the North Pole. During the same period the North Pole shifted over 65 degrees of latitude and over 180 degrees of longitude.

THE NORTH POLE AND GERMANY
(According to Alfred Wegener)

Geological Epoch	Position of the North Pole	Latitude of Germany
Recent	Lat. 90° N. Long. 0°	Lat. 50° N.
Quaternary	Lat. 70° N. Long. 10° W.	Lat. 69° N.
Pliocene	Lat. 90° N. Long. 0°	Lat. 54° N.
Miocene	Lat. 67° N. Long. 172° W.	Lat. 37° N.
Oligocene	Lat. 58° N. Long. 180° W.	Lat. 29° N.
Eocene	Lat. 45° N. Long. 180° W.	Lat. 15° N.
Paleocene	Lat. 50° N. Long. 180° W.	Lat. 20° N.
Cretaceous	Lat. 48° N. Long. 140° W.	Lat. 19° N.
Jurassic	Lat. 69° N. Long. 170° W.	Lat. 36° N.
Triassic Permian	}Lat. 50° N. Long. 130° W.	Lat. 26° N.
Triassic	Lat. 25° N. Long.155° W.	Lat. 3° S.
Permian	Lat. 30° N. Long. 140° W.	Lat. 15° N.

It is not necessarily to be assumed that polar shift has caused continental drift, or *vice versa*. A third possibility is that they have a common cause. Whatever the original cause may have been, it is plausible to assume that polar shift, causing changes in the speed of rotation of the different parts of the earth's surface, would cause corresponding changes in the rate of motion of the upper crust. On the other hand, changes in the distribution of the land masses would affect slightly the equilibrium and center of gravity of the earth, and thus gradually bring about changes in the polar axis. The earth is an oblate spheroid whose greatest diameter corresponds to the greatest circumference which must be the equator. The diametric difference of about 22 miles is much greater than the distance between the highest continental peak and the lowest oceanic level which is from 10 to 12 miles. Hence it is reasonable to suppose that there has been a good deal of action and reaction between continental drift and polar shift.[10]

There has been little change in the distribution of the great land masses, and in the location of the poles, since the advent of mankind, or, at any rate, during the later stages of cultural evolution. During the Tertiary epoch, extensive geophysical changes took place, which had their influence upon the evolution of the primates and the emergence of the human type.[11] During the Quaternary epoch took place the glacial periods, whose causes and effects upon mankind have been briefly discussed in Chapter VII. Minor climatic and topographical changes are continually taking place, such as increasing regional humidity or aridity, which have differential effects upon human and cultural evolution.[12] Climate, topography, the distribution of raw materials and of power, are permanent though variable factors. Geographic position is a factor which may increase in importance as cultural evolution proceeds. But its importance in earlier stages and at all times should not be underestimated.

The physical factors of the environment have the most direct and immediate effect during the earlier stages of cultural evolution. Food-gathering peoples must go to wherever their food is procurable.

[10] "Die einzige Verschiebungskraft, die man gegenwärtig genauer kennt ist die Polfluchtkraft, die bestrebt ist, die Kontinente relativ zu ihrer Unterlage äquatorwärts zu treiben. . . .

"Die Kräfte, welch die Kontinente verschieben, sind dieselben, welche die grossen Faltengebirge erzeugen. Kontinentiverschiebungen, Spaltung und Zusammenschub, Erdbeben, Vulkanismus, Transgressions-wechsel und Polwanderungen stehen untereinander zweifellos in einem grossartigen ursächlichen Zusammenhang. Das zeigt schon ihre gemeinsame Steigerung in gewissen Perioden der Erdgeschichte. Was aber Ursache und was Wirkung ist, muss erst die Zukunft enthüllen." (A. Wegener, *op. cit.*, pp. 173, 185.)

[11] J. R. de la H. Marett, *Race, Sex and Environment*, London, 1936.

"The evolution of the first human being occurred in response to the rising of the heads of the Tertiary limestone mountain-system above the hitherto unbroken carpet of forest with which it was formerly covered. This introduced a completely new kind of habitat to which physiological efficiency was the sole test of entry." (p. 127.)

[12] See, for example, Huntington's studies of the effects of increasing aridity upon culture. (E. Huntington, *The Pulse of Asia*, Boston, 1907; *Climate and Civilization*, New Haven, 1915; *The Human Habitat*, New York, 1927.)

In many parts of the world the location of this food supply fluctuates seasonally. In the temperate and colder zones plant food could not be depended upon the year around. In some regions the animal food also moved with the seasons. The North American plains Indians, who depended largely upon the bison for their food, had to follow the herds for many hundreds of miles southward in the autumn, and in the spring as far northward. In some parts of the warmer zones plant food is available the year around, so that seasonal migrations were not necessary. Generally speaking, the distribution of population was directly related in space and in time to the immediate food supply. Movements of population were also directly related to topographic factors, such as rivers, valleys, mountain ranges, passes through the mountains, sea winds, ocean currents, etc., which either facilitated or impeded these movements.

With the rise of agriculture, human dependence upon the physical environment became somewhat less direct. Stores of food could be accumulated to carry a community through the less fruitful seasons of the year. In a more fundamental sense the influence of the environment was equally great. The natural fertility of the soil now became of decisive importance. The population began to concentrate permanently, and to increase rapidly, in the more fertile regions, remaining relatively sparse elsewhere. With the rise of mining and metallurgy, the distribution of the mineral resources began to influence considerably the movement and density of population. In the latest stages of cultural evolution the rapidly increasing utilization of energy extraneous to human beings has accentuated greatly the importance of the extent and distribution of the sources of energy in a state of nature.

In fact, it is questionable whether it would be correct to say that, either theoretically or empirically, the physical environment has been more or less, as the case may be, influential for mankind as a whole over any considerable period or even at a given moment of time, than it has been influential at any other period or moment of time. The manner in which the environment has been influential has, however, varied greatly from time to time and from place to place. In some cases the later effect of an environmental situation has become the very reverse of its earlier effect. For example, seas and oceans were originally effective barriers against migration, communication, and diffusion of culture. The invention of sea-going vessels rendered them useful highways of travel.

The prospect is that in the future also the physical environment will continue to dominate production, though the manner of its influence may vary from time to time. In 1924 the geologist Penck estimated the potential population of the world from what then seemed the feasible production of food.

Penck also estimated the potential population of some of the political divisions of the world as follows: Brazil—1,200,000,000; Spanish America—1,200,000,000; white British Empire—600,000,000; Russia—600,000,000; China—600,000,000; United States of America—

ESTIMATE OF THE POTENTIAL POPULATION
OF THE WORLD

(According to Albrecht Penck)

World Population—1920-1,800,000,000   Potential Pop.—8,000,000,000

Eurasia	1,400,000,000 or 80%	2,080,000,000 or 26%
Africa	126,000,000 or 7%	2,320,000,000 or 29%
Australia	9,000,000 or 0.5%	480,000,000 or 6%
N. America	162,000,000 or 9%	1,120,000,000 or 14%
S. America	63,000,000 or 3.5%	2,000,000,000 or 25%
Total	1,800,000,000 or 100%	8,000,000,000 or 100%

600,000,000. The world's population is now overwhelmingly concentrated in the temperate zones. Eurasia contains 80% of it, whereas Africa and South America, the predominantly tropical continents, contain only 10.5%. According to the above estimate, the potential population, based upon the possible production of food which may be attained in the future, will give Africa and South America 54% of the total, whereas Eurasia will have only 26%. As Penck has expressed it: "Die Tropen sind das Gebiet der grossen Menschenanhaeufungen der Zukunft, waehrend es heute die gemaessigten Zonen sind." [13]

Penck did not take into consideration the distribution of raw materials, apart from food, and of natural energy, such as atomic energy which could be utilized as industrial power. In 1937 he explained to the present writer that he considered food the predominant factor, because if the temperate zones acquire a population greater than can be fed by the food products of these zones, it will cost more in materials and energy to transport tropically produced food to them than they can repay from their resources of materials and natural energy. Penck

[13] Albrecht Penck, *Das Hauptproblem der physischen Anthropogeographie*, Preussische Akademie der Wissenschaften, Berlin, 1924, p. 252.

also did not consider the effects of agricultural methods now being developed whereby plants are grown more rapidly in water, their growth is stimulated by chemicals, light, etc. The finer foods are made from cheap vegetable and animal products, a few other foods are already being synthesized from minerals, and vast amounts of textiles, building materials, drugs, dyes, etc., are already being replaced from synthetic and mineral sources. Whether or not these methods will turn the potential demographic balance in favor of the temperate zones still remains to be seen. Certain it is that these mineral and synthetic sources have demonstrated the possibility of a great increase of the total population of the world. At any rate, throughout all of these calculations and speculations the physical environment runs as a dominant, if not the predominant, factor which limits, directs, and stimulates in one way or another according to the relations between it and the cultural factors at any given time and place.

In Chapter XII I have mentioned the many ways in which science, invention and technology are hampered and frustrated by the dominant form of economic organization. With the progress of transportation and communication, through both invention and wider political organization, all parts of the world tend to become more alike as producers and consumers. Goods are often transported from the ends of the earth to every community, whether it be a mountain mining town or a fishing village on an island of the sea. Each exports its most salable products and imports those of other communities. However, this geographic division of labor, and equilibration of production and consumption, are hindered, not only by the remaining difficulties of transportation and communication, and local differences of taste, but also by the national policy of protectionism. This policy operates through tariffs and other artificial trade barriers, and by restrictions on migration. For example, the United States, possessing enormous natural resources, sits tight on its land like a landlord and reaps a "rent" of higher income per capita from its monopoly, instead of permitting the people of the world to share its land and natural resources. All the ways in which these cultural factors interfere with the environmental factors will be described later in this treatise.

To supplement and illustrate Penck's estimates of population, there are given below estimates of the world's population in 1930 by three international organizations:[14]

14 These figures are taken from the *Aperçu de la Demographie des divers Pays du Monde,* Institut International de Statistique; the *International Year-Book of Agricultural Statistics,* International Institute of Agriculture; and the *Statistical Year Book of the League of Nations,* cited by A. M. Carr-Saunders, *World Population,* Oxford, 1936, p. 17.

ESTIMATES OF THE POPULATION
OF THE WORLD IN 1930

Continents	International Institute of Statistics	International Institute of Agriculture	League of Nations
Europe	484,575,000	505,730,000	504,600,000
America	248,772,000	251,500,000	249,800,000
Africa	143,315,000	142,400,000	145,400,000
Asia	1,101,692,000	1,103,300,000	1,118,600,000
Oceania	9,925,000	9,880,000	9,800,000
World Total	1,988,279,000	2,012,810,000	2,028,200,000

More recent statistics, compiled since 1935, give the areas and the approximate densities of population of the five well populated continents as follows:[15]

CONTINENTAL AREAS AND ESTIMATED POPULATION

Continents	Area in square miles	Per cent	Estimated Population circa 1935-40	Per cent	Density per sq. mi.
Asia	16,281,909	34	1,080,301,480	54	66
Europe	3,780,103	8	512,773,807	26	136
Africa	11,508,588	24	143,900,107	7	13
N. America	9,363,868	19	176,629,611	9	19
S. America	7,047,656	15	92,888,595	4	13
Total	47,982,124	100	2,006,493,600	100	42

Needless to say, the population of a considerable part of the world is enumerated inadequately or not at all, so that these statistics can at best be only approximate. As of 1954, the population of the world was estimated at 2,689,000,000 by the *World Almanac, 1959*, New York. My own estimate as of 1950 was 2,170,000,000.[16]

These statistics do not vary greatly from those given by Penck. They indicate that if his prognostications are fulfilled, the density of

[15] *Rand, McNally Atlas of the World*, Chicago, 1938.
[16] See Maurice Parmelee, *Geo-Economic Regionalism and World Federation*, New York, 1949, Chapter XI entitled "A Geo-Economic Regional Classification."

population in Africa will increase nearly twenty times, so that it will be more than 200 per square mile; in South America, more than thirty times, over 300; and in North America, about seven times, about 125. The density of Eurasia will rise from about 80 to about 110 inhabitants per square mile.

Within the geographical setting which has been briefly described many human migrations have taken place. The physical factors for movement predominated in the primitive migrations. In other words, food-gathering peoples had to move often in order to find food. With the coming of agriculture a more stable and settled communal existence became possible. Since that time socio-economic factors have probably directly stimulated the greater number of migrations. Perhaps the most frequent cause has been an inadequate food supply due to increase of population. The food-gathering peoples had to move even without an increase of population. The economic opportunity to exploit new land has caused some human migrations. Defeat in war has sometimes led to mass expulsions, or to voluntary migrations by both the victorious and the conquered peoples, or by either of them. During historic times exploration and discovery led to the search for a higher standard of living by the spreading abroad of numerous migrants from the Phenician, Greek, Roman, Teutonic, Spanish, British, Russian, and many other peoples.

The evidences of migratory movements have been archeological remains, racial traits, oral traditions, linguistic and other cultural traces, and historical records. For prehistoric times the evidences have been mainly archeological. Racial traits have sometimes given slight indications of the movements and mingling of peoples. Among the paleolithic migrations of which there is archeological and racial evidence were the Aurignacian migration from northern Africa into Europe, and the Solutrean migration from central into western Europe. In early neolithic time there took place a migration of brachycephalic Alpines from western Asia into central and western Europe. During the copper age there took place a chalcolithic migration of nomads from the Russian steppes into southeastern Europe. The distribution of the Indo-European languages suggests a dispersion from the region of the Caspian Sea, perhaps in late neolithic time. Probably about the same time an Ugro-Finnic infiltration was taking place from northern Asia into northern Europe. Several waves of migration of different racial strains passed over the Bering Strait into America. The earliest of these may have taken place before the last glacial phase, but this is doubtful. The latest migrations were from 1,000 to 2,000 years ago. From North America migration took place over the Isthmus of Panama into South America. In this fashion the western hemisphere was populated, in most of its regions very thinly, from north to south, probably following the mountainous or dry western regions, which were easier to traverse and in which to find food than the primeval forest. During the past 2,000 years Oceania has become inhabited by migrations of Negrito and of Malay peoples.

Since agriculture has become widespread, the principal migrations have been by two types of people. The nomadic peoples who have adopted or who have clung to a pastoral life have wandered more or less continuously in search of water and pasturage for their herds and flocks. These movements have often been seasonal between the colder and warmer zones, and between the mountains and the plains. Somtimes they have been permanent migrations to other parts of the world. The maritime peoples, in the course of their voyages of trade and of exploration, have sometimes discovered lands hitherto unknown to which they have migrated in considerable numbers. During the past century easy and rapid means of transportation have facilitated a large migration over land and sea from the eastern to the western hemisphere of both agrarian and urban inhabitants who have settled more or less permanently in the two Americas. Similar, but less extensive migrations have taken place to South Africa, Australia, and New Zealand.

There are numerous historic examples of these two types of migration. Prolonged droughts in central Asia and Arabia caused migrations into more fertile regions, and conflicts with the settled and stable peoples which usually had a higher culture. These migrations sometimes caused others in turn, such as the great *Voelkerwanderung* of the 4th and 5th centuries A.D., when Slavic and Teutonic tribes, pressed by the Asiatics, in turn pressed upon the Romans. The other chief type of migration was illustrated by the Phenicians, Greeks, Romans, and modern Portuguese, Spaniards, Dutchmen, Englishmen, and Russians, when a seafaring or otherwise more highly cultured and powerful people, invaded its weaker neighbors or newly discovered lands, or at least pervaded them by traders, leading in many cases to colonial imperial rule.

Migration affects the migrants themselves, and also those with whom they come in contact. These contacts between individuals and groups give rise to corresponding contacts between the cultures which they represent. These cultural contacts result inevitably in a certain amount of cultural mingling and change. The former constitutes diffusion. The latter may give rise to invention. In almost all of the migrations which occurred prior to neolithic time the migrating groups carried with them a culture which contained as a minimum the following elements: the knowledge and use of fire; the art of flaking stone, and of working wood and bone; the use of skins; and a few crude implements of wood, bone and stone. From at least the middle paleolithic onward this common or almost universal culture contained linguistic, animistic, and artistic elements. Groups coming in contact through migration almost invariably experienced some modifications in arts, implements, and customs and beliefs. Such changes occurred also through inter-group communication short of mass migration. The conditions which determine modifications in the culture of a group at any specified time, and in any given environment, are its own cultural antecedents, its present status, its contacts, and its group psychology or collective consciousness. A cultural parallel noted between two groups may be due to diffusion, or to independent invention, or to convergent evolution. The latter is usually due to a series of invented and diffused elements.

Some writers have asserted that an additional important factor in the determination of a culture is racial hereditary nature and psychology. For example, Dixon contended that most of the great cultures have been due in each instance to a gifted people, so located as to become numerous, and favorably placed to receive the benefits of diffusion; but also where nature was not too kind. He alleged that the conditions for discovery are opportunity, observation, curiosity, need, and genius. He made the erroneous statement that discoveries and inventions are "essentially one-man affairs." [17] All of the available evidence goes to show that practically all discoveries and inventions are the cumulative results of the thought and effort of many persons. Furthermore, he exaggerated greatly the importance of "gifted" people, and of individual "geniuses."

As a matter of fact, social changes and technological changes are inextricably inter-related with each other. The former precipitate the latter, and *vice-versa*. The inventive tendencies, both of peoples and of individuals, are conditioned by the social factors which play upon them. "An important invention, like the airplane or television, is not the product of one inventive act by one heroic, titular inventor at one date. Instead that great invention is an agglomeration of a vast number of detail inventions, like the thousands that have been added to the auto." [18] Hence it is that inventions are not mysterious things which come out of the air, but have causes and display trends. They can to a certain extent be predicted by projecting into the future the trends which have manifested themselves. [19]

[17] Roland B. Dixon, *The Building of Cultures*, New York, 1928, p. 59. These unscientific and misleading notions and vagaries emanated from the former head of the department of anthropology in Harvard University.

[18] United States National Resources Committee, *Technological Trends and National Policy*, Washington, 1937, p. 18.

[19] S. C. Gilfillan, *The Sociology of Invention*, Chicago, 1935.

Gilfillan has reported the facts that about the year 1923 Connecticut was taking out nine times Arkansas's patents per white capita, and that the United King-

All of the data available demonstrate that there are no important racial or ethnic differences of a psychological nature among extant peoples which could in, of and by themselves give rise to important social and cultural differences. In other words, the social and cultural differences between racial and ethnic groups are much greater than the minor hereditary physical and psychological differences between them. This has been demonstrated repeatedly both in time and in space, in the past and in the present, and in all parts of the world. It has often happened that peoples of similar race have differed greatly in culture, while other people of relatively unlike races have resembled each other culturally. The Hindus of India are largely of Caucasian stock like the Europeans, and yet their caste system, religion, family organization, etc., differ vastly from European institutions.[20] The "Nordic" Germans, the "Mediterranean" Italians, and the "mongolian" Japanese, were drawn together temporarily by a similar fascist political, economic and social system during the world war of 1939-45.

Race and culture must be sharply distinguished and separated from each other. While all cultural traits arise out of and are conditioned and limited by human nature in general, within which there is a wide range for variation, no cultural traits arise directly, exclusively, or even in large part, out of specific racial peculiarities. The French anthropologist Boule has stated emphatically the distinction between race and history: "By race we should understand the continuity of a physical type, expressing affinities of blood, representing an essentially natural grouping, which can have nothing, and in general has nothing in common with the people, the nationality, the language, or the customs corresponding to groupings that are purely artificial, in no way anthropological, and arising entirely from history, whose actual products they are."[21] The Swiss anthropologist Pittard has discussed exhaustively the relation and distinction between race and history. He has refuted the fallacies underlying the racial prejudices according to which races not only differ greatly from each other, but certain races are vastly inferior to other races.[22] These fallacies and prejudices are, nevertheless, widely disseminated in the world today. The most brutal and stupid example was furnished by the national socialists in Germany who alleged that the Jews, who created

dom was taking out three times New Zealand's patents per capita, although the inhabitants of all these areas are of about the same race. (S. C. Gilfillan, "Inventiveness by Nation," *Geographical Review*, 20:301-4. 1930; "Inventiveness by Nation and State." *Patent Office Society Journal*, 12:259-67, 1930.)

[20] See my *Oriental and Occidental Culture*, New York, 1928.

[21] Marcellin Boule, *Les hommes fossiles*, Paris, 1921, p. 322.

[22] Eugene Pittard, *Race and History*, London, 1926, translated from the French.

a considerable part of German culture, are incapable of assimilating it, and slaughtered several millions of them during the war of 1939-45.

There are great intellectual and emotional differences between individuals. In any group of considerable size will be found a wide intellectual and emotional range. This range is approximately the same for all races. The mean or median point, if it could be calculated would in all probability be found to be nearly identical for all races. All of the inter-racial intelligence tests which have been applied confirm this conclusion. There are slight emotional differences between some of the races. Climatic environmental factors may have caused minor adjustments in the visceral processes, which may in turn have slightly influenced the affective traits. This is mainly conjectural and far from certain.[23] At any rate, it is safe to assume that race and human nature in general are constant factors in all cultures. They can be ignored in the sense that they are not the determinants of cultural variations. Human nature has certain wide limits beyond which variability is impossible. Within these limits variations of culture take place regardless of racial, ethnic or group heredity, and due to other factors which we must seek in each case as the true determinants.

There have been several theories of cultural evolution. The so-called "unilinear" theory of Herbert Spencer, L. H. Morgan, E. B. Tylor, and J. G. Frazer, is that approximately the same line of evolution has taken place in each group, even when a group has been largely and entirely separated from other groups. This theory assumes a large amount of independent invention. It also assumes that the evolution is progressive in the sense that it is in the direction of a greater variety and complexity of cultural phenomena.

The so-called "diffusionist" theory of F. Graebner, G. Elliot Smith, and W. J. Perry, minimizes the amount of independent invention, and replaces it with a great deal of diffusion. According to this theory, many groups have remained stationary because they have not been in contact with one of the few centers of invention and diffusion. These centers are progressive societies in the sense that they are headed toward greater variety and complexity of cultural phenomena. However, the progressive tendency in human society the world over is rather weak. In most places it can be stimulated only by the accident of contact and of communication with a progressive center. At any rate, so runs the theory of the diffusionists.

The so-called "cyclical" theory asserts that there is constant alternation and no permanent movement in any given direction. It is an ancient theory often stated in the past by philosophers. Recent

[23] See Maurice Parmelee, article entitled "Ethnic Factors in International Relations," the *Scientific Monthly*, 1914.

voluminous statements in many heavy tomes have been made by the Italian Pareto, the Englishman Toynbee, the German Spengler, and the Russian-American Sorokin. The former has expounded his cyclical theory of social change as an alternate predominance, in the governing groups of a society, of two classes of "residues." The one is the "instinct of combinations" absorbed in immediate and tangible interests. The other is the "persistence of aggregates," or subordination of individual and immediate interests to ideal ends. The cycle has three aspects. The political aspect is dominated by strong men (lions) devoted to ideal ends. The economic aspect is dominated by cunning men (foxes) devoted to saving wealth or to speculation. The ideological aspect is characterized by an alternation of skepticism (with what?) in the intellectual sphere. Or perhaps this aspect is characterized by a recurrence of skepticism. Such is the rather unclear and fanciful exposition of his cyclical theory of social change by the mathematician and economist Pareto.

According to Pareto, residues are inborn drives, such as instincts and sentiments, which often lead to non-logical conduct. From these residues are derived various forms of rationalizations, which he calls "derivations," to justify non-logical conduct, and "prove" non-logico-experimental ideas and beliefs. This is a very crude adumbration of human psychology. His theory of cyclical change was based upon too limited a range of social phenomena, and could not be applied to the whole of cultural evolution. In so far as there is a modicum of truth in Pareto's writings, it has been much better and more precisely expounded by the abler of the social psychologists and sociologists. His merit was more literary than scientific. A certain amount of historical data, deriving mainly from the classical Roman and medieval Italian periods, is rather discursively but somewhat entertainingly set forth.[24]

Sorokin's theory of fluctuations in forms of art, systems of truth, ethics and law, social relationships, war and revolution, though somewhat broader in scope, is even less scientific than that of Pareto, who maintained at least the semblance of scientific objectivity and seemed to be free from animistic superstitions. Sorokin alleges that there are two fundamental types of culture, namely, the "pure ideational," which is the truth of faith revealed by religion, and the "sensate," which is empirical "scientific" truth. Variants of there two types are the mixed idealistic or rationalism, the passive sensate and cynical or skepticism, and the ideational desperate (*sic*) or fideism. He professes to have proved fluctuations between these types by listing and

[24] Vilfredo Pareto, *The Mind and Society*, (*Trattato di Sociologia generale*), 4 vols., New York, 1935, translated from the Italian.

weighting many thinkers and writers between 600 B.C. and 1920 A.D., a very subjective method of measurement. He has little comprehension of causal factors. He asserted that the highest type of cultural integration is "logico-meaningful or internal unity," which is a meaningless and highly subjective interpretation of his own. His concept of immanent causation and inner logic of change is like that of Hegel, Spengler, and other metaphysicians.[25]

Sorokin's unscientific attitude is illustrated on nearly every page of his verbose tomes by such statements as the following: ". . . 'endocrinological, psychoanalytical' interpretation of man as a mere bag filled with filthy sex (Freud, . . . or some other variety of the 'physio-dirty' theory." "The full and complete truth is 'white' and is possibly accessible only to the Divine mind." [26]

As two of Sorokin's critics and reviewers have well said: "The 'logico-meaningful method' is neither logical nor meaningful, nor indeed a method . . . a suspicious mixture of logic, meaning, sensation, science, mysticism, and intuition." (Bierstedt). "In the history of ideas, 'fluctuation' seems to mean no more than that there has been a 'Dark Ages.' " "Throughout Sorokin seems generally arbitrary and often demonstrably wrong; with few exceptions he follows very conventional and antiquated judgments." (Randall).[27]

Another critic has summed up Sorokin's work as follows: "By omitting from consideration primitive society and all anthropological and archeological evidence as to the early history of man and culture Sorokin shortened the perspective on the past and can force the argument that history has been fluctuational rather than accumulative. By advancing his 'logico-meaningful' method, he can make truth and the interpretation of history a matter of personal feeling rather than validated observation. . . . By exemplifying science in its worst interpreters—the mystic popularizers and exploiters of its prestige—he can seek to deny the verity and utility of all science." [28]

Sorokin resembles, though on a much lower intellectual plane, the German mathematician Oswald Spengler who put forth a theory of the life cycle of civilizations passing through the phases of youth, middle age, old age, and death. In his principal work he alleged that

[25] P. A. Sorokin, *Social and Cultural Dynamics*, Vols. I, II, III, New York, 1937; Vol. IV, New York, 1941.

[26] P. A. Sorokin, *op. cit.*, Vol. II. pp. 115, 475. Such is the drivel which flows from the pen of a professor at Harvard University, and former head of its department of sociology.

[27] R. Bierstedt, "The Logico-Meaningful Method of P. A. Sorokin"; J. H. Randall, review of Sorokin's Vol. II; in the *American Sociological Review*, Dec., 1937, pp. 823, 922, 923.

[28] Elton P. Guthrie, "Sorokin: Counselor to Reaction," in *Science and Society*, Spring, 1939, Vol. III, No. 2, p. 238.

Occidental civilization is now approaching death.[29] His "Faustian" and "Apollonian" concepts are similar to Sorokin's "ideational" and "sensate" concepts. Such ideological concepts are much too rigid for cultural and social phenomena which are ever changing qualitatively as well as quantitatively.

A theory somewhat similar to that of the preceding writers is the theocratic and therefore hierocratic theory of the English historian Toynbee. In its religious character it is much akin to that of Sorokin, though Toynbee knows more of history and perhaps also of primitive culture than the former. According to Toynbee, 21 specific civilizations have arisen during the past 6,000 years, all of which, except the "Western," are extinct or in their terminal stages.[30] An English political scientist characterized his work as follows: "*A Study of History* reveals itself as a number of dogmatic assertions overlaid with a vast structure of pseudo-science." Toynbee asserts that "the true key to history is the growth of the higher religions." [31] Toynbee's ultimate conclusion was that "all men and women in the western world who have been baptized into Christ. . . . should call upon the Vicar of Christ to vindicate his tremendous title. . . . To the apostle at Rome our forefathers committed the destiny of western civilization, which was the whole of their treasure." [32] An American social scientist has characterized his work as follows: "Toynbee resolutely believes in the dominant role of God in History. God is the most active force in history, and the Kingdom of God is the goal of the historical development of mankind. The Incarnation of Jesus is the central fact of history." [33] An American political scientist said of him: "I do not find him a discoverer of the laws of history, nor do I find him a prophet who can pierce the future. His laws of history seem to me not science but poetry: his projections into the future are at once romantic and fuzzy." [34] Thus the grandiose conceptions of this verbose London professor shrink into a grotesque travesty of history in that he appealed to the pope of Rome to save civilization.

I have cited these four modern expositions of a cyclical theory,

29 Oswald Spengler, *Der Untergang des Abendlandes,* Munich, 1918-1922, 2 vols.; English translation, *The Decline of the West,* London, 1926-28.

30 Arnold J. Toynbee, *A Study of History,* New York, 1947. This volume is a condensation of three volumes published in 1933 and three volumes published in 1939. The six volumes were abridged by D. C. Somervell. By 1954 there were ten volumes conprizing 3,150,000 words. In 1956 was published a condensation of the later volumes.

31 R. H. S. Crossman, "The Faith of Arnold Toynbee," in the *New Republic,* New York, May 17, 1948.

32 Arnold J. Toynbee, *Civilization on Trial,* Oxford, 1948.

33 Harry Elmer Barnes, in the *American Sociological Review,* August 1947, page 480.

34 Max Lerner, in *PM,* New York, May 2, 1948.

not because they possess any intrinsic merit, but because they demonstrate that such a theory furnishes no adequate explanation of the vast cultural changes which have taken place. These changes are due in part to the numerous technological conditions of human existence. These inventions are largely ignored by any cyclical theory, which perforce fails to recognize the novel factors introduced by these inventions, despite whatever fluctuations caused by them may occur. Cultural changes are also due to the extensive mutations in social organization and institutions, in wealth and population, and sometimes to climatic change. The pervasive influence of the economic factors is in the main ignored or emphatically denied by the ideologists of the cyclical theory. The ultimate resultant of all these factors is that the cultural and social process moves in this direction or that, and is progressive or regressive, good or bad, according to whatever normative criterion is used. It is not cyclical in the sense that there is repeated recurrence to a previous situation on an all-inclusive or predominant scale.

Chapter XV

The Rise of Animism—Magic and Religion

IT has often been asserted that religion originated in the worship of nature. This notion has arisen out of the fact that many deities have been associated or identified with objects or forces of nature. The solar cult was widespread in the ancient world, and still exists in many parts of the world. Among the solar deities were the Egyptian Ammon or Ammon Ra, the Babylonian Marduk, the Persian Mithras, and the Japanese sun goddess Amaterasu-omikami. It was sometimes believed that the divine sun traveled in his chariot across the sky, and then returned at night in a boat across the river Ocean underneath the earth.

Over a large part of Asia Minor, and a smaller part of Europe, was disseminated a belief in a mother goddess called the Great Mother or the Earth Mother. This goddess personified fertility, reproduction, and the sexual life. She was often associated with the planet Venus. The Semitic mother goddess, worshiped in Babylonia and Assyria, was Ishtar the wife of Tammuz the god of vegetation, the Phenician goddess was Astarte, the Hellenic goddess was Aphrodite, and the Roman goddess was Venus.

These forms of so-called nature worship are much later than the origin of religion. They are based upon highly evolved animistic myths. These myths often were attempts to explain the processes and events of nature. They reflected some meditation concerning these natural phenomena. The solar myth attempted to explain the diurnal rise, movement, and descent of the sun, the alternation of light and darkness, of night and day. The myth of the mother goddess attempted to explain the cycle of seasons and their annual recurrence.

Long before these more or less rationalized myths had been invented, mankind had reacted in various ways toward the forces and processes of nature as well as of itself. Its emotional reaction was often that of fear. Its intellectual reaction was more crude and simple than these rather complicated and imaginative myths. These reactions gave rise to a wide range of beliefs and practices which have varied greatly from place to place and from time to time, but which still constitute a large portion of the mental content of culture, and have extensive effects upon its material aspects.

Many Mousterian burials, often accompanied by provision for the dead in a life hereafter, have been found. At Grimaldi on the Mediterranean coast, and in other caves and rock shelters in France and elsewhere, the dead were buried by their hearths with implements and other objects of their daily life. The Aurignacian cave paintings, which were usually of animals, seem to indicate magical beliefs. They may also indicate totemic beliefs. These data demonstrate that animistic ideas and beliefs extended as far back as the middle paleolithic and probably still earlier.

Animism originated from an anthropomorphic interpretation of the universe. This interpretation gave rise to the belief that all things, inanimate as well as animate, are conscious in somewhat the same way as human beings and other animals. This tenuous and diffused psychological animism has often taken the more specific form of a belief in spirits which are beings more ethereal than ourselves and other animals. This form of animism has sometimes been termed hyperphysical animism. It includes souls and ghosts, fairies and hobgoblins, angels and demons, gods and devils, and all the other hypothetical denizens of an imaginary animistic universe.

Out of animistic ideas and beliefs have arisen many activities which are intended to influence these animistic forces and beings. These activities divide into two main categories. The one category includes those destined to propitiate, conciliate, and persuade animistic beings. The other includes the activities directed toward coercing animistic forces. These categories mark the division between religion and magic. Religion includes beliefs in spiritual and supernatural beings, some of which are regarded as superhuman. These beings, and especially the latter group, are conceived of as deciding in varying degrees the fate of human beings for good or for ill. Hence it is of the utmost importance to influence these supernatural and superhuman beings to benefit mankind. Thus arise prayer, sacrifice, and praise and flattery of the gods. These religious beliefs and propitiatory activities are usually accompanied by the emotion or, better said, sentiment of awe. This sentiment is compounded largely out of the fear which is aroused by these powerful and mysterious spiritual beings. To this fear is added a touch of wonder, and also at times of admiration for these fantastic and imaginary creatures.

Some of these traits of the religious aspect of animism are well illustrated in the so-called "Lord's Prayer" of Christianity. This supplication begins with fulsome praise and flattery of the supreme deity of this religion. This deity is portrayed in a most anthropomorphic fashion as a great king and monocratic ruler. "Our Father, who art in heaven, hallowed be thy name, thy kingdom come, thy will be done, upon earth as in heaven." Having propitiated the Almighty, the prayer proceeds to business by requesting material goods and absolution from sin. "Give us this day our daily bread, and forgive us our debts as we forgive our debtors." In order to leave a pleasant taste in the divine mouth, the prayer returns to propitiation and adulation. "For thine is the power and the glory, forever, Amen." It should, however, be recorded that the Christian god, though alleged to be kind and merciful, has often hardened his heart, and has refused their daily bread to countless millions of his devotees, despite their humble supplications.

Magic includes beliefs in animistic forces which are more impersonal in their character than the spiritual beings of religion. Hence it is not so feasible to persuade or cajole these forces to assume an amiable attitude toward mankind. It may, however, be possible to coerce, or at least to direct, these forces toward the results desired by man. The methods used to attain these ends are of a magical character. They arise usually out of the observation of a coincidence, correlation, or succession of events which are erroneously assumed to be causally related to each other. Hence they display a crude resemblance to the methods of science. This fact has led some writers to conjecture that magic was a rudimentary form of science. They have even suggested that magic may not have been animistic in origin, but later became confused with animism and religion.[1]

Science may have been derived in part from magic. It may also be said to have preceded magic in a limited sense. Science is a development and extension of common sense in an uncommon fashion. A certain amount of common sense may have preceded magic, but the latter violates common sense continually by making the most improbable assumptions. The repeated failure of magic, and the occasional application of tests to determine its validity, encouraged the development of genuine science.

Magic, religion, and science resemble each other in that each involves a certain conception of the universe and of the nature of things. This conception gives rise to certain activities destined to

---

[1] For example, Read has contended that magic probably preceded animism, and was independent of it and of religion in its origin, and has defined the former as follows: "Magic may be defined as a connexion of events imagined to be constant and to depend upon the agency of some thing or activity possessing an efficacious quality or force (in fact unreal), and not to depend (as a connexion) upon the will of any particular person." (Carveth Read, *Man and His Superstitions*, Cambridge, 1925, p. 40.)

influence the universe, or, at any rate, some of the things in it. Beyond this point all resemblance ceases. Science is fundamentally antagonistic to magic and religion and to all forms of animism. It does not assume the anthropomorphic conception of the universe implicit in animism. It is not based upon casual observation of external and superficial similarities. It recognizes causal connections only after numerous observations, and, whenever possible, after experiments, under controlled conditions, which test any hypothetical causal relation. In the later stages of human thought came metaphysics which has often revived magical ideas of force and a quasi-animistic conception of the universe. As indicated in an earlier chapter, some of the contemporary workers in the physical sciences have been venturing into the dark realm of animistic and magical beliefs. Science has to guard itself at all times against the tendency of the human mind to try to overstep the boundary after it has reached the frontier of knowledge which has already been attained or is attainable.

The notion that magic was not originally animistic, and that there was a pre-animistic stage of human thought and belief, has arisen mainly out of the study of certain ideas and beliefs prevalent among various primitive peoples. Among them are the idea of *mana* or *atua* in Melanesia and Polynesia, and of *manitou* or *orenda* among certain North American tribes. The missionary bishop, Codrington, has characterized *mana* as follows: "The Melanesian mind is entirely possessed by the belief in a supernatural power or influence called almost universally *mana*."[2]

This belief is based upon the idea of a more or less immanent and non-personalized force in the universe. It has been named "animatism" by Marett.[3] The notions that religion is inherent in mankind, and that religious beliefs reflect spiritual realities in the universe, have led some writers with religious inclinations to contend that "animatism" preceded and was more fundamental than animism. Needless to say, there is no basis in fact for these notions. Religion is superstition just as much as magic.

Even if it is assumed that this "animatistic" idea preceded the more obviously animistic and anthropomorphic ideas which have been observed, and even where this idea is the sole or dominant feature of the ideational equipment of a people, it is not safe to assume that animatistic notions have not been held in the past and then have disappeared. This idea of an immanent force, though somewhat less

[2] R. H. Codrington, *The Melanesians*, Oxford, 1891.

[3] R. R. Marett, *The Threshold of Religion*, London, 2nd edition, 1914. This book reads as if its author was influenced by a partizan bias in favor of religion and against magic. He seems to have had an animistic point of view even though he was an anthropologist.

personified than other animistic conceptions, is by no means non-animistic. On the contrary, it is regarded as sufficiently conscient as to respond to the coercive or propitiatory methods of magic and of religion. This belief is, in fact, an illustration of a tendency of primitive thought which has often been noted by observers of primitive peoples. These peoples do not usually distinguish as sharply between the natural and the alleged supernatural as do their more civilized congeners. Hence the natural universal force or energy of modern philosophy might readily have a supernatural as well as a natural character in its primitive precursor or prototype.

The study of pre-literate culture has revealed a wide range of magical and religious beliefs and practices. The study of historical culture has revealed an equally great range of religious but a somewhat smaller range of magical phenomena, because science has supplanted magic far more than it has precluded religion. Repeated failure of magical methods must eventually arouse doubt as to the feasibility of coercing nature, while the advance of science is constantly extending the range of effective scientific methods of attaining desired ends. The failure of religious methods is not so readily demonstrated. It may well be that the gods or other spiritual beings to be propitiated are unwilling to listen or to be conciliated, even when approached with cajoling words, rich sacrifices, and fair promises. Because rain inevitably follows prayer sooner or later religionists usually fall into the common *"post hoc propter hoc"* fallacy of assuming that prayer has caused rain. Hence it is that religion persists, and retains respectability far into the scientific age, while magic is repudiated and reprobated as a black art, not only by science and technology, but even by its twin sister religion born of the same animistic parents. Religion has also been an effective instrument in the hands of a dominant class to maintain its power over and to exploit the lower classes. Especially in the later stages of cultural evolution, this has been the principal reason for the perpetuation of religion and its organization as an institution in churches and other religious bodies. This function of religion as a means of coercion and control by the ruling class will be expounded in later chapters. Religion thereby becomes a means of social control in the interest of an exploiting class, and a factor for the perpetuation of a predatory class system.[4]

4 "Religion is in its essence, a weapon of exploitation and enslavement; it is, in fact, from religion that all the other exploitative and authoritarian institutions draw their primary strength. The religious attitude is the core from which all authoritarian submission and degradation of the human spirit spring. . . . Religion furnishes the rationale by which parents and culture check a child's inquisitiveness and suppress his sexuality. It alienates a person from the world around him, and from himself." (Donald Calhoun, *Liberation*, July-August, 1957, p. 24.)

As a result of an extensive survey of magical and religious phenomena in both pre-literate and literate culture, Frazer has distinguished between two main types of magic. The one is sympathetic, homeopathic, or imitative magic. It is based upon the law of similarity which arises out of the association of ideas due to similarity which is real or assumed. The other is contagious magic. It is based upon the law of contact or contagion, which arises out of an association of ideas due to contiguity.[5] Needless to say, this is a rationalization and schematization by Frazer, and not by the magicians who practised these forms of magic, or those who believed or still believe in their efficacy.

The positive methods of magic are charms and the use of amulets. Its negative methods are taboos. Imitative magic has been used to injure and destroy, by means of an image; to facilitate conception and childbirth; in hunting and fishing, often by portraying in some manner the animal preyed upon; in eating or rejecting foods of various sorts; in influencing vegetation, usually in order to induce desired plants to grow; and in order to control the sun, wind, rain, and other natural elements. In fact, imitative magic is directed in large part toward the control of nature.

Contagious magic has attempted to injure and destroy by means of severed portions of the body; and to attain desired ends by means of impressions made by the body. It is much less extensive than imitative magic in the range of its methods. It is directed largely toward influencing persons rather than controlling nature. While Frazer has perhaps rationalized magic too much, his schema of its different types is a helpful guide through the vast maze of magical ideas and practices.

Magic and religion assume an almost unlimited possibility of influencing nature. This is partly due to a wholly inadequate conception of the vastness and complexity of the universe, and of the infinitesimally small role played therein not only by mankind but by the animate world in general. Religion has often assumed that a man may become a god. Many mundane kings, rulers of this world, have been derived, according to an oft-recurring myth, from male gods and magicians, rulers of the other world. Anthropocentrism has attained its apogee in the deification of men. Science, on the contrary, has an increasingly more adequate conception of the infinite size of the universe, and of the infinitesimally minor role played therein by man. It recognizes that mankind can influence nature only to a slight extent upon this planet, and not at all in any other part of the universe.

[5] J. G. Frazer, *The Golden Bough, A Study in Magic and Religion*, New York, 1922. This is a condensation of a treatise which appeared originally in many volumes.

Religion and magic differ as between themselves with regard to the extent to which nature can be influenced. Religion implies a somewhat greater variability and elasticity of nature than is recognized by magic. The self-conscious and personal powers whose existence is assumed by religion are very irresponsible and wayward beings. They may be greatly influenced by prayer, sacrifice, and adulation. It must, however, not be forgotten that they may at times refuse to be propitiated and conciliated at all. On the other hand, magic must recognize that the animistic but less personified forces which it postulates can be coerced up to a certain point but not beyond that point. They cannot be flattered and cajoled like the superhuman beings postulated by religion. Magic is, therefore, less capricious than religion, and at times approaches a recognition of some sort of an order in the universe, whereas religion encourages belief in a rather disorderly universe governed by wilful superior beings.

The preceding characterization of magic and religion renders more significant the meager indications of their prevalence in prehistoric times. Tylor thought that animism arose out of experiences which gave primitive men the idea of a human soul which could be separated from the body. Such experiences were dreams, shadows, reflections in water, etc.[6] Spencer also emphasized the idea of a human double in the form of a spirit.[7] According to this theory of the origin of animism, the concept of a spirit accompanying a body was then extended to animals and plants, and eventually to inanimate things. Durkheim and Levy-Bruhl have, however, criticized Tylor's theory as being too intellectualistic in its interpretation of primitive thought and behavior.[8] Levy-Bruhl has characterized primitive thinking as being "prelogical" and not genuine reasoning.[9] Pareto also has criticized incisively Tylor's and Spencer's theories of the origin of animism.[10]

Early man certainly did not commence with a theory of the animate nature of the universe. It is much more probable that his tendency was to act and react toward inanimate objects as he did toward animate beings. So that animism was in its inception the state of mind of a human being who has not distinguished between behavior toward persons and toward things. This hypothesis is rendered all the more plausible by the behavior of children who often treat

---

[6] E. B. Tylor, *Primitive Culture*, 2 vols., 7th edition, London, 1924.

[7] Herbert Spencer, *Principles of Sociology*, 3 vols., London, 1876-96, vol. I, 3rd edition, 1885.

[8] Emile Durkheim, *Les formes elementaires de la vie religieuse*, Paris, 1912.

[9] L. Levy-Bruhl, *Les fonctions mentales dans les societes inferieures*, Paris, 1910; *La mentalité primitive*, Paris, 1912.

[10] V. Pareto, *The Mind and Society*, New York, 1935, Vol. I, pp. 423-33, translated from the Italian.

inanimate objects as if they were animate. A rudimentary form of this state of mind may be present also in animals, which is manifested when they are attracted or terrified by moving things. In its purely subjective aspect animism may, therefore, have antedated the development of language. It could not have been rationalized and formulated in theories of the universe, and of the forces and beings therein, until language was highly evolved, thus rendering discussion and conceptual thought possible. Until this point was reached, magic and religion could not have commenced, or at least have attained, considerable development.

Reinach has called magic "the strategy of animism."[11] While this is an apt characterization, religion also is a form of animistic strategy. Both strategies have often been used at the same time in order to enhance the prospect of attaining the desired end. It has been asserted that magic is mechanistic as contrasted with religion. Magic is not mechanistic in the modern scientific meaning of that term. A mechanistic conception of the universe excludes every vestige of animism. It is science that has introduced this conception. A genuine mechanistic technology is based on science and not on magic, which bears only a spurious resemblance to science.[12]

The preceding considerations disprove the hypothesis that magic was a primitive form of science. They furnish no support for the hypothesis that magic antedated religion in its origin. It will never be possible to prove conclusively which of the two had priority. The Mousterian burials indicate a belief in the souls or spiritual personalities of human beings. Otherwise the dead would not have been buried at all, or, at any rate, would not have been given tools, weapons, etc., to use in the other world. These practices demonstrate the existence not only of animistic but of religious beliefs as far back as the middle paleolithic. The Aurignacian drawings and models of animals may indicate a belief in imitative magic. They may have been intended to stimulate the increase and aid the capture of animals

[11] S. Reinach, *Cultes, mythes, et religions,* 5 vols., Paris, 1905-23; *Orpheus, histoire generale des religions,* Paris, 1909.

[12] After having asserted that magic and religion represent two extremes in behavior dealing with the supernatural, Mrs. Benedict added the following somewhat contradictory statement: "Magic is technological and mechanistic, a compulsion of a passive universe to one's own ends; religion is animistic behavior and employs toward a personalized universe all the kinds of behavior that hold good in human relations." Elsewhere she has asserted that "man in all his mythologies has expressed his discomfort at a mechanistic universe and his pleasure in substituting a world that is humanly motivated and directed." (Ruth Benedict, articles on "Magic" and "Myth" in the *Encyclopedia of the Social Sciences,* New York, Vol. X, 1933, and Vol. XI, 1933.) There may be some psychological justification for the last assertion, though the distinction between magic and religion implied is in the main erroneous, because magic is no less animistic than religion.

which were eaten by men. They may also have been connected with the totemism which forms a part of the animistic beliefs and practices of many extant primitive peoples. Totemism is always associated with the division of a tribe into clans.[13] Whether such a form of social organization existed in paleolithic time, it is impossible to determine. In fact, the relation of paleolithic art to animistic beliefs and practices is wholly conjectural. The Aurignacian culture probably came to western Europe from elsewhere, so that it may have been as old in its origins as the Mousterian in Europe.

While it is useless to conjecture as to the precise or even approximate date of the origin of animistic beliefs and practices, it is safe to assume that animism extends a long way back into the past, that religion is comparatively old, and that magic is probably as old as and perhaps more ancient than religion. The extensive complex of animistic beliefs and practices found among primitive peoples, many of which survive among so-called civilized poeples, bespeak a long period of development. The idea of tabu is one of the most prominent of these beliefs. It has been defined as "a negative sanction, a prohibition whose infringement results in an automatic penalty without human or supernatural mediation."[14] This negative sanction arises out of the notion that certain objects or situations are permeated with a noxious automatic force. Contact with this object or situation is prohibited in order to avoid contagion. Other objects and situations are conceived of as permeated with a beneficial animistic force and regarded as sacred, so that a positive sanction commands contact with them. The objects and situations subject to tabu may also be regarded as sacred, but contact with them is sacrilegious and therefore harmful.

Upon the basic idea as to what is sacred and what is tabu are built up a large part of animistic practices. Fetishes are material objects which are supposed to possess a supernatural force or in which resides a spirit. Certain places came to be regarded as sacred because associated in some way with supernatural forces or beings. After mankind had invented writing and created a literature, a part of the latter came to be regarded as sacred because it was supposed to be of supernatural origin, or dealt with supernatural matters. Moslems

[13] "Among many primitive tribes divided into sibs (clans or gentes) the sib name is derived from an animal, plant or natural object; the sib mates display special aptitudes toward these creatures or things." (Alexander Goldenweiser, article on "Totemism," in the *Encyclopedia of the Social Sciences*, Vol. XIV, New York, 1934.) These totems are objects of enhanced emotional value for these clans. In some cases they are regarded with awe and reverence and almost worshiped. Totemism was prevalent in North America, Africa, Australia, and certain other parts of the world.

[14] Margaret Mead, article on "Tabu," in the *Encyclopedia of the Social Sciences*, Vol. XIV, New York, 1934.

will not step on a piece of printed paper because it may contain a quotation from their holy book—the Koran. Fetishes, holy places, and sacred books still play an important part in the extant religions of the world, even in the religions of the most civilized peoples.

The prohibition of blasphemy arises out of the fear of spiritual beings. At an early stage it was connected with the notion of the interchangeability of names with the things which they designate, thus giving names a potency in themselves. Among many primitive peoples has been prevalent the idea that persons can be affected for good or for ill through their names. This idea has sometimes led to the concealment of true names, in order to prevent their magical misuse. In most civilized countries there is a drastic tabu against taking the names of alleged great spirits in vain.[15] A similar tabu is sometimes extended to the names of great personages, such as kings, dictators, prelates, etc. Change of rank and status often leads to change of name, even when useless and inconvenient, as when an Englishman takes a new name when ennobled.

Like other phases of culture, animistic beliefs and practices are transmitted from generation to generation by tradition and in part by means of folklore. The latter contains both secular and sacred folk tales. It reflects the primitive view of the world, and to a certain extent conveys the wishful thinking of mankind. Myths are folk tales about the supernatural. They often stand to magic in the relation of theory to practice. Religious dogmas are myths. They are *a priori* in the sense that the animistic beliefs which they embody existed before the rationalization by means of which it is attempted to prove and to justify them. The theology of the so-called civilized religions therefore belongs in large part to mythology. The same may be said of a good deal of metaphysics which is largely a more extended rationalization of religion.

Animistic beliefs have given rise to an elaboration of ceremonial observance with which many of the animistic practices are accompanied or surrounded. Ceremonies in general are expressions or symbolizations of more or less fixed cultural patterns and standardized social behavior. Ceremonies may be classified roughly into two main groups, namely, the secular and the sacred ceremonies. Secular ceremonies vary greatly in importance. Among the most trivial are some of the ceremonies of etiquette. Etiquette itself is in part a survival of the ritual whose chief purpose was and often still is propitiation.

Among the most grave of these ceremonies are patriotic ceremonies, expressing the unity and common interests of a tribal or

[15] See Maurice Parmelee, *Criminology*, New York, 1918, pages 474-478, for a description of the laws against blasphemy and profanity and sabbatarian legislation in the United States and Great Britian.

217

national group, marriage ceremonies, and the like. The more important of the secular ceremonies are often accompanied by prayer, psalm singing, and other sacred ceremonies, because of the alleged significance of the supernatural which, it is assumed, communicates itself in some fashion to and emphasizes the importance of the secular ceremonies. This tends to blur the distinction between the more important secular and the sacred ceremonies, and to obliterate it completely in the minds of many persons. The consequence is that sentiments and practices connected with the group, initiation into or expulsion from the group, marriage, and other important aspects of life which are in their inception and essence secular, acquire a sacred character in the minds of the majority.

Many ceremonies are accompanied by rationalizations which in most cases are more recent than the ceremonies themselves. Few ceremonies are consciously and intentionally invented for a specific purpose. Ceremonies are likely to be survivals of archaic or obsolete practices which have lost their utility, but still possess a symbolic significance. A ceremony is, therefore, almost invariably more stable than its rationalization, which may be forgotten or changed.

Generally speaking, it may be said that the features of a social system which are essential and fundamental to it are likely to be regarded as sacred or semi-sacred. In a monarchy the king and royal family are regarded as, if not divine, almost superhuman. In a system of private enterprise the private ownership of the means of production comes to be regarded as sacred, or at least as a natural and absolute right which existed prior to the development of the institution of property. The importance and significance of these sacred or semi-sacred institutions are often emphasized by appropriate ceremonies, such as coronation of a king, laws prayerfully enacted to protect private property, marriage sanctioned by the priestly class, etc.

The ceremonies of an animistic cult are usually called its rites, and constitute the ritual of the cult. Ritual is a form of conduct prescribed for all devotees of a cult. Violations of it are often followed by overt or occult punishments. An individual also may develop a ritual of behavior obligatory for himself and accompanied by penalties for violations of it. Such an individual ritual usually arises out of a compulsion neurosis from which its victim is suffering. The great majority of these individual rituals have had no social significance. A few of them have been incorporated in the rituals of cults because they characterized influential members of these cults. Several of the so-called founders of religions doubtless suffered from such compulsion neuroses, and were able to transfer parts of their individual rituals to their cults. However, no religion has been invented out of whole cloth by one person. The most that one individual can do is

218

to modify slightly, and to impart a certain amount of impetus to an already existing religion.

The range of sacred ceremonies or rites has been very extensive, and a considerable portion of these rites still survive. Many have been the magical incantations by means of which it has been attempted to coerce the forces of nature. They have often been associated with the use of potions, charms and amulets. Some of the latter are of the nature of fetishes. In India today *mantras* or magical utterances are often used to ward off disease, stimulate fertility, increase the harvest yield, etc. Similar incantations are used in China to drive away the *feng-shui* or evil spirits. Many of the religious rites are connected with the sacrifice of human beings, animals or some form of property in order to propitiate spiritual beings; with methods of purification from the effects of impure or evil forces; and with forms of initiation into life, an age group, a different rank or status, a religious cult, a profession, such as the priesthood, etc.[16]

The so-called mysteries have included some of these rites connected with sacrifice, purification, and initiation, and many dramatic representations of myths of legendary heroes, divine or semi-divine in character. The theater and the dance, now mainly secular in their nature, originated in large part from the religious ceremonial and cult of the mysteries. The ancient and medieval mystery plays were among these portrayals of myths. Many of the ancient plays represented the mystery of death and resurrection, and symbolized the alternation of winter and summer, the decay and revival of vegetation. Among the representations of death and resurrection were the dramas of Osiris in Egypt, of Tammuz and Marduk in Mesopotamia, of Adonis in Syria, of Attis in Phrygia, and of Melgart or Melquarth in Tyre. In Greece the Orphic, Eleusinian, Delphic, and Dionysian mysteries dramatized various Hellenic myths. The medieval mystery plays centered largely around the passion of Jesus Christ. A few of these have survived to the present day, such as the passion plays repeated periodically in Germany and in the United States.

The Christian sacraments furnish instructive examples of the survival of magical and religious rites. The Roman Catholic Church recognizes and practices seven of these sacraments, namely, baptism, anointment or confirmation, the Lord's Supper or Communion or Eucharist, penance, extreme unction, marriage, and holy orders or ordination into the clergy. The sacraments of baptism, confirmation, ordination, and marriage, are rites of initiation. Baptism initiates into life itself, confirmation primarily into the membership of the

[16] *Cf.* A van Gennep, *Les rites de passage,* 1909. In this book this author has applied the term "dynamism" to the attitude toward the more or less impersonal forces called *mana, orenda, manitou* or *atua* by various primitive peoples.

Church, but also secondarily into the age period of adolescence and of puberty, ordination into the priesthood, and marriage into a sexual union sanctioned by the Church. The latter sacrament has a good deal of significance, economic and political, in addition to that of initiation into the sex life. The sacraments of penance, the Lord's Supper, and extreme unction are purificatory rites. The latter also commemorates departure from this life, and facilitates initiation under favorable auspices into the suppositious future life.

The Eucharist of today is a direct descendant of much of the cannibalism and human sacrifice of the past. Primitive men often ate their fellow human beings for magical reasons, namely, because they believed that they acquired thereby the strength and virtue embodied in the individuals who were ingested. Human sacrifice was often destined to furnish food for the gods, and thereby to placate them and put them in a good humor. The Eucharist reverses the latter process in its material aspect. According to the dogma of transubstantiation, the bread and wine of the communion service is transformed into the flesh and blood of Jesus Christ, and thereby men are able to eat a god.

The doctrine of transubstantiation is based in considerable part upon the alleged discourse of Jesus Christ as recorded in the sixth chapter of the gospel of St. John. He is reported to have said that his followers were to "eat the flesh of the Son of man, and drink his blood." This doctrine has been affirmed by many of the ecumenical councils of the Catholic Church, among them being the councils at Ephesus in 431 A.D., Nicaea in 787 A.D., and Trent in 1545-63 A.D. The church teaches that "in the Eucharist, the Body and Blood of the God-man are really, truly, substantially, and abidingly present." [17]

In the Protestant churches the Eucharist has degenerated into a symbolical rite. It is a sort of a mimicry of the "Lord's Supper" (the last repast of Jesus Christ with his apostles before his crucifixion). In partaking of this rite, however, many of the devotees imagine that they are attaining a mystical union with their divine lord and master.

The minor rites of the Catholic Church also reveal their animistic and often magical origin or background. The making of the sign of the cross resembles the gestures used by superstitious persons to protect themselves against the evil eye. Wetting any part of the body with the so-called holy water to be found at the entrance of every Catholic church has value because the water has acquired a magical potency by being blessed by the Pope. The ceremony of the stages of the Cross performed during Holy Week is a pale imitation of the medieval passion play.

[17] *The New Catholic Dictionary*, New York, 1929, p. 345.

220

The protestant or evangelical sects of Christianity have retained only two of the sacraments, namely, baptism, and communion or the Lord's Supper. These sacraments have become more symbolical in their character. It is not usually assumed that an infant will be damned if it dies before it has been baptized. As protestantism did not embrace the doctrine of transubstantiation, it is not believed that the bread and wine of the communion service have actually become the flesh and blood of Jesus Christ, thus diminishing somewhat the cannibalistic character of this rite. Closely associated with rites are the sacred days and periods during which many of them are performed. The Sabbath of Judaism, the Sunday of Christianity, and the Friday of Islam, are holy days, dedicated to the worship of a jealous monotheistic deity. Each recurs hebdomadally, and involves many taboos and prescribed services. The Day of Atonement of Judaism is associated with purificatory rites. The Lent of Christianity requires partial fasting during forty days, and the Ramadan of Islam requires complete fasting between sunrise and sundown during one lunar month, both of them being purificatory rites.

The sacred days or periods are in many cases seasonal. They may be associated with and celebrate the planting and harvesting of crops, the apparent turning of the sun in its annual course at the winter or summer solstice, the flooding of a river which causes fertility of the soil, as in the case of the Nile, the coming of the rainy season, the phases of the moon, or any other manifestation of nature which affects mankind for good or for bad. Each one is accompanied by appropriate rites which may be magical or religious or mixed in their origins. Some of them commemorate the mythology of a religion, as in the case of Holy Week, which celebrates the passion or sufferings and death of Jesus Christ and culminates in Easter which is the festival of his triumphant resurrection from death.

In fact, Christianity absorbed a large part of the pagan rites and festivals which preceded it. An instructive example is furnished by the fire festivals. Among them are Lent, Easter, Beltane (first of May in Scotland), Saint John's Eve (the midsummer solstice), Hallowe'en, Yule (the midwinter solstice), and the need-fire which may be utilized at any time to prevent a scourge. These festivals may have originated as imitative magic to insure that the sun would continue to furnish warmth and light. They became rites of worship when the sun had come to be regarded as a god. Or they may have originated as purificatory rites. In any case, at one time and another imitative magic, solar worship, and purification have been connected with these festivals. Two of them have become the most sacred of the Christian festivals. The one is Yule as the celebration of the legendary birth of Jesus Christ. The other is Easter as the celebration of his even more mythi-

221

cal resurrection from the dead. Lent also is observed by a large part of Christianity as a period of penitential fasting.

The cardinal Christian doctrine of vicarious atonement was derived from the primitive practice of transferring evil to a public scapegoat. Various magical methods were used to transfer evil conceived as vague maleficent forces or personified as malfeasant demons, to inanimate objects such as fetishes, to animals, or even to man. Sometimes these methods became public rites by which evils were expelled from the community. The public scapegoats might be animals, men, or even gods. In the Christian theology the man-god Jesus Christ has become the scapegoat for human ills by suffering and atoning vicariously for the sins of mankind.

As we have seen, it is impossible to determine whether a belief in impersonal forces which can be coerced preceded an anthropomorphic belief in personified spiritual beings which may be influenced if not coerced. Whichever of these animistic beliefs may have had the precedence in time, it is certain that the anthropomorphic conceptions extend a long way back. At an early date mankind began to personify the forces and some of the objects of nature, and to regard them as spirits or as inhabited by spirits. Thus arose the belief in the great spirits or gods of the sun, moon, stars, wind, rain, mountains, rivers, trees, and many other objects and forces of nature. While totemism in general was not a form of animal worship, some of the totemic animals were in course of time exalted into gods. As many of the forces of nature are maleficent in their effects upon mankind, there arose the belief in malevolent spirits or demons which often reside in human or animal bodies such as hobgoblins, witches, vampires, werewolves, etc. A belief in a great spirit of evil or a devil sometimes arose. Demonology and diabolism therefore constitute one aspect of nature worship in general. The worship of both benevolent and malevolent spirits probably gave rise in due course to the belief in an ethical dualism in the universe.

The processes of worship and of deification did not stop with non-human objects, but were extended sooner or later to certain human beings as well. The exaltation of heroes and leaders during their lifetimes and after has given rise to many eponymous heroes around whom have clustered numerous myths. To some of them was attributed a divine ancestry, and a certain number became gods. A large part of the pantheon of deities has been of human origin. According to the national epics some of them succeeded in defeating their rivals and became the gods of monotheistic religions. No religion can, however, become or continue to be monotheistic and spiritual in the sense that no material object is worshiped. Elements of demonology, diabolism, and of fetishism creep into every religion. The latter quickly develops into idolatry in one form or another. Even though an idol may at its inception be regarded as symbolical, it soon comes to be regarded in the minds of many of its devotees as the embodiment or the abode of a spirit. And even apart from overt idolatry, the concept of a spirit is inevitably anthropomorphic. Whether or not it is invested with arms and legs, it must feel, think, and have moral traits which are human and organic. A disembodied and immaterial mind, brain or heart is humanly inconceivable. In this sense all religion is idolatrous, even the most modern whose devotees labor under the delusion that their religion is wholly spiritual and fully purged of the crude idolatry of their barbarous ancestors. Despite their vain intellectual pretensions modern religionists are still wallowing in the barbarism of their paleolithic and neolithic ancestors.

Ancestor worship is a much more diffused and generalized form of worship of deceased human beings. In theory it includes the worship of all ancestors as such. In practice more reverence may be displayed toward one sex than the other, usually toward the male ancestors. Certain individual ancestors may be accorded an exceptional attention. But ancestor worship as such has rarely if ever resulted in deification. A deceased ancestor becomes a god in his capacity as a hero of some sort and not as an ancestor. Ancestor worship implies a belief in individual souls possessed by all human beings, or at least by one sex. In recent times it has been widespread among the Bantus of Africa, among many of the Melanesian tribes, in China, and in Japan where it was derived from China. It is connected with the belief in reincarnation in Africa, Melanesia, and Japan. This belief, to be discussed presently, was brought to Japan by Buddhism. Its provenance in Africa and Melanesia is not so easily traced.

When monocratic rule came into existence, divine traits were usually attributed to the monocrat, who may originally have been magician, priest, tribal chief, king, or a combination of two or more of these. Thus worship of a living human being originated and sometimes acquired great significance. It may have been due in part to the psychological tendency to attribute a supernatural character to anything that is exceptionally powerful. In many cases it was encouraged by the monocrat and his supporters in order to consolidate and perpetuate his power. It was one way in which theocratic rule came into existence. Another way was when the priesthood ruled in the name of a god in heaven or on earth. In these ways the identification of the human with the superhuman and the supernatural influenced social organization and social control. Until recently a divine or semi-divine character was attributed to many kings. Until the world war of 1939 to 1945 the Japanese mikado was venerated by his loyal subjects as the descendant of Amaterasu-omikami, the sun goddess. Devout Catholics believe that the Pope of Rome is inspired by God, and therefore infallible in all matters pertaining to the church. Recrudescent monocracy in Germany attributed semi-divinity to its dictator from 1933 to 1945. In this fashion does this belief become a bulwark of tyrannical rule.

The belief in souls possessed by and inhabiting many human beings or all of mankind preceded ancestor worship, hero worship, and the deification of men.[18] As we have seen, Tylor and Spencer thought that the belief in a human double arose out of the interpretation of dreams, and the observation of shadows and reflections. Whether the soul was regarded as a shadow or reflection, or as a manikin, and whatever may have been the origin of this belief, it has given rise to subsidiary animistic beliefs and many practices with regard to the individual soul. A necessary corollary is the belief in another existence after this mortal life is terminated. The Mousterian burials in which the corpse was furnished with food, tools, weapons, etc., indicate a belief in a life after death as far back as middle paleolithic time.

Arising out of both of these beliefs is the idea of reincarnation. According to this belief the soul may migrate from one human being to another, or to other animate beings, or even to inanimate objects. The transmigration of souls may be made qualitative in that the soul may rise to a higher or fall to a lower form of existence. Its fortunes in this regard may be influenced by rites of purification and of consecration. These rites may therefore have value not only for the present life but also for future lives. The soul regarded as a manikin may leave the body and return during this life, it may be deposited outside of the body for safety and then be recalled. According to this conception, it may be regarded as a somewhat etherealized form of matter. The ghost is a disembodied spirit which returns to its earlier corporeal haunts where it startles or terrifies its former bodily associates.

In another book I have discussed at some length the belief in metempsychosis or the transmigration of souls in India, its principal stronghold. The doctrine of metempsychosis is universally accepted. But it is not wholly satisfactory, because it involves effort if the individual is to attain to higher incarnations. Consequently, we find a doctrine of salvation by faith creeping into Hinduism, just as it has into many another religion, because it promises an easy way of attaining eternal bliss.

[18] With regard to religious theories of consciousness, I have said in another book: "Such theories are closely related to the religions doctrine of the soul and regard consciousness as something entirely distinct from matter. No such theory of consciousness can be regarded as scientific because there can be no inductive evidence of the existence of any such spiritual entity." (Maurice Parmelee, *The Science of Human Behavior*, New York, 1913, p. 282.)

The doctrine of metempsychosis, in some form or other, has been held by many primitive as well as civilized peoples. It has probably arisen spontaneously many times out of primitive animistic ideas which have made men feel a close kinship with animals and plants and even with inanimate objects. In India it takes the form of a cycle of existences whose ultimate goal is nirvana, or extinction through mergence with the infinite and absolute. This doctrine is akin to the maya doctrine, because it implies that this world is unreal, and its origin can perhaps be explained on similar grounds.

The doctrines of maya, metempsychosis, and nirvana lead naturally and inevitably to fatalism, because human destiny is preordained by whatever power or powers are conceived to preside over it. But fatalism is a doctrine which can never be wholly acceptable to human nature, which craves certain things too strongly to refrain entirely from trying to secure them. Yoga is an attempt to arrive at nirvana more speedily by skipping some of the reincarnations which may otherwise be necessary.

The belief in metempsychosis tends to break down the barrier between man and the remainder of the natural world. If the souls inhabiting human bodies also dwell at various stages in their careers in beasts, plants, and even inanimate objects, man may well have a feeling of close kinship with his organic and inorganic surroundings. It sometimes leads to an exaggerated form of Zoophilism. Some of the Buddhist sects kill no animals whatsoever. In accordance with the Indian doctrine of *ahimsa* (non-violence) many animals are not killed, but they are often left to starve to death.

These Oriental doctrines have led certain writers to opine that the East more than the West regards man as a component part of nature, and that the doctrine of the transmigration of souls encourages a feeling of unity with nature. Belief in the supernatural is even more widespread in the Orient, and anthropomorphism as prominent there as in the Occident. But the natural and the supernatural tend to be confused and to become merged into one another. So that in this sense the East has a feeling of an all-inclusive unity of the natural and the supernatural, of man and of nature. In this union the Oriental assumes in the main a fatalistic attitude of resignation toward these natural-supernatural powers which he little understands and has less hope of controlling. Among the common people these powers are usually personified, owing to the strong anthropomorphic tendency of the human mind everywhere, and gods and goddesses, fairies and hobgoblins abound throughout the Orient. In the intellectual class, however, especially in eastern Asia, belief in a personal deity is perhaps less strong than it is in the Occident, where the Jehovah-God-

225

Allah deity of Semitic origin, having vanquished other tribal gods, jealously maintains his monotheistic supremacy and monopoly.

In the West, on the other hand, science has been developing a new attitude toward nature. Based upon a much more extensive and accurate knowledge of natural phenomena has arisen a concept of a fundamental unity between man and nature which eliminates the supernatural by bringing all phenomena, human and non-human, animate and inanimate, under the same realm of law and order. Through an understanding of natural law man in the West has acquired a certain measure of control of the field of nature within his puny grasp and to this extent feels himself its master. To whatever he cannot control he endeavors to adapt himself, provided he does not become drunk with power and too arrogant in his attitude toward nature. The latter is perhaps exemplified in the cities of the Occident, monstrous creations by means of which mankind has been cut off almost entirely from nature, much to its injury. With this arrogance may be contrasted the supine yielding of the Orient to the forces of nature. The happy medium is somewhere between these two courses.

Many of the Westerners who are favorably disposed toward the East believe that the Occident has much to learn from Oriental religion. In its popular form religion is perhaps even more degraded in the East than in the West. In its more esoteric phases Oriental religion is more philosophic and less militant. While there is no evidence whatsoever for life other than our present mundane existence, if such a life is postulated the Oriental conception of it is on the whole more logical and humane. Christianity and Islam each professes belief in a deity who is responsible for both good and evil in the universe and who creates both good and bad souls. Thus God and Allah each is to blame for the illogical and unjust fate of the bad soul, which the deity has created.

The Oriental religions have not attained to the same grotesque extreme of ethical dualism. The Indian religions teach the doctrine of reincarnation, and through the spread of Buddhism this belief has reached eastern Asia. According to this doctrine the individual soul is eternal, and must attain its own salvation by working its way up from a lower to a higher plane. While Confucianism does not include a belief in reincarnation, its central doctrine of the self-development of the superior man is somewhat akin to this phase of the doctrine of reincarnation and encourages self-reliance and an austere self-discipline. From a scientific point of view the eternal soul of the doctrine of reincarnation is no more plausible than the immortal soul created by a Semitic deity. But Oriental religion may be able to temper somewhat the harshness and crudity of Christian and Moslem theology and render it a more satisfactory sedative for the many who are not yet

226

prepared in mind and character to accept the scientific conception of the universe.[19]

Certain individuals have devoted special efforts to purifying and consecrating themselves. A common method has been asceticism or denying the body some of the things which it craves, such as food and sex relations. The flesh is thereby purified and mortified at the same time, and the spirit is thereby exalted. Eremitism and monasticism deprive the individual of most of the joys of normal social life, and are usually accompanied by celibacy and a good deal of fasting. All of these methods are purported to promote spiritual perfection, and to bring the devotee close to the sacred. Mysticism includes all kinds of attempts to reach beyond and outside of bodily existence, and to perceive the supernatural world. Through some or all of these methods may be attained sainthood. This is a state of holiness in this life.

Animism has given rise to the professions of the magician and of the priest. While every one can perform at least some of the magical and religious practices, those who were proficient in the art of magic became the magicians to whom the community turned for assistance when seeking the aid of magic. The most primitive religious rites had no priests and temples. The priests probably were originally persons who were credited with exceptional powers, either as agents of more or less impersonal forces, such as manitou, orenda, atua or mana, or as representatives of personified spiritual beings. Thus the profession of priesthood came to be regarded as holy, and usually was accompanied by various taboos. Shrines and temples became sanctuaries because they also were and still are reputed to be sacred and holy places.

The functions of magician and of priest were often mingled in the same person. As the magic art declined, and religion gained the ascendancy, the priest supplanted the magician. Priests still perform many functions which are primarily magical in their character. Among the arts long practised by priests is that of divination through contact with supernatural sources. Many methods of divination have been used, such as the questioning of oracles, the reading of omens by means of scapulimancy, haruspicy, etc., astrology, and crystal gazing.[20] Nearly every sermon by priest or parson professes to be more or

[19] Maurice Parmelee, *Oriental and Occidental Culture, An Interpretation,* New York and London, 1928, pages 36, 64, 205-207, 364-365.

[20] Scapulimancy or omoplastoscopy is divination by means of the shoulder-blade. Haruspication or haruspicy is divination by the haruspex (Latin, priest-soothsayer) through inspection of the entrails of sacrificed animals. Astromancy, still very prevalent the world over, is foretelling the future by reading the stars. Omens have been derived from the flight of birds, the arrangement of the clouds, the falling of lots through the casting of dice or other numbered objects. Numerology, or the reading of fortunes through the combination of numbers, is still much used. In the

227

less prophetic. The notion of the priesthood that it is in contact with the supernatural and possesses revealed knowledge creates the priestly delusion of insight into the future, which incites it to mislead the public to an even greater degree than by preaching the doctrines and dogmas of religion.

Proselytizing is a function of the priests of the universal religions. The principal missionary religions have been Buddhism, Christianity, and Islam. This is largely because they, or at least the two latter, profess to be monotheistic religions whose deities claim the right to rule over the whole of mankind, and accuse all other deities of being spurious or evil.

It often happened that magicians became tribal chiefs and kings. Among many African peoples the king was the rain-maker. In other words, he was the magician who professed to be able to bring rain. If the king failed as a magician, he might be punished or even killed. In some cases, the magician-king developed into the priest-king, who might also come to be regarded as an incarnate human god. The sacred kingship probably attained its most extreme form in the monarchies of ancient Egypt and Peru. The life of the sacred king was regulated by many taboos, so that no act of his would disarrange the order of nature. These taboos often prevented the king from actually ruling. Eventually the spiritual functions were divorced from the temporal, and the civil and religious aspects of the kingship were divided. This was the situation in Japan for several centuries. While the Mikado performed religious ceremonies in Kyoto, the Shogun ruled the country from Tokio. At the time of the restoration in 1867, the Mikado regained his temporal power. Since that time he has been liberated from many taboos.

There have been departmental kings of nature, divine or semi-divine in repute, who professed to rule over various aspects of nature because of their attainments as magicians. Some of these kings ruled temporarily while their magical powers appeared to last. Sometimes a divine king was killed before his powers became weak, so that the control over nature would not be relaxed. A competent successor had already been chosen to take his place, so that the soul of the dying king-god would pass to him. In some cases the sacrifice of a human god led to sacramental cannibalism. His worshippers ate his body in order to acquire his physical, moral, and intellectual traits. In other cases, the human god was not eaten, because he was regarded as too sacred for this purpose. Or it may be more accurate to say because

Occident the commonest method of reading fortunes is by means of playing cards. Most of this fortune telling and soothsaying is now done by persons who are not priests, but who claim special skill in the art of divination. Hence they have something of the character of magicians.

of the taboos which applied to him. The same diversity of practice has been illustrated with regard to totemic or other sacred animals. Some of them were revered because they were eaten. Others of them were not eaten because they were regarded as too sacred. It is probable that most if not all of the animals which have been regarded as too unclean to be eaten were originally sacred animals which were not eaten because of the taboos attached to them. Some of these taboos persisted long after the myth of their divinity had been forgotten.

Trees are objects in nature to which spirits have often been attributed. The trees have been regarded as the bodies of the spirits, or as their abodes. Human beings have sometimes personified the spirits of the trees. Many of the rites associated with these spirits have been for the purpose of insuring the revival of nature in the spring. As already indicated, the myths of Osiris, Tammuz, Adonis, Attis, and Melgart, called for a man-god who annually died and was resurrected, thus representing and symbolizing the yearly decay and revival of life. There was often connected with these myths a myth of a great mother goddess who personified the reproductive forces of nature. Osiris, or each of his counterparts, was presented sometimes as the son, sometimes as the divine lover of the mother goddess. To Osiris was also attributed the goddess Isis who was regarded sometimes as his sister, sometimes as his wife. The annual resurrection of Osiris was a pledge of eternal life for the Egyptian people.

The sacred marriage, namely, the sexual union of gods, is one instance of the widespread use of sex in sympathetic magic. It has been generally believed that sex relations have great influence upon vegetation. Often it has been believed that the growth of plants is stimulated by sexual intercourse or its simulation. Elsewhere it has been believed that sexual continence accomplished the same end, because the strength thus conserved flowed into the vegetation. Chastity was also often practised by warriors in order to help them win, by hunters and fishers for similar reasons, etc.

The preceding survey demonstrates the great diversity and often contradictory nature of magical and religious practices, even when the fundamental animistic beliefs and ideas underlying them have been alike. This is well illustrated in the innumerable taboos which have existed, many of which still survive and play a potent part in social control. Among the taboos on persons have been those upon strangers, because they may possess magical powers; upon chiefs and kings, because they are believed to be charged with magical or spiritual power; upon warriors who are in spiritual danger from their alive or dead enemies; upon manslayers who may be haunted by the ghosts of their victims; upon hunters and fishers who may be haunted by the spirits of the animals which they have killed; upon mourners and others who come in contact with the dead whose ghosts may come back to haunt the living; upon women at menstruation and childbirth who are polluted by the catamenial and puerperal flow of blood; and various other categories of persons who are temporarily or permanently under taboos for everyone or for certain persons to whom they are related by blood, marriage, profession, status, or otherwise.

Magicians and priests are very likely to be under some degree of taboo, because of the supernatural powers which they possess, or with which they are in contact. Many words also are tabooed, because they are the names of kings and other sacred persons and of gods, all of whom are presumed to have spiritual powers; or personal names which constitute parts of the persons themselves; or names of relations; or names of the dead whose ghosts are feared; etc.; etc.

Many material things have been tabooed. Among them have been both sacred and unclean objects, which are alike in being dangerous, and often alike in being in danger. Blood has been tabooed, because it may contain a soul or other spirit; the head, because it may contain a spirit; sharp weapons after a death, because they may wound the ghost of the deceased; the hair, finger and toe nails, and spittle, which are difficult of disposal, and may be used by magical devices to injure the persons from whom they came; knots and rings, which involve the danger of being tied up and bound; various little known things, such as iron among primitive peoples, because of their novelty; and various foods through which may be acquired the undesirable traits of the animals or plants from whence they are derived.

There have been many taboos connected with food. Under certain conditions eating and drinking have been forbidden, because the soul may escape through the mouth. On the other hand, showing the face at certain times has been forbidden, because evil spirits may enter. It has often been forbidden to leave superfluous food, because it may be utilized against the eater by magical methods. On the other hand, eating food together, or transfusing blood, has often been regarded as establishing a sympathetic spiritual bond.

A cursory survey of animistic beliefs and practices conveys an impression of a welter of confusion and of conflict. Little or no order is at first apparent. The confusion of thought thus arising has been greatly accentuated by the numerous attempts at a teleological interpretation. For example, Frazer, who accumulated a vast mass of data concerning magic and religion, alleged that they have strengthened respect for life, government, property, marriage, and sexual morality, and have thereby increased security.[21] Perhaps as much can be said

---

[21] J. G. Frazer, *Psyche's Task*, 2nd edition, London, 1913.

for the contrary allegation. In any case, it is not necessarily to be assumed *a priori* that the right of private property, the sort of marriage which Frazer favored, and sexual morality as he conceived it, a wholly subjective conception, are worthy of respect. In similar fashion, Kidd alleged that religion has furnished an essential "ultra-rational sanction" for morality for which allegation there is not the slightest evidence.[22] In another work Frazer contended that Oriental religions turned mankind away from the public good to the salvation of the individual soul, thus contributing to the downfall of Greece and Rome, and that a reaction commenced in the middle ages and still continues against Oriental religions.[23]

While there is a modicum of historical truth in this contention, as illustrated in some of the individualistic features of Christianity, Frazer's presentation of it is much too tendencious. Magic and religion, and increasingly the latter during the later stages of cultural evolution, have furnished most pervasive sanctions for conduct, in particular through the promise of supernatural rewards and the threat of divine penalties. In addition to the fact that these claims are wholly invalid, these promises and threats are usually destined to maintain the domination of predatory individuals and classes upon their subject victims. Even some scientists are influenced by animistic beliefs. They must free themselves from intimidation by these minatory aspects of animism before they can describe and interpret these phenomena objectively.[24]

---

[22] Benjamin Kidd, *Social Evolution*, London, 1894.

[23] J. G. Frazer, *The Golden Bough, A Study in Magic and Religion*, New York, 1922.

[24] "Hell fire as a punishment for sin is a doctrine of cruelty. . . . Science can teach us . . . no longer to look around us for imaginary support . . . or to invent imaginary allies in the sky, but to look to our own efforts to make this a fit place to live in." (Bertrand Russell, *Why I Am Not a Christian*, New York, 1957.)

Chapter XVI

Sex, Marriage and the Family

NO aspect of human nature has been a greater mystery to man than his sexual nature. Connected with sex are powerful feelings and physiological processes which are difficult to explain. At the time of puberty and adolescence there develop most of the secondary sexual traits. At the same time come to fruition the sexual passions which give rise to some of the keenest sensations experienced by mankind. These impulses constitute one of the principal dynamic elements in human nature. With puberty there arrive at maturity the processes involved in the sex relation, which have already appeared in an adumbrated form during childhood. For the human female there begins at this time the catamenial function or menstruation. After conception comes pregnancy and then parturition.

These physiological and psychological transformations, largely connected with sex, were early noted by mankind. Many primitive peoples celebrated them by ceremonies aptly called *"les rites de passage"* in the French language. Many of the rites concerned the advent of puberty and adolescence for both sexes, and, soon after, the initial sexual union. Some of these ceremonies have persisted down to the present day. Corresponding with or related to transformations arose certain institutions. Some of them were concerned with the rearing of the young. The most prevalent had to do with the relations between the sexes. It is impossible to ascertain the form or forms taken by the sex relationship in the early stages of cultural evolution. Conjecture ranges all the way from complete promiscuity to strict monogamy. The truth probably lies somewhere between these two extreme theories, but may approach closer to the theory of promiscuity than to the theory of monogamy.

Against the theory of complete promiscuity it is argued that the rearing of the young required the care of the male as well as of the female parent, so that unions between individuals of the two sexes

232

must have been of some duration. There are reasons for thinking that the hominidae, like some of the primates to which they are closely related and many of the carnivorous species, are relatively non-gregarious. They may have lived in the earlier stages of cultural evolution in small family groups rather than in large communal groups. In the latter case, the young may have been reared by the group in common, as is true of many of the gregarious herbivorous species, so that the care of the individual parent, or, at least, of both parents, would not be necessary. However, it seems likely that individual care by the mother was always the general rule, at least through the period of suckling, while the infant depended upon its mother's milk for nourishment and the mother needed the relief of being sucked.

It is also argued that another limitation upon promiscuity was the powerful emotion of jealousy, which may have characterized man as it apparently characterizes some of the higher mammals. This emotion leads the male to try to monopolize the female or females of whom he has gained possession. It is possible that this trait evolved because of its survival value for the rearing of the young, since it furnishes a strong bond to hold the parents together. Jealousy and the necessity of rearing the young would be powerful forces for more or less permanent unions.[1] As to whether these were monogamous or polygynous unions, it is impossible to say. The numerical equality of the sexes must have been a strong factor for monogamy. The stronger males may have been able to gain possession of more than one female apiece.

The contrasted view to the above is that the hominidae lived in communal groups in which the young were cared for by the group in common. Those holding this view do not usually regard jealousy as a primitive trait or emotion, but rather as a secondary trait or sentiment which arose out of the sense of ownership after the women had acquired an economic value. Numerous facts indicate much promiscuity in the earlier stages of cultural development. Among these are the records of observers of many primitive peoples which indicate that promiscuity before marriage, and sometimes after marriage, was customary. Such institutions as group marriage, sexual hospitality, the *jus primae noctis*, sacred prostitution as an expiation for

[1] Among the writers who have expounded this point of view, or whose writings pointed in this direction, are the following: Charles Darwin, *The Descent of Man and Selection in Relation to Sex*, London, 1871, 2 vols.; Andrew Lang, *Social Origins*, and J. J. Atkinson, *The Primal Law*, London, 1903; E. Westermarck, *The History of Human Marriage*, London, 1891; N. W. Thomas, *Kinship Organizations and Group Marriage in Australia*, Cambridge, Eng., 1906; B. Malinowski, *The Family Among the Australian Aborigines*, London, 1913.

marriage, and other savage and barbaric customs may be vestiges of an earlier state of promiscuity.[2]

There is some biological and psychological evidence which indicates that sexual jealousy was an original and primary trait of man. This innate human trait has been accentuated and complicated by the development of the sense and concept of ownership as a secondary trait. Sexual jealousy as an original trait would, however, not be incompatible with a considerable amount of promiscuity. Until a female had been permanently appropriated by a male, she might have promiscuous relations. Hartland has presented an extensive array of facts with respect to the widespread practice of sexual liberty, not only among the unmarried, but often among the married as well. Upon these facts he based his theory that jealousy is not an original human trait but has arisen out of the sense of ownership.[3]

Some of the writers who hold the theory of jealousy as an original human trait admit that promiscuity has been widespread at many times and places. Westermarck, who held this theory, cited many such instances of promiscuity in his history of human marriage.[4] Malinowski, who was a follower of Westermarck, also recognized the influence of the sense of ownership.[5]

Whatever may have been the situation among early men, all forms of sex relationship have existed and still exist among the peoples of whom we have records. These include promiscuity, group marriage, polygyny, polyandry, and monogamy. Various combinations of these forms also exist. Promiscuity before marriage may exist

[2] Among the writers who have furnished data which have supported in one way or another this point of view are the following: L. H. Morgan, *Ancient Society*, New York, 1877; J. F. McLennan, *Studies in Ancient History*, London, 1876; W. Robertson Smith, *Kinship and Marriage in Early Arabia*, London, 1903; B. Spencer and F. J. Gillen, *The Native Tribes of Central Aristralia*, London, 1899, *The Northern Tribes of Central Australia*, London, 1904; A. W. Howitt, *The Native Tribes of South-East Australia*, London, 1904.

[3] "The wide prevalence of the opposite practice, namely, the sexual liberty recognized as the right of the unmarried both male and female, may be regarded as evidence of the small social importance attached to the gratification of the sexual instincts apart from the limitations imposed by the sense of ownership and the consequent growth of the ideal of chastity. The sense of ownership has been the seed-plot of jealousy. To it we are indebted for the first germ of sexual relations." (E. S. Hartland, *Primitive Paternity*, London, 1910, regulations Vol. II, pp. 102-103.)

[4] E. Westermarck, *op. cit.*

[5] "The idea of the individual sexual over-right and control over his wife is strongly present in the aboriginal mind. This right is undoubtedly realized as a privilege, and the natural tendency to keep his privileges for himself, or dispose of them according to his wish or interest, must create a strong opposition to any encroachment. In other words, the sexual act has its intrinsic value, and it is considered as an unquestionable advantage. And the right to this advantage constitutes a kind of private property." (B. Malinowski, *op. cit.*, pp. 126-127.)

for both sexes or for the male sex alone, accompanied by strict prohibition of promiscuity after marriage for both sexes or for the female alone. Or strict prohibition of promiscuity before marriage may exist for both sexes or for the female alone, accompanied by a certain amount of promiscuity after marriage for both sexes or for the male alone. There has been more liberty on the whole for the male than for the female, thereby giving rise to a double standard of sex freedom which has had a considerable influence upon sex regulation.

The general tendency has probably been away from promiscuity and toward monogamy. Jealousy, not only on the part of the male, but also upon the part of the female who resents the existence of other wives or sweethearts; the necessity of caring for the offspring, and parental affection for their young; the numerical equality of the sexes; the desirability of providing a tested companionship for old age; and the establishment of a social order in the place of individual power encourage these tendencies. The development of human personality may also have aided these tendencies in some ways, though in other respects it has probably been a force for greater freedom.

Reproduction as well as sex seemed inexplicable to primitive man. The physical relation between father and offspring was not recognized until comparatively late in cultural evolution. Traces of attempts to explain the pregnancy of the mother are to be found in the totemic beliefs still extant among some primitive peoples, in myths of supernatural birth and metempsychosis, and in metronymic and patronymic ideas and practices. Supernatural and mythical explanations of reproduction were inevitable until scientific knowledge had been acquired of the causal relation between sex and reproduction.[6]

The sexual function in woman was especially mysterious to early man. This was probably the chief reason for the development of a suspicious attitude toward the female on the part of the human male. The most striking feature of the female sexual function is the flow of blood in connection with puberty (the hymenal flow), the periodic catamenial function (the menstrual flow), and parturition (the puerperal flow). This may have been the principal cause for the notion, still more or less prevalent, that sex is unclean, especially in women.[7] This notion of the uncleanness of sex led to many sexual taboos to guard

[6] Many primitive explanations of reproduction in the absence of a knowledge of physiological paternity are given in E. S. Hartland, *Primitive Paternity, The Myth of Supernatural Birth in Relation to the History of the Family*, London, 1909-1910, 2 vols.

[7] See, for example, J. G. Frazer, *Balder the Beautiful*, London, 1913, Vol. I, Chap. 2, "Seclusion of girls at puberty"; *Taboo and the Perils of the Soul*, London, 1911, Chap. 4, "Tabooed persons," Sec. 3, "Women tabooed at menstruation and childbirth."

against the contagion of this uncleanness.[8] It has also played a part in the establishment of many exogamous and endogamous regulations of the sex relation, some of which still persist in the form of prohibitions against incest.[9]

Sex has played an important part in magic. Owing to a false analogy between sexual acts and the growth of vegetation, sex has often been regulated on the principle of homeopathic or imitative magic in order to insure a good harvest.[10] Sex has also played an important part in religion, perhaps even more important than in magic. Phallic worship has existed at many times and places. Sex has been attributed to anthropomorphic deities. Sacred prostitution has played its part in the worship of these deities.[11] In the attempt to propitiate deities has arisen the ascetic ideal of foregoing sexual pleasures in order to expiate sin and to attain purification.[12]

The Christian religion derived mainly from Judaism, which contains many of these magical and religious ideas with respect to sex. The notion of the uncleanness of sex plays a prominent part in the Hebrew religion. A considerable portion of the Jewish law is devoted to the regulation of sex with respect to its uncleanness. The following passages from the Old Testament illustrate this part of the Jewish law. *Leviticus* XV describes the uncleanness of the sexual issues of men and of women, and prescribes how they are to be cleansed. This passage reveals the notion of the greater sexual uncleanness of woman, and of how man may be defiled by her uncleanness. *Leviticus* XII specifies how women are to be purified after childbirth. It reveals the inferior position of women, and the belief in the greater uncleanness of sex in women, because it was more defiling to give birth to a female child than to a male child.

In the Christian religion these ideas, acquired from Judaism, developed into a form of asceticism which exalted celibacy. For example, in *Revelation* XIV, 4, it is said: "These are they which were not defiled with women; for they are virgins." Throughout the

---

[8] See E. Crawley, *The Mystic Rose, A Study of Primitive Marriage*, London, 1902. Descriptions of many of the rites connected with sex are given in A. van Gennep, *Les rites de passage*, Paris, 1909.

[9] See, for example, L. H. Morgan, *op. cit.*; J. F. McLennan, *op. cit.*; W. Robertson Smith, *op cit.*

[10] See, for example, J. G. Frazer, *The Magic Art*, London, 1911, Vol. II, Chap. 11, "The influence of the sexes on vegetation."

[11] See, for example, J. G. Frazer, *Adonis, Attis, Osiris*, London, 1907, Chap. 4, "Sacred men and women"; E. S. Hartland, *Ritual and Belief*, London, 1914, essay entitled "The Rite at the Temple of Mylitta."

[12] *Cf.* E. Westermarck, *The Origin and Development of the Moral Ideas*, London, 1908, Vol. II, Chap. 39. "In various religions we meet with the idea that a person appeases or gives pleasure to the deity by subjecting himself to suffering or deprivation. This belief finds expression in all sorts of ascetic practices." (P. 356.)

236

New Testament the dominant theme with respect to sex is that sex is unclean; that virginity and chastity are highly meritorious; that the flesh, by which is usually meant sex, is antagonistic to the spirit; and that marriage is a grudging and questionable concession to the flesh.[13]

The pristine Christian attitude toward sex is stated in the Pauline epistle, I *Corinthians,* VII: "It is good for a man not to touch a woman. Nevertheless, to avoid fornication, let every man have his own wife, and let every woman have her own husband. . . . I say therefore to the unmarried and widows, It is good for them if they abide even as I. But if they cannot contain, let them marry: for it is better to marry than to burn." The utterances of the greatest apostle of Christianity, Paul, did much to establish this ascetic doctrine in the Christian religion, and thereby to carry it into Occidental culture.[14]

In addition to the types of marriage mentioned in an earlier paragraph are successive marriage, and cousin marriage. In the former mating is first with the old in order to secure sexual education, and then with those of the same age. Cousin marriage is usually cross and not parallel. Cross marriage is with the offspring of the father's sister or the mother's brother. Parallel marriage is with the offspring of the father's brother or the mother's sister. Most or all types of marriage limit the range of choice for sex relations and mating. In the earlier stages of cultural evolution the predominant reason for such limitations probably was to maintain certain groupings based on kinship: "As Tylor indicated, savage matrimony is preponderantly a means for cementing group alliances between families or clans according to the social organization."[15] Kinship as a basis for social organization will be discussed in the following chapter.

Economic considerations, arising out of the division of labor between the sexes, have had much influence upon marriage and family organization. In fact, it is probably true that marriage arose almost invariably out of property relations. The economic value of the girl to be given or taken in marriage has given rise in many societies

[13] For a discussion of asceticism in Judaism, Christianity, Islam, and other religions, see W. G. Sumner, *Folkways,* Boston, 1907, Chap. 18.

See also, for a discussion of the Christian ascetic doctrine, E. Westermarck, *op. cit.,* Vol. II: "For a nation like the Jews, whose ambition was to live and to multiply, celibacy could never become an ideal; whereas the Christians, who professed the most perfect indifference to all earthly matters, found no difficulty in glorifying a state which, however opposed it was to the interests of the race and the nation, made men pre-eminently fit to approach their god." (P. 420.)

[14] In another book I have discussed at length many subjects relating to sex, among them being sexual jealousy, sex regulation, sex repression, the double standard of sex freedom, asceticism, prostitution, sex education, etc. (Maurice Parmelee, *Personality and Conduct,* New York, 1918.)

[15] R. H. Lowie, article on "Marriage," in the *Encyclopedia of the Social Sciences,* Vol. X, New York, 1933.

to bride purchase and patrilocal residence. Polygyny often reflects the rank and wealth of the husband in addition to or apart from whatever economic value the work of the multiple wives may have for the polygynous husband. In certain societies, as some of the modern industrialized societies, in which the economic value of the woman has become relatively small, the dowry has come into existence in order to induce the wary suitor to assume the responsibility for the care and support of a wife who has little economic value. However, the dowry existed prior to the rise of modern industry, as in some of the agrarian societies.

Female dominance has arisen usually, if not almost invariably, owing to the invention and practice of horticulture. The cultivation of plants necessitates a sessile society. In many of the earlier societies agriculture was almost entirely in the hands of the women. These two conditions placed the balance of power in the hands of the women in a few societies. In no such society did female dominance persist indefinitely or even for a long time. Superior male strength, the incapacitation of women owing to pregnancy and the catamenial function, and attacks from outside the society either by hostile men or savage beasts necessitating defense by the men, have usually sufficed to maintain male dominance in the long run. Many agricultural societies have been subjugated by pastoral and nomadic peoples which have never tended toward a gynaecocratic form of society. In modern times agriculture has become mechanized which has put it largely in male hands.

Monogamy usually prevailed in primitive societies which were democratically constituted, and in which the natural sex ratio had not been disturbed by warfare or any other destructive factor. The pristine, unconscious, and unintended democracy of primitive men rapidly disappeared as soon as exploitation and a class system made their appearance. As already indicated, polygyny sometimes appears as a mark of rank and wealth in a class society. But the approximate equality of the sexes is a powerful and permanent factor for monogamy. In the long run monogamy is the sanctioned mode of marriage even in class societies. The dominant class mitigates for itself the sternness of the monogamic dispensation by permitting and promoting concubinage. This is an institution fully authorized and sanctioned by the law and the prevailing ethical standards in certain societies, as at present in a few Oriental countries. In the Occident it no longer exists legally. It is nevertheless prevalent in the upper classes in a covert and more or less illicit form.

Concubinage has been defined as "marriage dissociated from juridic functions, more particularly in regard to property and succession. . . . The term may also be applied to secondary unions con-

238

tracted conjointly with regular marriage." [16] There are two forms which should be distinguished from each other. In the first meaning, concubinage, more or less sanctioned by law, has been widespread among the lower classes who are too poor to marry, or for whom, owing to their poverty, the property and succession rights guaranteed by marriage have no value and significance. In the English common law, and later in some of the United States, this form of sexual union was recognized for a time under the term "common law marriage." In the second meaning, concubinage, whether legal or illegal, can be prevalent only among the upper classes whose male members can afford to maintain more than one woman.

The combination of juridical monogamy with legal concubinage is transitional between polygyny in which the multiple wives are on a legal and social equality, and a system of monogamy which recognizes only one legal sex union. In the course of this transition concubinage is transformed from a legal and ethical form of union to an illegal, illicit, and immoral union. This transformation has taken place fully in Occidental society. There is little likelihood of a reversion to concubinage in the second meaning of the term, namely, reverting to a multiplicity of wives and-quasi-wives. On the other hand, the concept of individual economic independence for both sexes, now widespread in modern industrialized society, has weakened the legal basis for the distinction between juridical marriage and concubinage in the first meaning of the term, namely, sex union without legal sanction.

The biological family, arising out of the helplessness of the young during a more or less prolonged infancy which results in parental care, exists most often among the birds and mammals. It has never existed outside of the vertebrates. Its essential and unique feature is the living together of one or both parents with their offspring during the infancy of the latter. This association does not continue necessarily after the young have attained adulthood. The communal care of the young among certain insects, such as the ants, bees, wasps, and termites, does not create a family. This is true, among other things, because there is no recognition of individual offspring by their parents. The biological family of the birds and mammals falls short of being a family as a form of social organization or as an institution. During childhood it furnishes a little association with siblings and a little knowledge acquired from parents. It does not necessarily lead to association continued into and throughout adulthood. In fact, among the predatory animals this association almost invariably ceases as soon as the young are able to shift for themselves. Hence the first

[16] Robert Briffault, article on "Concubinage," in the *Encyclopedia of the Social Sciences*, Vol. IV, New York, 1931.

requisite for developing social forms out of the biological family, namely, continuous association, is lacking. However, this is only one of several requisites. There are many gregarious species whose members live in association with each other throughout their lives in family or larger groups which have developed none of the social forms, or, if at all, only in a rudimentary state.

In order that the biological family shall develop into the socialized family, it is essential that the kinship relationship be recognized and remembered throughout life, and that it shall be regarded as a bond of union between the members of a social group. As to the early human stages of this development, we can only conjecture. The concept of kinship could not originate until after language had developed to a considerable degree. Whether or not relations and bonds based on kinship made their appearance as between families living in isolation, and with only occasional and casual contacts with each other, we can never know. It seems more plausible to assume that these social phenomena first made their appearance within a horde made up of several families, and where speech already furnished a means of communication and a tool for the formulation of concepts. The most that we can do is to enumerate the types of kinship relationships and bonds which have existed among preliterate peoples which have been observed, and those which have persisted among literate peoples and during the historical period. It is doubtful if the primordial biological family persisted into the historical period in any part of the world. At any rate, it has not been observed and studied. Many types of the socialized family have existed among preliterate peoples and peoples of a literate culture. Each of these types has existed within a larger social group, and its character has been molded by this group. It can be studied most profitably in its setting in the larger social group. This will now be done with regard to several historical peoples and countries.

In China what is called the family is rather the greater-family.[17] According to Confucian doctrine, which systematized the theory and rules of Chinese social organization, a newly married pair is not a distinct and independent entity, as it is in the Occident. Usually it becomes a part of the husband's household under the rule of his father, the bride coming largely under the domination of her mother-

---

[17] "The Chinese family is seldom an independent unit, but a member of the greater-family. In the Chinese village, families bearing the same surname live together. The members of the greater-family generally number hundreds and sometimes thousands. They have a common ancestral temple which is the center of their social and religious life." (Ching-chao Wu, "The Chinese Family: Organization, Names, and Kinship Terms," in the *American Anthropologist*, July-September 1927, Vol. XXIX, No. 3, p. 316.)

in-law. When a household breaks up on account of the death of the father, or because it has become too unwieldy, or for any other reason, the kinship relations with the greater family are retained. The family is ruled by the family, the greater-family by a board of elders.

The greater-family is said to be stronger in southern China, where life is more settled than in the north. This type of social organization cannot maintain itself in a migratory population. The strong desire of the Chinese to be buried at home, due to their family sentiment, causes unequal distribution of population, because it is difficult to induce the inhabitants of the densely populated provinces to migrate to the thinly settled regions, such as Manchuria and Mongolia. Attempts at colonization have been hampered by this sentiment in favor of home burial.

The life of the greater-family centers around its temple, where a tablet of wood is placed for each member upon his death. The ancestors of the family are worshiped on certain festivals and family anniversaries. Owing to the overwhelming importance of ancestor worship, domestic religion is much stronger than personal religion. This accounts in part for the tolerance and catholicity of the Chinese in matters of religion, and their secular attitude toward many phases of life. Mysticism is not likely to proliferate under such conditions. The board of elders manages the affairs of the temple and administers the funds of the greater-family. It has a certain amount of judicial authority to settle disputes between family households, and to impose punishments, such as reproof and expulsion from the ancestral temple, and sometimes more drastic penalties.

Owing to the great importance of family relationships, and the varying significance of relationship to older and younger relatives, and through male and female ascendants, there are many more kinship terms in Chinese than in European languages. For example, there are five terms for uncle—namely, father's older brother, father's younger brother, husband of father's sister, mother's brother, and husband of mother's sister. The predominance of the family is emphasized also by placing the family name before the personal name, in contrast to the European custom of placing the surname last.

Everywhere and at all times the older is likely to be more influential than the younger generation. This is because of its superior knowledge and experience, and also because it has a long start over the younger generation. The power of the ascendants over their descendants is accentuated where the family system prevails, especially if accompanied by ancestor worship. The patriarchal authority tends also to increase the power of the males over the females. Marriage is enjoined upon every one as a duty, in order to perpetuate the family, and to breed descendants to worship at the shrine of the venerated

241

ancestors. Polygyny may be encouraged when the wife is childless by taking another wife, or a concubine, in order to secure offspring. Overpopulation may also result from the inordinate desire for children.

The situation in China at present, or in the recent past, before the Collectivist Revolution of 1949, is revealed by the legal status of the family and of marriage. According to Chinese jurisprudence, as reflected in the decisions of the supreme court, a man cannot share in the wealth of his family, or set up a separate establishment, without the consent of all of his surviving parents and grandparents. The consent of parents and grandparents is also required to invalidate a marriage. More or less elaborate betrothal and marriage ceremonies are prescribed. The institution of concubinage is recognized by the law. In case of destitution, the duty of support exists between father and son, grandfather and grandson, brothers, and husband and wife. The cult of the worship of the ancestors, and the inheritance of most of the family wealth, are transmitted through the male descendants.

Divorce may take place by mutual consent. But a recent civil code provides that if the husband is under thirty, or the wife under twenty-five, the consent of his or her parents, as the case may be, is also required. The seven ancient causes for the repudiation of a wife are still recognized, namely, childlessness, wanton conduct, neglect of duty toward her husband's parents, loquacity, thievishness, jealousy, and a grave disease. Exceptions are made when the wife has mourned for three years for the parents of her husband, when her husband has risen from poverty to riches, and when the wife no longer has a family to which she can return. Adultery on the part of the wife is probably the most frequent cause of divorce, because it is most fatal to the existence of the family.

Prior to the restoration of the Mikado in 1867, Japan was divided into 262 fiefs ruled by the daimyos or feudal lords, exclusive of the land belonging to the shogun. These feudal clans were unlike the Chinese greater-family, which has at no time been feudal or military. Ancestor worship has not existed, except to the slight extent that it has been imitated from China. Shinto is ancestor worship only to the extent of worshiping the sun goddess Amaterasu Omikami as the ancestress of the imperial family. The family as an institution has, nevertheless, been and is powerful. The authority of the father is great. The family ideal is to have many children to honor their parents and to work for them. This is the chief cause of overpopulation in Nippon. The position of the Japanese woman is somewhat similar to that of the Chinese woman. But nationalism is much stronger in Japan than in China. Patriotism encroaches somewhat upon family sentiment and loyalty. The impact of Occidental indus-

242

trialism has been greater upon Japan than upon China. This has been an influence somewhat disturbing to family relationships.

Hindu social organization is or was until recently dominated by the caste system, to be described in the following chapter. Within the barriers of caste the family plays a very important part. The greater-family is not formally organized as in China. But households often contain several related families and generations. A joint family system is widespread which assumes responsibility for the welfare of every member. It may also encourage idleness on the part of the more indolent, and sometimes leads to family dissension.[18]

The home is a religious center in India to a greater degree than in any other country. Even the building of a house is governed by religious rules. The preparation of the food, and much of the household work, is often accompanied by a ritual. The morning and evening prayers are more or less obligatory, and elaborate ceremonies required. Hindu religion, which embraces the whole of life, and is strongly personal as well as domestic, makes of the home a veritable sanctuary. While a Chinese home contains a shrine to the ancestors, no one of the religions of China has the personal and all-pervasive character of Hindu religion.

The influence of the woman in the Indian home is said to be very great. The same is probably true in China and in other Oriental countries. Whether or not it is greater than in the Occident, it is difficult to determine. Her career is restricted to the home much more than that of her Western sister. Her devotion to her husband is also said to be strong. It was symbolized in the past by the practice of suttee (cremation of the widow on her husband's funeral pyre), and at present by the degradation of the widow.

Hindu home life has an unusual degree of intimacy.[19] Indians have sometimes asserted that this is due to child marriage. The bond established early in life, though not necessarily consummated physically until later, and the courtship which comes after marriage, if at all, may have something to do with it. Home life is exceptionally important in India, partly because there are comparatively few distractions outside of the home. Recreation and a common social life

[18] An Indian social reformer said that the Hindu joint family "tends to cut at the root of all domestic affection, put a premium on idleness, weigh down personal exertion, encourage strife and jealousy, stifle notions of equity and justice, check self-assertion and individuality, and promote an over-exuberant growth of reverence of authority." (M. R. Jayakar, in *The Social Reform Advocate*, Madras, June 30, 1917.)

[19] See, for example, Sister Nivedita (Margaret E. Noble), *The Web of Indian Life*, New York, 1904; J. P. Jones, *India: Its Life and Thought*, New York, 1908. Miss Noble lived in northern India for several years, and Jones was an American missionary in southern India for many years.

are less organized than in the Occident. Several Westerners have asserted that Easterners are less individualized than Westerners. It is also asserted that there is greater difference in the Occident between the common herd and persons of ability—in other words, that there is more genius, and of a higher order, in the West than in the East. It is therefore assumed that the Orient is less advanced, its rate of progress less rapid, and its individual members more alike in character, that is to say, more homogeneous.

The facts which have been cited concerning the Oriental family lend some plausibility to these assertions. The Easterner is compelled by custom and public opinion, and sometimes by the law, to give more heed than in the West to the wishes of his family. He is guided by its head long after adulthood is attained. He may be forced or coerced often to sacrifice his own interests to those of his family. He is more likely to have to enter an occupation in accordance with the traditions and status of his family. In the Occident there is greater freedom of choice. Several occupations are often represented in the same family. Even the right of women to careers of their own is becoming more and more recognized. They are no longer regarded as animals for breeding purposes only. Under the Oriental family system there is a greater tendency for the individual career to be hampered by group interests, for the younger to be repressed by the older generation, and for women to be devoted exclusively to the rearing of children and the care of the home.

The seclusion of women in the home has existed in varying degrees at many times and places, in the Occident as well as in the Orient. It is far more characteristic of the East than of the West. At all times and places where it has existed, it has been primarily and mainly true of the women of the upper classes. The women of the lower classes usually have to work with the men in the fields and elsewhere. Their homes are too small to render possible the segregation of the sexes which a thoroughgoing seclusion of women requires. Like polygyny wherever it has existed, the complete seclusion of women is largely a luxury of the men of the upper classes.

The family system, which is almost always based upon patriarchal authority, enhances the power of the males over the females. It devotes the women specially to purposes of breeding, and cuts them off to a considerable extent from a broader social life. A complete seclusion of women is rare. But the family system in the Orient renders the life of the women much more secluded than that of the men.

All the historical evidence available goes to show that the male sex has in the long run been dominant. In the efflorescence of several civilizations, woman has for a time acquired more freedom, thus diminishing the degree of male dominance. Such periods occurred in

244

Babylonian, Egyptian, and Roman history.[20] It has even been asserted that during certain periods among several peoples the usual relations between the sexes have been reversed, so that female dominance has replaced the customary male dominance, and that alternation between male and female dominance has repeatedly taken place.[21] It is doubtful whether so complete a reversal in dominance has ever happened, if for no other reasons than that men are physically stronger, and women are hampered by the burden of childbearing.

Dominance by either sex results in certain assumptions with regard to sex differences, some of which are false, and a different status with respect to many matters of common interest. It is usually assumed that the dominant sex is stronger and more intelligent, the subordinate sex more beautiful and highly sexed. Man is physically stronger, but that his intellect is superior is debatable. It is impossible to pass judgment upon the comparative beauty of the sexes. This is a subjective question of taste based upon variable esthetic standards. Whether or not either sex is more highly sexed is partly a question of definition. The reproductive processes play a more important part in the life of woman.

The bound feet of the Chinese women constituted a striking and appropriate symbol of their seclusion. While this practice was forbidden by law shortly before the establishment of the republic in 1912, its victims still hobble along city streets and country roads. The origin of this custom is obscure, but was closely related to the seclusion

[20] Commenting upon this period in ancient Rome, Westermarck and Ellis pointed out that Christianity was largely to blame for the renewed subjection of women which followed:

"This remarkable liberty granted to married women, however, was only a passing incident in the history of the family in Europe. From the first Christianity tended to narrow it. . . . And this tendency was in a formidable degree supported by Teutonic custom and law." (E. A. Westermarck, *The Origin and Development of the Moral Ideas*, London, 1906, pp 652-4.)

"Nothing is more certain than that the status of women in Rome rose with the rise of civilization exactly in the same way as in Babylon and in Egypt. . . . The patriarchal subordination of women fell into complete discredit, and this continued until, in the days of Justinian, under the influence of Christianity the position of women began to suffer." (Havelock Ellis, *Studies in the Psychology of Sex*, Vol. VI, *Sex in Relation to Society*, Philadelphia, 1911, p. 395.)

[21] *Cf.* Mathilde and Mathias Vaerting, *The Dominant Sex, A study in the sociology of sex differentiation*, translated from the German, London 1923.

The Vaertings alleged that female dominance existed in ancient Egypt and Sparta, among the Kamchadales, Chamorros, Iroquois, Basque-Iberian stocks, Garos, Dyaks, Balonda, etc. In their eagerness to prove that there has been much female dominance, they often used historical and anthropological sources uncritically and misinterpreted many facts, as, for example, with respect to the influence of female rulers. Thus they implied that the greatness of England during the Elizabethan and Victorian ages was due to the female monarchs who then reigned.

of women. Few measures are better adapted to restrict their freedom of movement. Esthetic considerations were probably an after-thought, and constituted a rationalization to justify the custom. Only within the last few decades have upper-class Chinese women begun to appear in public. But foot-binding was prevalent among the proletarian and peasant classes as well.

How early the doctrine of the seclusion and subjection of women became a part of Chinese culture it is impossible to determine. The Li-ki, or Book of Rites or Ceremonies, was compiled after Confucius (born 551 B.C.), but is supposed to contain his teaching based upon the ancient traditional ethical ideas and customs. "The woman follows the man. In her youth she follows her father and elder brother; when married, she follows her husband; when her husband is dead, she follows her son." (Book IX, 10.) Drastic separation between the sexes is maintained. "The Master said: 'The ceremonial usages serve as dykes for the people against evil excesses. They exemplify the separation between the sexes which should be maintained, that there may be no ground for suspicion and human relations may be clearly defined.'" (Book XXVII, 33.) Propriety in the most important relation between the sexes is emphasized. "The observance of propriety commences with careful attention to the relations between husband and wife." (Book X, sec. ii, 13.) The separation between the sexes is extended to domestic and extramural affairs. "The men should not speak of what belongs to the inside of the house, nor the women of what belongs to the outside." (Book X, sec. i, 12.) "Outside affairs should not be talked of inside the home, nor inside affairs outside of it." (Book I, sec. i, pt. iii, c. vi, v, 33.)

As China is the classic land of the family system, the position of the women has been determined largely by this system. Its patriarchal character made boys more valuable than girls. When the pressure of population on the means of subsistence encouraged infanticide in the congested regions, it was female and not male infanticide which took place. Marriages are made by the parents, usually at a comparatively early age, sometimes through middlemen, and presumably in the interest of the family. The parties often do not see each other until it is consummated. Woman is not regarded as the companion of man, but as the mother of his children and his housekeeper.

According to Confucian theory, the wife has no rights which the husband must respect. The women, nevertheless, have much influence and authority within the home. During the first years of married life she is under the autocratic rule of her mother-in-law. After she has become a mother, especially if she bears male offspring, her influence increases until she in turn becomes the head of the internal economy

246

of a household. Barrenness, on the other hand, may result in her being supplanted by another wife. Mencius uttered the dictum that to leave no posterity is the worst of three lines of unfilial conduct. In ignorance of the biological laws of heredity, the wife alone is held responsible for sterility.

In the cities the life of the woman goes on largely behind the high stone walls of the Chinese house. While her physical seclusion is less, the mental seclusion of the peasant woman is as great as if not greater than that of her urban sister. For women as well as for men this mental seclusion can be broken only by means of the education which comes through the use of books, travel, and taking part in the broader social life outside of the home. This is as true in the Orient as in the Occident, whatever claims may be made as to esoteric and recondite sources of knowledge. The impact of Occidental culture is already having its effect in this regard in most parts of the Orient.

The overwhelming influence of Chinese civilization in eastern Asia caused the doctrine of the subordination and partial or complete seclusion of women to be adopted in an extreme form by Korea, and eventually in a milder form by Japan. Until recently Korean upper-class women were almost entirely secluded in their homes. In ancient Japan women were relatively free until Chinese influence manifested itself. While not secluded as much as in China and Korea, her status has been much inferior to that of man. A married woman cannot perform many important legal acts without the consent of her husband. She has fewer causes for divorce than he. Male heirs have superior rights over female heirs. Until 1922, women were forbidden by law to promote or even attend any political meetings whatsoever. Until after the war of 1939-1945 they did not have the suffrage, though in this regard their Western sisters are not far in advance of them. There is little indication as yet of the so-called women's movement which has been active during the last few decades in almost all Occidental countries.

The position of women in Japan is similar to many other phases of the present situation in that country. The rapid adoption of the Occidental economic system has created a demand for female labor in industry, especially in the textile factories, and as stenographers, clerks, and the like, in commerce and business in general. These changes have not as yet had much influence upon public opinion as to woman's status and functions. As we have already seen, the family system still dominates with its concomitant idea of rearing many children, as indicated by the rapid increase of population and opposition to birth control. Militarism may also have its influence, for it requires a sharp differentiation between the functions of men and

247

women. Woman still is regarded as primarily and principally a breeder of children and housekeeper. While the external form has changed in part, the spirit remains as of old.

The position of woman varies greatly in different parts of India. The cultural situation is less uniform than in Japan or China. There have been several indigenous cultures. Other cultures have been imported, and have met and mingled there. India is to a large extent a cultural and anthropological museum. The numerous castes vary considerably in their treatment of women. The situation is very complicated. Only a few outstanding facts can be stated.

The majority of the more than seventy million of Moslem inhabitants dwell in northwestern and eastern India, and since 1947 in Pakistan. Among them the custom of the "purdah" (curtain or screen), or physical seclusion of women, is prevalent. Hindus sometimes assert that Islam introduced the purdah into India, and that in ancient times the Indian woman was free. This belief is manifestly erroneous. It is fostered by Hindus who dislike Western criticism of the position of their women. There is evidence in the ancient literature, as well as historical evidence, that in certain parts of India women led a very secluded existence long before the advent of Islam.[22] It is, however, probable that Islam encouraged the custom and caused it to persist in an accentuated form even among the Hindus. In the Punjab and United Provinces purdah carts and palanquins containing women are often to be seen. But even in Moslem India the majority of the Hindu women, at any rate the lower-class women, are free from the purdah so far as appearing in public with faces uncovered is concerned.

In southern India there has never been any trace whatsoever of the purdah. The women move about freely and with no attempt at concealment. Whether or not this was characteristic of the indigenous Dravidian culture, it is difficult to determine. On the southwest coast there still survive traces of matriarchal institutions from an early date. However, in southern as well as in other parts of India, Hindu

[22] See the Vedic literature (probably 1500 to 1000 B.C.), and the *Ramayana* (probably composed by Valmiki in the fifth century B.C.). King Ashoka, in the third century B.C., speaks of his secluded female apartment (avarodhana). See the dramas of Bhasa and Kalidasa, and the *Kama Sutra* of Vatsyayana, who lived early in the Christian era. Some of these citations, however, refer only to the seclusion of women in royal and aristocratic families. Professor D. R. Bhandakhar, of Calcutta University commented as follows: "The general belief is that the seclusion of woman was unknown to ancient India and that the Purdah system was introduced into the country by the Mohammedans. But nothing is more erroneous." (*The Carmichael Lectures, 1923, Ashoka*, Calcutta, 1925.)

248

culture restricts woman's interests and activities to the home, where her mental seclusion is as great as in most Oriental countries.

Many of the peoples of the Malay States and of the East Indies are Mohammedan. Islam rests lightly on the Malay folk, whom it has not succeeded in completely subduing. The physical seclusion of women is not prevalent among them. In Java the women in their colorful garb move about freely in public. However, that does not mean that their activities are not almost entirely restricted to the home, and that their mental seclusion is not as great as in other Oriental countries.

In Burma the women move about freely, buying and selling in the markets and shops. The courting customs indicate a certain measure of freedom of choice. Burmese marriage is a sort of partnership. No religious ceremony is necessary. Divorce is free to both parties. Property is retained by each spouse. What is earned during marriage is divided in case the conjugal tie is broken.[23] Hinayana Buddhism has long held sway in Burma. Its gentle and humanitarian doctrines may account in part for the relatively high position of Burmese women. There are doubtless other factors which are not obvious on the surface.

As the breeder of children, and the physically weaker sex, woman has with few exceptions been more closely associated with the home than man. Temperamentally also she may crave home life more than man. If this be true, the seclusion of Oriental women is not as great a hardship as it appears to Western eyes. However that may be, in the course of social evolution there has been considerable variation in the extent to which woman has engaged in pursuits outside of the home. It is not improbable that she played an important part in the development of agriculture, and of certain of the early industries, while man was engaged in hunting, fishing, and fighting. In primitive society the basket makers, potters, weavers, embroiderers, leatherworkers, etc., were to a large extent craftswomen, and these trades were in part household industries.[24] In certain societies militarism was developed to such an excessive degree that man devoted himself almost exclusively to military pursuits, while woman took over practically all of the economic activities. A few such barbarous communities still survive in remote corners of the world.

As industry was removed more and more from the home, in the Occident as well as in the Orient these economic activities have usually been carried on by the men. The industrial revolution has, however, again furnished women with many opportunities for work

[23] *Cf.* H. Fielding Hall, *The Soul of a People*, London, 1898.
[24] See O. T. Mason, *Woman's Share in Primitive Culture*, New York, 1894.

outside of the home. The direction and control of industry and commerce still remain largely in the hands of the men, and the same is true of political activities. The Orient has as yet been only slightly touched by this great revolution. It will doubtless materially influence the position of the women within the near future.

As we have seen, marriage as a social institution has been determined largely by economic factors. Repression of sexual expression has not ordinarily been the sole or even the principal objective of this institution. In fact, many preliterate and literate peoples have provided outlets for sex expression outside of marriage. For example, some primitive and preliterate peoples have sanctioned premarital sex relations.[25] However, until modern times the inevitable tendency of all forms of marriage has been to curb, to a greater or less degree, one of the two functions of sex in the interest of its other function. The reproductive function has been favored and safeguarded owing to the economic considerations mentioned above, and also because kinship has in the past often been the basis for social organization. The other function, which I have termed its "play" function, has usually not been recognized and has often been discriminated against in spite of its important role in the life of mankind.[26]

Industrialization, the increasing economic independence of women, the decreasing importance of kinship as the basis for social organization, the decay of certain religions and ethical ideas, and other factors, are rapidly changing the character of the family, and are also having repercussions upon the institution of marriage not

[25] See, for example, Verrier Elwin, *The Muria and Their Ghotul*, Bombay, 1948.

The Muria are an agricultural tribe in the Central Provinces, India. The ghotul is the common dormitory to which boys and girls are sent usually before puberty, and where they remain for several years until marriages have been arranged for them by their families. According to Elwin, this tribe considers sexual relations good if according to rules which govern the temporary and often changed mating of the young.

See also Margaret Mead, *Coming of Age in Samoa*, New York, 1928.

[26] See Maurice Parmelee, *Poverty and Social Progress*, New York, 1916, Chapter 21 entitled "Eugenic Measures and the Improvement of the Human Breed"; and *Personality and Conduct*, New York, 1918, Chapter 9 entitled "The Play Function of Sex," and Chapter 18 entitled "The Organization of Sex Relations." In the latter book I have described "free contractual marriage" as to its temporary or permanent duration, as to whether it is exclusive or inclusive, as to whether reproduction is an object, and as to its economic aspects. Such a marital relationship would be more in accordance with the rapidly emerging collectivist economic and social organization in the world of today.

Havelock Ellis, in his *The Play Function of Sex*, London, 1921, which was published again as Chapter 6 of his *Little Essays of Love and Virtue*, New York, 1922, said: "The term seems to have been devised by Professor Maurice Parmelee."

250

only in Oriental countries but also in the Occident.[27] These changes are discussed more fully in the latter part of this treatise which deals with modern times and the outlook for the future.[28]

[27] According to certain American writers, the "companionate" marriage is now emerging which "is a union for companionship and mutual personal advantage." (Melvin M. Knight, "The Companionate and the Family—The Unobserved Division of an Historical Institution," *Journal of Social Hygiene*, 1924, Vol. X, pages 257-267. See also Ben B. Lindsey and W. Evans, *The Companionate Marriage*, New York, 1927.)

Judge Lindsey proposed "companionate marriage" nine years after I described "free contractual marriage" which is a far more satisfactory solution of the marital problem.

[28] See Maurice Parmelee, *Oriental and Occidental Culture*, New York, 1928.

In this book I have described at length Oriental marriage and family in the recent past. But the trend toward collectivism in the Orient as well as in the Occident is having a marked effect upon marriage and the family.

Chapter XVII

Kinship Bonds —Clan, Tribe, Caste

THE biological family consisting of two parents and their offspring is the most perfect kinship group because it is united by the two closest blood relationships, namely, the parental-filial and the sibling relations. The family as a social unit and all other social groups fall short of complete kinship in varying degrees. Sometimes the kinship relation has been very slight or non-existent, in which case it has been assumed to exist as the basis of social union. This fiction has been manifested by peoples ranging in size from small groups, such as hordes and clans, among primitive and preliterate men, up to large national populations. Only in comparatively recent times has there been a tendency to recognize that the most useful human bond is social and cultural, and sometimes territorial, instead of kinship, real or fictitious.

The two most important social groups among the preliterate peoples, were the tribe and the clan. The tribesmen usually claimed a kinship bond, often largely mythical, with their fellow members, sometimes tracing this bond back to an eponymous ancestor. The members of many tribes called themselves "men," thus distinguishing themselves as a tribe from all other human beings as if belonging to a different species. The clan a subdivision of the tribe, also claimed a genetic relationship, real or assumed between its members. Inasmuch as most clans were exogamous, the kinship bond could not be more than one-half, because the parents in each family belonged to different clans. In other words, in a tribe of exogamous clans the families crossed the boundaries between the clans. As to whether the clan evolved directly from the family or the horde, or arose as a division of a tribe, we can never know. It is doubtful if the clan could arise from families living usually in isolation, but related to each other by sex unions between their respective offspring.

Briffault contended that the rule of exogamy was introduced in order not to break up a maternal group by the pairing of its siblings.[1] This theory suggests that the clan may have originated as an enlarged maternal group. Briffault assumed that the primordial clan was maternal or matriarchal, that is to say, metronymic or matrilineal. Kinship and descent may have been traced originally through the mothers because of uncertainty as to fatherhood due to ignorance of the reproductive process or to promiscuity on the part of the women. Briffault also asserted that marriage was originally matrilocal, that is to say, that the man went to the woman's home, and that patriarchal marriage arose from the increase of wealth which rendered possible the purchase of wives.

Some anthropologists have suggested that the rule of exogamy was due to fear of incest. However, there is not the slightest evidence of an innate aversion to sexual intercourse between the closest blood relatives among men as well as among other animals. Such an aversion, wherever it has existed, was acquired as a result of social and cultural reasons for restraining coitus between parents and offspring, male and female siblings, etc. Among many primitive peoples this restraint was carried much further by forbidding all forms of social intercourse between certain relatives. On the other hand, there have been a few instances where incest has not only been permitted but prescribed, as in the case of certain royal families.

The theory of the matriarchal character of the biological or primordial family as a socialized group is rendered plausible by the obviousness of the kinship between a mother and her offspring, and by the uncertainty and dubiousness of fatherhood. Until the causal nexus between coitus and procreation was recognized, and more or less permanent mating established, fatherhood was not determined with certainty. In the meantime kinship was traced from generation to generation only through the mothers and their daughters. On the other hand, this theory may be controverted by the probability that male dominance existed from the outset, so that the ascendancy of fathers and sons would tend to make the primordial family patriarchal, patri-local, and patrilineal. In any case, both types of family have been found among the most primitive of preliterate peoples. Where the clan has been patronymic, it has sometimes been called the gens, according to the nomenclature used by the American anthropologist L. H. Morgan, who restricted the term clan to the metronymic clan alone. Other American anthropologists have used the term sib, with father-sib for the patrilineal and mother-sib for the matrilineal clan. These terms have usually been employed in describing totemic clans,

[1] Robert Briffault, *The Mothers, The matriarchal theory of social origins*, New York, 1931, abridged edition in one volume.

each of which considers an animal as its putative ancestor, or as its patron.

The clan may have evolved directly from the horde as soon as the latter had attained to a recognition of kinship. But inasmuch as all clans are endogamous or exogamous, almost always the latter, a single, isolated clan would have little significance. In fact, it could not long survive as an exogamous group. Hence it is probable that the clan originated within the tribe which arose from the union of two or more hordes. These formerly independent hordes may have become transformed into clans. Another possibility is that as the tribe increased in size it may have split into two or more divisions which became clans.[2]

The tribe probably evolved directly from the horde, and was almost always divided into clans. In some cases the tribe had a territorial basis. That is to say, it made a proprietary claim to a more or less defined area of land. It was usually characterized by forms of organization in addition to the clan. The latter had special reference to reproduction, and to sex relations. Some tribes were divided into two or more phratries which had special functions to perform. As these phratries sometimes coincided with the clans, so that a phratry contained two clans, it is possible that the phratry arose from the segmentation of a clan. Tribes were sometimes divided into two parts known as moieties, which had certain functions to perform.

With a territorial basis, and somewhat complex and varied forms of social organization, the tribe marked the beginning of political organization. In many if not all cases it was the precursor of the state and of the nation. There were, however, many different kinds of tribes which varied according to their physical environment and their cultural background. Thus there were fishing and hunting tribes, peaceful and warlike tribes, sedentary and migratory tribes, pastoral and agricultural tribes. In fact, much of the range of social and cultural phenomena existed in tribal organization. Some vestiges of clan and tribal organization have persisted into the literate culture.

During the neolithic period and later many tribes adopted agriculture, and settled permanently on the land. In some cases this marked the beginning of a development beyond tribal organization into a nation and a state. Many of these tribal groups became village communities characterized by a patriarchal organization, and often by communal or semi-communal ownership of the land. Other tribes,

---

[2] "The evidence from nearly all the unequivocally simplest tribes . . . (Shoshoneans, Yahgan, Andamanese, Chukchi) . . . seems to dispose of the hoary dogma that the clan is a truly archaic institution." (R. H. Lowie, *The Origin of the State*, New York, 1927, p. 69.) See also R. H. Lowie, *Primitive Society*, New York, 1920, pp. 150 *seq.*; and W. Schmidt, *Volker und Kulturen*, 1924, pp. 79 *seq.*

warlike and migratory in character, embarked on careers of aggression and of conquest, usually against the sedentary agricultural peoples which had descended from the tribes which had adopted agriculture. In this fashion were established some of the early states which were oligarchical or feudal in character. In other cases a nation and state grew out of the amalgamation of several tribes inhabiting contiguous territory.[3] The origins and early evolution of the state are described in Chapters XX and XXI of this treatise.

While the tribe was probably based originally upon the bond of kinship, there arose within the tribe many groupings which are independent of kinship. Among them have been friendship societies, age groups, secret societies, military groups, and rudimentary political groups. The division of labor was leading to occupational diversification, and economic and social classes began to appear even before the tribal level was surpassed.

It may be worth while at this point to describe briefly a preliterate group which has been observed by several anthropologists. Tikopia is a small, isolated island on the eastern edge of the Solomon Islands in the Pacific Ocean about ten degrees south of the Equator. It is about three miles in diameter, and has several villages around the coast. The inhabitants are Polynesians, but their habitat is not far from Melanesia.

The Tikopians have been little influenced by European contacts and missionary work. Their material culture is almost entirely indigenous, with only a few metal instruments introduced from outside. Malinowski has said that "the facts of family life and of territorial grouping; the extension of kinship bonds beyond the household and their integration into the clan system follows in Tikopia the universal scheme of kinship which, with minor and major variations, obtains in every human society."[4] However, as we shall see, it can no longer be said that there is a "universal" scheme of kinship.

The Tikopian community is divided into four clans containing 76, 66, 61, and 15 households each, a total of 218 households. The household may be somewhat larger than a biological family, and may contain relatives other than parents and offspring. There is a

[3] *Cf.* Franz Oppenheimer, *The State*, Indianapolis, 1914, translated from the German.

In this work Oppenheimer has attributed the origin of the state to conquest.

Thurnwald has contended that several factors should be recognized: "Keinesfall kann man die Entstehung des Staates auf die einfache und tendenzioese Formel von 'Eroberung' allein bringen." (Richard Thurnwald, "Das Gesellungsleben der Naturvoelker," in the *Lehrbuch der Voelkerkunde*, edited by K. T. Preuss, Stuttgart, 1937.)

[4] B. Malinowski, in his "Preface" to Raymond Firth, *We, The Tikopians, A Sociological Study of Kinship in Primitive Polynesia*, London, 1936.

language of kinship which indicates more or less precisely the degree and character of the kinship between given individuals. There are various taboos pertaining to kinship relations. Sex relations are prohibited within certain specified degrees of relationship. The taboos of avoidance between certain kin are intended in large part to prevent incest. There is a classificatory system which regulates mating in large part.

Though the clan structure prevails, the tracing of descent is not exclusively, or even predominantly, matrilineal, but is largely patrilineal. This is probably due in part to the fact that forms of organization other than those based on kinship have made their appearance. There is distinction of rank between chiefs of clans or villages and commoners. There is class distinction arising out of differences of wealth consisting of various forms of property, such as land, or, at least, the right to use land. There are mechanisms of population control, such as *coitus interruptus,* abortion, and infanticide. There is marriage by capture, which has apparently arisen out of the economic institutions pertaining to property rights.[5]

The truth of the matter is that while Tikopia is preliterate, it is not a primitive community possessing only a rudimentary culture. Kinship relations and organization are influenced by other types of social organization, and may become rather complicated in their character: "The complex series of social relationships formed on this basis comprises activity of a residential, an economic, a political, a juridical, a linguistic order, and constitutes a system of primary integration in the society."[6] In Tikopia the chieftainship and property rights in land are transmitted in the male line.

Firth, who lived in Tikopia for one year, has characterized Polynesian kinship grouping as follows: "Descent in Polynesia, that is membership of a named kinship group, is not reckoned everywhere in terms of unilateral consanguinity, but is conditioned to a large extent by residence. . . . It is difficult to see the kinship institutions of Polynesia arranged in a developmental series such as would be in accordance with their diffusion from a common centre. . . . Certain features which appear to be common to the whole area may be regarded as basic or characteristic. These include the branching or ramage type of kinship unit, a strong emphasis on the patrilineal

5 "We have in Tikopia a form of marriage which utilizes real capture as one of its mechanisms, and this not as a survival from a more primitive condition but as a custom which fits closely into the other existing institutions of the people. Different societies have each their own mechanisms for dealing with the problem of transferring the major allegiance of a woman from her parents to her husband." (R. Firth, *op. cit.*, p. 574.)

6 R. Firth, *op. cit.*, p. 577.

256

transmission of group interests coupled with a readiness to admit interest through the mother."[7] It must be remembered that Polynesia has a highly developed preliterate culture.

In the matrilineal family there is usually special emphasis upon the relationship between the mothers and daughters, and in the patrilineal family upon the relationship between the fathers and sons. According to Mead, the complicated Australian classificatory system is a compromise between the matrilineal and the patrilineal types of family.[8] In a classificatory system all of the members of an age and sex group in a clan, phratry, moiety, or tribe are on the same footing as to sex and mating relations with respect to the corresponding age and sex group in another clan, phratry, moiety, or tribe.

Wherever there is special emphasis upon the relationship between husband and wife, there is usually a bilateral kinship system. The kinship structure in general is likely in this case to be simple, as among very primitive peoples, and also in modern industrial society. In the latter case kinship bonds have lost a large part of their social significance, and the individual is much less bound by them. But the right of the inheritance of wealth still gives the family a good deal of economic significance. Types of the family, or rather of marriage, showing a strong emphasis on the husband-wife relationship, are the levirate in which a man marries his deceased brother's widow, the sororate in which a woman marries her deceased sister's widower, and fraternal polyandry. Polygyny usually reflects rank and wealth rather than emphasis upon the husband-wife relationship. Both polygyny and polyandry are rare, especially the latter, and group marriage as an institution has probably never existed.

We now come to one of the most extreme examples of social organization based upon kinship—real or mythical. An American anthropologist has characterized a caste as follows: "A caste may be defined as an endogamous and hereditary subdivision of an ethnic unit occupying a position of superior or inferior rank or social esteem in comparison with other such subdivisions." Kroeber goes on to suggest some of the origins of caste: "Conquest, race differences, religion, economic developments, all have contributed, and in varying degrees, to the growth of the several caste systems."[9]

As we have seen, a clan is exogamous, whereas a caste is endogamous. Castes are ranked and rated in relation to each other, whereas clans are essentially equal. A clan cannot exist by itself and alone,

---

[7] R. Firth, op. cit.

[8] Margaret Mead, "Family," in the Encyclopedia of the Social Sciences, Vol. VI, New York, 1931.

[9] A. L. Kroeber, article on "Caste," in the Encyclopedia of the Social Sciences, Vol. III, New York, 1930.

partly because it is exogamous and requires the presence of other clans with which to intermarry. A caste, because it is endogamous, is self-sufficient in so far as reproducing itself is concerned. A single caste has sometimes stood alone, as when there has been a royal caste, or a noble caste, while the remainder constituting the great majority of the society has not been characterized by caste. However, a solitary caste is not a system, so that a caste system has always included several castes which have uually contained in the aggregate the whole of a society. A single caste which included the whole of a society would not be a genuine caste or caste system. The relationships of superiority and of inferiority would not be possible in such a society, and these relationships are essential for a caste system.

The caste, like the tribe, is a collection of families bearing a common name. But the title of a caste sometimes implies that its members follow the same occupation. The caste usually claims common descent from a mythical ancestor, human or divine, while the tribe sometimes traces its ancestry to an animal which is its totem. The tribe, but not the caste, usually occupies a well-defined territory. The tribe is not always endogamous. The caste is not only always endogamous as a whole, but is sometimes divided into sub-castes each of which is endogamous.

The most noteworthy example of a caste system has been in India. Nothing like this system prevails in any other part of the world. There is no evidence that anything closely resembling it has ever prevailed at any other time or place. While isolated features of the Hindu system have existed and do still exist here and there, this extraordinary social classification is, and probably always will be, unique in its vast extent and great antiquity.[10]

A caste system is an hereditary classification according to special functions, the castes being hierarchically arranged with unequal powers, rights, and privileges. The Hindu system was, and still is in theory, fourfold. The castes are the Brahmans, or priests and teachers, the Kshatriyas, or warriors and administrators, the Vaishyas, or merchants, and the Shudras, or servitors and manual laborers. Each of these castes is supposed to inherit the traits which peculiarly fit it for its functions. The Bhagavad-Gita, one of the sacred books of the Hindus, composed probably early in the Christian era, in its eighteenth discourse, describes these traits as follows: "Of Brahmans, Kshatriyas, Vaishyas, and Shudras, O Parantapa, the duties have been distributed according to the qualities born of their own natures.

[10] The following description of the Hindu caste system is paraphrased from my book entitled *Oriental and Occidental Culture*, New York, 1928, Chapter VIII, "Indian Caste and Western Class."
The caste system was abolished in 1949 by the new constitution of India.

Serenity, self-restraint, austerity, purity, forgiveness, and also uprightness, wisdom, knowledge, belief in God, are the Brahman duty, born of his own nature. Prowess, splendor, firmness, dexterity, and also not flying from battle, generosity, the nature of a ruler, are the Kshatriya duty, born of his own nature. Ploughing, protection of kine, and trade, are the Vaishya duty, born of his own nature. Action of the nature of service is the Shudra duty, born of his own nature."

A caste system is a form of occupational division of labor. In a primitive or comparatively simple society it may serve this purpose fairly well. Before an educational system has developed, the most feasible method of transmitting professional knowledge may be from father to son, so that there is a specialization of occupations which appears to be hereditary. As knowledge accumulates, new methods of doing things are invented, and the range of information within each occupation becomes extensive, the situation becomes too complicated to be effectively handled by a caste system. This is particularly true with regard to the extremely technical methods of modern industry which have resulted from the development of science. They call for a minute differentiation of functions, and also for a high degree of flexibility to meet changes due to scientific discoveries and inventions. In the face of such demands, a hereditary classification breaks down completely. It can change only slowly and in the course of generations.

There is no reason to believe that there is a hereditary transmission of abilities which corresponds with a classification of occupations. There has always been some mixture of functional capacities. This is in accordance with biological knowledge which indicates that abilities of all kinds may appear in any social class. As the ancestors of the present castes were not selected for their special abilities, it is doubtful if there is even a slight preponderance of unusual fitness in each caste. There is also little or no evidence of a racial classification. The favorite theory of the Brahmans is that they are the descendants of the superior "Aryan" conquerors of northern India. The Hindu name for caste is *varna*, which means color. A Sanskrit scholar suggests that this name may have come from the garb: "Varna, once a common name for all classes, as, for example, white for the Brahmans, red for the Kshatriyas, yellow for the Vaishyas, and black for the Shudras, came to mean a caste in post-Buddhistic literature."[11]

Endogamy was widespread in the earlier stages of social evolution. Clans were sometimes endogamous. More often they were exogamous within endogamous tribes. Such restrictions may have been necessary to preserve the tribal organization. With the evolution of the nation and the state, endogamy has disappeared almost entirely.

[11] R. Shama Sastri, *The Evolution of Castes*, Mysore, 1916.

It is retained only by such archaic institutions as monarchy and hereditary aristocracy in order to protect their special privileges. Endogamy has also been practiced for the preservation of racial purity, so called. It is still used for this purpose to a certain extent. Even if there was originally a racial basis for the caste system, it was never very extensive. Any degree of correlation between race and caste has long since disappeared. As the Brahmanic religion, that is to say, the religion of the chief Hindu god Brahma, spread over the Indian peninsula, many primitive tribes were incorporated in the caste system, either as new castes or subcastes, or as parts of existing castes. Even the proud and exclusive Brahman caste has thereby received many infusions which have destroyed whatever racial homogeneity it may once have possessed.

The ban upon intermarriage has led to or has been accompanied by other restrictions upon intercourse between the castes. Interdining is forbidden between the Brahmans and the lower castes, and to a certain extent among the other castes. There are more than fifty million outcastes who have for one reason or another lost their caste status, or have never acquired such a status. Between these outcastes and the castes there exists "untouchability." This varies greatly in degree in different parts of India. The Hindu system not only divides the castes from each other and from the outcastes, but also establishes a high degree of repulsion between these groups. This division and repulsion are effected by means of occupational, connubial, commensal, and contactual restrictions on a wider scale and to a greater degree than in any other social system which has ever existed.

All of these restrictions were more or less common among primitive peoples. The repast has often been regarded as establishing a peculiar and intimate bond, perhaps because of the connection between nourishment and life. Hence it was not to be shared by persons of a different social status. The idea of pollution was implicit in many forms of taboo. It led to contactual restrictions between persons standing in certain relationships to each other. It is not easy to explain why such restrictions not only persisted or were revived, but also were expanded in India long after they had almost entirely disappeared among every other people which had attained a high degree of culture.

The Hindus allege that their caste system is Vedic in origin. This implies that it is also "Aryan," because the Vedas are supposed to belong to this culture. There is, however, no trace of the caste system elsewhere whenever the so-called "Aryan" culture is supposed to have prevailed, as in Iran and in Europe. Moreover, the Vedas do not describe a fully developed system. In the Rig Veda there is only one vague reference to four functional groups. "His mouth became Brahman, his arms became the Kshatriya, his thighs are the Vaishya, the Shudra was

260

produced from his feet." (*Rig Veda,* X, 90, 12.) There was a priestly class, but apparently it was not endogamous. It may have acquired its hereditary monopoly by clinging jealously to its functions of performing the sacred offices to the gods, and of repeating the mantras or charms by which the deities are supposed to be influenced.

It has been suggested that the caste system attained its full-fledged form after and to a certain extent as a result of the advent of Buddhism and Jainism. Buddhism, whose founder Gautama lived in the 6th century B.C., has always been opposed to caste. Jainism also opposed it during its early stages. Both of these religions condemned flesheating and advocated a strict vegetarianism, because they were strongly influenced by the doctrine of transmigration which preaches a close kinship between the human and animal worlds. The Brahmans were criticized for eating flesh, and also for the polygyny which they practiced to a considerable extent. In the course of their long struggle for the ascendancy, they gradually gave up the eating of meat, and relinquished most of their polygynous rights as concessions to the new reforming religions. But vegetarianism increased the rift between them and the other castes which still ate flesh, thus reinforcing the ban against intermarriage and interdining. If this theory is correct, the new religions were successful in extending zoophilism, but indirectly and unintentionally strengthened the caste system. Partly for this reason, Buddhism was eventually driven from the land of its founder, but spread far and wide in Ceylon, Burma, Siam, Tibet, Indo-China, China, Mongolia, Korea, and Japan. Jainism succumbed in large part by accepting the caste system and many other features of Brahmanic religion, and remained an Indian religion.

It has also been suggested that the caste system was in part Dravidian in its origin. This is contrary to the favorite Hindu theory that "Aryan" culture and the Vedic religion carried the caste system to southern India. This system incorporates certain primitive features. It is possible that these features persisted in southern India, and were absorbed into the caste system. The historical record for the Dravidian culture is even more scanty than for the Vedic culture. Few data are available for the study of the origin and evolution of the caste system. Suffice it to say that this system has displayed itself in its most aggravated form in southern India. This may have been due to the fact that it was the place of its origin. Or it may have been due to the zeal of certain converts to Brahmanism, or to oppression on the part of conquerors from the north.[12]

Whatever may have been the origin of the Hindu caste system,

[12] Dr. Slater expressed the opinion that the Dravidian culture was democratic, and probably not dominated by a caste system. (Gilbert Slater, *The Dravidian Element in Indian Culture*, London, 1924, p. 181.)

its peculiar and outstanding feature is its religious character. The castes are, or were originally, trade guilds. In other parts of the world guilds usually have no religious aspect. The Hindu system apparently originated with the sacerdotal class. This was able to impress a religious character upon the whole system. The doctrine of transmigration, prevalent in India, has aided this process by justifying the inequalities of castes as penalties and rewards for conduct in previous existences.

The status of the caste system in India may be indicated by a few figures. According to the census of 1921, the population of India, excluding Burma, was about 306,000,000. Of these 217,000,000 were Hindus, who were divided as follows: Brahmans, 14,000,000; non-Brahman castes, 143,500,000; outcastes, 53,000,000; recently Hinduized tribes, 6,500,000. The census recognized only the first of the four traditional castes. The lines of demarcation between the other three have become so vague that it is often difficult to determine whether an existing caste or sub-caste is Kshatriya, Vaishya, or Shudra. Even the distinction between caste and outcaste sometimes becomes vague, for the outcastes have formed castes among themselves, and the degree of their untouchability varies. The census enumerated several thousand castes and mutually exclusive sub-castes. There were 54 castes numbering more than a million each, six of which were over five million each. These were the Brahman, Chamar, Rajput, Ahir, Jat, and Maratha castes.

The Oriental caste system may be contrasted with the Western class system. The former is undemocratic because it denies equality of opportunity to individuals. It debases manual labor by degrading the laborer in the lowest caste. It hampers the free and full development of the individual and of the highest type of individualism. On the other hand, it hampers the evolution of a larger social unity by standing in the way of the political and juridical development of the state and nation, and by suppressing a broadly humanitarian point of view. Hinduism, of which it is an integral part, is itself not a world religion which contemplates the inclusion of the whole of mankind, because a Hindu is born a Hindu and cannot become one in the course of his lifetime.

The Western class system is primarily economic. The three main classes are the capitalist, the middle or bourgeois, and the proletarian or working class. The lines of demarcation are somewhat vague. An individual may belong to more than one class at the same time. Theoretically there is freedom of movement from one class to another. In practice it is impossible for the vast majority of proletarians to raise themselves to the economically higher classes. Economic insecurity is characteristic of the status of the vast majority under the class system.

262

This is to a certain extent inevitable under any competitive system. The proletarian is not assured of a position in his trade for life. The same is to a less extent true of the economic status of the bourgeois and of the capitalist. By means of trade unions and collective bargaining the proletariat is trying to assure itself of security. Corresponding organizations have been developing in the other classes. Much social legislation is directed toward assuring a minimum standard of living for the workers. On the other hand, the class system utilizes the efficiency derived from competitive individualism. It is sufficiently elastic to furnish the possibility of experimentation and progressive change.

The caste system assures the individual's economic status for life. It is a sort of hereditary trade union. His caste protects the low-caste man within his rights as much as the high-caste man. It protects him against the greatest risks of industrial and competitive life. It may serve as a sort of automatic poor law. But it lacks the flexibility of the class system. It is adapted only to a comparatively primitive type of economic and social organization. It will break down completely and disappear in the face of the economic and social evolution of the Orient.

In this connection may be mentioned the rapid disappearance in modern times of the Japanese caste system. The principal Japanese castes were the following:

1. The Kuges or aristocrats of the mikado's court.

2. The Daimyos or feudal lords. They constituted the aristocracy of the shogun's court who did not usually intermarry with the Kuges, perhaps because of the rivalry between the two courts.

3. The Samurai or military caste. Their appointments were hereditary, and they were forbidden from marrying with the lower castes.

4. The Heinui or commoners. They were divided into the three main castes of farmers, artisans, and merchants.

5. The Etas or "untouchables." They lived in segregation, could not marry the higher castes, and could eat, drink, and associate only with their caste fellows.

While the Japanese caste system resembled in a measure the Hindu system in its outward appearance, a basic difference was that the Japanese system was feudal and not theocratic and hierocratic. No priest arrogating divine powers dominated it with the aid of supernatural threats. It was not embedded in a religion as an integral part of it with a sacerdotal sanction. While the feudal and military domination may have been as complete in its own manner, it proved to be easier to dislodge. This was because of the strong national consciousness which transcended caste in binding the Japanese together. In India caste consciousness is the stronger. It serves to disunite the

263

Indians. When Occidental pressure to open the ports to foreign trade became too insistent to resist, Japan was compelled to present a united front to the demands of Western nations. This meant the disappearance of the dual rule of shogun and Mikado.

In October 1867, the shogun, who for nearly three centuries had been in practice the real ruler, resigned. The mikado was restored to his pristine power. To complete the centralization of authority, the 262 feudatory fiefs were abolished. The Daimyos were retired to private life on pensions. In 1871, an imperial decree abolished all caste distinctions. In 1876, the Samurai, of whom there were about 400,000, were deprived of their military pensions and sword-wearing privileges. In 1890, was opened the first parliament. It embodied a restricted form of representative government, which was later somewhat expanded. For several decades after the restoration of the mikado, the Japanese government was largely oligarchic. Political power was mainly in the hands of the Genro or Elder Statesmen. This was a small group of the principal feudal lords, whose long established prestige died hard, with a few newly created nobles.

Though a caste system no longer exists in Japan, there still remain vestiges, and institutions which resemble caste. Prejudice lingers against the Eta, or formerly untouchable outcastes. Owing to this prejudice, they are still under pressure to dwell apart by themselves to a certain extent. Ethnically they do not differ from the population at large. The Japanese government is trying to break up their communities, which contain about 1,200,000 inhabitants, so that discrimination against them will disappear.

There are about a dozen families of imperial descent. In 1884, a peerage was established. It contained five grades, namely, prince, marquis, count, viscount, and baron. It now includes descendants of the former courtiers or Kuges, descendants of the former feudal lords or Daimyos, recently created peers, and Korean peers. There are about 950 Japanese and 80 Korean peers. Like the titled class in England, and in other capitalist countries where an hereditary aristocracy survives, the Japanese peerage was constantly being recruited from among the commoners of wealth, and might intermarry with commoners. Japan is rapidly moving toward the Western class system in which the distinction between capitalist and proletarian is of far more significance than any gradation of caste.

In this chapter, as in the preceding one, Oriental social and cultural conditions are described as they existed prior to the worldwide war of 1939 to 1945, and before Russian communism had a widespread influence in the Orient as well as in the Occident.

The preceding discussion has demonstrated that kinship as a basis for union has decreased greatly in importance. Only within the narrow limits of the family is it still significant. Even there it no longer serves to hold close relatives together for all their lives.[13] In the political units, from village to nation, the bond of union is territorial, social, and cultural. The largely fictitious notion of common ancestry is still believed by many inhabitants of nations which claim racial or ethnic unity. It is true only in the tenuous sense that all human beings are remotely related in their hominoid origin. As mankind becomes more alike socially and culturally, the basis for union will become social and cultural, and not always even territorial, instead of a mythical blood relationship.

---

[13] A Polish-British anthropologist was mistaken when he said: "Kinship controls family life, law, social organization and economics, and it deeply influences religion, morality and art." (Bronislaw Malinowski, article on "Kinship" in the *Encyclopaedia Britannica*, Vol. 13, 1942.)

Apart from the family, kinship cannot be said to influence any other aspects of society greatly, and most of them only slightly or not at all.

Chapter XVIII

The Sources of Social Control

NO conscious and overt means of social control have been observed in any animal species. In a state of nature even the most predatory animal will not molest another except to secure a direct and immediate benefit such as food or sexual gratification.[1] In other words, anarchy prevails throughout the animal world. Hence it must be assumed that mankind also commenced in a state of anarchy which does not necessarily mean disorder. Social control developed in the course of cultural evolution, because many forms of conflict, of exploitation and of invasive conduct came into being as a result of this evolution.[2]

While social control presumably was lacking during the early existence of mankind, control of individuals by individuals probably existed from the outset. The original condition favoring such individual control must have been superior physical strength, the control of the weak by the strong. Stronger men could control weaker men, the male sex could dominate the female sex, the adults could discipline the children, and the young and middle-aged adults could repress the old adults. Such forms of control are to be observed in many parts of the animal world, such as all of the primate species and many other mammalian species. In fact, all species whose young require parental care display a certain amount of parental training and discipline which is in most cases maternal, but in some cases is also paternal. Human infancy is exceptionally long, so that parental control is unusually protracted.

The traits which give rise to these individual forms of control

[1] P. Kropotkin, *Mutual Aid, A Factor in Evolution*, London, 1902.

[2] See Maurice Parmelee, *Personality and Conduct*, New York, 1918. Chapter II, "Invasive and Non-Invasive Conduct."

"Invasive conduct includes acts which are unmistakably harmful to others. Non-invasive conduct include acts which do not injure others, or which are not unquestionably harmful to others." (Pp. 8-9.)

266

constitute a part of man's mammalian and primate heritage. They are among the anatomical, physiological, and psychological traits which furnish the organic basis and setting for the emergence of social and cultural phenomena. These phenomena are, in the first instance, psychological, and always remain so. Culture contains in addition, however, the material consequences of cultural evolution, such as tools, houses, and books, which become a part of the cultural heritage.

The problem is as to whether social control developed spontaneously out of these forms of individual control or was the product of certain institutions and forms of social organization. If the former were true, it may be asked why many animal species did not develop social control. Was it because no animals have displayed as strong tendencies toward control by the individual as has mankind? However the latter may be, it is plausible to assume that social control did not arise solely and entirely spontaneously out of individual control, though the latter may in many cases have furnished the starting point for the former. Social control developed almost entirely or in large part in the course of cultural evolution like many other social phenomena which do not characterize the animals. In fact, it could perhaps not come into existence until something in the nature of organized society already existed.

According to an American sociologist, "leadership or authority is the original source and directing agency in social control."[3] Leadership of a sort makes its appearance in certain mammalian groups, such as ungulate herds, without resulting in social control. Another American sociologist has asserted that social control is by (1) physical force, and (2) human symbol-devices, and that the conditioned reflex is the earliest form of social control.[4] However, animals also have conditioned reflexes. In fact, this is no more than saying that habit is the original form of social control.

Individual traits, such as the conditioned reflex, habit, and the impulse to dominate, play their part as basic and primordial factors in social control, as in other social phenomena. But social control cannot be said to be caused immediately and directly by them, or to be due to them alone, any more than marriage as a sacred rite or a civil contract can be said to be caused by the sexual instinct; the family as a form of social organization or institution by the parental

[3] Jerome Dowd, *Control in Human Societies*, New York, 1936, p. 3.
[4] F. E. Lumley, *Means of Social Control*, New York, 1925. "In a delicately articulated society, a highly complex order, these reflexes and the series of them which we call instincts, cannot always be allowed to discharge according to their nature: some of them have to be inhibited, some have to be re-attached." (p. 24) According to Lumley, the "want-expressions" of the growing young have to be controlled.

instincts; tribal, national or civil warfare by pugnacity; and privately owned and inherited wealth by individual greed.[5] Every form of social organization and institution furnishes individual traits opportunities to express themselves, but cannot be attributed solely to them. All forms of social organization, and most if not all institutions, exercise control of some sort in varying degrees.

The preceding considerations suggest that we must seek for the sources and origins of social control not in the individual traits, many of which mankind shares with the animals, but in the culture which mankind alone has brought into being. As explanations of specific social phenomena individual psychological traits often cancel out. That is to say, they are found universally without invariably giving rise to these social phenomena. In fact, many of them rarely if ever give rise to these phenomena. For example, the universally distributed individual traits of the so-called instinct of or innate tendency to pugnacity and the emotion of anger often cause conflicts between individuals, but almost never cause war. Warfare between groups is a social phenomenon due to various causes in different kinds of culture. There have been religious, racial, dynastic, civil, national, and imperialist wars. Rarely if ever is a war due to the individual traits which give rise to conflict between two individuals or a small number of individuals, but rather to the type of culture to which the warring groups belong.[6]

Many phases of human culture involve social control, ranging from severe and narrow restrictions upon the individual to a very mild degree of coercion. Among these phases of culture are the following:

1. Custom, folkway, public opinion, and moral ideas.

2. Magic and religion.

3. Institutionalized forms of parental authority, leadership, sex dominance, age dominance (gerontocracy), and of the family.

4. The governmental functions of the clan, tribe, caste, nation, and state, and the legal systems which arise therefrom.

5. Types of rule or public authority, such as monocracy (king, tyrant, dictator), oligarchy, democracy.

---

[5] See Maurice Parmelee, *The Science of Human Behavior, Biological and Psychological Foundations*, New York, 1913. Chapters XI, "The Nature of Instinct; XII, "The Neural Basis of Instinct; XIII, "The Principal Human Instincts and General Innate Tendencies."

[6] "War in our own civilization is as good an illustration as one can take of the destructive lengths to which the development of a culturally selected trait may go. If we justify war, it is because all peoples always justify the traits of which they find themselves possessed, not because war will bear an objective examination of its merits." Ruth Benedict, *Patterns of Culture*, New York, 1946, p. 29.

6. Class dominance arising out of the division of labor and specifically out of the accumulation and inheritance of wealth, which is perhaps the most pervasive and powerful in the long run.

While these phases and forms of culture are described in more or less detail in other chapters, in this chapter we will attempt to follow the current of social control which flows through all of them.

We may conjecture that at the commencement of cultural evolution the adults, and parents in particular, exercised control over the young, the male sex may have dominated the female sex to a certain degree, and the young and middle-aged adults may have coerced the old in a measure, though habits of obedience acquired in childhood may have restricted considerably the coercion of the old. All of these spontaneous forms of control were manifestations of superior physical force, and could have had no social sanction. Violations of habits acquired by all or most of the members of a family or horde may at times have called forth hostile reactions from some or most of the members of the group. Here again there could have been no social sanction for such reactions at the outset.

Sumner defined customs and folkways as group habits, laws as group habits enforced by police power, ethics as a corpus of rules, and morals as "the sum of taboos and prescriptions in the folkways by which right conduct is defined," "right" being the differentia of moral.[7] The term "group habit" can be used only by analogy, as habit is a psychological term for a trait which can characterize only the individual. With this clearly understood, it is not very objectionable to define customs and folkways as group habits. It is much more objectionable to define laws as group habits. Many of them are antithetical to habits which are widespread.

The development of language was essential for the inception of social control. Until early men could talk, they could not possess ideas as to the regulation of conduct. At any rate, they could not share these ideas in common, so as to furnish a basis for group sanctions and group action which constitute genuine social control. When a requisite degree of intercommunication was attained, customs and folkways could be recognized which in many cases were based upon and arose out of habits which were widespread in the group. The conscious and collective recognition of these customs and folkways probably constituted the starting point of public opinion which were gradually extended to many other subjects. Implicit in custom, folkway, and public opinion is the idea that certain things should be done and other things not done. Here was the starting point of the ideas

[7] W. G. Sumner, *Folkways*, Boston, 1907. See also W. G. Sumner and A. G. Keller, *The Science of Society*, New Haven, 1927-28, 4 vols.

of right and wrong which were extended from forms of conduct to ideas, beliefs, ways of thinking, etc. In other words, this was the germ of the concept of morality and of an elaborate system of moral ideas which eventually was organized and rationalized in an ethical code. Many factors in addition to custom and folkway have influenced and sometimes determined these moral ideas and ethical codes, among them being magic, religion, and forms of social organization.

The development of language rendered possible the socializing of control and authority over the young. Parental authority may have been the first to be recognized and sanctioned. With the emergence of certain social groups based upon kinship, such as the larger family, the caste, and the clan, other types of authority over the young made their appearance, such as the authority of the grandparents or of the uncles on the maternal side. Parental authority has also usually been predominantly maternal or paternal, more often the latter, at any rate in the later stages of cultural evolution. Sometimes all of the adults of a kinship group exercised a certain amount of authority over the individual young persons. With the rise of the tribe and later of the state, collective authority was instituted over the young as a group. Many social groups have imposed rites of initiation which must be experienced before the young can attain adulthood in the sense of sharing in all of the rights and duties of the members of the group.

In similar fashion, the development of language rendered possible the recognition and sanctioning of sex dominance (male or female) and of age dominance, both of which, and especially the former, probably existed prior to the beginning of cultural evolution. Class domination, which has become of the utmost importance in the later stages of cultural evolution, could not have existed at the outset. It has arisen out of a widespread and detailed division of labor and a high degree of concentration of wealth. The first condition does not necessarily result in class domination. It is the inevitable result of the second condition when wealth is concentrated in the ownership of a relatively small class.

Leadership also could be recognized and sanctioned after language made intercommunication possible. However, the sort of leadership which is most effective as a means of social control manifested itself later as one feature of various forms of social organization (*e.g.,* monocracy, oligarchy, aristocracy). Furthermore, leadership has often been as much a means of anti-social as of social control.

Whether or not there were other forms of pre-cultural individual control which were transformed into social control after language and other phases of culture came into being, it is impossible to ascertain. The cases which have been mentioned, namely, parental authority,

270

sex dominance, age dominance, and leadership, are sufficient to illustrate the process. Underlying and implementing every cultural and social phenomenon are physiological and psychological processes. Such processes existed before and can exist independent of social and cultural processes. The reverse situation cannot arise because social and cultural processes cannot exist independent of the physiological and psychological processes. Nevertheless, the former should be distinguished to a certain extent from the latter processes. While they do not constitute a "super-organism,"[8] and can never be divorced from their physiological and psychological base, they do constitute, "super-organic" processes which are often absent when these physiological and psychological traits are functioning. Hence it is preferable to define collective identical behavior as custom or folkway and not as group habit, though the latter is not necessarily erroneous but is subject to misunderstanding.

Assuming that control which was social in the strict sense of the word did not arise until the commencement of cultural evolution, and that very little of such control could come into existence until after speech had developed to a considerable degree, we are still far from determining when social control commenced, and in what order the various forms of social control made their appearance. Until the beginning of the historical period, we can indulge only in conjecture and inference with regard to these questions.

Adult and parental control over the young may have been the first to reach the social and cultural level. However, male dominance may have reached this level at as early a time. Both of these could arise within the horde. As we have seen in an earlier chapter, we can never know as to whether mankind lived originally in families or in hordes. In the former case, social control probably developed along patriarchal lines with male parental authority and male dominance strongly emphasized. In other words, it was recognized that man had the right (based in the first instance on superior physical strength) to dominate his mate and his children. In the latter case, adult authority over the young may have been more diffused and male dominance less clearly defined. However, it is conceivable that during the early stages of cultural evolution human association fluctuated between the family and the horde.

During certain periods and over certain areas, owing largely to the sparse distribution of food, each family lived by itself more or less isolated from other families. At other times and places, owing to a more plentiful food supply or to favorable physical features, such

8 I have already criticized the theory of the "super-organic" in Chapter VII.

as a river valley, rock shelter, or cave, spring of water, supply of wood or stone for the manufacture of implements, etc., a horde might come into existence. A horde might originate as a congregation of isolated individuals. Such a horde would be characterized by sexual promiscuity. It would have no clearly defined form of social control at the outset. It seems more likely, however, that the horde was constituted ordinarily of a grouping of families brought together by a favorable physical environment.

The horde furnished a much better *milieu* than the isolated family for the origin and development of the early phases of culture. The two most important of these cultural phases were language and the division of labor. Language was a pre-requisite for most if not all of cultural evolution. The division of labor rendered possible many forms of social control which could not have arisen spontaneously or more or less directly out of the primordial parental-filial and sexual relationships. Hence it may be assumed that if human association had continued indefinitely and solely in isolated families, it would never have exceeded these two primordial relationships and would have resulted in little or no culture.

From the horde consisting of a collection of families arose the clan, tribe, and other organized groups based upon kinship—real or assumed. Each of these forms of social organization has exercised a high degree of control over its individual members. Even before any of these organized groups came into existence, certain forms of social control had in all probability emerged within the horde. Adult control of the young and sex dominance have already been mentioned. Leadership as a form of social control probably also appeared soon after the congregation of families as a horde. Such leadership might be exercised by an individual of exceptional strength, prowess, or cunning, who acquired a tacit or explicit recognition of his commanding position. Or a few such individuals might form an oligarchy which would dominate the group. In some cases the old members of the horde, or the old men in particular, might become an oligarchy because of their greater experience and prestige. This was the earliest appearance of the gerontocracy, or rule by the aged, which later played some part in certain forms of social organization.

The division of labor furnished a new and radically different basis for segregation and classification, namely, skill. No longer could age, sex, or superior physical strength alone be the exclusive source of control and seat of authority. However, this is not to say that skill became at once, or in a relatively short time, or even in due course of time, the sole basis of classification. On the contrary, skill has almost always had to compete with superior physical strength, or age, or sex,

272

or kinship relations, whether of the family or of caste, for the ascendancy in determining the source of control and the seat of authority. The class system, while originating in part from the division of labor and its concomitant specialized skills, has in the long run been molded and dominated by factors which are wholly irrelevant so far as skill is concerned, primarily by biological descent through which also the transfer of wealth from generation to generation has taken place.

Observation of extant or recently extinct primitive peoples renders it probable that custom was stronger and more persistent in primitive or preliterate communities than in some of the more complex societies. In the latter are usually more personal freedom and a higher tempo of change. As Westermarck has said: "In primitive society custom stands for law, and even where social organization has made some progress it may still remain the sole rule for conduct. . . . The laws themselves, in fact, command obedience more as customs than as laws."[9] Mrs. Benedict has spoken in similar fashion: "The fact of first-rate importance is the predominant role that custom plays in experience and in belief, and the very great varieties it may manifest." "Society is only incidentally and in certain situations regulative, and law is not equivalent to the social order. In the simpler homogeneous cultures collective habit or custom may quite supersede the necessity for any development of formal legal authority."[10]

Many of the laws of the higher stages of social evolution have developed out of the customs of the community. Even in the most complex societies changes in the laws are largely determined by changes in the customs. Law grows out of custom when explicit penalties, recorded orally or in writing, are prescribed for violations of custom. Social control attains the level of government when it becomes formally organized in some degree and operates by law.

Customs exist in every human group. There will always be a slight tendency on the part of a community to react against violations of these customs. However, there has already been much variation as to the number of customs which are sanctioned by religious beliefs and magical practices, violations of which are repressed or at least discountenanced by the group as a whole. The trend is for fewer customs to receive supernatural sanction. In many of these cases only personal reactions will be possible against them and not social reactions sufficiently strong to constitute social control. Here is the borderline between personal and public opinion.

[9] E. Westermarck, *The Origin and Development of the Moral Ideas*, London, 1906, Vol. I, pp. 161, 164.
[10] Ruth Benedict, *op. cit.*, pp. 2, 233.

The primary causes of the customs of any group are to be found in the innate traits of human beings and in the features of the environment. The customary relations between the sexes, between parents and offspring, etc., are determined in large part by the general innate tendencies and feelings. The food customs are determined to a large extent by the environment. If the available food is in the form of wild beasts, various hunting customs arise. If the environment causes frugivorous habits, customs with respect to the gathering and the apportioning of the fruit come into being.

Secondary causes of customs make their appearance when, largely due to the evolution of language, religious and magical ideas and practises and moral ideas develop. At some point in his career upon this planet man began to think about the nature and causes of his environment and of himself. His thinking was at first not for purposes of philosophic speculation. It was for a pragmatic reason. He wanted to influence the forces of nature for his own benefit and to attain certain ends. As a result of this thinking there arose the animistic ideas which underlie all religious and magical beliefs and practices. These ideas have already been described in Chapter XV. They will now be discussed with specific reference to social control.

Animistic ideas are to the effect that the events which take place in nature, and the occurrences which happen to or in man, are caused and governed by beings which are conceived to be more or less like the beings of the animate world, and often like man himself. Hence it is to the interest of man to influence these supposititious spiritual beings to regulate the affairs of the universe, or at least of that part of the universe which concerns him, in such a manner as to promote the safety and happiness of man. There have been numerous methods of influencing these alleged spiritual beings. They may be classified in two main groups, though the distinction between the two is not absolute and they shade into each other. These are the magical and the religious methods.

The magical methods attempt to coerce these spiritual beings to do the will of man. The religious methods are intended to persuade these hypothetical beings to do what is desired by man. These differences in methods probably arose in part out of differences of opinion as to the nature of these spiritual beings. Magical methods postulate that these imaginary beings can be coerced. Religious methods assume that they may or may not be coerced but which may possibly be persuaded. In many cases the coexistence of both of these orders of animistic beings has been postulated. For these reasons magical and religious methods have often accompanied each other, and have been practiced at the same time and place.

Magic may be classified as contagious and imitative. The contagious methods are those which purport to influence something through something else which has at one time been in contact with the first thing. An attempt may be made to injure an enemy by doing injury to something which was at one time a part of him, such as nail parings, hair, etc. The imitative methods are supposed to bring about desired events by causing other events which resemble in certain respects the desired events. An attempt may be made to stimulate the fertilizing of the seed in order to secure a good harvest by going through the process of human sexual fertilization. Civilized man may discern that both of these magical methods are based on false analogies. In the pre-scientific age this was not apparent. Even to the present day it has not been clear to many human beings.[11] The gradual disappearance of magic has come about, in the first place, as a result of the repeated failure of magical methods to attain the ends desired, and, second, owing to the spread of scientific knowledge with regard to the true causes of the events which take place in nature.

Magic has to a large extent arisen from a process of mental association. In fact, many of those who have practiced magic have lost sight of or have never been conscious of the animistic basis of magic, and have been governed entirely by the apparent similarities. It has been the weakness of magic that these mental associations have been with respect to superficial resemblances which have not necessarily involved any causal relations.

Religious methods have been and are attempts to persuade the hypothetical animistic beings. They are propitiatory methods. They have included prayer, oblations and sacrifices of all sorts, and adulation of these imaginary beings in various forms of ceremonial worship. Religion also has arisen in large part out of mental association with respect to superficial resemblances. Man has assumed, because of external resemblances between occurrences caused by man or by other animate beings and the other events which take place in nature, that these natural events are caused by spiritual beings similar to animate beings. Religion has, however, one great advantage over magic which has enabled it to outstrip magic. This advantage is that the repeated failure of religious methods does not in itself discredit religion. It is always possible to assume that the god or gods are not listening or are unwilling to grant the requests of man. Religion does not have to meet the pragmatic test to the same extent as magic.

The idea of taboo is one of the most prominent of animistic

---

[11] In eastern New Guinea, among the Kuman aborigines, there are three categories of magic, namely, "beneficent magic which gets results" such as love incantations, planting invocations, etc.; "protective magic" against evils and dangers; and "malignant magic" to injure others. (Jens Bjerre, *The Last Cannibals*, New York, 1957, translated from the Danish, pp. 138-140.)

beliefs. It has been defined as "a negative sanction, a prohibition whose infringement results in an automatic penalty without human or supernatural mediation."[12] This negative sanction arises out of the notion that certain objects or situations are permeated with a noxious animistic force. Contact with this object or situation is prohibited in order to avoid contagion. Other objects and situations are conceived of as permeated with a beneficial animistic force and regarded as sacred, so that a positive sanction commands or recommends contact with them. Still other objects and situations subject to taboo may also be regarded as sacred, but contact with them is sacrilegious and therefore harmful.

Upon the basic ideas as to what is sacred and what is taboo are built up a large part of animistic practices. Innumerable taboos have existed a few of which have been mentioned. Many of them survive and play a potent part in social control. Among them have been taboos on many persons and on many things. A cursory survey of animistic beliefs and practices conveys an impression of a welter of confusion and conflict. Little or no order is at first apparent. The confusion of thought thus arising has been greatly accentuated by the numerous attempts at a teleological interpretation. Magic and religion, and increasingly the latter during the later stages of cultural evolution, have furnished pervasive sanctions for conduct, in particular through the promise of supernatural rewards and the threat of divine penalties.

All forms of behavior arise, in the first instance, in the course of the struggle of the individual for existence. Each individual must overcome the difficulties in the way of its existence if it is to survive. It must secure the food it needs, it must not succumb to the climate, it must defend itself against its enemies. The individuals which act in such a manner as to attain these ends will survive. Those who fail to do so will be eliminated. A selective process takes place in which some individuals survive and are perpetuated, while others perish and are eliminated. In this fashion the struggle for existence determines what forms of behavior are to persist. It is no less a struggle even though it assumes other than physical forms in the later stages of cultural evolution.

In every human group conflict arises between the interests of the individual and of the group. Every person experiences impulses and desires which if gratified would injure other persons. If not restrained these individual impulses would give rise to continual warfare between individuals which would prevent social organiza-

[12] Article on "Tabu," *Encyclopedia of the Social Sciences*, Vol. XIV, New York. 1934.

tion.[13] These impulses and desires arise out of the innate tendencies and feelings, which are the principal psychological factors in the determination of human behavior.

These tendencies and feelings lead sometimes to social and sometimes to anti-social behavior. The pugnacious tendency and the emotion of anger often give rise to acts of violence. These acts are usually injurious to society, though sometimes they are committed in the defense of society. Sexual impulses also sometimes give rise to acts of violence which are anti-social in their character. But the sexual impulses usually arouse a tender emotion which stimulates sympathetic feelings and often leads to acts of kindness. The parental instincts and emotions cause numerous acts of self-sacrifice, and are powerful social forces. However, these instincts and emotions sometimes lead to anti-social acts, as when a parent injures many persons in behalf of his or her offspring. In similar fashion many other innate tendencies and feelings sometimes lead to social behavior, and under other conditions to anti-social behavior. Some of these dynamic forces lead more frequently to social behavior, and other forces more often to anti-social behavior. Every human trait may be manifested either in a social or in an anti-social manner.

Social groups, as well as individuals, are engaged in a struggle for existence. The survival of individuals is of primary importance, because there could be no groups without individuals. In every social or partially social species the survival of the individual depends in part upon the survival of the group to which it belongs. The behavior of the members of the group must in the long run promote the survival of the group. Social instincts, sympathetic feelings, and intellectual activities which are socially directed, tend to be preserved and encouraged in the social struggle for existence. On the other hand, anti-social instincts and feelings, and intellectual activities which are anti-socially directed, tend either to be eliminated, or, when too deeply rooted in human nature to be eliminated, to be restrained.

This control of anti-social tendencies in most individuals comes in part from within. Certain human traits exercise a restraining influence over the anti-social tendencies of other traits. The sympathetic feelings may ameliorate somewhat the impulse to do injury to others which is encouraged by the pugnacious tendency. But this

[13] See Maurice Parmelee, *Personality and Conduct*, New York, 1918. Chapter II, "Invasive and Non-Invasive Conduct."

"The proposed criterion is as satisfactory theoretically as any . . . , and is the most practical because it is concrete and can be given the pragmatic test. In the long run it is possible to ascertain fairly accurately whether or not a form of conduct is invasive." (Pp. 10-11.)

internal control often is not sufficient, giving rise to the need for an external control.

Habit is an important form of control. It is primarily an internal and not an external form. Even though each habit belongs to an individual and is formed by him, nevertheless the character of the habits formed depends largely upon social influences. In organized society many habits are drilled into individuals, so that the directed or compulsory formation of habits becomes a potent means of social control.

Custom is another important means of social control which varies in considerable part from habit. Certain customs are also the habits of many individuals. In Occidental culture the custom of eating with knives and forks is also the habit of the great majority of individuals because the acts involved are repeated so often as to become habitual. In China and Japan eating with chopsticks is both the customary and the habitual way. Other customs do not involve habits. While it is customary to marry, it can hardly be said to be habitual, because the vast majority of individuals do not marry more than a very few times at most.

Custom often brings about uniformity of behavior in matters in which uniformity is essential, or, to say the least, desirable. In order to avoid disorder and accidents it is well to have a custom on the public highways that vehicles shall always pass to the right or to the left. However, custom may also do social injury by causing an excessive degree of uniformity, and by obstructing desirable changes.

Public opinion exists when the majority of a group have the same opinion about a certain matter, or when a majority of those who have a definite opinion agree, or when a powerful minority is able to impose its opinion upon an ignorant or an indifferent or even an unwilling majority. When public opinion concerns matters of conduct, it often has a powerful coercive influence. In many cases an individual will suffer bodily injury if he acts contrary to the public opinion of the group to which he belongs. Even when bodily injury is not inflicted, he will usually experience mental discomfort which will deter him from acting contrary to public opinion.

Public opinion is closely related to custom. Some customs are due to public opinion as to how certain things should be done. On the other hand, many customs become established first, and then give rise to public opinion. While it is impossible to ascertain which comes first in the majority of cases, it is likely that usually the custom becomes established without any conscious forethought. Public opinion follows as an attempt to rationalize the customary mode of conduct.

278

When public opinion with regard to matters of conduct becomes strong, and involves the belief that certain forms of conduct are right and other forms are wrong, there arise moral or ethical ideas. Theologians and metaphysicians have usually averred that the concepts of right and wrong existed in the first instance and were then applied to forms of conduct. Whatever may be thought of such *a priori* reasoning, these ideas have a restraining force because violations of them usually bring in their train penalties of various sorts.

Religion often plays an influential part in regulating human conduct. Its representatives teach and preach the existence of powerful spiritual beings which desire and command men to act in specified ways. They assert that if men do not act accordingly they are liable to suffer severe penalties. To the extent that these religious doctrines are believed they influence human conduct. Religious organizations, such as the churches, have often acquired a vast amount of power over human actions. The rules of conduct specified by religion are usually the same as those which have already been developed by public opinion and have become moral or ethical ideas. When these ideas and religious beliefs are identical, religion reinforces the accepted standard of morality. Sometimes, however, the religious rules of conduct come from other sources. Ruling classes have almost invariably utilized religion to maintain their power.

Magical ideas have also played a part similar to that of religion in regulating human conduct, especially in the earlier stages of social evolution. They still have a good deal of influence among primitive peoples and among the more ignorant classes in civilized countries. Magic resembles religion in that it assumes the existence of spiritual beings. As has already been indicated, it differs from religion in that it uses coercive rather than propitiatory measures in its efforts to influence these imaginary powers. In either case human conduct is regulated with reference to the alleged nature and desires of these mythical beings.

In the earlier stages of cultural evolution there was usually no organized mechanism for social control. Ordinarily it was effected through individuals who were wreaking personal vengeance for injuries done to themselves or to their relatives. At the same time they were giving expression to the public opinion, customs, moral ideas, religious beliefs, and magical ideas of their group. The earlier forms of social organization, such as the tribe, had a rude mechanism for administering social control.[14] A highly organized mechanism came

[14] See G. C. Wheeler, *The Tribe and Intertribal Relations in Australia*, London, 1910.

into being with the rise of the state and government. Government usually operates under a legal system. Law is based in large part upon custom, public opinion, moral ideas, religion, etc. The state through its government has administrative and judicial means for enforcing its laws. All forms of social control are eventually expressed to a considerable extent through the law and its enforcement. The most drastic and coercive portion of law is the criminal or penal law. The acts prohibited by this branch of the law are crimes.

Social control furnishes the restraint upon the anti-social tendencies of the individual which is essential for the preservation of society. Utility for the survival of society is in the long run the determining factor with respect to these forms of social control, just as it is the ultimate determining factor throughout the struggle for existence. The conditions which determine the criterion of social utility are continually changing. The forms of social control must change accordingly. Forms of social control which are suitable for one type of social grouping may not be suitable for another type, and may even lead to its destruction. So that these forms change greatly from time to time and from one group to another.

It often happens, however, that forms of social control which no longer have social utility, sometimes indeed which have never had social utility, persist for a time, even though they are injuring society. This can happen only when they are not fatal in their effects. There is reason to believe that many social groups have been destroyed as social organisms by injurious forms of social control. Religion and despotism, sometimes each by itself, but often in unison, have at many times and places developed drastic forms of social control which have been injurious to a large part of the membership of the group. Such control has sometimes persisted for a long time. When this has been due to despotism or oligarchy, it has been in the interest of a few at the expense of the many. When it has been due to religion, it has resulted from the influence of beliefs to the effect that the spiritual beings feared by man demanded these drastic measures. When the two have worked in unison, the despot or oligarchy has usually been regarded as representing by "divine" right these imaginary beings, and therefore delegated to enforce their wishes. Despots and oligarchs have often found it useful to reinforce their own secular authority with this supernatural sanction.

Hence it is that there are two aspects to social control and regulation. Society must be preserved against the anti-social tendencies of its individual members. On the other hand, an excessive amount of social control may lead to the destruction of the group itself, because of the injury it does to its members. Even when it does not destroy the group, more control than is essential for social survival

280

limits the liberty of individuals unnecessarily. The restriction of individual liberty is inevitable in so far as it is essential for social survival. It becomes unnecessary when it is carried beyond this point. Individual liberty and social control always have been and always will be in conflict with each other to a certain extent.[15]

[15] In my two books on crime I have described at length how the state through its legal and penal institutions exercises control over its citizens:

Maurice Parmelee, *Criminology*, New York, 1918. See especially Chapter III entitled "Crime and Social Control."

Maurice Parmelee, *The Principles of Anthropology and Sociology in Their Relations to Criminal Procedure*, New York, 1908. See especially Chapter III entitled "Society and the Criminal."

Chapter XIX

The Forms of Social Control

THE preceding chapter has revealed a profound distinction between two forms of social control. This distinction is not always superficially evident. The first form arises out of and is exercised by the collective authority of the social organization at any time and place. This may be a clan, tribe, community, state or nation. The collective authority arises out of the universal or predominant sentiments of the individual members of the organization. At what times, in how many places, and to what degree such an authority has actually existed is difficult to determine.

The second form of social control arises out of the domination of one or more groups by another or other groups within a social organization. The historical evidence seems to indicate that this second form has been by far the most prevalent. In fact, it is doubtful if a genuine collective authority has ever existed. Gerontocracy, sex dominance, chattel slavery seldom as a transitional form from slavery to freedom, caste, theocracy, oligarchy, monocracy, timocracy, plutocracy, class dominance, wage slavery arising out of the class system, the state as an agency of power, and other forms of group dominance and exploitation have limited and prevented a genuine collective authority. By means of threats of supernatural or mundane punishments the dominating minority has often intimidated and coerced the dominated majority into believing that the system of exploitation under which they suffered was inevitable and the best for them. Or by means of the instruments of propaganda in the hands of the dominating minority the dominated majority has been persuaded into this belief, sometimes by the promise of celestial rewards. It must be remembered, therefore, that what appears to be collective authority very often conceals what is in reality one form or another of group domination. Many forms of group control are social only in this limited sense, and may even be anti-social in their ultimate effect.

Inasmuch as preliterate peoples do not possess the art of writing, and the state has not yet evolved a penal code, a code of criminal procedure, courts of public justice, in other words, law and its mechanism in the formal sense of those terms, cannot exist among them. Many acts which in civilized communities are punished by the law are in primitive groups subject to private revenge. For example, homicide is often reacted against by retaliation on the part of the family or friends of the victim. In a sense these acts also are crimes in the primitive group. Private retaliation is sanctioned by the public opinion of the group and is even expected by it. Failure to exercise such retaliation would be regarded as indicating, to say the least, cowardice, if not graver culpability. On the other hand, these acts are not reacted against by the group as a whole. In this sense they cannot be regarded as crimes and as manifestations of social control.

Observation of preliterate peoples and study of the oldest codes of law indicate that the earliest crimes probably were somewhat as follows:[1]

1. Treason.
2. Witchcraft.
3. Sacrilege and other offenses against religion.
4. Incest and other sexual offenses.
5. Poisoning and allied offenses.
6. Breaches of the hunting rules.

The offenses listed above are crimes in the sense that they are punished by the group as a whole. While there is no written law it is understood in the group that such acts are to be publicly punished. Whenever a member of the group has committed or is suspected of having committed such an act, an investigation or ceremony is held to determine the facts. This is a crude prototype of a trial by a court of justice. This primitive judicial process may be the gathering of evidence from witnesses by the elders of the group. It may be an ordeal inflicted upon the suspected person. Or it may be an incantation performed by a magician which is supposed to reveal the truth. When the accused person has been found guilty by one or more of these methods, appropriate punishment is imposed upon the culprit by the group as a whole or by its authorized agents.

Treason is most likely to occur in connection with war. If the group, whether it be a horde, a clan, or a tribe, is in conflict with another group, and one of its members aids and abets the enemy, or even merely refuses to fight, he is punished for this crime which menaces the integrity and survival of the group. The nature of trea-

[1] See H. Oppenheimer, *The Rationale of Punishment*, London, 1913; S. R. Steinmetz, *Ethnologische Studien der ersten Entwicklung der Strafe*, Leyden, 1894, 2 vols.

sonable acts varies according to the organization of the group and the character of the environment.

Oppenheimer has asserted that "witchcraft is probably the first in point of time, and certainly the most universal, of all primitive crimes."[2] It is doubtful if witchcraft as a crime is any earlier or perhaps any more universal than treason. It is probable that since a very early time, and almost if not quite universally, the practice of some forms magic has been punished. Not all magic has been punished. Magic may be divided into the so-called "white" and "black" magic. The white or good magic is the kind which benefits the group, by bringing needed rain, by destroying the enemy, etc. The black or bad magic does injury to the group, by blighting the crops, by bringing illness, etc. The bad magic is punished by the group. A good magician merits reward from the group, while a bad one suffers punishment. To be a magician at all is likely to arouse suspicion. The lay public cannot be certain that the magician is not using his power surreptitiously against the public. Hence the persistent suspicion against witchcraft which has lasted down to the present day, even in civilized communities where belief in magic still lingers.[3]

Sacrilege is the religious correlative of witchcraft as a crime. If instead of or in addition to the somewhat impersonal powers postulated by magic, spiritual beings of a more personal character, such as gods, are assumed to exist, which cannot be coerced but can be pleased or offended, it is to the public interest that these beings should be pleased and not offended. Otherwise they may wreak divine vengeance upon the group.[4] Hence it is that those who have committed acts which are supposed to offend these sensitive deities must be punished in order to avert divine vengeance. This belief is the cause of the legislation against blasphemy, profanity, violation of so-called "holy" days, and the like, which has persisted down to the present day even in civilized countries.

Incest as an early crime may have originated as a violation of the rules of exogamy. This explanation is suggested by the fact that the scope of forbidden relationships among many primitive peoples is much wider than among civilized peoples. The origin of exogamy may have been due to an inborn aversion to sexual intercourse be-

[2] H. Oppenheimer, *op. cit.*, p. 73.

[3] See, for example, Margaret A. Murray, *Witchcraft in Western Europe*, 1921. The term "witchcraft" is derived from the Anglo-Saxon word "wit"—to know, so that "witchcraft" means the "craft of the wise." A pagan religion and magic art survived into modern times which Christianity strove to suppress by persecution.

[4] The Hebrew Yahveh spoke vengefully in the Mosaic law to those who offend him: "For I the Lord they God am a jealous God, visiting the iniquity of the fathers upon the children unto the third and fourth generation of them that hate me." (*Exodus*, XX, 5.)

tween near of kin. However, it is much more likely that it was caused by an acquired aversion to sexual intercourse between persons who have been closely associated with each other during early youth, and perhaps also to the greater attractiveness owing to novelty of mates chosen from another group.[5]

The regulation of sexual relations varies greatly among preliterate peoples. There is variation from a high degree of freedom approaching promiscuity to strict regulation. On the whole, there seems to have been little sexual morality in the civilized sense of the term. Apparently there was little regulating of sexual relations because they are alleged to be right or wrong in themselves, as is often the case among civilized peoples. Adultery, seduction and rape were more likely to be regarded as private than as public wrongs, because they are violations of the proprietary interests of husbands and fathers. Even when these and other sexual offenses were treated as public wrongs, it was in many cases for religious and magical reasons. It was often believed that there is a causal relationship between sexual acts and the success of the group in warfare, hunting, the gathering or cultivation of plant foods, etc.

A great deal of magic and religion has centered about sex not only among preliterate peoples but in civilization as well. This is due to the mysterious character of sex to those who have no scientific knowledge of its nature. It is due also to the unaccountable and powerful erotic feelings it arouses and to the inexplicable physiological processes with which it is connected, especially in the female sex in connection with menstruation and reproduction.

The Christian attitude toward sex illustrates magical and religious ideas with respect to sex. The principal source of Christianity is in Judaism which contains many of these magical and religious ideas. The notion of uncleanness of sex plays a prominent part in Hebrew religion. A considerable portion of the Jewish law is devoted to the regulation of sex with respect to its uncleanness. In the Old Testament *Leviticus* XV describes the uncleanness of the sexual issues of men and women and prescribes how they are to be cleansed. *Leviticus* XII specifies how women are to be purified after childbirth. In the New Testament these ideas imported from Judaism developed into a form of asceticism which exalted celibacy. In *Revelation* XIV, 4, it is said: "These are they which were not defiled with women; for they are virgins." Throughout the New Testament the dominant theme with respect to sex is that sex is unclean; that virginity and

5 See the discussions in E. Westermarck, *History of Human Marriage*, London, 1894, Chaps. XIV, XV; *The Origin and Development of the Moral Ideas*, London, 1906, Vol. II, Chap. XL; and in J. G. Frazer, *Totemism and Exogamy*, London, 1910, 4 vols.

285

chastity are highly meritorious; that the flesh, by which is usually meant sex, is antagonistic to the spirit; and that marriage is a grudging and questionable concession to the flesh. All of this is emphatically stated in the Pauline epistle, I *Corinthians* VII, which says: "It is good for a man not to touch a woman. Nevertheless, to avoid fornication, let every man have his own wife, and let every woman have her own husband." In the Christian religion the magical notion of the uncleanness of sex has been combined with and has reinforced the ascetic ideal of propitiating the deity by expiation and purification through chastity.[6]

The action of poisons and of curative drugs is mysterious to preliterate man. He is prone to attribute their effects to supernatural properties. If he believes that these properties have been imparted to them by magicians, and if their effect is harmful, as in the case of poisoning, he will regard poisoning and similar offenses as black magic and will punish them as such. As Oppenheimer said, "primitive toxicology is a branch of magic."[7] The public punishment of poisoning is due not so much to respect for human life as to fear of black magic.

It is of the utmost importance to a primitive group in the hunting stage to maintain the hunting rules, because hunting is the main source of food. Some of these rules have obvious utility, as when they conserve the supply of animal food. Other rules are manifestly absurd to civilized man, as when incest is prohibited because it is supposed to interfere with success in hunting. Here again magical and religious ideas are having their influence. Totemic regulations probably in many cases originated as primitive game laws. Later they acquired a magical or religious character which obscured their original purpose and often destroyed their utility.[8]

The preceding survey of some of the principal primitive crimes suggests the origin and early evolution of penal treatment as a form of social control. Back of these primitive reactions, both private and public, can be discerned fundamental human traits of mind and of character, such as the powerful emotion of fear and various inborn reactions to remove the causes of fear, the overwhelming emotion of anger and various innate reactions to injure the object of anger. From the standpoint of control which is genuinely social there can be discerned in the category of public punishments both errors of

[6] For an extensive discussion of the religious and magical regulation of sex see Maurice Parmelee, *Personality and Conduct*, New York, 1918, Chaps. VIII-XVIII especially Chapter VIII on "The Sex Relation" and Chapter XII on "The Double Standard of Sex Freedom."

[7] H. Oppenheimer, *op. cit.*, p. 88.

[8] J. G. Frazer, *op. cit.*

286

commission and errors of omission. The errors of commission were and still are due to the persistence of customs which are no longer useful, and to the influence of magic and religion. The errors of omission are illustrated in the comparatively little protection afforded by primitive public justice to human life and limb and to the preservation of wealth. This lack of protection is probably due in part to a low respect for human life and to a rudimentary development of property rights. As indicated above, offenses against human life and sometimes also against property are often reacted against privately with the sanction of the community.[9]

These offenses which were privately punished later developed into either crimes or torts. Thus arose the distinction between the criminal and the civil law. Magical and religious ideas also had a considerable influence, as they still have, to act as a restraint upon these offenses spontaneously without regard to private or public punishment, because of the automatic consequences feared from the violation of these ideas. In this fashion the taboo system, described in the preceding chapter, has been a restraining force because of the dire consequences feared from any breach of the taboo.

We have seen that in primitive communities social control operates through custom, public opinion, tradition, magic and religion. Law in the political meaning of the term cannot exist in such communities. The above-mentioned factors continue to exercise a powerful influence in barbarous, semi-civilized and civilized societies. But there are at least two new important factors for social control. The first is the art of writing which makes possible an accurate, permanent record of laws in the place of the inaccurate, word-of-mouth record of tradition. The second is the state which evolved from the simpler clan and tribal organization. The organization of the state brought into being a centralized government over a definite area of considerable extent and a large number of people. It created executive and legislative authorities for the promulgation and enactment of laws, and judicial authorities for their interpretation and administration, to a degree which was not possible in the simpler forms of social organization. Written law became one of the most important agencies of social control.

Some of the offenses of which the law takes cognizance were formerly subject to private vengeance. Many of the offenses in primitive society were subject to the so-called *lex talionis* or law of retaliation (an eye for an eye, a tooth for a tooth, a life for a life, etc.).

---

[9] For example, Lowie says of the Plains Indians of North America that "even homicide was a tort, not a crime," but that "transgressions of the hunting regulations . . . were treated as an attempt against the public," (*i.e.*, a crime). (R. H. Lowie, *The Origin of the State*, New York, 1927, p. 104.)

Without social regulation private vengeance is likely to become excessive, and to give rise to disorder. Blood feuds arise between families, hordes, clans, and sometimes tribes, and long continue to cause much loss of life.[10] With the rise of the state, society attempted to regulate this prolific source of disorder. Such regulation was attained, not necessarily by making private vengeance public, but by specifying through the law the limitations of private vengeance, and by establishing courts of justice to decide when private vengeance might be exercised.

Many of the ancient penal codes were devoted in part to describing the offenses in which the victim might take private vengeance, and the kind of vengeance which was permissible. A judgment of a court in such a case permitted the victim to wreak vengeance if he chose to do so, but did not usually require it of him. As time went by, the practise of compounding for these offenses developed. It became possible for the offender to escape vengeance by making a money payment (Anglo-Saxon, *bot* and *wergild*)[11] to the victim.[12]

From the early social and legal institutions of private vengeance and of the composition of wrongs there developed much if not all of the civil law and a part of the criminal law. In some of the cases in which it came to be recognized that it was to the public interest that the offender be punished, the victim failed to exercise his right of vengeance, so that the offender escaped punishment. These offenses gradually became public wrongs or crimes, and are now punished under the criminal law. The scope of the criminal law has expanded with the increased complexity of the life and organization of the community.

Primitive society is more or less democratic. It is too simple to permit of great differentiation of status. A hereditary caste system, or a class system based on the rights of property and inheritance, has not developed or is still rudimentary. The elders, magicians, priests, and chiefs may have much influence. But it is ordinarily impossible for one individual or class to dominate for long. From the tribal organization there arose more or less permanent village communities, cities, and especially the state and the nation. There also arose the autocratic and despotic power of kings. As a result of the increasing complexity of the political organization due to the development of the state, of the economic organization due to the extension of the division of labor, and of the exploitation which arose out of the private ownership of property, there appeared ruling classes.

---

[10] Cf. H. E. Seebohm, *On the Structure of Greek Tribal Society*, London, 1895, pp. 41-45.

[11] According to the Standard Dictionary, *bot*=profit, *wer*=man, *gild*=payment.

[12] Cf. Frederic Seebohm, *Tribal Custom in Anglo-Saxon Law*, London, 1902.

288

Despots and ruling classes have created many new crimes and have enforced the criminal law in the most drastic fashion. Throughout the long and turbulent period during which nations and states were being formed, which in some parts of the world has lasted down to the present day, dictators and oligarchies have exploited the masses partly by means of the criminal law. Centralized power may have been necessary at certain times and places to bring into being a strong and effective government. But, on the one hand, the modern democratic movement, inspired in part by a humanitarian ideal, has ameliorated the law, and has diminished the extent to which it is used as a means of exploitation. On the other hand, after the European War of 1914 to 1918, totalitarian government crushed democracy and established dictatorial and oligarchical rule in Italy under the name of Fascism, in Germany under the misleading guise of National Socialism and in several other countries.[13] While the World War of 1939 to 1945 defeated these totalitarian governments it remains to be seen whether or not they will continue to be suppressed.

Despots and ruling classes have been greatly helped by religion. It has almost always been to the interest of the priestly class to league itself with dictators and oligarchies and to give them religious sanction for their tyrannical acts. In many of the nations which evolved from a tribal organization the tribal god developed into a powerful and often jealous, wrathful and vindictive deity. These anthropomorphic traits are repeatedly attributed to the Jewish Yahveh in the *Old Testament* and to the Christian God in the *New Testament*:

"I the Lord thy God am a jealous God, visiting the iniquity of the fathers upon the children unto the third and fourth generation of them that hate me." (The second Commandment of Moses.) Exodus 20:5.

"The Lord shall swallow them up in his wrath." Psalms 21:9.

"To me belongeth vengeance and recompence." Deuteronomy 32:35.

"Do we provoke the Lord to jealousy?" 1 Corinthians 10:22.

"The wrath of God abideth on him." St. John 3:36.

"Vengeance is mine; I will repay, saith the Lord." Romans 12:19.

Hence it was all the more desirable to avoid giving offense to this spiritual being who was not only powerful but also jealous, wrathful and vindictive. Any act which could in any sense be construed as offending the deity was severely punished. The priests have almost invariably encouraged the suppression of sins by penal measures because it has enhanced their power and prestige. And the acts stigma-

[13] See Maurice Parmelee, *Bolshevism, Fascism and the Liberal-Democratic State,* New York, 1934.

289

tized as sins have usually been the acts which menace the power and interests of the dictators and ruling oligarchies.

Kings have been aided in wielding their power by the divinity which has been attributed to them partly because of their exalted position. As a divine or semi-divine person, and as the viceregent of the deity upon earth, a king could punish offenses against himself as being also against the deity. Hence were derived the notions of the divine right and power of kings, justice as emanating from the king, crimes regarded as "breaches of the King's peace," etc.

There are many ancient penal codes of which historical records are extant. Among them are the criminal laws of ancient Egypt; the the Babylonian code of Hammurabi; the oldest extant Hindu code, the Manava Dharma Sastra; the Hindu laws of Manu; the so-called Mosaic laws in the Hebrew scriptures, especially the Pentateuch; the ancient Greek law of Draco (B.C. 621) and of Solon (B.C. 539); the Twelve Tables of Rome; the Ta Tsing Leu Lee of China; the Tai-ho Ritsu of Japan; the Moslem criminal law in the Koran; the early Germanic criminal law quoted by Tacitus the Latin historian; the Lex Salica, probably the earliest Germanic code of which a written record is extant; the Ruskaia Pravda, an ancient Slavic criminal code in the oldest Russian law book; the ancient English laws in the Domesday Book; the ancient Irish law, or so-called Brehon law; the laws of ancient Mexico; the laws of ancient Peru; and various others.[14]

Each of the many systems of law developed more or less independently, though most of them have been influenced by other systems. Some of these legal systems are in barbarous and semi-civilized countries, and other systems in civilized countries. The legal systems of countries possessing culture of Mediterranean or European origin are derived almost entirely from the Roman civil law and the English common law. The systems of Roman origin cover most of Europe, South and Central America, and smaller areas elsewhere. The systems originating from the common law cover most of the British Empire and of the United States.

In the early stages of cultural evolution many injurious acts were punished by private vengeance, usually with the approval of the community. Most of these acts later became either public or private wrongs under the law. The acts regarded as harmful to the com-

---

[14] Brief summaries of some of these codes are in the following works: L. T. Hobhouse, *Morals in Evolution*, 2nd ed. rev., London, 1915, Chap. 3; H. Oppenheimer, *The Rationale of Punishment*, London, 1913, Part II, Chap. 3; E. Durkheim, *De la division du travail social*, Paris, 1893, Chap. 4. See also the treatises on the evolution of custom and law by Maine, Maitland, F. Seebohm, etc. The text of some of these codes is in A. Kocourek and J. H. Wigmore, Editors, *Sources of Ancient and Primitive Laws*, Boston, 1915.

munity became crimes or public wrongs, to be punished under the criminal law. Those regarded as harmful only to individuals became torts or private wrongs to be redressed under the civil law. It has usually been assumed that no questions of moral turpitude are involved in torts. There has always been more or less shifting of wrongs back and forth between the criminal and the civil law. An act which was at one time regarded as a private wrong may at another time be regarded as a public wrong, and *vice versa*.

The differentiating of the criminal from the civil law can be traced in both the Roman and the English law. The Romans developed more fully the law of torts, the law of contracts, the law of testamentary succession, etc., than they developed the criminal law. This explains why the Roman law is sometimes called the Civil Law (*Jus Civile or Corpus Juris Civilis*). However, the term civil law usually applies to that branch of the law which deals with private wrongs, contracts, etc., as distinguished from the criminal law.

The first written records of Roman law which are extant are in the fragments of the Twelve Decemviral Tables (*Lex Duodecim Tabularum*). These tables were prepared about the year 450 B.C., or half a century after the birth of the Republic. They apparently constituted a codification of the existing laws. The eighth table is the *tabula de delictis* which contains the criminal section of this code. Some of these delicts were crimes in the modern sense of the term, namely, offenses against the public. Among them were murder, perjury and nocturnal disturbances. Capital punishment in different forms was prescribed for all of these offenses. Other offenses were regarded as private wrongs against individuals and punished by retaliation and compensation. When Roman jurisprudence became well developed, delicts were divided into four classes:—(1) Theft (*furtum*); (2) Robbery (*vi bonorum raptorum*); (3) Injuries to property (*damnum injuriae per legem Aquiliam*); (4) Injuries to the person (*injuriae*). These classes included the two principal types of offenses in every system of criminal law, namely, (1) Crimes against property; (2) Crimes against the person. Later under the Empire in the code of Justinian (A.D. 483-565), crimes were classified, based upon the manner of prosecution, as (1) *Publica justicia;* (2) *Extraordinaria crimina;* (3) *Privata delicta*.[15]

The English criminal law developed from several sources. It was derived in part from the prehistoric inhabitants of the British Isles. Almost no records survive of their legal system. The best record extant is of the ancient Irish or so-called Brehon law, which remained in force in an archaic form through several centuries of the Christian

[15] R. R. Cherry, *Lectures on the Growth of Criminal Law in Ancient Communities*, London, 1890.

era.[16] Like every system of punitive law, the early English criminal law was based largely upon the principle of retaliation, the *lex talionis*. In the Anglo-Saxon and in the early English law many offenses against persons and property were compounded. If an offender failed to pay the compensation imposed upon him, he was outlawed. This meant that he lost all rights of person and of property and could be killed with impunity. Outlawry became a public punishment imposed and enforced by the courts.

For several centuries the Romans held Britain as a colony. They introduced their law as well as other phases of their culture. But not much of their law remained behind when they evacuated Britain in the fifth century of the Christian era. Later Roman law had some influence indirectly through the relations between England and the Continent, especially through the canonical law which influenced English equity jurisprudence greatly. However, Roman jurisprudence had comparatively slight influence upon the evolution of the English common law.

The common law had its roots mainly in the Anglo-Saxon jurisprudence. After the establishment of the king's peace it was developed by the decisions of courts and the statutes enacted by Parliament. In its evolution was exemplified the transition from the time when the majority of offenses were private wrongs or torts, to be punished by blood-feud or composition, to the time when many of these offenses became public wrongs or crimes to be punished by the State. The common law furnishes an example of the more or less spontaneous and unintended development of organized social control.

In the common law there evolved a three-fold classification of crimes:—(1) Treason; (2) Felony; (3) Misdemeanor. Treason was at first one of the felonies, and then became differentiated. It is by definition an act directed at the existence of the State itself. In the early English law many acts directed against the king and members of the royal family were treasonable. The same is still true of some of these acts. Needless to say, acts against the royal family should not be classified as treasonable because they do not menace the existence of the State itself in a constitutional monarchy. Such criminal laws are examples of the abuse of monarchical power.

The felonies were originally the offenses which were unemendable, that is to say, which could not be compounded because of their heinousness. They were punished by the forfeiture of the criminal's estate, and often of his life. There were seven felonies recognized by the common law. Three were against the person—murder, manslaughter, and rape. Four were against the property of individuals—arson, bur-

[16] See Lawrence Ginnell, *The Brehon Laws*, London, 1894, and R. R. Cherry, *op. cit.*

292

glary, theft or larceny, and robbery. Three other crimes—wounding, mayhem, and false imprisonment—have at one time or another been called felonies. To these so-called common law felonies have been added by means of statutes enacted by Parliament numerous other felonies. The total number of felonies is now very great.

The misdemeanors, originally called "transgressions" or "trespasses," were and are the crimes less grave than the felonies. In recent years has been recognized a group of petty offenses which are distinguished both from the felonies and from misdemeanors, because they are tried by a modern method of summary procedure without a jury.

The Roman law and the English common law furnish the basis for the legal systems of all countries of Mediterranean or Occidental culture. They illustrate the manner in which the criminal law furnishes the most drastic and the civil law a somewhat less drastic means of social control. Earlier in this chapter it was noted that there is some shifting back and forth between the criminal and the civil law, owing to changes in social conditions and public opinion. Formerly it was customary to imprison debtors for failure to pay a debt as if they were criminals. Today the law usually regards such failure as a violation of a contract.

The concept of property is gradually changing. It is being increasingly recognized that the right of private property is giving rise to monopolistic practices which accentuate greatly the inequality in the distribution of wealth. These and similar practices, not yet stigmatized as crimes in capitalist countries, are sometimes called "white collar" crimes.[17] The common man does not yet realize the far-reaching economic consequences from these practices because these consequences are not immediately obvious. He is more outraged by murder, rape and kidnapping. But as Mannheim has said: "In the future, we shall have to get used to the idea that not only protection of property, but also the protection *against* property falls under the scope of the criminal law."[18] Soviet Russia is as yet the only country in which this is fully recognized.[19]

Earlier in this chapter it has been suggested that primitive peoples may have possessed a rudimentary form of democracy. In modern times there has been a so-called democratic movement. To say the least, there

[17] See articles by E. H. Sutherland entitled "White Collar Criminality," "Is 'White Collar Crime' Crime," in the *American Sociological Review*, February 1940 and April 1945, and "Crime and Business," in the *Annals of the American Academy of Political and Social Science*, September 1941; and book entitled *White Collar Crime*, New York, 1949.

[18] Hermann Mannheim, *Criminal Justice and Social Reconstruction*, New York, 1946.

[19] Harold Berman, "Principles of Soviet Criminal Law," in the *Yale Law Journal*, May 1947, pp. 803-836.

has arisen a concept of a social system in which there are no preferential distinctions of wealth and of status between individuals at birth. In a democratic society there would be an equality of rights, of opportunities, and of duties between all of its members. Innate differences between individuals give rise to differences of income and of authority. In a democracy no artificial social distinctions would enhance these differences and perpetuate them from generation to generation. No hereditary classification, such as a caste system, could exist in a democratic society. No group, owing to its status or wealth or both, could dominate another group.

It is often alleged that the ancient Greek city states were democracies and even "pure" democracies in the sense that they did not utilize representative government. The same has been alleged of the Roman Republic organized about 500 B.C. of city states contemporary with the Greek states. Both the Greek and the Roman states possessed many slaves who had no rights whatsoever. Not even all of the free inhabitants were citizens with the right to vote because of preferential distinctions of birth and of wealth.

Slavery probably originated after agriculture began to develop. Warlike tribes captured prisoners in order to use them in carrying on agricultural and some industrial occupations. In the Homeric period in Greece the sources of slavery probably were (1) Capture in war, (2) Piracy and kidnapping, (3) Slave trade, (4) Birth when slavery had become hereditary, (5) Sale of children and freemen selling themselves. Slavery persisted into the golden age of Greece.

Greece became imperialist for a time before it succumbed under Roman rule. The Roman Republic became a vast empire which ruled most of the known world for many centuries. However, the experience of a small group of individuals, never more than a few thousand in each city state, expressing their desires and choices by means of a popular suffrage, may have left a tradition which had a slight influence in later ages. It was a step away from autocracy and the narrowest form of oligarchy, but did not set a pattern for democracy on a national or a worldwide scale.

During the Middle Ages there were slight traces of democracy in the free cities of the Hanseatic League, in the cantons of Switzerland, and later in the Dutch Republic (*circa* 1579-1795). The Reformation was a revolt against ecclesiastical authority. It may have reflected to a slight extent the doctrine of primitive Christianity of the equality of men before the deity. But historical Christianity has not translated it into political and social realities. The Christian nations have not been more democratic than the non-Christian peoples by virtue of their religion but owing to economic and social forces.

294

Insofar as democracy has actually materialized it has come not so much through an effort to attain a democratic ideal as through the efforts of depressed social groups and classes, such as chattel slaves, feudal serfs, peasants, or wage slaves, to free themselves from subjection to their respective rulers. The bourgeois revolutions of the seventeenth and eighteenth centuries expressed the growing power at first of the merchants, and then of the industrialists as well, against the vested rights of the feudal nobility and against monarchical authority.

The English Revolution of 1688 gave the middle class a good deal of power. The invention of the steam engine in the eighteenth century rendered possible large-scale production and strengthened the manufacturers and industrialists. The industrial revolution, which commenced in England, gave the decisive blow to feudalism. The French Revolution freed the bourgeoisie politically and removed the remaining restrictions upon private enterprise. The American War of Independence made the middle class supreme in the northern states. The Civil War of 1861 to 1865 destroyed chattel slavery and the plantation system in the southern states. These revolutionary changes suppressed feudalism throughout most of the Occident. It became possible to produce anything in almost unlimited quantities, except insofar as the intrinsic nature of capitalism as a scarcity economy imposes restrictions.

The middle class was formerly the mercantile class with an economic and social status between the feudal lords and their serfs. It now became merged with the capitalists. The latter became the heirs of the feudal monopolists and established their own monopolies. Capitalism is monopolistic in the sense that a privileged few own the means of production. Economic power leads in turn to a preponderant political influence. The capitalist class is able to exploit the proletarian class. The workers, though nominally free, are actually at the mercy of the capitalists because they own the tools of production even less than the handicraftsmen under the earlier feudalism. This situation sets the stage for the proletarian revolution. On the one hand, the proletariat is becoming more class conscious and aware of its power. On the other hand, the ownership of wealth and the control of production are becoming more and more concentrated in the hands of a few.

The proletarian revolution would greatly transcend the bourgeois revolution in importance. The transition from the capitalist to the classless society would be far more radical than from the feudal to the bourgeois system. In the latter case the exploitation of one class by another persisted and merely changed its form somewhat. In the former case it would perforce disappear entirely. Capitalism has little more

295

organization than feudalism, though its form is different. A classless society would require a socialized system including a planned society, whereas capitalism is in the main anarchic, chaotic, and disorganized. These subjects will be discussed in later chapters.[20]

[20] Bernard has classified the methods of social control as the *exploitive* methods, such as revolution, non-violent coercion, regimentation standardization, custom, law, social reform, and education. (L. L. Bernard, *Social Control in Its Sociological Aspects*, New York, 1939.)

Human exploitation and injury by the business world are becoming more apparent. They will probably lead to more regulation of monopoly, competitive wastes, false and misleading advertizing, unsound finance, speculative profits, unearned increment, instigation of war, and other methods of plundering the public.

296

Chapter XX

The Origins and Nature of the State

IN Chapter IX on the linguistic prerequisite of culture we have noted that all known human groups have had a highly developed language however rudimentary their culture may have been in other respects. In Chapter XI on language and writing we have seen that in Europe and Asia there are about 25 linguistic families. In North America and South America about 75 each have been distinguished, but this large number may be reduced with further study. In Africa at least five have been determined and there are several more which have not been identified. These 200 more or less families are very different from each other. They indicate either great diversity of origin or that some of them may have had a common origin from which they have widely varied. Such diversity of origin or high degree of variation suggests great antiquity. This is also suggested by the anatomical changes in the vicinity of the mouth mentioned in Chapter IX which seem to have been caused by or at least associated with speech and which would require a long time to develop.

This is very perplexing. If all branches of mankind evolved or invented or acquired in whatever fashion fully developed language long ago, why did they not advance more rapidly in other phases of cultural attainment? Mrs. Langer assumes that language developed very rapidly. "Whether there were many beginnings of language or few, or even only one, we cannot tell; but wherever the first stage of speaking, the use of any denotative symbol, was attained, there the development of speech probably occurred with phenomenal speed." She goes on to aver that language "might well transform the entire mode of living and feeling, in the whole species, within a few generations," and uses the power-engine as an example of rapid and far-reaching change.[1]

It is reasonable to assume that mankind could speak before neo-

[1] Susanne K. Langer, *Philosophy in a New Key*, New York, 1948, pp. 115-16.

lithic time, but how far back in paleolithic or eolithic time we cannot determine. In Chapter VII on the threshold of cultural evolution we saw that eoliths are found mainly in the pliocene horizon or the last of the Tertiary period. Paleolithic remains are found throughout most or all of the Quaternary period. This was an age of glaciations which probably lasted from 500,000 to 1,000,000 years and which terminated from 12,000 to 17,000 years ago. In Chapter XII on the origins of social organization we have surveyed briefly the paleolithic and neolithic periods. The neolithic period commenced at least as early as 6000 B.C. or more than 8,000 years ago. The glaciers probably delayed cultural evolution in its material phases. But the glaciers covered only a portion of the earth's surface. Furthermore, there were inter-glacial intervals which were relatively warm. So that the glaciers do not constitute a conclusive explanation of the slow advance of culture during paleolithic time.

During the latter part of the paleolithic or early in the neolithic there developed the pastoral culture of migratory peoples moving with their flocks of domesticated animals from place to place wherever pasture was available. At about the same time or soon thereafter the invention or discovery of agriculture resulted in the rural culture of more or less permanently located communities. These sessile communities sometimes tempted the mobile pastoral groups to attack them for purposes of plunder, thereby giving to the pastoral groups a somewhat warlike character as contrasted with the more pacific character of the village communities which were tied to the soil.

Early in the neolithic there began to arise in certain favorable spots the urban culture of cities. Some of these places were fertile river valleys, such as the valleys of the Nile and of the Euphrates, the valleys of the Ganges and of the Brahmaputra, the valleys of the Hoang-ho and of the Yangtze-kiang. In such places nature could support a relatively dense population without a highly developed mechanism of production. Surplus wealth could accumulate as a material basis for civilization. These urban communities were also tempted to dominate and exploit the village communities in their vicinity, though they themselves were subjected at times to exploitation by the pastoral groups.

In Chapter XVII have been described the kinship bonds and relations of tribes, clans and castes. These relations were often changed and sometimes supplanted by the relations between master and subject groups and individuals which arose from war and conquest. Amalgamation between groups sometimes also resulted from these relations. Out of these diversified and often conflicting processes and relations arose the political form of social organization commonly known as the state.

298

In Chapters XVIII and XIX have been described various forms of social control. In the later stages of cultural evolution some of the more drastic forms of social control have been exercised by the state. The first question is as to how far back in cultural evolution the form of social organization now known as the state came into existence. This in turn raises the question as to what we mean by the state. An American political scientist has said that "because political institutions follow no generally fixed order of development, it is misleading to speak of the evolution of the State."[2] This depends in part upon how we define the state. No form of social organization or social institution comes into existence full-blown at its inception. It develops gradually through a process which may or may not be called its evolution.

A writer on the modern state has defined it as follows: "The state is an association which, acting through law as promulgated by a government endowed to this end with coercive power, maintains within a community territorially demarcated the universal external conditions of social order."[3] Here is described a group of human beings within territorial limits characterized by or possessing an agency of social control called a government which operates through directives of behavior known as laws. How this type of "association" came into being is not indicated.

In Chapter XIX I have indicated that there are two forms of social control which differ profoundly from each other. The first arises out of and is exercised by the collective authority of the social organization in which it exists. The second arises out of the domination of one or more groups by another or other groups within a social organization. The available data suggest that the second form has been the most prevalent.

Oppenheimer emphasized the second form of social control when he said: "Every state was or is a *state of classes.*" He asserted that the state has been "a social institution, forced by a victorious group of men on a defeated group, with the sole purpose of regulating the dominion of the victorious group over the vanquished, and securing itself against revolt from within and attacks from abroad." And again he asserted: "Everywhere we find some warlike tribe of wild men breaking through the boundaries of some less warlike people, settling down as nobility and founding its State."[4] While these assertions per-

[2] Article on the "State," by George H. Sabine, in the *Encyclopedia of the Social Sciences*, New York, 1934, Vol. 14, page 329.

[3] R. M. MacIver, *The Modern State*, Oxford, 1926, page 22.

[4] Franz Oppenheimer, *The State, Its History and Development Viewed Sociologically*, Indianapolis, 1914, pages 5, 15, 16, first published in German in 1908 in Berlin.

haps are too sweeping, they suggest one of the origins of the state. A similar theory is that the state originated in the struggle between the races. Its principal exponents have been Ludwig Gumplowcz (1838-1909) and Gustav Ratzenhofer (1842-1904). These theories that the state originated in conflict characterize the state as an agency of power, of force, and often of violence. This is why sovereignty is often presented as the outstanding feature of the State.[5] The state as an agency of social and public welfare has received much less recognition.

In pre-literate tribal society kinship is the usual and principal bond of union. To what extent a common habitat served as a bond of union cannot be determined with precision. Kinsfolk would be likely to dwell together. Whether or not they would dwell together in one place for an extended period would depend largely upon the available food and shelter. A river valley with a continuous water supply, with ample game to be hunted in the vicinity, and perhaps also with caves and rock shelters at hand, as in the Dordogne valley in Southern France, would furnish a site for a more or less permanent settlement. Long continued use of a site would give rise to a rudimentary sense of ownership which would resent and repel intrusion by other groups and individuals. This may have been the beginning of property in land as distinguished from property in things made by the hand of man. It may also have been the beginning of group authority over or control of an area with territorial limits. This may have been the germ of the concept of sovereignty which later became an outstanding characteristic of the state.

Lowie has gathered together bits of information from pre-literate peoples which seem to illustrate origins of the state or stages in its development. He has asserted that "territorial sentiment, at first subordinate to the blood tie, was intensified to the point of assuming the dominant role." His conclusion with regard to the "territorial tie" as distinguished from the "blood tie" is as follows: "That local contiguity is a real basis for union on primitive levels may thus be taken as an established fact."[6]

Among many primitive peoples have been observed groupings or associations according to various rubrics or categories. MacIver has defined an association as "an organization of social beings . . . for the pursuit of some common interest or interests."[7] However, most of these associations have not included the whole of a given population. They have been organized on the basis of sex, or age, or status, or mili-

[5] The Encyclopedia Britannica (14th edition), 1942, has no article on the state but refers to the article on sovereignty.

[6] R. H. Lowie, The Origin of the State, New York, 1927, pp. 54, 115.

[7] R. M. MacIver, Community, New York, 1924, p. 23.

[8] Op cit., p. 93.

tary activities, or they have been secret societies whose purposes presumably have not been known. Lowie has reached the conclusion that "associations uniting *all* members of an area evidently prepare the way for the political integration of that area, while associations of more limited scope are proportionately less effective in that regard." [8]

The rise of chieftainship among some primitive people may have played a part in the development of the rudimentary state. The chieftain may have originated as the old man of the horde or tribe, as the leader in intertribal warfare, as the priest who interceded with the gods, as a magician who was supposed to possess exceptional supernatural powers, or in some other fashion. He would become the symbol or the agent of the sovereignty of his group. If the chieftainship became hereditary so that it was transmitted from generation to generation in one family, the concept of sovereignty would become emphasized and strengthened.

In most of the primitive peoples which have been observed the chieftainship, where it has existed, has been hereditary. The rule of descent has been that of the community, namely, patrilineal or matrilineal. The chief has sometimes been the principal judge and lawgiver of his people. Here were the germs of political institutions. In some cases the chief has been the economic leader of his community, perhaps because he was its wealthiest member. This may have marked the beginning or an early stage in the development of economic classes. Thus the chief united in himself some or all of the attributes of religious, magical, political, military, and economic leadership. As an English anthropologist has expressed it: "The essential fact about chieftainship, wherever it occurs, is that it serves as a means of concentrating the activities of the community under the direction of one person. The chief is not merely the representative and leader of the community; he is also frequently the symbol of its corporate unity." [9]

The preceding discussion is largely conjectural. There is little if anything definitive which can be said concerning the evolution of the state in prehistoric times. It may even be questioned as to whether anything remotely resembling the state came into existence prior to historic times. In that case it would be possible only to discuss the prehistoric development of the conditions which rendered possible the eventual emergence of the state.

The most important condition doubtless was agriculture which arose in the more fertile areas. Agriculture rendered possible a settled and more numerous population. It encouraged the rise of a political organization within well defined territorial limits. Such an organization is likely to have a city as its focal point. As has already been

[9] I. Schapera, Article on "Chiefs," *Encyclopaedia Britannica*, 1942, Vol. 5, page 464.

noted, many cities are located in river valleys or on harbors on the sea coast. Some cities are located on trade routes or near mines. The ancient city of Anau may have risen on a trade route between China and Mesopotamia. It is 20 miles east southeast of Ashkabad in Turkmenistan. Four different cultures have been excavated, two each in two kurgans or mounds. The earliest inhabitants of Anau were grain cultivators. By hand they made geometrically decorated pottery which parallels Chinese pottery. This fact suggests that its inhabitants were in touch with China. It has been estimated that Anau I dates back to about the period 3,900-3,300 B.C. The region is semi-arid and subject to droughts during which the site seems to have been deserted. In Anau I copper was rare but pottery was abundant. In Anau II copper was abundant and the pottery was monochrome. Anau IV, which was apparently about 750 B.C., had already reached the iron age.[10]

Nothing is known of the political organization of Anau and of its region. In some of the river valleys, such as the Nile, the Euphrates and the Tigris valleys, extensive empires had arisen. The same was true elsewhere in Asia Minor and in northern Africa, and later in Mexico, Central America and northern South America. No historical record is extant of the rise of any one of these early empires. Presumably a chief who had acquired religious, magical, military or economic leadership had extended his power not only over his own immediate community but also over extensive adjoining territory. A peasantry is a sessile population bound to the land it cultivates. It cannot readily abandon this land to move against the encroachments of a neighboring ruler. Its only alternative is to succumb to his rule and to pay the tribute imposed upon it.

Another factor for extensive power entered upon the scene. The migratory hunting and pastoral peoples were tempted by the accumulated wealth of urban and of rural agricultural populations to raid and plunder these populations. In some cases they imposed their rule more or less permanently upon these agricultural and urban folk. This became a new and additional factor for dividing a people into classes of the rulers and the ruled. Later similar methods were used by seafaring peoples which conquered for purposes of trade and exploitation. The culmination of this early period of imperial growth was the Roman Empire which used both terrestrial and marine methods of conquest and which at its apogee covered most of the then known world.

The Egyptian royal dynasties commenced about 3100 plus or minus 100 B.C. The great pyramids of Giza, which were burial monuments of the kings of the 3rd and the 4th dynasties, were constructed about 2800 to 2700 B.C. Babylon was founded prior to 2234 B.C. be-

[10] Harold Peake and H. J. Fleure, *Peasants and Potters*, 1927.

cause astronomical observations were made in that year which identify it. Sumeria was an earlier kingdom in a portion of Babylonia. Nineveh, the capital of the Assyrian Empire was founded by Ashur in 2245 B.C. There were also early empires in Iran such as Elam. Troy in western Asia Minor was founded by 1500 B.C. or earlier. Carthage in northern Africa is reputed to have been founded about 826 B.C. Still later came Macedon in northern Greece. Probably all of these and other kingdoms and empires were of a despotic nature. What of the relations of these early states in the Near East to China and India in the Far East?[11]

There were Sumerian cities in existence before 3500 B.C. in lower Mesopotamia near the Persian Gulf. It is possible that they were city states. As an English specialist concerning Sumeria has said: "That the Sumerians, the earliest inhabitants of Babylonia, had long lived under the rule of State-law is to be inferred not only from the great antiquity of their settled dwelling in cities, but from the survival of certain very early documents concerned with sales of land and slaves."[12] Little is known as to the origin of the Sumerian people, of its language, and of its culture. Their cities became a part of the empire known as Babylonia. Sumerian history has been divided into several periods. The first period was prehistoric to about 3500 B.C. Its second period was early Sumerian from before 3000 B.C. to about 2500 B.C. During the third to the sixth periods inclusive Sumerian culture influenced various dynasties, such as the Semitic, Akkadian and Amorite, and the Kassite. The seventh period included the time of Assyrian domination and the New Babylonian Chaldean empire from 1150 B.C. to the capture of Babylon by Cyrus of Persia in 539 B.C.

Under Hammurabi of the Ur Amorite dynasty, who reigned *ca.* 1728-1686 B.C., was promulgated a legal code most of which has been preserved. It went beyond tribal custom and "was compiled from a mass of existing Sumerian law under which highly civilized cities had certainly lived for many centuries."[13] The code recognized three classes, namely, the aristocrats, the freemen, and the slaves. It legalized complete private ownership of land. It made provision for contracts of sale, lease, barter, gift, etc.

To the north of Assyria and Babylonia was the Hittite empire which ruled over much of Asia Minor and Syria between the years 2000 and 1200 B.C. The origin of the Hittites is not known. Their rulers spoke a language which resembled the European languages. All

[11] The following paragraphs are paraphrased, abbreviated and brought up to date from my book entitled *Oriental and Occidental Culture* published in 1928.

[12] C. J. Gadd, article on "Babylonian Law," *Encyclopaedia Britannica*, Vol. 2, 1942, p. 862.

[13] C. J. Gadd, *op. cit.*

these nation-states of the ancient Near East were under despotic rule.

In the Honan and Kansu provinces, ranging across northern China for a distance of about 1200 miles have been found many late neolithic sites. A significant phase of this culture, called Yang Shao, is the polychrome pottery which characterized it. This pottery resembled the pottery found in the earliest Anau culture in Central Asia. Similar pottery has been found at many sites in the Near East, such as on the eastern borders of Iran, in Babylonia prior to 3500 B.C., in Asia Minor probably about 2500-2000 B.C. at Tripolje in southwestern Russia, and in Thessaly from 2000 B.C. At Anau it may have appeared somewhat earlier, so that it may have ranged in time from about 4000 to 1500 B.C. It may have appeared in China by 3000 B.C. in the Yang Shao culture which may have commenced about 3500 B.C. It is unknown where this polychrome pottery originated. It seems likely that it was dispersed from some point in western Asia. In that case it must have traveled the long distance from Anau in Russian Turkestan across Chinese Turkestan to northern China. As the discoverer of the Yang Shao culture has said: "The distance from Honan to Anau is very great, but the two regions are connected by a highway of migrations which extends between the Tibetan highlands in the south and the Siberian taiga (forest region) in the north. These vast expanses of steppe and desert which form a nearly continuous belt from the Pacific to the Black Sea have, according to the researches of Pumpelly and Huntington, during certain periods enjoyed a climate much more genial than the present." [14]

Certain philologists have noted resemblances between the Sumerian and the Chinese scripts which have suggested a common origin, possibly in central Asia. There apparently was a correlation if not a connection between the ceramic and the linguistic origins throughout the Near and the Far East. So far as we can judge from the scanty data available, the Chinese culture was partly indigenous in its origin and partly derived from elsewhere. It apparently assumed its characteristic form in the middle and lower reaches of the Hoang-ho or Yellow River, and spread eastward into what are now the Chihli and Shantung provinces, and southward toward the Yang-tse-Kiang. If linguistic relations furnish any guide, Tibet, Annam, Siam and Burma belong to the same culture complex, because the languages of those countries are of the same family as the Chinese tongue.

The Chinese appear never to have been pastoral, but have as a people always been agriculturists and village and town dwellers. In other words, their ancestors apparently passed directly from the hunting to the agricultural stage. Such a civilization could readily develop

[14] J. G. Andersson, *An Early Chinese Culture*, Peiping, 1923, pp. 35-36.

in the fertile valleys of the Hoang-ho and of the Yang-tse-Kiang, especially the former.

For the historical period, China has, with the exception of a few doubtful tombs, only literary evidence of the antiquity of its culture. The Chinese histories begin with the mythical Five Rulers, commencing with the legendary date of 2852 B.C., each of whom is alleged to have reigned an incredibly long time. The first more or less authentic dynasty was the Hsia (2205-1766 B.C.), followed by the Shan or Yin dynasty (1766-1122 B.C.). Until the latter date, what now constitutes China consisted of several independent kingdoms. Outside of these kingdoms were regions inhabited by unconquered savage and barbarous peoples.

During the Chóu or Chow dynasty, which reigned for nearly a millennium, (1122-249 B.C.), China became a federation of states ruled by feudal lords owing a loose allegiance to the emperor. Many wars took place between the different states. The efforts to unify China have continued without entire success down to the twentieth century. For the first two thirds of this dynasty we have the historical record compiled by Confucius (born 551 B.C.) in the Shu-king. While wars and political dissensions were rife, it was nevertheless the classical and constitutional period during which Chinese culture acquired its characteristic form which served as a unifying bond, and eventually spread to Japan, Korea and other contiguous countries.

The Chóu-li (circa 1100 B.C.), a code compiled near the beginning of this dynasty, provided for the ministries of the government, established the different classes, prescribed the order of precedence, and in many other ways regulated Chinese life. This was six centuries after the Code of Hammurabi which performed a similar function in Mesopotamia. This is a sort of measure of the time-lag between these civilizations. In its essential features the Chóu-li was followed down to the twentieth century. It has perhaps had more influence upon a larger number of people over a longer period of time than any other book. During this dynasty also the Chinese classics were edited and compiled, in part by Confucius, which have guided the Chinese people down to the present day. These classics and the Chóu-li probably constitute the oldest classical literature which is extant in more or less complete form, the only possible exception being the Vedas of India, soon to be discussed. Fragments only survive of the older Egyptian literature and of the still older literatures of the ancient civilizations of the Mesopotamian Valley, which may have been the first to come into existence.

In northern and central India the neolithic culture was followed by a copper age. Little trace has been found of a bronze age. Important remains of copper have been discovered at three sites, Harappa in the Punjab southwest of Lahore in the old bed of the Ravi, a tributary of the Indus River, and Mohen-jo-daro and Chandhu-daro in Sind, south of Larkana, in the old bed of the Indus. All of them appear to be the sites of what were large cities.

The most significant objects found at these sites are stamp-seals, painted pottery, and copper coins. On the seals are as many as sixteen characters which resemble characters in the Sumerian syllabary dating from about 3000 B.C. These include most of the characters on these seals. In the earliest stratum at Mohen-jo-daro were found the pottery, and copper coins with pictographic signs. The earliest of the coins are unlike coins found anywhere else. Some of them bear pictographs which suggest Iranian affinities. The pottery resembles a painted pottery found at Susa in Elam which has been assigned to the fifth millennium B.C. The latest chalcolithic culture, using both stone and copper implements, was in the last city at Mohen-jo-daro which was abandoned apparently about 2500 B.C. The Indus valley culture resembled the early Sumerian and Babylonian culture. The early Indian and Mesopotamian cultures may have represented cognate developments having a common origin. At any rate the excavations at Mohen-jo-daro, Chandhu-daro, Harappa, and also at Taxila, indicate an advanced urban civilization in ancient India.

The resemblance between the stone objects, brick work, funeral pottery, and pictographs discovered at Harappa, Chandhu-daro and Mohen-jo-daro, and Sumerian remains found in Mesopotamia, has suggested either that the Indus culture was derived from Mesopotamia, or that the Sumerian culture originated in India. Phases of the Sumerian culture have been found at Susa in Iran and at Anau in Turkmenistan. At both of these sites the cultural series goes back continuously to neolithic strata. It is possible that the Sumerian culture originated in Central Asia, and reached India by way of Mesopotamia.

Another feature of Indian prehistory which suggests cultural relations with other parts of the world is furnished by the megalithic monuments. These consist mainly of dolmens found in many parts from the Narbada River to Cape Comorin. They are very numerous in the Deccan in central India. There are said to be over 2000 in the Bellary district alone. These monuments were used mainly for funerary purposes. Hence they were constructed by peoples who practised burial. During the iron age, when most of these monuments were erected, burial and cremation were practised sometimes side by side in central and southern India. Since that time the Hindu custom of cremation has prevailed. Megalithic monuments have been traced all the way from India along the north coast of Africa and the west coast of Europe to Scandinavia. They have also appeared in remote parts of the earth, such as Japan, America and the southern Pacific. These facts have given rise to the hypothesis of a single megalithic race which originated this custom. It has also been suggested that it may have originated in India, possibly with the Dravidians of southern India.

The Dravidians of central and southern India speak languages which have not been connected with any other family of languages, east or west or north. In Baluchistan is a Dravidian language called Brahui which suggests that the Dravidians may have entered India from the northwest. Apparently they mixed with the aboriginal inhabitants. At an early period they were settled in villages the organization of which is not known.

We have already mentioned the ancient sites at Harappa and Mohen-jo-daro in northwestern India where cities existed perhaps as long ago as 3000 B.C. North of Harappa is Taxila at Sarai Kala, near Rawalpindi, where a city existed probably as early as 2000 B.C. The first two cities, and perhaps the third also, represented a culture which may have been derived from Mesopotamia. While it probably left its mark on Indian civilization, it seems to have in large part disappeared from this region, or at any rate to have become merged in the culture which became dominant.

Between the years 2400 and 2000 B.C. there began to penetrate from the north the so-called "Aryan" culture entering through the passes of the northwest frontier. It is often assumed that it was brought into India by an "Aryan" people. It is more probable that several peoples shared this culture. Aryan, or Indo-European, as they are more generally called, languages spread through Iran into India, and westward and northward over most of Europe. Suffice it to say that there gradually developed the social system now known as Hinduism. It was probably due in part to external forces and in part to indigenous elements. At first it was dominant in the Punjab and in the valleys of the Jumna and the Ganges. Then it worked its way southward during the centuries until 1500 B.C. and even later. When the Manava-dharma-shastra or Manu-smriti (Code of Manu) took its present shape (between 200 B.C. and 200 A.D.), Hinduism was dominant from the Himalayas to the Vindhya range in central India. Eventually it spread over the whole of the Dravidian south, though absorbing some of the Dravidian culture.

The Aryans apparently had a tribal organization when they penetrated into India. The Aryan village developed into the village community. While it had no written constitution, it had a social organization of its own. Occasionally a tribal chieftain succeeded in extending his power over so many communities and so large an area as to become a king. From time to time powerful Indian states were established, usually by strong leaders. No one of these states has survived. For long periods a large part of the peninsula has been under foreign domination. The native rulers were usually Kshatriyas or members of the military caste. Sometimes they were Vaishyas or members of the merchant caste. In very few cases were they Shudras or members of the servile caste. In occasional instances, as in the case of the Peshwas of the Mahratta region, they were Brahmans, or members of the priestly caste.

Among the Indians, whose whole culture is permeated with religion, and whose social organization is characterized by gross inequalities between the different castes, it was to be expected that the upper castes would usually rule. Through it all the Brahmans have retained their ascendancy, though they were not the military, political and economic leaders. This situation is reflected in Indian law, which has remained largely punitive. In the so-called laws of Manu, which still serve as a guide to the Hindus, most of the provisions are explicitly repressive. There is little suggestion of restitution. Torts or private wrongs are not distinguished from crimes or public wrongs, which in Indian law are violations against religion. In Occidental jurisprudence, on the contrary, torts far exceed crimes in number, and civil law has attained a high degree of development in comparison with criminal law, whose scope has in some respects been limited rather than expanded.

The historical period in India presents a grave difficulty of chronology. We have seen that Chinese chronology goes back 4000 years or more with a good deal of accuracy. Egyptian chronology goes back 5000 years or more. Even as far back as 2000 years, Indian chronology becomes very vague. And yet a relatively advanced culture existed there long before that time. It has usually been explained by the fact that the Hindus believe in nirvana or a future state of peace and bliss, when the consciousness of the individual will be obliterated so that time becomes meaningless. Hence time relations in the present existence seem to them to be of little significance.

The lack of a chronology was probably due in part to political conditions. India has at no time been united under a single strong central government. Consequently, there was no dynasty desirous of keeping a record of events in order to enhance its renown, like the dynasties of China and Egypt. Such records as were kept by local rulers were intermittent and did not give an unbroken chronology.

Other factors which interfered with the keeping of a chronology were the widespread practice of cremation, the limited use of writing, and the character of the Indian classics. Cremation destroys effectually the records of individual lives often found in funerary monuments, which have in Egypt and in many other countries furnished valuable historical data. It discourages the remembrance of the dead or soon

308

turns these memories into myths, unless convenient methods of keeping a written record exist, which was not the case until the era of printing and of books arrived.

Long after writing was introduced, texts were handed down verbally, partly because of the lack of suitable writing materials. The palm leaf is not durable in contrast to papyrus, which made possible permanent written records in Egypt. The principal Indian texts are the Vedas or "Books of Knowledge," consisting mainly of sacred lore, and the two great epics, the Ramayana and the Mahabharata, consisting mainly of myths. All of the Indian literature is permeated with religion and is largely mythological, so that there is little room for an historical record.

In default of an orderly record, a few important events of the 4000 years or more since "Aryan" culture entered India may be noted. The first 1000 years and more are shrouded in darkness. During this period the Vedic literature was taking shape, probably from 1500 B.C. onward. The Ramayana and Mahabharata were probably evolving from 500 B.C. Gautama Buddha was born about 563 B.C. Alexander the Macedonian invaded northern India from 327 to 324 B.C., leaving several Greek garrisons behind. This invasion had considerable cultural significance in bringing Indian in contact with European culture. Chandragupta Maurya conquered Magadha in 322 B.C., and established the Mauryan dynasty. His grandson, Ashoka, who reigned from 274 to 237 B.C., embraced and propagated Buddhism with great zeal. His dominion extended from the Hindu Kush Mountains to approximately Lat. 15° N., and was one of the greatest of any Indian ruler.

The preceding rather fragmentary survey does not throw very much light on the origins and early development of political institutions because much light is not available. It does indicate clearly that sufficient data are not yet available to weigh with any degree of precision the relative influence upon each other of eastern and western culture during the prehistoric and early historical periods. Two regions stand out with peculiar prominence because of the antiquity and continuity of the cultural series there exposed. In Egypt a relatively high culture existed more than 5000 years ago and was preceded by a well marked neolithic culture. There are also many paleolithic sites which may or may not have been connected with the neolithic.

The ancient Egyptian culture apparently included a fully developed state. An Egyptologist has characterized it as follows: "The king exercised his power through ministers at all periods and through feudal chiefs: in times of royal weakness the latter were practically independent."[15] This description suggests that the development was

[15] *Encyclopaedia Britannica*, 14th edit., 1942, article on "Egypt," Vol. 8, p. 53.

from the tribal through the feudal to the more or less unified state with occasional reversions to the feudal organization. When these changes took place it would be impossible to determine. As indicated above, the first dynasty commenced between 3500 and 3000 B.C. Whether this was earlier than a corresponding political development in the Mesopotamian region, it is impossible to determine.

In the Mesopotamian region arose a civilization which was perhaps as old as or even older than the Egyptian. To the northeast at Anau, on the eastern border of the Iranian plateau, the cultural series goes back through agricultural and pastoral stages to the neolithic. The lowest strata perhaps date back as far as 5000 or 6000 B.C. It has sometimes been suggested that the domestication of food and of draught animals and the art of agriculture originated in this region. There is also some evidence that agriculture originated in Egypt. It is not impossible that it developed independently in both regions and was invented in still other localities.

These two regions lie to the west of the greatest natural barrier in the world. The Hindu Kush, the Pamirs, the Kwenlun, the Karakoram, and the Himalaya ranges form a continuous mountainous wall, while the Tien-shan and Altai ranges extend to the northeastward. The barrier is reinforced with the aid of the deserts of eastern and southern Iran, Baluchistan, Turkestan, and Mongolia. This great barrier more or less effectually separated India and eastern Asia from the Occident, and India from eastern Asia. Asia Minor, Mesopotamia, Arabia, Egypt, and Iran belong to the cultural series represented in its later stages by the Mediterranean culture which has spread over the whole of Europe, the western hemisphere, and certain other extensive areas. The cultural area represented by Anau lies to the west of the great barrier, but this ancient city apparently exercised some influence in both directions.

Chinese culture may have been derived in the first instance from a type of culture developed in northern or central Asia eastward of the great barrier. A peculiar feature of this culture was an aversion to milk as a food, which is still characteristic of eastern Asia, whereas it is and has been eaten by Indo-Europeans, Semites, Scythians, Turks, and many other peoples.[16] Until modern times there was very little contact between Chinese and Mediterranean culture. The Chinese culture developed along the lines of a powerful family organization based on ancestor worship, the sacredness of the family, filial devotion, and marriage enjoined on every one as a duty to the ancestors. The resulting subjection of the individual to the family accounts in large part for the racial and national continuity of the Chinese and the

[16] B. Laufer, "Some Fundamental Ideas of Chinese Culture," *Journal of Race Development*, 1914, Vol. V, pp. 160-4.

tenacity of their culture. This culture became dominant throughout the world of the yellow peoples. The predominance of the family organization probably detracted somewhat from the development of a corresponding power of the state.[17]

The only phase of the "Aryan" culture of which we can be certain is linguistic. Indeed, this is the only sense in which the term has any meaning. Northern India is linguistically Indo-European, whereas there is no such linguistic connection between China and the Occident. Ethnically also it is closely related to the white race in features, hair, etc. The only outstanding physical difference is a darker skin color. However, the culture which now dominates India was in all probability largely developed at home. Its religion permeates its culture to a degree unequaled by any other religion. Its social organization is based upon the amazing caste system, the like of which has never existed at any other time or place. This religion and caste system have probably in a measure taken the place of the state as methods of social control and delayed the political development of India.

There has probably been a certain amount of correlation between the authority of the family and the power of the state. An American sociologist has differentiated three types of the family in its relation to the state.[18] The trustee family had the maximum strength and was correlated with a weak external political authority. It existed in Greece from the Homeric period to about 800 B.C., in Rome from the tribal period to about 450 B.C., and in western Europe from 500 A.D. to about 1200 A.D. The domestic family was of medium strength. It existed in Greece from 800 B.C. to about 500 B.C., in Rome from 450 B.C. to about the beginning of the Christian era, and in western Europe from 1200 A.D. to about 1700 A.D. The atomistic family has the maximum weakness and is, according to this writer, correlated with a strong centralized state, a somewhat questionable generalization. It existed in Greece from 500 B.C. to the end of the classical period or about 300-200 B.C., in Rome from 1 A.D. to about 500 A.D., and in western Europe from 1700 A.D. to the present day. However, there are other factors, to be discussed in a later chapter which affect the significance of the family in its relation to the state.

---

[17] I have described the Chinese greater family and the Indian joint family systems in Chapter 6 of my *Oriental and Occidental Culture*, New York, 1928.

[18] C. C. Zimmerman, *Family and Civilization*, New York, 1947. While this writer has assembled some historical data of value, his conclusions and generalizations are often open to serious question probably because he is an ardent protagonist for what he calls the "trustee" family.

311

Chapter XXI

The State as an Agency of Power

THE greater part of the development of the state has taken place in the Occidental world. Its early development was in regions which border on the Orient. In the Mediterranean region north of Egypt and west of Asia Minor arose in the 4th millennium B.C. a culture commonly known as the Egean civilization. At various times during a period of nearly 3,000 years it covered all or parts of the Egean Archipelago, Crete, Cyprus, the Hellenic peninsula, the Ionian isles, and western Anatolia. It has been described as follows:

"A people, agreeing in its prevailing skull forms with the Mediterranean race of North Africa, was settled in the Aegean islands from a remote Neolithic antiquity, but, except in Crete, where insular security was combined with great natural fertility, remained in a savage and unproductive condition until far into the 4th millennium B.C. In Crete, however, it had long been in close contact with Egypt and had developed a certain civilization, and at a period more or less contemporary with Dynasties 11 and 12 (2200-2000 B.C.) the scattered communities of the centre of the island coalesced into a strong monarchical state, whose capital was at Cnossus. There the king, probably also high priest of the prevailing nature cult, built a great stone palace, and received the tribute of feudatories. . . . The Cnossian monarch had maritime relations with Egypt, and presently sent his wares all over the southern Aegean. . . . A system of pictographic writing came into use early in this Palace period. . . . The absence of fortifications . . . suggests that at this time Crete was internally peaceful and externally secure. . . . The acme of this dominion was reached about the end of the 3rd millennium B.C." [1]

[1] *Encyclopaedia Britannica*, 14th edit., 1942, Vol. 1, page 215.

The Egean civilization as represented and manifested in what has sometimes been called its fountainhead, namely, Crete, has been designated as the Minoan civilization after Minos, a legendary king of Crete. The contemporaneity of the Minoan with the Egyptian civilization is set forth in the following table:

Minoan periods	Egyptian dynasties	Approximate dates
Early Minoan	Dyn. 1-11 (Old Kingdom)	B.C. 3100-2100
Middle Minoan	Dyn. 11-17 (Middle Kingdom)	2100-1580
Late Minoan	Dyn. 18-20 (New Kingdom)	1580-1100

At Cnossus anthropologists have excavated a deep neolithic layer. Above it were the remains of the bronze age. In the island of Cyprus, where there is copper, the bronze age probably lasted from before 3000 B.C. to about 1200 B.C. Iron was introduced about 1100-1000 B.C., perhaps from the north.

The Egean civilization was characterized by an indigenous script which has not been deciphered, an highly developed ceramic and pictorial art, a distinctive architecture, and in its later stages in some parts of its area by the dome or "beehive" tombs. The Cretan palaces were of great size built on elevated spots. They dominated lower towns of meaner houses. This may indicate that the monarchy existed at all periods. Traces have been found of what may have been an earlier matriarchate. The shrines were in the palaces which renders it probable that the kings held religious power and may have been the high priests. Tablets found at Cnossus were apparently used for the registration of the population, the keeping of accounts, and similar records. They indicate a comparatively high economic and political development. There were, however, no traces of a currency though there was an extensive maritime commerce.

The early Minoan civilization attained its peak about 2100 B.C. This was followed by a decline which culminated in a general disaster at about 1600 B.C. The cause of this disaster is unknown. It may have been a war or an earthquake. Soon after there came a renaissance during the late Minoan period at about 1580 B.C. On the Hellenic and Asiatic mainland were built fortified citadels at Mycenae, Tiryns, Thebes, and at Troy (Hissarlik) in western Anatolia. These citadels were centers or outposts of Egean civilization. They indicate that warfare against invaders or between these centers was prevalent. The more or less legendary Trojan War which is reputed to have taken place in about 1200 B.C. was of the latter type.

The Egean civilization was subject to intrusion from outside.

About 2000 B.C. was introduced on the Hellenic mainland a ceramic style known as the Minyan pottery. It came from an unknown source and people. There were references to or hints of the Egean civilization in Hittite tablets about 1400 B.C. The iron which came in about 1100-1000 B.C. may have been used by invaders from the north, the so-called Dorians, to overthrow the Egean civilization. Cyprus was conquered by Egypt for a time during the 18th dynasty or about 1500 B.C. There were also influences from Asia Minor, earlier from Babylonia and later from Phenicia. Still later there were Mycenaean colonies in Cyprus.

In Crete after the late Minoan period the monarchy disappeared. There was oligarchical rule by an aristocratic group advised by a council of elders. The population was divided into two classes—the citizens and the serfs. The Cretan boy was trained as a warrior as in Sparta. Some of the Cretan law was incorporated in Greek law. Thus did the Egean civilization contribute to the Hellenic civilization which succeeded it. Like all cultures it did not disappear *in toto,* but was gradually transformed and merged into a culture of a somewhat different type.

Many if not most states have originated from urban concentrations of population engaged in trade, industry, and in some cases to a certain extent in agriculture. Whether ruled by a chieftain, a king, an oligarchy, an aristocracy, or with some semblance of democracy, many of these city states or their rulers extended their rule over the neighboring agricultural population to form a national state. Some of these city and national states were invaded by nomadic pastoral peoples for loot. In at least a few cases the conquerors maintained their rule for long periods. The Hyksos or shepherd kings who ruled Egypt during the 16th and 17th dynasties (B.C 1720-B.C. 1580) were, to start with at least, such alien rulers. The empires of history have often been formed by a process of invasion and conquest.

Oppenheimer has asserted that "the cause of the genesis of all states is the contrast between peasants and herdsmen, between laborers and robbers, between bottom lands and prairies."[2] This is partly a question of the definition of a state. Probably many city states and some national states arose without conquest from outside, though with domination of the majority of inhabitants by the proprietors of land and the owners of serfs and slaves. However, the six stages in the development of a state which Oppenheimer distinguished probably took place at least in part in the case of many states:[3]

[2] Franz Oppenheimer, *The State, Its History and Development Viewed Sociologically,* Indianapolis, 1914, p. 53.
[3] F. Oppenheimer, *op. cit.,* pages 56, 64-5, 70, 71, 78, and 80.

(1) "The first stage comprises robbery and killing in border fights, endless combats broken neither by peace nor by armistice."

(2) "The peasant, through thousands of unsuccessful attempts at revolt, has accepted his fate and has ceased every resistance. . . . The herdsman now appropriates only the surplus of the peasant."

(3) "The third stage arrives when the 'surplus' obtained by the peasantry is brought by them regularly to the tents of the herdsmen as 'tribute,' a regulation which affords to both parties self-evident and considerable advantages."

(4) "The fourth stage (territorial) . . . adds the decisive factor in the development of the state, as we are accustomed to see it, namely, the union on one strip of land of both ethnic groups."

(5) "The lords assume the right to arbitrate, and in case of need, to enforce their judgment."

(6) "The necessity of keeping the subjects in order and at the same time of maintaining them at their full capacity for labor, leads . . . to the sixth stage, in which the state, by acquiring full intra-nationality and by the evolution of 'Nationality,' is developed in every sense."

Partly or wholly through these stages there came into being the feudal state in which the peasant agriculturist lived in serfdom, bound more or less indissolubly to the soil, and required to pay tribute in goods or services to his conquering master. This situation existed in many of the territorial states. There came into being also the maritime state which included a somewhat different type of domination. "The maritime State is the scene of the development of movable wealth; the territorial State is the embodiment of the development of landed property. The final issue of the first is *capitalistic exploitation* by slavery, the outcome of the latter is, first of all, the *developed feudal State*." "The maritime state . . . came into being from piracy and trade."[4]

Some of these maritime states developed into sea empires. "If any region in the world was naturally adapted to teach the advantages of sea-enterprise it was the coast of the Aegean."[5] Here were archipelagoes, strings of islands which furnished convenient stepping-stones from one mainland to another. Even where there were no islands the distances were not too great for the small sailing craft of that time to traverse. By establishing trading centers on harbors, contact could

[4] F. Oppenheimer, *op. cit.*, pages 118 and 158.
[5] R. M. MacIver, *The Modern State*, Oxford, 1926, page 61.

be made with the inland region which might soon be dominated from the fortifications of the trading center. Thus came into being the Phenician colony at Carthage on the northern coast of Africa in the 9th century B.C., and Hellenic colonies in the Italian peninsula. Aeneas, the legendary Trojan prince, is reputed to have arrived in Italy in 1182 B.C. and to have become the traditional king of Latium. Presumably he bore with him the Egean culture. While this legend may be wholly fictitious, it reflects the historical process of conquest, colonization and domination over the indigenous agricultural population. An Italian writer has poetically described the universal truth contained in this legend.

> "The peasant world has neither government nor army; its wars are only sporadic outbursts of revolt, doomed to repression. Still it survives, yielding up the fruits of the earth to the conquerors. . . . Of the two Italys that share the land between them, the peasant Italy is by far the older; so old that no one knows whence it came, and it may have been here forever. *Humilemque videmus Italiam;* this was the low-lying, humble Italy that first met the eyes of the Asiatic conquerors as the ships of Aeneas rounded the promontory of Calabria."[6]

Greek colonies persisted for many centuries in southern Italy and Sicily. Tradition has it that Rome was founded by Romulus in 753 B.C. This legend is wholly fictitious. But it is true that at an early date a city arose on the site of Rome which eventually became the center of an empire including a large part of the then known world. During part of the time it was acquiring its empire it was a republic governed mainly by a senate. About the time of Julius Caesar (100-44 B.C.) it became an autocracy governed by a lengthy succession of emperors.

Prominent in the development of the state has been the role played by warfare. There is no reason to believe that war, or rather the tendency to prosecute it, is inherent in human nature. There is little evidence of warfare among primitive peoples. Conflicts may readily arise between individual human beings. Groups in personal contact with each other may become involved in conflict. But no individuals or groups of individuals will spontaneously undertake hostilities against other groups whom they do not know personally and who are removed from them in space. Antipathies between peoples usually are the results rather than the causes of war. It is only when their greed is incited by the prospect of plunder, or their fear is aroused by attack, or their anger by an artful propaganda, that

[6] Carlo Levi, *Christ Stopped at Eboli*, New York, 1948, page 97.

316

they will become belligerent enough to embark upon an offensive against people whom they have never seen and toward whom they could not have the emotions either of love or of hate. Otherwise they will not fight unless they belong to an organization in which resides the authority to order and compel them to fight people against whom they have no animosity. Such an organization is the state whose sovereignty includes the power to sacrifice the lives and well-being of its own subjects and citizens as well as to slaughter as many as it can of the inhabitants of the countries and peoples which it attacks.

Many of the early centers of culture were in locations shielded by natural barriers such as in river valleys, on elevated spots which could be easily fortified, on islands, and even in locations surrounded by a swamp. As we have seen, these cultural centers have often been raided for plunder by hunting and pastoral peoples from ancient times down to comparatively modern times. Such were the raids by the Bedouins on the Syrian coast, by the Scythians north of the Black Sea on the Balkan Peninsula and on the southern Caucasus, by the Mongolians on China, by the Kabyle tribesmen on the north African coast, and, perhaps the most extensive and prolonged of all, of the Huns on Europe.

Some wars have had the result of partially displacing one people by another racially or culturally or both. This was probably true of invasions of peoples speaking Semitic languages from the Arabian peninsula into Mesopotamia and Syria in the 3rd millennium B.C. A similar spread took place of Aryan or Indo-European speaking peoples from an unknown source into Persia, India and Europe in the 3rd and 2nd millennia B.C. Germanic tribes spread westward and southward in Europe about the beginning of the Christian era. Turkish tribes invaded Asia Minor and southeastern and central Europe during the Middle Ages. Most of these wars have not been attempts to exterminate whole populations. Wars of extermination have been rare. They have been for conquest and exploitation without necessarily exterminating the conquered population.

Wars of invasion and conquest have often been caused by the growth of population of the invaders which impelled them to seek more land and natural resources. Some of them, however, have been caused solely by the greed for plunder. Whether pressure of population or the desire for loot was the cause of the invasion, the invaders have usually taken the best land but permitted the indigenous population to cultivate the remainder. Sometimes the latter population has been reduced to the status of slaves or serfs.

Wars have also arisen from the expansion of political systems. City states have often extended their rule over adjoining territory. Empires have extended their power to control centers of wealth and

317

of culture and to establish strong frontiers. At one time and another this has been true of Egypt, Babylonia, Assyria, the Hittite empire, Persia, Rome, and Macedonia under Alexander. Plunder and tribute from the conquered peoples have usually been among the motives of the conquerors. Sometimes conflict has arisen between conquering generals giving rise to civil war. In Rome many of the conquering generals seized the imperial throne so that the history of Rome was to a considerable extent the annals of a military dictatorship.

The Crusades illustrate some of the causes or occasions and forms of warfare. They commenced ostensibly as holy wars to capture the so-called "Holy Sepulcher" of Jesus from the infidels. The first Crusade began in 1095 A.D. From 1099 A.D. when Jerusalem was captured by the Europeans until 1187 when it was captured by Saladin, the sultan of Egypt and Syria, the Crusaders were most successful. The Crusades continued for another century until the eighth Crusade came to an end in 1291. Thus for two centuries these invasions of the East by the West were causing conflict and turmoil. They came toward the end of the feudal period when the feudal lords were seeking new fields to plunder. The pressure of population in Europe caused many of the landless and propertyless common people to welcome new adventures. The merchants, though not instigating these feudal forays, were interested in commercial opportunities which might arise from them. The Crusades were in the main predatory commercial and colonizing expeditions.

These wars were probably most important as a part of the struggle between the East and the West. They were attempts to check the victorious advance of the Turks. The eastern or Byzantine empire was in greatest danger and repeatedly appealed for help from the west. In this regard the Crusades were complete failures. The Turks continued their victorious march to the Danube. In less than two centuries after their close, they captured Constantinople in 1453 and crushed the eastern empire. The most lasting effect probably was that these wars broadened somewhat the culture of the West.

Colonization has taken place since prehistoric times. Colonial expansion played its part in the earlier forms of imperialism. Roman imperialism was in part colonization in its intent and character. The vainglorious invasion of India by Alexander the Macedonian in the 4th century B.C. was solely an imperialist adventure. It failed as a permanent conquest. The Greek garrisons eventually withdrew. It did, however, establish a cultural contact with the Occident which influenced not only India but also China and other Oriental countries.

The discovery of a new hemisphere at the close of the Middle Ages, and the exploration of extensive regions in Africa and Asia hitherto unknown by Europeans, gave rise to an era of colonization

318

which far surpassed, both in extent and significance, the colonial expansion of ancient times. In order to take possession of and then to retain control of and connection with their colonies, the colonizing European nations required large navies and sometimes also armies. At one time or another since the discovery of the western hemisphere, Spain, Portugal, Holland, and France have possessed powerful navies.

Nor has the Occident alone had its imperialist enterprises. Japan has had several of them. For a time during its early history it ruled Korea. Later it conquered the island of Hokkaido to the north, and made conquests in northern Manchuria. In 1592 the Japanese general Hideyoshi undertook to conquer China as well as Korea, but died before he could attain his purpose. In modern times Japan has been incited to militarist adventures in Korea, Manchuria and China proper by its excessive and growing population, its rapidly developing capitalism, which is seeking markets for its products, and by the example of Western imperialism.

While Japan has been the most prominent exponent of modern Oriental imperialism, China was an imperialist nation in the past. Much of the territorial growth of China proper was by force of arms. Tonkin and Cochin-China were conquered about 214 B.C. Chinese armies marched as far west as the Caspian Sea during the Han dynasty (206 B.C.-A.D. 221), and conquered a considerable part of central Asia. They entered northern India, and as one result Buddhism came to China. Korea was conquered during the T'ang dynasty (A.D. 618-907). Burma was first invaded about A.D. 224, and again about the year 1280 by Kublai Khan, the Mongolian conqueror of China. In 1766 began a war which made Burma a tributary state until Great Britain acquired complete suzerainty. French imperialism in Indo-China and British imperialism in Burma have been the successors of Chinese imperialism. Within the last few decades Chinese punitive expeditions have vied with similar British expeditions into Tibet, which each would like to make its vassal state.

Indian states and other Oriental countries also have had imperialist adventures. Any nation which acquires great military strength is likely to become imperialist. If the modern rise of nationalism in the Orient brings militarism in its train, it may give rise to a recrudescence of imperialism which will gravely menace the Occident, because the Orient has the advantage in numbers.

The attempt at domination of the East by the West began at the outset of the 16th century with the Portuguese in the lead. Vasco da Gama rounded the Cape of Good Hope and reached Calicut in 1498. The viceroy Albuquerque came in 1503 and in 1510 established the first European colony at Goa. The Philippine Islands were visited by Magellan in about 1520 and occupied by the Spanish during the 16th century. The Portuguese acquired extensive territories in India until the Dutch arrived in 1595 and competed successfully with them.[7] The French came at the beginning of the 17th century, and later conquered extensive territories until defeated by the English at Plassey in 1757, after which their power dwindled rapidly. Dutch, French, and British East India companies were formed to carry on trade. The English began to come early in the 17th century, and eventually acquired suzerainty over the whole of India with the exception of the small Portuguese colony at Goa and five French colonies comprising less than 200 square miles.

Oversea commerce with China began at Canton about A.D. 300. For centuries it was controlled principally by Arabs, though it included some Hindu traders. The Portuguese reached China in 1516 and Japan in 1541. The Dutch reached China in 1604, the British in 1607, and the Americans in 1784. The Russians were in communication with China overland. The first treaty between China and a European power was concluded with Russia in 1689.

Seafaring trade brought the West to the East on a somewhat extensive scale. Western seafarers and merchants were seeking for raw materials which could be secured only in the Orient, markets for finished products, and cheap labor with which to manufacture goods. They sometimes met opposition and contempt. This was particularly true of China. The Chinese had conquered all of their neighbors. For many centuries they were almost entirely isolated from the rest of the world. This situation had developed in them an arrogant attitude toward foreigners. Their emperor considered himself the ruler of the whole world. When George III of England sent Lord Macartney to China in 1792 to negotiate a commercial treaty, and demanded treatment as an equal, the Emperor Chien Lung dispatched the following message to the English monarch: "It behooves you, O King, to respect our wishes and by perpetual submission to our Throne in the future to bring prosperity and peace to your people. Tremble and obey."

Whatever arrogance the East displayed was more than matched by the aggressiveness of the Westerners. They were usually better armed than the Orientals and possessed a power on the sea unequaled by any Oriental nation. Their firearms were of larger caliber and longer range and their ships of greater burden. The peaceful pursuit of trade soon developed into invasion and conquest, often aided and abetted by a Christian zeal which regarded all Oriental religions as false and evil. In the course of four centuries a large part of the Orient passed under Occidental domination. During the first half of the 20th century India, Burma, the Malay States, Northern Borneo, eastern

---

[7] Cf. Henry H. Hart, *Sea Roads to the Indies*, New York, 1951.

New Guinea, and minor possessions elsewhere were under British sway, with British influence strong in Nepal, Bhutan, and Siam, and menacing in Tibet. France was ruling Indo-China and minor possessions elsewhere. Holland possessed most of the East Indies. The United States ruled the Philippines. Russia dominated all of northern Asia from the Urals to the Pacific. In fact, nearly three fifths of the area of Asia and one half or more of its population were under Occidental suzerainty. An even larger proportion of the area and population of Africa was under European domination.

Even where suzerainty was not declared, a certain measure of domination was secured. China, in addition to losing several important ports, was for a time divided into several "spheres of influence" by the leading Western powers. Extraterritorial rights for foreigners and control of the customs duties were imposed upon Japan, China, and several other Oriental countries. Western capital invested in Eastern railways, factories, etc., has levied a heavy tribute and has often interfered with the political affairs of these countries. Up to the worldwide war of 1939 to 1945 the only Oriental country which had succeeded in freeing itself entirely from these restrictions was Japan. It did so by imitating the material aspects of Occidental culture —in other words, by equaling and sometimes beating the West at its own game of force and aggression. Thus did Western empire, political and economic, spread over practically the whole of the East, and presented the most extensive display of imperialism in the history of mankind. Not even Rome in its more powerful days equaled it.

This extraordinary situation was not entirely intentional. The West did not by a premeditated and concerted design conquer the East. It came about partly through the frequent resistance of the East to Western advances, and its unwillingness to adjust itself to international finance, trade, and industry which was developing under the rapid scientific and technical progress of the West. In some Oriental countries the laws were of such a nature that foreigners could not live and do business under them, thus giving rise to the demand for extraterritorial rights. Sometimes these countries isolated themselves entirely or gave only very limited rights of residence to foreigners. For more than two centuries Japan excluded all foreigners, with the exception of a few Dutch merchants who were permitted to live on a small island in Nagasaki harbor. In Canton the foreigners were banished to a mudbank in the Pearl River, which they filled in and then built the city of Shameen. At Shanghai they were assigned the swampy strand of the Whangpoo River, where they built the stately International Settlement.

Balked and irritated by such discriminations against them, by the indifference and somnolence of the Orient, and its inefficiency

321

according to Occidental standards, Western powers often went on to conquer where it was at first intended only to trade. Their traders were in many cases preceded or accompanied by missionaries of a militant Christianity which wished to conquer the East with the dominant religion of the West. However, Western imperialism was due even more to greed and aggressiveness than it was to missionary zeal and a desire for fair exchange in trade, which could not be restrained from exploiting by force the physically and materially weaker East.[8]

Western imperialists have often rationalized their imperialism on the basis of the postulate that they are morally as well as intellectually superior to the Orientals. As the raucous imperialist poet Rudyard Kipling has vulgarly expressed it:

> Ship me somewheres east of Suez where the best is like the worst,
> Where there ain't no Ten Commandments, an' a man can raise a thirst.

This belief was more elegantly phrased when Lord Rosebery, a former Liberal prime minister (1894-1895), asserted that the British Empire was "the greatest secular agency for good known to the world." Certain benefits derived from British and other colonial rule are not to be denied, but they were benefits which were forced upon and not solicited by these peoples. An excellent commentary on the self-assumed "white man's burden" has been furnished by the eminent English economist, John A. Hobson:

> "Imperialism is a depraved choice of national life, imposed by self-seeking interests which appeal to the lusts of quantitative acquisitiveness and of forceful domination surviving in a nation from early centuries of animal struggle for existence. Its adoption as a policy implies a deliberate renunciation of that cultivation of the higher inner qualities which for a nation as for an individual constitutes the ascendancy of reason over brute impulse. It is the besetting sin of all successful States, and its penalty is unalterable in the order of nature."[9]

[8] I have discussed Western imperialism in the East at length in my *Oriental and Occidental Culture*, New York, 1928. See especially Chapter XII entitled "The Attempt at Domination by the West," and Chapter XIII entitled "The Missionary Invasion of the East."

[9] *Imperialism*, New York, 1902.

See also P. T. Moon, *Imperialism and World Politics*, New York, 1927; S. Nearing and J. Freeman, *Dollar Diplomacy, A Study in American Imperialism*, New York 1925; R. W. Dunn, *American Foreign Investments*, New York, 1925; and George Marion, *Bases of Empire, A Chart of American Expansion*, 3rd edition, New York, 1949.

322

The imperialist use of military and naval power has been due mainly to the following causes:

1. Colonial expansion.
2. Search for markets.
3. Attempts to maintain the balance of power between nations.
4. National aggrandizement.

Colonial expansion is closely related to the second cause for the imperialist use of military and naval power. The vast increase in the productive capacity of the Occident since the industrial revolution has resulted in a surplus production of many manufactured commodities which cannot be disposed of in the domestic markets owing to lack of adequate purchasing power on the part of the great mass of the consumers. This situation has intensified greatly the search for foreign markets on the part of the leading industrial nations of the world. It has often been said that "Trade follows the flag." It would be nearer the truth to say that the flag follows trade. The conquest of colonies has usually been for the more or less conscious purposes of utilizing them as markets for the surplus products of the country claiming ownership, sometimes as a source of raw materials, and also sometimes as a reservoir of cheap labor.

Colonization schemes are usually intended to secure exclusive control of the markets concerned. The conquering nation may succeed in doing so for a time. It does not necessarily gain thereby in the long run. As soon as a colonial market becomes large and profitable, its retention entails a heavy expense. There is great danger of losing it because other nations become covetous. Before long there is likely to be a war over the colonial possession which may cost more than the colony is worth. When it becomes sufficiently strong, the colony itself is likely to revolt against exploitation. This is what happened in almost all of the American colonies of European countries. If a colony wins independence or a high degree of autonomy, its market is no longer the exclusive possession of the quondam mother country.

Some colonies have served as outlets for the surplus population of their mother countries. This has usually been true only of colonies situated under climatic and topographical conditions more or less suitable for Europeans. Even in these colonies, the purpose of supplying an outlet for surplus population was not usually the original and primary consideration. Ordinarily commercial considerations alone have determined colonial policies in their inception. The recognition of the utility of colonies as a safety valve for the pressure of over-population in the mother-country has come later and has sometimes influenced these policies. Most of the colonies and dependencies in

323

Africa and Asia have not been regarded as havens of refuge for emigrants from European countries.

Attempts to maintain the balance of power between nations have taken place ever since the evolution of large and powerful states. The most notable instance of a balance of power has been in modern Europe. The rapid industrial development of European countries has accentuated economic rivalry among them. It has furnished the means for offensive and defensive measures far surpassing anything that was possible in earlier times.

European history has consisted largely of these attempts to maintain a balance of power among themselves. Whenever this balance has been disturbed and rendered unstable, it has usually led to a war or series of wars which has again restored the balance. It has sometimes been maintained by an empire exercising control over Europe. When the imperial power has decayed, a period of instability has resulted. At other times the balance of power has been maintained by several nations more or less equal in strength. When one of them has grown much stronger, the balance has again become unstable and warfare has often ensued.

The attempts to maintain a European balance of power have arisen in part out of international relations within the continent of Europe. These relations have been partly economic, but also political in the sense that each nation has tried to aggrandize itself at the expense of the others. Religious and dynastic considerations sometimes played a part in the past. The balance of power has been greatly influenced also by the conflicting interests of these nations outside of Europe. These interests have been almost entirely economic and have arisen principally out of colonial expansion and the search for markets.

National aggrandizement is the most imponderable factor for the imperialist use of military and naval power. Sea power has perhaps been utilized less than military power upon the land for purposes of national aggrandizement. This is due in part to the fact that military power is more obvious to the eyes of the great majority of the population than the somewhat remote naval power on the sea. Nevertheless sea power has been an important factor for national aggrandizement in some countries. When a British audience sang "Britannia rules the waves," it contributed as much to their consciousness of national greatness as songs of military prowess among other peoples.

The evolution of large-scale factory production and of the modern capitalist system has resulted in large surpluses of manufactured goods and of other forms of capital. During the past 100 years the business men of the Occident have been strenuously en-

324

deavoring to secure foreign markets for their commodities and new fields for the investment of their surplus capital. Although modern business enterprise has been partly international, it has been conducted in the main along national lines. These national groups have often been organized in powerful trusts, mergers, or cartels which have concentrated all the force and influence of a national industry.

These groups have desired not only colonial expansion, but also spheres of influence, concessions, monopolistic control of raw materials, protective tariffs, subsidies, exemption from taxation, and similar advantages. They have been able to manipulate patriotic sentiment through the press and by other means of publicity, and to place many of their representatives in important political offices. They have influenced and controlled governments. Many aggressive acts by governments have been instigated by business men seeking their own ends. The policy of colonial expansion and of foreign trade and enterprise in general arising out of this situation is the modern form of imperialism which may be appropriately termed economic imperialism. It is an extension into the international field of the same predatory methods which prevail at home in all capitalist countries.

The rapid increase of population in Europe during the last century and a half gave rise to a good deal of emigration. The desire to provide suitable homes for their surplus population has been one of the causes for the search for colonies by European nations. It is doubtful, however, whether this has been the principal cause. A large part of these emigrants have gone to the United States, which has furnished opportunities for economic prosperity to many of these Europeans. Since the early part of the 19th century more than 20,000,000 of these emigrants have settled in the United States. Many of the remaining emigrants have gone to other countries of the western hemisphere, most of which are independent republics and not European colonies.

Colonial expansion has been due in large part to the desire to secure an outlet for the export of manufactured goods and of surplus capital, and to gain possession of sources of raw materials. The desire to exploit cheap native labor has also sometimes played a part. Ever since trading has become extensive in its scope, nations have endeavored to control regions where they have discovered commercial opportunities. The recent discovery of vast unexplored and unexploited regions by explorers and traders has stimulated greatly the race for colonies and spheres of influence as outlets for the export of commodities and of surplus capital. Morocco and Tripoli in Africa, China and India in Asia are illustrations.

In the events which led up to the European War of 1914 to 1918, in addition to the controversy over the ownership of Alsace-Lorraine, and the fact that the rich coal and iron fields in the region and in northern France were coveted by both Germany and France, the desire of the central European empires to secure additional colonies and spheres of influence played an important if not a decisive part in precipitating the war. Balked in its attempt to secure control of Morocco in Africa, Germany turned its attention to the opportunities for exploiting Asia Minor which had already intrigued it, and thereby aroused the jealousy and fears of Great Britain in India and of Russia in central Asia.

These facts demonstrate that colonial expansion for commercial purposes has been a powerful force for war. Many nations have tried to seize and exploit colonies in such a fashion as to profit at the expense of other nations. Nationalism renders it difficult to secure a general recognition of the truth that a condition essential for permanent success in international trade, as in every form of trade, is that all parties to the trade should benefit therefrom.

Nationalism has played an important role in politics, war and imperialism. Indeed, nationalism itself is a comparatively modern phenomenon. At least until the neolithic period mankind lived in small groups of a few score, or a few hundred or at most a few thousand of individuals. These groups, usually called tribes, had to move fairly often in search of food. They could not develop the attachment to the soil originally called patriotism. It was not until agriculture was invented during the neolithic that a more or less permanent attachment to the soil became possible and that food supplies became available for much larger agglomerations of population.

Then came the city state which was both a political and a territorial entity. Its territorial base rendered possible the rise of patriotism. Some of these city states expanded by peaceful or by forcible methods to become empires. Or the city state was overwhelmed by barbarians from outside who were able to establish an empire. In both cases there could be no patriotism or nationalism on the part of the vast majority of the subject population. Among these empires of antiquity and also of more modern times were those of Egypt, Crete, Babylonia, Assyria, China, Persia, Rome, Arabia, Turkey, Spain, Holland, Great Britain, and latest of all the United States.

In some of these areas had arisen the feudal system of land tenure. Typically this was based on grants of land by an emperor or king to local chiefs who had rendered military services. These local lords sublet their lands to their tenants or vassals in return for agricultural or military service or rent in agricultural products or money. These fiefs or feuds, from which the system derived its name, were therefore cultivated by serfs whose service was more or less closely attached to the soil of the estate of their lord. Feudalism arose usually in an economy in which money was little used. It was therefore less easy to dispose readily of property than of services. A characteristic form of feudalism existed in Europe during the Middle Ages. Its rise has been described as follows:

"In the absence then of a strong state, of blood ties capable of dominating the whole life and of an economic system founded upon money payments there grew up in Carolingian and post-Carolingian society relations of man to man of a peculiar type. The superior individual granted his protection and divers material advantages that assured a subsistence to the dependent directly or indirectly; the inferior pledged various prestations or various services and was under a general obligation to render aid. . . . The leading features of feudalism in its fully developed form are the system of vassalage and the institution of the fief."[10]

In the 12th and 13th centuries economic exchange with the use of money, in other words, commerce rather than barter, was becoming more prevalent, and the cities were growing. Hence there was less need for feudalism or it was less suitable in the urban regions. In the rural regions it persisted in several European countries until comparatively recent times. It terminated in France approximately at the time of the French Revolution which began in 1789, in Germany in 1848, and in Russia during the European war of 1914 to 1918 owing to the Bolshevist Revolution.

Feudalism has also existed in one form and another in China, Japan, several Moslem countries, and elsewhere. Wherever it has existed, its effect has been to localize government somewhat. This does not mean that it has not existed frequently or usually under an imperial or a monarchical regime. It has, however, usually meant a certain amount of decentralization of authority and government because the local lord has ruled over his own feudal estate.

Tribalism was submerged primarily by the advance of agriculture and industry and by the rise of empires covering extensive territories. In some regions subsidiary factors were the spread of intertribal or universal religions, such as Buddhism, Christianity and Islam, and of literary languages such as Sanskrit, Greek, Latin and Chinese. These factors rendered communication between tribes more facile and tended to obliterate some of the differences between them. Between tribalism and nationalism came feudalism or empire or both together. Feudalism did not usually persist long by itself. A monarchical or imperial overlordship above the feudal lords was almost certain to

[10] K. Breysig, "Feudalism," *Encyclopedia of the Social Sciences*, New York, 1931, Vol. 6, pp. 204-205.

arise in course of time. A lord who had acquired exceptional power usually extended his domination over his fellow lords and became a duke, a king, or an emperor. Here and there were city states a few of which grew into empires, such as Rome, Carthage, and Athens.

The explorations of the 15th and 16th centuries resulting in the discovery of the western hemisphere and of maritime routes to the Orient gave an enormous stimulus to trade. Vastly more mobile capital was poured into commercial channels. The middle class, composed largely of merchants rose greatly in importance. The interests of this class were opposed to the decentralized feudal system. It required order and organization on a wider scale. Hence the middle class allied itself with the kings in order to destroy the anarchy and decentralization caused by feudalism. This alliance strengthened the kings greatly and in some cases led to monarchical absolutism and tyranny.

A national dynastic state may have been said to come into existence when the balance of power between the feudal order and the monarchy turned in favor of the monarchy. This did not mean that feudalism had disappeared immediately. It persisted in varying degrees and for varying periods largely in the rural regions. The first national dynastic state may be said to have arrived in England in 1485, at the end of the War of the Roses, and the beginning of the reign of Henry the 7th. A similar turning point came in France a century later in 1589, at the beginning of the reign of Henry the 4th, the first Bourbon king. In similar fashion national dynastic states arose in Portugal in 1498, in Spain in 1555, and in Sweden in 1630. In one of its phases the French Revolution of 1789 emphasized and formulated the concept of the national state and enunciated the doctrine of national self-determination.

The art of printing was introduced into Europe from the Orient during the 15th century. Paper had been imported somewhat earlier.[11] These inventions rendered possible the growth of a vernacular literature which aided greatly the rise of a national consciousness and sentiment. In the economic field the commerce of each nation became national in the sense that it was organized to compete with other nations. Each national government was trying to aid the commerce of its subjects by hook or by crook. Very often this resulted in making international competition in trade little better than piracy. This was illustrated in the struggle to command the sea.[12]

[11] Maurice Parmelee, *Oriental and Occidental Culture, An Interpretation,* New York, 1928, pp. 80-81.
[12] The following paragraphs are paraphrased from my book entitled *Blockade and Sea Power,* New York, 1924, Chap. XV, "Sea Power and Imperialism," and Chap. XVI, "The Freedom of the Sea."

As a consequence of the rapid development of maritime commerce near the close of the Middle Ages, there were many attempts to appropriate seas. When Venice became a powerful maritime state, it claimed the ownership of the Adriatic Sea. The Baltic Sea was claimed at one time and another by several Scandinavian countries and Poland. In the 16th and 17th centuries Spain and Portugal claimed the right, under the authority of Papal edicts or bulls, to divide between themselves the Atlantic, Pacific and Indian Oceans.

The last of these claims was abandoned two centuries or more ago. Such attempts to appropriate the sea now have an historical significance alone. One of the latest of these attempts, though abandoned in its original form, was succeeded by the greatest sea power of modern times, if not indeed of all times. England's attempt in the 17th century to appropriate certain maritime areas resulted in this sea power.

When the Stuart dynasty came to England from Scotland at the beginning of the seventeenth century (1603), it brought with it the doctrine of the ownership of the sea. The Scottish and Dutch fishermen had clashed on the fishing grounds of the North Sea. Hence the Stuart monarchs were desirous of establishing the claim to ownership which would furnish a legal basis for excluding the Dutch fishermen. Thus began a series of attempts during the 17th century to establish English ownership over several bodies of water, such as the North Sea, the Irish Sea, the English Channel, and so forth, and to enforce alleged rights of tribute, of salute to the English flag, and the like, which gave rise, among other things, to three wars with Holland. There had been earlier vague precedents. The mythical tale of the Danish-English King Canute (died A.D. 1035), who commanded the tide not to rise, and other legends, furnished the basis for this claim. These claims were assembled and used by Selden in his treatise, written under and for the sake of the Stuarts, in which he attempted to substantiate this English claim to the ownership of the sea.[13]

While the early claim led to little attempt at enforcement, the claim as revived by the Stuarts had far-reaching results for about a century. It soon went much beyond a claim to fishing rights alone. This was a time when, as a result of the discovery of vast new regions and the consequent development of oversea trade, dominion over the sea had acquired a much greater value and significance. The Stuart monarchs used this claim also for the purpose of stimulating the patriotic feelings of the English when they desired to prosecute a foreign war in order to aggrandize their own royal house or to distract the attention of the people from internal difficulties. These enter-

[13] John Selden, *Mare Clausum Seu de Dominio Maris*, London, 1635.

prises were, however, unhappy in their consequences to themselves as well as to the English people. The reign of Charles I ended with his execution (1649) because he had engaged in civil war. The Commonwealth (1649-1653) and the Protectorate with Oliver Cromwell as Lord Protector intervened before the restoration of the Stuart dynasty with Charles II in 1660. The dynasty itself lost the throne at the opening of the eighteenth century in the year 1714. With it disappeared this claim to ownership over specific areas of the sea.

Naive claims to ownership of the sea have vanished with very few minor exceptions. Their disappearance has been due in part to the fact that their naivety was even more obvious than similar claims to the land. While the land is usually inhabited by human beings who make use of it and can thereby establish a claim to its use and ownership, the sea is an uninhabited and almost barren waste. It furnishes abundance of space for transit for every one, and a claim to absolute ownership is therefore unjustifiable even on the part of the nations which make the largest use of the sea. But the disappearance of these naive claims to ownership by no means signified a cessation of attempts to exercise power upon and sometimes over the sea. In fact, in the evolution of modern imperialism sea power has played a role perhaps even superior in importance to military power upon land.[14]

While naval power was increasing there was at the same time developing the theory of the so-called "freedom of the sea." This is a fairly ancient theory. In the Roman law the sea was called common and free. But the meaning of the term has varied greatly from time to time and so far no genuine freedom has existed. In their attitudes toward this theory nations have followed, as usual, the policies which they conceived to be to their own interest. For several centuries Rome had a powerful rival in Carthage on the African side of the Mediterranean. It is possible that the theory of the freedom of the sea was incorporated in the Roman law out of a desire to check the growth of the naval power of its great adversary. Commercial considerations also may have played a part. The advantages of a free exchange of commodities between the different parts of the Roman empire and the remainder of the known world may have been discerned. However, these considerations and the theory itself did not restrain imperial Rome from using naval power whenever it saw fit to do so.

The modern theory of the freedom of the sea is usually dated

[14] This was the opinion of the American navalist and imperialist, Admiral A. T. Mahan. See, for example, his *The Influence of Sea Power upon History, 1660-1783*, Boston, 1890; *The Influence of Sea Power upon the French Revolution, 1793-1812*, Boston, 1892, 2 vols.; *Sea Power in Its Relation to the War of 1812*, Boston, 1905, 2 vols.

from the famous work of Hugo Grotius (1583-1645). In his *Mare Liberum* he argued in favor of the freedom of the sea in the interest of mankind. His book influenced to a considerable extent the development of international law with respect to the sea. It is, however, enlightening to note the circumstances under which Grotius wrote his book, and the specific purposes which he apparently had in mind. The first edition of *Mare Liberum* was published anonymously at Leyden in 1609. Six years earlier James I of the Stuart dynasty had ascended the throne in England and put forward the doctrine of the British ownership of the seas in the vicinity of the British isles. This doctrine was propounded and put into effect at first because the fishermen from Scotland, from whence the Stuart dynasty came, had conflicted with the Dutch fishermen on the fishing grounds in the North Sea. Hence it was to the interest of Holland to maintain the theory that the sea should be an open and common ground for fishing.

Other circumstances furnished a justification for this theory even more than the fishing rights. The preceding century had been characterized by extensive exploration and discoveries which made possible an enormous expansion of commercial enterprise. Certain nations which were interested in taking advantage of these opportunities for trade, or sometimes rather for wholesale robbery on land and sea, claimed the ownership of extensive areas of the sea. The most extravagant of these claims was the one put forward by Spain and Portugal under the alleged authority of a Papal bull to divide the waters of the western hemisphere and of the East Indies.

The Dutch merchants and mariners, in search of trade and profit, were at that time pushing their way into various maritime regions claimed by these Catholic Powers. While the Dutch lawyer Hugo Grotius may have been influenced to a certain extent by humanitarian considerations, it is highly probable that his argument in behalf of the freedom of the sea was inspired largely by a nationalist and patriotic desire to remove these obstacles in the way of the navigation and commerce of his country. This seems all the more probable in view of the fact that Grotius did not consistently advocate the freedom of the sea throughout the whole of his career. When he went to London as one of the Dutch commissioners to protest against the English claims to ownership over the North Sea, he was the Grotius of *Mare Liberum*. Later in his career when he was the ambassador of the Swedish queen in Paris, he displayed great reluctance to advocate this theory because Sweden at the time was making extravagant claims to ownership over the Baltic Sea.

As we have seen, the earlier naive claims to ownership of the sea have disappeared almost entirely. The discussion of the freedom of the sea by Grotius and his successors, such as Puffendorf, Van Bynkerhoek, de Vattell, von Martens, Azuni, Bluntschli, etc., has encouraged its partial recognition by international law. It has also given rise to lip service to this theory from all the civilized nations of the world. This is often even more true of the nations possessing great naval power, whose professions of recognition of and loyalty to this theory are prone to wax in vehemence with the growth of their naval power.

The European war of 1914 to 1918 and the world war of 1939 to 1945 have added air to military and naval power. This has raised the question of the freedom of the air. The atomic and hydrogen bomb and bacterial warfare have increased enormously the dangerousness and destructiveness of war. Total war threatens the extermination of most of mankind and the destruction of almost all of human products. It accentuates immeasurably the gravity of all of the phenomena arising out of or connected with warfare, such as nationalism, patriotism, navalism, militarism on land and in the air, imperialism, colonialism, and all other violent manifestations of force. It complicates greatly the problem of the sovereign state as an economic and political instrument of destructive power. It emphasizes the fact that the state has been mainly an instrument of violence, warfare, conquest, plunder and exploitation. In later chapters will be described the more peaceful and less predatory aspects of the state. Unless its social functions expand greatly before long, the sovereign state as the most dangerous form of social organization will destroy mankind.

Chapter XXII

The First Age of Imperialism from Sargon (ca. 2341 B.C.) to Alexander (323 B.C.)

THIS treatise is not a comprehensive, and even less a detailed history of mankind. It is an attempt to trace the main stages of cultural evolution in so far as the available data render it possible. For this purpose many pages of history are barren. Many peoples have come and gone, many states have risen and fallen, without leaving an appreciable impress upon the course of this evolution. Here and there in space and in time events have occurred, factors of the physical environment have been present, social influences have coalesced, peoples and their cultures have collided and combined with varying degrees of amalgamation and unification, so as to produce cultural variations and sometimes innovations. Sociologists have made considerable use of anthropological data concerning primitive peoples, but much less use of the rich store of historical data concerning literate peoples. And yet during the brief space of historical time of a few thousand years many more cultural changes have taken place than during the hundreds of thousands of years of prehistoric time which witnessed only the beginnings and early stages of cultural evolution among the comparatively few and widely dispersed human beings.

Food production as distinguished from food gathering was commenced at various places during neolithic time. This happened in regions where the soil was favorable for cultivation, such as river valleys, grasslands, wind-blown loess deposits, and other fertile spots. The first agricultural tool was the digging stick, which is still used by the most primitive peoples. Then the stone celt, or hand-ax, was fastened to a handle and used as a hoe. Later came the plow drawn by oxen which rendered field agriculture possible.

During the neolithic period also was taking place the domestication of animals. The dog was probably domesticated as early as late paleolithic time. Then followed the domestication of swine, cattle, sheep, goats, fowl, asses, horses, camels, elephants, and cats, not necessarily in the above order. Most of these species were tamed and domesticated from 6000 to 4000 B.C. Agriculture arose from 8000 to 5000 B.C. These two achievements together rendered possible a settled community life as distinguished from the nomadic existence of hunting and pastoral peoples.

There were food producing cultures in Mesopotamia, Iran, Anatolia, Syria, and Egypt, in other words in southwestern Asia and northeastern Africa. They developed somewhat later in Europe. When they commenced in India and China is uncertain. Wherever agriculture arose small aggregations of human beings, or villages of peasants, came into existence. At first these villages were self-sufficient in the sense that they produced enough food and other necessities for their own subsistence without producing a surplus.

At the same time were developing the industrial crafts some of which had their origins in paleolithic time. Among them were the manufacture of stone and wooden tools, the making of pottery and basketry, the textile industry, the art of cookery. New forms of food were produced, such as cheese from curdled and dried milk, bread by the baking of cereals, preserved meats by drying and smoking the flesh of animals, fermented beverages from grains, fruits and berries. Some of these crafts rendered possible the construction of more or less permanent shelters and houses from wood, clay or stone.

When these crafts and industries reached a point of development where they could produce more than enough to supply the immediate needs of the village population, an economic surplus came into existence. This was most likely to happen in the valleys and on the flood plains of large rivers where a fertile soil produced an abundance of food not only for the tillers of the soil but also for an additional population. Hence it was that the first cities arose in Mesopotamia and Egypt about 3500 B.C. They did not arise in Crete and India before 3000 B.C., possibly somewhat later, and perhaps still later in China.

It may be assumed that the nascent city was composed of craftsmen who had congregated at a site favorable for their crafts because the raw materials were readily available or because the power of water or wind could be utilized. They exchanged their products for the excess food produced by the inhabitants of neighboring villages. Thus for a time at least the relation between an urban center and its surrounding villages was that of a more or less equivalent exchange of tools, clothing, bricks, etc., for food, wool, flax, and other agricultural raw materials. The use of metals increased greatly the productive capacity of labor. First copper was cold-hammered into useful shapes.

When the fusibility of metals was discovered, it became possible to shape not only a soft metal like copper but also to make bronze, an alloy of copper and tin, and to work with the harder metals. The greatest achievement of metallurgy was the fusing of iron probably between 1500 and 1000 B.C. Water control to prevent floods and irrigation to promote crops were also important factors for the increase of wealth in the river valleys where the early urban cultures flourished.

With the increase of wealth the simple first-hand exchange of manufactured commodities for food did not continue indefinitely. The urban dwellers sought to secure and retain most or all of the economic surplus. The result of these endeavors was to reduce the rural inhabitants to an inferior status of tenancy, serfdom, or even of slavery. The city inhabitants had better weapons, were more highly organized and had the beginnings of literacy. They could claim more influence with the spirit world because they could construct more imposing shrines and temples for their gods.

Another factor for the subordination of the peasant inhabitants of villages may have been of decisive importance. The clan and tribal organizations of primitive peoples persisted in many peasant villages. As we have seen in an earlier chapter, chieftainship arises in various ways in the clan or more often in the tribe. When a tribe subdued neighboring tribes the chief of the conquering tribe was likely to become a king over the territory of the conquered as well as of the conquering tribe. To the king was early attributed the traits of a divine being. In Egypt the cities grew up around the tombs of the divine rulers. In Mesopotamia they arose around temples of the priests. It has not yet been determined around what centers arose the extinct cities of the early third millennium B.C. in the valley of the Indus River. In Crete the early cities seem to have arisen around a building which was both the palace of a king and a temple. But in all these regions industrial and commercial factors must have played an important part in determining the size if not the original location of cities.

Conflicts between cities in Mesopotamia and in Egypt resulted in the unification in each region of groups of cities, each group being under one governmental control. Thus arose national states. The control was by means of a standing army or a military reserve which was ready at any time to maintain and to extend the territory of a state. The extension of territory was due mainly to economic factors. The cities needed for their industries various raw materials such as timber, metals and other mineral products, textile materials, etc. The search for these materials was ever carried farther afield. Conquest was the most effective way of securing and safeguarding these materials. Roads were needed to maintain communication with the newly acquired territory. These roads had to be protected from attack by other states and from brigands. This furnished an additional reason for a permanent military establishment.

In some cases this process of expansion continued until a powerful state conquered and more or less absorbed weaker states thereby creating an empire. In other cases outlying nomadic or pastoral peoples, attracted by the wealth of the cities and urban states, raided and looted these wealthy centers and sometimes maintained domination over them for a period of time. The first type of empire was usually due to a combination of conquest and more or less peaceful penetration. The second type of empire was due entirely to conquest and was maintained by an alien domination.[1] Both of these types of empire existed during the early period of imperialism in Mesopotamia, Asia Minor, and Egypt.

We have already noted that the first cities of importance arose in Mesopotamia and Egypt about 3500 B.C. There were earlier urban centers probably of smaller size. One of them was at Anau in Russian Turkestan near the border of Iran. Its urban culture apparently began between 4500 and 4000 B.C. But Anau disappeared entirely from the map and its culture did not belong in the main current of cultural evolution, unless it contributed something to the development of agriculture or some of the crafts. Toward the close of its existence it may have been a trading center between the west and east Asiatic cultural regions.

The Mediterranean civilization arose in the vicinity of the Mediterranean Sea. The other two great civilizations arose somewhat later in India and in China. In a book on Oriental and Occidental culture I distinguished between these cultures as follows:

"The latter (Occidental culture) originated and has had its principal development in the Mediterranean area. It has spread over the whole of Europe and the Western Hemisphere and has been carried wherever men of European origin have established colonies. The former is represented chiefly in the Indian and Chinese cultures, which are so sharply defined and distinctive that it is hardly possible to speak of an Oriental culture.

"This illustrates a fact of great importance—namely, that the East is much less unified than the West, both culturally and geographically. Just as the Himalaya range thrusts its great bulk between India and China, so are they rigidly separated from each other culturally. The West has had its own continuous, more or less uniform, and rapid development. The East has had several coeval lines of

[1] "Many times have barbarous nomadic peoples entered the territories of settled tillage peoples to raid, despoil, conquer, and rule. . . . Predatory nomadism has been an outstanding fact of recorded, and doubtless of unrecorded history." (Hutton Webster, *History of Civilization*, Boston, 1947, Vol. I, p. 375.)

development and in recent times has remained comparatively unchanged."[2]

Too much writing about history has consisted of information about dates, dynasties and kings, and their military victories. Dates are important in so far as they indicate the sequence in time of conditions and events because they often throw light upon causal relations. Kings illustrate the fact that throughout history the many have usually been dominated by the few. Military conquests constitute one of many methods by which men have exploited mankind. But dates, rulers, and wars are of genuine significance only in so far as they aid in understanding the course of cultural evolution.

On the broad flood plains and delta of the Euphrates and Tigris rivers and in the narrow valley of the Nile, during the prehistoric period prior to 3500 B.C., there arose numerous peasant villages and some small cities. During the millenium between 3500 and 2500 B.C. there arose in Mesopotamia the early Sumerian culture. During this period were developed or crystallized the customs, laws, religious beliefs and practices, social institutions, economic practices, and political and military organizations which characterized and dominated the near and middle east during ancient historical time. A parallel development was taking place in Egypt. About 3100 (plus or minus 100) B.C. was established at Memphis in lower Egypt near the modern city of Cairo a kingdom now designated as the old kingdom.[3] Upon the decline of this kingdom about a millennium later was established a kingdom at Thebes, near the modern city of Luxor, which is now designated as the middle kingdom, and which lasted from about 2130 until about 1780 B.C. These two cultural regions, namely, Mesopotamia and Egypt, were about 800 miles apart as the crow flies, a vast distance in those days. The difficulty of communication was increased by the Arabian desert which lay between. The communication, such as there was, from Egypt was through Syria to the great bend of the Euphrates and then to lower Mesopotamia, a distance of more than 1,200 miles.

The Egyptian kingdoms were much more enclosed and isolated in the narrow confines of the Nile valley than the Mesopotamian kingdoms. A Semitic king, Sargon the Elder of Akkad or Agade (ca. 2341-2285), conquered all of lower Mesopotamia and a part or all of Syria and extended his rule to the Mediterranean Sea. This was the first empire of which we have any record. However, it disintegrated after Sargon's death. His dynasty ended about 2160 B.C., probably because

[2] Maurice Parmelee, *Oriental and Occidental Culture, An Interpretation*, New York, 1928, p. 11.

[3] The first astronomical date which could serve as a check upon historical dates in Egypt was 1850 (plus or minus 3) B.C.

337

this empire was not well organized. Later the kings of Ur, a city southeast of Akkad ruled lower Mesopotamia for a time.

About this time Semites from the Arabian peninsula began to filter into Mesopotamia and to adopt its culture. Eventually they gained the ascendancy and established a kingdom, or empire as it is often called, with its capital at Babylon. This was the first Babylonian dynasty whose best known monarch was Hammurabi who reigned about 1728 to 1686 B.C.[4] and who promulgated the code of laws described elsewhere in this book.

The Semitic invasion of Mesopotamia illustrates the second type of imperialism due to alien domination mentioned above. It continued the first age of imperialism which lasted about two millennia. It was followed by a second age of imperialism which began with the invasion of Asia by Alexander the Macedonian and lasted eight centuries to the fall of Rome in 476 A.D. This included the most important part of Roman imperialism. After the disintegration of the Roman empire imperialism on a grand scale was more or less in abeyance for a millennium. At the close of the Middle Ages the European type of imperialism arose with the era of exploration. Its characteristic features will be described later in this treatise.

During the latter part of the third millennium B.C. Indo-European peoples began to move southward and eastward into Asia Minor, Mesopotamia and even as far south as Egypt. These peoples were partly nomadic and pastoral with perhaps a certain amount of peasant-village culture. They may have been encouraged to migrate by a change of climate in central Europe which decreased the amount of forest and grass lands. They were certainly attracted by the more fertile land and the accumulated wealth to the south of them. They conquered or mixed with the peasant-village peoples they encountered on their way so that they did not approach the urban centers as pure Indo-Europeans, either biologically or culturally.

The first to arrive were apparently the Hittites who came from somewhere in Southeastern Europe into Anatolia. However, they did not establish an empire until several centuries later. The Hurrites who were partly Indo-European, coming from the region between the Caspian and Black seas ruled from about 1800 to 1400 B.C. in the upper Euphrates-Tigris area. The Kassites came from Persia by way of

---

[4] At the Oriental Institute of the University of Chicago the beginning of Hammurabi's reign is put at 1796 B.C. The reign of Sargon the Elder is estimated by Professor I. J. Gelb of this institute to have lasted 56 years from 2341 to 2285 B.C. "Sargon of Agade, by his sweeping conquests, created the first historic empire. . . . Mankind by this time had passed from the petty robbery, murder, and border feuds characteristic of primitive society to organized warfare, in which state was ranged against state." (Hutton Webster, op. cit., Vol. I, page 134.)

338

the Zagros mountains into lower Mesopotamia about 1550 B.C. and founded a dynasty which lasted until about 1150 B.C. The Hyksos, who were a mixture of Indo-Europeans, Hurrites and Semites, coming from Syria and Palestine, in the 18th century B.C. invaded Egypt and ruled there until about 1600 B.C. They were formerly designated as the shepherd kings and were supposed to have been Semites who came into Egypt from Arabia. About the middle of the second millennium B.C. the Achaians began to filter into the Hellenic peninsula and other Indo-European peoples into Bithynia.[5]

The Hittite empire lasted from about 1400 to 1200 B.C. It was a military and priestly domination by a victorious minority over a native peasant population. The Hittites probably introduced the horse into Anatolia. Their power was derived in large part from the horsedrawn chariot and bronze weapons. The rule was shared by the nobles and the priests. The kings were probably elected from the nobility. Their industries and much of their culture in general were borrowed from the Mesopotamians. For a time they ruled over vassal states in Mesopotamia and Syria and as far west as the Egean coast. They were constantly threatened by Egypt and Assyria. Toward the end of their domination they were also threatened by invaders from the northwest who were probably new Indo-European migrants from southeastern Europe. Inasmuch as their script has been only partially deciphered, little is known as to their disappearance as a ruling people.

After the overthrow of the Hyksos dynasty in Egypt it was ruled by native kings some of whom expanded their kingdom for a time into an empire. About the year 1400 B.C. Egypt was ruling over Palestine and Syria to the north and Abyssinia to the south. But about the same time was arising a country which was later to conquer Egypt.

Assyria was at first a dependent province to the north of Babylonia on the upper reaches of the Tigris. The Assyrians were partly of Semitic descent and their language was Semitic. However, they borrowed a good deal of the Babylonian culture. About the year 1100 B.C. Babylonia was being attacked by Semitic invaders from the Arabian peninsula. The Assyrian monarch took advantage of this situation and conquered Babylonia. For a time Assyria ruled from the Persian Gulf to the Mediterranean Sea. After the death of this king, Tiglath-pileser I, the short-lived first Assyrian empire disintegrated.

Some three centuries later an adventurer named Pul who had seized the Assyrian throne and called himself Tiglath-pileser II, con-

[5] See V. Gordon Childe, *The Aryans: A Study of Indo-European Origins*, 1926; George Poisson, *Les Aryens: etude linguistique, ethnologique, et prehistorique*, 1934; Albrecht Goetze, *Hethiter, Churriter, und Assyrer*, 1936; E. A. Speiser, *Ethnic Movements in the Near East in the Second Millennium B.C.*, 1933; John Garstang, *The Hittite Empire*, 1929.

quered Babylonia again. Preceding empires had usually left conquered states under their native rulers as tributary kings. This time Assyria organized its empire in provinces with a *satrap* or representative of the emperor governing each province. Under this system government was more centralized which was intended to prevent subject peoples from rebelling. This innovation in government was imitated by several future empires. Even with this more centralized government the Assyrian empire did not survive for very long.

In 672 B.C. Assyria conquered Egypt. At its greatest extent this empire included Babylonia, Media to the east, most of Asia Minor, Syria, as well as Egypt. The latter rebelled after twenty years of subjection. Babylonia followed suit after another score of years. Then came another invasion from the north by a people known to history as the Scythians. In 606 B.C. the Medes and Babylonians captured and destroyed Nineveh. Assyria disappeared forever as a kingdom or empire as other empires arose.

The second Babylonian, or Neo-Babylonian or Chaldean, as it is sometimes called, empire lasted only from about 625 to 538 B.C. It included all of the first Babylonian empire of 1,500 years earlier and some additional territory. To the east lay the plateau of Iran where were living the Medes whose ancestors had come from the north a few centuries earlier, and the Persians who may have come from India. At any rate, the latter spoke an Indo-European language and bore cultural resemblances to the Indians. At first the Medes dominated this plateau. Then about 558 B.C. a tributary Persian prince, who has become known to history as Cyrus the Great, rebelled against the Medes and established an independent Persian kingdom. Persia soon conquered not only Medea but by 538 B.C., Babylonia, and then Lydia in western Asia Minor, Egypt, and extensive territories to the east including even some of northwest India. By the commencement of the 5th century B.C. the Persian Empire included all of the earlier empires, all of Asia Minor, and even included a part of Thrace and Thessaly in Europe.

The Persian empire was modelled in part after the Assyrian empire. It was divided into satrapies each of which was governed by a satrap or representative of the emperor. An extensive system of good roads was built to maintain communication between all parts of the empire and to facilitate trade. The principal road was more than 1,500 miles in length from Susa the capital city near the Persian Gulf to Sardis near the Egean Sea. These roads served to unify the empire and to delay it from disintegrating as rapidly as had some of the earlier empires.

The Persians sent three large expeditions into Europe in attempting to conquer Greece in 492, 490, and 480-479 B.C. They were the

340

first and the last attempts of Asiatic powers to conquer Europe until one millennium later the Huns and two millennia later the Turks invaded Europe. But the Greeks in Ionia and elsewhere in Asia Minor were restive under Persian rule. At the commencement of the 4th century B.C. Sparta made war against Persia in an attempt to free the Asiatic Greeks but failed partly because of its enemies in Greece. Shortly thereafter Philip of Macedon extended his power to the north into Thrace and to the south over Thessaly. In 338 B.C. he invaded Greece and at Chaeronea defeated Athens and Thebes. He was then declared at a congress of the Greek states at Corinth as their leader for a war against Persia. In 336 B.C. Philip was assassinated. In 334 B.C. his son Alexander (B.C. 356-323) commenced his invasion of the Persian empire.

After his vast conquests of the ancient empires Alexander the Macedonian died in 323 B.C. before he could integrate these conquered lands in a strongly centralized empire. His generals fought among themselves for the succession but no one gained the imperial throne. Alexander's empire fell apart into three large kingdoms and several smaller ones. The kingdom of the Seleucids (descendants of Seleucus (B.C. 365?-281) a Macedonian general and nobleman) included Babylonia, Syria, and the western part of Asia Minor. The kingdom of the Ptolemies (descendants of Lagus, a general of Alexander) included Egypt, Palestine and the Lebanon. The Antigonids, descended from Antigonus (382-301 B.C.) an older half-brother of Alexander, ruled Macedonia and neighboring European territories. The monarchies which were smaller in territory or in population or less important in other ways included Bactria, Parthia, Armenia, Pontus, Cappadocia, and Bithynia. Some of the Greek city-states regained their independence and formed leagues for mutual protection but with a good deal of internal dissension.

In preceding chapters have been described briefly the Minoan or Egean culture which became merged into the Hellenic and through it into the general Mediterranean culture. The earliest stages have been briefly described of the Indian and Chinese cultures which for several millennia had little contact with Mediterranean culture. The Chou dynasty which ruled a good deal of what is now known as China from about 1122 to 225 B.C. was more of a feudalistic than an imperial regime. The first Chinese emperor was Shi Huang Ti of the Chin dynasty who reigned until 210 B.C. Feudalism disappeared in large part, the land was distributed to the peasants, and universal military service was established. There is less evidence of imperialism in ancient India though the Mauryan dynasty ruled most of India from about 321 to 184 B.C.

Some of the principal features and effects of the first age of imperialism may be summarized. It is, however, not easy to distinguish between the effects of imperialism and the effects of forces which were at work before imperialism and which continued at work during the imperialistic period. Imperialism accentuated somewhat the mingling of peoples and of cultures which was already taking place before imperialism and which would have continued even without imperialism. It expanded the stage upon which was being performed the exploitation of millions of individuals and of scores or hundreds of peoples. Imperialistic wars stimulated slavery because prisoners of war could be retained as slaves when it was more profitable to do so than to kill them. Also as many of the conquered peoples could be enslaved as was found profitable. Often the enslaved included the better educated and more skilful of the conquered who could thereby create more wealth for their owners. They also included many field laborers for agriculture and unskilled workers to perform common labor on residences, temples, pyramids and other funerary monuments, and public buildings in general. For example, Herodotus (Greek historian of the 5th century B.C.) alleged that the construction of the great pyramid of Khufu (Cheops) at Giza of 2,300,000 blocks of stone, averaging $2\frac{1}{2}$ tons each, required the labor for 3 months of each year for 10 years of 100,000 men who could have been little if any better off than slaves. In these different instances the slaves would belong to private masters, to the priestly class, to the noble class, or to the king or emperor who was the supreme ruler.

The same applied to property other than chattel slavery. Some of the land in the conquered territory was often taken over by the ruler or given by him to his soldiers. The native inhabitants, if not transported, then became the slaves or at least the serfs of the new owners. The mobile capital, such as tools and domesticated animals, if not confiscated and taken elsewhere, was often used, even while still in the hands of its original owners, to produce wealth much of which was claimed by the new owners. In so far as the necessities for survival were concerned, such as food, clothing and shelter, only enough was left in the hands of the subject population to enable them to go on producing a surplus of necessities, comforts and luxuries for their masters.

At this point it may be well to survey the evolution of the right of property. Among contemporary primitive peoples several types of property ownership have been observed. Among hunting peoples the right of private property is usually restricted to weapons and other movable goods. Ownership of land is almost always collective. It is held by families, clans or tribes. If held by a family or clan it is usually under a vaguer tribal ownership. This ownership restricts hunting on the land to the members of the collective unit so that trespassers from

342

other tribes are excluded. With the beginning of agriculture private ownership of pieces of land near the village began to be recognized. However, there were occasional redistributions of the land so that the private ownership was not as lasting and absolute as in later stages of cultural evolution. This did not come until a permanent peasant economy based upon a rather intensive cultivation with the plow had come into being, in other words, a type of agriculture higher than the rudimentary digging stick and hoe culture. "Although no dates can be set for the appearance of any of these conceptions of property, it seems clear that primitive peoples probably maintained a system of mixed property rights, with collective rights outweighing individual rights. The individual's right of private property, it may be said, is never absolute, for other individuals either may claim a right of use when occasion demands or may share in its disposal under certain rules." [6]

It will be noted from the above that property among primitive peoples was based mainly upon use, namely, that the individual or group actually using the land or movable goods also had the right of ownership. This fact must be correlated with the fact that labor was expected from almost all members of a primitive group. The only exceptions were chiefs and magicians and medicine men who were supposed to protect the group from the natural and supernatural dangers which menaced it. These exceptional persons might also possess property rights in land and other goods which they did not actually use. The general rule of universal service and property based upon use was doubtless due to the fact that the margin between income and bare subsistence was very slight, so that there was no surplus to allow for a leisured and propertied class.

This situation was perpetuated for countless ages in part because of the primitive restrictions on technology. While human inventiveness and imitation and diffusion played their part in technological advance during eolithic, paleolithic and neolithic time, these factors were limited by the tradition that methods used in the past should be continued, and perhaps even more by the belief that inventions and skillful use of them were due to supernatural forces. Owing to this belief magic rather than experiment with the physical world was used to attain the ends desired. These factors explain in large part the very slow advance of technology during most of the hundreds of thousands of years which have elapsed since the beginning of the eolithic age.

Changes in this situation, in particular with regard to the right of private property, occurred when an economic surplus arose which

[6] Ralph Turner, *The Great Cultural Traditions*, Vol. I, New York, 1941, page 75. See also Richard Thurnwald, *Economics in Primitive Communities*, London, 1932, translated from the German.

permitted the existence of a class of owners who did not actually cultivate the land and create the goods from which they lived. As we have seen, this happened first in fertile regions such as river valleys where a peasant economy based on a field agriculture became established. The owners and persons other than the cultivators of the soil themselves who drew their sustenance therefrom were free to live in idleness or to engage in specialized crafts, to undertake business enterprises as in trade, or to embark on military adventures destined to deprive more cultivators of the right of property in the soil into which they had poured their blood and sweat.

During the 4th and 3rd millennia b.c. the Sumerian urban culture in Mesopotamia traveled a long distance toward formulating rights of property many of which were not based upon use for production or even for consumption purposes. According to the code of Hammurabi, land and chattel goods could be bought, sold, rented and bequeathed. Contracts to attain these ends were recognized and enforced by the law and courts. Much of the land, however, was held by the king, by the temples, and by nobles to whom it had been given by the king in return for military service and which could not be alienated by the nobles. To that extent the right of individual private property was limited.

In Egypt the right of private property was not as clearly defined as in Sumeria and Babylonia. All of the land belonged to the king. Permission to use it was given in return for certain payments or services to the king. However, this right to use it could apparently be sold, rented and bequeathed. The Egyptian system of land tenure was manorial in the sense that the ultimate ownership was vested in the king. Chattels were subject to unrestricted private ownership with rights of use and sale.

Turner has summed up the principal effects of the early imperialism in Mesopotamia and Egypt as follows: "The first age of imperialism brought the organization of culture patterns in areas much greater in size than those of the original urban cultures, as well as innovations, which, while they did not disrupt the ancient traditions, gave urban culture as a whole a more secure base." [7] It may be futile to conjecture what would have happened had there been no imperialism. It is perhaps questionable that it put urban culture on a more secure basis. It may have increased the extent of the confiscation and expropriation of the economic surplus by persons and groups who did not create this surplus. It probably accentuated the degree of hierarchy in the structure of the social classes by extending slavery and increasing the number of types of citizens. It doubtless increased the com-

[7] Ralph Turner, *op. cit.*, Vol. I, page 244.

plexity of the political system thereby preparing the way for some of the governmental forms of the future.

On the other hand, imperialism served the purpose of bringing different cultures into contact with each other, though this contact was often in the form of armed strife. We have noted that the Mesopotamian and Egyptian cultures were for many centuries almost entirely isolated from each other. In between were minor cultures such as the Syrian and Semitic cultures. Both of them were invaded and conquered at times by Mesopotamian rulers. About the year 1400 B.C. Syria was ruled for a time by Egypt. In the 7th century B.C. Egypt was conquered by Assyria though the conquest lasted for only about 20 years. Such contacts led inevitably to a certain amount of imitation. Sometimes the blending of traits from different cultures gave rise to innovations. Whether or not this cultural diffusion and the innovations resulting from it could have been attained except by way of the militant and warlike paths of imperialism, it is impossible to say.

Imperialism often arose out of a human activity which is in itself peaceful though it has repeatedly led to violence and warfare in modern as well as ancient times. When the urban culture arose it required the interchange of the products of the crafts located in the cities with the raw materials produced in the rural areas. As Turner has expressed it: "When trade of this kind between the cities and outlying regions became continuous, the kings sent out military expeditions to protect it, and thereby united economic and political factors in that combination which the world has learned to call *imperialism.*" This led to the "cycle of imperialism" which he has described as "Peaceful trade, easy conquest, organized exploitation, border warfare, counterattack, brilliant victory, recurrent disorder, sudden defeat, bloody vengeance and expropriation. . . ."[8]

Imperialism is the second of the two main forms of social conflict. Or rather it is an amplification of the earliest form, namely, the struggle between the social classes which commenced as soon as the economic surplus began to accumulate, the never-ending struggle between the proprietors and the expropriated, the haves and the have-nots. Sometimes it was a struggle between those who had more and those who had less though not entirely destitute. While there is very little historical or literary evidence of the condition of the working class and of attempts on its part to revolt in ancient times, there are a few fragmentary suggestions. The Mesopotamian "Epic of Gilgamesh" is about a mythical Babylonian king. "Gilgamesh, ishakku of Uruk or Erech, who ruled for one hundred and twenty-six years, oppressed his people by forcing them to labor excessively in

[8] Ralph Turner, *op. cit.*, Vol. I, pages 222 and 224.

345

building the walls of the city. For relief the people appealed to the goddess, Aruru, ..." [9] From the Seventh to the Twelfth Dynasties inclusive (*ca*. 2280-1780 B.C.) Egypt was a feudalism dominated by the nobles and priests. About 2200 B.C. a social revolution took place during which nobles were killed and lawlessness was widespread according to the written records left by the priests and nobles. During the Twentieth Dynasty (*ca*. 1200-1090 B.C.) another revolution took place during which soldiers as well as workers robbed the temples and tombs. Both of these revolutions apparently happened because the ruling classes did not permit the masses to have enough food. There is much more evidence of the class struggle in ancient Rome and Greece.

However, there were very few revolts against the established social order throughout ancient times. The social hierarchy maintained its dominance with crushing force upon the lower classes. At the top were the priestly class, and the noble class or military aristocracy. The first acquired its power originally through the universal belief in hobgoblins, or supernatural beings such as gods and devils, a belief which still is almost universal. The priests attributed to themselves the ability to influence these animistic beings by magical or religious means. Owing to an almost complete ignorance of the natural causes of phenomena on the part of mankind, they have been able to acquire and retain a vast control over the minds and actions of men. Hobgoblinism persists today in the forms of monotheism, polytheism, demonism, angelism, spiritism, and the almost universal belief in human souls. The priests of old were also able to amass much treasure in their temples and shrines and to acquire the ownership of much land. This wealth enhanced greatly their power. Modern science has curtailed somewhat the power of the priestly class, because it has weakened the belief in the supernatural powers of the priests. But it has as yet made little inroad upon hobgoblinism in the forms of religion and magic.

Wherever the kingship existed, the king was usually the chief priest or chief noble or both. The nobles formed a military aristocracy which maintained its power by force of arms rather than that of superstitions. The distribution and concentration of power shifted somewhat from place to place and from time to time as between the priesthood, the military class, and the monarchy. At all times the rule was oligarchic with a tendency to become more and more timocratic as wealth accumulated.

[9] *The Babylonian Story of the Deluge and the Epic of Gilgamesh*, British Museum, 1920. This epic written on cuneiform tablets was found at Nineveh in the library of the Assyrian king Ashurbanipal or Sardanapalus who reigned about 668 to 625 B.C.

346

A small literate class was closely associated with and to a certain extent identical with the priestly class. Many of these literates were scribes who were employed in keeping temple records and writing down the meager lore of ancient times. In Mesopotamia the Sumerian cuneiform system of writing was developing from pictographic writing probably between the years 3500 and 2700 B.C. The Egyptian writing developed, probably a little later than in Mesopotamia, from its pictographic form which began during the First Dynasty (*ca.* 3100 plus or minus 100 B.C.). By the Fourth Dynasty (*ca.* 2720 to 2560 B.C.) there had evolved two kinds of script, namely, the hieroglyphic which was used almost entirely by the priests for sacred writings, and the hieratic which was a cursive form of the hieroglyphic used by scribes for secular purposes, such as the writing of accounts and contracts. Nearly two millennia later, about the 7th century B.C., there appeared the demotic which was an abbreviated form of the hieratic script. Apparently it was used at first by merchants and later for all ordinary purposes.

A mercantile class was growing in size and influence during ancient times. The merchants formed the first group which engaged in business enterprise and were the forerunners of the capitalists who were to become the masters of most of the modern world. They were rendered possible as soon as a standardized medium of exchange came into being. This happened after the invention of metallurgy furnished a supply of refined metal which could serve not only as a medium of exchange but also as a measure and sometimes as a storehouse of value. Copper, which is a soft metal fusible at a comparatively low temperature, was at first hammered into the desired shape when cold. It was fused at least as early as the 5th millennium B.C. because fused copper beads were found at Mesopotamian and Egyptian sites of that period. Bronze, an alloy of copper and tin, was produced later. The effective use of refined iron did not come until just before the beginning of the 1st millennium B.C. One or another of these refined metals was used as a measure of value and medium of exchange long before money in the form of stamped coins was first minted in Lydia. Money made capital mobile by rendering it possible to move wealth readily by transferring it from person to person and from place to place. That trade and other business activities had already developed considerably by the beginning of the 2nd millennium B.C. is indicated by the elaborate provisions with respect to buying and selling, contracts, mortgages, and the like, in the code of Hammurabi.

The above-mentioned classes ruled jointly or severally over the workers. The latter consisted usually of peasants, urban craftsmen, and slaves. The earliest cities were enlarged villages which in Mesopotamia were built around temples administered by priests and in Egypt

347

around the tombs of divine rulers who were the chief priests when alive. In Crete the early cities were around a building which was apparently both a palace and a temple. At Mohenjo-daro in the Indus valley the largest structure was a bath, 170 by 90 feet, which may have been a sacred place. It seems likely that priests were the first rulers of the earliest cities. They were able to deprive the peasants of much of their economic surplus by requiring contributions to the local deities, namely, to themselves, by imposing taxes, and by collecting interest on loans to the peasants. It is not known how early the ownership of the land passed from the cultivators themselves to members of the ruling classes who did not take part in the cultivating. It is certain that landlords of whatever ruling class existed already in Egypt and Mesopotamia as early as 3000 B.C. The peasants already were serfs in the sense that they were required to cultivate the land for the benefit of their landlords and were not free to leave it.

The craft workers appear to have been at the start subject to priestly control. Gradually they acquired some freedom, especially the more skilled workers, probably because their skills were of great value for the ruling classes. Some of the crafts became organized, perhaps in order to take part in the management of production, both in Mesopotamia and Egypt. In Assyria the crafts were organized in guilds which acquired some rights and measure of freedom. However, the common unskilled laborers remained entirely unorganized. They were subject to forced labor in the gangs which built the pyramids of Egypt, the ziggurats or step temples of Mesopotamia, and the other monuments to the vanity of the gods, the priests, and the kings. At times the peasants also were forced into these labor gangs, usually in the seasons when agricultural labor was not heavy.

Apparently there was little if any slavery prior to neolithic time, and only a little in the village cultures which arose during the neolithic age. It was not until human labor acquired value as a commodity to be exploited that slavery became significant. This was the case when there was an economic surplus which could be and was exploited. Captives of war were no longer slaughtered but enslaved. Debtors who could not pay their debts became slaves. The children of slaves were born into slavery. Freemen sometimes sold their children into slavery. As slaves human beings had the same legal status as chattels, namely, that they could be purchased, sold, borrowed, and pledged as security. Generally speaking, their masters had the power of life or death over them. Under imperialism their condition probably worsened perhaps because so many of them were aliens from foreign lands captured in war. The economic value of slaves stimulated a trade which consisted in kidnapping human beings in foreign countries or in distant parts and then selling them in the urban marts.

348

In ancient times there were temple and palace slaves, galley slaves who rowed the galleys and were chained to their seats, craft slaves who acquired some skill in the crafts, rural slaves who worked in the field, gang slaves who worked on the construction of walls, temples, tombs, palaces, canals, etc., and domestic slaves who did menial labor in homes. With the passage of time the types of slave service varied. Galley slavery disappeared when sails replaced oars. Temple slavery decreased as theocratic rule diminished. Whenever slavery ceased to be economically profitable for the master classes, so-called free labor took the place of slave labor and wage slavery supplanted chattel slavery mainly because it was found that wage slaves were more productive than chattel slaves and could yield their employers a higher margin of profit even though they had to be paid wages.

Throughout ancient times and in the main down to the present day the attitude of the ruling classes has been that they belonged to a different and superior species. This attitude was generally accepted without question by the working class because it was subjected to upper class propaganda to the effect that this was the social order prescribed, ordained and sanctioned by the gods. The Christian injunction—"Render unto Caesar that which is Caesar's"—reflected the acceptance of imperial rule.[10] The Pauline exhortation to a runaway slave to return to his master recognized and accepted a social order in which the dominance of the upper classes was absolute.[11]

---

[10] When Jesus Christ was asked, "Is it lawful to give tribute unto Caesar, or not?", he replied, "Render therefore unto Caesar the things that are Caesar's, and unto God the things that are God's." (St. Matthew, XXII, 17, 21. Repeated in St. Mark, XII, 17; and St. Luke, XX, 25.

[11] St. Paul said in his epistles: "For there is no power but of God: the powers that be are ordained of God. Whosoever therefore resisteth the power, resisteth the ordinance of God: and they that resist shall receive to themselves damnation. . . . Render therefore to all their dues: tribute to whom tribute is due; custom to whom custom; fear to whom fear; honor to whom honor." (Romans, XIII, 1, 2, 7.)

"Servants, be obedient to them that are your masters according to the flesh, with fear and trembling, in singleness of your heart, as unto Christ." (Ephesians, VI, 5.)

"Let as many servants as are under the yoke count your own masters worthy of all honor, that the name of God and his doctrine be not blasphemed." (I Timothy, VI, 1.)

"Exhort servants to be obedient unto their own masters, and to please them well in all things; not answering again." (Titus, II, 9.)

St. Peter said: "Submit yourselves to every ordinance of man for the Lord's sake: whether it be to the king, as supreme; Or unto governors." (I Peter, II, 13.)

Chapter XXIII

The Middle Age of Imperialism to the Fall of Rome
(476 A.D.) and the Byzantine Empire to 1453 A.D.

TOWARD the close of the first age of imperialism, which was predominantly Asiatic, there arose the imperial power which created
what may be called the middle age of imperialism and which was
Mediterranean and European in origin. From about the 11th to the
9th century B.C. the Etruscan people migrated into Italy by way of the
Tiber river, probably coming from Asia Minor. Partly because their
writing and language, which apparently was not Indo-European, have
not yet been deciphered, little is known of their origin and early
history. By the 6th century B.C. they ruled most of northern Italy and
the west coast as far south as the bay of Naples where they came in
contact with the Greek cities. Etruria consisted mainly of more or
less independent and fortified cities which were united in a sort of
confederacy. The Etruscan culture was largely Asiatic but their art
was somewhat influenced by the Greeks who were penetrating Italy
from the south.

At about the close of the 2nd millennium B.C. the imperialist wars
in Asia Minor drove some migrants into the western part of the
Mediterranean. About 1100 B.C. the Phenicians, who were a trading
and seafaring people, began to colonize the western Mediterranean
especially western Sicily and northern Africa. Some wealthy refugees
from Tyre who were fleeing from the conquering Assyrians founded
Carthage about 853 B.C. By the 6th century B.C. the Carthaginians
ruled over an empire which included the north African coast west of
Cyrenaica, Sardinia, western Sicily, the Balearic Isles, most of southern
Spain, and some of the European and African coasts outside of Gibraltar. Carthage was a plutocracy with a republican form of government.

During this period the Greeks were colonizing from the Hellenic
peninsula all the way around the Egean Sea, the Sea of Marmora,
and along the Black Sea, southern Italy which came to be known as

Magna Graecia, and eastern Sicily. After the Greeks finally defeated the Persians in 480 B.C., Athens acquired an imperial power over a good deal of Greece, and around the Egean and the Sea of Marmora. The Athenians colonized without extending citizenship to their subject territories which they exploited by imposing heavy taxes. While it ruled despotically abroad, the very limited Athenian democracy rested on the backs of slaves and *metics* or foreign residents. In 431 B.C. commenced the Peloponnesian war between Athens and Sparta which lasted until 404 B.C. This war weakened Athens to such a degree that it lost its imperial power. It left Sparta supreme in Greece though without enabling it to establish an empire of its own.

Early in the 1st millennium B. C. certain Indo-European peoples called the Italic tribes came across the eastern Alps and spread southward into Italy. Among them were the Latins, the Sabines, the Samnites, and the Umbrians. Latium is a small plain between the lower Tiber and Mount Alban. The Latins had doubtless mixed with the indigenous population by the time they arrived. They founded or held about thirty villages on this plain where they farmed. On the south bank of the Tiber are seven hills where several villages were built by different peoples, among them the Latins. Eventually these villages combined into the city of Rome. Several roads led away from here which enhanced its importance as an urban center. From the late 7th to the late 6th century B.C. the Etruscans ruled the city and brought to it some of their culture. During their rule Rome acquired commercial contacts with the Mediterranean world. Greek products were imported and Greek artisans worked on its public buildings.

During the Etruscan rule the *patricians,* who were the family heads in the warrior *gentes* and large landlords, were socially differentiated from the *plebeians,* who were poor farmers, traders, foreigners, and others who were not *patricians.* The latter had all the political privileges and the duty of furnishing military service. The Etruscans also extended slavery, introduced forced labor, and organized the artisans into guilds similar to those in Assyria. By these measures they concentrated the wealth and increased the military power of Rome.

Near the close of the 6th century B.C. the patricians, aided by the Greek enemies of the Etruscans, expelled the Etruscan royal family. Etruria was eventually weakened by Celtic inroads from the north and finally absorbed by the rising Roman republic. About 500 B.C. the Roman patricians organized a so-called republic of which they had complete control. Instead of a king there were two consuls each of whom could command the army and could veto the acts of the other. The senate, composed entirely of patricians, was the legislative and supervisory arm of the Roman state. The *comitia curiata* was an assembly of the families which was supposed to ratify the acts of the consuls. But its decisions could be vetoed by the senate so that it had little or no power. In fact the Roman republic from its inception was an organized timocracy of wealth in land. The proportion of the patricians to the total population gradually fell from one-tenth to one-twentieth.

During the 5th and 4th centuries there was a long continued struggle between the patricians and the plebeians for the control of the republic. Some of the plebeians who were engaged in trade acquired considerable wealth. They wished to acquire political privileges by becoming eligible for the consulship and for other public offices. The poor plebeians, especially the small farmers, wanted land reform. There were certain political reforms. The principal one was the creation of the tribunate composed of five, later of ten, tribunes of plebeian origin who were supposed to represent the interests of the plebeians. However, the main outcome of this struggle was that the wealthy plebeians acquired most of the political privileges which they desired. The timocracy, therefore, changed somewhat in the composition of the group which wielded political power because it possessed wealth of whatever sort, but continued to be no less of a timocracy. Political power and activity continued to be related to the possession of wealth as has usually been the case in the history of mankind.

During the 4th century B.C. Rome gradually extended its rule over Italy. This was accomplished in part by a series of wars with various Italic tribes which had settled in different parts of the peninsula. It had three wars with the Samnites who inhabited the Apennine region to the east and southeast of Rome. These wars took place in 343-341 B.C., 326-304 B.C. and 298-290 B.C. In 338 B.C. Rome fought with about thirty Latin cities which revolted against its domination. By the end of the third Samnite war (290 B.C.) Rome dominated the whole of the peninsula except some Greek cities in the south. From 280 to 275 B.C. it fought a war with Pyrrhus, king of Epirus, a Greek country opposite southern Italy on the eastern side of the Adriatic Sea. This war completed Roman domination of the southern part of the peninsula.

There is no reason to believe that the Romans set out with the intention of conquering Italy and a large part of the remainder of the known world. Its success was probably due in the first instance to the fact that it was located near the mouth of the only navigable river in peninsular Italy which was about half way between the northern and southern ends of the peninsula. It used imperialist methods with its conquered territories. It established military and civilian colonies at strategic points so that by 200 B.C. they extended from the Po River in the north to the toe of Italy in the south. It constructed a network of roads connecting most of the colonies with each other. This was for military purposes though these roads doubtless had great value for travel and trade. It followed a policy of divide and rule, thereby keeping its conquered populations weak. For example, after the last and great Latin war of 340 to 338 B.C., Rome dissolved the Latin league whose public land became Roman. Most of its cities became subjects of Rome and were not allowed to communicate with each other, except through Rome, in political and commercial matters. The more favored cities were admitted to the Roman state and their inhabitants became Roman citizens.

Rome was now to embark upon its career of imperialism outside of Italy. The western Mediterranean had long been controlled by the Carthaginians who would not permit the ships of other nations to sail on it. Carthage held the western half of the island of Sicily and there was danger that it would occupy the eastern half as well which was held by the Greek ruler of the city of Syracuse on the east coast of Sicily. This furnished a pretext for Rome to attack Carthage. The first war between them, known as the first Punic (Phenician) war, took place from 264 to 241 B.C. Rome captured Sicily and a little later Sardinia and Corsica. In the meantime Carthage gained a strong foothold in the Iberian peninsula. In 218 B.C. the Carthaginian general Hannibal marched from Spain across the Alps into Italy and defeated the Romans in 216 B.C. at Cannae on the east coast of Italy. The second Punic war was prolonged until 201 B.C. by which time Carthage had lost all of its European possessions. Rome had now become a predatory power determined to destroy Carthage as expressed in its war cry "Carthago delenda est."[1] The third Punic war from 149 to 146 B.C. resulted in the complete destruction of Carthage. The great city of Carthage was razed to the ground. Now Rome ruled the territory all around the western Mediterranean.

Rome fought wars with Macedonia which had helped the Carthaginians in 215 B.C., 196 B.C., and 171-168 B.C. In 146 B.C. it annexed Macedonia. In 129 B.C. it annexed Pergamum a small Greek kingdom on the west coast of Asia Minor. It continued its career of conquest so that by the end of the republic in 27 B.C. its dominion extended to the east as far as Persia, to the south as far as Nubia, to the west as far as Spain, and to the north as far as the Rhine and Britain. Rome now ruled most of the western world.

The unified administration of this vast area gave a great impetus to business enterprise. Trade could now flow freely over the whole of the so-called republic which was later to become an empire in name as well as in fact. The central government took an active part in this

[1] "Carthage must be destroyed."

enterprise. It leased state-owned properties such as fisheries, mines, timber regions, salt works, etc. It built roads, harbors, bridges, lighthouses, temples, etc. from some of which it derived revenues such as tolls. It farmed provincial revenues. It loaned funds to provincial and municipal administrations. It manufactured munitions which were used in its wars. The capital which it used in these enterprises it derived mainly from the booty which it seized in its wars. So that in its inception as well as in its subsequent development Roman enterprise, both public and private, was a system of exploitation.

Private enterprise developed a system similar to that of modern capitalism. The Roman law evolved the concept of the corporation. There were municipalities, craft guilds, priestly fraternities, business concerns, etc. These legal entities were at one time and another called *universitates* (one out of many), *collegia* (gathered together), and *societates* (social groups). Then as now these artificial collective persons had rights and duties similar to those of natural persons. They could own property, make contracts, litigate, and engage in many activities. As Sohm has said, "Roman law contrived to accomplish a veritable masterpiece of juristic ingenuity in discovering the notion of a collective person; in clearly grasping and distinguishing from its members the collective whole as the ideal unity of the members found together by the corporate constitution; in raising this whole to the rank of a person (a juristic person), and in securing it a place in private law as an independent subject of proprietary capacity, standing on the same footing as other private persons."[2]

The business associations were syndicates organized by Roman business men. They included the *socii* or promoters or enterprisers, the *participes* or subscribers who furnished the initial capital, and the *partes* or ordinary investors in the enterprise. The analogies need hardly be pointed out between these groups and the promoters and managers, the initial subscribers with favored or privileged shares, and the holders of ordinary or common shares of contemporary corporations.

The dominant special interests' groups at succeeding stages in the rise of Rome were somewhat as follows. In the 5th and 4th centuries B.C. the patricians dominated. In the 3rd century B.C. the patricians and such of the plebeians as had acquired wealth dominated. By the end of the 3rd century B.C. there was a senatorial oligarchy representing the patricians, who constituted the hereditary and usually wealthy aristocracy, and the parvenu aristocracy of plebeians who had amassed wealth through trade, speculation, or by whatever means. By this time Rome was dominated by a mature timocracy.

[2] R. Sohm, *Institutes of Roman Law*, Oxford, 1907, translated from the German.

During the late Roman republic the social classes included a senatorial nobility descended from magistrates such as consuls and others who had held high office, the *equites* or equestrians or knights who were wealthy business men, the poor citizens, and the slaves. The working classes could be subdivided from the bottom up as being the slaves, the freedmen who had been slaves, the free urban workers, and the peasants who still retained ownership of their small farms.

Throughout this period the *latifundia* or large estates were growing in size. This took place partly and perhaps largely through the mechanism of debt. The small peasant farmer could not compete with the large landlord who in many instances was using slave labor. He went into debt because of a bad harvest or period of business depression, mortgaged his farm, and in default of payment was sold out. He then became the serf or slave of his landlord or joined the landless proletariat in the cities.

Debt has always arisen whenever and wherever there have been great differences of wealth and has always accentuated these differences. Debt is usually contracted with the understanding that it must be repaid with an increase in value known as usury or interest. The creditor is usually safeguarded by a pledge of the person or property of the debtor in case of default. The first sort of pledge has often resulted in slavery and has been one of the most prolific causes of human enslavement. It probably has ranked only second to the capture of prisoners of war as a cause of slavery. Wherever enslavement for defaulting the repayment of a loan has existed, it has been a constant menace to most of the free population. Debt has usually been a means of enriching the wealthy and pauperizing the poor. It has reinforced the tendency of property holders to become also the holders of political power. At times attempts have been made to restrain these effects of debt by treating all loans as philanthropic deeds to be repaid without usury. Even when recognized by law these efforts have had little success. In the post-medieval period imprisonment for debt was substituted as a slight amelioration of slavery and persisted into the 19th century, A.D. However, this measure affected primarily bankrupt and financially ruined members of the middle and upper classes.

In modern times the permanent indebtedness of many persons is an essential element of capitalism. It takes the form of long term mortgages and bond issues which absorb free surplus capital. The struggle between the debtor and creditor classes is waged around the question of inflation and deflation, or of rising and falling prices, or of cheap and dear money.

As I have said in another work: "The debt structure of capitalism arouses various serious problems and creates a complicated situation. The relationship between debtors and creditors is an acute problem of

355

adjustment. . . . This situation reveals the source of one of the principal causes of inflexibility and rigidity in the capitalist system, especially in the later stages of its development. Debts are to be repaid in the currency in which they were borrowed. If prices have fallen in the meantime, the purchasing power of money has risen, and debtors have to pay more than they received. If prices have risen, the purchasing power of money has fallen, and debtors have to pay less than they received. Generally speaking, creditors profit during deflation and lose during inflation. The latter situation is not so serious in so far as the incidence of the loss is concerned, because the creditors are on the whole more affluent than the debtors. The creditors are usually busy making profits from speculative enterprises during inflation and do not greatly feel the partial loss of the loans they have made. The former situation is much more serious because the debtors are on the whole less affluent and can ill endure the strain of repaying their artificially inflated debts. . . . Corporate debt obligations in the form of bonds and note issues constitute the largest part of the private long-term indebtedness. In 1929 the corporate long term debts formed 65 percent of the private long-term indebtedness . . . and in 1933 the corresponding percentage was 62."[3] Later in this treatise we shall return to the part played by debt in determining the distribution of wealth.

Wealth has been the principal factor in determining social differentiation. We have seen that as goods accumulated the unequal distribution of property arose. When wealth began to be inherited it became a potent cause of classes. Furthermore, property has made the social classes more lasting and permanent. Wealth has been the most common basis of high rank. It has often been the basis of nobility and of royalty. Members of this exalted rank have usually been appointed to official positions. Its exclusiveness and purity have been safeguarded by the practice of endogamous marriage. Old and distinguished ancestry has had much more influence than the personal traits and abilities of individuals.[4] The amount of native ability which has been suppressed in the lower classes and among the slaves is

[3] Maurice Parmelee, *Farewell to Poverty*, New York, 1935, pp. 37, 39, 40, and 41.

See also Max Radin, article entitled "Debt," in the *Encyclopedia of the Social Sciences*, New York, 1937, Vol. V, pp. 32-38. "Speculation, economic instability, the corporate structure, inflation and bankruptcy are as important in the modern debt problem as was the reduction of the debtor class to a semi-servile condition in ancient society." (P. 38)

[4] Gunnar Landtman, *The Origin of the Inequality of the Social Classes*, London and Chicago, 1938. "Wealth is in point of fact a more important factor, with regard to the rise of classes, than merely personal qualities, for the reason that it preserves in a higher degree than these to coming generations the position attained by a preceding one." (P. 75)

incalculable. Even when not intentionally suppressed it has been rendered ineffective through lack of opportunity for expression. In its place mankind has suffered immeasurably from the blundering, whether well or ill intentioned, and stupidity of numerous kings, lords, priests, and owners by acquisition or by inheritance of great wealth. Furthermore, the possessors of wealth have usually despised the manual labor from which they are liberated and have had contempt for the laborers. This attitude of the ruling class has tended to depress the working classes to still lower levels. The propaganda of the ruling class has with rare exceptions induced the workers to accept their lowly state as inevitable if not justified.

The Roman republic was named after the two Latin words *res* (affair) and *publica* (public). In modern times the word republic has come to mean a form of the state which is representative of a considerable part of the people and which is to that extent democratic. However, this was true of none of the ancient republics and of very few if any of the medieval republics. The Roman republic was controlled mainly by the patrician class throughout its five centuries of existence. The even older Carthaginian republic was a plutocracy. The Athenian republic may have represented the free citizens but did not represent the large slave class and the foreign born inhabitants however long they may have lived there. Throughout most of the course of history republics have differed from monocracies only in that power has resided in a small oligarchy instead of in one individual, nominally or actually.

The Roman empire came into existence as the immediate result of the struggle for power of a few individuals. After the destruction of Carthage in b.c. 146, the senatorial oligarchy proved to be incapable of ruling effectively over the vast empire which Rome had conquered. Several victorious generals set up partial or complete dictatorships. Among them were Marius (b.c. 157-86), Cinna (b.c. ?-83), Sulla (b.c. 138-78) who was declared permanent dictator by the Senate in b.c. 81, Pompey (b.c. 106-48), Crassus (b.c. 115-53) and Julius Caesar (b.c. 100-44). The three latter formed the first "triumvirate." After the first two died Caesar ruled supreme in fact though not in name. He did so by assuming all of the important offices such as consul, tribune, censor, praetor, quaestor and aedile. In b.c. 44 he was assassinated in the Senate for overthrowing the republic by his former favorite Brutus (b.c. 85-42) and Cassius (b.c. ?-42). Soon thereafter was formed the second "triumvirate" composed of Octavian (b.c. 63-a.d. 14), the grand-nephew and adopted son of Julius Caesar, Marc Antony (b.c. 83-30), and Lepidus (b.c. ?-13). By b.c. 30 Octavian had defeated his two colleagues and maintained a virtual dictatorship.

Like his uncle, Julius Caesar, Octavian observed the outward

357

forms of a republic. However, the Senate gave him the titles of Augustus (majestic) and Princeps (first citizen), and as a victorious general he had the title of Imperator. By the time he died in 14 A.D. he was being worshiped as a divinity. He had organized the empire so that there was a much more effective control over the provinces than the Senate had been able to attain. He was succeeded by four Julio-Claudian emperors who were related to him by blood or marriage and who reigned from 14 to 68 A.D. They were Tiberius, Caligula, Claudius and Nero. Then came the three Flavians from 68 to 96 A.D., namely, Flavius Vespasian, who began his career as a common soldier and his sons Titus and Domitian. The latter reduced still more the power of the Senate. The six Antonines, Nerva, Trajan, Hadrian, Antoninus Pius, Marcus Aurelius, and Commodus ruled from 96 to 192 A.D. Under Trajan the empire reached its greatest extent.

During this period the Roman army numbered about 400,000. It had a good deal of influence upon the choice of emperors. Sometimes the Praetorian Guard stationed just outside of the walls of Rome and sometimes the legions on one or another of the frontiers of the empire exercised a decisive influence and a victorious general was placed on the imperial throne. Sometimes an emperor was able to secure the succession to the throne of a member of his family. In a few instances the Senate had some influence. During the third century, from 192 to 284 A.D., the army almost invariably chose the emperors. There were more than thirty emperors many of whom are now known as the "barrack" emperors and some of them as "phantom" emperors because they reigned for so short a time. Almost all of them were assassinated or died in battle. As might be expected, during this century there was much disorder in the empire and economic conditions became very bad. The disorder was due largely to the facts that the form of government was too primitive to rule so vast an empire and that the succession to the imperial throne was so uncertain.

In 284 A.D. a soldier Diocletian (A.D. 245-313) came to the throne. He introduced the system of two emperors, each being Imperator Caesar Augustus, one to rule in the west the other in the east. Each designated an heir known as Caesar. The empire was divided in four prefectures—East, Illyricum, Italy, Gaul—each being ruled by an emperor or an heir. The prefectures were divided into thirteen dioceses, and the dioceses into 119 provinces. This made a highly organized and more effective method of administration of the empire. It also made the succession to the throne more certain. The emperors assumed the title of Dominus (Lord) as well as Imperator. They were worshiped as divine beings and became the sole source of law. The Senate sank to the level of a municipal council for the city of Rome.

Constantine I (A.D. 272-337) became emperor soon after Diocletian and in 330 A.D. moved the capital to Byzantium where the predominant cultural influence was Greek. The eastern or Byzantine or Greek empire lasted until conquered by the Turks in 1453 A.D. The western empire began to disintegrate soon after the death of Theodosius I in 395 A.D. In 410 A.D. Alaric, the king of the Visigoths sacked Rome. Germanic kingdoms were set up in Italy, Gaul and Spain. The period of Teutonic domination of Europe had set in. In 476 A.D. Odoacer (434?-493), a German general in the Roman army, overthrew the western empire and ruled over all of Italy, thus completing the Teutonic conquest.

The immediate cause of the fall of the western Roman empire was the Teutonic invasion. The more profound causes were the economic conditions created within the empire. Earlier in this chapter has been mentioned the rise of capitalism in the Roman republic during and after the Punic wars which took place between 264 and 146 B.C. Wars usually accentuate the extremes of wealth and poverty. Manufacturers and merchants are able to sell their wares at high prices to governments at war which have urgent need of them. At the same time many poor people are being devastated by war. But in times of peace as well as of war the process of enrichment and of impoverishment goes on. We have seen that the *latifundia* or large landed estates had grown to such a degree that the small farmer had almost disappeared in Italy. The same process was taking place elsewhere in the republic and later in the empire. The expropriated peasants were becoming *coloni* or serfs of the landlords, bound to the land, or were swelling the number of unemployed laborers in the cities.

Rome had become the money center of the world. The moneyed class drew a large tribute for performing banking functions for the world's trade and industry. Like the finance capitalists of today they shared in the creation of trade monopolies which raised prices for the consumers. As in modern times, there was a close alliance between these moneyed interests and the government. Roman law dealt mainly with property and was almost entirely in the interest of the wealthy. The government was often in need of funds for its predatory wars as well as to carry on its peacetime administration. It secured these funds partly by looting conquered territories, partly by imposing heavy taxes, and partly from farms, orchards, forests, mines, and other state-owned properties. The taxes were usually farmed out to collectors who derived a lucrative income from squeezing all they could from the poor taxpayers. In its search for funds the government often debased the currency thereby pushing up the price level. The government made several attempts to control prices. To the extent that price inflation was due to currency debasement such price control was certain to fail. It can be successful only when price inflation is due to speculation and monopolistic restrictions which limit supply. As the power of the emperor became more absolute, his personal properties became more extensive.

An American historian of the Middle Ages has described these economic conditions in a chapter entitled "The Roman Empire in Prosperity and Decay." "The government was controlled by an oligarchy of rich capitalists, government contractors, army sutlers, and wealthy landowners. . . . By the fifth century, when the Germans began to invade the Empire . . . practically the whole Empire was owned by a powerful landed aristocracy. The free farmer and the free artisan had almost vanished away. . . . The emperor was by far the largest landed proprietor in the Roman Empire, and was possessed of estates in almost every province. In the case of Egypt the whole country was imperial property. . . . In every newly conquered region portions of territory were reserved for the crown; confiscation, forfeiture, and escheat increased the number. In its entirety the imperial domains were known as *res familiaris,* or the fisc. Certain kinds of properties by their very nature pertained to the fisc, such as mines, quarries, salt springs, immense tracts of forest. The imperial government kept its hand upon the important natural resources of the Empire."[5]

Thompson summarizes the economic reasons for the decline and fall of the Roman empire by citing "the increasing cost of administration, rise of prices, decline of purchasing power and corruption of the coinage, the escape of the rich from taxation by privilege or evasion which necessarily increased the burden on those who were not so successful, monopolies and unfair competition, consumption of capital and impossibility of saving, growing poverty of the masses, indolence of the proletariat, decline of production owing to the increasing discouragement and apathy of the producing classes, whether farmers, tradesmen, or artisans, decay of civic spirit, political turmoil like revolts of upstart emperors in the provinces, sometimes culminating in the secession of many provinces for years together, peasant rebellions, brigandage, expensive wars like those with Persia, almost all of which were disastrous. Antiquity had little perception of the nature or working of economic or social forces, though it cannot be boasted that modern governments have advanced far in these matters."[6]

These economic conditions in ancient Rome were not entirely different from economic conditions which prevail in modern times.

[5] James Westfall Thompson, *Economic and Social History of the Middle Ages (300-1300 A.D.)*, New York, 1928, pp. 33-37.

[6] *Op. cit.*, pp. 37-38.

Roman imperialism was a system of exploitation which was certain to yield decreasing returns in course of time. This happened when the supply of capital and of labor, which consisted largely of slave labor secured as prisoners of war, decreased as wars of conquest and the looting arising from them decreased or ceased. This was true by the time the empire attained its greatest extent during the second century A.D. The laborers, who were largely slaves or serfs, were allowed only a bare subsistence so that they lacked the incentive to increase their output which is possessed only by workers who are free at least to the extent that their remuneration bears some relation to the amount which they produce. Increasing purchasing power and a consequently expanding market occurred only rarely in ancient times, as indeed has also been true to much the same degree in modern times. As an historian of the ancient world has said: "It very seldom happened in the evolution of the Ancient World that the market for goods was expanding and its buying power steadily increasing. . . . When it did happen—in the Fifth and Fourth Centuries B.C. in Greece, in the early Hellenistic Period, in the early Roman empire—ancient technique and capitalistic organization made rapid progress. But this firmness and growth of the market never lasted long."[7]

Technological progress in the Roman empire as well as elsewhere in the ancient world was very slow partly because the ruling classes—priestly, monarchical and imperial, noble, military, and timocratic and plutocratic—despised labor. It was slow even more because the ruling classes depended in large part upon hypothetical supernatural forces for prosperity, and the subject classes in the even greater ignorance in which they were kept supinely accepted this attitude of their rulers. Many of the ancient philosophers regarded the phenomenal world as unreal. Some of them considered interference with nature as pernicious and thought that contact with matter is corrupting. They believed that knowledge is obtainable only through meditation or contact with an alleged spiritual reality. Consequently, they failed in the main to gather factual information by means of observation of nature and by experimentation. A few of them, such as Aristotle in the fourth century B.C., did some observing of nature, but of experimentation there was almost none. In so far as there was any technical progress, it was due to an accidental stumbling, so to speak, upon a new or different way of doing things, or to an entirely pragmatic solution of an urgent practical problem. It was not due to a search for principles or laws of nature or a demonstration of causal relations which could then be applied to the solution of practical problems. We shall discuss later the ideology of ancient thinking.

[7] M. I. Rostovtzeff, "The Hellenistic World and Its Economic Development," in the *American Historical Review*, Vol. 41, (1936), p. 252.

In modern times science has developed to the point of stimulating and guiding technology to a high degree, especially in the Occidental world. It has had little effect as yet upon other aspects of human culture in which supernaturalism and hobgoblinism still prevail. For example, at the present time of writing, in one of the principal centers of modern technology, the city of Chicago, a leading newspaper is publishing "The Greatest Story Ever Told," which purports to be the tale of the miraculous conception and life of Jesus Christ. In similar fashion political and economic organization still retain the weaknesses detected by historians in the ancient world. In another work I have described some of these weaknesses as follows:

"The capitalists withdraw from immediate circulation a part of the revenue from the sale of their commodities in the form of profits from their enterprises or of interest upon capital which they have loaned. If they expended all their incomes at once by purchasing commodities or paying for services, the situation would be somewhat relieved and the crisis might be averted. But the incomes of some capitalists are so great that they cannot readily spend all upon themselves. Most capitalists, small as well as large, save part of their incomes in order to increase their present capital and their future incomes, and also in order to assure economic security for themselves and their families.

"If the flow of new capital into the production and distribution of goods always equaled the amount saved, the situation might be slightly more stabilized. But the eagerness of the capitalists to make money while profits are large leads them to expand production with precipitate haste during the upward phase of the business cycle until the saturation point in relation to the purchasing power of the public is reached and passed. Then comes the even more precipitate shrinking of production with the disastrous consequences which have been described."[8]

Needless to say, there were important differences between business, profit making, capitalism, the business or trade cycle, and other phases of economic activity in the ancient world and in modern times, especially in the Occident. However, in their essential features they were similar. "An extensive maritime and merchandizing trade was controlled by a profit making system which in the Roman Empire had come to include both, as a money changing process, and an elaborate machinery for speculation and investment. With the collapse of the Roman Empire this business system was virtually wiped out in northern and western Europe, but in the area controlled by Constantinople a substantial trade tapping the Orient and the western

[8] Maurice Parmelee, *Farewell to Poverty*, New York, 1935, pp. 219-220.

362

Mediterranean continued to be organized and directed by profit-seekers. After the crusades the center of the business system gradually shifted to the Italian cities and later to Holland, where through steady advance in profit making machinery its modern expansion began."[9]

Though business cycles have been studied only very recently there are evidences of them in ancient times. The phases usually described were the most striking events in the cycle, namely, the crises manifested in trade. As an American student of cycles has said: "Trade crises must be as old as trade itself and must have affected the fortunes of increasing numbers as trading grew in social importance. The early crises of record were commonly attributed to what would now be classed as random causes, such as governmental aggressions, riots, wars or 'acts of God.' As economic activities became more highly organized, random factors continued to make business troubles; but new sources of difficulties appeared within business itself. For example, the outstanding feature of the Mississippi bubble and the South Sea scheme, which ran their parallel courses to disaster in 1720, was a mania for speculation. In the later crises of the eighteenth century commercial miscalculations were held responsible in increasing degree. By the close of the Napoleonic wars it was realized that 'commercial crises' are recurrent, and economists began to devise explanations which applied not merely to a particular case but to crises at large."[10]

There is ample reason to believe that Christianity was an important factor in the decline and fall of the Roman empire. This is clearly indicated in the following excerpts from Thompson:

"It is a mistake to think that the Early Church initiated any movement of a revolutionary social nature, or even of a thorough-going reforming nature. . . . It accepted slavery as a matter of course. . . . The Church never challenged the justice of the relation of master and servant. It did far less than is usually believed in regard to the contempt of the ancient world for labor. . . . It was Stoicism, not Christianity, which refined the Roman law in the third century and moderated some of its most inhumane features. . . . Stoicism was more universal in its aspect of humanity than early Christianity. . . . Stoicism was not intolerant; Christianity was . . . Stoicism never ridiculed; Christianity did . . . Stoicism taught love of all humanity; the love of the early Christians was for and among themselves only. . . .

"The Dark Ages were at least as much due to the corruption of the Church as to the decay of Roman civilization or the barbarian invasions. . . . The Church in the Roman Empire was a dissolving

[9] Encyclopedia of the Social Sciences, New York, 1937, Vol. 3, p. 81, article entitled "Business" by D. M. Keezer.

[10] Wesley C. Mitchell, "Business Cycles," in the Encyclopedia of the Social Sciences, New York, 1937, Vol. 3, p. 92.

and disintegrating influence of the first magnitude. . . . After Christianity became the established religion of the Roman Empire, whatever social and economic program of reform the Church may have cherished went by the board. Wealth and political power made it conservative. . . . There is not a word of protest against selling Christian slaves, to say nothing of pagan German and Slavonic captives in war, to Christians. . . . The monasteries were great slave owners. We find Church slaves in Spain, France, Germany, Italy, England, all through the Middle Ages. . . . Worst of all the Church created slavery where it had never existed under Roman law. It made conspiracy and treason punishable not only by the enslavement of the culprits, but also by condemnation of their descendants to perpetual slavery. . . . The right of asylum was sometimes denied to slaves. No slave could be a plaintiff in court. Even an emancipated slave was so incapacitated. . . . As for the treatment of slaves, the clergy were as brutal as lay masters."[11]

In another book I have described "the attributes of Christianity which have rendered it one of the most aggressive, intolerant, and domineering of religions, and which explain its long history of persecuting unbelievers, its religious wars, its Inquisition and its Crusades, and its extensive proselytizing activities, some of which have been carried on with the aid of the mailed fist. These attributes are its jealous and ambitious deity, its belief in a peculiarly Christian character which is superior to human nature in general and which is incarnated in the partially mythical figure of Jesus, its cut-and-dried formula for salvation than which there is no other way to be saved, and its grotesque and wholly unscientific conception of evil. Every religion grows out and is a part of a complex of economic, political, and social factors and conditions. The intrinsic character of Christianity has harmonized well with the commercial greed and the political imperialism of the Occident. . . . These belligerent attributes constitute the main body of historical Christianity and have had the most influence in the affairs of mankind."[12]

An historian of civilization has stated the distinctive Christian doctrines as follows: "There were, first, the distinctively Christian doctrines of a triune God and the Incarnation and, second, those doctrines derived from antecedent Judaism, including the belief in the fall of man through the sin of Adam, in a personal devil, in angels and archangels, in the resurrection of the body, in a last judgment, and in a heaven and a hell. The few went to heaven; the many —all non-Christians, all heretics, and all Christians who died in a state

11 J. W. Thompson, *op. cit.*, pages 60-86.
12 Maurice Parmelee, *Oriental and Occidental Culture, An Interpretation*, New York, 1928, pages 236-7.

of mortal sin—went to hell. The future life, so vague and shadowy in pagan thought, was real indeed to the medieval mind, and the hold of the church over its children lay very largely in the fact that it could promise them so much in the way of eternal bliss and threaten so much in the way of eternal ill." While this historian is much too indulgent to Christianity he admits that "the church did not carry its pacific policy so far as to condemn attacks upon heretics and infidels; such enemies of God deserved to be exterminated."[13] He is referring in particular to the Roman Catholic church in medieval and practically all of modern times. Most of what he says still applies to the Greek Catholic church and to the Evangelical churches as well. This includes the mysterious mathematical formula of three equalling one and one equalling three, the hobgoblinism which characterizes Christianity no less than other religions and more than some of them, and the Christian view of the future life as punishment for the wicked and "pie in the sky" for the pious.

The Greek Catholic or Orthodox church was closely associated with the Byzantine empire which became an Oriental despotism. The eastern empire survived the western empire by ten centuries because of its wealth and resources, its profitable commerce, its strong navy and army, and its easily defended capital. It was further removed from the European tribes which menaced Rome for centuries. The Persian empire made several attempts to recover its former territories without much success. It was the coming of the Arabs with their new religion of Islam in the seventh century which slowly undermined the Byzantine empire.

For many centuries Byzantium led the world in commerce partly due to its favorable location. In its business affairs it used bills of exchange, letters of credit, and contracts of partnership and insurance just as the Babylonian business men had used them two millennia earlier. The gold "bezant" was not debased until rather late in Byzantine history thus furnishing a stable basis for trade and industry. In course of time Venice and other Italian trading cities increased their commerce with the west as well as the east so greatly as to rival Byzantium successfully. The final blow came when the Ottoman Turks captured Byzantium or Constantinople in 1453 thus putting an end to the last surviving vestige of the middle age of imperialism a whole millennium after it had virtually terminated.

[13] Hutton Webster, *History of Civilization*, New York, 1947, pages 443 and 467.

Chapter XXIV

Science and Technology in the Ancient World

IN Chapter XV we have discussed the rise of animism and have noted that animistic ideas and beliefs are still widespread not only among the more or less illiterate masses of mankind, but also among the more educated groups. Even some of the modern scientists are permeated with these beliefs and the emotions which accompany them. For example, a well known contemporary scientist has said that "I cannot believe that God plays dice with the world," that "the sensation of the mystical is the sower of all true science," and that a "deeply emotional conviction of the presence of a superior reasoning power, which is revealed in the incomprehensible universe, forms my idea of God."[1] It is wholly unscientific to deduce from an "incomprehensible universe" an anthropomorphic deity which reasons and is amiably disposed toward mankind. Religious rationalizing is the inevitable result of the vain attempt to harmonize religion and science. Scientists are at times all too human in the expression of their emotions.

Animistic beliefs, as manifested in religion and magic, have constituted one of the principal factors to delay the development of science and of technology. As an historian of culture has said: "Perhaps no single factor has had a greater influence in the general development of civilization than the very early fixing of attention on the imagined daimonic universe, for by diverting attention from

[1] Albert Einstein (1879-1952), quoted by Lincoln Barnett, "The Universe and Dr. Einstein," *Harper's Magazine*, April, May and June 1948. Similar quotations from Einstein elsewhere in these articles also published in book form. (See also Leopold Infeld, *Albert Einstein, His Work and Its Influence on Our World.*)

The contemporary American physicists, the late R. A. Millikan (1868-1953) and A. H. Compton (1892-   ), have made similar statements. For example, the latter has said: "I think that not only did God condone our act in dropping the bombs, but that it was only with His help and inspiration that the job was done in time." ("God and the Atom," *American Magazine*, October 1950, p. 118.) All three are Nobel Prize scientists.

physical nature, emotion was given such free play that thought was mainly fantasy. Even when thinking became systematic in the mythologies and early philosophies it was still mainly fantasy."[2] This can be illustrated in all of the leading cultures of the present day. Mankind, even in minute part, has not yet faced the universe in which it is an infinitesimal speck in space and a fleeting moment in time, and in which it attempts vaingloriously to play an anthropocentric role.

In many of the earlier cultures learning was largely in the hands of the priestly class. The main intellectual interest of this class was and is to describe the universe in terms of the animistic beings and powers which are alleged to control it. This interest was not likely to lead to science except in so far as it resulted in a belief in some sort of order in the universe, though this order might be wholly inconsistent with observation of phenomena. This is well illustrated by astrology which observes a certain order in the movements of the heavenly bodies and assumes an orderly correlation between these movements and certain mundane human phenomena. However, science has revealed that the heavenly bodies do not move in the (Ptolemaic) manner assumed by the astrologers and that the correlation which is alleged does not exist.

For certain practical purposes it was essential to count. Hence the art of mensuration developed and later became an important tool in scientific research. People need to measure distances, number and quantities in weight or bulk of commodities, durations of time, and other tangible and intangible phenomena; and mensuration became more essential as culture evolved from its most primitive forms to its agricultural and village stages and then to its urban stage. In the cities the priestly and other ruling classes began to accumulate wealth. As trade developed the merchants had to keep records and accounts of their transactions.

In Sumeria the earliest accounts which have been found are of grain, sheep and beer. The Sumerians and the Babylonians developed measures of quantity, area, distance, and time which were more complete than other early systems. The smallest unit of linear measurement was called the finger which was about two-thirds of an inch. The foot was 20 fingers or between 12 and 13 inches. The cubit was the length of the forearm or between 18 and 20 inches.

The Babylonians devised a calendar in which the year was based on the movement of the sun and the month on the movement of the moon. The year was computed as 360 days. As the lunar months did not correspond with the solar year the priests inserted extra days into

[2] Ralph Turner, *The Great Cultural Traditions, The Foundations of Civilization*, New York, 1941, Vol. I, pp. 114-115.

the calendar from time to time. The Babylonian hebdomadal week resulted from connecting a day with each of the seven obviously movable celestial bodies, which were supposed to be gods, or at least to have gods controlling or associated with them. These were the sun, moon, Mercury, Venus, Mars, Jupiter, and Saturn. The hours and the minutes may have been derived from the Sumerian system of numbers, based on a unit of 60. The Babylonians invented the gnomon or sun dial.

The mathematics of the Mesopotamian countries arose from a numbering system in which the principal units were 1, 10 and 60. Thus 600 was 60 x10, 3,600 was 60^2, and 36,000 was 60^2x10, so that the system was both decimal and sexagesimal. With this system the Sumerians were able to add and substract. By the beginning of the second millennium b.c. the Babylonians were able to multiply large numbers and also to deal with fractional quantities. They made a beginning with geometry, though not always accurately. For example, they computed the circumference of a circle by multiplying the diameter by 3 instead of 3.1416 or π, which was calculated later. They also made a slight beginning with algebra, especially in their astronomical calculations. However, their rudimentary mathematics arose mainly from practical needs and were not theoretical or abstract. They did, however, render possible the concept of accuracy. They prepared the way for the time when mankind would begin to recognize that phenomena are not governed by animistic beings but are subject to natural laws and can not be influenced by religious practices and magical methods.

Mesopotamian medicine was dominated almost completely by animistic beliefs. Diseases were supposed to be caused by specific spirits. Their treatment was largely by exorcism by priests. Various concoctions were used which were supposed to drive forth these maleficent spirits. The prevention of disease was by means of spells and incantations.

The Sumerian and Babylonian priests made many observations of the heavens. But apparently they did not regard the celestial bodies as physical objects. The sun, moon, planets and stars were gods or manifestations of gods. Consequently, they did not develop a genuine science of astronomy, though they made progress in observing the regular movements of the heavenly bodies, and developing the pseudo-science of astrology in which this regularity was applied but erroneously interpreted. It was assumed that these movements in the heavens indicated the will of the gods which was the cause of all mundane phenomena. The priests divided the heavens into twelve regions now known as the signs of the zodiac. These included a belt around the zenith and extending to about 8° on each side of the ecliptic, includ-

368

ing all the visible planets. In each region was a constellation for which it was named. In the spring the sun was in the constellations Aries (ram), Taurus (bull), Gemini (twins); in summer in Cancer (crab), Leo (lion), Virgo (virgin); in autumn in Libra (balance), Scorpio (scorpion), Sagittarius (archer); and in winter in Capricornus (he goat), Aquarius (water-carrier), Pisces (fishes). However, owing to the precession of the equinoxes during the four to five millennia which have passed since the Sumerian or Babylonian priests observed the heavens, the sun is no longer in the constellation designated for that sign but in the following constellation. Thus in the first zodiacal sign of spring, namely, Aries, the sun is no longer in Aries but in Taurus. The planets also have changed their position relative to the earth. However, these changes have not discouraged the belief in astrology. Probably the majority of mankind still retains this belief. It is widespread in India and elsewhere in the Orient,[3] and even in the Occident there are many believers. For example, all four of the newspapers in Chicago with large circulations publish horoscopes and astrological advice daily. One of them characterizes the month under the zodiacal sign Aries as follows: "Stars vary; A.M. less stimulating than P.M Romance, family affairs on 'touchy' side." Astrology in ancient times was often used to foretell public events as illustrated by the following astrological forecasts: "If the west wind is blowing when the new moon is first seen, there is likely to be an unusual amount of illness during that month." "If Venus approaches the constellation of Cancer there will be respect for law and property in the land; those who are ill will recover, and pregnant women will have easy confinements." Astrology and other forms of divination were and still are based on the assumption that there are animistic forces in the universe which control the life of mankind in general and of individual human beings in particular. In modern times astrology has been used more often to divine the future of individuals and not so often to foretell public events.

The Sumerian and Babylonian priests also practised liver divination or hepatoscopy usually with a sheep's liver. It has been traced as far back as the reign of Sargon of Akkad who is reputed to have reigned from about 2341 to 2285 B.C. Hepatoscopy was apparently based on the beliefs that the liver is the seat of life because it is filled

[3] See my book entitled *Oriental and Occidental Culture*, New York, 1928, p. 77.

The precession of the equinoxes is a slow motion of the equinoctial points on the ecliptic (the plane passing through the center of the sun which contains the orbit of the earth) from east to west, causing the time between the successive equinoxes to be appreciably shorter, caused by the attraction of the sun and moon upon the equatorial protuberance of the earth. One period of precession takes 25.868 years.

with blood, and that the liver of the sacrificial animal assumed the same character as the soul of the god to which the sacrifice was made. Hence if one understood the signs on the liver one could enter into the soul or mind of the god and thus ascertain what he proposed to do. This was done by a Babylonian priest known as a *baru* who was skilled in reading these signs. However much hepatoscopy may have failed to foretell the future, it probably contributed to the study of animal including human anatomy, though not as much as hunting, butchering, torture, and surgery. Other forms of divination were also used by the Mesopotamians, among them being oneiromancy or divination through dreams.

Egyptian mensuration was similar to that of Mesopotamia. Their methods of measuring time, as in their calendar, distance, area, and weight, were not unlike the Mesopotamian methods. Their mathematics were even less developed than the Sumerian and the Babylonian mathematics. Their numbering system was based on 10. They could multiply only by adding and could divide only by subtracting. Their geometry was rudimentary. Their mathematics arose entirely as a means of solving practical problems in agriculture, industry and commerce. They were not concerned with logical methods, general principles or abstract problems. On the whole the Egyptian science of mathematics was somewhat inferior to the Mesopotamian.

The Egyptian priests observed the heavens as did their Sumerian and Babylonian fellows. Their observations also did not result in a science. They regarded the celestial bodies as gods. The sun was said to cross the sky in a boat and then to travel over an ocean under the earth to come up in the east at dawn. The positions of the heavenly bodies were supposed to indicate the relations between the gods but not between human beings. Perhaps partly for this reason astrology as a method of divination did not develop to the same degree in Egypt. In Egypt also astrological speculation, dream interpretation, and omenology were widespread, especially after 1200 B.C.

In medicine the Egyptians were a little in advance of the Mesopotamians. They had three types of medical practitioners—the physician, the surgeon, and the exorcist or magician. Various methods of treatment were used such as exorcism, incantations, sleep in a sacred place such as a temple where the patient was exposed to the influence of the spirits which inhabited it, manipulation, and certain substances used as drugs. Among the latter were turpentine, rancid fat, vinegar, swine's teeth, flyspecks, date blossoms, and lizard's blood. Their drugs displayed no knowledge of chemistry. Their surgeons were able to perform only simple operations. The nearest approach of Egyptian medicine to science was an appreciation of the importance of a knowledge of the heart, as is indicated in the Ebers Papyrus,

370

the principal source of information about Egyptian medicine. However, the extent to which this ancient system of medicine was dominated by animistic and magical ideas is indicated in this compendium of Egyptian medicine where it says that the physician "imbued his own excrement and urine, the very pen he wielded, the ink he used, and the papyrus he wrote upon with Healing Magic." [4]

In neither Mesopotamia nor Egypt was there the slightest beginning of a social science. In both regions it was universally believed that the world is governed by animistic beings, so that the only order which could exist was divinely ordained by them. The most that mankind could do was to try to ascertain this order and to abide by it. Inasmuch as divinity was often if not usually attributed to the mundane rulers, the order which prevailed was to a large extent the one promulgated by those rulers. This order required as the moral attributes of individuals such traits as submission to superiors in a class society, respect for property, peaceableness, nonviolence against superiors, and the like. In other words, it was assumed that class status must be accepted, that labor is inferior, and that poverty is the common lot of the vast majority of mankind. Since these were conceived as necessary aspects of the divine moral order, it was inconceivable that they could be changed. These were traits to be expected in a predatory class society based upon exploitation and violence, and have by no means disappeared in the world of today. The next four chapters describe the origin and development of social status and class which stratify human beings, not in accordance with individual traits, but usually according to wealth acquired by hook or by crook, whether by inheritance, theft, warfare, commercial chicanery, business enterprise, political corruption and trickery, or actually produced by the individual by mental effort or muscular labor. To say the least, a large part of the wealth of the world has not been acquired, owned and enjoyed by those who actually produced it.

The moral ideas of a stratified society are presented in more or less secularized form in the code of Hammurabi who reigned in Babylon probably from 1728 to 1686 B.C. This code was apparently based on earlier Sumerian codes. The earlier priestly judges were replaced by magistrates who were appointed from the owners of land by royal grant, who owed military service to their monarch. The Sumerian and Babylonians were apparently the first to define and regulate by law the right of private property. Two types of property in land were recognized, namely, royal grants as payment for military service, and land acquired by purchase, lease, mortgage, or inheritance. The code also regulated wages and fees with respect to workmen, tenants, and professional men.

[4] Cyril P. Bryan, *The Papyrus Ebers*, London, 1930, pp. 37-38.

371

Other important topics covered by the code of Hammurabi were domestic relations, slavery, and crime. In the family the husband and father had dominant rights. Both the obligations and the rights of slaves were defined. The treatment of crime was based upon the *lex talionis*. Class distinctions were recognized in the penal treatment accorded to slaves, freemen, priests, and nobles and princes. Slaves were punished severely, but crimes against them only lightly. A crime against a priest or prince was much more severely punished than an offense against a freeman.[5]

Early in the third millennium B.C. several large cities were flourishing in the valley of the Indus River, among them being those at the sites now known as Mohenjo-daro, Chandhu-daro, and Harappa. These cities became entirely extinct, possibly owing to floods. They were apparently in contact with Sumerian culture as indicated by metallic and ceramic remains found in both countries. No literary or other remains indicate any rudimentary science in this early Indian culture. Certain seals and figurines suggest their gods. Cubical stones may have been used as weights, indicating a system of measurement. While the remains of no temples or palaces have been found, this does not mean that they did not have priests and rulers. This culture was more or less on a level with the Mesopotamian. While these cities disappeared completely and their ruins have been discovered only within the past half century, it is possible that some elements of this culture became merged with the later Hindu culture.[6]

In the case of the Indus Valley culture and several others of that age, little or nothing is known of their scientific knowledge and attainments, because their languages and scripts, if any, have not been deciphered. This is true of the Egean culture which originated in Crete. During the two centuries from 2000 to 1800 B.C. and again between 1600 and 1400 B.C. the Minoan culture in Crete reached a relatively high point. The material remains seem to indicate that it derived many of its traits from Egypt, and very few from Mesopotamia. Records on clay tablets indicate that they had a decimal system of numeration similar to that of Egypt. Digits were represented by upright lines, tens by horizontal lines, hundreds by circles, and thousands by spurs. Their religion was apparently less oppressive than the Egyptian, at least it did not dominate art to the same degree as in Egypt and Babylonia.[7]

[5] See Pierre Cruveilhier, *Introduction au code d'Hammurabi*, 1937.

[6] See Ernest Mackay, *The Indus Valley Civilization*, 1937; and Sir John H. Marshall, *Mohenjo-Daro and the Indus Civilization*, 1931. See also my *Oriental and Occidental Culture*, New York, 1928, pp. 25 and 28.

[7] See Gustave Glotz, *The Aegean Civilization*, 1925; J. D. S. Pendlebury, *The Archaeology of Crete: An Introduction*, 1939.

Little also is known of the scientific ideas of certain peoples which established states in Anatolia and vicinity. The Hurrite empire from perhaps as early as 1800 to 1400 B.C. was established by a people which probably came from the Caucasus but spoke a non-Indo-European language. For a time they were ruled by a small group of Indo-Europeans known as the Mitanni. Usually political power was in the hands of the Hurrite nobles, who fought on horseback. The Hittites, whose language was proto-Indo-European, maintained an empire in Anatolia from 1400 to 1200 B.C. They organized a military feudalism based upon the horsedrawn chariot and bronze weapons. Their priests shared the rule with the nobles. Both the Hurrites and the Hittites were ruling over a native peasant-village population. Their agriculture and industry were organized more or less as in Mesopotamia.[8]

Much of the cuneiform and hieroglyphic writings of these peoples has not yet been deciphered. In 1947 at Karatepe in Cilicia were discovered bilingual inscriptions in hieroglyphic Hittite and Phenician which are aiding this work of decipherment. A specialist in the languages of this region and period has summarized its history tentatively as follows:

"As can be seen from the foregoing, we know little about the extent of early Hurrian migrations between 1700 and 1500 B.C. We may try to reconstruct the story in the following way. Around 1700 B.C., after the reigns of Samsi-Adad I in Assyria, Hammurabi in Babylonia, and the 12th dynasty in Egypt, a great migration of Hurrians started from an area somewhere between Lake Van and the Zagros Mountains. The Hurrians invaded Mesopotamia and Assyria, and through Syria and Palestine some of them reached Egypt as a part of the Hyksos invasion. They seem also to have caused disturbances on the flanks of their north-south route. On the one side they may have been influential in pushing the Kassites into Babylonia from their homes in the Zagros Mountains. On the other side Hurrian pressure toward Anatolia is attested in Hittite sources. In time various Hurrian tribes formed themselves into an organized state with its center in Mesopotamia. The later traces of Hurrians in Babylonia, Assyria, Anatolia, Egypt, Syria, and Palestine are witnesses to a greater expansion in the past, when Hurrians occupied or held sway over large portions of the Near East."[9]

In other countries deciphered writings furnish a much more de-

8 See Albrecht Goetze, *Hethiter, Churriter, und Assyrer*, Oslo, 1936; E. A. Speiser, *Ethnic Movements in the Near East in the Second Millenium* B.C., 1933; *Mesopotamian Origins: The Basic Population of the Near East*, Philadelphia, 1930.

9 I. J. Gelb, *Hurrians and Subarians*, Oriental Institute of the University of Chicago, 1944, page 70.

tailed record of the cultures of the past. Cuneiform writing on clay persisted in Mesopotamia, somewhat simplified, at least as late as the second half of the second millennium B.C. At the same time the hieratic script was being used in Egypt. The invention of the alphabet increased greatly the utility of writing. The date of this invention has been pushed back repeatedly, and may be again to a still earlier date. From a few brief inscriptions it has been ascertained that inhabitants of Sinai who were working for Egyptians in copper mines adapted some Egyptian hieratic symbols to express certain sounds in writing of their Semitic language. By adding new signs they had about thirty phonograms, of which eighteen are found in later alphabets derived from the Sinaitic one. The original alphabet was about the 19th or 18th century B.C., and within two or three centuries the Phenician and Aramaic scripts were derived from it. From these two alphabets were developed in course of time the Greek, Roman, Brahmi, Arabic, and nearly all other alphabets from Manchu in the East to Icelandic runes in the West.[10]

Writing probably was invented to meet the practical need of keeping accounts. As wealth accumulated and property rights and obligations became established, it was necessary to maintain a record of the properties and dues involved. In other words, writing was at the outset an instrument of administration or business, not of learning. Next it was used to transcribe and record codes, sacred books, and other literature, such as myths, incantations, and the like, which were at that time conceived to be learning, and important to the priestly class. In this fashion it served to conserve ancient tradition, rather than to record new knowledge. Much later, when religion, the priesthood, despotism, and the exploitative and predatory activities of a ruling class, were no longer able to suppress all freedom of thought, writing became a powerful and essential tool in the hands of scientists, because it enabled them both to make a permanent record of the results of their research, and to communicate it to their fellow scientists, contemporary and future, thereby informing and stimulating them.

Iron in its very rare natural nickel alloy from meteorites was known in earlier historic and probably also in prehistoric time; but this form was too scarce to be important. Until about the middle of the second millennium B.C., iron was generally regarded as a sacred or precious metal, because of its scarcity. Its smelting from ore was apparently invented about 1400 B.C. in Anatolia or Armenia, imitating

[10] See Martin Sprengling, *The Alphabet: Its rise and development from Sinai inscriptions, Oriental Institute*, University of Chicago, 1931; and David Dillinger, *The Alphabet*, 1948.

the process used earlier for fusing copper and perhaps for making bronze from mixed ores of copper and tin. Iron requires higher temperatures. Until iron ore could be reduced by heat and the iron separated from the slag, it could not became plentiful and widely used in the industrial arts and in making armor and weapons. The iron age began in Mesopotamia about 1200 B.C., but Egypt did not smelt the metal until four centuries later.[11] Though the rise of metals was indispensable for science, we can hardly call metallurgy or other ancient inventions science. Their discovery was accidental, or simply worked out by ingenious and inventive persons who when confronted with practical problems devised ways or better ways for dealing with them.

During the fifth and fourth centuries B.C. there arose in Greece a small amount of more or less free thinking about the nature of the universe and of man. This culminated in Aristotle (384-322 B.C.) who attempted to gather and classify all the known facts about man and his environment. While many of his alleged facts were errors, nevertheless the inductive method which he used might conceivably have led to an efflorescence of science, which did not actually take place until two millennia later.

Alexander's conquests in Asia and Africa carried Hellenic culture into those regions, to be mingled with the indigenous civilizations. Some of the results or accompaniments of this mingling were new means of transportation, an extension of long distance trade, a world market extending from western Europe and western Africa to India and central Asia, and from the Danube to Somaliland, a spread of the money economy which had commenced in Lydia about 600 B.C., and an increase in the number of cities. By the end of the Hellenistic age commercial relations extended as far east as China.

The blended Hellenistic and Oriental culture came eventually under the domination of Rome. "The Hellenistic Age is usually reckoned as about three hundred years in length, reaching from the death of Alexander in 323 B.C. to the Roman conquest of Egypt in 30 B.C. During this period the Graeco-Oriental world of city-states, federations, and kingdoms about the eastern Mediterranean came into contact with the great power—Rome—which had arisen in the western Mediterranean, and the contact led to their annexation and incorporation into the Roman Empire. Politically, the Hellenistic Age then comes to an end; culturally, it does not. The spirit of Hellenism

---

[11] "Just when a generally applicable technique of iron-smelting was discovered is not clear. . . . But it is from about 1100 B.C. that iron tools and weapons began to be used widely in Palestine, Syria, Asia Minor and Greece, spreading thence to other countries." (S. Lilley, *Men, Machines, and History*, London, 1948, p. 21.)

lived on and for many centuries continued to permeate much of the ancient world."[12] Many elements of it survive in European and American culture, especially in geometry, art, and literature.

Among the primitive elements which have been identified in early Greek culture were a general belief in animism, which has existed among all primitive folk as well as cultural peoples down to the present day, and in particular a belief in daimons or guardian spirits which accompanied individuals. Along with these beliefs were the practise of omenology and prophetic utterances by priests and sorceresses or sibyls. However, the priests did not acquire much power in Greece. Consequently, a few individuals could more readily acquire a secular outlook than was the case among peoples where the priesthood was dominant. Furthermore, there were no sacred books claiming supernatural origin and authority to enchain the minds of men, such as the Egyptian Book of the Dead, the Chinese Tao-teh-king, the Zoroastrian Zend-Avesta, the Hindu Vedas, the Jewish Old Testament, the Christian New Testament, and the Moslem Koran. The Homeric poems constituted the epic and not the bible of the Greeks. Philosophy became partially divorced from religion. Socrates was executed, not because he was irreligious (he believed in his personal daimon), but because he taught religious doctrines which were contrary to the prevalent beliefs. His method of teaching was too prone to arouse scepticism. He was accused of corrupting the minds of the youth.

Greek intellectual achievements originated in part in Ionia. The influence of the Egean environment left its mark on many phases of Hellenic culture. The mingling of land and sea, the sea-faring life, the trade which it rendered possible, all were stimulating factors in Greek life. The sea-borne commerce from country to country discouraged provincialism and probably encouraged individualism in the Greek character. The Greeks borrowed the north Semitic alphabet. The first Greek inscriptions are from about 750 B.C. Greek freedom was based on citizenship in the *polis*, not on a bill of rights or on theories of the equality of all humans, as in some parts of the modern world. The execution of Socrates symbolizes the failure to recognize the liberty of the individual as such, and not as a member of a certain order or as having a certain status. Slaves and *metics* (foreigners) did not possess this liberty.

The great literary and intellectual period in Greece came in the 5th and 4th centuries B.C. Prose writing became an instrument of intellectual discourse. In the 5th century Herodotus described the Persian war and Thucydides the Peloponnesian war. Socrates ques-

[12] Hutton Webster, *History of Civilization*, Boston, 1947, page 232.

376

tioned many things which had usually been assumed. Greek philosophy began to ask such questions as what exists, what causes change, etc. The concept of the natural as distinguished from the supernatural began to be recognized. More than two millennia would have to pass before scientists would discern that there is no supernatural but that all phenomena are natural.

The Greek philosophers began to try to explain the universe in terms other than supernaturalism. Instead of assuming, as does the Hebrew-Christian Bible, a primeval chaos from which the chief god fashioned the world which mankind perceives, they conjectured that the universe consists of an original indestructible element which has existed always and is always changing. Thales (B.C. 640-546) of Miletus, a seaport in western Asia Minor, thought that this element was water. Other philosophers thought that it was air or fire or earth. However mistaken they were, they had at least conceived of an orderly universe governed by natural law. Heraclitus (ca. 500 B.C.) of Ephesus, near Miletus in Ionia, thought that everything is changing all the time—, "παντα ρει" "everything flows," as he expressed it. Democritus (ca. 400-357 B.C.) of Abdera in Thrace surmised that matter consists of indestructible particles, thus anticipating the modern atomic theory. We cannot fully explain why these cosmological theories appeared during this period and in this region. Such theories inevitably gave rise to a skeptical attitude toward the prevalent religious beliefs. However, very few held these heterodox ideas. Then as now the vast majority were dominated by the customary animistic beliefs. This original Greek thinking was to have more significance for the future than it had at that time.

The sophists or teachers of wisdom during the 5th century and later, leaving aside the often contradictory speculations of the cosmologists, concerned themselves with knowledge pertaining to mankind, such as logic, epistemology or the study of the nature and limitations of human knowledge, a natural and secular ethics not based on religion, and displayed something of a social point of view. They assisted in freeing the Greek mind in a measure from its bondage to religion and the past. The most famous of these teachers was Socrates (469-399 B.C.) who differed somewhat from the sophists because he was inclined to believe in a universal moral order, and because he emphasized individual virtue rather than social well-being. However, his insistence that man should know himself contributed toward intellectual freedom. Socrates' most famous pupil, Plato (428-348 B.C.), represented a retrogression from the sophist conception of relative human knowledge in that he believed in a theistic perfect god, in universal forms or noumena as opposed to phenomena, in absolute truth, and attempted to describe an ideal state dominated by a small ruling class.

377

Epicurus (341-270 B.C.) taught at Athens that pleasure is the *summum bonum* and pain the *summum malum*. His was an exceptionally humanitarian doctrine far in advance of his time. While he recognized the existence of gods, he denied that they had anything to do with mankind. Consequently, he opposed fear of gods and also fear of death which he said is fear of the after-life. He believed that the human body disintegrates into atoms similar to those conjectured by Democritus. Epicureanism was so contrary to traditional religion that it never attracted a large following. But it constituted a landmark in the progress of human thought.

Zeno (336-264 B.C.), a Hellenized Phenician from Cyprus, taught at Athens and founded the Stoic school. He believed in a supreme deity whom he regarded as rational, but he recognized other gods as well. He accepted the state, private property and slavery as institutions belonging to the natural order of society, though he also conceived of an ideal republic. His central thought was that human conduct should be guided by reason, which is presumably an offshoot of the divine reason. There was a suggestion in his teachings that the deity is the father of mankind so that all men are brothers. This was a new idea in the ancient world. Later Stoicism had much influence upon the upper classes in the Roman Empire, and through the apostle Paul it had some influence upon Christianity.

As we have already seen earlier in this chapter, for more than two millennia Sumeria, Babylonia and Egypt had been making a few contributions to scientific knowledge. We know little or nothing about similar contributions in China and India. The Greeks made considerable advances in several fields of science. In fact, they went almost as far as was possible without such instruments as the microscope, telescope, thermometer, barometer, mechanical timepiece, and delicate balance. They had no adequate system of quantitative measurement, except of length, volume, weight, and angle. Lacking these facilities they speculated a great deal but added little to the factual description of the universe. They thought about nature but did not really investigate it. They had institutes for instruction and for aiding scientists where there were collections gathered from nature. But they made little practical application of such information as they acquired. This probably explains in part why they did not invent the tools of research which did not come into existence until nearly two milleninia later. It was because science and technology were not acting and reacting upon each other that science came to a standstill and technology did not advance. As we shall see presently, this was due primarily to certain of the social and economic institutions of the Greeks which also characterized most of the ancient cultures.

378

Before attempting to explain later in this chapter the impasse reached by the Greeks let us review briefly their scientific accomplishments.

In mathematics the Greeks were hampered by the lack of a convenient system of numerals. They wrote numbers with the letters of the alphabet which was even more clumsy than the Roman system of notation. Neither had the sign for zero. The so-called Arabic numerals apparently were invented in India and were introduced into Europe by the Arabs in the early middle ages. The zero sign and decimals may have been invented in Babylonia and imported into India before being brought to Europe by the Arabs. Owing to the lack of these convenient devices the Greeks did not accomplish much in arithmetic, though they had the abacus, still used in the Orient and Russia, to aid in computing numbers by a decimal system. In plane and solid geometry, however, they accomplished a great deal. About 300 B.C. Euclid of Alexandria wrote his book on plane geometry which is still used. They also invented trigonometry, the geometry of conic sections and made a beginning with algebra. Later the Arabs developed algebra to a high degree, and plane and spherical trigonometry.

In astronomy the Greeks made some advance beyond the Babylonians and Egyptians, who had been interested in observing the heavenly bodies mainly in order to construct a calendar and to practise omenology and prophecy in the form of astrology. The Orientals had devised a lunar calendar and knew the five visible planets, namely, Mercury, Venus, Mars, Jupiter, and Saturn. With the sun and moon these planets formed the seven mobile heavenly bodies as distinguished from the apparently immobile fixed stars. The Greeks were less interested in astrology and more in describing and explaining the universe as they conceived it. Practically all of the ancient astronomers assumed a geocentric universe, namely, a universe which revolved every day around the earth as its center. This Ptolemaic geocentric universe was generally accepted until the Copernican system was expounded in the sixteenth century A.D. The only known exception was Aristarchus of Samos in the third century B.C. who believed that the earth rotates every day and goes around the sun every year, and he was accused of impiety because of his heterodox views.

The principal representative of early Greek science was Aristotle (ca. 384-322 B.C.), a pioneer scientific investigator. He assumed that there are individual and universal essences, that the universe is composed of four elements, namely, earth, air, fire and water, and that there are four qualities, namely, coldness and hotness, dryness and wetness. He sought for the causes of natural phenomena, nature's

379

p.rpose and laws, and thought he discerned evidences of design. He distinguished inorganic from organic matter. He discovered that the female sex contributes to the origin and development of the offspring in generation. He collected and described many specimens. He made many biological errors, but also some genuine scientific discoveries. He developed formal logic in the form of the syllogism. But his major premise was based on intuition. Hence tradition approved by social sanctions and his teleological point of view aided religion as much as science. He sublimated ethics in religion. He asserted that a middle class government is the best and a working class government the worst. He inveighed against revolution and upheld the right of private property. He considered agriculture the only sound basis for the social economy. He condemned usury or interest for the use of money or capital. He favored the unequal distribution of wealth, and the enslavement of human beings without rational "souls." "Aristotle's *Politics* is partly a polemic against Plato's *Republic*. It sets out to prove that private property is natural, because it is more in harmony with human nature than communism; that slavery is not contrary to nature, as the natures of men are unequal, and therefore that the doctrines of communal possession, of freedom and equality, cannot appeal to the law of nature on their behalf."[13] For these reasons a large part of Aristotelianism was incorporated in medieval Christian theology.

Generally speaking, it may be said of Greek science that their mathematics originated in commercial calculations as among all peoples, but it developed into a science of abstract concepts which was very useful two millennia later when it began to be applied to technology. Their astronomy was of a spherical universe rotating around a stationary earth. They did a little descriptive work in geology and geography. In biology they speculated as to the evolution of organisms due to chance and not purpose, but did not by any means divorce themselves from the teleological point of view exemplified by Aristotle. In zoology they dissected a few animals which gave them a slight knowledge of anatomy. In physiology they devoted a little study to the functions of the sense organs. Their medicine was almost as inexact and as ineffective as that of most ancient peoples. They believed that many diseases were caused by the humors, namely, the blood, the black and yellow bile, and the phlegm. As therapeutic measures they used bloodletting, sweating and purging. The two latter may have been useful at times. They had some knowledge of the value of dieting and of the healing power of certain natural forces, such as sunlight.

[13] Max Beer, *Social Struggles in the Middle Ages*, Boston, 1924, translated from the German, p. 117.

380

The Hellenic culture was a product of urban communities ruled by a relatively few free citizens, often headed by an oligarchy or a "tyrant." An aristocratic character was indicated by the dominant social attitudes which were the principal sources of the ethical theories of the Greek philosophers. Politics and war were the main occupations of the upper class just as in every other nation until modern times, with agriculture the most respectable normal occupation. The ruling citizens subsisted mainly from the labor of others, many of whom were slaves. In fact slavery was inevitable in a society of this character. Because labor was associated almost exclusively with the socially inferior classes it was regarded as degrading. Perhaps partly for this reason the Greeks had little taste for technology. Poverty and illiteracy as well as slavery were not regarded as abuses which should be extirpated. On the contrary, they were looked upon as the natural order of things. Furthermore, the Greeks had a very masculine outlook upon life, so that women played little or no part in their intellectual, political and public life. The Greeks were pious in their attitude toward their gods, but not priest-ridden. They were patriotic in their attitude toward their own city states. Their upper class probably had more interest in intellectual subjects than any people up to that time.

The Greeks also had a concept of beauty as an absolute form. Beauty is now considered relative to the observer, due entirely to the pleasurable sensations received by those who perceive it, and no more absolute than the pragmatic concept of good or evil, right or wrong. The Greeks of certain cities created with unusual frequency works of art still regarded as beautiful by mankind. As I have said in another book: "Our concept of beauty arises out of sensations which are pleasing to us for various reasons. A symmetrical design is apprehended by the eye and visual nerve centers with little effort. It is, therefore, reposeful, and conveys the impression of harmony. Certain rhythms in sound give a pleasing stimulus to the auditory nerve centers. Many nerve stimuli are regarded as beautiful because they arouse instincts and their correlated emotions which are pleasant. . . . The sight and touch of the loved one are beautiful, because they arouse pleasing sexual instincts and emotions. . . . The concept of beauty has grown out of these and other simple factors which are combined in endless complicated ways, so that it is often difficult to explain how and why beauty is apprehended in a given case. But enough has been said to indicate that beauty is purely subjective, and its perception is related to and determined by the inborn and acquired traits and the experience of the individual."[14]

[14] Maurice Parmelee, *The New Gymnosophy, The Philosophy of Nudity as Applied in Modern Life,* New York, 1927, pp. 145-146.

The Greeks did in a sense discover man. But they did not discover mankind. Slaves, serfs, peasants, manual workers were hardly human to the thoughtful and educated Greek, as indeed has been the case among practically all peoples down to the present day. Even among those professing the highest culture there has been little compunction about slaughtering millions of men in warfare. During the twentieth century many more millions of human beings have been butchered for racial, economic, political and occasionally religious reasons. There is as yet little sentiment for *Homo sapiens* as a single species of the Primate order. It is, therefore, not surprising that the world is not much closer to democracy than were the Greeks two millennia ago. As an historian of civilization has said: "Greek democracy never faced, let alone solved, the main problem of modern democratic politics, namely, the organizing of the continuous production and distribution of wealth so that citizens shall not only participate in making the significant decisions which affect their lives but also share in the social services and the opportunities for cultural activities which such production and distribution make possible."[15]

The Greeks probably were the first self-conscious thinkers. They raised certain intellectual problems and issues some of which had not been formulated before. They thereby helped to release mankind from the pattern of primitive thinking. They took mankind one step away from the daimonic universe of fantasy in which it had always lived and in which it still lives in the main.

Hellenism penetrated Rome through the Greek cities in southern Italy and Sicily. Insofar as art, literature, philosophy, and, to a certain extent, religion were concerned, Roman culture came to be permeated by Hellenism. This was true all the more as all of the Greek regions became gradually absorbed into the Roman empire. As the Roman poet Horace (B.C. 65-8) said: "Captive Greece captured her conqueror rude." Thus Hellenism may be said to have dominated Rome culturally, though not politically, for about six centuries from B.C. 300 to 300 A.D., when Christianity became dominant under Constantine. The Greek influence disappeared to a large extent from the West during the early and dark Christian centuries, and was brought back to Europe by the Arabs. At Byzantium it was partly preserved largely because the Greek language was the vernacular of the eastern empire, and facilitated reading the ancient Greek texts.

During the Hellenistic period the mystery religions of the near east and of Europe came into contact with each other and became blended. In Egypt the worship of Isis the nature goddess, and of her brother and consort Osiris, celebrated the renewal of life every year.

[15] Ralph Turner, *The Great Cultural Traditions, The Foundations of Civilization*, New York, 1941, Vol. I, p. 465.

In Phrygia the worship of Cybele, or Magna Mater (the great mother) as the Romans called her, and Attis her consort performed the same function of commemorating fertility. The myth of the annual death and resurrection of Osiris and of Attis offered many centuries before the similar Christian myth a promise of eternal life after death, which appealed to the devotees of these mystery religions. In Persia Zoroastrianism taught that there is a god of light and goodness, Ahura Mazda (Lord Wisdom), and a god of darkness and evil, Ahriman. The conflict between these divine personifications of good and evil was also embodied in Judaism and carried into neo-Judaism or Christianity, explaining the dualistic character of Christian ethics. From Zoroastrianism there arose another mystery religion, Mithraism. Mithra was an old Indo-Iranian deity who was also a god of light though subordinate to Ahura Mazda. Some of the Mithraic ceremonies were similar to later Christian ceremonies, such as the communal meal of bread, water, and consecrated wine, holy water ablutions as in baptism, anointing, progressive degrees of membership, and litanies to the sun. Indeed, some of the references to the Hebrew-Christian deity in the Bible suggest that he was conceived as a sun god. For example, in Psalms CIV the Lord God is apostrophized as follows: "Who coverest thyself with light as with a garment: who stretchest out the heavens like a curtain: Who layeth the beams of his chambers in the waters: who maketh the clouds his Chariot: who walketh upon the wings of the wind:" (2-3).

In ancient Greece also there were mystery religions. In Eleusis, an Attic town twelve miles from Athens, was celebrated in the autumn the worship of Demeter, a goddess of vegetation, and her daughter Persephone. It was one of the many commemorations of the death and seasonal revival of vegetation the world over before a scientific explanation of this cyclic phenomenon existed and was widely accepted. This rite also seemed to encourage a belief in human resurrection after death. The Orphic mysteries celebrated in various parts of Greece consisted mainly of the worship of Dionysus, a god of vegetation, who represented the reproductive power of nature. This rite also encouraged the hope of human redemption. In the ecstasies of these rites the Greeks seemed to feel that they had acquired a personal acquaintance with divinity and an intuitive knowledge of reality. The deity was believed to be the universal reason, and a moral universe was the universal good. Nature was regarded as a cosmos and the distinction between nature and a super-nature persisted. As has already been indicated, these beliefs stood in the way of a free and unrestricted efflorescence of science and of a concomitant development of technology. There were a few sceptics. Epicurus (B.C. 341-270) of Samos has already been mentioned. Lucretius (B.C. 95-55) the Roman author of "De rerum natura" denounced religion as superstition. Lucian (*ca.* 120-200 A.D.), the Greek sophist, in his "Dialogues of the Gods" satirized faith in deities who were only magnified human beings. Thus they anticipated the modern concept of gods as imaginary anthropomorphic beings. But it required nearly two millennia for this concept to attain any degree of currency. In the meantime the mystery religions, especially the Greek, had played some part in European mysticism, particularly through their influence upon Christianity, as we shall see in a later chapter.

We may now return to the problem mentioned above of the impasse in the development of science and technology reached by the Greeks two millennia ago. This problem concerns not only Greece but all the peoples of the Mediterranean region. Sumeria, Babylonia, and Egypt had taken the first rudimentary steps in science two millennia before the Greeks, and yet they also reached the same impasse. What were the causes of this long delay of 2,000 years from Mesopotamia to Greece and of another 2,000 years from Greece to modern Europe? The debasement of labor due to human exploitation which hampered technological development, and the animistic beliefs which obstructed the rise of science, remained in full force until within the past two or three centuries, and are still very strong today. Other factors must have become involved in order to give rise to the efflorescence of science and technology within the past century or two. We discuss this subject in Chapter XXXI of Part II of the present treatise.

The Mediterranean region comprising western Asia, northern Africa, and southern Europe, is not well supplied with such natural resources as metals, coal, timber, water power, oil, and precipitation. Here and there are plentiful supplies of certain resources. For example, Italy has no coal but an ample supply of so-called "white coal" or water power, about half of which has been developed in modern times.[16] Much of Asia Minor is well watered and wooded, and has some metal resources. Within the past few decades oil resources have been discovered and exploited in Mesopotamia and Iran. But these somewhat scattered resources, even if they had been more or less fully exploited in ancient times, would hardly have furnished the basis for a high technological development.

As the population of Europe increased and tended toward the north, the rich iron, coal and timber resources of northern Europe were utilized to a small extent with the aid of the rudimentary technology then available. But under the feudalism which dominated Europe for many centuries, the master class possessed almost unre-

---

[16] See Maurice Parmelee, *Geo-Economic Regionalism and World Federation,* New York, 1949, Chapter VIII entitled "Climate and Natural Resources."

stricted power over the subjugated mass under various forms of slavery and serfdom. The ownership of the land by the feudal lords was the decisive factor in the exploitation of the masses. Production was in the handicraft stage. The tools of production were small and inexpensive and could be readily procured by the workers. To this extent the workers possessed a small amount of freedom. But the scope for individual enterprise was narrowly limited by the preponderant rights of the nobility and monarchy, so that there was little opportunity for the worker to gain more than a meager living.

Toward the close of the Middle Ages there arose in European cities a class which was the mercantile class in an intermediate economic and social status between the feudal lords and their serfs. This was a period of exploration and discovery, of colonization, and of the worldwide extension of trade in which this mercantile class played an active part. About the time of the discovery of America in 1492 A.D., there commenced the first important stage of modern capitalism, namely, its mercantile stage, which lasted through the 16th and 17th and part of the 18th centuries. During this stage capitalism had comparatively little need of science and invention. With the coming of the industrial revolution and the mechanization of industry, commencing with the invention of the steam engine in the 18th century, perfected by James Watt from 1765 to 1776, this need increased greatly for a time. In order to compete successfully with handicraft and secure the profits from large-scale production, the capitalists encouraged mechanical inventions. The inducement of private profit even led some of the capitalists to establish research laboratories in order to discover new methods which they could utilize and new products which they could exploit profitably. An incidental by-product has been a small increment to scientific knowledge.

While the second important stage of capitalism, its industrial stage, was running its course, it not only had to produce a much larger supply of consumption goods for a rapidly increasing population, but also to build up the equipment of the machine age. For a time there was ample scope for private enterprise and capital expansion. As the new structure approached completion, the opportunities for the profitable investment of surplus capital decreased, and the disparity between productive capacity and the effective purchasing power necessary to distribute the products increased. The fundamental contradiction between capitalism as a scarcity economy and the machine and power age has become increasingly acute. The profit motive is in large part incompatible with technical efficiency. Capitalism sometimes aids in a haphazard fashion, but usually restrains scientists, inventors, engineers, and technicians in general. Bound hand and foot by the financial restrictions of a capitalist economy, they cannot carry out projects which are not only feasible but are most efficient and productive from a technical and social point of view. Capitalism utilizes scientific and technical progress only when profits are increased thereby. Many patented inventions are purchased and suppressed by capitalists because their utilization would decrease profits in the immediate or near future. Monopolies often smother inventions in order to save the cost of new installations. Capitalists are interested primarily in cheap labor and not in educated and trained labor as such. In all these ways capitalism frustrates science, invention and technology.[17]

Science has given rise to a technology by which it can be applied. Physical technology is already highly developed because it was profitable and therefore useful to capitalism during its period of expansion in its industrial stage. Social technology scarcely exists even in a rudimentary form. This is partly due to the fact that social science itself cannot attain a high development under the present order and could not do so under any preceding order. It is also because a social technology can function hardly at all under capitalism.

The so-called science of economics has been permeated almost entirely by the ideology of capitalism. In similar fashion the still more nebulous science of politics has been dominated by the political correlative of capitalism. Sociology has been largely a study of reforms within the framework of the capitalist system. Some of the sociologists have applied the term inaccurately and inappropriately to a program of these remedial and preventive measures, which embraces only a small portion of the life of society.

Science has arisen in considerable part out of the pragmatic impulse, and has eventually been applied. Between the initial impulse and the ultimate application there should be a period of unbiased and objective study and research during which what may be characterized as pure science can prevail. Otherwise the end sought is likely to influence the conclusions reached, which will in turn vitiate their application. Scientists should always guard themselves against being influenced unduly by whatever system under which they happen to live and work.

In the physical sciences it is comparatively easy to maintain an objective and impersonal attitude. Physics, astronomy, mathematics, chemistry, etc., have no obvious and little direct bearing upon the fortunes of mankind, but are beginning to have much indirect influence. It is much more difficult to retain an impersonal attitude in the social sciences. The anthropocentric and egocentric point of view

[17] Maurice Parmelee, *Farewell to Poverty*, New York, 1935. See especially Chapters VI, "The Profit Motive *versus* Technical Efficiency"; XVIII, "The Contradictions of Capitalism"; and XXII, "The Development of Social Technology."

is very likely to intrude and to bias the attitude of the social scientist. The ideology of the dominant social system is almost certain to color his thinking in some degree. Up to the present this ideology has been permeated with the animistic beliefs of the organized religions which are very useful for the upper classes because they tend to make the lower classes more acquiescent with their humble lot. Hence it is not surprising that much of alleged social science is shot through with religious and class rationalizations.

During the efflorescence of ancient Hellenic culture there lived in China two men who reflected and to a certain extent influenced the Chinese cultural situation. Kung-fu-tze (B.C. 551-478), latinized as Confucius, was declaring that "all men are brothers," and, when asked what should be done for the people, replied: "First relieve their poverty, then educate them." [18] A century later his principal disciple and expounder, Meng-tze (B.C. 372-289), latinized as Mencius, was declaring that all men are born equal, however great the emperor, however wise the philosopher, and however humble and stupid the common man.[19] Confucianism as a system of ethics rather than a religion resembled the Stoicism of the West which was its contemporary. Its egalitarian and humanitarian doctrine might have furnished the basis for the development of a genuine social science. Chinese culture was superior to European culture throughout the Middle Ages down to modern times. And yet China also displayed no efflorescence of science. Were the reasons for this failure the same in Oriental as in Occidental culture?[20]

It is difficult enough to explain why events take place in cultural evolution. It is often even more difficult to explain why they do not happen. A complete and conclusive explanation as to why science did not develop in the East is out of the question. In India an exceptionally ardent interest in religion, a strong tendency toward cosmological and metaphysical speculation, and an intense desire to transform the personality by methods which encourage introspective rather than objective habits of thinking were antithetical to the inductive and experimental methods which are essential for science. In China ancestor worship early acquired a firm grip and promoted the stability of the Chinese culture. But the excessive filial reverence which it inspired gave rise to a conservatism and self-satisfaction on account of one's family which effectually prevented the radical departure from tradition which science and its application require.

[18] *Analects*, 12.5., and 13.9. See H. G. Creel, *Confucius, the Man and the Myth*, New York, 1949.

[19] *Mencius*, 4 (2) .32., and 6 (1) .7.

[20] The following paragraphs to the end of this chapter are paraphrased from my *Oriental and Occidental Culture*, New York, 1928, pages 84-88.

It must be remembered that science is a very recent factor in the Western world, and might easily have failed to develop at all. As we have seen, the Greeks in Asia Minor and the Hellenic peninsula, influenced from Indian, Mesopotamian, Egyptian and Egean sources, made a small beginning, and then came a long interlude. The Roman Empire, somewhat like its great contemporary, the Chinese Empire, spread a political and military order throughout the West. Its authority was highly centralized, so that it did not foster a spirit of free research and investigation.

It was succeeded by the Roman Catholic church, which was and is the most centralized and institutionalized religion in the world. Under its hierarchical and theocratic rule there was little freedom for independent thought. It was largely responsible for the gloomy centuries of the Dark and Middle Ages. Monastic ideals and a static philosophy prevailed, and the universities existed largely for the training of monks and priests. The sort of contemplation and meditation encouraged was hardly more fruitful than that of the Indian yoga systems. For two thousand years science was almost at a standstill, about the only exceptions being a few contributions from the Arabic culture, which were by-products, so to speak, of the sudden and rapid spread of Islam. But no more than Christianity was Islam capable of stimulating science to develop to its full fruition.

Then came a concatenation of events which played their part in preparing the way for the coming of science, such as exploration leading to the discovery of America and of both eastern and western routes to the Orient, the invention of printing, the renascence of learning, the revival of the ancient classics, the revolt against the church, and the increase of wealth and leisure. These and many other factors aroused men's minds and broadened their outlook. The ancient Greek custom of questioning and investigating was awakened again. Unlike the speculative cosmologies and metaphysics of the East and of the medieval philosophers, the scientists sought first the pertinent data and then based their theories thereon.

The empirical method led to an inductive logic, which in turn gave rise to habits of thinking and reasoning radically different from those of the Orient. While India dreamed in its mental seclusion, and China plodded along its well-worn path in its geographical isolation, men of the West were beginning to realize that religious dogmas, metaphysical hypotheses, human fantasies, ethical doctrines, political theories, and social and economic systems must bow their heads before what the American psychologist William James called "the irreducible and stubborn facts" of science.

Science is derived in part from intellectual curiosity as to the nature of observable phenomena and whatever may lie back of them, and in part from attempts to attain practical ends, which, however blundering and ineffective they may be, result in accidentally bringing to light new data. Thus astrology aided the development of astronomy, alchemy of chemistry. Science is in turn applied to the attainment of these ends. The application of modern science has encouraged the hope of controlling nature in so far as is possible. When such control is or appears to be out of the question, it is supplemented or replaced by adaptation to nature. Thus the motives of control or of adaptation are increasingly influencing the Occidental world under the guidance of science. They encourage a mental flexibility, and an open-mindedness toward change and progress, such as has never before existed to the same degree.

In the East man still retains in the main an attitude of resignation toward the natural forces which he knows no way to control, though he tries to influence them by means of religion and magic. Droughts, floods, famine, disease, an excessive birth-rate, and like evils, are fatalistically accepted instead of striven against as in the West. Since the Oriental assumes that nothing can be done with nature, the attainment of perfection becomes his ideal, rather than adaptation to the environment.

In India the ideal is to acquire holiness, saintliness and divinity. Consequently, this vast peninsula is overrun with sadhus, sannyasins, and yogis. In China the craving for holiness is much less prevalent than in India. Indeed, it may be said to exist only to the extent that Buddhism has succeeded in introducing it. But another ideal of perfection wields a powerful influence. Instead of the gods, the revered ancestors constitute an archetype to be copied. Traditionalism and formalism expressed in elaborate ceremonies, a code of formal courtesy which is a ritual of technicalities, the observing of "face" and of "good" form which constitutes "propriety," play an important part in the character and conduct of the Chinese gentleman and "moral" person.

While these traits exist in a measure everywhere, and are changing in the Orient as a result of the impact of Occidental culture and of its technology in particular, in the West there is greater latitude and more opportunity for adaptation and adjustment on the part of the individual. The Chinese ethical code has played a large part in the perpetuation of Chinese civilization. But its ideal of perfection is too narrow to afford such opportunity for the development of individual types. And yet the greater flexibility and adaptability of the West have in some respects socialized its ethics more than has taken place in the East.

One of the outstanding contrasts between the East and the West is with regard to standards of precision and accuracy. Every European

389

and American country accumulates numerous statistics concerning many matters of scientific and social significance. In China there have been so far only vague and widely varying estimates of population. In India the principal source of precise and reliable information has been the Indian census, which was entirely due to the British administration. Japan has already copied the Occident with characteristic thoroughness, so that many statistics are published by its governmental departments, scientific organizations, and the like. This indifference to quantitative measurement and size is another indication of the comparative absence of a scientific attitude of mind in the East. However, this does not mean that the Orient is not alive to many qualitative distinctions whose significance is perhaps not fully appreciated in the Occident.

The concept of evolution now has much influence over the Western mind. To it is often given a teleological interpretation which colors the prevalent ideas of social and cultural progress. Even certain religious sects have accepted the theory of evolution in its erroneous teleological misinterpretation. So far as science is concerned, evolution is solely a name for a process of change. Its first great exponent, Herbert Spencer, recognized this and indicated clearly that evolution is correlated with and balanced by involution, since it is inconceivable that change in a certain direction could go on indefinitely in space and time. This fact was dimly perceived by Indian sages two to three thousand years ago, though they failed to describe this process of change accurately and in detail, as has been accomplished to a considerable extent by Western scientists. These sages of old and scientists of today are, however, at one in realizing that there can be no purpose or end in this infinite and universal process of change.

Chapter XXV

The Origin of the Social Classes

BY the social classes are usually meant groupings of human beings in terms of power, wealth, prestige and status. These groupings may or may not be hereditary. Wherever they are hereditary, an individual's status is rigidly fixed from birth and remains so throughout his life. He inherits whatever power, prestige and wealth, or lack of them, belong to his class. When they are not hereditary, the status of the individual may shift during his lifetime. In other words, he may pass from one class to another. The shift may be upward or downward. It may be due to skill, craft or to fortuitous circumstances. Even if status is not ostensibly hereditary, it is likely to be so in effect through the ownership and inheritance of wealth. In fact, throughout the course of cultural history, the status accompanied by power and prestige, or by the lack of them, of the vast majority of human beings has been inherited even though it was overtly not hereditary. Social mobility has on the whole been very restricted.

Among the groups which are of high status by birth are the royalty and the nobility. The latter is sometimes known as the aristocracy, though this term may be applied to those who are preeminent by wealth or by culture and not necessarily by birth. The priesthood has in many cases been hereditary, but the priestly status has often been acquired after birth. It has almost always been associated with the classes which are predominant by birth and not by individual traits and achievements. The sacerdotal interests have almost invariably been interwoven with those of the ruling classes for reasons which will be stated.

Among the groups which are of low status by birth are the slaves and the serfs. The slave belongs, so to speak, body and soul, to his master. He represents the lowest level of the artificial gradations of status which mankind has created in the course of its exploitative and predatory career on this planet. Warfare, rapine, debt, and certain kinds of business enterprise have resulted in enslaving a vast multitude of human beings who have been deprived of every human right including the supreme right of existence. During the world-wide war of 1939 to 1945 many millions lost all of their rights culminating in their slaughter. Nor was this exceptional. The wage slavery of the past two centuries or more has been little different from the slavocracies of ancient and modern times. Furthermore, the forces for slavery have been no respecters of persons in so far as ability and character have been concerned. The persons of productive and of creative capacity, and of stable and social character have been enslaved as readily and as quickly as their opposites when the predatory and exploitative forces have engulfed them. The similarity between chattel slavery and the wage and pauper slavery of modern capitalism will be discussed later.

Under serfdom the agricultural worker is usually bound to the soil which he cultivates and therefore to the proprietor of that soil. This became possible when the land fell under the ownership of persons who did not themselves cultivate the soil but who nevertheless were enabled by custom and law to confiscate much of the fruits of the soil and its cultivator. This was true of the helotage of Sparta, of the colonate of Rome, of the vassalage and villeinage of medieval feudalism, and of peasant tenantry at many other times and places. Under their thinly disguised capitalist equivalents both slavery and serfdom persist down to the present day. As I have said in another book: "Under various forms of slavery or of serfdom the master class has possessed almost unrestricted power over the subjugated mass. Even when the ownership of human beings (chattel slavery) has not been formally recognized, a monopoly or virtual monopoly of wealth or a control over the means of subsistence has in effect enslaved the masses." "The monopoly arising out of the ownership of land persists and is still of preeminent importance. The monopoly arising out of the ownership of the tools of production has attained an equal importance. The right of inheritance perpetuates these monopolies from generation to generation. The workers, from being chattel slaves and feudal serfs, have become wage slaves, which is a no less dire form of slavery. Even the slightest measure of responsibility acknowledged by the slave-owner and feudal lord for the sustenance of his slaves or serfs is not recognized by the capitalist, who may hire or fire his employees at will. Inasmuch as under the inexorable operation of the capitalist system the worker can procure no work and wage elsewhere, the alleged freedom of the worker to work when and where he chooses and to compete freely for his work and wage is a hollow

392

farce. When, as often happens, no work and wage are procurable, the wage slave becomes a pauper slave or perishes from starvation."[1]

A caste system is the most inclusive system of hereditary groupings. Royalty and nobility may form parts of a caste system. A complete system includes the whole of a given population which I have defined in another book: "A caste system is a hereditary classification according to special functions, the castes being hierarchically arranged with unequal powers, rights, and privileges. . . . A caste system is a form of occupational division of labor. In a primitive or comparatively simple society it may serve this purpose fairly well. Before an educational system has developed, the most feasible method of transmitting professional knowledge may be from father to son, so that a hereditary specialization of occupations is a natural result. But as knowledge accumulates, new methods of doing things are invented, and the range of information within each occupation becomes extensive, the situation becomes too complicated to be effectively handled by a caste system. This is particularly true with regard to the extremely technical methods of modern industry which have resulted from the development of science. They call for a minute differentiation of functions, and also for a high degree of flexibility to meet changes due to scientific discoveries and inventions. In the face of such demands a hereditary classification breaks down hopelessly, because it can change only slowly and in the course of generations. The same is true of commerce, government, and various cultural pursuits."[2]

The accumulation of private wealth created the plutocratic or timocratic class which is ostensibly not hereditary. But since the right of inheritance of property carries the power and prestige of wealth from generation to generation plutocracy is in effect hereditary. As a necessary corollary, the laboring class of the landless peasant and the wage worker is also hereditary even when these peasants and workers are not serfs or chattel slaves. Since the industrial revolution and the rise of capitalism there has perhaps been a little more vertical mobility between these classes. There has arisen a middle class known as

---

[1] Maurice Parmelee, *Farewell to Poverty*, New York, 1935, pp. 155, 156-7. In the latter part of the present treatise, capitalism as the modern equivalent of slavery and serfdom will be described in detail, including such modifying and ameliorating factors as have been introduced.

[2] Maurice Parmelee, *Oriental and Occidental Culture, An Interpretation*, New York, 1928, pp. 106-107.

In this book I have described at length the Indian caste system and the manner in which it is rapidly disintegrating at present. See especially Chapter VII.

The Indian Constituent assembly in the Constitution of India adopted on October 2, 1949, made the "untouchability" of the outcastes a criminal offense, and forbade its practice in any form. Freedom of religion is guaranteed by this Constitution.

the bourgeoisie between the rapidly disappearing nobility or hereditary aristocracy and the working class now known as the proletariat. It includes not only the capitalists themselves, but also their henchmen, retainers and dependents. Among the capitalists are not only the large landlords, masters of industry, big merchants, and bankers and financial magnates who exercise an extensive control over industry, commerce and agriculture, but also the small farm owners and the petty business enterprisers.

In the higher ranks of the bourgeois henchmen and retainers are the corporation lawyers, factory and business managers, consulting engineers and technicians, public relations counselors and advertising agents. In the lower ranks are most of the lawyers, the plant and store managers and foremen, and the less important technicians. Belonging in the main to the higher or lower ranks of the henchmen are the professors and teachers, the ministers of religion and magic, the physicians, and the politicians. Whether or not hired by the owners of the means of production, these professions consciously or unconsciously share their interests and work for the maintenance of their economic system of private profit. On the borderline between the bourgeoisie and the proletariat are the tenant farmers who dream of becoming farm owners, and the white collar petty retainers who cherish vain hopes of clambering into the capitalist group. The increase of class feeling and the intensification of the class struggle will probably go on apace in the near future as indeed it has already dominated the political scene for more than a century.

In the ancient world the hierarchy of classes was illustrated in each of the leading countries by a fundamental pattern. At the top was the imperial or royal dynasty. The nobility was represented in India by the princes, in China by the ennobled officials, in Iran by the warrior-nobles, in Egypt by the tributary nobles, in Rome by the senators, etc. In each country there was at least one lower privileged order, such as the landlords in India, the provincial officials in China, the warrior-knights in Iran, the merchant-knights in Rome, etc. The priestly class was often at or near the top rank. It was privileged because it had learning which was supposed to be essential in this world or in the next for mankind or at least for the privileged classes. Also to it were often attributed magical and supernatural skills. Among these sacerdotal groups were the pre-literate medicine men and sorcerers, the Indian Brahmans, the Confucian literati, the Iranian magi, the Jewish rabbis, and later the Christian priests and Moslem mullahs. Monastic orders often formed specialized divisions of the priestly class. Entrance into the privileged classes was usually by birth, but sometimes by military prowess, or by purchase of office or rank in which case the accumulation of wealth was a necessary preliminary.

394

At the base of this hierarchy was the vast mass of the workers under the yoke of this regimented social order. Class was usually marked by dress, etiquette, manners, education, and occupation. Rivalry and conflict between the privileged classes was much more usual than the struggle between the exploiters and the exploited which is a comparatively recent phenomenon on a large scale. Sometimes aristocracy and monarchy have been opposed to each other though usually they have cooperated in ruling the exploited laboring classes.

With this introduction concerning the nature of social classes in general we may turn to the problem as to how social differentiation arose in the first instance. It is not to be assumed that it was due entirely or even in large part to differences between individuals. Certain it is that in all of the social groups which have been observed there are many kinds of individuals. Hence it is not unreasonable to assume that social forces rather than individual differences have given rise to social classes.

Inborn differences between individuals do not and cannot of themselves give rise to social inequality though they may furnish a starting point for such inequality. It is inequality of opportunity which gives rise to social inequality. This arises from the nature of the social organization at any time and place. It must contain class domination and subordination the sources of which must be sought in cultural history. In the lower stages of social evolution such domination and subordination may be enforced by custom and convention. In the later stages it is certain to be enforced by laws which explicitly or by their inevitable consequences separate the social classes and discriminate between them.

Some of the socially undeveloped peoples which have been observed have lived in a natural environment where there was an ample supply of food and the other necessaries of life which could be secured with little effort. This has been true in certain tropical environments where the food hung on trees or bushes ready to be picked. Even where the environment has not been tropical, in certain regions there has been an abundance of fertile soil which could be readily cultivated and of animal food which could be easily hunted or fished or bred. Under such conditions the necessities of existence, however great their intrinsic value, would have little or no economic value. Even the helpless such as the very young and the old could be cared for without much exertion on the part of the able-bodied. The question therefore arises whether or not it was a certain degree of scarcity of these consumable goods which first gave rise to social differentiation or at least was an important factor in giving rise to such differentiation. Such a scarcity of some or all consumable goods would furnish an incentive to some individuals to secure possession of these goods, now having economic value. They would use physical and mental means to attain these ends and would safeguard their property by means of customs, conventions and laws which would seem to justify such possession. This would furnish an economic basis for social differentiation. We shall discuss later in this treatise to what extent these economic factors have caused social inequality.

Age and sex are biological causes for differentiation within human groups. However, they do not give rise to social classes. Men and women, old and young, children and adults are found in all human groups. While they do not form social classes, they give rise to a certain amount of social differentiation which resembles the class domination and subordination which develop later in social evolution.)

(Owing partly to the greater physical strength of men and partly to the fact that women are at rather frequent intervals handicapped by menstruation and childbearing, women have always been subject to domination by men to a certain extent. Among many primitive peoples and also many peoples at higher cultural levels much of the hardest drudgery of work has devolved upon the women. This was true of the plant food gathering at the most primitive levels and of the cultivation of plants at the lower levels of agricultural evolution. At the same time the men did most of the hunting and fishing and all of the fighting for their families, clans, tribes and nations. Certain rights were denied to women at many times and places, such as the right to eat certain kinds of food. Women have usually been excluded from taking part in public affairs. When property in land came into being women were almost invariably prevented from owning land. In other words, property in land was inherited only by sons and not by daughters. Where old men were revered, old women also sometimes were revered to a certain extent. In a few exceptional cases they were permitted to take a small part in public affairs, such as being present at meetings of the councils of the elders. Wherever the position of women improved as they reached old age, it was probably due in large part if not entirely to the fact that they had passed childbearing and the climacteric.) As has been noted in an earlier chapter, among many primitive peoples as well as many peoples at higher cultural levels it was believed that women were impure because of the menstrual and puerperal flow of blood. The old women could no longer be impure for this reason.

Children have always been more or less under the domination of adults. Usually it is the domination of their parents. Very often paternal authority is greater than maternal authority. In metronymic clans or tribes the maternal uncle has sometimes exercised the greatest authority over his sister's children. Among many primitive peoples as well as peoples at higher cultural levels there have been initiatory

rites to mark the transition from childhood to adulthood. This inita-
tion is usually about the time of puberty. For the boys it often takes
the form of an ordeal the purposes of which is to reveal the degree of
courage and fortitude of which the boy is capable. For the girl the
initiatory ceremony is usually somewhat milder. Among many peoples
it has been customary for the initiates to take new names, thereby indicating the change in the character and status of the young person.

Old persons have sometimes had a certain amount of influence
and even of authority owing to their age. Among some primitive peoples a council of the elders was the only form of government. Under
such conditions the older generation would be regarded with reverence
and even with awe. Gerontocracy by the old men was especially prevalent in Australia and Melanesia. The old women were rarely ever
given authority. Gerontocracy is more likely to prevail where ceremonial observances are highly respected. It is weakened by the military activities of the younger men and by men's secret societies.

It has more generally been true that with the decline of vigor
and strength the old have been treated with neglect and even with
scorn. Among some peoples they were abandoned to perish or were
killed. This was particularly true of tribes leading a nomadic existence, such as hunting or pastoral tribes, where the old would have difficulty in keeping up with the tribe. However, the old have never been
a superior or an inferior social class any more than the women. All
persons who live long enough attain old age and every human group
has its quota of the aged. Whether discriminated in favor of or against,
their status is determined primarily by a biological and not by a social
factor.

Personal differences between the individual members of a human
group may give rise to a certain amount of differentiation which may
or may not be called social. Such personal traits as physical strength,
courage, skill in making the things of value for a human group, alleged influence with supernatural powers, and many other unusual and
exceptional traits may give an individual prestige, influence and even
power within his group. Thus the brave warrior and the skilful hunter
acquires fame within his tribe or whatever his group may be. His renown may be visibly indicated by trophies which are worn as badges
of honor. Among primitive peoples the trophies of the warrior were
skulls, scalps, and other parts of the bodies of the vanquished foe. The
trophies of the hunter were feathers, horns, and other parts of the
hunted animals. Painting or tattooing the body might set forth the exploits of the successful individual. In some cases the personal prestige
and precedence attained by successful persons might be transferred in
a measure to their offspring. However, until a superior social class
began to develop such precedence could not become hereditary.

While exceptional personal ability could not bring about social classes, and was indeed in a sense an obstacle in the way of such differentiation because the exceptional man stood by himself within his group, the division of labor or the specialization of certain industries and professions was an important cause of social classes. The earliest division of labor was between the sexes. As we have seen, this could not lead to the formation of classes. Among the most primitive peoples there could have been little or no specialization because there were no highly developed skills and each family or household was a unit serving its own needs.

The highly developed skill of paleolithic peoples in chipping and shaping stone implements has led some anthropologists to think that stonecutting may have been the earliest specialized occupation. There may have been an early specialization among craftsmen in less durable materials, such as wood and bone, examples of whose work have not survived. However that may be, several specialized occupations must have arisen during the early stages of cultural evolution. If these occupations had remained on an equality in the esteem of the public, they would not in themselves have given rise to social classes in the sense of human groups having a different status from each other. Observation of primitive peoples has, however, revealed a wide variation in the degree of social esteem accorded to the specialized occupations. A good deal of this social discrimination between occupations persists to the present day when so-called "white collar" jobs are rated more highly than manual labor.

Activities requiring a high degree of courage and strength as well as skill have almost invariably rated high in social estimation. This has been peculiarly true of warfare though warfare can hardly be considered an occupation in any social and economic sense. It does not create anything of value though unavoidable at times for protection against enemies. Furthermore, it is intermittent in character. Nevertheless, the warrior group has always stood high in social esteem. Hunting and fishing are genuine occupations which have also been rated high for similar reasons but more specially because of the skill required. Occupations requiring a great deal of skill, such as carpentering, have usually been rated high. Among the more primitive peoples tattooing had a high rating as an occupation.

Certain occupations have rated low in social esteem for reasons extraneous to the skill required. In some cases it was because they were regarded as feminine occupations. Cooking has often been contemned for this reason, and agriculture also because in its early stages it was almost exclusively a feminine occupation. This may have been true also of weaving which has been rated low at certain times and places in spite of the fact that it is an occupation requiring a good deal of skill. Other occupations have been contemned because of their real or alleged uncleanliness. Among them have been working with swine, tanning, and butchering. Some occupations have been regarded as unclean at certain times and places because their craftsmen were reputed to be sorcerers. Among them have been barbers and smiths. At other times and places smiths have been in high repute because of their skill. It is possible that they acquired the reputation of being sorcerers because iron was often regarded as having magical qualities and was sometimes used as a charm before it became plentiful and widely used.

Occupations have often become hereditary in the male line of descent. This has encouraged the rise of some sort of caste system which is the most rigid type of social classification. The superior class has almost invariably despised manual labor in general. This is because with the accumulation of wealth upon which superior class status is usually based this class has been able to own slaves and to hire the inferior class to do its work. Consequently, it has had a strong incentive to dissociate itself as completely as possible from the occupations of the lower classes.

The amalgamation of tribes through conquest and subjugation has been an important factor for social inequality. The conquering tribe became the superior and dominant class. This class included the nobility and royalty wherever royalty existed. We have already discussed this process in connection with government and imperialism. Very often a part of the conquered tribe was enslaved. This resulted in a tri-class system consisting of the noble, common and slave classes. It corresponded with the modern tri-class system of upper, middle and lower classes. Besides these classes is the priesthood which in some repects is a distinct class but which is in its interests and functions closely assimilated with the upper class whose interests it almost invariably serves.

In an earlier chapter have been described the animistic beliefs of primitive men which are in large part still retained by the vast majority of human beings. Unable to explain natural phenomena scientifically, early men assumed that vague generalized or more definite individualized supernatural forces were causing or controlling these phenomena. They wanted to increase the wild animals which they hunted, to precipitate the fall of rain for vegetation, to prevent and cure disease, to prolong life, to injure their enemies, to fend off evil spirits, etc. They thought they could attain some of these ends by coercing or propitiating these supernatural forces. Thus arose the coercive methods of magic and the propitiatory methods of religion. Both of them are based on animistic beliefs. Both of them are more or less mingled in the animistic practices of mankind down to the present day. Scientific knowledge has gradually narrowed the scope of these practices. But presidents of the United States, prime ministers of England, and many other of the world's potentates appeal to god and providence, while the vast majority of mankind believe in gods and goddesses, angels and devils, demons and hobgoblins, spirits and souls. Hobgoblinism or animism is still one of the most widespread of human beliefs which stands in the way of the utilization of science in the affairs of mankind.

It is possible that among primitive peoples every one was originally his own priest and magician. It is more probable that the earliest practitioners of the sacerdotal arts were the fathers or heads of families and the chiefs of clans and tribes. This custom persisted in some communities where the family was strongly organized. For example, in ancient Rome the *pater familias* was the family priest as well as secular head. The *lares* and *penates*, or protecting spirits of the family, were worshiped daily at the family meal. In course of time specialization arose in order to perform the rituals, incantations, and other arts deemed necessary or useful in order to influence or coerce the supernatural powers which man often feared and sometimes reverenced. Thus it came to pass that the social order or profession known as the priesthood included and still includes not only the religious officiants and celebrants, such as clergymen, parsons and priests, but also magical practitioners, seers, prophets, rainmakers, healers, sorcerers, exorcists of demons, oneiromancers, thaumaturgists, and all others who professed and still profess to have special skills in relation to the supernatural world.

The priesthood arose in the first instance because of the almost universal belief that mankind needs superhuman aid to overcome the dangers which menace it. The priests (used as a generic term) are still maintained by the popular belief in their ability to coerce or to mediate with supernatural powers. They have at various times and places professed to be able to read omens, to interpret dreams, to predict future events, to perform miracles, and to kill enemies by sorcery. They have, to be sure, often failed to attain their objectives. The more shrewd have provided escape clauses by stipulating that the prospective beneficiaries were to fulfill certain conditions. The less shrewd or the more unlucky have suffered by losing part or all of their reputations and at certain times and places have been killed for their failures. In the long run they have commanded veneration and awe because of their professed abilities. This awe has been exacerbated by the bodily decorations or vestments of the priest, the imposing character of the edifices, such as temples and churches, devoted to animistic practices, and the portentous nature of the rituals utilized in hobgoblinism or

400

animism which arouse the emotion of fear in the superstitious and simpleminded devotees.

In view of the tremendous hold that hobgoblinism has had upon the mind of mankind down to the present day it is not surprising that the priesthood has often been of the ruling class or at least on an equality with and in cooperation with the rulers. The chief and the priest have often been combined in one person because both offices have power.[3] The most extreme form of this combination has been the king-priest who was regarded as divine. This was the case in ancient Egypt and in several other of the ancient monarchies. Even when government became more or less secularized and no strife existed between the government and the priesthood because the latter had been forced to accept a curtailment of its power, the priesthood has reenforced the state by attributing to it an alleged supernatural sanction.

During the lower stages of cultural evolution slavery was rare among hunting and fishing peoples. It was somewhat more prevalent among pastoral peoples. It was most prevalent among agricultural peoples with fixed habitations. This was because slave labor had almost no value for peoples which lived solely by hunting and fishing, had limited value for pastoral peoples, and was most useful for agricultural peoples.

Slavery was probably extra-tribal in its origin. In any case, the sources of many of the slaves was extra-tribal. A large part of the enslavement took place as a result of conquest in war.[4] At first some of the captives may have been preserved temporarily by cannibalistic tribes to be eaten. Or they may have been kept to be sacrificed in religious and magical rites. It is not likely that captives were enslaved on a large scale until their labor had acquired economic value. They were killed immediately or sometimes freed and adopted into the tribe. When, however, the rise of agriculture rendered their labor valuable, all the able-bodied captives were likely to be enslaved. In fact, the desire for cheap slave labor may have become an economic

[3] Gunnar Landtman, *The Origin of the Inequality of the Social Classes*, London and Chicago, 1938.

"Among certain peoples the priests heighten their authority by attaching themselves to the kings and noble classes in the community, while at the same time, they are said in return to support the ruling system." (P. 184) "The increased authority which religious and magical power confers upon a ruler has contributed to the extreme degree of autocracy which has signalized the potentates of not a few semi-civilized and barbarous peoples." (P. 323)

[4] "Regarding the origin of slavery, we seem thus to be entitled to assume that captivity in war constitutes its veritable and dominant source, at least so far as we can conclude from the condition of the peoples known to us." (G. Landtman, *op. cit.*, p. 286.)

401

motive for warfare so that some of the wars of primitive and barbarous peoples may have been little more than slave capturing enterprise. To that extent warfare became very similar to the slave trade. Even without warfare the kidnapping of members of another tribe or people, or the slave trade proper, became an important source of slaves for several millennia. The commerce in slaves persisted until the 19th century A.D. Denmark declared it unlawful in 1792 and England and the United States in 1807-1808. The Congress of Vienna denounced it in 1815. But it persisted until the end of the 19th century when the slave trade in the interior of Africa was suppressed by the concerted action of several European countries.

Slavery itself lasted somewhat longer. England abolished it in its colonies in the West Indies in 1833. The United States abolished it in 1865 by the Thirteenth Amendment to the Constitution. Brazil abolished it in 1888 just before the establishment of the republic in 1889.

We cannot know the precise relation in time and in extent between extra-tribal and intra-tribal slavery. It is doubtful if kidnapping and the slave trade played so extensive a part in the latter. Moral ideas, customs and laws would tend to limit forcible abduction and enslavement within the tribe or nation. However, the development of the economic process of loaning wealth, whether real or monetary, for a consideration created the economic relation between creditor and debtor. If the debtor was unable to repay his creditor, the only recourse of the latter was to take possession of the person of the former and to use his labor to produce wealth with which to reimburse himself. Sometimes the debtor himself or a member of his family was seized by the creditor as a sort of pawn who could be redeemed by the payment of the debt. The pawn was then in a state of temporary enslavement which might develop into permanent slavery if the debtor was never able to liquidate his debt. Thus slavery as an outcome of the economic process of loaning wealth for profit became established as an economic institution and was recognized by custom, sanctioned and justified by the ethical ideas of the ruling class, and enforced by law. For example, the code of Hammurabi (*ca.* 1700 B.C.) sanctioned the right of a debtor to bind his wife and offspring out to service or to sell them as slaves, but not for more than three years. Thus were the property rights of the wealthy ruling class safeguarded.

An additional source of intra-tribal slavery arose when enslavement came to be used as a punishment for crime. However, this was probably much inferior to war, kidnapping and the slave trade, and debt, as a source of slaves. These criminal slaves belonged to the ruler or the state and their labor was used on public works or they were sold to private owners. Remnants of this form of slavery still persist in some modern countries as in the United States where prison labor is utilized on public undertakings and where it is sometimes hired out to private employers. This has resulted in the "peonage" system in those states in which convicts have been almost literally sold body and soul to the purchasers of their labor, though contract labor is prohibited by the Constitution of the United States. As I have said in another book: "The Thirteenth Amendment, ratified by the states in 1865, reads as follows: 'Neither slavery nor involuntary servitude, except as a punishment for crime whereof the party shall have been duly convicted, shall exist within the United States, or any place subject to their jurisdiction.' The Supreme Court of the United States has defined the meaning of the word slavery as it is used in this amendment as follows: 'Slavery implies involuntary servitude—a state of bondage; the ownership of mankind as a chattel, or at least the control of the labor and services of one man for the benefit of another, and the absence of a legal right to the disposal of his own person, property and services.' (*Plessy v. Ferguson*, 163 U.S. 537.) It is evident that the Constitution expressly permits penal servitude as a form of punishment. It is also evident that, according to the opinion of the Supreme Court which has been cited, contract labor is expressly prohibited, because it involves 'the control of the labor and services of one man for the benefit of another.' " [5]

Slavery as an industrial system has been described by an historian of ancient civilization as follows: "There is little scope for slavery in most primitive communities unacquainted with cattle-raising or farming; as a rule slaves will be kept only when they can be gainfully employed. Under pastoral conditions slaves are useful as cowherds, swineherds, and shepherds, but no need exists for many workers. Moreover, the nomadic life of pastoralists forms a bar to the keeping of slaves. Where agriculture is the principal or only occupation, forced labor becomes much more profitable, for on a given plot of land every additional worker means, as a rule, an increased yield. The settled life of agriculturists also makes it easier to maintain oversight and control over bondmen. Thus slavery develops into an industrial system, with the slave class recruited from prisoners of war and their descendants, persons kidnapped or purchased from the outside, poor men who voluntarily sell themselves into servitude, and debtors and criminals. . . . Early civilization owed much to slavery, for it facilitated the accumulation of wealth and out of war-captives and their offspring it helped to create the class of workers, as distinct from warriors, who at first were the only freemen." [6]

Professor Webster's last assertion is open to grave question. Neither he nor any one else can prove that these war-captives who were en-

[5] Maurice Parmelee, *Criminology*, New York, 1918, page 431.
[6] Hutton Webster, *History of Civilization*, Boston, 1947, Vol. I, pages 60-61.

slaved facilitated the creation and accumulation of wealth more as slaves than they would have if they had remained as freemen who had ceased fighting. Slavery is the most extreme of the many forms of exploitation invented by mankind by means of which certain human beings have despoiled and often persecuted and tortured a vast number of their fellows. In so far as productivity is concerned, free laborers who have acquired most or all of their own product have ordinarily been much more productive than slave laborers who have had little incentive to produce.

In the Euphrates-Tigris valley slavery seems to have existed at least as early as the beginnings of agriculture. The Babylonians not only made slaves of their prisoners of war but organized warlike expeditions to capture more prisoners for enslavement. Their slaves consisted mainly of war captives, their descendants, and slaves purchased abroad. The Sumerian ideograph for slave used by the Babylonians means "male of foreign land." The Assyrians used similar methods to secure their slaves. The unskilled slaves became so numerous that sometimes they were sold for less than sheep. They were branded like cattle and sometimes mutilated to prevent their escape. The code of Hammurabi prescribed death for any one who helped a slave to escape. However, the condition of many of the freemen was little or no better than that of the slaves so that some of them sold themselves or their children into slavery.

Egypt seems to have had fewer slaves than Babylonia and Assyria though it was a very fertile agricultural country. This does not mean that there was more freedom in Egypt. The Egyptian kings were absolute monarchs with power of life and death over their subjects. The priesthood was very powerful and wealthy. In the 20th dynasty (ca. 1100 B.C.) the priests owned about one-seventh of the arable land. The scarcity of slaves may have been due in part to the fact that Egypt was somewhat isolated from other countries and was not so much engaged in international wars. Consequently, it did not have so many prisoners of war to enslave. However, the rulers summoned corvées of forced labor to build temples, pyramids, and other public works and such labor was little better than slavery.

Slavery existed in Greece during the Homeric age which lasted from the close of the Egean age about 1100 B.C. to the beginning of recorded Greek history about 750 B.C. The slaves were war captives or foreigners purchased from Phenician traders. The landless peasants worked for wages and were little better than serfs. There were much fewer slaves than later in the history of Greece. Many of the peasants fell into debt because they were unable to pay the rent to their landlords and were sold into slavery. In the 5th century B.C. Athens had a free population of about 200,000 which included the resident foreigners

404

who were not citizens. The Athenian citizens took a small step toward democracy partly because some of them were freed from the necessity of working by the slaves they owned. This furnished them leisure for the arts and for political activities. The Attican economy was based largely on slavery. "While most of the industries of Athens were carried on by free labor the city contained a large body of slaves. They worked on large estates owned by wealthy men, toiled in mines and quarries, served as oarsmen on ships, and were employed also in household tasks and handicrafts. Most of them were non-Greeks, recruited from the barbarous tribes of Asia Minor, Thrace, and the lands about the Black Sea." [7] It is estimated that about one-fourth of the population of Attica were slaves and that about one-sixth were aliens. However, even though Greek culture depended partly on slavery, it did not honor labor. The chief occupations of the citizens were government and war; so that slaves were ranked very low in public estimation.

In Sparta slavery assumed a much harsher form. The ruling class was not much more than one-tenth of the total population. The helots or slaves were about four or five to each Spartan. They belonged to the government but were assigned or farmed out to till the soil of the Spartan citizens. A Spartan could kill a helot without trial. When their numbers threatened or were supposed to threaten Spartan security, many of them disappeared secretly. In wartime they were furnished light armor. During the Peloponnesian War they put them into heavy armor and then became alarmed. The Athenian historian Thucydides (*ca.* 471-399 B.C.) described what happened. "They (the Spartans) proclaimed that a selection would be made of those helots who claimed to have rendered the best service to the Spartans in the war, and promised them liberty. The announcement was intended to test them. . . . So (the Spartans) selected about two thousand, who . . . were supposed to have received their liberty, *but not long afterwards the Spartans put them all out of the way, and no man knew how any of them came to their end.*"

Slaves were very numerous during the latter part of the Roman republic. Many of them were captured in war who were sold by the state or given to rich nobles. There were also manhunts on the frontiers. The slaves revolted several times. In 135 B.C. 70,000 slaves held Sicily for four years. In about 105 B.C. there was another slave revolt in Sicily. In 73-71 B.C. took place a gladiatorial revolt against Rome. Its leader, the Thracian captive Spartacus who had been made a gladiator like many slaves with about 70,000 gladiators and fugitive slaves resisted Rome for three years. These revolts were suppressed with great cruelty. During the last century of the republic Pompey

[7] Hutton Webster, *op. cit.*, Volume I, page 225.

and Caesar are reputed to have sold into slavery more than one million Gauls and Asiatics. Ordinary slaves became as cheap as beasts of burden.

During the empire slavery decreased greatly. The main reason was that with the establishment of a stable imperial rule over a large part of the known world, foreign warfare decreased greatly. There were also certain ameliorating forces in the later Roman culture. The civil law was becoming more exact, impartial, and liberal. It limited the use of torture to extort confessions from persons accused of crime. It decreased the authority of the *pater familias*. It prescribed that a master who killed his slave should be treated as a murderer. These tendencies were encouraged by the Stoic philosophy which was then prevalent among the upper classes. It taught that all men are born free and that slavery violates natural right. Many slaves were manumitted or were permitted to buy their own freedom by means of money which they themselves had earned. Some of the more intelligent and better educated of the freedmen entered the imperial civil service which had been established by the first emperor, Augustus. Many of the slaves captured in Asia Minor and elsewhere were educated persons. Under the eastern Byzantine Roman empire, however, from about the beginning of the 4th century A.D., the state became very autocratic and the slaves, while not so numerous and perhaps better treated than formerly, had no legal rights.

Slavery also had some influence upon the decline of population which took place during this period in Rome. Barbarian raids sometimes carried off into the north much of the population of the border provinces. The Emperor Marcus Aurelius Antoninus (121-190 A.D.) compelled a German people, the Quadi, to surrender 50,000 Roman captives who would otherwise have died in slavery. Slavery also caused a decline of population within the empire because the masters were permitted to expose the infants of slaves since it was cheaper to buy slaves from the captives of the Roman legions on the borders than to rear them from infancy. Slave labor competed with free labor which could not rear large families and was often forced to expose its infants.

Roman slavery gradually merged to a large extent into serfdom. Slaves ceased to be human chattels but became attached to the soil apart from which they could not be sold. Many free peasants also became serfs because they lost title to whatever land they had owned by becoming indebted to the large land owners. In this fashion Roman slavery was transformed into the feudal serfdom which characterized most of Europe during the Middle Ages.

Slavery existed among the Arabs and was recognized by and incorporated in the Moslem religion which regulated it somewhat.

Only non-Moslems captured in lawful warfare or kidnapped in a foreign land could be enslaved. The manumission of slaves was regarded as having religious merit. A slave woman who bore children for her master was freed and her children were free. In the Koran its author Mohammed (570-632 A.D.) said: "Feed your slaves with food of that which you eat and clothe them with such clothing as you wear, and command them not to do that which they are unable to do." With such restrictions slavery did not assume its most extreme form in the social system of Islam. It was not human chattelhood in the form taken by Negro slavery in America a millennium later.

Slavery has apparently arisen spontaneously in various parts of the world. When the Spaniards invaded Mexico in 1519 A.D., Aztec society included many serfs and slaves. The latter were prisoners of war, persons who had been enslaved as punishment, and children who had been sold by their parents. Though there had been no communication between the eastern and the western hemisphere, and no conceivable contact except by migration at a much earlier period, slavery arose in much the same fashion in both hemispheres. It was due to warfare, to the private ownership of land and tools—producers' and consumers' goods, to the concentration of power in the hands of a few, and to the innate predatory and exploitative traits of human beings. The same is true of many other phases of human culture.

Chapter XXVI

Class Dominance

THE student of cultural evolution faces the difficult problem not only of describing all of the important factors which have played a part in this evolution, but also of weighing as far as is feasible the relative importance of these factors. To accomplish the latter task it is essential to measure the extent and duration of each of these factors. Some of them are permanent, some are subject to more or less change, and some have disappeared in large part or entirely.

The human biological traits described in earlier chapters are relatively unchangeable and permanent. The same is true of the human psychological traits which have been described at some length, such as instincts or inborn tendencies to action, emotions and intellect. These traits may, however, be influenced considerably in the direction they take by the culture within which they are functioning. Human beings belong to one and the same species as is demonstrated by the fact that all human varieties interbreed. These varieties differ little among themselves, much less indeed than the varieties among many other animal and plant species. The differences are mainly external and superficial. Typical of them are pigmentation of the skin and shape of the hair.

The significance of this universal human similarity is that the influence of the biological and psychological factors can be discounted to a large extent. That is to say, they must be recognized as at work in much the same way among all peoples and races and in all cultures. The differences between these cultures cannot be explained by fundamental biological and psychological differences between the races and peoples concerned. We have to look elsewhere for these explanations.

The ecological factors are of prime importance and here we find vast differences between the various regions of the world. In temperature the range is from arctic cold to equatorial heat. In rainfall the precipitation ranges from nil in certain desert areas to an average rainfall of 420 inches a year in Assam. In altitude the range is from below sea level in a few relatively small areas to nearly 30,000 feet above in the Himalaya Mountains. The topography varies in many respects, as, for example, as to whether the land surface is flat, hilly or mountainous. The most potent single factor in the long run is the chemical composition of the soil which renders it fertile. This factor in conjunction with temperature and precipitation determines the habitability of a given area and the density of its population.

Above the lowest cultural levels two features of the environment assume great importance. The one is the distribution of the natural resources. As soon as mankind began to mine and refine metallic ores and to weld the metals thus derived into useful forms, the areas where these ores are concentrated became densely populated even where the adjoining soil is not very fertile. In similar fashion the areas in which are concentrated coal, and more recently mineral oil, have also become densely populated, largely because these fuels are used in the reduction or fusing of metallic ores, and more recently also because they are used in generating steam power.

The other feature of the environment which in course of time assumed great importance was the existence of navigable water. With the invention of the boat and especially of the sea-going ship towns and cities began to arise at harbors along the coast. Water highways became established from port to port and also along navigable rivers. These water routes became important means of communication. They increased greatly the facility of trade because water transportation is usually less expensive than land transportation. Maritime and riverine trade also has been an important factor for the diffusion of culture.

Assuming the more or less uniform human biological and psychological factors and the widely varying ecological factors we come to the cultural factors which also vary widely. Among them are the various forms of social organization and of social control and the institutions which have evolved. In studying them we have to take into account their extent and duration in order to distinguish between those which have been evanescent or intermittent and limited in extent and those which have been widespread and more or less permanent.

We also have to consider the social processes which have operated in the course of cultural evolution. Among them are invention and diffusion, the division of labor or occupational specialization, technological change, the accumulation of scientific knowledge, the selection and survival of institutions and of forms of organization and of control, conservation and revolution.

At the opposite extreme from the institution of slavery described in the preceding chapter is the nobility or the upper free class which when endogamous forms a caste. This class probably arose through extra-tribal amalgamation or through intra-tribal differentiation. In the first case the members of a conquering tribe became a hereditary privileged class as against the members of the conquered tribe who were relegated to the status of an inferior if not servile class. The conquering tribe often was a nomadic and war-like tribe of herdsmen which invaded a sessile agricultural population of peasants. According to Oppenheimer: "The peasant is attached to his ground . . . , yields to subjection, and pays tribute to his conqueror, that is the genesis of the land states of the old world. . . . In the new world . . . the hunter is the conqueror of the peasant." He asserted that the first land state was founded about 1800 B.C. by a nomad people which ruled Egypt from the 15th to the 18th dynasty. "The incursion of the Hyksos, whereby for over five hundred years Egypt was subject to the shepherd tribes of the eastern and northern deserts . . . is the first authenticated foundation of a state." [1] The Hyksos probably did not rule Egypt more than two centuries. They may have been a mixture of several nomadic peoples. About the same time in the 18th century B.C. the Kassites, a warlike tribe of eastern mountaineers invaded Babylonia and ruled it for several centuries.

Oppenheimer, writing more than half a century before the present treatise, did not have the benefit of later researches. In Chapters XX, XXI and XXII we have seen that the state must have antedated 1800 B.C. by many centuries. There were city states in Mesopotamia and in Egypt several centuries at least prior to 3000 B.C. Written records were kept by the Babylonians and the Egyptians earlier than 3000 B.C. Prior to that date there may have been national states in Egypt and possibly also in Mesopotamia. Soon after the middle of the third millennium B..c, Sargon the Elder, king of Sumer and Akkad, established an empire which probably extended from the Euphrates to the Mediterranean. About 2500 B.C. a culture was flourishing in the Indus valley with what were at least city states at Mohenjodaro, Harappa and probably at other sites. The code of Hammurabi, king of Babylonia, formulated about 1700 B.C., reflects many centuries of political and legal development. Mena (or Menes) was king of upper and lower Egypt about 3100 B.C. The pyramids at Giza of the kings Khufu (whom the Greeks called Cheops), Khafra and Menkaura were built about 2800 to 2700 B.C. It is certain that not only city states but also national states of considerable territory existed more than a millennium before the Hyksos shepherds invaded Egypt and established a dynasty.

More than two millennia later when the Teutonic tribes were

[1] Franz Oppenheimer, *The State, Its History and Development Viewed Sociologically*, Indianapolis, 1914, (first appeared in German in 1908), pp. 52, 63.

410

invading the Roman empire some of the Germanic warriors who had been common freemen at home became nobles in the former Roman empire because as conquerors they became the possessors of landed estates which had belonged to the former Roman nobles. In fact, the distinguishing trait of the nobility has usually been the ownership of much land.

Nobility arose through intra-tribal amalgamation mainly as a consequence of the accumulation of wealth in the hands of a few. Inheritable property is the most secure basis for the permanence of privileged classes. Transition from one class to another has usually been difficult and sometimes impossible. Occasionally an individual through heroism in warfare, prowess in hunting, or through some other form of achievement, has succeeded in hoisting himself from a lower into an upper class. But these individual achievements are not inheritable so that they do not assure the position of his descendants in the upper class. It is secured by property, especially by real property the title to which is rendered inalienable by laws of entail which restrict the inheritance of land to particular individuals or to a particular class. In many places laws of primogeniture have limited the inheritance of land and of titles to eldest sons thus conserving great estates and making the noble class relatively small and exclusive.

Nobility may have originated also through extra-tribal amalgamation. In the long run, however, more of it has probably resulted from intra-tribal differentiation. This has consisted mainly in the accumulation of wealth in the hands of a few individuals and families. With this wealth the noble class has been able to live in better dwellings, wear better and sometimes distinctive clothing, eat superior food, and have various outward distinguishing class insignia such as distinctive head dresses and coiffures, colors, tattooing, sunshades, elongated ear lobes, long finger nails, bound feet, the latter of which indicate freedom from manual labor. The noble gentleman often has the privilege of a plurality of wives. While the noble class often is endogamous, the noble gentleman may take a lower class woman as concubine if not as wife. In medieval Europe the feudal lord had "le droit du seigneur" or right to deflower the virgins of his fiefdom, usually at the time of their marriage. The noble class usually has its characteristic ceremonial observances. It may even speak a distinctive language. It may be protected by taboos which give to it a semi-sacrosanct status.

Wherever slavery is prevalent the noble gentleman owns many slaves who are to him as so many sheep or cattle. Under feudalism the feudal lord has his serfs at his command. Even where slavery and serfdom do not exist, the wealth of the noble class enables it to employ numerous servants. So that the noble class is always freed largely

411

or entirely from labor, especially from manual labor. The appropriate pursuits of the noble gentleman are warfare, hunting, and sports which usually simulate warfare. His freedom from labor breeds in him a contempt for labor, especially for manual labor. Corresponding to this contempt for labor is the servile attitude of the lower classes which have had the slave psychology instilled into them. This psychology reconciles these classes to their humble status. Awed by the old and distinguished ancestry of the noble class and its visible prestige, this servile attitude is an almost insuperable obstacle to revolt. Until very recent times rare have been the attempts on the part of the lower classes to deprive the upper classes of their privileges. The present writer said to a London cockney lift boy: "How would you like to be a lord?" "Oh, I'd like it very much, sir," he replied with a servile grin, "but since I can't be a lord, I wish I were the friend of a lord."

The nobility has always played a preponderant part, or at least a part far out of proportion to its numbers, in government. In the Roman republic most of the senators and higher magistrates came from the *nobilitas* or patrician families which usually owned large estates. In fact, most of the republics of which we have an historical record were ruled by an hereditary aristocracy or oligarchy. The history of government is very largely a record of the alternation between monarchical and oligarchical rule. Sometimes a single family, usually of the nobility, has gained control and its head has been the king and has transmitted his authority to his heir. Such a concentration of power in one individual and family is likely to arouse a certain amount of rivalry and jealousy on the part of the other noble families. While royalty and nobility have a common interest in maintaining their inherited privileges they may become competitors and sometimes enemies over the question of the division of power. Consequently, republic has replaced monarchy and vice versa in a good many countries.

A few of the republics of ancient and of modern times are listed as follows:

List of Republics

Carthage	B.C.	850-146
Greek city states		700-146
Rome		539-29
Venice	A.D.	600-1796
Genoa		1000-1802
Lombard free cities		1183-1530
German free cities (including the Hanseatic League)		1241-1630
Switzerland		1291-
Netherlands		1609-1805

412

United States of America	1776-
France, Republic I	1792-1804
Republic II	1848-1852
Republic III	1871-
Latin-American republics at various dates beginning with	1810-
China	1911-
Russia	1917-
Germany and Austria	1918-
Finland, Esthonia, Poland, Latvia, Lithuania, Turkey, at various dates beginning with	1918-

Until modern times the franchise or suffrage in republics was usually if not invariably in the hands of a small minority. Slaves were invariably excluded. The same was true of serfs bound to the soil. The city republics which controlled any adjoining territory or more distant colonies did not usually grant the right to vote to its neighboring or colonial inhabitants. Even within the republic itself property qualifications often limited the franchise considerably.

The suffrage has usually been a function of citizenship. There has, however, been much variation as to the proportion of a given population included as citizens. Citizenship arose originally out of membership in a greater family, clan or tribe. In other words, a varying degree of blood relationship was the unifying bond between the citizens of a given state or nation. However, this bond became too weak to be effective when the state or nation attained considerable size. Eventually citizenship became a territorial instead of a personal concept. In other words, persons became citizens in the first instance because they were born or lived within the territory of a nation. By means of naturalization they can transfer their citizenship from one nation to another. In Rome citizenship was first restricted to the patrician class and later extended to the plebcians. Territorial citizenship arrived fully with the *Constitutio antoniana* of A.D. 212 which extended citizenship to the whole Roman empire. In Athens the reforms of Solon in the 6th century B.C. abolished distinctions of birth but distinguished four classes of citizens on the basis of property. "The modern concept of citizenship, as inherited by the territorial and national state from the ancient and medieval municipality, represents a combination of two elements. One of them is the notion of liberty derived from ancient moral philosophy and medieval rights of personal status, while the other is the concept of membership in a political unit, involving cooperation in public decisions as a right and sharing of public burdens, chiefly military service and taxation, as a duty. . . . As shown by the terminology of common and inter-

413

national law, another important source of citizenship is the allegiance of a vassal seeking the protection of a feudal lord." [2]

In both Rome and Athens the suffrage was a function of the citizenship of all adult males. The same concept prevailed among the Germanic peoples of the early Middle Ages. In their folkmoots or tribal assemblies all male adult members of the tribe had a vote. In Renaissance Italy also the suffrage was a function of citizenship, though the latter was often narrowly limited and sometimes was hereditary in certain families, so as to form an oligarchy in control of a republic. In the socially stratified society of the later Middle Ages the right of the vote was often attached to a special status, usually the ownership of land or a specified income. In England male adult suffrage did not become widespread until the nineteenth century. The same was true in the United States where in the middle of the twentieth century the poll tax in several states made the suffrage dependent upon the ability and willingness to pay this tax.

There have been several concepts as to the nature and basis of the suffrage or as to its justification. Two of these concepts have already been mentioned. They are the suffrage as a function of citizenship and the franchise as a privilege usually based on the ownership of land. The first concept has usually prevailed wherever citizenship has been widespread or universal. The second concept has invariably prevailed wherever a small oligarchic and aristocratic class has ruled as under feudalism. Until modern times these two concepts have been the only ones which have been effective.

That all human beings are born equal and should have the rights of citizenship and of the suffrage is an old theory. However, it had no practical effect until the French Revolution and other modern revolutions. Even then it was paid only lip service in the main. The female sex was almost entirely excluded from the suffrage until after the beginning of the twentieth century. This was in accordance with what has usually been the position of women. As we have seen in the preceding chapter, women have been dominated by men mainly owing to their inferior physical strength and to their disabilities arising out of child bearing. Schroeder has suggested that male dominance has been due in part to the ascendancy of man in phallic worship, owing to his visible sex organs, and to the habitually recumbent position of woman beneath man in coition.[3] The distinction between men and women is biological and not social in origin. Class lines which are social often cut across sex lines which are bio-

2 Carl Brinkmann, in the *Encyclopedia of the Social Sciences*, Volume 3, 1930, page 471.

3 T. Schroeder, "Psycho-Genetics of Androcratic Evolution," in the *Psychoanalytic Review*, Vol. II, No. 3, July 1915, pp. 277-285.

414

logical. The suppression of a class is usually associated with some suppression of the female sex. So that women's rights are more or less bound up with human rights in general. Women have almost invariably had fewer educational advantages and economic opportunities than men.

There have, however, been some variations in women's rights which were not necessarily associated with variations in the rights of the lower classes. For example, in Babylonia women had some rights which were very rare until modern times. "It is a remarkable fact that Hammurabi's code and later Babylonian regulations gave to married women more rights than they have enjoyed in many civilized countries almost until our own time. Wives were allowed to engage in business, to appear as witnesses, and, in certain cases, to hold and dispose of property. They were still subordinate to their fathers and husbands, but the old patriarchal authority was on the wane." [4]

In ancient Egypt also women seem to have had a comparatively large amount of freedom. "The status of women was even higher in Egypt than in Babylonia. They had full rights of ownership and bequest, could engage in business on their own account, and in sexual matters enjoyed much liberty. The many surviving love songs indicate that women wooed men as often as men wooed women; in these songs, indeed, the 'sister' speaks out more frequently than the 'brother.'" This freedom seems to have been correlated with, if it did not arise out of, a social system which was not as stratified as it was at that time in Babylonia and later in India. "Egypt had no caste system such as developed in India and no such marked social divisions between freemen as were found in Babylonia. Moreover, the number of slaves seems never to have been great, and the role of slavery as an industrial system was comparatively insignificant at all periods of Egyptian history." [5] The relatively free position of Egyptian women may have been due partly to the fact that the metronymic family was predominant so that children took their mother's name and property was inherited in the female line of descent.

In China since the beginning of Chinese civilization, some four to five millennia ago, the greater family, somewhat like a clan, has apparently been the basis of social organization. The family is patronymic. Until marriage a daughter is subject to her father. Upon marriage she becomes subject to her husband and is taken to live in his paternal home, where she is to a large extent ruled by her mother-in-law. If she becomes a widow, she is subject to her eldest son. Within the home, however, the women are more or less autono-

[4] Hutton Webster, *History of Civilization*, Boston, 1947, Vol. I, page 135.
[5] H. Webster, *op. cit.*, Vol. I, pages 158-9 and 157.

mous. The traditional Chinese social system was divided among the scholars, farmers, artisans, and traders. The officials were selected from among the scholars. The civil service examinations were open to all persons regardless of class. There was no hereditary noble class with a few exceptions such as the descendants of Confucius. Chinese life was more egalitarian than in most ancient civilizations.[6]

During the second millennium B.C. a people who spoke an Indo-European language were migrating into India from the northwest. Their women seem to have ranked relatively high. "The family had a patriarchal organization. Women held a high position, much higher than in later times. Neither the practice of child marriage nor the custom of 'suttee,' requiring a widow to immolate herself on the funeral pyre of her husband, was followed in the Vedic Age. An elected chief ruled each tribe and led it in war. There was a priesthood, but without the exclusive privilege afterward enjoyed by Brahmans. There were social classes, but no real castes."[7]

A similar development took place in Greece. In Homeric society at about the beginning of the first millennium B.C. women ranked fairly high and were not kept secluded as they were later in certain parts of Greece. In fact, the society described in the Homeric "Iliad" and "Odyssey" resembled the Indo-Aryan society described in the "Rig-Veda." Later the position of Greek women degenerated. This was particularly striking when Athens was at its apogee. "Women did not share in this social life. Until her marriage, usually at an early age, an Athenian girl lived a virtual prisoner. . . . Women had few legal rights, for their divorces, as well as their marriages, were arranged by their male relatives, and they could not in their own persons inherit property. Their education was neglected, usually including nothing more than instruction in household management. This inferior position of women at Athens affords a marked contrast to the refinement of life and manners among the men."[8]

In early Roman society women were much subjected to men. "The wife had few, if any, rights as against her husband: he could chastise her, divorce her, or put her to death for unfaithfulness. . . . Upon her husband's death she and her unmarried daughters came under the authority of a son or the next nearest male relative of the husband. . . . This patriarchal system, with its subordination of wife and children to the family head, has been found in different parts of the world, but among no other people was it carried to such lengths

[6] Cf. Maurice Parmelee, *Oriental and Occidental Culture*, New York, 1928, for social organization and the position of women in China, India and Japan. See especially chapters VI, VII and VIII.

[7] H. Webster, *op. cit.*, Vol. I, page 105.

[8] H. Webster, *op. cit.*, Vol. I, page 224.

as among the early Romans." Later this rigorous system was some-what tempered both by custom and by law, at least for the women of the more affluent groups. "During late republican times and under the empire women of the upper classes were often highly educated." [9]

Christianity did not improve the position of women. "As Christianity became dominant throughout Europe, women were deprived of that freedom which they had attained in Rome and had enjoyed to some degree under Anglo-Saxon law. . . . Canon law institutionalized male dominance reflecting the influence of the strongly patriarchal family law of the Old Testament and of Germanic law." [10] As for the chivalry under medieval feudalism in Europe, which was a sort of christianization of knighthood because it made the knight a "soldier of Christ," it introduced a form of gallantry toward upper class women which was in effect a romantic degradation of women in general. The chivalric knights continued to despise and oppress the lower classes which were under the yoke of feudalism.

In another book I have discussed the part played by Christianity in the history of the Occident. Its influence in general is summed up in the following two paragraphs:

"The preceding description reveals the attributes of Christianity which have rendered it one of the most aggressive, intolerant, and domineering of religions, and which explain its long history of persecuting unbelievers, its religious wars, its Inquisition and its Crusades, and its extensive proselytizing activities, some of which have been carried on with the aid of the mailed fist. These attributes are its jealous and ambitious deity, its belief in a peculiarly Christian character which is superior to human nature in general and which is incarnated in the partially (or totally) mythical figure of Jesus, its cut-and-dried formula for salvation than which there is no other way to be saved, and its grotesque and wholly unscientific conception of evil. Every religion grows out of and is part of a complex of economic, political, and social factors and conditions. The intrinsic character of Christianity has harmonized well with the commercial greed and the political imperialism of the Occident, as will presently be indicated.

"Needless to say, there have been and are other aspects of Christianity which some of its apologists eagerly push to the fore in order to cover up what has been described. The Christian mystic, like all mystics, is absorbed in his autosuggestively and hypnotically induced inner vision. The gentler and less aggressive believer is attracted by its more amiable tenets and engages in charitable deeds. The more

[9] H. Webster, op. cit., Vol. I, pages 263-4, 307.

[10] B. J. Stern, in the Encyclopedia of the Social Sciences, Vol. 15, 1934, page 444.

thoughtful adherent is appalled and shocked by the gross inconsistency of its ethical dualism and endeavors to smooth it away, often by means of casuistry. Thus it is argued that while God is responsible for the possibility of evil, he has given man free will so that the individual is responsible for choosing evil rather than good. But these phases of Christianity have had comparatively little influence upon missionary work, which is due almost entirely to the attributes described above. These belligerent attributes constitute the main body of historical Christianity and have had the most influence in the affairs of mankind." [11]

With respect to the effect of Christianity upon women in particular I said in the same book:

"In so far as woman has acquired greater freedom in the West, it has been due not to Christianity but to social and intellectual evolution. The economic changes of the last century or two have increased her independence greatly. Science has discovered effective contraceptive measures which enable her to control procreation and thus to eliminate the danger of unwanted pregnancies. By such means is a single standard of sex freedom being gradually approximated in the Occident, and only in a similar fashion can it be attained in the Orient as well. Until that time comes the double standard will be openly recognized and applied." [12]

In his treatise on the evolution of moral ideas Westermarck has described how in the Roman empire marriage was on a contractual basis, thus giving married women considerable personal liberty. He indicated how the Christian doctrine with respect to women destroyed this liberty in large part. (See *Ephesians,* v. 22 *sqq.* and 28; I Peter, iii, 5 *sqq.*; I Corinthians, xi, 8 *sqq.*; I Timothy, ii, 11 *sqq.*) He asserted that the influence of this doctrine has persisted to the present day:

"It is difficult to exaggerate the influence exercised by a doctrine, so agreeable to the selfishness of men, and so readily lending itself to be used as a sacred weapon against almost any attempt to extend the rights of married women, as was this dictum of St. Paul's. . . . And in more modern times Christian orthodoxy has constantly been opposed to the doctrine which once sprang up in pagan Rome and is nowadays supported by a steadily growing number of enlightened men and women, that marriage should be a contract on the footing of perfect equality between husband and wife." [13]

[11] Maurice Parmelee, *Oriental and Occidental Culture*, New York, 1928, pages 236-7.

[12] Maurice Parmelee, *op. cit.*, page 166.

[13] E. Westermarck, *The Origin and Development of the Moral Ideas*, London, 1906, Vol. I, pages 654-5.

The extensive economic, political and social changes of the 19th and 20th centuries prepared the way for an increase of women's rights and freedom much more than any ethical, humanitarian, philosophical or religious concepts, theories or doctrines, however ancient some of them may be. This increase was indicated by and to a certain extent culminated in the extension of the suffrage to women in many states and countries. Wyoming Territory adopted woman suffrage in 1868, and the states of Colorado, Utah and Idaho during the decade following 1890. Finland adopted it in 1906, Norway in 1913, Denmark in 1915, and Sweden in 1921. Russia adopted it immediately after the Soviet Revolution in 1917, and Germany immediately after the end of the war in 1918. The United States adopted it by an amendment of the Federal Constitution in 1920. England adopted it fully in 1928. The Chinese soviet republic adopted it in 1931. Other countries which adopted it after the close of the European War of 1914 to 1918 are Australia, New Zealand, Canada, Mexico and Brazil. Since the close of the World War of 1939 to 1945 it has been adopted by France, Japan, and certain of the Balkan states. It seems probable that before long the right of women to vote and thereby to become almost full-fledged citizens will be widely recognized.

Another extension of the suffrage to both men and women which has already been introduced in the Soviet Union is the lowering of the voting age from 21 to 18. Advocates of this change for men argue that because men usually become eligible for military service at 18 they should also be granted full rights of citizenship. Another agrument for both men and women is that by the age of 18 they should have formed opinions on public questions which enable them to vote intelligently. The argument that there should be no taxation without representation through voting is not so pertinent in this connection because in many jurisdictions taxation, as, for example, of income or inheritances, may begin at a much lower age than 18 when the citizen is not yet able to vote intelligently. But the extension of the rights of citizens without racial, religious, property or any other kind of discrimination is becoming more widespread the world over.

The extension of the political rights of citizenship is one phase of the breaking down of class dominance. It has not been accompanied by a corresponding degree of breakdown of economic dominance. This is readily apparent when the criteria of class are considered. The principal criterion is the ownership or non-ownership of the instruments of production. Over a large part of the world the ownership of land, machinery, means of transportation such as ships and railroads, and means of communication, is still in the hands and control of a small upper class. Owing to the narrow concentration of wealth there is a marked contrast in the standard of living of the upper and the lower classes.[14] This difference gives rise to differences in the psychological and cultural traits of the classes which in turn cause varying ideologies of class. The control of schools and of the press by the upper class enables this class to mould and determine to a large extent the ideology of the lower classes. These classes are likely unwittingly to use such political rights as they have acquired in the interest of the upper class. While labor, the original and principal factor of production, is nominally free in most jurisdictions, because chattel slavery has largely disappeared, the laborer often is unable to produce and to promote his own welfare because the opportunity to do so is under the control of the owners of land and of capital. Unless he has this freedom of opportunity, his political rights of citizenship and of the suffrage are of little value to him. The awareness of this lack of freedom has aroused the laboring class from time to time to rebel and to struggle against the domination of the upper class. This is the class which appears obscurely and inadequately described in the pages of history.

More than a century ago in their "Communist Manifesto" Marx and Engels asserted: "The history of all society that has existed hitherto is the history of class struggles." [15] With the scanty historical data available it is not easy to determine to what extent this assertion is justified. In earlier chapters I have mentioned a few references in the literature of the ancient empires, such as Babylonia and Egypt, to the misery of the exploited classes and expressions of pity for them. But these classes were illiterate and had no means of expressing themselves. They had no way of rebelling collectively against exploitation and individual resistance was of no avail. There was probably little overt struggle on the part of the working class prior to modern times. As I have indicated in the preceding chapter, class struggle in the past has usually been among the upper and privileged classes and not between them and the working class.

The Jewish law was modelled largely upon the Babylonian law. For the Hebrews the chief rule of punishment was the *lex talionis* (eye for an eye and tooth for a tooth). It sanctioned slavery and discriminated against women. It contains no suggestion whatsoever of social justice or of a humanitarian outlook upon mankind. On the contrary, it often commands war and vengeance in the spirit and on behalf of its jealous and vengeful tribal deity—Yahweh. There are numerous exhortations to piety and an occasional one to charity. In

---

[14] For ample evidence of the concentration of wealth in the United States, see Maurice Parmelee, *Poverty and Social Progress*, New York, 1916; and *Farewell to Poverty*, New York, 1935.

[15] Karl Marx and Friedrich Engels, *The Communist Manifesto*, London, 1847, translated from the German.

Leviticus written *ca.* 5th century B.C. the pious Jew is admonished in Chapter 25 to relieve "thy brother who is poor," and to "Take no usury from him, or increase": by which is meant no interest on money loaned to a fellow tribesman. But *Deuteronomy* (written *ca.* B.C. 625) in Chapter 23 after repeating the admonition not to "lend upon usury to thy brother;" adds that "Unto a stranger thou mayest lend upon usury." In Chapter 25 of *Leviticus* the Jew is urged to buy "heathen" bondmen and bondmaids. Elaborate provisions are made for the redemption of Jews who were enslaved for debt or for some other reason. In "jubilee" years some of these native slaves may be freed entirely. In Chapter 24 of *Deuteronomy* the Jew is instructed that "Thou shalt not oppress an hired servant that is poor and needy. . . . At his day thou shalt give him his hire, neither shall the sun go down upon it."

Many of the apologists for Judaism and Christianity have alleged that the so-called "prophets" conceived a rather high standard of social justice. For this claim there is not the slightest shred of evidence. These semi-mythical Jews were no more capable of foretelling the future than any other human beings. The confused collections of writings which have been brought together under their names consist of hodgepodges of myth, history, piety, denunciation of enemies, vengeance, bombastic visions of future greatness for Israel, with a very rare and casual mention of the widespread oppression of the poor. For example, the 3rd and 4th chapters of *Amos* rebuke those "who store up violence and robbers in their palaces" and who oppress the poor and needy but does not indicate who are the poor and needy. *Micah*, in the 1st and 2nd chapters, is more specific in that it denounces the taking of fields by violence and is apparently referring to landgrabbing by princes. "Hear, I pray you, O heads of Jacob and ye princes of the house of Israel. . . . Who hate the good and love the evil. . . . And they covet fields and take them by violence; and houses and take them away." Both of these "prophets" are attributed to the 8th century B.C.

Israel was for a large part of its career as an independent nation a theocratic state or combination of states in which the priests ruled. The Jewish tribal god, Yahweh, demanded their exclusive worship when neighboring nations worshiped many gods. The legendary hope of a messiah (the anointed) who would achieve political domination of the world rendered the Jews intolerant of other peoples as well as exclusive (the chosen people). Their kings, when monarchy prevailed, were priests or under priestly domination. The Jews were not touched at all by Greek influence until near the close of their independent existence when Palestine became an integral part of and was completely absorbed in the Roman empire during the 1st century of the Christian era. Consequently, they had no knowledge whatsoever of the theories of the natural rights of men uttered by Plato, Aristotle, Zeno the Stoic, and other Greek thinkers. They were also untouched by the beginnings of science among the Greeks. The Jews formed a small tribal unit on a narrow strip of the eastern Mediterranean coast who never played a significant part in history. Their subsequent prominence was due to the fact that the form of neo-Judaism known as Christianity spread over the whole of the Occidental world for reasons which were wholly fortuitous so far as the Jews themselves were concerned. Their culture was derived in large part from the empires and nations of much higher culture which surrounded them, such as Egypt, Babylonia, Assyria, the Hittite empire, and Phenicia. At one time and another they were conquered and ruled temporarily by Egypt, Babylonia, Assyria, and Persia. The Hebrew culture amalgamated the Babylonian world outlook and the Egyptian social outlook with the Yahweh cult of western Semitic peoples.[16] The Egyptian social outlook included class status, the inferiority of labor, poverty as a static condition with no social amelioration or justice whatsoever. The Babylonian culture included the same features but probably had a somewhat broader outlook because it was less isolated geographically than Egypt. This amalgamation was dominated by the Jewish priestly class.[17] Under the ancient theocracy this sacerdotal plutocracy exploited the peasants and the urban poor with little or no restraint in accordance with the Oriental pattern of upper class domination. Though this did not put an end entirely to priestly exploitation, Rome terminated the existence of Israel as a national state until it was revived in the 20th century A.D. with a very different outlook upon the world.

[16] Hamburger has traced the evolution of the law of equity through Sumerian, Babylonian, Mosaic-Hebrew (probably derived from Babylonian) , Greek, Roman, to modern law. (Max Hamburger, "Equitable Law," *Social Research*, December 1950, pp. 441-460.)

See also Hamburger, *The Awakening of Western Legal Thought*, London, 1942; Fritz Schultz, *History of Roman Legal Science*, London, 1946; Huntington Cairns, *Legal Philosophy from Plato to Hegel*, Baltimore, 1949.

[17] See Ralph Turner, *The Great Cultural Traditions, The Foundations of Civilization*, New York, 1941, Vol. I, especially pages 214 and 343-6.

Chapter XXVII

Social Stratification

THE pattern of the ancient Oriental culture arising in the urban centers included a hierarchy of social classes, a marked differentiation of the literate intellectual tradition and ideology from the illiterate intellectual tradition and ideology, and the concentration of the ownership and control of the gradually increasing economic surplus in the hands of the relatively small upper classes. This was the most important feature of the pattern in the long run. During the first age of imperialism there was opposition to the centralized imperial authority by conquered rulers and ruling classes and occasional rebellion against it by them after each conquest which was sometimes successful. This was not class conflict or a phase of the class struggle because the rebels were no less despotic and predatory than their conquerors, only less fortunate.

An illustration of civil war which was not a part of the class struggle occurred in Egypt under Amenhotep IV who reigned about 1375-58 B.C. This monarch conceived an overweening admiration for the solar god Ra or Aton (or Aten) and changed his name to Ikhnaton (or Akhenaten). He moved the capital from Thebes to Akhetaton, the modern Tell-el-Amarna, and tried to suppress the priests of other gods, especially of the chief god Amon (or Amen.) His religion was for the aristocracy and not for the common people. He was as theocratic as the priests and apparently had no conception of social justice. He has often been given unmerited praise as the inventor of monotheism. This form of religion does not foster humanitarianism and social justice unless it encourages the concept of the unity of nature. As compared with polytheism, it has often caused an excessive degree of intolerance as in the cases of the Semitic religions— Judaism, Christianity and Islam. Ikhnaton lost much of the territory of Egypt perhaps because of the civil strife. After his death the capital was moved back to Thebes and the priests won. He was succeeded one after the other by two sons-in-law of no historical significance, the latter of whom, Tutankhamen, is now remembered solely because his tomb, when excavated in 1922-24 yielded a rich harvest of furniture and *objets d'art,* which had been overlooked by grave robbers for 3250 years.

This ancient cultural pattern evolved mainly in Egypt and Mesopotamia. The Egyptian record begins at least as far back as 3000 B.C. It continued more or less continuously to evolve for three millennia before being greatly modified by Greek and Roman influences. Egyptian culture had probably greater internal stability than its Mesopotamian counterpart because it was more isolated from the remainder of the world.

The Mesopotamian record is prehistoric prior to 3500 B.C. The early Sumerian culture began before 3000 B.C. and continued until about 2500 B.C. It was absorbed among other dynasties by the Akkadian dynasty, the Gutium dynasty, the third Ur dynasty, the Isin and Larsa dynasties, and the first dynasty of Babylon which lasted from about 2150 to 1740 B.C. The Kassite dynasty ruled from about 1740 to 1150 B.C. Then followed the Assyrian domination and the new Babylonian empire until Cyrus the Persian conquered Babylon in 539 B.C.

In the first Persian empire, the successor of the Babylonian and Assyrian empires, under the Achaemenian dynasty (*ca.* 559-330 B.C.), the Persians treated conquered peoples, such as the Jews, as slaves. Under the domination of the king-emperor as overlord, the satraps ruled the provinces autocratically. Under the Parthian empire (B.C. 250-224 A.D.), which for a time was the chief rival of the Roman empire, feudalism was prevalent under the Iranian landed nobility. In the later Persian empire, under the Sassanian dynasty (A.D. 226-651), which conquered Parthia, the satraps ruled the provinces, a caste system was widespread, and the priestly hierarchy and feudal lords supported the dynasty and exploited the common people.

The history of this dynasty records a rebellion against this sort of rule. Mazdak (*ca.* A.D. 470-530), who was chief priest at Nishapur, proclaimed himself a prophet. He preached the equality of man, the abolition of private property rights, free love, vegetarianism and the simple life. Apparently he had some conception of social justice. Whether it was original with him or derived from a Greek or Roman writer is not known. He converted King Kavadh I who was imprisoned by the nobles who feared the impact of these strange, new ideas upon their privileges. Kavadh escaped and regained his throne. But his crown prince, who became Chosroes I and reigned from A.D. 531 to 579, executed Mazdak and thousands of his followers, thus putting an end to their abortive revolution which was primarily a revolt against the exploitation of peasants by the Persian feudal lords.

The early economic pattern of villages in Mesopotamia and elsewhere usually was that the land belonged communally or individually to the peasants who actually cultivated it. Agriculture probably originated in several, perhaps many, parts of the world. According to Peake, one of its places of origin was in or near Syria from whence it spread to Egypt, Mesopotamia, Asia Minor, Persia, and the Indus basin.[1] The village community is a permanent agricultural settlement which has been observed in many parts of the world. It existed in China at least as far back as the 3rd millennium B.C., and in India since the Vedic period. In Europe it was prevalent among Slavonic peoples and to a certain extent among Teutonic folk.

The village community was often on a kinship basis with one or more greater family or clan. Sometimes it was tribally organized on a patrilineal basis under a tribal chief or headman. The community usually had common pastures which could be used by all of its members. The arable land was divided into strips or fields which were either rotated in use to all the inhabitants or were individually owned by the members. The community has varied in many other respects. But it has at all times been a permanent agricultural community which was able to maintain itself and usually to produce a surplus of agricultural products to exchange for commodities which it was unable to produce.

In course of time, however, the village community came under the domination of individuals, groups, or classes outside of itself. For example, about the middle of the 3d millennium B.C. equestrian pastoral peoples from the steppes between the Dnieper River and the Hindu Kush mountains invaded many agricultural areas in Asia Minor, Mesopotamia, Persia, and India, and made themselves the lords of the indigenous peasant population from whom they wrested tribute. These invasions may have been due to insufficient pasturage in their original habitat. The desire for loot also doubtless played a part. The imposition of foreign rule as one of the origins of the state has been discussed in an earlier chapter. However, such domination came often, probably in the majority of cases, from within. In earlier chapters on the origins of the state and of the social classes I have described some of the methods and processes by which this domination came into being. The most effective and far-reaching of these methods and processes have been those which have given an upper class a virtual monopoly of the economic surplus. One of these methods has been taxation.

In the ancient world tax liability was usually a mark of some degree of bondage. Often it was the obligation to perform services which was complete for chattel slaves and in varying degrees for serf

[1] Harold J. E. Peake, *The Origins of Agriculture,* London, 1928.

and bond servants. Sometimes it was in the form of fees, charges and levies to be paid in commodities at irregular intervals. Gradually these compulsory contributions became periodic. With the invention of metallic currency about the 9th or 8th century B.C. these contributions could be more readily standardized. In Periclean Athens (5th century B.C.) taxes were imposed mainly on slaves and foreigners. Under feudalism and monarchy they have invariably been levied with little regard for equity upon the poor and helpless while the well-to-do have escaped. They have, therefore, formed one of the most effective methods of "grinding the faces of the poor." Many of these poor fell into slavery owing to inability to pay their taxes, just as many of them became slaves because they were unable to pay their debts to individuals. Only very gradually did there emerge the social ideas and ideals of justice and equity to change in a measure the basis of taxation. Only very recently have they had any appreciable effect. And they have not yet molded the tax structure in many parts of the world.

There are at least three ideas or principles as to equitable taxation. The first is that the revenue from taxation should be used for the public welfare, not for the benefit of the upper classes or certain favored individuals. The second is that taxes should be adjusted to ability to pay. The third is that taxes should be commensurate in large part to the material income which the tax payer derives from the society to which he belongs. In other words, if the income which society enables or permits him to acquire is large his tax should be correspondingly large.

The first principle is not always easy to apply because there may be difference of opinion as to what form of expenditure of public revenue is most suitable for the public welfare. A graduated income tax is best adapted for applying the second and third principles. Most indirect taxes, such as a salt tax, are most unsuitable because they are equally onerous upon both rich and poor. A fourth principle of equitable taxation, which may prove to be as important as the first three principles in the long run, is that it shall prevent great inequality in the distribution of wealth. A graduated income tax can have considerable effect toward this end. The most effective tax for this purpose is a heavily graduated inheritance tax which is asymptotic to 100 percent for large accumulations of wealth, thereby preventing the inheritance of great fortunes.

In the ancient world property in land, whether individually or communally owned, at first arose out of or was based upon actual cultivation of it by the peasant villagers themselves. The increase in capital goods caused an increased production which in turn led to a larger economic surplus. There arose a struggle for this surplus which was only in part a struggle between the upper and lower classes. Among the contestants and rival claimants were monarchs, feudal lords, priests, and military chieftains, all of whom belonged to the ruling classes. Not least among these rivals were the owners of these capital goods or capitalists. They had acquired this ownership either by manufacturing these capital goods or by purchase or exchange. Having control of these valuable means of production they could levy a tribute for their use in the form of rent. As land also came into their possession they could collect rent for its use. Or they could purchase slaves or employ wage laborers to utilize the tools, crude machinery of that day, means of transportation, and other forms of capital, to produce manufactured goods for barter or sale. The traders with means of transportation at their command were able to distribute and sell these commodities. Thus arose business enterprise which has dominated the economic scene until modern times. The profits from such enterprise have created the fortunes of the past and present. A wealthy as distinguished from a poor class could not have come into existence otherwise. Monarchs, feudal lords, priests, and soldiers could not have brought this class into being because they do not create wealth. However, as the retainers of the capitalists, manufacturers, merchants, and later, after the invention of money, of the bankers and financiers, they have protected their patrons while these patrons were engaged in their acquisitory and predatory pursuits. These retainers have been amply rewarded in the overflow from the coffers of the rich.

There has been difference of opinion among historians and economists as to the nature and time of origin of capitalism. Sombart, the German economist, asserted that early capitalism lasted from the 13th century A.D. to the middle of the 18th century, full capitalism from 1750 to 1914, and late capitalism since 1914. He excluded capitalism from ancient and early medieval times. He described capitalism somewhat abstractly as follows: "In systems dominated by the idea of acquisition the aim of all economic activity is not referred back to the living person. An abstraction, the stock of material things, occupies the center of the economic stage; an increase of possessions is basic to all economic activity." "Since the guiding principle of capitalism is gain, there is production only if prices yield profit, if they offer to the individual enterprise the prospect of economic success."[2]

In another book I have described the basic similarities between medieval and modern capitalism and their ancient prototypes.

"Capitalism is not entirely unlike systems which have preceded

[2] Werner Sombart, article on "Capitalism" in the *Encyclopedia of the Social Sciences*, Vol. 3, 1937.

it. Private ownership of the means of production existed under feudalism and many earlier systems. Private business enterprise has existed in commerce ever since markets came into being. To a much smaller degree it characterized production prior to the capitalist era. Private profits have always accompanied business enterprise and have constituted its object and justification.

"Modern capitalism differs from the earlier economic systems in degree more than in kind. Its efflorescence was due to the coming of the machine age, rendering possible private enterprise on a large scale. In the earlier handicraft system the workman usually owned his tools. While these constituted a primitive form of capital, his status was much more that of a laborer than it was that of a capitalist. His income was almost exclusively payment for his labor and services. To that extent it constituted wages. But ownership of his means of production gave him a small degree of independence similar to that of the capitalist."[3]

Whatever the name given to this process, it has been more or less the same since neolithic times. It is the competition for the excess of commodities produced over the minimum required for a bare subsistence. It has been the main factor in creating the stratification of status or of class. Where status prevails, as in a caste system, there is little or no social mobility. In a class system there is some mobility. In the ancient world the stratification was largely of status. The slaves, whether of the field, gang, or domestic variety, were in the vise of a virtually immutable status. The peasants were often bound to the soil which they could not leave. The craftsmen were often born into their crafts and could choose no other craft than the one inherited from the preceding generation.

It has been thought that the so-called guilds of craftsmen in the ancient world indicated some independence of action and freedom of choice which made these guilds analogous to modern trade unions. In Babylonia and Assyria these guilds were apparently associations of merchants whose social position was very different from that of the craftsman. Later in Greece there were associations of traders and also of craftsmen for social, religious, and economic ends. During the Hellenistic period there arose an extensive organization of trade and industry in western Asia and Egypt. Some of this organization was under governmental supervision. In Rome there arose professional corporations, especially under the empire. In late Rome and Byzantine times the guilds became compulsory public service corporations in the 4th century A.D. They were called *corpora* in Rome and Byzan-

---

[3] Maurice Parmelee, *Farewell to Poverty*, New York, 1935, pages 57-58. See Part I entitled "A Critique of Capitalism" and Chapter V entitled "The Economic Theory of Capitalism."

tium and *collegia* in the provinces. All merchants and craftsmen were members of these guilds. Their members, known as *corporati* and *collegiati,* were descendants of former members so that the guilds constituted hereditary castes. Slaves could not be members of guilds but could be owned by guilds. The emperor controlled the guilds through the prefects and other public officials.

The main purpose of this state control was to insure food and other necessities for the population of the empire. For this purpose the services and property of the members of the guilds were at the disposal of the state. However, this did not mean state socialism. After the members of a guild fulfilled their public duties, they could and did work for private gain. However onerous their public duties may have been, the monopolies possessed by their guilds upon their occupations were greatly to their advantage because they were protected from competition from outside. After the division of the empire in 395 A.D. and the capture of Rome in 410 A.D. by Alaric the Visigoth the guilds disappeared almost entirely in the west. In the Byzantine empire they gradually lost their hereditary character and the property of the members was no longer subject to public service. During the three to four millennia from early Babylonia to the end of the eastern Roman empire in 1453 there is no evidence that the guilds conducted any collective bargaining in behalf of wage-workers or engineered a strike. They were usually and mainly organizations to aid the business enterprises of their members who were craftsmen of various sorts, merchants, shipowners, bankers, and other urban inhabitants, but usually not farmers and other rural dwellers.

Among the upper and ruling classes were the kings and royal families, nobles, landlords, merchants and other business men, and the retainers of the ruling classes, such as priests, scribes, and soldiers. At times some of these retainers, such as priests and soldiers, were able to seize power and become rulers. Some of the Roman emperors began their careers as common soldiers. As recently as the 20th century A.D. common soldiers have become kings and dictators, as, for example, in Germany, Italy, Spain, Iran and Albania. A striking comparison between ancient Rome and modern England reveals that after more than 2,000 years an hereditary nobility was still the ruling class:

"A modern investigator reports that in the hundred and twenty-five years preceding the first Labour government of 1924, of the three hundred and six men reaching cabinet rank, one hundred and eighty-two, or sixty percent, were hereditary titled aristocrats. So in Rome. . . . In something under two hundred years down into the second century before Christ, Mommsen has listed sixteen Roman families that furnished one hundred and forty of the two hundred patrician

429

nobles who attained consular rank. . . . In both England and Rome it was necessary for the nobles to dominate the popular legislative bodies. In each case the foundation of power, as has been suggested, was social prestige."[4]

The same likeness exists between ancient and modern times in the means used by the ruling classes to secure and maintain power. Among these means is the theory that government is of divine origin. This may be expressed in the belief that the ruler, whether king or dictator, is of divine origin or at least has received his power and authority from a divine source. Thus the king of England and many other 20th century rulers have ruled by the "grace of God" as they and their retainers have pretended. The representatives of religion have sedulously maintained this fiction. They portray a deity ruling in the spirit world of whose divine sway mundane government is supposed to be a copy. Christian hymnology furnishes many pictures of this divine ruler and war chief, as illustrated in the following bit of sacred doggerel:[5]

> Let thrones and powers and kingdoms be
> Obedient, mighty God, to Thee!
> And, over land and stream and main,
> Wave Thou the scepter of Thy reign!

In England the State Church, the Church of England, owns a vast amount of land and other property from which it derives a large income in rents and dividends, in addition to the contributions received from its adherents. The head of this church, the Archbishop of Canterbury, ranks next to the royal family. His position corresponds to that of the Pope of Rome, though he may not be quite so powerful. But whether state churches or not, all religion organized in churches, with very few exceptions, supports the established power and authority, regardless of its nature. The cardinal rule of the church in its relation to government is the biblical injunction in the New Testament: "Render therefore unto Caesar the things which are Caesar's, and unto God the things which are God's."[6] Furthermore, the general effect of all religion, whether organized or not, is to encourage a subservient acceptance of established authority, regardless of its nature. This is because religion postulates a belief in a

---

[4] H. J. Haskell, *This Was Cicero: Modern Politics in a Roman Toga*, New York, 1942.

[5] See Maurice Parmelee, *Oriental and Occidental Culture, An Interpretation*, New York, 1928. In Chapter XIII, entitled "The Missionary Invasion of the East," I have given similar examples of sacred doggerel which portray the divine belligerent and militant traits.

430

spiritual power, more or less personal and therefore anthropomorphic in its character, which is a prototype of earthly government. Mankind has yet to accept the ineluctable facts that it is existing for only an instant of eternity upon an infinitesimal speck of an infinite universe which is wholly indifferent to its insignificant fate. If and when these facts are generally recognized, men will no longer believe the fables that a "beneficent Providence rules" and that a "good God provides," and leave matters to a mythical deity, but will judge impartially and rationally the established authorities and will make such changes as seem desirable.[7]

Other institutions and means by which the ruling classes have maintained their power both in ancient and modern times are the law, police power, military agency, official bureaucracy, taxation, religious and patriotic liturgical and ceremonial observances, controlled learning or scholarship, and propaganda. A large part of the law has always been devoted to safeguarding the rights of private property. The police and military agencies are used to suppress any attempt to rebel against the ruling classes. The bureaucrats are the servile retainers of the rulers. Taxation is often used to shift the distribution of wealth in favor of the upper classes. Liturgies and rites such as baptism, the sacrament, ordination, inauguration, coronation, flag ceremonies, and the like, are often used to arouse the enthusiasm of the populace for wars, colonial and imperialist expeditions, and other ventures which are injurious to the lower classes, however profitable they may be for the upper classes. By means of a discriminatory patronage the schools and the scholarship of the learned are controlled in the interest of the ruling classes. Propaganda of all sorts has been used from ancient times until the 20th century A.D. when almost all of the newspapers are under the control of big business. An instructive comparison has been made between propaganda at the birth of the Roman empire and in the 20th century. It concerns the struggle for power between Octavian (B.C. 63-14 A.D.), the grand-nephew of Julius Caesar, later known as Augustus and Princeps, who is now regarded as the first Roman emperor because he reigned from B.C. 31 to 14 A.D., and his former ally and chief rival Mark Antony (83-30 B.C.).

"The manner in which nations were roused to war and the

---

[6] *St Matthew*, 22:21. See also *St. Mark*, 12:17, *St. Luke*, 20:25.

[7] The United States Senate and House of Representatives employ chaplains to open their sessions with prayer. On October 6, 1949, the Senate chaplain supplicated his deity as follows: "O God, . . . Save us from the fatal folly of attempting to rely upon our own strength. In a world so uncertain about many things we are sure of no light but Thine, no refuge but in Thee." (*Congressional Record*, Vol. 95, No. 186.)

methods by which they prosecuted it in the first century before Christ differed very little from the twentieth century of our era. . . . Public opinion had to be won, and every sort of intrigue was to be used if there was any chance of its success. Spies, bribery, scurrility, personal attacks, foreign and domestic alliance, the dissemination of handbills in the enemy's camp, promising rewards or defaming the foe, the falsification or suppression of reports from the front, all bulk large in the politics of the civil war that consumed the republic and created the empire phoenix-like, from the ashes."[8]

In Chapter XXII on the first age of imperialism are briefly described the Hittites who ruled over much of Asia Minor and Syria between the years 2000 and 1200 B.C. In fact, they probably ranked next to the Egyptians and the Babylonians and Assyrians in the power which they wielded. Their ancestors apparently came from the north. It seems probable that the intrusive ancestors of the Hittites became so completely amalgamated with the much larger autochthonous population as to lose their original physical ethnic traits. In so far as their language has been deciphered, it seems to have been Indo-European in origin. They wrote it with a pictographic script which they may have derived from the Babylonians from whom they borrowed much of their culture.

About B.C. 1800 the Hittite kingdom extended to the Mediterranean Sea. They made invasions of Syria, southern Armenia, and Mesopotamia. About 1550 B.C. they overthrew the Babylonian dynasty to which Hammurabi had belonged. About B.C. 1385 they established an empire which lasted for two centuries. For a time it was the most powerful kingdom in the Near East. They also formed a confederation which did not last very long. Finally they succumbed to the rising power of the Assyrians. A well known encyclopedia offers the following questionable explanation for the fall of the Hittite empire: "The rise and fall of their empire follows a familiar pattern: in the early period the Hittites were nomadic and aggressively militant, but in the later period wealth and luxury sapped their strength and they became weak and corrupt. . . . There is good evidence that they maintained close relations with other peoples of Asia Minor, at times heading confederacies."[9] This moralistic explanation is no more satisfactory an explanation for the fall of the Hittite empire than it is for the fall a millennium and a half later of the western Roman empire, or, for that matter, of any empire at any time.

The records and archives discovered in 1906-1907 near the modern

[8] Kenneth Scott, "The Political Propaganda of 44-30 B.C.," in the *Memoirs of the American Academy in Rome*, Vol. XI, 1933.

[9] *Encyclopedia Americana*, Vol. 14, 1948.

village of Boghazkeui in Anatolia in the ruins of the ancient city of Hattushash, which was at one time the capital of the Hittite kingdom, indicate that the Hittites had a strict military and political organization with many detailed regulations. They had a code regulating prices which indicates that their commerce was well developed. Their punitive law was not as severe as the law of the Babylonians, the Assyrians, and the Hebrews. The Old Testament often mentioned them as the "children of Heth" and usually with animosity. It alleged that the Lord made the following covenant with Abraham: "In the same day the Lord made a covenant with Abram, saying, Unto thy seed have I given this land, from the river of Egypt unto the great river, the Euphrates." (*Genesis,* 15:18. Written *ca.* B.C. 850). In the next three verses are enumerated many peoples who are to be dispossessed including the Hittites. Later the Hebrews were ordered by their tribal deity to destroy these peoples: "And when the Lord thy God shall deliver them before thee, thou shalt smite them, and utterly destroy them; thou shalt make no covenant with them, nor shew mercy unto them." (*Deuteronomy,* 7:2. Written *ca.* B.C. 625.) But the Lord failed to aid them to carry out these genocidal designs. This was one of the numerous vainglorious assertions by the Hebrews, not unlike many statements made by other peoples. Biblical scholarship indicates that Hebrew history, which is mainly fictitious, as recorded in *Genesis,* and the re-writing of Hebrew law in *Deuteronomy,* were intended to convey the impression that Hebrew prowess had caused the downfall of the mighty Hittite empire. The Hebrews had little or nothing to do with this downfall. The Hittite empire was apparently a federation of different peoples dominated by the Hittite king of Hattushash. It may have been weakened by invasions of tribes from the west and north. At any rate, its records ceased about B.C. 1200 after which Assyria became the dominant power in that region.

For several thousand years prior to the discovery of America in the 15th century A.D. cultural evolution in the western hemisphere was independent of the eastern hemisphere. "Because of their isolation the American Indians had to work out for themselves many practical arts and inventions. Their tools and weapons were of polished stone, copper, and, among the Aztecs and Incas, occasionally of bronze. The use of iron was unknown to them. They cultivated maize, or Indian corn, from Canada in the north to Patagonia in the south; its importance in their economy was comparable to that of rice among the Chinese or of wheat among Occidental peoples. They had the common dog, which they brought with them from Asia, the turkey, the guinea pig, and, in South America, the llama and the alpaca, but no other domesticated animals. The majority of them lived in clans and tribes, ruled by headmen and chiefs; some of them formed tribal confederations; and the Aztecs and Incas established real states."[10]

Whether or not the Aztecs and Incas formed "real states," as Webster alleges, depends upon how we define a state. The most highly developed culture in pre-Columbian America was probably the Mayan culture in Central America, Yucatan and southern Mexico. The earliest identified date corresponds to 291 B.C. At first there were large cities in Central America, later in Yucatan and southern Mexico. The archeological remains include temples, pyramids, altars, paved roads, and palaces which may have been the residences of priests and nobles. About the year A.D. 1000 three cities near the tip of the Yucatan peninsula—Mayapan near the present city of Merida, Uxmal and Chichen Itza—formed a confederation. These three cities apparently ruled the Mayan territory for a time. Then it broke up into divisions under chiefs who were often fighting with each other. This warfare weakened the Mayans to such a degree that they were easily conquered by the Spaniards between the years A.D. 1527 and 1547.

The Mayan pictographic script has not been fully deciphered as yet, so that little is known as to their social and political organization. Like the other inhabitants of the Western Hemisphere they were apparently still in the tribal stage of cultural evolution. The monumental structures, such as pyramids and temples, suggest that the chiefs and priests had sufficient authority to force large numbers of the population to labor on the construction of these edifices. The Mayas apparently came from the north. The earliest identified date mentioned above was on a monument in what is now the Mexican state of Vera Cruz. In this fertile region of middle America a large population arose in which the usual phenomena of class dominance and stratification made their appearance.

After the Mayan tribes there came from the north tribes of the Nahuatlan linguistic family. The earliest probably were the Toltecs who left some monuments such as the great pyramid of Cholula near Puebla and the pyramids of Teotihuacan near Mexico City. They seem to have been influenced somewhat by the Mayan culture. The Toltecs controlled the central plateau of Mexico for several centuries. They were conquered by other tribes from the north. The last was the Aztec tribe which was composed of 20 clans. Each clan had a representative in a supreme council of 20 members. The tribe had a dual executive one of which was civil and the other was military and religious. The rank of military chief, who was also a priest, became hereditary in one family in about the year 1375. In about 1325 A.D. the Aztecs built a city called Tenochtitlan on a lake near what is

10 Hutton Webster, *History of Civilization*, Boston, 1947, Vol. I. page 75.

now Mexico City. With two other tribes they formed a confederation in which they were dominant. Their war chief commanded the confederate army and their war god was regarded as superior to the gods of the conquered tribes. For about a century this confederation dominated an extensive territory between the Gulf of Mexico and the Pacific Ocean. In 1521 A.D. a Spanish army under Hernando Cortez captured Tenochtitlan and substituted Spanish for Aztec rule. A few years later the Spaniards conquered the Mayans and extended their rule over the whole of Mexico and Central America.

Aztec social organization was apparently feudal in its character. The nobles paid no taxes but rendered military service. The freemen had to serve as warriors under their lords. Prisoners of war were enslaved. Many of them were slaughtered as sacrifices to the Aztec gods. Some of them were eaten. Many criminal offenders were enslaved, also children who were sold by their parents. Marital infidelity and remaining unmarried were punished by the man becoming a serf and the woman a prostitute. These traits indicate the militant character of Aztec society. Their war chief Montezuma (or Moctezuma) came the nearest to being an "emperor," as he has sometimes been called.

South of the Isthmus of Panama the most advanced culture was that of the Incas whose territory extended along the Pacific coast from Ecuador to Chile. Their name applied at first only to the ruling family. "All authority centered in the Inca ruler, who as the son of the sun god enjoyed reverence akin to worship. Politically he was an emperor and religiously, a god. The purity of the divine blood was preserved by his marriage with his sister. Through his officials he distributed the arable land and its produce among the people in accordance with their needs. There was no individual ownership of land; a peasant could neither sell nor bequeath his holding. The Inca's officials likewise saw to it that every person lived in a fixed district, followed a definite occupation, and did a proper share of the work. Those who refused to perform their allotted tasks were severely punished. Unemployment was nonexistent, for the idle population could always be kept busy on roads, aqueducts, fortifications, and other useful enterprises. An all-powerful state, in conjunction with a state church, thus constantly supervised and controlled the activities of its members. One result of this regimentation was social security. The aged and the infirm were cared for, want and misery were unknown. Another result was a habit of passive obedience and a lack of initiative which prevented any determined resistance to the Spanish invaders."[11]

[11] Hutton Webster, *op. cit.*, Vol. I, page 82. See also Philip A. Means, *Ancient Civilizations of the Andes*, New York, 1931; and *Fall of the Inca Empire*, New York, 1932.

The Inca social organization has often been called state socialism. It is obvious that it resembled modern socialism scarcely at all,
partly because it was not democratic in any sense of the word. The
tribal deity was the sun god whose chief priest was an official of high
rank, often a brother of the Inca who was himself a sacrosanct ruler
of absolute authority. The governors of the provinces were hereditary
chiefs. The lower officials were drawn from a few families. The boys
of these prominent families were trained for official positions at the
capital which was near the modern city of Cuzco in Peru. The government was in effect an hierarchical oligarchy of these families with
the Inca at its head. This ruling caste was supported by the products
of land reserved for this purpose. The remaining land was apportioned for cultivation to the peasants. All products were property of
the state. Taxes were paid in manufactured goods. There was also
tribute in the form of work on public enterprises or service in the
army. There was no money and very little trade, all of which was
in the form of barter.

It is probable that the Inca rule was imposed upon the clans and
tribes of that part of South America by a conquering tribe. The
legendary accounts of this conquest prevalent among the natives are
not to be trusted. The indications are that social processes were taking
place in the western hemisphere similar to those in the eastern
hemisphere, but two to three or more millennia later. There is no
evidence that these social phenomena in the west were derived from
or influenced by similar phenomena in the east, so that all of the
western culture was indigenous. Practically all of the migration from
the eastern into the western hemisphere was by way of the Bering
Strait. These migrants were in the paleolithic, or at most in the lower
neolithic stage of cultural evolution. Over most of the western hemisphere they evolved a culture no higher than the lower neolithic in
pre-Columbian days. A few Polynesians may have drifted across the
Pacific Ocean but brought with them no higher a stage of culture.

There are practically no historical records of pre-Columbian
America. The Mayans and the Aztecs had only a pictographic script.
The Inca people had no script whatsoever. The scanty data are derived from the silent testimony of the archeological remains, the traditions of the natives,, and the more or less inaccurate descriptions of
the predatory Spanish invaders and *conquistadores*. There were movements of population from areas with scanty food to more fertile areas.
This probably explains the successive invasions of middle America
from the north. The invaders did not have the horse to aid them in
these invasions. They did not have the sheep and the ox to enable
them to lead a nomadic, pastoral life. In a few cases an invading tribe
succeeded in imposing itself upon the tribes which it had attacked or

436

upon which it had encroached. In this fashion social strata of the conquerors and the conquered came into being. This was the situation in the Aztec territory. It was probably also what had happened in the Mayan and Inca territories.

These autochthonous American peoples developed agriculture. Maize was their principal cultivated plant from which much of their food was derived. The Aztecs and Incas lived on temperate highlands. The Mayas inhabited damp lowlands which perhaps explains why the southern cities such as Copan, Quirigua and Palenque were deserted even though monumental structures had been built there. None of these peoples used iron and the Mayas did not have copper. The only pack-animal was the camel-like llama in Peru. The sheep-like alpaca and the llama were the only domesticated wool-bearing animals. The plow, the potter's wheel, and wheeled vehicles had not been invented. The true arch with a keystone was unknown, but the corbelled arch of overlapping stones was used. No alphabet or syllabary was invented in the western hemisphere. The Mayas and the Aztecs made some discoveries in arithmetic and astronomy and devised a calendar. Such scientific knowledge was known only to the priests and the aristocrats. The Spaniards effectually destroyed all of this indigenous culture.

PART II

EMERGENCE OF MODERN CULTURE

Chapter XXVIII

The Transition from Rigid Status to Class Mobility

DURING the last three chapters the terms class or social class were somewhat loosely used to denominate a variety of human groupings. The most important division among these groups is between those whose members are bound by a status from which they can escape never or rarely ever, and those whose members can move from one group to another. The gradual transition from the rigidity of status to the mobility of class is one of the most significant aspects of social evolution.

In a condition of status there is almost no social mobility. Tribe, clan, caste, slavery, serfdom, royalty and nobility are characterized by status. All are hereditary, except in a few cases such as an elective kingship. Even nationality is inherited as a form of citizenship. It may be superseded by super- or inter-nationality or world citizenship. It is already subject to change by naturalization.

/ Class permits of more or less mobility. It is not inherited though the advantages or disadvantages of a specific class often persist from generation to generation. Ownership of wealth tends to perpetuate the membership of a family in an upper class. This has been more true of the ownership of land than of mobile wealth which may be readily dissipated. The transition from status to class has sometimes taken place in connection with the accumulation of wealth though not necessarily./Other considerations and factors have to be taken into account. However, organized industry and trade, especially on a large scale and resulting in large accumulations of individual wealth, have constituted one decisive factor.

This transition from status to class has occurred many times in history in isolated cases or to a more or less limited extent. The counter-change from class to status has rarely occurred. Until comparatively modern times the most frequent change has been from one form of status to another.

Commerce was developed on a far-reaching scale with the aid of transport by pack animals on land and by boat on the river Nile in Egypt and on the rivers Euphrates and Tigris in Mesopotamia. River transportation and agriculture on the rich alluvial soil of these river valleys were probably the two principal factors in producing the dense population and high culture of these ancient countries. The ass was domesticated by the pre-dynastic Egyptians and the Sumerians. To what extent it was used for agriculture and for transportation is uncertain. The horse did not come until later. It belonged to the Asiatic steppe culture. From thence it spread eastward into China and westward into Europe from whence it entered southwestern Asia and Africa. As a steed it was useful for nomadic horsemen for shepherding and driving their flocks and herds and for moving from place to place in search of fresh pasture. It also was useful for raiding and looting agricultural and settled communities. Later it played a decisive part in warfare as a charger or harnessed to a chariot.

It is impossible to state with certainty when the horse arrived in Mesopotamia and Egypt. The *Encyclopedia Britannica* (1942) asserts in its article on the horse that it first appeared in Babylonia about 2000 B.C., and that the Hyksos, a nomadic folk, introduced the horse when they conquered Lower Egypt in the 18th or 17th century B.C. In its article on Persia this encyclopedia asserts that about 1700 B.C. the horse appeared in Babylonia, Egypt and Greece where it was used in the war-chariot, and that the "Aryans" had already used the horse for riding. The *Encyclopedia Americana* (1948) in its article on the horse asserts that the Metropolitan Museum of Art in New York City has an Assyrian shell cylinder dating from about 4000 B.C. which shows horses and wheeled chariots in battle. The above statements sound contradictory. However, it is possible that the ass or other members of the *equidae* family, such as the onager, may have been used and depicted at an early date.

This much is fairly certain. About the middle of the 2nd millennium B.C. peoples speaking Indo-European languages moved into Anatolia, Mesopotamia, Egypt, Iran and India. They brought with them the charger and the chariot which they used in warfare. Some of their leaders established principalities and kingdoms in Mesopotamia, Syria and Palestine. The Hyksos apparently ruled much of Egypt for about two centuries. The horse appeared in Crete during the latter half of the 2nd millennium B.C. There were horse-drawn chariots in Greece about 1000 B.C.

The Indo-European Medes and Persians came into Iran about the middle of the 2nd millennium B.C. or soon after. Aided by the horse they imposed a rule of warrior minorities on the indigenous population. The Persians had a military aristocracy and a hereditary priesthood, so that their rule was based on a regime of status. The Zoroastrian religion which arose later was an expression of the interests and ideals of the Persian military aristocracy and hereditary priesthood in terms of a supernatural universe. In the 6th century B.C. the Persians created their vast empire, the greatest in extent up to that time. Their success was due in part to the effectiveness of the Persian cavalry charge. After their victory the Persian emperors, such as Cyrus (558-528 B.C.), Darius I (521-485 B.C.) and Artaxerxes I (465-425 B.C.), used the priesthoods of the conquered nations to maintain their power. However, Persian Zoroastrianism was too abstract to become the permanent popular religion. It spread mainly under the forms of Mithraism which was permeated with the more concrete folk religions, as was Christianity which arose a few centuries later.

Like many other religions Zoroastrianism included the doctrine of ethical dualism. Inasmuch as there are certain mundane and celestial conditions and factors which benefit mankind and other conditions and factors which injure human beings, it was to be expected that this doctrine would arise rather early in cultural evolution. Like many social inventions it probably arose spontaneously in several places and spread by diffusion. In its Persian expression it took the form of a belief in Ahura (Lord) Mazda (Wisdom), or Ormuzd, the power of good, who is opposed to Ahriman, the power of evil. Such a belief is likely to be used by earthly potentates to justify their usurpation of power. The rulers can claim not only divine power but righteous divine power, thus adding an ethical sanction to overt force.

During the 2nd millennium B.C. China was invaded by a people from the west which established the Chou dynasty (ca. 1122-225). The Chou ruler was the son of Heaven, which was the supreme deity, and its chief priest. The nobles also were priests so that the dominant power was a theocratic oligarchy. The Chou aristocracy maintained its power because it had a monopoly of weapons, which indeed has been true wherever there has been monocratic or oligarchical rule which has been almost everywhere. A small slave group of war captives appeared. The Chinese also developed a doctrine of ethical dualism. *Yang* means good spirits, and also sun, light, and male. *Yin* means evil spirits, and also moon, darkness, and female, *Yang* represents the positive and *yin* the negative force in human life. The ancestor cult strengthened the stability of the Chinese social system. While it was not worship in the same sense and to the same degree that heaven was worshipped, the reverence displayed toward their ancestors discouraged any divergence from ancestral customs and beliefs.

In India the hardships and sufferings of mundane existence have been ameliorated, or at least tolerated, by a widespread acceptance of mysticism. Release has been sought in meditation, loss of identity, and reincarnation. This attitude of abnegation and defeatism has encouraged social conservatism and has helped to perpetuate the caste system. As I have said in another book: "The mystic believes that he stands in a peculiarly intimate and personal relationship with the world spirit, whatever it may be called. He alleges that he has become one with this spirit, or that it is in some mysterious fashion in him. Mystics appear the world over, and are likely to belong to the psychological type which turns its imagination inward and creates a world of its own. They are unwilling to face frankly and grapple with the difficult problems of the world into which we have been unwittingly pitchforked, or perhaps they are incapable of doing so. They seek escape in a world of their own creation." [1]

Another way of escaping from the misery and evil of human life has been through the media of the intercessionary religions, such as the Hinduism of Krishna, the eighth incarnation of the great god Vishnu, the Buddhism of Amidha Buddha, one of the avatars of the Buddha, and the Neo-Judaism of Jesus, the putative savior, who professed to be the son of Jehovah. "Jesus, Krishna, and Amidha Buddha alike intercede with the chief god, whatever his name may be, to save men from the evil consequences of their conduct. It is often asserted that these likenesses are due to imitation, that Jesus was derived from Krishna, and that Buddhism became a religion of salvation by mediation through intercourse with Christianity in the region of northwestern India, Kashmir, and Afghanistan. Even though a certain amount of borrowing may have taken place, these likenesses indicate fundamental similarities of human nature." [2]

There were several of these savior gods in ancient times. The oldest of which we have any record was Tammuz who was apparently of Sumerian origin and who was also a god of the Babylonians and Assyrians. He was a propitiatory god who interceded for human beings who worshipped him. He probably interceded with Marduk the Babylonian chief deity and sun god with whom he was sometimes identified. Tammuz was the god of vegetation. He died every winter or spring and then was resurrected, thus symbolizing the annual cycle of death and revival of plant life. His wife was Ishtar, the principal Babylonian female deity, who was a goddess of war and of fertility. Legend had it that she killed her husband and then restored him to life.

Osiris was the Egyptian ruler of the dead, god of agriculture and also of health and of light. In the latter respect he rivaled Ammon or

[1] Maurice Parmelee, *Oriental and Occidental Culture, An Interpretation*, New York, 1928, page 58. See especially Chapter III, "The Religious East," and Chapter IV, "Indian Quietism and Occidental Activism," for a discussion of Indian mysticism.

[2] Maurice Parmelee, *op. cit.*, pages 52-53.

444

Ra or Ammon Ra, the Egyptian sun god. He suffered annual death and was resurrected. His wife as well as sister was Isis, the principal Egyptian goddess, who was reputed to have invented agriculture and who symbolized fertility. His death was avenged by his son Horus. The belief in and worship of Osiris may have been imported from Syria.

Adonis was a Semitic god of vegetation who experienced annual death and resurrection. His Phenician incarnation was sometimes identified with the Babylonian Tammuz. Later he was adopted by the Greeks who made him into a beautiful youth loved by Aphrodite the goddess of love, who was also the goddess of vegetation and of fertility and was identified with the Phenician Astarte and the Roman Venus.

Attis was the Phrygian god of vegetation. Like many of these gods he died and was resurrected in the spring. He was the consort of Cybele the Great Mother and goddess of fertility of Anatolia.

Mithras was the Iranian sun god who mediated between the supreme deity, Ahura Mazda or Ormuzd, and mankind. Belief in him may have originated in India where Mithra was the god of light. Mithraism was widespread throughout the Roman empire and was the principal rival of Christianity which borrowed or imitated many of the Mithraic rites. In fact, if the Emperor Constantine had not made Christianity the state church for political reasons in the 4th century A.D., Mithraism might be the dominant religion of the Occident today.

Another religion from which Christianity borrowed directly or through Mithraism was the Krishnaism of India. Krishna was the eighth incarnation of Vishnu, one of the Vedic trinity of which the other members were Brahma and Shiva. About 1200 B.C. it was already believed in India that Krishna was born of a virgin when his putative parents went to a city to pay their taxes, that angels sang at his birth, that wise men came with gifts, that it was rumored that a king was born. The local ruler, fearing that his throne would be usurped, ordered all new-born male infants to be slain. His father escaped into a foreign country where Krishna was reared by shepherds. Among his miracles were the straightening of the body of a hunch-backed woman, feeding a large crowd with a small amount of food, healing lepers, and raising the dead. At his death he ascended into heaven promising to return. All of these marvelous incidents are repeated in the Christ myth. More than a millennium before Jesus, Krishna was alleged to have taught brotherhood, justice, mercy, compassion and humility, though none of these traits have had much influence either in India or in Christendom. His character as a savior god is revealed in the Bhagavad-Gita or Song of the Adorable One which is incorporated in the Mahabharata, the war epic which was evolving as

445

early as 500 B.C. though the Bhagavad-Gita may have been incorporated somewhat later. In the eighteenth or last chapter faith in the Lord Krishna is exalted as the best method of salvation. Thus spake the Lord to his faithful disciple Arjuna: "Abandoning all duties come unto Me alone for shelter; sorrow not, I will liberate thee from all sins." In the twelfth chapter Krishna said: "They who follow this eternal law as spoken above, endued with faith and regarding Me as the highest goal and devoted, are exceedingly dear to me." Centuries later similar statements claiming a divine authority and redemptive power were attributed to the Jewish Messiah by what seems to be more than a coincidence.

The savior gods of four other religions much closer in space to Palestine than India, namely, Osiris, Attis, Adonis and Mithras, were reputed to have been born of a virgin. Their birth was set at the time of the winter solstice and the rise of the constellation Virgo, namely, the same time as the Christian Christmas. The time of their resurrection and also in some cases of their deaths was reputed to be the vernal equinox, namely, the same time as the Christian Easter. Numerous other similarities between these religions and Christianity may be noted. "In one or another of these four religions we find the derisions, the flagellation, the crying out from the place of execution, the vinegar-soaked sponge, the soldiers casting dice for the garments of the condemned man, the women at the place of execution, the grave in the rock, and the resurrection. Even the cross, which has the shape of a sword hilt, was used as a religious symbol long before the time of Christ. . . . Each new religion has been founded on one or more older religions. Abundant proof of this is to be found in 'The Golden Bough,' the result of Sir J. G. Frazer's long and intensive research into the subject." [3] In this respect religion does not differ from other phases of human culture.

Similar gods and goddesses appeared in Greece and Rome whose myths have originated in western Asia. Dionysus was a Greek god the belief in whom may have come from Phrygia or Thrace. He was originally a tree god or god of vegetation and also the god of fertility. As such he experienced periodic death and resurrection. He became specialized as the god of the vine. In Rome he was known as Bacchus who was also a law-giver and god of peace. A similar goddess was the Greek Demeter who was the goddess of agriculture and of fertility. In Rome she was called Ceres and specialized as the goddess of grain and harvests.

The dozen or more gods and goddesses which have been mentioned and briefly characterized, namely, the Sumerian-Babylonian

[3] Wallace Stockwell, *A Shield Has Two Sides, Light on the dark side of the shield*, Chicago, 1946, p. 31.

446

Tammuz and Ishtar, the Egyptian Osiris and Isis, the Phenician Adonis and Astarte, the Phrygian Attis and Cybele, the Iranian Mithras, the Indian Krishna, the Jewish Messiah, the Greco-Roman Dionysus-Bacchus, and the Greco-Roman Demeter-Ceres, represent religions which arose in space in an area stretching from the Indian sub-continent to the Mediterranean Sea, and in time from at least as far back as the 3rd and 2nd millennium B.C. to the 3rd or 4th century A.D. Many of them originated as nature deities of trees or of vegetation in general. This explains why, like plant life, they die and are born again each year. This also explains why the god or his consort symbolizes fertility.

The resurrection of the patron god is a hopeful sign for his human devotees for if plant life did not revive in the spring mankind would perish. In this sense and to this extent all of these gods were saviors of mankind because they inspired the revival of plant life. In a more special sense three gods which may originally not have been gods of vegetation, namely, the Indian Krishna, the Iranian Mithras and the Jewish Messiah were redeemers of a portion or all of mankind which obeyed their behests. Buddhism also, which originated in northern India or Nepal, furnished if not a savior god at least a kind and merciful deity in the person of one of the facets of the many-sided Buddha known in Japan as Amidha Buddha and in China as Amitabha. Along with this god, though not necessarily as his consort, went the Indian god Avalokiteshvara who was reputed to be the son of Amitabha but who became transformed into the goddess of mercy and pity known in China as Kuan-yin and in Japan as Kwannon.

Largely owing to the Indian caste system the Indian religions have never been proselytizing and militant religions. While Buddhism originated in or near India it has not been widely prevalent in that country, except from the 3rd century B.C. to the 4th century A.D., probably because it was a reaction against the caste system in the intention of its founder Gautama (ca. 563-483 B.C.). Indian Buddhism was eventually absorbed by Hinduism and Gautama deified as the Lord Buddha became the 9th incarnation of Vishnu just as Krishna had been his 8th incarnation. The later Buddhist conquests were to the east and north, principally in Burma, Siam, China and Japan.

While Krishnaism, embedded in the caste system, did not spread beyond India, it was doubtless imitated in considerable part by Mithraism and the neo-Judaism which later became known as Christianity.[4]

---

[4] "The (Mithraic) ceremonies included ablutions with holy water, a communal meal of bread and wine, and litanies to the sun—all sufficiently like the Christian sacraments to seem to Christians deliberate counterfeits, the work of devils. . . . An initiation through bodily ablutions, or baptism, supposed to regenerate the soul; a communal meal believed to produce a mystical union with a dying and reviving

The two latter religions were the principal rivals of each other in the Mediterranean region. Mithraism was probably the more widespread of the two and might have become the dominant religion of the Occident. As stated above, the decisive factor in favor of Christianity was its adoption for political reasons as the state religion by the Roman Emperor Constantine I (A.D. 272-337). Whether this made much difference in the history of the Occident is a debatable question because the two religions were much alike in their doctrines, dogmas and hierarchical organization.

All of these religions of the Mediterranean region were polytheistic as indeed are all religions everywhere, as I have said in another book: "Christianity, for all its boasted monotheism, has an inexplicable doctrine of a divine trinity in which, by means of a mysterious mathematics, three are one and one god becomes three. The Christian God has a son who himself ranks high as a deity. The angels and demons derived from Zoroastrianism and Judaism, especially Satan the arch-devil, form a host of minor deities, while human beings themselves with their immortal souls are godlike in comparison with the poor dumb beasts. Islam also has its complement of angels and good and bad jinns or genii midway between men and angels, while Mohammed and some of the saints (e.g., Ali and his sons Hassan and Husein, all of whom were martyrs) waver on the brink of godhood. In fact, no religion ever has been entirely monotheistic, and no religion can become so, because when it reaches that stage it passes over into a form of monism which is a philosophy rather than a religion." [5]

Every polytheistic system is a hierarchy. There is always a chief deity or supreme being—Shang-ti of the Chinese, Brahma of the Hindoos, Ormuzd of the Persians, Marduk of the Babylonians, Yahveh of the Jews, God of the Christians, Allah of the Moslems, Zeus of the Greeks, and Jupiter of the Romans. But this supreme being is usually or always relatively or absolutely inapproachable. This is a distressing situation for weak and insecure human beings, fearful of the many dangers of this life and of an hypothetical after-existence who crave the aid and protection of the divine powers. Hence some of these religions have evolved beliefs in lesser deities which will intercede for these hapless humans, such as Amitabha and Krishna, Mithras and Messiah. In return these saviors exact obedience to themselves and to their master deities which usually means adherence to a prescribed moral code and way of life. Needless to say, this code was

redeemer-god; and the assurance of salvation for faithful initiates: these Christian beliefs and rites were of a familiar type." (Hutton Webster, *History of Civilization*, Boston, 1947, page 332.)

[5] Maurice Parmelee, *op. cit.*, page 52.

448

determined predominantly by the interests of the ruling groups for whom the popular belief in redeemer gods was a useful means of keeping the common people and laboring class subservient to their rulers.

Some of these deities may have had human prototypes. A Nepalese or north Indian prince named Gautama may have been the origin of the Buddhist god. A Jew named Jesus with Messianic pretensions may have become the Christian god. At least four writers, namely, the English historian John M. Robertson, the German philosopher Arthur Drews, the Danish literary critic, historian and biographer Georg Brandes, and the American mathematician William Benjamin Smith, have written books to disprove the historicity of Jesus.[6] However, it is irrelevant for our purpose as to whether any of these human prototypes existed. What is significant is that these intercessionary or redemptive religions arose in large part if not entirely because the vast majority of mankind were bound in a condition of status with little or no hope for release in their mundane existence.

The above-mentioned facts concerning these redemptive cults indicate that religion has not been, and indeed could not be, a factor for releasing human beings, including most of mankind, from a rigid condition of status. On the contrary, as has repeatedly been pointed out in this treatise, religion has consistently, with very minor and insignificant exceptions, been a force for keeping most of mankind in a subservient status. It has done so by dire threats of vengeance and punishment, on the one hand, and, on the other hand, by holding forth illusory hopes of happiness either in the present mundane life or in an hypostatized future existence. What then have been the factors which have enabled a considerable part of mankind to pass from a rigid condition of status to a more flexible and mobile condition of class? Very few so far have passed into authentic democratic society where the barriers neither of status nor of class exist.

Perhaps the answer to the foregoing question is to be found in the clues suggested by a well known historian of civilization: "The development of Athens into a commercial empire, the growth of the plutocracy in the Roman Republic, the disintegration of Roman society in the 4th and 5th centuries A.D., the breakdown of feudalism

---

[6] J. M. Robertson (1856-1933), *Christianity and Mythology*, 1900, *Pagan Christs*, 1903; A. Drews (1865-1935), *Freie Religion*, 3rd edit. 1921; W. B. Smith (1850-1934), *Der vorchristliche Jesus*, 1906, *Ecce Deus*, German edit. 1911, English edit. 1912; G. Brandes (1842-1927), *The Jesus Myth*, published serially in the *Haldeman-Julius Monthly*, 1925-1926.

Jesus (Greek of Joshua, Yeshua in Hebrew), Christ (Chrestos the anointed in Greek), the Messiah (Moshiach the anointed in Hebrew). The Christian myth is the one of the many Hebrew messianic myths which happened to conquer the Occident.

and the origin of the national states, the rise of the bourgeoisie following the Commercial Revolution, that greatest of all social and economic revolutions—the Industrial Revolution of the late 18th and 19th centuries—and the growth of modern imperialism with the expansion of European civilization throughout the world are well-known examples of social and economic transformations which have produced their accompanying programs of social reform." [7]

Some writers have attempted to explain the difference in the status of the rulers and the ruled, and between the classes in a class society, by the innate differences between individuals and races.[8] This explanation is not valid in an undemocratic society where there is inequality of opportunity. If a genuinely democratic society ever comes into existence, namely, a society in which there are no differences of status, no classes, and equality of opportunity for all, it will be possible to test this explanation and determine to what extent differences of achievement are due to individual differences, or to racial differences. The principal factors for stratification according to status or class have been and are still mainly economic in character. The fundamental factor is the private ownership and inheritance of wealth. Alongside of these private owners and inheritors of wealth are their retainers and henchmen who intentionally or unwittingly perform various services for their employers which are necessary if this wealth is to be retained. Among these retainers are soldiers, policemen, bankers, lawyers, priests, magicians, bookkeepers, and numerous civilian government officials ranging from chiefs of state to tax collectors and rat catchers.

The transition from status to class, and from class to a classless democracy is caused or at least accompanied by status or class consciousness and class conflict and struggle. The transition from status to class has happened quite often and the reverse change from class to status has occurred less frequently. The transition from class to a classless democracy has not happened at all on a large scale, unless it has taken place in part in Soviet Russia and Soviet China within the 20th century. It should result in a complete disappearance of class consciousness and class conflict and struggle. How to trace and explain these transitions is not easy.

The available evidence seems to indicate that there was no wide-

[7] H. E. Barnes, "Social Reform," *Encyclopedia Americana*, Vol. 25, 1948, page 166.

[8] Among these writers were the English Francis Galton, the French R. Vacher de Lapouge, the German O. Ammon, H. Guenther and E. Fischer, and the American Madison Grant. During the World War of 1939 to 1945 the German Nazis led by A. Hitler attempted to apply these ideas by their genocidal slaughter of Poles, Russians, Jews, *et al.*

450

spread or general transition from status to class in Egypt and Mesopotamia. The fixed order of royalty, nobility, priesthood, landlord and military or soldiery on the one hand, and peasant, serf, wage slave, and chattel slave prevailed throughout ancient times and has persisted in large part down to the present day. Occasional and sporadic revolts there may have been, but no evidence of a widespread class consciousness and conflict accompanied by an ideology of class relations arising out of and accompanying such a consciousness and conflict.

Europe derived much of its early culture from Egypt and Mesopotamia, probably more from the former than from the latter. The Egyptian culture influenced Europe by way of Crete and the Egean culture which has been described in Chapter XXII. The latter culture in turn influenced the barbarian tribes which had come mainly from the north into Greece. The Minoan age in Crete was a bronze culture which began as early as B.C. 2500 and lasted at least a millennium. The Minoan rule has sometimes been called a thalassocracy because it apparently dominated the neighboring sea. The environment was favorable for navigation with plenty of sunlight and fair winds. Along the lengthy coasts of the surrounding waters were numerous indentations suitable as ports and places of refuge. An extensive trade flourished in the eastern Mediterranean and Egean seas. The Cretan script has not yet been deciphered so that little is known about the Cretan language which apparently was not Indo-European. Consequently, not much is known of the origin of the Minoan culture.

About the year 1600 B.C. there arose on the mainland of Greece a culture known as the Mycenaean. Two of its principal centers were at Mycenae and Tiryns in the Peloponnesus. The Mycenaean age probably lasted at least 400 years. Whether its culture was indigenous or brought there by invaders from the north or elsewhere is uncertain. It was doubtless influenced by the Egean culture of which indeed it formed or became a part. A characteristic feature of the Mycenaean culture was the fortress (*acropolis*) on an eminence around which grew up a village or town. The fortress belonged to a hereditary warrior nobility and dominated the neighboring peasants. When near the sea coast it was apparently sometimes a center of piracy. Thus the acropolis became the center of the Greek city (*polis*) which was born in an atmosphere of warfare.

In the Mycenaean society there was usually a chieftain (*basileus*) who was a sort of hereditary or elective king chosen by the warrior nobility. He was also the chief priest. The subject orders of society included the peasants, craftsmen, hired men, and slaves. Later, perhaps after the Mycenaean age, the early monarchy disappeared in most of the Greek states. It was succeeded by an oligarchy of the nobles whose claim to govern was based on birth and land ownership. There was a council (*boulē*) of nobles which elected a magistrate (*archon*) for a limited term. This archon was similar to the consul of the Roman republic several centuries later.

The Minoan age and the Cretan thalassocracy may have been destroyed by the descendants of Cretan colonists in the Peloponnesus who attacked their ancestral land. The Mycenaean age may have been terminated by an Achaean invasion from the north. The Homeric epics seem to be describing the rule of Achaean chieftains. The Achaean invasion came during or at the end of the Mycenaean age. It was followed by the Dorian invasion (*ca.* B.C. 1200-1150) from the north which terminated the Achaean rule and established a military caste of rulers which made the natives their serfs.

Migrations and invasions have been common features of the life of mankind. There were Celtic invasions of Galatia in Asia Minor and later of Gaul and of Britain. Migration is often due to pressure of population and the consequent search for food. It is always due to the search for better living conditions. When the invasion is by a nomadic people it may consist only of plundering raids on land and sea. When it is by a people in search of a permanent home it is likely if successful to lead to a caste system, or at least to superior and inferior groups on a basis of status. During periods of migration and invasion economic, social and political conditions are unsettled. In a settled world the cultivation of the soil is likely to improve and more or less peaceful trade to flourish.

Greece is not very fertile. Only about one-fifth of its soil is arable. It was formerly more fertile. Its present aridity is due to the fact that its forests were cut down which caused the springs to dry up. Thessaly in the north is more fertile than the remainder of Greece. The Ionian, Achaean and Dorian migrants may have invaded Greece because the lands from which they came were even less fertile than Greece. This seems doubtful, especially with regard to the migrants from Asia Minor. It is perhaps more likely that these invaders were attracted by the wealth accumulated by the Minoan and later by the Mycenaean age. Whatever the reasons may have been, these invasions led gradually to the close of these ages, if indeed they did not actually cause their end. At any rate they led to a period of more or less disorder. During the preceding ages there had been a good deal of peaceful trade in the Egean area. During the period of disorder there was a good deal of piracy. Also the Phenician traders began to penetrate into this area. Later they were to found Carthage in northern Africa in the 9th century B.C. and reach the western Mediterranean.

Egean including Hellenic trade revived in the 8th century B.C.

452

During the 7th and 6th centuries it was stimulated by the invention of coinage in Lydia. Partly owing to this revival of trade came Greek colonization to the west mainly in Italy and Sicily, and to the east along the shores of the Hellespont, Propontis, and the Euxine. The other principal cause probably was the growth of population in Greece itself. The Greek colonies were usually independent of the mother country. In this respect they were not like the later Roman colonies and the colonies of modern times. The only exceptions were the Athenian colonies during the imperial period of Athens about to be mentioned.

The Dorian invaders of Greece were originally mountaineers whose form of government was primarily aristocratic. Their principal representatives were the Spartans who dominated Laconia in the southern Peloponnesus. They subjugated the native population and made them helots or serfs. The Ionian invaders were dwellers of the seacoast. Many of them were traders and accustomed to maritime travel. Their principal representatives were the Athenians of Attica in southeastern Greece. While their form of government was primarily aristocratic, they developed a limited type of democracy. However slight this was, it had some significance with respect to the transition from status to class. Sparta became a military aristocracy. Athens was for a short time in the 5th and 4th centuries B.C., not more than a century, an imperialist aristocracy. Both of these states exploited the economic surplus produced by the lower classes so that both of them in reality were timocracies. In fact, all the Greek states, like practically all states down to the present day, failed to solve the problem of organizing the production and distribution of wealth so that all their inhabitants as well as citizens could share in it freely.

The Greek states, however, were not theocracies. In the monarchical period the kings and also the nobles were priests in the sense that they performed religious rites and were the official media between the gods and the people. Later the priests were hierophants in the sense that they showed or explained the religious rites and administered the temples. There were also no sacred writings. This is not to say that the Greeks were not religious. They had an elaborate pantheon of gods and believed in the intervention of these divinities in the affairs of men. However, the absence of sacred writings, and of a powerful priesthood with vested interests permitted a little more freedom of thought on the part of the more intellectual and better educated of the population. It was also less easy for the oligarchs and timocrats to use religious means to impose their will upon the people.

The earliest glimmerings of the concept of social justice probably came in Greece. In the 8th century B.C. the Bœotian didactic poet Hesiod, in his "Works and Days" criticized plutocracy and the ex-

453

ploitation of labor. However, he did not advocate any far-reaching changes in social organization. His writings were devoted mainly to describing the work of the farmer and to exhorting the peasant to be industrious and do his duty, so that they were not at all revolutionary.

The extension of Greek trade over a large part of the Mediterranean and Euxine accompanying the expansion of Greek colonies resulted in a commercial class. This class joined in a somewhat incongruous union with the landless peasant or serf and poor landholder to oppose the dominant landed aristocracy. Many of the peasants and small landholders were heavily indebted to the landed aristocracy. Some of them had become enslaved because of their debts. Many of them could not pay the rent demanded by their landlords.

During the 7th century B.C. Athens was ruled by the Eupatridae or nobles who represented the landed aristocracy. In about 594 B.C. Solon (ca. 638-558 B.C.) became archon or chief magistrate, a position similar to that of a king though not hereditary. Owing to the pressure from the landless peasants and merchants he abolished the Attic law of debt through loans on the security of the debtor's person. He restored to freedom those who had been enslaved for debt. On the other hand, he refused the demand for the division of the land. He established an oligarchy or hierarchy of the landed proprietors by dividing them into four classes according to wealth and income. He also created a council of four hundred (boulē) which may have prepared the way for a small amount of democracy. His regime was predominantly timocratic in character. But he had to yield a little in what was perhaps the first class conflict in Greece if not in the world.

Solon's rule was followed by that of the tyrant Peisistratus (ca. 605-527 B.C.) who ruled Athens from B.C. 541-527. He was succeeded by two sons who brought his tyranny into disrepute. The Peisistradae were examples of the tyrants who arose in various Greek states in the 7th and 6th centuries. They were unconstitutional and illegitimate rulers in the sense that they had seized power without any previous social sanction or recognition. Tyranny was usually an expression of more or less popular discontent of some sort. The tyrant was, therefore, ordinarily the champion of an economic or political, national or racial cause. Tyranny in ancient Greece was something like Caesarism in Rome, despotism in medieval Italy, and dictatorship in modern times. It helped to break down the power of hereditary aristocracy and to this extent encouraged democracy, though it was often followed by oligarchy based on wealth and land ownership. The tyrants also usually fostered the popular cults, and thereby rendered religion more democratic. They may also have served to break down the barriers between the Greek city states, most of which were small.

454

Partly owing to the expansion of trade mentioned above and the wealth resulting from it came the great cultural efflorescence in Greece during the 5th and 4th centuries B.C. However, in the 6th and 5th centuries B.C. there was unemployment due perhaps to the competition between free and slave labor. This was one of the many indications that the Greeks had not solved the problem of organizing the production and distribution of wealth so that all of the rather limited number of citizens, to say nothing of the much larger number of inhabitants, could share in it more or less according to need. Their failure was no greater than that of all nations down to the present day, even the highly industrialized nations in which want often exists in the midst of plenty. Then as now only a few had the leisure to follow intellectual pursuits either because they were wealthy or because they were the retainers of and patronized by the wealthy. The most famous members of this small group were Plato the philosopher and Aristotle the scientist whose views on political organization reflect in a measure the current thinking on this subject.

Plato (*ca.* 428-348 B.C.) came of a wealthy and distinguished Athenian family. During his youth he was a disciple of the philosopher Socrates (469-399 B.C.) who was much concerned with ethical questions. After a certain amount of travel he established a school of philosophy at Athens known as the Academy. His political opinions were expressed mainly in his "Republic." He regarded an aristocracy of birth as the "rule of the best" and therefore the most preferable. A timocracy or rule by the wealthy was his next choice. He did not object to a military state if under a certain amount of civilian control. He regarded an oligarchy of plutocrats as evil, even though he did not object to a timocracy. This was a distinction in name more than in fact. The plutocrat had usually acquired his wealth by the vulgar pursuit of trade while the timocrat had ordinarily inherited his wealth. He denounced democracy as the rule of the rabble. A tyranny he considered the worst form of rule. In other words, he was for domination by the upper classes while the lower classes were to be subjected to their rule.

Aristotle (384-322 B.C.) was the son of a physician who was connected for a time with the court of the Macedonian king. For 20 years (367-347 B.C.) he was a disciple of Plato at the Academy. For 12 years (347-335 B.C.) he was at the Macedonian court where he is reputed to have been the tutor of Alexander. During the latter part of his life he conducted a school at Athens known as the Lyceum (335-322 B.C.). He examined the constitutions of many Greek states and arrived at certain conclusions. He favored a royalty provided there was a good monarch, a hazardous supposition. He also favored an aristocracy. He seems, however, to have considered a constitutional democracy which included all of the citizens, who were in Greece a minor portion of the inhabitants, as the best form of government. He disapproved of an oligarchy and a tyranny. Like Plato and most ancient thinkers and writers, he approved of slavery. While he did not ignore economic problems completely, as did Plato, he paid little attention to them like most ancient writers.

What then was the Greek democracy, to what extent if any did it cause a transition from status to class, and what significance if any did it have for modern political development? Greek citizenship was usually acquired and transmitted by birth. The so-called Law of Pericles restricted the franchise to Athenian descent on both sides. Often there was an additional property qualification. The Greek city-states were small compared with nation-states. They usually had not more than 10,000 to 20,000 citizens and sometimes even less. Outside of the citizens was a larger number including the inhabitants who could not fulfil the birth and property requirements for citizenship, the foreigners, and lowest of all the slaves who had no rights whatsoever. Ancient democracy was therefore limited by the privileges of birth and wealth whereas modern democracy implies and sometimes exemplifies no such restrictions. The assembly (*ecclesia*) governed directly and not through representatives. This was feasible with a limited number of citizens many of whom living in the rural portion of the state could not or would not attend. There were at first no distinctions between the legislative and the executive functions of government both of which were performed collectively by the assembly or by some of its members. There was no organized party system. There was also no civil service. It is possible, however, that the generals (*strategoi*) and the wealthy citizens had an undue influence in the assembly. In the 5th century B.C. the general (*strategos*) Pericles (*ca.* 490-429 B.C.) was the leading Athenian statesman. Under such conditions a stratocratic despotism or oligarchy may readily be established by the military leaders. The rise of democracy often causes a decline of military efficiency. Consequently, soldiers are likely to favor monocratic or oligarchic rule of some sort. This may be a monarchy which is virtually under the control of the military men or a stratocracy—despotic or oligarchic in character. The two often merge into each other. Many victorious generals became Roman emperors. Perhaps the majority of royal dynasties have descended from military conquerors.

During the 5th and 4th centuries B.C. certain important changes took place in Greek or at least in Athenian democracy. The lot was substituted for election to public office. This eliminated the influence of wealth and military prestige but did not necessarily result in more efficient public officials. The property qualifications for citizenship were abolished. It became customary to pay public officials for their services which rendered it possible for poor persons to hold public office. Partly for this reason there arose a group of professional politicians which played an important role in public affairs. Indeed by the 4th century the generals had largely reverted to their only appropriate and legitimate role as professional soldiers while the statesmen were being drawn from the ranks of the professional politicians.

The foregoing brief description demonstrates that ancient democracy and oligarchy differed from each other only in form and degree and not in kind. Oligarchy was based usually on land ownership and wealth. Admission to the democratic society was based on birth and often also on property qualifications. Most of the unskilled and much of the skilled labor was slave labor which had no political or any other human rights. Manual labor was regarded as degrading as indeed is more or less true in every class society. The limited number of citizens managed the state and were sometimes paid to do so. Within these narrow limits there was so-called "pure" democracy in the sense that the citizens present at a meeting of the assembly decided directly and at first hand some or all matters of state.

A certain amount of representative government developed in the leagues or federations of Greek states which arose from time to time. They probably originated in the amphictyony which was an association of neighboring communities around the shrine of a god. It existed for carrying on in common religious rites and festivals and had little or no political significance. Such was the Delian amphictyony on the Egean island of Delos in the 7th century B.C. and later. Such also was the Delphic amphictyony at Delphi a few miles north of the Corinthian gulf. Just after the Persian wars in 478 B.C. was established the Delian league which in the 5th and 4th centuries was a political confederacy of offense and defense. It was usually dominated by Athens which was then in its imperialist period. Other federations existed until the Roman conquest of Greece in the 2nd century B.C.

Alexander, the Macedonian adventurer, during his invasion of Asia acquired the megalomaniac delusion of eastern potentates and deified himself. More than three centuries later the Roman emperors began to acquire divinity. Twenty centuries later the sacred monarchy was at its last European gasp in Germany in 1918 A.D., and at its last Asiatic gasp in Japan in 1945 A.D.

In Chapter XXIII has been briefly described the rise of the Roman republic. The struggle between the patricians and plebeians in the 5th and 4th centuries B.C. arose because the plebeians engaged in trade who had acquired wealth desired certain political privileges. The small farmers wanted land reform. The principal outcome of this struggle was that the wealthy plebeians acquired political rights. The

457

timocracy which wielded political power changed somewhat in composition but continued to be a timocracy. The wealthy business men became the equestrian knights with an hereditary status.

In the 4th century B.C. Rome embarked on its imperialist policy which lasted for many centuries. There were a few isolated attempts to reform the dominant system of status. "The Gracchi brothers (in the 2nd century B.C.) made an attempt to check the growing power of the Roman plutocracy, but the vested interests proved too strong for their efforts." [9] In Chapttr XXV have been mentioned a few revolts of slaves during the 2nd and 1st centuries B.C. But there was little transition from status to class during the many centuries when Rome was the greatest power in the world. There were not even the slight glimmerings of democracy which manifested themselves in the Greek city states.

Athens, which had emerged from the Persian wars in a more or less dominant position, attempted to combine imperialism with democracy in the 5th and 4th centuries B.C. This was indeed one of the causes of the Peloponnesian War because not only Sparta but other Greek states resented the imperialist policies of Athens. For example, it went so far as to transfer the treasury of the Delian league to Athens. While maintaining a small measure of democracy at home it denied it completely to its colonies none of whose inhabitants were granted Athenian citizenship. Within a few decades it had to relinquish its hold upon these colonies.

The principle and technique of representative government were not developed in detail in ancient times. Without this technique it was impossible to have democracy except for a small community in a limited area. Throughout ancient times the vast majority of human beings were in a condition of more or less rigid status, most of them in a subject status. There were comparatively few transitions to class. Probably the principal factors for such mobility were commercial and other economic activities. The private accumulation of wealth enabled a few individuals to pass from a lower status to an upper class. However, this upper class was likely to harden into an upper status like the equestrian knights in Rome. In later chapters will be explored the ways in which economic activities have stimulated mobility between social groups.

[9] H. E. Barnes, "Social Reform," *Encyclopedia Americana,* Vol. 25, 1948, page 166.

Chapter XXIX

Feudalism and Land Tenure

THE land is the source of almost everything of human value. All the food, with the exception of marine food, comes from the soil—directly in the form of edible plants or indirectly as edible animals. Mineral and wooden products originate in the earth. Hence the ownership and control of the land are of vast import for human welfare. They are also closely related to economic and political organization and determine in large part the politico-economic institutions which prevail at a given time and place.

Paleolithic man lived by hunting, fishing and plant gathering. This manner of life did not usually permit of permanent settlement on the land. Certain favored spots, such as rock shelters, caves, and riverine or marine sites, were inhabited for long periods, though not necessarily by the same groups. Paleolithic man usually led a wandering life in search of the animals and plants which he consumed. There was not much occasion for a sense of ownership to arise in such a migratory existence. However, certain primitive peoples claimed large areas as their hunting grounds and resented or opposed the intrusion of members of other groups. Among the Australian aborigines these areas were sometimes as large as 100 square miles. Where the food is scanty such restrictions are more likely to arise. This is not individual ownership of the land. It is rather group ownership, a rudimentary form of collective ownership by a limited number of persons.

During the neolithic period the early agriculturists cultivated the soil superficially without fertilizing it. Consequently, the soil was soon exhausted and its cultivators forced to move on. Permanent property rights could hardly arise under such conditions. As mankind learned to enrich and conserve the soil by fertilizing and rotating the crops, agricultural settlements and villages became more permanent and property rights in land more valuable. This increase in value incited

459

predatory aggression of various sorts as has been described in earlier chapters. Sometimes a nomadic pastoral tribe conquered a sessile agricultural people usually of a more complex culture. Sometimes dominance has arisen through the development of credit instruments, debt and taxation which delivered much of the rural population into the clutches of the urban financiers and capitalists. By many other devious methods a small group has gained ascendancy over the large mass. Thus there have been the royalty, nobility, gentry (gentleman and lady), the sometimes hereditary priesthood, boyars, brahmans, landlords, capitalists, etc., exploiting and oppressing the slaves, helots, serfs, villeins, muzhiks, peons, peasants, proletarians, etc. Invariably the ruling predatory class has rationalized its position by inventing the myth of the superiority of its own blood, race and family, thereby attempting to justify its usurpation of power. Inevitably the master class, which professes to be "well born" and to have an exceptional capacity to rule, has had a contempt for labor in order to distinguish itself as completely as is practicable from the subject class, which it stigmatizes as "ill born" and incapable of ruling itself.

As I have pointed out repeatedly, in nearly every society which has existed to the present day, labor, and manual labor in particular, has been regarded as menial, and the laborer has been looked down upon as inferior and ill-born. The gentility of the master class is well described in the series of excerpts in the next two paragraphs which has been somewhat paraphrased.[1]

The gentleman (and lady) must be well-born. No gentleman works, especially not for a living, which means that he must have inherited wealth. The theory has been elaborated by Veblen in his *Theory of the Leisure Class*. All through historic times manual labor has been a bar to gentility, as well as all forms of menial labor, whether manual or not. The taint of labor descends from grandfather to grandson. Most of the professions, especially the learned ones, are barred from gentility. The reason is revealed by Veblen's principle of gainful employment. No profession is genteel when it is practiced for a living. Merchants were completely barred from feudal and ancient gentility. In the Occident the gentlemanly professions have been the armed forces, in other words, the warlike profession, diplomacy and statecraft, and the church down to the grade of vicar, all of which are manifestations of power, secular and sacred. The ordinary priest is not a gentleman, he may have been born of the common people. In Europe the class struggle has raged violently within the clerical profession. The teacher has never been a gentleman. In the past he was usually a priest. Since the feudal period the

[1] *Encyclopedia of the Social Sciences*, New York, 1937, article entitled "Gentleman, Theory of the."

460

Occident has assiduously cultivated the theory and the art of manners. Today manners (not genuine courtesy) form an essential attribute of the gentleman.[2] In France in 1640 A.D. Faret formulated the rules for politely slighting inferiors. Manners are determined, as Pareto has shown, by historic forces not directly comprehended by the gentleman, who eats with his fork because gentlemen eat with forks, he does not know why. Moralists have contended that "the clothes do not make the man." They do, however, make the gentleman.

The ethics of the gentleman are ethics of combat, of competition in a struggle for eminence and distinction and are, therefore, antithetical to humility, self-effacement, altruism, and abnegation. Montesquieu remarked that the ideal of the gentleman is not virtue but honor, the honor of the battle-field, of the duel, of the gambling table, of sport. The ethic of the gentleman at all times and in all places is part Nietzschean and part Machiavellian. Gentlemen may espouse minorities as a matter of conscience, but the minority must never be small enough to count as queer or eccentric. The ethic of the gentleman is a technique of prestige and prestige requires good standing with majorities. Many of the genteel manners and morals have persisted to the present day. They are gradually yielding to the pressure of industrialization, mechanization and political ideologies striving for a classless society. In a few countries the gentility is already being dispossessed of their inherited wealth, mainly in land, which is the indispensable material basis for the practice of their mores.

Land tenure has varied greatly in time and in space. As agriculture developed and more or less permanent communities arose where the soil was fertile and otherwise favorable, in many places, but not everywhere, the tenure was communal. The villagers took turns in cultivating the strips or portions into which the village land had been divided. The village community was usually on a kinship basis with a headman from the village clan. Sometimes the community was under the suzerainty of a lord or king to whom tribute had to be paid in the form of goods or services. The pastures were usually held in common for the grazing of the cattle of the villagers. The village community has been described in greater detail in Chapter XXVII.

Elsewhere individual property rights in land arose. Even where this was the case, "common" rights were often retained in pastures which all the villagers could use. This common right usually persisted until a lord or king seized this land and enclosed it for his own

[2] See Maurice Parmelee, *Criminology*, New York, 1918, pp. 223-4 and 487, for the distinction between genuine and formal courtesy or manners or politeness or civility. See also my *Personality and Conduct*, New York, 1918, especially Chapter I entitled "The Spontaneous Expression of Human Nature," and Chapter XIX entitled "The Development of Personality."

use. Furthermore, the right of the state to eminent domain has always persisted. In that sense and to that extent unlimited private property right in land has never existed. But the enclosure of the "commons" extended greatly the concept of private property in land. Karl Marx has described this process in England. "Communal property (to be clearly distinguished from the State lands) was an old Teutonic institution which lived on under cover of feudalism. We have seen how the forcible seizure of the common lands, accompanied for the most part by the transformation of arable into pasture, began in the fifteenth century and lasted on into the sixteenth. But by that time the process was effected by individual acts of violence against which the legislature fought, though vainly, for a hundred and fifty years. The eighteenth century shows that the law itself became the instrument by which the theft of the people's land was achieved." [3] According to Marx, from 1801 to 1831, 3,511,770 acres, or about 5,500 square miles, were stolen from the common people by the landlords in England.

Land tenure has often been determined by military or political conquest where the conquerors have dispossessed the native population which has been exterminated, driven away, or more usually reduced to a servile status. Property rights in land have been correlated with family and clan organization, forms of government, technological levels attained, prevalent types of economic activity, and sometimes with religion as when sanctuaries, temples, churches, monasteries and convents have laid claim to land. The extent in space of land tenure has ranged from royal or imperial ownership of all the land of a nation, as in ancient Egypt or in the Inca empire, through ownership of large areas by feudal lords, to individual private ownership, though the latter also has sometimes meant the ownership of large tracts of land by individuals.

The financial mechanism of debt and credit is also likely to affect land tenure. A money economy often causes urbanization and entrepreneurial farming. Something of this sort occurred during the first age of imperialism in the eastern Mediterranean region, but was interrupted for many centuries by migrations of agricultural peoples from the north. Between about 4000 and 1000 B.C. urban civilizations of kindred economic and social structure extended from eastern Turkestan and northwest India to the Aegean. Economic innovations consisted of the intensive use of interest-bearing loan capital, in the form of weighed out metal money and allotted food stuff money, and craft production for the market. . . . The most important centers were Mesopotamia, where loan capital played an important role, and Egypt, where forced labor was emphasized. . . . Toward the end of the second

---

[3] Karl Marx, *Capital, A Critique of Political Economy*, Vol. I, Hamburg, 1867, Chapter 7, Section 24. English translation, London, 1887.

millennium B.C. the Mediterranean basin and the Near East as far as the Indian frontier were settled by peoples whose social and economic organization was that of the agricultural civilization of the iron age. They replaced the overthrown empires by military communities of free farmer tribes with private family tenure of land and without a developed market and interest-earning money economy." [4]

Feudalism is a form of political organization related to or based upon a type of land tenure conjoined with a sort of social classification which has recurred frequently from ancient to modern times. It is, however, somewhat difficult to define, because it has varied greatly in form from time to time and place to place. The *Standard Dictionary* (1946) erroneously limited it to Europe by defining "feudalism" as "The medieval European system of land tenure on condition of military service," and "feudal system" as "a politico-social system in force throughout Europe from the 9th to the 15th century, founded on the tenure of feuds, or fiefs, given as compensation for military services rendered by chiefs and by them sublet by allotments to their subordinates and vassals." The *Encyclopedia Britannica* (1942), in its article on feudalism states its principles as follows:—"The chief of these are: the relation of vassal and lord; the principle that every holder of land is a tenant and not an owner, until the highest rank is reached, sometimes even the conception rules in that rank; that the tenure by which a thing of value is held is one of honorable service, not intended to be economic, but moral and political in character; the principle of mutual obligations of loyalty, protection and service binding together all the ranks of this society from the highest to the lowest; and the principle of contract between lord and tenant, as determining all rights, controlling their modification, and forming the foundation of all law."

Some historians have asserted that feudalism first appeared in Egypt: "The monarchy of the Pyramid Age declined in strength, and with its decline the nomes, which had once been city-states, regained a large measure of self-government. Beginning with the Seventh Dynasty, Egypt split up into a number of small and almost independent principalities with only a nominal allegiance to the Pharaoh. Egypt thus affords the first example of a feudalized society such as afterward developed in ancient China and medieval Europe. Feudalism spelled disorder and civil warfare, which continued for hundreds of years. Peace, prosperity, and good government were restored under the kings of the Twelfth Dynasty, who occupied the throne for over two centuries (from about 2000 B.C.)" [5]

A somewhat similar development took place in Mesopotamia.

[4] *Encyclopedia of the Social Sciences*, New York, 1937, article on "Land Tenure."
[5] Hutton Webster, *History of Civilization*, Boston, 1947, Vol. I, pages 152-3.

"From geographically limited principalities under the authority of district rulers in Egypt and city kings in Babylonia there arose through a process of warlike accumulation the empires of Egypt and Mesopotamia, both of which have served as a pattern for the economic and social organization of the other eastern urban civilizations down to about 1000 B.C."[6] Land tenure in Babylonia at about 2000 B.C. has been described as follows: "The agricultural land was privately owned; if ever a stage of collective ownership existed, that stage had long since been passed. The proprietors were the king and the members of the upper class, so that the possession of land formed a social distinction, as in modern England. Even the royal officials received grants of land in lieu of services. . . . Most farmers, the actual tillers of the soil, were tenants, who paid to their landlord what seems an exorbitant rent of one-third or one-half of the crop."[7] Whether or not these tenants were bound to the soil so as to constitute serfs is uncertain. Some of the artisans and craftsmen were slaves who were hired out by their masters. The free artisans probably formed guilds to secure their mutual economic and social benefits as did the artisans of China and India.

Ancient Egyptian feudalism was due to a breakdown, probably during the 7th dynasty, of the central national authority which became distributed among local chieftains and princes. Thty paid a more or less nominal allegiance to the kings of the 12th dynasty. The same apparently happened in several parts of the world due to causes which were not identical everywhere. In China the ancient clan organization apparently furnished a basis: "The earliest definite and credible information concerning feudal tenures refers to the time of King Wu Wang, the founder of the Chou dynasty (about 1100 B.C. according to the corrected chronology." Fiefs were granted to royal relatives, soldiers, and other favored personages. "The constitution of the clan, demanding on the one hand the unrestricted power of the eldest in distributing the common property to the members under his supreme control, and on the other the common right of usufruct on the part of all the members together with the maintenance of the ancestral sacrifices, forms the bases upon which Chinese feudalism developed. The old Chinese state was conceived as a large family, and its character was shaped according to this notion. . . . The earlier type of feudalism disappeared (about the 3rd century B.C.) and was replaced by a unified empire under the control of a much stronger central power, whose public functionaries were in charge of the administration of the different provinces. Nevertheless, feudalism constantly endeavored

[6] *Encyclopedia of the Social Sciences*, 1937, article on "Land Tenure."
[7] Hutton Webster, *op. cit.*, Vol. I, page 137.

to reassert itself. . . . Only gradually did it disappear as a constituent element in the organization of the state."[8]

Chinese feudal lords were supplanted by provincial governors who might be transferred by the central government from one province to another and were, therefore, not rooted in the soil. The first Chinese emperor, Shih Huang Ti (246-210 B.C.) and his successors were despots who ruled through an appointive bureaucratic hierarchy of literati. This was the emperor who burned the books, apparently in order to make a clean break with the past, and who built the Great Wall to protect China from Mongol invasions from the northwest. But as an historian has said: "Powerful feudal lords sometimes reduced the imperial authority to a mere shadow; ambitious military adventurers fought with one another and with the emperors for supremacy; and the country was repeatedly overrun by barbarous invaders from central Asia."[9] In spite of these difficulties the Han dynasty lasted from 206 B.C. to 220 A.D., or more than four centuries.

Japanese feudalism is sometimes traced back to the earlier Chinese feudalism, but without adequate justification. Chinese culture began to influence Japan in the 7th and 8th centuries A.D. after the main period of Chinese feudalism had passed. Confucianism encouraged the ancestor worship already prevalent in Japan. It may thereby have strengthened the Japanese clan organization. For reasons which are somewhat obscure the mikado (mi = sublime, $kado$ = gate) began to lose his power to the chieftains of the leading clans. In 1192 A.D. the head of the Minamoto clan, Yoritomo, usurped the royal and imperial power under the title of shogun (sho = general, gun = army). The shogunate lasted for nearly seven centuries until 1867 when the last Tokugawa shogun surrendered and thereby restored the mikado to power.

Though the shogun exercised great power the period of the shogunate was characterized by many feudal features. "Two-thirds of the arable land was parceled out among less than three hundred nobles (daimyos), who held their estates from the shogun, in return for military service when called upon. The daimyos lived in fortified castles and enjoyed all the rights of petty sovereigns, levying taxes, coining money, administering a rude justice, keeping armed forces, and indulging in constant warfare with one another. Their knights, or retainers, were called samurai. Far beneath this warrior class came farmers, artisans, and traders, the last standing lowest in the social scale. The commoners, though much more numerous than the samurai, really counted for nothing, except to pay the taxes and labor for the

[8] *Encyclopedia of the Social Sciences*, New York, 1937, article on "Feudalism."
[9] Hutton Webster, *op. cit.*, Vol. I, page 92.

465

comfort and luxury of their superiors. It was all quite like the contemporary feudalism in western Europe."[10]

It can hardly be said that there was a feudal period in India, though the caste system bears at least one resemblance to feudalism about to be mentioned, and a large part of the peasants have not owned the land they till. Of the culture of the pre-Aryans of the Indus valley we have only archeological remains. The peoples speaking Indo-European languages who penetrated from the north apparently were tribally organized with a patriarchal family. The caste system began to arise for reasons which are rather obscure.[11] It resembled the feudal system in that it consisted of hereditary social groups, the upper castes and the lower castes, corresponding in the feudal system to the nobility and the gentry on the one hand, and the serfs and often also slaves on the other hand. In other respects, however, Indian society was not feudalistic. Most of the population was agricultural, many of the inhabitants living in village communities which were economically more or less independent. Joint families were often organized in village units with common grazing fields and woodlands. Social stratification came to be based in a measure on the length of tenure of land. The craftsmen were ordinarily organized in guilds.

This somewhat idyllic situation broke down as invaders entered India and established states with centralized and concentrated authority in the place of the pristine tribal society. It is uncertain as to whether the ownership of the land was vested in the king so that the cultivators of the soil became tenants, or the peasants themselves were the proprietors. In any case the cultivators had to pay a rent or a tax or tribute to the king. A village community might pay this tribute collectively. Tax collectors acquired the right to revenue from the land which eventually became the right to the land itself. The members of this landlord class came to be known as "zamindars" and have levied tribute on the poor peasants for many centuries until modern times.

During the first age of imperialism (see Chapter XXII) centralized imperial rule over large areas put an end for the time being to most of the earlier forms of feudalism. During the middle or later portion of the middle age of imperialism (see Chapter XXIII) a form of feudalism, or at least of serfdom, developed out of the colonate which arose after 300 A.D. in the Roman empire. Prior to that time there had been no feudalism in the full sense of the word in Greece or Rome. For example, in Sparta the helots were serfs or slaves who tilled the soil to which they were bound. They were kept in subjection

[10] John B. Wolf, *History of Civilization*, Boston, 1947, Vol. II, page 316.
[11] See Maurice Parmelee, *Oriental and Occidental Culture*, 1928, Chapter VII entitled "Indian Caste and Western Class."

by the soldiers of the military state in which the power was too centralized to be a feudal state.

In the Roman empire the landlords divided their estates into small tracts which they leased to tenants who were known as *coloni*. Toward the end of the 3rd century A.D. many coloni became insolvent on account of war and heavy taxation. To maintain agricultural production the Emperor Diocletian (A.D. 245-313) who reigned from A.D. 284 to 305 ordered the coloni to stay on the farms of their landlords for life. The Emperor Constantine (A.D. 272-337) issued in A.D. 332 a rescript punishing the coloni who left their holdings and ordered that their children be permanently attached to the soil.[12] Thus the coloni or tenants became serfs and were later absorbed by medieval serfdom. Even before the coloni there were already servile tenants in Egypt and some of the eastern provinces of the Roman empire. The reasons for the rise of this servile status were probably similar to those in the Italian peninsula, namely, indebtedness of the peasantry, and also war, decreasing fertility of the soil, and insufficient man power to produce the food needed by the urban population and the army.

Many centuries earlier there had been some transition from status to class, in Greece in the seventh and sixth centuries B.C. and in Rome somewhat later. By status we mean a rank or social position into which an individual is born and cannot leave so that it is closed. By class we mean a social group which is open in the sense that the individual can move from class to class so that his rank may be acquired and not inherited. With the rise of a mercantile class a larger portion of the population was free to move from one class to another. However, a large number of slaves still remained. There was also a small group of aristocrats whose high rank was inherited and not acquired. So that there was comparatively little social mobility and status remained the predominant form of social standing.

After Islam came into being in the 7th century A.D. and made its extensive conquests, feudalism arose in Moslem countries. Moslem feudalism grew mainly out of the disposition and administration of lands conquered by the Arabs. In each Moslem country the monarch

[12] "Diocletian dealt with this agrarian problem by simply ordering the tenants to remain on their farms for life; Constantine went further and ordered that their children after them should also be permanently attached to the soil. The *coloni* thus fell into the condition of serfs, unable to leave their holdings in search of employment elsewhere and often compelled to work for their landlord a certain number of days every year without recompense. If a tenant fled from the land he was brought back by force, and if the land was sold he and his family went with it. . . . This system of serfdom had long prevailed in some parts of the Near East and in North Africa. It was now extended to Spain, Gaul, Britain, and other European provinces, and during the Middle Ages it became general throughout western Europe." (Hutton Webster, *op. cit.*, Vol. I, pp. 322-323.)

467

retained more control over the land than in feudal Europe. Fiefs were given to soldiers and courtiers. Moslem feudalism was more of a money economy, because Islam was closely akin to commerce, and not so closely knit as European feudalism. This was partly due to the fact that Islam originated among the Arabic Saracens, a commercial people.[13] Saracen was followed by Ottoman feudalism which was extended to Egypt.

In Italy were the latifundia or large land holdings owned by private proprietors or by the crown. In Rome and the other cities were large unproductive classes, namely, the legions, the functionaries, the bourgeoisie, and the city mobs of proletarians. It was the problem of feeding these unproductive groups as well as the causes of the decline in fertility, such as too frequent cropping of the soil, which led to the imperial laws of Diocletian and Constantine cited above. Thus the originally free coloni were bound to the soil and became a part of the colonate.

Let us now look a little more closely at the characteristic features of the feudal system. The serfdom which characterizes it is not the personal servitude of the domestic slave subject to every whim of his owner but is a form of group servitude regulated by custom. "By and large, serfdom has been the mark of low grade economies, where the ruling classes were more anxious about the labor supply than the land supply. Feudalism, transplanted by conquest, tended to simplify peasant class structure at the expense of its privileged elements."[14]

Under the feudal system the land is held by one person from another. If there is a monarchy the land is vested in the king who makes grants to lords, knights, soldiers, and others. These in turn grant smaller pieces of their land to those who actually work it and produce food from it. The status of these agricultural laborers has varied at different times and places from more or less free tenants and

---

[13] Saracen was the name given by the Greeks to the Arab nomads who conducted caravans through the desert. Webster has described the commercial provenance of Islam as follows: "Islam arose among the mercantile communities of Arabia, and Mohammed, himself a successful business man, had encouraged trade as being pleasing to God. The merchant occupied an honorable social position, and the bazaar, or trading quarter, had a place in every Moslem city. . . . The geographical setting of the Arab Empire facilitated its commercial development, for now a solid block of Moslem territory stretched from the Atlantic eastward into the heart of Asia. The Arabs controlled the old caravan roads along which the products of inner Africa and the Far East reached the Mediterranean." (Hutton Webster, *op. cit.*, Vol. I, p. 433.)

The Arabs also traded by water in the Mediterranean, down the Atlantic coast of northern Africa, throughout the Indian Ocean, and as far east as China. This explains the spread of Islam far beyond the bounds of the Arab empire of the 7th to the 13th centuries A.D. to India, the East Indies and China.

[14] *Encyclopedia of the Social Sciences*, New York, 1937, article on "Serfdom."

cottars to villeins and serfs more or less bound to the soil. While at the Norman Conquest (1066 A.D.) all land was vested in the king, later in England came copyholding according to which holdings were recorded by the courts so that the copyholder could secure a copy of the record. Later there were leases to the tenants which created the question of the ownership of improvements. "The equitable claim of a tenant to be recouped for his improvements arose as soon as the lotting of farms became general." [15] Still later yearly tenancies became more or less permanent. Gradually peasant proprietorship became prevalent in Europe, though in some countries there was a good deal of metayage or share-cropping or share-renting.

In Europe the feudal system grew up in Carolingian and post-Carolingian society (named after Charles, A.D. 742-814, known as Charlemagne, who was king of the Franks from 768 to 814, and Emperor of the West from 800 to 814). We have already seen that feudalism, or something resembling feudalism in land tenure and relation between the owner and user of the land, had already existed in Egypt, Mesopotamia, China, Japan, India, the Roman empire, and in Moslem countries. However, as we have already noted, it is not easy to define feudalism or to determine its immediate causes wherever and whenever it has existed. That it invariably involves exploitation of one group by another where each group has inherited its status is evident. But the same can be said of slavery. We will cite some of the features which have been attributed to feudalism though not all of them distinguish it from slavery. Generally speaking feudalism is an economic system in which there is comparatively little exchange of commodities and use of money. "One of the essential characteristics of feudalism is that prestige and social worth sprang less from the free disposal of property than from the free disposal of human forces. . . . The leading features of feudalism in its fully developed form are the system of vassalage and the institution of the fief." [16]

An historian of European feudalism has described it as follows: "By feudalism is meant the delegation or appropriation, the seizure or exercise of public authority by the private individual, in a greater or less degree over territory of greater or less extent. It was the bearing of rule, the administration of justice, the imposition of taxes by a proprietary noble, layman or cleric, baron or bishop or abbot, within a fixed territory and over all the population therein. In such a polity the substance of government was particularized. The crown retained only a vague overlordship (suzerainty), a mere ascription of authority, and the king was reduced to a shadow. . . . The peak of power of Europe of the feudal age was attained between 1150 and 1250. Feudal-

[15] *Encyclopedia Britannica*, 1942, article on "Land Tenure."
[16] *Encyclopedia of the Social Sciences*, New York, 1937, article on "Feudalism."

ism was a form of government, a structure of society, an economic regime based upon landed proprietorship." [17]

Thompson has described some of the forces which brought about serfdom in Europe: "The same process that happened in ancient Rome worked over again. The rich grew richer and the poor poorer. When the mortgage was foreclosed the freeman, perforce, became a tenant farmer. If again he fell behind in his obligations he lost his freedom and was reduced to serfdom. . . . The ruinous weight of the *heerban,* or compulsory military service, was a potent influence in depressing freemen to a state of dependency, even to serfdom, on the lands of great abbeys and great nobles and accordingly an influence which induced the hardier to seek the frontier." [18]

The political and social situation under European feudalism Thompson has described as follows: "Kingdoms were mere agglomerations of fiefs. Fiefs were agglomerations of manors. Political thought was wholly local—of a province or a county or a fief. The two ruling classes, clergy and nobles, were an order (*ordo*), a caste, alike in every kingdom. The peasantry, serfs and villeins, were also a caste, but a lowly class, bound to the glebe lands of their lords. They, too, were alike in status and condition in every kingdom. Thus the political ideas of men functioned along vertical lines, the man below, whether noble or serf, looking to the man above him; the man above, again whether noble or serf, looking to the man below him. There was no sense of either social or territorial amplitude, no sentiment of nation or of country." [19]

The land tenure phase of European feudalism was apparently derived from the Roman law of property and serfdom from a Teutonic custom and institution. "The remote roots of feudalism are to be found in the former Roman patrimonial proprietorship, which the Church and the Germans imitated and continued, and in the old Germanic concept of personal loyalty of all the members of the primitive *comitatus,* or war-band, to its chief. Thus Rome contributed the property relation, the Germans the personal relation. Their fusion together formed the essential nature of feudalism." [20]

We have seen that feudalism had already existed in Egypt and elsewhere long before the Roman law of property had evolved and Teutonic customs had any influence outside of northern Europe. However, it is possible that it had its most complete development in Europe. It seems to have arisen partly if not largely because of the

[17] James Westfall Thompson, *Economic and Social History of the Middle Ages (300-1300)*, New York, 1928, p. 240.
[18] J. W. Thompson, *op. cit.,* p. 232.
[19] J. W. Thompson, *op. cit.,* p. 248.
[20] J. W. Thompson, *op. cit.,* p. 700.

470

disorder which prevailed in Europe after the fall of the western Roman empire.[21] As the French historian Taine (1828-1893) has said: "When we clearly represent to ourselves the condition of humanity in those days we can comprehend how men accepted readily the most obnoxious of feudal rights. . . . People accordingly lived, or rather began to live, under the rude, iron-gloved hand which used them roughly but which afforded them protection."[22]

Religious institutions played an important part in European feudalism. The lands owned by the churches and monasteries were held in fief and subinfeudated by the latter. Much land was given to these institutions, especially the monasteries, partly for religious but also for secular reasons. Consequently, these institutions were deeply interested in maintaining the feudal system. In spite of the vow of poverty taken by the monkhood and the nuns, many of the monasteries and convents became very wealthy not only because of the donations received by them but also because they had many privileges and their cost of production was low. In fact, they were often able to underbid the secular producers. This gave rise to a certain amount of economic anticlericalism which was one of the causes of the Protestant Reformation. The denial of the vow of poverty was circumvented by the legal fiction that these religious institutions were corporations. Through this device the monks and nuns could live in luxury, and many of them did so.

In medieval literature the charge of avarice and of covetousness was often made against the monks, nuns, and priests or regular clergy. However, the basic reason for the economic collapse of the monasteries and convents doubtless was the gradual disappearance of the manorial system because the monastic economy was founded on this system. The medieval church was a feudalized church. It was not only a state within a state but a super-state also because it claimed a divine authority. It commanded a large revenue because it imposed the tithe, or one-tenth of their incomes, upon its adherents, and also charged fees for many of its services. It was in order to prevent the loss of much of its property that it prohibited the marriage of its priests and created a celibate clergy. This celibacy was ordained for the first time by the Lateran Council in 1059 A.D. This was in recognition of the fact that if its priests had offspring, they would be strongly tempted to alienate as much of the church property as they could for the benefit of their children.

In its attitude toward serfdom the church was not merely conservative but also reactionary. It never objected to the slave trade. In

[21] The Western Roman empire ended when the German chieftain Odoacer deposed the last emperor in 476 A.D.
[22] H. Taine, *Ancient Regime*, p. 8.

471

fact, during the eleventh century and later chattel slavery existed on church lands even in the papal states. The church was less inclined to free its serfs than secular owners. Consequently, ecclesiastical pretensions of altruism and humanitarianism must be regarded with much reservation. The charitable activities of which it boasted were often due to poverty caused by its own practices of economic exploitation. The clerical which was also the scholastic attitude toward labor was that it is a commodity to be bought and sold either as a slave or as a serf or as a wage worker. In the latter case the worker's pay was to be measured not by the value of his product but by his minimum needs, which would always keep his wages low unless a scarcity of labor forced them up.

Numerous competent authorities have commented on these traits of the church. A French historian has said: "The clerics of the Middle Ages showed almost as much cruelty to the peasants and burghers as did men of the sword. In fact, the feudal conception prevailed in the Church, which consisted of the priesthood." [23] Two British legal historians have said: "There is plenty of evidence that of all landlords the religious houses were the most severe—not the most oppressive, but the most tenacious of their rights; they were bent on the maintenance of pure villein tenure and personal villeinage." [24] An American historian of the Middle Ages commented repeatedly on these traits of the church and monastic establishments: "The arm of the medieval Church was long and its heart hard." As to the monastic establishments, by the 13th century, "wealth, idleness, vice had gradually worked their corruption and decay like that of all the others." "The condition of ecclesiastical serfs was inferior to that of serfs on lay lands. . . . Peasant insurrections against the excessive fiscal exactions of the Church were not uncommon in the thirteenth century." "To the end of the Middle Ages it (the Church) remained politically and spiritually autocratic, socially and economically aristocratic." [25]

The church displayed these traits in its internal organization. It was divided into an independent upper class and a dependent lower class. Its hierarchy was made up almost entirely of members of the nobility. The parish priests were almost invariably village serfs who had to be emancipated by their feudal lords and masters before they could enter holy orders. A few of these priests proved to be men of

[23] Achille Luchaire, *Social France at the Time of Philip Augustus*, (reigned from 1180 to 1223 A.D.).

[24] F. Pollock and F. W. Maitland, *History of English Law*, Vol. I, p. 378, 2nd edition, 1898.

[25] J. W. Thompson, *op. cit.*, pp. 619, 622, 681, and 684. See especially his Chapter 24, "The New Monastic Orders," and Chapter 25, "The Church as Feudal Society."

472

talent in spite of the servile position into which they were forced by the hierarchy of nobles. In this occupation as in all others there was an enormous waste of human talent due to the discriminations of birth and of family which are not determined by talent. Even a freeman of the 9th and 10th centuries could only become a vassal of a noble, or enter the church in one of the lower orders, or become a serf.

At the end of the Middle Ages when economic changes brought about the decay of feudalism the church was the last to free its serfs. Idealism and humanitarianism influenced the church even less than the secular proprietors in this movement of emancipation. This was wholly in accordance with historical Christianity. "Christian teaching of the brotherhood of man logically involved the condemnation of the slave system, but while the Church always encouraged emancipation as a meritorious act, it never sought to abolish slavery or the serfdom into which slavery gradually passed. As long as the Christians formed a forbidden sect, they claimed toleration on the ground that religious belief is voluntary and not something that should be enforced by law. This attitude changed after Christianity triumphed in the empire and had the support, instead of the opposition, of the government. The Church, backed by the state, no longer advocated freedom of thought, no longer relied exclusively on persuasion as a missionary method, but resorted to compulsion and repression. Nonbelievers were imprisoned, exiled, and, on occasion, executed. Persecution was this time successful, and the use of force to put down divergent opinion henceforward marked the history of the Church for many centuries." [26]

In order to understand the rise and effects of European feudalism it is necessary to take a look at the dark ages which preceded it and which followed the fall of the western Roman empire due in part to the invasions from the north. An historian of the ancient world characterized this period as follows: "The invasions of the fifth and sixth centuries remain the most terrible catastrophe that ever befell so great a civilized society. It took long to restore order. The seventh and eighth centuries, after the invasions themselves had ceased, are a dreary period of confusion, lawlessness, and ignorance,—the lowest point ever reached by European civilization. The whole four hundred years, from 400 to 800, are properly called the *Dark Ages*. During these long centuries there was no tranquil leisure, and therefore no study. There was little security, and therefore little labor." He described the situation at the end of this period as follows: "In 800, the West was ignorant and poor. There was much barbarism in the most civil-

26 Hutton Webster, *op. cit.*, Vol. I, p. 350.

ized society. Roads had fallen into neglect, and there was little communication between one district and another. Money was little heard of. Trade hardly existed. Almost the only industry was a primitive kind of agriculture." [27]

Another historian of the ancient world characterized this period as follows: "How dark was the age which now ensued we can judge from the appalling decrease of population, the result of the wars, the plagues and famines that followed the wars, and the widespread disorder and lawlessness. The city of Rome, which in the great days of the empire counted probably a million inhabitants, contained only a twentieth of that number by the opening of the seventh century. Many cities completely disappeared." And again he said: "The barbarian invasions of the fourth and fifth centuries had ushered in a Dark Age for western Europe, but darker still were the ninth and tenth, when each locality had to organize for its own protection, organize or perish. In these circumstances of dire necessity feudalism took root, developed, and saved western Europe from complete dissolution." [28] As we have seen, similar institutions had arisen elsewhere under similar conditions, as, for example, in Egypt after its Pyramid period, in China in its early days, in the eastern part of the Roman empire while it was declining, and in the latter part of the Arab empire. In each case the central national or imperial authority had more or less broken down and men of rank and wealth in each locality had taken over most of the governmental functions.

It may be worth while at this point to discuss briefly the historical background of the rise of feudalism in Europe. In Chapter XXIII I have described the internal causes of the fall of the Roman empire. An historian of ancient times referred to them as follows: "The great Empire . . . was suffering from an inner decay, whose symptoms at first hidden were fast becoming more and more evident. In the first place, the decline of farming, so noticeable before the fall of the Republic, had gone steadily on. In spite of the heavy taxes imposed upon it, land had continued to pass over into the hands of the rich and powerful. . . . At the same time the financial and business life of the cities was also declining. The country communities no longer possessed a numerous purchasing population. Hence the country market for the goods manufactured in the cities was so seriously reduced that city industries could no longer dispose of their products. They rapidly declined. The industrial classes were thrown out of work and went to increase the multitudes of the city poor. City business was also much hurt by a serious lack of precious metals for coining

[27] Willis M. West, *The Ancient World from the Earliest Times to 800* A.D., New York, 1913, pp. 596-597, and 632.
[28] H. Webster, *op. cit.*, Vol. I, pp. 376 and 470.

money. Many of the old silver and gold mines around the Mediterranean now seem to have been worked out." [29] These economic conditions of nearly 2,000 years ago resemble those of today, in its concentration of wealth and shortage of purchasing power, which illustrates how long it takes for mankind to solve some of its gravest problems.[30]

To the north of the Roman empire were the barbarian peoples which had from time to time threatened it. As far back as 382 B.C. an army of Gauls had captured Rome and plundered and burned it. But for several centuries there was a relative amount of peace between the north and the south. The first Roman emperor, Augustus, reigning at the beginning of the Christian era, decided not to try to conquer any more of the north. As Gibbon, writing in the latter part of the 18th century somewhat quaintly expressed it: "The northern countries of Europe scarcely deserved the expense and labor of conquest. The forests and morasses of Germany were filled with a hardy race of barbarians, who despised life when it was separated from freedom; and though, on the first attack, they seemed to yield to the weight of the Roman power, they soon, by a signal act of despair, regained their independence, and reminded Augustus of the vicissitude of fortune." [31]

There was a good deal of peaceful penetration of the Roman empire by the northern barbarians before and during the invasions. Some of them served as mercenary soldiers in the imperial armies. A good many came into the empire as colonists in vacant regions, sometimes as *coloni* or serfs. Some of them became slaves. There were several causes for the invasions, the principal one being the desire and need for land, as has been pointed out by an historian of civilization: "The love of adventure and of fighting for fighting's sake, the prospect of plunder in the rich Roman cities, the attraction which the warm and sunny Mediterranean basins seems always to have had for northern peoples—these were minor causes of the invasions. But land hunger principally explains them, even as it explains those other great 'wanderings of the nations' which in earlier times carried men of Indo-European speech to India and Persia, to Greece and Italy, to Gaul and Spain and Britain. When the soil, as men know how to use it, can no longer sustain increasing numbers, the inhabitants must either migrate or starve—the grim alternatives that confronted the Germans in antiquity. They chose to migrate, even though to do so

[29] J. H. Breasted, *Ancient Times, A History of the Early World*, Boston, 1917, pp. 667-668 and 670-671.

[30] In my *Farewell to Poverty*, New York, 1935, I have described at length how often there is not sufficient purchasing power widely distributed to dispose of the products of industry. See in particular Chapters XV entitled "The Business Cycle," and XVIII entitled "The Contradictions of Capitalism."

[31] Edward Gibbon (1737-1794), *The Decline and Fall of the Roman Empire*, Vol. I, Chapter I.

meant war, and their gradual movement southward from their seats on the Baltic brought them finally to the boundaries of the Roman Empire." [32]

The invasions were begun by the West Goths or Visigoths who had migrated from the Baltic region to southwestern Russia. In 271 A.D. they conquered Dacia just north of the Danube. This was the last province added to the empire by the emperor Trajan (A.D. 56-117). During the 4th century the Huns, a Mongoloid people from central Asia poured into Europe. Among other regions they occupied what is now known as Hungary. Partly because of the pressure of the Huns the Visigoths crossed the Danube in 376 A.D. and defeated the Romans at Adrianople in 378 A.D. Then more Visigoths and also East Goths or Ostrogoths poured into the provinces south of the Danube. During the next few decades they moved about in the Balkans, Greece and Italy. Under the leadership of the Visigothic king Alaric they captured and sacked Rome in 410 A.D. But they moved on into southern Gaul and northeastern and southern Spain and established the first kingdom within the Roman empire which lasted from 415 to 711 A.D. in Spain and 415 to 507 A.D. in Gaul. In the meantime the Vandals had migrated from northern Europe through southwestern Europe into northern Africa and had established a kingdom with its capital on the site of ancient Carthage which lasted from 429 to 534 A.D. In 455 A.D. they landed at Ostia at the mouth of the Tiber River and captured and sacked Rome, thus unwittingly avenging the ancient Carthaginians, and then sailed back to Africa with their loot.

In 451 A.D. an alliance of European peoples defeated Attila, the king of the Huns, at Chalons in what is now France, thus preventing the conquest of Europe by the Huns. The Burgundians established a kingdom in southern Gaul which lasted from 443 to 534 A.D. In 486 A.D. King Clovis of the Franks defeated the last of the Roman legions at Soissons, thus destroying the final vestiges of Roman power in western Europe. Clovis adopted Catholic Christianity in 496 A.D. and is reputed to have founded the Frankish kingdom which later absorbed a large part of western Europe. In 493 A.D. Theodoric, the king of the Ostrogoths, established a kingdom which included all of Italy and Sicily and a part of what is now Yugoslavia, and which lasted until 553. Later the Lombards established a kingdom in northern Italy which lasted from 568 to 774 A.D.

In 711 A.D. the Arabs and Berbers entered Spain. At the same time the Arabs were besieging Constantinople from 711 to 718 A.D. without success. In 732 A.D. the Arabs were defeated at Tours in western France by Charles Martel the Frank. This stopped their advance

[32] Hutton Webster, *op. cit.*, Vol. I, page 360.

northward. During the rest of their stay in Europe they remained in the Iberian peninsula from four to eight centuries. Toledo was captured by the Spaniards in 1085 A.D. and Granada four centuries later in 1492 which meant the end of Moorish rule in Europe.

By the beginning of the ninth century the Franks had absorbed a large part of western Europe in what amounted to a Frankish empire. This fact was recognized by the Romish pope when he crowned Charlemagne, the king of the Franks, as Roman Emperor in 800 A.D. It is not easy to explain why within a century this Carolingian empire began to disintegrate and break up into feudal fiefs. When Charlemagne died in 814 A.D., he was succeeded by his son Louis who ruled until 840 A.D. Upon his death his three sons quarreled and fought over their inheritance. The empire was divided into three parts in 843 A.D. The east Frankish kingdom eventually became modern Germany. The west Frankish kingdom later became modern France. The central kingdom lacked geographical and linguistic unity and became parts of the modern countries of Holland, Belgium, Switzerland, France, Italy, etc. A much more important reason for the break down of the Frankish empire was that a new series of invasions was destroying this brief lived empire in much the same way that the invasions of four or five centuries earlier had destroyed the western Roman empire. Moslem pirates from their foothold in North Africa and the Iberian peninsula were looting the coasts of Italy, Sicily and France. Slavic peoples were pushing their way into eastern Germany. The Magyar people in Hungary made inroads from the east. Most extensive were the invasions of the Northmen of Scandinavia.

As contrasted with the disorder caused by the factors mentioned above, feudalism brought a certain amount of order, as was pointed out with perhaps too much emphasis by Thompson: "The relief which Europe felt from the misery of the later Carolingian epoch by the growth of feudalism must be appreciated. In spite of abuses, feudalism was better than disorder verging on anarchy, and in the baronial court even the serf had standing." A few pages further on Thompson again emphasized the order created by feudalism: "It was only when feudalism became an ordered regime—at least as reasonably regulated as human government in any age may be—that life in the chateaux became more refined and more comfortable. By that time, too, military architecture had so advanced that the castles had ceased to be mere blockhouses and had become ample, even tremendous, edifices of stone." [33]

Thompson asserted that the principles upon which feudalism was based were as follows: "The principles upon which feudalism rested

[33] J. W. Thompson, *op. cit.*, pp. 251, 255.

477

were different and of higher morality than the autocracy and slavocracy of the later Roman Empire. Feudalism reduced the earlier excessive and barbaric individualism to obedience to law and order, crystallized in institutions of suzerainty, vassalage, fidelity, service, the duties of contract. In its finest form it produced a new civilization. . . . The only capital was land, and it was fixed, not mobile, a fact deeply responsible for the static condition and fixity of social structure in feudal society. . . . In its best days feudalism probably enforced the law about as effectively and as honestly as modern society does. . . . The ancient German principle that the State was subordinate to the law was at odds with the classical tradition that law was made by the State." [34]

Here again Thompson may have over-estimated the degree and kind of order created by feudalism, and especially the German contribution to it whose fundamental principle was, so he alleged, that "great private wealth owes something to society." (Page 703). As a matter of fact, feudalism was as aristocratic, as exploitative, and as predatory as most of the forms of social organization which have existed down to the present day. Feudal society consisted of two exploiting and predatory groups, namely, the clergy and the nobility, and the great mass of the common people, mostly rural laborers, whom they exploited. Indeed, another historian characterized the feudal system as "confusion roughly organized" and condemned European feudalism as follows: "Europe has paid a heavy price for the feudal aristocracy; to some extent Europe continues to pay that price. As a system of government feudalism was about the worst possible. . . . One wonders how society managed to hold together in the days when monarchs were weak and nobles were turbulent and strong." [35]

Thompson did, however, recognize the seamier side of feudalism in the following words: "The manorial system was the lower side of feudalism. It was the relation of the landed proprietary class to the servile, villein, and slave dependents dwelling as farm laborers upon the estates of that class, or the relation of the noble to the non-noble class in medieval society. . . . Manorialism became fixed by the end of the ninth century, while feudalism did not acquire form and fixity before the eleventh. . . . The life of the common people in the Middle Ages was almost wholly rural and agrarian. There was little modification of it until the eleventh century, when commerce and industry began to develop, chiefly owing to increasingly intimate contact with the Mediterranean lands and the East." The similarity between the feudal manor and its predecessor, the Roman villa, he indicated as

[34] J. W. Thompson, *op. cit.*, pp. 701, 702, 703, 706.
[35] Hutton Webster, *op. cit.*, Vol. I, p. 483.

follows: "The Roman villa was a great farm owned by a rich landed proprietor, on which were villages of both slaves and servile dependents (*coloni*) who worked the fields for him and got little more than subsistence for their labor. The slave was a chattel. The serf was a former freeman sunk to economic dependence and bound to the glebe. . . . He was a prisoner for debt, working off but never cancelling the obligation by his daily toil in the open air upon his lord's lands. His holding was called a tenure (from Latin *tenere*, 'to hold'), but in law the tenure held the serf, not the serf the tenure. It fixed his status legally as a bondman, and socially as a dependent." [36]

The German tribes were composed mainly of noblemen and freemen. There were comparatively few slaves, much less in proportion than in the Roman empire. This was due primarily to economic reasons because slave labor would not have been as profitable as free labor in the early Teutonic economy. The nobles were in the main the chieftains of the tribes. After the Germans had conquered a large part of the Roman empire during the 5th and 6th centuries, so that there was a Visigothic and Ostrogothic Balkans, a Visigothic Gaul and Spain, a Vandal North Africa, a Lombard and Ostrogothic Italy, beside a papal Rome and Byzantine Italy, the so-called free German village community became a servile village community with a lord and master who became virtually independent when the feudal period was reached. A king was then needed only as the apex of the hereditary nobility, a *primus inter pares,* but no longer the sovereign lord. This situation prevailed in the main until the rise of nations described in the next chapter. The higher clergy was selected mainly from the nobility. As indicated earlier in the present chapter, many abbots, bishops and other prelates were also feudal lords. Consequently, the nobility and the higher clergy presented a united front in exploiting their serfs. The lower clergy came largely from serfdom, and were more likely to identify themselves with the interests of their servile relatives.

The manorial economy was more or less inconsistent with slavery which declined after the 8th century. A relatively few slaves were domestic servants. At the Domesday survey (1086 A.D.) in England, only 9 percent of the dependent population on the crown lands were slaves. Slavery declined not owing to humanitarianism but for economic and social reasons. "Serfdom had developed in two ways. Slaves became serfs when they were treated no longer as human chattels but were attached to the land and might not be sold off it. Freemen became serfs when for any reason they lost title to their farms but still

[36] J. W. Thompson, *op. cit.*, pp. 726-727, 730.

remained on them and cultivated them for the proprietor. For former slaves serfdom represented a step upward in the economic scale; for former freemen it represented a step downward."[37]

We must now consider the reasons for the decline of European feudalism. After developing gradually during several centuries, and flourishing for from one to two centuries, it began to decline during the 11th century. The serfs began to be replaced by tenants holding and using the land by lease. After 1100 A.D. serfdom decreased more rapidly but in varying degrees in different parts of Europe. Predial serfdom, that is to say, a serfdom which involved attachment of the serf to the soil, could not survive the economic and social changes which were taking place in Europe. These changes have been briefly summarized as follows: "Politically, feudalism tended to pass away when kings grew strong enough to put down private warfare, execute justice, and maintain order everywhere in their dominions. Economically, feudalism could not withstand the great changes of the later Middle Ages, when reviving industry and commerce led to an increase of capital, the growth of markets, and the substitution of money payments for payment in services. Flourishing cities arose, as in the days of the Roman Empire, freed themselves from the control of the nobles, and became the homes of a powerful middle class of traders, manufacturers, bankers, and professional men. The middle class was always antifeudal."[38]

The shortage of money during the Middle Ages encouraged feudalism and the manorial system because rents and wages had to be paid largely in produce and personal services. This shortage seems to have been due in part to the fact that much money had been sent to the Orient to pay for such luxuries as silk and spices. Apparently there was not an equivalent movement of money to the Occident. Another reason for the shortage was that the mines of the precious metals in western Europe ceased to produce during the time of the invasions from the north. Paper money as a substitute for specie was not introduced until the 17th century, though it had been used in China since the 12th century. Furthermore, debasement of many of the coinages in existence and counterfeiting limited the amount of money available for commerce and industry.

However, money is at most only of secondary importance, and may in the future become wholly unimportant. In another book I have pointed out that there are several possibilities with respect to the measure of value upon which the future medium of distribution may be based. "Gold, silver, or any scarce commodity or combination of commodities is wholly unsuitable for this purpose. Commodities

[37] Hutton Webster, *op. cit.*, Vol. I, p. 486.
[38] Hutton Webster, *op. cit.*, Vol. I, p. 482.

480

cannot be measured in terms of themselves. The value of gold and silver is unstable and variable because it is subject to the supply of and demand for precious metals, the fiscal policies of governments, the balance of trade between nations, and various other incalculable factors. Scarcity does not in and of itself furnish stability to a measure of value. A scarce article is at best only a rubber 'yardstick' which continually expands or contracts. The frequent great and sudden fluctuations in the exchange value of money disrupt price and income standards. Monetary inflation and deflation constitute one of the principal causes of the economic insecurity which afflicts mankind."[39]

In modern times the socialists have advocated labor as a standard of value, so that the man-hour would become the unit of value. However, it cannot be assumed that the productivity of the man-hour of one worker is equivalent to the productivity of the man-hour of another worker. Furthermore, a kind of labor skill which is very productive at one stage of technological evolution may become almost valueless at another stage. The technocrats have proposed that energy extraneous to human beings should be the standard of value, so that the erg or the kilowatt would become the unit of measurement.

Either of these methods of measuring economic value or a combination of both of them may be feasible in the future when economic organization is more socialized and when the instruments for measuring the amount of energy expended have been perfected. However, neither of these methods could have been used in the past partly for technical and partly for ideological reasons. Until very recently the labor of the common man has been regarded as of negligible value. Furthermore, it has been regarded as legitimate that a large proportion of whatever is produced should be siphoned off for the small dominant land and capital owning class. Money, therefore, in the form of coins or more recently of paper whose value is guaranteed by a government has been an important aid to commerce and industry down to the present time. During the latter part of the Middle Ages the supply of money increased somewhat. It did not become sufficient for commercial and industrial purposes until the discovery of the western hemisphere resulted in bringing silver to Europe from the mines in Peru and Mexico.

More fundamental than the money economy, however, were the growth of cities, the increase of trade, the Crusades, the guild system, the rise of the nation, the strengthening of the monarchy, and modern imperialism, all of which in one way or another weakened feudalism and collectively put an end to most of it in Europe. The detailed story of how this happened would be equivalent to the complete

[39] Maurice Parmelee, *Farewell to Poverty*, New York, 1935, p. 396.

history of medieval and modern Europe. In the present chapter we shall touch upon them very briefly and deal with some of them more fully in later chapters.

We may trace the decline of European feudalism in France. As we have seen, feudalism arose in this country after the fall of the Carolingian rule. "On the ruins of the Carolingian Empire in France, the debris of whose administrative, social, and economic institutions were everywhere visible, a violent and powerful proprietary nobility by force, usurpation, and fraud slowly built up a new form of government, a new condition of society, a new economic regime, wholly feudal in its genius and natural in the circumstances."[40] This development took place mainly during the tenth and eleventh centuries. During the twelfth and thirteenth centuries the monarchy began to gain in power. "The king was a feudal noble himself, the highest in the realm. He never attacked feudalism, but he never permitted its excesses. His concept of government was a strictly regulated feudal form of administration. In putting this into practice he cut to the roots two of the gravest abuses of the age—private war and judicial duels. He made the royal authority prevail over the feudal authority. . . . The towns also felt the weight of the crown. . . . Feudal litigation frequently culminated in war, for the logic of feudalism in extreme cases justified rebellion of the vassal or forcible coercion of the vassal by the suzerain. . . . Serfdom steadily declined."[41]

During the same period feudalism was on the decline also in Germany, though German feudalism had been somewhat different from French feudalism. "Out of this political and economic struggle between the towns and the feudality was destined to come a great and constructive movement in the middle of the thirteenth century, which was to have far-reaching influence upon the history of commerce and trade in medieval Germany. This was the formation of the city-leagues. . . . Politically Germany was given over to sectionalism and feudal particularism on a large scale—a condition precisely the opposite from that which obtained in France. The burgher population in the walled towns was able to protect itself against the overbearing ways of the petty feudality. But the rural peasantry had not such protection."[42]

Medieval Italy did not become feudalistic to the same degree as western and central Europe. This was probably due mainly to the fact that there were many old cities in which commerce and industry were predominant. The wealth invested in these activities was more powerful than the wealth invested in land. Furthermore, the peninsular shape of Italy with its long coastline rendered possible its merchant

[40] J. W. Thompson, *op. cit.*, p. 303.
[41] J. W. Thompson, *op. cit.*, pp. 496-8.
[42] J. W. Thompson, *op. cit.*, pp. 513-16.

marine and the maritime nature of its leading mercantile republics. On the Mediterranean there was intense commercial rivalry between the Moslems, the Italians and the Greeks which often took the form of naval expeditions and buccaneering enterprises. These commercial and predatory activities encouraged the economic backwardness of northern Europe while they helped to save southern Europe from feudalism. They also prepared the way for the Crusades which we have discussed in Chapter XXI.

The Crusades were superficially religious expeditions intended to rob the "heathen" Moslems of the "Holy Sepulcher." Christian pilgrimages to Palestine began as early as the 4th century. The Crusades were ostensibly mass pilgrimages with an aggressive intent, but were also or soon became mainly military adventures in search of gain in the form of loot. The seven or eight Crusades which took place from time to time between the years 1095 and 1291 A.D. became less and less religious and more and more secular in character. In fact, they were or soon became early forms of capitalistic enterprise. Profiting from these enterprises were emperors, kings, princes, nobles, as well as many commoners—mostly merchants. Many vassal nobles went crusading thus enabling their sovereign lords to increase their power over their fiefdoms. To that extent feudal government was breaking down and monarchical government was taking its place.

The increase of international trade stimulated in part by the Crusades had many results such as the development of banking, the use of letters of exchange, the rise of stock companies, the taking of usury by indirection, and the development of commercial law. All of these changes were inconsistent with and often contradictory to feudalism. They involved the extensive use of mobile capital whereas under feudalism most of wealth consisted of real estate. An indirect result of the Crusades was that Europe became better acquainted with the Orient, thus broadening its horizon and outlook. They also furnished the starting point for the period of discovery which led to the discovery of the western hemisphere and other unknown parts of the world.

The principal factor in the great decline of European feudalism was the successful rivalry of the towns and cities with the feudal lords. "The germ plasm of the town is to be found in clusters of merchants, who settled down under the shelter of castle or monastery, and whose protection was gradually extended over the local dependent population, whom they ultimately raised to their own level. . . . Everywhere the gradual conquest by the bourgeois of the rights of local public authority dispossessed the older feudal jurisdictions. . . . The fundamental common principle is that these urban centers were derived from the same generative and active principle, namely, trade. . . .

483

There were no more servile tenures; each owner was free. Wealth determined the burgher class and gave status."[43]

After the beginning of the 11th century there arose in these medieval towns and cities the merchant and artisan guilds which controlled capital and regulated labor, which governed the production and distribution of wealth, and which fixed prices and wages. They developed into aristocracies of the master merchants and artisans and were the forerunners of the modern capitalist corporations. The bourgeoisie and their guilds had a common interest in cooperating with the king in depriving the feudal lords of their power. Thus the modern centralized monarchy and nation came into being and led in turn to modern imperialism. Whether or not there was less oppression and exploitation of the common man is a moot question. Nationalism led to patriotism and chauvinism and imperialism to colonialism.

During the latter part of the feudal period there was a great rise in prices and wages. This was due at least in part to the increase in the amount of money in circulation. The inflation tended to impoverish the feudal nobility whose income consisted mainly of relatively fixed rents. The bourgeoisie, on the other hand, was profiting by the rise in prices. Some of the rich bourgeois purchased the land at bargain prices of the land-poor feudal nobility. Thus economic factors were at work to extinguish or at least to transform feudalism in many parts of Europe, especially in western Europe.

[43] J. W. Thompson, *op. cit.*, pp. 775-7.

484

Chapter XXX

The Rise of Modern Nationalism from the Medieval Period

Chapter XXII has described how the empires of the first period of imperialism, and to a large extent of the second period of imperialism as well, arose out of the expansion of city-states. These small states had arisen in turn out of a primitive tribalism in which the bond of union was an authentic or supposititious common descent. Such a bond of union often persisted in the city-states. But in certain areas a large and more powerful city-state conquered some of its neighbors and then continued to grow through conquest or mere accretion until it attained imperial dimensions with an almost absolute rule over its subject territories. Thus arose the ancient empires of Egypt, Mesopotamia and Rome in which common descent was no longer regarded as the bond of union. Even less was that the case when a migratory pastoral people conquered a sedentary agricultural population and established an imperial rule. This happened in Mesopotamia when the Akkadians, who were probably Semitic desert nomads from the Arabian peninsula, conquered the Sumerians during the third millennium B.C. Later in the same millennium Sumeria was again invaded by another Semitic-speaking people, the Amorites, who came from Syria and may not have been pastoral. In the early part of the second millennium B.C. Babylonia was invaded and conquered by the Kassites, a people from the mountains of Elam in western Persia. At about the same time Egypt was conquered by the Hyksos, a shepherd people from Arabia and Palestine.

Similar invasions and conquests have been common enough in other parts of the world and in later times. In the Orient may be mentioned Mongol invasions of China which led to the building of the Great Wall. The Huns, a Mongol nomadic tribe from Central Asia, swept over eastern and central Europe in the fourth century A.D. and were not decisively stopped until the battle of Chalons in France in

485

451 A.D. The semi-barbarous Aryans invaded India about 1500 B.C. and probably obliterated the Indus valley civilization which may have been derived in part from the Mesopotamian, in particular the Sumerian civilization. During the early Christian centuries Germanic tribes swept over the Roman empire. In the western hemisphere tribes from the north conquered the Mayan people in central America nearly a millenium ago. In many of these cases the conquerors were absorbed culturally by the more complex culture and larger population of the conquered. During the last few hundred years most of the habitable area of the world has been occupied by a large sedentary agricultural and industrial population, too large to be conquered by the few surviving remnants of nomadic tribes. Under the influence of nationalism these sedentary peoples are now trying to conquer or at least to dominate each other by means of devastating wars, due partly to economic and ideological differences.

Primitive communities have usually ranged in population from 50 to 1,000 or 1,200 inhabitants. Beyond the last number they cannot maintain daily or customary face-to-face relations with each other. To become larger a community has to have one or more of three conditions. It must be in a region suitable for agriculture and have suitable tools of cultivation; or it must be a center for the exchange of commodities, namely, located on a highway of commerce; or it must have developed an industry, usually because some or all of the raw materials required by the industry are at hand. It is almost certain that these larger communities have come into existence only within the last 8,000 years because these three conditions have been fulfilled within less than that period of time.

In the small primitive community only such informal types of social control existed as arise from face-to-face relations, though some individuals acquired prestige which enabled them to exercise power. Among them were the old men, tribal chiefs, magicians, and priests. As large aggregations of populations arose in fertile river valleys such as those of the Nile, Euphrates, Tigris, Indus, Ganges, Hoang-ho and Yangtze-Kiang, more formal methods of enforcing social control became necessary because the face-to-face relation was no longer universal or customary. Thus arose many city-states and a few empires. In some regions and at certain periods of time arose the feudal system which has been described in the preceding chapter. Feudalism was not as extensive in space as a vast empire nor as limited as a city-state. In some cases it resulted from the disintegration of imperial power. It sometimes developed into or was followed by nationalism.

It is not altogether easy to explain why nationalism has become so prominent in the present age. It has, indeed, presented at least one very striking contradiction. "While the present age has seen such a contraction of space and time as to produce an international mind (if not an international conscience), never before has nationalism been so dominant and so aggressive. The sense of nationality did not exist among the Greeks, for whom the city-state formed the political unit, or among the Romans, who created a dominion embracing many diverse peoples. It found no expression during most of the Middle Ages. Only toward the close of the medieval period did it arise in western Europe, particularly in England, France, and Spain. It long remained rudimentary. Even in the eighteenth century the thinkers of the Enlightenment exalted, not national feeling, but cosmopolitanism." [1]

In the preceding chapter we have seen that under the feudal system there were numerous small principalities ranging in size from a few score to a few thousand square miles at most. Their lords were usually the vassals of a king who ruled nominally over a large number of fiefs. Because each feudal lord had his own army and waged warfare with whomsoever he wished, and administered justice according to local customs and rules or his own will, the king had little or no authority. Under such circumstances nationalism could not readily arise. In Europe two international agencies served for a time as obstacles, namely, the Romish church and the so-called Holy Roman Empire. Transition to nationalism took place as follows: "Under feudalism a man's 'country' was the neighborhood where he lived. His duties were owed, not to his sovereign, but to his lord. There was personal loyalty but no patriotism. Differences between peoples were largely obscured by the existence of the Roman Church and the Holy Roman Empire, both international agencies, and by the use of Latin as the common language of all cultivated persons. The new monarchies, by breaking down feudalism, promoted the growth of nationalism. Allegiance to the sovereign and to the state that he represented gradually replaced allegiance to the feudal lord. Clergy, nobles, city people, and even peasants began to think of themselves as having a common 'fatherland,' and the sense of corporate national life was immensely strengthened by the development of English, French, Spanish, and other vernacular tongues. Another very important influence in arousing national self-consciousness in England and France was the long struggle between these two countries known as the Hundred Years' War (1337-1453 A.D), and in Spain the contest of the Christian states with the Moslems brought about a similar result. Patriotism always thrives in wartime." [2] The latter contest lasted for four centuries from the capture of Toledo by the Christians

[1] John B. Wolf, *History of Civilization*, Boston, 1947, Vol. II, p. 636.
[2] Hutton Webster, *History of Civilization*, Boston, 1947, Vol. I, pp. 512-513.

in 1085 to the capture of Granada in 1492 A.D. which drove the Moslems from the Iberian peninsula.

The frontiers of the nations which arose in Europe were delineated only in part by geography. The Pyrenees separate France and Spain and Italy is separated in part by the Alps from the rest of Europe. But generally speaking the mountain ranges and the principal rivers do not serve as boundaries. Ethnically the European nations are more or less confused, though the racial differences are not as great as is usually supposed. Linguistically also these nations have more or less internal diversity, though a common language should, presumably, be the strongest bond of union. Perhaps these nations are most unified as to religion, though here again there is a good deal of diversity. At any rate, we have to look for certain historical factors, rather than geography and race or such cultural factors as language and religion, to explain the composition of these states. These factors may be economic and political in character. Much the same situation exists elsewhere in the world, though geographical factors may have had more influence in determining national frontiers in certain other regions, as, for example, in Asia where the Himalaya Mountains and other mountain ranges have constituted almost insurmountable barriers until recently when aviation began to overcome them.

The decline of feudalism and the rise of the national states came about in various ways in different parts of Europe. In England the feudal lords came into conflict with King John, whom they accused of having failed to fulfill his feudal obligations, at the beginning of the 13th century. In 1215 A.D. he was forced to sign the Magna Carta by a coalition of nobles, clergy, and townspeople. Most of this document is devoted to guaranteeing the special privileges of these three groups. The serfs who formed most of the population were mentioned only once. While it has sometimes been called a "Great Charter of Liberties," it was mainly a settlement of the disputes between these two predatory parties struggling for power and property. The popular rights of *habeas corpus,* of trial by jury, and of no taxation without representation, were supposed to be safeguarded by this charter. However, it was several centuries before these rights were generally recognized. The king had not the slightest intention of carrying out the charter. Immediately he induced the pope to declare the charter null and void. He died a year later, in 1216, and the nobles, who were the principal beneficiaries of the charter, managed to make it effective for a time. In the long run, however, their interests were contrary to those of the urban bourgeoisie. Nevertheless, they cooperated temporarily in building up parliament in order to limit the powers of

488

the king and in particular in order to retain the right of voting tax funds to the king.

Then came the so-called War of the Roses which was a fight for the throne between two branches of the royal family, namely, York whose insignia was a white rose, and Lancaster designated by a red rose. The war lasted from 1455 to 1485 when the Lancastrian leader became King Henry VII and married a Yorkist wife, thus founding the Tudor dynasty. This war was disastrous for the feudal lords because many of them were killed and their class thereby weakened. Furthermore, the business activities of the middle class urban bourgeoisie were hampered by the national disorder. Consequently, the townspeople sided with the king and helped to build up a strong monarchy which ruled more or less despotically for the next century or two. For the common people, therefore, it was like jumping from the frying pan into the fire to pass from feudal to royal rule. The centralization of power and of government began with the conquest of England by Duke William of Normandy in 1066. He forcibly united the petty Anglo-Saxon and Danish states which existed or had existed in England, such as Kent, Sussex, Essex, East Anglia, Northumbria, Mercia, and Wessex. King Egbert (801-839 A.D.) of Wessex had already compelled some of these kings to recognize his suzerainty. This process continued under the Tudor dynasty. Thus such nationalism as arose was brought about under the pressure of the force and violence which were centralizing the authority and administration of government. The expansion of England into Great Britain was accomplished by the incorporation of Wales by Henry VIII in 1536, the union of Scotland with England in 1707, and the union of Ireland with Great Britain in 1801. This expansion resulted in a greater British nation. But it did not result in an integrated national feeling, even though these four members of the British union do not vary greatly in culture, and not even in language because English is almost universally known and understood. On the contrary, Scotland and Ireland have always been restive members and after World War I the larger part of Ireland seceded to become the republic of the Irish Free State.

The national unification of France was perhaps more difficult than that of Great Britain, but resulted in a more highly developed form of nationalism. Feudalism was unusually strong in France. As late as the twelfth century there were about 40 feudal principalities. The feudal lords acted like independent rulers, coining their own money and carrying on their own wars. A few of these rulers were prelates of the church—bishops, abbots, and the like. Most of them were counts or dukes. The duchy of France was centrally located between the Seine, Meuse and Loire rivers and included the city of Paris. In 987 A.D. the last Carolingian king of the west Franks died without

489

an heir. The feudal lords elected Duke Hugh Capet of France as their nominal sovereign. Though he had no real power he was strategically located geographically. The forces against feudalism described in the preceding chapter were working in the interests of his dynasty. "By hook or crook, by conquest, by fraud, by marriage, by inheritance, by forfeiture, they drew all the separate sovereignties into their own hands, until at length their possessions had become indeed identical with a kingdom embracing most of the territory between the Rhine, the Alps, the Pyrenees, and the sea. The Capetians created modern France."[3]

The last sentence quoted is somewhat of an exaggeration because no dynasty could create a nation unaided. Every nation has been due to a concatenation of historical circumstances. By the 14th century most or all of such regions as Flanders, Normandy, Brittany, Champagne, Burgundy, Poitou, Guienne, Languedoc, and Dauphine had become incorporated in the French nation. It had a vernacular spoken by most of its inhabitants, the Roman law, a common coinage and army. "Feudalism as a political force practically disappeared with the Hundred Years' War (1337-1453 A.D.), although the nobles retained their social rank and privileges until the French Revolution. Meanwhile the kings, especially Louis XI (1461-1483), steadily enlarged the royal domain, until by the end of the fifteenth century the unification of France was almost complete."[4] The power of the French kings increased so that Louis XIV, who reigned more than 70 years from 1643 to 1715 A.D., could say with a good deal of truth, "L'etat, c'est moi." The influence of the French Revolution of 1789 upon nationalism will be discussed later in this chapter.

The unification of other European countries and their nationalization came about in various ways as will be illustrated in a few cases. About the end of the fifteenth century, as a result of the discoveries of its explorers, Portugal began to acquire its colonial possessions in Africa, Asia and America, some of which it retained to the nineteenth century. At the same time Spain also was building up a colonial empire in the same three continents. For a time the Spanish kings held the title of Holy Roman Emperor and acquired possessions in the Netherlands, central Europe and southern Italy which later they lost. After it freed itself from the Spanish yoke in 1581 Holland joined in the race for colonies. At about the same time England embarked upon its imperialist career. The wealth derived from their colonies served to unify each of these nations and to enhance the power of their monarchs. The latter consequence encouraged the belief in the divine rights of kings to rule and made absolutism wide-

3 Hutton Webster, *op. cit.*, Vol. I, p. 520.
4 Hutton Webster, *op. cit.*, Vol. I, p. 524.

spread for a time in Europe. Imperialism in its modern European and American forms will be described in Chapters XXXII, XXXIII and XXXIV.

In Germany feudalism decentralized the country perhaps more than in any other country, even more than in France. The East Frankish kings of the Carolingian dynasty descended from Charlemagne became extinct by A.D. 911, one century after his death. Thereafter the more important German feudal lords elected a king from among themselves. However, they did not pay him much obedience. In the 10th century there were five large German feudal principalities, namely, Bavaria, Franconia, Saxony, Swabia, and Lorraine. In 962 A.D. King Otto I was crowned by the pope as emperor of what was known thereafter as the Holy Roman Empire. This did not result in consolidating Germany into one national state, perhaps because the German emperors devoted much of their attention and military strength to interfering with Italian affairs. In 1273 the imperial title passed to Count Rudolf of Hapsburg who conquered Austria and founded the Austrian dynasty. The imperial title remained in his dynasty until Napoleon extinguished the title in 1806 after he had been elected Emperor of the French in 1804.[5] Until the 19th century Germany remained divided in more than 300 feudal states, varying greatly in size, and under the nominal suzerainty of the Holy Roman Emperor. These feudal rulers were princes, archdukes, margraves, counts, archbishops, bishops, etc. During the 17th, 18th and 19th centuries the kingdom of Prussia gained in power and territory in comparison with the other German states and succeeded in 1871, at the close of the Franco-Prussian war, in consolidating all of these states in the new empire of Germany.

Italy had a similar experience in that it remained divided in many states until the 19th century. This was probably due in part to the fact that the pope claimed the right to temporal rule over a good deal of territory in the central portion which divided the peninsula into a northern and a southern part. During the 19th century many revolutions took place in Europe inspired in large part by the French Revolution of 1789. Italy took part in some of the revolutions which gradually unified the country. By 1870 it had defeated the pope and in that year Rome became the capital of a unified Italy.

---

[5] Count Rudolf (1218-1291) of Hapsburg was a petty feudal lord. It is therefore surprising that he should have been elected German and Holy Roman emperor. The explanation seems to have been that the feudal lords who were the electors did not want a strong emperor who would try to control them. In 1278 Rudolf defeated and killed Ottokar, the king of Bohemia, who had been his principal rival for the German imperial throne. From that point on the Austrian empire was built up by conquests in war, marriage, and other more or less violent methods, like all empires.

The Austrian empire arose in the course of several centuries as a result of bringing together by force under one ruler several peoples of different languages and cultures. Under such circumstances the empire could not become a unified national state and fell apart in 1918. Much the same was true of Russia which since the 17th century united under one autocratic imperial rule many peoples who, however, were little unified as a nation. What will happen under the socialist regime in power since 1917 remains to be seen.

An American historian characterized western Europe at the beginning of the 16th century as follows: "Feudalism as a governmental system had largely disappeared and the Holy Roman Empire was little more than a name, but the monarchs waxed ever more powerful and the national states which they created are among the dominant political entities of today. In the emergence of national states the historian finds another great dividing line between the medieval and the modern world."[6] He exaggerated the part played by the monarchs, for many factors created the national states. During several centuries the kings wielded great power which they have now lost. But the national states continue to dominate the situation, partly due to the emotional factors which they embody, but more particularly owing to economic changes such as were brought about by the commercial revolution described briefly in the preceding chapter. "The growth of commerce in the later Middle Ages had created a town-dwelling, merchant class, whose interests, like those of the kings, were opposed to those of the feudal nobility. This 'third estate' in parliaments or diets voted money and power to kings in return for royal attacks against the baronial impositions upon trade. At the same time changes in the art of warfare that brought foot soldiers with bows and arrows or pikes on the battlefield to challenge the feudal cavalry, and cannon to batter down the feudal castle wall, made this money count heavily in political life."[7]

Most of the feudal political units were too small for the new commercial system because the barriers of tax imposts levied between the numerous feudalities seriously impeded trade. The commercial city states which had arisen beside feudalism were also too small to meet the new needs. The geographical discoveries of this time expanded both the economic and political outlook. From the mines in the western hemisphere came much gold and silver to implement the extended trade. This increase in currency also inflated European prices. This inflation impoverished the feudal lords who had to depend upon relatively fixed incomes from the rents paid in money or kind by their serfs and tenants. This weakened the nobles in relation to

[6] H. Webster, op. cit., Vol. I, p. 530.
[7] J. B. Wolf, op. cit., Vol. II, p. 51.

492

the kings. "The cheapening of bullion and the rise in prices swelled the profits seeking investment; the growth of an international banking system mobilized immense resources at the strategic points. . . . They formed together the departments of an international clearinghouse, where bills could be readily discounted, drafts on any important city could be obtained, and the paper of merchants of almost every nationality changed hands."[8] Thus arose an international banking and commercial system which would have been impossible under feudalism. It is still hampered by political nationalism.

The Protestant Reformation helped the rise of the national state to power. It weakened the claim to supremacy and in some parts of Europe broke completely the authority of the Pope and the Romish church over the secular, and in some Catholic countries even the religious rule. The latter countries formed treaties or concordats with the pope which gave their kings and governments supervision over their national churches. Thus these Catholic kings were almost as supreme as the Protestant kings who were the religious as well as secular heads of their state churches.

The theory of the national state which has dominated modern times was expressed by Machiavelli in the following words: "The state is an end in itself and owes allegiance to no law other than that of its own interests." In his principal work he advised kings how to gain and maintain absolute power over their subjects.[9] During the 16th, 17th and 18th centuries most of the countries of Europe were absolute monarchies. The doctrine of the divine right of kings persisted or was revived from ancient times. The Egyptian king had been the "Son of the Sun." The Greco-Macedonian kings and the Roman emperors had received divine honors from their subjects. The medieval kings were the Lord's anointed. The Chinese emperor was the "Son of Heaven" until 1911, and the Japanese emperor was the "Son of Amaterasu-omikami the Sun-Goddess" until 1945. The German emperor claimed divine rights to rule until 1918.

For a time such parliaments as were in existence were in abeyance. In England it began to regain its power during the 17th century, in France not until the end of the 18th century. However, the power even of these absolute monarchs was not complete. "These absolute kings lived in a contractual society in which provinces and classes rather than individuals held rights against the monarch. Their despotism was limited by these contracts, which formed the basic constitutions of their states. No absolute monarch could have reached into the pocketbooks of his subjects for money or into their homes for soldiers with the assurance of a twentieth-century government; but they could

[8] R. H. Tawney, *Religion and the Rise of Capitalism*, New York, 1947, p. 69.
[9] Niccolo Machiavelli (1469-1527), *The Prince.*

imprison the subject and punish him for his opinions as no liberal regime can do in our day. To identify their power with that of a modern dictator, however, is to misunderstand the limits of absolutism in the Old Regime." [10] The modern state, even without an absolute monarch or dictator, can and does exercise a legal tyranny over its subjects or citizens and a lawless anarchy toward the rest of the world. There are at least two causes for this internal tyranny and external anarchy. The first and most fundamental, but less obvious, is the ultimate power which rests in the hands of a small predatory dominant business class to whose interest it is to perpetuate this tyranny and anarchy. The second is the sentiment of national patriotism which is fostered by the dominant class and which makes the masses docile to be exploited by this predatory class. This sentiment arises out of deep-seated emotions which have manifested themselves in different forms at various stages in cultural evolution and may change their forms again.

Like the other primates the human species is more or less gregarious. The human individual is impelled not only to satisfy his cravings for food and sex but also to seek the satisfaction derived from association with his congeners which has been described in the psychological chapters in this treatise. Human nature is, therefore, ambivalent in that it is both individualistic and social, a combination which does not always harmonize. In the various groupings which have existed the proportions between these two somewhat incompatible tendencies have fluctuated, but it is doubtful if the individualistic traits have ever gained the upper hand. "On the one hand the individual found personal survival chiefly through the survival of his group; on the other hand the group protected itself by destroying those individuals who endangered its existence. Between this hammer and anvil was forged the powerful feeling of in-group loyalty. Under its spell the individual lost all sense of fairness, forgot all rational judgment, and, deeply stirred by emotion, rushed headlong into action with no regard to consequences whatever. But this action was tremendously satisfying, for in it self was identified with society; in other words, the individual felt that he was serving a high social purpose." These traits are fully exemplified in national patriotism. "To an extreme degree the patriotic fervor obstructs all rational conduct; as an enduring emotional fixation it orientates individual behavior about social purposes." "The patriotic fervor obscured knowledge in group excitement. And the sentimental mood made experience only the point of departure for feeling. As elaborated by the literate few, liturgical, meditative, and decorative learning failed to attend

[10] J. B. Wolf, *op. cit.*, Vol. II, p. 55.

to observed experience of the physical and social worlds in a systematic manner. In all these ways the role of a knowledge of the objective world in human affairs was obscured, and men followed the uninformed paths of necessity, worship, in-group loyalty, and sentiment; thus they made ignorance, motivated by emotions, the essential guide to action."[11]

In the last quotation Turner is referring in particular to the preliterate and early literate stages of cultural evolution. However, his statements apply almost word for word to the national patriotism of the world of the 20th century A.D. Under its influence humans behave in a sentimental mood of group excitement, without knowledge, without rational judgment, without a sense of fairness, and in a spirit of blind worship. And this is much more destructive and catastrophic than in the past because mankind now has far more deadly forces to unleash in its ignorance and blindness.

In another book I have described how patriotism reaches its deadliest level in wartime: "The sentiment of patriotism is greatly exaggerated in time of war and renders a people almost entirely incapable of appreciating the mental attitude of the enemy to whom they are induced, by the powerful emotions of fear and of hatred exacerbated by wartime hyperesthesia, to attribute the most infamous motives. The result of this situation is a dangerous form of ethical dualism in time of war which results in a most distorted view of the actual situation. The enemy peoples which have hitherto usually been looked upon with friendship, or, to say the least, with indifference, are now regarded as possessing most of the evil traits which characterize mankind."[12]

More than two millennia ago Aristotle (B.C. 384-322) studied the constitutions of 158 Greek cities. He concluded that with a good king monarchy is the best and with a bad king one of the worst forms of government. The worst form he considered a working-class government. He was inclined to favor a government by a middle class of wealthy property owners. He alleged that the success of government depends upon the virtue of the people. Apparently he believed that this virtue resides largely or entirely in a wealthy class. According to Aristotle, therefore, the objectives of a people's patriotism, in so far as they are symbolized and personified in individuals, would be a king, good, bad or indifferent, or a predatory and exploitive wealthy class, or both. He condemned usury or the taking of interest on loaned money, defended private property and wealth, condemned Plato's

[11] Ralph Turner, *The Great Cultural Traditions, The Foundations of Civilization*, New York, 1941, Vol. II, pp. 1279-1280, 1286.

[12] Maurice Parmelee, *Blockade and Sea Power, The Blockade, 1914-1919, and Its Significance for a World State*, New York, 1924, pp. 249-250.

communism, justified chattel slavery, and advocated a form of education which would instill uniform opinions in all citizens of the state. Plato's communism consisted of a common ownership of property but under the oligarchic rule of an aristocratic intellectual class. Aristotle contemplated a purely secular state unlike most conceptions of the state which have been theocratic down to the present day.

As a consequence of the conquests of Aristotle's pupil Alexander (B.C. 356-323), were established the Hellenistic monarchies. "The central organ of the Hellenistic monarchy was the kingship. Greek hero worship united with the oriental conception of the divine king to create the practice of deifying rulers. Thus the Hellenistic kings, regardless of their antecedents, became divine, and their power was regarded as having a supernatural basis. The king and the state were one."[13] The principal example was Egypt. Under the pre-Hellenistic monarchy the king or *pharaoh* was the falcon god, Horus, the son of the sun-god Re or Ra and the chief priest of all the gods. The conquering Hellenistic Ptolemies received from the Egyptian priests the *pharaonic* consecration as sons of Re. At first the whole of Egypt was the private property of the Ptolemy who administered through a ruling class of Greeks, Macedonians and Grecized Asiatics. Estates were given to members of this ruling class as tenants some of whom later became owners. "Under Greek and Macedonian leadership the traditional urban social pyramid developed toward a complete political centralization, a caste system, and a regimented economy. Political power, social prestige, and the possession of wealth were concentrated in the hands of small ruling groups. These groups were everywhere distinguished more by economic and political privileges than by racial and national unity. Outside Egypt the members of these groups generally enjoyed the privileges of municipal self-government on the Greek model. The professions and occupations tended to become hereditary, so that most forms of labor approached the status of serfdom. . . . The Hellenistic monarchy was the mature form of the exploitive state; it was, indeed, a planned exploitation."[14]

When the Romans conquered Egypt about the beginning of the Christian era the emperor became the titular heir of all the land. An historian of the Roman empire has characterized the situation in Egypt as follows: "Everything was for the State and through the State, nothing for the individual, except the mere possibility of a grey existence which saved the worker from starvation. Nowhere in the whole evolution of mankind can be found so far-reaching and so systematic limitations as those which applied to private property in

---

[13] Ralph Turner, *op. cit.*, Vol. II, p. 620.
[14] Ralph Turner, *op. cit.*, Vol. II, pp. 622-623.

Ptolemaic Egypt." [15] Needless to say, these limitations on private property did not imply collectivism for the benefit of the whole populace, in the modern sense, but a sort of capitalism managed by the state for the benefit of the ruling class.

During Hellenistic times there took place in China a struggle between state management of capitalism and economic *laissez faire* under the Han dynasty (B.C. 202-A.D. 220) which established the Chinese empire. "The government took over the operation of the iron and salt industries and went into the business of distributing the most essential commodities; the system was state capitalism, designed to increase the imperial revenue." Eventually *laissez faire* was restored. "These developments meant the restoration of private property in land, the revival of landlordism, the abolition of the state monopolies, the dependence for revenue upon the land and the peasants—accounted for under a national census—and the re-establishment of a condition not greatly different from serfdom among the peasantry." Thus the Chinese economy swung from one extreme to the other in its form of exploitation of the masses, from a highly centralized exploitation for the benefit of the emperor and his court, retainers, and henchmen, to a diffused exploitation by many merchants, landowners, industrialists and capitalists. "The Chinese empire created by the Ch'in and Han Dynasties consisted of a vast number of peasant villages loosely knit together under an aristocracy whose members justified their rule by a decorative learning made possible only by a continuous exploitation of the villagers. Thus the China of the next two thousand years was born." [16]

Under the Han dynasty came a considerable part of Chinese military imperialism. As I have said in another book: "During the Han dynasty the imperial form of government was developed and the boundaries extended as far south as the provinces of Kwangsi and Kwangtung. The Chinese, with the exception of the Cantonese, often call themselves the Sons of Han. During this dynasty China had relations with India, whence came Buddhism, Asia Minor, and the Roman empire." [17] Tonking and Cochin-China were conquered at the beginning of this dynasty and Chinese armies marched as far west as the Caspian Sea and conquered much of central Asia. Korea was conquered under the T'ang dynasty (A.D. 618-907). Burma was invaded about A.D. 224 and again by Kublai Khan about A.D. 1280. In fact,

[15] M. I. Rostovtzeff, "The Foundations of Social and Economic Life in Hellenistic Times," *Journal of Egyptian Archaeology*, Vol. 6, 1920, pp. 161-171.

[16] Ralph Turner, *op. cit.*, Vol. II, pp. 821, 826.

[17] Maurice Parmelee, *Oriental and Occidental Culture*, New York, 1928, p. 22. See also p. 279.

British imperialism in Burma and French imperialism in Indo-China were the successors of Chinese imperialism. As late as the 20th century Chinese punitive expeditions have vied with similar British expeditions into Tibet.

Religion organized as a church has often claimed independence of or authority over the state. "From the first the Christians regarded the church and the state as separate bodies, and this dualism was never given up. Until Constantine the church was at war with the Roman state; after him the two bodies shared authority over society, but questions as to their relation remained to be settled." The Emperor Constantine tried to solve this conflict by making Christianity the state cult or church in A.D. 313 by the so-called Edict of Milan which however put paganism on an equality with Christianity. This did not satisfy the church which professed to have supernatural and divine authority. "In line with this theory the church argued that the use of coercive power by the church was justified only when the state was directed by the church or served the church; in effect, therefore, the state ought to be the slave of the church."[18] This conflict has persisted down to the present day. In most Occidental countries a more or less effective separation between church and state has been reached.

The first amendment of the Constitution of the United States, adopted on December 15, 1791, reads as follows:—"Congress shall make no law respecting an establishment of religion, or prohibiting the free exercise thereof; or abridging the freedom of speech, or of the press; or the right of the people peaceably to assemble, and to petition the Government for a redress of grievances." All the state constitutions have a similar provision. Article I, Section 3 of the New York State Constitution reads in part as follows:—"The free exercise and enjoyment of religious profession and worship, without discrimination or preference, shall forever be allowed in this State to all mankind." In spite of these constitutional guarantees of religious liberty it is constantly being violated in this country. "Christianity has been officially recognized as the national religion in many ways. This happens every time that an official function is accompanied by a religious ceremony, as, for example, when Congress is opened with prayer. It is recognized in Thanksgiving Day proclamations by the President and in many other state documents. But the United States has been judicially declared to be a 'Christian' country in numerous decisions of many of the highest courts of the land, a few of which I will cite."[19]

The above brief survey of several forms of coercive social organ-

18 Ralph Turner, *op. cit.*, Vol. II, pp. 1199, 1200.
19 Maurice Parmelee, *Criminology*, New York, 1918, p. 471. In this book I have not only cited these judicial decisions, but have described many other violations of religious liberty in the laws against blasphemy and profanity, sabbatarian legisla-

ization, such as tribalism, urbanism, theocratism, feudalism, monarchism, imperialism, and nationalism, has indicated that the individuals or groups toward whom the masses were supposed to direct their loyalty has varied from time to time. In every case, however, whomsoever these groups and individuals have been, they have exploited the masses who have felt loyalty and affection toward their exploiters only under the delusion that they were being benefited. The predatory individuals and groups have often succeeded in creating this mass delusion because they have almost invariably had education and all other means of communication entirely at their command. Sometimes the masses have benefited accidentally and marginally, so to speak, from the efforts of the dominant groups to enhance and enrich themselves. This happened to a certain extent from the mercantilism which resulted from the rise of nations. "The kings and their ministers sought to build up the national wealth, power, and prestige by the encouragement of manufacturers and agriculture, the creation of a merchant marine, the establishment of foreign trading monopolies, and the acquisition of markets in undeveloped countries across the ocean. All this implied a close oversight of private enterprise by the public authorities. . . . The possession of large and flourishing colonies was considered essential to the successful operation of the mercantile system. Colonies were regarded simply as estates to be worked for the advantage of the mother country. They would provide raw materials, markets for manufactured goods, and opportunities for the profitable investment of capital. The home government tried, therefore, to prevent foreigners from trading with the dependencies."[20] The masses of the successful mercantilist countries usually prospered in a small measure along with their dominant classes. The masses of the unsuc-

tion, religious discrimination in military conscription, the laws against suicide, etc.

On April 3, 1951, the session of the U. S. Senate was opened by its chaplain with the following prayer: "Eternal God, we thank Thee for this shrine of the Nation's faith where, facing vast human issues committed to our hands, relying on a strength and a wisdom not our own, we come humbly to confess: In God we trust." The last phrase is inscribed on most of the coins of this republic.

On March 30, 1951, U. S. Attorney General J. Howard McGrath, a Roman Catholic, declared to the National Catholic Educational Association, meeting in Cleveland, Ohio, that the principle of separation of church and state is a distortion of the intent of the first amendment of the federal constitution, quoted above, and that there "must not" be "any fence between" church and state in the United States. (*The Christian Century*, April 11, 1951, Chicago, Illinois.)

For numerous examples of the interference of the Roman Catholic church in affairs of the state in America and Europe, see Paul Blanshard, *American Freedom and Catholic Power*, Boston, 1949; Avro Manhattan (pseud.) *The Vatican in World Politics*, translated from the Italian, New York, 1949. Many other churches interfere with affairs of state but not to the same degree as the Romish church.

[20] J. B. Wolf, *op. cit.*, Vol. II, pp. 104-105.

cessful countries did not prosper and almost invariably suffered, while the colonial peoples were the most exploited of all.

Mercantilism is an appropriate economic accompaniment of political nationalism. It includes among other things the fallacious doctrine that real wealth consists of money. This leads to the notion that exports should exceed imports in order to secure a so-called "favorable" balance of trade. This results in turn in so-called "protective" tariffs on imports. Underlying all of this is the theory that a nation can benefit itself by injuring other countries. Mercantilism is, therefore, a policy of robbing Peter to pay Paul. The supreme expression of this theory is a war in which a country endeavors intentionally and deliberately to injure another country or other countries under the delusion that it is benefiting itself thereby. The most disastrous of such wars have taken place during the 20th century A.D.

The modern nationalist movement has certain other aspects which should be noted. Nationalism has sometimes freed national groups which were being oppressed by being incorporated involuntarily in an empire or being exploited by a powerful national neighbor. This phase of nationalism was due largely to the influence of the French Revolution. "There had been patriotic loyalty to national kings and sentiments of love of country in the preceding epoch but it was not until the French Revolution that nationalism became a driving political force. First in France when the Revolution struck down all provincial differences and made all Frenchmen brothers, and later in the rest of Europe, this doctrine became a force of great moment for political life. Stated most simply it was an overpowering desire that people of like kind, interest, and culture should live under common political institutions."[21]

Because so many ethnic, linguistic, religious and cultural groups were being oppressed by more powerful groups, nationalism came to be associated somewhat spuriously with liberalism, democracy and even radicalism in the form of socialism. Thus freedom of opinion, speech, assembly, the suffrage, the press, and often of private enterprise, became incorporated in nationalist policies and programs. "In central Europe, Italy, Poland, Belgium, and the Balkans the idea of nationalism was the guiding principle for these men of liberty; in France and England political liberalism and democracy were most important. By the 1840's the new theory of socialism or social radicalism joined liberalism, nationalism, and democracy to disturb the political climate of the day." "The men of the period after 1848 boldly reckoned on nationalism, liberalism, and even democracy as realities that could not be ignored and used these movements to create new

21 J. B. Wolf, *op. cit.*, Vol. II, p. 171.

500

states and to organize new forms of governments. It was this generation that made the compromises that brought liberalism, nationalism, and democracy out of the ranks of revolutionary dogma and made them into supporters of the national states."[22]

This somewhat unnatural alliance between nationalism and liberalism reached its apotheosis immediately after the European war of 1914 to 1918. President Woodrow Wilson of the United States had made eloquent pronouncements about self-determination and the rights of small nations which had aroused the hopes of the Poles, Czechs, Letts, Finns, Hungarians, Rumanians, Serbs, Greeks, and other more or less oppressed or ambitious minor peoples for independence or enlarged territory. The complete or partial dissolution of the Russian, German, Austro-Hungarian and Turkish empires furnished the opportunity in the post-war settlements to set up several new national states. Thus arose the "balkanization" of central and southeastern Europe which created new problems and increased the confusion and anarchy of national states which already existed.

Liberalism has been a cloak for bourgeois exploitation by advocating free private enterprise as a form of "freedom," in spite of the fact that such enterprise usually results in wage slavery because the employer can hire and fire at will, and because it renders inevitable the business cycle during which long periods of depression cause unemployment and destitution for a large proportion of the workers. This is not genuine freedom for them. Political democracy is a delusion without economic democracy. In its broadest sense liberalism is an attitude of mind characterizing a rather small minority of humans. It is tolerant and undogmatic and therefore openminded to new ideas and ways of doing things. It believes that truth is relative and not absolute. When consistent, in this aspect it opposes the absolute truth of religion. It tends toward a libertarian philosophy of non-coercion or non-violence as much as possible without going to the extreme of anarchism.

Liberalism displays itself in varying degrees in all phases of human thought and activity, such as politics, economics, religion, education, the fine arts, etc. It opposes intolerance, dogmatism, and persecution of minorities, and advocates the civil liberties of thought and opinion, assembly, publication, and action for social change which is legal when possible but may be illegal when legal means for advocating social change and taking action to bring it about do not exist.

In all countries where a certain measure of political democracy or representative government has been attained, there is always at least one party, whatever its name may be, which tends to be slightly

[22] J. B. Wolf, *op. cit.*, Vol. II, pp. 202, 215.

liberal in its point of view, policy, and program. Such a political party is neither extremely conservative nor extremely radical but moderate and therefore middle-of-the-road. It is reformist in the sense that it advocates rather mild measures of reform in the hope that by such means some of the economic and political problems of society will be solved.[23]

Liberal democracy postulates in theory, but not necessarily in practice, the equality of all citizens before the law. Certain civil liberties are recognized and to some extent safeguarded. Among them are freedom of speech, of publication, and of assembly. The police powers and economic functions of the state are limited, while the nominal legal rights of the individual are expanded. There is a strong tendency toward a *laissez-faire* policy both in political and in economic affairs.

The liberal-democratic state, in its economic aspect, is based upon the private ownership of the means of production and free business enterprise. In its economic organization it is a form of capitalism. In its political aspect it is based upon the party system and parliamentarism. These involve the popular election of representatives and the control of the executive by the legislative and judiciary branches of the government. As contrasted with the theocratic, feudalistic and monarchistic types of the state, it is the secular or lay state. It is also the civil state based in theory, but very little in practice, upon the will of the people.

The liberal-democratic state has modified the status of war and of peace. A secular state is not interested in carrying on religious wars. Monarchism, wherever it still persists, is too weak to instigate dynastic wars. On the one hand, the orderly development of capitalism and its international and worldwide ramifications required peace and fostered a pacifist trend during the 19th century. On the other hand, capitalist interests in different countries are often opposed to each other. Certain groups of capitalists in all countries, the armament manufacturers in particular, incite wars or at least military preparedness which instigates war. The munitions manufacturers are business men like other business men, eager to make money regardless of human welfare.[24] However sinister and repulsive is the traffic in arms, it is an integral part of the capitalist system. Nationalist and imperialist war is inevitable so long as capitalism creates large war profits for

[23] The following paragraphs are paraphrased from my books entitled *Bolshevism, Fascism and the Liberal-Democratic State*, New York, 1934, Chapter I, "The Attack upon Democracy and Parliamentarism"; and *Farewell to Poverty*, New York, 1935, Chapter XXVII, "Democratic State Control."

[24] See, for example, H. C. Engelbrecht and F. C. Hanighen, *Merchants of Death*, New York, 1934; and George Seldes, *Iron, Blood and Profits*, New York, 1934.

the profit-makers. In spite of the fact that they have professed the principles of the civil liberties, the equality of all citizens before the law, etc., the liberal-democratic states have had many wars during the 19th and 20th centuries which have been almost entirely economic in origin. They have maintained large standing armies and navies and have fostered militarism and navalism which have been nationalist in sentiment. Their wars have been fought not by mercenaries and only in part by conscripted soldiers, but to a certain extent by citizen volunteers who have represented and responded to the exacerbated national sentiments of their peoples.

The European War of 1914 to 1918 habituated many peoples to violence and emergency dictatorships. It overthrew several monarchies and discredited political democracy and parliamentarism for their inefficiency in wartime. In many other ways it weakened the cult of liberty. At the same time it increased greatly the spirit of nationalism. This is not necessarily incompatible with the liberal-democratic state. But an intense nationalism tends to place the interests of the nation and of the state above those of the individual. Thus it violates most of the principles of democracy. On the other hand, the European War stimulated an opposing current of internationalism which also menaces the liberal-democratic state.

After the European War came a period of prosperity during the 1920's which was more or less favorable to liberal democracy. The intense and prolonged economic depression which followed during the 1930's still further discredited political democracy and parliamentarism. The liberal-democratic state is incapable of coping effectively with the industrial and commercial stagnation and the widespread unemployment which ensue from the business cycle characteristic of and peculiar to capitalism. This weakness renders it still more vulnerable to attack on the part of its opponents. These attacks have come from both extremes. Russia, since the Bolshevist Revolution of 1917, has passed from an undeveloped capitalist stage to state socialism. Hence it has not become a liberal-democratic state as was intended by some of the anti-tsarist revolutionary groups. Temporarily it is under the dictatorship of the proletariat until it is freed from the danger of attack from outside. The unitary Bolshevist or communist party corresponds to all the capitalist parties of the liberal-democratic countries. For example, at the middle of the 20th century in the United States the monolithic Republican-Democratic party was the correlative of the communist party in Russia. It was almost as "totalitarian" as the latter party which represents communism as those parties represent capitalism. If and when Russia is safe in a world in which collective security prevails, it can pass from state socialism to communism in a classless society in which differing views as to the policies of the communist cooperative commonwealth can be represented and advocated by political parties.[25]

At the opposite extreme, Italy was under the domination of the fascists from 1922 to 1943. Fascism brought capitalism to its highest monopolistic stage, abolished the party system and parliamentarism, in effect if not in form, eliminated democratic control over the executive branch of government, suppressed the labor movement and most of the civil liberties. As its leader, Benito Mussolini (1883-1945), crudely expressed it: "We have buried the putrid corpse of liberty." Germany followed the example of Italy from 1933 to 1945 under the misleading name of national socialism. The national socialists added nationalist and racialist doctrines so extreme in their nature that national socialism is even more incompatible with liberalism than is fascism. The German nazis injected into their creed racialism as a political principle which played only a small part in the program of the Italian fascists. Soon after the European War of 1914 to 1918 many other European and American countries succumbed to totalitarian dictatorships, among them being Hungary, Turkey, Portugal, Spain, Brazil, and some of the Latin-American countries where dictatorships have been common and where parliamentary government has not attained a stable footing.

The libertarian features mentioned above have furnished the facade for liberal democracy. But the most important feature of a state is not its outward appearance. It is the nature of the control hidden therein. The dominant control in the liberal-democratic states is economic. As Laski has rightly said: "So long as the State expresses a Society divided into economic classes, it is always the servant of that class which owns, or dominates the ownership of, the instruments of production." Laski also suggested the origin of state education as follows: "Education becomes a state-matter instead of one of purely private concern as soon as industry requires a corps of workers who can read and write." [26] It is this control by the small class of the monopolists of land and of capital which has defeated and brought to naught the libertarian and egalitarian aspirations of the liberals and democrats of the 18th and 19th centuries. In the place of an educated people is a small educated class. In the place of individual liberty is the so-called "natural" right of private property. In the place of progress to an ever higher order of human welfare are worldwide

[25] Worldwide collective security has not and cannot be attained through the leagues of sovereign nations founded in 1919 and 1945. For a blueprint of a genuine world federation which would bring global peace and prosperity, see my *Geo-Economic Regionalism and World Federation*, New York, 1949.

[26] Harold J. Laski, *The State in Theory and Practice*, New York, 1935, pp. 295, 297.

504

poverty and insecurity for the vast majority of the dispossessed and non-propertied workers. The principal outcome of industrial and finance capitalism under the acquiescent regime of liberal democracy has been the unparalleled concentration of wealth and disparity of income giving rise, on the one hand, to excessive riches, and, on the other hand, to widespread and hopeless destitution for the masses.*

It is generally believed that popular literacy in the Occident was due to the invention of printing. Although this invention rendered possible the mass production and cheap distribution of written matter, it did not of itself bring about widespread literacy. It is characteristic of any slavocracy that the servile class, whether made up of chattel slaves, feudal serfs, outcastes, or wage and pauper slaves, is not given access to the fountain of knowledge. Such knowledge is likely to give the slaves of whatever category and status ideas with regard to freedom, rights, human and cultural standards, and the like, which will menace the interests and privileges of the master class.

It is, therefore, an interesting and important question as to why literacy became prevalent in the modern western world. The answer is to be found mainly in the industrial revolution. In order to be able to read instructions and operate machines in the factory, to keep books in the counting house, to maintain records in the warehouse, to account for sales in the shop, a knowledge of reading, writing, and arithmetic became essential. Geography acquired some utility in connection with worldwide commerce. Grammar and spelling also were not to be spurned, especially for the clerical help who had to write the business correspondence, the amanuenses, the typists, the stenographers, and the secretaries.

Common school education, therefore, was due primarily, not to any fanciful notions as to the cultural rights of the wage and pauper slaves, but to the needs of modern capitalism. While a few of the idealists and ideologists of the French Revolution, such as Condorcet, indulged in vain dreams of the political enlightenment of the populace, most of the bourgeois leaders knew what they wanted and were determined to get it.[27] The industrial revolution and the rise of modern capitalism at first required political democracy in order to give ample scope to private business enterprise unfettered by feudal lords or absolute monarchs. The democratic revolution freed the middle or bourgeois class and made it dominant in the Occident. It did not loosen the chains of the wage and pauper slaves but merely changed their masters in part.

With regard to common school education, the master class could

* See Note 28.

[27] J. S. Schapiro, *Condorcet and the Rise of Liberalism*, New York, 1934, Chapter XI entitled "Popular Education."

not permit this education to serve as a threshold to political literacy and social understanding, for this would endanger its own privileges and prerogatives. Now and again it has introduced a little vocational training. But this training has been intended to prepare the worker for tasks of a routine nature which would not arouse independence of thought or of action. In any case, such training is almost entirely superfluous under capitalism. There is always at hand a large reserve of cheap labor in the vast mass of the pauper slaves. From this starvation class the capitalists can recruit wage slaves whenever a transient phase of capitalist prosperity or a war calls for an enlarged labor force.

Striking and ample proof of the last statements is furnished by the wealthiest country with the highest standard of living and the most efficient capitalist economy—the United States of America. According to a report of the Joint Committee on the Economic Report of the Senate and House of Representatives of the U.S. Congress, the distribution of families and individuals, by income level, for the United States, in 1948, was as follows:

Income	Percentage
Under $1,000	17
$1,000 to $2,000	16
$2,000 to $3,000	20
$3,000 to $5,000	30
$5,000 to $10,000	15
$10,000 and over	2

Half or more of these families and individuals did not have an "adequate standard of living." "The Bureau of Labor Statistics has estimated that in 1947 the minimum budget necessary for a family of four persons to maintain an 'adequate standard of living' varied from a low of $3,004 in New Orleans to a high of $3,458 in Washington, D.C., in the 34 cities studied. Using similar methods, the Social Security Administration estimated that a budget for an elderly couple living at the same level would have required $1,365 a year in Houston, Texas, and $1,767 a year in Washington, D.C., in June 1947." [28] In view of these facts, it is not inaccurate to speak of a large bare subsistence, starvation, pauper class in the richest country in the world. In con-

[28] *Low-Income Families and Economic Stability*, Joint Committee on the Economic Report, 81st Congress, 1st Session, Washington, 1949, p. 2.

These conditions of destitution are even more prevalent on a worldwide scale. "80% of the world's goods are available to only 20% of the world's population, and 50% of the world's population lives in subhuman misery." *World Council for the Peoples' World Convention*, Paris, 1955.

trast, the National City Bank of New York, in its April 1951 Letter, reported that the profits after taxes of 3,304 leading corporations in the United States were $10,468,449,000 in 1949 and $13,563,279,000 in 1950, an increase of 30 percent in one year. This increase was largely due to the Korean war which began in 1950, and the war economy reinstated in the United States on a more or less permanent basis on a vaster scale than ever before in the history of mankind. The Federal Trade Commission and Securities and Exchange Commission reported that the net income after taxes of manufacturing corporations of 21 industry groups was $9,021,000,000 in 1949 and $12,864,000,000 in 1950, an increase of 43 percent in one year.

In every slavocracy the principal ideological barrier against the acquisition of political intelligence and social understanding by the slaves is a slave morality. This is instilled into and imposed upon the servile class by any and every means at the disposal of the masters. Religion and the church have always been most useful for this purpose, because they invest the servile virtues with a divine sanction and impress them upon the minds of the ignorant slaves with the awe-inspiring pomp of mystifying ritual. The school, the press, radio, television, and other means of communication and propaganda are utilized whenever they reach the servile class.

Under capitalism the cardinal virtues of the slave morality are to work hard and long, to be punctual, and to be thrifty. It is not surprising that Benjamin Franklin has become a paragon of virtue. Some of his adages were. "Time is money;" "Credit is money;" "Money begets money." Similar utterances in praise of thrift by other American worthies reflect the pecuniary ideology of capitalism.[29] An earthly reward for the practice of these alleged virtues being conspicuously absent for the masses, much emphasis is laid upon the dubious prospect of a heavenly reward in a hypothetical after-life. As the satirical song of the Industrial Workers of the World graphically expressed it: "You will eat bye and bye; Work and pray, live on hay; you'll get pie, in the sky, when you die, (that's no lie)."

Tht slave morality is ably supplemented by patriotism — the ethic of nationalism. Here the school can be of great utility. National morality can be effectively imparted through the teaching of a distorted history and a so-called "civics." Patriotism extends considerably the

[29] "Economy makes happy homes and sound nations. Instill it deep." (George Washington.)

"Save, and teach all you are interested in to save; thus pave the way for moral and material success." (Thomas Jefferson.)

"Save your money and thrive, or pay the price in poverty and disgrace." (Andrew Jackson.)

"Teach economy. That is one of the first and highest virtues. It begins with saving money." (Abraham Lincoln.)

scope of the slave morality. By means of it the slaves are induced not merely to work hard and long, but to make the supreme sacrifice of their lives at the behest of their masters.

An inevitable corollary of a slave morality is a master morality. Every slavocracy is characterized by ethical dualism. The master morality sanctions abundant leisure, ostentatious expenditure, conspicuous waste, and the other features of luxurious living for the master class. This is one of the danger spots of a slavocracy. If the slaves begin to rationalize, they may discover the inconsistency of a dual ethical standard. If they become envious of the good fortune of their masters and resentful on account of their own misery, a revolution may be imminent.

Capitalism has perpetuated the forms of political democracy. Their principal function has been to serve as a cover for the exploitation of the masses. So long as a people is politically illiterate, the machinery of government can readily be manipulated by the masters. Even though the workers have been taught to read, they are effectively quarantined against dangerous ideas. The press is devoted largely to murder trials, divorces, kidnappings, sports, comics and the movies. Most of the other literature purveyed for the masses has been subjected to a fairly thorough antiseptic bath of direct or indirect censorship exercised by publishers, advertisers, business organizations, priests and parsons, and professional and patriotic moralists.

In a socialized system increased production would be distributed to the workers of the classless society and would not accentuate the concentration of wealth and disparity of incomes. Higher labor productivity would be reflected in a higher standard of living or shorter hours of labor, and not in technological unemployment. Capitalism could no longer frustrate science and technology. Work would become more and more automatized, so that it could no longer stupefy and brutalize the worker by a mechanical routine. The deadening effects of the minimum of routinized labor which could not be eliminated would be almost entirely neutralized by very short hours of labor and abundant leisure.

The automatization of production renders a large part of manual skill obsolete. The skilled specialized worker will be replaced in large part by the more generalized worker. The traits required are a broad knowledge of machinery and productive methods, relatively high intelligence, good judgment, accurate perception, alertness, sustained attention, quick reaction to signals, careful watch of instruments, observation of changes, and prompt adjustment to new circumstances.[30]

[30] "With the advent of the Power Age, the tendency toward specialized men and universal machines is gradually changing toward special single-purpose ma-

508

This generalized worker requires the sort of education which will give him polytechnical literacy, a kind of vocational training which scarcely exists under capitalism.

It may be desirable at this point to compare bourgeois, nationalist education under capitalism with collectivist education under socialism or communism. Lenin set forth the fundamental purpose of education to train the individual to become a citizen of the communist commonwealth: "The school must train the communist who possesses a broad general education, who is capable of connecting theory with practice, of connecting every step of his instruction, education and training with participation in the common struggle of all toilers against the exploiters—who possesses the polytechnical outlook and is thus capable of becoming a good specialist in a definite branch of socialist construction." Lunacharsky, who was the commissar of education of the Russian Socialist Federation of Soviet Republics from 1917 to 1929, told me in 1928 in Moscow that the aim of communist education is not to develop the individuality as such but to assimilate it in the social whole. However, he added that the personality may be developed by many and varied means. Here is recognized a distinction between individuality and personality which must be borne in mind in dealing with education as well as many other phases of Soviet life and activities.

In accordance with the mechanization and rationalization of industry, Soviet education is mainly polytechnical. Karl Marx emphasized the need for such education more than a century ago. "The division of labor in the automatic factory is characterized by the fact that labor there has lost all specialized character. But as soon as all special development ceases, there develops the need for universality, the tendency of the individual toward an all-round development." [31] An authoritative statement sets forth the theory underlying polytechnization in Russian education. "The Soviet worker must not only gain a practical knowledge of this or that process of labor but must understand also the theory of the process, the theory of organization of production in general, the theory of the national economy and politics, in order to be able to approach his work from a general viewpoint, to be master rather than slave to the machine, to be a rationalizer and inventor, to be active in the political and social life." [32]

Polytechnical education furnishes the pupil a broad understanding of the methods and processes by means of which the material equip-

chines and all-round 'universalized' mechanics." (Walter Polakov, *The Power Age* New York, 1933, p. 112.)

[31] K. Marx, *Poverty of Philosophy*, 1847, Chapter XI, Section 2.

[32] *Socialist Construction in the U.S.S.R.*, Moscow, 1933, Vols. I-II, pp. 50-51. Published by the Society for Cultural Relations with Foreign Countries.

ment of our civilization is produced. It is far more scientific than the bourgeois conception of labor education prevalent in capitalist countries which is largely handicraft. As illustrated in the above quotations from Marx and Lenin, the communists recognize that the increasing use of automatic, mechanized processes decreases the importance of narrowly specialized skilled labor. The workman of the future will need to be attentive and alert and to have the knowledge to direct the machines and to correct them when they go wrong. Thus the laborer will become the master rather than the slave of the machine, and its intelligent director rather than a routinized automaton. Stalin has indicated how work can be organized under communism. "To educate, to help grow, to offer a prospect, to promote in time, to transfer in time to another position if the man does not manage his work, without waiting for him to fail completely; carefully to grow and train people; correctly to distribute and organize them in production, to organize wages so that they will strengthen the decisive links of production and urge people on to higher skill—this is what we need in order to create a large army of industrial-technical forces." [33]

All instruction in the Russian schools is based upon science. Supernatural, nationalist, patriotic, racialist, and romantic features are banned. For the first time in the annals of mankind a state has based its ideology (in theory though not always in practice) upon science, and not at all upon daimonic, theocratic, ecclesiastical, dynastic, imperialist, ruling class, nationalist and patriotic assumptions and dogmas. A realist attitude toward the world is developed in the pupils. Emphasis upon the past is limited (perhaps too much so) as compared with the present and future, so that the past will not acquire a predominant influence over the minds of the young. Thus the power of tradition is diminished. The same pedagogical principles are applied through the press, theater, literature, and art upon the adults as well as the young.

By these means the communists hope to train a populace which will be indifferent to the blandishments of the demagogue, and unmoved by passionate appeals based upon religion, race, or nation, and by the seductions of imperialist, nationalist, militarist, navalist, heroic and romantic adventures, which down to the middle of the 20th century have caused the slaughter of untold millions of humans and the destruction of vast quantities of wealth produced by human sweat and blood. They wish to transfer the emotions hitherto directed in these channels by statesmen and politicians, priests and parsons, publicists and moralists, orators and journalists who represent a ruling class

[33] Joseph Stalin, "The Problem of Technique," speech to the executives of the Russian iron and steel industry, Moscow, December 26, 1934; *Economic Review of the Soviet Union*, New York, January 1935.

which never intends to admit all and sundry to its exclusive membership, to the inclusive mankind of a classless society.

Along with this transference of emotional energy, in Soviet Russia there is an education in public affairs intended to make the masses politically literate and enlightened. If this end is attained, leadership of any sort becomes much less essential and may become entirely unnecessary. The communist theory is that any worker and ordinary citizen should be competent to deal with affairs of state. Lenin once said that their aim would be attained when a chambermaid could run the government. Subsequent events have demonstrated that this was not an idle dream. In Moscow I was walking through the corridor of my hotel with a Russian friend. Calling my attention to one of the hotel maids he said: "She is a member of the local soviet elected by the workers." It had not occurred to me that while engaged in her prosaic tasks she was also concerned with affairs of state.

Several writers on nationalism identify or at least connect it closely with liberalism, democracy and even socialism. A voluminous writer on nationalism has said: "In the eighteenth century contemporary Europe took shape. . . . The old order, with its traditional religious foundations which had claimed eternal validity, was slowly crumbling. . . . In search of a new basis for society, European thought crystallized around the three concepts of liberty, humanity, and patriotism." [34] To associate patriotism, which is the most brutal and inhuman aspect of nationalism and which advocates and justifies the slaughter of an unlimited number of the enemy nation in time of war, with humanity and liberty is either to make an egregious error or to recognize tacitly the capacity of the human mind to entertain incompatible and contradictory concepts at the same time. [35]

The term "liberalism" has been used only during the past century or so. An American historian has said that "liberalism comprehended a belief in the power of reason to regulate the conduct of life, in critical views of dogmatic beliefs, and in an experimental attitude toward problems in government and society." Some of these traits existed sveral millennia ago in the minds of at least a few humans. This historian described the rise of modern liberalism as follows: "The beginnings of liberalism can be traced to the sixteenth and seventeenth centuries, the period when feudal society was disintegrating and modern society was emerging. Capitalist enterprise during the Commercial

---

[34] Hans Kohn, *The Idea of Nationalism, A Study in Its Origins and Background*, New York, 1944, p. 455.

[35] During the war which commenced in Korea in 1950, which was rationalized and justified by the usual demagogic claim that it was being fought for freedom and democracy, one of the military operations of the United States army was officially named, correctly as well as brutally, "Operation Killer."

Revolution was creating a new economic system. The consolidations of territory and of power into sovereign states was creating a new political system. The revival of the ancient classics, and especially the birth of modern science in the Copernican Revolution, was creating a secular culture far different in outlook from the theological culture of the Middle Ages. All these changes had in them the germinating principle of liberalism." [36] Schapiro also asserted that the changes caused by the industrial revolution and the French Revolution gave an impetus to liberalism which stands for the principles of the "essential goodness of man" as opposed to the Christian doctrine of the inherent sinfulness of man, the "efficacy to the appeal to reason," the "equality of all human beings," the "worth and dignity of the individual," the "classless society" (but not that brought about by the proletarian revolution), and the state as the "guardian of human liberty."

It is obvious that nationalism contradicts all of the attributes of liberalism. It implies when it does not assert the inferiority of other nations, it appeals almost exclusively to the emotions and not to reason, it usually permits gradations of citizenship among its own nationals, it tolerates when it does not create a class society, and it ranks with the empire, the church, and with all of the master classes as an oppressor of human liberty. Its spurious virtue of patriotism has violated human worth and dignity by obliterating them in wartime. The nearest approach between liberalism and nationalism took place when certain liberal forces espoused the cause of certain national groups, such as colonies and refugees, which were being persecuted and oppressed. But this did not mean endorsement of nationalism by liberalism. And Schapiro himself recognizes in his last chapter that the liberalism of the 19th and 20th centuries has been of the bourgeois variety which can only incidentally and almost accidentally aid liberalism in its most fundamental sense. "It is an historic truth that in both the political and social spheres the bourgeois liberals aimed to advance chiefly the interests of the middle class. Yet in the process of doing so, they unwittingly and inevitably created political machinery that served wider interests; inaugurated policies that benefited the nation as a whole; and proclaimed a political and social philosophy which, in the end, was to be turned against the very class whose interests they championed." [37]

Nationalism creates, or rather perpetuates a state of anarchy among the nations of the world. Anarchy has been abolished in theory as between individuals. It exists not only in theory but also in fact as

[36] J. S. Schapiro, *Liberalism and the Challenge of Fascism, Social Forces in England and France (1815-1870)*, New York, 1949, pp. 1, 2.

[37] J. S. Schapiro, *op. cit.*, p. 397.

between nations. It is put into effect in practice by capitalism, which thereby aids and abets the anarchy of nationalism. All nations have displayed a willingness to go to war, if capable of doing so, whenever their sovereignties have been threatened. They have often done so even when their national honor, so called, has been offended. Nationalism and its ethical complement, patriotism, have caused the slaughter of an incalculably large number of humans and the destruction of an enormous quantity of wealth which might otherwise have contributed to the welfare of mankind.[38]

Even with respect to the rights of small nations, the idea of national sovereignty has been exaggerated. In so far as these small nations have been oppressed by more powerful countries, and the fundamental rights of their citizens to freedom of speech, of the press, of religion, of language, and of cultural development have been restricted, these rights are worthy of recognition and defense. These rights are more than national rights. They are fundamental human rights. They can be more effectively safeguarded by means of an international organization which will limit greatly, if not entirely wipe out, the independent sovereignties of all nations, both great and small.

During the great wars of the 20th century a good deal of emphasis has been laid upon national and colonial rights, and upon nations and colonies as distinct political entities, in most of the declarations of the warring nations of both sides. It would be more logical to put this emphasis upon the rights and interests of the people involved as groups of human beings. In order to safeguard these human rights and interests an international political organization is needed.[39]

Such an international organization would aid greatly in solving the difficult problem of the improvement and development of the economically backward regions of the world. It would place and keep the exchange of commodities, namely, the trade of the world upon the basis of a competition which would be free from national barriers, restrictions and hindrances. As soon as a world federation of geo-economic regions comes into being the regulation of trade would perforce be in the interest of mankind as a whole and not of any

---

[38] An eminent American social scientist has characterized nationalism in the following drastic fashion: "Born in iniquity and conceived in sin, the spirit of nationalism has never ceased to bend human institutions to the service of dissension and distress. In its material effects it is altogether the most sinister as well as the most imbecile of all those institutional incumbrances that have come down out of the old order." (Thorsten Veblen, *Absentee Ownership and Business Enterprise in Recent Times*, New York, 1923, pp. 38-39.)

[39] See my *Farewell to Poverty*, New York, 1935, especially Chapters XIII entitled, "Economic Imperialism and the Search for Markets," and XIV entitled "National Sovereignty and War."

513

national groups. There can no longer be the conflicting national methods of regulating trade which have caused so much confusion and disaster.[40]

International economic relations have been much disturbed by the great variation in the different parts of the world between levels of living, the price of labor or wages, and the cost of production. Surplus capital has sought areas of low living levels in order to reap the profits accruing from a low cost of production. Economic imperialism has been encouraged and the laborers of the areas of low living levels have been exploited, especially where they have been colonial areas. The cheap products of their labor have been used to compete with the products of more costly labor in the areas of higher levels of living, and have thereby tended to undertake and pull down these higher living levels.

This is a problem of worldwide scope which cannot be entirely solved until levels of living and the price of labor have become approximately equal the world over. The cost of production may continue temporarily to vary somewhat the world over owing to the unequal distribution of natural resources and variations in other factors of the natural environment. If national economic barriers are removed the tendency in the long run will be for the equilibration of the costs of production, as well as for the levels of living and the price of labor the world over. The utilization of atomic energy may greatly hasten this equilibration.

The most important function of the world federation of geo-economic regions, in the long run, is likely to be planning. This does not mean, however, that it would have to prepare these plans in detail. It would be the function of each regional government to prepare a social and economic plan for its own region in all matters within its jurisdiction. The world federation would fit together these plans and create of them a master plan for the world as a whole. It would have a high degree of control over the production and distribution of raw materials, especially those which are limited in quantity and localized in space. This control can be exercised through a federal board for the allocation of raw materials.

The world federation would exercise a certain measure of control over the investment of surplus capital. Among the purposes of this control would be those of guiding surplus capital into productive and not speculative investments, of preventing national or regional economic discrimination, of obviating national diplomatic and private

[40] The next few paragraphs are paraphrased from my *Geo-Economic Regional-ism and World Federation*, New York, 1949-50. See especially Chapters II entitled "The Nature of Geo-Economic Regionalism," and V entitled "Functions of the World Federation."

exploitation of foreign investments, of stabilizing the industries dealing in raw materials, of equilibrating profits and losses in the world-wide capital investment field, of stabilizing prices in the raw materials market, and of liquidating satisfactorily the international debt situation which has resulted from highly speculative investment policies, economic depression and war. This control could be exercised through a federal investment corporation or administration which would set up a common pool of surplus capital derived from all parts of the world, to be allocated to private firms or to governmental projects, regional or national, the world over, with an equilibration of its profits and losses.

Nationalism may be checked by the greatly increased dangerousness of weapons not only for armed forces but also for the whole of the civilian population. Fear of uranium and hydrogen bombs and radioactive fallout from them, and of biological and chemical warfare may drive mankind to adopt world federation, though the appeal of reason has not yet attained that end. Collectivism also should check nationalism because it includes a planned and rationalized economy which cannot be limited by national boundaries.In fact, it is an open question as to whether world government can come before most or all of the world has become collectivist. If such be the case, then collectivism, disarmament, world federation and peace must go hand in hand. So long as capitalism and the anarchy of free private enterprise dominate a considerable part of the world, it is doubtful if nationalism and war can be overcome.

Chapter XXXI

Science, Invention and Technology in the Modern World

IN Chapter XXIV we have discussed science and technology in the ancient world and have noted that animistic beliefs, as manifested in religion and magic, constituted one of the principal factors against the development of science and technology. The same has been true in the main throughout the modern world, though with certain important differences. The vast majority of humans still believe that the universe was created by a god, or rather by a group of deities, for, as I have pointed out elsewhere, a wholly monotheistic religion is psychologically impossible. In Chapter XV I have said: "No religion can become or continue to be monotheistic and spiritual in the sense that no material object is worshiped. Elements of demonology, diabolism, and of fetishism creep into every religion. The latter quickly develops into idolatry in one form or another." And I have quoted from an earlier book passages indicating the unscientific character of the religious theories of consciousness.[1]

The persistent belief that the universe had a creator or creators is an example of the anthropomorphic character of much of human thinking. Because man creates certain things with his hands, therefore the universe must be the handiwork of some one—a god or gods or spiritual beings of some sort. Such naive reasoning ignores at least two insuperable objections to such a belief. The first is that if the universe, which presumably includes everything, was created by a "creator" existing in some indefinable fashion outside of it, who created the "creator"? This question reveals a logical impasse from which there is no escape for the believers in a created universe. The second insuperable objection is that if time is eternal it had no be-

[1] Maurice Parmelee, *The Science of Human Behavior, Biological and Psychological Foundations*, New York, 1913. See especially Chapter XV entitled "Consciousness."

ginning and will have no ending. How then could the universe have ever begun in time? But finite and mortal man has difficulty in graping the concept of eternity. He dreams vaguely and vainly of a universe which began at some point in time and which will presumably terminate at a later point in time. A similar logical difficulty arises with regard to space. It is as impossible to conceive of unoccupied space as it is to conceive of eventless time before and after the universe is alleged to exist. The only way to solve these logical difficulties is to abandon belief in this hypothetical and wholly imaginary *deus ex machina* and to conceive, as best we may with our very limited understanding, of an eternal universe which never began and will never end, and which occupies space at all times.

By means of these religious beliefs man has revealed his egotism, which with the evolution of culture has become overweening, his extreme cowardice, and his sadistic impulses to slaughter even his own congeners who do not share his beliefs. In all these respects mankind is different from if not inferior to all other living beings. The human animal alone inflicts pain on its fellows consciously, intentionally and purposively, and with a callous disregard for suffering. No other animal murders countless numbers of its own congeners for national, racial, religious, political or economic reasons. No other animal condemns most of its congeners to some form of slavery (chattel, wage, etc.) in order to exploit their labor. Only the human animal conceives of itself vaingloriously as the center of or at least the most significant or important thing in the universe. It alone conceives of powerful deities in its own image. It is so fearful of a cold and inanimate universe that it vainly seeks security by imagining that these deities are specially concerned with protecting and safeguarding it.[2] All of these things the vast majority of humans continue to believe and to do, including some of the scientists themselves, as I have shown in Chapter XXIV, in spite of the fact that science has demonstrated that *Homo sapiens* is a fleeting speck of dust in an infinite and eternal universe. Is it any wonder that science and the technology based on it were hampered, frustrated and delayed for many thousand of years?

It may be said that these animals have not equaled some of man's

[2] On the danger of attacking the "sacred cow" of religion an English astronomer has commented as follows: "Religion is but a desperate attempt to find an escape from the truly dreadful situation in which we find ourselves. Here we are in this wholly fantastic Universe with scarcely a clue as to whether our existence has any real significance. No wonder then that many people feel the need for some belief that gives them a sense of security, and no wonder that they become very angry with people like me who say that this security is illusory." (Fred Hoyle, "The Expanding Universe, The Nature of the Universe, Part V," *Harper's Magazine*, April 1951, p. 91.)

constructive achievements. The fact remains that they are innocent of human destructiveness and brutishness. The so-called "law of the jungle" should be called the law of the man-made jungle.

These anthropomorphic beliefs are not only of theoretical but also of great pragmatic significance. The vast majority of humans who believe that the universe was created by supernatural beings, are constrained to believe that these gods continue to meddle with the events occurring within it, including the infinitesimally petty affairs of mankind. Consequently, they call upon these mythical beings to help them, whether it be to procure food for themselves or to destroy their enemies. Religion dominated mankind down through medieval time. "The philosophy underlying medieval civilization was based exclusively on Christian theology and morality. It had as its goal the Kingdom of Heaven rather than the conquest of nature. The effect of this philosophy on science and technology was indeed profound: in the field of science the modern scholar is inclined to think 'disastrous' would be the better word. Science in the Middle Ages was totally different from modern science in concept as well as in method. Science was no longer the handmaid of philosophy; instead, both were made to serve religion. . . . The Bible and the Church Fathers reigned supreme until well into the thirteenth century." [3]

The inevitable consequence of these religious beliefs has been and still is that mankind has trusted in large part to these mythical deities for things which it needed and desired. Not until mankind recognizes that it must accomplish for itself whatever can be accomplished in a universe of natural law and forces, and which is not dominated by the whims of irresponsible deities, will it succeed in procuring whatever is feasible under natural law. In modern times a few, a mere handful of individuals, have freed themselves from these religious myths entirely or in a sufficient degree to enable them to develop science, a human invention of vast import. Science has in turn rendered possible an extensive development of technology, for most of technology is the result of and dependent upon the precise knowledge of science. "During many periods in history craftsmen and engineers had to proceed by trial and error, collecting and evaluating facts in their own workshops. . . . The modern scientist studies, measures, and calculates the forces of nature and thus provides the engineer and technologist with physical data." [4] Forbes is also right in asserting that the conquest of nature has been due mainly to science and technology and not to political factors as is mistakenly assumed by many historians who ignore scientific and technological

[3] R. J. Forbes, *Man the Maker, A History of Technology and Engineering*, New York, 1950, pp. 104-105.
[4] R. J. Forbes, *op. cit.*, p. 1.

518

achievements almost completely. "The story of man's conquest of nature is the story of his discoveries and inventions rather than of his political achievements. . . . In no field of human action can we speak more truly of evolution." [5] It might be added that these political achievements have often served to postpone these discoveries and inventions for long periods of time.

In Chapter XXIV we have also discussed how upper-class contempt for manual labor in ancient times frustrated science and technology. This was due to the fact that such labor was performed almost exclusively by slaves and menial servants. This frustration was also due to the fact that with an ample supply of cheap labor it seemed superfluous to the ancients to supplement human energy with inanimate prime movers. This attitude characterized even the scientists of that day because they were almost invariably members of the upper-class or at least dependent upon it. "Greek scientists had a horror of manual work and despised those who had to engage in it. There was no urge whatever to develop power resources. It looked as if the slaves were a sufficiently plentiful source of energy." [6] Consequently, most of the applied science was by anonymous slaves and handicraftsmen. The degrading effect of slavery prevented many discoveries and inventions, in fact, postponed them for thousand of years.

During the long paleolithic ages primitive men had used only crude stone and wooden implements and were able to gather only enough food to feed a relatively small human population. Why these paleolithic men did not invent agriculture and pottery, and why neolithic men did invent them are among the most difficult problems of the human past. Changes in the human species or changes in the human environment or both must have taken place in order to render possible the transition from the paleolithic to the neolithic culture. In Chapter III I have discussed the emergence of mankind and in Chapter VII the threshold of cultural evolution. In Chapters IV, V and VI I have described the evolution of the human traits and forms of behavior which have rendered culture possible.[7] Among them are a relatively large brain with a deeply convoluted cerebral cortex, an erect posture, the prehensile hand with opposable thumb, bi-focal and stereoscopic eyes, vocal organs suitable for speech, etc. Each of these traits is possessed in some degree by other animals. It was the combination—fortuitous in so far as any teleological design was concerned—of these traits in the human species which furnished the basis for the emergence of culture for the first and probably for the last time upon this planet and perhaps in the universe, because we do not have to assume that eternity means endless repetition. Even if such repetition

[5] *Op. cit.*, pp. 4-5.
[6] R J. Forbes, *op. cit.*, p. 62.

takes place in the course of eons of time, it can be of no practical significance whatsoever for the temporary denizens of this planet, only a subject of idle speculation for it can be neither proved nor disproved.

In Chapter VII I have described the pleistocene or quaternary environment in the northern hemisphere mainly inhabited by mankind because it contains the larger part of the global land surface. This environment was to a certain extent dominated by the movements forward and backward of four glacial periods. These periods probably lasted about one million years. A glacial period may not seem conducive to cultural evolution. However, the geological evidence seems to indicate that during more than half of these million years the glaciers were retreating and the temperature was higher than it is now when we may be coming out of the last glacial period. I have correlated the paleolithic periods, which probably also lasted about a million years, with the glacial periods. If the geological chronology is approximately accurate, the lower paleolithic was seven times as long as the middle paleolithic and the latter four times as long as the upper paleolithic. The lower paleolithic alone lasted more than three-fourths of the time. While there was a little acceleration the course of cultural evolution was very slow down to the close of paleolithic time.

Man of the wholly modern type was in existence at least as far back as the opening of the upper paleolithic period, some 30,000 to 40,000 years ago, probably earlier. The Cro-Magnon man and the negroid Grimaldi man of that period probably have direct descendants living today, the former in France and the Canary Islands and the latter in Africa. The men of the Aurignacian and Solutrean phases of the upper paleolithic displayed great skill in flaking and chipping stone implements and in carving objects of bone. Before the close of the upper paleolithic came the domestication at least of the dog and perhaps a rudimentary pottery. But a rapid cultural accumulation did not begin before the neolithic. Since this marked change cannot be accounted for by human changes it must have been due to environmental changes the nature of which is not entirely clear. Probably the passing of the last glacial period had something to do with it. "Under the changing climatic conditions during the retreat of the glaciers early modern men learned how to utilize the growing processes of plants and animals so that a more secured food supply became available, and from this circumstance flowed developments that almost completely reorganized the daily life of common men."[8]

During the neolithic period at least three types of culture arose,

[7] See Maurice Parmelee, *The Science of Human Behavior, Biological and Psychological Foundations*, New York 1913.

namely, the hoe culture, the nomadic culture, and the peasant-village culture. The first was the lowest level of agriculture combined with hunting. The second was a pastoral culture based on the domestication of animals. The third combined the cultivation of plants with the domestication of animals and the craftsmanship of some of the early industries. It has been described by Turner as follows: "The period that brought the invention of cultivation, domestication, and the domestic crafts and arts is aptly described, therefore, as the 'first great age of progress' in history. For the masses, indeed, it was the only important period of social and cultural change between the old stone age and modern times. In the main, until the rise of machine production and industrial cities, all social and cultural developments were merely superimposed upon the peasants and nomads, who lived, worked, believed, and died in the manner of their ancestors, generations without end. Upon the continued performance of routines of life organized in neolithic achievements, rested the order, stability, and wealth of all subsequent cultures. In these routines was taken up that burden of labor in the fields, on the plains, and at the simple crafts which was to be the lot of common men until very recent times. Even in the most advanced industrial nations, it should be recognized, the masses of the population are only a few generations away from the organization of life that came into existence at least seven thousand years ago."[9] From the peasant-village culture arose the city-states, nations and empires, often invaded formerly and somewhat influenced by the nomadic-pastoral culture. The urban culture arising out of the commercial and industrial revolutions dominates the situation today.

In Chapter XXIV and elsewhere in preceding chapters we have seen that prior to B.C. 3000 various tools had been invented and certain methods of production discovered. Among them were agriculture utilizing the hoe, sickle and plow; irrigation in river valleys such as those of the Nile, Euphrates, Tigris, Indus, and probably the Hoang-ho, involving collective action by the peasants, mathematics and astronomy in estimating the time of periodical floods, civil engineering in planning and constructing the irrigation channels; pottery necessary for preserving surpluses of food; textile manufacture utilizing the spindle and loom; ground and polished stone of the neolithic industry used by carpenters and other craftsmen; some copper mining; smelting and casting and the beginning of bronze; wheeled vehicles and harness for animal traction, and sail boats for transportation.

Up to neolithic time humans apparently lived in a state of what

[8] Ralph Turner, *The Great Cultural Traditions, The Foundations of Civilization*, New York, 1941, Vol. I, p. 51.

[9] *Op. cit.*, pp. 66-67.

has sometimes been called "primitive communism," though differing greatly from the communism of today which requires a complicated system of production and of distribution. There was so little surplus of food over and above the subsistence level that there could be no great differences of wealth. With the inventions and productive methods of neolithic and post-neolithic time, however, a surplus of food gradually accumulated which rendered possible the manufacture of many things other than food, and also a much greater inequality in the ownership of wealth. "It was now possible to feed groups such as craftsmen and merchants from the surplus harvest, thus leaving those groups free to produce clothing, tools, and other durable goods that the peasants had formerly been obliged to make for themselves."[10] Furthermore, then as now any one who acquired a surplus was in a favorable position to accumulate more. Thus a class division between those who possessed wealth and those who lacked it began to arise, as has been described in Chapters XXV, XXVI and XXVII. Differences in wealth and power between different members of the community increased apace. "Men used the advantage given them by copper weapons to force others to pay them tribute or rent for the land or to become their serfs. Having dominated local communities in this way, they built armies from them and went on to conquer surrounding districts—till great empires were built up."[11]

Thus arose the first age of imperialism described in Chapter XXII. It was due in large part to what has sometimes been called the "first industrial revolution" during the 2,000 or 2,500 years prior to 3000 B.C. An Orientalist gives some tentative prehistoric and early historic dates for Mesopotamia. There is archeological evidence from the prehistoric neolithic and chalcolithic (copper-stone) periods. The latter may have lasted from about 5000 to 3000 B.C. This Orientalist excavated a site at Tepe Gawra in Iraq near the Iranian frontier which has 26 cultural levels 20 of which are prehistoric. The latest is about B.C. 1500. The 13th is in the 5th millennium B.C. Sumerian history began about 3000 B.C. Writing and metallurgy appear early in the 3rd millennium B.C., or earlier in a rudimentary form. Babylonian historical information is available from early in the 2nd millennium B.C. Historical information about Assyria is available from the beginning of the 1st millennium B.C. [12]

An Egyptologist furnishes somewhat more precise dates for prehistoric and early historic Egypt. The prehistoric Faiyumic and

---

[10] R. J. Forbes, *op. cit.*, p. 22.

[11] S. Lilley, *Men, Machines and History, A Short History of Tools and Machines in Relation to Social Progress*, London, 1948, p. 9.

[12] E. A. Speiser, "Ancient Mesopotamia: A Light that did not Fail," *National Geographic Magazine*, January 1951.

Merimdean neolithic cultures were about B.C. 5000 ± 500. The Tasian and Badarian chalcolithic cultures were about B.C. 4500 ± 500. The Mesopotamian stimulation came about B.C. 3250 ± 150. By this time many city-states had been formed in the Nile valley which had combined in two kingdoms, namely, lower Egypt in the delta region whose capital near modern Cairo was either Memphis or Heliopolis, and upper Egypt to the south whose capital near modern Luxor was Thebes. These kingdoms were unified under the 1st dynasty at about B.C. 3100 ± 100 with its capital at Memphis. The first astronomical date is fixed at B.C. 1850 ± 3, so that up to that point the dates are somewhat variable. The 2nd dynasty terminated about B.C. 2700. The 3rd to the 6th dynasties inclusive lasted from about B.C. 2700 to B.C. 2200 and is designated as the old kingdom during which the greater pyramids were built.[13] The three largest at Giza near ancient Memphis and modern Cairo were constructed under the 4th dynasty which reigned about B.C. 2650 to B.C. 2500. These huge pyramids, which still survive more or less intact after four and one half millennia, are exceeded in size only by the great pyramid of Teotihuacan near Mexico City built by the Toltecs about 1,000 years ago. Under the 5th and 6th dynasties smaller pyramids were constructed not far south of Giza at Sakkara and Abusir. More were built later so that the total number of these monuments to the vanity of rulers is more than 70. However wasteful they were, they give some indication of technology during the first age of imperialism. "One marvels at the engineering skill which they display and at the craftsmanship of the masons working with only stone and copper tools, but most of all one marvels at the immense resources controlled, directed, and wasted by one man in the creation of monuments so useless and unprofitable."[14]

Such human waste has occurred often in the doleful annals of mankind, either to minister to the arrogance of emperors, such as those of the Ming and Manchu dynasties in China and of the Mogul dynasty in India, or to the useless worship of mythical deities, such as the temples and cathedrals of Europe and America. However, what concerns us at the moment is the technological significance of the Egyptian pyramids. The great pyramid of Khufu (Cheops) is 775¾ feet square. It contains 2,300,000 blocks of stone, some of which weigh 350 tons, and totalling 5,750,000 tons, or 2½ tons apiece. The enormous amount of work required to quarry, shape, transport and hoist into place these millions of blocks can readily be imagined. Herodotus (Greek historian of the 5th century B.C.) reports a tradition that 100,000 men (slaves or serfs or peasants) were employed in moving

[13] John A. Wilson, *The Burden of Egypt, An Interpretation of Ancient Egyptian Culture*, Oriental Institute, Chicago, 1951.

[14] H. Webster, *History of Civilization*, Boston, 1947, Vol. I, p. 152.

these blocks for 3 months of each year for 10 years. However great a waste this labor was, it may have contributed a little to the technique of construction. This technique did not change greatly for two millennia. "Apart from architectural forms, it can almost be said that, after the Great Pyramid, the masonic craft remained static as regards mechanical and technical processes until the advent of the Greeks and Romans."[15] This brings us to the difficult and serious problem of the long retardation in the development of science and technology and of the fluctuations in their rate of development before their modern phase. We know that for many centuries the small ruling class of kings, nobles, priests, land-owners, and capitalists produced nothing and lived well from the work of the slaves, serfs, peasants and craftsmen who produced everything but received only a bare subsistence. The latter class had the only practical experience of the techniques then in existence but no incentive to improve them because their masters would seize any increase of products. On the other hand, the master class knew only the art of government which at that time was solely an art of exploitation. "Thus, with one class possessing the requisite knowledge and experience, but lacking incentive and leisure, and the other class lacking the knowledge and experience, there was no means by which technical progress could be achieved."[16]

About a millennium and a half after the pyramid age came the iron age. We have seen in Chapter XXIV that we do not know when the smelting of iron was invented. It may have been about B.C. 1400 in Armenia or Anatolia. But iron tools and weapons were not widely used in the eastern Mediterranean region until about B.C. 1100. Iron is much more plentiful and widely distributed and vastly more useful than copper or bronze which were essentially luxury metals. During the next few centuries iron tools became available for the farmer thus increasing greatly the output of agriculture. The food surplus rendered possible a larger number of industrial craftsmen who had better iron tools with which to work. The makers of iron tools furnished them to farmers as well as to craftsmen. Thus tools of iron, which were much more efficient than tools of wood, stone, copper or bronze, became more widely disseminated. The amount of wealth produced increased greatly. As in the past, much of this increase went to the wealthy because they owned slave craftsmen and peasant serfs, or because they had loaned money to craftsmen, peasants and merchants, or because they were emperors, kings, priests, nobles, landlords and soldiers who claimed and obtained tribute by force. But some of it doubtless fed and clothed an increased population, probably at a

[15] Engelbach, in *The Legacy of Egypt*, edited by S. R. K. Granville, Oxford, 1942, p. 148.
[16] S. Lilley, *op. cit.*, p. 18.

little higher standard of living. Because these iron tools were cheaper as well as more efficient than the earlier tools they could be more widely possessed. The situation created a market and stimulated commerce and transportation of goods from their place of manufacture to the markets, some of them quite distant.

It has also been contended that the iron age caused a certain amount of democratization by making the use of tools more widespread. For example, Athens became a center of industry and commerce and by B.C. 450 had developed a form of citizenship with more or less equal rights. However, all slaves, women and foreigners were excluded so that Athenian citizenship was shared by only a small minority of its inhabitants. Furthermore, even though production was at first by free independent craftsmen, the growth of the export trade gave rise to a factory system which utilized slave labor which success in war, piracy and the indebtedness of many peasants made available. Slavery was not only an obstacle to political progress but also delayed greatly the utilization of non-human prime movers. For example, the water wheel was little used not only in Greece but in the Roman empire so long as victories in war furnished a plentiful supply of slaves.[17]

The utilization of animal and inorganic prime movers was long delayed by the debasement of labor. Sailing was invented before B.C. 3000 and was widely used because it enabled men to travel long distances over water, though galley slaves were also used for this purpose. The wheel also was invented before B.C. 3000. Then animal power was used to draw wheeled vehicles which were in use in Sumeria as early as B.C. 3500. Animal traction of vehicles and plows was rendered possible by the harness. However, the early harness included a band around the horse's throat which forced his head up and back and thereby decreased his pulling power greatly. It is strange that traction from a yoke resting on the shoulders of the animal was apparently not invented, at any rate in Europe, until the 10th century A.D. The use of horseshoes also began about 900 A.D. in Europe, thus making available the full power of the tractive animal. It is not known when the windmill was invented but it did not come into general use in Europe until the 12th century A.D.

An historian of the Roman empire has commented on the lack of technological advance in the 3rd and 4th centuries A.D. as follows: "The problem remains. Why was the victorious advance of capitalism stopped? Why was machinery not invented? Why were the business

[17] "The slaves were the backbone of the economic life of the Empire, especially in commerce and industry, where they supplied the labor employed by the owners of the various workshops." (M. Rostovtzeff, *The Social and Economic History of the Roman Empire*, Oxford, 1926, p. 100.)

systems not perfected? Why were the primal forces of primitive economy not overcome? They were gradually disappearing: why did they not disappear completely?"[18] The implication seems to be that technology did not progress because capitalism was stopped. This historian several times referred to lack of purchasing power as impeding capitalism. For example, elsewhere in his book referring to the 2nd century A.D. he said: "The market for industry was now limited to the cities and the country districts of the Empire. The future of ancient industry depended on their purchasing power, and while the buying capacity of the city *bourgeoisie* was large, their numbers were limited, and the city proletariate grew steadily poorer."[19] Like most historians and economists he did not recognize that this is a permanent and ineradicable obstacle and that under capitalism purchasing power is usually inadequate to distribute the goods which could readily be produced, even under the capitalist system, to say nothing of an economic system on a much higher technological plane with a method of distribution capable of furnishing the whole population the goods they need and desire. In another book I have described these fundamental traits of capitalism at length. Among the contradictions in its financial structure are the following: "Withdrawal of profits reduces buying power and disturbs market relations, because effective demand cannot absorb actual or potential supply. Inasmuch as the price level must average higher than the cost of production, business enterprise does not promptly release as much purchasing power as the distribution of its products requires." Other contradictions are involved which apply more particularly to modern capitalism.[20]

Another inherent phase of capitalism which limits its ability to progress to an ever higher stage of economic development is its ambivalent character in that it contains both competitive and monopolistic tendencies. These opposing tendencies give rise to contradictions among which are the following: "Capitalist 'freedom,' namely, free private enterprise, does not promote the freedom, or, in the long run, the well-being of most individuals. Free competition between individuals is prevented by private property in and the inheritance

[18] M. Rostovtzeff, *op. cit.*, p. 484.

[19] *Op cit.*, p. 305.

[20] Maurice Parmelee, *Farewell to Poverty*, New York, 1935, p. 266. See especially Chapters XV to XVIII inclusive, entitled "The Business Cycle," "Unemployment and Wages," "Capitalistic Production and Waste," and "The Contradictions of Capitalism."

Historians and social scientists should take care not to be influenced unduly by the economic and political systems under which they live. Rostovtzeff was inspired by an animus against Soviet Russia from which he was a refugee.

of land and capital which destroy equality of opportunity, and which also decrease greatly the efficiency of management. 'Pure' competition, even in its capitalist sense, is deranged and limited by the monopolistic features which inevitably creep into capitalism because of its ambivalent character."[21]

More directly related to the subject of this chapter is the inability of capitalism to make a full and consistent use of science, invention, and technology which not only creates additional contradictions but accentuates some of the contradictions in its financial structure, especially with respect to inadequate purchasing power. "Capitalism utilizes science, invention, and technology to promote profits, but otherwise frustrates them by neglect or suppression. Capitalism gives rise to technological unemployment, but opposes shorter hours and distribution of work because it fears increased labor costs. Reduction of wages in order to diminish labor cost increases capital cost by decreasing purchasing power which in turn reduces sales and output. The power age decreases capital investment and labor in relation to the amount produced, thereby lowering the effective demand. To that extent the market becomes more restricted for both capital and consumption goods. Mechanization of industry renders fixed capital charges high in comparison with labor cost."[22]

The decline of the Roman empire decreased the supply of slaves because they were no longer being secured by means of war and conquest. During this decline which lasted for several centuries arose the system of feudalism in Europe which has been described in Chapter XXIX. In this system the serf took the place of the slave. While no more free than the latter in many respects, the serf was not quite so much separated from his lord in class and status as was the slave, regarded as less than human, from the emperor who became "divine" like an Oriental despot, in the later days of the empire. Hence the serf had a little more independence and the lord of the manor had some knowledge of and more interest in the productive processes. The craftsmen also were no longer slaves. These changed conditions were

---

[21] Maurice Parmelee, *op. cit.*, pp. 265-266.

Monopoly in the United States has been described in the following books: G. W. Stocking and M. W. Watkins, *Monopoly and Free Enterprise*, New York, 1951; *Monopoly Today*, Labor Research Association, New York, 1950. Just before the war of 1939 to 1945 the Temporary National Economic Committee published many reports which indicated the extent of concentration in the American economy, especially in manufacturing.

[22] Maurice Parmelee, *op. cit.*, p. 268.

The above quotations from my *Farewell to Poverty* apply more particularly to the effect of the capitalism of the modern power age upon science and technology which will be discussed later in this treatise.

somewhat more encouraging for inventiveness and for substituting animal and inorganic sources of power for the comparatively limited human energy. These conditions constituted the principal cause for the increase during the middle ages of machines and the great utilization of animal, wind and water power. "These three sources of power, at last rationally used, made a tremendous difference to the world. Before their arrival a high level of civilization could only be provided for a few, on the basis of huge numbers of slaves, used not as workers, but as sources of power, as engines. . . . These new sources of power, therefore, provided the basis for the development of a high level of civilization without slavery, and as they were developed slavery died out."[23]

Nearly three millennia earlier Egypt had passed through a feudal period. During the so-called first intermediate period between the old and the middle kingdoms, namely, from the 7th to the 10th or 11th dynasties, the kings lost much of their authority to the lords of the nomes, which were formerly city states, of which there were about 42. This period lasted about two centuries from B.C. 2200 to 2000.[24] But it is doubtful if even under feudalism the Egyptian worker had enough freedom to be able to exercise any degree of independence and initiative. The same was probably true elsewhere in ancient times.

Two inventions which increased greatly the possibility of invention were paper and printing. Both of them seem to have been invented in China but did not have far-reaching effects there, perhaps because the Chinese script was so clumsy and complicated and the alphabet so numerous that very few could devote their lives to mastering it. The printing of books in substantial quantities in Europe commenced about 1450.[25] Because many craftsmen and other workers could learn to read the relatively easy European languages and to procure readily the inexpensive printed books, it became possible for them to acquire a good deal of technical knowledge which had hitherto been inaccessible for them. "This was a revolution comparable to that brought about by the introduction of iron. Iron democratized physical tools; printing did the same for the tools of thought. This

[23] S. Lilley, op. cit., p. 40. This does not mean that slavery has died out entirely throughout the world, as we have seen in an earlier chapter. See, for example, Bruno Lasker, Human Bondage in Southeast Asia, Chapel Hill, N. C., 1950. This book describes slavery, serfdom, peonage, debt bondage, and compulsory public service in Indochina, Indonesia, Burma, Siam, Malaya, British Borneo, and the Philippines. The Economic and Social Council of the United Nations has a committee of experts on slavery.

[24] John A. Wilson, op. cit.

[25] Maurice Parmelee, Oriental and Occidental Culture, An Interpretation, New York, 1928, pp. 80-81. See also T. F. Carter, The Invention of Printing in China and Its Spread Westward, New York, 1925.

was an important factor in the increasing rate of invention which came in the following centuries."[26]

We now come to the commencement of the five centuries of modern times. During this period the number of the fundamental kinds of implements and of machinery at the disposal of mankind has increased from 3 to 4 times while the amount of goods which can be produced with their aid has increased vastly more. During the same period the rate of invention has risen with rapidity. If we go back to the beginning of the period of invention, which lasted from about B.C. 5000 to 3000 during neolithic and chalcolithic times, we find that we are now equipped with at least 30 times as many fundamental tools, while the volume of goods which can be produced is incalculably greater and is limited only by an economic organization which is incapable of utilizing to the full the technical equipment already available.[27]

Earlier in this chapter we have seen that the autocratic Roman empire based largely on slave labor discouraged inventiveness almost completely. The feudal system encouraged a small amount of inventiveness because authority was more dispersed and the serfs had a small amount of freedom. However, the inventions achieved called for more division of labor and production on a larger scale than was possible under feudalism which was based almost entirely upon small scale agricultural production. Two forms of social organization might render this possible, namely, capitalism with the incentive of private profits but no plan, which actually developed after the middle ages, and collectivism with a planned economy which can remove all restrictions from inventiveness and all obstacles from production, which has commenced only during the first half of the twentieth century.

During the 15th century began the great expansion of trading known as the commercial revolution. As we have seen, it was due in large part to improved methods of transportation, exploration, discovery and colonization. It rendered it possible for a community to specialize in its productive activities and to procure some of its necessities from other communities. It resulted in large-scale industry which required a higher degree of mechanization. The great increase of sea-going commerce required more accurate methods of navigation. While the latitude could be determined more or less accurately by observation of the stars, the directions being determined by the points of the compass, the longitude could not be determined without a mechanical clock on board ship registering Greenwich time which could be compared with sun time. A mechanical clock is said to have

[26] S. Lilley, *op. cit.*, p. 47. See also his chapter entitled "Iron, the Democratic Metal (1100 B.C.-A.D. 500)."

[27] See Chapter XXIV entitled "Science and Technology in the Ancient World."

been invented during the 13th century while the spring clock was invented in about 1490 A.D., and the pendulum clock in approximately 1657 A.D.

The commercial revolution stimulated in part many inventions in various industries, such as the textile industry, milling, mining, paper making, and most branches of metallurgy. The great increase in the use of power-driven machinery stimulated the search for new prime-movers or improvements of the old ones, such as water wheels and windmills. The first of the new prime-movers was steam which after much experimentation by many inventors was made effective in Watt's steam engine in the latter part of the 18th century. Electricity arrived as a prime-mover in the 19th century and atomic energy in the 20th century. Early in the nineteenth century the steam engine was applied successfully to travel upon the sea in steamships and upon land on the railroads. At the close of the 19th century it was applied to travel upon roads in automobiles. During the latter part of that century and the beginning of the 20th the oil-burning internal combustion engine using the explosive expansion of gas within a cylinder was applied to the automobile and rendered aviation on a large scale possible. This is because this engine is of very light weight in relation to the amount of power it generates.

The English revolution of 1640 destroyed much of what remained of the feudal system and rendered it possible for England to become the first highly industrialized country during the 18th century. The French revolution of 1789 swept away the feudal remains and enabled France to become industrialized. Industrialization advanced rapidly in the United States after independence was gained in 1783. Some of the social effects were harmful. Many hand workers were thrown out of employment. Hours of work were long—12 to 16 hours—and factory conditions were bad. The workers were at first helpless and could only riot ineffectually against the machines. Not until the workers began to unite in trade unions and political movements in their behalf commenced, did their conditions improve.

On the other hand, the economic result was a vastly greater production of commodities. As always heretofore, these products were very unevenly distributed. At first the workers did not benefit at all by this increased production. Then gradually the standard of living even of the working class began to rise slightly. An indirect result was that the population began to increase rapidly largely because of the fall in the death-rate due to the higher standard of living and the advance of medical science. The centralization required by large-scale production resulted in the growth of monstrous cities. The steamship and the railway rendered possible the worldwide distribution of these products.

530

The rapid increase of population demanded a much greater supply of food. This in turn required a mechanization of agriculture. As has often happened, the need stimulated the inventiveness which created the machines in the form of mechanized plows, seeders, rakes, reapers, threshers, and the like. In the United States in 1787 it required the surplus food produced by 19 agricultural laborers to feed one urban dweller. By the middle of the 20th century 19 agricultural workers could feed 66 urban dwellers. Each agricultural worker could support three-and-one-half workers engaged in manufacturing, transportation, and other non-agricultural occupations which are involved in large-scale production and in raising the standard of living. The invention of mechanical refrigeration about 1870 was also important for feeding large industrial populations because it rendered possible the preservation of food for transportation and for storage.

Until the 18th century wood was the principal material from which machinery was constructed. Wrought iron could as yet be produced only in small quantities and cast iron was too brittle for most purposes. Consequently, iron was utilized usually only for cutting edges and bearing parts. Toward the close of the 18th century the method of producing malleable wrought iron by a puddling or stirring process was greatly improved. It became possible to produce large quantities for the manufacture of machines, rails and later iron ships, automobiles and aeroplanes. In the aeroplanes lighter metals are predominantly used. During the 19th century was perfected a method of making steel, a form of wrought iron of great toughness and tensile strength, which is now widely used in the manufacture of machines and especially of tools. Its properties have been multiplied by alloying it with small amounts of non-ferrous metals such as tungsten, chromium, manganese and nickel.

During the second half of the 19th century was perfected a method of producing aluminum in an electrical furnace. Bauxite, the ore from which this light metal is derived, exists in huge quantities in the earth's surface. In its pure form or alloyed with other non-ferrous metals, such as copper (duralumin) and magnesium, it has acquired great commercial importance, especially in the aviation industry. In the 20th century plastics are becoming useful for many purposes because they are light-weight, inexpensive to produce, and their raw materials are almost unlimited because some of them are organic products which can be cultivated.

The lathe in its many forms is the most important of machine tools. During the 19th century it developed into a machine of great precision. This rendered possible the manufacture of interchangeable parts which are exactly alike. Otherwise the mass production of automobiles and of many other manufactured articles would have been

531

impossible. The only kind of mass production which was possible earlier was of articles of only a single part such as pins and nails. It was not necessary for two specimens of such an article to resemble each other closely. The enormous output of the past century has been due mainly to these two types of mass production. Among the many other methods and tools recently introduced may be mentioned tungsten carbide used in making high-speed tool-steel which has increased cutting speed greatly; grinding instead of cutting to secure a finish of high precision; oxygen flame cutting; automatic machinery, such as die-casters; the photo-electric cell or "electric eye"; the tractor; the internal-combustion turbine; synthetic chemical products, such as used in plastics; etc. During the past century or so have been invented innumerable other mechanical and electrical devices some of which are producers' goods and others are consumers' goods. Machines to produce the latter have increased greatly since the beginning of the 20th century, and have raised the standard of living actually for the privileged class and potentially for the masses.

During the two wars of 1914 to 1918 and 1939 to 1945 there was an increase in the tempo of inventiveness and of technological advance, especially during the latter war. Among other things this was illustrated in many improvements in flying and in the release of atomic energy. The volume of products increased greatly though most of this increase was of products wasteful and injurious to mankind. This wartime increase was due mainly to full employment and to an economy more or less planned under government control. Between these two wars there came, however, one of the worst economic slumps in the annals of mankind during which production decreased about 50 percent, there was widespread unemployment, and technological advance almost ceased. The only exception was Soviet Russia where many new inventions were applied. As Lilley has explained: "These results were achieved by a conscious approach to the problem of mechanization. The objective of plenty for all could be reached only through raising production by the most advanced techniques. The raising of the technical level was not left to individuals, but was undertaken by the State and became one of the main political tasks. Inventors were given every possible encouragement; apparatus, laboratories, and so on, were lavishly provided. Education was directed to providing a maximum of skilled engineers, scientists and inventors. Workers were given facilities to enable them to use their intimate knowledge of the job for the purpose of inventing improvements. Hundreds of thousands of inventions came from workers."[28] However,

[28] S. Lilley, *op. cit.*, p. 140.

In my books entitled *Bolshevism, Fascism and the Liberal-Democratic State*, New York, 1934; and *Farewell to Poverty*, New York, 1935; I have given statistics of

the level of production was so low in Tsarist Russia, Soviet Russia was so hampered by hostile intervention during its first decade, and the destruction of the war of 1939 to 1945 was so great that the standard of living remained for a time below that of the leading capitalist countries.

In addition to human muscular energy, there are three forms of natural energy, namely, (1) gravitational, (2) chemical or electromagnetic, and (3) nuclear energy. "Apart from sailing ships and a very imperfect harnessing of animals, till two thousand years ago man's own muscles provided the only source of power. Athens became a very rich city because on an average each freeman had the muscles of half a slave to work for him. But in 1935 the 1,231 million h.p. of engines of all types in the U.S.A. were equivalent to some *seventy* slaves available to work for every man, woman and child in the country. Britain was a little less well off with the power equivalent of about fifty slaves per head. Since then the number of these power 'slaves' has been steadily increasing." [29] For example, the volume of electrical energy produced in the United States increased more than three times from 91,111,548,000 kilowatt hours in 1930 to 291,032,277,000 kw. hrs. in 1949, while the population increased less than one-fourth. In 1955 it was about 546,000,000,000 kw. hrs. The standard of living at any time and place depends upon the amount of power available and the efficiency of the tools and machines energized by this power to produce the goods which make up this standard. For example, in 1830 with a sickle and flail it required 57.7 man-hours to produce a bushel of wheat. In 1930 with a combine harvester it required only 3.3 man-hours. In fact, all the factors are in being to provide a high standard of living for the whole of mankind, namely, adequate man-power, an almost unlimited and inexhaustible supply of non-human energy to be utilized as prime movers, an already large number of tools and machines for the mass production of useful commodities, and human inventiveness capable of creating many more of these productive implements if given the slightest incentive and encouragement.

Why then is the vast majority of mankind still living in dire misery? Why has no nation yet attained a genuinely high standard of living? Why is mankind overtaken every few years by man-made catastrophes such as economic crises and depressions and wars? Why have the few comparatively slight advances made by mankind been fol-

---

Russian production up to 1935. Lilley has given similar statistics up to 1939. Reliable figures are not yet available to show Russian production during and after the war of 1939 to 1945. Owing to the threat from the west, the Soviet Union has been burdened with the maintenance of vast armaments since 1945 which have reduced the volume of consumption goods.

[29] S. Lilley, *op. cit.*, p. 180.

lowed by long periods of stagnation and regression? Why has human inventiveness been so little used? The answer, or a part of it, is to be found on nearly every page of this treatise. Most of the time and in most places, at least since the dawn of history, the prevailing economic system has been guided and controlled primarily by the search for private profits and not by the motive of supplying the needs of mankind. In other words, it has not been a genuine social economy. The satisfaction of human wants has been attained only incidentally and usually very inadequately as a sort of an accidental epiphenomenon of the hunt for profits. As profits require scarcity, a plentiful supply of any commodity has rarely ever been attained. In this search for profits predation and exploitation have almost invariably been used and have often resulted in monopoly of one sort or another and in war as an instrument of acquisition. What have been the effects upon technology of these man-made handicaps to human progress and well-being?

For many tens of thousands of years mankind lived in the eolithic and paleolithic stages of culture described above in Chapter VII and VIII. Why human progress was so slow during this long period is an almost insoluble problem. Perhaps there were some man-made obstacles of which we do not know. Probably the glaciers had something to do with it, as we have already noted. In any case, the rate of invention doubtless is cumulative and accelerative in the sense that each invention renders its successors somewhat easier to be born, provided no man-made obstacle interferes. Not until the neolithic period did the tempo attain any degree of speed. During that period were invented or greatly improved the useful arts of agriculture, pottery, basketry, weaving, mining, smelting, casting, etc. During the latter part of the neolithic and the chalcolithic period, from about b.c. 5500 to 3000, were invented or improved such agricultural implements as the hoe, sickle, flail, and plow; for pottery the bow-drill and wheel; for weaving the spindle and the loom; mainly for working copper and making bronze, the bellows and smelting; ground and polished tools of various sorts; for transport the sail, harness and wheeled vehicle. However, after this period of fairly rapid advance of two millennia or more there came a hiatus of about one millennium during which there were no inventions of fundamental importance. In fact, the same rate of technical progress in relation to the technical level already attained was not reached again until the beginning of modern times about five centuries ago. In other words, for about four and one-half millennia there were only a few short outbursts of technical progress while most of the time there was relative stagnation. Why did the natural and ever-present forces for progress not operate at much the same rate throughout this long period? The ineluctable conclusion is that man-made artificial obstacles hindered this progress most of the time.

534

The comparatively rapid progress of neolithic and chalcolithic time created a considerable surplus for the first time in the annals of mankind. As we have seen in Chapters XXV to XXVIII it transformed a more or less egalitarian society into a class society which did not encourage invention because the master class had an ample supply of labor at hand and did not feel the need of labor-saving devices. It was, however, concerned with making changes in the art of government which would make its exploitation of labor more effective. During the iron age the relative invention rate, namely, the rate of technical advance relative to the technical level already reached, rose somewhat reaching a low peak during the heyday of Greek culture described in Chapter XXIV. However, industrial slavery increased greatly and the small Greek states were constantly warring with each other so that the invention rate soon dropped. A couple of centuries or so later this rate rose again to a small peak during the Hellenistic period when Alexander's conquests led to the spread of Greek culture over a large part of the Mediterranean area. Then came the long period of the Roman empire described in Chapter XXIII when there was an ample supply of slave labor procured largely through conquests in war which discouraged invention. For another millenium or so the relative invention rate was practically at zero. However, the decline of the Roman empire and the invasions of the barbarian tribes from the north decreased the supply of slaves and caused a labor shortage. Furthermore, the northerners introduced a form of social organization in which the craftsmen had greater latitude and therefore more incentive to invent. About the beginning of the second millennium A.D. came a rise in the relative invention rate which during the period of feudalism carried it to a peak somewhat higher than the earlier peaks. During this period the use of water and wind power was considerably increased. The horseshoe (900 A.D.) and an improved harness (1225) greatly increased the use of animal power. Among other inventions were the magnetic compass (1195), mechanical clock (1232),[30] wheelbarrow (1250), modern rudder (1250), spinning wheel (1298), lathe (1350), cast iron (1400), spring clock (1490), powered town water supplies (1500). Needless to say, most of the dates are approximate.

As we have seen earlier in this chapter, feudalism could encourage invention only to a very limited extent. It could permit only small-scale production and mainly agriculture. Consequently, about the 14th or 15th century there came again a slump in the relative invention rate which lasted for a century or two. More division of labor and large-scale mass production were needed to stimulate this rate. They

[30] The *Encyclopedia Britannica* ascribes the invention of some sort of clock to Pope Sylvester II in A.D. 996.

were furnished by modern capitalism utilizing the free labor supply of the growing cities. With the incentive of private profits capitalism continued to furnish this stimulus until comparatively recently. Now the question is whether it is not more of an obstacle than it is a stimulus.

Feudalism and capitalism furnish illustrations of how an economic system may vary greatly in its effect upon technical progress at different stages in its development. Lilley has expressed these facts well in the following conclusions: "The form of society has a very great effect on the rate of inventions and a form of society which in its young days encourages technical progress can, as a result of the very inventions it engenders, eventually come to retard further progress until a new social structure replaces it." The converse conclusion is that "technical progress—invention and the spread of the use of invention—is a fundamental factor in determining social structure and in bringing about the necessity for a change from one social structure to another." [31]

Among the innumerable inventions of methods and machines of modern times some of the more important are listed below:

Some of the More Important Modern Inventions[32]

Invention	Date A.D.
Railways at mines	1546
Screw-cutting and mandrel lathes	1550
Turret windmill	1580
Pendulum	1581
Knitting machine	1589
Cementation steel	1614
Barometer	1643

[31] S. Lilley, op. cit., pp. 189-190.

Lilley presents enlightening graphs on pages 184, 187 and 193, depicting respectively the "score" of inventions since B.C. 5500, the relative invention rate since B.C. 5500, and a detailed relative invention rate since 1700 A.D. Many of the inventions mentioned herein are described in his book.

In my Farewell to Poverty I have said: "During the mercantile stage of capitalism a good deal of wealth was concentrated in the hands of the principal merchants. Trading on a large scale and over an extensive area could not be carried on without a considerable accumulation of capital to acquire ships, vehicles, and animals of burden, to maintain trade routes, and to purchase large stocks of goods. Under industrial capitalism manual tools were supplanted in large part by machines which the individual worker is too poor to own." (P. 15.)

[32] Some of these inventions are listed in the World Almanac, 1951, pp. 464-465; and 1957.

Clock, pendulum	1657
Balance spring	1658
Newcomen engine	1712
Mercury thermometer	1714
Smelting with coke	1717
Flying shuttle	1733
Cast steel	1740
Carding machine	1748
Chronometer	1766
Spinning jenny	1768
Pen, steel	1780
Watt rotative engine	1781
Balloon	1783
Cotton gin	1793
Hydraulic press	1796
Breast water-wheel	1799
Whitney's interchangeable manufacture	1800
Jacquard loom	1804
Electroplating	1805
Fulton's "Clermont" steamship	1807
Stephenson's locomotive	1814
Milling machine	1818
Planing machine	1820
Galvanometer	1820
Electromagnet	1824
Automatic spinning mule	1825
Water turbine	1827
Friction match	1827
Hot blast in smelting	1828
Reaper	1831
Screw propeller	1836
Harvester	1836
Telegraph	1837
Vulcanized rubber	1839
Steam-hammer	1839
Babbitt metal	1839
Stethoscope, binaural	1840
Ether, anesthetic	1842
Practical arc lamp	1844
Rotary printing press	1845
Turret lathe	1845
Sewing machine	1846

Compressed air in mining	1849
Pin, safety	1849
Airship	1852
Elevator, with brake	1852
Practical maize planter	1853
Bessemer steel	1856
Spectroscope	1859
Universal milling machine	1861
Pneumatic tool	1865
Open hearth steel	1867
Combine seed drill	1867
Dynamite	1867
Typewriter	1868
Refrigerator car	1868
Oleomargarine	1868
Automatic lathe	1870
Tool steel	1871
Telephone	1876
Gas engine	1876
Sheaf binding harvester	1878
Lamp, incandescent	1878
Lamp, arc	1879
Linotype	1880
Public electric lighting	1881
Rayon	1883
Steam turbine	1884
Bicycle	1884
Pen, fountain	1884
Daimler's petrol engine	1885
Electric welding	1886
Gramophone	1887
Kodak	1888
Motor car	1889
Multi-spindle lathe	1890
Gas mantle	1893
Cinematograph	1895
Oxygen, from liquid air	1895
Radio telegraphy	1896
Diesel internal combustion engine	1897
High-speed tool-steel	1898
Oxygen cutting and welding	1900
Percussive coal-cutter	1901

Aeroplane	1903
Thermionic valve	1904
Radio, vacuum tube triode	1907
Thermit welding	1908
Duralumin	1909
Lamp, mecury vapor	1912
Conveyor belt mass-production	1913
Jigger-type conveyor in mining	1913
Tractor spread	1914
Magnesium from brine	1915
Radio telephony	1918
Centrifugal casting	1920
Insulin	1922
Pumpless absorption refrigerator	1923
Beam radio	1924
Autogyro	1925
Tungsten carbide tools	1926
Television	1926
Talking cinematograph	1928
Modern gyro-tiller	1930
Heat-and-power electricity generation	1935
Cotton-picker	1936
Hydro-mechanical mining	1937
Nylon	1937
Underground gasification of coal	1938
Significant development of gas-turbine	1939
Helicopter	1941
Jet-propelled aeroplane	1941
Quality control, full development	1941
Radar developments over a wide field	1943
Release of atomic energy	1943
Synthetic penicillin	1946
Aureomycin	1948
Neomycin	1949
Izoniazin	1952
Polio vaccine	1953

Most of the above inventions are of capital goods utilized in producing goods for consumers. They have rendered possible the enormous increase in volume of consumption goods in recent times. Many of these methods and machines were invented in part or entirely several times. The dates in the above list are the most important usually being when the invention began to be used to a significant degree.[33]

Lilley's intensive graph of the relative invention rate since 1700 A.D. indicates that it rose quite steadily until about 1890. Then it slumped and has not gone as high again, though it went up somewhat during each of the two wars of 1914-1918 and 1939-1945. The causes of a slowing down of this rate can hardly be scientific and technological because the inherent possibilities for technical advance are almost unlimited. It seems likely that the causes for this decline are social. We have already noted that the sale of manufactured and agricultural products has often been restricted. Sometimes this is unintended as when not enough purchasing power has been distributed to absorb all that is being produced. In the case of other commodities it is intended because a monopoly has been formed to limit production and maintain a high price level. When there is no incentive to increase production there is little or no inducement to invent more productive methods. When there is widespread unemployment labor is plentiful and cheap and there is little or no incentive to invent labor-saving devices. In fact, monopolies often discourage new inventions and suppress those which may compete with them. In 1934 the American Bell Telephone Company owned 9,234 patents of which it was using only 4,225 and suppressing 5,009 or more than half. The Federal Communications Commission estimated that 3,433 or 68.5 percent of the latter might be socially useful. Many examples of such suppression are given in *Technological Trends* published in 1937.[34] Inasmuch as modern industrial research is expensive it can be carried on only by large private corporations or by government. Unless a corporation has reason to believe that it will derive profits from such research it will not engage in it however socially useful it may be.

These facts explain why the Soviet Union has had a high relative invention rate while the rest of the world was slumping. It has a

[33] "Social study of invention, and especially of its duplication, shows that it is a highly social product and part of an endless mutually causative network. The principle of functional equivalence reinforces this idea, showing that the general background of social forces brings forth unlike but equivalent solutions, as well as identical ones, making doubly inevitable in modern times that the world will get the economic effects of an invention, if possibly not the device itself." "The further tentative generalizations we started off with may also be verified, that whereas a regression or cataclysm may have purely social causes, a wide advance of civilization cannot take place, whatever its causes, without a string of inventions to implement it." (S. C. Gilfillan, "Invention as a Factor in Economic History," *Journal of Economic History*, April 1947, pp. 262-288. See also his *The Sociology of Invention*, Chicago, 1935.)

[34] U. S. National Resources Committee, *Technological Trends and National Policy, Including the Social Implications of New Inventions*, Washington, 1937.

social and economic organization which permits of the distribution of all the commodities which it is technically possible to produce. It has no waste of man-power through unemployment. Its industry is not controlled by private monopolies. Its government encourages invention and technological advance with the ultimate purpose of producing plenty for every one. Of the recent inventions mentioned above at least four are utilized only in Soviet Russia, namely, heat-and-power electricity generation, cotton-picker, hydro-mechanical mining, and Kapitza's turbine refrigerator.

Another reason for the recent high relative invention rate in the Soviet Union probably is that it has encouraged scientific research regardless of its immediate application to practical problems. Such research of a fundamental nature is in the long run of great value in furnishing information which renders possible the invention of useful methods and articles. This has been well illustrated recently by physical research which led to the release of atomic energy, and chemical research which led to the invention of many medical drugs, plastic articles, and other useful products.

If and when the Soviet Union is free from the external menace of war, it should be able to pursue unhampered its ultimate aim and ideal of producing an abundance for all of its inhabitants. The same should be equally true of Soviet China. It will then be possible to determine more or less definitively the relative importance of competition and of cooperation in stimulating invention and technological advance and in increasing the volume of production. Earlier in this chapter I have commented on the relatively egalitarian character of primitive social organization. It was destroyed when an economic surplus was accumulated during the neolithic and chalcolithic periods which incited the more predatory elements to seize it and to establish the class society. An American anthropologist has commented upon the relative importance of cooperation and of competition in primitive economic life: "One of the most striking aspects of primitive labor is the cooperation which characterizes it . . . the voluntary association of a group of men or women whose objective is the completion of a specific, definitely limited task. . . . Work organizations of this kind, free or compulsory, temporary or permanent, organized or informal, are found everywhere in the primitive world; for everywhere man has apparently recognized the efficacy of group over individual effort. . . . The data amply prove that man works neither by nor for himself; that a spirit of mutual aid and of a kind not unlike that suggested by Kropotkin does exist." [35]

[35] Melville J. Herskovits, *The Economic Life of Primitive Peoples*, New York, 1940, p. 461.

Competition in individual effort will always exist and some of it is socially as well as individually useful. But the divisive effects of economic classes and of national and imperial states have not only destroyed or prevented most of an over-all human cooperation but have also given rise to the most dire of conflicts, as has been amply demonstrated in this treatise.

Chapter XXXII

The Modern Age of Imperialism from the Discovery of America (1492)

THE first age of imperialism has been briefly described in Chapter XXII. It may be dated from Sargon of Akkad (Agade) to Alexander the Macedonian or two millennia (*ca.* 2340-323 B.C.). There were doubtless more or less successful attempts at conquest for a thousand years or more earlier. So far as we have historical evidence, Sargon was the first ruler to bring a large territory containing diverse peoples under one rule. He conquered all the way westward from the mountains of Elam to the Mediterranean Sea and northward into Asia Minor. Of the earlier attempts at empire prior to Sargon we have no historical record. The Akkadian empire was followed at various intervals by the Amorite, Hittite, Assyrian and Chaldean or Babylonian empires in Mesopotamia and southern Asia Minor. From the 16th to the 12th centuries B.C. there was an Egyptian empire which extended some of the time into Asia Minor. The Phenicians and Cretans were engaged in imperialistic adventures in the eastern and middle Mediterranean Sea. From the 6th to 4th centuries B.C. the Persian empire extended over practically the whole of Mesopotamia and Asia Minor and some of the time included part of Egypt.

The second age of imperialism has been described in Chapter XXIII. Most of it was dominated by the Roman *imperium* which commenced under the republic with conquests on the Italian peninsula over Etruria and other Italian peoples, Carthage, Greek states, Gaul, England, and other territory in Europe, Asia and Africa. It lasted for eight centuries until the virtual division of the Roman empire in 395 A.D. between the two sons of Theodosius, the capture of Rome in 410 A.D. by Alaric the Visigoth, and the overthrow of the last western emperor by Odoacer in 476 A.D. Then followed a millennium of feudalism and the rise of modern nationalism during which empire with the possible exception of the Byzantine Empire, described in Chapter XXIII, was more or less in abeyance in the Occident for reasons which are not entirely in evidence on the surface of things, but which have been discussed in Chapter XXIX and XXX. This chronology ignores the rise of empires in India, China, Japan, and in the Western Hemisphhere, not because they were unimportant but because they illustrate much the same forces and processes of predation, exploitation and conquest, as the empires in the Mediterranean area. Furthermore, the historical data concerning them are much less adequate than the data concerning the Mediterranean empires. In any case, it would be impossible to arrange a chronology which would apply to all of these areas, because they were more or less isolated from each other or entirely so, as is illustrated in the following examples.

In Chapter XX has been described the culture in the Indus valley (*ca*. 2500 B.C.) the principal centers of which were Mohenjo-daro and Harappa. This culture may have been an extension by conquest of the Mesopotamian culture, or *vice versa*. About a millennium later the Aryan tribes entered India from the north and gradually conquered or at least infiltrated the indigenous population. The Maurya dynasty (*ca*. 321-184 B.C.) founded by Chandragupta immediately after the death of Alexander gradually extended its rule over most of India. About 250 B.C. its king, Asoka, ruled from the Hindu Kush and the Himalaya mountains to nearly as far south as Madras. The succeeding dynasties ruled varying degrees of this vast territory, among them being the Sunga (184-72 B.C.), Kanva, Kushan, Andhra, and Gupta (A.D. 320-480) dynasties. The Mogul dynasty (A.D. 1526-1760) was founded by the conquering Moslem Tatar king of Kabul, Baber. This was an alien rule followed by the even more alien British *imperium*.

The earliest Chinese dynasty of which there is any evidence whatsoever was the Shang dynasty which ruled sometime during the second millennium B.C. Then China was invaded from the West by the Chous, a people who established a dynasty on the legendary date of 1122 B.C. The Chou government was of a somewhat feudal type, and there were several more or less independent states so that the situation was not unlike the feudal period in Europe. In the 3rd century B.C. the king of the state of Ch'in conquered the other Chinese states and became the first Chinese emperor, Shih Huang Ti, who tried to burn all Chinese literature so as to make a complete break with the past. The short Ch'in dynasty (221-208 B.C.), under which the Great Wall was built to keep out invaders from the west was followed by the Han dynasty (206 B.C.-220 A.D.), under which the Chinese empire was consolidated and united. About six more dynasties followed with a few intervening periods of disunion. Three of these dynasties were particularly imperialist in character. Under the T'ang dynasty (618-907 A.D.) the

Chinese empire was the largest in the world, stretching from the Pacific Ocean to the Caspian Sea and from the Himalaya to the Altai mountains. The Yuan or Mongol dynasty (1279-1368 A.D.) imposed foreign rule upon the Chinese, and the Ch'ing or Manchu dynasty (1644-1911 A.D.) introduced alien rule until overthrown by the first republic of China in 1912.

The first Japanese emperor, Jimmu Tenno, is said to have ascended the throne in 660 B.C. Japan was then a small territory of only a few hundred square miles, including the province of Yamoto on the principal island of Honshu. Gradually it expanded so as to include the whole of the Japanese archipelago. For several centuries it was more of a feudalism than it was an empire. For many centuries no attempt was made to conquer alien territory. But Japan has had its imperialist adventures. For a time during its early history it ruled Korea. Later it conquered the island of Hokkaido to the north, and made conquests in northern Manchuria. In 1592 the Japanese general Hideyoshi tried to conquer China as well as Korea, but died in 1598 before he could succeed. From 1636 A.D. to 1867 it isolated itself completely from the remainder of the world. Its recent imperialism in China and Korea belongs to the modern age of economic imperialism to be discussed later.

In the western hemisphere the first historical date (*ca.* 291 B.C.) belonged to the Maya culture and empire of Central America which was overthrown later for unknown reasons. The Inca empire of South America probably came into being early in the Christian era and lasted until the Spanish conquest by Pizarro in 1531. The Toltecs were a tribe that invaded Mexico from the north and conquered a large part of its area. The Aztecs conquered central and southern Mexico about 1325 A.D., and ruled until the Spanish conquest by Cortez in 1519. While we have few data concerning these four American empires, they seem to indicate that the same factors and processes of predation, exploitation, and conquest were at work as in the eastern hemisphere. Perhaps the main difference was that the imperialist stage was reached two or three millennia later in the western hemisphere, and had therefore not developed so far in the western as in the eastern hemisphere.

With this brief historical survey of the preceding imperialist ages already described in Chapters XXII and XXIII we may now proceed to a description of the third or modern age of imperialism in order to ascertain its characteristics and to determine wherein it differs from the earlier ages of imperialism. In the present chapter will be described the attempt of the Occident to dominate the Orient.

An outstanding difference between ancient and modern imperialism is the vastly greater geographical extent of the latter. This was due partly to the development of the art of navigation which made long sea and ocean voyages possible, though this development was stimulated in part by the desire to explore and exploit distant lands. The magnetic compass was first used in Europe about 1195 A.D. though it was probably invented earlier somewhere in the Orient. The modern rudder hinged to the center of the stern was invented about 1250 A.D., and took the place of an oar over the side or a paddle over the stern, thus aiding considerably the maneuvering of the vessel. Sailing to windward and tacking became more feasible also because of changes in the shape of the ships which made the keel deeper. More sail coverage and flat sails increased the sailing power as well as aiding in tacking.

The cross-staff was invented in the 14th or 15th centuries and the astrolabe in the 15th century. These instruments aided in measuring the altitude of planets and stars and thus determining the latitude of a ship. They were somewhat difficult to use because of the movements of a sailing vessel. The sextant invented in the 17th or 18th century obviated these difficulties.

A mechanical clock is needed to determine the longitude of a ship at sea. Such a clock was invented about 1232 A.D. and a spring clock about 1490 A.D. Their accuracy, however, was greatly diminished by the movements of a sailing ship. Not until the chronometer was invented about 1766 A.D. was it possible to keep accurate Greenwich time while at sea which could be compared with the sun time determined by observations each day. The art of cartography was developing but the longitude indicated was often less accurate than the latitude.

About the end of the 15th century vegetables and fruit began to be used on shipboard to prevent scurvy on long voyages. Other changes might be noted in the size and shape of ships. For example, the high poop deck which had been used as a sort of fortress in fighting was lowered so that it impeded the progress of the vessel to a smaller degree.[1]

The first important attempt at domination of the East by the West was Alexander's vainglorious invasion of India in the 4th century B.C. While it failed as a permanent conquest and the Greek garrisons eventually withdrew, it established a cultural contact with the Occident which had far-reaching consequences not only for India but also for China and other Oriental countries, because India influenced China in religion, art, science (mathematics in particular), and philosophy. Overland trade between the East and the West continued. The Romans traded with China through the Parthians, and there were other commercial relations.

[1] Cf. S. C. Gilfillan, *Inventing the Ship*, Chicago, 1935.

The attempt at domination of the East of special significance for our purpose commenced at the outset of the sixteenth century, with the Portuguese in the lead. The navigator Vasco da Gama rounded the Cape of Good Hope and reached Calicut in 1498. The viceroy Albuquerque came in 1503 and in 1510 established the first European colony at Goa. The Philippine Islands were visited by Magellan and occupied by the Spanish in the sixteenth century. The Portuguese acquired extensive territories in India until the Dutch arrived in 1595 and competed successfully with them. The French came at the beginning of the 17th century, and later conquered extensive territories until defeated by the English at Plassey in 1757, after which their power rapidly dwindled. Dutch, French, and British East India companies were formed to carry on trade. The English began to come early in the 17th century, and eventually acquired suzerainty over the whole of India with the exception of the small Portuguese colony at Goa, and five French colonies comprising less than two hundred square miles. These were trading empires and resulted in almost no migration and colonization.

Oversea commerce with China began at Canton about A.D. 300. For centuries it was controlled principally by Arabs, though it included some Hindu traders. The Portuguese reached China in 1516 and Japan in 1541. The Dutch reached China in 1604, the British in 1607, and the Americans in 1784. The Russians were in communication with China overland, and the first treaty between China and a European power was concluded with Russia in 1689.

Seafaring trade brought the West to the East in a decisive fashion. Western seafarers and merchants were seeking for raw materials which could be secured only in the Orient, markets for finished products, and cheap labor with which to manufacture goods. These were in the main legitimate ends. However, they sometimes met opposition and contempt. This was particularly true of China. The Chinese had conquered all of their neighbors and for many centuries were almost entirely isolated from the rest of the world. This situation had developed in them an arrogant attitude which has rarely ever been equaled. Their emperor considered himself the ruler of the whole world. When George III sent Lord Macartney in 1792 to negotiate a commercial treaty, and demanded treatment as an equal, the Emperor Chien Lung dispatched the following message to the English monarch: "It behooves you, O King, to respect our wishes and by perpetual submission to our Throne in the future to bring prosperity and peace to your people. Tremble and obey."

Whatever arrogance the East displayed was more than matched by the aggressiveness of the Westerners. They were usually better armed than the Orientals, and possessed a power on the sea unequaled by any Oriental nation. Their firearms were of larger caliber and longer range and their ships of greater burden. The peaceful pursuit of trade soon developed into invasion and conquest, often aided and abetted by a Christian zeal which regarded all Oriental religions as false and evil. Thus in the course of four centuries a large part of the Orient passed under Occidental domination. Until the middle of the 20th century India, Burma, the Malay States, northern Borneo, eastern New Guinea, and minor possessions elsewhere have been under British sway, with British influence strong in Nepal, Bhutan, and Siam, and menacing in Tibet. France has ruled Indo-China and minor possessions elsewhere. Holland has possessed most of the East Indies. The United States ruled the Philippine Islands for half a century, and still exercises a partial protectorate over them. Russia dominates all of northern Asia from the Urals to the Pacific. In fact, nearly three fifths of the area of Asia and one half or more of its population have been under Occidental suzerainty up to the middle of the 20th century.

Even where suzerainty was not actually declared, a certain measure of domination was secured. China, in addition to losing a few important ports, was for a time divided up into several "spheres of influence" by the leading Western powers. Extraterritorial rights for foreigners and regulation of the customs duties were imposed upon Japan, China, and several other Oriental countries. Western capital invested in Eastern railways, factories, etc., has levied a heavy tribute and has often interfered with the political affairs of these countries. The only country which succeeded in freeing itself entirely from these restrictions is Japan, and it has done so by imitating the material aspects of Occidental civilization—in other words, by equaling and sometimes beating the West at its own game of force and aggression. Thus has Western empire, political and economic, spread over practically the whole of the East, and presented the most extensive display of imperialism in the history of mankind. Not even Rome in its palmiest days equalled it.

This extraordinary situation did not come into being intentionally. The West did not by a premeditated and concerted design conquer the East. It came about partly through the frequent resistance of the East to Western advances, and its unwillingness to adjust itself to international finance, trade, and industry which was developing under the rapid scientific and technical progress of the West. In many Oriental countries the laws were of such a nature that foreigners could not live and do business under them, thus giving rise to the demand for extraterritorial rights. Sometimes these countries isolated themselves entirely or gave only very limited rights of residence to foreigners. For more than two certuries Japan excluded all foreigners, with the exception of a few Dutch merchants who were permitted to live on a small island in Nagasaki harbor. In Canton the foreigners were banished to a mudbank in the Pearl river, which they filled in and then built the city of Shameen. At Shanghai they were assigned the swampy strand of the Whangpoo River, where now stands the former International Settlement.

Balked and irritated by such discriminations against them, by the indifference and somnolence of the Orient, and its inefficiency according to Occidental standards, Western powers often went on to conquer where it was at first intended only to trade. But this imperialism was due even more to Western greed and aggressiveness, which could not be restrained from exploiting by force the physically and materially weaker East.

Whether or not this imperialist outcome could have been avoided it would be useless to discuss. It would also be superfluous to describe in detail Western political and economic imperialism, concerning which there is an extensive literature.[2] Its dangerousness is too obvious to require proof or extended comment. Occidental historians and other writers, with characteristic arrogance, usually call the European War of 1914 to 1918 the "World" War. It was a war which originated solely in Europe between rival groups of European powers and should have been settled by them alone. With the exception of Japan, which had already entered the European game of balance of power, the Oriental nations which became involved were dragooned into it by Western imperialism. It concerned them only indirectly—namely, in so far as they were the pawns and spoils over which their alien rulers were quarreling and fighting. To call such a war the World War is a misleading piece of inaccuracy. Only a myopic view of the world which regards the Orient as a caudal appendage of the Occident could be guilty of this egregious error, so insulting to the East.[3]

The manner of contact between the two cultures has therefore not been of such a nature as to promote the most satisfactory kind of assimilation and interpenetration. The Westerners, coming as conquerors and exploiters, have assumed a supercilious and contemptuous

[2] See, for example, P. T. Moon, *Imperialism and World Politics*, New York, 1927; S. Nearing and J. Freeman, *Dollar Diplomacy, A Study in American Imperialism*, New York, 1925; R. W. Dunn, *American Foreign Investments*, New York, 1925; and especially J. A. Hobson, *Imperialism*, New York, revised edition 1938, which is an excellent survey of the whole subject.

[3] My books are among the very few concerning this war which do not commit this error. I have invariably called it the "European" War. The war of 1939 to 1945 was more nearly worldwide in extent because it included fighting in Asia and Africa as well as in Europe, in the Pacific and Indian as well as the Atlantic oceans.

attitude toward Oriental culture. The Easterners have heretofore usually assumed a subservient or at least deferential manner toward these alien rulers and exploiters. While this manner may be due in part to Oriental politeness, it arises mainly out of fear of Occidental might and belligerence. But it conceals a contempt and hatred for the West which fully equal the corresponding feelings of the Western imperialists for the East.

This situation is aggravated by racial prejudices and antagonisms. Orientals are on the whole of a darker color than Occidentals. The dominant Western powers in Asia are British and American. Great Britain ruled India and other extensive territories. In recent years the United States has been England's principal rival in eastern Asia, not by conquest but by the more subtle method of heavy investments of capital in Oriental enterprises. Hence it is that the Anglo-Saxon influence is the most powerful throughout the world. Anglo-Saxon peoples are predominantly or, at any rate, traditionally of the lightest-colored race, the so-called Nordic. The "Nordics" are therefore for the moment on top, and can display to the full their dislike for the dark-skinned peoples.

Anglo-Saxon antipathy toward the dark races is exemplified in the laws to exclude Oriental immigrants enacted by the United States, Canada, Australia, New Zealand, South Africa, etc. While these laws are intended primarily to keep out cheap labor, racial prejudice also plays its part. This was strikingly illustrated in the clause excluding the Japanese in the immigration law passed by the United States Congress on the 12th of April, 1924. The Japanese Government had displayed its willingness to recognize the economic reasons for restricting immigration. In accordance with the "gentlemen's agreement" of 1907, the Japanese Government prevented laborers from going to the United States. As a consequence, the excess of incoming over outgoing Japanese during the years 1908 to 1923 was only 8681, and this number included merchants, students, tourists, government officials, and others who are permitted to enter. Under the immigration restriction act the annual quota for Japanese immigrants would have been only a little over one hundred. It was therefore a wholly gratuitous insult to discriminate against the Japanese nation by specifically excluding its nationals.

Physical and mental racial differences have not yet been sufficiently studied to warrant definite conclusions. Most of the assertions made with regard to the alleged inferiority or superiority of various races have no scientific justification whatsoever, and are based on preconceived notions, casual observations, misinterpreted anecdotes, mistaken assumptions as to the causes of cultural differences, and racial and national prejudices. An extensive investigation of a

550

rigorously scientific nature is necessary before reliable conclusions can be reached.[4]

Many of these allegations of racial inferiority have been made concerning the negroes, and because some of the Oriental peoples also are dark-colored, it has been assumed that these assertions could be applied to them also. Whether or not such allegations against the negroes are justified is very debatable. Inasmuch as negro blood is not much more prevalent in Asia than in Europe and much less so than it is in America, this question is of no more significance for the Orient than it is for the Occident. There are many dark-skinned peoples which are not negroid. Many egregious errors are made in this connection. An important official of the Department of State of the United States Government asserted that the Chinese are of a much higher type than the Indians, and added that this is not surprising, because the Chinese are of a lighter color and therefore more closely related to us. Ethnically the great majority of the Indians belong primarily to the Caucasian race, so that we are, on the contrary, more closely related to them than we are to the Mongolian peoples. A cursory examination of the head form, hair, features, and bodily anatomy is sufficient to prove this obvious fact.

During long residence in the Far East and two protracted journeys around the world, I have discussed this back-thrust of imperialism with educated and cultured representatives of several Oriental countries who are alarmed and incensed by this outburst of race prejudice and discrimination against their peoples. They fully realize that it indicates a belief prevalent in the Occident that they are racially and culturally inferior. The feeling of resentment thus aroused does

[4] Ginsberg has made a careful survey of this subject, which he has summarized in the following words:

"There may be differences in respect of both intellectual faculty and temperamental disposition as between different races, but the extent to which these differences are due to innate constitution is at present uncertain. The stress laid in recent biology upon hereditary factors must not be interpreted as implying a denial of the importance of environmental factors. In regard to social evolution, moreover, cultural development and change appear to be largely independent of germinal change. A great many social changes take place of vast importance in the history of civilization which cannot be shown to be connected with any changes in racial type. Further, it seems unwarranted, in the light of the present state of ethnological psychology, to place races on a scale of *genetic* superiority or inferiority. The genetic basis of behaviour is difficult enough to determine within a well-defined group. Such an attempt becomes wellnigh hopeless when made in reference to whole races. We may therefore say with the distinguished American biologist, Professor T. H. Morgan, that 'a little goodwill might seem more fitting in treating these complicated questions than the attitude adopted by some of the modern race propagandists.' " (Morris Ginsberg, *The Problem of Colour in Relation to the Idea of Equality*, in the *Journal of Philosophical Studies*, Vol. I, No. 2, London, 1926.)

not encourage them to welcome and to assimilate whatever is beneficial in Occidental culture, but turns them back toward their own culture, thus accentuating the cultural dissimilarity and antipathy between the East and the West.

This contemptuous attitude toward the Orient is manifested at its worst by the European and American residents in the East, most of whom are intensely imperialist. Their ignorance of and indifference toward the culture of the peoples among whom they live is little short of appalling. The term "native" as used by them is often intentionally insulting, and the phrase "going native" as applied to Westerners who adopt Oriental customs is always intended as a severe criticism and condemnation. Contempt for strangers is common the world over, but the foreigners in the Orient succeed in surpassing it in their contempt for the natives. This is due not only to provincialism and prejudice but also to a desire to dominate the peoples whom they are trying to rule and exploit by setting themselves as far apart from them as possible by their dress, manners and customs. A foreigner who does not follow this policy is therefore a traitor to their cause. And yet an Oriental who carries with him to the Occident his own dress, manners, and customs is very likely to suffer from chauvinism and intolerance, though Westerners are constantly doing the same with impunity in the Orient.

This tension is greatly accentuated by the belief prevalent among imperialists that they are performing an altruistic mission in ruling the Orient. This notion is based upon the postulate that they are morally as well as intellectually superior to the Orientals. As the raucously imperialistic British poet Rudyard Kipling has vulgarly and insultingly expressed it on page 322.[5]

This belief was more elegantly phrased when Lord Rosebery, a former Liberal prime minister, asserted that the British Empire is "the greatest secular agency for good known to the world." Certain benefits derived from British and other colonial rule are not to be denied, but they are benefits which were forced upon and not solicited by these peoples. onsequently, it is not surprising that colonial officials and other imperialists are irritated and angered by the lack of appreciation of their alien rule displayed by its unwilling recipients, nor is this lack of appreciation any more surprising. The best commentary

---

[5] Kipling also wrote these imperialist lines:

> God of our fathers, known of old,
> Lord of our far-flung battle-line,
> Beneath whose awful Hand we hold
> Dominion over palm and pine—
> Lord God of Hosts, be with us yet,
> Lest we forget—lest we forget!

on the self-assumed "white man's burden" has been furnished by the English economist, John A. Hobson:

"Imperialism is a depraved choice of national life, imposed by self-seeking interests which appeal to the lusts of quantitative acquisitiveness and of forceful domination surviving in a nation from early centuries of animal struggle for existence. Its adoption as a policy implies a deliberate renunciation of that cultivation of the higher inner qualities which for a nation as for an individual constitutes the ascendancy of reason over brute impulse. It is the besetting sin of all successful States, and its penalty is unalterable in the order of nature."[6]

Until the Occident ceases its attempt at domination, accompanied by unctuous professions of doing good or by more frank and truthful assertions of pecuniary gain and political power as its motives, it will not be possible for the East and the West to profit by an entirely free and mutually helpful exchange of their cultures.

In spite of its tremendous social and political prestige and its close association with Occidental imperialism, Christianity has had little success in the Orient, even though it is a religion of Semitic origin. Leaving aside the case of the Philippines, where Roman Catholicism was forced upon a primitive people by a despotic European government, Ceylon, a small and unimportant country where a hybrid mixture of Asiatic and European culture prevails, is the only place where the proportion of Christians approaches 10 percent. Next comes Korea with less than 2 percent. And Korea has long been culturally decadent and has no vital religion of its own, the upper classes favoring Confucianism and the lower classes Buddhism. The almost complete failure of the Christian offensive on the Orient is a striking fact worthy of careful consideration.[7]

The missionary spirit is much stronger in the Occident than in the Orient, and is correlated with the more aggressive spirit of the West. Both Christianity and Islam are belligerently proselytizing religions, partly because each is monotheistic and professes that its god should dominate the whole world, but also owing to other tenets soon to be mentioned. The contrast between the Occidental and Oriental religions with regard to their proselytizing zeal is of considerable significance in relation to their respective cultures and their contact and assimilation with each other.

Three religions profess to be universal religions—namely, Buddhism, Christianity, and Islam. Judaism at one time entertained the

---

[6] *Imperialism*, revised edition, 1938, London, p. 368.

[7] Prior to the war of 1939 to 1945, census figures and estimates indicated that the percentages of Christians were less than one percent in China (perhaps 4 to 5 percent Moslem), less than 1½ percent in India and Burma, and barely one third of one percent in Japan.

hope that its Jehovah would some time rule the world. But Jehovah never became much more than a tribal god. The Jews persisted in considering themselves a people chosen by divine preference over other peoples, and to whom the deity was to send a messenger, the Messiah. With such a narrow and exclusive outlook Judaism could never become a great missionary religion.

Christianity derived its deity from Judaism. Jehovah and God alike are monarchs, wielders of brute force and avid for power. However, God is the greater king who contemplates dominion over the whole earth in a not too remote future, whereas Jehovah was never quite so ambitious. In one of its aspects Christianity is as monarchistic, militaristic, bombastic, and domineering as Judaism. The phrase "kingdom of God," with its variant "kingdom of Heaven" in the gospel of Matthew, appears more often than any other phrase in the four pospels.

> Let thrones and powers and kingdoms be
> Obedient, mighty God, to Thee!
> And, over land and stream and main,
> Wave Thou the scepter of Thy reign!

On the other hand, Christianity has also professed the doctrine that God is a father as well as king. He is called the "Father" about three hundred times in the New Testament. Inasmuch as Christians believe that the Messianic hope has been fulfilled, they are willing to extend the fatherhood of God and the ministrations of his son to the rest of mankind. The idealized character of Jesus furnishes a concrete object toward which to direct personal loyalty, perhaps more so than in most religions. Thus Jesus also becomes king and martial leader to be followed into battle like God himself.

> Great God! whose universal sway
> The known and unknown worlds obey;
> Now give the kingdom to Thy Son;
> Extend His power, exalt His throne.

> The Son of God goes forth to war,
>   A kingly crown to gain;
> His blood-red banner streams afar!
>   Who follows in His train?

Christian hymnology, derived mainly from the Psalms, attributed to the warlike Jewish king David, and the New Testament, furnishes abundant evidence of the belligerent character of this religion. While some of the hymns reflect its more amiable tenets, speak of God as love, and dwell upon a peaceful though rarely if ever upon a con-

554

templative or thoughtful life, a large proportion of them are filled with the dust and din, the boasting and bellicosity of war. The Christian is repeatedly characterized as a warrior.

> The Christian warrior, see him stand,
> In the whole armor of his God.
> Soldiers of Christ, arise,
> And put your armor on.
>
> Gird thy heavenly armor on,
> Wear it ever night and day;
> Ambushed lies the evil one:
> Watch and pray.

The bellicose spirit of Christianity is to be explained in large part, if not entirely, by its strong sense of evil and sin in the world. This it derived from Zoroastrianism and Judaism, but has considerably intensified and amplified it. In the cruder forms of this doctrine, evil is personified in numerous hobgoblins, genii, demons, and the like, whose weaker magic is pitted against the superior magic of God and his followers, as is illustrated in this characteristic bit of sacred doggerel.

> And though this world, with devils filled,
>   Should threaten to undo us,
> We will not fear, for God hath willed
>   His truth to triumph through us.

In Luther's famous hymn which describes God as a "mighty fortress," the arch-fiend Satan is depicted in the most uncomplimentary terms.

> For still our ancient foe
> Doth seek to work us woe;
> His craft and power are great,
> And, armed with cruel hate,
> On earth is not his equal.

The principal battle hymn of Christianity presents this religion arrayed in the full panoply of pomp and power against the evil one.

> Onward, Christian soldiers!
>   Marching as to war,
> With the Cross of Jesus
>   Going on before.
> Christ the Royal Master
>   Leads against the foe;
> Forward into battle,
>   See, His banners go!

These hymns graphically mirror those features of Christianity which have made it a belligerent religion, for the sacred poetry and music of a religion reflect its most dynamic traits. Sung by myriads of Protestant believers, they have spurred them on to renewed efforts to fight the devil and convert the benighted heathen from their wicked ways by moral suasion if possible, by force if necessary.

It is generally believed by Christians that theirs is a missionary religion because Jesus is reputed to have said to his disciples: "Go ye therefore, and teach all nations, baptizing them in the name of the Father, and of the Son, and of the Holy Ghost." (Matthew XXVII, 19.) "Go ye into all the world, and preach the gospel to every creature. He that believeth, and is baptized, shall be saved; but he that believeth not, shall be damned." (Mark XVI, 15, 16.) Here, then, is a formula for salvation through belief and the ceremony of baptism mercifully held forth to all mankind, but short shrift for the recalcitrants who refuse to be saved.

The foregoing exposition indicates clearly the important part played in Christian theology by the dogma of the dualism of good and evil in the universe. Hence the Christian life must be a constant struggle against evil under the command and leadership of God the incarnation of good. A hymn written for the convocation of missionaries, therefore, begins appropriately as follows:

> Assembled at Thy great command,
> Before Thy face, dread King, we stand;
> The voice that marshaled every star,
> Has called Thy people from afar.

This ethical dualism permits of no shading. Good is light and evil is darkness. The heathen incarnate evil, or, at any rate, are under its influence. They must be fought and, if possible, saved, whether they wish it or not, partly for their own sake but much more for the glorification of God the inexorable king. The self-righteous Christian, therefore, goes forth to struggle against but also for the wicked heathen, in order to exalt his ruthless deity.

> Scatter the gloom of heathen night,
>   And bid all nations hail the light.
> The heathen in his blindness,
>   Bows down to wood and stone!
> Shall we, whose souls are lighted
>   With wisdom from on high,—
> Shall we, to men benighted,
>   The lamp of life deny?

The preceding description reveals the attributes of Christianity which have rendered it one of the most aggressive, intolerant, and domineering of religions, and which explain its long history of persecuting unbelievers, its religious wars, its Inquisition and its Crusades, and its extensive proselytizing activities, some of which have been carried on with the aid of the mailed fist. These attributes are its jealous and ambitious deity, its belief in a peculiarly Christian character which is superior to human nature in general and which is incarnated in the partially or wholly mythical figure of Jesus its cut-and-dried formula for salvation than which there is no other way to be saved, and its grotesque and wholly unscientific conception of evil. Every religion grows out and is a part of a complex of economic, political, and social factors and conditions. The intrinsic character of Christianity has harmonized well with the commercial greed and the political imperialism of the Occident, as will presently be indicated.

Needless to say, there have been and are other aspects of Christianity which some of its apologists eagerly push to the fore in order to cover up what has been described. The Christian mystic, like all mystics, is absorbed in his autosuggestively and hypnotically induced inner vision. The gentler and less aggressive believer is attracted by its more amiable tenets and engages in charitable deeds. The more thoughtful adherent is appalled and shocked by the gross inconsistency of its ethical dualism and endeavors to smooth it away, often by means of casuistry. Thus it is argued that while God is responsible for the possibility of evil, he has given man free will so that the individual is responsible for choosing evil rather than good. But these phases of Christianity have had comparatively little influence upon missionary work, which is due almost entirely to the attributes described above. These belligerent attributes constitute the main body of historical Christianity and have had the most influence in the affairs of mankind.[8] They cannot be rationalized away by the sophistry of the Christian devotee.

Mohammedanism was derived in part from Judaism and Christianity. Its formula for salvation consists in submission (islam) to Allah the one god. All human beings who submit and fight for this religion can be saved, thus making it universal in its appeal. Those who do not submit may be exterminated by the faithful, who attain religious merit thereby. Moslems who secure converts increase their chances of going to paradise. All of these traits and its extreme simplic-

[8] Edward Gibbon (1737-1794), *The Decline and Fall of the Roman Empire*, Volume I, Chapters XV and XVI, has described these attributes of Christianity. "The church of Rome defended by violence the empire which she had acquired by fraud; a system of peace and benevolence was soon disgraced by the proscriptions, wars, massacres, and the institution of the holy office." (P. 504.)

ity render Islam even more aggressive than Christianity. The Moslem is rarely ever troubled by philosophic doubt, which makes him very sure of himself. During the first millennium of its existence—namely, from the seventh to the seventeenth century—proselytizing zeal aided by the force of arms and an efflorescence of Arabic culture carried it throughout northern Africa, into southern Europe, over most of Asia Minor, and into central Asia. The conquest of a considerable part of India and several centuries of Moslem rule firmly established it there, where it has a larger following in Pakistan than in any other country. As it carries with it a smaller cultural content than Christianity, it is readily accepted by peoples of a simpler culture without affecting materially their own culture. This explains in large part its success in Malaysia and the East Indies.

It is usually assumed by missionaries and their supporters and sympathizers that the extent to which the Orient has adopted Occidental civilization is to be credited entirely to Christianity. This fantastic notion is due to the egregious error made by many Christians that civilization and Christianity are identical, and that all of the credit for the social progress which has resulted in civilization should be given to this religion. Japan alone furnishes ample disproof of this mistake on the part of the missionaries, for while it has adopted a good deal of Western culture, especially on its material side, Japan has completely repudiated Christianity. The true situation in this regard cannot be understood until it is clearly recognized that no cultural system can be attributed to any one religion, because every culture is derived from many and diverse sources. In its relation to Christianity this is much more true of Occidental culture, which had a very complex origin in Rome, Greece, Egypt, and other parts of the Mediterranean area, than it is of the Hindu culture, which originated to a much greater degree from the Brahmanic religion, and of the Chinese culture, which was formulated to a considerable degree by the Confucian ethics and religion. And yet a missionary propagandist has asserted that "the peoples of the West have derived their ideals of justice, freedom, opportunity, cooperation, and progress from no other religion than that of Jesus Christ." [9] The prevalence of this erroneous belief tends to increase the aggressiveness of the missionary attack upon the Orient and other non-Christian parts of the world.

An Indian critic of missions has said that the Orient concludes that the Western political method is first to send missionaries, second traders, and third gunboats.[10] While this method has not usually been followed consciously and intentionally, it has nevertheless often worked

[9] R. E. Hume, *The World's Living Religions,* New York, 1924.
[10] J. J. Cornelius, "An Oriental Looks at Christian Missions," in *Harper's Magazine,* April, 1927.

558

out in this fashion. Missionary work has been both the forerunner and the follower of Occidental imperialism. The establishment of political power has usually resulted in a large influx of missionaries. This cycle is well illustrated in India. The acquisition of power by Catholic countries—namely, Portugal and France brought numerous Romanist missionaries. The establishment of British rule brought many Protestant missionaries. If the Orient should attempt successfully to acquire political power in the Occident, it is not impossible that such an outbreak of imperialism would incite a proselytizing spirit even in the non-missionary religions of the East, because religion is useful to imperialists as it is to all exploiters.

The presence of missionaries and the establishment of missionary institutions, such as churches, schools, hospitals, and the like, have often furnished excuses for aggressive measures to secure more power. This was graphically illustrated in the case of British missions in China. Protection for these missions as well as for trade interests has been one of the reasons for demands for extraterritorial rights, spheres of influence, and the like, and the British Government has ever been ready on the slightest provocation to send gunboats for the protection of its missionaries and their institutions. The United States Government has been less aggressive in China, has never claimed a sphere of influence, and has advocated an open-door policy. But the American missionary investment is larger than the British, and is even larger than the American commercial investment. So that American missionary interests have influenced its diplomatic policy greatly. The Catholic missionary investment in China is larger than the Protestant, and as much of it is French, the French Government has been active in demanding diplomatic protection for Catholic missions.

The missionaries have reciprocated, perhaps unconsciously, by being very chauvinistic, and often endeavoring indirectly when not directly to instill into the minds of their neophytes the benefits of Western rule as well as religion and culture. With comparatively few exceptions their influence has been against nationalist movements, even when those movements were not directed against their own or other Christian governments. Thus in Turkey the missionaries always opposed the nationalist movements of the Armenians (the Huntchagist movement) and other subject races. In India this attitude was imposed upon the missionaries, whether they wished it or not. A missionary society, in order to secure permission from the British Government to carry on its work, had to sign a declaration "that all due obedience and respect should be given to the lawfully constituted Government, and that while carefully abstaining from political affairs, it is its desire and purpose that its influence, in so far as it may be properly exerted, should be so exerted in loyal cooperation with the

Government of the country concerned, and that it will only employ agents who will work in this spirit." (British Memorandum A, Article 5: iii.) Individual missionaries also were required to sign this declaration. While missionaries may not take part in nationalist movements, they should remain neutral with respect to all political matters instead of becoming the agents, in a measure, of Western governments.

Needless to say, religious proselytizing is as legitimate as political propaganda, and missionaries are entitled to protection as much as traders, tourists, and other foreigners. But the correlation between missions and imperialism and their interaction upon each other are significant facts for cultural relations. They have resulted in a so-called "missionary statesmanship" in which missions and imperialism have specifically and more or less openly worked hand-in-glove for the joint spread of Christianity and political power. This is a conscious recognition of the subtle influence which is always at work, for the missionaries cannot help but recognize that the success of Christianity in the Orient depends entirely upon political power. Even where Western rule prevails, as it did in India, it is not likely to succeed. Lacking such power it is certain to fail. This was strikingly illustrated in Japan, where under complete national independence Christianity was a dead issue. Hence it is not surprising that Orientals come to regard missions as the vanguard and accomplice of imperialism. In China the nationalist movement has turned against or at least its back upon the missionaries and their religion, and the same is true to a smaller degree of the nationalist movements in India and other Eastern countries. Thus the cooperation between missions and imperialism has proved to be fatal for Christianity, though it is doubtful if it could in any case have conquered the Orient.

The point has already been reached where missionaries can hope to have much success only among groups which expect to gain material advantages by changing their religion. This was chiefly true among the lower castes and outcastes of India who improve their social status thereby. Christianity and Islam were vying with each other to win neophytes from these lower social strata. The constitution of independent India has abolished the castes and thereby destroyed the appeal of these religions to the former outcastes.

The death-knell of a highly successful missionary enterprise in the Orient has already sounded. The missionaries and their supporters and sympathizers often aver that their new activities are as truly missionary as the old. But education is due to scholarship, medicine to science, and sport and athletics are derived from the traditions of pagan Greece and our barbarous Teutonic ancestors. Social work is inspired by the modern humanitarian movement which is due mainly to factors other than Christianity. The elevation of the position of women is due

560

to the same movement. In fact, while engaged in such work missionaries are conveying various features of Occidental culture in general and not its religion in particular.

Japan has been the only modern Oriental power strong enough to follow an imperialistic policy. It was incited to do so by its excessive and growing population, its rapidly developing capitalism, which is seeking markets for its goods, and by the example of Western imperialism. Korea was the most striking example of its imperialism. It has also been notably imperialistic in its policy toward China, having taken Formosa and the Pescadores after the Sino-Japanese War of 1894, and territories in the province of Shantung and in southern Manchuria a few years later. This phase culminated in the notorious twenty-one demands of 1915 when the European War had distracted the attention of the Western powers away from China.

While Japan has been the most prominent exponent of modern Oriental imperialism, China was one of the most imperialist of nations in the past. Much of the territorial growth of China proper was by force of arms. Tonking and Cochin-China were conquered about 214 B.C. Chinese armies marched as far west as the Caspian Sea during the Han dynasty (206 B.C.-A.D. 221), and conquered a considerable part of central Asia. They entered northern India, and as one result Buddhism came to China. Korea was conquered during the T'ang dynasty (A.D. 618-907). Burma was invaded about A.D. 224 and again by Kublai Khan about the year 1280. In 1766 began a war which made Burma a tributary state until Great Britain acquired complete suzerainty. So that French imperialism in Indo-China and British imperialism in Burma are the successors of Chinese imperialism. Within the last few decades Chinese punitive expeditions have vied with similar British expeditions into Tibet, which each would like to make its vassal state.

Indian states and other Oriental countries also have had imperialistic adventures. Indeed, any nation which acquires great military strength is certain to become imperialist. If the nationalist movement in the Orient brings militarism in its train, it may give rise to a recrudescence of imperialism which will gravely menace the West, for the East has the advantage of numbers. In any case, it will seriously interfere with their cultural relations.

Chapter XXXIII

The Cost of Economic Imperialism

IN his book entitled *Imperialism, The Highest Stage of Capitalism,* first published in 1917, during the European War of 1914 to 1918, and just before assuming the leadership of the Russian Revolution, Nikolai Lenin (Vladimir Ulyanoff) defined it as follows: "Imperialism is capitalism in that stage of development in which the domination of monopolies and finance capital has established itself; in which the export of capital has acquired pronounced importance; in which the division of the world among the international trusts has begun; in which the partition of all territories of the globe among the great capitalist powers has been completed." (p. 81.) This definition was applied to the latest phase of the imperialist struggle when the whole world was subjected to this strife and just before the Bolshevist revolution removed part of the world from the arena of this conflict.

An American economist and sociologist defined it much more broadly so as to include its earlier ages. "Imperialism is the stage of economic and political development during which a ruling class conquers and exploits beyond the boundaries of the civil state." After defining civilization as "a period of class exploitation," Nearing characterized imperialism as follows: "Imperialism is a phase of civilization. Empire building therefore begins, as civilization begins, at that point in culture history where pastoral tribesmen or agricultural villagers develop trade and thus lay the foundations of the civil state. The imperial pattern begins when groups of people pass from barbarism into civilization." However, later in his treatise he described the imperial ruling class in terms which seem to refer more particularly to the modern age of economic imperialism. "The imperial ruling class is a business class, or a class engaged in business ventures. It must search for raw materials. It must discover and exploit markets. It must find profitable investment outside the glutted home field." [1] While im-

[1] Scott Nearing, *The Twilight of Empire, An Economic Interpretation of Imperialist Cycles,* New York, 1930, pages 16, 37, and 72-3.

perialism has always from the very outset been inspired by the objectives of loot, slaves, cheap labor, raw materials, etc., one or more of them, it was not always seeking a foreign market for its products, and still less often a profitable investment abroad because its home field was not always glutted. The latter objectives developed later in history, especially with the development of mobile capital.

An English economist and sociologist differentiated modern from ancient imperialism in a book first published in 1902 and characterized by Lenin as "the chief English work on imperialism." "The notion of a number of competing empires is essentially modern. The root idea of empire in the ancient and medieval world was that of a federation of States, under a hegemony, covering in general terms the entire known recognized world, such as was held by Rome under the so-called *pax Romana.* . . . Thus empire was identified with internationalism, though not always based on a conception of equality of nations." Hobson characterized modern imperialism more particularly in relation to the British empire. "The distinctive feature of modern Imperialism, from the commercial standpoint, is that it adds to our empire tropical and sub-tropical regions with which our trade is small, precarious and unprogressive." This has happened in the interest of a small group which is exploiting the public. "Imperialism, as we see, implies the use of the machinery of government by private interests, mainly capitalists, to secure for them economic gains outside their country. The dominance of this factor in public policy imposes a special character alike upon expenditure and taxation." This policy leads inevitably to militarism and often to war. "The economic root of Imperialism is the desire of strong organized industrial and financial interests to secure and develop at the public expense and by the public force private markets for their surplus goods and their surplus capital. War, militarism, and a 'spirited foreign policy,' are the necessary means to this end. This policy involves large increase of public expenditure." [2] As he pointed out, this policy means an expensive militarism in the present and ruinous wars in the future.

Hobson pointed out that there can be no limit on production if there is an effective demand for everything produced. "There is no necessary limit to the quantity of capital and labor that can be employed in supplying the home markets, providing the effective demand for the goods that are produced is so distributed that every increase of production stimulates a corresponding increase of consumption."[3] This statement has been made repeatedly in the present treatise by

[2] John A. Hobson, *Imperialism*, London, 1902, revised edition 1938, pages 6-7, 38, 94, and 106.
[3] *Op. cit.*, p. 29.

pointing out that there must be sufficient purchasing power to distribute the goods which have been or can readily be produced.

After tracing the sequence of conquest, tribute, trade and financial imperialism, Nearing described what he called the imperial cycle:[4]

1. Nucleus of imperial power.
2. Expansion.
3. Survival struggle among empires.
4. Supremacy of one empire.
5. Dissolution of the imperial organization.

According to Nearing, imperialism uses its economic surplus (above a bare or very moderate subsistence for the vast majority of its population) for[5]

1. Defense.
2. Productive building.
3. Unproductive building.
4. Conspicuous consumption.
5. Bread and circuses. (*Panem et circenses.*)
6. Decoration and culture.

Nearing's generalizations still apply in the main in the modern age of imperialism. The British empire may be used as an example of the imperial cycle. It commenced as a small island power in the 16th century. It struggled successfully against the Spanish, Portuguese and Dutch empires in the 16th, 17th and 18th centuries. It expanded through the 19th century when it became not the only empire but the most powerful one in the world. During the 20th century it is rapidly disintegrating. The original causes of its rise in power were that its insular position protected it from invasion on land; that it was a junction point of Atlantic coast trade routes; that it is well supplied with harbors for maritime trade; that it had two rich mineral deposits, namely, coal and iron; and that the relatively early victory of English business over landed interests in the revolution of 1642, as contrasted with 1789 for France, gave England an early start as compared with other countries in the scramble for loot, trade and colonies. England was also aided by its early start in the industrial revolution. "Machine industry broke in on the sequence of the imperial cycle. It also added greatly to the power of the imperial ruling classes by developing industry, transport, merchandising and trade at the expense of agriculture, and by greatly enriching the business class as

[4] S. Nearing, *op. cit.*, p. 36. "As trade develops, sporadic piracy and intermittent plundering expeditions are replaced by an organized war-making machine. The army and navy become professional functions of the ruling class." (P. 59.)

[5] *Op. cit.*, p. 80.

564

compared with the agricultural class. . . . . The industrial revolution laid the basis for an intensified imperialist survival struggle."[6]

The economic surplus is still being spent in much the same way as in the past. In the second half of the 20th century the more powerful nations are spending for offense as well as defense more than ever before in the history of mankind. Among the expenditures are walls, forts, armaments and munitions, the equipment and maintenance of armies, the care of crippled and aged veterans, in other words, the costs of past as well as future wars. Among these costs should be included the wealth destroyed by war, the waste of human energy which might be productively employed, and many other losses due to war. Productive building includes roads, market-places, harbors, docks, canals, ships, railroads, airplanes, factories, warehouses, dwellings, etc. Unproductive building includes temples, churches, palaces, pyramids, sphinxes, burial mounds, statues and other monuments to conquerors, dictators, emperors, kings, generals, and the other parasites, oppressors and exploiters of mankind. Vast sums have been spent in appealing to mythical gods and goddesses and in trying to induce them to aid imperialist adventures. Divine aid is invoked upon every imperialist war.

Conspicuous and wasteful consumption has always characterized the wealthy beneficiaries of imperialism. At the other extreme are bread and circuses for the poor and needy. Even in the richest of modern nations it is often necessary literally to give bread to the starving victims of an economic system so unstable and inefficient that it is characterized by frequent periods of economic depression. The modern "circuses" for the poor are celebrations on national holidays appropriately punctuated with martial music and fireworks simulating "bombs bursting in air," public receptions to conquering heroes returning from sanguinary slaughter for which they are lauded by a misguided public, military, naval and aerial parades, religious processions in honor of imaginary deities and canonized saints, athletic exhibitions imitative of war, and academic ceremonies. Even the latter are inappropriately and incongruously colored by special emphasis upon the patriotic, the warlike, and the religious, all of which are wholly inconsistent with the scholarly and educational functions of academic institutions. It is by arousing these militant, vindictive and bellicose emotions that the masses can be induced to tolerate and endure if not to support the additional exploitation of being forced to contribute time and money, if not also one's life, to an imperialist war.

Nearing also named the causes of imperial disintegration:[7]

---

[6] S. Nearing, *op. cit.*, pp. 131-3.

1. Urbanization.
2. Imperial overhead costs.
3. Civil war.
4. Foreign war.
5. Colonial revolt.

The growth of cities has been one of the inevitable consequences of cultural evolution. Until the Middle Ages it was due largely to commerce. In modern times the industrial revolution has made industry equally important as a factor for concentrating population in urban centers. On the other hand, agriculture has become so highly mechanized in the industrialized nations that only a small part of the population is needed to cultivate enough food to supply the large urban population. Consequently, urbanization, however harmful these monstrous cities may be in other respects, can be attributed only in small part to imperialism, and it will probably be no more than a minor factor for imperial disintegration.

Every imperialist enterprise furnishes profits for a small privileged class, and several private fortunes are made therefrom. A much larger number of lucrative positions are created for members of the privileged class. Not all parts of the ruling class are benefited evenly by each imperialist adventure. In the past it is probable that the merchants profited the most. In modern times the manufacturers have been greatly benefited. But these profits have been secured at the expense of the masses at home, to say nothing of the foreign victims. First comes the heavy expense of conquest, or at least of securing a protectorate over the foreign region to be exploited. Then follows the continued expense of retaining control of the conquered territory by means of armed forces. This heavy expense of armament is borne entirely or in large part by the common people, and only in a relatively small degree by the privileged class.

The exploitation of the foreign or colonial victims of imperialism is even more drastic, especially if they belong to the so-called "lower races." "The condition of the white rulers of these lower races is distinctively parasitic; they live upon these natives, their chief work being that of organizing native labor for their support." "The vast majority of whites admittedly live their own life, using natives for domestic and industrial service but never attempting to get any fuller understanding of their lives and character than is required to exact these services from them or to render official services in return."[8]

More than forty years ago I described the heavy costs for a nation as a whole of a protectionist economic policy and of wars most of

[7] S. Nearing, *op. cit.*, p. 79.
[8] John A. Hobson, *op. cit.*, pp. 282, 301.

which are due to imperialist designs.[9] Tariffs for the restriction of imports are imposed for the purpose of conserving home markets. In the long run they lead inevitably to the loss of foreign markets. This is because of the so-called "favorable balance of trade" which is created. No country can continue indefinitely with either a favorable or an unfavorable balance of trade. In the end imports and exports must balance. If a protective tariff succeeds in excluding imports, in course of time the exportation of goods and of services from that country must also cease. If the possession of foreign markets is desirable, this form of industrial warfare is folly. Furthermore, it interferes with the international division of labor which increases greatly the total production of the world.

Colonization schemes also are usually for the purpose of securing exclusive control of colonial markets. A nation may succeed in doing so for a time. Usually it does not gain by it in the long run. As soon as a colonial market becomes large and profitable, it costs a great deal to retain it, and there is much danger of losing it. This is because other nations become covetous and soon there is likely to be a war over the colonial possession, which will cost more than the profits derived from the colony by the groups which are exploiting it. Or the colony itself, when it becomes large and strong enough, may revolt against exploitation and win freedom or a high degree of autonomy under which its markets are no longer the exclusive possession of the mother country.

The payment of the cost of a war hangs over a people long after the war is ended. No modern government can carry on a war very long without going into debt. This is usually done by the issue of long-term bonds, which are purchased in the main by capitalists and upon which interest has to be paid for many years. The question as to who pays in the end for these bonds depends upon the incidence of the taxes by means of which they are liquidated. Up to the present time they have been paid for in the main by the poorer classes upon which indirect taxes eventually fall. Wars in general have been paid for mainly by the working class. One of the results of modern warfare has been to furnish another means of transferring wealth from the poor to the rich. These bonds have furnished relatively safe investments at fairly good rates of profit for the capitalists. For many years after a war the poor are contributing heavily to pay the interest to

[9] The next few paragraphs are paraphrased from my *Poverty and Social Progress*, New York, 1916, pp. 205-207. The imperial masters even use their colonial subjects as cannon fodder in wars which do not concern these victims. In the war of 1939 to 1945 Great Britain enlisted half a million colonial troops, of which 350,000 came from Africa, the happy hunting ground of the imperialists. (*The Economist*, London, April 14, 1951, p. 844.)

the capitalists and ultimately to pay back the principal.[10] During a war the profits from manufacturing munitions and other war goods are exorbitantly high because a belligerent government has urgent need for such goods.

According to estimates by several official sources in Washington, D. C., and by American University, Washington, the total military cost of the World War, 1939-45, was $1,116,991,463,084, and the property damage was $230,900,000,000. The military costs of the principal belligerents were estimated as follows.[11]

United States	$330,030,464,000
Germany	272,900,000,000
Soviet Union	192,000,000,000
United Kingdom	120,000,000,000
Italy	94,000,000,000
Japan	56,000,000,000
	$1,064,930,464,000

According to a report made by several international agencies the total military and civilian dead due to this war were 22,060,000 and the wounded were 34,400,000. These losses are incalculable in monetary terms but are no less real in terms of wasted manpower than the military costs and destruction of wealth mentioned above.

According to the Treasury Department the debt of the European War of 1914 to 1918 owed to the United States as of July 1, 1950, was $16,129,875,915. According to the Office of Foreign Transactions of the Department of Commerce the aid extended to all foreign countries

---

[10] This is the normal course of events unless a government repudiates its debt obligations directly or by means of inflation and depreciation of the currency. Since ancient times many governments have defaulted and repudiated their debt obligations. (Max Winkler, *Foreign Bonds, An Autopsy, A Study of Defaults and Repudiations of Government Obligations*, Philadelphia, 1938.)

The aggregate amount of principal and interest of intergovernmental war debts, incurred during the European War of 1914 to 1918, to be received or paid after July 1, 1931, was $52,741,547,000. Of this amount the United States was to receive $20,822,691,000. (H. G. Moulton and L. Pasvolsky, *War Debts and World Prosperity*, Washington, 1932.)

In December 1934, the total funded war debt payable to the United States was $11,704,487,464.44; and the total defaulted interest was about $630,000,000.

The net cost of the European War to the United States Government from April 6, 1917, to June 30, 1933, has been calculated at $40,583,062,000. To this was added the loss through default and repudiation on the foreign debts owed to the United States Government, whch were valued on June 30, 1933, at $8,500,000,000 on a 4 per cent basis. (U. S. Department of Commerce, *Statistical Abstract of the United States, 1934*, Washington, 1934.)

[11] *The World Almanac and Book of Facts*, New York, 1951, p. 521.

568

by the United States from July 1, 1940, to June 30, 1950, amounted to $80,142,000,000. All of the "lend-lease" up to the end of the war in 1945 was military aid to allies. Since then most of the aid has been military to satellites and allies of the United States in accordance with the so-called "Truman Doctrine" of containment of communism and by means of the "Marshall Plan" which implements this doctrine. Even the economic aid has been mainly if not exclusively to strengthen these satellites and allies for military purposes, *i.e.,* to fight the communists.

If wars were paid for by heavy assessments upon the rich at the time of a war, or by the issue of bonds to be paid for by direct taxes upon the rich, such as inheritance and income taxes, a war would no longer be a means of making the poor poorer by making the rich richer. Although the workers would gain nothing from a war, and would still be slaughtered at the behest of their capitalist or feudalistic masters, they would not lose as much as they do now, and the rich would not become richer at their expense. If such were the case, there would be much less warfare. The rich usually control governments. Under these conditions it would less often be to the interest of the rich to make war.

Heavy expenditure in times of peace between wars is caused by the menace of military, naval and aerial warfare. So long as international relations are based upon the notions that a nation is sovereign and that the economic interests of nations conflict, war will continue to be an imminent danger. Every nation must maintain itself in a state of military and naval preparedness. Standing armies and navies are inevitable. There must be continual expenditure for munitions and other equipments of war. The services of fighting men who are being withdrawn from the production of wealth must be remunerated. As no government can safely, from a military point of view, refuse to give pensions to veterans and their dependents, for a long period after every war there must be heavy expenditure for the payment of pensions. All these expenditures arising out of international wars are paid for in the main by means of taxes whose incidence falls upon the poorer classes.

These facts reveal the tragic irony of war for the working class. Every war is fought and paid for in the main by the workers. They are forced to slaughter their fellow wage-earners of other countries. Their masters are the only beneficiaries therefrom.[12] The only war from which the workers can hope to gain anything whatsoever is not an international war but the class war. It is the war of the working

[12] Hobson asserted that imperialistic finance creates public debt in order to furnish good investments for the capitalists. (J. A. Hobson, *Imperialism,* revised edition, London, 1938, p. 108.)

class against its exploiters, the capitalists. All dynastic, religious, feudalistic, nationalist, fascist, and imperialist wars can do nothing but
grave harm to the workers. However, the capitalists control not only
governments but most of education, the press, and other means of
publicity. When they wish to instigate a foreign war in order to
enhance their profits, to pull out of a depression and resume the
taking of profits, or to distract the attention of the workers from domestic and internal affairs, it is not difficult for them to mislead the
public into the belief that such a war is a patriotic duty. This is not
to say that capitalists as individuals like war as a means of securing
their profits. Many of them would doubtless prefer peaceful means.
Rather than lose their prospective profits, however, they more or less
unconsciously rationalize an alleged justification for war on patriotic
grounds.

The accompanying tables indicate part of the enormous cost of
war, but not the destruction of wealth and the waste of man power.
Table 1 gives the expenditures of the United States Government for
the fiscal year July 1, 1950, to June 30, 1951, as $68,000,000,000 of
which $48,000,000,000 or 70 percent were for past, present and future
wars, though much of it is listed hypocritically under the misleading
term "defense."

Table 2 estimates the expenditures for the fiscal year 1951 to
1952 at $72,000,000,000 of which $61,000,000,000 or 85 percent was
for war purposes. The recommended new obligational authority for
1952 would increase the appropriations for war purposes by $22,210,-
000,000. But a considerable part of this sum would be spent during
the year or two immediately following 1952.

The following figures are for purposes of comparison with the
Federal expenditures for the fiscal years 1951 and 1952. The Federal
budget for the fiscal year 1939 just preceding the beginning of the
war of 1939-45 was $8,965,555,000, of which $1,784,699,000 or 20 percent was for past and future wars. The Federal budget rose to
$98,702,525,000 for the fiscal year 1945. The public debt rose from
$40,440,000,000 in 1939 to $252,770,000,000 in 1949, the great increase
being due entirely to the war expenditures. The gross national product
rose from $91,339,000,000 in 1939 to $279,800,000,000 in 1950.[16]

In 1939 the expenditure for war was about 2 percent of the
gross national product of 1939. In 1951 it was about 17 percent and in
1952 about 22 percent, of the gross national product for 1950. The
newspapers of May 13, 1951, indicated how this vast expenditure was
extending the warlike and imperialist activities of the United States
the world over. "By obtaining rights to British occupied air fields in

[16] U.S. Department of Commerce, *Statistical Abstract 1950*, 1951, pp. 261, 309,
338.

570

Tripoli, Egypt, Cyprus, Jordan, and, possibly, Iraq, plus strips already available in Turkey, the United States air force hopes to control the eastern Mediterranean if war comes to the middle east."[20]

Table 1

Expenditures of the U. S. Government for past, present and future wars, fiscal year July 1, 1950 to June 30, 1951[13]

Summary of all appropriations for all purposes made by the U. S. Congress from January 3, 1950 to October 31, 1950 for the fiscal year ending June 30, 1951	$67,966,083,088
Department of Defense	$26,213,931,250
Veterans Administration	6,822,963,700
Interest on public debt (in the main)[14]	5,675,505,000
Mutual defense assistance	5,678,023,729
Economic cooperation to supplement military aid	2,250,000,000
Assistance to the Republic of Korea	140,000,000
International development	26,900,000
Atomic Energy Commission (in the main)[15]	907,832,400
American Battle Monuments Commission	9,170,000
Displaced Persons Commission	8,000,000
Government in occupied areas of Germany	27,000,000
Philippine rehabilitation	10,000,000
War Claims Commission	61,471,000
Total expenditures for war purposes	$47,870,997,079
Percent for war purposes of total appropriations	70.4

[13] Source: U. S. Treasury Department, Fiscal Service, Bureau of Accounts, Digest of Appropriations for the Support of the Government of the United States for the service of the fiscal year ending June 30, 1951, Washington, 1951, pp. 544-563.

[14] Inasmuch as the public debt was $40,440,000,000 in 1939 and rose to more than $250,000,000,000 after the war of 1939-45 with an interest rate of about 2¼ per cent, about $910,000,000 of the interest on the public debt may be attributed to the pre-war debt.

[15] Inasmuch as most of the expenditure of the Atomic Energy Commission, at least up to 1955 was for producing atomic bombs and other war purposes, it is legitimate to list this appropriation under expenditures for war purposes.

[20] *Chicago Tribune*, May 13, 1951.

Table 2

Estimated expenditures of the U. S. Government for past, present and future wars, fiscal year July 1, 1951 to June 30, 1952[17]

(In millions)

	1952 estimated	Recommended new obligational authority for 1952
Estimated expenditures for all purposes for the fiscal year ending June 30, 1952	$71,600	
Military services	$41,421	$60,971
Veterans' services and benefits	4,911	4,426
Interest on the Public Debt	5,897	5,897
Military and economic assistance (present programs and proposed legislation)[18]	7,112	10,664[19]
Atomic Energy Commission	1,277	870
Total estimated expenditures for war purposes	$60,618	$82,828
Percent for war purposes of estimated expenditures for all purposes	84.7	

The mounting costs of war are shown by the movement of the public debt of the United States. From $65,000,000 and a per capita of $2.06 in 1860, it rose to $2,756,000,000 and a per capita of $75.42 in 1866. This was due to the Civil War of 1861 to 1865. From $1,225,-000,000 and a per capita of $12.02 in 1916, it rose to $25,482,000,000 and a per capita of $242.54 in 1919. This was due to the European

[17] Source: The Budget of the U.S. Government for the Fiscal Year Ending June 30, 1952, Budget Message of the President and Summary Budget Statements, Washington, 1951.

[18] On May 24, 1951, President Truman recommended to the Congress of the United States to increase its appropriation for foreign aid as follows: "Three weeks ago I transmitted to the congress a request for 60 billion dollars for the United States defense establishment during the fiscal year ending June 30, 1952. I am now recommending for the fiscal year ending June 30, 1952, a mutual security program as follows: (1) Military assistance to other free nations in the amount of 6.25 billion dollars. (2) Economic assistance to other free nations in the amount of 2.25 billion dollars, primarily to support expanded defense efforts abroad. These amounts compare with 5.3 billion dollars appropriated for military assistance, and 3.0 billion dollars for economic assistance, in the current fiscal year."

[19] Include $1 billion in new lending authority for the Export-Import Bank.

War of 1914 to 1918 in which the United States took part during 1917 and 1918. From $42,968,000,000 and a per capita of $325.59 in 1940, it rose to $269,422,000,000 and a per capita of $1,907.62 in 1946.[21] This was due to the World War of 1939 to 1945 in which the United States took part from 1941 to 1945.

In an earlier chapter I have pointed out that civil war takes place either between rival predatory groups of the ruling class or between the ruling class and their exploited and rebellious slaves, serfs, tenants, wage slaves (proletariat), and other victims. The former type was probably the more prevalent in the past because the subject classes were in the main ignorant, were imbued by the slave psychology which had been sedulously instilled into them by their masters and buttressed by the threats of a minatory religion formulated in the interest of their masters, and had almost no opportunity whatsoever to secure weapons to use against their oppressors. In spite of these almost insuperable obstacles there were several revolts of the slaves in the Roman republic and empire, and from time to time there have been sporadic uprisings of serfs, tenants, wage-earners, and other victims of exploitation, which have been ruthlessly suppressed and have, therefore, been almost wholly ineffective. Not until modern times have the subject classes begun to acquire the knowledge, technique, and leadership essential for effective resistance against their exploiters.

Conflicts between rival groups of exploiters whose special interests and privileges have clashed have often arisen and have sometimes led to civil war. Among these conflicts have been.

1. Monarchy *versus* theocracy (priesthood).
2. Monarchy *versus* nobility (feudalism).
3. Dynasty *versus* dynasty (rival claims of legitimacy).
4. Church (clergy) *versus* state.
5. Civil *versus* military government.
6. Fascism (bourgeois private monopoly) *versus* liberal (bourgeois private enterprise) democracy.
7. Landlords *versus* finance.
8. Industry *versus* finance.
9. Private (bourgeois) finance *versus* government fiscal treasury.

Most of the above interests are exploiting the masses all of the time and the remaining few are doing so much of the time. Many of these conflicts are colored by imperialist designs on both sides. How-

[21] U.S. Dept. of Commerce, *Statistical Abstract 1950*, Washington, D.C., p. 338; and *Historical Statistics of the United States, 1789-1945*, series P132-143, pp. 305-306. Washington, D.C., 1949.

ever, these designs do not entirely coincide. The public is certain to suffer and pay a large part of the cost whichever side wins in any of these conflicts. Whenever such a conflict results in war the masses are almost certain to pay the bulk of the cost in blood and wealth. In any case, armed conflicts between rival groups are likely to weaken the national economy and thereby lead to imperial disintegration.

Colonial revolts have from time to time weakened empires. The most famous example was the American revolution of 1776 to 1781 whereby thirteen colonies in North America won their freedom from England thereby depriving the British empire of a vast territory. Soon after during the 19th century followed the revolts of the Latin-American colonies against Spain and Portugal. Even when an armed revolt has not taken place, colonies have sometimes become so strong or their mother countries so weak that they have been able to break away peacefully. This happened in the middle of the 20th century when India, Burma, and Ceylon were able to secede from the British empire after Great Britain had been greatly weakened by the war of 1939 to 1945.

In the past nomad hordes have sometimes invaded more settled communities and ruled them for a time. Such imperialist wars are not likely to happen again because the nomad groups are now much weaker than the settled communities. However, wars of conquest by powerful nations against their weaker contemporaries have occurred down to the present day. Furthermore, many wars against imperial rivals or potential rivals have also occurred and continue to occur. In fact, these have been the characteristic wars of modern times. As will be subsequently discussed, the question now arises whether these imperialist wars will continue or whether the wars of the future will be class wars.

History has shown that imperial decay in the past has led to feudalism. That is to say, the powerful centralized imperial government has broken down into numerous petty local governments. This happened in Europe after the decline and fall of the Roman empire, in Egypt, China, and elsewhere. Whether future class wars will create a different situation remains to be seen.

Owing partly to some of the improvements in navigation it became possible for Columbus to cross the Atlantic in 1492, and for Vasco da Gama to sail around the Cape of Good Hope, visit Calicut in India, and return from 1497 to 1499. Thus began the conquest by peoples of European origin during the next four centuries of all of the western hemisphere, most of Africa, and a large part of Asia. Such conquest resulted variously in the annexation of colonial dependencies, the declaration of protectorates over desirable regions, the claim of exclusive spheres of influence, or at the very least the de-

574

mand for exclusive concessions to exploit the natural resources, the labor, or the markets of the conquered or intimidated backward region.[22]

The cultural impact of these conquests was very great, as has been pointed out by an American historian of modern times. "The cultures of Asia had very little in common with the culture of the West until European armies rudely battered down the walls that separated the Orient and the Occident and forced non-Europeans either to accept Western domination or to graft Western culture onto their own. It was the colonial expansion of Europe that gave the idea of global history a unified meaning. Historically speaking, the colonial expansion of European whites is but a thing of yesterday. Begun by the Portuguese and Spaniards in the sixteenth century and continued in the seventeenth and eighteenth centuries by the Dutch, French, English, and Russians, it has culminated during the past hundred-odd years. Between 1500 and 1800 the American continents were occupied and settled; since 1800 Asia, Australia, Africa, and the islands of all the seas have provided the chief areas of European penetration."[23]

Capitalism often fails to create sufficient effective demand in the form of a widely distributed purchasing power to absorb the supply available in the domestic market. Hence the business man looks abroad for a market for his unsalable surplus or for what can readily be produced if a market can be found.[24] In similar fashion, the capitalist and financier seeks abroad for a field of investment for his surplus capital which cannot be profitably invested at home. The search for profits therefore becomes a pseudo-economic factor for expanding international trade just as it is often a similar factor for the expansion of domestic trade. There arises a certain amount of trade which is artificial in the sense that it is an uneconomical method of distribution. It is wasteful to transport goods hither and thither when they can be produced more economically at home. Only when they can be procured more economically from abroad is foreign trade justifiable according to the standards of a genuine social economy. Profit-seeking is a pseudo-economic factor in both domestic and international commerce in so far as it moves goods around without creating space and time values.

In a purely competitive system of private business enterprise this

[22] See Maurice Parmelee, *Blockade and Sea Power*, New York, 1924.

[23] John B. Wolf, *History of Civilization*, Boston, 1947, Vol. II, p. 298.

[24] The instability of foreign trade as a basis of domestic prosperity is demonstrated by the index of world trade of the League of Nations. On the basis of 1929 as 100, the value in terms of gold of imports and exports fell to 80.8 in 1930, 57.7 in 1931, 39.1 in 1932, 35.2 in 1933, and 33.8 in 1934. (*Monthly Bulletin of Statistics*, Geneva, April, 1935.) In other words, during this period of depression, two-thirds of the world trade had disappeared within five years.

pseudo-economic factor could influence trade little or not at all. The distribution of goods would be determined mainly, or entirely, by the ultimate cost of production. But capitalism has created many forces, financial and political in nature, which have adulterated to a large extent its own professedly competitive character. These factors derange considerably the distribution of goods according to the ultimate cost of production.

International trade is normal and healthy when it consists in distributing raw materials from their sources of origin to the countries where they are not found in a state of nature or cannot be produced. It consists also in distributing finished products from the regions where they can be most economically manufactured to the countries where the cost of production is higher or to new countries where these industries are not yet developed.

International trade is abnormal and not healthy from an economic point of view when it is due solely to the export of surplus capital. The export of a certain amount of capital, namely, loaning, to a country in the early stages of industrial development may be justified. If this industrial development is economically sound, it should soon be able to pay its own way. If international borrowing nevertheless continues, it usually means that surplus capital unable to find profitable investment in the older countries is seeking it in the countries which are less industrialized. The result is to throw international economic relations into a chaotic condition.

The imperialist use of military and naval power has taken place ever since prehistoric times. Colonial expansion played its part in the earlier forms of imperialism, such as Roman imperialism. The discovery of a new hemisphere at the close of the middle ages, and the exploration of extensive regions in Africa and Asia hitherto unknown by Europeans, gave rise to an era of colonization which far surpassed, both in extent and significance, the colonial expansion of ancient times. In order to take possession and then to retain control of and connection with their colonies, the colonizing European nations required large navies and sometimes also armies. At one time or another since the discovery of the western hemisphere, Spain, Portugal, Holland, and France have possessed powerful navies.

Colonial expansion is closely related to another cause for the imperialist use of military and naval power. The increase in the productive capacity of the Occident since the industrial revolution has resulted in a surplus production of many manufactured goods which cannot be disposed of in the domestic markets owing to lack of adequate purchasing power. This situation has intensified greatly the search for foreign markets on the part of the leading industrial nations of the world. It is often said that "Trade follows the flag"; it would be nearer the truth to say that the flag follows trade.[25] The conquest of colonies has usually been for the more or less conscious purpose of utilizing them as markets for the surplus products of the country claiming ownership, and also sometimes as a source of raw materials.

Colonization schemes are usually intended to secure exclusive control of the markets concerned. The conquering nation may succeed in doing so for a time. It does not necessarily gain thereby in the long run. As soon as a colonial market becomes large and profitable, its retention entails a heavy expense. There is great danger of losing it because other nations become covetous. Before long there is likely to be a war over the colonial possession which may cost more than the colony is worth. When it becomes sufficiently strong, the colony itself is likely to revolt against exploitation. If it wins independence or a high degree of autonomy, its market is no longer the exclusive possession of the quondam mother country.

Some colonies have served as outlets for the surplus population of their mother countries. This has usually been true only of colonies situated under climatic and topographical conditions more or less suitable for Europeans. Even in these colonies, the purpose of supplying an outlet for surplus population was not usually the original and primary consideration. Ordinarily commercial considerations alone have determined colonial policies in their inception. The recognition of the utility of colonies as a safety valve for the pressure of over-population in the mother country has come later and has sometimes influenced these policies. Most of the colonies and dependencies in Africa and Asia have not been regarded as havens of refuge for emigrants from European countries.

Attempts to maintain the balance of power between nations have taken place ever since the evolution of large and powerful states. The most notable instance of a balance of power has been in modern Europe. The rapid industrial development of European countries has accentuated economic rivalry among them. It has furnished the means for offensive and defensive measures far surpassing anything that was possible in earlier times. This has been as true of naval power upon the sea as of military power upon the land. The evolution in the size and speed of ships and the possibility of protecting them by means of armor plate and of equipping them with guns of long range and of great destructive power have rendered it possible for navies to become an important element in the game of maintaining the balance of

[25] Speaking of the export of surplus capital, Davies says that "Trade follows the bond." (A. E. Davies, *Investments Abroad*, New York, 1927.) This writer has described how often international debts are not repaid. "The borrowing nations of the world pay interest on their loans just about to the extent that their creditors advance them the wherewithal to do so." (A. E. Davies, *op. cit.*, p. 20.)

power between European nations, even though most of them are contiguous by land.

European history consists largely of these attempts on the part of the European nations to maintain a balance of power among themselves. Whenever this power has been disturbed and rendered unstable, it has usually led to a war or series of wars which has again restored the balance. This balance has sometimes been maintained by an empire exercising control over Europe. When the imperial power has decayed, a period of instability has resulted. At other times the balance of power has been maintained by several nations more or less equal in strength. When one of them has grown much stronger, the balance has become unstable and warfare has often ensued.

The attempts to maintain a European balance of power have arisen in part out of international relations within the continent of Europe. These relations have been partly economic, but also political in the sense that each nation has tried to aggrandize itself at the expense of the others. Religious and dynastic considerations sometimes played a part in the past. The balance of power has been greatly influenced also by the conflicting interests of these nations outside of Europe. These interests have been almost entirely economic and have arisen principally out of colonial expansion and the search for markets.

National aggrandizement is the most imponderable factor for the imperialist use of military and naval power. Sea power has perhaps been utilized less than military power upon the land for purposes of national aggrandizement. This is due in part to the fact that military power is more obvious to the eyes of the great majority of the population than the somewhat remote naval power on the sea. However, in some countries sea power has been an important factor for national aggrandizement. When a British audience sings "Britannia rules the waves," it contributes as much to their consciousness of national greatness as songs of military prowess among other peoples.

The evolution of large-scale factory production and of the modern capitalist system has resulted in large surpluses of manufactured goods and of other forms of capital. The business men of the Occident have been strenuously endeavoring to secure foreign markets for their commodities and new fields for the investment of their surplus capital. Although modern business enterprise has been to a slight extent international, it has been conducted in the main along national lines. These national groups have often been organized in powerful trusts, mergers, or cartels which have concentrated all the force and influence of a national industry.

These groups have desired not only colonial expansion, but also spheres of influence, concessions, monopolistic control of raw materials, protective tariffs, subsidies, and the like. They have been able to manipulate patriotic sentiment through the press and by other means of publicity, and to place many of their representatives in important political offices. They have influenced and controlled governments. Many aggressive acts by governments have been instigated by business men seeking their own ends. The policy of colonial expansion and of foreign trade and enterprize in general arising out of this situation is the modern form of imperialism which may be appropriately termed economic imperialism. It is an extension into the international field of the same predatory methods which prevail at home in all capitalist countries.

The rapid increase of population in Europe during the last century gave rise to a good deal of emigration. The desire to provide suitable home for their surplus population has been one of the causes for the search for colonies by European nations. However, this has not been the principal cause. A large part of these emigrants have gone to the United States, which has furnished opportunities for economic prosperity to many of these Europeans. From 1820 to 1945 inclusive, 38,461,395 immigrants entered the United States, most of them from Europe.[26] Many other European emigrants went to other countries of the western hemisphere, most of which are independent republics and European colonies.

Colonial expansion has been due in large part to the desire to secure an outlet for the export of manufactured goods and of surplus capital, and to gain possession of sources of raw materials. The desire to exploit cheap native labor has also sometimes played a part. Ever since trading has become extensive in its scope, nations have endeavored to gain possession of regions where they have discovered commercial opportunities. The recent opening up of vast unexplored and unexploited regions by explorers and traders has stimulated greatly the race for colonies and spheres of influence as outlets for the export of commodities and of surplus capital. Morocco and Tripoli in Africa, China and India in Asia are illustrations.

If we turn to the events which led up to the European War of 1914 to 1918, we find that in addition to the controversy over the ownership of Alsace-Lorraine, and the fact that the rich coal and iron fields in that region and in northern France were coveted by both Germany and France, the desire of the central European empires to secure additional colonies and spheres of influence played an important if not decisive part in precipitating the war. Balked in its attempt to se-

[26] U.S. Dept. of Commerce, *Historical Statistics of the United States, 1789-1945*, series B 304-330, pp. 33-36, Washington, D.C., 1949.

cure control of Morocco in Africa, Germany turned its attention to the opportunities for exploiting Asia Minor which had already intrigued it, and thereby aroused the jealousy and fears of Great Britain in India and of tsarist Russia in central Asia. Similar purposes led to the World War of 1939 to 1945, as well as the fear that the example of a successful communism in Soviet Russia might lead to a worldwide overturn of capitalism.

These facts demonstrate that colonial expansion for commercial purposes has been a powerful force for war. They do not mean that commerce in itself is necessarily a destructive force. International trade has been an important factor in the development of modern civilization. The civilized nations have sent their manufactured products and surplus capital to the industrially backward regions of the world and have received in return the raw materials available in those regions. The economic development of the United States and Canada is an excellent example of the beneficial aspects of international trade and finance. Europe furnished part of the capital by means of which the natural resources of North America have been developed, while Europe has received in return vast supplies of raw materials. The development of North America could not have taken place so rapidly without this interchange of capital for raw materials.

It is a condition essential for permanent success in international trade, as in every other form of trade, that all parties to the trade should benefit therefrom. This truth has often been ignored in colonial expansion. Many nations have tried to seize and exploit colonies in such a fashion as to profit at the expense of other nations. While both the European War of 1914 to 1918 and the World War of 1939 to 1945 furnished additional evidence of this truth, they also accentuated national feeling greatly. Nationalism renders it difficult to secure a general recognition of this truth. Numerous schemes for protective and preferential tariffs, import and export prohibitions, and economic discriminations of various kinds were proposed during and between these wars. Some of them were incorporated in the peace treaties. The outlook for freedom of competition in international trade is very dark at present.

Many wars have been fought for the possession and control of raw materials. Whenever a nation has possessed all or most of the world's supply of a raw material, there has always been a strong incentive to establish a monopolistic control and to force prices upward to the disadvantage of the rest of the world. This may be accomplished by limiting the output, or by imposing heavy export duties, or by limiting the privilege of exploiting the production of these raw materials to its own nationals. The struggle for raw materials will become more and more acute as the world's natural resources diminish and population increases, and will require a global control of their exploitation.[27]

All these facts clearly demonstrate that there is a fundamental defect in the political organization of the world which must be removed before these economic wastes and contradictions can be obviated. This defect is the idea of absolute sovereignty which permeates the theory of the national state upon which most of the political organization of the world is now based. The crudest expression of this concept in modern times is to be found in the German literature about the state. The philosopher, Hegel (1770-1831), and the historian, Treitschke (1834-1896), for example, uttered fulsome praise of the "great state" which they regarded as the supreme end of human achievement. If they had meant a world state which would abolish all national distinctions, it would result in the negation of national sovereignty. Treitschke, at any rate, had in mind a great Teutonic state so powerful as to overrun weaker states regardless of their national sovereignties, and to make itself dominant in the world. This notion of the great state has pervaded imperialist ideals and programs whenever and wherever they have existed.

[27] See Maurice Parmelee, *Blockade and Sea Power*, New York, 1924, especially Chapters XV-XVII, entitled "Sea Power and Imperialism," "The Freedom of the Sea," and "The Balance of Power and Economic Imperialism."

Chapter XXXIV

The Rise of American Imperialism in the 20th Century

IN the middle of the 20th century the military-strategic imperialism of the United States became worldwide in its ramifications as the immediate consequence of the war of 1939 to 1945. This is not to say that American imperialism had not existed earlier. In fact, it goes back at least as far as the origin of the new nation in the 18th century. Nor am I referring merely to expropriation of the territory belonging to the aboriginal inhabitants as much as land can belong to any group of individuals, namely, by occupation and use, and the extermination of many of these aborigines. The expansion of the United States in the North American continent was in the face of and partly against the imperialist designs of Great Britain, France and Spain.

The United States began as a small and weak nation. It had, however, at least three great advantages for rapid development of size and power. In the first place, it had a large continent over which to expand. This continent contains huge natural resources which have furnished the raw materials for an enormous industrial development. Second, it lies between the two great oceans, thus giving it the advantage in its rivalry for sea power with Great Britain. Third, it was fairly isolated and immune from invasion from Europe. This isolation and immunity have greatly decreased with the rise of air power and the invention of atomic weapons, both in the 20th century.

The government of the United States through its Monroe Doctrine of 1823 declared that it would not permit further colonization of or intervention with American countries by foreign nations. The immediate occasion was a secret treaty of the Holy Alliance of Austria, Russia, Prussia and France to put an end to representative government. While the Monroe Doctrine was intended to protect the new American republics from European interference, it was also an effort to maintain the hegemony of the United States in the western hemisphere and later to assert its domination. No later than 1897, in a controversy over Venezuela, Secretary of State Richard Olney bombastically declared to the imperialistic British government: "Today the United States is practically sovereign on this continent, and its fiat is law. Its infinite resources combined with its isolated position render it master of the situation and practically invulnerable against any or all other powers."

In its struggle for sea power with Great Britain the United States at first advocated the freedom of the sea. This is the inevitable tactic to be followed by a nation weak in sea power. It took no part in the carving up of Africa by European nations during the latter half of the 19th century.[1] But it did share in the struggle for the trade of China which became acute early in the 19th century. China, and a little later Japan, were opened up for foreign trade by the rival imperialist nations, Great Britain and the United States. The so-called "open door" policy was maintained in order to keep China open to all the rivals because if any one of them had attempted to monopolize the China trade it would almost certainly have resulted in warfare among the rivals. "The Open Door policy as employed by Great Britain and inherited by the United States, was part of the diplomacy of imperialism. It was imperialist because its objectives were imperialist prizes. It was a policy designed to preserve and even extend foreign domination and exploitation of China and the Chinese."[2] China was kept in debt to these imperialist powers, British, French, Russian, German and American, which took control of its customs duties in order to "guarantee" the payment of the debt. Furthermore, foreign settlements were established in its cities, its ports were occupied by foreign warships, and its nationals lived under extraterritoriality in China.

Under the presidency of Theodore Roosevelt (1901-09) the United States Government used the game of balance of power to weaken its imperialist rivals in the Far East. Russia was played against Japan and the Russo-Japanese War of 1904-05 was instigated. The peace treaty was negotiated in the United States. An historian has asserted that President Theodore Roosevelt's "purpose was to give Japan a free hand in Korea, to render her assistance, both morally and financially in her fight to loosen the clutch of Russia in Manchuria, with its menace to American commercial and industrial interests, to prolong the war for a sufficient length of time to exhaust both Russia and

[1] However, Liberia, though nominally independent and a member of the United Nations, is virtually a dependency of the United States where the Firestone Rubber Company has leased 1,000,000 acres until 2025. Its capital, Monrovia, is an important naval base of the United States.

[2] George Marion, *Bases of Empire, A Chart of American Expansion*, 3rd edition, New York, 1949, p. 90.

Japan, and to leave a weakened Russia and a strengthened Japan facing each other at the end of the war, thereby equalizing the Manchurian balance of power. A war from which both powers would emerge financially, economically, and physically drained . . . would better serve the economic and commercial interests of the American Republic." [3]

In the meantime, the Spanish-American War of 1898, ostensibly directed at Spain's mistreatment of its colonies, had resulted in the United States taking possession of the Philippine Islands, annexing Puerto Rico, and extending a protectorate over Cuba. Even if conquest was not the immediate purpose of this war, it extended greatly the geographical scope of American imperialism. The Filipinos were already rebelling against Spain and continued to do so against the United States until 1902.

A characteristic American method of imperialism has been its so-called "dollar diplomacy" which was defined by President William H. Taft as follows: "This policy has been characterized as substituting dollars for bullets. . . . It is an effort frankly directed to the increase of American trade upon the axiomatic principle that the government of the United States shall extend all proper support to every legitimate and beneficial American enterprise abroad." This diplomacy became increasingly a diplomacy of investment rather than of trade. And it was a diplomacy of gaining strategic positions by means of financial influence. "The tendency of the businessmen and diplomats was, quite naturally, to seek exclusive commercial and financial privileges within their respective spheres."[4] President Griswold of Yale University also concluded that dollar diplomacy "was an attempt to force American capital by diplomatic pressure into a region of the world where it would not go of its own accord." In the rivalry of investment diplomacy the United States had a great advantage over other imperialist nations in that during and after the European war of 1914 to 1918 it attained financial supremacy which it has retained after the World War of 1939 to 1945 and which has put the whole world more or less at its mercy, not only because of its dollar diplomacy, but also because of its violent method of arming its satellite nations and equipping its military, naval and air bases the world over to crush communism by blood and bombs.

The people of any imperialist country, which has to pay the heavy price for its imperialism, is nevertheless induced to believe that it is to the "national interest" to increase foreign trade, especially export trade, and foreign investment, by propaganda carried on by the churches, newspapers, schools, radio and other means of communica-

[3] E. H. Zabriskie, *American-Russian Rivalry in the Far East, 1895-1914.*
[4] A Whitney Griswold, *The Far Eastern Policy of the United States,* 1938.

584

tion, and by means of a heavy barrage of advertisements, to the effect that private enterprise and business are essential to morality and freedom, and that, conversely, any form of collectivism (socialism and communism) is identical with immorality and slavery. The public has not yet learned that capitalism is incapable of distributing all of its products and is therefore seeking a market for its surplus by imperialist methods for which the public has to pay. The result is perpetual war with occasional truces during which the rival imperialist powers are in a state of balance and the weak exploited countries are too subdued to resist.

As already indicated, imperialism does not necessarily result in annexation and colonization. Hobson has referred to "the sliding scale of diplomatic language," in which are used such terms as "hinterland, sphere of interest, sphere of influence, paramounty, suzerainty, protectorate, veiled or open, leading up to acts of seizure or annexation." If annexation takes place it is hypocritically hidden under such terms as "lease or leasehold," "rectification of frontier," "concession," "League of Nations "mandate" or United Nations "trusteeship." [5]

Since the close of the World War of 1939 to 1945 American imperialism has acquired a new aspect or an additional phase which is trying to conceal its original and fundamental character. It is now cloaked under a great crusade, an almost "sacred" crusade, against Soviet communism and Russian "imperialism." The communism is there and is the gravest threat which capitalism has ever encountered. Of the alleged imperialism there is not the slightest evidence. Even if there were any evidence it would be of trivial importance in comparison with the overwhelming weight of evidence of American imperialism. The United States has secured numerous military bases the world over during and since the termination of the war of 1939 to 1945. Many of them are within a very short striking distance, a few miles or a few hundred miles, of Soviet Russia. In contrast Russia has no armed bases within many thousands of miles of the United States with the possible exception of bases in eastern Siberia which can strike only at the barren and frozen wastes of northern and western Alaska.

I have already indicated that the imperialism of the United States was gradually developing for a century and a half before it reached its great efflorescence immediately after the World War of 1939 to 1945. As two American writers have said: "Across Mexico and Central America, through the countries surrounding the Caribbean, as far west as the Philippines, in China and Turkey, the pioneers of the American Empire have been active during the past generation, laying economic and political foundations." [6]

[5] John A. Hobson, *Imperialism*, 3rd edition, London, 1938.
[6] Scott Nearing and Joseph Freeman, *Dollar Diplomacy, A Study of American*

For the post-war efflorescence of American imperialism there were the perennial causes of modern imperialism, namely, raw materials, cheap labor, markets for surplus products, investment opportunities for surplus capital, and the "merchants of death," the munitions industries, whose profits are derived from the perpetual armament and frequent warfare necessitated by imperialism.[7] In addition there was the menace of Soviet communism. The latter factor changed somewhat the mode of expression of American imperialism. It became more military and strategic in its nature. It secured army, navy and air bases the world over. In this regard it became more like the British imperialism of the 19th and first half of the 20th centuries.

The planning of a total war economy commenced in 1947. By 1955 there was an estimated arms investment of $200 billion of planes, warships artillery, tanks, guided missiles, ammunition, stores, bases, etc., with an annual replacement cost of $20 billion after 1955.[8]

More than $9,000,000,000 had been appropriated by Congress for military bases around the world. In Europe there are bases in England, Belgium, France, Luxembourg, Norway, Germany, Austria and Greece. In Africa they are in French Morocco, Algeria, Tunisia, Liberia and Egypt. In the Middle East they are in Turkey, Syria, Lebanon, Iraq, Palestine, Yemen and Saudi Arabia. In the Orient they are in India, Pakistan, Burma, Australia, the Philippines, Korea, and Japan. The above-mentioned are but some of the bases. They are on numerous islands of the Pacific and on several of the North Atlantic, thus making these two oceans virtually American lakes. Without annexation of territory within a few years military-strategic control had been secured of most of the world outside of Soviet Russia, China and their allies. The vilification of these countries which accompanied this control created a favorable psychological atmosphere for the outbreak of a most disastrous war. And yet on October 25, 1945, President Harry S. Truman stated American foreign policy in this false and misleading fashion: "We seek no territorial expansion or selfish advantage. We have no plans for aggression against any other state, large or small. We have no objective which need clash with the peaceful aims of any other nation."

Table 3 shows the military-strategic empire, that is to say, territory under effective military control and domination, of the United

Imperialism, New York, 1927, p. 219. See also R. W. Dunn, *American Foreign Investments*, New York, 1925.

[7] *Cf.* H. C. Engelbrecht and F. C. Hanighen, *Merchants of Death*, New York, 1934; George Seldes, *Iron, Blood and Profits*, New York, 1934.

[8] *U.S. News and World Report*, March 14, 1952. See also *Collier's*, May 27, 1955, Shadow Plants—Our Secret Weapon"; "Operation Ready is a twin-barreled program, and its string of shadow plants is only half the story, the other half is Layaway."

States since 1945. It includes all of the western hemisphere except Argentina. While the bases which control much of Europe and Asia and all of Africa are not represented in this table, they constitute a decisive part of this control. The grand totals of the table indicate that the post-war empire is eleven times as large as the pre-war empire as to population and fourteen times as large as to land area. It approximated 247 million of population, 13 million square miles of land area, and 96 million square miles of water area. With the United States itself it includes over 400 million of population and 16 million square miles of land area. The population and area dominated by the American military-strategic bases would increase greatly these totals.

In 1939 the U.S. army including the air force, was 268,000, and in 1954 the armed forces numbered 3,300,000. In 1958 more than half-a-million of the armed forces were "over seas." (*Life Magazine*, Dec. 23, 1957.) The Selective Service Act of 1954 conscripts American youth aged between 18½ and 26 years for 24 months and 6 years in the reserve, with exemptions and qualifications for health, family, occupational and educational reasons. The peacetime armed forces are limited to 5,000,000.

Table 3

Military-Strategic Empire of the United States
after the World War of 1939-45[9]

Western Hemisphere—Sphere of special influence and strategic domination

	Land Area in square miles	Population
North America	4,440,000	11,895,000
Middle America	1,095,000	43,495,000
South America	6,130,000	81,080,000
Hemisphere Total	11,665,000	136,470,000
Atlantic Theater—Water area, 26,495,000 sq. mi. in U.S. sphere.		
Atlantic Total	820,000	1,905,000
Pacific Theater-Water area, 70,000,000 sq. mi. wholly in U.S. sphere.		
Pacific Total	345,000	19,120,000
Asia Total	210,000	89,085,000

[9] Source: Revised from George Marion, *Bases and Empire, A Chart of American Expansion*, New York, 1949, 3rd edition, pp. 164-7.

587

| | Area in square miles | | |
	Water	Land	Population
Western Hemisphere		11,665,000	136,470,000
Atlantic	26,495,000	820,000	1,905,000
Pacific	70,000,000	345,000	19,120,000
Asia		210,000	89,085,000
Total Strategic Empire	96,495,000	13,040,000	246,580,000
Pre-War Empire[10]		900,000	22,000,000
Total Expansion	96,495,000	12,140,000	224,580,000

With a minimum standing peace-time armed force of three and one half to five million, more thoroughly mechanized than ever before, the United States would have far more than is required by defense alone. In a few years it would have in reserve a highly trained armed force several times as great. With this armed force it could hold in submission the capitalist part of the world and would threaten and sooner or later attack the collectivist world. The Senate Committee on Armed Services in its 1951 report on the "Universal Military Training and Service Act" expressly designated the communist nations as the enemy to be crushed, thus indicating the official purpose of the United States Government to extirpate communism, and to maintain capitalism by brute force regardless of the desires of the peoples of the world. "Since 1939, 10 nations have fallen under the boot of international communism. . . . The grim fact is that the United States is now engaged in a struggle for survival. The dimensions of that struggle cannot be measured." (pp. 2-3.)[11]

The United States had already asserted its supremacy by force by manufacturing and using for the first time in warfare the atom bomb in 1945. In June 1951 the chairman of the Atomic Energy Commission declared that most fissionable material was being used to manufacture weapons, although atom-fueled electric power might be produced for peaceful purposes; that atom bombs were being produced

[10] Estimated in P. T. Moon, *Imperialism and World Politics*, New York, 1926. All of the pre-war empire was in the western hemisphere, except the Philippines and a few small Pacific Islands, and Liberia in Africa; including principally Alaska, Hawaii and Puerto Rico, and the nominally independent dependencies Cuba, Haiti, Dominican Republic, Nicaragua and Panama.

[11] *Chicago Sun-Times*, June 8, 1951. Owing to "security" (a euphemism for "belligerent") control, not before 1955 was atomic energy considered for peaceful uses.

on a mass basis; that the hydrogen "super-bomb" would soon be produced; and that Russia could be defeated in war.[12] No more conclusive evidence could be cited that the government of the United States has deliberately constituted itself the enemy of mankind by manufacturing these weapons for the mass slaughter of humans and the wholesale destruction of wealth.[13]

Not content with menacing the world with its own armament the United States has been subsidizing profusely the armaments of its allies and satellites. Soon after the termination of the war of 1939 to 1945 it began to re-arm its principal vanquished enemies, Germany and Japan, in order to attack its allies, Russia and China, whom it now regards as its enemies. At the same time it took the lead in 1949 in organizing the western European nations in an offensive alliance against Russia known as the North Atlantic Treaty Organization (NATO). Its leading militarist, General Dwight D. Eisenhower, commanded the armed forces of this alliance. In June 1950 it invaded Korea in an undeclared and most destructive war, to which the United Nations gave very lukewarm support, because the Koreans were trying to unify their country after being divided at the 38th parallel of north latitude at the close of the war in 1945.[14]

However overpowering may seem the brute force of American imperialism, it will not last forever. In the preceding chapter have been discussed the causes of the disintegration of empires. The last

[12] Senator William Langer of North Dakota commented: "I submit that this doctrine of groveling before the threat of Communism everywhere is a false doctrine. It is we, not the Russians, who are looked on as being trigger-happy. We are considered pompous, reactionary, cruel and selfishly rich." *Congressional Record,* 1951.

[13] A very pious American nuclear physicist made this brutally egregious assertion: "I think that not only did God condone our act in dropping the bombs, but that it was only with His help and inspiration that the job was done in time. I consider it a true act of Providence that the ability to make and use atomic bombs first became available to a nation whose primary international concern was a free and stable world." (Arthur H. Compton, "God and the Atom," *American Magazine,* October 1950, p. 118.)

[14] Early in 1951 the Assembly of the United Nations accorded a vote of confidence of 44 to 7 nations to the United States concerning Chinese aggression in Korea. But the 44 nations have an aggregate population of about 590 million while the 7 nations have approximately the same number. Furthermore, the European votes were given under strong pressure from the United States. And more than one billion humans were not represented at all because they have not been admitted to the UN.

The UN Relief and Rehabilitation Committee reported that in less than a year the U.S. armed forces had killed or wounded 3,000,000 Koreans out of a population estimated in 1949 to be about 29,000,000, and that the destruction in Korea was worse than any man-made catastrophe since the sack of Carthage in B.C. 146 by the Romans and in A.D. 698 by the Arabs. (See the *National Guardian,* New York, June 13, 1951, and the *1951 Britannica Book of the Year,* p. 403.)

great empire was the British empire whose undisputed supremacy did not persist much more than a century. This supremacy arose out of sea power. American imperial domination also arises mainly out of sea power to which have recently been added air power and nuclear missiles. The forces most likely to cause disintegration of the American empire are imperial (military) overhead peacetime costs, internal unrest with the menace of civil war, external dissension among the satellites (colonial and otherwise) and allies of the imperial master (the U.S.A.), and the heavy costs in blood and wealth of foreign wars which can never be recovered.[15]

Sea-going vessels made possible deep-sea fishing and maritime commerce. These two important economic pursuits gave to the sea a new value and significance. Attempts were made by nations to appropriate the sea and thereby secure a monopoly of the profits to be derived from deep-sea fishing and maritime commerce. The desire to enforce these claims was the principal motive for the construction of navies and the patrolling of appropriated waters. Seafaring discoverers often claimed title for their countries to seas as well as lands discovered by them, and such claims by discovery were made the basis of legal ownership over these marine areas.

Another early factor for the construction of navies and the development of naval power was piracy. Pirates, like highway robbers, harassed commerce and made travelling dangerous, thus giving rise to the problem of policing the sea and maintaining order thereon. All nations with a sea coast were forced to take measures to free neighboring waters from pirates. This police duty furnished some justification for the claim to ownership of those waters. It was much more difficult to police the ocean and other vast marine areas more or less remote from organized government upon land. Piracy was eventually stamped out, not so much by policing the sea as by closing all the havens of refuge and sources of supplies which the pirates had been utilizing. This came to pass as soon as all the important ports of the world were under governments which recognized the international obligation to permit no craft not engaged in legitimate commerce from making use of their port facilities. Thus piracy was stamped out by means of international cooperation and not by national ownership of the sea. In the future the prevention of piracy will doubtless be an international police function rather than a task for the individual national states.

As a consequence of the rapid development of maritime commerce at the beginning of the Middle Ages, there were many attempts to appropriate seas. When Venice became a powerful maritime state, it

[15] The following paragraphs on sea power and blockade, the freedom of the sea, and the balance of power, are paraphrased and brought up to date from my book entitled *Blockade and Sea Power*, New York, 1924.

claimed the ownership of the Adriatic Sea. In similar fashion Genoa claimed the Ligurian Sea. The ownership of the Baltic Sea was claimed at one time and another by various Scandinavian countries and Poland. In the sixteenth and seventeenth centuries Spain and Portugal claimed the right, under the authority of Papal bulls, to divide between themselves the Atlantic, Pacific, and Indian Oceans.

These claims were abandoned centuries ago. Such attempts to appropriate the sea have only an historical significance. But one of the latest, though abandoned in its original form, is worthy of special note, because it was succeeded by the rise of the greatest sea power of modern times, if not indeed of all times. It was the attempt on the part of England during the seventeenth century to appropriate certain maritime areas.

When the Stuart dynasty came to England from Scotland, at the beginning of the seventeenth century, it brought with it the doctrine of the ownership of the sea. Scottish fishermen had conflicted with Dutch fishermen on the fishing grounds in the North Sea. The Stuart monarchs wished to claim ownership which would furnish the legal basis for excluding the Dutch fishermen. This began a series of attempts during the seventeenth century to establish English rule over various bodies of water, such as the North Sea, the Irish Sea, the Channel, and so forth, and to enforce alleged rights of tribute, of salute to the English flag, and the like, which gave rise, among other things, to three wars with Holland.

There had been earlier vague precedents of English rule over the sea. These precedents were gathered together and utilized by Selden in a treatise,[16] written under and for the sake of the Stuarts, in which he attempted to substantiate this English claim to the ownership of the sea.

While the early claim led to very little attempt at enforcement, as revived by the Stuarts it had far-reaching results for about a century. It soon went far beyond a claim to fishing rights alone. This was a time when, as a result of the discovery of vast new regions of the world and the consequent development of oversea trade, dominion over the sea had acquired a much greater value and significance. The Stuart monarchs made use of this claim also for the purpose of stimulating the patriotic feelings of the English when they wanted to prosecute a foreign war in order to aggrandize their own royal house or to distract the attention of the people from internal difficulties. These enterprises were, however, unhappy in their consequences to themselves, as well as to the English people. The reign of Charles I ended with his execution in 1649. The Protectorate and Commonwealth intervened before the restoration of the Stuart dynasty with Charles II. The dynasty

16 John Selden, *Mare Clausem seu de Dominio Maris*, London, 1635.

591

itself disappeared with Queen Anne in 1714, and with it this claim to ownership over specific areas of the sea.

English belief in the value of sea power preceded this attempt on the part of the Stuarts to appropriate and enforce ownership over the sea, and increased greatly with colonial expansion and the growth of militarism in modern times. It has been flamboyantly described by a British writer: "The sea must be kept. That has been the maxim and watchword of national policy throughout the ages, and the recognition of its truth was by no means confined to rulers and statesmen. The people at large have always been convinced and as resolved that the supremacy or dominion on the sea should be maintained as were those in whose hands was placed the guidance of the affairs of the state." [17]

These naive claims to ownership of the sea have vanished with a few minor exceptions. Their disappearance has been due in part to the fact that their naivety was even more obvious than similar claims to the land. While the land is usually inhabited by human beings who make use of it and can thereby establish a claim to its use and ownership, the sea is an uninhabited and almost barren waste. It furnishes abundance of space for transit for every one, and a claim to absolute ownership is therefore unjustifiable even on the part of the nations which make the largest use of the sea. But the disappearance of these naive claims to ownership by no means signified a cessation of attempts to exercise power upon and sometimes over the sea. In fact, in the evolution of modern imperialism sea power has sometimes played a role even superior in importance to military power upon land.

The increase in the size and speed of ships, and the possibility of protecting them by means of armor plate and of equipping them with guns of long range and of great destructive power, has rendered it possible for navies to play an important part in the game of maintaining the balance of power between European nations, even though most of these nations are contiguous by land. The most notable example has been Great Britain which, partly because it is somewhat isolated from the continent of Europe, has usually played its part in maintaining the balance of power by naval measures. It has almost invariably refrained from entering upon formal alliances in the many groupings of nations which have taken place upon the European mainland. It has always stood ready to throw the weight of its naval power upon the one or the other side, when it thought that its interests dictated such intervention. It was an exceptional departure from its traditional policy when Great Britain joined in forming the Triple Entente in 1906, and then entered the European War of 1914 to 1918 and developed great military power.

[17] T. W. Fulton, *The Sovereignty of the Sea*, Edinburgh and London, 1911.

All of these factors for the imperialist use of sea power, as well as one or two factors peculiar to this case, were illustrated in the most notable example of modern sea power. The first argument usually put forward in defense of British sea power was the necessity of procuring food for the inhabitants of the British Isles. Inasmuch as Great Britain is isolated by the sea and is incapable of producing sufficient food for its own population, naval power is needed so long as it may be cut off from its sources of food by an enemy. To this extent British sea power is not imperialist in its character and is justified for purposes of defense. But this factor alone did not explain or justify the existence of a fleet so great as that of Great Britain.

The second argument used in justifying the size of the British navy was the alleged necessity of maintaining connection with British colonies. Inasmuch as the British Empire was scattered the world over, it was necessary not only to possess a fleet large enough to maintain constant communication with all the numerous colonies, but also a sufficient number of coaling stations, and the ownership or control of such strategic points as Gibraltar, Malta, Cyprus, the Suez Canal, Aden, Singapore, Hong Kong, and so forth, to render it impossible to cut these connections even in the case of a war with the leading naval powers of the world. In other words, so long as the British Empire was accepted not only as an actual fact but as a necessary fact, there was probably sufficient justification for the British fleet. This justification stands or falls in accordance with the more fundamental question of the justification for the British Empire and British imperialism.

Modern British industry was developed largely on the basis of its mineral resources of coal and iron. Its coal deposits were estimated in 1913 at about 180,000,000,000 tons. Its production in 1949 was about 203,000,000 tons. At that rate of production its coal deposits would not be exhausted for about eight and a half centuries. Its iron ore deposits were estimated in 1942 at 3,400,000,000 tons. Its production in 1949 was about 13,400,000 tons. At that rate of production its iron ore deposits would be exhausted in 250 years, or about 2200 A.D. Great Britain is already importing iron ore. In 1949 it imported about 8,7000,000 tons.[18] Coal is the only natural resource with which it is generously supplied.

The British Isles are unable to produce enough food and many other essential raw materials to maintain the British population. Great Britain has become a highly industrialized nation, devoted mainly to manufacture of finished products from raw materials which

[18] *Statesman's Yearbook, 1950*, pp. 99-100; and the *Encyclopaedia Britannica, 1942*, article on "Iron and Steel." Estimates of mineral reserves must be regarded as very tentative because they are constantly being revised in the light of new discoveries.

are in large part imported. The search for markets has been one of the most important features of British colonial and imperial policy and a powerful factor for the development and maintenance of British sea power. Principally in order to dispose of its manufactured products, as well as in some cases to secure control of sources of raw materials Great Britain has either sought for colonies or has retained them when British explorers, mariners, and traders have, so to speak, stumbled upon them.

This situation has been a justification for British imperialism to the extent that imperialist methods are necessary to safeguard sources of raw materials and to secure markets for finished products. Even if this justification is admitted in so far as the past is concerned, it will not hold good in the future, provided freedom of trade is guaranteed and safeguarded to such a degree that no country is in danger of being cut off from its sources of raw materials and from its markets for finished products.

While naval power has continued to increase, there has at the same time developed the theory of the so-called "freedom of the sea." This is not a new theory. In the Roman law, the sea was called common and free. But the meaning of the term has varied greatly from time to time, and no genuine freedom has existed up to the present.

With respect to this theory, nations have followed, as usual, the policy which they conceived to be to their own interest. For many years, Rome possessed a powerful rival in Carthage on the other side of the Mediterranean. The theory of the freedom of the sea probably was incorporated in the Roman law out of a desire to check the rise of the naval power of its great rival. Commercial considerations also may have played a part. Imperial policy may have discerned the advantages of a free exchange of commodities between the different parts of the Roman Empire and the remainder of the known world. But these considerations and the theory itself did not restrain Rome from developing naval power when it saw fit to do so.

The modern theory of the freedom of the sea is usually dated from the Dutch work of Grotius entitled *Mare Liberum*. Grotius advocated the freedom of the sea in the interest of mankind, and his book influenced to a considerable extent the development of international law with respect to the sea. It is, however, significant to note the circumstances under which Grotius wrote his book, and the specific purposes which he apparently had in mind. The first edition of *Mare Liberum* was published anonymously at Leyden in 1609. Shortly prior to that date, in 1603, the Stuart dynasty had ascended the throne in England, and put forward the doctrine of the British ownership of the seas in the vicinity of the British Isles. This doctrine was propounded and put into effect at first because the fishermen from Scot-

594

land, from whence the Stuart dynasty came, had conflicted with the Dutch fishermen on the fishing grounds in the North Sea. It was to the interest of Holland to maintain the theory that the sea should be an open and common ground for fishing.

Other circumstances furnished a justification for this theory even more than the fishing rights. The preceding century had been characterized by extensive exploration and discoveries which made possible an enormous expansion of commercial enterprise. Certain nations which were interested in taking advantage of these opportunities for trade, or for wholesale robbery on land and sea, claimed the ownership of extensive areas of the sea. The most extravagant of these claims was the one put forward by Spain and Portugal under the alleged authority of a Papal bull to divide between themselves the waters of the Western Hemisphere and of the East Indies.

The Dutch merchants and seamen, in search of trade and profit, were at that time pushing their way into various areas claimed by these Catholic nations. While the Dutch lawyer Hugo Grotius may have been influenced to a certain extent by humanitarian considerations, it is probable that his appeal in behalf of the freedom of the sea was inspired largely by a patriotic desire to remove these obstacles in the way of the navigation and commerce of his country. This seems all the more probable in view of the fact that Grotius did not consistently advocate the freedom of the sea throughout the whole of his career. When he went to London as one of the Dutch commissioners to protest against the English claims to ownership over the North Sea, he was the Grotius of *Mare Liberum*. Later in his career when he was the ambassador of the Swedish queen in Paris, he displayed great reluctance to advocate this theory because Sweden was at the time making extravagant claims to ownership over the Baltic Sea.

As has been pointed out, the earlier naive claims to ownership of the sea have disappeared almost entirely. Furthermore, the discussion of the theory of the freedom of the sea in works of Grotius and his successors such as Puffendorf, Van Bynkerhoek, de Vattel, von Martens, Azuni, Bluntschli, etc., has resulted in its partial recognition by international law, and has also given rise to lip service to this theory from all the civilized nations of the world.[19] This is even more true of the nations possessing great naval power, whose professions of recognition of and loyalty to this theory are prone to wax in vehemence with the growth of their naval power.

The controversy over the principle of the freedom of the sea during the European War of 1914 to 1918 involved several points of

[19] A detailed historical account of the development of this theory is in the following work: P. B. Potter, *The Freedom of the Seas in History, Law, and Politics,* New York, 1924.

595

interest with regard to sea power. It illustrated the conflict between the interests of neutrals and of belligerents upon the sea in time of war. It is to the interest of neutral nations to use the sea as freely in time of war as in time of peace. If belligerent nations use their rights of blockade, they hamper neutral commerce. Furthermore, almost every war illustrates the conflict between the interests of seafaring and non-seafaring nations with respect to the freedom of the sea. As nearly every nation was swept into the World War of 1939 to 1945, the rights of neutrals were almost completely forgotten.

It is often contended that sea power is comparatively bloodless and therefore relatively harmless as compared with military power on land. This theory is comforting to the nations which possess great naval power, and is likely to arouse a self-righteous attitude on their part toward the nations which possess great military power on land. The sea is an almost barren waste, so that it is impossible to slaughter many humans upon the sea, or to destroy as much wealth as is available for this purpose upon land. However, these facts do not prove that sea power is ever beneficent, or, to say the least, innocuous in its effects.

Blockade is an exercise of sea power which may lead indirectly to the loss of many human lives. The Spanish conquest of the Netherlands and the religious persecution which resulted therefrom was possible owing to the great naval power which Spain then possessed. Sea power has been used as much as and perhaps even more than military power on land for purposes of exploitation of undeveloped territories. The history of colonial expansion furnishes abundant evidence of this fact. There is even less justification for sea power than there is for military power on land. Inasmuch as the land is inhabited by humans and is covered with wealth, there is some justification for the exercise of power over this population and wealth by means of government, which should be administered by the local population so that they are selfgoverning, and which must rest in the last analysis upon force. The sea, on the contrary, is uninhabited and contains little of value. Hence the sea should be a neutral area and not subject to the sovereignty of any nation.

In view of these facts, it is obvious that great naval power is incompatible with freedom of the sea. However pacific may be the purpose of the nation possessing such power the very existence of a powerful navy will inevitably in course of time lead to violations of the freedom of the sea. In this regard, there is little difference between great naval and military power. A large standing army is a perpetual menace to peace because, however pacific may be the spirit of the people possessing it, and however sincere their belief in its necessity for defensive purposes, it is certain eventually to give rise to war. In the first place it brings into existence a military class whose interest it is to foment war in order to aggrandize itself. Second, a standing army is a menace to peace because of the jealousy, rivalry and fear which it arouses in other countries. If for no other reason, to say the least for self-defense, other nations are certain to develop similar armed forces. Third, apart from and in addition to self-defense, national pride and ambition are likely to encourage the development of military power.

In addition to the imperialist argument that a worldwide colonial empire requires a mastery of the sea, the British claim to naval supremacy was that freedom of the sea was safeguarded and maintained by the British navy, by which was usually meant that it policed the sea without discriminating between the merchant ships of different nations. Whether or not this assertion was true, this claim did not meet the fundamental issue. No such national claim to supremacy either upon land or upon sea can be continued indefinitely without harmful consequences. Just as it is dangerous for the most righteous man to possess unlimited power which will eventually undermine his character and be abused by him, so it is dangerous for the most righteous nation to possess a similar power which it will inevitably abuse at some time or other. Even if this righteous nation never abused its power, such a claim to supremacy invariably irritates other nations and leads eventually to emulation or retaliation which gives rise to war. The self-complacence of any nation which believes that it is not misusing naval or military supremacy is in itself a grave menace to the safety of mankind.[20]

After the termination of the European War of 1914 to 1918 the even greater British post-war navy exacerbated the naval program and ambitions of the United States. The ground for this development had been prepared before this war by a group of navalistic writers, the most notorious and pernicious of whom was the American Admiral Mahan. Throughout his writings upon sea power he was an ardent advocate of force and displayed great admiration for German militarism as well as British navalism. He was an excellent example of the close kinship between the spirit of navalism and the spirit of militarism. His central thesis was in effect a reiteration of the classic saying *"si vis pacem— para bellum."* The falsity of this saying has been disproved many times. But this did not deter Mahan from misinterpreting and misusing historical facts in support of his navalistic propaganda. The fallacious character of his theory was well illustrated two years prior to the outbreak of the war, in a book in which he exalted forcible methods of maintaining peace, and made the following assertion: "The

[20] See Maurice Parmelee, *Blockade and Sea Power, The Blockade, 1914-1919, and Its Significance for a World State*, New York, 1924.

597

German Empire, which owes its existence to its army, has, thanks also to its army, known forty years of unbroken peace, of the sheathed sword."[21] When the German armed hordes swept over Belgium and Northern France in August, 1914, it was obvious that the "pacific" influence of German militarism alleged by Mahan did not preserve peace indefinitely, but, on the contrary, precipitated what was up to that time the worst of wars.[22]

The influence of British navalism upon Germany and also upon the United States, was not exceptional. In neither case was the country influenced to be exonerated entirely from blame. But the bulk of the blame must rest upon the nation which instigates such rivalry. It has always been true and will invariably be true, that great military and naval power not only accentuates nationalist feeling at home, but also aggravates it abroad and thus incites rivalry.[23]

In addition to the damage wrought by great naval power in arousing hostile rivalry and giving rise to war, it is inevitably an instrument of injustice and of oppression in time of peace. Like great military power, it is a potential coercive force which may be put into action at any time to accomplish the ends of the nation possessing it. Its existence must be tacitly recognized by the small countries and other nations not possessing great military and naval power. However polite may be the verbiage used in diplomatic relations, a large navy or a large army looms, a dark and sinister menace, behind the great power and signifies far more emphatically than the diplomatic language that its will must be obeyed. Even short of war, the purposes of a great power may be attained by means of "pacific" blockades,[24] confiscation of customs revenues, and like measures, put into effect by its navy.

The problem, therefore, presents itself of attaining the useful and necessary functions which have so far been partially accomplished by the great national navies, while avoiding their baneful effects. Among

[21] A. T. Mahan, *Armaments and Arbitration*, New York, 1912, p. 17.

[22] Mahan's principal works on sea power are the following: *The Influence of Sea Power upon History, 1660-1783*, Boston, 1890; *The Influence of Sea Power upon the French Revolution and Empire, 1793-1812*, Boston, 1892, 2 vols.; *The Life of Nelson, the Embodiment of the Sea Power of Great Britain*, Boston, 1897, 2 vols.; *Sea Power in Its Relation to the War of 1812*, Boston, 1905, 2 vols.

[23] Some of the navalistic works which exhibit the influence of Mahan and exemplify the chauvinism aroused by war are the following books: Gerard Fiennes, *Sea Power and Freedom*, New York, 1918; W. O. Stevens and Allan Westcott, *A History of Sea Power*, New York, 1920; H. F. Kraft and W. B. Norris, *Sea Power in American History*, New York, 1920; H. C. Bywater, *Sea Power in the Pacific, A Study of the American-Japanese Naval Problem*, London, 1921; M. W. W. P. Consett, *The Triumph of the Unarmed Forces*, London, 1923.

[24] J. B. Moore has described many instances of pacific blockade in his *Digest of International Law*, Washington, 1906, Vol. VII, pp. 135-142.

these functions are the policing of the sea against piracy, the prevention of discriminatory use or monopolization of fishing regions and other valuable areas of the sea, such regulation of maritime traffic as is necessary, and the promotion of the safety of navigation against the perils of the sea.

The first step toward a real freedom of the sea is the internationalization of all waterways which are essential to worldwide commerce and transportation. This means, in the first place, that such commanding strongholds as Gibraltar and the Suez Canal in the hands of the British, the Panama Canal in the hands of the United States, the Dardanelles and the Bosphorus in the hands of the Turks, the Sound in the hands of Denmark, should no longer be under the control of individual nations. However freely these nations may permit international commerce to make use of these waterways in time of peace, there always exists the menace that the nation in control may put an end to this freedom. It is much the same as if a householder were to place a loaded cannon in front of his house and then inform his neighbors that, while they might, as a rule, use the street freely, it was his intention to close the street when he so desired. The principle of freedom should, therefore, be applied to waterways essential for international navigation and commerce as much as to the high seas, even though these waterways are contiguous to territory under national domain. This principle should be applied not only to such waterways as have already been mentioned, but also to important inland waterways, such as large rivers which are more or less essential to international commerce.[25]

The second essential for a genuine freedom of the sea is a limitation of naval armament on the part of individual nations. This is closely related to the development of a world federation of geo-economic regions which will take over the police powers of the individual nations in so far as international affairs are concerned and substitute for the national military and naval forces an international federal military and naval force for this international police function. Such a world federation will perform the necessary and useful functions heretofore performed by the great navies and armies.[26]

The rapid development of flying has transferred a considerable part of warfare to the air. Nations are attempting to appropriate and control the air like the sea, so that air power will correspond to sea power. What I have said concerning the sea, therefore, applies to the air as well as to the sea, for the air should be as free as the sea. It will be the duty and function of the world federation to guarantee

[25] Cf. P. M. Ogilvie, *International Waterways*, New York, 1920.
[26] See Maurice Parmelee, *Geo-Economic Regionalism and World Federation*, New York, 1949, Chapter 4.

and safeguard the freedom of the air as much as the freedom of the sea, in order that this common medium of communication and transportation may be used by mankind for all peaceful and productive purposes.

It was sometimes alleged during the European War of 1914 to 1918 that it was fought for the rights of small nations. Similar assertions have been made in connection with other wars. When the Napoleonic wars ended and the monarchs of the Grand Alliance which had fought against Napoleon met at the Congresss of Vienna they announced that "Nations will henceforth respect their mutual independence; no political edifices shall henceforth be erected on the ruins of formerly independent States; the object of the War, and of Peace, is to secure the rights, the freedom and the independence of all Nations." But the Treaty of Vienna of 1815 which resulted from their deliberations ignored almost entirely the principle of nationality.

European history consists largely of the history of attempts on the part of European nations to maintain a balance of power among themselves. Whenever this balance has been disturbed and rendered unstable, it has usually led to a war or series of wars which has again restored the balance. The balance of power has sometimes been maintained by an empire exercising control over Europe. When the imperial power has decayed, a period of instability has resulted. At other times the balance of power has been maintained by several nations more or less equal in strength. When one of these has grown much stronger, the balance of power has again been rendered unstable.

Attempts to maintain the balance of power can be traced throughout recent European history. Such wars as the Crimean of 1854 to 1856, the Franco-Prussian of 1870 to 1871, and the Russo-Turkish of 1877 to 1878 were followed by treaties and alliances which were directed toward maintaining a stable balance of power. Territory has been apportioned, small countries have been kept in existence and made neutral in order to serve as buffer states, and colonial policies have been dictated by this effort to maintain a stable balance. The most recent examples of such a treaty were the Treaty of Berlin of 1878 and the Treaty of Versailles of 1919, which apportioned the territory and determined the national boundaries of a considerable portion of Europe.

Immediately after the World War of 1939 to 1945 the United States Government assumed the role of global policeman at a terrible and tragic cost not only to the people of the United States, but of the whole world. It expects to suppress communism and to maintain capitalism by military might. The small number of politicians and generals who direct and control this government are ignorant of or oblivious to the fact that the issue between these two economic and

600

political systems must be decided in the long run not by brute force but by their relative success in providing a high and stable standard of living for mankind. Whatever may be the faults and weaknesses of the communist regimes, they do not justify the U. S. Government from following an inflammatory and incendiary policy of warmongering, spy- and witch-hunting, red-baiting and vilification against these communist governments.[27] That this militarist-imperialist adventure will fail disastrously is demonstrated not only by history but by the logic of events. This failure will probably be due to the factors mentioned earlier in this chapter, namely, the imperial overhead peacetime costs, the internal unrest with the menace of civil war among a people not wholly convinced of the wisdom of a militarist-imperialist policy, the external dissension among satellites and allies of the American imperial master who are not entirely immune to communist persuasion, and the appalling costs in blood and wealth of foreign wars from which no belligerent can gain victory.

The empires of Babylonia, Egypt, Assyria, Persia, Rome, and that of Great Britain, to which we have devoted special attention in this chapter, have passed into history. And yet the American empire sets forth upon the same road of brutal folly. The Russians witness with alarm that they are being surrounded by American air bases in Greenland, Iceland, Canada, Western Europe, Greece, Turkey, Spain, northern Africa, the Middle East, the Philippines, Hawaii, Alaska, and numerous islands of the sea. The Europeans watch with foreboding American preparations for war because they know that when the United States attacks Russia Europe will be the most bombed area in the world. The Asians are angered and terrified by the wholly unprovoked and savage destruction of Korea by American armed forces. With unparalleled arrogance the United States government dictates policy to practically all of the western hemisphere and to some of the eastern hemisphere. That this will be its own nemesis sooner or later can hardly be questioned, because it has already created a vast amount of ill will against the United States and its nationals the world over.

What is much worse, the United States government, while professing to be fighting for political freedom, is standing in the way of the freedom and economic welfare of a large part of mankind as well as menacing the peace of the whole world. As has been well said: "Moreover, we forget too easily that freedom has a different meaning

---

[27] See, for example, U.S. House of Representatives, Committee on Un-American Activities, "Report on the Communist 'Peace' Offensive," April 1, 1951; Albert E. Kahn, *High Treason, The Plot against the People*, New York, 1950, especially Chapter 17 entitled "The Red Specter." The latter book furnishes ample evidence of the warmongering and red-baiting of the U.S. Government.

for two-thirds of the human race still submerged in a basic struggle against hunger, poverty, and disease. To them freedom has largely an economic meaning: freedom from antiquated systems of land holding or taxation, freedom from the crushing effects of poverty. They have had little opportunity to know the meaning of political freedom, and Communism is attractive largely because it talks in the economic terms they can understand."[28]

The United States government is rapidly destroying such political and personal freedom as the American people has heretofore enjoyed.[29] Ahead looms the police and garrison state which threatens to supplant the American republic and obliterate the last vestiges of democracy. It may also mean the end of Occidental culture as it has developed during the past two and a half millennia.

[28] *Steps to Peace, A Quaker View of U.S. Foreign Policy*, American Friends Service Committee, 1951, p. 12.

[29] *Cf.* Walter Gellhorn, *Individual Freedom and Governmental Restraints*, 1956.

Chapter XXXV

The Politico-Economic Development of the State

IN Chapters XVIII and XIX we have seen that except in isolated cases, and in some primitive groups, social control has not originated because an individual has been able to impose his will upon a group of any size for any length of time. It has arisen rather because customs and traditions, public opinion and moral ideas, have come into being concerning specific forms of conduct. These forms are enforced by certain groups of individuals to whose interest it usually is to require conformity to such forms. Hence it is reasonable to suppose that these groups of individuals have influenced and prescribed the patterns of conduct to which the community or society is compelled to conform. As in the case of all social phenomena, there has been the unconscious and unintended growth of certain ways of doing things modified intentionally at times by interested parties who were advantageously situated to influence and exploit the course of events.

Social control has, therefore, been group rather than individual in the sense that a group or class, relatively small in number, has exercised it. There has been no genuine collective social control in the sense that all members of the community or society have partaken in specifying the scope of social control and in administering it. In Chapters XXV to XXVII inclusive we have discussed the origin and nature of the social classes. Among them have been the magicians and priests of the theocratic society, the chiefs and kings of the monocratic society, the nobles and feudal lords of the aristocratic society, the tyrants and timocrats of the oligarchic society, the landlords and capitalists of the plutocratic society, and the owners of the chattel slaves and employers of the wage slaves of the slavocratic society in many times and places. These have been some of the exploitative and predatory classes. Among their victims have been not only the chattel and wage slaves, but also the proletariat and peasantry, tenants and serfs, bondmen and sometimes freedmen as well, conscript soldiers

603

and laborers of the corvée, and the outcastes, pariahs and mendicants of many lands.

Within historic time, to say the least, there has been no classless society in which genuine collective social control could exist. There has also been no socialized economic system in the interest of the whole community. There have been states whose economies have been planned in an authoritarian military fashion for the benefit of the dominant classes, such as ancient Egypt during certain periods and pre-Columbian Peru. But up to the present the state has been primarily an agency of power, as described in Chapter XXI, and of exploitation in the interest of the privileged classes. Liberals under capitalism who characterize private exploitation and enterprise as free have little conception of authentic collective social control and of a genuine cooperative social economy. These are adumbrated in the forms of collectivism emerging during the 20th century in Russia and China and to a less degree in such countries as England. Their fate depends upon the outcome or the inevitable conflict between capitalism and collectivism. If the latter prevails it may be possible for the state as an agency of power to "wither away" as Karl Marx foretold.

Modern political democracy is a product of the French Revolution of the 18th century and of the industrial revolution of the 18th and 19th centuries. Parliamentarism was developed in England in the 17th century. The French Revolution emphasized liberty and equality which led to widespread publicity for these two democratic principles. The industrial revolution and the rise of capitalism at first required political democracy in order to give ample scope to private business enterprise unfettered by feudal lords or absolute monarchs. The liberal-democratic revolution freed the middle or bourgeois class and made it dominant in the Occident. But it did not bring liberty and equality to the vast mass of the workers.[1]

The liberal-democratic state, in its economic aspect, is based upon the private ownership of the means of production and free private business enterprise. In its economic organization it is a form of capitalism. In its political aspect it is based upon the party system and parliamentarism. These involve the popular election of representatives and the control of the executive by the legislative and judiciary branches of the government. It is opposed to feudalism, absolutism, and clericalism. As contrasted with the feudalistic, monarchistic, and theocratic types of the state, it is the secular or lay state and also the civil state based in theory though usually not in practice upon the will of the people.

Liberal democracy postulates, in theory at least, the equality of

[1] Some of this chapter is paraphrased from my book entitled *Bolshevism, Fascism and the Liberal-Democratic State*, New York and London, 1934.

all citizens before the law. Certain civil liberties are recognized and to some extent safeguarded. Among them are freedom of speech, of publication, and of assembly. The police powers and economic functions of the state are limited, while the rights of the individual are expanded. There is a tendency toward a *laissez-faire* policy both in political and in economic affairs.

The liberal-democratic state has modified the status of war and of peace. A secular state is not interested in carrying on religious wars. Monarchism, wherever it still persists, has become too weak to instigate dynastic wars. The orderly development of capitalism and its international and world-wide ramifications call for peace and have encouraged a pacifist movement. Nevertheless, capitalist interests in different countries are often opposed to each other. Certain groups of capitalists in all countries, the armament manufacturers in particular, incite wars or at least military preparedness which instigates war. National groups of capitalists are tempted to induce their governments to wage wars which they think will be to their interest by marauding the capitalists and peoples of other countries. Thus capitalism is ambivalent in its attitude toward war.

The liberal-democratic states have had many wars which have been almost entirely economic in their origin. They have maintained large standing armies and have fostered a militarism which is nationalist in sentiment. Their wars have been fought not by mercenaries and only in part by conscripted soldiers. Some of the soldiers have been citizen volunteers who have represented the exacerbated national sentiments of their peoples whipped to a white heat by propaganda. They have perpetrated, or at least have taken part willingly, in the two greatest wars of all time and have encouraged the invention and manufacture of the most lethal weapons.

The European War of 1914 to 1918 habituated many peoples to violence and emergency dictatorships. It overthrew several monarchies and discredited political democracy and parliamentarism in a measure for their inefficiency in wartime. In other ways it weakened the sentiment of liberty. At the same time it increased the spirit of nationalism. This is not necessarily incompatible with the liberal-democratic state. But an intense nationalism tends to place the interests of the nation and of the state above those of the individual. Thus it violates the democratic principle of the supreme worth of the individual. On the other hand, the European War led to the ill-fated League of Nations, a partially opposing current of internationalism which also menaces the liberal-democratic state which is essentially nationalist.

After the European War came a period of prosperity which was in the main favorable to liberal democracy. However, the intense and prolonged economic depression which followed still further discredited political democracy and parliamentarism. The liberal-democratic state was unable to cope effectively with the industrial and commercial stagnation and the widespread unemployment which ensued. This weakness rendered it still more vulnerable to attack on the part of its opponents.

Russia, the largest country in area not only of Europe but also of the world, has, since the Bolshevist Revolution of 1917, passed entirely from an undeveloped capitalist stage to state socialism. Hence it has not become a liberal-democratic state as was intended by some of the anti-tsarist revolutionary groups.

The current extensive changes require a drastic revision not only of political but also of economic theories. These changes have been too much ignored both in practice and in theory. Conditions favored the establishment of fascist dictatorships in several countries of which Italian fascism was the prototype and model. Bolshevism first attained control in Russia. Communist ideas are spreading among the proletarian workers and intellectual radicals of many countries, and conquered China in 1949. Bolshevism cannot claim a monopoly of international communism, nor can fascism of the nationalist state. But these somewhat extreme international and nationalist movements are having much influence at the time of the present writing.

These two political and economic systems challenge political democracy and representative government. Bolshevism, sometimes called Leninism, is a form of Marxism which advocates an extensive use of violence in order to hasten the revolutionary processes, but proposes to return to democracy eventually. Fascism harks back to the traditions of ancient Rome and of the medieval city state in Italy, and borrows from papist hierarchical and modern nationalist institutions. In the form of German national socialism, it reverts to the traditions of the ancient Teutons. It is the supreme expression of chauvinist nationalism. While similar in many of their methods, bolshevism and fascism differ fundamentally in their ultimate aims and philosophies.

The world war of 1939 to 1945 suppressed fascism in Italy and national socialism in Germany for the time being. However, the germs of fascism exist in all capitalist countries because fascism, when fully developed, is the extreme form of monopoly capitalism, which is the last stage of capitalism. In the worldwide struggle between communism and capitalism fascism in varying degrees is likely to arise in the surviving capitalist countries. Hence a description of the traits of fascism is not obsolete, and may be put in the present tense.

As methods, bolshevism and especially fascism utilize force to an almost unlimited degree. Through control of the press, theater, schools, etc., they carry on an intensive propaganda. They organize the young

606

from the earliest age and attempt to control the leisure time of the workers, thus reducing considerably the field for spontaneous social activity. Reacting against the inefficiency of parliamentarism, they have restricted political democracy, reduced representative government, and established oligarchical dictatorships which approach despotic rule.

In each case this situation has been attained through a party organization which forbids other parties. This monopolistic party contains a small minority of the population, maintains a rigid discipline over its membership, and is directed by a hierarchical oligarchy. It controls its respective government completely. Its program is not only political, but includes economic reorganization and many cultural ends.

The contrast between the party system in the liberal-democratic countries and the communist party is not as great as is usually assumed. The parties in the former countries are entirely or predominantly capitalist, and therefore, correspond collectively to the communist party. This is strikingly the case in the most powerful surviving capitalist country, namely, the United States. The two principal parties—the Republican and the Democratic—form one monolithic capitalist party, quite as dominant as the communist party in the Soviet Union. The Republican-Democratic Party had by the middle of the Twentieth Century completely suppressed not only the American communist party but also all other parties left of center. So that there is a capitalist party dictatorship in effect in the United States which is as drastic as the communist party dictatorship in Soviet Russia. While the organization of this monolithic capitalist party is not as hierarchical or as unitary in appearance as that of the communist party, it has so far been quite as effective in maintaining in America the capitalism inherited from Europe as the communist party in maintaining communism, or rather state socialism which is destined to become communism, in the Soviet Union.

With regard to ultimate purposes, bolshevism socializes the means of production, organizes state production and distribution, abolishes nationalism, and attempts to incite a world revolution. Its philosophy is materialist and its logic dialectic. It combats religion and glorifies science which it often uses for its own ends. It implies fundamental changes in ethical ideals and cultural standards, and has already considerably modified the ideology of the Russian people. For the first time in the annals of mankind Soviet Russia has made science the basis of its ideology and not religion, ethics or any form of metaphysics.

Fascism maintains private ownership of the means of production, and attempts to regulate economic life through guilds of employers and of workers. It is intensely capitalist as well as nationalist. It has no characteristic philosophy, apart from a faint tinge of pragmatism. Hence it is very opportunist, and often makes sudden and sometimes startling changes of policy. It only slightly modified the ideology of the Italian people during its ascendancy in Italy from 1922 to 1943, and its ultimate significance for the transformation of culture is far more limited than that of bolshevism.

The current struggle between bolshevism, fascism, and the liberal-democratic state, which is the political organization of capitalism in Western Europe and America, raises many interesting and important questions. Among them are those of personal freedom, the relation of the individual to the mass, the relation of youth to adulthood, the relations of the sexes to each other, the solution of the conflict of the classes, personal and party dictatorships, leadership and the succession of authority, the degree and manner of using force, national and international organization, voluntary and compulsory social organization, the means of social control, the conflict between science and religion, the future of the state, and other more or less controversial problems of the day. Most important of all at present is the fundamental problem of economic organization.

In most countries the state is, in theory at least, the supreme power and the government its organized manifestation. In point of fact, the state, which in modern times is supposed to represent the entire population, has usually been controlled by a comparatively small group. This group may be ethnic, namely, one race dominating other races. It may be a priesthood controlling a theocratic state. It may be a hereditary dynasty or nobility. It may be one or more of the castes of a caste system. Usually it has been an economic group such as slave-owners, feudal landlords, or capitalists owning and controlling the means of production and gaining private profits therefrom.

Lenin defined the state as follows: "The state is the instrument of the suppression of one class by another." He also declared that "the state is the product and the manifestation of the irreconcilability of class antagonisms." [2] This is in accordance with the communist theory that the state is the organ of exploitation by a ruling class. Hence the communists conclude that with the disappearance of classes the state itself will disappear. The communist theory of the state lends justification to the dictatorship of the proletariat. In any case, the dictatorship by a party is historically congruous with the domination by various groups mentioned above. The outstanding difference is that the bolshevist party proposes eventually to include the whole population whereas the above-mentioned groups can by their very

[2] N. Lenin, *The State and Revolution*, Chicago, 1924, p. 4. First published in Russian in 1917.

nature never include more than a small proportion of the population. Chapter XXI has described "The State as an Agency of Power."

Liberal democracy, in name at least, seems to sponsor the largest amount of liberty. It professes to maintain freedom of thought, of speech, of publication, and of assembly, in other words, all of the so-called civil liberties. It also professes to maintain economic liberty. In a comparatively simple agricultural community and where industrial production is largely by handicraft, liberal democracy may succeed in promoting economic liberty for the great majority. With the development of large-scale machine production it became no longer possible for the average worker to own the means of production. The workers are now largely at the mercy of the capitalists who own the machines. By uniting and bargaining collectively they have endeavored to defend themselves against the advantageous position of their employers. But technological advance has rendered such measures somewhat ineffective. It is now possible to produce all that the capitalist system is capable of distributing by means of its mechanism of prices and markets with a comparatively small amount of the available labor supply. There is a large labor surplus which can find little or no employment and therefore gradually starves to death by malnutrition or survives at the miserably low subsistence level afforded by charity, public or private. The existence of this labor surplus also lowers the wages and standard of living for the whole of the working class. Under these circumstances economic liberty in the liberal-democratic system has become a tragic farce. The many millions in the liberal-democratic countries, such as the United States and France, who are unemployed or have miserably low incomes have no liberty or individual rights which have any practical value.

The above statements are amply demonstrated by numerous statistical data. For example, a special study in 1946 by the Federal Reserve Board and the United States Bureau of Agricultural Economics showed that one-fifth of the American families had incomes of less than $1,000 per annum apiece, one-half had incomes of less than $2,000 per annum apiece, and that two-thirds of these families had incomes of less than $3,000 per annum apiece. Furthermore, it was found that the wealthiest 10 percent of American families owned 60 percent of all liquid assets, namely, government bonds, savings accounts and checking accounts, while the poorest 50 percent of American families owned only 3 percent of these liquid assets.[3]

[3] U.S. Department of Commerce, *Survey of Current Business*, July 1946, pp. 10-11. This study showed "the very great concentration of Government bond and deposit holdings in the hands of a relatively small part of the population." Similar figures for 1950-51, reflecting monetary inflation, are given in Chapter XLII.

The National Bureau of Economic Research made a study of national income which indicated that income payments before deduction of federal income taxes from 1919 to 1938 were so unequally distributed that one percent of the population received 14 percent and 5 percent of the population received 26 percent of these payments. As to the sources of these payments it was found that the upper one percent received less than 7 percent of the total of wages and salaries but almost 70 percent of the total dividends. The rent, interest and dividends combined accounted for more than one-third of the incomes of the upper 5 percent but less than one-tenth of the incomes of the lower 95 percent.[4]

The above statistics indicate that in the richest country in the world with the highest average standard of living the great majority have inadequate incomes to maintain a comfortable living standard and there is great inequality in the distribution of the ownership of wealth. Nevertheless, the capitalist propaganda alleges that there is a widespread distribution of wealth in the United States. This is true only in a very limited sense. What is much more significant is the extreme concentration of wealth in the hands of relatively few people under capitalism. For example, in 1951 the American Telephone and Telegraph Company announced that it had 1,000,000 stockholders. Needless to say, each of the vast majority of these stockholders owned only an infinitesimal amount apiece. Even though this company asserted that no one stockholder owned more than one-half of one percent of the capital stock, inasmuch as 35,000,000 shares of stock have been authorized at a par value of $100, and on December 31, 1949, 25,261,183 of these shares were outstanding, it would have been possible for one stockholder to own 126,305 shares worth $12,630,500 at par.[5] At this rate less than 200 stockholders could own most of the great wealth of this giant corporation. In any case, the over-all figures for 20 years collected by the National Bureau of Economic Research, cited above, demonstrate conclusively that the income from the ownership of property, namely, rent, interest and dividends, is highly concentrated in the hands of comparatively few people. These are the parasites who through no merit or socially useful service of their own, but through inheritance or marriage, speculation or skullduggery, business booms and busts, wars and other catastrophes and fortuitous events, by hook or by crook, acquire ill-gotten fortunes running into the millions of dollars, whereas the highest salaries for services presumably of social value run only into the hundreds of thousands.

[4] Simon Kuznets, *National Income: A Summary of Findings*, National Bureau of Economic Research, New York, 1946, p. 13. Some of these figures are slightly revised in a 1950 report of the Bureau cited in Chapter XLII.

[5] John Moody's *Manual of the Securities of Public Utilities*, 1950.

The failure of liberal democracy to provide an adequate standard of living for the vast majority has also resulted in destroying in large part the civil liberties. The capitalists in power have been chiseling away these rights and thus preparing the way intentionally or unconsciously for the coming of the authoritarian state under capitalism. With the proletarian and lower middle classes much weakened economically and ideologically there can be little opposition to the rule of the capitalists. This is a class dictatorship which contemplates no termination because the capitalist class can never include the whole of mankind. Under capitalism there can be no "withering away of the state" as an agency of power.

The foregoing discussion indicates that economic well-being and genuine liberty for the great majority can come neither through a theoretically unrestricted individualism nor through the authoritarianism of monopolistic capitalism. It is becoming increasingly clear and more widely recognized that these ends can be attained only under a genuine socialized system, which neither of the above-mentioned is.

Autocracies, tyrannies, dictatorships, and oligarchies have been common enough in the past. They have almost invariably been theocratic in their nature in that the mundane ruler was supposed to have derived his authority from a divine potentate. Machiavelli gave to the theory of autocracy a more secular character in his doctrine of the hereditary "good prince" or benevolent despot. At various times of crisis when governments have been overthrown or greatly weakened dictatorships have arisen. Some of the dictators have endeavored to establish hereditary dynasties, the most notable instance being Napoleon. Under fascism and national socialism the *duce* and *Fuehrer* have arisen out of the common people and the leadership is not necessarily hereditary.

The first serious objection which may be raised against the principle of unbridled leadership is that no human being can be an expert in every field of activity. No one can exercise leadership with wisdom in every field, or even wisely delegate authority to subordinates or deputy leaders in various fields. The danger is that the so-called leadership will be little more than a technique of playing upon the emotions, passions, and prejudices of the people, in other words, the art of demagogy. This was strikingly illustrated by two modern leaders. Mussolini was a man of great willpower and strong personality. But he won his victory with no constructive program and maintained his power by means of a constantly shifting policy of opportunism rarely ever equaled in history. Hitler's verbose and incoherent *Mein Kampf* is filled with vague and more or less inconsistent ideas. But he was an eloquent and persuasive orator who by constant repetition of a few

611

simple ideas, which are in the main erroneous, won the support of many millions of Germans. As a leader he was little more than a "stuffed shirt." But he became an almost mystical symbol of authority and leadership whom his stronger colleagues had to support in order to retain their control of the government. In some quarters in Germany there was talk that he was a new messiah. Despite the great disparity between these two leaders, both attained power not so much through their own statecraft as through the political illiteracy of the Italian and German peoples, neither of which was well habituated to democratic and parliamentary institutions. Thus a people can become the victim of demagoguery because of its own political ignorance and economic misery.

The second serious objection to this principle of leadership is the difficulty of determining the succession of authority. In a hereditary monarchy the succession is determined automatically by birth because the authority passes to the hereditary heir. In a republic the succession is by election for a limited period. In a dictatorship for life there is great uncertainty as to the succession. The duce or Fuehrer is an uncrowned, nonhereditary king for life. Preparations were made for this eventuality in these two countries. In Italy the dictator was to be chosen by the *Gran Consiglio Fascista,* and in Germany by the *Grosser Senat* of the party. But both regimes collapsed before these methods could be put to the test.

Another difficulty is that the successors are not likely to have as much prestige as the original leaders who have come into power with unquestioned authority and under a quasi-charismatic aura. The authority of the leader will at times hang upon a slender thread, and a socially wasteful and harmful struggle for the leadership involving loss of life and property will readily break out. Neither fascism nor national socialism had a sufficiently extensive and consistent body of doctrines to carry it along independent of whatever leader happened to be in power. Under the original leader, in each case an exaggerated exaltation of the dictator amounting almost to deification was necessary in order to keep the regime going. The increasing complexity of the economic functions of government renders the parliamentary leader incompetent under liberal democracy. A more technically trained leadership is needed. Neither fascism nor national socialism furnishes any guarantee of securing technically competent leadership. Both of them utilize the principle of leadership for purposes of exploitation rather than for socially constructive statesmanship. The same often happens under liberal democracy as well.

According to the Marxian theory of dialectic materialism, history is not determined by the leader. Each social system has the leaders which it creates and deserves. While the personal influence of the leader is one factor in a given situation, he is not independent of the masses in making his decisions. A leader who loses contact with the masses is no longer a leader. He has a following only in so far as the masses consider that he is leading in the direction of certain chosen ends. However, this is a situation which varies from time to time and from place to place according to the degree of literacy, the dissemination of knowledge and the means of communication.

The communist theory of leadership differs not entirely in kind but largely in degree from liberal-democratic theories of leadership. Communism and liberal democracy are agreed in theory that the ultimate seat of authority is in the people. But the communists contend that this theory cannot work out in practice under liberal democracy because the favored position of the capitalists gives them a preponderant power. Bolshevism liquidated capitalism almost entirely in Russia. The bolshevists then engaged in combating other forces which suppress the spontaneous and direct expression of the will of the masses, such as the church and religion, parental and pedagogical authority, and the ponderous inertia of bureaucratism.

The Freudian psychoanalysts believe they have discovered that mankind requires a social substitute for the father and that the Oedipus complex is inevitable. This theory is gratifying to a ruling class which wishes to impose an authority from above on the masses. The bolshevists do not consider this mental complex inevitable. They believe that they can eliminate absolutism from the family in order to free the young from a blind respect for and servile subordination to their parents. Without attempting to destroy affectionate relations between parents and offspring, they endeavor to develop in children a feeling of dependence upon and responsibility to the community as a whole rather than to their parents. In similar fashion they are eliminating authoritarianism from the schools so that the pupils will not become unduly subject to pedagogical authority.

The instruction in the Russian schools is based upon science. All supernatural, nationalist, patriotic, racialist, and romantic features are banned. A realistic attitude toward the world is developed in the pupils. Emphasis upon the past is limited as compared with the present and future, so that the past will not acquire a predominant influence over the minds of the young. Thus the power of tradition is diminished. The same pedagogical principles are applied through the press, theater, literature, and art upon the adults as well as the young.

By these means the bolshevists hope to train a populace which will be indifferent to the blandishments of the demagogue, and unmoved by passionate appeals based upon religion, race, or nation, and by the seductions of militarist, imperialist, and heroic adventures.

They wish to transfer the emotions hitherto directed in these channels by statesmen, politicians, priests, teachers, publicists, orators, and journalists who represent a ruling class which never intends to admit all and sundry to its exclusive membership, to the inclusive mankind of a classless society.

The foregoing survey indicates that fascism and national socialism have furnished no promise of efficient leadership. Under the pressure of grave economic problems the parliamentary system has proved to be in the main incompetent in the liberal-democratic countries. Their parliaments are composed largely of lawyers, politicians, and careerists of one sort and another, and the wars engendered by capitalism furnish their quota of military adventurers and heroes.[6] Vocational representation might improve the situation somewhat. It already exists in fact in Russia, and did exist for a time in name but not in fact in Italy and Germany in which countries representative government was virtually abolished. Under capitalism the lure of profits and large salaries attracts a large part of the technical skill and exceptional ability while much talent finds no scope for expression. Communism offers in theory an admirable scheme for the full utilization of technical skill and of all kinds of talent for social ends with the minimum amount of leadership required by a politically literate and enlightened populace. Soviet Russia is trying to apply this scheme. If permanently successful, it will furnish an object lesson of a socialized system of the utmost value to mankind.

Parliamentarism has taken on somewhat different forms in various parts of the world. The chancellor of the erstwhile German Empire was the prime minister of the chief of state who was the emperor ruling directly. The cabinet of ministers was not responsible to the Reichstag. It was dependent upon the latter only to the extent that it had to secure the legislation that it desired.

The British prime minister is the only connection between the crown and the cabinet. In theory he directs the whole government. But the tradition of the unwritten constitution compels the king to appoint as prime minister the leader of the dominant party. Hence the government is determined by the balance of power in parliament.

The French "president du conseil" is the mandatory of the parliamentary majority. He is formally invested by the chief of state who is the president of the republic. The former and his cabinet of ministers are entirely at the mercy of the balance of power in parliament.

The British two-party system makes the government relatively stable. A dissolution of parliament occurs only when the opposition

---

6 In the United States several war heroes have been elected President, among them being Washington, Jackson, Grant and Eisenhower. Many of the Roman emperors emerged from the soldier class.

defeats the party in power decisively. The French parliament also is dissolved rather infrequently. But it contains many parties, so that cabinets are formed by coalitions of small parties. Usually they are weak and unstable and the ministry changes frequently. The permanent bureaucracy furnishes continuity to the governmental activities. This is true in varying degrees in all governments.

After the European War of 1914 to 1918 most of the new states adopted the French system with proportional representation in order to give to each small minority a representation in proportion to its strength. The socialist parties have not been strong enough to dominate and there are numerous class-interest and nationalist parties. Consequently, the weakness of the French parliamentary system has been widely reproduced. Several European countries have been under fascist dictatorships. In 1933 Portugal became a "unitary and corporative republic" somewhat after the Italian fascist model, and in 1936 Spain became a military dictatorship.

In the western hemisphere the type of government which may be called the presidential regime is predominant. This governmental type originated in the United States and has been copied more or less closely by most of the Latin-American countries. The president is elected for a term of years and has extensive executive powers. He appoints the cabinet ministers, who are responsible only to him, and many other officials. Through a limited veto power he exercises a certain degree of control over legislation.

In Canada the British model is followed. In Latin-American countries the principal variations from the presidential regime are in Uruguay, Ecuador, and Honduras. In Uruguay the executive power is divided between the president and the national council of administration. In Ecuador the parliament elects many of the most important officials, may nullify presidential decrees as unconstitutional through a council of state, and may retire from office the cabinet ministers who, though appointed by the president, are responsible to the parliament and may be dismissed from office by it.[7] After the European War of 1914 to 1918 Brazil adopted a constitution creating the "integral state" which somewhat resembled the "unitary and totalitarian" state of fascism and national socialism. It gave the government a certain degree of control over associations of employers and of employees. After the World War of 1939 to 1945 Argentina adopted a fascist form of government, until its dictator Peron was expelled in 1955.

Several forms of parliamentarism exist within the general framework of the liberal-democratic state. They have succeeded in varying degrees to meet the requirements of that type of state. But liberal

[7] B. Mirkine-Guetzevich, *Les Constitutions des Nations Americaines*, Paris, 1932; F. Garcia-Calderon, *Les Democraties Latines de l'Amerique*, Paris, 1920.

democracy has been associated with a capitalist economic organization. Its ideal is the government that governs least. Hence its demands of the state are not extensive or high. So long as capitalism functions moderately well, the efficiency of the state is not of crucial importance. It is at times of crisis and stress that the weakness of the liberal-democratic state becomes most evident.

The European War of 1914 to 1918 constituted a crisis during which parliamentary institutions broke down to a considerable extent in many countries. The prolonged and acute economic depression which ensued was a period of stress which the liberal-democratic state has not adequately met. Pressure has been brought to bear upon it from both sides. The widespread distress among the workers has called for extensive measures of relief which the state has been able to furnish to a comparatively limited degree. The capitalists also have demanded assistance to stimulate stagnant enterprises by means of financial credit, subsidies, regulation of foreign trade, manipulation of currencies, and like measures, which have been more or less unavailing to attain their ends.

The liberal-democratic conception of the state as a political organization whose principal function is to maintain order, but which is expected to perform relatively few economic and social functions, has attracted to governmental activities a large percentage of lawyers who have little knowledge of statesmanship and of political adventurers and careerists who are ignorant of everything. Technical skill and ability have usually found a more adequate and profitable scope in private life. As the largest financial rewards are in private business enterprise, the latter has attracted a high proportion of the best organizational and administrative ability. Parliaments largely composed of lawyers and politicians are little competent to deal with economic and social problems when circumstances force these problems upon the attention of a liberal-democratic government, as during an economic depression, or in time of war.

The communist theory of the origin of the state, and of the state as the organ of exploitation and domination by the ruling class, is a unilateral and inadequate theory. Various factors have been involved in the origin and evolution of the state as has been demonstrated in Chapters XX and XXI. It is an administrative as well as a coercive organ. Even in Marxian literature the theory of the state is not so simple. Engels himself asserted that the state originated as an administrative organ and then developed into a coercive agent. "In what did the chief characteristic of the old state consist? Society had created for itself definite organs, originally by simple division of labor, for the provision of its common interests. But these organs, at the head of which is the power of the state, had in course of time, and in the

616

service of their own separate interests, transformed themselves from the servants of society into its masters. And this is true not only of the hereditary monarchy, but also of the democratic republic." [8]

While the state may disappear in large part as a coercive agent, it is becoming enlarged as an administrative organ.[9] The bolshevists limit the term unduly both in its historical significance and its functional activities, as when Lenin said that "the state is the instrument of the suppression of one class by another," and Bukharin that "the organization of the state is altogether an organization of the 'ruling class.'"[10] In Russia the soviet state has already assumed enormous proportions. It is an instructive lesson for the whole of mankind as to what its course of development is likely to be.

Even if classes disappear entirely, the state in some form will persist as a coercive agent over the individual. With the advent of economic security, a much higher standard of living, widespread scientific enlightenment, and political literacy, a large part of the anti-social conduct of today will disappear. Theft, for example, is due mainly to poverty and the great disparities of wealth. Under a socialized system stealing would not be possible in most cases. Money as a medium of exchange having a more or less permanent though fluctuating value will disappear and will be replaced by a new medium of distribution which will probably consist of purchasing certificates issued in proportion to the quantity of commodities produced and to be exchanged for them. Securities representing the ownership of capital and debt claims will no longer exist. Objects of great intrinsic value will no longer be subject to private ownership. The numerous forms of deceit, such as false advertising, permissible under a regime of private enterprise and sanctioned by the capitalist principle of *caveat emptor* will be impossible.

And yet it is hardly conceivable that the time will ever come when individuals will not invade the rights and interests of others. There will always be at least a few abnormal persons who will need restraint. Under exceptional circumstances some normal persons also may need restraint. There are certain types of conduct which are difficult to classify as to whether or not they are invasive. A well-known case is the use of alcoholic beverages, which has been a problem for Soviet Russia as well as for capitalist states. Under any system

[8] F. Engels, Introduction to Marx's *The Paris Commune*, New York, 1902, pp. 17-18.

[9] "State interference in social relations becomes in one domain after another, superfluous, and then dies out of itself; the government of persons is replaced by the administration of things, and by the conduct of processes of production." (F. Engels, *Socialism, Utopian and Scientific*, London, 1892, pp. 76-7.)

[10] N. Bukharin, *Historical Materialism*, New York, 1925, p. 151, translated from the third Russian edition.

617

delicate adjustments are at times necessary between social control and individual freedom. Some sort of central arbiter is needed for these cases.

The state is also needed to protect the individual against the omnipotence of public opinion and custom. In pre-state tribal society, tradition, public opinion, and custom were often more tyrannical than the state itself. With the spread of enlightenment the power of convention and of fashion will decrease. The right of the individual to dissent in matters which are not vital or relevant to the maintenance of the social system should at all times be recognized and upheld against the pressure of mob psychology. This right has great social value because it is a prolific agent for change and progress.

The state as a central organ of authority to perform a minimum amount of coercion will always be necessary. Lenin's hope that under socialism "people will grow accustomed to observing the elementary conditions of social existence without force and without subjection," [11] will doubtless be largely though not entirely fulfilled. Some degree of control will always be needed to perform most of the present functions of the state. Among them are the maintenance of highways and of means of transportation and communication, police regulation, harmonizing of conflicting individual interests by means of a system of jurisprudence, and education. A socialized system of production and of distribution of commodities will enormously increase its administrative functions, as the bolshevists themselves in effect recognize.[12]

Marxist writers often speak as if production and distribution will eventually be turned over to autonomous collective organizations which may grow out of the labor unions and cooperative societies of today. They look forward to this stage as the ultimate disappearance of the state as an administrative organ. It is hardly conceivable that these autonomous organizations or gilds can successfully meet the needs of a large population over an extensive area without some sort of general organization which will coordinate and unify their activities. Whether this general organization is called the state or the cooperative commonwealth, it will be the successor of the state of today. It will be the collectivist, socialist, and communist government and state of tomorrow, which may or may not be organized in the form of gilds. The latter is a technical problem to be solved by experiments such as are being carried on in Soviet Russia.

[11] N. Lenin, *op. cit.*, p. 59.

[12] "We know that the classes themselves have risen organically, as Engels described, from the division of labor, from the organizational functions that had become technically necessary for the further evolution of society. Obviously, in the society of the future, such organizational work will also be necessary." (N. Bukharin, *op. cit.*, p. 309.)

618

The state is still a political organization ruling a definite territory and people, exercising coercion, and performing certain economic and social functions, in Soviet Russia as in capitalist countries. If the bolshevist ideal, which is shared by some of the liberal democrats, that nations should disappear and be replaced by a worldwide political organization, is attained, some of the functions of the state will disappear. International warfare will die out and armies and navies need no longer be maintained and administered. There will no longer be any foreign and diplomatic relations to be administered. Regulation of foreign trade will no longer be necessary. Under a unified economic administration the standard of living will tend to become equal the world over. Thus will be eliminated a fruitful cause for the maladjustment of economic relations.

A genuine world organization can with difficulty come into existence under capitalism. National power is a profitable tool utilized by the capitalists to secure every possible advantage for themselves. Fascism and national socialism have been striking illustrations of this fact. Soon after the European War of 1914 to 1918 I wrote that "an essential prerequisite for the establishment of a genuine and permanent world state is an international movement similar to the modern socialist movement, which would eliminate the possibility of economic discrimination and would restrain effectually the powerful groups which today are almost certain to manipulate an international political organization." [13] Subsequent events, especially those pertaining to the League of Nations and the United Nations, have corroborated the essential accuracy of this forecast.

The foregoing survey indicates that the bourgeois liberal-democratic state is already in an unstable equilibrium and has become more or less self-contradictory. While clinging to the theory that the government which governs the least is the best, it is subjected to severe pressure to perform many social and economic functions for which it is not well fitted. The bolshevist and fascist theories of the state are more self-conscious than the liberal-democratic theory, partly because they are of more recent origin. The fascist-nazi state professed to be strong, but was in reality a puppet in the hands of the big capitalists. The bolshevists profess to abolish the state, but are actually building up an extensive organization which will direct and administer the economic as well as the political life.

The outcome of this situation depends mainly upon what happens to capitalism. The fate of the bourgeois state of today, namely, the state as an agency of power, and the fate of capitalism are inextricably bound up together. If capitalism is destined to disappear, fascism

[13] Maurice Parmelee, *Blockade and Sea Power*, New York, 1924, p. 338.

and national socialism, which constitute its most monopolistic phase will no longer be possible. The way will then be clear for the genuinely efficient collectivist state. This will combine the libertarian feature of liberal democracy with the economic functions of capitalism. The only other possibility is a combination of state socialism in certain economic activities, such as transportation, banking, mining, the heavy industries, with capitalism in the other branches of production, such as the light industries, agriculture, etc. Whether such a hybrid combination can long persist is questionable. Soviet Russia's experience with the NEP (New Economic Policy), which lasted only from 1921 to 1929, seems to indicate that any considerable degree of socialism will soon eliminate the remnants of capitalism.

These circumstances set the stage in modern times for the advent of fascism and dictatorships of various sorts. Fascism professed to establish the strong state in which the interests of the individual are subordinated to those of the nation, as if the nation were an entity distinct from and superior to the individuals of which it is composed. The state thus becomes a sort of Moloch to which are to be sacrificed the individuals under its domain. Power is centralized in a personal dictator or small oligarchy. Democracy and other liberal institutions, such as the civil liberties, are denounced and in large part eliminated. Parliamentarism disappears or remains merely as a form.

These measures purport to result in the extinction or at least the collaboration of the classes and the elimination of the class struggle. A casual inspection of the actual situation is sufficient to indicate that the classes are not obliterated and that there is no genuine collaboration among them. Fascism and national socialism championed the cause of capitalism and maintained the privileges of the capitalists to the highest degree. The contradiction between the interests of the workers and of the capitalists was accentuated and not diminished. By suppressing the labor movement, fascism and national socialism reverted to the early days of capitalism when the workers were forbidden to organize. It was only during the nineteenth century that they won this right with great difficulty in England and in some other countries.

The genuine strong state would represent the interests of the whole of its people, and would be an effective instrument for attaining its collective purposes. The fascist-nazi state represented primarily and predominantly the capitalist class and discriminated against the much more numerous proletarian classs. In Germany it discriminated against certain racial elements as well. As compared with the liberal-democratic state, it reenforced and concentrated capitalism so as to give to it a monopolistic power which the proletarian class could for the time being in no way resist.

620

The Program of the Communist International asserts that "the state, being the embodiment of class domination, will die out in so far as classes die out, and with it all measures of coercion will expire." Lenin declared that "the state is the product and the manifestation of the irreconcilability of class antagonisms. When, where, and to what extent the state arises, depends directly on when, where, and to what extent the class antagonisms of a given society cannot be objectively reconciled. And, conversely, the existence of the state proves that the class antagonisms are irreconcilable." [14] These assertions are based upon the theory of the "withering away of the state" of Marx and Engels.

In the countries where capitalism has developed most highly, such as the United States and Great Britain, the functions of government, especially its economic functions, have been correspondingly limited. In the countries where capitalism has not developed highly, most of which are predominantly agrarian, there has been more room for the expansion of a governmental bureaucracy. The peasantry is usually more or less under the domination of semi-feudal landlords. There are parliamentary institutions in most of these countries. They are usually under the control of the bureaucrats, because the peasants are too ignorant to know how to vote and the landlords absent themselves a good deal of the time. These bureaucratic governments display mild tendencies toward a paternalistic form of state socialism because in the absence of a vigorous capitalism they initiate and operate certain public services and utilities.

Under socialism the state has the whole economic system under its management, thus requiring a vast administrative mechanism or bureaucracy. A capitalist economy also has a vast administrative mechanism which may be called its bureaucracy. Capitalism entails enormous social losses which are eliminated by socialism, among them being the wastes of competition, of salesmanship, of advertising, of the trade cycle, of unused and misused labor, etc. But capitalism contains within itself one powerful factor for efficiency in the desire and the necessity in the long run of making profits. Otherwise a capitalist enterprise is doomed. The success of the capitalist depends upon ingratiating himself with the public and "serving" it to the extent of inducing it to purchase his commodities, though these commodities are often not the best which might be had for the price paid and sometimes are actually harmful to the purchaser. The success of the retainers of the capitalists also depends upon their ability to aid their employers in attaining these ends. This is why salesmanship is

[14] V. I. Ulianov (Nicolai Lenin), *The State and Revolution, Marxist Teaching on the State and the Task of the Proletariat in the Revolution*, Chicago, 1924, p. 4. First published in Russian in 1917.

one of the most pecuniarily remunerative forms of ability under capitalism.

The problem of bureaucratism cannot be finally and fully solved until a functional plan of operation of a socialized system has been devised.[15] Such a plan would include, among other things, a method of choosing the workers for their respective tasks on the basis of fitness. As far as possible, the work would be rationalized, mechanized, and automatized, so that the laziness, carelessness, ignorance, and inefficiency of the worker could not make it go wrong and to that extent it would be fool-proof. It remains to be seen to what extent a social and educational technology can be developed which will insure industry, alertness, knowledge, good judgment, initiative, and originality on the part of the worker when those qualities are needed.

The situation with regard to the efficiency of government is altogether different in a collectivist from a capitalist society. The spoils system consisting of buying votes, corrupting the press, bribing officials directly or indirectly for political favors or rewarding them with lucrative businesss positions, distributing jobs to party workers and members, awarding contracts at high rates, giving or selling franchises at low prices, and class legislation of various sorts, disappears completely under collectivism. No one is interested any longer in creating or securing jobs, public or private. There is work for everyone. An income is assured to every person. As the profit system has been abolished, there are no contracts and franchises to be bought and sold. The press cannot be corrupted and officials bribed or rewarded, because private business no longer exists. As classes have disappeared, there can be no more class legislation.

There is no longer any occasion for special training for the public service in the socialized commonwealth. Public service and private enterprise are merged in the administration of the entire unified system. The general education and vocational training prepare citizens for all branches of the administration. The duality of point of view, of interests, and of loyalty, as between the public service and private enterprise, which often gives rise to conflict under capitalism, disappears entirely under collectivism.

The question now arises as to the form of the administration which will include the political state and the management of the economic mechanism of the socialized and planned order. This administration must be so organized as to utilize fully expert knowledge and technical skill. At the same time it must contain adequate safeguards

[15] See Maurice Parmelee, *Farewell to Poverty*, New York, 1935, Part II, "Evolution of the Social Commonwealth," from which the following paragraphs are paraphrased.

against the concentration of power in the hands of a small oligarchy or of a personal dictator. The final seat of authority must at all times be in the people. In other words, the administration must be democratic at bottom, however much power may be delegated to its representatives by the people.

The division of governmental powers in the capitalist countries is intended primarily to restrain the masses and to give the decisive control to the dominant class. In a liberal-democratic state where there is universal suffrage the popular will is more likely to express itself through the legislative branch of the government. Hence it is essential for the vested interests to limit the legislature narrowly by the executive and judicial branches. The so-called balance of power between the three governmental branches is largely a myth.

In the American type of government, which may be called the presidential regime, the president is not chosen by the direct vote of the people. He is elected for a term of years and has extensive executive powers. He appoints the cabinet ministers, who are responsible only to him, and many other officials. Through a limited veto power he exercises a certain degree of control over legislation. The courts have the power to interpret the Constitution. They are able thereby to nullify much legislation and to restrict narrowly the legislature. The makers of the American Constitution, who had no intention of establishing a genuine democracy, did their work only too well.

In the liberal-democratic state the political organization is democratic in form and theory whereas the economic system is feudal in almost every respect. This contradiction is resolved through the domination of the government by the feudal interests. The liberal-democratic government is in practice very little more democratic than and almost as feudal as liberal capitalism. When the liberal-democratic state was transformed into the fascist state of monopolistic capitalism, even the pretense and form of democracy disappeared, so that the fascist government was fully as feudal as capitalism.

In a socialized system it becomes possible, perhaps for the first time in the history of mankind, to correlate a democratic political organization with the economic system, because the latter is collectivist and the means of production are under social control. The form of government arises out of, is related to, and is harmonious with, the planned production, organized work, and effective distribution which constitute a functional economic whole.

A planning board will coordinate and plan all forms of production. In this fashion will be harmonized in a well-integrated whole the functions performed under capitalism by enterprisers, business managers, technical directors, trade unions and other vocational and

623

professional bodies, and various political bodies such as parliaments, ministries, commissions, bureaus, etc. The capitalist scheme is ill-organized, unplanned, and contains many internal conflicts.

The ultimate authority of the socialized system will be vested in the parliament chosen by the entire adult population. The representation will be proportional. It will also be vocational, at any rate in the early stages of the evolution of the socialized system. It need be only broadly territorial in so far as there are important geo-economic differences which require representation of the various geo-economic areas by those most familiar with them. When the system is highly developed and working smoothly and more or less automatically, and the populace has become politically literate, it may no longer be necessary to make the representation vocational. Any intelligent, educated, and experienced citizen will then be competent to serve as a representative in a parliament which will act only on matters of general policy. All questions requiring special knowledge will be referred to the boards of experts or the administrative boards.

Under capitalism representation is often demanded for the consumers or the "public." This is because conflict often arises between the interests of the consumers and those of the producers, in spite of the fact that the consumers and the producers are in the main the same persons. In a socialized system this antagonism between the citizen as consumer and himself as producer and worker will disappear entirely. The antagonism is a gratuitous and irrelevant incident of the class struggle which arises out of the vested rights in land and capital. The owners of these rights are able to exploit the consumers some of whom are their own employees who are thereby involved unwittingly in exploiting themselves. The elimination of the class struggle will make the consumers entirely identical with the workers and the producers. There will no longer be any occasion for a representation of the citizens as consumers distinct from their representation as producers and workers.

The parliament will legislate as to such broad matters of policy as constitutional amendments and changes in social organization, the standard of living, hours of labor, length of service, norms and forms of social control, educational methods, and will stand ready to meet any new social, economic, and political situation which may arise. It should at all times safeguard the civil rights and liberties which should be greatly extended under a socialized system and which should protect minorities and individuals from undue pressure from the majority. On the other hand, a great deal of legislation which arises out of property rights and the class struggle, or which relates to taxation and other financial matters, will disappear entirely. The tendency will be toward a simplification of democratic processes. Such

624

democratic procedures as the initiation of legislation by the public and the referendum of laws to the public, and the recall of representatives by their constituents can be given their full effect. There will probably be little occasion to make use of them.

There will be a much more realistic party alignment with respect to principles, programs, and policies when private plunder and covert class designs are no longer possible. Demagogic personal ambitions can hardly appeal to and influence a politically literate electorate. Politicians and parliamentary careerists will disappear. The spoils of office to nourish them will no longer exist. Each citizen will have his career primarily in his work in the functionalized social system. Any political activities in which he partakes can only be incidental to his career. Political activities will, in any case, be merged to a large extent with economic and other social activities.

The judicial function will shrink greatly in scope and importance. The contested cases which arise out of vested rights and class interests will disappear entirely. Almost all the litigation which arises out of the law of contracts and the law of torts will no longer be possible. At least nine-tenths of the civil actions will disappear from the courts. As practically all the economic causes of crime will no longer exist in a society where almost all forms of theft are impossible, the number of criminal cases will also decrease greatly.

Most of the questions which are now decided by the slow and blundering methods of incompetent legislatures will be solved by the automatic functioning of the socialized system. Technical decisions requiring specialized knowledge will be relegated to the bureaucracies of experts and technicians. They will operate under the authority of the economic, educational, scientific, and cultural councils.

These are a few suggestions as to the main lines of development of the organization of a planned social order. The details of organization can be worked out only in practice and through experimentation and experience. The problem is much more simple than that of a competent government and of an efficient economic system under capitalism where conflicting class interests create a perennial internecine warfare.[16]

[16] A capitalist weekly journal has commented upon how easy it would be to turn the United States into a Socialist state:

"It's not to be hard to turn U.S. into a socialist state. There's a lot of socialism, a diminishing amount of capitalism in the setup now.

"*Profits* are socialized up to 70 per cent. *Wage rates* are under control of Government officials. *Prices* are, too. *Rents* in many areas are set by an act of Government, not by the market place. *Money* is Government controlled.

"*Seizure*, Government operation, is just the final step."

(*U.S. News & World Report*, April 18, 1952, Vol. XXXII, No. 16.)

Chapter XXXVI

The Nature of Capitalism

STRANGE as it may seem, few social scientists have subjected capitalism as an economic and social system to critical analysis. They often misconceive its intrinsic nature. An American economist has defined it as "a system making general use of capital equipment." The leading German historian of capitalism has described it as "an economic system significantly characterized by the predominance of capital." Every economic system utilizes genuine capital. Collectivism uses it even more than capitalism which creates much fictitious, monetary and paper capital. Such definitions lead only to confusion of thought and of action.

Social scientists in general have displayed little historical hindsight and almost no scientific foresight. Most of them are dominated by the existing system upon which they are dependent and cannot see it in its evolutionary setting. They think of it as a permanent and relatively immutable economic system. The next few chapters describe the finance, corporate and monopoly phases of capitalism, and the rapid disappearance of competition. They depict the accumulation of surplus capital and of debt, and the inadequacy of purchasing power which limits production narrowly. Science and technology are hampered and partly frustrated by the search for profits. The business cycle becomes more violent as capitalism becomes more mature. The export of surplus capital extends these conditions into the international field and precipitates imperialist wars. As the economic frontier is approached or reached, the contradictions inherent in capitalism become more acute and threaten its existence. The social anarchy and warlike disorder characteristic of capitalism are attaining a state of chaos.

Capitalism is hastening toward its dissolution. It has already been overthrown in large areas of the world. Looming up in the future is the new social order. Its structure can be partially discerned. Science and technology, which are shattering the old order, are furnishing a

626

basis for the new order. The outlines of the emerging social common-wealth can be foreseen in so far as that is possible within the limits of scientific prevision. Planned production, organized work, effective distribution, and rationalized consumption are implicit in the scientific and technological factors already in existence. A political organization correlated with a planned economy is indicated. Geo-economic regionalism is designated as the geographical framework for the worldwide system. The cultural consequences from a genuine functional organization of mankind will far exceed those resulting from any antecedent revolution.[1]

The term "capital" is the collective name for all the material means of production, such as tools, machines, buildings, etc. Under the capitalist system it is more often used as the name for the value in monetary terms of all the means of gaining profits. It includes not only the means of production, but also such facilities for gaining profits as business reputation and good will, advertising opportunities, sales methods, etc. In other words, it includes all the business organization which brings commodities to the market and sells them. Under capitalism these facilities are even more important than the means of production. Only through successful salesmanship in the market place can the purpose of capitalism, namely, the acquisition of profits, be attained.

Much of the so-called "capital" of capitalism is quasi- and pseudo-capital. To the extent that this system distributes goods as well as produces them, it attains a useful social purpose. But a large part of its distributive apparatus is superfluous and socially wasteful. It is becoming increasingly incapable of distributing the goods which can readily be produced. Capitalism is rapidly breaking down as a system of distribution.

In addition to the quasi- and pseudo-capital mentioned above, money and credit have become commodities which are bought and sold. Banking and other financial institutions are devoted in large part to the traffic in these forms of quasi- or pseudo-capital. Under capitalism their control and manipulation have an extensive influence upon the economic welfare of mankind. To the extent, therefore, that it is based upon and operates by means of these spurious and fictitious forms of capital, the capitalist system belies its own name. Neverthe-less, they are not only characteristic but essential features of this system.

The three fundamental and essential traits of capitalism are private ownership of the means of production, private enterprise, and private profits. In its ultimate nature it is an acquisitive system. In

[1] Part of this chapter is paraphrased from my book entitled *Farewell to Poverty*, New York, 1935.

this regard it resembles the activities of the predatory animals and of human robbers. It differs from these activities in two respects. First, it is an organized system of predation. Its activities are legalized and are carried on to a large extent peacefully. Second, it is a productive system in so far as production leads to profits. Profit and not production is the prime motive and dominates in the long run. The capitalist as producer has no incentive to produce unless he can derive profits therefrom. In fact, he cannot produce indefinitely without profits. Within the narrow limitations of this system, production is inevitably subordinated to the acquisition of profits. The main purpose of any economic system, namely, the creation of goods for mankind, becomes a mere incident to the pecuniary interests of a small class. The capitalists become the exploiters of the vast majority whose most vital interests are at the mercy of the fortuitous chance of profit making on the part of this small class which has acquired a monopolistic control of the means of production, namely, land and capital.

It is a singular as well as a significant fact that economists have written very little about capitalism *per se*. They are unable to see the forest on account of the trees. They write with the tacit assumption that capitalism as the dominant economic system is permanent. By so doing they violate the fundamental postulate of every science, namely, that nothing is permanent, and that in every field of phenomena is taking place a process of constant change ordinarily called evolution. These economists are like a zoologist who studies the saurians of mesozoic time with little knowledge of what has preceded and with less appreciation of what may follow.

Capitalism is not entirely unlike systems which have preceded it. Private ownership of the means of production existed under feudalism and many earlier systems. Private business enterprise has existed in commerce ever since markets came into being. To a less degree it characterized production prior to the capitalist era. Private profits have always accompanied business enterprise and have constituted its object and justification.

Modern capitalism differs from the earlier economic systems in degree more than in kind. Its efflorescence was due to the coming of the machine age, rendering possible private enterprise on a large scale. In the earlier handicraft system the workman usually owned his tools. While these constituted a primitive form of capital, his status was much more that of a laborer than it was that of a capitalist. His income was almost exclusively payment for his labor and services. To that extent it constituted wages. But ownership of his means of production gave him a small amount of independence similar to that of the capitalist.

The industrial revolution of the eighteenth and nineteenth cen-

628

turies deprived the workman of his ownership. Only the rich, or large accumulations of capital under corporate ownership, can own the machines and buildings required for modern large-scale production. The workman depends upon the capitalist for an opportunity to produce and to earn a living. When the factory closes down, the workman can only walk the streets and starve. Large-scale production has also invaded agriculture. The small farmer and peasant, even though he still owns his means of production, finds it increasingly difficult to make a living.

The machine age of the nineteenth century was the period of efflorescence for capitalism. The building up of the new machine system and the exploitation of undeveloped regions furnished it great opportunities for expansion. Production has increased enormously and not only has paid huge profits to the capitalists but also has raised considerably the standard of living of the workers. But the construction of the machine system and the exploitation of new countries are temporary conditions. It is questionable whether capitalism can function so successfully under more stable and permanent conditions.

Since the commencement of the twentieth century has come the extensive use of electricity in industry and also in agriculture. By means of high-tension (high-voltage) transmission it is possible to carry electricity a long distance from its place of generation. In the United States it is already carried more than two hundred miles, and this distance may be greatly extended. This renders possible the distribution of water and of steam power transformed into electricity, over a wide area. It has already resulted in a rapid growth in the size and efficiency of power-producing factories. Electricity can now be produced and distributed at a low cost. The machine age is merging into the power age in which with an abundant supply of power most of the industrial and agricultural processes can be mechanized.

The last fact is of peculiar significance for the future of capitalism. The increasing application of power has accentuated the tendency already introduced by the use of machinery to reduce the number of man-hours required to produce a given quantity of commodities. The rational adjustment to this situation is to reduce the hours of labor and to increase leisure time. The capitalist resists this solution because he wishes to keep down his labor cost and to maintain and increase his rate of profit. The inevitable consequence is an increase of unemployment which reduces purchasing power. Decrease of production follows, which leads to economic depression with all its disastrous consequences. This is one of the inherent contradictions of the capitalist system. It is rendered much more acute by the power age which is succeeding the machine age. Its repercussions upon capitalism will be described.

The fundamental traits usually ascribed to capitalism by its exponents, proponents, and apologists are economic freedom, as exemplified by unrestricted competition; creativeness, as embodied in its productive capacity; elasticity, as demonstrated by its tendency to change; and rationality, as illustrated by its accuracy in keeping accounts. To what extent the capitalist system actually possesses these traits will become more evident in the course of this discussion.

According to the economic theory of capitalism, the factors of production are land, labor, capital, and business enterprise or management. Land is not only a factor of but a prerequisite to all production. It is, however, distinguished by the economists of capitalism not so much because it is a genuine productive force as because it has become privately owned. As such it is a source of private income.

Labor also is a primary and essential factor of production. It has to be remunerated in order to be kept in existence. Under capitalism a considerable part of the labor is unproductive. This unproductive labor has to be performed in order to keep this system in existence. Those who perform it usually do so in order to earn a living, regardless of its unproductivity. They are remunerated well or ill, as the case may be.

Capital, in the strict sense of the term, consists of capital goods or the concrete apparatus of production created by labor. The term is also used to designate the monetary value of this apparatus. Under capitalism it almost invariably includes quasi- and pseudo-capital which is useful for gaining profits, but which has little or no value for production. Hence the distinction is sometimes made between acquisitive capital, which includes all forms useful for gaining profits, and productive capital.

Business enterprise sometimes organizes the factors of production, promotes the division of labor, and undertakes new forms of production. To this extent it is productive. All business enterprise is directed in the first instance toward gaining profits by selling goods and services and only incidentally toward production. Much of it is entirely spurious in that it produces nothing. It often destroys wealth or prevents it from being produced.

According to capitalist economics, the shares in distribution are rent, wages, interest, and profits. These shares correspond respectively to their factors of production. Rent is determined by the diminishing returns from the successive units of land utilized. As an original endowment of nature and not a creation of mankind, it is entitled to no share in distribution. The monopolistic control arising out of the right of private property enables its owners to collect a rent which approximates the difference between the amount produced on the superior units and the marginal unit of land utilized.

According to the classical economists, wages are determined by the marginal productivity of the least efficient unit of labor employed. Competition between the laborers tends to bring the wage scale down to this level. The difference between this minimum and the amount produced by the more efficient units of labor forms a surplus out of which rent, interest, and profits are paid.

In similar fashion, the rate of interest or usury is determined by the marginal productivity of the last unit of capital which is applied. Interest is said to be a reward for the abstinence practiced by the capitalist who saves part of his income instead of consuming all of it. As most of the saving which results in the formation of capital, in whatever sense we use that term, is performed by the rich or by corporations, comparatively little abstinence of an irksome nature is involved.

According to capitalist theory, profits constitute the reward received by the business enterpriser for the risk he has assumed and the skill he has displayed in organizing and managing a business venture in the hope of gaining a profit. As it consists of whatever is left over from the surplus not paid to labor after rent and interest have been deducted from this surplus, the enterpriser's profit is a form of residual income.

Profits constitute the share in distribution most characteristic of and peculiar to capitalism. The recipient of this share has in the course of his evolution come to belie more and more the flattering but never wholly deserved reputation accredited to him by capitalist theory. Veblen has traced this evolution through the "captain of industry" and "entrepreneur" to the "Captain of solvency." "The prototype rather than the origin of the captain of industry is to be seen in the Merchant Adventurer of an earlier age, or as he would be called after he had grown to larger dimensions and become altogether sessile, the Merchant Prince. In the beginning the captain was an adventurer in industrial enterprise—hence the name given him; very much as the itinerant merchant of the days of the petty trade had once been an adventurer in commerce. . . . In the manuals the captain of industry still figures as the enterprising investor-technician of the days of the beginning, and as such he still is a certified article of economic doctrine under the caption of the 'Entrepreneur.' . . . The popular ideal came to be the prehensile business man rather than the creative driver of industry; the sedentary man of means, the Captain of Solvency." [2]

A considerable part of capitalist economics is devoted to the

[2] T. Veblen, *Absentee Ownership and Business Enterprise in Recent Times,* New York, 1923, pp. 102, 107, 113-14.

Veblen quotes the following: "In the beginning the Captain of Industry set out to do something, and in the end he sat down to do somebody."

631

discussion of economic value. It is generally recognized that this value originates in the use value of commodities for human beings. The form of value with which these economists are particularly concerned is exchange value in a market. Exchange value arose originally as a result of the division of labor in a primitive economy. The commodities resulting from this division of labor were exchanged directly by barter between the producers who were collectively also the consumers of these goods. The exchange value existed primarily and exclusively for these producers and consumers and was identical with the use value for the consumers. With the rise of trade and of industrial enterprise these goods acquired an exchange value but not a use value for the traders and enterprisers. While the use value for the ultimate consumer always remains the basis of this exchange value, it is the exchange value in the market and not its ultimate use value which is of particular concern for the merchant and enterpriser, in short, for the capitalist. It is this somewhat artificial market value which engages the attention of the orthodox economist rather than the use value which is solely of human and social importance.

The capitalist conception of value is presented in its most characteristic form in its theory of marginal utility. According to this theory, the economic value of a class of goods is determined not by the average cost of production, but by the cost of its marginal unit. This unit is the last one produced at the greatest cost to meet the market demand. This cost and the utility which it creates establish the value and fix the price of every unit of its class. The difference between the cost of production of the marginal unit and of the other units constitutes a surplus from which profits are derived. This surplus renders private property in the means of production a valuable right. No capitalist would be interested in owning these means if he could not secure profits thereby.

Certain economists allege that when capitalists form pools, combinations, trusts, cartels, and the like, which monopolize and control production, prices are fixed by the average cost of production and not by the cost of the marginal unit. This is an obvious fallacy. If monopoly prices do not average above the average cost of production, there is no surplus from which profits can be derived. Capitalists would quickly abandon such unprofitable enterprises or gladly turn them over to the state.

According to capitalist theory, changes in the relation between supply and demand cause changes in economic value. If the supply increases through the discovery of natural resources, or through technological improvements, or through a rise in the efficiency or quantity of labor, the value decreases in accordance with the decrease in the cost of production of the marginal unit. If the demand increases, the

632

cost of production of the new marginal unit is higher. Hence the value rises. If the supply and the demand increase or decrease to the same extent, their respective changes offset each other and there is no variation in the value or the prices of the goods.

The orthodox economists assert that this theory proves that under the undisturbed operations of capitalism each so-called "factor" of production receives precisely the amount which it produces. Many of them also allege that it is only right and ethical that this should be the case.

Capitalism will never again operate in its unmitigated and unadulterated competitive form. The capitalist theory of value arose under a regime of scarcity. Under a regime of plenty, value in the capitalist sense will disappear. The capacity of goods for gratifying human wants will then be recognized as their only genuine value. Production will be determined by this value, and not by the possibility of gaining profits through scarcity.

The least that can be said concerning these economists is that they are remarkably blind or at least indifferent to the many unfavorable traits of capitalism, even in its best form. They are still more blind to its inherent contradictions which constitute the germs of its own destruction and give to capitalism a very brief viability. The ideal capitalism portrayed by some of these economists has not materialized. Capitalism has not only failed to promote the freedom and well-being of most individuals but has also lost the security of some of the older systems without a corresponding gain. Nevertheless the economists of capitalism continue to portray it as if it were the only possible economy. They fail to depict a genuinely social economy.

In theory, capitalism promotes economic freedom, liberty of competition, elasticity in adjustment to new conditions, and rational modes of procedure. Under the automatic operation of the laws of supply and demand, capitalism is supposed to produce the largest possible amount of goods to meet human needs and desires. In practice, capitalism soon discloses numerous fundamental contradictions which defeat these ends in large part if not entirely. Some of the more general of these contradictions will now be mentioned. Most of them will be demonstrated in due course.

Capitalism subordinates the two primary economic processes, namely, the production and distribution of wealth, to the private ownership of wealth and accumulation of profits. It thereby frustrates the fundamental ends of any economic system by preventing the major part of potential production and causing excessive disparity in the distribution of what little is produced.

Some of these contradictions arise out of the conflict between the competitive and the monopolistic tendencies of capitalism. Capitalist "freedom," which is limited to private business enterprise, does not promote the freedom, or, in the long run, the well-being, of most individuals. Free competition between individuals is prevented by private property in and inheritance of land and capital. This artificial right destroys equality of opportunity. It also decreases greatly the efficiency of management. "Pure" competition, even in its capitalist sense, is deranged and limited by the monopolistic features which inevitably creep into capitalism.

In addition to and in part arising out of the more general contradictions are the more specific contradictions. Many of the latter are related to the financial structure of capitalism. The withdrawal of profits reduces buying power and disturbs market relations, because the effective demand cannot absorb the actual or potential supply. Inasmuch as the price level must average higher than the cost of production, business enterprise does not promptly release as much purchasing power as the distribution of its products requires.

Many of the contradictions of capitalism arise out of its inability to make a full and consistent use of science, invention, and technology. Capitalism utilizes science and technology to promote profit. Otherwise it frustrates them by neglect or by suppression. The power age decreases capital investment and labor in relation to the amount produced. It thereby lowers the effective demand created by labor and thus restricts the market for both capital and consumption goods. In the long run, science and technology threaten the survival of capitalism.

The foregoing contradictions can in a measure be summed up in what may be termed the final contradiction of capitalism. Having passed through its early mercantile stage, capitalism reached its apogee during its period of industrial expansion. It is now passing into the monopolistic stage of finance capitalism. The proletarized masses are fast becoming more or less equally divided between the relatively over-worked wage-earners, paid on the basis of a bare subsistence minimum, and the undernourished and starving unemployed or paupers who are kept alive if at all upon the meager doles of public and private relief. A situation so anomalous cannot endure indefinitely. The final contradiction of capitalism, which curtails its efficiency as a productive and distributive mechanism by more than half, can be resolved only under an economic system which will release the productive forces from their chains and will distribute work and income to the entire population.

Many persons are already dimly or more or less acutely aware of this anomalous situation. Some of them recognize that "pure" *laissez-faire* capitalism has in considerable part disappeared. This is due not only to the comparatively slight encroachments of government upon

634

private enterprise. It is due much more to the monopolistic tendencies inherent in capitalism itself. Nevertheless, they cling to the dubious notion that capitalism contains features worthy of preservation, such as incentive to effort and opportunity for individual initiative. Hence they advocate a combination of collectivism and capitalism. Such a hybrid economic organization would create a new set of contradictions.

Assuming that the exploitation of natural resources (coal, oil, metals, atoms, water power, etc.), transportation, and the capital goods industries (the so-called "key" or "basic'" industries) are under governmental ownership, control, and management, the consumption goods industries and commerce would remain open for private enterprise and exploitation. Some persons believe that all forms of economic activity which display monopolistic tendencies should be under governmental control. In the field of private enterprise capital accumulation would continue to take place. In course of time this would become so great as to furnish the capitalists sufficient incentive to engineer a revolution to overthrow the semi-socialized state in order to secure a wider scope for private enterprise and the investment of capital. This would be especially true if private corporate enterprise was permitted, which would inevitably develop monopolistic power and constitute an *imperium in imperio*. Whether the state could take adequate measures to protect itself against this danger is doubtful.

The most effective measure which the state could take would be to abolish the private inheritance of the means of production. This would promote free individual competition and to this extent would be in accord with the capitalist ideal. It would at the same time destroy much of the incentive to private enterprise. The state would then become the heir of capitalism. All privately owned, controlled, or utilized means of production would speedily revert to the state, which would be compelled to operate them, thereby entering the field open to private enterprise. Before long all this field would be occupied by the state, which would become entirely collectivist.

The contradictions of semi-collectivism may be summed up as follows. In a hybrid capitalist-collectivist state, capital accumulation would instigate the capitalists to overthrow the semi-socialized state. The abolition of private inheritance, though in accord with the capitalist ideal of individual competition, would destroy much of the incentive to private enterprise. It would soon make the state absorb capitalism.

As a system of economy, capitalism is inefficient in many respects. The profit motive is often opposed to technical efficiency. Out of this opposition arise some of these contradictions. Capitalist economics furnishes a detailed and in part accurate analysis of the functioning of capitalism. It ignores or minimizes almost to the point of suppression these causes of inefficiency, in spite of the fact that they are rapidly becoming of life and death importance. The bankruptcy of capitalist economics renders it wholly inadequate in the face of the present situation.

The capitalist or business man or enterpriser is the characteristic type of the capitalist system. His psychology is predominantly that of the trader and merchant. He is interested in exchange but not in the exchange of commodities of equal monetary value. He strives to exchange his commodities for those of a greater monetary value, thereby gaining a profit. He is, therefore, intensely individualistic, and social considerations mean naught to him.

In a pure system of barter each party to an exchange usually benefits by securing something which he needs or desires more than what he surrenders. By this means the advantages arising from the division of labor are distributed to all persons who partake of it. The capitalist exploits these advantages to his own profit by trading in them. Under a monetary system pecuniary profit becomes possible through the acquisition of a monopolistic control of one sort or another. For this profit no service or commodity of equivalent value is necessarily or even usually rendered.

The capitalist does not limit himself to trade in commodities. He borrows and loans money at a profit, thus becoming usurer and financier as well as merchant. He also invades the field of production. He is, however, interested solely in producing goods which are salable and not those which have the greatest intrinsic value. Vendibility and not productivity is his ultimate goal. Though he may never appear in the market place in person and may operate entirely through middlemen, it is as vendor of his own products that he is chiefly of significance in the capitalist scheme of things. Hence advertising, publicity, trade connections, "good will," trade marks, and salesmanship are much more important for the capitalist as producer than scientific knowledge and technical skill. It is not surprising that salesmanship is one of the highest paid forms of ability under capitalism.

Labor also becomes a commodity to be bought and sold under capitalism almost as much as under slavery or feudalism. From the laborer the capitalist demands as long and intensive labor as possible. Time and human sweat acquire a monetary value. The industrial revolution by destroying handicraft not only enabled the capitalist to profiteer in the field of production but delivered the laborer into his hands as a wage slave.

The economic theories of capitalism are predominantly those of individual profit and not of social welfare in any far-reaching and fundamental sense. Exchange, market conditions, monetary relations, and the like, play a prominent part in capitalist economics. The meas-

636

ure of value becomes price instead of the satisfaction of human wants (use value). This has been true of the writings of the classical economists from Adam Smith and Ricardo down to the present day. They have developed no *social* economics of the production, distribution, and consumption of goods in the interest of human beings as individuals and of mankind as a collective whole. They have usually assumed that the normal operation of the capitalist system would attain these social ends. Subsequent events have completely disproved this assumption. In the face of an extensive and prolonged breakdown of the productive and distributive system they stand speechless or propose puerile and inadequate remedies.

The goal of a genuine social economy is a balanced load of production which will steadily and swiftly deliver and distribute an adequate supply of goods for the satisfaction of human wants. Capitalism is as little capable of performing this function as is a paleolithic knife of cutting a diamond.

In accord with his economic theories are the political and ethical ideas of the capitalist. The state exists to protect the right to acquire profits and not for the welfare of society. Thrift, business honesty, punctuality, etc., are virtues for the capitalist. Benjamin Franklin is his paragon. For his employees he preaches a slave morality in which work is a virtue for which there may be only a hypothetical reward after death. However orderly, methodical, and precise he may be in his private enterprises, he requires a state of chaos in the economic world in order to attain his ends. The absence of social planning resulting in business crises and depressions furnishes him an admirable opportunity for speculative profits.

Every field of human activity has its technology in the sense of the most efficient methods of attaining the ends sought. The term is usually applied to the methods of producing objects of human value. There is also a technology of the distribution of these objects. Unless they can be distributed they have no value. There should be a technology of their consumption which has so far been almost completely ignored.

While capitalism has a technology of its own, it is directed primarily toward gaining private and individual profits. It is concerned with the technology of production only in so far as profits can be derived thereby. It is not a social technology because it is not concerned wholly or even primarily with the production and distribution of goods for social ends. The capitalist as such is not interested in science, invention, technology, and art except if and in so far as they can be manipulated in order to fill his purse. The scientific and technician types are represented by the scientist, inventor, engineer, and artist, not by the capitalist. They are interested in science for the sake of knowledge and in technology for the sake of attaining creative and constructive ends most efficiently.

In so far as science, invention, technology, and art have progressed under capitalism, they have been incidental and almost accidental by-products. The capitalists have encouraged the technology of production somewhat in the hope of gaining more profits thereby. They have aided the technology of distribution and consumption much less. A social technology which would harmonize and synthesize production, distribution, and consumption is almost non-existent and can be developed only in a socialized system. Its goal would be the production of a supply of goods adequate to furnish a high standard of living to the whole of mankind, with the least possible expenditure of labor, the distribution of these goods on an equitable basis to all human beings, and their consumption with the least possible waste.

During certain periods capitalism has stimulated science and technology to a certain extent; at other times, hardly at all. In ancient Greece the development of science was the work of an upper class whose leisure was purchased at the cost of the slavery of a much larger number. During the Dark and Middle Ages the monks and schoolmen made some contributions to science and technology. Timekeeping for prayers in medieval monasteries encouraged the new mechanical conception of time. Among other things it resulted in the invention of the modern mechanical clock by Pope Sylvester II toward the end of the tenth century. This in turn transformed timekeeping into time-serving and time-rationing. It rendered more feasible the determination of quantities of energy, the measurement of automatic action, standardization, and fineness of articulation. Without the accurate measurement of time the modern industrial system would not be possible.

More important perhaps than the invention of the clock was the attempt of the medieval schoolmen to bring all phenomena under a reign of law which they conceived to be ordained by God. Whether or not their theological postulates were correct, this attempt encouraged somewhat the idea of an orderly universe. Medieval Christianity thereby aided the development of scientific method.

Much more important than these religious and clerical influences were such powerful forces as the increase and migrations of population, exploration and discovery, colonization, the worldwide extension of trade, etc. The capture of Constantinople by the Ottoman Turks in 1453 stimulated a search for new routes to the Orient, which in turn led to the discovery of America. About this time commenced the first great stage of modern capitalism, namely, its mercantile stage, which lasted from two to three centuries.

During this period capitalism had comparatively little need of

638

science and invention. With the coming of the industrial revolution and the mechanization of industry, commencing with the invention of the steam engine in the eighteenth century, this need increased for a time. In order to compete successfully with handicraft and secure the profits from large-scale production, the capitalists encouraged mechanical inventions. Some of the capitalists even went so far as to establish research laboratories in order to discover new methods which they could utilize and new products which they could exploit profitably. An incidental by-product has been a small increment to scientific knowledge.

As the second great stage of capitalism, its industrial phase, has run its course, it has not only had to produce a much larger supply of consumption goods for a rapidly increasing population, but also to build up the equipment of the machine age. For a time there was ample scope for private enterprise and capital expansion. As the new structure approached completion, the opportunities for the profitable investment of surplus capital decreased and the disparity between productive capacity and purchasing power increased.

The fundamental contradiction between capitalism as a scarcity economy and the machine and power age as an economy of abundance has become increasingly acute. According to capitalist economics, the price of a commodity varies inversely with the quantity available at a given time and place in relation to the population. Free goods, that is to say, goods unlimited in quantity, have no price and therefore no value in the capitalist sense. Air and often water cost nothing. A fall in price may stimulate the sale for a time, as has happened in recent years with automobiles and radios. But a point is reached for each commodity when further increase in production means a decrease in profits not only per unit but *in toto*. When profits vanish, capitalism comes to an end. Hence the numerous attempts by capitalists in recent years to limit production and thereby bolster up profits. While modern industrialism and the machine age arose and the power age commenced under capitalism, the last will eventually disappear, whereas the former three will go on forever. Capitalism could endure permanently only under the conditions which prevailed in the pre-machine age. Science, invention, and technology, temporarily and partially utilized by capitalism, have proved to be its nemesis.

The widespread distribution of electricity will decentralize industry to this extent that factories will no longer be concentrated in large urban centers as much as in the past. The machine with an individual drive by its own motor may render feasible, though not necessarily desirable, the dissemination of some industries in homes. Large-scale production will not necessarily decrease. In a few industries a saving in the cost of transportation of the finished product may cause the breaking up of large factories into smaller units and their distribution over a wide area. In most industries this saving would be more than balanced by increased cost in the transportation of the raw materials, in the transmission of power, and in greater overhead expenses.

Even if industry became greatly decentralized, it would not mean a return to *laissez-faire* capitalism with free competition between many small producers. The construction of power plants and systems requires the concentration of much capital. The power companies usually possess a monopolistic control. With little or no competition they furnish a necessary commodity and service. This enables them not only to charge a monopolistic price at a high rate of profit. They are also able to discriminate in favor of the consumers whom they wish to aid as producers and against those whom they wish to ruin. As electricity is becoming more and more the form of power used, industrial success depends to an increasing degree upon its availability and cost.

The widespread distribution of power may revive a limited amount of small-scale production in a few industries where local distribution of the product is not only feasible but cheaper than from a large factory. This would not necessarily mean the revival of petty private enterprise. It is perhaps more likely to be the revival of sweated home industry. Even if the worker or small capitalist could meet the initial cost of installation of machinery, he would then encounter the problems of securing his power from the monopolistic power companies, and his raw materials from sources which are also likely to be monopolistic. Last but not least he would have to compete in the market with the large producers in order to dispose of his products. Before long he would probably become the exploited employee of the big interests rather than a petty enterpriser. Neither in the form of small-scale private enterprise nor of sweated home industry is the decentralization of industry likely to compete to any great extent with the potential and actual economies of mass producion and distribution.

The power resources of the world are great, but they are not unlimited. At any rate, this must be assumed as long as no method has been discovered of deriving energy readily and cheaply from the air or water or plant life or atoms, or some other inexhaustible source. The coal, oil, and gas resources will be consumed and cannot be replaced. All the water power will eventually be developed and cannot be expanded. The world's power resources should be utilized in accordance with a long-term program of development and consumption. Such a program is impossible or only partially feasible under a capitalist economy. Capitalists are interested only in profits which are immediate or in the near future. They are utterly heedless of the waste of natural resources. The impossibility of a far-reaching power program is one of the principal reasons why not only social technology but even physical and mechanical technology cannot be fully developed under capitalism.

The preceding considerations render it increasingly evident why the profit motive is in large part incompatible with technical efficiency. Capitalism sometimes aids in a haphazard fashion but usually restrains scientists, inventors, engineers, and technicians in general. Bound hand and foot by the financial restrictions of a capitalist economy, they cannot carry out projects which are not only feasible but are most efficient and productive from a technical and social point of view. Capitalism utilizes scientific and technical progress only when profits are increased thereby. Many patented inventions are purchased and suppressed by capitalists because their utilization would decrease profits in the immediate or near future. Monopolies often smother patents in order to save the cost of new installations. Capitalists are interested primarily in cheap labor and not in educated and trained labor as such. In all these ways capitalism frustrates science, invention and technology.

Capitalism induces the accumulation of capital rather than an abundance of consumption goods. This tendency is rapidly becoming accentuated. It is partly due to the spontaneous operation of the capitalist system and partly to deliberate attempts to limit production in order to safeguard and increase profits.

One of the reasons why capitalism prevents the development of a social technology is that it renders impossible the accurate measurement of many features of a socially efficient economy. Among them are feasible productivity, potential demand, possible consumption, and use value. Prices, wages, interest, rent, and profits, are vague as concepts and far from precise as measurements of anything. Prices are varying at all times and sometimes fluctuate violently, so that they can give little indication of intrinsic or use value. Wages only rather remotely measure the productivity of labor or the ability of the individual worker. Interest, rent, and profits are determined largely by a monopolistic control arising out of property rights, and have little relation to the productivity of capital, land, and enterprise or managerial ability.

The amount which it is feasible to produce is estimated by the orthodox economists within the numerous restrictions and the narrow limitations of a capitalist economy instead of within the free scope and flexible adjustments of a socialized economy. The potential demand for and the possible consumption of many commodities cannot be determined because of the limited purchasing power of the public. In a socialized economy purchasing power, *i.e.,* the medium of distribution, would expand as rapidly as productivity. The inability of capitalism to measure accurately many things of great social significance is one of the numerous reasons why capitalism cannot create an economy on a scientific and technical basis.

The power age is intensifying the opposition between the capitalist profit system and technology. The use of electrical power has accelerated mechanization, augmented the automatic character of machinery, and emphasized the use of chemistry and of chemical apparatus. It has rendered it possible to start and stop each machine independently by throwing a switch. In a factory operated by steam power there is an elaborate system of belts and shaftings, so that in order to stop one machine it is often necessary to stop a large number. The electrical eye, the thermostat, and various other instruments are replacing the human machine tender. The automatic factory is coming into existence in which not only physical labor but also the routine work of directing the machines are being supplanted by non-human mechanisms. A technological revolution is taking place which is throwing a large part of labor out of work. Under capitalism the inevitable consequence is widespread technological unemployment. Furthermore, the character of the labor still utilized is rapidly changing.

The Florentine, Niccolo Machiavelli (born 1469), cited a maxim which runs as follows: "The cause of every man's success in life is owing to the temperature of his mind in conformity to the times in which he lives." This adage applies to institutions as well as to human beings. Science, invention, and technology are not sufficiently in conformity with the principles, spirit, and methods of capitalism to attain their highest fruition in the capitalist era. On the other hand, capitalism cannot master its internal contradictions and rigidities sufficiently to take full advantage of technology and create new industries to supply new wants as rapidly as these wants manifest themselves.

Chapter XXXVII

Finance and Monopoly Capitalism

IT was to be expected that the accumulation of surplus capital would give rise to devices and a mechanism for the profitable manipulation of this capital, even though it could not be utilized for the benefit of the community as a whole. The profits arising from this manipulation may accrue to the owners of the surplus capital or they may accrue to the manipulators. In either case the purpose of the capitalist system would be attained, namely, the acquisition of profits by capitalists or business enterprisers or both.[1]

The banks have long served as a repository for capital in a fluid form. They have furnished a relatively safe place of deposit for funds. They have often paid a small rate of interest for the right to make use of these funds. With the aid of these funds they have extended credit facilities to business enterprises and other borrowers. They have acted as a sort of reservoir for gathering liquid capital which they have put at the disposal of commerce, industry, and agriculture. These services have long been regarded as legitimate functions of the banks. The bankers have usually been amply rewarded for their services. When conducted with wisdom, prudence, and caution, as well as with honesty, banking has performed a useful function not only for capitalism but for society as a whole.

As liquid capital increased in volume, many depositors wished to invest their deposits in securities which would yield a higher return than could be paid by the banks. It was natural that they should turn to their bankers for advice. In many cases the banker acted as an agent in purchasing or selling these securities and charged a commission for his services. Some of these bankers began to purchase security issues at wholesale from corporations and governments, sell-

---

[1] Most of this chapter is condensed, paraphrased and brought up to date from my book entitled *Farewell to Poverty*, New York, 1935; see especially Chapters VII to X on financial, corporate, and monopoly capitalism, and the public utilities.

ing them at retail at a profit to investors. Thus arose the investment banker, who is a commission merchant and trader in securities.

As soon as the banker became a merchant, he could no longer advise his depositors impartially. He was prejudiced in favor of his own securities which he was trying to sell. This commerce in securities was so profitable that before long some of the bankers began to manufacture securities in order to increase the scope of their trade. They became promoters of business enterprises, or at least cooperated with and were the associates of the promoters. In this fashion many of the railway consolidations, large trusts, holding companies, and industrial mergers of this country have been organized by the large investment banking houses.

As directors of these corporations the investment bankers have been in a position to decide what securities were to be issued by these corporations, and at what prices they were to be sold. In many cases their decision has been that these securities were to be sold to themselves at a considerable discount from their nominal value, and then sold to the public at a higher price by themselves and their subsidiaries. In order to retain this profitable business they have used many devices to maintain their control of these corporations. Among these devices are voting trusts, interlocking directorates, exclusive financial agencies, holding companies, etc.

The power of the investment bankers has arisen from their control over a vast amount of liquid capital, not only in their own banks but in many commercial banks, trust companies, and savings banks. They have also secured control over many of the large insurance companies which are among the greatest purchasers of securities in the country. The power of the "money trust" or "financial oligarchy," as it has often been called, comes almost entirely from their manipulation of other people's money. The money which they themselves risk is very small in comparison. Their control over a corporation is often secured by a pyramiding of stocks which gives them complete control on the basis of a comparatively small investment. In other cases, their control of credit facilities or over customers' proxies delivers a corporation into their hands without any investment whatsoever on their own part.

These profitable activities, for which the public has paid heavily, have enhanced greatly the fortunes of the big bankers, and have to this extent directly aggravated the maldistribution and the concentration of the ownership of wealth. Much worse consequences have resulted from these activities. Banker-management has almost always been disastrous for the corporations which the bankers have controlled. This has not been merely because bankers are no more omniscient and infallible than other human beings, and that as bankers

644

they are no more competent to manage railways, steel mills, textile factories, power plants, etc., than any one else. It has been so all the more because the bankers, as financiers, have been more interested in speculation, investments, and promotion than in competent management. Even when they have employed technical experts to manage these properties, their financial depredations have often resulted in over-capitalization and excessive debt obligations which have seriously hampered the corporations upon which they have preyed.

Even more disastrous than banker-management has been the concentration of money and credit control by finance capitalism. The much-vaunted competition and freedom for business enterprise have been to a large extent suppressed by this control of money and credit. Almost all businesses require credit from time to time. With most of the banks directly or indirectly under the control of the big financiers, the small business men can usually be easily crushed by withholding credit from them when they do not act in accordance with the dictates of big business. This suppression of competition and of freedom of enterprise constitutes one of the contradictions of capitalism.

The investment bankers have also often encouraged and stimulated speculation, and thereby increased financial instability. They are able to do so through their control over banks, trust companies, and insurance companies. They can influence the money market greatly by lending or refusing to lend on the stock exchanges. Easy money encourages the prices of securities to rise. Tight money usually makes these prices fall. If the bankers were solely or mainly interested in financial stability, they could readily use their power to this end. But they are usually interested in influencing the prices of certain securities from the manipulation of which they expect to derive profits. They influence the general trend of prices in the securities markets and the prices of these securities in particular in order to gain these anticipated profits. Instead of promoting financial stability, they contribute to the confusion and instability which already exist in these markets.

It is alleged that the stock exchanges perform at least three useful functions, namely, to furnish a market place for securities, to obtain capital for business enterprises, and to promote stability by smoothing down some of the more violent fluctuations in prices. The first function they doubtless perform. This is not as essential as is contended. Two-thirds of the industrial stocks held by American investors are not listed on the exchanges. There will always be a market for securities, whether there are exchanges or not.

The exchanges perform the second function to a very slight extent. In the early stages of the development of the great industries the necessary capital has been obtained almost entirely outside of the exchanges. It is usually not until an enterprise is well on its way that the financiers get hold of it, "reorganize" it, issue large amounts of paper in the form of capital stock and debt obligations, and list this paper on the exchange to manipulate for their own profit. Then begins the game of "making a market" for these securities, which has little relation to their real value. Thus are encouraged speculation, not enterprise, the piling up of debts, and not the creation of wealth.

The stock exchanges do not and cannot in the long run determine the prices of securities which are in the last analysis and ultimately determined by the values which lie back of them. By anticipating price changes, the exchanges may sometimes make changes come about more gradually. But the speculative forces in exchanges create many fluctuations which more than counterbalance the stabilizing influence of the exchanges. Much of the time, and especially during periods of inflation, they mislead the public almost entirely as to fundamental features of the economic situation.

The principal significance of the stock exchange is that it reflects in a somewhat grotesque and exaggerated form the financial aspect of capitalism. Speculation is inherent in capitalism and has always endangered the production and distribution of the most necessary commodities. A corner in wheat may raise the price of bread so high as to bring many millions to the verge of starvation. There have been many periods of "frenzied finance" in the past. The beginning of corporate enterprise caused such a period in England. Speculation, stock-jobbing, stock-watering and swindling were widespread. In 1719 commenced the boom in the stock of the South Sea Company. Its shares rose quickly from £100 to £1,000. Then the bubble burst and the shares fell as rapidly as they had risen.

The accumulation of surplus capital furnishes additional fuel for speculation when a period of inflation commences. This capital lying idle in the banks can now be profitably used for speculative purposes. The rise in prices creates a fictitious capital which serves as a basis for expansion of credit and for collateral loans. Many new issues of capital stock and of bonds are placed on the market. Overcapitalization and an unjustifiable increase in the volume of debt obligations ensue. The capital structure becomes top-heavy. Inventories are inflated by the rise in prices. Purchasing power is buoyed up for a time on this unsound basis. During the midwar period of prosperity (1918-1929) it was supplemented by the instalment plan of purchasing. This continues until the bottom drops out of the market. Then a financial crisis ensues and the period of depression sets in.

Money, banks, and stock exchanges constitute a part of the paraphernalia of capitalism. Money serves as a "medium of exchange" and a "standard of value." Banks serve as a reservoir for capital which they distribute to business enterprise. The exchanges furnish a market place for securities. All this is useful and inevitable under capitalism. In course of time there arose a traffic in money and securities as if they are commodities in themselves and not merely representative of genuine wealth. This traffic has obscured the true nature of money and securities and has given them an exaggerated role to play. The financier is like the industrialist and merchant in that his sole purpose is the quest of profits. Unlike them he produces no wealth whatsoever, whereas, incidental to their profit-seeking activities, they sometimes produce commodities and give to them place value.

All orthodox economists are prone to regard money, which is a secondary aspect and merely a tool of the financial structure of capitalism, as a primary cause of economic conditions. They often forget that not gold and money, but effective demand and available supply, are determining price levels and market relations. Much more often they completely fail to realize that demand and supply are narrowly limited by the conditions inherent in and inevitable under capitalism. While they talk and write voluminously about demand and supply, they do not recognize their real nature under a system which checks demand by making it effective only through pecuniary purchasing power, and decreases supply by failing to utilize a large part of the available capital equipment and labor; and also by frustrating science and technology, and by wasting huge quantities of both capital and consumers' goods. In like fashion they fail to recognize the true causes of the business cycle, the excessive maldistribution of wealth, the so-called favorable balance of trade, etc. Their view is so beclouded by the pecuniary aspect of capitalism that they cannot see that it fails in large part to perform the most elementary functions of any economic system.

The secondary role played by money is strikingly illustrated in connection with the controversies which invariably arise between the defenders of "sound money" and the proponents of monetary inflation whenever there is a depression or financial stress of any sort. The ineffectiveness of a stable currency to remedy the fundamental and fatal defects of capitalism has been repeatedly demonstrated during recent years. Government after government, after clinging desperately for a time to the gold standard in the hope that its magic effect would prove to be a panacea, has plunged in despair into the turbid waters of inflation. Even though this measure sometimes affords a slight temporary relief, readjustment to the new monetary standard soon takes place and then the situation is no better and often worse. This is because monetary measures of and by themselves can have little effect upon the underlying situation.

Another controversy which is certain to arise at a time of depression or of financial crisis is with regard to the rights of creditors and the liabilities of debtors. Capitalism has created a situation so anomalous with regard to debt claims and obligations that it is impossible to adopt a consistent and wholly logical policy. Whatever measure is applied is certain to injure one group or another, and it is difficult to gauge the gain and the loss. The defenders of "sound money" are the vociferous champions of the legal and moral rights of the creditors. The proponents of monetary inflation usually embrace the cause of the debtors whose debt burden becomes in proportion much heavier and sometimes crushing, when widespread deflation takes place, in the forms of income other than the proceeds from debt service. The development of the financial structure of capitalism has rendered monetary relationships very intricate and complex. It is almost impossible to follow through all the ramifications of the effects from measures for the adjustment of debts.

Finance capitalism faces this dire situation quite as helpless as mercantile capitalism and industrial capitalism. The financiers can perhaps be a little more active than the merchants and the industrialists, whose hands are tied by their own system. But the activity of the financiers can be only mischievous. At best they can accomplish nothing to set things going, and at the worst they can aggravate the situation somewhat by their greed for speculative profits.

The Roman law developed the concept of the corporation. In ancient Rome there were many corporations, such as craft guilds, municipalities, priestly brotherhoods, business associations, etc. At one time and another these legal entities were called *societates* (social groups), *universitates* (one out of many), and *collegia* (gathered together). Then as now these artificial collective persons had rights and duties similar to those of natural persons. They could own property, make contracts, litigate, and engage in many activities. As Sohm has said: "Roman law contrived to accomplish a veritable masterpiece of juristic ingenuity in discovering the notion of a collective person; in clearly grasping and distinguishing from its members the collective whole as the ideal unity of the members found together by the corporate constitution; in raising this whole to the rank of a person (a juristic person), and in securing it a place in private law as an independent subject of proprietary capacity, standing on the same footing as other private persons."[2]

During the Dark and Middle Ages the corporate form of organization was more or less in abeyance, being used chiefly by the church. The rise of modern capitalism brought it back into extensive use. In England the Russia or Muscovy Company was founded in 1555, the

[2] R. Sohm, *Institutes of Roman Law*, Oxford, 1907, translated from the German.

Royal Exchange was opened in 1571, the Senegal Adventurers Company was chartered in 1588, the Levant or Turkey Company was organized in 1592, and the East India Company in 1600. Many of these early corporations were for purposes of trade, and some of them, like the East India Company, were granted monopolies. All of them sought the investment of capital by the public in their enterprises. The East India Company announced that "noblemen, gentlemen, shopkeepers, widows, orphans, and all other subjects may be traders, and employ their capital in a joint stock."

In days of old, kings were identified with their governments and wielded a power almost unheard of in these days when the few remaining specimens of the kingship have degenerated to a shadow of their former greatness. In many countries the monarch had extensive regulatory powers over commerce, industry, and agriculture. In some countries the king alone had the right to utilize inventions and to produce new commodities. This power was often used to protect the pre-capitalist handicraft system and feudalism against these disturbing influences by prohibiting the utilization of inventions and the production of new commodities. These negative measures helped to perpetuate the existing system, but hampered technical and economic progress. Sometimes a king would decree a monopoly in a certain industry in favor of himself in order to replenish the royal exchequer. In other cases royal patents were granted to develop new industries or to promote exploration and discovery in order to find new markets.

In spite of these royal prerogatives, the English common law was very hostile to monopolies. It prohibited forestalling, engrossing, and regrating. The first consists in buying up secretly and in advance by going outside of a market town to purchase goods on their way to market. Engrossing means to buy in large quantities in order to secure a monopoly. Regrating consists in reselling in the same market.

The Tudor and Stuart dynasties acquired the habit of granting to their favorite courtiers patents of monopoly in certain trades and commodities.[3] This practice became so oppressive that Parliament opposed it vehemently, partly in order to free private business enterprise. In danger of losing her throne on this account, Queen Elizabeth revoked all patents of monopoly on November 28, 1601. In 1602 a court held a monopoly for the manufacture of playing cards contrary to common law and illegal. It stated that monopolies cause increase

---

[3] Lord Coke (1552-1634) defined a monopoly as follows: "A monopoly is an institution or allowance by the King by his grant, commission or other wise, to any person or persons, bodies politic or corporate, of or for the sole buying, selling, making, working, or using of anything, whereby any person or persons, bodies politic or corporate, are sought to be restrained of any freedom or liberty that they had before, or hindered in their lawful trade."

of prices, deterioration in quality, and unemployment and beggary. James I continued to grant monopolies until an anti-monopoly law was enacted in 1624. In 1689 Parliament abolished the royal right to grant monopolies.[4]

The advantages of the corporate form of organization for capitalism are that it enables a large number of persons to pool their capital and unite in a business enterprise, that the liability of each stockholder is limited to his investment in the enterprise, and that the life of a corporation is perpetual or at any rate is not limited by the lives of any individuals. In all three of these respects it differs from the partnership which cannot include many individuals, involves unlimited liability for each partner, and is limited in time by the lives of the partners.[5]

With the rise of large-scale factory production the corporate form of organization became very useful for industrial enterprises. It brings together large quantities of capital and centralizes its control and management. Its utility in these regards to capitalism has given rise to many encomiums from persons imbued with the capitalist ideology. In 1910, the late President Woodrow Wilson, in an address to the American Bar Association, said: "I regard the corporation as indispensable to modern enterprise." He added that it should be recalled to "the service of the nation as a whole." In 1911, the late President N. M. Butler of Columbia University said to the Chamber of Commerce of the State of New York that "in my judgment the limited liability corporation is the greatest single discovery of modern times, whether you judge it by its social, by its ethical, by its industrial or, in the long run,—after we understand it and know how to use it,— by its political, effects."

Within the framework of capitalism the corporation is essential, or at least useful, for large-scale enterprises. It would be not only superfluous but a cumbersome nuisance in a socialized system. In a genuine social economy the capital needed would be set aside before distribution in accordance with a preconceived plan. It would no longer be necessary to collect capital by the hit-or-miss fashion of setting up a corporation to serve as a catch-all for the miscellaneous savings of a large number of individuals. Butler descended to greater absurdities when he went on to say: "Even steam and electricity are far less important than the limited liability corporation, and they would be reduced to comparative impotence without it." On the contrary, freed from the corporate bonds of capitalism, our power equip-

---

[4] W. H. Price, *The English Patents of Monopoly*, Boston, 1906.

[5] A corporation is called a joint-stock company with limited liability in England, a société anonyme in France, and an Aktien-Gesellschaft mit beschraenkter Haftung (A. G. m. b. H.) in Germany.

ment would have a vastly greater scope for usefulness. Butler's "greatest single discovery" is a passing phase of an ephemeral and rapidly perishing capitalism. Power will always furnish the material basis for the higher civilization of the future.

The inherent nature of corporate organization accentuated by the corporation laws enacted in large part under the influence of corporate interests has fostered a high degree of centralization of corporate control. Sometimes this control is in the hands of one man, thus constituting a dictatorship. In many cases it is in the hands of one man, thus constituting a dictatorship. In many cases it is in the hands of a very few men, thus constituting an oligarchy. In all cases the tendency of corporate organization is away from individual initiative, free competition, democratic control, and management in the public interest even to the extent that the public is involved as shareholders.

In many cases promoters are secretly interested in property which is being transferred to or will be purchased by the new corporation which they are organizing. In addition to the usually excessive remuneration they receive for the work of organizing the corporation, they anticipate profits from this sale which, unknown to their investors, they are engineering from both sides as sellers as well as purchasers. Under cover of the legal principle of *caveat emptor,* which applies to securities as well as to commodities, they can in many ways mislead their clients with impunity, so that the prospectus of any new corporate enterprise should be regarded with the utmost caution.

One of the worst abuses of corporate management is the writing up or watering of stock. This takes place when capital stock is issued as fully paid up when the consideration for it is largely inadequate or wholly fictitious. Stock is fully paid up when it has been paid for at its par value. The paid-up stock is the only sound financial basis for the credit of a corporation. In many of the cases where promoters have received issues of stock for little or nothing in return for their services or alleged services, in accordance with a preconceived arrangement they return part of these issues to the corporation where it becomes so-called "treasury stock." Nothing has been paid for this stock which is, therefore, almost wholly fraudulent, but which nevertheless becomes a part of the capital structure of the corporation. Other methods by which capital stock is watered are re-appraisals of corporate property; values arbitrarily placed on stock dividends; values placed on bonus stocks paid to officers of the corporation, promoters, or others; splitting of the stock already issued ("cutting a melon"); and capitalizing earnings.

These are very dubious and questionable additions to capital value and at worst wholly fictitious. A re-appraisal is likely to be influenced by a desire to magnify the value of corporate property in order to appear to justify the issuance of new stock. Stock dividends at best represent earnings and not capitalization; at worst they do not even represent earnings. Bonus stocks are likely to have little or no capital value back of them. At any rate, nothing has been paid in return for them except services or alleged services. The splitting of stock is based upon an alleged but often dubious increase of corporate resources. To capitalize present or past earnings is very risky, because there is no assurance that future earnings will continue at the same or higher rates.

The theory upon which is supposed to be based the payment of bonuses is that such extra compensation stimulates the officers to greater efforts which will enhance the profit of a corporation. According to this theory, the payment of extra compensation is not justifiable if there are no profits or if no dividend is paid to shareholders. It has often been questioned whether such huge payments are justifiable at any time, in other words, whether the services of any human being are worth so much. The disclosures of the Federal Trade Commission and the United States Securities and Exchange Commission during the 1930's aroused widespread public indignation, especially because many millions of persons were unemployed, on relief, and on the verge of starvation.

This question cannot be divorced from the much broader and more fundamental question of the justification of the stupendous individual profits gained under the profit-making system. Under this system it is possible for a speculator in the securities or commodities exchanges, a banker, a broker, a merchant, an industrialist, or a real estate speculator, to amass a fortune of hundreds of millions in the course of a comparatively few years. Otherwise there could be no multimillionaires or billionaires. The question is usually not raised as to whether these enormous profits are justified by their services. It cannot be justified according to any conceivable criterion in the case of speculation, and its justification may be seriously questioned in all others. Still more may it be questioned in the cases of the heirs of these great fortunes who have done nothing whatsoever to amass them.

The officers of these large corporations are themselves financiers, industrialists, merchants, etc., who control these corporations. It is consistent with the inherent nature of the profit-making system that they should share in these profits. Whether their shares are called salaries, bonuses, or some other name is immaterial so far as the fundamental question at issue is concerned. If they do not receive their shares in one way, they are certain to receive them in some other manner so long as the profit-making system survives. What they receive is a mere bagatelle compared with the huge profits and incomes of the big capitalists, whose henchmen and retainers they are.

The investment bankers have been largely responsible for the stock-watering and over-capitalization which have swollen their fortunes as promoters and underwriters at the expense of the public. They have attempted to defend their practices by contending that potential earning power and not tangible assets should determine corporate capitalization. This argument sounds plausible and misleads the public while dividends are being paid and the stock market is going up. Under capitalism, depression is certain to follow prosperity. Then dividends cease, the stock market falls, the water is squeezed out of the stocks, and the gullible public discovers that it has been robbed. This serves to accentuate the violence and the range of the movements on the stock market which bear little relation to production, distribution, income, and the welfare of the masses. But these stock movements are extremely valuable for the bankers, brokers, and other financiers because the activity of the market, both upward and downward, furnishes abundant opportunities for speculative profits.

This situation has accentuated the deceit and hypocrisy which have at all times been inherent in capitalism. As a corporation lawyer has said: "Nothing in the whole wide world usually is more misleading today than the dollar sign on a stock certificate." [6] Vendibility is the end-all of capitalism. In order to secure the largest possible profits the vendor is not only permitted, but encouraged and incited, to resort to all manner of deception and chicanery. The principle of *caveat emptor,* the most characteristic feature of capitalist jurisprudence, protects him in his activities. Apart from such obvious and clumsy methods as short-changing and false measurements, he is rarely ever restrained. Even when he runs foul of the law, which is legislated in the main in his interest, its own refinements and the aid of lawyers usually save him from the consequences.

Corporate organization has facilitated the exploitation of the public and the taking of profits on a scale which far surpasses anything hitherto achieved by landlords, merchants, manufacturers, and financiers. This has been due to its concentration of economic power which has become apparent even to representatives of capitalist jurisprudence and economics. A corporation lawyer and an economist have recognized, though not to a sufficient degree, this corporate concentration of power, in these words: "The rise of the modern corporation has brought a concentration of economic power which can compete on equal terms with the modern state—economic power versus political

6 I. M. Wormser, *Frankenstein, Incorporated,* New York, 1931, p. 150.

653

power, each strong in its own field."[7] What these writers fail to recognize is that it is not a case of two rival systems of power, each sovereign in its own realm, but of the dominant economic power expressing itself in a political form.

The principal economic and social significance of the corporate form of business organization is that it has in large part divorced the control of property from its ownership, in other words, has deprived the owners of much of the control over their own property, and that it has concentrated economic power to a high degree. This has freed the directors and executive officers from most of their responsibility not only to the public at large but also to the owners in particular. It has facilitated the exploitation of the proletariat not only as wage and salary earners but also in so far as they have been able to invest their petty savings in corporate securities. It has also facilitated the exploitation and progressive absorption of the small capitalist interests by big business, thus bringing capitalism to its cannibalist phase in which there is no mercy even for the little brothers of the rich. This absorption and the concentration of power resulting therefrom are the principal factors for the monopoly capitalism which is rapidly coming into being.

Many states in the past and present have maintained monopolies which are to be distinguished from the purely royal monopolies of the past. These governmental monopolies have existed in order to procure revenue, or to regulate the consumption of harmful products, or for both fiscal and regulatory purposes. Among the harmful commodities which have been regulated are opium and spirits. Among the commodities which have been subjected to state monopoly are salt, tobacco, and matches. In some countries such enterprises as lotteries are monopolized by the state partly for regulatory and partly for fiscal reasons. No government in a capitalist country has, however, gone so far as to intrude to any considerable degree upon the field of private business enterprise.

The modern corporate monopoly has come into being as a result of large-scale production utilizing steam, water, and electrical power and substituting machinery for manual work. In the United States manufacturing developed rapidly after the Civil War of 1861 to 1865. Individual enterprises and partnerships were replaced by corporations some of which became very large. Many corporations were combined in order to eliminate competition and secure the advantages of monopoly. The first method of combination utilized was the trust. The trustees took the place of the former corporation directors. Trust certificates or certificates of interest were issued to the stockholders in

[7] A. A. Berle, Jr., and G. C. Means, *The Modern Corporation and Private Property*, New York, 1932, p. 357.

return for their shares of stock which were held in trust by the trustees. The actual owners of the stock lost their voting rights, and the control was highly centralized in the hands of a few individuals.

The trust has been almost entirely abandoned, largely on account of legal action against it. In some states a voting trust for a limited period is permitted. It has been utilized most often for the reorganization of railways.

The holding company has been defined as "any company, incorporated or unincorpated, which is in a position to control, or materially to influence, the management of one or more other companies by virtue in part at least, of its ownership of securities in other company or companies."[8] This definition does not state that the control exercised by a holding company is based upon the ownership of the major part of the capital invested in these companies. In most instances this is not the case. One of the great advantages of the holding company is that usually it acquires control with comparatively little investment and therefore of risk. It may be acquired by means of an option to purchase a majority of the stock in the other companies. Or it may be acquired by purchasing the majority of a class of stock to which the voting right is limited. Or it may be acquired by a process of stock pyramiding.

The holding company may be concerned only with draining profits from its vassal companies, and may take no part, at any rate overtly and ostensibly, in their management. Or it may act as a parent operating company. The latter type has been most characteristic of the railway holding companies. In many cases control has been attained by means of a lease of a railroad. Partial combinations have also been reached by traffic agreements.

The most extreme form of combination is attained when two or more companies become fused into each other. The fusion may take the form of a merger in which the assets of one or more corporations are transferred to another corporation so that the former are merged into the latter. Or there may be an amalgamation by statutory means in which the assets of two or more corporations are consolidated. Or the assets of one or more corporations may be purchased by another corporation. In all of these cases the fusing corporations become in effect one concern even though the old outward corporate forms and names may be retained for trade or legal reasons.

The holding company is at present the dominant type of combination in the United States. It is the usual method of forming industrial combinations. This is because it has certain advantages over fusion. Among its minor advantages are the ease with which it

[8] J. C. Bonbright and G. C. Means, *The Holding Company*, New York, 1932, p. 10.

655

can be organized and also the ease with which its properties can be divorced when that seems desirable. Its administration need not be highly centralized. More important is the advantage that its liabilities may be insulated by giving its creditors debt claims against its vassal companies. The pressure of an accumulation of debts will then fall upon the vassal company which may fail without overthrowing the holding company itself. By this means the holding company evades its financial obligations. Its activities and even its existence can be concealed at least in part by secrecy, which is often an advantage in avoiding legal prohibitions.

The two principal advantages of a holding company are its relative freedom from governmental regulation and its ability to retain and extend its control by means of stock pyramiding. This extraordinary device renders it possible to control a vast amount of wealth with a relatively small investment. There are, however, limitations in practice. Competition is likely to arise among the financiers themselves for the rich booty from promoting, reorganizing, and underwriting, and from the speculative profits which may be derived from the manipulation of these enormous issues of stock in the securities markets. The exploited public may succeed in arousing some resistance, however weak, which may lead to governmental interference and regulation.

The principal obstacle in the way of unlimited exploitation on the part of these financial adventurers probably lies elsewhere. Their sole interest in the corporations which they subjugate is to squeeze as much money as possible out of them. Technical efficiency in the management of these corporations means nothing to them except in so far as it may increase their profits. They are in most cases wholly incompetent to administer them. The effects of their control vary considerably in different fields of business. In some fields these corporations may be able to stumble along after a fashion in spite of the incompetent management. In other fields they are likely to fail eventually and to collapse, bringing down the houses of cards erected by the financiers.

One of the two principal advantages of the holding company is that it can be readily used as a legal device for escaping social control. This has been demonstrated on an extensive scale in the field of the public utilities. There is a traditional legal doctrine that a common carrier or a public utility is "affected with a public interest," and therefore peculiarly subject to governmental regulation and control. The courts have decided that a holding company is not a common carrier or public utility, and consequently not affected with this public interest. By using the holding company as their form of corporate

656

organization, the public utilities, and to a less extent the common carriers, have evaded a great deal of governmental regulation.

The promoters of a holding company, as of every other form of combination, are usually interested in attaining monopolistic power as far as possible, in taking advantage of the economies of large-scale production, and in improving and broadening market facilities, because all these factors contribute to profits. As in the case of many of the public utility holding companies, it may furnish expert services to its subsidiaries, though usually at a high charge. It may organize horizontal combinations of companies in the same line of production, or vertical combinations which bring together the producers of the raw materials and of the finished products, or circular combinations which unite companies whose products supplement rather than directly compete with one another, such as a general foods company.

A holding company is particularly concerned with the financial aspects of the companies it controls. It endeavors to pool the voting power, to centralize the financial activities, and to secure the credit and finance the capital requirements of its subsidiaries. The result usually is to unify the financing of the whole concern. This result is attained by substituting the securities of the holding company for those of its vassal companies. Almost invariably this means capital inflation and has the same effect as watering the stock. The large issues emitted by holding companies give the public the impression of large values, and it is often misled into investing in them, much to its subsequent regret. Although this sort of financing is by no means limited to holding companies, it is peculiarly characteristic of them. The capital inflation serves a very useful purpose to those in control by concealing excessive earnings, which might otherwise be heavily taxed or might lead to governmental regulation.

The holding company has certain disadvantages as compared with fusion, mainly lack of stability. The creation and maintenance of separate corporate organizations are somewhat expensive. The looseness of the organization uniting the holding company, especially if it is not also a parent operating company, with its subsidiaries may give rise to administrative and managerial difficulties. Creditors and minority stockholders who have reason to believe that they are being cheated out of their property are likely to form protective committees, bring legal actions, and create other obstacles. This situation may become so menacing as to give rise to the danger of dissolution against the wishes of the controlling interests.

The principal factor in the instability of the holding company is its top-heavy financial structure. The pyramiding of stocks which has usually played an important part in its creation increases the

657

proportion of debt obligations in its capital structure. Capital inflation almost invariably takes place, usually during and often after its organization. Inability to perform its debt service or some other financial crisis is likely to bring down the shaky structure. This may happen to a merger or amalgamation as well. A holding company is somewhat more vulnerable in these regards.

In its voluminous report on the public utilities the Federal Trade Commission has described in great detail the numerous malpractices of the holding companies. Among them are the pyramiding of companies owning or controlling the operating companies, with highly speculative organizations; loading the fixed capital account of public utilities in order to establish a rate for excessive returns; writing up fixed assets without regard to the cost thereof; exaction of payments from affiliated or controlled companies for services in excess of cost or value of such services; gross disregard of prudent financing in excessive issues of obligations, imperiling solvency; manipulating security loans to deceive security holders or potential purchasers of securities; putting funds in the call-loan market with a result of stimulating speculation; misstatement of earned surplus; deceptive or unsound methods of accounting; issuance of special voting or management stock giving control at small cost to promote the interests of selfish cliques; evasion of state laws; evasion of federal income taxes, and other practices.

During the Wilson administrations (March 1913 to March 1921) there was some legislation against combinations or for their regulation. But the federal courts were displaying an increasing disinclination to sustain such legislation. In 1920 the United States Supreme Court acquitted the U. S. Steel Corporation from the charge of being a monopoly. This decision was perhaps a reflection of the growing opinion, at any rate in the business world, that unbridled competition is less desirable than combination. This opinion in turn may be a recognition that capitalism has a monopolistic tendency, even though it is supposed to be based upon competition. So long as capitalism survives, governmental regulation is certain to be determined in the long run by the relative strength of these two contradictory capitalist tendencies. This contradictory situation is likely to arise in any predatory system. Wolves unite in packs at times to carry on their depredations. Criminals in this country have found it increasingly profitable to unite in gangs which not only prey upon the public but in which the big gangsters exploit the petty gangsters. In similar fashion, the capitalist pendulum swings between cutthroat competition and monopolistic combination. In either case, profit-making is the primary motive and the principal activity.

This is illustrated in the methods used in order to attain a monopoly and in utilizing monopoly power in order to exploit the public. Many of these methods have been disclosed in the course of the numerous anti-monopoly trials in the courts. Among them are price-cutting; paying rebates to customers, which is an indirect method of price-cutting; espionage upon the affairs of competitors; bribing railway officials and others in order to secure secret information concerning the business of competitors; and dumping goods at a lower price outside of the customary sales territory. As the counsel of the Standard Oil Company said in one of its trials, "Competition is a state of war."

The English common law opposed private monopolies because they may give rise to a socially dangerous control over human necessities. It endeavored to maintain and enforce competition by prohibiting restraints of trade. Partly for this reason the *laissez-faire* theory of business enterprise has received its most extreme expression in British and American writings on economics. Ruthless and rugged individualism has had few obstacles placed in its way. It has manifested itself in the most extreme ambivalent forms of competition and of monopoly.

On the continent of Europe the tradition of governmental control is much stronger. The continental economists have been inclined to recognize the inevitability of monopolistic tendencies, and to favor regulation rather than suppression. Capitalism has attained its highest continental development in Germany, where there was a strong tendency toward mutual organization. Early in the eighteen seventies, cartels began to arise in Germany. A German economist has described the cartel as "an association based upon a contractual agreement between enterprises in the same field of business which, while retaining their legal independence, associate themselves with a view to exerting a monopolistic influence on the market."[9]

Many of the German cartels are based upon price agreements which fix prices in order to eliminate price-cutting. Some of the cartels are based upon production agreements which restrict output, especially during periods of depression, in order to prevent prices from falling. Territorial cartels operate by dividing the territory between the concerns signing the agreements.

The more loosely formed cartels trust to their members to observe the agreements without supervision. The more highly organized cartels create special bodies in the nature of trade associations to supervise the enforcement of the agreements. There are several general cartels (Mantelkartell) which regulate the output of entire groups of products.

From time to time there has been an international cartel among

[9] R. Liefmann, article on the "Cartel," in *Encyclopaedia of the Social Sciences,* New York, 1930, Vol. 3. This writer said that the word cartel is derived from *charta,* meaning contract in Latin.

steamship companies with respect to freight and passenger rates. Such a cartel is likely to arise after a rate war which has cut the rates down to a low point. Also a few international cartels have been formed in industries in which a small number of producers are scattered over several countries.

The German cartels, of which there have been many thousands, approach most closely to the more loosely formed American types of combination, such as the community of interest agreement and the pool. The Interessengemeinschaft, or pooling of profits, is sometimes used as a substitute. Few if any German trusts and holding companies have been formed. However, a few amalgamations and mergers have been entered upon.

A German economist has found the medieval roots of the cartel in the feudal system of caste and special privilege. He asserted that it causes higher prices for the public, and promotes the survival of obsolescent plants which is harmful to the public and eventually to the industries concerned.[10] In these respects the cartel is similar to the American pools and trade agreements.

A holding company may be created by stock pyramiding. For example, an operating company has its capital structure divided among $100,000 of bonds, $100,000 of non-voting preferred stock, and $100,000 of par value common stock. Investment bankers, or other promoters, buy half of the common, and organize a holding company to which they sell the $50,000 of common for $20,000 of bonds, $10,000 of non-voting preferred, and $20,000 of common stock issued by the holding company itself. They sell the bonds, the preferred stock, and $10,000 of the common stock. With the remaining common, they control the holding company, which controls the vassal operating company, so that an investment of $10,000 controls $300,000. By such methods huge wealth can be controlled by relatively small sums.[11]

---

[10] M. Bonn, *Das Schicksal des deutschen Kapitalismus*, Berlin, 1926. Another German economist has published a history and defense of the cartels from an exclusively business point of view: H. Levy, *Industrial Germany, A Study of Its Monopoly Organizations and Their Control by the State*, New York, 1935.

[11] "In the case of the Middlewest Utilities Company pyramid, the equity of the top Insull interests in one instance, the West Florida Power Company, amounted to only .07 of one percent of the book investment of the Florida company, yet absolute control was exercised." (U.S. *Federal Trade Commission*, Public Utilities Release, No. 264, May 28, 1935.)

Chapter XXXVIII

Competition and Capitalist Waste

THE economic theory of capitalism postulates competition as one of its fundamental traits. Every orthodox economist extols the supposedly competitive nature of an ideal capitalism. The predatory aspect of capitalism seems to confirm this doctrine. The crudest and most primitive form of competition is to be found among the predatory animals. Each starts on an equality with the others. To no individual is given an artificial advantage. There are no rules of the game. The strongest win, whether it be by physical strength or weight, by shrewdness or by slyness, by hook or by crook. In a broader and looser sense of the term, the whole organic world is competitive. In the universal struggle for existence the fittest survive at the expense of those plants or animals which are less fit to survive.[1]

Capitalism does not appear to be wholly predatory in the most direct and primitive sense of that term. It is entirely predatory in the sense that it manifests exploitation in all its phases. Another fundamental trait of capitalism is private property, especially the private ownership of the means of production. Private property is made doubly strong by the right of the inheritance of property. This right gives to the owners and their heirs an advantage over the propertyless which limits greatly the freedom of competition of the latter. Whether owing to a sense of justice or a lack of shrewdness, no non-human animal species has yet devised a means of limiting individual competition by giving an artificial, unearned, and unmerited advantage to a restricted number.

Capitalism probably is no less predatory because it cloaks some of its predation under the semblance of an artificial order. By the exercise of force it creates an outward appearance of peace and

---

[1] Much of this chapter is paraphrased and brought up to date from my book entitled *Farewell to Poverty*, New York, 1935; see especially Chapters XI, XV, and XVII on competition under capitalism, the business cycle, and capitalist production and waste.

prosperity for a part of the time. But it conceals none too successfully the continuous exploitation of the mass by a privileged class and the perennial class struggle which arises therefrom. This exploitation is fully as predatory as the predation of the animals, if not more so.

Capitalism is by no means unique in this regard in the annals of mankind. As far back as there is any record, organized society has not only tolerated but even fostered human exploitation. Whether it be under a theocracy or gerontocracy, a monarchy or oligarchy, a caste or class system, the ownership or control and use of property have given a relatively small group the opportunity to exploit the great majority. Nor has the right of ownership been limited to inanimate things and plants and animals alone. It has been extended to human beings as well. Under various forms of slavery or of serfdom the master class has possessed almost unrestricted power over the subjugated mass. Even when the ownership of human beings (chattel slavery) has not been formally recognized, a monopoly or virtual monopoly of wealth or a control over the means of subsistence has in effect enslaved the masses.

Under feudalism the ownership of the land by the feudal lords was the decisive factor in the exploitation of the masses. Production was still largely in the handicraft stage. The tools of production were small and inexpensive and could be readily procured by the workers. To this extent the workers possessed a small amount of freedom. But the scope for private enterprise was limited by the preponderant rights of the nobility and monarchy, so that there was little opportunity for the worker to gain more than a meager living.

The middle class was formerly the mercantile class which had an economic and social status between the feudal lords and their serfs. The English Rebellion of 1640 and Revolution of 1688 were directed against certain feudal and monarchical rights and privileges in behalf of the middle class. The invention of the steam engine in the eighteenth century rendered possible large-scale factory production. The Industrial Revolution commenced in England. The French Revolution freed the bourgeoisie and removed the final restrictions upon capitalist enterprise. The American War of Independence made the middle class supreme in the North. The Civil War of 1861 to 1865 destroyed the feudalism of negro slavery and the plantation system in the Southern States. Medieval feudalism was suppressed, and agriculture, industry, and commerce liberated. It became possible to produce anything in any quantity.

The mercantile class now became merged with the capitalists. The latter became the heirs of the feudal monopolists and established their own monopolies. Capitalism is inherently monopolistic because only a privileged few can own the means of production which are in

662

large part machinery, factory buildings, and other bulky and expensive forms of capital equipment. Economic power leads in turn to a preponderant political influence. The capitalist class is now able to exploit the proletarian class almost without restraint. The workers, nominally free, are actually at the mercy of the capitalists because they own the tools of production even less than under the earlier feudalism. Not until the means of production are owned by all the workers alike can capitalism and its monopoly of power cease and collectivism begin.

The foregoing historical survey indicates that modern capitalism does not differ entirely in kind or in degree from the economic systems which have preceded it. As Hobson has said: "The historical foundation of capitalism is rent, the product of labor upon land over and above what is requisite to maintain the laborers."[2] The monopoly arising out of the ownership of land persists and is still of preeminent importance. The monopoly arising out of the ownership of the tools of production has attained an almost equal importance. The right of inheritance perpetuates these monopolies from generation to generation. The workers, from being chattel slaves and feudal serfs, have become wage slaves, which is a no less dire form of slavery. Even the slightest measure of responsibility acknowledged by the slave-owner and feudal lord for the sustenance of his slaves or serfs is not recognized by the capitalist, who may hire or fire his employees at will. Inasmuch as under the inexorable operation of the capitalist system the worker can usually procure no work and wage elsewhere, his alleged freedom to work when and where he chooses and to compete freely for his work and wage is a hollow farce. When, as often happens during a business depression no work and wage are procurable, the wage slave becomes a pauper slave or perishes from malnutrition and slow starvation.

Owing to these numerous and narrow restrictions, competition in its most fundamental human sense can exist only to a very limited extent under capitalism. Free competition between individuals is prevented by the right of private property and still more so by the right of inheritance which destroys equality of opportunity. In the pecuniary economy of capitalism the owner and heir of wealth has notable advantages over the penniless individual. However great may be the innate superiority of the latter, he can overcome this pecuniary lack with difficulty if at all. The right of inheritance also decreases greatly the efficiency of management—a subject to be discussed elsewhere in this treatise. Under the initial conditions of artificial inequality between persons created by these rights, capitalist freedom for private

2 J. A. Hobson, *The Evolution of Modern Capitalism*, New York, 1926, p. 4.

enterprise is highly advantageous for the possessors of wealth. This freedom does not promote the freedom or, in the long run, the well-being of most individuals.

Even though capitalism is fundamentally monopolistic rather than competitive, the question may be raised as to whether capitalism is competitive in more superficial senses of that term. The most competitive aspect of capitalism is perhaps the process by which prices are fixed in the market. Here take place at least two forms of competition. There is competition among the vendors. There is also a struggle which may be termed a form of competition between the sellers and the buyers. If there is a plentiful supply and many vendors, there is likely to be acute competition among them, and the buyers procure the goods at their own prices. If the supply is limited, the competition between the buyers and the sellers becomes more acute. A third form of competition may also arise, namely, competition among the buyers for the limited supply. These various forms of competition manifest themselves in bargaining and in the higgling of the market. The ultimate result is the fixation of the prices at which sales and purchases are actually made.[3]

The market is the most vital and the most sensitive place in the capitalist system. Here is ascertained and registered the vendibility of goods. As vendibility is the primary end of production under capitalism, the productive process is governed thereby. Here also is determined the return from business activities. Inasmuch as the ultimate purpose of capitalism is the acquisition of profits, and not the satisfaction of human wants, the final decision as to what and how much shall be produced is reached in the market place.

According to the theory of an ideal capitalism the profit-making purpose of capitalism will also attain the end of satisfying human wants in so far as that is possible at any given time and place. Within this limitation there will be a supply to meet the demand and a demand to absorb the supply as long as there are wants to be satisfied. In its actual operation capitalism has always fallen far short of attaining this end, often by more than half. The effective demand as expressed in purchasing power has usually been insufficient to absorb the actual supply and has invariably been unable to absorb the po-

---

[3] Veblen has asserted that owing to monopolistic business organization the competitive production of goods has in large part disappeared, and competition between sellers and buyers is the chief form which remains: "Competition as it runs under the rule of this decayed competitive system is chiefly competition between the business concerns that control production, on the one side, and the consuming public on the other side; the chief expedients in this businesslike competition being salesmanship and sabotage. Salesmanship in this connection means little else than prevarication, and sabotage means a businesslike curtailment of output." (T. Veblen, *Absentee Ownership*, New York, 1923, p. 78.)

664

tential supply which is not produced because it cannot be marketed. At no time has capitalism been capable of distributing all the goods which might readily be produced.

The next question which may be raised is whether there is a competition between the so-called factors of production for the largest possible share of the return from the sales in the market place. The answer depends upon the theory as to the manner in which these shares in distribution are determined under capitalism. According to the marginal productivity theory, each unit of land, labor, or capital utilized receives a share in proportion to the amount it has produced. In other words, labor receives in the long run all that it has produced, and the same is true of capital and of land.

This theory tends to put these three factors on the same footing. It ignores the facts that land is an original factor which existed long before labor and capital made their appearance, and that capital is the product of past labor. In like fashion it ignores the fact that the so-called shares of land and of capital are received by the land-owner and the capitalist by virtue of their monopolistic control of these productive factors, and not because they have created the land and the capital. The marginal productivity theory does not seem to favor the theory that there is a competition between the factors of production. It implies rather that their shares are predetermined by their relative productivity. The question may, however, be raised as to whether it is possible to dissociate the various products of these three factors, because the total product is their joint product. It is, for example, inconceivable that anything at all could be produced if either land or labor were withdrawn entirely.

The marginal productivity theory says nothing about a fourth share in distribution which is ordinarily recognized, namely, the profits which go to business enterprise or management. This share often fluctuates greatly and is commonly known as the residual share. These fluctuations display little relation to the amount actually produced. Despite the attempts at inductive confirmation, the marginal productivity theory remains somewhat ideological. It is nevertheless gratifying to the champions of capitalism because it seems to justify the manner in which wealth is distributed under that system.

The bargaining and the exploitation theories of distribution are more realistic in these respects. They recognize that the relative strength of the possessors of the productive factors varies considerably and sometimes greatly at different times and under different conditions. These theories recognize the feature of monopolistic control which is often present, especially with respect to land and capital. They also recognize the conscious and purposive element which may enter in through legislation or through collective action on the part

665

of laborers, or of landowners, or of capitalists. With regard to competition, these theories suggest that the determination of the shares in distribution is in part competitive in spite of the monopolistic control arising out of the private ownership of land and of capital.

The marginal productivity theory may also recognize bargaining in a measure and even exploitation to a slight extent as playing a part in determining the shares in distribution. It must perforce regard them as very secondary in importance as compared with productivity. To recognize exploitation in any considerable degree would imply an ethical condemnation of capitalism. This would be an indiscretion on the part of the capitalists.

The marginal productivity theory may well prove to be a boomerang against capitalism. It seems to justify capitalist distribution of wealth. If it indeed be true, the cure of the major evils of capitalism is hopeless. It perpetuates forever the excessive concentration of wealth and the extreme disparity of incomes. Increasing population and large-scale production at an ever higher technical level enhance the marginal productivity of land and capital and minimize the corresponding productivity of labor. This situation limits still more narrowly the distribution of purchasing power. This in turn restricts production, increases unemployment, and piles up surplus capital which cannot be utilized. These factors accentuate the business cycle with its rapidly recurring and prolonged periods of depression which constitute the major disorder of capitalism.

The marginal productivity theory might be equally true under collectivism and yet no one of these evils would arise. The product of the land would go, not to a small group of proprietors who dominate it by force or monopolize it through vested rights which arose out of conquest, but to the whole of mankind to whom the land was originally given by nature, if, indeed, it can be said to belong to anyone. The product of capital, which is itself the product of past labor, would go not to the capitalists who by inheritance or exploitation have acquired a monopoly of it, but to the workers collectively. A rise in the marginal productivity of land and capital would redound to the benefit of the masses and not of a small class. There could be no concentration of wealth and little disparity of incomes. There would be an adequacy of widely distributed purchasing power. Production would not be restricted by the inherent nature of the economic system itself. Work would be equitably divided. Surplus capital would be profitably utilized. There would be no more of the violent fluctuations of the business cycle but a consistent progress to higher levels of production and distribution.

The logic of the marginal productivity theory points to the conclusion, which is amply demonstrated on other grounds, that permanent prosperity, namely, an economy of abundance, is inherently impossible under capitalism. The fluctuations of the business cycle can only continue to become more violent in their character. The accentuation of the business cycle may lead to the rapid disintegration and complete disruption of the capitalist system. The only other alternative is stabilization at a depression level, namely, a scarcity economy for the vast majority. A temporary period of such stabilization may intervene before the final collapse of capitalism.

Some of the orthodox economists themselves admit that the "pure" competition of capitalism has become a transparent myth. They are beginning to recognize that corporate and finance capitalism are deranging and gradually eliminating the few competitive features which have ever characterized capitalism. They even recognize that capitalism is passing into its cannibalistic phase in which the petty bourgeoisie is being expropriated. Corporate organization and management are depriving many small capitalists of the control and often of the ownership of their capital.

The most striking manifestation of monopoly is its invasion of the market. This is the sacred place of capitalism, its *sanctum sanctorum*, its holy of holies, where profits, its most precious possession, are won. According to capitalist theory, the market is a most sensitive place where are promptly registered all the competitive factors of supply and demand, buyers and sellers, capital and labor. Through the complicated mechanism and intricate pattern of the market are supposed to be reflected and expressed all these competitive forces which result in the fixation of prices.

The present tendency among orthodox economists to recognize and even to condone monopoly capitalism is a far cry from the economics of Adam Smith. In his *Wealth of Nations* (1776), Smith disapproved even of the joint-stock company of his time because he discerned the monopolistic tendency of corporate organization. He would doubtless be horrified by the Standard Oil Company, the Steel Corporation, and similar creations of large-scale capitalism.

The failure of capitalist economics to recognize the monopoly which has at all times been fundamental in capitalism is perhaps its most unrealistic feature. This monopoly arises out of the private ownership of land and of capital. This blindness on the part of the orthodox economists is readily explicable. It is due to the fact that this monopoly is the crucial feature of capitalism. The loss of this monopoly would cause the capitalist system to collapse. Hence the tendency, which is largely unconscious, on the part of these economists to conceal this monopoly at the heart of capitalism from the vast majority who are victimized by it. Hence also the futility and sterility of capitalist theories of the shares in distribution and of price. These theories are attempts, mainly unconscious, to rationalize and to justify this monopoly and the shares in distribution which arise out of it.

The orthodox economists have for some time past recognized the more superficial forms of monopoly and are now beginning to recognize the rapid disappearance of the forms of competition which lie on the surface of capitalism. Some of them are commencing to justify the outward forms of monopoly capitalism which are emerging. It is contended that the wastes of cutthroat competition are eliminated and that the economies of large-scale production and of technical progress are more fully utilized. This may be true to a certain extent. A much more important question is whither this movement is tending. Is it toward a complete capitalist monopoly, perhaps under some form of fascism? If the big capitalists looked always at their main interests in the long run, they would invariably act collectively and thus maintain their monopoly. But capitalism is fundamentally anarchic. Individual greed will probably at all times induce some of the capitalists to violate the collective monopoly by endeavoring to secure larger shares of the rich plunder for themselves, instead of sharing it in common with their fellow-exploiters.

In the interest of big business, attempts are now being made to prove that free competition gives the inefficient enterprisers the opportunity to cause a great deal of waste. This is doubtless true. But under monopoly capitalism the ablest enterprisers are working for individual and class objectives and not for social ends. The chief significance of monopoly capitalism in the long run probably is that it is preparing the way for a socialized economic system by organizing production and distribution on a large scale. When and how this transformation will take place still remains to be seen.

In the United States a common saying is "from shirtsleeves to shirtsleeves in three generations." The implication that wealth is not long retained in American families has probably never been true in a high percentage of cases. It is much less true today. Trusts *in perpetuo* are forbidden by law. But many family fortunes are tied up in personal trusts. By including several infants among the beneficiaries of a trust, such a trust can be made to last approximately a century. By this means private fortunes are conserved and the concentration of wealth is perpetuated.

The inheritance of property is the most powerful and most fundamental vested right, which, as Veblen once said, is a "legal right to get something for nothing." It is of the utmost significance for capitalism in general and for monopoly capitalism in particular. It curtails freedom of competition to the highest possible degree. It aids greatly in the accumulation of large masses of wealth under one ownership or control. It protects these large fortunes from being

668

dissipated. It perpetuates them from generation to generation. It becomes thereby the chief support of monopoly capitalism.

The business cycle is even more disastrous to human welfare than international warfare, though it occurs in times of peace. This recurrent alternation of periods of so-called prosperity and of depression is the most salient feature of modern capitalism and one of its major defects. It is generally true of capitalism that prosperity brings depression as its inevitable consequence, expansion leads unavoidably to contraction, and inflation gives rise to an ineluctable deflation. This situation promotes a chronic state of instability which causes an incalculable amount of social waste. It accentuates economic insecurity and intensifies the concentration of wealth and the disparity of incomes. It thereby hampers a consistent progress to higher levels of production and of distribution. The business cycle reveals in a grotesque and lurid fashion many of the fundamental contradictions of capitalism.

Prior to modern capitalism the economic crises which took place were those of exceptional scarcity. They were due mainly to bad harvests, wars, earthquakes, epidemics, and other catastrophes. Subject to these exceptional disturbances, the earlier economies, such as feudalism, were stabilized on a low production basis with a bare subsistence level for the vast majority, and relative abundance only for the small dominant class or caste of exploiters.

With the development and expansion of trade, crises began to manifest themselves which were not due to catastrophes, exceptional scarcity, or even average scarcity. On the contrary, these commercial crises came in the normal course of events and were due to relative abundance rather than to scarcity. By the commencement of the nineteenth century it was recognized that these commercial crises are recurrent and perennial. Attempts began to be made to explain them as characteristic features of the capitalist system.

The salient features of the prosperity phase of the business cycle are as follows:

1. Expansion of old and new business enterprises, especially in the capital goods industries. This transforms a good deal of circulating into fixed capital.

2. Rising prices.

3. Higher interest rates.

4. More employment and higher (nominal) wages. But technological progress sometimes checks employment and may decrease it, even during prosperity.

5. Expansion of private and public expenditure.

6. Increased speculation in the securities and commodities markets, with an accentuation of unsound finance.

7. Expansion of loans and discounts.

The depression phase of the business cycle presents a reverse picture with the following features:

1. Contraction of business enterprise, commencing usually in the capital goods industries. Accumulation of liquid capital which cannot find profitable investment.

2. Falling prices.

3. Lower interest rates.

4. Less employment and lower (nominal) wages.

5. Contraction of private and public expenditures. But widespread destitution may increase governmental expenditures for relief and public works.

6. Decreased speculation in the securities and commodities markets.

7. Contraction of loans and discounts.

When business has fallen into its self-created depression, the business men accentuate it by attempting monopolistic price-fixing, by enforcing the payment of contractual debts in an appreciated currency, by protective tariffs, by lowering the fiscal revenue, and by various other measures which are inconsistent with recovery. Just when the government is in greatest need of an enhanced revenue to finance emergency relief and public-work projects, and to foster private business enterprises by means of subsidies, the capitalists encourage taxation which can be passed on to the consumer, such as import, sales, and excise taxes, thereby decreasing purchasing power. At the same time they oppose even more vehemently than usual heavy taxes on the higher income brackets and sharply graduated inheritance levies which would check the accumulation of surplus capital which is now more futile and wasteful than ever. These are among the numerous insoluble contradictions in which capitalism becomes involved.

The orthodox economists approach most closely to a genuine explanation of the business cycle when they touch upon profit-making as a factor. They are prone to treat the subject gingerly and with caution. It is a dangerous subject for them as retainers of the capitalist system to discuss, because profits constitute the supreme end of capitalism. They sniff around profit-making tentatively, but dare not attack the question of its relation to the cycle frankly and without reserve.

The capitalist crises have assumed serious proportions since the arrival of large-scale production. They are due to a lack of equilibrium between production and consumption. They are crises of relative over-production as contrasted with the crises of under-production of the preceding economy of scarcity during depression. The production is excessive in relation to the available purchasing power and the effective consuming power which results from it. The production is, however, not greater than the potential and absolute consuming power of the public. In fact, under-consumption actually exists on an extensive scale in spite of an adequate productive capacity. It is solely due to the inability of capitalism to distribute the products efficiently and fully.

The prime motive of the capitalist is to gain profits. So long as he is able to sell his products at prices above the cost of production, he continues to produce. When the public is no longer able to absorb his output at this price level, he decreases his production. He discharges some or all of his employees, thereby increasing unemployment and diminishing the already inadequate purchasing power of the public. When this situation becomes general, a crisis arises and a period of depression ensues. This period is prolonged until the accumulated stocks of commodities fall to such a point that the effective purchasing power of the public can absorb a new supply. At this point commences the upward phase of the business cycle, or so-called period of prosperity, during which employment, production and sales increase.

Why is there this shortage of purchasing power which starts the downward phase of the business cycle and which is accentuated by increased unemployment? The capitalists withdraw from immediate circulation a part of the revenue from the sale of their commodities. This is in the form of profits from their enterprises or of interest upon capital which they have loaned. If they expended all their incomes at once by purchasing commodities or paying for services, the situation would be somewhat relieved and the crisis might be averted. But the incomes of some capitalists are so great that they cannot readily spend all upon themselves. Most capitalists, small as well as large, save part of their incomes in order to increase their present capital and their future incomes, and also in order to assure economic security for themselves and their families.

If the flow of new capital into the production and distribution of goods always equaled the amount saved, the situation might be slightly more stabilized. But the eagerness of the capitalists to make money while profits are large leads them to expand production with precipitate haste during the upward phase of the business cycle until the saturation point in relation to the purchasing power of the public is reached and passed. Then comes the even more precipitate shrinking of production with the disastrous consequences which have been described.

This situation is inevitable because private enterprise is an essential feature of capitalism and cannot be socially regulated and planned. Under the most favorable conditions, there are fluctuations in production which have no technical, economic, or social justification. The amount produced often falls far below productive capacity and never attains a sufficiently high level to furnish an adequate standard of living for the masses. Production is wholly unrelated to the genuine needs and desires of mankind. On the one hand, unemployment and destitution give rise to widespread poverty. On the other hand, the fluctuations of the business cycle furnish many opportunities for speculative enterprises which have little or no relation to production. The more astute of the business men take advantage of these opportunities and build up large fortunes. Thus the concentration of the ownership of wealth and the disparity in the distribution of incomes are greatly accentuated.

The lack of coordination between productive capacity and the capitalist system of production and distribution has been enhanced by the technological progress of the past century or more, especially during the last few decades. Owing to this progress, it is possible to produce the same amount with a proportionally much smaller application of labor. Unless the amount produced is increased to a corresponding degree, or the hours of labor are reduced, unemployment is the inevitable result. This leads in turn to diminution of purchasing power, decrease of production, more unemployment, and so on around the vicious circle.

During the nineteenth century these effects of technological progress were counterbalanced in a measure by several temporary factors. Technical equipment had to be manufactured for industry and to a large extent also for agriculture. In the new countries, such as the United States, a complete equipment had to be produced. Science and invention not only improved and renovated the equipment of the old industries but also created many new industries. For a time the economically backward countries in the Orient and elsewhere imported many industrial products from the Occident. These conditions demanded a good deal of capital and labor. They compensated in part if not entirely for the rapid increase of wealth and of population, and for the economies in the expenditure of capital and labor due to technological progress. All these phenomena were caused in the last analysis by science and invention.

These compensatory factors have disappeared in large part. The new as well as the old industrial countries have attained a high level of technical equipment. The rate of creation of new industries has slowed down greatly. These industries cannot absorb all the capital and labor left idle by technological progress. The economically backward countries are becoming industrialized and are taking a constantly decreasing proportion of commodities from the Occident.

Many countries have tried to protect themselves against economic depression by raising their import tariffs, admitting only contingents of goods, and controlling foreign exchange. Some countries have tried currency inflation, hoping to stimulate their export trade thereby. This has been of little avail because most of the countries threatened with dumping have imposed compensatory taxes. The undeveloped countries have great needs but little purchasing power. In any case, they are now developing themselves and offer little promise of foreign markets. In the United States it was attempted to stimulate buying at home by means of the instalment plan. This only deferred a little the effects of inadequate purchasing power. It helped to precipitate the crisis of 1929 and to render it more acute by augmenting debt obligations. Fiscal difficulties in many countries have led to heavy taxes which constitute an additional obstacle to private enterprise.

In the effort to revive profits there has been widespread destruction of goods in many parts of the world. At times production has been curtailed by trade agreements, trusts, cartels, and in some countries by legislation. While the vast majority of mankind is in urgent need of a much higher standard of living, capitalism has restricted production to far less than can be readily produced. It has practiced what Veblen has called "sabotage" or "a conscientious withdrawal of efficiency."[4]

Since 1900 economic equilibrium has not been restored under the capitalist system. Up to 1914, America was an outlet for the surplus labor of Europe. It is so no longer. The European War of 1914 to 1918 was caused primarily by the search for markets for surplus production. Warfare for this purpose has become futile. The former foreign markets are becoming industrialized. Russia is almost entirely withdrawn as a market, and China in large part. India now produces its own textiles and the Lancashire textile industry is moribund. Japan, owing to its low labor cost and highly rationalized industrial system, is competing successfully for the export trade as against the Occidental industrial nations.

The present world situation is that, with the exception of the Soviet countries, the markets overflow in peacetime with unpurchasable goods while a large part of mankind is on the verge of starvation. Besides the many who have not the financial means to buy are those who can buy but refrain from doing so because of the uncertainty and in some cases because they are awaiting lower prices. The surplus capital which cannot find profitable investment accumulates in the banks and elsewhere. The thesaurization of wealth takes place which renders it socially useless for the time being and much of it is totally

[4] T. Veblen, *Absentee Ownership*, New York, 1923, pp. 218, 285.

wasted. Preparation for war and warfare are the only solutions which capitalism has for these problems.

Private property and profits are feasible only when there is a scarcity of goods. A relative or absolute over-abundance of goods destroys profits. It renders private ownership valueless because it destroys the exchange value of property, however much intrinsic value it may have. These facts indicate that capitalism can function only under a regime of scarcity. As mankind approaches the era of abundance, capitalism becomes less and less workable. Even if it could continue to work, it would cease to be profitable for the capitalists themselves. Hence they will eventually abandon it of their own accord, if they are not expropriated before that time arrives.

Capitalism contains the germs of its own destruction. The limited degree of freedom and encouragement which it has given to science and invention has prepared for its demise. Capitalism and its political correlative, liberal democracy, have played a part in building up the present system. The technical transformation of production is rapidly and inevitably bringing into existence a new system more or less independently of the concerted action of men. A directed economy and capitalism are incompatible. The new technical methods and organization require a planned economy. The cyclic nature of the capitalist economy indicates an inherent instability which would not be present in a planned and socially regulated economy. This instability is inevitable under capitalism.

The present business cycle does not belong to an indefinite series. It manifests symptoms of being one of the last in the career of capitalism. The exploitation and depletion of natural resources, progressive industrialization of the whole world, increasing spread between potential productive capacity and actual purchasing power, and accumulation of surplus capital seeking profitable investment, are rendering it difficult for capitalism to extricate itself from a depression by developing new industries, creating new wants, waging imperialist wars, fostering foreign markets, tampering with the currency, manipulating prices, stimulating speculation, or by utilizing any other of its favorite devices for promoting profitable business transactions.

Such artificial stimuli as war, inflation, and emergency governmental enterprises are becoming much less potent to stimulate flagging industry and commerce, maintain agriculture on a profitable basis, decrease technological unemployment, and augment inadequate purchasing power. The capitalist system is not so much attacked from without as it is disintegrating from within. Even if it is not overthrown by violence, it will rapidly be supplanted by a socialized system which is not only workable but far more efficient as a system of the production and distribution of wealth. The advance of science, invention, technological progress, the application of power, and rapid industrialization menace it far more than the class struggle, rise of the proletariat, revolutionary socialism and communism, military and civil dictatorships, or agrarian and handicraft movements.

Many of the contradictions of capitalism are illustrated in the business cycle. The withdrawal of profits reduces purchasing power and disturbs market relations, because the effective demand cannot absorb the actual or potential supply. Inasmuch as capitalism cannot function unless the price level averages higher than the cost of production, business enterprise does not promptly release as much buying power as the distribution of its products requires. Saving and investment expand the capital goods industries until a plethora is attained. The latter and a simultaneous or subsequent plethora in the consumption goods industries give rise to a depression. Wide fluctuations in the capital goods and durable commodities industries accentuate the business cycle. The accumulation of capital promotes and impedes production simultaneously or in rapid succession. Falling prices discourage the investment of capital when most needed during depression. Rising prices encourage the investment of capital when least needed during prosperity.

The fluctuations of prices in the course of the business cycle enhance the opportunities for speculation. The latter has stimulated the amassing of great fortunes. It has accentuated the concentration of wealth in the hands of a few. At a time of panic and crisis and during the succeeding period of depression many business men and others are forced to liquidate their enterprises and sell their property because they have failed or are in danger of failure. Bankruptcies and bankruptcy sales are numerous. There is excellent opportunity for speculation by the shrewd investor with money. At such a time he can buy securities, land, buildings, etc., at low prices, often much below their value. In this fashion many of the great fortunes have been in large part accumulated.

A crisis furnishes such excellent opportunities for speculation that there is reason to believe that some of the panics and crises have been created, or at least stimulated, by speculators who were in a position to profit therefrom. Speculators have in certain cases manipulated stocks of railways and of industrial concerns in such a fashion as to reap large profits therefrom. Speculation in land has been a prolific source of profits. The upward and downward movements of the price level during the business cycle afford abundant opportunity for speculation of all sorts. In fact, the amassing of large fortunes has been due far less to the productive ability of the rich than to their skill in speculation and speculative investment which has served only to disturb and hamper the orderly evolution of the economic system.

The business cycle is, however, not so beneficial to the capitalists and business men engaged in less speculative enterprises. Many of them lose part or all of their property and some of them are forced out of business entirely through failure and bankruptcy. Various methods of preventing the alternations between the periods of prosperity and of depression and thereby wiping out the business cycle have been proposed. It has often been suggested that a business barometer be devised which would indicate to what extent business enterprise is expanding. Several methods of business forecasting have been applied to detect whether an unpurchasable surplus of goods is accumulating. If business men were influenced in their policies by the indications of such a barometer, the excessive expansion of business enterprise leading to relative overproduction might be somewhat mitigated. Business men can, however, never be greatly influenced in this fashion. So long as the lure of profits exists, most business men will take the gambling chance to bring on over-production. Even with an excellent barometer of trade, supply and demand can never be well adjusted to each other under private business enterprise.

The fact of central importance in the business cycle is that under capitalism production outruns effective demand as measured by purchasing power. Hence arises an unpurchasable surplus of capital and of consumption goods. As a consequence, production slows down. This situation continues until this surplus disappears and effective demand outruns the current production. In the meantime there has been an enormous waste of goods and of labor. The total loss is much greater. Not only has much of the accumulated goods been wasted but the glut of capital impedes the production of new goods. To put it concretely, if one-fourth of the accumulation of goods is wasted, this is not the total loss. The glut of capital has prevented the production of a quantity as great or very much greater.

This situation is so obvious that it is described in one way or another in practically every treatise on classical economics. It stands out clearly even though the writers themselves may not be aware of it. The business cycle is much better understood than several other phases of the capitalist system. Among these phases are the manner of fixation of the shares in distribution, the concept of value, etc. Nevertheless, the orthodox economists continue to repeat that the business cycle still is more or less of a mystery. They allege that it must be studied a good deal more before it can be clearly understood.[5] They are unwilling to admit that the cycle has been explained in its fundamental and salient features. Further study can only add refinement of detail to what is already known. This unwillingness to accept

[5] For example, the National Bureau of Economic Research, New York.

the obvious explanation is due to psychological factors. They hesitate to face the fact that the business cycle is unavoidable and unpreventable under capitalism. Hence they pursue their hopeless search for an explanation which will furnish or suggest a solution of the problem under capitalism.

There is no economic security for anyone, not even for the rich, under capitalism. For the vast majority the only way of earning even a bare subsistence is to procure a job, if and when that is possible. The service rendered may be productive, though much of the work performed under capitalism produces nothing whatsoever of intrinsic value. Whether productive or not, many human beings are often deprived not only of the opportunity to work (and perchance to produce), but also of the right to sustain a miserable existence thereby. The social loss entailed by the failure to utilize productive capacity and the human misery created by robbing many men and women of their only means of livelihood and abandoning them to the precarious and capricious assistance of private and public charity have no bearing upon the conditions of employment under capitalism. When employment, productive or unproductive, ceases to be profitable to the capitalists because the effective demand for goods and services arising out of available purchasing power is satiated, the employment itself ceases.

For the helpless workers the situation is all the more tragically ironical because the more productive the worker becomes with the aid of science and technology, the less his services are needed and the smaller are his chances of employment. The worker as producer is forced to become the enemy of himself as consumer. Technological progress is creating an ever-increasing mass of the unemployed. Capitalism might abandon its unfortunate victims to perish. But this would be too risky. A starving mob may precipitate a revolution. It is more prudent to set aside a small fraction of profits to keep surplus labor barely alive, and thereby safeguard the profits of a dying capitalism. By these means its demise may be somewhat postponed.

The last stages of capitalism are characterized by a diminishing class of wage-earners remunerated as always with a very low standard of living, and a growing class of paupers kept alive at the lowest subsistence level. The latter class constitutes a reserve of surplus labor which can be utilized whenever war or any other exceptional contingency calls for a larger number of workers. The wage and pauper slavery of capitalism is almost as complete and hopeless as was the chattel slavery of the negroes in the southern states, the serfdom of feudalism, and the degradation of the untouchables in a caste system. It affords even less economic security than chattel slavery or feudal serfdom, for the slave-owner or feudal lord assumed at least a slight measure of responsibility for his slave or vassal. According to capitalist ideology, the worker has no right, legal or moral, to a job, in contrast to the sacred rights of property.

The problem of unemployment is becoming so acute that even some of the capitalists are disturbed by it. A British economist of the Manchester school wrote a defense of free trade in which he described the growth of unemployment under capitalism. "The great machine has been improved so fast that fewer men are needed to work it; and since only those who receive wages for work or interest from profits can purchase its products, we have the machine continually producing more than customers are ready to buy. Our system of trade has developed so fast that we are no longer able to manage it."[6] The dean of the graduate school of business administration of Harvard University said that "the only sound remedy for unemployment is work, and capitalistic society fails miserably if able-bodied men are persistently unable to get work."[7] He asserted that corporate capitalism should provide work. These trite remarks furnish no solution. And no capitalist solution is possible because widespread unemployment is inevitable under capitalism for reasons which are stated above.

A large proportion of those who are unemployed for any length of time never again become self-supporting. There is a constant stream of workers passing from wage slavery to pauper slavery. This process is to a certain extent selective. The less efficient, the older, and the partially incapacitated by ill health are somewhat more likely to be pushed down into pauperdom. But the business cycle throws into unemployment many of the most efficient as well. When widespread cessation of business and production comes, there can be little discrimination between the more and the less efficient. The total loss in all grades of labor which could be utilized in a socially profitable manner is incalculably great. This loss is due solely to the instability of capitalism and its inability to put to work all the available labor and capital. Prolonged unemployment causes deterioration in the skills of workers. It weakens their self-reliance and power of initiative by stimulating a sense of inferiority and an attitude of despair. It diminishes greatly the constructive and creative capacity of mankind.

An obvious device for mitigating somewhat the disastrous effects which result from the inability of the capitalist system to utilize technological progress in a socially beneficial manner is a reduction in the hours of labor and a shortening in the years of labor. This would distribute work more equitably, enhance purchasing power, and increase

---

[6] A. L. Bowley, *A Short Account of England's Foreign Trade in the Nineteenth Century*, London, 1893, p. 144. A Cobden Prize essay at Cambridge University.

[7] W. B. Donham, *Business Adrift*, New York, 1932, p. 111. This is almost as fatuous as the remark of the late President Calvin Coolidge that "there is a great deal of unemployment because many men are out of work."

678

leisure time and the cultural advantages which flow therefrom. Nevertheless, the capitalists have always opposed the reduction of the hours of labor because they fear that it will increase their labor cost and diminish their profits. This has been one of the major issues in the class struggle. A bitter fight has been necessary on the part of the workers, sometimes aided by social legislation, to force the capitalists to lower the hours of labor since the commencement of the nineteenth century from sixteen to fourteen, to twelve, to ten, and to eight hours a day. The eight-hour work day has not yet been fully and firmly established in every field of employment.

This measure is at best only a temporary amelioration of the situation under capitalism. A reduction of the hours of labor stimulates technical improvements because the capitalists wish to balance the increased cost of labor by diminishing the amount of labor needed. The consequence is a speedy reversion to the same state of affairs. At present many countries hesitate to reduce the hours of labor because they fear that it will put them at a disadvantage in international competition. Whether they are right or not, these matters cannot be regulated on an international scale except within a world federation. Free competition has sacrificed the workers in the interests or alleged interests of the capitalists. The workers are sometimes told that it is their patriotic duty to accept lower wages so that their country can complete successfully in the world market. International trade competition, by underbidding prices and dumping goods, has a tendency to force down wages and the standard of living the world over. Capitalism has always demanded this freedom to exploit the workers. Nevertheless, whenever it gets into trouble, it runs to the state for aid in the form of subsidies, tariffs, and favorable legislation of various sorts.

Many economists have recognized explicitly or by inference that capitalism exists primarily, not for the production and social distribution of wealth, but for the acquisition of private profits. Instead of being sensitive to human needs and social welfare, capitalism is dominated almost exclusively by the money-making prospects of the profiteers. The vast army of wage and pauper slaves can do nothing to start the wheels of industry unless the monopolists of land and of capital anticipate and foresee their unearned increment over and above the costs of capitalist production.

Since capitalism exists primarily for profits and not for production, the huge losses in actual production which take place under it cannot be attributed to mismanagement of the system. Some mismanagement characterizes every human institution. But these losses are the direct and inevitable consequences of the capitalist system. The recurrence of an economic crisis at frequent intervals and the fact that capitalist society is in a state of depression for approximately half of the time prove conclusively that depression is an inherent and inextirpable trait of capitalism. Though the labor force and the capital equipment remain the same, production falls off from 20 to 40 or more percent.

The loss owing to depression is trivial compared with the loss in potential production, even when capitalism is in its so-called prosperity phase. In other words, at all times capitalism produces far less than could readily be produced with the available productive factors. This loss is incalculably great and is cumulative in its effect. By its continual frustration of science and technology, capitalism is constantly slowing down the rate of development of a more productive mechanism and system. In so far as it is possible to calculate this loss, a measure is furnished which can at best only underestimate the inefficiency of capitalism as an economic system.

The industrial exploitation of the United States and of Canada has been the greatest, or at least the most spectacular, achievement of capitalism. Aided by a vast territory, the richest natural resources in the world, the surplus labor and capital of Europe, and the rapid progress of science and technology, it brought these two new countries in little more than a century to the front rank of industrial nations. No state hitherto was equal to this feat. Whether or not another kind of economic system could have accomplished it in America is an academic question. The socialist government of the U.S.S.R. is industrializing the largest country in the world at a rapidly accelerating tempo. If Soviet China survives and grows stronger and more efficiently organized, it may accomplish the same feat in another vast country. Capitalism is not the only economic system which can attain a high industrial level. It may, indeed, be limited to a low level in comparison with the future achievements of a socialized system.

Private enterprise may have been best adapted for the earlier stages of the development of large-scale production. Capitalism functions most efficiently in an expanding economy. If it can continue to do as well as or better than any other system, it should and probably will survive. If and when it breaks down in part or entirely, the state is forced to take over its activities and become the heir of capitalism. The latter now presents the strange paradox of want in the midst of plenty. Scarcity is necessary in order to secure profits and maintain the private ownership of capital. The technology of production renders scarcity superfluous. Hence scarcity must be artificially induced in order to perpetuate the profit-making system.

The greatest human need is an uninterrupted flow of an abundant supply of goods to the consumers. Capitalism now faces the most crucial dilemma of its career. It must do grave injury to the common

680

welfare of mankind in order to perpetuate itself, or give way by force or otherwise to another system in which science and technology will have full scope to operate for the benefit of mankind. This dilemma is clearly illustrated in the present status of production in the United States, which is industrially the most developed and technically the most advanced country in the world.

The consumption of certain commodities, such as food and clothing, is more or less narrowly limited by the size of the population. The potential consumption of other commodities, which may or may not be absolute necessities, is much more flexible. The capitalist system fails even to supply mankind fully with the necessities. Hunger, starvation, and inadequate clothing and housing are widespread even in the richest countries. This is especially true at a time of economic depression when the system breaks down and ceases to function to a considerable extent. It is also true when capitalism is at the height of its so-called prosperity.

In a desperate attempt to augment their shrinking profits during depressions, the capitalists try to cut down their costs of production by introducing labor-saving devices with the aid of technology and by lowering wages. Both these measures decrease purchasing power and aggravate the situation. Science and technology are prevented from producing an abundance for mankind by the inability of capitalism to distribute this abundance. Bewildered by the unforeseen consequences from the application of technology which they are too ignorant to explain, some of the capitalists demand its restriction.

It is often alleged in behalf of capitalism that the business incentive, *i.e.,* the lure of profits, is necessary to stimulate the production of wealth. In other words, this all-important social function of producing an ample supply of goods for the whole population is to be attained by indirection. The very reverse has actually taken place. Capitalist production is narrowly restricted, and the vast majority receive minimal incomes. The much-vaunted capitalist incentive has resulted in crushing the individual initiative of the great mass of the wage and pauper slaves. An incalculable amount of human talent and genius has been wasted.

If all business incentive were always directed toward producing wealth, the situation would be somewhat improved, though production would still be far below what might readily be produced under a socialized system. But a large part of business activity is not directed toward production at all, even as an indirect method of gaining profits. It is directed solely toward "making money" in the sense of transferring the ownership of wealth from someone else to one's self. In other words, it is a pure and unmitigated form of predation. It includes a large part of commercial and financial activities and many

681

services which are wholly supernumerary so far as production is concerned. The experts who really direct industrial production are remunerated not in profits but in salaries. This situation has become more acute with the refinement and expansion of the technique of capitalism, especially its financial technique.

An important aspect of this capitalist disorder is the intermittent utilization or repression of science and technology. When labor costs rise, more machinery and power are used and industry is rationalized to a higher degree. If the cost of the labor is low, less machinery and power are used. In either case, the supreme end is the largest possible net profits, not increased production and a higher standard of living for the workers. Human beings are used merely as means of production like machinery, and are employed and discharged as an incident to the quest for profits.

A Cambridge University scientist has stated the haphazard experience of science: "Science was not developed in the past for the purpose of human welfare, but partly to increase profits and partly to secure military superiority. There is no reason to suppose that this has changed. The very structure of scientific research in any capitalist country shows the contrary. The greatest amounts of money and time are spent in applying scientific research to war. Heavy industry, light industry come next, then medicine and agriculture. Sociology and psychology receive practically nothing. This cannot fail to react on pure science."[8] The only country in which the dominant regime encourages and supports science and technology wholeheartedly is Soviet Russia.

Technology and capitalism are in conflict with each other not only because the latter is a scarcity economy. The power age decreases capital investment and labor in relation to the amount produced. It thereby lowers the effective demand and restricts the market both for capital and consumption goods. The mechanization of industry renders fixed capital charges high in comparison with labor cost. The pressure of unused capacity on profits increases as capital investment rises and labor cost falls. Consequently, a recession of business not only causes unemployment, decreases purchasing power, and deflates prices, but also often wrecks capital structure. It thereby accentuates economic instability and exacerbates the violence of the business cycle.

Capitalism can utilize science, invention, and technology to pro-

[8] J. D. Bernal, "If Industry Gave Science a Chance, " *Harper's Magazine*, February 1935. Reprinted as a chapter in a symposium by English scientists entitled *The Frustration of Science*, New York, 1935, with a Foreword by Frederick Soddy.

See also Julian Huxley, *Science and Social Needs*, New York, 1935. Huxley demonstrated that the effect of the existing social order on science is frustration because those in control of industry are interested in science only to the extent that it promises immediate profits.

682

mote profits up to a certain point. Beyond that point they become disruptive forces within the capitalist system. Attempts are made to restrain these forces by production control. This is a first step toward planning under capitalism. Such control increases unemployment and decreases purchasing power. It thereby defeats its own end and checks any incipient tendency towards capitalist planning.

The capitalists may nevertheless be forced to adopt a certain measure of planning in order to prolong the life of the profit system. Such planning would include concerted control of output, price regulation, a ruthless suppression of all proletarian movements, and a reduction of all salary and wage scales to a bare subsistence minimum. These measures were already foreshadowed or partly in force in the countries where fascism prevailed, such as Italy and Germany. They may safeguard for a time a dwindling rate of profits. If the capitalists fail to attain a sufficient unity of action to put these measures into effect, capitalism may collapse before they have squeezed from the dying system the last vestige of profits.

Even this degree of planning would not be genuine economic planning. Capitalist planning is directed toward the maintenance of a scarcity economy in the interest of the monopolists of land and of capital. Genuine economic planning is directed toward the creation of an economy of abundance in the interest of mankind.

Chapter XXXIX

The Contradictions of Capitalism

BEFORE proceeding with the description of a social order planned in the interest of the whole of mankind and not only of a privileged class it may be well to state the contradictions of capitalism. The latter has been the dominant economic system in modern times. The only serious breaches in this system up to the time of the present writing have been the Russian revolution of 1917 and the Chinese revolution of 1949. The following capitalist contradictions are so obvious and so outstanding that a summary statement of them should be sufficient.[1]

The greatest economic contrast in the world, caused by the private monopoly of land and of capital, is between riches and poverty. On the one hand is the extravagant and ostentatious luxuriousness not only of the millionaires but of the wealthy class in general. On the other hand is the low standard of living not only of the proletariat but of a large part of the middle class as well. Nowhere is the difference so great as in the United States, because this is the richest of all countries.

This contrast is manifested in its extreme form in the most depressed groups. Among them are the unskilled laborers, many of the factory and mine workers, agricultural and other seasonal laborers, the tenant farmers and sharecroppers, the "poor white trash" and Negroes of the southern state, and the homeless vagrants the country over. The standard of living of these groups approximates that of the coolies of China and the outcastes and untouchables of India. At a time of depression a large part of the working population is forced down to this lowest of all human levels. Pauper slavery takes the place of much of the wage slavery. These are the realities which lie back of statistics of wealth and income, of production and distribution.

In the United States and Occidental countries in general this

[1] I have described these contradictions at length and in detail in my *Farewell to Poverty*, New York, 1935, *passim*.

684

greatest of all contrasts is accentuated by the contradictions which proliferate under capitalism. Many of them may now be summarized. The first seven are the more general in their character:

1. Capitalism assures economic security to no one, not even to the capitalists themselves, thereby failing to fulfil the first requisite of any economic system.

2. Capitalism subordinates the two primary economic processes, namely, production and distribution, to the private ownership of wealth and accumulation of profits. It thereby frustrates the fundamental ends of any economic system by preventing the major part of potential production and causing excessive disparity in the distribution of what little is produced.

3. Capitalism cannot master its internal complexities and rigidities sufficiently to take full advantage of technology and create new industries to supply new wants as rapidly as these wants manifest themselves.

4. Inasmuch as abundant production destroys scarcity and therefore profits, capitalism stimulates production so long as it is profitable, namely, as the products are vendible, and then checks it.

5. Capitalism promotes accurate bookkeeping and rationalizes industry and agriculture within its own narrow limitations as a scarcity economy. At the same time it prevents social accounting and planning, thereby maintaining anarchy in the economic world.

6. Production and consumption are antagonized so that the citizen as producer is arrayed against himself as consumer, and vice versa. As producer he seeks high income, as consumer he desires low prices.

7. It is generally true of capitalism that prosperity brings depression, expansion leads to contraction, inflation gives rise to deflation, thereby creating a chronic state of instability which causes much waste and hampers consistent progress to higher levels of production and of distribution.

Capitalism is ambivalent in that it contains both competitive and monopolistic tendencies. These opposing tendencies give rise to the five contradictions which follow:

MONOPOLY VERSUS FREE COMPETITION

8. Capitalist "freedom," namely, free private enterprise, does not promote the freedom, or, in the long run, the well-being of most individuals.

9. Free competition between individuals is prevented by private property in and the inheritance of land and capital which destroy equality of opportunity, and which also decrease greatly the efficiency of management.

685

10. "Pure" competition, even in its capitalist sense, is deranged and limited by the monopolistic features which inevitably creep into capitalism because of its ambivalent character.

11. Corporate organization and management deprive many small capitalists of the control and often of the ownership of their capital, and thereby proletarize them.

12. Though capitalism is international in theory and business enterprise is worldwide, capitalists utilize nationalism to secure monopolies and discriminatory privileges, thereby giving rise to international warfare.

Many detailed contradictions arise out of the general contradictions. Some of them are related to the financial structure of capitalism and give rise to a complicated series of rigidities and inconsistencies:

CONTRADICTIONS IN THE FINANCIAL STRUCTURE OF CAPITALISM

13. Withdrawal of profits by capitalists reduces buying power and disturbs market relations, because effective demand cannot absorb actual or potential supply.

14. Inasmuch as the price level must average higher than the cost of production, business enterprise does not promptly release as much purchasing power as the distribution of its products requires.

15. Saving and investment expand capital goods industries until a plethora is attained and depression ensues.

16. Wide fluctuations in the capital goods and durable commodities industries accentuate the business cycle.

17. The accumulation of capital promotes and impedes production simultaneously or in rapid succession.

18. Capital accumulation leading to foreign investments stimulates imports in payment of interest and principal without creating adequate purchasing power to absorb these imports, thus putting additional pressure of supply on the domestic market.

19. Falling prices discourage investment of capital when most needed during depression.

20. Rising prices encourage investment of capital when least needed during prosperity.

21. Debt increases more rapidly than capital and purchasing power, and hampers production and accentuates maldistribution.

22. Long-term debts make prices more rigid when they should fall, because debt service is very inflexible compared with other forms of income.

23. Capitalism encourages taxation which can be passed on to

686

the consumer, such as import, sales, and excise taxes, thereby decreasing purchasing power. It opposes heavy taxes on the higher income brackets and sharply graduated inheritance levies which would check the accumulation of surplus capital. Even if the latter taxes were imposed, the revenue therefrom would force the government into business, thus competing with private enterprise. It would thereby create the contradiction of semi-collectivism.

24. Capitalism accentuates depressions by monopolistic price-fixing, enforcing contractual debts, tariffs, lowering the fiscal revenue, etc.

25. While thrift as a protection for the future is forced upon the individual by the economic insecurity of capitalism, saving often becomes a social menace more than a productive factor by causing a glut of monetary capital which clogs the wheels of business enterprise.

The inability of capitalism to make a full and consistent use of science, invention, and technology not only creates additional contradictions but accentuates some of the contradictions in its financial structure, especially with respect to inadequate purchasing power:

CAPITALISM VERSUS SCIENCE, INVENTION, AND TECHNOLOGY

26. Capitalism utilizes science, invention, and technology to promote profits, but otherwise frustrates them by neglect or suppression.

27. Capitalism gives rise to technological unemployment, but opposes shorter hours and distribution of work because it fears increased labor costs.

28. Reduction of wages in order to diminish labor cost increases capital cost by decreasing purchasing power which in turn reduces sales and output, namely, large-scale production.

29. The power age decreases capital investment and labor in proportion to the amount produced, thereby lowering the effective demand. To that extent the market becomes more restricted for both capital and consumption goods.

30. Mechanization of industry renders fixed capital charges high in comparison with labor cost. Recession of business not only causes unemployment, decreases purchasing power, and deflates prices, but also often wrecks capital structure. Instability is thereby accentuated and the violence of the business cycle exacerbated.

31. Production control, the first step toward planning under capitalism, by increasing unemployment decreases purchasing power. It thereby defeats its own end, and any general tendency toward capitalist planning is checked.

The final contradictions arise out of the decline of capitalism and the rise of a hybrid semi-collectivism:

THE FINAL CONTRADICTIONS OF CAPITALISM
AND SEMI-COLLECTIVISM

32. The only alternatives are stabilization at a depression level, namely, an extreme form of a scarcity economy; or the rapid disintegration and complete disruption of the capitalist system. A continuous and permanent prosperity, namely, an economy of abundance, is inherently impossible under and diametrically opposed to capitalism. A temporary period of stabilization at the depression level, as under fascism, may intervene before the final collapse of capitalism.

33. Having passed through its early mercantile stage, and reached its apogee during its period of industrial expansion since 1800 A.D., capitalism is now passing into its final monopolistic stage of finance capitalism. The proletarized masses are fast becoming more or less equally divided between the wage-earners, paid on the basis of a bare subsistence minimum; and the starving unemployed or paupers, kept alive if at all on the meager doles of public and private relief, in order to avert the danger of a hungry mob which might precipitate a revolution. A situation so anomalous cannot endure indefinitely. The final contradiction of capitalism, which curtails its efficiency as a productive and distributive system by more than half, can be resolved only under an economic order which will release the productive forces fully and will apportion work and distribute income to the entire population.

34. In a hybrid capitalist-collectivist state, which may serve as a transitional stage, capital accumulation would instigate the capitalists to overthrow the semi-socialized state. The abolition of private inheritance, though in accord with the capitalist ideal of individual competition, would destroy much of the incentive to private business enterprise and would soon make the state the heir of capitalism. The lack of equilibrium arising out of this imbalance would soon result either in throwing society back into the contradictions of capitalism from which it is trying to extricate itself, or in pushing it forward to a thoroughgoing collectivization. This would replace the chronic and anarchic disorder of capitalism with the integration and harmony of a self-consistent socialized system.

Chapter XL

A Social Economy—Planning

SCIENCE has given rise to a technology by which it can be applied. Reciprocal action is ever operative between science and the technology which is its applied aspect. Physical technology is already highly developed. Social technology scarcely exists even in a rudimentary form. This is partly due to the fact that social science itself cannot attain a high development under the present order which is mainly a state of anarchy. It is also because a social technology can function hardly at all under capitalism because it requires a social order in which to function.

The so-called science of economics has been permeated almost entirely by the ideology of capitalism.[1] The still more nebulous science of politics has been dominated by the political correlative of capitalism. Sociology has been largely a study of reforms within the framework of the capitalist system. Some of the sociologists have applied the term social technology inaccurately to a program of remedial and preventive measures, which embraces only a small portion of the life of society.

A good deal of science has arisen out of the pragmatic impulse to attain useful ends, and has eventually been applied. Between the initial impulse and the ultimate application there should be a period of unbiased and objective study and research during which what may be termed pure science can prevail. Otherwise the end sought is likely to influence the conclusions reached, which will in turn vitiate

[1] An American economist has characterized well the meaninglessness of much of this pseudo-science: "The seeming clarification of price theory has tended to introduce into the language of economic speculation a pretentious but desiccated mumbo-jumbo of unimportant maxims which it may masquerade as profound only to those not able to see through the pale cast of elementary mathematics with which it is sicklied over. We are left with a monument of babble to social science Ignorabimus. . . . There can no more be a science of bookkeeping than there can be a science of etiquette." (Robert A. Brady, *American Economic Review*, June 1951, p. **436.**)

their application. Scientists should always guard themselves against being influenced unduly by whatever social system they happen to live and work under.

Science is the same everywhere and for all human beings in so far as it is genuine, namely, an accurate description of observable phenomena. The ideology of individual scientists varies according to their inherent traits and social environment. These factors enhance or diminish the value of their scientific work, as the case may be. Science as an organon of verified data, interpreted and explained so far as feasible, goes on from generation to generation independent of, or, at any rate, superior to, the vagaries of the individual scientists who contribute to it.

In the physical sciences it is comparatively easy to maintain an objective and impersonal attitude. Physics, astronomy, mathematics, etc., have no obvious and little direct bearing upon the fortunes of mankind. It is much more difficult to retain an impersonal attitude in the social sciences. The anthropocentric and egocentric point of view is likely to intrude and to bias the attitude of the social scientist. The ideology of the dominant system is almost certain to color his thinking in some degree.

The difficulty of developing a pure social science is the initial obstacle in the way of the development of a social technology. A much more serious obstacle at present is the fact that capitalism cannot utilize a social technology. Capitalist production is by its very nature unplanned. The distribution of wealth is determined largely by monopolistic privileges and powers which take no cognizance of social interests. Consumption can be rationalized only to a slight extent because the vast majority of the consumers are at the mercy of the unplanned production and great disparity in the distribution of wealth imposed upon them by capitalism. Slightly more planning may be present in the political organization. As the political is the reflection and correlative of the economic organization, it can have little social value and significance under capitalism.

The term planning is often used, but with much variation in its meaning. During the depression which commenced in 1929 many persons turned toward Soviet Russia in the hope that planning might be the magic method which would drive away the deadly pall. Even a part of the business world, puzzled by the fact that Russia had not suffered from a depression, directed its myopic vision in that direction with the hazy notion that some form of planning adapted to capitalism might bring back prosperity and profits. These gentry do not realize that genuine economic and political planning is impossible except under social control and for the social interest. An economic system dominated by private enterprise and competition or capitalist

690

monopoly in which the vast mass of the people is exploited by a small privileged class lacks social control and does not function in the social interest.

A government is planned in the sense that it is based upon laws and usually upon a constitution. It is national in its jurisdiction. It performs a few economic and social functions as well as its immediate political functions. But capitalism narrowly limits the functions of government and corrupts and undermines its efficiency in the performance of these functions. Furthermore, capitalism renders government incapable of genuine social and economic planning because it wishes private business enterprise to reign unchecked and supreme.

The only economic and social planning of any practical significance up to date has been in Russia. It has become a commonplace to say that the Soviet system is a planned economy. The bolshevists reiterate it on every possible occasion and point the finger of scorn at capitalism as an unplanned economy. All theories of a socialized system are based upon the concept of social planning. These considerations lend practical as well as theoretical importance to the question as to what extent and in what ways the Soviet system is already a planned economy.

Economic planning consists of at least two parts. The first is the planning of the current economy to provide the supply of goods day by day for immediate consumption. The second is the planning of the capital equipment not only to replace the worn-out or obsolete producers' goods but also to expand or diminish the equipment in accordance with changes in population or in standard of living.[2]

It is the second phase of planning to which reference has almost invariably been made in the descriptions of Soviet planning both by bolshevists and others. The low order of economic development in Russia has forced the bolshevists to concentrate attention upon capital construction. They have neglected the planning of the current economy perhaps more than has been required by the need for building up the new system. As the latter approaches its completion, the former can be developed to the point where it will furnish a high standard of living and ample leisure to the whole of a classless population. Out of this development is arising a social technology not only in the economic sphere but in the cultural realm as well which renders possible a functional organization of society in all its aspects.

Economic and social planning is not business, capitalist, or class planning. Corporate and monopoly capitalism has destroyed *laissez-faire,* competition and small private enterprise in large part. Corporate

[2] See Maurice Parmelee, *Farewell to Poverty,* New York, 1935; Chap. XXIV, "Planned Production," from which some of this chapter is paraphrased and brought up to date.

capitalism can plan business more extensively than petty enterprise and can prepare the way in a measure for genuine planning.

It is sometimes contended that planning should be "strategic," that is to say, partial, at any rate for a time. It is argued that if land and natural resources, the capital goods industries, transportation, in other words, all the "key" industries, are socialized and planned, other economic activities, such as the consumption goods industries, can be safely left in private hands. Some persons believe that the business incentive to make profits therein contained is beneficial to society. A partial, strategic planning immediately creates the contradiction of semi-collectivism. This contradiction compels either a more or less rapid advance to a complete and all-inclusive planned order, or retreat to capitalism and the disorder of anarchy.

Under capitalism the precise measurement of many economic and other social phenomena is difficult or impossible. Among them are prices, wages, costs, productive capacity, money, value, supply, demand, volume of trade, etc. This is largely due to the mutability and instability which characterize these erratic phenomena. Most of them are at best vague and uncertain as quantities, and in some cases also as concepts. It is also due in part to the difficulty of securing reliable and adequate data under a regime of private enterprise which operates in part under a cloak of secrecy.

Under a socialized system, science and technology will not be neglected, frustrated, or suppressed as they often are under capitalism. Scientific discoveries and new inventions will be fully applied in order to raise the standard of living, lengthen the span of human life, and diminish toil. The widespread utilization of science and technology will encourage more precise and accurate modes of thinking and ways of acting which will almost spontaneously eliminate religion and magic.

A planned society requires a good deal of statistical and other data for its successful operation. But certain kinds of statistics now much used will have little if any utility. Among them are statistics of price, cost of living, currency, banking, etc., which reflect conditions which will in large part disappear. A self-consistent planned society will in many respects be simpler and easier to direct than the contradictory and chaotic society of capitalism. After the initial problems are solved and a social technology devised its operation will become largely automatic.

The mechanical and physical technology to produce an abundance of commodities for the whole of mankind is already available. Its implications are helpful for developing a social technology which will furnish an efficient method of distribution. This social technology will also include a political organization correlated with the economic system, appropriate educational institutions, and the other essential features of a socialized system. North America is an admirable scene for the new system. It possesses the richest natural resources of any continent. The United States and Canada have the most highly developed technical equipment in the world. The new system can be introduced with the least possible degree of economic dislocation and social disorder. The experience of Soviet Russia furnishes numerous valuable suggestions to render this doubly certain.

Modern capitalism was rendered possible by the enormous increase in the volume of production due to technology, which was in turn due to science. The division of labor was prevalent as far back as paleolithic time. Even prior to the invention of the steam engine standardized mass production on a small scale had existed at certain times and places where the factory system had arisen. Capitalism in its later stages is in part the spurious and unintended offspring of science and technology. Toward these parents it has often displayed an unfilial attitude by hampering and frustrating them. Science and technology for the first time received full recognition and unrestricted application in Soviet Russia where science, and not theology or metaphysics, furnishes the ideology of the Soviet commonwealth.

The United States has many advantages over Soviet Russia in its higher technical development, skilled working population, and greater natural resources. The capitalist system alone stands in the way of a planned economy at a much higher level of production than has ever existed. In its fallacious and misleading study of productive capacity the Brookings Institution greatly under-estimated potential productive capacity. It did so because it assumed all the limitations of capitalism in which vendibility, and not use and serviceability, is the prime mover to production. On the other hand, by concluding that American production could have been 19 per cent greater in 1929, it over-estimated capitalist capacity to produce.[3] Within its own limitations, capitalism could have produced no more than it did. It has again produced as much and more, but under the stimulus of war and its aftermath.

Under capitalism much of the capital equipment is used only a part of the time. In many cases it would not be profitable to introduce the best technical methods. Under a socialized and planned system the capital equipment would usually be operated at full capacity. Consequently, the cost of investment in automatic and semi-automatic plants and processes would be small in relation to the capacity output. Under capitalism human labor is relatively cheap. No humanitarian

[3] E. G. Nourse and Associates, *America's Capacity to Produce*, Brookings Institution, Washington, 1934.

693

or cultural considerations restrain its masters, the capitalists and profiteers, from driving labor to the utmost limit of endurance whenever that is the most profitable mode of production for the masters. Only collective action by labor has served as a minor restraint. Under a socialized system no one can profit from the exploitation of labor. There is every incentive to substitute machinery and automatic processes for labor, thereby increasing human leisure and the cultural consequences which flow therefrom.

Under capitalism many inventions and patents have been suppressed for financial reasons. So long as a capitalist can make more profits with cheap labor and a restricted production, he will try to purchase the patent and suppress the invention which renders possible the production of a larger quantity with less labor. Under a socialized system the decisive question with regard to every invention is whether it will save labor in the long run. If so, it is applied at once. If not, it is postponed until such time as when its application will save more labor than it costs.

Under a planned economy, factories and other productive plants are located in the best possible positions with respect to sources of raw materials, supply of power, transportation facilities, and regions of distribution and consumption. The locating of these plants is at present influenced by national, political, military, "national defense," financial, competitive, monopolistic, "cheap" labor, and other capitalist and pseudo-economic considerations which are irrelevant from a technical and economic point of view.

The fate of agriculture under a regime of private enterprise is amply demonstrated in the United States. The pioneers who carved their homes out of the wilderness destroyed a vast amount of natural resources. They razed the forests to the ground in an indiscriminate and wholesale fashion. As a result, the fertile soil was washed away from large areas of land into the silt-filled rivers. Many impoverished families are trying to wrest a miserable livelihood from the worn-out soil when an abundance of fertile land still remains to supply adequate food for the nation's population. The government is trying to rebuild the forests and to check soil erosion. Under a planned economy the most fertile land would be used for the present and the submarginal land would be reserved for gradual improvement and for future use if the population increases sufficiently to demand it.

The agricultural output could be greatly increased by concentrating the crops on the most fertile soils; by applying power and large-scale mechanical production to staple goods, such as cotton, wheat, corn, rye, oats, barley, rice, etc.; and by utilizing fully the discoveries of agrobiology. As an agrobiologist has said, "the ruthless application to the best lands" in the United States of the best available

694

agricultural methods "would throw four-fifths or more of our farm lands out of use and expel four-fifths of our farm population from the open country."[4] Although this is technically feasible at once, it is economically and politically impossible and would be a great disaster under capitalism. The superfluous 80 per cent of the farmers would be deprived of their present inadequate means of subsistence and would have no other means available. Capitalist industry already has a large reserve of surplus unemployed labor. The millions of dispossessed farmers would perforce be added to the already enormous and constantly increasing (except in time of war or of a fleeting period of peace-time prosperity) class of the starvation and pauper unemployed. There is no solution for this problem under capitalism and no possibility of planning, partly because the planning of one branch of the economic system must be correlated with the planning of the whole.

The principles of genetics have already been applied to improve the breeds of cattle, hogs, sheep, etc. The average milch cow produces much more milk than formerly. Under a planned economy these principles could be applied far more effectively and completely. The live-stock industry, like all branches of agriculture and industry, would be under the most competent scientific direction, whereas much of it at present is in the hands of farmers who have little or no scientific knowledge.

Capitalism reduces the economic system in large part to a destructive state of warfare instead of a constructive system of production. This is inevitable because of the diametrically opposed interests of the exploiters—the monopolists of land and capital, and the exploited —the wage and pauper slaves who are exploited both as laborers and as consumers. Both sides in this class struggle indulge in sabotage. The capitalists often restrict production in order to increase their profits by creating an artificial scarcity. The workers often lower the efficiency of their labor consciously or unconsciously because they know they are working in the interest of the small class of employers and not in their own interest and for the community as a whole. Furthermore, they know that efficiency will diminish the number of jobs and help to bring themselves to unemployment and destitution. Capitalism is by its very nature a contradictory system filled with conflicting interests and torn by strife.

When judged in relation to the means of production and of dis-

[4] O. W. Willcox, *Reshaping Agriculture*, New York, 1934.
This writer is a competent agrobiologist, but he displays much ignorance of economics. This is illustrated by his contradictory statement that if the new principles of agrobiology were applied, the ideals of socialism could be attained without losing the incentive of capitalism.

695

tribution at its disposal, capitalism is by far the most inefficient economic system which has ever existed. Not even the primitive economies fell so far short of producing and distributing what was then possible. Capitalism produces only a small fraction, not more than a fourth or a fifth or even less, of what could now be readily produced with the available productive forces and with much less human toil. It destroys part of what is produced. It distributes what little survives so unevenly that much of it does not reach the people who need it most, but goes to a privileged few who need it least. When measured in terms of use, serviceability, and human welfare, many of these products are wasted. No other system has fallen so far short of what it could accomplish with the means of production and distribution available to it in its own time and place. Science and technology have furnished capitalism the opportunity to become preeminent. Its inherent contradictions have prevented it from attaining this exalted rank.

The much-vaunted competition of capitalism also gives rise to much waste. Competition is a form of warfare among the capitalists themselves. It is paid for in the end by the community at large. Even in the monopolistic industries in which the cost of production and of service is reduced to the minimum, the public does not necessarily benefit from these economies. The excessive capitalization and the high rates of profit invariably give rise to abnormally high prices. Whether competition or monopoly prevails under capitalism, productive efficiency, use value, serviceability, and human welfare are not and cannot be the prime objectives.

Capitalism has already made some use of science and technology. It does so whenever profits can be gained thereby. Otherwise it neglects or suppresses discoveries and inventions or applies them much less than is technically feasible. In the long run, capitalism is the mortal foe of science and technology because they promote abundance whereas it depends for its existence upon scarcity.

Capitalism has used the conveyor belt, straight-line processes in manufacturing, high-speed steel, the internal-combustion engine, the destructive distillation of coal, turbine prime movers, the high-power transmission of electricity, the photo-electric cell, various kinds of farm as well as factory machinery, a good many household electrical devices, etc. But its utilization of science and technology is narrowly limited by its productive capacity which in turn is limited by the relatively small amount of purchasing power which it releases. And yet the possibilities for the expansion of science and technology are almost unlimited.

The ordinary sources of power are as yet little exploited. Only a small part of the potential water power has been harnessed. The

696

coal supply should last for several thousand years. There is a large reserve of low-grade coal which it is not profitable to mine at present. Coal can be converted into liquid fuel by several processes, some of which are already being used in Europe. There are extensive deposits of shale and oil sands from which gasoline can be obtained when the oil wells are exhausted.

There are sources of power which have hardly been touched as yet. Giant windmills have been designed to pump water into huge reservoirs which could be used to operate turbines and thereby generate electricity. Whether or not the tides can be used extensively as a source of power is still debatable. Volcanic heat is already being used in Italy, and this use may be capable of expansion. There are other sources of heat inside the earth which may eventually be drawn upon. If all the non-recurrent sources of energy become exhausted and water power proves to be inadequate, alcohol and other hydrocarbons can be manufactured synthetically from all vegetable growths.

The sun as a direct source of energy has hardly been used at all. It is an inexhaustible source whose rays can be harnessed fairly readily. Photo-electric cells generate electricity from the sunshine. Every square foot of sunlight carries about 200 watts of energy. Batteries of photo-electric cells placed on top of buildings and in other exposed places can gather this energy.

Most portentous of all is the atomic energy the existence of which science has revealed and has made technically applicable. It is inexhaustible and unlimited in quantity and available in most parts of the world. It has at first been used for wholesale human slaughter and the widespread destruction of wealth. With more scientific research it can readily be made applicable to most forms of production. By lowering considerably or greatly the cost of production, including the cost of labor by substituting inorganic energy for human labor, it will hasten the equilibration of these costs the world over, as well as the standard of living at a higher level. Such an equilibration will render more feasible the realization of the worldwide social-economic system which is contemplated in this book.

The electrification of industry has had far-reaching results. The electric motor, large and small, has taken the place of the steam engine to a large extent. By equipping each machine with its own motor the complicated system of belts and pulleys has been abolished from the factories in the main. Many tasks formerly done by hand are now performed by small motors. Apart from and in addition to the mechanization of industry, many processes have been electrified. For example, electrical spot welding is taking the place of riveting in many industries. The automatic factory is coming into existence in which all processes will be mechanized and will be controlled by electrical devices. Before long agriculture also will be mechanized and electrified to a considerable extent.

The new science and technology of electronics is already having a marked effect upon productive processes. The electron is a sub-atomic unit which is constantly moving at great speed. Each atom contains one or more electrons. There are many electrons which have broken away from atoms or have never united in an atom and are free and at large in the universe. Electrons can be directed and controlled to a certain extent and thus compelled to perform useful services. They are already being used in ultra-speed photography, talking motion pictures, radio, television, the electric eye, the cathode ray, etc. The electron tubes and other electronic devices can duplicate the organic functions of seeing, hearing, smelling, tasting, and feeling. Their sensitivity is often greater than that of the human senses. A photo-electric cell or electric eye can "see" by ultra-violet or infra-red light, both of which are invisible to the human eye. Radio devices can detect sounds which the human ear cannot hear. These electronic devices furnish an unremitting automatic control for non-electrical as well as electrical processes.

Science now stands on the threshold of discoveries which will render possible even greater technological changes. Hitherto mankind has used in the main materials furnished by nature. Before long it will become increasingly possible to produce materials which will possess the traits of durability, flexibility, lightness, etc., required for industrial processes. The lighter metals, such as aluminum and magnesium and their alloys, are continually taking the place of the heavier metals. Iron and steel are being used less for structural purposes, though retained for tools and working surfaces. The study of crystalline structure is resulting in new kinds of fine metal in which the crystals will be arranged so as to give the greatest strength in the desired direction. Changes are also coming in the use and in some cases in the composition of stone, bricks, cement, pottery, glass, and other stony materials. The supply of new light materials will revolutionize the principles of architectural construction.

Similar changes are taking place in the materials for clothing. Artificial silk made from wood already exists. Artificial wool and synthetic silk are adumbrated. It should soon be possible to produce a light, porous texture from cellulose materials by molding and pressing which would obviate spinning, weaving, and sewing. The cost of production should be so small that laundering and repeated use would be superfluous.

These are but a few suggestions of what is coming if mankind can free itself from the bondage of capitalism. As an English scientist has said: "The present time marks the beginning of a transition from

698

the use of materials extracted out of nature to materials constructed by men. If science can be used to its full capacity, the former will become relatively less and less important. Man has not obtained full control over Nature until he can produce materials with the properties he desires instead of doing the best he can with the materials that are already there." [5]

The prerequisites for a planned economy are now obvious. It cannot come into existence so long as the monopolies of land and of capital, or vested interests and special privileges of any sort, survive. While these monopolies persist, any attempt at planning is certain to be perverted in the interest of the monopolists and will result eventually in a more drastic exploitation of their victims. Technical difficulties will at once arise in the form of the lack of purchasing power, the frustration of science and technology, the inefficiency of public administration under a regime of private enterprise, the insufficiency of authority in the hands of those who are trying to plan an economy on a nation-wide, continental, or worldwide scale.

In view of these considerations all talk of planning under capitalism is not only futile but even mischievous. A planned economy is incompatible with and impossible under capitalism. Not until the last vestiges of capitalism have been swept away can planning on a comprehensive scale commence. In Soviet Russia the first five-year plan did not commence until the semi-capitalist New Economic Policy was terminated, and the second five-year plan did not commence until the NEP had been liquidated. Not until all political power is vested in the people can planning be undertaken with safety. Pending the liquidation of the class of exploiters this power must be held by the proletariat in trust for the coming classless society.

Practically all the literature of planning, outside of Soviet Russia, has been produced by engineers who have little or no comprehension of economic problems and by economists and sociologists whose vision is limited and in part blinded by capitalist concepts. Most of this literature can be discarded and ignored as valueless so far as genuine social and economic planning is concerned. It is worse than useless because it confuses the issues and obfuscates the truth.

Economic planning consists of two main parts. The planning of the current economy provides the supply of goods day by day for immediate consumption. The planning of the capital equipment not

[5] J. D. Bernal, "If Industry Gave Science a Chance," in *Harper's Magazine*, New York, February 1935, p. 259.

Bernal was careful to point out that these changes are impossible under the present economic system: "Introduced in our present economic era, such inventions would be an unmitigated disaster. Millions of people would be thrown out of work. Whole countries would be devastated. An orgy of speculative finance would certainly follow."

only replaces the worn-out or obsolete producers' goods but also expands or diminishes the equipment in accordance with changes in population or in the standard of living.

The second phase of planning has exceptional importance at the inception of a planned economy. In Soviet Russia the low order of economic development inherited from the Tsarist regime by the bolshevists forced them to concentrate almost exclusive attention upon capital construction during the first five-year plan. They neglected the planning of the current economy perhaps more than was required by the need for building up the new system. After several five-year plans they began to devote more attention to the current economy by producing more consumption goods. Neglect of the current economy is unnecessary in the United States and the other highly industrialized nations where the capital equipment already is adequate for the maintenance of a relatively high standard of living for the whole population.

In a socialized system whatever is needed for the replacement and expansion of the capital equipment is provided for in the plan of production and is withdrawn in terms of raw materials, finished goods, and services before distribution takes place. This renders saving out of individual and group incomes unnecessary and eliminates this factor for confusion from the process of distribution. The outgo of consumption goods is devoted in the first instance to provide an adequate subsistence for everyone. The surplus over and above this subsistence minimum can be distributed equally, or differentially according to a social standard of individual productivity. The basis for the distribution of this surplus, whether equal or differential, may vary according to the stage of development attained by the socialized system. It is in part a problem for social technology to solve in the light of its bearing upon the basic processes of production. In the last analysis it is a question of policy to be decided by a democratic society through its political mechanism.

Standardization is much more feasible under a planned economy. Under capitalism new forms and models are often produced with little or no improvement solely for the purpose of stimulating sales and thereby increasing profits. This motive disappears entirely in a socialized system, so that this waste can be eliminated. Standardization need not be applied completely or at all to commodities where there is consumers' choice. If esthetic tastes and individual preferences play an important part, as many forms can be produced as are demanded by the public. Standardization applies more particularly to the impersonal objects where efficiency alone is important. Clothing, objects of adornment, and the like, which have an intimate personal significance, can be produced in a variety of forms and styles.

700

The reform of the calendar can be accomplished more readily under a planned economy than under capitalism in which there are many divergent and conflicting interests. This is one of the many instances in which a logical and orderly procedure can take the place of a traditional and often disorderly procedure. The bolshevists have been experimenting with the calendar in Soviet Russia and have already tried several forms of it. Their experience is of great value for the eventual worldwide reform of the calendar. Its practical significance for a planned economy is too obvious to require comment. A logical division of time is the first requisite of planning. It is of special importance for the organization of work.

The purpose of economic planning is to achieve capacity operation on the basis of a balanced load so as to assure a steady and adequate flow of goods to the consumers. In other words, the amount to be produced during a specified period of time—one year, two years, etc., as the case may be—will be determined beforehand. Then the machinery of production will be set in motion to produce this quantity at a certain rate of speed. In order to avoid waste of capital goods, the machinery will be operated so far as possible at capacity. Unlike capitalism which has a large equipment of capital goods standing idle a good deal of the time, a planned economy will have just enough to produce the requisite output, with a small reserve for emergency needs. In like fashion, capitalism often has a large surplus of consumers' goods which cannot be distributed because inadequate purchasing power has been alloted to the masses of the population, in spite of the fact that they are in urgent need of these goods which remain unused in idle inventories and warehouses.

The kinds of goods and the quantities to be produced will be determined almost entirely by consumers' demand and choice. This will be registered more precisely than at present. Under capitalism it is impossible to ascertain how much has been produced and consumed of many kinds of goods. Each private enterprise is interested primarily in producing to sell and not to satisfy human wants. It often keeps no accurate record of how much it has produced. This is particularly true of farms, small enterprises in general, and industries which have not been highly mechanized and automatized. Consequently, the government or private investigators find it difficult to ascertain how much has actually been produced.

In a planned economy an accurate record of production can easily be maintained because the whole productive system will be under one management. The system of distribution by means of purchasing certificates will readily, and in the main automatically, register the amount consumed. The records of production and of consumption will no longer be kept in terms of a measure of value so unstable and

701

fluctuating as existing monetary systems. Under capitalism the value of money is subject to the supply of and demand for the precious metals, the fiscal policies of governments, the balance of trade between nations, and other more or less incalculable factors. In a planned economy the records for most goods will be of the goods themselves. For a few goods and for services the records will be in terms of a new medium of distribution which will measure the actual cost of production instead of vendibility in a capitalist market. The symbol required in return for goods distributed according to individual choice will represent a definite quantity of something readily measurable and immutable, such as a unit of energy, or relatively unchangeable, such as labor. Whenever a standard of value is needed this symbol can be used. The economic value of goods will vary only as their cost of production decreases because technology, unhampered by capitalism and its financial structure, is becoming more efficient.

The plan of production for the period of the balanced load will take into consideration anticipated changes in population. Suitable adjustments will be made to this demotic factor for change.

The plan of production will also be influenced by the policy of conservation of non-renewable raw materials and natural resources. Even though substitutes are being found or manufactured for many of these raw materials, it is wise to conserve the original supply as long as possible. Bassett Jones has said that the production of non-renewable raw materials tends to become asymptotic to zero. That is to say, the production always approaches zero without attaining it. A conservation policy can postpone more or less indefinitely the attainment of zero. Jones also asserted that the production of renewable raw materials tends to become asymptotic to the maximum. This may be true in theory. In a planned economy no more will be produced of any kind of commodity than can be consumed. In many cases this will be far less than could be produced. He contended that the production of the mixed type of goods, *i.e.,* the many kinds that are manufactured from both non-renewable and renewable materials, tends to become asymptotic to a quantity between zero and the maximum which can be attained.[6] This is probably true, but applies also in practice to many of the renewable raw materials.

The plan of production will provide for the replacement of worn-out capital goods. The rate of depreciation can be calculated much more accurately than at present. Under capitalism there is great uncertainty as to how much capital equipment will be needed and used. If a period of prosperity manifests itself, production increases and the capital equipment is used to a greater degree. If a period of depression

[6] Bassett Jones, *Debt and Production*, New York, 1933.

702

puts in its appearance, the capital equipment is much less used but may deteriorate from disuse to an indeterminate extent. None of these conditions can be foreseen. In a planned economy the volume of production and consequent wear and tear on the capital equipment during the period of the balanced load can be foretold to a nicety in most cases. The erratic and often violent fluctuations in production and consumption, use and disuse, which are characteristic of and inherent in capitalism, will no longer disturb the steady and harmonious operation of the productive mechanism.

Planning for the introduction of improved equipment and methods is somewhat more complicated. On the one hand must be considered to what extent the increase in production therefrom is desirable. On the other hand must be considered to what extent it saves labor. If an increased production is not important, and the labor involved in producing the new improved equipment would not be saved in producing the subsequent consumers' goods for some time to come, it may be preferable to prolong the use of the old equipment for a time. If increased production is highly desirable, and the labor expended in manufacturing the new equipment is soon saved, the new equipment should be introduced at once.

Planning for increased production of consumers' goods in proportion to the population is the most complicated of all. Here it is a question of choice between more goods with more work and more leisure with less work. As soon as a high standard of living for the entire population is attained under a planned economy, it becomes much less important to produce an increased volume of goods per inhabitant. It then devolves upon the citizens of the socialized system to decide whether or not they wish to sacrifice more time and toil in order to have more goods to consume. This is not a technical question which can be decided by the planning board. It is a question of the most far-reaching human and social import which must be submitted by the board to the citizenry. The ultimate decisions as to volume of production, hours of work, and standard of living must be reached by a democratic procedure provided for in the political organization of the socialized system. The technical details as to the administration of these decisions can then be safely left to the technical boards.

Economic planning will in most cases be nationwide in scope at its inception. As soon as possible it should be extended so as to include the whole of a geo-economic region administered as one planning unit. This is the most economical and most effective basis for planning. Eventually should arise a world planning organization. This will deal with economic problems which are worldwide in scope. Among them are the allocation and distribution of geographically limited raw materials; marine, terrestrial and aerial navigation and transportation;

postal, telegraphic, telephonic, and radio communication; inter-regional and intercontinental travel; the distribution of power and its sources in so far as such distribution is feasible; and the production and distribution of certain foods, such as tropical fruits, coffee, tea, etc., and other agricultural products which are limited to climatic zones.

Soviet Russia has much to teach the capitalist world concerning a planned economy. It has an extensive organization for local, state, and federal planning. This organization still runs too much along traditional political, national, linguistic, and racial lines. These traditional lines should eventually be entirely obliterated so that the planning can be organized solely upon a geo-economic basis.

Capitalism has been most successful in its early stages and in the development of new countries with large natural resources. The United States and Canada are notable examples. With very little state planning and under intensive capitalist exploitation they have in less than a century attained the vanguard of nations in technical equipment. The fundamental reason is that capitalism functions most efficiently in a rapidly expanding economy. If Russia had had a different type of political regime and as effective a capitalist exploitation, it might also have attained a high technical development. Theoretically, state planning should be more successful than capitalist planning in building up a new economic and technical equipment, as the bolshevists have demonstrated. It is of much greater practical importance that a permanent efficient state administration of a highly developed system be devised. It is becoming more and more evident that technological unemployment and the lack of purchasing power resulting therefrom render capitalism incapable of operating such a system efficiently. Hence it is highly desirable to ascertain whether or not the bolshevists have succeeded in devising a plan for the current economy of a going concern.

Soviet Russia has carried over into its present stage of state socialism much of the capitalist paraphernalia, even though it has eliminated all the essence and substance of capitalism. Among these paraphernalia are the currency system, the purchasing power of money, the financial and credit system, the price level, the wage level, etc. The Soviet government has continued to buy and sell, pay wages, reckon state (not private) profits, levy taxes, borrow money, etc. By juggling the national income under the terms of taxes, loans, profits, etc., the government is trying to attain by indirect and rather confused methods the simple objective of dividing the national income into two portions, one for capital construction and the other for immediate consumption.

The failure of the bolshevists up to the present to devise and

704

put into operation a functional economic plan is not due wholly to the facts that they have had great difficulties to overcome and not much time to develop such a plan. It is due in considerable part to the fact that their economic policy is greatly influenced by political considerations. Mass political training has been one of their principal objectives. This explains why the workers are often given so large a share in the management that the discipline of labor is greatly weakened and the output considerably lessened. The temporary division of functions and of authority between trade unions, consumers' cooperative societies, the Soviet government, and the communist party renders the system too complicated for the highest efficiency in administration.

A more fundamental political reason why Soviet Russia is stumbling and blundering along with capitalist forms and mechanisms, after the essential features of capitalism have been eliminated, is the communist theory of the withering away of the state. Nowhere in Marxist, bolshevist, or communist literature has a practicable and detailed program for organization under communism been presented. This is not due to the opportunistic attitude that such a program must be worked out when the time comes. The Program of the Communist International presents a somewhat detailed plan for the transitional period of state socialism. It has no such plan for its ultimate objective, namely, worldwide communism. The reason is apparent in the following assertion: "The state, being the embodiment of class domination, will die out in so far as classes die out, and with it all measures of coercion will expire. . . . In communist society no social restrictions will be imposed upon the growth of the forces of production." (Chapter III.)

The abolition of unnecessary social restrictions is highly desirable. But social planning and organization are hardly conceivable without some sort of centralized administrative authority. This means that the state as a form of political organization and of economic administration will be retained. The experience and experiments of the bolshevists will aid greatly in determining the future form of the state. When the mass political education has prepared the people for democratic social control, a more effective economic and political organization will arise.[7]

The preceding criticisms of Soviet planning are in no sense intended as disparagement of the genuine and very great achievements of the bolshevists. In certain fields they have already demonstrated the superiority of socialist over capitalist methods of production. The

[7] I have discussed the errors and failures of the bolshevists at length and in detail in my book entitled *Bolshevism, Fascism and the Liberal-Democratic State*, New York, 1934. See especially Chapters IX, X, and XI.

Soviet economy is amply protected against the devastating effects of the trade cycle which has its alternations of speculation and inflation with deflation and widespread unemployment. This explains in large part the success of the earlier five-year plans and presages the success of the later quinquennial plans. The experience of Soviet China will also be of great significance.

Chapter XLI

Organized Work and a World Calender

IN many of the earlier social systems the occupational division of labor was largely hereditary. Prior to the advent of vocational schools, or a system of apprenticeship, the most feasible method of transmitting vocational knowledge was from father to son. A hereditary specialization of occupations was the natural result. Wherever the family system still is dominant, as in portions of the Orient, a hereditary division of labor is prevalent.

A caste system is a hereditary classification according to special functions. The castes are hierarchically arranged with unequal powers, rights, and privileges. Each caste is supposed to inherit the traits which peculiarly fit it for its functions. There is no reason to believe that there is a hereditary transmission of special abilities to correspond to the classification of occupations. Special abilities of all kinds may appear in any social class. As the ancestors of each caste were not selected for their special abilities, there is unlikely to be even a slight preponderance of unusual fitness in each caste.

The Indian caste system was, and still is in theory, fourfold. The castes are the brahmins or priests, the kshatriyas or warriors and administrators, the vaishyas or merchants, and the shudras or servitors and manual laborers. There has always been some confusion of functions. Under British rule this confusion became greater. Many of the sub-castes are still limited by custom and religion to their special occupations. But the independent republic of India is trying to rid itself of the cumbersome caste system.

The Occidental class system is not hereditary in name. But the inheritance of property tends to perpetuate the class status of the individual. The two main classes are the capitalist and the proletarian. The former contains the owners of the means of production and the latter the unpropertied wage-earners. Theoretically there is freedom of movement from one class to another. In practice it is impossible for

707

the vast majority of the proletarians to raise themselves to the economically higher but relatively small class.

The technical methods of modern industry which have resulted from the development of science have rendered the situation too complicated to be handled effectively by a family or caste system. Modern industrial methods call for a minute differentiation of function. They also require a high degree of flexibility to meet changes due to scientific discoveries and inventions. Traditional methods no longer have prestige. In the face of such demands a hereditary classification of occupations breaks down completely. It can change only slowly and in the course of generations. The same situation has arisen with regard to commerce, government, and various professional pursuits.[1]

In the days when handicraft was predominant the craftsman required a long training to acquire the necessary skill. This was usually secured during a period of apprenticeship. The crafts often were highly organized in guilds which regulated the conditions of apprenticeship. The machine age changed this situation greatly. A large part of the craftsmanship became obsolete and superfluous. Most of the pauper slaves. From this starvation class the capitalists can commodity, such as a pair of shoes or an article of furniture, was split up into numerous routine tasks, oft-repeated and requiring little training and skill. In so far as production was automatized, extraneous energy was substituted for human labor. The highly skilled type of work and of worker was largely eliminated under capitalism. There is always at hand an enormous reserve of cheap labor in the vast mass of the pauper slaves. From this starvation class the capitalists can recruit wage slaves whenever an evanescent outburst of capitalist prosperity or a war calls for an expansion of the labor force. Usually these wage workers can be readily prepared for and adjusted to their routine tasks.[2]

Under these circumstances there is little occasion to train the worker and to organize work under capitalism. In any case, it is hardly possible to organize work under any system of private enterprise because each entrepreneur is responsible for and has control over only a small fraction of the productive system. There have been little attempts at vocational training, usually in the public schools. There has been no system of free industrial training in all kinds of work. Such training would, in any event, be largely wasted under capitalism.

[1] See my *Oriental and Occidental Culture*, New York, 1928, Chapters VI, "Oriental Familism and Occidental Individualism," and VII, "Indian Caste and Western Class."

[2] See my *Farewell to Poverty*, New York, 1935, Chap. XXV, "Organized Work," from which much of this chapter is paraphrased and brought up to date.

The workers have to take whatever jobs they can get, with no regard to their own preferences and with little regard to their fitness and adaptability.

The principal attempt to improve the efficiency of the worker has been by means of what is ordinarily called scientific management. Its chief exponent stated its utility as follows: "The useful results have hinged mainly upon (1) the substitution of a science for the individual judgment of the workman; (2) the scientific selection and development of the workman, after each man has been studied, taught, and trained, and one may say experimented with, instead of allowing the workmen to select and develop in a haphazard way; and (3) the intimate cooperation of the management with the workmen, so that they together do the work in accordance with the scientific laws which have been developed, instead of leaving the solution of each problem in the hands of the individual workman."[3] Closely related to scientific management are the psychological tests which have been devised to determine the kind of work for which an individual is best fitted. The vocational guidance which has been developed to a small extent can utilize these tests.

The immediate effect of scientific management in the factories and shops where it has been applied has been to increase the production per man-hour. This has invariably increased the profits of the employers. It has also raised the wages of the employees. But the wages have risen much less than the profits. While the employees have been given bonuses and higher wage rates as incentives to produce more, and sometimes in order to hold workmen trained under scientific management, this increase has been far from commensurate with the rise in the profits of their employers. Scientific management has done nothing to lessen the inequality in the distribution of wealth; indeed, it has probably enhanced this inequality. It has often introduced the piece-work system in its worst form, and has made pace-makers of the workers whom it has trained.

As the application of scientific management becomes more widespread, competition between the employers brings down their rate of profits. In similar fashion, competition between the workers brings down their rate of wages. Scientific management has much the same effect upon the working class as the introduction of machine methods of production. It increases the amount produced per man-hour but gives the workers a smaller proportionate share of the product. As a result of the rise in efficiency it drives many workers out of their jobs and causes technological unemployment. Inasmuch as new industries

[3] F. W. Taylor, *The Principles of Scientific Management*, New York, 1911, p. 60.

cannot arise fast enough to absorb these unemployed workers, the application of science under capitalism tends in part to augment pauper slavery instead of contributing entirely to raise the standard of living for mankind. Technological unemployment supplements and increases "normal" unemployment under capitalism due to chronic shortage of purchasing power caused by syphoning off of private profits.

The labor movement has displayed hostility to scientific management. The latter has been regarded as a scheme for speeding up the workmen in a factory or shop. It has been opposed in order to restrict output upon the theory, usually fallacious, that by diminishing the output the wages can be increased. It is inimical to the labor movement because scientific managers usually require that workmen under their tuition and directions shall not be members of trade unions. This requirement is based upon the ground that hours of labor, rates of wages, and every other feature of the work must be regulated according to the principles of scientific management, otherwise such managment cannot succeed. Whatever arguments of efficiency may be made in behalf of autocratic control, workingmen and especially organized workingmen are certain in the long run to react violently against such control. Though they may submit to it for a time, owing to ignorance or to the bonuses they are receiving, the clash comes in the end unless the managers make concessions.

Scientific management tends to extend the mechanical process to human beings. It makes the workers to a higher degree mere cogs in the machine and reenforces their slavery to the capitalists. Such workmen are not prepared to take their places as members of a democracy. It may dehumanize and brutalize some of them to a considerable degree. It sacrifices them to attain an efficiency which can benefit their masters alone.

Scientific management under capitalism does not solve the problem of the unequal distribution of wealth, but accentuates it. Such management is undemocratic and often brutalizing in its character. As Hobson has said: "Were the full rigor of scientific management to be applied throughout the staple industries, not only would the human costs of labor appear to be enhanced, but progress in the industrial arts itself would probably be damaged. . . . For not only would the arts of invention and improvement be confined to the few, but the mechanization of the great mass of workmen would render them less capable of adapting their labor to any other method than that to which they had been drilled. . . . It would become even more difficult than now for a majority of men, accustomed in their workday to mechanical obedience, to stand up in their capacity as citizens

710

against their industrial rulers when, as often happens upon critical occasions, political interests correspond with economic cleavages." [4]

In a socialized system the valuable features of scientific management could be utilized and its detrimental features eliminated. Increased production would be distributed to the workers of the classless society and would not accentuate the concentration of wealth and disparity of incomes. The higher productivity of labor would be reflected in a higher standard of living or shorter hours of labor, and not in technological unemployment. Capitalism would no longer frustrate science and technology. Work would become more and more automatized so that it could no longer stupefy and brutalize the worker by a mechanical routine. The deadening effects of the minimum of routinized labor which could not be eliminated would be almost entirely neutralized by short hours of labor and abundant leisure.

The automatization of production renders a large part of manual skill obsolete. The skilled specialized worker will be replaced in large part by the more generalized worker. The traits required in this type of worker are a broad knowledge of machinery and productive methods, relatively high intelligence, good judgment, accurate perception, alertness, sustained attention, quick reaction to signals, careful watch of instruments, observation of changes, and prompt adjustment to new circumstances. This generalized worker requires the sort of education which will give him polytechnic literacy, a vocational training which scarcely exists under capitalism.

In a socialized system the hours and years of work can be determined entirely by social needs and productive capacity. As soon as all reasonable social needs are supplied, no more time and labor will be required of the individual. At any given place and time the hours and years of work will depend upon the standard of living designated as desirable by the community and the productive capacity available. The decision as to standard of living will be made democratically through the political mechanism of the socialized system. The technical organization composed of boards of experts will calculate the hours and years of labor required to maintain the stipulated standard of living.

The labor cost of replacement and obsolescence will diminish greatly under a socialized system. Consumers' goods will be much more substantially made and therefore more durable. New models will not be introduced simply in order to stimulate sales for profiteers, and will not be purchased by consumers simply in order to "keep up with

[4] John A. Hobson, "Scientific Management," in the *Sociological Review*, London, July 1913, pp. 211-12.

711

the Joneses." As soon as the capital equipment has been modernized and has been made as nearly 100 per cent automatic as is feasible, it will rarely be necessary to introduce new types of machinery. As most of this machinery wears out slowly and will not have to be thrown out on account of obsolescence before it is worn out, as it often is now, the cost of replacing capital goods will fall to a minimum.

Whatever the number of hours which will be socially necessary, the period of service will not commence until the citizen has received an ample general education and vocational training. The general education will render him politically and culturally literate and qualify him to exercise his rights and privileges as a member of a democratic commonwealth. The vocational training will generally reveal his special aptitudes and determine his choice of an occupation. Inasmuch as inclination usually coincides with special aptitude, free choice of occupation will be the general rule. The only exceptions will occur when too many individuals wish to enter an occupation than is socially necessary or too few in other occupations. In the first case entrance examinations will limit the number admitted to favored occupations. In the second, workers will be allocated by the vocational boards.

Even with these exceptions, there will be far more freedom of choice of occupations than at present when most persons have to take whatever jobs they can get, whether they like them or not. There will be much fewer misfits than at present when most persons enter occupations with no demonstrated fitness for them. Under capitalism there are many square pegs in round holes. Even when they have exercised a choice and are more or less fitted for their chosen occupations, they are often forced out of them because the occupation is overcrowded or because a business depression brings about widespread unemployment. During the prolonged depression which commenced in 1929 construction work decreased very greatly and the great majority of architects were unemployed. Many of them were forced into other occupations even though well trained for their chosen profession. The same situation existed in many other professions.

The plan of production will determine the number of workers required in each occupation. The choice of vocation will ordinarily be free. Under capitalism the so-called freedom of choice is almost entirely mythical. The general education and vocational training in a planned society will bring to fruition the inborn capacities.

Whenever an excessive number of candidates desire admission to an occupation, the number admitted will be regulated by competitive examinations. Those eliminated by these examinations will have their second and third choices for other occupations. The residue

712

of workers will be drafted into the least popular occupations. Their restriction of choice will be compensated for by shorter hours of labor. Favoritism based upon birth, wealth, and social status will disappear entirely in a classless society.

Every worker will have an abundance of leisure time in which to pursue any favorite avocation by himself or in cooperation with others. Free societies will be spontaneously formed and free enterprises undertaken for any purposes whatsoever, provided they are not anti-social. It will also be permissible to furnish capital equipment to these free enterprises. This will not endanger the socialized system provided the ownership and the ultimate control of this capital is social and no private and individual profits can be derived from its free use. Freedom of organization and of enterprise under these conditions will render the social system flexible, and introduce a factor for change and progress. Cooperative scientific research, inventive experimentation, exploration, artistic and literary pursuits, recreational activities, and many other cultural enterprises will be encouraged and promoted thereby. New forms of activity which cannot now be foreseen will arise under the stimulus of the free society.

The ideology and pseudo-ethics of income as a reward for work constitute the basis of slave morality. It is almost impossible to dislodge and overcome this ideology and spurious ethics under the present system. They support the fallacious ideas that work is meritorious and an end in itself, instead of the only sound theory, namely, that work is useful and justifiable only when it produces something of intrinsic value to mankind. Inasmuch as work will be divorced from income, all pecuniary motives and considerations will be eliminated.

The socialists and communists have long advocated the separation of work from income because they believe that collectivism would soon bring into being so great an abundance of goods that it would be unnecessary to limit the income of any one. The technocrats also favor this separation partly because they believe in the coming economy of abundance. They advocate it also as a measure of efficiency. It will be possible to plan production much more accurately if the incomes of all citizens have been fixed beforehand. The incomes of adults will be equal, and those of children will be smaller in proportion to their needs.

Each occupation will have its own hierarchy chosen for achievement. Under the supervision of this hierarchy selection for promotion from the rank and file will take place. From the higher ranks of these occupations will be chosen the supreme technical, economic, and professional boards which will constitute the highest authorities within the occupations. The administrative bodies of the various branches of production will be made up in large part of representa-

713

tives from these boards. Industry, agriculture, transportation, mining, etc., will be administered by those who are most familiar with the processes involved in each of these productive activities. Success in climbing the occupational ladder will furnish ample incentive for achievement.

The organization of work which will be possible in a socialized system will not only eliminate unemployment and the worry and loss of time suffered while seeking for employment, but also most of the square pegs in round holes. It will not only make the worker much happier in his occupation but will increase his efficiency and social productivity greatly. The abundant leisure time will furnish him ample opportunity for avocational pursuits some of which will be of social value.

In a socialized system many unproductive occupations which proliferate under capitalism will disappear. Most of the occupations connected with trade will no longer be necessary. Among them are shop salesmen, commercial travelers, advertising workers, bookkeepers, accountants, etc. The distribution of consumers' goods will be greatly simplified and automatized to a large extent, so that comparatively few workers will be necessary for this purpose. For similar reasons most of the occupations connected with banking and finance will disappear. The legal profession will almost entirely disappear. Most litigation arises out of the law of contracts and the law of torts or private wrongs. With the abolition of private enterprise most contracts will disappear. With the abolition of private property in the means of production most torts will disappear.

On the other hand, the scientists, inventors, artists, and technicians of all sorts will have unlimited opportunities to exercise and express their creative and productive abilities in a socialized system. They will no longer be the servitors and at the mercy of the profiteers. They will be the servants but also the leaders of the collective commonwealth.

The Gregorian calendar utilized everywhere in the Occident is a clumsy and illogical way of reckoning time. The months are uneven in length and bear no relation to any natural division of time, not even the lunar cycle. They do not indicate readily the number of days between one day of the year and another. An artificial division of the year into more or less equal parts such as 12 or 13 months has little or no utility for any purpose whatsoever. The days of the solar cycle should be numbered from 1 to 365 or 366. Each day in every year would then correspond numerically to the corresponding day in the solar cycle.

The solstices and equinoxes, which are important solar and terrestrial events and phenomena, can be designated as days of the year.

714

If the year commences as at present on January 1, the approximate dates for these solar events will be as follows: spring equinox d81, (d = day, Latin, *dies*), summer solstice d172, autumn equinox d264, winter solstice d355. The initial day of the calendar year might be made to coincide with one of these terrestrial phenomena. In leap years the extra day might be added at the close of the year as the 366th day. Or it might be intercalated without a number but with an appropriate name, such as midyear day, at a convenient point, such as midway through the calendar. The former method would perhaps cause less confusion because it would not create a break in the continuity of the numerical series of days.

The week also is a purely artificial division of time. It may have originated as the period of time between periodically recurring market days. It has varied considerably as to length. Some form of the week may have utility in indicating the alternation between work days and rest days. It should, however, conform precisely to the organization of work and rest at any given time and place. This organization has varied greatly and the week should vary accordingly.

The hebdomadal week, which the Occident inherited from Western Asia and which dates back to prehistoric antiquity, is functioning badly under the economic conditions now prevalent. It prevents a flexible work program which can readily be adjusted to the rapidly increasing productivity of labor. Five and a half days of work out of seven corresponds most closely to a 5-day week with one rest day in each 5-day period. Five days of work out of seven stand between a 4-day and a 3-day week with one rest day out of each. The continual reduction in the hours of labor caused by technological progress calls for a shorter week, or for fewer hours of labor per day, or both.

Soviet Russia has experimented with at least two forms of the week. In 1929 was introduced the continuous 5-day week, or what might be called the individual 5-day week because it did not cover the same period for all individuals. Each person had one rest day out of five days, but not all persons were having their rest days at the same time. In a factory or office or farm one-fifth of the labor force were resting while the other four-fifths were working. Each fifth of the force received its rest day in the course of the five days. In other words, the rest day was staggered. This rendered possible the continuous operation of the factory or enterprise by the four-fifths of the labor force at work on any given day.

After being in operation for two or three years in Soviet Russia, the continuous 5-day week was set aside for the time being. In 1931 a 6-day week was introduced with the rest days falling on the 6th, 12th, 18th, 24th, and 30th days of each month. In the months with 31 days each, the last week of the month became 7 days and a day was added to the annual vacations of the workers. A corresponding adjustment was made for the end of February. Under this system the names of the days of the hebdomadal week, namely, Monday, Tuesday, etc., were soon discarded and a given day was identified as the day of the month. The rest day was called "weekhodnoi," which means literally "going out."

Owing to the pressure of World War II, on June 26, 1940, the hebdomadal week with Sunday as the day of rest was restored. The 7-hour working day, provided for in the 1936 Soviet Constitution (Section 119) was lengthened to 8 hours, except for a few dangerous occupations for which the 6-hour working day was retained.[5]

Soviet Russia has great advantages in reforming the calendar. There is no religious opposition to overcome such as exists in countries where the Christian Sunday, or the Jewish Sabbath, or the Moslem Friday, or any other day of the week or month or year, is considered a holy day. There are no mythological or other sentiments to appease with regard to the names of the days of the week and of the months. There are no vested economic interests or other predatory groups and classes which are desirous of maintaining a long work week in order to exploit labor. It is generally recognized that abundant leisure is desirable for every one, and is, indeed, one of the social objectives of the soviet system. A centralized state authority would render feasible the introduction of a new calendar uniformly and at one time.

Soviet Russia is, however, not in a position at present to achieve a thoroughgoing and permanent calendar reform. The appalling destruction caused by the war from 1941 to 1945 requires excessive exertion for reconstruction by all its citizens. Its capital equipment is far from adequate to produce a high standard of living for all of its inhabitants which is the avowed purpose of the Soviet Union. When the development of the new system is farther advanced, the U.S.S.R. may return to the continuous 5-day week, and then can shorten the week and the daily hours of labor as the socially necessary work decreases. Its experience will be instructive with respect to the eventual worldwide reform of the calendar.

The World Calendar Association of New York City and the Rational Calendar Association of London are advocating a calendar which would divide the year into four seasons of 91 days each, or 13 hebdomadal weeks. Each season would contain two months of 30 days each and one month of 31 days. There would be a Year-Day every year and a Leap-Day in leap years. These could be intercalated between seasons at the beginning and in the middle of the year. A

5 Vladimir Gsovski, "Elements of Soviet Labor Law," U.S. Department of Labor, Bureau of Labor Statistics, *Monthly Labor Review*, March and April 1951.

minor advantage would be that each day of each season would fall on the same day of the hebdomadal week. But this calendar fails to solve any of the serious problems involved because it retains the uneven months and the uneconomic hebdomadal week.

No calendar is satisfactory which does not take adequate account of the division of time between work and leisure. This can be done by a modified form of the week. After recording the astronomically and cosmically determined facts with regard to the length of the day and of the year, the calendar should be flexible enough to register changes in the relation between work and leisure by changes in the form of the week.

No universal system of dividing the seasons can be prescribed or even recommended. Theoretically the summer solstice should come midway in summer and the winter solstice midway in winter. In similar fashion the spring equinox should come midway in spring and the autumn equinox midway in autumn. But the seasons as distinguished by temperature, moisture, vegetation, etc., and not as determined by the earth's position in relation to the sun, are actually determined by latitude and also greatly influenced by the lines of isotherm. Generally speaking, summer predominates in equatorial regions and winter in polar regions, so that the greater the distance from the equator the shorter becomes the summer and the longer becomes the winter.

In the eastern half of North America at approximately latitude 40° summer begins about the first of June or only 20 instead of 45 days before the summer solstice. In similar fashion winter begins about the first of December and continues through March or all of four months. Spring and autumn are somewhat less than three months each. In this region, therefore, winter extends from d335 to d90, spring from d91 to d151, summer from d152 to about d258, and autumn from d259 to d334. The seasons are in length approximately as follows: winter—121 days, spring—61 days, summer—107 days, autumn—76 days. In other latitudinal and isothermal regions the seasons vary even more in length. In some regions summer and winter follow each other in such quick succession that spring and autumn approach zero in length. The ancient Greeks recognized only three seasons, namely, spring, summer and winter. The Hindoo year has six seasons, each of two months' duration.

The permanent hebdomadal week should not persist much longer. It obstructs a flexible work program which can be adjusted to the increasing productivity of labor and the rising standard of living. A standard week cannot be prescribed because the length of the week, frequency of recurring rest days, number of special holidays, as well as the number of hours worked per day vary greatly in different places and at different times. The vast populations of China and of India have never had a high level of living and productivity of labor. Soviet Russia, Great Britain, France, Germany, etc. have had their level of living and productivity of labor lowered by the widespread destruction of the war of 1939 to 1945. The circumstances as to work requirements and the most suitable week vary considerably as between these countries and the United States with its relatively high standard of living and productivity of labor.

A 5-day week with one rest day in each week would create 73 weeks in each year with one day over in leap years. A 4-day week with one rest day in each week would yield 91 weeks with one day over in each year and two days over in leap years. A 3-day week with one rest day in each week would yield 121 weeks with two days over in each year and three days over in leap years.

The primary consideration is the aggregate number of hours of labor required to maintain a given level of living for a given population. The type of week would then depend upon the length of the work day—whether 8 hours or 7 hours down to 4 hours or even less per day; the length of the annual vacation; the number of public holidays; whether or not the rest day is staggered so as to permit continuous and therefore more productive utilization of the capital equipment; the length of the working life, whether 45, or 40, or 35, or fewer years; and also how large a proportion of the population belongs or should belong to the available and actual labor force.

Let us see what sort of week might be suitable for the labor requirements of the United States. The vast majority of its inhabitants do not have as high a level of living as could be readily given them with the potentially available labor force, the already existent capital equipment, the vast natural resources, and the available scientific knowledge and technical skill. We cannot estimate precisely what are the labor requirements to furnish every inhabitant of the United States a satisfactory standard of living. These requirements will be decreased considerably as soon as atomic energy can be used productively. We can, however, estimate roughly how much labor is actually being used productively and how much is being used wastefully or not being used at all.

The Fair Labor Standards Act of 1938 established 2,080 hours as a normal year's work. (United States Code Annotated, Title 29, Section 207) More than 40 hours in a week must be paid at the penalty overtime rate of $1\frac{1}{2}$ time. Many industries give at least 2 weeks of vacation which reduces the normal year's work to 2,000 hours. If 5 out of every 7 days are worked, 8 hours are the daily work period.

Large sections of labor are exempted from this law, such as agricultural labor, seamen, many trade employees, employees of carriers, such as railways, over which the Interstate Commerce Commission has jurisdiction. For example, the average number of hours paid for per employee per week of class I railroads was 49.0 in 1940, 54.2 in 1943, and 45.3 in 1950. The increase in 1943 was due to the war. The decrease in 1950 was due to the 40-hour week adopted for the non-operating railway workers. We may nevertheless assume that the 40-hour hebdomadal work week and 2,000-hour work year are standard and normal for the United States. However, many persons in the potential labor force are not working at all, and much labor is used unproductively or wasted. An incomplete estimate of this idleness and waste can be made.

The Brookings Institution has estimated that the average annual percentage of industrial unemployment was 24 percent during the 20 years 1919-38.[6] The National Unemployment Census of 1937, a year of moderate prosperity in which the national income climbed 10 percent from $66.9 billion in 1936 to $73.6 billion in 1937, revealed that the total unemployment in 1937 was about 25 percent. Under the present system of private profit, therefore, unemployment reduces the year's work from 2,000 to 1,500 hours, and to much less in unprosperous years.

About half of the working population is engaged in commercial and financial activities and in many services whose work is largely or wholly supernumerary so far as actual production is concerned. It includes most of the salesmen, financiers, lawyers, advertisers, speculators, and other retainers and camp followers of capitalism, whose efforts are directed toward the acquisition of profits rather than genuine production. "According to the Sixteenth Census of the United States, manufacturing industries in 1939 employed 9,750,000 persons; agriculture, 9,695,000; and the distributive trades, 9,606,000. Adding employment in the service trades to wholesaling and retailing gives a total of over 12 million, or more than one-fourth of all employment in the country in 1939."[7]

A comparison of the distribution of the national income in 1917 and 1932, in which years it was approximately the same, indicated that in 1917 the producers constituted two-thirds of the workers and received one-half of the national income in the form of wages, salaries, and farm incomes. The "overheaders" constituted the remaining third of the workers and received the other half of the national income. In 1932 the producers had fallen to one-half of the working population and received only one-third of the national income. The overheaders

[6] Spurgeon Bell, *Productivity, Wages, and National Income,* The Brookings Institution, Washington, 1940.

[7] U.S. Department of Commerce, "Domestic Commerce," June 1947, page 3.

had risen to half of the working population and received two-thirds of the national income. While the total costs of operation remained the same, the costs of overhead rose 128 percent from 1917 to 1932. For every dollar of income received by the producers in 1932 the over-headers received $2.30. An excess of overheaders are being supported by the producers.[8]

It is a very liberal assumption that these overheaders do as much as 1,000 hours of genuinely productive labor per annum per capita. Only a minor portion of the huge army of salesmen is needed to distribute the goods produced. Salesmanship and advertising are venal arts of manipulation with little or no regard for the welfare of the ultimate consumer. The total cost of merchandising goods is from a quarter to one-half of the price paid by the ultimate consumer.[9] This reduces the average year of genuinely productive work for the working population to not more than 1,000 hours in prosperous times, if average unemployment and wasteful overhead work are deducted.

Sickness and accidents cause at least 3 percent and perhaps as much as 4 percent of lost working time. This reduces the average year's work to not more than 940 hours in prosperous years. In years of depression, when unemployment may rise as high as 40 percent, the annual average may drop to only 640 hours.

This brings us to the somewhat surprising discovery that the American economy is being maintained not by 2,000 but only 1,000 or even less hours per annum of genuinely productive labor per capita of the actually working population. This does not include the portion of the population which is not at present in the available labor force but which should belong to it, in other words, the potential labor force. This should include all adult able-bodied Americans between certain ages who are not performing some socially useful function, such as homemaking, the breeding and rearing of children, scientific research, inventing useful devices, etc.

According to the census of 1940, in the United States there were 101,102,924 persons 14 years old and over, who were evenly divided between males and females. A little more than half, or 52,789,499, were in the available labor force, of whom 46,765,014 were in the age group 20-64 inclusive. Deducting those under 20 years of age, who were or should be in school, and those over 64 years, who were or should be retired, there were 77,344,357 persons in all in the age group 20-64 inclusive who should contribute productive labor.

About 60 percent of the women in this age group were married, many of whom were housekeepers. American housekeeping is mechanized to a considerable degree. It is doubtful if these housekeepers

---

[8] W. Rautenstrauch, *Who Gets the Money?* New York, 1934.

[9] Maurice Parmelee, *Farewell to Poverty*, New York, 1935, Chap. XXX.

averaged more than 1,000 hours of productive labor per annum, even if the time spent in child breeding and rearing is included. The following census data render this assumption highly probable.

In April 1940, before the United States entered the war, there were 26,605,800 families with male head married and wife present, with 23,438,860 wives not in the labor force. Of these wives, 9,081,300, or 39 percent, had no children under 18, and 5,740,000, or 24 percent, had only one child under 18. In 1946, shortly after the war which had increased the number of women in the available labor force, there were 28,800,000 such families with 23,400,000 wives not in the labor force. Of the latter, 8,970,000, or 38 percent, had no children under 18, and 5,590,000, or 24 percent had only one child under 18. In both years nearly two-fifths had no child and more than three-fifths not more than one child under 18.[10]

The remaining non-employed adult population of the age group 20-64 inclusive, namely, somewhat more than 7,000,000 in 1940, averaged far below 1,000 hours per annum of genuinely productive labor. It is almost certain that the adult population not in the available labor force averaged considerably less than 800 hours of productive labor per annum.

While the foregoing is a rough computation based on the crude statistical data which alone are available, it is very probable that the overall average for the American adult population is not more than 800 hours per annum of genuinely productive labor. The elimination of many of the contradictions and wastes of the present economic system, such as unemployment, unproductive labor, the business cycle, war, etc., would enable the actual and potential labor force to produce a higher level of living and abundant leisure for all of the American population with an annual average of not more than 800 hours of labor. With the utilization of atomic energy as a productive force, this average will diminish. As Dr. Robert Bacher, former scientist member of the U. S. Atomic Energy Commission has said: "Atomic energy is almost certain to revolutionize our extraction of energy from nature."[11]

The preceding discussion of the labor requirements of the United States brings us to a consideration of the sort of arrangement of the week as a periodic alternation between work days and rest days which might meet these requirements more or less satisfactorily. A 5-day week would divide the year into 73 weeks, with one day extra in leap year to be called leap-year-day. A 16-hour work week, 4 hours of work daily for 4 days and then a day of rest for 50 weeks in the year would yield 800 hours of productive labor per individual worker. The remaining 23 weeks or 115 days would be vacation time. This would

[10] Bureau of Census, *Population,* Series P-S, No. 20, February 1946.
[11] *Science Illustrated,* August 1947, page 109.

be a feasible arrangement provided the present average working life of about 45 years is maintained.

The working life is, however, certain to decrease for both social and economic reasons. When it falls from 45 to 40 years, the average hours of work per annum would be 900 which would be 56¼ weeks of the 5-day week. This would decrease the vacation to 16¾ weeks or about 83 days. If the working life falls from 40 to 35 years, the annual average of hours of work would be about 1,029 hours which would be 64⅓ weeks. This would decrease the vacation to 8⅔ weeks or about 43 days. If it should fall from 35 to 30 years, the annual average of hours would be 1,200 hours which would be 75 weeks, or more than the total length of the year.

Before this point is reached the week would have to be lengthened from 5 to 6 days, or the hours of work per day would have to be raised from 4 hours upward. The latter method would perhaps be the easier way of making the adjustment. If would be unfortunate because 4 hours of work can readily be accomplished between meals so that the work period would not be interrupted by eating. However, this adjustment may never be necessary because of the increasing productivity of labor. This would render it possible to lower the working life not only to 30 years but even to 25 or to 20 years.

Similar calculations can be made with respect to a 4-day week with one rest day in each 4 days. With a 4-hour work day an annual labor requirement of 800 hours would be met in 67 out of 91 weeks. This would leave 24 weeks or 96 days of vacation time. An annual labor requirement of 890 hours would be met in 74 weeks with a vacation of 17 weeks or 68 days. An annual labor requirement of 1,000 hours would be met in 83 weeks with a vacation of 8 weeks or 32 days. An annual labor requirement of 1,145 hours could not be met by this type of week because it would require 95 weeks. The daily hours of labor would have to rise if the 4-day week was to be retained.

The type of week best suited for the United States is a domestic question which should be solved democratically by its people. It would be determined mainly by the standard of living desired, the amount of leisure desired, the productivity of its labor force, and the stability of its economic system. The latter depends in part upon the extent to which its production is planned. In similar fashion the people of each country or region must solve this question in accordance with its economic conditions and requirements. The United Nations Organization cannot set up a standard week for the world while these conditions and requirements vary so greatly from country to country.

In the meantime the UNO can adopt at once the day with its hours counted from one to 24, and the year with its days reckoned from one to 365 and 366 in leap years, and use the latter in dating its publications. When the economic situation becomes more or less alike the world over, and when the UNO or a genuine world government has acquired sufficient authority to do so, it can establish a standard week as a part of the world calendar.

The first requisite of a planned economy is a logical division of time. It is highly probable that worldwide production will have to become more and more planned in order to produce a steady and abundant flow of goods. The UNO should take the lead in devising, adopting for its own use, recommending to its member nations, and eventually establishing by its own authority a rational and workable world calendar. It is as reasonable as it would be for the UNO to standardize measures of weight, length, surface and volume, as in the metric system; currencies and other measures of value; or any other units of measurement which are utilized the world over.

Chapter XLII

The Effective Distribution of Wealth

IN this treatise it has been repeatedly stated that under capitalism insufficient purchasing power is distributed to furnish a market for the wealth which can be readily produced. This is a far-reaching factor perpetuating indefinitely the failure of capitalism to satisfy the needs and wants of the vast majority of the inhabitants living under this system. In the United States, the richest country in the world, the great disparity in the distribution of its national income is revealed by a study of the average annual income shares from 1919 to 1938 inclusive. The top one percent of the population received 13.1 percent of the countrywide income, the top 5 percent received 24.7 percent, while the lower 95 percent received only 75.3 percent of the national income.[1]

Some indication of the large incomes received by some of the persons in the top one percent is furnished by the figures published annually by the United States Securities and Exchange Commission.[2] In 1950 seventeen companies with sales ranging from $1,020,000,000 up to $7,531,000,000, averaging $2,088,470,000 per company, paid their top officials from $100,000 up to $652,156, averaging $264,365 per official.

However, these incomes were small in comparison with the incomes of multi-millionaires in the form of rent, interest, dividends and profits from property ownership which range upward into the millions instead of the hundreds of thousands of dollars. The United States Treasury Department has reported the following figures for 1947 for income returns before taxes for incomes ranging from $500,000 to $5,000,000 and over:[3]

---

[1] Simon Kuznets, *Shares of Upper Income Groups in Income and Savings*, National Bureau of Economic Research, New York, 1950, p. 6.

[2] *Business Week*, New York, May 19, 1951, p. 68.

[3] U.S. Treasury Department Press Service, No. S. 2670, May 1, 1951. See also *Statistics of Income, Part I*, Washington, April 10, 1950, p. 13.

724

High Income Returns before Taxes in the United States, 1947

Income before taxes	Number of returns
$5,000,000 and over	6
$4,000,000 to $5,000,000	1
$3,000,000 to $4,000,000	8
$2,000,000 to $3,000,000	12
$1,500,000 to $2,000,000	23
$1,000,000 to $1,500,000	64
$ 750,000 to $1,000,000	84
$ 500,000 to $ 750,000	218

Though these high incomes were greatly reduced by the income tax, even after taxation they averaged several hundred times as large as the average income of more than half the families in the United States as shown in the next table. In 1950 the personal income tax was 91 percent of the excess of taxable income over $200,000 with lower rates below $200,000 ranging down to 20 percent. An income of $1,000,000 before taxes netted about $220,000 after taxes, and an income of $5,000,000 before taxes netted about $600,000 after taxes.

The Federal Reserve Board studied the income grouping of consumer spending units in the United States in 1950. It defined spending unit as "all persons living in the same dwelling and related by blood, marriage, or adoption, who pooled their incomes for their major items of expense."

Incomes of Spending Units in the United States in 1950

Money income before taxes per spending unit	Percentage of all spending units
Under $1,000	13
$1,000 to $1,999	17
$2,000 to $2,999	19
$3,000 to $3,999	19
$4,000 to $4,999	12
$5,000 to $7,499	14
$7,500 and over	6
	100

The above table indicates that more than half of the families were living on less than $3,000 per annum after taxes were deducted, more than three-tenths on less than $2,000, and more than one-eighth on less than $1,000. The Bureau of Labor Statistics reported that the total annual cost in October 1950 of the city worker's family budget in 34 large cities ranged from $3,453 in New Orleans and $3,507 in Mobile, to $3,926 in Washington, D.C., and $3,933 in Milwaukee. This budget was designed to describe a "modest but adequate" standard of living for a family of four persons—an employed father, a housewife not gainfully employed, and two children under 15 years of age.[4] Hence considerably more than half of the population of the United States were existing below an adequate standard of living. This conclusion is confirmed by the fact that the Census Bureau reported that the median earnings of all families and single individuals in the United States in 1949 was $2,739.

The Federal Reserve Board found that in the spring of 1951 the proportion of liquid assets held by each tenth of the nation's spending units when ranked by size of liquid asset holdings was 65 percent for the highest tenth, 17 percent for the second highest tenth, one percent for the sixth tenth, and less than one percent in the aggregate for the lowest four tenths.[5] In other words, four-fifths of these spending units had only 18 percent of these liquid assets, and one-half of them owned less than two percent. The vast majority had inadequate protection against the economic insecurity of life in the country in which capitalism has been most successful.

The injustice of such a situation is too obvious to require comment. Equally grave is the inefficiency of an economic system which cannot distribute the wealth which can readily be produced at the present stage in the development of the arts and sciences. In order to promote profits, capitalism must perpetuate scarcity, even though abundance is feasible. Inasmuch as the price level must average higher than the cost of production in order to yield profits, business enterprise does not promptly release as much purchasing power as the distribution of its products requires. The withdrawal of profits reduces buying power and disturbs market relations, because effective demand cannot absorb actual or potential supply. Saving and investment expand the capital goods industries until a plethora is attained and depression ensues. The accumulation of capital promotes and impedes

[4] U.S. Department of Labor, Bureau of Labor Statistics, *Family Budget of City Worker, October 1950*, Bulletin No. 1091, March 1951, p. 1.

[5] *Federal Reserve Bulletin*, June 1951, pp. 630, 632, 636, 637.

The liquid assets included all types of United States Government bonds, checking accounts, savings accounts in banks, postal savings and shares in savings and loan associations and credit unions, but excluded currency.

production simultaneously or in rapid succession. Debt increases more rapidly than capital and purchasing power. It thereby hampers production and accentuates maldistribution. While thrift as a protection for the future is forced upon the individual by the economic insecurity of capitalism, saving often becomes a social menace more than a productive factor by causing a glut of monetary capital which clogs the wheels of business enterprise. Capitalism assures economic security to no one, not even to the capitalists themselves. It forever denies a high standard of living to the vast majority of mankind.

An attempt to attain economic security and a wider distribution of wealth under capitalism is by means of social insurance, including old age pensions. Security legislation has been enacted in several European countries, such as Germany, Great Britain, Holland, Sweden, Denmark, and France, and by several states and the federal government in the United States. The principal dangers against which social insurance usually purports to furnish protection are those which menace the proletarian class in particular. These include unemployment, sickness, accidents, and old age.[6]

Many kinds of state insurance schemes are now in existence. A government may establish an insurance system and finance it entirely. Or it may subsidize a commercial insurance agency to furnish insurance facilities at low rates to the poorer classes. It may require the employers to bear part or all of the cost of the insurance against dangers for which they are at least in part responsible, such as unemployment and accidents. It may make the insurance compulsory upon the workers, so that they have to insure themselves. The government may enforce this requirement by levying the cost of the premiums in part or entirely upon the wages of the insured before their wages are delivered to the earners. Or the state insurance may be entirely voluntary. These and various other forms of insurance are to be found in the governmental systems of today.

Insurance stimulates the accumulation of capital by encouraging thrift on the part of individuals, or saving by employers or by the state. Such accumulation is desirable or not according to the relation between the amount of capital in existence and the natural resources and available supply of labor. If capital is limited in proportion to the other factors of production, it may be desirable to accumulate more of it. If capital is plentiful, it may be much more desirable to raise the standard of living of the lower classes. The savings of the poorer classes constitute a very minute source of capital. A rise in

6 See my *Poverty and Social Progress*, New York, 1916, Chapters XXII, "The Question of Thrift," and XXIII, "Social Insurance and Pensions;" and *Farewell to Poverty*, New York, 1935, Chapter XXVI, "Effective Distribution," from which much of this chapter is paraphrased and brought up to date.

their standard of living is usually a greater social gain than an increase of capital.[7]

In a scarcity economy saving causes under-consumption and depresses industrial activity. The wealth saved is converted into capital and is used to produce more wealth. As the income for consumption purposes has been diminished, it is not possible to market all that is produced. Consequently, there arises a state of relative over-production. The capitalist economists usually call this situation over-production. Fundamentally it is a state of under-consumption, because under-consumption for the purpose of saving has led to over-production.[8]

Insurance does not prevent poverty because it does not change the conditions which give rise to poverty. An extensive literature concerning insurance, and social insurance in particular, has arisen in recent years. Many of the writers represented in this literature labor under the delusion that insurance prevents poverty, and that social insurance furnishes a solution for the problems of poverty and dependency. On the contrary, social insurance is desirable only to the extent that it is preferable to poor relief. It is a remedial measure. Like every remedial measure it is temporary in its effect.[9]

Social insurance is closely related to certain remedial measures which are sometimes called forms of social insurance. They appear to be so in the sense that they are intended to safeguard the poorer classes from certain dangers. In this fashion society or the state is trying to insure the welfare of these classes. In the strict sense of the word they are not forms of insurance, because they lack the mutuality and saving which characterize insurance. These measures remove the burden of the cost of this protection directly from the shoulders of the poor and place it at least in part upon other classes. The poor are protected against such dangers as accidents, sickness, unemployment,

[7] "The cure prescribed for the workers is that they shall not only be chary of consuming the goods which they live by producing, but equally abstain from consuming high-class goods, the production of which would call for labor which could not be superseded by machinery. And their saved money is consequently to be invested in the production of only the kind of goods or services which, so far as parsimony prevails, must of necessity be forthcoming, and are for the most part only too easily multiplied. Thus their very savings do but go to facilitate the crises which throw them idle." (J. M. Robertson, *The Fallacy of Saving*, London, 1892. p. 72.)

[8] "Over-production or a general glut is only an external phase or symptom of the real malady. The disease is under-consumption or over-saving. These two imply one another." (J. A. Hobson, *The Evolution of Modern Capitalism*, London, 1913. p. 314.)

[9] The Webbs have said that insurance has "one fundamental drawback which stands in the way of its being any real alternative to the proposals of this book. *Insurance does not prevent.*" (Sidney and Beatrice Webb, *The Prevention of Destitution*, London, 1911, p. 160.)

728

old age, etc., without any direct contributions from their own incomes. Such protection is supposed not to lower their standard of living. It is not certain in every case that they do not pay for it in the end. Among these measures are workmen's compensation laws and noncontributory pensions.

All these measures form a part of what is ordinarily called social legislation. What is social legislation as distinguished from other kinds of legislation? Almost all legislation is social in the sense that it affects all society. In modern constitutional democracies, comparatively little legislation is openly and directly for the benefit of individuals and classes, though there is a good deal of indirect class legislation. What is ordinarily meant by social legislation is legislation in the interests of the poorer classes. This seems to be contrary to the democratic idea in modern government. It is justified by its supporters on the ground that these classes are at a disadvantage in the existing economic organization, which is undemocratic at least to that extent, and should be aided by political means. If this is granted, there can be no objection to such legislation on political grounds.

Social legislation includes a great deal of labor legislation, such as regulation of the hours of labor, minimum wage legislation, prohibition of the sweating system, child labor legislation, and woman labor legislation. It includes factory legislation with respect to sanitary conditions, overcrowding, protection against fire, etc. It also includes tenement house legislation because this affects the poorer classes in the main.

Very little if any social legislation can accomplish anything in the way of preventing poverty. Such legislation may benefit individual members of the poorer classes. However much individual workers may be improved physically and mentally, so as to become more efficient workmen, such an increase in efficiency will not lessen the amount of poverty unless there is a corresponding change in the economic organization of society. So long as wealth is distributed according to the present method, so long as the distributive mechanism fetters the factors of production, and so long as industry does not expand adequately in response to an increase in the labor supply, poverty cannot decrease.

Social legislation is likely to stand in the way of effective preventive measures. In the first place, this may happen by distracting the attention of well-meaning reformers, desirous of lessening the amount of poverty, from more fundamental measures. Many humanitarians today have realized the ineffectiveness of philanthropy, but labor under the delusion that they have found sufficiently effective measures in social legislation. They think so because they exaggerate greatly the ultimate results from such legislation. They are not yet

729

capable of appreciating the need for and the much greater results from fundamental changes.

In the second place, social legislation may be used as a concession and a sop, in order to avert more fundamental measures. Capitalist interests often use philanthropy for this purpose. When philanthropy no longer serves this purpose, it becomes necessary for capitalism to make further concessions in the form of social legislation. Much of this legislation since 1880 has been a sop to the workers, in order to induce them to desist from pressing their demands for more drastic social measures.[10]

Social insurance measures and old age pensions, whether contributory or non-contributory, are always lower than the prevailing rates of income and standard of living and to that extent depress the average. This is inevitable under capitalism. If all the sick and the injured, the unemployed and the superannuated workers received full pay, it would require a large contribution from the employers, perhaps equal to their profits. The employers would pass on a large part of this burden to the workers, either directly by cutting wages or indirectly by raising the prices of their goods. If the state had to carry this burden, it would mean a large increase in the tax rates. Much of this increase would have to be borne by the workers. Furthermore, it would require large funds of monetary capital which it would be impossible to invest profitably. As Robertson has said: "The old idea of a National Insurance Fund is out of the question. Even apart from any perception of the general Fallacy of Saving, it is widely admitted that such a fund would be unworkable. It is hard enough for private insurance companies to go on investing their funds profitably, without the Government attempting to compete with them as an investor on a gigantic scale."[11]

In recent years it has become even less feasible to operate social insurance schemes on a large scale. This is notably the case with respect to unemployment. Insurance on an actuarial basis can no longer be effective against mass unemployment. Not only has it attained an enormous volume but has become even less predictable than it was in the past. Any insurance system set up before the depression which began in 1929 would have broken down completely. In so far as the needs of the unemployed have been relieved, it has been by means of inflationary measures which cannot long endure because

---

[10] This was indicated in the speech from the throne to the German Reichstag in 1881, when the first social insurance legislation was enacted: "His majesty hopes that the measure (accident insurance) will in principle receive the assent of the federal governments, and that it will be welcomed by the Reichstag as a complement of the legislation affording protection against Social-Democratic movements."

[11] J. M. Robertson, *op. cit.*, p. 143.

730

they soon defeat themselves. Fictitious capital which soon loses even its appearance of value furnishes no permanent basis for dealing with emergency conditions. The insecurity and economic risks under capitalism have become far too great to be met by any system which capitalism itself can create.

The problem of old age also is becoming too difficult for capitalism to handle. In 1900 about 4 percent of the population of the United States was over 65 years of age. In 1950 the percentage had risen to 7.5. The longevity of the American people rose from about 49.25 years in 1900 to 67.5 years in 1950. If the span of human life continues to lengthen, the proportion of the aged will continue to increase. Before long as much as 10 percent or more of the population may be over 65 years of age. Capitalism is incapable of caring for this large army of the superannuated. So long as capitalism persists, the vast mass of the unemployed, the aged, the children, and the sick and disabled may be abandoned more and more to slow starvation. Civilization may revert to barbarism and savagery when the three gaunt specters of famine, disease, and war again take their heavy toll. The span of life may reverse its course and begin to shrink instead of to expand.

Social insurance, old age pensions, and similar patchwork measures can do little to mitigate the insecurity of human existence under capitalism. In the Soviet Union the situation is the reverse. All the workers are protected against all the contingencies. These include cessation of work, namely, unemployment (now very rare), sickness, accident, maternity, and old age. Pensions are paid to men at age 60 with 25 years of service, to women at 55 with 20 years of service, and to workers in underground and other hazardous occupations at 50 with 20 years of service. The annuity ranges from 50 to 60 percent of earnings. This is a defect which should be corrected as soon as the Soviet economy has developed enough to render possible a high standard of living.

The Soviet economy still uses the monetary system inherited from capitalism, which should be superseded by a more accurate and stable system. Even after reaching the stage of state socialism the bolshevists have continued to act and also to think in terms of money, credit, prices, wages, taxes, loans, etc. In fact, they have retained practically all the external paraphernalia of the capitalist state. Though they have eliminated the essential features of capitalism, they have continued to use its forms and mechanisms. Whether or not this was inevitable during the transitional period in a country so backward as Russia is not easy to determine. Suffice it to say, these clumsy and cumbersome methods of distribution should be swept away as rapidly as possible.

731

Production cannot be planned and a stable and orderly economy is impossible so long as capitalism persists. With its highly developed productive capacity the United States is in a much better position to create the new economy than was Russia at the time of its revolution. As one of the bolshevist leaders, Leon Trotzky, said: "Soviet America will not have to imitate our bureaucratic methods. Among us the lack of the bare necessities has caused an intense scramble for an extra loaf of bread, an extra yard of cloth by every one. In this struggle our bureaucracy steps forward as a conciliator, as an all-powerful court of arbitration. You, on the other hand, are much wealthier, and would have little difficulty in supplying all of your people with all of the necessities of life." [12]

The first step toward the establishment of the socialized economy is a system of distribution which is effective as well as equitable. The basis for such a system is laid when the private ownership of the means of production, private enterprise, and private profits are abolished. Soviet Russia has already laid this basis but has not yet devised an entirely effective method of distribution. In the United States there are much talk and writing and many government reports on planning which ignore the necessity of abolishing the profit system. These are but empty words. Until the social distribution of wealth is attained, it is futile to talk of planning. A planned production cannot function properly unless it is geared into a system of distribution of its products which is both effective and equitable.

The new system must be solely a mechanism of distribution and not primarily a mechanism of exchange as under capitalism. In other words, market relations and the ideology which arises out of them must disappear as rapidly as possible. This is most feasible in the highly developed countries such as the United States, Germany, and Great Britain. Here the problem of transition is comparatively simple. As the Program of the Communist International rightly says, in such countries "having powerful productive forces, highly centralized production, with small-scale production reduced to relative insignificance, and a long established bourgeois-democratic political system, . . . unregulated market relations (need) to be given comparatively small scope," and a "rapid rate of Socialist development generally, and of

<hr />

[12] L. Trotzky, "If America Should Go Communist, " in *Liberty*, New York, March 23, 1935, p. 22.

Trotzky went on to say: "Moreover, your needs, tastes and habits would never permit your bureaucracy to divide the national income. Instead, when you organize your society to produce for human needs rather than private profits, your entire population will group itself around new trends and groups, which will struggle with one another and prevent an overweening bureaucracy from imposing itself upon them." (Pp. 22-3.)

collectivization of peasant farming in particular" can be attained.[13]

The basic distribution will take place regardless of the organization of work. That is to say, a high standard of living will be assured to all citizens of the socialized commonwealth irrespective of what productive functions they perform. Whatever is produced over and above this universal basic income will be distributed equally or differentially as may seem desirable at different times. During the early stages of the new system it may be necessary or advisable for a time to remunerate greater ability and skill more highly than inferior ability. So long as the pecuniary standard of valuation characteristic of capitalism survives, it may be necessary to use differential remuneration as an incentive to effort and achievement. This is still true in Soviet Russia where the piece-work system of payment is prevalent. Other incentives are rapidly taking the place of the pecuniary motive which should disappear entirely after a universal high standard of living is attained.[14]

When an abundant supply of most goods has been obtained, so that all reasonable demands for these goods are satisfied, differential incomes will become useless and valueless and will no longer be desired by anyone. Under these conditions the medium of distribution which will replace money will no longer be necessary, except possibly for a few relatively scarce goods. In a modified form it may be retained merely as a record of goods distributed and consumed.

According to various proposals the medium of distribution will be issued against available goods and services, non-transferable, canceled at the point of distribution of goods and services, and valid for a limited period at the end of which it will be canceled whether used or not. It will be issued every thirty days or thereabouts to everyone, except young children, feeble-minded and insane persons, and others incapable of using it, for whom custodial care will be provided. It will designate the goods or services obtained by their functional numbers, and their consumers by function and sex, in each case indicating whether the purchase was before, during, or after the consumer's

---

[13] *Program of the Communist International*, Chapter IV, Section 8.

[14] See Harry F. Ward, *In Place of Profit, Social Incentives in the Soviet Union*, New York, 1933. Among the incentives described are socialist accumulation, social ownership, social approval and disapproval, the new attitude toward work, creative purpose, workers' rationalization, participation in the government, improvement of material conditions, and new antagonisms (against religion, nationalism, bureaucratism, etc.) The last two mentioned are characteristic of the period of transition. Among the incentives which influence the workers while they are constructing the capital equipment of the communist commonwealth are payment by results (piece-work), socialist competition, the *vstrechny* or counter-plan prepared by the workers to outdo the plan of production, *khosraschet* or cost accounting, and shock work by the *oodarniks* or shock brigadiers who are striving to increase production.

period of service. The places of origin and of consumption of the goods and services rendered will be indicated by numbers which show their geographical locations.[15]

As the medium of distribution will be non-transferable, it is not likely to be stolen, given away, or permanently lost. Its validity will be limited to the period of the balanced load or one complete industrial cycle, which in North America will probably be about two years. It cannot be saved indefinitely, but must be used to secure the full quota or ration of goods and services or forfeited to the extent that it is not used.

Whether or not all these details need to be recorded remains to be seen. The medium of distribution will record the selective choices of goods and services by the consumers. It will thereby furnish a guide for the plan of production for the next period of the balanced load. This plan will be adjusted to the estimated increase of population and expansion of the standard of living. The record furnished by the medium of distribution will also indirectly influence the length of the labor service. This length will vary in accordance with the expansion or contraction in the aggregate demand for goods and services. Small changes in the length of the labor service of, let us say, not more than five percent either way, can safely be left to the technical boards to decide for the period of each balanced load. Proposals for greater changes in the length of service will be decided by the electorate. In this fashion the citizens can express their preferences collectively for more consumers' goods and services or for more leisure time and less labor.

The amount of the medium of distribution issued will correspond to the aggregate of consumers' goods and services available during the period of the balanced load. The aggregate of consumers' goods will equal the total production less the producers' goods withdrawn before distribution for replacement or for expansion of the capital equipment. The medium of distribution will at all times be adequate to distribute all the consumers' goods and services available for distribution. The absolute under-consumption and relative over-production which constantly arise on a grand scale under capitalism cannot occur in a socialized system.

Many universally used goods and services will require no medium of distribution. Even under capitalism this is already true in a number of cases where formerly payment was required each time the good or service was utilized. Examples are public roads and bridges, police and fire protection, etc. The cost of these services is now paid for

[15] For example, New York—Long. 73°, Lat. 40°, will be in Region 7340; Chicago—Long. 87°, Lat. 41°, in Region 8741; and Los Angeles—Long. 118°, Lat. 34°, in Region 11834.

through taxation. The same might be done with other goods and services, such as heat, light, and local transportation, which everyone uses. The cost of collecting the payments is often greater than the cost of providing these goods and services. This is true of gas and electricity furnished in small quantities for residential and household use. The utility company or municipal plant must install a meter for each household. These numerous meters must be read by the inspectors at least once a month and whenever there is a change of tenancy. The readings must be recorded, the accounts calculated, and the bills dispatched. The many small payments must be collected and recorded, which involves much more accounting. A similar situation exists with respect to local transportation. In the subways, for example, an agent is stationed at each stopping place to sell tickets or at least to make change. The tickets or the coins must be collected, counted, recorded, and accounted for.

This waste is inevitable under capitalism because otherwise the harvest of profits cannot be reaped. In a socialized system all this waste can be swept away and great economies effected. In fact, there is scarcely any reason for using a medium of distribution at all except for goods and services where there is individual choice. Very little loss through excessive use is likely to be entailed thereby. Few people will ride more than is useful in the subways and streetcars simply because they no longer have to pay for it. A little electricity may be wasted through carelessness. This waste can be checked in large part by automatic devices for turning off the current when not in use. Almost all the vast and onerous burden of salesmanship will be swept away. Shops and salesmen will disappear almost entirely. Practically all the universally utilized goods and services and most of those subject to individual choice will be ordered by and delivered directly to the consumers from their places of origin without the intervention of the clumsy and cumbersome mechanism to promote vendibility which is necessary under capitalism.

There are several possibilities with respect to the measure of value upon which the new medium of distribution will be based. Gold, silver, or any scarce commodity or combination of commodities is unsuitable for this purpose. Commodities cannot be measured in terms of themselves. The value of gold and silver is unstable and variable because it is subject to the supply of and demand for precious metals, the fiscal policies of governments, the balance of trade between nations, and other incalculable factors. Scarcity does not in and of itself furnish stability to a measure of value. A scarce article is at best only a rubber "yardstick" which continually expands or contracts. The frequent great and sudden fluctuations in the exchange value of money disrupt price and income standards. Monetary inflation and deflation constitute one of the principal causes of the economic insecurity which afflicts mankind.

The socialists have usually advocated labor as a standard of value. The man-hour would become the unit of value. The amount of toil suffered in producing a commodity is unquestionably the cost of production from any and every human point of view. It should, therefore, indicate its value. But there are different grades of labor from a social point of view. Some grades of labor produce more wealth than other grades of labor. Hence it cannot be assumed that the man-hour of one worker is equivalent to the man-hour of another worker.

It has been suggested that different labor levels be recognized which will be rated in relation to each other at a ratio corresponding to their relative productivity, so far as that productivity can be determined. One labor level might be rated at twice the value of another labor level, etc. The kilo-man-hour (kmh.) would be the time-rate based on 1000 productive hours averaged for the group to which a worker belongs. The kmh. of one group would have a fixed ratio in its relation to the kmh. of another group. Practical difficulties, however, arise in applying such a standard of value. The productivity of many kinds of labor cannot be measured quantitatively, and their qualitative value cannot be related to each other at any fixed ratio. The productivity of labor varies considerably from time to time according to the stage of technological evolution attained. Labor which is very productive at one stage may become almost valueless at a higher stage of technology.

The technocrats have proposed that energy extraneous to human beings be recognized as the standard of value. The erg or the kilowatt would become the unit of measurement. The cost of a commodity would then be measured by the amount of extraneous energy expended in producing it. "Instead of having an elastic type of 'value' as at present, goods, under Technocracy, would possess a measurable energy cost, and would be distributed on that basis. Thus the total cost of all goods and services produced would be the total amount of energy used in their production. The total currency is a certification of the total net energy consumed; the income of the individual in a Technocracy is arrived at by dividing the total adult population into the total certification of consumed energy." [16]

Energy as a yardstick has the great advantage of being unchangeable and therefore entirely stable. An erg or a kilowatt is always the same, regardless of time and place. For the highly mechanized and automatized forms of production it furnishes an accurate and readily

[16] *Some Questions Answered*, issued by Technocracy, Inc., New York, 1934, pp. 9-10.

736

applied means of measurement. In the forms of production in which labor still plays an important part it is not so readily applied. Services cannot be measured by the energy yardstick. This may not be a serious objection because practically all services such as medical or educational service will be socialized.

It may prove to be necessary to combine man-hours and ergs in measuring cost of production. Another consideration which may influence the valuation of commodities is the scarcity of certain non-recurrent raw materials, such as the rare metals (radium, platinum, etc.), which play a part in the production of certain commodities. The unpleasantness or dangerousness of certain kinds of work may also have to be considered. As the Continental Committee on Technocracy has said: "Obviously 'difficulty', which takes the place of the 'dollar cost' of the price system, is the important item in estimating the price of most commodities. Energy cost and man-hours are still important measures of difficulty in industry, but will become less and less so as technology, released from the restraint of present financial procedures, advances." [17]

Needless to say, use value, which is the only intrinsic value of a commodity and has nothing to do with cost of production and scarcity, is a subjective quality which cannot be measured by any yardstick. All these methods which attempt to measure cost of production and economic "value," which is the rating given to a commodity or service by the economic system and has nothing to do with its intrinsic value, decrease in importance and significance as the era of abundance is approached. They may eventually become entirely superfluous. As Trotzky has said: "Only when Socialism succeeds in substituting administrative control for money will it be possible to abandon a stable gold currency. Then money will become ordinary paper slips, like trolley or theater tickets. As Socialism advances these slips will also disappear, and control over individual consumption—whether by money or administration—will no longer be necessary when there is more than enough of everything for everybody!" [18]

The fate of the citizen as a wage slave under capitalism is hard indeed. If he can get work at all to keep body and soul together, he is forced to toil for long hours, usually under unhealthy conditions, for a pittance. His fate as a consumer is not much better. He is deprived of a considerable part of his income, small enough at best, to pay for the costs of salesmanship and advertising. With what little remains he is able usually to procure goods which are at best shoddy and of inferior quality, and at worst are harmful and dangerous. He is subjected to a constant stream of deliberate and calculated mis-

[17] *The Plan of Plenty*, New York, 1934, p. 7.
[18] Leon Trotzky, *op. cit.*, p. 22.

information which is intended to influence his choices as a buyer. Salesmanship and advertising are venal arts of manipulation in the interests of the manufacturer and the merchant with no regard for the welfare of the ultimate consumer.

As Veblen has rightly pointed out, a large part of the so-called cost of production is sales cost. Salesmanship diverts purchasing power from one line to another. It does not increase the total of sales, in other words, the aggregate amount of goods distributed and consumed.[19]

The commercial ideology and apologetics of capitalism have tried to justify advertising and ennoble it by attributing to it a very dubious spiritual significance. A president of the United States made the startling but questionable assertion that advertising is aiding in the salvation of mankind: "Advertising ministers to the spiritual side of trade. It is a great power that has been entrusted to your keeping which charges you with the high responsibility of inspiring and ennobling the commercial world. It is all part of the greater work of the regeneration and redemption of mankind."[20]

Governments have at times made attempts to regulate the quality of some commodities. They have usually been such commodities as foods, beverages, and drugs which endanger the health and sometimes the lives of the community if not of good quality. Even in the case of these goods of such vital importance to the physical welfare of mankind, the profit-making interests often succeed in balking the governmental efforts to regulate effectively or at all. With large funds at their disposal these private interests can control the press and many other forms of publicity, maintain lobbies, and influence legislators and other public officials directly as well as indirectly. In the face of corporate and monopoly capitalism government is almost helpless.

Governments have rarely made attempts to regulate the quality of goods which are not of such immediate vital importance. The capitalist juridical principle of *caveat emptor* has reigned supreme. In the earlier days when there was not a large choice and most goods were locally produced the consumer was in a better position to judge the quality of the articles he was purchasing. Under present conditions of large-scale factory production it is no longer possible for the consumer to judge wisely the quality of most of the goods submitted to his choice. Very often it is the ware whose publicity makes the biggest noise and not the one of the best quality which secures the largest number of sales.

[19] Thorsten Veblen, *Absentee Ownership and Business Enterprise in Recent Times*, New York, 1923, pp. 300, 392.

[20] The late President Calvin Coolidge at the annual convention of the American Association of Advertizing Agencies in Washington, October 27, 1926.

The combined effects of all these factors have rendered the situation with regard to consumption hopelessly confused under capitalism. The constant and erratic variations of incomes, prices, cost and standard of living disturb greatly the steady development and fixation of norms of consumption. The demand for commodities is correspondingly erratic and causes a good deal of waste through over-production or under-consumption. Most goods are much inferior in quality to what could readily be produced at very little or no increase in the genuine cost of production. As most persons have very small incomes, they are compelled to purchase in small quantities and at high retail price. Their choices are influenced and manipulated, according to no rhyme or reason, by salesmanship and advertising, by mercurial fashions, and by meretricious standards of external appearance established by the leisure class and imposed upon the servile classes in their vain struggle to improve their standard of living by aping the upper classes.

This confused situation is reflected in capitalist economics. In recent years has arisen an extensive literature on salesmanship, merchandising, marketing, wholesale buying and selling, retail selling and buying, advertising, and the like. Some of this literature professes to belong to the science of economics and to the economics of consumption in particular. As such it is almost entirely spurious. It belongs almost exclusively to the technique of manipulating the consumer and selling him something. Apart from this objective it is not in the least concerned with either the art or the science of consumption. It is hardly above the intellectual level of stock prospectuses and "pep" sales talks. Nearly every American university has its school of business or commerce purveying this counterfeit "Science" of economics.

According to the orthodox economic theory prices are fixed by the higgling in the market. They have only an indirect relationship to costs of production in that these costs must be more than covered by the prices in the long run. At any given time and place the prices are determined by the relative advantages of the vendors and the buyers. This process can be seen all the time even in the most petty retail trade in the bargaining which is characteristic of Oriental and certain other countries. In many Occidental countries prices are supposed to be fixed in the sense of being temporarily stable and not varying from one transaction to another. There are, however, many price variations which are more apparent than real and are intended to mislead the consumers. Merchants often raise the prices of goods at first to exorbitant heights from which they are soon dropped down to so-called "reduced" levels. Bargain sales, "fire" sales, holiday and seasonal sales are filled with these wares at "reduced" prices, and the purchasers are fooled into thinking that they are getting something for nothing.

Shops put forward "leaders" or goods at unusually low prices which serve as a bait to entice purchasers into the shops where they are cajoled into buying much more expensive wares. Premiums and prizes are given with many commodities for the same purpose. Charge accounts and instalment buying are devices to induce consumers to commit themselves to purchasing goods even when they are financially not in a position to do so.

Needless to say, every vestige of this technique of salesmanship and advertising will disappear in the social commonwealth. No one will any longer have any pecuniary interest in selling anything to anybody. Prices will be fixed by the costs of production. Most goods will be standardized and need not be displayed at all or only in one or two central depots. They will be recorded and briefly described in catalogues. They can be ordered from the warehouses and will be delivered promptly by mail, pneumatic tubes, or some other automatic device, to the consumer at his residence or place of work. The unstandardized goods for which there is consumers' choice, such as clothing, personal adornments, household furniture, books, art objects, etc., will be on display in a few show places. By these methods almost all the present clumsy and wasteful system of distribution of commodities will be swept away. The consumers themselves will be saved a great deal of time and bother thereby, and will be assured of better goods at lower cost.

It is hopeless to expect any improvement of the situation with respect to the art of consumption under capitalism. Consumption can be rationalized only in the social commonwealth. Its citizen will be assured of an ample income and ample leisure in which to enjoy it. The young will receive a rearing and education which will enable them to appreciate and utilize a wide range of material goods without injury to themselves and to others.[21]

At the same time many things now extensively used will gradually disappear because they are useless and often harmful. Among them are unnecessary, unhealthy, and uncomfortable clothing, useless structures built largely for show, ugly and uncomfortable furniture, much trumpery bric-a-brac intended for decoration, and many superfluous and injurious kinds of food and drink. Some of these are due to abnormal and artificial appetites which are stimulated by the present social order, as for many indigestible foods and poisonous drinks, such as alcoholic beverages, and for opium, morphine, tobacco, and other stimulants and sedatives.

At present much of the expenditure of most persons whose in-

[21] The remainder of this chapter is paraphrased from my book entitled *The New Gymnosophy*, New York, 1927, published since 1931 under the title *Nudim in Modern Life*, 5th revised edition, 1952.

comes are appreciably higher than a bare subsistence minimum is for the purpose of displaying their purchasing power, and thereby their economic and social status. Whatever satisfaction may be gained in the form of prestige, adulation, and power in the present order, ostentatious expenditure will be pointless and futile in the democracy of the social commonwealth. Pecuniary emulation will disappear when differential incomes have been eliminated.

In the social commonwealth it will be possible for the first time in history to develop both a science and an art of consumption. Capitalism has developed the science and art of production in so far as they assist in producing goods to be sold. It has no interest in the use value of goods after they are sold. As Corey has rightly said: "Capitalist production aims to make profits. Consumption is subordinate to production, and consumption grows incidentally, as a mere by-product of the accumulation of capital." [22]

A mankind inured to scarcity, accustomed to a long drudgery of toil, devitalized by a low standard of living and chronic fatigue, and dulled by worry and misery, is ill prepared to utilize an abundance of goods and ample leisure. It has been compelled to devote most of its energies to activities which are means to ends. Those ends have usually been the objectives of the master class. The slave morality has sanctioned this meaningless drudgery for the masses. Freedom from exploitation and unceasing toil will enable them for the first time in history to devote their energies to activities which are ends in themselves, as well as being in some cases means to secondary ends.

During the period of transition to the era of plenty, it may be necessary to furnish some training and instruction in the consumption of goods and the enjoyment of leisure. When a generation has grown up under the new regime, special instruction for this purpose will no longer be necessary. The ample educational facilities of the social commonwealth will develop the personality of the individual to such a degree that he will spontaneously and without special guidance choose his own ways of spending his time and consuming his income. He will devote part of his leisure time to pure enjoyment with no ulterior end in view, and a part of it to congenial avocational activities, some of which will have social value. The release of a vast amount of human talent which is frustrated and crushed at present will result in many new forms of activity which cannot now be foreseen.

The new science and art of consumption will aid the citizens of the social commonwealth in making their free and democratic choices as to how much time and toil they wish to devote to the production of more goods in preference to more leisure and a smaller abundance

[22] Lewis Corey, *The Decline of American Capitalism*, New York, 1934, p. 147.

of goods. The researches of the scientific and technical boards in the field of the consumption of goods and of the utilization of leisure time will be at the disposal of the citizens. Mankind will then be guided by a technique of consumption as well as of production.

The hours of labor will be arranged in relation to eating, out-of-door life and exercise, and the sunlight. As no more than four hours of work, and probably less, will be required of a person in any one day, it will be possible to do this stint between meals, thus avoiding the indigestion caused by hurried eating when tired and by work soon after the meal. During the warm seasons, all or at least a part of the forenoon or afternoon will be free. Several hours will be available for basking unclothed in the sunlight in the open. During the cold seasons, as far as it can be arranged by interchanging services which have to go on all the time, several hours will be free in the middle of the day, in order to bathe in the sun whenever it appears.

The dominant ideals of Occidental civilization include a large population, much of which is crowded into monstrous cities, the production of huge quantities of material goods, the intensive exploitation of natural resources and of human labor, the extensive use of physical force in industry and in warlike activities, and the employment of science and invention mainly for these purposes. In this crudely materialistic welter the criterion is quantity rather than quality. The promotion of human happiness is greatly hampered. The development of personality is ignored. Man's intimate relation with nature is forgotten.

In contrast to the above, the social commonwealth will be dominated by ideals whose criterion is quality rather than quantity. A happy mankind will be regarded as more important than a vast population, life in a close relation to nature as preferable to the current urban existence, and the development of personality as more valuable than the expenditure of an enormous amount of physical force. In the past the realization of these ideals has been regarded as utopian. Science and technology have now made them readily attainable as soon as the production and distribution of wealth have been socialized.

During the past ten thousand years has arisen our civilization. It has become largely urban in its character. Man himself has changed very little during that period. The extant remains of *Homo aurignacensis,* who lived in Europe 25,000 or more years ago, indicate a type substantially the same as the human type of today. While his social environment and his manner of life have changed greatly, man's physical traits have remained essentially the same. Hence has arisen an acute maladjustment between man the air-and-light animal, and his civilized and urbanized existence. In the social commonwealth the human body will be given its proper dignity which will aid greatly in restoring mankind to a more natural existence. This will imply and connote many other important and beneficent changes for the individual and for society.

The city of the future will be far more spacious than the warrens and sties in which human animals now huddle together and breed like rabbits and swine. It will be flooded with air and light. Possessing an abundance of foliage, it will combine the advantages of city and of country. The rural folk also will be leading a more natural and healthy existence. While they are surrounded by nature today, they cut themselves off very largely from its beneficent influence by their clothing and manner of life. The social commonwealth will enable mankind not only to develop and enrich all that is of value in our existing culture, but also to recover much that we have lost through our artificial civilization.

Chapter XLIII

The Political Aspect of a Collectivist Economy

HOWEVER brutal and unjust capitalism may be, that is no reason in itself why it should not persist indefinitely. Other brutal and unjust systems have survived for many ages. If capitalism is disintegrating, it is because it is inefficient as an economic system, and contains many inherent contradictions which are threatening its viability. Capitalism is inefficient because it can produce far less—much less than half—than the available productive capacity renders possible. It often frustrates science and technology which could readily and speedily expand this productive capacity. It is subject to violent and frequent fluctuations (the business cycle) which are becoming more accentuated. Capitalist prosperity brings depression, expansion leads to contraction, inflation gives rise to deflation, thereby creating a chronic state of instability. Capitalism is ambivalent in that it contains both competitive and monopolistic tendencies which are mutually incompatible.

Having passed through its early mercantile stage, and reached its apogee during its period of industrial expansion, capitalism is now passing into its monopolistic stage of finance capitalism. The proletarized masses, into which the lower middle class is being pushed, are becoming divided between the wage slaves, paid on the basis of a bare subsistence minimum, and the unemployed or pauper slaves, on the meager and capricious doles of public and private relief, in order to avert the danger of a hungry mob which might precipitate a revolution.

A situation so anomalous cannot endure indefinitely. The only alternatives are stabilization for a time at a depression level, namely, an extreme form of a scarcity economy, or the rapid disintegration and disruption of the capitalist system. A continuous and permanent prosperity, namely, an economy of abundance, is inherently impossible under and diametrically opposed to capitalism. A temporary period of stabilization at the depression level, as under fascism, may intervene before the final collapse of capitalism.

Liberal democracy professes to maintain freedom of thought, of speech, of publication, and of assembly, in other words, the civil liberties. It also professes to maintain economic liberty. In a comparatively simple agricultural community and where industrial production is largely by handicraft, liberal democracy may succeed in promoting economic liberty for the great majority. With the advent of large-scale machine production it became no longer possible for the average worker to own the means of production. The workers are now largely at the mercy of the capitalists who own the machines. By uniting and bargaining collectively they have endeavored to defend themselves against the advantageous position of their employers. Technological advance has rendered such measures almost ineffective. All that capitalism can distribute with its mechanism of prices can be produced by a small part of the available labor force. A large labor surplus can find little or no employment. It survives at the low subsistence level afforded by public or private charity. This labor surplus lowers the wages and standard of living for the whole of the working class. Under these circumstances economic liberty, in the liberal-democratic sense, has become a tragic farce. The many millions in the liberal-democratic countries, such as the United States, England, and France, who are unemployed or have low incomes have no liberty or individual rights which have any practical value.

The failure of liberal democracy to provide even a moderate standard of living for the vast majority has also resulted in destroying the civil liberties in large part. The capitalists have been chiseling away these rights and preparing the way intentionally or unconsciously for the coming of the authoritarian state under capitalism. With the proletarian and the lower middle classes much weakened, there can be little opposition to the rule of the capitalists. This is a class dictatorship which contemplates no termination because the capitalist class can never include the whole of mankind.

The authoritarian capitalist state professes to remedy the faults of liberal democracy. In fascist Italy and nazi Germany, in the first half of the 20th century, it failed to do so, and made the economic situation even worse for the masses. It destroyed what vestiges of liberty survived in the liberal-democratic state. Freedom of the press, of assembly, and of voluntary organization disappeared entirely. The women lost their newly acquired liberty. The class struggle was temporarily obstructed by the complete subjugation of the largest class which contains most of mankind. The doctrine of the "leader" carried this process still farther by subjecting almost everyone to a small oligarchy. Italy reverted to extreme severity in the treatment of

745

criminals. In Germany came the stupid and brutal racial limitations which soon culminated in genocide.

When we turn to bolshevism, what seems at first a paradoxical situation presents itself. Here also as under authoritarian capitalism we find militarism, dictatorship, terrorism, the suppression of civil liberties, and the frequent use of undemocratic methods. But the bolshevist system differs in all its fundamental traits from capitalist authoritarianism. Nowhere in communist literature is there a word against liberty and democracy as such. On the contrary, the ultimate purpose of bolshevism is invariably set forth as the freedom of the individual and the protection of his rights, while authoritarianism in all its forms is denounced.

The authoritarian methods used by the bolshevists are intended to be temporary and should terminate as soon as the ends sought are attained. The dictatorship of the proletariat will cease with the termination of the class struggle. The permanent subjugation of one class by another, as under authoritarian capitalism, is not contemplated. On the contrary, class distinctions will disappear because all the classes will be merged in an all-inclusive mankind in which there will be no groups of exploiters and of the exploited. In similar fashion, discrimination as between races and nationalities will disappear. All of them will enjoy an equal freedom. This is already illustrated in the Soviet policy toward the many racial and national entities in Russia.

The bolshevists recognize that discrimination against races and nations as such furnishes a basis for exploitation. Capitalist enterprise the world over, both in colonial expansion and at home, has utilized and accentuated such discrimination to diminish wage rates, to furnish scapegoats for the evils it causes, to reenforce class distinctions, and in general to establish its slavocracy more firmly. Even though capitalism had been overthrown, racial prejudices and discriminations would soon lead to a new class system, which would give rise to political, social and even to economic exploitation, under the cover of collectivism. During the transitional period these prejudices would encourage the prolongation of differential income. Even if equality of incomes became established, the freedom of occupational choice of the oppressed groups would be restricted. More extensive forms of discrimination would soon follow.

Collectivism is warring against the class of the exploiters and not against racial, national, or linguistic groups. In the collectivist society the individual is judged by his personal traits, and not by his racial or national origin. Only if and when he joins the class of the exploiters can he be judged and condemned as a member of a group.

The scientific attitude advocated by bolshevism destroys ab-

746

solute standards, and repudiates spiritual authoritarianism promoted by the dogma of an almighty deity. Dialectic materialism itself implies never-ending change and development. The accusation which has perhaps been the most plausible is that bolshevism strives to submerge the individual in the mass and to standardize him. There has been a tendency in this direction during the revolutionary period which has not yet terminated. All this is contrary to the fundamental tenets of collectivism, whose purpose it is to promote to the highest possible degree the freedom of the individual. Such measures can be justified, if at all, only temporarily as revolutionary means. Under collectivism the "submergence of the individual in the mass" can take place only to the minimum extent to which every individual must be adapted to the social system under which he lives. The submergence is far less than under authoritarian capitalism, where the individual is intentionally and systematically submerged to a high degree.

The liberal-democratic conception of the state as a political organization whose principal function is to maintain order, but which is expected to perform relatively few economic and social functions, has attracted to governmental activities a large percentage of lawyers and of political adventurers and careerists of various sorts. Technical skill and ability have usually found a more adequate scope in private life. As the largest financial rewards are in private business enterprise, the latter has attracted a high proportion of the best organizational and administrative ability. Parliaments largely composed of lawyers and politicians are little competent to deal with economic and social problems when circumstances force these problems upon the attention of a liberal-democratic government.

The foregoing survey indicates that the liberal-democratic state is already in an unstable equilibrium, and has become more or less self-contradictory. While clinging to the theory that the government which governs the least is the best, it is subjected to severe pressure to perform many social and economic functions for which it is not well fitted. The bolshevist and fascist theories of the state are more self-conscious than the liberal-democratic theory, partly because they are new. The fascist-nazi state professed to be strong, but was in reality a puppet in the hands of the big capitalists. The bolshevists profess to abolish the state, but are actually building up a powerful organization which will direct and control the economic as well as the political life.

The outcome of this situation depends mainly upon what happens to capitalism. The fate of the state of today and the fate of capitalism are inextricably bound up together. If capitalism is destined to disappear, fascism and national socialism, which constitute its

747

most monopolistic phase, will go with it. The way will then be clear for the genuinely strong state of communism. This will combine the libertarian features of liberal democracy with the economic functions of capitalism. The only other possibility is a combination of state socialism in certain economic activities, such as transportation, banking, mining, the heavy industries, with capitalism in the other branches of production, such as the light industries, agriculture, etc. Whether such a hybrid combination can long persist is questionable. Soviet Russia's experience with the NEP (New Economic Policy), which lasted only from 1921 to 1929, seems to indicate that any considerable degree of socialism will soon eliminate the remnants of capitalism.[1]

In the countries where capitalism has developed most highly, such as the United States and Canada, the functions of government, especially its economic functions, have been correspondingly limited. In the countries where capitalism has not developed highly, most of which are predominantly agrarian, there has been more room for the expansion of a governmental bureaucracy. The peasantry is usually more or less under the domination of semi-feudal landlords. There are parliamentary institutions in most of these countries. They are usually under the control of the bureaucrats, because the peasants are too ignorant to know how to vote and the landlords absent themselves a good deal of the time. These bureaucratic governments display mild tendencies toward a paternalistic form of state socialism because in the absence of a vigorous capitalism they initiate and operate certain public services and utilities.

The question now arises as to the form of the administration which will include the political state and the management of the economic mechanism of the socialized and planned order. This administration must be so organized as to utilize fully expert knowledge and technical skill. At the same time it must contain adequate safeguards against the concentration of power in the hands of a small oligarchy or of a personal dictator. The final seat of authority should at all times be in the people. In other words, the administration should be democratic at bottom, however much power may be delegated to its scientific, technical and professional experts by the people.

The technocrats have emphasized the importance of utilizing technical skill. They have been barren of proposals as to the organization of the socialized system. The chief administrative body, composed of equal numbers of executive and technical personnel from every branch of the productive and distributive system, is to be the

---

[1] For a lengthy discussion of the subject matter of this chapter, see my *Bolshevism, Fascism and the Liberal-Democratic State*, New York, 1934.

748

technate: "All essential functions would be a part of this all embracing, non-democratic, non-political organization: the American Technate. The Technate bears no resemblance to a political state; it is a technological control of the continental area, functional in structure, socially integrating and synchronizing all operations on the balanced load basis necessary for the maintenance of the highest standard of living permissible on that area." [2]

This technocratic statement goes on to say that "political government as we know it today would not exist under Technocracy for the reason that the function of political government has simply been to act as an arbiter among the vested interests; i.e., those groups which act on prescriptive authority." This is a partial and distorted representation of the truth. Government has usually been not the arbiter between vested interests but the tool of one vested interest in exploiting the rest of society. The abolition of vested interests does not, however, mean the complete disappearance of government and the state under technocracy. This is as fallacious an assertion as the Marxist theory of the "withering away of the state" in the classless society.

The technocratic statement contains a fundamental contradiction. It characterizes the technate as non-democratic and non-political. And yet it asserts that the chief administrative body will contain representatives of all branches of the administrative personnel. Inasmuch as this personnel will include all the workers and citizens, this body will be democratic as well as political. It will closely resemble a soviet congress or any genuinely democratic parliament on a vocational basis.

The division of governmental powers in the capitalist countries is intended primarily to restrain the masses, and to give the decisive control to the dominant class. In a liberal-democratic state where there is universal suffrage the popular will is most likely to express itself through the legislative branch of the government. Hence it is essential for the vested interests to limit the legislature narrowly by the executive and judicial branches. The so-called balance of power in liberal-democratic government is largely a myth.

In the American type of government, which may be called the presidential regime, the president is not chosen by the direct vote of the people. He is elected for a term of years and has extensive executive powers. He appoints the cabinet ministers, who are responsible only to him, and many other officials. Through a limited veto power he exercises a certain degree of control over legislation. The courts have the power to interpret the Constitution. They are able thereby to nullify much legislation and to restrict narrowly the legislature. The

[2] *Some Questions Answered*, issued by Technocracy, Inc., New York, 1934, p. 19.

makers of the American Constitution, who had no intention of establishing a genuine democracy, did their work only too well.[3]

In the liberal-democratic state the political organization is democratic in form and theory whereas the economic system is feudal in
almost every respect. This contradiction is resolved through the domination of the government by the feudal interests. The liberal-democratic government is in practice little more democratic than and almost as feudal as liberal capitalism. When the liberal-democratic
state is transformed into the fascist state of monopolistic capitalism, even the pretense and form of democracy disappear, so that the
fascist government is fully as feudal as capitalism.

In a socialized system it becomes possible, perhaps for the first
time in the history of mankind, to correlate a democratic political
organization with the economic system, because the latter is collectivist
and the means of production are under social control. The form of
government arises out of, is related to, and is harmonious with, the
planned production, organized work, and effective distribution which
constitute a functional economic whole.

A planning board will coordinate and plan ahead all forms of
production. In this fashion will be harmonized in a well-integrated
whole the functions performed under capitalism by enterprisers, business managers, technical directors, trade unions and other vocational
and professional bodies, and various political bodies such as parliaments, ministries, commissions, bureaus, etc. The capitalist scheme is
ill-organized and contains many internal conflicts.

The ultimate authority of the socialized system will be vested
in the parliament chosen by the entire adult population. The repre-
sensation will be proportional. It will also be vocational, at any rate
in the early stages of the evolution of the socialized system. It need be
only broadly territorial in so far as there are important geo-economic
differences which require representation of the various geo-economic
areas by those most familiar with them. When the system is highly
developed and working smoothly and more or less automatically, and
the populace has become politically literate, it may no longer be
necessary to make the representation vocational. Any intelligent,
educated, and experienced citizen will then be competent to serve as
a representative in a parliament which will act only on matters of
general policy. All questions requiring special knowledge will be referred to the boards of experts or the administrative boards.

[3] John B. Wolf, *History of Civilization*, Boston, 1947, Vol. II, p. 124.
"The delegates to the Federal Convention . . . were . . . at least as solicitous
for the rights of property as for the rights of man. . . . The Constitution . . . was
essentially a conservative document, a bulwark of the middle class against the level-
ing tendencies of farmers and artisans."

Under capitalism representation is often demanded for the consumers or the "public." This is because conflict often arises between the interests of the consumers and those of the producers, in spite of the fact that the consumers and the producers are in the main the same persons. In a socialized system this antagonism between the citizen as consumer, and himself as producer and worker, will disappear entirely. The antagonism is a gratuitous and irrelevant incident of the class struggle which arises out of the vested rights in land and capital. The elimination of the class struggle will make the consumers entirely identical with the workers and the producers. There will no longer be any occasion for a representation of the citizens as consumers distinct from their representation as producers and workers.

The parliament will legislate as to such broad matters of policy as constitutional amendments and changes in social organization, the standard of living, hours of labor, length of service, norms and forms of social control, educational methods, and will stand ready to meet any new social, economic, and political situation which may arise. It should at all times safeguard the civil rights and liberties which should be greatly extended under a socialized system and which should protect minorities and individuals from undue pressure from the majority. On the other hand, a great deal of legislation which arises out of property rights and the class struggle, or which relates to taxation and other financial matters, will disappear entirely. The tendency will be toward a great simplification of democratic processes. Such democratic procedures as the initiative of legislation by the public and the referendum of laws to the public, and the recall of representatives by their constituents can be given their full effect. There will probably be little occasion to make use of them.

There can be a much more realistic party alignment with respect to principles, programs, and policies when private plunder and covert class designs are no longer possible. Demagogic personal ambitions can with difficulty influence a politically literate electorate. Politicians and parliamentary careerists will disappear. The spoils of office to nourish them will no longer exist. Each citizen will have his career primarily in his work in the functionalized social system. Any political activities in which he partakes can only be incidental to his career. Political activities will, in any case, be merged to a large extent with economic and other social activities.

The judicial function will shrink greatly in scope and importance. The contested cases which arise out of vested rights and class interests will disappear entirely. Almost all the litigation which arises out of the law of contracts and the law of torts will no longer be possible. At least nine-tenths of the civil actions will disappear from the courts. As practically all the economic causes of crime will

751

no longer exist in a society where almost all forms of theft are impossible, the number of criminal cases will also decrease greatly.

Most of the questions which are now decided by the slow and blundering methods of incompetent legislatures will be solved by the automatic functioning of the socialized system. Technical decisions requiring specialized knowledge will be relegated to the bureaucracies of experts and technicians. These bureaucracies will operate under the general authority of the economic, educational, scientific, and cultural councils.

These are a few suggestions as to the main lines of development of the organization of a planned social order. The details of organization can be worked out only in practice and through experimentation and experience. The problem is much more simple than that of a competent government and of an efficient economic system under capitalism, where conflicting class interests create a perennial internecine warfare.

Scientific prevision is limited by the extent to which factors for change are already explicit, or at least implicit, in any field of phenomena. To predict outside of these limits is at best superfluous and useless and at worst misleading and mischievous. Recent predictions of future population illustrate such unwarranted attempts at prevision. Birth and death rates are peculiarly susceptible to economic and social factors. In making these predictions the demographers have usually considered the medical factors almost solely. They have ignored the impending social and economic changes whose effects upon population can be only dimly foreseen. Such predictions are theoretically supererogatory and practically inapplicable. They reveal on the part of their makers a static rather than a dynamic conception of society, a belief that the existing social order is relatively permanent and immutable, and a failure to recognize that social changes in the past have had a far-reaching influence upon the increase, decrease, and migration of population.

Technological advance will continue to accentuate the contradictions of capitalism which will soon be unworkable. However, the capitalists will not willingly surrender their monopolistic privileges and vested rights. The proletariat is the only class which can be entirely revolutionary because it has nothing to lose. The peasants and farmers are still bound by their petty rights to the land. The middle class, even the lower middle class, may still derive some advantages from serving as retainers of the capitalists. But most of the proletariat is politically illiterate and dominated by the slave morality instilled into it by its masters. This creates the revolutionary dilemma, namely, a working class which unwittingly betrays its own interests.

This dilemma furnishes gradualism its golden opportunity. The

752

gradualists are mostly liberal intellectuals with vested interests which they fear to relinquish. They recognize that the old order must go. But they wish to be sure that the new order is functioning efficiently before they surrender their precious rights. Hence the outpouring of social reform and other gradualist programs, which would precipitate mankind into the contradiction of semi-collectivism. They argue that the capitalists can be induced by persuasion to give up their privileges. They ignore the fact that no master class in the history of mankind has done so except through compulsion. It would be contrary to human psychology for the capitalists to act otherwise. The gradualists render the confusion of their theories worse confounded by advocating the rich balm of compensation for the confiscation of expropriated wealth.

In the United States the tempo of technological advance is exceptionally fast. The capitalist crisis is developing here even more rapidly than in most of the industrial countries. But the proletariat and the other oppressed and exploited groups are less prepared to meet the crisis than are their fellows in most of the European countries. There is no revolutionary group as competent as were the bolshevists in Russia. There have been little thought and planning concerning the tactics and technique of the revolution and of the transition. When the present system falls, a provisional revolutionary government will have to carry on until the new order begins to function. The nature of that provisional government can be foreseen even less than in similar revolutionary situations in the past. These problems render the impending revolutionary and transitional period more incalculable than the subsequent constructive program.

The high technological development in the United States renders it feasible to introduce a planned social economy more readily than has been the case in the U.S.S.R. An intermediate "NEP" period of semi-collectivism may be unnecessary. It may be possible from the outset to plan for the current economy, that is to say, to provide the goods day by day for immediate consumption, as well as to plan for the capital equipment. The superficial paraphernalia of capitalism can be dispensed with more quickly than in the Soviet Union.

The technological preparation already achieved renders it possible to foresee the salient features of the planned economy. Many of its details will have to be worked out in practice through experimentation. Some of the blunders committed in Soviet Russia can be avoided. The ultimate cultural consequences can only very dimly be foreseen. Though tentative and subject to modification under the test of experience, the following plan is not utopian. All its features are explicit or at least implicit in the present technical, economic, and social situation. Because they are exceptionally mechanical-minded

753

the Americans are well prepared to grasp its technical implications, though not so capable of understanding its economic and social significance.

The first requisite of a planned economy is a logical division of time.[4] The hours of the day will be counted from one to twenty-four. The months will be abolished. They perform no useful purpose, under any economic system. The days of the year will be counted from 1 to 365, and 366 in leap years. The permanent hebdomadal week will be abolished. It prevents a flexible work program which can readily be adjusted to the increasing productivity of labor.

At the inception of the new order the following work schedule will probably suffice. The year will be divided into 73 weeks of 5 days each. A 16-hour work week, 4 hours of work daily for 4 days and then a day of rest, for 50 weeks in the year will yield 800 hours per individual worker. The remaining 23 weeks will be vacation time. The week may be uniform in time for all or it may be individual. In the latter case, one-fifth of the workers will rest while the other four-fifths work. In other words, the rest day will be staggered in order to keep the productive system in operation all the time and obviate the wastefulness of idle capital equipment. The vacation time will be staggered in similar fashion.

It is now rare for anyone in the United States to work more than 8 hours a day for 300 days in the year, making a total of 2,400 hours per annum. Most persons work on a shorter schedule. Unemployment, disease, etc., cause an enormous loss of work. Many members of the leisure class work not at all. The average for the individual actual or potential worker at present is less than 800 hours per annum. Moreover, much of this work is unproductive because it is devoted to acquiring profits and not creating use values.

In the social commonwealth all the work will be productive. Science and technological progress, no longer restrained and frustrated by capitalism, will rapidly increase the productivity of labor. Before long it will be possible to reduce the hours of labor considerably below 800 per annum.

The period of service will commence between the ages of 20 to 25 and will continue for 20 to 25 years, thus terminating between the ages of 40 to 50 years. As the social need for labor decreases, the period of service will be shortened and will terminate at an earlier age.

The years before the period of service commences will be devoted in the first instance to education and vocational training. Inasmuch as this training will be carried on largely in connection with productive enterprises, the transition from the period of preparation to

4 See Chap. XLI.

754

the period of service will be easy and natural. Within the limits of age (20 to 25 years), the transition will take place when the individual is ready for it. The assignment to a vocation will be determined in part by individual choice and in part by examination.

The latter part of the period of preparation will be devoted also to mating and childbearing, when the youth are best fitted for these functions. Social care and education of the children and communal housekeeping will enable the young women to go on with their vocational training and to enter upon their period of service. By performing their procreative function during their youth they will be more free during their maturity for avocational activity and achievement.

The planned economy will be directed not only by the physical and mechanical technology, but also by the new social technology. Production will be based upon the principle of the balanced load now operative in engineering. The amount and nature of the goods produced will be determined mainly by the demand during the preceding period of the balanced load. Suitable adjustments will be made for changes in population, variations in the standard of living, technological progress, and capital replacement and expansion. Standardization will be applied to impersonal objects where efficiency alone is important. Commodities subject to consumers' choice and preference will not be standardized completely or at all.

Scientific research will be maintained by the social commonwealth to extend the boundaries of knowledge and to apply it by means of technology. Through the higher institutions of learning and a competitive system will be secured the experts who will become the members of the scientific and technical boards which will direct and manage the planned economy. Here will be furnished ample incentive for achievement for the talented citizens of the commonwealth. This incentive will extend throughout the ranks of the workers. Achievement in both vocational and avocational activities will be recognized and rewarded by social prestige and the assignment of more important functions.

The acquisitive ideology and pecuniary standard of valuation characteristic of capitalism will disappear, and be replaced by a more social ideology and normative standard. Incentives to effort and achievement have varied greatly in different social systems, and will continue to vary in the future. It is puerile to assume that the profit motive is the sole incentive. As I have said in another work: "The tendency to work involves many different kinds of activity. Work may be defined as being effort devoted to the production of things of value. Like play, it is due in part to the physiological need of the organism to expend a certain amount of energy. . . . Various compounds of instincts, intellectual characteristics, and feelings arise which play a part in directing the tendency to work. Among them may be mentioned esthetic traits, such as the so-called architectonic sense, ambition to secure wealth, power, etc., certain altruistic sentiments, etc. This effort is also directed and its character determined in part by numerous factors of the physical and social environment of the individual."[5] Incentives and activities will arise in the new social environment which we cannot now foresee.

The basic distribution of wealth will take place regardless of the organization of work. A high standard of living will be assured all citizens throughout their lives. Over and above this basic distribution, incomes may be equal or differential. This is largely a technical problem to be decided at successive stages of the evolution of the new system. With an increasing abundance of goods the tendency will be toward an equality of incomes. Money as a medium of exchange will soon disappear and be replaced by an effective medium of distribution. Its features can be readily determined in practice.

The physical distribution of goods will be attained largely by the direct transmission of commodities from the place of production to the ultimate consumer. In this fashion most of the clumsy and wasteful mechanism of shops and merchandising will be eliminated. This mechanism has arisen primarily to promote vendibility and make profits and not to satisfy human wants. The latter end is accomplished inefficiently and inadequately. In the social commonwealth the citizen will be offered a wide range of commodities briefly described in a catalogue. Upon ordering any of these goods they will be delivered promptly at his residence and charged to his account. In the relatively few cases where the citizen wishes to inspect a commodity before purchase, he will be able to do so at one of the depots where goods subject to consumers' choice and preference will be on exhibition.

The educational system of the social commonwealth will make its citizens politically literate. It will prepare them to become self-respecting and self-reliant members of a democratic and self-governing community. As such, they can no longer be misled and victimized by demagogues, dictators, and oligarchs. The only kind of leadership to which they will respond will be that of knowledge and ability.

The state as a coercive organ will diminish greatly in importance in the social commonwealth. Most of the causes of crime will disappear. Class warfare cannot exist in a classless society. International

[5] Maurice Parmelee, *The Science of Human Behavior, Biological and Psychological Foundations*, New York, 1913, p. 252. See Chapters XI on "The Nature of Instinct," XII on "The Principal Human Instincts and General Innate Tendencies," and XIV on "The Nature of Intelligence."

756

wars will disappear as the nations adopt a socialized system and unite in a world federation of geo-economic regions.

As an administrative organization the state will increase greatly in importance. For the first time in history it will be possible to correlate closely the political with the economic organization. Indeed, with the abolition of private business enterprise the distinction between economic and political will become vague and of little significance. Most of the economic activities will be highly automatized under the direction of the scientific and technical boards. There will be few economic matters concerning which the citizens will need to take direct political action.

The framework of the state will be defined by the constitution adopted by the citizens. The supreme authority in the social commonwealth will be vested in the parliament chosen by and representing all the citizens. It will decide all ultimate questions of social importance and serve as the final court of appeal. The arbitrary and fundamental distinction and separation between the executive, legislative, and judicial functions of government have arisen primarily out of the class structure and coercive nature of the state. In the classless society they can have only a superficial and purely administrative significance. A balance of powers between the different branches and functions of government will no longer be necessary.

The executive function of government will decrease with the diminution of the coercive nature of the state. The judicial function of government will shrink greatly because the conflict of class and group interests will disappear in the cooperative commonwealth. The police power of the state will be exercized only in such minor conflicts as may arise between individuals. They will be adjudicated through such courts as may be necessary. These courts will handle the rare cases of citizens who refuse to perform their service to the state.

The administrative realization of the legislative acts and judicial decisions of parliament will be carried out under the direction of the scientific, economic, and cultural councils. These permanent bodies will supervise all phases of the collective life and activities of the commonwealth. Among the technical and administrative boards will be the planning board, the educational and public health boards, the administrations of mining, manufacturing, agriculture, transportation, etc., with such subdivisions as may seem desirable.

The members of these councils and boards will be recruited from the ranks of the citizens who have qualified through vocational training, competitive tests, and occupational attainments. They will constitute expert bureaucracies selected solely on the basis of individual ability and achievement. Distinctions of birth, wealth, and social status

757

will no longer exist. There will be equality of opportunity for all to attain the most important and responsible positions. There will be a similar freedom for achievement in avocational activities. Social prestige will be an incentive and a reward in both the vocational and the avocational fields.

The civil liberties, the right of free association, and the rights of criticism and of dissent will be guaranteed to the citizens by the constitution of the commonwealth. The vigilance of a democratic parliament will protect the rights of minorities. In this fashion the dangers of regimentation and of an excessive social crystallization will be averted. The factors for change and for progress will be assured.

The movement of population in the social commonwealth cannot be predicted. Whether or not it will be necessary or advisable to regulate the increase of population cannot be foreseen. The same may be said with regard to eugenic measures. Most discussions of eugenics and of the sterilization of the "unfit" have assumed an exclusively class point of view and have displayed ignorance of or a reckless disregard for biological knowledge. These demographic problems will be solved in conformity with the social relationships and in the light of the augmented knowledge of the future commonwealth.

The construction of the social commonwealth involves far-reaching changes. It is nevertheless a simpler and easier task than the reconstruction of capitalism with all its numerous contradictions and inconsistencies. It will solve the fundamental economic problems, namely, those of security, a universally high standard of living, and ample leisure for all. Other human and social problems can then be more readily solved.

The elimination of poverty will not prevent all pain and sorrow. Defects and ailments of body, mind, and character will always cause suffering. Friction and maladjustment in personal relations will never cease to give rise to unhappiness. There will always be enough and to spare of human misery.

The elimination of poverty will nevertheless diminish pain and misery far more than any other single change. The social system which it implies will in other respects as well be far more conducive of happiness than the existing order. The social commonwealth will carry mankind a long way toward the free and spontaneous expression of human nature which constitutes the normal life.

758

Chapter XLIV

War and Social Anarchy

WARFARE is often attributed to inborn instincts and emotions. The inference drawn from this belief is that since these traits are innate little or nothing can be done to prevent war. This is similar to common beliefs with regard to other social phenomena such as crime, poverty, prostitution, gambling, and the like. Individual humans are said to be "good" or "bad," "virtuous" or "vicious," "moral" or "immoral," "righteous" or "evil," "upright" or "wicked," "godly" or "sinful," "pure" or "impure," "just" or "unjust," "chaste" or "unchaste," "industrious" or "lazy." To reform myriads of "bad" individual humans is indeed a hopeless task, even for the combined efforts of priests, parsons, prigs, prudes, theologians, metaphysicians, teachers, publicists, journalists, orators, politicians, and statesmen. It is doubly hopeless if these obdurate humans have been endowed by an omniscient and omnipotent deity, for some inscrutable reason of its own, with hereditary sinfulness, as has been preached by some religious sects. For example, the Calvinists have alleged that only those who are elected by God are saved, and that "fallen" men are incapable of true faith and repentance.

Human behavior is psychologically determined in the sense that simple and compound reflexes, instincts and habits; sensations, feelings, emotions, and consciousness; and images, ideas, intelligence and reasoning; all or most of these psychological traits are involved in such behavior. In other words, conative, affective, and cognitive factors are the immediate determinants of behavior. But all of these traits are influenced, conditioned and partly determined in their overt manifestation by the factors not only of the physical but also of the social environment. Thus not only the climatic factors of temperature and precipitation, and the topographical factors of soil, altitude, and land and water in their relations with each other, but also the cultural factors of social organization, institutions, customs and traditions, are

759

conditioning the manner in which these traits are expressing themselves.[1]

Ethical judgments as to psychological traits are inept and misleading. These traits are the product of organic evolution and have been selected for survival in the struggle for existence. As such they are neither good nor bad. They can be appraised only in relation to the part they have played in the life of mankind, and in determining cultural phenomena.

Within the narrow limits of this chapter I cannot give a comprehensive picture of war. In his voluminous treatise Wright has given a comprehensive though somewhat eclectic discussion of the history, analysis, causes, control and prevention of war.[2] Davie described its evolution among primitive peoples, attributing it largely to the need or desire of tribes for the ownership or at least control of territory from which they derived their sustenance.[3] Nef has written a history of industrialism in Europe from 1494 to 1950 in relation to armaments and battles. He has furnished evidence that there have been more inventions during peacetime than during wartime, that many weapons were invented in the first instance for hunting and not for warlike purposes, and that the great industrial revolution came during the "Great Peace" from 1815 to 1914. But he concluded with the moralistic argument that war is caused by man's evil nature and can be prevented only by reforming this nature, thus ignoring many of the social and economic causes of war.[4]

Let us consider some of the human instincts and emotions which may play a part in war. There are a number of simple reactions which may be mere reflexes and not instinctive. Among them are the following acts which characterize infants very early in life: Crying, sneezing, snuffling, snoring, coughing, sighing, sobbing, gagging, vomiting, hiccuping, starting, moving the limbs when tickled, touched, or blown upon, etc. If any one of these reactions is a simple reflex, it is not an instinct according to the definition of instinct which I have given elsewhere.[5]

---

[1] I have discussed these internal and external determinants of behavior in several of my books, especially with respect to criminality: "Criminal conduct is, therefore, like every other kind of conduct, the outcome of the cooperation of these internal factors in the determination of human behavior with the forces of the environment. In order to understand the criminality of criminals it is necessary to study both these internal factors and the external environmental forces." (Maurice Parmelee, *Criminology*, New York, 1918, p. 39.)

[2] Quincy Wright, *A Study of War*, Chicago, 1942, 2 vols.

[3] M. R. Davie, *The Evolution of War*, New Haven, 1929.

[4] J. U. Nef, *War and Human Progress, An Essay on the Rise of Industrial Civilization*, Cambridge, Mass., 1950.

[5] Maurice Parmelee, *The Science of Human Behavior, Biological and Psycho-*

"An instinct is an inherited combination of reflexes which have been integrated by the central nervous system so as to cause an external activity of the organism which usually characterizes a whole species and is usually adaptive."

If any one of these reactions is an "inherited combination of reflexes," it falls under my definition, for every one of these actions is external. There are a number of more complicated actions which appear early in the life of the infant and which are more certainly instinctive in their character. Among these are the following: Sucking, biting, clasping, carrying to the mouth of an object, smiling, turning the head aside as a gesture of rejection, holding head erect, sitting up, standing, locomotion, vocalization, etc.

We now come to very complex forms of behavior, and it may be questioned whether some of them are distinct instincts. Among them have been named the following: Imitation, emulation or rivalry, pugnacity, anger, resentment, sympathy, the hunting instinct, fear, appropriation or acquisitiveness, constructiveness, play, curiosity, sociability, shyness, secretiveness, cleanliness, modesty and shame, sexual love, jealousy, parental love.

It is doubtful if imitation can be considered an instinct, since it does not involve any specific reflexes or mode of behavior. In the course of imitation any kind of act may be performed, Imitation is caused by suggestion and is like instinct only in that the tendency to imitate is inborn. Much the same can be said of emulation or rivalry. It does not involve any specific reflexes or mode of behavior. In the course of rivalry any kind of act may be performed. It is to a certain extent imitation, but imitation which is stimulated in part at least by the instinct of pugnacity.

Pugnacity is in all probability an instinct, since it usually involves a well-defined mode of action. But anger and resentment are emotions which accompany pugnacious acts, and as such cannot be called instincts.

Sympathy is primarily a state of feeling. Various acts result from this state, but they are very diverse in character, and so far as sympathy implies external action, it is a general innate tendency.

The tendency to hunt may be an instinct, because it involves a well-defined mode of action.

Fear is an emotion rather than an instinct, but it usually accompanies an instinctive act, the most frequent one being flight.

Appropriation or acquisitiveness is probably an instinct. Con-

logical Foundations, New York, 1913, p. 226.

See William James, Principles of Psychology, New York, 1896, Vol. II, who believed that many reflexive actions are instincts.

structiveness may possibly be an instinct, though it involves a good many different kinds of action.

The tendency to play is inborn, but it involves so many different kinds of action that it can hardly be regarded as a distinct instinct. It is rather a general innate tendency.

Curiosity may have an instinctive basis, but in man is in large part an intelligent phenomenon.

Sociability and shyness are inborn, but are so general that it is doubtful if they are distinct instincts.

Modesty and shame are not instinctive but arise from certain cultural traits which I have described elsewhere.[6]

Sexual love is an emotion. But the sexual instinct is one of the most powerful of the instincts. Jealousy is an emotion which is aroused when sexual love is violated or the sexual instinct is thwarted, and may accompany various instinctive acts usually pugnacious in their character.

Parental love is an emotion. But the parental instincts which cause parents to care for their young are very powerful instincts.

The difficulty involved in determining in the case of many of these modes of behavior whether or not they are instinctive is that we do not know what nervous mechanism is involved. All of the modes of behavior which have been discussed are probably inborn, with the exception of modesty and shame, but we cannot be sure in every case whether there is involved a sufficiently definite combination of reflexes to justify calling it an instinct. Where, however, there is a great variety of acts grouped under one name, as in some of the above cases, it is doubtful that it is an instinct, but rather a general innate tendency which involves a good many different kinds of instinctive acts.

Angell[7] asserted that the generally recognized instincts in man are the following: "Fear, anger, shyness, curiosity, affection, sexual love, jealousy and envy, rivalry, sociability, sympathy, modesty (?), play, imitation, constructiveness, secretiveness, and acquisitiveness." Elsewhere he said that instincts "represent structurally performed pathways in the nervous system, and stand functionally for effective inherited coordinations made in response to environmental demands."[8] In view of this statement it is strange that he included as instincts such general tendencies as imitation and play, which do not represent any specific pathways or coordinations in the nervous system, but

---

[6] See my *Personality and Conduct*, New York, 1918; and *The New Gymnosophy*, New York, 1927; later published under the title *Nudism in Modern Life*, 5th revised edition, 1952. In these books I have distinguished artificial from genuine modesty or humility.

[7] James R. Angell, *Psychology*, New York, 1908, p. 349.

which manifest themselves through many reflexes and combinations of reflexes. I have already commented upon all in his list with the exception of affection and envy. Both of these are emotions which are often accompanied by instinctive actions.

McDougall[9] gave the following list of what he considered the principal human instincts: Flight, repulsion, curiosity, pugnacity, self-abasement, self-assertion, parental, reproductive, gregarious, acquisitive, constructive. I have already commented upon most of them. Flight is undoubtedly an instinct and usually the instinctive act which is in mind when fear is spoken of as an instinct. Repulsion is probably a distinct instinct. Self-abasement and self-assertion are probably innate tendencies, but it is hard to say whether they are sufficiently specific to be called instincts. McDougall associated with each of these instincts an emotion which is aroused by it. He also discussed some of the general innate tendencies.

Several writers have tried to classify the instincts according to the ends which they accomplish, as, for example, according to whether they preserve the individual, the species, or society. Some distinction may be made between instincts according to the above criterion. And yet the instincts are so closely bound up together that such distinctions should not be emphasized. The instincts, like all other organic traits, are, so far as they have any end, directed toward the general end of increasing the amount of living matter. The preservation of the individual, the species, and of society in the long run aid each other and accomplish this general end. Often it is impossible to determine whether an instinct preserves one of these three any more than it does the other.

Playful activities are widespread among animals. Play may be defined as the expenditure of energy for the sake of pleasure without being directed toward any useful end. While no useful purpose can be the immediate object of play, it may serve such an end in the long run. Playful activities are most frequent among the young, who often spend all their time in play. The simplest theory of play is the Schiller-Spencer surplus energy theory. According to this theory, animals play in order to get rid of what energy they have left over after they have completed the activities necessary for existence. An organism cannot remain healthy unless it performs its functions to a normal degree. To do so it has to expend a certain amount of energy. It is stimulated to perform these functions by the necessities of existence. If these necessities require it to expend enough energy to become normally tired, it will not need to expend any more energy.

The surplus energy theory of play may explain why animals ex-

[8] *Op. cit.*, p. 339.
[9] W. McDougall, *Social Psychology*, Boston, 1909, chap. III.

pend energy in ways which are not immediately useful. But this theory does not explain the forms these activities take. If play is more than the expenditure of surplus energy, it might be only formless activity. However, playful activities assume definite forms which are suggestive of their nature and origin. The significant thing is that they resemble certain instinctive activities. Thus the plays of the boy seem to reveal the presence in him of the hunting and combative or pugnacious instincts, while the little girl playing with her dolls may reveal an early awakening of the maternal instinct. Imitation has a good deal to do with determining the playful activities of the young. Often these activities are nothing more than imitations of the activities of their elders. But when such playful activities are spontaneous, that is to say, do not copy the activities of the adults among whom these young live, it is usually possible to detect likenesses to instinctive activities. A test is to separate entirely from the earliest age the young of a species from the adults of the same species and then observe the playful activities which spontaneously manifest themselves among these young. For example, if a number of very young puppies are isolated from other dogs, as soon as their eyes are open and their legs are strong enough to move around easily, they will fight each other in play, thus revealing an early awakening of the combative instinct. But the instinctive impulse will not display itself in its full strength, for they will not usually hurt each other, but will merely go through the motions of fighting. The inborn, integrated series of reflexes upon which the combative instinct is based is already beginning to function, though not yet with the facility and force it will display as maturity is reached. As has been shown by Groos,[10] playful activities take the form, to a large extent, of early manifestations of instinctive impulses which will attain full force as maturity is reached. And as has been pointed out by Groos and others, such playful activities have utility for the young after they have grown up and for the species, because in these playful activities skill is acquired in the practice of the instinctive activities which will have utility later in life. Though playful activities have no immediate utility, they may have great utility for the future.

The playful activities of adults also are to a large extent the manifestation and expression of instinctive impulses. In most games are involved opposition and conflict, which are manifestations of the combative instinct. In modern civilized society some instinctive impulses find their expression for most individuals only in the form of play. Few people need to hunt for purposes of securing subsistence, which was the original cause for the growth of the hunting instinct,

[10] Karl Groos, *The Play of Animals*, translated from the German, New York, 1898. *The Play of Man*, translated from the German, New York, 1901.

764

but many indulge in hunting for purposes of play. While the utility of playful activities, the forms of which are determined by instinctive impulses, has been shown for the young, it is perhaps unfortunate that the same should be true to so great an extent for adults, for if playful activities differed greatly from purely instinctive activities, there would be greater variety in human behavior, and human personality would be correspondingly more complex.

Very different kinds of activities are included under the rubric of play. If, therefore, an instinct is as I have defined it, namely, an integrated series of reflexes, play is not a specific instinct. The inborn physiological characteristics require that surplus energy be expended, and the instincts furnish well-worn grooves into which the expenditure of this energy may fall. Playful activities often are also instinctive activities, but taken together they do not constitute a distinct instinct.

Emulation or rivalry is much the same kind of a phenomenon as imitation or play. It does not involve any one integrated series of reflexes, and in the course of emulation an individual may use many different kinds of behavior. Emulation is to a large extent imitation stimulated in part by the combative or pugnacious instinct. Other instincts are involved according to the subject of emulation or rivalry. If it is rivalry in love, the sexual instinct plays a part. If it is rivalry in economic activities, the instinct of acquisition plays a part. Under the rubric of emulation are certain complex groups of activities which as groups are similar to each other. These groups include many activities which are instinctive.

Another so-called instinct is the "instinct of workmanship." [11] The tendency to work involves many different kinds of activity. Work may be defined as effort devoted to the production of things of value. Like play, it is due in part to the physiological need of the organism to expend a certain amount of energy. It is also and in large part due to the needs of subsistence which force the individual to expend effort in order to secure the things needed. In human society this takes the form of economic pressure in the economic struggle for existence. This effort is directed and its character is determined in part by numerous internal factors. Among them are instincts such as the so-called instinct of contructiveness, and various feelings and emotions. Furthermore, intellectual factors play a more and more important part, especially among humans. Various compounds of instincts, intellectual characteristics, and feelings arise which play a part in directing the tendency to work. Among them may be mentioned esthetic traits, such

[11] Thorsten Veblen, *The Instinct of Workmanship and the Irksomeness of Labor*, in the *Am. Jour. of Sociology*, Vol. IV, No. 2 (Sept. 1898) , pp. 187-201; *The Theory of the Leisure Class*, New York, 1899; *The Instinct of Workmanship*, New York, 1914.

as the so-called architectonic or constructive sense, ambition to secure wealth, power, etc., certain altruistic sentiments, etc. This effort is also directed and its character determined in part by numerous factors of the physical and social environment of the individual. So that this so-called "instinct of workmanship" is very complex in its character and causes, and far from being a distinct instinct.[12]

Some of the psychological traits discussed above may lead to conflict and predation between humans. Among them are such instincts and general innate tendencies as pugnacity or combativeness, rivalry or emulation, hunting, acquisitiveness, and repulsion or flight, and such emotions and innate states of feeling as anger or hatred, fear, jealousy, greed, and envy. But these traits are manifested in the first instance between individual humans. Unless conditioned by training or experience to do so, it is hardly possible for an individual to act pugnaciously toward or to feel fearful or jealous of a collective entity like a tribe, people, nation, race, or state. Not until the individual has been induced to personalize in some measure this collective entity can he experience any of these inimical traits toward it. Only after being for a time under propaganda to this end can this happen. The consequence was that in the past when means of communication were very limited most of the inhabitants of warring countries did not feel hostile toward each other. Indeed, they were often hardly aware that a war was in progress.

In modern times means of communication have become much more plentiful. Journalism in particular is able to reach the majority of the inhabitants of a literate civilized nation. It is possible in a comparatively short time to arouse in many of the inhabitants the sentiments of fear and of hatred against the enemy. In this fashion these psychological traits become secondary factors for warfare of which they were not the original causes.[13]

One of the most pernicious effects of the outbreak of war is the heavy pall which falls between enemy countries. This pall is caused partly by the severance of direct communication. But it is due even more to the fact that most of the news and other articles published by

[12] See my criticism of Veblen's theory of the instinct of workmanship in my *Science of Human Behavior*, New York, 1913, p. 252.

In this book I have described all of these instincts. See especially Chapters XI to XIII inclusive.

[13] *Cf.* L. L. Bernard, *War and Its Causes*, New York, 1944. Bernard discusses war as a social institution with special reference to the psychological factors which play a part in its causation.

An institution is a complex of beliefs, ideas or activities, such as law, custom, tradition, or the like. Because war violates most of these attributes of organized society, it is hardly entitled to be called an institution, though laws, customs and traditions may arise with respect to warfare.

the press are so partisan in their character as to furnish a notably one-sided picture of the actual situation. Whether this feature of journalism in time of war is encouraged by the belligerent governments or not, the result is the same in giving the public a distorted view of the feelings and motives of the enemy. Furthermore, the sentiment of patriotism is greatly exaggerated in time of war and renders a people almost entirely incapable of appreciating the mental attitude of the enemy to whom they are induced, by the powerful emotions of fear and of hatred exacerbated by wartime hyperesthesia, to attribute the most infamous motives.

The result of this situation is a form of ethical dualism in time of war which results in a distorted view of the actual situation.[14] The enemy peoples which have hitherto usually been looked upon with friendship, or, to say the least, with indifference, are now regarded as possessing most of the evil traits which characterize mankind.

During the European War of 1914 to 1918, blockade as well as other belligerent measures were used as weapons in the class struggle. The war showed how effectively blockade measures could be utilized in coercing whole peoples, and this lesson has already been used in attempting to suppress extensive political and economic movements. The most notable instance was the blockade of Russia beginning with the year 1917 whose purpose it was to suppress the attempt to establish a communist system in that country. A similar blockade which succeeded in attaining its object within a few months was the blockade of Hungary in the year 1919. Since the world war of 1939 to 1945 a form of blockade called the iron curtain has been used against communism.

Whatever may be thought of communism, or of any other political and economic system, recent events have demonstrated that capitalism is at all times far from ideal, and is capable of precipitating mankind into the most frightful catastrophes. Whether or not a better system is feasible cannot be ascertained without trial and experimentation. The above-mentioned attempts on the part of the dominant nations of the Occidental world to suppress far-reaching political and economic experiments have resulted in a loss to social progress, for it is now impossible to determine how successful these experiments might have been had they not been interfered with. Blockade was an effective weapon for these dominant nations to use in accomplishing their designs because it could be applied more or less unobtrusively against the governments which they did not wish to recognize.

There is a sort of poetic justice in blockade because it distributes in a measure the burden of war over the whole of a belligerent nation. The combatants are limited to the male half of the population, and

[14] Maurice Parmelee, *Blockade and Sea Power*, New York, 1924, Chapter XIV entitled "Ethical Dualism in Wartime."

767

even to a comparatively small part of that half. These men are forced to endure the horrors of the battlefield, and to be killed, blinded, crippled, and maimed in many ways for the sake of their compatriots. The distress of mothers, fathers and wives is insignificant in comparison with the suffering of these victims of the folly of mankind. In fact, war is a holocaust of young men.

When there is no blockade, the non-combatant portion of the population live in comparative comfort. From this point of view, there is some justification for asserting that every belligerent nation should be blockaded in order that the women and children and non-combatant men may be forced to share to at least a small degree the suffering and sacrifice which inevitably fall upon the combatants. Especially just is it that women and older men, who for patriotic reasons wish to send the boys and young men to their horrible fate, experience some of this suffering.

Furthermore, blockade is the most effective teacher of the horrors of war to the whole population. When everyone in a country feels the pinch of hunger, or is at least forced to give up some of the comforts and luxuries of life, they will not be so ready again to rush into war for the defense of national honor or other puerile reasons, or even when they think material advantages may be gained by means of waging war.

Blockade may have value as a concrete expression of disapprobation of a nation's policy. But when a blockade is declared in the course of a war between nations, it loses this value entirely or almost entirely because patriotism renders most individuals incapable of regarding their own nation as in the wrong. For example, there were numerous indications of the hurt surprise and indignation which the Germans felt in the course of the European War of 1914 to 1918 because many nations declared war against them. There were few Germans who accepted the contention of their enemies that their nation was ethically in the wrong. The same was almost as true during the World War of 1939 to 1945. On the contrary, they were strengthened in their opinion that they were the victims of an infamous conspiracy against them on the part of many of the other nations of the world. If a blockade is to have ethical significance, it must be under an international sanction, and should be declared and administered in such a fashion as to obviate all suspicion of national ambition or revenge. Otherwise it is as immoral as all other forms of warfare between nations.[15]

---

15 Nef terminates his discussion of war by an appeal to God on the last page of his book: "When the mind of man has presented humanity with weapons that would be safe only in the hands of God, is it not evident that the only hope of staying the power of these weapons lies in redemption through Him." (J. U. Nef,

The effects of war upon all social phenomena are complicated so that it is difficult to analyze and measure them precisely. War has both limiting and expanding immediate effects upon crime. There is difference of opinion as to its ultimate effects.[16]

Statistical records indicate that criminality often diminishes apparently during time of war. This is due in large part to the fact that many of those who would otherwise be engaged in criminal activity volunteer for military service or are drafted into the armed forces. Consequently, their tendencies toward murder, theft, etc., are furnished an outlet in the opportunities to kill, to plunder, etc., in the course of warfare. War therefore becomes, in a measure, a substitute for crime for these persons. But this apparent diminution of criminality during time of war is probably due in part to the fact that the repression of crime is usually weakened during time of war, so that many crimes are not pursued and punished. This may explain why the criminality of women and of children as well as of men sometimes appears to diminish during time of war.

Some writers, however, allege that war diminishes crime by acting as a moral influence. Their opinion is that war stimulates a condition of emotional excitement under which many desires and impulses which would otherwise assume a criminal form are turned into patriotic, national, and social channels, and result in efforts in behalf of the public welfare. War also stimulates courage and leads to deeds of valor. There may be a measure of truth in this idea, especially when the war is for the purpose of carrying out a popular ideal. But warfare inevitably engenders hatred and vengeance toward enemies, which more than counterbalances this so-called moral influence of war. Furthermore, war arouses far more fear than courage.

Militarism has an influence upon crime during times of peace as well as during wartime. Military service is reputed to have both a moral and an immoral influence upon conscripts and volunteers. It is alleged that military training furnishes discipline for the character. It encourages obedience, orderliness, regularity, etc. But military organization is of such a nature as to develop servility in the common soldiers, and a domineering spirit in the officers. It also tends to develop contempt for and brutality toward the civilian class.

Furthermore, the conditions under which military service is usually performed are harmful, especially for the young conscripts. These youths are torn away from their homes at an impressionable age. They are thrown into garrison life in large cities and elsewhere in

op. cit., p. 416.) Many would-be scholars and scientists have not yet learned that human problems can be solved only by mankind and not by a mythical deity.

[16] Cf. Maurice Parmelee, Criminology, New York, 1918, pp. 99-105.

which they may readily acquire vices and diseases which will affect their conduct throughout the remainder of their lives.

The extent to which such conditions prevail in military service depends in part upon the manner in which an army is organized and the attention which is paid to conditions of living for the soldiers by those in charge of the army. If an army is as democratically organized as is possible for a military body, and if the government provides beneficial living conditions for the soldiers, these injurious conditions will be reduced to a minimum. Even if this end is attained, it is doubtful if the benefits derived from military service can counterbalance its injurious effects.

It has been asserted that the criminality of the soldier class is higher than that of the civilian population. This appears doubtful when the criminality of the soldiers is compared with that of the male civilian population of about the same ages. Wherever it is true, the difference usually is not great, and is probably due in part at least to the fact that the soldier is guilty of various military offenses, such as insubordination and malingering, which the civilian cannot or will not commit. In some places the criminality of the soldier class is below that of the civilian population, owing to the strict discipline maintained over the soldiers. This fact, however, does not disprove the harmful effects of military service, for these effects may display themselves later in the lives of the soldiers, after their military service is ended.

The indirect but much more far-reaching effects of war and militarism upon crime are the spirit of lawlessness and the violence encouraged by war, and which usually persist for some time after a war ends and may cause an increase of crime. The history of every nation furnishes more or less evidence of this condition. War arouses the passions of hatred, vengeance, and envy, and requires the committing of many deeds of violence. It is not surprising that it should lead to lawlessness and violence.

The payment of the cost of a war hangs over a people long after the war is ended. No modern government can carry on a war very long without raising special funds. These funds are secured usually by issuing long term bonds, which are purchased in the main by capitalists and upon which interest must be paid for many years. The question as to who pays in the end for these bonds depends upon the incidence of the taxes by means of which they are paid. Up to the present they have been paid for in the main by the poorer people who are most of the ultimate consumers, upon whom indirect taxes almost invariably fall. So that wars have been paid for mainly by the working classes, and one of the results of modern warfare has been to furnish another means of transferring wealth from the poor to the rich; for these bonds have usually furnished safe investments at fairly good rates of profit for the

770

capitalists, while for many years after a war the poor are contributing heavily to pay the interest to the capitalists, and ultimately to pay back the principal. If wars were paid for by heavy assessments upon the rich at the time of the war, or by the issue of bonds to be paid for by direct taxes upon the rich, such as inheritance and income taxes, a war would no longer be a force for making the poor poorer by making the rich richer; for while the poor would not gain anything through the war, they would not lose as much as they do now, and the rich would not become richer at their expense. If such were the case, there might be less war; because the rich usually have much influence with governments, and under those conditions it would no longer be to the interest of the rich to have war. Up to the present time war profits have outweighed war taxes for the rich.

Heavy expenditures between wars are caused by military warfare. So long as international relations are based on the theory that the economic interests of nations conflict, war will continue to be an imminent possibility for every nation. Consequently, every nation must maintain itself in a state of preparedness for war. This means constant expenditure for munitions and other equipments of war, and for the services of fighting men who are withdrawn from the production of wealth. As no government can safely, from the military point of view, refuse to give pensions, for a long period after every war of any extent there is heavy expenditure for the payment of pensions. In most cases these expenditures are paid for by means of taxes whose incidence falls at least in part upon the poorer classes.

War and militarism are, therefore, factors for creating economic conditions which encourage crime. They accentuate the inequality in the distribution of wealth, and swell the size of the poorer classes which contribute most heavily proportionately to the criminal class. Furthermore, war increases the instability of commerce and industry by disturbing the normal processes of manufacture and trade. Even the smaller wars cause world-wide disturbances in the stock markets and in the prices of many commodities, while a great war is almost certain to bring on a world-wide panic, crisis, and to accentuate a period of depression. This instability in economic conditions, by rendering the economic status of many persons insecure through loss of employment, loss of property, etc., increases the incitement and the temptation to acquire criminal habits. Furthermore, the great fluctuations in prices in the stock markets and elsewhere furnish shrewd speculators excellent opportunities to amass great fortunes, and enhance the inequality in the distribution of wealth.[17]

War and militarism impede the progress of civilization, and delay

[17] See my *Poverty and Social Progress*, New York, 1916, pp. 404-405.

771

the coming of the time when crime will be diminished. Social progress requires the continual extension of cooperation in the form of the division of labor, in order thereby to augment the sum total of human achievement. The principle of the division of labor has already been widely applied in many fields of human activity, such as economic affairs, science, art, etc. It has so far been applied only to a slight extent in political affairs. Nationalism is still the fundamental principle in political organization, and stands as a barrier against the division of labor and cooperation, not only in political matters but also often in economic activities. It is a serious hindrance to the diffusion of culture, and an obstacle to the unification and organization of mankind into a coherent social organism. Not until internationalism supersedes nationalism, and a world state or federation comes into being, can civilization attain the highest rate of progress.

In the English common law there evolved a three-fold classification of crimes, namely, (1) Treason; (2) Felony; (3) Misdemeanor. Treason seems at first to have been regarded as one of the felonies, but in course of time became differentiated. It is by definition an act which is directed at the existence of the state itself. In the old English law many acts directed against the king and members of the royal family were treasonable, and the same is still true of several of these acts. As to whether or not these acts should be classified as treasonable depends upon whether or not they are in reality directed against the state itself, and this in turn depends upon the nature of the state. In the majority of these cases it has not been justifiable to classify acts against the royal family as treasonable, for they have not menaced the existence of the state itself, and such criminal laws have been examples of the abuse of monarchical power.

The laws against treason are inevitable in any political state, because a government must create and enforce such laws for its own preservation. But such laws should make treasonable only overt acts directed toward the overthrow of the state, and not such offenses as against a royal family, the church, etc. They should not penalize the advocacy of changes in the form of government.

The laws against treason and sedition acquire special importance in war time. During a war a country is in danger from its external foes. Consequently, these laws must be executed with rigor upon its internal foes, whereas in times of peace it is possible to treat treasonable offenses with comparative leniency. There is danger of these laws being stretched too far even in time of war, so as to cover criticisms of the policy of government and of the men in power, which may be loyally made, and which may have utility in exposing defects in the conduct of the war by the government. While a censorship of information having military value is essential for the prosecution of a war, a

772

censorship of opinions under the laws against treason is intolerable in a democratic state.

There are at least three ways in which business and industry are injured in the course of a war. First, there is the direct interference with industry in the area covered by the military operations. This loss is likely to be small compared with the other losses. Second, there is the loss of certain foreign markets and usually to a certain extent of the home market as well. The markets of foes are closed to each other during warfare, and usually for some time thereafter. They may become closed by blockade or otherwise to neutral nations as well, thus causing them injury. The home market also may become smaller, because people may lessen their expenditures during war time and the supply of peace time commodities may decrease. Third, there is a loss or shortage of raw material and other necessary products coming from the countries of belligerents. All of these losses, except those from direct interference (and even that one sometimes), fall upon neutral as well as belligerent nations.

As to the effects of these losses upon the working class, wages may fall or they may rise, unemployment may increase or it may decrease. The loss of foreign markets and of certain parts of the home market tend to lower wages and increase unemployment. But there are compensating factors. War usually drafts into the armed forces a considerable number of men, thus lessening the supply of labor. War usually creates a big demand for munitions and other equipments of war which stimulates their production. These compensating factors may counteract the forces which lower wages and increase unemployment, though increased wages may be more than counterbalanced by the monetary inflation which often results from war.

The general economic results from war may be summarized as follows. War is almost certain to reduce the aggregate production of wealth, thus making society poorer at the end of a war than at its beginning. This is due to the destruction of property by military operations and to the cessation in the production of wealth during the war. Most of the goods produced for war purposes are worthless at the end of the war. The working class is almost invariably poorer at the end of a war, though the wealthy class is likely to be richer owing to excessive war profits.

The means of production available at the end of a war are likely to be smaller. Owing to the reduction in the supply of wealth, there may be a shortage of capital. Owing to the destruction of human life, there may be a shortage of labor. This loss of life may sometimes appear to be a blessing in disguise. War has been one of the forces for restricting the growth of population. Even if it is somewhat beneficial where there is excessive pressure of population, the relief it brings is at best only temporary. The vital reproductive force soon replaces any loss of population, and this force is likely to be artificially stimulated by the government at such a time. Furthermore, the loss of life caused by war is largely of adult laborers, many of them skilled, whose rearing and training are lost to society. Infanticide would be a more economical method of reducing population, while contraceptive methods are the most humanitarian means of restricting the increase of population.

In order to reconstruct what has been destroyed by war, and to bring the supply of wealth back to the normal; production is almost certain to be brisk after a war, within the limits placed by the available capital. Because the supply of labor has lessened, the surviving laborers are likely to get better wages and to suffer less from unemployment. There comes a period of prosperity which is beneficial both for the employer and for the worker. It is indeed a sad commentary upon capitalism that the period immediately following a war often is preferable to many a period of depression during times of peace. This is what has led many to think that war is beneficial because of the stimulus it apparently gives to manufacturing and trade. It is ironic that capitalism requires human slaughter and the destruction of wealth to stimulate production. This industrial activity after a war is largely due to an effort to get back to the condition which existed before the war, by making good the losses mentioned above. It is almost certain to be followed by a depression even greater than would have ensued had there been no war.

Cultural factors usually play an important part in bringing about decadence and degeneration. Certain religious, moral, and economic institutions have served as arresting and retrogressive forces, as when a rigid caste system impedes progress, or a class system on an economic basis, in which certain classes are being exploited to an excessive degree by other classes. Cultural relations may play a similar part in various ways, as when one nation is threatened by a stronger one, and when a weaker people is subjected or enslaved by a stronger people. Migrations of peoples may cause an excessive degree of ethnic heterogeneity, thus impeding cultural development.

War has played a considerable part in causing racial and national decadence and degeneration. It has caused a process of reversed selection in which the physically superior individuals have been killed off while the weaker individuals have survived, thus leading to racial degeneration. On the other hand, war may also have been a beneficial selective force by eliminating in part certain unsocial and anti-social types, such as the turbulent, the refractory, and the unsympathetic.

Certain features of modern civilization are forces for decadence. The pressure of a complex civilization gives rise to neurotic tendencies

774

which manifest themselves in certain forms of art and literature, in an increase of suicide, and in other ways. It is alleged that national virility is often sacrificed for advancement along certain cultural lines, as illustrated in modern humanitarianism, the decline of patriotism, antimilitarism, pacifism, individualism, evolution along certain esthetic lines, etc. With respect to the United States, it is asserted that immigration has caused an excessive degree of ethnic and cultural heterogeneity, and that there is a large abnormal element in the immigration to America composed of defective, dependent, and criminal immigrants.

The co-existence in human nature of the traits which are ordinarily called humanity and cruelty is a strange anomaly. It manifests itself in many forms in individual cases and at different times and places. Primitive man may display cruelty toward all humans not belonging to his own small social group, and yet show the tenderest regard for his own offspring. The criminal may murder his victim in cold blood, and yet devote a loving care to an animal pet. The peoples of modern civilized nations are displaying concern over the welfare of the poor, and yet rush into wars with each other which cause untold suffering and loss of life.

This apparent anomaly can be explained only by the evolution of human nature in general. In the course of this evolution traits have developed which seem incompatible with each other. On the one hand are traits which promote the preservation of the individual. These include the aggressive tendencies which aid the individual in defending himself and impel him to prey upon others. These aggressive tendencies may be grouped under the head of the instinct of pugnacity or the combative instinct, and the affective state which ordinarily accompanies it is the emotion of anger. The sexual and the parental instincts may also impel the individual to commit aggressive acts against those who attempt to thwart his desires.

On the other hand, certain traits impel the individual to perform acts which promote the welfare of the species. The sexual and parental instincts and their accompanying states of feeling impel the individual to do things for the persons toward whom those instincts are directed, and in these acts are the germs of altruism. It is alleged that there are also social instincts which impel individuals to do things for their fellows, apart from the sexual and parental relationships. There is no specific social instinct, but a number of traits described in earlier chapters in this treatise make man social.

The numerous instincts and feelings which play a part in causing humanity and cruelty are combined in many complex forms of sentiments. The indirect and therefore unexpected and sometimes abnormal ways in which these traits may lead to humanity or to cruelty further complicate their analysis. These are fundamental in human nature, and will remain as permanent forces for humanity and for cruelty.

Religious devotees often allege that religion is a powerful force for humanity. Christianity like all religions has been a force both for and against humanitarianism. The attitude of mind required by every religious faith is such as to render impossible an all-inclusive humanitarianism. Religion will always be to a certain extent a force against humanitarianism. This is because a religious faith requires an unquestioning belief in its doctrines, and demands that they be set above other truths as of a sacred character. Partly for this reason religious ideas are usually held by believers with a high degree of emotional intensity, and differences of religious belief often serve as a serious barrier between individuals and groups, because of the emotional conflict which they bring about. Especially hostile is the religious devotee to the non-religionist who rejects his "sacred" beliefs. Other ideas are held with emotional intensity by individuals and by groups, but this is peculiarly true of religious ideas, because these are regarded as of supreme importance by those who believe in them.

We can illustrate this point best by comparing religion with science. A scientist may hold a scientific idea with a degree of emotional intensity which equals the fervor of the religious believer. But that is an individual peculiarity. According to the spirit and method of science no idea is sacred. Every scientific idea, however firmly established, may be attacked and overthrown. The mental attitude encouraged by science permits free intercourse without restriction between all parts of mankind, while the mental attitude not only encouraged but required by religion will always serve as a barrier to the most extensive form of humanitarianism.

On the other hand, most if not all religions have taught certain doctrines which have had a humanitarian influence. Christianity is the complex of religious beliefs and practices which from time to time and from place to place have been called Christian. This historical Christianity is alone of importance for the interpretation of social evolution, and not the beliefs attributed to the legendary person after whom this religion was named, or to any other individual real or mythical.

Christianity has exerted an influence for humanitarianism principally through two of its doctrines, namely, the doctrine of the sanctity of human life, and the doctrine of universal brotherhood. Neither of these doctrines was original with Christianity. The doctrine of the sanctity of human life is based upon the idea of an immortal soul possessed by every human. This idea existed not only in many of the more civilized religions but is to be found among the religious be-

776

liefs of many primitive peoples. It indeed constitutes one of the primitive animistic beliefs. The doctrine of universal brotherhood had also been held by various individuals and religions before Christianity, as, for example, by the Stoics. But coming as a new religion into the pagan world it emphasized these ideas anew and may have been a force for humanitarianism for a time.

Christianity had not been in existence more than two or three centuries before asceticism began to play an important part in it, and has ever since remained a powerful force against humanitarianism. It has attempted to suppress the normal place of sex in human life. Consequently it has lowered the position of woman, and has done much to destroy the joy of living for innumerable humans by encouraging puritanical ideas and practices.

Then Christianity became hierarchically organized in the form of a church. For more than a thousand years its history was blackened by the incredible inhumanity of its wars, crusades, and persecutions, and by its stupid and brutal opposition to the higher forms of culture. Not even the partisans and apologists of the Catholic Church have been able to deny, where they have been at all unbiased, that during this dark and bloody period it was a powerful force against humanitarianism. Christianity then took the form of a strong and militant religion at its worst, carrying its doctrines at the point of the sword. During this period it applied its doctrines of the sanctity of human life and of universal brotherhood only to Christians, and not always even to them.

The above discussion has been a brief analysis of the principal causes of the modern humanitarian movement, especially in its relation to war. It is important to understand the causes of this movement, if practical measures are to be taken to further it. If the religious theory mentioned above is correct, the principal and perhaps the only measure to be taken is to preach religion. If the moral theory is correct, the principal and perhaps the only measure to take is to deliver lectures on ethics. But if my theory is correct entirely or in the main, then to talk about peace will not prevent war, and to tell the economic classes to love one another will not abolish industrial warfare. The only effective measures in the long run will be those which direct the forces of industry, commerce, and science in such a fashion as to make the personal interests of individuals and the collective interests of social groups as nearly alike as possible, and the educational measures which will disseminate the kind of knowledge described above. Many ideas which circulate as religious or as moral ideas, or sometimes in both forms, did not originate as such, but came from science, or arose out of the conditions which have been brought into being by economic and other changes. If the ideas are correct and will aid the progress of humanitarianism, they may gain currency more easily under religious or an ethical form. But the fundamental causes of humanitarianism should never be forgotten.

The modern humanitarian movement has arisen out of certain human traits influenced and directed by the conditions and ideas which have become prevalent during the last few centuries. Like every movement it is a product of social evolution in general and can be understood only in the light of analysis of social evolution. It is one phase of and an inevitable result from the universal world culture which is coming into being. No unilateral theory can account for it.[18]

During the 19th and 20th centuries there has been a rapid increase both of population and of the amount of economic commodities produced over most of the civilized world. This situation raises the important question as to whether the increased production was caused by the increase in population or *vice versa*. The usual opinion seems to be that the population increased somehow or other and then stimulated the increase in production. If this were true and there was reason to believe that continued increase in population would continue to increase the production, it would be a powerful argument in favor of increasing the population. But if, on the contrary, the increase in population has resulted from the increase in production, it is not safe to advocate continued increase of population, unless there is assurance of continued increase of production.

It may appear as if the population must have caused the increase in production, because the increase in population has resulted to a considerable extent from a reduction of the death rate rather than from a rise in the birth rate. This reduction has come about in part from the advance of medical science, from better hygiene and sanitation, etc. But a more careful analysis shows that these causes are due, in large part if not entirely, to increase in production. The advance of medical science has been a part of the modern scientific movement, which was an important cause of the industrial revolution and its resulting changes, and then was stimulated by the vast increase in wealth which followed that revolution. Better hygiene and sanitation are a part of the higher standard of living which has resulted from this great increase of wealth. The lessening of war, in so far as it has decreased, chiefly during the 19th century though during the 20th century it has been on the increase, has been due in the main to the vast extension of the principle of the division of labor in modern trade and industry which has increased the interdependence of the nations of the world, thus making war more disastrous in its results. Even though the increase of population may be due immediately to the re-

[18] See Maurice Parmelee, *Poverty and Social Progress*, New York, 1916, Chapter XVII entitled "The Modern Humanitarian Movement."

778

duction of the death rate, it can be traced ultimately to the increase in production.

In the past famine, pestilence, and war have been the great factors for the restriction of the increase of population. This is still true to a considerable extent. War is being caused sometimes, as so often in the past, by the pressure of population. One of the causes of war during the last few centuries has been the desire for colonies. This desire rises in a country when it has become relatively overpopulated, so that there is need either for a place to which some of the population can migrate or for a market for its manufactured products in return for which it can secure food stuffs to feed its excess population. So that pressure of population, as well as lust for loot and profits, leads to war. In similar fashion pressure of population leads to disease, and disease is killing off many millions of humans before their time. Many are dying for lack of food, either by literally starving to death or by being weakened by continued under-nourishment.

Nevertheless, largely because of the vast increase in wealth during the past century or two, population has increased greatly. How much longer this increase can continue it is impossible to prophesy. It cannot go on forever. If it is not checked by other means, these three gaunt agents of death ever stand ready to put an ultimate limit to the population of the earth. The practical question therefore is whether it is to be left to regulate itself automatically or is to be regulated by conscious, artificial means. The automatic method is not humane and is excessively wasteful, so that the artificial methods of regulating population by contraception are preferable.

Many discriminatory economic measures have constituted a prolific cause of war. War in turn has often led to such measures. The only way to destroy completely and forever the vicious circle between these discriminatory measures and war is to eliminate these measures. Among them are export and import duties, excessive internal taxes upon goods of foreign origin, the dumping of surplus products at cut prices for the purpose of underbidding a competing nation, national regulation of international waterways, and the monopolization of sources of raw materials. An international government would have to maintain equality of competition among nations on the basis of free trade. If a country adopted a policy which aroused international friction, the injured parties could bring the case to the international courts to secure protection from discriminatory practices.

There remains a question of fundamental importance. Is a genuine international state or world federation possible under capitalism? Modern capitalist enterprise has been somewhat international in its character. Financiers of different countries have sometimes cooperated in carrying out large undertakings, usually in unexploited areas of

779

the world. Theoretically capitalism should be international in its character. If the principles of the division of labor and of freedom of trade, both of which are compatible with capitalism in theory but are constantly violated by capitalists in practice, were applied on a worldwide scale, capitalism would perforce be international.

The supreme purpose of capitalism is the acquisition of the largest possible amount of profits. Efficiency in production, the amount produced, the division of labor, freedom of trade, mean nothing in comparison with this supreme end. Capitalists utilize every possible advantage in order to defeat their competitors. Whenever possible they create a monopoly to their own interest. The nation furnishes the means for gaining certain monopolistic advantages. Business men often attempt to manipulate patriotic sentiments, governments, and the national state in general, as weapons in the rapacious struggle of business and finance. They would not willingly relinquish the advantages of the national state for a genuine international organization which would be entirely impartial and would eliminate all possibility of discrimination between national groups.

During the European War of 1914 to 1918 the border neutrals served as economic buffers between the belligerent states. The commerce and shipping of the whole world were more or less deranged. The blockade interfered artificially with trade balances and gave rise to fluctuations in currency exchange. In this fashion it prepared the way and was partly responsible for the serious financial crisis which followed the war in all parts of Europe, and the industrial maladjustment throughout the world. The blockade, as conducted by both sides, not only injured the countries against which it was directed, but also reacted unfavorably upon the countries which had used it as a weapon.

Blockade is one of the most striking manifestations of sea power and the most far-reaching in its effects. Economic imperialism is in part the most important indirect result from the exercise of sea power, which is in turn its principal instrument. Imperialism is based upon nationalism and the absolute sovereignty of the national states. It arises out of the efforts of the national states to expand territorially and commercially at the cost of their rivals. The ultimate cure for imperialism of all kinds and the wars which arise therefrom is the world state.

The League of Nations established in 1919 by the Entente Allies at the close of the European War was not a genuine world state. The international conferences which subsequently took place could not check imperialism and war, even when professedly in behalf of disarmament. The so-called "Disarmament" Conference which convened in Washington in November 1921, was called by a president of the

780

United States who represented a political party one of whose principal tenets is not to concede one atom of American national sovereignty. Such a principle is an absolute barrier against even a first step toward the establishment of a world state. In the background of this conference were controversial questions concerning mineral oil concessions, trade opportunities in China, and the like. The same or similar questions dominated the other international conferences, such as those at Paris in 1919, Brussels in 1920, London in 1921, Rapallo, Cannes and Genoa in 1922, Lausanne in 1922 and 1923, Locarno in 1925, and London in 1933. Thus was repeated the old game of the balance of power played upon a somewhat more extensive scale.

Such conferences, though they may incidentally bring about partial and temporary limitation of armament, are certain to result primarily in trade deals, distribution of concessions, apportionment of spheres of influence, military and naval alliances, and similar tactics of imperialist and capitalist rivals who dread and fear each other to such a degree that they are willing to compromise. At present the capitalist nations are willing to cooperate because of their vastly greater fear of communism in Russia, China and elsewhere, which is already sounding the death knell of capitalism. The best that can be said for the conferences prior to the war of 1939 to 1945 is that they gave some publicity to the idea of the limitation of armament. The same can be said of the extinct League of Nations, and also of the moribund United Nations which furnished a few samples of more or less genuine international cooperation, and encouraged the development of international law.

Here is a task for the capitalist foreign offices of the world, far more important than trade promotion, diplomatic intrigue, colonial expansion, and like activities to which they have ordinarily devoted their efforts. During recent years most of these foreign offices have established special sections in the interest of national trade. No one of them has created a section for promoting the foundation of a world state.

Many trusts, combinations, mergers, syndicates, cartels, and other monopolistic organizations, organized mainly along national lines, were already in existence prior to the European War of 1914 to 1918. That war gave a tremendous stimulus to business enterprise and caused a temporary period of industrial expansion and so-called prosperity which increased greatly the wealth of the capitalist world. The increased wealth of both the old and the new capitalists was used to increase their control of the economic process. The nationalism accentuated by the war furnished these capitalists a valuable tool to be utilized in securing every possible advantage that national power could

781

give them. At the cost of whatever war they deem necessary to safeguard their interests, they will fight for war profits and against their dreaded foe—communism.

The munitions manufacturers instigate war because their profits are enormous in war time.[19] They are business men like other business men, eager to make money regardless of human welfare. However sinister and repulsive is the traffic in arms, it is an integral part of the capitalist system. Nationalist and imperialist war is inevitable so long as capitalism creates large war profits for the profit-makers.

After the termination of the wars intended to spread the principles of the French Revolution of 1789, which degenerated into the Napoleonic wars of conquest, the 19th century was a relatively peaceful period. By the beginning of the 20th century the balance of power in Europe had become sufficiently deranged to lead to the European war of 1914 to 1918, or the German war, as it might be called. Germany had advanced rapidly industrially and sought colonies and spheres of influence to furnish it markets for its products which it had not secured during the first modern scramble for colonies. The war was, therefore, primarily between Germany and its imperialist rivals.

Following the European war of 1914 to 1918 a form of monopolistic capitalism conquered Italy in 1922 under the name of fascism, and Germany in 1933 under the name of national socialism. This form of capitalism was by no means opposed to the more competitive type of capitalism prevalent in liberal-democratic countries. In fact, it was a further development of the latter type, and is likely to supplant the competitive type of free enterprise.[20] Nevertheless, it led somewhat illogically to the war of 1939 to 1945, which was also a war to check Germany's designs of conquest which threatened to upset the balance of power in Europe. However, immediately after this war the capitalists of both types began to unite under the leadership of the most powerful capitalist country, the United States, against their common foe of communism. By 1951 or 1950 their erstwhile military foe, western Germany, was permitted to rearm itself and in 1954 Japan was forced to rearm in order to fight against Soviet Russia. And even fascist Spain was admitted to the fold for the same reason. For such conflicting and contradictory motives are wars fought.

The two principal wars of the first half of the 20th century were, therefore, singularly inept and futile. They were not primarily wars of antagonistic ideologies. However, they led to several important

[19] See, for example, H. C. Engelbrecht and F. C. Hanighen, *Merchants of Death,* New York, 1934; George Seldes, *Iron, Blood and Profits,* New York, 1934.
[20] See Maurice Parmelee, *Bolshevism, Fascism and the Liberal-Democratic State,* New York, 1934.

782

events not intended or foreseen by their protagonists. The first war caused the breakdown of the Tsarist regime in Russia which rendered possible the Bolshevist revolution and the establishment of the Soviet Union. The second war destroyed the Japanese power in China and rendered possible the foundation of the second Chinese republic upon a collectivist basis. It precipitated the commencement of a partially socialist regime in Great Britain and strengthened the social democratic forces in several other countries. It brought about a widespread revolt against colonialism and western imperialism in Asia. Thus while war is itself a state of anarchy, the economic, political and social shock of war sometimes gives rise to far-reaching changes which may or may not be constructive in their nature.

In the second of the first two of the great wars of the 20th century the western hemisphere, which had hitherto been relatively isolated from European wars, became seriously involved for the first time. The fundamental reason is that the capitalist forces which dominate the western hemisphere, alarmed at the spread of collectivist ideas and institutions in Europe and in Asia, have allied themselves with the capitalist interests in western Europe in order to attack communism in the Soviet Union and in China under the usual guise of self-defense. In any case, long-range aviation and the uranium and hydrogen bombs have rendered armament in any part of the world a menace to all of the rest of the world. For example, American armament can destroy a buffer state in a distant part of the world, as happened to Korea in 1950 and after. America can no longer stand apart from wars which originate in Europe, the modern home of warlike anarchy. Thus the garrison state of permanent conscription, heavy armament and militarism is spreading across the Atlantic Ocean from east to west. War, hot or cold, is threatening to maintain social anarchy permanently over the world. The next few chapters will discuss how a global order may be created to prevent this anarchic situation.

Chapter XLV

What Is Geo-Economic Regionalism?

GEO-ECONOMIC regionalism is not sectionalism, nationalism, continentalism, or racialism. It does not necessarily involve linguistic, ethnic, or cultural homogeneity. Although it has political, administrative and juridical aspects, it does not necessarily eliminate national states, but changes their status greatly. It contemplates regions organized in accordance with the basic physiographic features of the earth—climate, soil, sources of natural energy, mineral resources, topography—and the economic factors created by mankind within the natural environment.

Regionalism postulates interdependence between the regions rather than self-sufficiency of each region. It renders feasible social and economic planning on a regional and worldwide scale. Within the scope of this planning are the flow of commodities, transportation and communication, movements of population, and certain important phases of the production and distribution of wealth. The geo-economic regions furnish the most effective basis for a world federation which can coordinate and harmonize the various regional plans into interregional economic activities, and can promote a worldwide division of labor for an abundant production of wealth. Geo-economic regionalism furnishes the geographical framework for the worldwide system.[1]

Geo-economic regionalism is not exclusively or at all:

(1) Political	(6) Continental
(2) Administrative	(7) Linguistic
(3) Juridical	(8) Ethnic
(4) Sectional	(9) Racial
(5) National	(10) Cultural

[1] I have described the subject matter of Chapters XLV, XLVI, and XLVII, in greater detail in my book entitled *Geo-Economic Regionalism and World Federation*, New York, 1949.

Political, administrative and juridical regionalism is usually concerned with regional divisions within a country. This is merely an administrative tendency toward decentralization. It has little or no bearing upon geo-economic regionalism.

If regionalism were applied the world over, it would have political, administrative and juridical aspects and functions. However, if limited to these aspects and functions, it would not necessarily have an advantage over the similar functions now being performed by national governments. Geo-economic regionalism has a much broader basis. It takes into consideration the forces of the natural environment, and the economic factors which have evolved partly as a result of those natural factors. Regionalism may also perform an important planning function. While regional organization would have certain political, administrative and juridical functions to perform, it would share these functions with local organizations on the one hand, and a world organization on the other.

Regionalism is not based at all upon sectionalism and nationalism. Regional boundaries would not be determined by national boundaries, and would not always coincide with them. In fact, regionalism may prove to be useful as a check upon the more violent manifestations of both sectionalism and nationalism.

Regionalism is not continentalism. In some cases regional boundaries may coincide with continental boundaries, but this would not always be the case. Most of the continents naturally divide into two or more regions. A region may overlap two or more continents. This may be the case in the vicinity of the Mediterranean, where a region might overlap Africa, Asia and Europe.

Regionalism does not necessarily have anything to do with linguistic, ethnic and racial distinctions. A region may include a population diversified as to all three of these traits. The basis for the regional unity would rest upon the characteristics of the environment, the economic factors involved, and the feasibility of a common plan.

Regionalism does not necessarily imply a uniform cultural development. However, a certain degree of cultural uniformity may be desirable.

The Purposes of Geo-Economic Regionalism

The term "regionalism" may be used in various senses. Regionalism may be advocated and put into effect for several different purposes. Certain of these purposes are wholly unsuitable for regionalism on a worldwide scale. Other purposes do bear upon this question. They should be recognized and used as criteria in planning for a worldwide regional organization.

Self-sufficiency

Prior to the war of 1939 to 1945, economic self-sufficiency, called autarchy in its most extreme form, was the objective of many nations. In some cases the purpose was to be armed for an offensive war of conquest. In other cases it was in order to be prepared for a defensive war against invasion and subjugation.

The effective and permanent application of geo-economic principles and plans is not possible in a world in which nations and peoples and parts of the world are in danger of attack and conquest. Geo-economic regionalism must, therefore, be based on the assumptions that each nation has ceded at least a portion of its national sovereignty, that national disarmament has taken place, leaving only domestic police forces, and that a central world authority has been created. Under the aegis of such an authority, a geo-economic regional plan can safely be put into operation. Having made these assumptions, self-sufficiency is not necessarily the chief purpose of regionalism. Absolute self-sufficiency is in any case impossible of attainment; self-sufficiency can be at best only relative. In certain parts of the world, regions may have a rather high degree of self-sufficiency. In other parts, regions may be so specialized in their economic activities and forms of production that they are dependent to a high degree upon other regions. Self-sufficiency can, therefore, not be regarded as the sole or even as the chief purpose of regionalism.

Interdependence

Any worldwide plan of regionalization must recognize from the outset that mineral and other natural resources are unevenly distributed over the world. Differences in soil fertility, sources of natural energy, and topography also give rise to great differences in the character of the economic activities and the productivity of the various geographical parts of the world. Any such plan must recognize the mutual interdependence of the regions as a much more important consideration than the relative self-sufficiency of which certain of the nations or regions may be capable. Such a plan also recognizes the principle of the division of labor on a worldwide scale.

Planning

Much has been written upon regionalism in the United States. Most of these writings assume (1) that a region must have a high degree of homogeneity, and (2) that it must be a suitable areal unit for social and economic planning.

The first of these assumptions applies to a much smaller degree

786

to regionalism on a worldwide scale, because of the wide divergencies within as well as between the different regions of the world. The second assumption is worthy of careful consideration. A region within a worldwide scheme should be, insofar as is compatible with the other purposes of regionalism, a suitable areal unit for regional planning. The plans of the various regions should fit into an over-all worldwide plan, just as the plans for the various regions of a regionalized United States should fit into an over-all national plan.[2]

Common Problems

Closely related to the idea of regional planning in American regionalism is the thought that a region should be an area characterized by the same or similar problems. This idea has some significance for regionalism on a worldwide scale. However, this is not the primary or principal basis upon which to delineate regions.

Administrative efficiency

The political aspect of geo-economic regionalism requires at least three assumptions: (1) The organization of the world on a regional basis would not entirely supplant the present organization on the basis of states and nations. Numerous administrative as well as legislative functions would continue to be performed by the national governments. (2) A geo-economic region should not be regarded as identical with a group of nations. A region may include several countries with portions of other countries, or it may be composed of portions of two or more countries, or it may be only a part of one very large country of diversified character. The guiding principles in delineating the regional area should be such principles as have already been suggested; e.g., interdependence, planning, common problems, and other principles to be suggested below. (3) The powers to be exercised by the regional organization or government should arise out of the functions to be performed by it. These will be determined by the principle or principles on the basis of which the region has been delineated.

This means that many administrative functions would be left to the nation, and to the local governments, such as provinces and counties, as has been the case in the past. In fact, since the regional organization should be concerned in the main with major questions of policy, it is not likely that a regional government would ever have a multiplicity of detailed administrative functions to perform. Partly for this reason it is not likely that difficulties would arise from the fact

[2] Maurice Parmelee, *Farewell to Poverty*, New York, 1935. See Chapters XXIV, XXVIII, and XXIX.

that regional and national boundaries would not, in many cases, coincide. In other words, the regional organization would be functioning for an area which might include parts of several countries having certain economic characteristics or interests in common without interfering at all or only in a minor degree with the majority of the functions performed by a national or local government.

Federalization of the World

One of the criticisms often made of the League of Nations of 1919 to 1939 was that it was so constituted as to be little concerned with worldwide economic problems. The International Labor Office was created to study and consider such problems with respect to labor. During the latter part of its short existence, the League of Nations was trying to strengthen its work on the economic side by setting up various economic and financial committees. In any case, neither the League of Nations nor the International Labor Office had any power with which to enforce anything which either or both international bodies might have considered desirable.

In a worldwide regional organization, each regional government should be concerned in large part with the economic matters of concern to its own region. The federal government would be made up of the representatives of the federated regional governments. Regional policies and plans could then be brought to the federal government for consideration, integration in a unified whole, and approval. In this fashion, adequate attention would be given for the first time in the history of the world to the economic problems, not only of the various parts of the world, but of the world as a whole. Geo-economic regionalism would thereby furnish a far more adequate basis for the federalization of the world than nations and empires.

Economic Systems

A possible obstacle to the above-mentioned program will suggest itself. The Soviet Union, and, since 1949, the Chinese People's Republic, may not fit into this plan. Inasmuch as the Soviet Union has an economic and political system radically different from the rest of the world, certain difficulties may arise. However, there are several mitigating circumstances. The Soviet Union as it now stands is composed of one vast stretch of contiguous territory. It is feasible to regard it as one region, and to give to it the recognition to which it is entitled in the federal world government.

During the years preceding the war of 1939 to 1945, the Soviet Government displayed an inclination to cooperate with the League of Nations, and to support the policy of collective security. It is unlikely

788

that the Soviet Government will try to hinder genuine attempts to promote collective security by means of a more effective organization of the world. While it is naturally as much interested in disseminating communist ideas as are the bourgeois governments in maintaining capitalism the world over, the Soviet Government needs protection through collective security so that it can develop and strengthen its own system in peace. The Constitution of the Soviet Union provides that any country or area in any part of the world which chooses to adopt the Soviet system may join the Soviet Union as one of its integral units, however far removed geographically this country or area may be from the present territory of the Soviet Union. Since no non-contiguous country or territory has so far seen fit to join the Soviet Union, this possible obstacle to geo-economic regionalism has not yet arisen.

The case of the British Empire is entirely different from that of the Soviet Union. The British Empire is scattered over several or all of the geo-economic regions of the world. This in itself is not an obstacle to a worldwide regionalization of the world. As we have seen, a region may include only parts of certain countries. The British Empire might be distributed through several different regions. No obstacles are likely to arise insofar as the Dominions are concerned, because they are already autonomous states with complete, or almost complete, self-government. The situation is rather different with respect to the Crown Colonies, some of which are of considerable size, such as the Kenya Colony and Tanganyika. This raises the whole question of the administration of colonies and of so-called backward regions. Their assignment to regions should depend upon their geographic location. Their administration, until they become capable of self-government, insofar as all matters of local and national administration are concerned, would have to be assigned by mandate to a regional government, or to the federal government, but probably to the former.

Regional Restraints Upon Nationalism

One of the advantages to be derived from the fact that a region would ordinarily include several nations and parts of nations, and that its boundaries would not always coincide with national boundaries, is that it would serve as a salutary check upon nationalism. The fixation of emotions upon the nation has given rise to some extremely harmful results. The same applies in a narrower sense to sectionalism and provincialism. By leaving to a nation at least a nominal existence, with certain national or local administrative functions, it can continue to serve as the channel for the expression of patriotic emotions. National disarmament, the limiting of the sovereign power of the state, and the setting up of regional and world authorities would deprive nationalism of its potentialities for harmful expression.

The question may arise as to whether the region would not in course of time become the object of a similar fixation of emotions with these harmful results following in its train. A safeguard against this possibility is the fact that a region, owing to its relatively large size, is likely to be somewhat diversified as to language, racial and cultural traits. However, it might not be desirable for a region to be too diversified. Extreme diversities in customs, manner of living, standards of behavior, etc., may render somewhat difficult the administration of a region as a whole. In its economic aspects this is mainly a matter of great divergencies in levels of living.

Future Possibilities of a Region

The regions may vary greatly as to area because of the vast differences in the resources and productivity of the land. Nearly half of the land surface of the world is of comparatively little value. The differences in size of population as between regions might be even greater than those of area. Some consideration should be given to the demographic future of a region. This involves the application of certain population indexes, in particular indexes of human fertility. There should, however, be considered also the future probabilities in the productive utilization of the land, and of the exploitation of the natural resources.

The regional division of the world should not be carried so far as to distinguish a large number of regions. Just as the forty-eight states of the United States of America are too numerous for regional treatment, so fifty or sixty or more regions are too numerous for the most efficient treatment of the fundamental economic problems of the world.[3] Great differences in the present or future population of the various regions could be adjusted and compensated by proportional representation in the federal world government.

Flow of Commodities

Foreign trade occupies a position of disproportionate importance in political and economic discussion. This is partly due to the fact that under the prevailing economic system there is a marked tendency toward the accumulation of surplus capital which seeks a profitable

[3] Odum and Moore divided the United States into six regions. (H. W. Odum and H. E. Moore, *American Regionalism*, New York, 1938.) Newbigin divided it into seven regions and McCarty into ten regions. (Marion I. Newbigin, *A New Regional Geography of the World*, New York, 1929; H. H. McCarty, *The Geographic Basis of American Economic Life*, New York, 1940.)

790

investment abroad. This capital takes the form either of commodities manufactured at home and then sold abroad at a profit, or of pecuniary capital loaned abroad from which comes interest, and eventually, under favorable conditions, the repayment of the loan. Because more private profits are usually made from the exportation than from the importation of commodities, there is a widespread belief in the fallacy that an excess of exports over imports is a favorable balance of trade, and that conversely an excess of imports over exports is an unfavorable balance of trade. The disproportionate importance attached to foreign trade is indicated by the fact that the value of imports into the United States is ordinarily equal to only about 5% of the value of the domestic retail sales, and rises toward, but does not exceed, 10% in a year of expanded economic activity.[4]

The whole concept of foreign or of international trade is, from an economic point of view, purely artificial. If no nations existed, or if all countries were under one government, or if the whole world constituted one trade area with no such artificial barriers as tariffs, export and import restrictions, subsidies, quotas, rationing, and the like, there would not only be no foreign trade but commodities would flow freely in response to the economic forces of supply and demand. The absurdity of this concept is demonstrated by the fact that there is no "foreign" trade within the United States, but an enormous volume of it within Europe exclusive of Russia, even though this portion of Europe is only two-thirds as large as the United States.

The federal and regional governments should promote such a free flow. This will be the case if the regional organization of the world is based on the idea of interdependence. The idea of self-sufficiency might encourage the tendency on the part of a region to monopolize its raw materials, and to try to develop industries which are not well suited to its natural environment. The former idea would discourage these tendencies, and would encourage the promotion of the largest flow of commodities.[5]

It may now appear as if the flow of commodities is of no importance in delineating the various regions of the world. Apart from the question of the relative weight which should be given to interde-

[4] In 1929, a year of expanded economic activity, this percentage that imports were of domestic retail sales was 9. In 1935, 1939 and 1944, it was 6. In 1943 and 1945 through 1949 inclusive, it was 5. In the peacetime years 1929, 1935 and 1939 the exports were not much larger than the imports. During the seven war and post-war years 1943 through 1949, exports were two or three times as large as imports because of military and civilian aid to foreign countries by the United States. (U.S. Dept. of Commerce, *Statistical Abstract of the United States*, 1950, pp. 841, 891.)

[5] Maurice Parmelee, *Bolshevism, Fascism and the Liberal-Democratic State*, New York, 1934. See Chapters, X, XXVI and XXVII.

pendence as opposed to self-sufficiency, the direction and extent of the flow is of some importance from the point of view of efficiency of administration. Hence statistical indexes as criteria should be used to give some weight to the flow of commodities. For example, in the years 1935-37, the exports of the United States went to the different parts of the world in the following percentages:

Europe	42.7%
Asia	16.7%
Canada	15.3%
Southern	
North America	9.2%
South America	8.5%
Oceania (Australia)	3.2%

During the same years the imports of the United States came from the different parts of the world in the following percentages:

Asia	30.0%
Europe	28.7%
Canada	14.4%
South America	13.3%
Southern	
North America	9.6%
Africa	2.4%
Oceania (Australia)	1.6%

This does not mean that the relatively high percentage of the foreign trade of the United States with Europe or with Asia is an argument in favor of putting the United States in the same region with Europe or with Asia. On the other hand, since Canada is contiguous with the United States, the comparatively large amount of the trade between these two countries, which is especially noteworthy when considered in terms of its per capita relation to the small population of Canada, may be an indication of common interests and common problems which would furnish a favorable basis for a regional union between the United States and Canada. The same consideration would apply in a smaller degree to the trade relations between the United States and southern North America.

Levels of Living

A disturbing factor in international economic relations has been the great variation in the different parts of the world between levels

792

of living, the price of labor or wages, and the cost of production. Surplus capital has sought areas of low living levels in order to reap the profits accruing from a low cost of production. This has been disturbing in several ways. Economic imperialism has been encouraged and the laborers of the areas of low living levels have been exploited. The cheap products of their labor have been used to compete with the products of more costly labor in the areas of higher levels of living, and have thereby tended to undermine and pull down these higher living levels.

This is a problem of worldwide scope which cannot be entirely solved until levels of living and the price of labor have become approximately equal the world over. The cost of production might continue temporarily to vary somewhat the world over, owing to the unequal distribution of natural resources and variations in other factors of the natural environment. The tendency in the long run would be for the equilibration of the costs of production, as well as of the levels of living and the price of labor the world over. The utilization of atomic energy may hasten this equilibration.[6]

In setting up a worldwide federation of geo-economic regions, due weight should be given to the above-mentioned considerations. At first sight, however, their significance for the delineation of regions is not entirely obvious. Do these considerations mean that each of the various regions should be more or less uniform and homogeneous as to the prevailing level of living and price of labor? This would mean regions of high levels of living and regions of low levels of living. Should, then, the products of the regions of low levels of living be barred entirely or in part from the regions of high levels of living in order to avoid undermining the high levels of living? This would be a serious check upon the free flow of commodities the world over.

The solution of this dilemma is perhaps to be found through worldwide and regional planning of production which would endeavor to distribute the industries in such a fashion as to concentrate the industries most compatible with low levels of living in the areas of these levels pending the time in a more or less distant future when the levels of living have become equilibrated for the world as a whole. Through such planning, it may be feasible to have within a region a combination of highly developed and efficient industries with a temporary fringe of less developed and inefficient industries. In any case, this would probably be inevitable in the regional division of the world, owing to the concentration of natural resources in certain areas, and to the vast extent of the relatively unproductive areas of the world to be apportioned among the different regions.

[6] See Boris Pregel, "Peacetime Uses of Atomic Energy," *Social Research, An International Quarterly of Political and Social Science,* New York, March 1947.

Geographic barriers have had a predominant influence in the past in bringing into being economic and cultural regions. While means of transportation and of communication have vastly improved, geographic barriers must be recognized in delineating geo-economic regions.

The most obvious of these geographic barriers are the great expanses of water—the oceans. However rapid maritime and aerial transportation may become, it is hardly likely that areas separated by oceanic distances will be included in the same region. A much shorter distance across water is not necessarily an obstacle. It is conceivable that Europe, or at least its southern portion, will be joined with northern Africa in the same geo-economic region.

Mountain ranges have been effective and sometimes almost insuperable barriers to transportation and communication. In this case also the improved means of transportation and communication have decreased greatly the effect of these mountain ranges as barriers. However, there is at least one mountainous barrier which will probably continue to serve as an effective division between regions, namely, the series of lofty and massive ranges which cross south Central Asia in a generally east to west direction. An extension of this mountainous barrier running to the northeast may also serve as a regional boundary.

These natural barriers also have an indirect effect in their influence upon climate, soil, and upon the productivity of the areas adjacent to them. When these additional factors are taken into consideration, other mountain ranges, such as the series of ranges which runs near the western coast of North America, and a similar series of ranges which runs near the western coast of South America, might also serve as regional boundaries. However, in the western hemisphere these boundaries are more likely to run east and west across its width which is narrow in comparison with its much elongated north and south length.

While a certain degree of self-sufficiency would characterize every region, this should not be the principal or decisive consideration in delineating a region. Interdependence should be recognized in the case of all regions, not only because it is inevitable in varying degrees, but also because it is a necessary condition of and conducive to the worldwide division of labor. Each region should be, insofar as other considerations permit, a suitable areal unit for social and economic planning, and may also have common problems to a certain extent.

While regional administrative efficiency is desirable, it should not be a preeminent consideration in delineating regions. The regional government would not have many detailed and administrative functions to perform. Any large region can secure competent personnel to set up an efficient administration. A more important consideration is that a region shall constitute a suitable unit for inclusion in a federation of the world. This means primarily that its representatives can bring to the federal government a fairly unified policy and plan for their region, to be fitted into a worldwide plan which would incorporate the plans of all the regions.

Diversity of economic systems as influencing the delineation of regions would decrease in importance as time goes by. The economic organization of the world would tend to become more or less similar. If great diversification were to persist, the divergent systems would have to work out a *modus vivendi* by which they could continue to exist side by side, and to cooperate in a federal union. Regionalism as a restraint and check upon nationalism, sectionalism, and provincialism, would have less importance as these emotional and sentimental manifestations of local pride diminish.

The future possibilities of a region should be kept in mind at its inception and thereafter. This includes a consideration of its demographic tendencies, and also of its productive possibilities. The latter depend upon the course of invention, technological change, and the exploitation of natural resources. A notable instance is that of African potential water power. This may render possible an extensive industrialization and a dense population.

In distinguishing geo-economic regions, should we be guided by one master principle, or by a master principle and several minor principles, or by several minor principles alone? The foregoing survey of the various criteria which may be utilized has not revealed any one criterion which may serve as a master principle, or even as a master principle with several minor principles. It seems probable, therefore, that several criteria should be utilized as minor principles. These criteria should perhaps be weighted in relation to each other for the whole world or for certain parts of the world.

In order to test the possibilities of using a master principle alone or with several minor principles, let us take production as the master principle. Under the guidance of such a principle, the coal and iron region in Germany, France, Belgium, and Great Britain might be distinguished as a geo-economic region. In similar fashion, the coal and iron region in the United States and Canada might be recognized. To take a different type of production, the grain belt in the United States and Canada might be recognized as a region. In similar fashion, the grain belt extending from central Europe through a considerable part of European Russia might be recognized.

There are, however, several objections to the use of production as the sole or predominant principle in distinguishing regions. Insofar

795

as the extractive industries are concerned, they are engaged in producing raw materials which are limited in supply. The amount produced annually is much inferior in value to numerous vegetable and animal products whose supply can be renewed from year to year. According to the statistics of the League of Nations, the annual production of minerals of all kinds in the world has a value less than that of milk or meat alone. Some of these minerals are very durable and can be used over and over again. This applies to the metals and various stony materials. However, the fuels, such as coal and oil, and the fertilizers, can be used only once. Furthermore, there are not many areas of the world in which one kind of production is the exclusive or predominant form over a very large area. If production were taken as the master principle, it would be difficult to distinguish a limited number of geo-economic regions, each of which would contain a relatively vast area. Such a region would be characterized by a variety or a multiplicity of kinds of production.

The boundaries of geo-economic regions would be subject to change. There are likely to be errors in the original regionalization which could be corrected upon subsequent investigation and experience. Inventions, the exhaustion of certain natural resources, population changes, and other changes would render modifications desirable in regional boundaries. As these boundaries will not necessarily be identical with national boundaries, there should be no emotional opposition to such changes due to nationalism. In fact, the territorial changes advocated and sometimes brought about by nationalist forces should be excluded entirely in a world organized in geo-economic regions and under a federal world government.

Having adopted a tentative regional division, the next step is to apply as many tests of its accuracy as possible. The most effective tests are statistical indexes which reveal various aspects of the regions. A trial-and-error application of as many of these indexes as are feasible and are significant may reveal certain respects in which such a division of the world is not the most suitable.

Geo-Economic Regional Indexes

There are several difficulties in the way of utilizing statistical indexes. For many portions of the world, statistics are lacking in large part or entirely. Where the statistics are available, they do not always permit comparison. Generally speaking, statistics are assembled by national governments and apply to the national area, and not to a larger area which might approximate a region.

796

Physiographic Indexes

Climate is the paramount factor in the natural environment. Soil is of great importance for the recurrent forms of production, namely, the cultivation and rearing of vegetable and animal products. Mineral resources are important, but not comparable in the long run with climate and soil. Sources of natural energy are of lasting importance. Topography, of which the distribution of land and water and the relief of the land are the outstanding features, is a significant permanent factor.

Statistics with respect to all these features of the natural environment are available, and may be used as indexes. However, much work in this field has already been done by geographers and geologists. It may not be profitable to devote much time and effort to this kind of statistical investigation.

Population Indexes

Statistical indexes as to the density, distribution, migration, and fertility of population should be applied. A large part of the population of the world is concentrated in Europe, India, China, Japan, Java, and in the northeastern portion of the United States. The statistics of the distribution of population should include statistics of the distribution between the rural and urban areas. The fertility indexes should throw some light upon the future possibilities of population in the various geo-economic regions.

Production Indexes

Numerous statistics of production in agriculture, manufacturing, mining, etc., are available, of which the most significant should be chosen. These statistics will furnish some indication of the world-wide division of labor and how that division takes place as between the different regions of the world. The future possibilities for production of each geo-economic region should also be indicated by means of statistical indexes. In this connection the physiographic indexes described above can be utilized. These include statistics with respect to climate, soil, mineral resources, and sources of natural energy. Closely related are the demographic indexes which reveal the available and potential labor supply.

Indexes as to the Flow of Commodities

There are numerous statistics of international trade which give a fairly good indication of the inter-regional flow of commodities.

These indexes reflect the relative degree of interdependence between the different regions.

Indexes of Levels of Living

Statistics of wages, prices, and employment are available which give some indication of the levels of living which prevail in the different regions of the world. These statistics also furnish some information as to the habits of consumption in the different parts of the world.

Methods of Procedure

A combination of the more important of these indexes, which could serve as a master index, would be very useful. Such an index might be a "man-resources" index, which could be a measure of the productivity of an area or region. However, there are various difficulties in the way of devising an index made up of two or more variables. In addition to the difficulty of securing accurate, adequate and comparable statistics for all parts of the world, there are certain special difficulties involved. There is the problem of selecting the most significant two or more indexes. There is also the problem of determining how much weight is to be given to each of these indexes. It cannot be assumed that they will necessarily be equally important. Assuming that these difficulties are overcome, it may appear to be a simple matter to add together the indexes of the two or more variables to arrive at the master index for an area or region. However, another difficulty immediately arises which may become insuperable if more than two variables are involved. The difficulty consists of the fact that the weight as well as the quantity of a variable may change in relation to changes in the other variable or variables involved.

Let us assume that we are trying to devise a "man-resources" master index. As an index of the human factor, we may take the number of men between the ages of eighteen and sixty. For the resources index, we may take the number of square miles of arable land. Even for a master index as simple and as limited as a combination of two indexes, it is not easy to correlate them. It is not to be assumed, for example, that doubling the number of men per square mile of arable land will necessarily double the amount produced, or even increase it by 50 per cent. Some method of correlation would have to be used to determine the genuine significance and value of this master index at every point on the scale. If a third variable were added, such as, for example, the number of women between certain ages for the human factor, or the mineral resources such as coal, or iron, or mineral oil for the resources factor, the difficulties would be multiplied for each additional variable. However, in spite of these difficulties, it may be worthwhile to explore the possibilities of devising a master index such as a "man-resources" index.

Having ascertained what statistical indexes are available for the whole or most of the world, by nations, or by whatever the local unit of area may be (province, state, county, etc.), the next step is to apply each one of these indexes—ten, twenty, or thirty of them, as the case may be—to the world as a whole. After applying each index, the results should be inspected in graphic or cartographic form. Areas of similarity of concentration, or dissimilarity, in several varying degrees, and borderline areas, should be noted. If we commence with a tentative rough-and-ready regional division of the world, a glance at these graphs will at once reveal whether or not each of these regions displays any characteristic feature of similarity or dissimilarity with respect to this index.

This procedure should be followed for each of the indexes utilized. The next step is to superimpose one index upon another. After each superimposition, inspection will reveal whether or not a pattern of any sort is distinguishable. The number of such superimpositions which are possible increases with an almost geometric ratio, according to the number of indexes used. For example, for five indexes, there are ten possible superimpositions of one index upon another; for ten indexes, there are forty-five superimpositions; for twenty indexes, there are one hundred and ninety superimpositions. Consequently, where a large number of indexes are used, it will probably not be feasible to utilize every possible combination or superimposition of them.

A more feasible method would be to work out a graphic representation for each group of indexes such as the population indexes, the production indexes, etc., and then to superimpose each representative graph upon each of the other representative graphs. Whichever method is used, the result should be a first approximation of regional divisions. After inspection of this first approximation, a selection of indexes for a combination of groups of them will be the next step. Superimposition of the representative graphs, which should result from this process of selection and of combination, will reveal new patterns, which will in turn furnish a second approximation of regional divisions. This procedure can be followed for as many approximations as may be feasible, or may seem desirable.

These statistical methods have been applied in part in the studies of regionalism in the United States. One outcome of the application of such methods is the disclosure of areas of homogeneity with respect to one or more variables. Areas of high productivity and of low productivity are revealed. Areas of high levels of living and of low levels of living are revealed. An area of high productivity is very likely to be also an area of high level of living, and vice versa. In the American studies of regionalism, homogeneity has usually been assumed as the sole or the principal criterion for regionalization within the nation. In a worldwide regional scheme, homogeneity is not necessarily the sole or principal criterion. For some purposes, indeed, diversity is highly desirable. For other purposes it is, to say the least, not objectionable. To the extent that regionalism is to be used as a restraint and check upon nationalism, a relatively high degree of diversity is desirable. To the extent to which the flow of commodities of transportation systems are to be considered, diversity within a region is not necessarily objectionable.

The statistical methods described above will reveal areas of homogeneity and of diversity with respect to one or more variables and with respect to groups of variables. They may also give some indication of the extent to which certain variables are complementary to other variables, or are contradictory to other variables, or are in positive or inverse correlation with each other. When these indexes or groups of indexes are superimposed upon each other, patterns more or less fundamental will be revealed. All of this information is valuable, and can be used at the inception of a worldwide regional scheme, and later when readjustments of this scheme may prove to be desirable. However, the criteria as to the purposes of regionalization which will have to be applied cannot always be measured or characterized in quantitative or statistical terms.

The diversities of language, race, and culture within a region, which may exist in a worldwide regional scheme, would not be greater than have existed and do now exist within the British, or the French, or the Dutch, or the Belgian, or the Portuguese empire. No such diversities could be greater than those which existed within the military alliance between the so-called "Aryan" Germans and the "non-Aryan" Mongoloid-Malay-Japanese during the war of 1939 to 1945. When we consider the purposes of such a regional scheme, namely, universal disarmament, world federation, effective social and economic planning for all parts of the world, mutual interdependence of the whole of mankind, it is inconceivable that geo-economic regions, coordinated by a world federation, could at worst be as ineffective for attaining these ends as the empires and military alliances, and the conflicting national sovereignties, of the past and of the present.

Chapter XLVI

What Are the Geo-Economic Regions?

THE geographers use the term "geographic region," also called a "natural region," in the sense that the regional traits have been determined entirely by nature. The economic geographers and the economists speak of an "economic region," which suggests an area whose characteristics have been influenced to some extent by man. Or the term may be applied to an area which may or may not as yet have been influenced by man, but which constitutes a distinct entity from the point of view of economic productivity or other activities. An example of the latter is an area containing mineral resources not yet exploited. An economic region may, therefore, be an agricultural region or an industrial region, an urban region or a rural region. The term "geo-economic region" signifies an attempt to combine and co-ordinate the geographical criteria with the economic criteria of a region. The concept of the geo-economic region may be extended so as to include political considerations which have an economic significance.

A geographic region may be demarcated according to certain of its natural features. Its physiography or topography embraces the distribution of land masses and water areas, and the relief of the land. The climate includes such important factors as precipitation and temperature. Other important features are the soil, the minerals, the sources of natural energy, etc. All of these natural features have economic significance. The geographer is often influenced by his awareness of this significance in choosing the criteria to be used in delineating geographic regions.

The above discussion indicates that a geo-economic region is determined and demarcated in the first instance by geographic and economic factors. It is, therefore, a composite product of those factors. The political factor, however, cannot be entirely ignored. The use of the word "political" has been avoided in this term, partly because it would make it long and clumsy, but also to obviate the misconception that the concept resembles the German ideas of *Geopolitik*. Whether we should use the term "geo-economic-political" is an open question. It might prevent some criticism from persons who insist, correctly up to a certain point, that political factors must be recognized. On the other hand, one of the chief merits of the geo-economic concept is that it demonstrates that geographic and economic factors should be recognized as fundamental in the political as well as the economic organization of the world—much more than has so far been recognized.

The primary service which the geographer can render is to describe the so-called natural regions, and to explain how they came into existence. Owing to the composite nature of the geo-economic region, it is not necessarily uniform in its geographic features. In fact, geographical diversity may have utility in such a region, *e.g.*, as a basis for a well-balanced economy. Many factors and conditions must be considered in delineating a geo-economic region, such as self-sufficiency, interdependence, planning, administrative efficiency, future possibilities, flow of commodities, levels of living, etc. The geo-economic regionalist is, so to speak, trying to create a harmonious melody out of the diverse sounds with which he must deal.

The relief features of the earth are not in themselves of great importance. The exceptionally high regions of the world, such as those over 10,000 feet, are not well suited for human habitation and activities. The most extensive area of this nature is the Tibetan plateau in central Asia. The only other area of considerable extent over 10,000 feet in altitude is in the Andean highlands extending a long way from north to south. The other areas of this nature are scattered here and there in North America, Europe, and Africa. By far the larger part of the land surface of the earth is under 5,000 feet in altitude. In most places, it is suitable for human habitation. Activities are determined not so much by the altitude as by other physical conditions, such as the precipitation, temperature, character of the soil, and accessibility.

Precipitation is one of the most decisive factors in determining suitability for human habitation and activity. Areas having an annual average rainfall of ten inches or less are characterized as arid and desert. An average annual rainfall of from 10 to 20 inches characterizes semi-arid areas. An average annual rainfall of from 20 to 80 inches characterizes the areas in which the great majority of mankind dwells. Within these areas are produced the larger part of the food and fodder crops, and also most of the textile and fiber crops. In most of the areas characterized by a very high rainfall, there is not a dense population. The principal exceptions are in Malaysia, Burma, India, and the northwest coast of North America.

802

Temperature is not of so decisive importance as precipitation. However, no area of very cold temperature is suitable for a dense population, partly due to the fact that all such areas are characterized by a low precipitation. Areas of high temperature may or may not be suitable for a dense population as determined by other factors, the principal one being precipitation.

Studies of climatic efficiency indicate that the conditions which promote the highest degree of efficiency in man, and the most suitable conditions for the growth of plants and animals, combine the suitable range of temperature with adequate precipitation and a moderate amount of seasonal and diurnal variability. A world map of climatic efficiency, based upon the stimulating effect of climate as inferred from work in factories, indicates that the regions of highest efficiency are to be found in two major and two minor areas. The major areas are northwestern Europe and in the central latitudinal zone of North America, ranging from the east coast to about two-thirds across the continent. The minor areas are along the Pacific coast of North America and areas of very small size in New Zealand and Tasmania.

Areas of secondary climatic efficiency are in central, eastern and northern Europe, central and northern North America, southern South America, the Japanese Islands, and the extreme southern tips of Australia and Africa. These areas of primary and secondary climatic efficiency correspond very closely to the areas of the greatest economic activity and, to a considerable extent, also to the areas of dense population. A large part of Asia lies in an area of tertiary climatic efficiency, and much smaller areas in the other continents. The remainder of the earth's surface is characterized by still lower conditions of climatic efficiency.

The geographic distribution of some of the most important crops and agricultural activities indicates that the areas of secondary and even of tertiary climatic efficiency perform useful services for the feeding and clothing of mankind. Wheat is the most important and also the most widely distributed of all the cereal crops. It is grown mainly in a cool and rather dry climate. The major wheat areas are in central and northern North America, western and central Europe, northern India, eastern and central China, southeastern South America, and southern Australia. Most of these areas are in semi-arid regions.

Rice is almost as important a cereal crop as wheat. It requires conditions entirely different from wheat. Rice can be grown only under conditions of high temperature and abundant moisture, either from rainfall or irrigation. The major rice producing areas are in southern and eastern India, Malaysia, the coastal area of China and Indo-China, and Japan. Minor rice producing areas are to be found over most of eastern and southern Asia and Malaysia, and along the eastern coast of South America.

The largest, though not the most important, cereal crop is corn or maize, much of which is used as fodder for animals. The largest corn-producing area is in the United States which produces nearly three-fourths of the world's crop of corn. Other major corn-producing areas are in central Europe, southern South America, South Africa, and Mexico. Minor corn-producing areas are in China, northern India, and along the east coast of South America. Corn requires a higher precipitation than wheat, namely, between 25 and 50 inches of rainfall, and a somewhat higher temperature. It is more likely to be found within the areas of primary or secondary climatic efficiency.

The major areas for cattle raising and dairying are in northwestern Europe, eastern and central United States, southern South America, and northern India. Minor areas are scattered over most of Europe, most of central and southern North America, the larger part of South America, parts of central and southern Africa, southern and eastern Asia, much of Malaysia, and parts of Australia. While the major areas are located in regions of relatively high climatic efficiency, this may be due as much or more to the demand created by a dense population than to the climatic conditions. The same is probably even more true of the breeding of swine. The major areas for this purpose are central United States, northwestern Europe, and eastern Asia. Minor areas are scattered over the United States, Europe, eastern Asia, eastern South America, northern South America, southern Africa, southern Australia, New Zealand, and the Philippine Islands.

Water power is a source of natural energy which may be of increasing importance in the future, provided it is not supplanted by atomic energy. The world total of developed water power in 1936 was about 60 million horsepower. North America had 26 million horsepower, of which the United States had over 17 million and Canada nearly 8 million. South America had 1,100,000 horsepower, of which 700,000 was in Brazil. Europe had 27,200,000 horsepower, of which 6,000,000 was in Italy, 5,250,000 in France, 2,900,000 in Norway, 2,800,000 in Switzerland, 2,550,000 in Germany, and 1,874,000 in Sweden. Asia had 5,400,000 horsepower, of which 4,240,000 was in Japan, and 500,000 in India. Africa had only 175,000 horsepower, and Oceania, 6,000 horsepower.

According to the figures for potential water power based on ordinary minimum flow, the distribution is very different from the present developed power. North America is estimated to have 77 million horsepower; South America, 74,000,000; Europe, 74,000,000; Asia, 148,000,000; Africa, 274,000,000; and Oceania, 24,000,000. North America, South America, and Europe have almost the same amount of potential water power. Asia has about twice as much as each of these three continents. Africa has nearly twice as much as Asia, though at present it has an insignificant amount developed. The cost of developing potential water power is a factor of decisive importance. It remains to be seen whether its huge potential water power will make Africa one of the most important industrial areas in the future.

If we glance at the distribution of potential water power according to countries, we find that in North America the United States with 33,500,000, and Canada with 25,500,000, have the larger portion. In South America, Brazil with 36,000,000. In Europe, Norway with 16,000,000, U.S.S.R. with 14,000,000, France with 6,000,000, Spain with 5,700,000, and Italy with 5,400,000. In Asia, U.S.S.R. with 64,000,000, India with 39,000,000 and China (including Manchuria) with 23,000,000. In Africa, the Belgian Congo with 130,000,000, French Equatorial Africa with 50,000,000, Cameroon (French mandate) with 18,000,000, and Nigeria and Cameroon (British mandate) with 13,000,000.

The delineation of regions has usually been based largely upon environmental factors such as topographical relief, precipitation, temperature, water power, and mineral resources. The human factor is represented in the total population and in the density of population of each area. Size, or density, of population has not been given much weight in demarcating these regions. The quality of a population as to its educational level and industrial skill, has usually not been considered at all. Nevertheless, a delineation based on environmental features brings out certain focal points or areas, such as a fine harbor, a rich mineral deposit, or a fertile agricultural area. Some of these focal points or areas are almost certain to become the nuclei of geo-economic regions. There are such areas in Europe, North America, eastern and southern Asia, and probably also in southern Africa, and in temperate South America.

Theoretically, a man-resources index should be devised which can be used in rating and ranking the different parts of the world. For certain purposes such an index would be useful. The question which concerns us here is as to whether such an index will be useful in delineating geo-economic regions. If such regions are to be demarcated upon the theory that some regions are superior and other regions inferior in the composition and quality of their population, and in the excellence of their physical environment for human habitation and for production, such an index would have great utility. Or a demarcation of these regions might be based on the theory that each region should contain a mixture of superior and inferior elements in the composition of its population and in the character of its geographic conditions.

It is questionable if either of these theories can be regarded as furnishing the guiding principle for the delineation of geo-economic regions. Neither self-sufficiency nor interdependence constitutes an infallible guide in the delineation of these regions. If an area, which on other grounds is suitable to be considered a geo-economic region, has a well-balanced and many-sided economy which renders it more or less self-sufficient, its self-sufficiency may be an additional reason for regarding it as a suitable region.

This is the situation in North America, which possesses an abundance of natural resources in the way of coal and metal reserves and plentiful water power, and at the same time has extensive agricultural resources. There are, however, large areas of the world which are poorly supplied with mineral resources, but have adequate agricultural resources. This is the situation in a part of South America, and also of Africa. On the other hand, northwestern Europe and a part of central Europe constitute one of the two greatest industrial areas of the world. This area possesses rich mineral resources, but has inadequate agricultural resources. Here are at least three types of geo-economic conditions, each of which may furnish a suitable basis for constituting a geo-economic region.

There are certain parts of the world which do not rank very high as to total population and density of population, such as tropical South America, central Africa, and Oceania. On the basis of other geo-economic considerations, one or the other of these areas may rank much higher. For example, Egypt would rank low according to most physiographic criteria. And yet inadequate precipitation is more than counterbalanced by the annual flood of the Nile. This furnishes adequate food supplies for the dense population of the valley of the Nile, owing to the rich loam which this flood spreads over the valley.

Central Africa has no coal reserves. However, its large energy reserves in the form of potential water power may more than counterbalance the lack of power derived from fuel. If present day experiments in cheap and effective methods of transmitting electricity over long distances are successful, central Africa may become a source of power for the Mediterranean region and other far-distant areas. In fact, technological progress along many different lines, as, for example, bio-chemistry applied to the cultivation of plants, may change materially the geo-economic and demographic situation of several of the regions of the world.

In view of these considerations, neither self-sufficiency nor interdependence in and of itself can be regarded as of primary importance in constituting a region. The important considerations are convenience for planning, administrative efficiency, the future possibilities of a region, the direction and size of the flow of commodities, and perhaps also the prevailing levels of living in relation to other regions—though the latter consideration may be of varying importance, according to the state of the technical arts. In connection with all of these considerations, the human factor is of great importance, but a difficult one to measure.

A population index of considerable significance, especially with respect to the future possibilities of the various regions, is a fertility index. Probably the best type is one which is based upon the ratio between the number of small children in relation to the number of women of child-bearing age. This index should be related to the expectation of life in a given area, which in turn depends upon the ratio between births and deaths. For example, according to the United States census of population of 1930, about 370 children under 5 years of age per 1,000 women of 15 to 45 years of age were necessary to maintain a stationary population. According to the 1930 census, expectation of life in the United States was 61 years. If the ratio of children under 5 years of age to women from 20 to 45 years is taken as an index, about 440 children under 5 years per 1,000 white women of 20 to 45 years were necessary to maintain a stationary population. Such an index of fertility is superior to the average size of family or the number of births per 100,000 population.

In 1940 there were 283 children under 5 years of age per 1,000 women of 15 to 49 years old. In 1910 there were 397 children under 5 years of age per 1,000 women of 15 to 49 years old. In 1940 the life expectancy of the white female was about 67 years and of the negro female was about 55 years. In 1910 the life expectancy of the white female was about 53 years and of the negro female is not known. All these figures should be interpreted in the light of such vital statistics as are mentioned above.[1]

The necessary statistics are available for devising a human fertility index for some of the more progressive nations of the world. For large areas of the world's land surface and for a large proportion of the world's population, such statistics are not available. It is doubtful if this index can be used at present as one of the indexes of utility for the delineation of geo-economic regions. However, it is possible that in the future when more and better statistics are available such indexes can be used to relocate regional boundaries and perhaps to subdivide some of the regions with very large populations.

The ocean trade routes give some indication of the flow of commodities between the different parts of the world. The most important, as measured by the value of commodities, is between Europe and

[1] U.S. Dept. of Commerce, Bureau of the Census, *Differential Fertility 1940 and 1910*, Washington, D.C., 1945, p. 3; *Statistical Abstract of the United States 1950*, p. 81.

the United States. This trade consists of exports of both manufactures and of raw materials and foods from each side of the Atlantic. No other part of the world exports large amounts of manufactured goods. Other ocean routes in order of importance according to the value of the commodities are from Europe to the Far East by way of the Mediterranean, between Europe and South Africa and Australia, and across the Pacific.

The distribution of predominant occupations also reflects the distribution of raw materials, as well as climate and soil. The industrial regions are concentrated mainly in northwestern Europe and in northeastern United States. Minor industrial regions are scattered through the remainder of Europe and of the United States, and are found in Brazil and Argentina in South America, and in Japan, China, India, Australia, and New Zealand. Farming regions are found mainly throughout Europe and north central Asia, eastern Asia, southern Asia, eastern and central United States, Mexico, the northeastern and southeastern parts of South America, the northern rim of Africa, and in portions of central and southern Africa. Pastoral industries, or forestry, or both, are found over most of the remainder of the earth's surface. Mining industry is scattered widely according to the location of mineral resources.

Regional classification with respect to agriculture is of great importance for the present, and probably is the most important for the more distant future. In all agricultural classifications the very cold areas, the desert areas, and the mountainous and excessively high areas can be excluded as of little or no agricultural value. Some of these areas are of significance because they contain mineral resources or forest products.

Most of North America lies within the temperate zone. This continent contains large areas highly suitable for agriculture. Large quantities of the cereals, fodder crops, vegetables, cotton, and meat and dairy products can be raised. In the more tropical portions, valuable crops can be produced, such as fruit, sugar cane, certain kinds of vegetables, cocoa, coffee, etc.

Almost all of the continent of Europe is within the temperate zone. Two-thirds of this continent lies within the favorable temperature belt of from 40 degrees Fahrenheit to 60 degrees Fahrenheit, of annual average temperature. Consequently, a large part of its area is cultivated, and its agricultural population is very large in comparison to its size. Cereal and dairy products are the outstanding agricultural products of this continent.

Asia is so vast and varied in character that it is more difficult to characterize it from an agricultural point of view. A large part of

808

this continent is composed of mountains and plateaus which are relatively unsuitable for agriculture. The lowland portions of the continent, however, are large enough to produce more agricultural goods than any of the other continents. These productive areas are mainly within the monsoon zone which extends through the tropical southern portion of the continent into the eastern temperate portion. The cereal crops are of outstanding importance, especially rice in the southern portions of the continent. Dairy products are of great importance, and tropical fruits in the southern portion.

Africa has as yet a relatively small amount of cultivated land. Most of its area suitable for cultivation lies within the tropical zone. However, much of this land is somewhat elevated so that it may be more suitable for agriculture than its low latitude indicates. It remains to be seen how important Africa will be in the future agricultural production of the world.

South America also has a relatively small area of cultivated land. About three-fourths of the continent is within the tropical zone. Most of its agricultural production at present is in the temperate southern portion which is comparatively limited in extent. It remains to be seen how important the much larger tropical portion of this continent will become from an agricultural point of view.

Europe, North America, and the eastern and southern portions of Asia are of outstanding importance for agriculture. Africa will probably assume a more important position in the future, though it may never succeed in rivaling the above mentioned regions. South America will probably always occupy a lower rank than these four continents. Australia will always be of small importance for the world's agriculture.

Climatic conditions favorable for human beings correspond in considerable part to a highly developed agriculture. This is not merely a fortuitous coincidence. Conditions which are favorable for human habitation and efficiency are usually also favorable for agriculture. However, there are exceptions both ways. Man can live in the mountains at relatively high altitudes, or in desert regions, without injury to health and retaining a considerable amount of efficiency.

Valuable crops can be raised under conditions of temperature and precipitation which, while not necessarily injurious to health, may be disadvantageous from the point of view of efficiency. These considerations indicate that many areas can be used both for human habitation and for raising food or other agricultural products which are not of the highest order for both purposes. A coincidence of the most advantageous conditions, both for agricultural production and for human habitation and efficiency, characterizes certain limited areas as of exceptional importance. Most extensive areas which are not so advantageous are complementary to the areas of primary importance.

As already stated, the major areas with respect to climatic efficiency are in northwestern Europe and in a central zone of North America ranging from the east to about two-thirds of the way across the continent. Much more extensive areas of secondary climatic efficiency are in central, eastern, and northern Europe, central and northern North America, southern South America, the Japanese Islands, and the southern tips of Australia and Africa. Other areas of the same degree of climatic efficiency may be identified in central and southern Africa, and in several parts of Asia.

The distribution of mineral resources is not necessarily connected with conditions favorable for agriculture and for human habitation and efficiency. However, the largest reserves both of iron and of coal exist in North America and Europe. There is also a large reserve of coal in China. The other mineral resources are scattered more widely and without any significant relation to climate.

The reserves of petroleum also are widely distributed. North America is of importance as a source of this form of fuel and of energy. Europe does not occupy a prominent position in this regard. The middle east has a large supply. With respect to potential water power, neither North America nor Europe occupy positions of exceptional importance. Asia possesses a much larger undeveloped reserve, but Africa is outstanding with the largest reserve of potential water power.

The foregoing considerations suggest that certain central, or focal, areas can be distinguished from which geo-economic regions can be planned and plotted, so to speak, by means of a process of approximation. Two such major areas are found in North America and northwestern Europe, respectively. Two similar areas also of great importance are found in eastern Asia and southern Asia. An area of much less importance is found in southern South America.

An American geographer has distinguished seven conspicuous regions as outstanding according to four world patterns, namely: (1) the pattern laid down by nature, (2) the facility pattern laid down by man, (3) the activity pattern with its political units, (4) the pattern of ideas and ideals. These regions are western Europe, eastern Europe, eastern Asia, the East Indian region, India, southeastern South America, and the United States.

"These seven regions taken together contain most of the people of the world, most of the natural resources, most of the established facilities, most of the social institutions and activities, and most of the ideas which are promoting or retarding the welfare of the world. They are the major parts of the international

810

scene, the pivot areas in any world order, and the regions of supreme interest in world recovery."[2]

The question of the optimum size of a geo-economic region should now be considered. The decision as to this question would help to determine the optimum number of geo-economic regions for a world federation. There is an upper and a lower limit as to the number of regions which it would be desirable to delineate. If the number were as high as sixty or seventy, there would be as many regions as there are nations in the world. While the regional boundaries might be determined somewhat more logically than the existing national boundaries, little would be gained from having as many regions as there are nations.

On the other hand, if there were no more than 5 or 6 regions in the world, each region might be too large and unwieldy for administrative and planning purposes. The optimum number of regions lies somewhere between these two extremes, but probably nearer to the lower than to the upper limit. The regions will not necessarily be approximately equal in land area. Population, climate, agricultural productivity, mineral resources, and other conditions, as well as land area, should be taken into consideration in determining the size of any geo-economic region.

As has been indicated, the criteria and purposes of geo-economic regionalism have an important bearing upon both the size and the delineation of a region. If a large natural area has a high degree of self-sufficiency so that it forms a comparatively well unified production and economic unit, this may be the decisive consideration in creating a region out of this area. Large areas in the world, however, are dependent to a rather high degree upon other parts of the world. These areas may become regions because each one of them has common problems to be met by means of planning, and can be administered with a high degree of efficiency.

Future possibilities should be given some weight in considering the suitability of any large area for becoming a geo-economic region. If such an area is likely to increase greatly in density of population, or vice versa, this probability should be given due weight. In the interest of the world as a whole, it would be preferable not to have a preponderance of the population of the world concentrated in one or two regions, especially if these regions were contiguous. This situation might lead to a domination of the world federation by one or two

[2] Charles C. Colby, "Regional Aspects of World Recovery," in *The Annals of the American Academy of Political and Social Science,* November 1941, Volume 218, page 142.

such regions. Demographic changes result almost entirely from changes of a material or technological character.

The exhaustion of important mineral resources in certain areas of the world may lead to a decrease of population in those areas. It is almost certain to happen before long in Great Britain, namely, England, Scotland and Wales. It has been estimated that its population will drop from about 50,000,000 (48,841,000 according to the 1951 census) to about 33,000,000 in 1976, and that its percentage of those aged 65 and over, which was 7.2 in 1931, will be 17.5 percent in 1976.[3] "This rapid decline in the birth rate is as wide as the European sphere of civilization. A stationary population in Great Britain, France, Germany and the Scandinavian countries will be reached, it is now estimated, within ten years, and a few years later decline will set in."[4]

The development of potential water power may result in the concentration of population in areas now sparsely populated. This may happen in central Africa, which possesses a large reserve of potential water power. Technological changes which can be only dimly foreseen will have marked effects upon the distribution of population, both in the way of increasing the density of population in certain areas and decreasing that density elsewhere. The productive use of atomic energy will be one of these changes.

Recent demographic changes in certain of the leading countries in the way of retardation of the rate of increase or of absolute decrease in population, have given rise to the belief that, as a result of widespread use of birth control methods, the worldwide increase of population will cease, and that the population of the world will become more or less stabilized. While this may be the present tendency, we cannot be certain that it will continue indefinitely. Improved methods of agriculture based on agrobiological and biochemical principles may furnish much more food for human consumption. Technological progress in industry will certainly render possible the production of a much greater abundance of manufactured products. The possibility of another period of increase of the world's population should not be overlooked.

While important changes in the future should not be ignored, they are not insuperable obstacles in the way of a regionalization of the world which is subject to modification from time to time as these

[3] Grace G. Leybourne, "An Estimate of the Future Population of Great Britain," *Sociological Review*, London, April 1934. In making these calculations it was assumed that no migration movements would take place and that the mortality rates would remain much the same.

[4] O. E. Baker, "The Population Prospect," *Scientific Monthly*, August 1934, p. 169.

changes render it desirable. Such modifications may affect the total number of regions, thereby changing the size of the regions and also modifying the location of the boundaries between the various regions.

Other criteria which may be considered in the delineation of regional boundaries are the flow of commodities, comparative levels of living, and means of transportation and communication. The direction and the degree of the flow of commodities to and from a more or less central, or focal, point within an area may serve as a criterion as to where the boundary of a region should be located. In other words, the imaginary line at which, or the zone of limited extent within which, the flow of commodities changes so that it is directed toward the focal point of one region, as contrasted with the focal point of an adjoining region, may serve as a guide in locating the natural boundaries.

Whether or not levels of living can serve so readily to delineate regional boundaries is questionable. So long as levels of living vary greatly in different parts of the world, it may sometimes be desirable to segregate in a measure the areas of a high level from those of a low level. However, in many cases, it will probably be impossible to do so without violating other important criteria and purposes of geo-economic regionalism. This difficulty cannot be entirely overcome until the level of living has become more or less equal the world over. As transportation is of considerable importance within each region, a lofty mountain chain such as the Himalayas may serve as a boundary between areas which in other respects might belong to the same region.[5]

There are certain natural barriers which indicate boundaries between regions. In northern Africa there is the extensive Libyan and Egyptian desert which separates the north African portion of the Mediterranean region from the Afro-Asiatic region. The broad belt of the Sahara separates central and southern Africa from the remainder of the eastern hemisphere. This desert belt passes beyond the Red Sea, across the peninsula of Arabia and Mesopotamia, across Iran and into northwest India. Farther to the north in Asia lies another broad and very lengthy desert belt, commencing at the Caspian Sea. It extends eastward with an interruption where it is crossed by the Altai Mountains. Further to the east it extends across Mongolia to Manchuria and northern China. In the heart of Asia lies the elevated plateau caused by the Himalaya mountain system and its subsidiary mountain ranges. In the northern part of South America is an extensive tropical jungle region which extends most of the way across the continent.

[5] Maurice Parmelee, *Oriental and Occidental Culture*, New York, 1928. See Chapters II, XIX, and XXII.

An indication of the potential demographic growth of regions is furnished by pioneer areas. A world map of pioneer belts indicates the areas of pioneer experimentation, actual or potential.[6] The following pioneer belts are designated: a narrow belt running west by north in western Canada, starting not far north of the boundary between Canada and the United States; a belt running along the western slope of the Rocky Mountains in the United States; a very extensive and broad pioneer belt extending all the way from northern Scandinavia across Russia and Siberia to Manchuria and the Pacific Coast of Siberia. Narrow pioneer belts run along the northern border of Russian Turkestan and the western border of China. Several pioneer belts, somewhat limited in extent, are included in eastern and southern Africa. An extensive pioneer belt is indicated in South America, running along the eastern slope of the Andes and then crossing southern Brazil and extending up the east coast into the eastern bulge of South America. A pioneer belt rather limited in extent is indicated in the southern portion of South America. A series of pioneer belts runs intermittently around Australia which is, at most points, not very far removed from the coast. In other words, this series of belts is along the border of the great arid region in the interior of Australia.

These pioneer belts, and several others in various parts of the world, are described in detail in a symposium by thirty-six authors, which is a sequel to the above mentioned book.[7] While the future of pioneer settlements cannot be predicted with certainty in their early stages, nevertheless these settlements throw a good deal of light upon the probable extension and development of regions. The permanently established communities of the Western Hemisphere are derived almost entirely from pioneer immigration from Europe. Similar movements of population have been taking place elsewhere in the world. It is estimated that during the two decades between 1911 and 1931 the population of Manchuria increased by 10,000,000 inhabitants, mainly due to Chinese immigration.[8]

The criteria for delineating geo-economic regions should not be racial, ethnic, linguistic or cultural. These human differences are irrelevant in so far as satisfying the fundamental and universal needs of mankind is concerned. These criteria should be mainly of the nature of physiographic indexes, population indexes, production indexes, indexes as to the flow of commodities, and indexes of the levels of living. Under the head of physiographic indexes should be taken into consideration temperature, precipitation, altitude, climatic effi-

[6] Isaiah Bowman, *The Pioneer Fringe,* American Geographical Society, New York, 1931, p. 50.

[7] *Pioneer Settlement,* American Geographical Society, New York, 1932.

[8] Bowman, *op. cit.* p. 281.

ciency, mineral resources, fertility of the soil, water power, topography, and accessibility.

The other indexes arise in large part from the physiographic indexes. The demographic indexes are so determined because the size, density and increase of population depend in large part on the fertility of the soil. The production indexes are determined in considerable part by the mineral resources. The indexes as to the flow of commodities depend mainly on topography and accessibility. The indexes as to the level of living are determined by all of the preceding indexes.

In addition to the indexes which have been mentioned and arising largely out of them, should be considered future prospects as to production, population, the flow of commodities, the levels of living, and also the extent to which a geo-economic region possesses common problems and can practice planning to solve these problems.

In view of the above considerations, it is obvious that geo-economic regionalism is not exclusively or at all political, administrative, juridical, sectional, national, continental, linguistic, ethnic, racial or cultural. On a world-wide scale its purpose is not regional self-sufficiency but the regional interdependence which is necessitated by the uneven distribution of mineral and other natural resources over the world. While it should strive for administrative efficiency, it is even more important that it should promote planning for the solution of common problems. It should facilitate the federalization of the world. It should place regional and federal restraints upon nationalism. It should promote the flow of commodities for useful and human purposes, and not merely for the accumulation of private profits, by maintaining world-wide freedom of transportation and communication. It should encourage a consistent rise in the levels of living by stimulating a constantly increasing world-wide volume of production.

By applying the above criteria the present writer has delineated 14 geo-economic regions.[9] These regions he has named Temperate North America, Caribbean, Tropical South America, Temperate South America, North Europe, Mediterranean, Central Africa, South Africa, Afro-Asia, South Asia, East Asia, Malaya, Oceania, and Soviet Union. The last-named region is the only one containing only one nation. However, this is justified by the area and population of the Soviet Union and by the fact that the Soviet Union is in itself a federation of nations.

The accompanying table gives the relatively habitable area in square miles, the approximate population, the density of population per square mile and the econographic index weighted according to

[9] Maurice Parmelee, *Geo-Economic Regionalism and World Federation,* New York, 1949.

815

area for each of these 14 regions. The econographic index is based upon four important physiographic conditions of each of these regions, namely, temperature, precipitation or rainfall, average elevation or altitude, and coal reserves in terms of 10,000 tons per square mile.

Geo-economic regions of the world proposed by Parmelee[10]

Region	Relatively habitable area in 1000 square miles	Approximate population in millions	Density of population per square mile	Econographic index weighted according to area
1. Soviet Union	5,090	180	35	123
2. North Europe	1,070	270	252	551
3. Mediterranean	940	154	164	174
4. Afro-Asia	1,200	58	48	82
5. East Asia	1,600	310	194	334
6. Malaya	1,340	255	190	202
7. South Asia	1,480	412	278	112
8. South Africa	2,000	26	13	198
9. Central Africa	4,440	100	23	69
10. Temperate North America	4,770	162	34	441
11. Caribbean	2,080	56	27	111
12. Temperate South America	1,770	21	12	232
13. Tropical South America	4,640	58	13	81
14. Oceania	2,480	100	40	158
	34,900	2,162	62	

These regions vary considerably in area and in size and density of population. The largest in relatively habitable area is more than 5 times as large as the smallest. The largest in population is nearly 20 times the smallest. The largest in density of population is 23 times the smallest. The highest econographic index is 8 times the lowest. However, these differences are far less than the differences which now exist between the many nations of the world in area, population, etc. Similar excessive differences exist between the political divisions within many nations. For example, in the United States, Nevada has less than 2 percent of the population of New York. On the other hand, Texas has 213 times the area of Rhode Island.

[10] The statistics in this table are as of the middle of the twentieth century. My book entitled *Geo-Economic Regionalism and World Federation* contains a a world map delineating these fourteen geo-economic regions, p. 103.

816

The differences between the 14 geo-economic regions delineated by the present writer are also indicated by the next table which indicates the ranking of these regions as to relatively habitable area in square miles, approximate population, density of population per square mile and econographic index weighted according to area.

Relative ranking of the geo-economic regions

Rank from highest to lowest	Relatively habitable area in square miles	Approximate population	Density of population per square mile	Econographic index weighted according to area
1.	Soviet Union	South Asia	South Asia	North Europe
2.	Temp. No. Amer.	East Asia	North Europe	Temp. No. Amer.
3.	Trop. So. Amer.	North Europe	East Asia	East Asia
4.	Central Africa	Malaya	Malaya	Temp. So. Amer.
5.	Oceania	Soviet Union	Mediterranean	Malaya
6.	Caribbean	Mediterranean	Afro-Asia	South Africa
7.	South Africa	Temp. No. Amer.	Oceania	Mediterranean
8.	Temp. So. Amer.	Central Africa	Soviet Union	Oceania
9.	East Asia	Oceania	Temp. No. Amer.	Soviet Union
10.	South Asia	Trop. So. Amer.	Caribbean	South Asia
11.	Malaya	Afro-Asia	Central Africa	Caribbean
12.	Afro-Asia	Caribbean	Trop. So. Amer.	Afro-Asia
13.	North Europe	South Africa	South Africa	Trop. So. Amer.
14.	Mediterranean	Temp. So. Amer.	Temp. So. Amer.	Central Africa

Such geo-economic regions and a world federation of these regions will not abolish the nations which will remain as they are and will continue to perform most of the functions they have performed heretofore. However, so far as the regions and the federation are concerned, the nations will, so to speak, vanish. The regional authorities will perform the functions assigned to them for their respective regions impartially and without regard to the nations or parts of nations contained within the region. In similar fashion, the world federal authority will perform its functions for the world and mankind as a whole regardless of national boundaries. The important question therefore is, what are the appropriate functions to transfer from the national governments to the regional authorities and from such loose organizations as the defunct League of Nations and moribund United Nations to the world Federal Authority? Needless to say, these functions should be broader in their scope than a function

817

which is purely national. For example, an appropriate national function is that of teaching the national language to the young which, in the case of many nations, is spoken only by one nation.

To demarcate the regions in such a fashion that each region would have approximately the same population as every other region would be as impossible as it is to demarcate them so that each will have approximately the same area. In any case, it would be futile to do so. The main considerations in delineating a geo-economic region are that it constitutes an extensive area of contiguous, or more or less contiguous, territory; and that it contains a rather large population, part of which is concentrated in urban centers and areas with a type of population capable of organizing and carrying on the planning and administrative functions of a region. The differences in population of the various regions could be reflected in the World Federation by giving to each region a representation which would correspond in a measure with its population.

According to the essential features of a region mentioned above, all of the fourteen regions in the above classification can fulfill these essentials with the possible exception of Central Africa. In each of these regions there is at least a nucleus of a population which is more or less accustomed to rule itself and to carry on the necessary functions of a region. Central Africa may be an example of a potential region which should be under the administration of the World Federation until such time as it is prepared for, and capable of, undertaking the task of organizing and carrying on a regional authority. In this status its position will be no worse and probably much better than as the colonial possession of several imperialist powers.

An objection which may be raised is that some of these regions are mixed as to race, and that others of them are inhabited predominantly, or exclusively, by the peoples of the darker races. These objections, based mainly upon the dubious notion that the white race is superior to the dark races and should rule those races, may wreck any attempt at a regional classification of the world. They are presented as so-called political realities, and as insuperable obstacles to geo-economic regionalism. However, geographic and economic realities are quite as real as political considerations, and are much more important and lasting.

When classified as to econographic index, 1,000 being the highest possible index, these fourteen regions may be divided into four groups. The highest group includes the regions named North Europe, Temperate North America, and East Asia, ranging in index from 551 down to 334. These three regions are mainly in the north temperate zone and possess a large part of the world's mineral resources and

818

most fertile land, though they include barely one-fifth of the world's relatively habitable area.

The second group includes Temperate South America, Malaya, South Africa, and Mediterranean, ranging in index from 232 to 174. These four regions are mainly sub-tropical and temperate. The third group includes Oceania, Soviet Union, South Asia, and Caribbean, ranging in index from 158 to 111. This group is largely sub-tropical and partly sub-temperate. The lowest group includes Afro-Asia, Tropical South America, and Central Africa, ranging in index from 82 to 69. This group is mainly tropical and equatorial.

Chapter XLVII

The World Federation of Geo-Economic Regions

THE nation has usually been an ethnic, linguistic, and cultural entity. Geographic and economic conditions and factors have sometimes been recognized but have usually not had a decisive influence in determining the boundaries of a nation. Global organizations of nations are suitable for various cultural purposes such as scientific, literary, artistic, and recreational purposes. Most people, however, even many scholars, and educated persons, are still dominated by the myth of the nation as a more or less permanent political entity, and can conceive only of a world federation of nations.

The nation is not the suitable unit for membership in a world federation for economic and political purposes. This is partly due to the fact that geographic and economic factors have played a minor part in determining national boundaries. It is also due to the fact that the existing nations vary too greatly in area and population from each other and are too numerous for an efficient administration of the economic and political functions which should be exercised by any world organization.

These defects of the nation as a suitable unit for membership in a world federation for economic and political purposes have been demonstrated twice on a world-wide scale. In the ineffectual League of Nations which existed approximately from 1919-39 and in the United Nations Organization which has been in existence since 1945, the absolute sovereignty of each nation was and is retained. The Charter of the latter organization says: "The Organization is based on the principle of the sovereign equality of all its Members." (Chapter I, Article 2)

The League of Nations had 45 members on March 31, 1944. The United Nations already include 80 or more members. A few are large and powerful but most of them are small and weak. China with more tnan 600 million inhabitants is over 4,000 times as populous

820

as Iceland with only 140,000. Several of the Latin-American countries have less than one million inhabitants apiece. National sovereignty provokes war, and prevents an effective world organization to solve the economic and political problems of mankind. The geo-economic region which limits national sovereignty and furnishes a suitable unit of organization for a world federation is a practicable solution. The geo-economic regions are of much greater permanent and fundamental importance, and for these as well as other reasons, more suitable than the nations to be the member units of a world federation.

The purposes of a world federation should be directed toward satisfying universal human needs regardless of racial, ethnic, linguistic, and cultural differences. These needs are, in the first place, economic in that they include food, clothing and shelter required by every human being, and a consistently rising level of living unimpeded by war and the disturbances caused by an anarchic economy such as the business cycle. These needs are, in the second place, political in that they require the protection of the whole of mankind from war and the other dangers which menace it, such as disease, poverty and starvation.

Regions delineated in accordance with geographic and economic considerations, each of which would contain one or more nations or parts of nations, would constitute suitable members for a world federation competent to attain the economic and political purposes outlined above. They would obscure the common humanity of mankind much less than the nations which now obstruct cooperation on a global scale. These geo-economic regions would possess no absolute sovereignty such as is claimed by each of the nations of today. They would not be characterized by the nationalism, patriotism and chauvinism which characterize all nations and which determine in considerable part national policies and programs. The boundaries of these regions could be readily changed in accordance with demographic and economic changes, whereas at present any proposal to change national boundaries is very likely to lead to war.

The proposal to divide the world into several large regions may arouse the fear that these regions would constitute super-states. This fear has been accentuated by the rise in modern times of totalitarian regimes which have stamped out civil liberties and have, on the whole, lowered the prevailing levels of living. There is also apprehension about increasing political machinery, some of which may be superfluous. These fears may strengthen the unwillingness of each nation to renounce a single iota of its absolute sovereignty.

No one of these fears with respect to regions is valid. The region would not have absolute sovereignty over the territory within its borders as the nation has had in the past. Its functions and power

821

would be limited, on the one hand, by the nation, and, on the other hand, by the World Federation. The regions cannot become super-states presenting the danger of eventual destructive inter-regional wars similar to the international and imperialist wars of the past and present. The police powers of the nation would be limited to the enforcement of its purely national and local functions. The police powers of the region would be limited to the enforcement of its regional functions. The police powers of the World Federation would be limited to the enforcement of federal functions and to maintaining the constitutional relations between the regions.

There is no reason to believe that the regional organization and government would be any less democratic than the average of the nations of the world. It should be somewhat above the national level in this regard. The political machinery created by the regional organization would not be an absolute increase in the political organization of the world. Inasmuch as the regional government would take over some of the political functions of the national governments, the net increase would be smaller than the apparent increase. Even assuming that there is a net increase, it would be fully justified by the useful functions which the regional government would perform in the world economy and polity.

The national and local governments would retain authority in matters of exclusively national and local concern. Among them are the regulation of marriage and the family, the administration of education, religious institutions, and almost all other matters which require an elaborate machinery for administrative details. The national and local governments would also have autonomy in most fiscal matters, e.g., national and local taxation. They would be restrained from imposing customs duties and other restraints upon the regional and inter-regional flow of commodities. They would also be required to make *pro rata* contributions to defray the expenses of the regional governments and of the world federation.

The principal problem in the creation of a regional organization is to distinguish and to segregate the matters of regional from those of national scope. These are largely matters of production in the basic industries, namely, agriculture, the extraction of mineral raw materials, and the manufacture of finished products. The regional government may also be given limited powers of intervention in the regulation of movements of population. However, these demographic problems can be solved in the long run most satisfactorily through the regulation of production.

The manner in which economic problems of international and worldwide importance can be regulated through the regional organ-

822

izations may be illustrated in many ways. The United States had recently a surplus of from one to two years' supply of wheat. The surplus was so great that there were restrictions on the production of wheat because there was not sufficient space in warehouses to store the wheat. At the same time, there was and is urgent need of wheat in many parts of the world.

Let us assume that after a worldwide regional scheme had been established, there are regional organizations for Europe and for North America. The European regional government will estimate the European requirements for wheat, the existing wheat production, and will also consider whether a large production of wheat in such an area as Italy is desirable. It may be concluded that Italy is better suited for the cultivation of fruits and vegetables. Having made these estimates, the European regional government will negotiate with the North American regional government with respect to whether or not North America can furnish to Europe the wheat it requires to make up its deficit. As a result of such negotiations, the North American regional government will plan to produce a sufficiently large crop of wheat to supply Europe and other deficit regions of the world in return for products of those regions. In similar fashion, the production of other raw materials and of manufactured goods can be planned in each region, and for the world as a whole, through the regional plans and inter-regional negotiations, which will be coordinated by the world federation of the regions.

A world wide regional and federal organization would eliminate restraints upon and disturbances in production caused by national boundaries, which are almost entirely artificial. This situation is well illustrated in the relations between the United States and Canada. The potato growers of Maine are much concerned over the competition which they receive from the potato growers of New Brunswick. As a consequence, there are elaborate international negotiations with respect to this agricultural product. And yet the potato growers of Maine receive more competition from the potato growers of Idaho. Since this competition is within the same nation, it does not cause the unnecessary restraints and disturbances which it causes in the former cases. The same situation exists with respect to the manufacture of pulp in the United States and Canada, in spite of the fact that

[1] See, for example, B. B. Wallace and L. R. Edminster, *International Control of Raw Materials*, Brookings Institution, Washington, 1930. These authors describe the Canadian embargoes on pulpwood which were intended as restrictions to promote the domestic industry to the disadvantage of the paper industry in the United States. In other words, they were export restrictions to protect a national industry rather than for the conservation of raw materials.

the pulp manufacturers of the different parts of the United States compete with each other as much as, or a great deal more than, they compete with the pulp manufacturers of Canada.[1]

Canada and the United States furnish an excellent example of a natural area with common forms and methods of production, uniform levels of living, and an homogeneous culture. In varying degrees all the nations of the world have the same or similar economic interests, however widely their cultures may differ from each other in other respects.

Freedom of competition is generally assumed to be a fundamental principle of capitalism. It is, in fact, contradicted by the monopolistic tendencies inherent in capitalism which make capitalism ambivalent in this respect.[2] Nevertheless, it is generally recognized that freedom of competition should be fostered and promoted. Accordingly, national boundaries should not place artificial restraints upon this freedom.

There have been several attempts to promote freedom of competition and the free flow of commodities on an international scale. During its short existence, the League of Nations made a few attempts in this direction. The only result was an international agreement signed on March 16, 1928 by a few nations with respect to hides, skins, and bones. Wallace and Edminster, in their book on the international control of raw materials cited above, have described various forms of control—national, private, and mixed—in the interest of national and private monopolies. They described in detail the Chilean control of sodium nitrate, the Japanese camphor monopoly, the Franco-German potash combine, the Brazilian scheme for the valorization and control of coffee, the British export restrictions on rubber, the Canadian embargoes on pulpwood, and colonial discriminatory export duties.

There have been various attempts to encourage freedom of competition and of international trade by means of bilateral and multilateral agreements. This is an uncertain, piecemeal, and inadequate method of attaining these ends. At best, such an agreement is likely to be accepted by only a part of the nations of the world. Even in peacetime such agreements are subject to repudiation. In wartime, they are almost certain to break down completely. This system of negotiation and barter between nations has not only proved inadequate, but, in certain instances, has had harmful results. As an American economist has said, "the system of bilateral trading (barter) which these two governments (German and Italian) have done much to foster has a tendency to make raw material purchases distinctly more

[2] Maurice Parmelee, *Farewell to Poverty*, New York, 1935. See especially Chapter XVIII entitled "The Contradictions of Capitalism."

expensive than need be." He concluded that "the less the movements of resources and goods and the location of industries have to be influenced by political boundary lines, the better for economic welfare."[3]

An economist who was long connected with the League of Nations has made an exhaustive survey of the results of these international trade agreements. He concluded that large scale production, requiring a worldwide search for raw materials, calls for a unified worldwide economic system in conflict with the eventually supplanting nationalism. Among other things, he described the various agricultural marketing schemes, and imperial marketing agreements.[4]

The regional government would have supervision over the national and local governments within its region in all matters coming within the jurisdiction of the regional government and of the World Federation. It would restrain the national and local governments from legislative and administrative acts which interfere with these regional and worldwide functions. In all matters of national and of local importance, the national and local governments would continue to take such action as they see fit. The nation would be autonomous within these limits in much the same way as a State in the United States and a Province in Canada.

Each of the regional governments would serve as the agent of the World Federation within its region. It would enforce the federal laws which pertain to its region. It would safeguard against any national or local developments which menace the humanitarian and democratic ideals of the World Federation. While each nation would choose the educational system peculiarly adapted to its cultural needs, it should not be permitted to include therein chauvinistic, militaristic, imperialistic, racialistic, and anti-democratic teachings which threaten the very existence of the Federation.

The regional government would have jurisdiction in matters pertaining to the whole of its region. It would have supervision over or administration of some of the economic activities within the region, in particular those activities which have an inter-regional significance. Governmental supervision over and regulation of these economic activities already exist in varying degrees in many countries. In the United States, for example, are the conservation agencies of the Departments of Agriculture and of the Interior, the Federal Trade Commission, the Federal Communications Commission, the Federal

[3] Eugene Staley, *World Economy in Transition*, New York, 1939, pp. 112, 118. In another work, Staley has described thirty-nine schemes of commodity control, in many cases for the restriction of production, which have existed in recent years by means of cartels and combines, often aided by national governments, to maintain monopolies. *Raw Materials in Peace and War*, New York, 1937.

[4] J. B. Condliffe, *The Reconstruction of World Trade*, New York, 1940.

Power Commission, the Securities and Exchange Commission, the Federal Deposit Insurance Corporation, the Social Security Administration, the Interstate Commerce Commission, etc. Regional supervision and administration would, therefore, be in the main an expansion of the already existing national supervision and regulation.

It would be premature to attempt to specify all of these economic functions, or to indicate the precise degree of regulatory authority, at the present stage. Some of them may be tentatively suggested:

1. The conservation of the natural resources of the region.
2. The supervision of the exploitation of the mineral and other limited raw materials, including some authority to allocate these raw materials to the industries of the region in conformity with the regional plan.
3. Supervision over the production and distribution of staple agricultural commodities, such as wheat, corn, rice, cotton, etc.; and certain foods, such as tropical fruits, coffee, tea, etc., and other agricultural products which are limited to climatic zones, to provide for current consumption as well as "buffer" stocks.
4. Supervision over the production of natural energy derived from water, coal, oil, etc., as well as atomic energy; including a certain degree of authority to distribute this energy to the industries of the region.
5. Supervision over the investment of surplus capital in new and expanding industries in accordance with the regional plan.
6. Indirect supervision over the manufacture of finished commodities. The varying degrees of supervision over the exploitation and allocation of raw materials, agriculture, and production and distribution of natural energy, and the investment of surplus capital, will probably be sufficient to direct the manufacturing industries in accordance with the regional plan. This plan will endeavor to maintain a suitable balance between the capital goods and the consumption goods industries in order to diminish thereby the fluctuations within the business cycle.
7. Supervision over, and partial or complete administration of, all means of transportation and of communication within its region.
8. The maintenance of standards as to levels of living, health, labor conditions, and social security, to be set up by each regional authority for its own region.

The supervision over, and in some cases administration of, the phases of regional life and activity enumerated above would be in accordance with a social and economic plan devised by the regional authority and revised from time to time. This plan would be submitted to the World Federation for approval before it can be put into effect. The Federation would ensure that the various regional plans do not conflict with each other, and that all of them can be fitted into a unified social and economic plan for the whole world.

If the world were divided into a number of large regions, without the simultaneous creation of a central world authority, little would be gained thereby. The fear that each region would become a super-state with sovereign rights within its own territory would be fulfilled. The various regions would soon begin to clash over real or imaginary conflicts of interests. Rivalries, jealousies, and, in course of time, hostilities between the regions would commence. Even though planning might take place within each region, no unified worldwide plan could come into operation. Geo-economic regionalism, if it is to be successful, implies the creation of a central world authority. The most suitable form for such an authority will be a federation of the regions of the world. Within the scope and under the jurisdiction of a world federation, inter-regional rivalries, jealousies, and conflicts of interests can be resolved.

The vital and necessary relationship of regionalism to world federation calls for a consideration of the nature and functions of the government of a world federation. The ineffective League of Nations of 1919 to 1939 furnished no criterion whatsoever. It was precisely what its name indicated—a league of nations, and not a federal union of regions, or a world state of any sort. The United Nations Organization of 1945 and after is a slightly improved version of the League of Nations.

A just criticism of the League of Nations was that it provided for no regional organization of the world. Even if it had had any power, it could not have legislated and administered efficiently for all parts of the world. At Geneva it was far removed from many regions of the world. It had no subsidiary bodies, such as regional governments, in closer touch with the conditions and problems of each region. It was like a head without sensory organs through which to acquaint itself with the conditions of the world, and a body without limbs with which to implement its administration of the affairs of the world.

The four essential features of a world state, whether involving geo-economic regionalism or not, are (1) the renunciation of absolute national sovereignty, (2) national disarmament, (3) the prevention of discriminatory economic measures, and (4) democratic institutions. The reasons why the first two features are essential are so obvious that they do not need elaboration here. If the third feature is not safeguarded and guaranteed from the outset, however favorable may be the outlook for a world state at its inception, discriminatory economic measures are almost certain to disrupt the state in course of time.

The reasons for the fourth feature are not as obvious, and may be controverted on various grounds. It may be asserted that not all peoples of the world are prepared for democratic institutions. It may be said that a democratic government is not efficient. Recent world events may be cited as justification for the latter contention, e.g., the failure of so-called democracies to prevent economic "booms" and "busts," to say nothing of devastating wars. It may also be said that no one knows what democracy is, and that there is too much difference of opinion as to the nature of democratic institutions to make democracy one of the essential features of a world state from its inception. Without attempting to answer all of these objections here, the absence of this feature is almost certain to give rise to discontent in some of the most influential parts of the world, and to become before long a disruptive force.

As in the case of the regional government, it would be premature to enumerate in full and with finality the functions of a world federation. Nevertheless, some of the functions which it will almost inevitably have to perform by its very nature should be mentioned.

Planning Functions

The most important function of the World Federation, in the long run, is likely to be planning. This does not mean, however, that it would have to prepare these plans in detail. As already indicated, it would be the function of each regional government to prepare a social and economic plan for its own region in all matters within its jurisdiction. The World Federation would fit together these plans and create of them a master plan for the world as a whole.

Economic and Financial Functions

The World Federation would have a high degree of control over the production and distribution of raw materials, especially those which are limited in quantity and are localized in space. This control can be exercised through a federal board for the allocation of raw materials. Among the purposes of this control would be the following:

(1) To prevent the waste and exhaustion of natural resources which result from unregulated competition.
(2) To avoid the exploitation of consumers by producers.
(3) To prevent the monopoly of consumption by a few nations.
(4) To obviate the elimination of producers, owing to a protracted lack of profits, where the production may be useful and necessary in the long run.

(5) To prevent wasteful, destructive rivalry for private or national economic control.

(6) To prevent the loss of capital goods, and the lowering of living standards, by avoidable shifts of production from one area to another.

(7) To allocate raw materials in accordance with the federal master plan based upon the regional plans.

(8) To create reserve or "buffer" stocks for bad years. This will apply particularly to agricultural products. These stocks will be in the nature of the "ever-normal granary."

(9) To prevent national accumulation of raw materials for war purposes.

The World Federation would exercise a certain measure of control over the investment of surplus capital. Among the purposes of this control would be those of guiding surplus capital into productive and not speculative investments, of preventing national or regional economic discrimination, of obviating national diplomatic and private exploitation of foreign investments, of stabilizing the industries dealing in raw materials, of equilibrating profits and losses in the world-wide capital investment field, of stabilizing prices in the raw materials market, and of liquidating satisfactorily the international debt situation which has resulted from highly speculative investment policies, economic depression, and war. This control can be exercised through a federal investment corporation or administration which would perform the following functions and attain the following ends:

(1) It would set up a common pool of surplus capital derived from all parts of the world, to be allocated to private firms or to governmental projects, regional or national, the world over.

(2) It would aid greatly to prevent private monopolies.

(3) It would tend to stabilize not only the industries dealing in raw materials, but also those engaged in manufacturing, by spreading out profits and losses. This would equalize the rate of return for all investors, regardless of their national, corporate, or individual character. It should also tend to stabilize prices.

The World Federation would have the power to issue a world currency. Whether or not the national governments should be entirely deprived of the power to maintain their own currency systems is a question for discussion. It can, however, hardly be questioned that there is an urgent need for a world currency which will serve as a standard of value, medium of exchange, and money of account, as between all parts of the world. Whether or not this world currency should be issued through a world bank established and maintained by the Federation, or by a fiscal agency of the Federation, are questions of detail.

The World Federation would have supervision over all interregional transportation and communication. While the regional governments would administer or supervise these facilities within their own regions, the Federation would ensure that no restraints are placed upon the transportation of goods and the travel of individuals between regions. The Federation would ensure that the regional systems of transportation and communication are integrated with each other so that they form an efficient unified system for the world as a whole. Supervision over the vast oceanic bodies of water between the regions would fall under the jurisdiction of the world government. This is not the same thing as guaranteeing the freedom of the seas over which there has been so much controversy.[5] When war has been eliminated, and rival and potentially hostile navies no longer exist, there would be no danger of violations of freedom for travel and transportation upon the oceans and seas.

Demographic Functions

The World Federation would have a certain amount of authority to regulate the flow of population. Insofar as this flow regulates itself through the forces of the supply and demand of labor, the Federation need take no action. Modern industrial development has, however, displayed a tendency to concentrate population to an excessive degree in industrial centers and in cities. The effects often are not only to bring about the unhealthy conditions due to congestion of population, but also a decline in the prevailing level of living. In such cases, the Federation would have the authority to take action along at least two lines. The first, or negative, line is to restrain additional population from moving into the congested area. The second, or positive, line is to furnish opportunities elsewhere for a higher level of living for some of the inhabitants of the congested areas. Neither of these lines of action would involve tearing people away from their homes and forcing them to settle elsewhere, as has often happened because of war and conquest.

The Federation should also concern itself with the relative increase of the different races. In the light of vital statistics, worldwide planning would include allocation of the fruitful areas of the world for the future in accordance with the respective size and rate of increase of these races, namely, the White, Negro, and Mongolian races.

[5] Maurice Parmelee, *Blockade and Sea Power*, New York, 1924. See especially Chapter XVI entitled "The Freedom of the Sea."

This authority, however, would not involve the power to enforce migration to certain areas, or exclusion from other areas. Inasmuch as most human beings prefer to live with people of their own race and culture, it would suffice in many cases for the Federation to designate certain areas as destined primarily for the use of one or the other of the races, and facilitate the migration to these areas of the designated races.

When the level of living has attained a uniformly high standard the world over, the movements of population in search of better living conditions will cease. Whether or not this uniformly high standard of living will depress the birth rate to such a degree as to bring about a stable or decreasing population, remains to be seen. It is doubtful that with the spread of hygienic and medical information, the high birth rates of certain of the races will persist. The problem of population is likely to settle itself more or less effectively without much intervention on the part of the World Federation. The prevention of war will also eliminate the stimulation of population increase for the purpose of providing *Kanonen Futter* (cannon fodder) for future wars.

Legislative and Juridical Functions

The constitution of the World Federation should contain a "Bill of Rights" specifying precisely and in detail the rights of the individual, commonly known as the civil liberties. The Federation would ensure the preservation of these liberties in all parts of the world. This function would be administered largely through the regional governments. There should always be the right of appeal to the federal courts in cases where the regional government may have failed to safeguard these liberties.

Citizenship should be entirely under the jurisdiction of the World Federation. All rights pertaining to citizenship would be safeguarded and administered by the Federation. All inhabitants of the world would become citizens of the World Federation. They may continue to be designated and enumerated for census purposes as residents of a region and of a nation or of a local area. World citizenship would prevent national governments from depriving individuals and groups of the rights of citizenship for racial, religious, and other irrelevant reasons, and from driving them into exile.

All questions of jurisdiction and other controversies which may arise between the regional governments would be adjudicated and decided by the federal courts. For this purpose, the Federation would maintain tribunals whose composition should differ radically from the vast majority of the tribunals of today. They should be composed largely, if not entirely, of economic and other experts, and of technicians of various sorts competent to pass upon the questions at issue —which are almost invariably economic and technical in character.

So long as there are so-called "backward" peoples, not yet capable of participating in the planning and administrative activities of the various regions, the World Federation would have the function of supervising these areas, or of assigning them by mandate to the regional government within whose region or contiguous to whose region a backward area is located. This is a temporary function of the Federation which would cease to exist when all of these less advanced peoples become competent to take their full share in the activities of the regional governments.

The constitutions of the World Federation and of the regional governments should be based upon democratic principles and create democratic institutions. The question will arise, however, as to the extent to which national and local governments can vary their forms of organization from those of the federal and regional governments. These national and local governments cannot exercise powers and functions which are reserved to the regional governments and to the World Federation. They cannot pursue a policy which is opposed to and will hinder the exercise of the functions performed by the federal and regional governments. Within the limitations set, the World Federation would guarantee as much freedom as is feasible for the choice of the form of government and of economic organization for each national entity. If a nation should adopt some form of collectivism, such as state socialism or communism, it would be permitted to do so, provided the system adopted did not violate the "Bill of Rights," and render impossible regional and worldwide planning.

This is a delicate problem for the World Federation. On the one hand, freedom of choice to maintain national and local traditions, customs, and beliefs, or to vary from these established institutions, furnishes a valuable discipline for groups of people as well as for individuals. This freedom may lead to a considerable amount of experimentation in different forms of political and economic organization which may be of great value to mankind. On the other hand, there will always be the danger that forms of economic and political organization will be adopted which will overtly or indirectly conflict with the functions of the federal and regional governments. Each one of these cases will have to be decided by itself. The Federation should not try to force all national and local governments into the same mold. This might result in the creation of disruptive forces which would break down the system of federal and regional governments, and bring mankind back to the era of sovereign states, nationalism, imperialism, racialism, militarism and navalism, culminating in warfare and the international anarchy which prevails today.

As a safeguard against violations of federal security measures, such as the control of armaments, and to discourage attempts to make war, penal action should be possible against individuals as well as states and nations. In accordance with the precedent established at the Nuremberg trials in 1946, official position in a national government or orders from a superior should not be a defense against violations of federal law. The head of a state could no longer cause with impunity the mass murder of thousands and millions of human beings. A federal criminal tribunal should be created to deal with these offenses.

Regional and Federal Constitutions

The creation of regions and of a federal union would necessitate the writing of constitutions. The United Nations should be instrumental in setting up these new political entities. In fact, they cannot come into being without the assent of these nations. These constitutions should, however, not be used as means of revenge and punishment. This was one of the fatal mistakes in the creation of the League of Nations.

In another book, shortly after its establishment, I described this error and the other fatal defects of the League:

"The League of Nations was created by means of the Covenant which constitutes Part I of the Treaty of Peace between the Allied and Associated Powers and Germany, which was signed at Versailles, June 28, 1919. The constitution of this League, which professes to exist 'in order to promote international cooperation and to achieve international peace and security,' is therefore a part of a treaty drafted by a conquering military alliance of nations and imposed upon a defeated nation. . . . In fact, throughout the Treaty the League is utilized repeatedly by the Entente Allies to carry out many of the conditions imposed upon the defeated enemy. . . . This brief survey of the constitution of the League is sufficient to indicate that it falls very far short of being a genuine international state. It must first of all free itself from its degrading servitude to the Principal Allied and Associated Powers and their pernicious instrument, the Treaty of Versailles." [6]

Since each regional government would have the same powers and functions as every other regional government, however much the regions may vary among themselves, all the regions could have the same type of constitution. This would provide for a regional legis-

6 Maurice Parmelee, *Blockade and Sea Power*, New York, 1924, pp. 339-40, 349.

lature elected by the popular vote of the inhabitants of the region. The constitutions of the democratic nations furnish many examples from which a selection could be made of the most suitable methods. The methods adopted should, however, discourage the choice of the regional legislators on the basis of nationalism, sectionalism, and provincialism. The aim should be to secure a legislature which would legislate in the interest of the region as a whole. It should not be made up of the representatives of nations, sections, and provinces as such, whose tendency would be to act solely or principally in the interests of their respective localities.

It may be contended that instead of an areal or territorial basis for the right of suffrage, an occupational basis may be used for electing the regional legislators. In an enlightened community in which most of the inhabitants are aware of the social and economic interests of their community, an occupational basis for the exercise of the right of suffrage is superfluous. Occupational representation might, however, be recognized in the planning and administrative branches of the regional government. The question of occupational representation is subject to further discussion. It raises a rather difficult problem not only of occupational but also of class interests. It may or may not be desirable to recognize these interests in the constitution of the regional government.

The areas of the so-called "backward" peoples furnish temporarily a problem of exceptional treatment. The world government would have the power to mandate supervision over these backward areas to the appropriate regional governments. In a mandated area the regional government would have more extensive and more detailed powers and functions of administration than in the non-mandated parts of a region.

The regional government would have administrative branches corresponding to its functions. The conservation of natural resources and the exploitation of raw materials are so closely related to each other that these two functions might be administered by one department or board consisting of two divisions. The supervision over the production and distribution of agricultural commodities should perhaps come under a separate branch of the government, because these commodities can be reproduced and involve questions of permanent land utilization.

The supervision over the production and distribution of natural energy derived from water, coal, oil, etc., should probably be under a separate branch somewhat similar to the Federal Power Commission in the United States. It would prevent the production of atomic energy for destructive purposes in war and promote its production for constructive purposes in peace.

834

The supervision over and partial or complete administration of all means of transportation and communication would be under the transportation branch of the regional government.

The supervision over maintenance of standards with regard to levels of living, labor conditions, and of social security would be under one or more social welfare branches of the regional government.

The planning function of the regional government would come under one or more research branches. The organization of these research and planning activities should utilize the best available scientific and technical talent within the region or attracted into the region from outside.

The regional government would also have a financial branch which would exercise, in the first instance, a certain amount of supervision over the banking and other financial institutions of the region. Whether or not this financial branch should also set up a system of regional banking, to be financed and administered entirely or in part by the regional government, is a matter for further consideration. The financial branch would have at least a supervisory power for the planning and guidance of capital investment within the region. The fundamental aims should be the orderly development of the resources of the region, and the diminution of the speculative aspect of capital investment. The Federal Reserve system in the United States furnishes a number of suggestions as to methods of guiding and influencing the financial market. The influence and supervisory power of the financial branch of a regional government should, however, go beyond those of the Federal Reserve System.

The constitution of the World Federation would provide for a federal legislature made up of the delegates from the various regions. The number of delegates from each region would depend, at least in part, upon the population of the region. Whether or not these delegates should be chosen by a popular plebiscite, or by the regional legislatures, is a matter for discussion. It would simplify the procedure and perhaps not make it less democratic to have these delegates chosen by the regional legislatures.

The administrative functions of the World Federation would be relatively small because the regional governments would perform most of these functions within their own regions. There would be a federal planning board to which would be submitted for study and coordination the various regional plans. There would be a fiscal branch which would institute a world currency or world unit of account in order to eliminate the disorderly and chaotic condition created by the many national currency systems of the world. Whether or not it would be desirable for this financial branch to set up a world banking system is a matter for discussion.

835

This branch would have a certain degree of supervision over the investment of surplus capital the world over. This supervisory power may be exercised by setting up an investment corporation or authority to create a common pool of surplus capital to be allocated on a regional basis to private firms or to governmental projects. This power of supervision over capital investment would be utilized by the Federation to stabilize not only the industries dealing in raw materials, but also those engaged in manufacturing capital goods, so as to spread out profits and losses. By so doing, the Federation would diminish to a considerable degree the disastrous effects of the business cycle.

One of the most essential lines of investigation is a study of the basic raw materials—not from a strategic, but from an industrial point of view. The United States Bureau of Mines recently made a study of resources of metals and of non-metallic minerals from the point of view of military strategy. This Bureau should be asked to make such a study from the point of view of the most efficient division of labor and of the highest possible production for the world as a whole. Among these basic or important minerals are iron, tin, copper, zinc, lead, antimony, nickel, tungsten, chromium, mercury, vanadium, titanium, magnesite, manganese, molybdenum, aluminum, asbestos, phosphates, nitrates, potash, sulphur, mica and graphite. Coal, oil, and the other natural fuels should be studied in the same fashion. As soon as the conditions essential to the creation of a World Federation are established, namely, the restriction of national sovereignty and universal disarmament, it will no longer be necessary to study these raw materials from the point of view of defending a country against attack or, in the case of certain nations, of preparing for the conquest of other nations.

A similar situation will exist with regard to animal and plant products, such as animal fibers (wool, horsehair, etc.), furs, textile fibers (cotton, flax, jute, kapok, etc.), timber, rubber, etc. The purpose should be also to create a situation in which it will not be necessary for the United States Department of Agriculture to study how to get rid of surpluses of valuable agricultural products, such as cotton, wheat, etc. This department should be asked to make plans for the most effective worldwide division of labor for the production of these animal and plant products.

Much research can be carried on in ascertaining what statistics are available, and which of these statistics are suitable for use as indexes with respect to regional boundaries. The United States Geological Survey, as well as the Bureau of Mines, can be called upon for assistance with regard to physiographic indexes. In regional studies of the United States, more than 700 indexes have been utilized. Among these are eighty or more indexes of population, a hundred or more indexes with respect to the land and its use, a hundred or more with respect to agricultural equipment and production, about fifty-five with respect to industrial production, about thirty with respect to water power, approximately forty with respect to income indicating levels of living, and more than two hundred miscellaneous indexes which may be termed cultural.

While it is not possible to find so many indexes applicable to the whole world, and, in any case, many of them would have no particular significance for worldwide regionalization, some effort should be devoted to find suitable indexes and to apply them. Even if they are not decisive in fixing regional boundaries at the outset, owing to political considerations and compromises which may have to be made, it will, nevertheless, be worthwhile to make these statistical surveys. As time goes by, and as these political considerations and compromises become of decreasing importance, it would be possible to correct the boundaries more in accordance with the important and fundamental geo-economic factors revealed and measured by these statistical indexes. The shifting of a regional boundary would not give rise to the uproar now caused by a proposed or actual shift of a national boundary.

Many of the schemes for international planning which have been prepared are financial in their character. Some of them have been for the purpose of stimulating international trade. While international trade is of value insofar as it contributes to the worldwide division of labor, it should not be regarded as an end in itself. Financial arrangements are not matters of primary or of fundamental importance. The task of immediate primary importance is to plan and then to set up a regional and federal organization of the world which will promote the most efficient division of labor and a high level of production, resulting in a high level of living.[7] Having determined the structure of such a worldwide organization for these ends, it will then be time enough to devise appropriate financial arrangements. Such a procedure will also, in all probability, meet satisfactorily the problem of excess production of raw materials stimulated by war in certain parts of the world.

The Regions and the World Federation

The wide variation in population between the regions raises the question of the regional representation in the federal assembly. Let

[7] The International Monetary Fund and the International Bank for Reconstruction and Development, which in 1949 had about forty member nations, are controlled by the governments of these nations in proportion to the capital subscription of each of these countries.

us assume that it is at the rate of one delegate for each 5,000,000 inhabitants. Of the fourteen geo-economic regions outlined in my book on World Federation, the two regions smallest in population—Temperate South America and South Africa—would have only four and five delegates each. The most populous regions—South Asia and East Asia—would have eighty-two and sixty-two respectively. The federal assembly would have about 430 members, or nearly the same as the United States House of Representatives, which has 435 members. If this is too large for efficiency there could be one delegate for each 10,000,000 inhabitants, or about 215 delegates.

In order to mitigate this preponderating influence of the most populous regions, it has been suggested that there should also be a federal senate. Each region would have at least two senators. For each 25,000,000 inhabitants over the first 25,000,000, a region would be given an additional senator. Temperate South America and South Africa would have only two senators each. South Asia and East Asia would have seventeen and thirteen respectively. The federal senate would have ninety-seven members. The United States Senate has ninety-six members. However, it would probably not be desirable to have a bicameral federal legislature, because a unicameral legislature is usually more efficient and equally democratic.

Similar principles may be applied to the regional legislature. There might be one delegate in the regional assembly for each million inhabitants of the region. There need be no regional senate. To the regional assembly might be assigned the function of electing the regional delegates to the federal assembly.

The peoples of the various regions should be represented, and not their nations and states. This is partly because the regional boundaries will not necessarily coincide at all places with the national boundaries. The nation or state, as such, cannot be represented in the regional legislature as the region can be represented in the federal legislature. Furthermore, some of the existing nations (Iceland, Luxembourg, etc.,) are so small in population or area or both that they are not, in justice to the rest of the world, entitled to representation as national entities.

There is a much more serious objection to recognizing the state or nation *per se* as electoral units within the region. One of the purposes of geo-economic regionalism is to restrain nationalism, and to replace it in part by an attitude toward and loyalty for the region, in the first instance, but for the World Federation in the main. In other words, humans should reach the point, through regional and world organization, where they feel themselves citizens not only of a nation, which rightfully claims some of their respect and loyalty, and with which they have close cultural ties, but also of a world federation which includes all of mankind. Diminution of national chauvinism

838

will result in a net gain of genuine patriotism not only for one's own country but for mankind as a whole.

In several of the regions, there will be a large nation with a preponderant population united with several smaller nations in one region. This will be the situation in East Asia and Malaya, with China as the preponderant nation; in South Asia, with Hindustan; in Tropical South America with Brazil; and in North America with the United States. However, the three most populous regions—South Asia, East Asia and North Europe—will have considerably less than half of the representatives in the federal assembly. No small group of regions is likely to control the World Federation.

Provincialism, sectionalism, nationalism, and imperialism will obstruct regional interests and sometimes manipulate regional affairs in the interest of the dominant nation. It will take time to overcome these obstacles. However, they will be removed much more rapidly when regional and federal legislators represent the people and are no longer the emissaries of national governments and ambassadors of "sovereign" states. At present, small nations cannot defend themselves against aggression on the part of the large states. There can be no lasting international security within the framework of sovereign states because of the vulnerability of the small nations.

The World Federation should be able to do much to prevent the obstruction of regional by national and imperial interests. This consideration should be kept in mind in organizing the World Federation and designating its functions and powers.

The World Capital

The location of the seat of the World Federation has a bearing upon the relations of the regions with each other. If its seat, which would become, in effect, the world capital, were located in the western hemisphere, it would be removed from the scene of the most acute and violent international conflicts of modern times. On the other hand, it would be far away from most of the regions of the world. The western hemisphere has a population of only about 285,000,000 inhabitants as contrasted with the eastern hemisphere with a population of about 1,880,000,000 inhabitants. This is the main objection to New York, which has been chosen as its seat by the United Nations Organization.

An argument in favor of Istanbul as the world capital is that it stands on the border between the Orient and the Occident. A more practical argument is that it is close to four regions, namely, North Europe, the Soviet Union, Afro-Asia, and the Mediterranean Region, and is nearer South Asia than any point in the Western Hemisphere. Cairo may be a still more convenient location for the world capital. An island, such as Malta (95 sq. mi.), Crete (3199 sq. mi.), or Cyprus (3584 sq. mi.), might be made federal territory and the world capital. It would probably not be desirable to locate the world capital permanently in any western European city, such as Geneva, Paris, London, or Berlin.

It has been proposed that the world capital should be moved periodically, perhaps every ten years, from one region to another, so that in due course it would be located in each of the regions in rotation. It has also been suggested that the buildings occupied by the World Federation in each region, after the world capital had migrated to another region, could become the seat of a regional university.

A Common Language

Another matter which has a bearing upon the relations between the World Federation and the regions is the question of the language, or languages, to be used by the World Federation. The League of Nations used at least two official languages, namely, English and French. Each of the more numerous peoples is likely to demand that its language be adopted as the official language, or one of the official languages, of the World Federation. The Chinese may claim that Chinese should be adopted because they constitute the most numerous people in the world. The Indians may make a similar claim for their tongue. English may be advocated upon the ground that it is the principal language of commerce and of travel the world over. On one ground or another, claims may be made for the French, Russian, Spanish, and other languages.

A possible compromise is an artificial language, such as Esperanto. Another possibility is a simplification of one of the living languages. Basic English is an example of such a simplification. It has a vocabulary of 850 English words which can be combined in such a fashion as to make a fairly comprehensive and effective tool of expression. Whatever the final choice may be, it is highly desirable that there should be some medium of expression which would eventually become world-wide in the sense that it would be used in any part of the world. This does not mean that such a world-wide, or universal, language would supplant the existing languages. On the contrary, without necessarily being or becoming the mother tongue of any considerable group, it could exist alongside of the living languages and mother tongues of the various peoples of the world as an auxiliary common medium of communication. It is, therefore, essential that a universal

840

language should be easy to learn. An artificial language has this great advantage.[8]

Regional Agencies and Powers

In delineating the geo-economic regions of the world, the functions which will in all probability be performed by the regional authority in each region should be kept in mind. Two major assumptions should be made with respect to these functions. On the one hand, it is assumed that all matters which are solely or predominantly of local importance are to be left within the jurisdiction of the nation or the state. On the other hand, it is assumed that there will be a federation of all the regions which will have within its jurisdiction all matters of world-wide importance. The functions of the regional authority will, therefore, be those functions which are of regional but not of worldwide significance or importance.

The time is certain to come, sooner or later, when a world organization based upon regions will be formed. In delineating these regions, it will be helpful to keep in mind these functions which in all probability will be performed by the various regional authorities, as well as the fundamental geographic and economic factors and conditions which have been described earlier in this book.

Federal Agencies and Powers

In delineating regions it will be helpful also to keep in mind the probable functions of the World Federation of Regions. Four assumptions may be made as to the conditions essential for the establishment of the World Federation. As already stated, these assumptions are (1) the renunciation of absolute national sovereignty, (2) national disarmament, (3) the prevention of discriminatory economic measures, and (4) democratic institutions.

The first three of these assumptions will be attained in part by the formation of the regions. However, they cannot be obtained fully without the establishment of the World Federation. Without such a Federation it would be possible for the region to claim an absolute sovereignty corresponding to that of the nation, to arm itself, and to

[8] Stuart C. Dodd, "On Measuring Languages," *Journal of the American Statistical Association*, March 1949, pp. 77-88. Dodd asserts that an international auxiliary language should be idiomless, uninflected, without synonyms and homonyms, phonetic in spelling, uniform in pronunciation everywhere (no dialects), with every letter unique in shape and sound, and have the order of the words obey rules without exception.

introduce discriminatory economic measures against other regions. This would mean that the region would become a sort of super-state and that the world would be dominated by a few great powers to a much greater degree than has been the case in the past. The World Federation would furnish the necessary guarantee that the region would not become a super-state in these senses. Supreme military and police power would be in the hands of the World Federation. It would be in a position to prevent anything in the nature of economic discrimination between the different regions. It would also be one of the functions of the World Federation to maintain and encourage the development of democratic institutions in all parts of the world.

Owing to these considerations, the functions of the World Federation will be somewhat more varied than those of each region within its own jurisdiction. The regional functions are entirely, or almost exclusively, economic in their character. The World Federation will have political and demographic as well as economic functions to perform.

Proposals have been made with regard to the formation of international corporations to operate in various economic and financial fields during and after the war of 1939 to 1945. There have been suggested an international commodities corporation, an international reconstruction finance corporation, and cartels in certain commodity and development fields. Some of these international corporations may come into existence before the formation of a World Federation.[9] When the Federation is formed, such international corporations should be brought under its supervision. The regional authorities concerned should also have a certain amount of supervision over these international corporations insofar as these corporations carry on activities within their respective regions. In view of the likelihood of the eventual formation of regional governments and a World Federation, the above considerations should be kept in mind in organizing any of these international or global corporations.

As already stated, the administrative functions of the Federation will be relatively small because the regional governments will perform most of these functions within their own regions. There will be a federal planning board, a fiscal branch, and a board, or commission, to exercise supervision over the investment of surplus capital the world over.

The World Federation will have a board or commission of territorial administration which will have supervision over the areas to be administered by the federal government, or through a mandate

[9] The International Bank for Reconstruction and Development and the International Monetary Fund are already in existence.

by a regional government. This will furnish the best possible solution of the colonial problem. Each nation will surrender to the World Federation whatever claim it may have in the way of sovereignty over a colonial territory. The existing administration of the territory at the time of this transfer will immediately become responsible to the World Federation. The legislature of the World Federation can then decide as to whether the territorial administration is to be continued under its own aegis or through a mandate to one of the regional governments. Positions in the territorial administration will be filled thereafter by means of examinations open to all citizens of the World Federation.

The World Federation will have a board or commission to supervise transportation and communication the world over. The function of this commission will be not so much to administer as to ensure that the means of transportation and communication in the various regions are coordinated in such a fashion as to create a worldwide system which will discriminate against no one of the regions and which will facilitate the flow of commodities and the transportation of individuals.

The World Federation will have a board or commission of migration and population to perform the demographic functions of the Federation. The work of this commission would be, in the first instance, to watch the growth, movement, and distribution of population and to make recommendations to the federal legislature as to what measures may be taken to encourage a distribution of population in accord with the development and exploitation of natural resources.

The World Federation will have a board or commission of social welfare which will be concerned with the labor conditions, health conditions, and social security of the population of the world. The function of this commission will be mainly to watch over the performance of similar functions by the regional governments in their respective regions.

The establishment of a regional organization in any part of the world should be regarded as only preliminary to a world federation of regions. The immediate prospect is a league of the United Nations dominated by the great powers. In theory, no nation will yield any of its sovereignty. In practice, the small nations will be controlled by the large nations even more than in the past. The armed might of the great powers may prevent some small and moderate-sized wars. The situation will be that of an armed truce. If a genuine world federation of region is not created soon, a war more devastating than the European War of 1914 to 1918 and more terrible than the World War of 1939 to 1945 is almost certain to take place in the now emerging atomic era. In this future war not only atomic, hydrogen, and cobalt bombs, but even more lethal biological and chemical methods of warfare will be used to destroy a large portion of mankind and much of its wealth.[10]

[10] My book entitled *Geo-Economic Regionalism and World Federation*, New York, 1949, describes at length a world federation of geo-economic regions.

The Peoples' World Convention (PWC), is a democratic means of bringing into existence a genuine World Federation by working from the "grass roots" upward.

Chapter XLVIII

The Play Function of Sex

MAN has always been a serious problem to himself, and many have been the interpretations he has placed upon the different parts of his nature. Records and evidences of these interpretations we find in magical and religious practices and beliefs; in mythology; in tradition, custom, law, and social organization; etc. Perhaps most inexplicable have been the powerful emotions such as anger, jealousy, envy, etc., and man has formulated many myths in his attempts to explain them.

There is no part of man's nature which has been a greater mystery to him than his sexual nature. Connected with sex are powerful feelings and processes which it is difficult for man to explain. During puberty and adolescence there develop most of the secondary sexual traits. At the same time come to fruition the sexual passions which give rise to some of the keenest sensations experienced by man, and which constitute one of the principal dynamic elements in man's nature. With puberty there arrive at maturity the processes involved in the sex relation, which have already appeared in an adumbrated form during childhood. For the female there begins at this time the catamenial function (menstruation), and after conception comes pregnancy and then parturition.

Man has had numerous hypotheses with respect to the nature of sex, and has regulated it in many and diverse ways. He has done the same with respect to other human traits. Inasmuch as his sexual nature includes what constitutes the most powerful group of instincts and emotions apart from the nutritive function, this has been especially true of it. We shall consider the nature of the sex relation in the light of modern scientific knowledge.

It is impossible to ascertain the form or forms taken by the sex relationship in the early stages of human evolution. Conjecture ranges all the way from promiscuity to monogamy or polygamy. The truth doubtless lies somewhere between these two extremes, but probably approaches closer to the theory of promiscuity than to that of permanent mating.

As against the theory of complete promiscuity it is argued that the rearing of the young required the care of the male as well as of the female parent, so that unions between individuals of the two sexes must have been of some duration. There are reasons for thinking that the hominidae, like some of the other primates to which they are closely related and many of the carnivorous species, are relatively non-gregarious, and therefore lived in the earlier stages in small family groups rather than in large communal groups. But if the hominidae lived in large groups the young may have been reared by the group in common, as is true of many of the gregarious herbivorous species, so that the care of the individual male parent would not be necessary.

It is also argued that another limitation upon promiscuity was the emotion of jealousy, which may have characterized man as it characterizes many of the higher mammals. This emotion would lead the male to monopolize the female or females of whom he had gained possession. It is possible that this trait evolved because of its survival value for the rearing of the young, since it furnishes a bond to hold parents together.

Jealousy and the necessity of rearing the young would therefore be forces for more or less permanent unions.[1] As to whether these were monogamous or polygynous, it is difficult to say. The numerical equality of the sexes was doubtless a factor for monogamy. But the stronger males were probably able to gain possession of more than one female apiece.

The contrasted view to the above is that the hominidae lived in communal groups in which the young were cared for by the group in common. Those holding this view do not usually regard jealousy as a primitive trait, but rather as a secondary trait which arose out of the sense of ownership after the women had acquired an economic value.

Many facts, indeed, suggest a high degree of promiscuity in the earlier stages of human social development. Among these are the records of observers of many primitive peoples which indicate that promiscuity before marriage and sometimes after marriage was cus-

---

[1] Among the writers who hold this point of view, or whose writings seem on the whole to point toward permanent mating, may be mentioned the following: Charles Darwin, *The Descent of Man and Selection in Relation to Sex,* London, 1871, 2 vols.; Andrew Lang, *Social Origins,* and J. J. Atkinson, *The Primal Law,* London, 1903; E. Westermarck, *The History of Human Marriage,* London, 1891; N. W. Thomas, *Kinship Organizations and Group Marriage in Australia,* Cambridge, Eng., 1906; B. Malinowski, *The Family Among the Australian Aborigines,* London, 1913; *Sex and Repression in Savage Society,* London, 1927: *The Sexual Life of Savages* (2 vols.) , London, 1929.

tomary. Furthermore, such institutions as group marriage, sexual hospitality, the *jus primae noctis* in some cases, perhaps sacred prostitution as an expiation for marriage, and many other savage and barbaric customs may be vestiges of an earlier state of promiscuity.[2]

There is biological and psychological evidence that sexual jealousy may have been an original and primary trait of man. But this trait has doubtless been greatly accentuated and complicated by the development of the sense of ownership as a secondary trait. In any case, sexual jealousy as an original trait would not be incompatible with a considerable amount of promiscuity, for until a female had been permanently appropriated by a male she would naturally have promiscuous relations.

Hartland has presented an array of facts with respect to the widespread practice of sexual liberty, not only among the unmarried but frequently among the married as well. Upon these facts he based his theory that jealousy is not an original trait of man but has grown out of the sense of ownership. The following quotations are of interest in this connection:

"The wide prevalence of the opposite practice, namely, the sexual liberty recognized as the right of the unmarried both male and female, may be regarded as evidence of the small social importance attached to the gratification of the sexual instincts apart from the limitations imposed by the sense of ownership and the consequent growth of the ideal of chastity. The sense of ownership has been the seed-plot of jealousy. To it we are indebted for the first germ of sexual regulations. To it in the last resort, reinforced by growing physiological knowledge and sanctioned by religion, is due the social order enjoyed by the foremost nations of Europe and America."[3]

"The view thus implied of what we should call serious offenses against virtue is not, it is true, universal. But it is common enough and distributed widely enough to lead the student seriously to ask whether the masculine passion of jealousy can be as fundamental and primitive as it is sometimes asserted to be. If the answer be, as I believe it must be, in the negative certain hypothetical reconstructions of the history of marriage will need reconsideration."[4]

---

[2] Among the writers who have furnished data which have supported in one way or another the theory of promiscuity, may be mentioned the following: L. H. Morgan, *Ancient Society*, New York, 1877; J. F. McLennan, *Studies in Ancient History*, London, 1876; W. Robertson Smith, *Kinship and Marriage in Early Arabia*, London, 1903; B. Spencer and F. J. Gillen, *The Native Tribes of Central Australia*, London, 1899, *The Northern Tribes of Central Australia*, London, 1904; A. W. Howitt, *The Native Tribes of South-East Australia*, London, 1904; R. Briffault, *The Mothers* (3 vols.) , London, 1927.

[3] E. S. Hartland, *Primitive Paternity*, London, 1910, Vol. II, pp. 102-103.

[4] *Op. cit.*, Vol. II, pp. 242-243.

Some of the writers who hold strongly to the theory of jealousy as an original human trait admit that promiscuity has been widespread at many times and places. For example, Westermarck, who held this theory, cited many such instances of promiscuity in his history of human marriage.

A follower of Westermarck, Malinowski, also recognized the influence of the sense of ownership. He first indicated the existence of physiological jealousy:

"In the first place, we may assume in this society, as in the whole of mankind and in the majority of higher animals, a physiological basis for jealousy in the form of an innate instinct; a natural aversion of an individual towards an encroachment on his sexual rights as far as possible—within certain variable limits. That among the Australian aborigines such instincts of jealousy are not absent, that they are, on the contrary, very strongly developed, is evident from nearly all the facts quoted and all general considerations. It is proved by the high esteem in which in some tribes chastity is held; by the fact that fidelity is required in all other tribes, and that it yields only to custom."[5]

Malinowski then recognized the influence of the sense of ownership:

"The idea of the individual sexual over-right and control over his wife is strongly present in the aboriginal mind. This right is undoubtedly realized as a privilege, and the natural tendency to keep his privileges for himself, or dispose of them according to his wish or interest, must create a strong opposition to any encroachment. In other words, the sexual act has its intrinsic value, and it is considered as an unquestionable advantage. And the right to this advantage constitutes a kind of private property. The feeling of jealousy exists here in its economic sense: the proprietor of a certain object begrudges the use of it to any one whom he does not invite to it, or who is not otherwise entitled to the privilege. And this seems to me one of the strongest probable sources of jealousy, besides the natural physiological impulse of aversion, mentioned above."[6]

Whatever may have been the situation among early men, all forms of sex relationship have existed and still exist among the peoples of whom we have records. These include promiscuity, group marriage, polygyny, polyandry, and monogamy. Various combinations of these forms also exist. For example, we find promiscuity before marriage for both sexes or for the male sex alone, accompanied by strict prohibition of promiscuity after marriage for both sexes, or for the female alone. Or we find strict prohibition of promiscuity before marriage for both sexes or for the female alone, accompanied by a certain amount of

[5] B. Malinowski, *The Family*, etc., p. 125.
[6] *Op. cit.*, pp. 126-127.

848

promiscuity after marriage for both sexes or for the male alone. As the above examples illustrate, there has been on the whole more freedom for the male than for the female. The causes for this difference will be indicated in a later chapter.

The most that can be said in any attempt to generalize is that there is apparently a tendency away from promiscuity, and toward monogamy. Jealousy not only on the part of the male but also on the part of the female who resents the existence of other wives or sweethearts, the necessity of caring for the offspring and parental affection for the young, the numerical equality of the sexes, the desirability of providing a well tested companionship for old age, and the organized government enforcing more or less permanent relationships, in the place of individual power, encourage these tendencies. The development of human personality has perhaps also aided such tendencies in some ways, though in other respects it has probably been a force for greater freedom.

In the course of human social evolution many other factors have made their appearance which have influenced sex relations and have enhanced the complexity of the problems involved. Some of the more important of these factors I shall mention, especially those which are playing a part in civilized society and are still giving rise to sex regulations.

As the human mind evolved, and especially as language developed, man began to meditate and speculate upon the nature of sexual phenomena. The phenomena connected with reproduction must have seemed extraordinary to him, and many have been the hypotheses formulated by him to explain them. For many ages the physical relation between father and offspring was not recognized. Vestiges of attempts to explain the pregnancy of the mother are to be found in the totemic beliefs still extant among many primitive peoples, in myths of supernatural birth and metempsychosis, and in matronymic and patronymic ideas and practices.[7] Superstitious and mythical explanations of reproduction were inevitable until scientific knowledge had been acquired of the causal connection between the sex relation and reproduction.

In similar fashion early man attempted to explain the mysteries of the sex relation, which is a critical experience for man on account of the intensity of the feelings involved. Especially mysterious is the sexual function in woman, and this was doubtless the principal cause for the development of a peculiar mental attitude on the part of the

---

[7] A vast amount of data with regard to primitive explanations of reproduction in the absence of a knowledge of physiological paternity is given in E. S. Hartland, *Primitive Paternity, The Myth of Supernatural Birth in Relation to the History of the Family*, London, 1909-1910, 2 vols.

male towards female. Perhaps the most striking feature of this function is the flow of blood in connection with puberty (the hymenal flow), the periodic catamenial function (the menstrual flow), and parturition (the puerperal flow). This was probably the chief reason for the notion still more or less prevalent that sex is unclean, especially in woman.[8]

This notion of the uncleanness of sex led to many sexual taboos to guard against the contagion of this uncleanness.[9] It has also played a part in the establishment of many exogamous and endogamous regulations of the sex relation,[10] some of which still persist in the form of prohibitions against incest.

It was to be expected that sex would play an important part in magic. For example, owing to a false analogy between sexual acts and the growth of vegetation, sex has often been regulated on the principle of homeopathic or imitative magic in order to insure a good harvest.[11]

It is not surprising also that sex has played an important part in religion. Phallic worship has existed at many times and places. Sex has been attributed to anthropomorphic deities and sacred prostitution has played its part in the worship of these deities.[12] In the attempt to propitiate deities has arisen the ascetic ideal of foregoing sexual pleasures in order to expiate sin and to attain purification.[13]

Another important factor in the regulation of sex has been the economic subjection of woman. On account of her inferiority to man in physical strength, woman has doubtless always been more or less subject to him. But in the early stages of the evolution of human society before the division of labor had been carried far enough to cause much differentiation in occupations and professions, woman

[8] See, for example, J. G. Frazer, *Balder the Beautiful*, London, 1913, Vol. I, Chap. II, "Seclusion of Girls at Puberty"; *Taboo and the Perils of the Soul*, London, 1911, Chap. IV, "Tabooed Persons," Sec. 3, "Women Tabooed at Menstruation and Childbirth.'

[9] A searching study of this subject has been made by E. Crawley, *The Mystic Rose, A Study of Primitive Marriage*, London, 1902, revised edition 1927. Descriptions of many of the rites connected with sex are given in A. van Gennep, *Les rites de passage*, Paris, 1909.

[10] See, for example, L. H. Morgan, *op. cit.*, J. F. McLennan, *op. cit.*, W. Robertson Smith, *op. cit.*

[11] See, for example, J. G. Frazer, *The Magic Art*, London, 1911, Vol. II, Chap. XI, "The Influence of the Sexes on Vegetation."

[12] See, for example, J. G. Frazer, *Adonis, Attis, Osiris*, London, 1907, Chap. IV, "Sacred Men and Women"; E. S. Hartland, *Ritual and Belief*, London, 1914, essay entitled "The Rite at the Temple of Mylitta.'

[13] *Cf.* E. Westermarck, *The Origin and Development of the Moral Ideas*, London, 1908, Vol, II, Chap. 39. "In various religions we meet with the idea that a person appeases or gives pleasure to the deity by subjecting himself to suffering or deprivation. This belief finds expression in all sorts of ascetic practices." (P. 356.)

was probably very little if at all upon an inferior plane economically. As the pastoral, agricultural, and later stages in economic evolution took place, woman became in a large measure a form of property. Marriage by purchase came into being and to the natural jealousy of man was added the artificial property right to subjugate woman in marriage.

The preceding survey has revealed some of the principal factors in the organization and regulation of the sex relation in the past. Some of these factors persist today. In the Occidental world the dominant religion is Christianity. This religion originated from an extensive folk culture arising from many sources. Some of the elements of this culture still persist in this religion. For example, the myth of supernatural birth is embodied in Christianity in the form of the legend of the virgin birth of Jesus.

In the Christian religion the magical notion of the uncleanness of sex has been combined with and has reenforced the ideal of propitiating the deity by expiation and purification through chastity. Thus the ascetic ideal has played a prominent part in Christianity and has influenced the regulation of sex down to the present day. Owing to this ascetic ideal the sex relation *per se* still has a certain amount of stigma attached to it, and its legitimacy is usually admitted by the conventional morality rather grudgingly only for purposes of procreation, and not always even for that purpose.

Sex is no more and no less mysterious to science than any other part of human nature or any other object in the universe. Magical and religious interpretations can, therefore, play no part in a scientific exposition of the nature and functions of sex.

The primary function of sex is reproduction. This function has existed as long as sex itself. Without it the human species would soon perish. Furthermore, the continued existence of the species requires not only the sexual acts but also care of the young, and this second requirement is likely to react upon the relations between the sexes and the ways in which the sexual functions are fulfilled.

In the higher animals, and in the warm-blooded vertebrates in particular, sex has acquired a second function, which is in its way as important as the first function. This is due to an efflorescence of the sexual impulse, largely through the affective traits of the warm-blooded animals. The feelings are much more highly developed in the warm-blooded animals than they are in the cold-blooded animals, owing to the more complex vascular system of the warm-blooded animals. Consequently, a great expansion of the extent and scope of sexual feeling has been possible in the warm-blooded animals.

The original seat of sexual feeling is in the sex glands. According to the theory of glandular action, some of the glands, including the sex glands, send out so-called "hormones" to other parts of the organism. Probably through the stimulation of the nerve centers caused by the hormones sent out from the sex glands, sexual feeling is aroused throughout the organism. It is not yet possible to state whether, if these hormones exist, they are in the form of discrete particles or of a chemical solution.

The results from this organic state of feeling are many and varied. The importance of sexual feeling is indicated by the recognition it has received in psychology. According to one psychological theory all feelings of pleasure are sexual in their origin. This theory may be wrong, but many pleasurable feelings, perhaps the majority of them, are sexual in their origin. Furthermore, sexual feeling is one of the most acute, perhaps the most acute, form of feeling and of pleasure. A good deal of pain also is, indirectly at any rate, due to sex. This pain is caused by undue repression of sexual impulses, or in some other way connected with sex.

The complexity of the results from the state of feeling stimulated by sex is so great that it is difficult to give a name to this secondary function of sex. I choose to call it the "play aspect" of sex, or the "play interest" in sex. My reason for using the word "play" is that this function of sex gives rise to much behavior whose motive is not practical in the sense that work is motivated by practical ends, so that in this respect it is like play. Even though this name does not indicate fully its scope, I shall call this function of sex the play function.[14]

The play aspect of sex is developed to a considerable degree among all of the higher animals. Among many of them it is a strong social force, and adds considerably to the pleasure of their life. But sex is on the whole more exclusively for reproduction among the animals than it is among men. This is illustrated by the rut. Owing to the rut sexual feeling is acute at certain times among many of the animal species, but is more or less quiescent at other times.

The rut seems to have disappeared entirely or in large part among men.[15] Sexual feeling is more or less evenly diffused over the whole of human life, in which the play function is a constant factor. Furthermore, the human intellect makes the play aspect a conscious end to a much greater degree than is possible for any animal, while many human ideas become associated with sexual feelings, thus forming sentiments which exercise a powerful influence over the life of man.

[14] This term was used for the first time in my *Poverty and Social Progress*, New York, 1916, pp. 310ff. Two years later appeared my *Personality and Conduct*, New York, 1918, Chapter IX entitled "The Play Function of Sex."

Dr. Havelock Ellis said in 1921: "The term seems to have been devised by Professor Maurice Parmelee." (*Little Essays of Love and Virtue*, London, 1922.)

[15] *Cf.* E. Westermack, *The History of Human Marriage*, London, 1891, Chap. II, "Human Pairing Season in Primitive Times."

Much of human achievement has been due to the play function of sex. Suffice it to say that many military, political, and economic achievements have been due to male gallantry in behalf of women, or to sexual rivalry among men. Furthermore, the play function is often an indirect cause of achievement. Much of art, literature, and religion is a symbolic interpretation of sexual feelings and desires, where these feelings and desires have been sublimated and the results of the sublimation are being manifested in these forms. The extensive role played in the life of man by this function of sex has been more or less fully revealed in recent years by the study of the unconscious, subconscious, co-conscious, or subliminal aspect of human nature. Psychoanalysis has furnished a valuable technique for this study.

In spite of these facts, certain ideas are more or less prevalent at present which deny the existence, or, to say the least, the utility of the play function of sex. The first of these ideas is that reproduction is the only natural, legitimate function of sex, and that the use of sex for any other purpose is animal, bestial, licentious, and immoral, and that a human being who recognizes any other function of sex and practices it reverts to the animal plane. The above facts indicate the precise opposite of this idea.

Among the lower animals sex is exclusively or almost exclusively for purposes of reproduction. Higher in the animal scale there develops the secondary function which I have called the play function of sex. This function plays an increasingly important role. It reaches its highest fruition in man, and is therefore most distinctively human in its character.

It is not animal and bestial to recognize the play function of sex and its need for a full scope. On the contrary, it is human, social, and cultural, in the best sense of those terms, to foster this valuable trait of mankind. Those who deny the play function of sex convict themselves of bestiality by so doing, because they are denying what is most distinctively human in favor of what is more distinctively characteristic of the beasts; while those who attempt to provide suitable and adequate opportunity for the exercise of this human trait in the life of mankind are furthest from the brutes.

A second idea, which arises to a large extent out of the first idea, is that each generation should live exclusively for the sake of succeeding generations. Several criticisms may be made of this idea. In the first place, there are no scientific or philosophic reasons why there should be any future generations. No facts have ever been discovered which prove that anything of moment in the universe apart from man's own interests depends upon the continuance of the human species. So far as any scientific or philosophic considerations are involved, it would be entirely justifiable for the present generation to devote itself exclusively to its own interests, and to make no effort to perpetuate itself by means of reproduction.

Even if it is assumed on religious or moral grounds that there should be succeeding generations (and this assumption is made by most persons), it would still not be necessary for the present generation to sacrifice itself entirely in the interest of future generations. If the present generation assumed that a complete self-sacrifice was obligatory, it would place itself in an inconsistent and logically fallacious attitude toward altruism. It would not be altruistic for the present generation to transmit to future generations a tradition of a duty which, if performed, would in turn destroy the enjoyment of life for those generations also. If this obligation rests upon the present generation, it must rest upon future generations as well, so that it would be the highest altruism not to bring those generations into the world under the burden of such an obligation.

In the second place, even if it is assumed that there should be future generations, and that each generation must sacrifice itself at least in part for its descendants, it is not necessary to assume that this sacrifice must be complete. If this were the case, only the last human generation could derive any enjoyment out of life, because it would have no descendants for which to sacrifice itself, and there would be no justification for the existence of the preceding generations. So that even the persons who believe in the duty of propagation can be hedonists to the extent of believing that each generation is entitled to some enjoyment.

Ideas opposed to the play function of sex are to be expected wherever duty and morality are worshipped as ends in themselves, as is the case in countries with a Puritanical cultural background. Owing to these ideas, it is customary to regard parenthood as a duty, but to look with suspicion upon the play function of sex because, perchance, pleasure may be derived from the exercise of this function. So long as it is believed that there is opposition between the two functions of sex, it will be impossible to harmonize them in the life of mankind.

The first step toward harmonizing these two functions is to regard parenthood not as a duty but as a privilege and a source of pleasure. As I have already indicated, there is no scientific or philosophic reason for regarding the perpetuation of the species as a duty. Rarely, if ever, also, is there any social and humanitarian reason for regarding reproduction as a duty, because it is ordinarily the tendency of population to increase more rapidly than is desirable for society.

On the other hand, parenthood may be and is under suitable conditions a source of much pleasure. Under the stress of poverty and similar conditions of misery it may be a source of more pain than pleasure. But ordinarily the satisfaction of the instincts and emotions

854

connected with parenthood more than repays all of the pain and discomfort caused by parenthood. There is every reason to consider parenthood a privilege rather than a duty, and its value to the individual as a privilege will doubtless be enhanced in the future by the increasing pressure of population upon natural resources. This pressure may become so great that society may be forced to prohibit each couple from having more than three or even two children.[16]

The second step toward harmonizing the two functions of sex is to recognize that they may reinforce each other, and will do so when properly exercised. The play function ordinarily leads in course of time to reproduction, and then, if the play aspect of the relation between the parents is strong, it is almost certain to be made stronger by the bond of mutual parenthood. It happens much more rarely, if ever, that reproduction without the play aspect leads to a development of the play function of sex. This is due to the fact that so far as the individual is concerned the play function normally comes first in point of time. This situation is explained by the following scientific facts.

While there is a sexual instinct, there is no specific parental instinct. That is to say, human beings feel a distinct impulse toward a definite form of behavior with respect to sex, namely, the satisfying of erotic feelings. But they do not feel, and could not feel a distinct impulse toward a definite form of behavior with respect to parenthood, because there is no single act on the part of the individual which is sure to cause parenthood. On the contrary, parenthood is the outcome of a long process which goes on automatically and independently of the acts of the individual. The process of reproduction begins as a result of sexual intercourse, but the individual can do nothing more to bring about this result. Then after pregnancy has commenced, the process is entirely automatic.

It is nevertheless true that reproduction stimulates certain instincts and emotions in the parents which lead to a strong affective attitude toward their offspring, and to various kinds of acts in behalf of the offspring. So that while there is no distinct parental instinct, there are various instincts and emotions which are stimulated by reproduction, and which are connected with parenthood.

If these two measures to harmonize the functions of sex are taken, sexual relations will under normal conditions begin on the play basis and culminate in parenthood, which will in turn reinforce the play

---

[16] I have discussed the problem of population at considerable length in my *Poverty and Social Progress*, New York, 1916, Chap. XII, entitled "The Growth of Population and the Increase of Wealth," and Chap. XIII, entitled "Population and Poverty;" and in my *Farewell to Poverty*, New York, 1935, Chap. XXIX, entitled "Population and Geo-Economic Regionalism."

aspect of the union. This result is much to be desired from the point of view of the interest of the child, because, if the play function is strong, the parents are not likely to separate, and thus the child will have the benefit of the care of both parents.

If, however, the sex relation begins without the play aspect, and is merely for the purpose of reproduction, it is almost certain to arouse a repugnance which can never be overcome. In such a case reproduction is not likely to reinforce the play function, and the parents are likely to separate, so that the children will not have the benefit of the care of both parents. And even if the parents do not separate under such conditions, the environment in the household of a mismated couple is not favorable to a good rearing for the offspring.

These facts indicate that both functions of sex are based upon powerful instincts which are deeply rooted in human nature, that they involve many feelings, and that numerous ideas and sentiments are connected with them. However important the reproductive function may be, the play function can claim a little superiority from a cultural point of view, because it is a later product of mental and social evolution. To say the least, the play function is a more conscious and intelligent element in the human mental makeup, because it is associated with more complex ideas and sentiments than the reproductive function of sex.

The significance of the above facts is that the play function of sex has been an important factor in the evolution of civilization, and has done much to enrich human personality. It is, therefore, an indication of profound ignorance of human nature and of cultural evolution to attempt to organize and regulate sex relations without any regard to this function of sex.

And yet there has been much regulation of this sort for magical and religious reasons, on account of the economic position of woman, and in behalf of the reproductive function of sex. Regulations arising out of the economic dependence of woman are inevitable so long as that condition exists. Inasmuch as the same impulses are involved in both the reproductive and the play functions of sex, though often in a different form, it is impossible to regulate sex to any degree in the interest or alleged interest of reproduction without interfering seriously with the play function.

It is characteristic of the play function of sex that it must act spontaneously so far as the individual is concerned. That is to say, there can be no immediate directing or regulating as to the object or objects toward which the sexual impulses of the individual will direct themselves. To interfere with sexual relations and acts in the name of reproduction is to interfere with the spontaneous operation of the play function.

The above remarks, however, are not meant to imply that the play function cannot be much influenced indirectly. As a matter of fact, early environment and training, the ideas possessed by an individual, and many other factors, influence the play function greatly. The wise method of trying to influence either of these two functions of sex is to do so by indirect means, and to be very careful to influence neither function in any way which will do injury to the other.[17]

[17] I have discussed the play function of sex at length and in detail in my books entitled *Peronality and Conduct*, New York, 1918; and *The Play Function of Sex*, 1960.

In the latter book I have proposed a future public institution to be called the *amatorium*. It will be the first public recognition of the play function of sex which has always been ignored or has been banned and suppressed so far as feasible by the state, church, and public opinion. This institution will furnish the opportunity to express the play function of sex to many men and women who are prevented by economic and social conditions from enjoying and benefiting by such expression. It will aid greatly in removing the stigma usually attached to sex. It will obviate much prostitution, and will encourage heterosexuality in the place of of homosexuality and narcissism.

Chapter XLIX

The Regulation of Sex

THE first step toward describing the inevitable limitations upon the spontaneous expression of human nature is to formulate a criterion for the social control of the individual. It would be desirable to suppress all conduct injurious to mankind. But it would require omniscience to discern all socially harmful conduct.

Some of the acts which now appear to be beneficial to society may in the long run prove to be detrimental. Conduct which is injurious to one individual may prove to be beneficial to the remainder of society. On account of these complicated problems, there will always be disagreement with respect to the social value of many kinds of conduct. Consequently, it is often difficult to decide which acts should be subjected to social control.

We shall use as a criterion for social control the distinction between invasive and non-invasive conduct. By invasive conduct I mean acts which are unmistakably harmful to others. Non-invasive conduct includes acts which do not injure others, or, to say the least, which are not unquestionably harmful to others.[1]

It is easy to classify many kinds of conduct as either invasive or non-invasive. Injuries to the person are obviously invasive of the rights and welfare of others. Among these injurious acts are to be included not only homicide and wounding, but also acts which do injury less directly. For example, it is invasive to make unnecessary loud noises which violate the sense of hearing and put a strain upon the nervous

[1] So far as I know, no other writer has stated this criterion, though several of the writers on social regulation have doubtless had it in mind. For example, John Stuart Mill said that "the individual is not accountable to society for his actions, in so far as these concern the interests of no person but himself," but "for such actions as are prejudicial to the interests of others, the individual is accountable, and may be subjected either to social or legal punishment, if society is of opinion that the one or the other is requisite for its protection." (J. S. Mill, *On Liberty*, London, 1863, p. 74.)

system; or to create insanitary conditions which breed the germs of diseases which menace the public. To deprive other persons of their property by theft or by destruction is obviously invasive. On the other hand, most of the habitual modes of conduct are non-invasive in the sense that they do no obvious or unquestionable damage to other persons. In many cases a person's conduct may do injury to himself, but this does not necessarily make it invasive.

There remain many instances which are not so easy to classify. For example, it is impossible to determine whether or not certain types of conduct are invasive until science has ascertained as to whether or not the conditions created by such conduct are insanitary to the extent of menacing the health of the community. The justice of the private ownership of certain property, such as land, capital goods, and inherited wealth, may be questioned, and this question may render dubitable the invasiveness of depriving the owner of this property. The conduct of an individual may be primarily and directly injurious only to himself, and therefore apparently non-invasive. But he may have other persons dependent upon him who will be injured indirectly by his conduct, which fact indicates that his conduct is nevertheless invasive. Furthermore, it is sometimes contended that every form of conduct which is harmful to the individual is also harmful to society, because the individual is a member of society, and such conduct is therefore invasive.

However, in spite of these doubtful cases, I believe that this criterion is the most feasible both in theory and in practice. The proposed criterion is as satisfactory theoretically as any that the limited intelligence and the relative knowledge of man can devise, and is the most practical because it is concrete and can be given the pragmatic test. In the long run it is possible to ascertain fairly accurately whether or not a form of conduct is invasive.

Even though this is the best criterion, it is constantly being violated. Conduct which is directly invasive is almost invariably subjected to social control. But it often happens that a form of conduct which is indirectly invasive is not subjected to social control for a long time because the public has not yet discovered its invasive character. For example, many insanitary practices were not repressed until science had revealed their deleterious effects.

It probably happens even more frequently that non-invasive forms of conduct are repressed. Such repression may be due to religious beliefs or moral ideas. Or it may be due to the dominance of a ruling class which is legislating in its own interest. Much of the sumptuary legislation in the past has been due to this cause. For example, a dominant class may require a subject class to wear a distinctive dress in order to indicate its servile status.

However, the principal cause for the repression of non-invasive conduct probably has been human intolerance for variation and change. After custom and public opinion have established customary modes of conduct, most individuals resent and try to repress variations from these modes of conduct, even when such variations are not invasive and may even be beneficial to society.

As a rule the public dislikes personal idiosyncrasies, however innocuous they may be. It is constantly trying to impose its own conventional standards of taste and esthetic judgments upon the individual. Thus it is that the public and its methods of social control themselves become invasive in their repression of the individual, and thereby are guilty of violations of personal liberty.

There will always be violations of this criterion of social control. On the one hand, the invasiveness of certain kinds of conduct will be obscure. On the other hand, it will never be possible to obviate entirely the deeply rooted tendency to persecute personal idiosyncrasies and innocuous variations from the conventional and the customary. But these violations can be greatly lessened. The progress of science, especially in its study of mental and social phenomena, will reveal more and more fully the true nature of invasive conduct. The rise in the average intelligence and knowledge due to the spread of educational facilities and the increased intercommunication between human beings will broaden the outlook and mental vision of the average human being and will thereby diminish intolerance for what is different, what is new, and what is idiosyncratic.

The more obvious of the gravely invasive acts are stigmatized as criminal by the law and are penalized. Other acts which are not so obviously invasive may or may not be penalized by the law. These acts are usually called vicious. Vicious acts like criminal acts are regarded as immoral and harmful to society. But ordinarily they are not considered immoral so generally as criminal acts, and they are not or are not supposed to be so harmful to society as criminal acts. In other words, vicious acts may be defined as the minor anti-social acts, and therefore differ in degree but not in kind from crimes.

Furthermore, vicious acts do not ordinarily affect other people directly in an injurious manner. Consequently, it is usually more or less futile to try to repress them by direct measures, because there is no one who has been immediately injured by these acts who is anxious to procure their repression. Hence it is often feasible to act viciously in secret, so that it is almost impossible to enforce penal legislation against such conduct. Some of the criminal conduct also escapes repressive legislation, but this is true of a much larger proportion of the vicious conduct. It is usually assumed also that the repression of vicious conduct is not so essential to the preservation of the existing system of society as is the repression of crime.

These are the principal differences between crime and vice. These differences are not absolute. For example, some forms of vicious conduct are more harmful to society than many crimes, and are in the long run more fatal to the existing social system. However, these differences indicate that indirect methods are as a rule more likely to eliminate vicious conduct than direct, repressive methods. These indirect methods are designed to remove the causes of vice, and will therefore have more effect in the future than in the present. Consequently, they have little immediate value, but direct repressive measures are likely to fail and may cause harm by their failure.

It is a serious problem as to when the regulation of vice by means of penal law is justifiable, if, indeed, it is ever justifiable. There are several general or more or less general objections to such regulation. It is indirectly if not directly a form of sumptuary legislation, and as such is distasteful as a restriction upon personal liberty. Owing to lack of public support it is often impossible to enforce such legislation. This results in a general disrespect for law, and leads almost inevitably to the corruption of police. A dishonest and inefficient police is a great danger to society.

Penal repression of vice is also likely to give rise to confusion in the minds of the public as to the distinction between crime and vice. As to whether or not such confusion is undesirable depends largely upon the public attitude toward crime. If the public would view crime purely from a social and ethical standpoint and not from a religious point of view, this confusion might not cause any harm. Inasmuch as there is a religious element in the public attitude toward crime, it is dangerous to confuse crime and vice, because such confusion is almost certain to lead to attempts to repress vice too harshly, and to regard vice as sinful as well as immoral. When the theological concept of sin has been replaced by the social and ethical concept of immorality, it will become less harmful to identify vice with crime.

Hence it is that these questions must be considered before deciding whether or not it is wise to repress any form of vicious conduct by penal methods. Furthermore, there are other methods of social control, and public opinion is often a safer and more effective means of control in the long run than the penal law. The prevention of vicious conduct is of far more importance than its immediate repression, and the work of prevention can usually be carried on as well if not better without the aid of repressive measures.

I shall now enumerate the sex regulations prevailing in the civilized world, classifying them in an orderly fashion. Some of these regulations exist everywhere in the civilized world, others of them exist only in certain parts of the civilized world.[2]

The first group includes the sexual offenses against the person. Strictly speaking, the only offense in this group is rape. In some legal jurisdictions sexual intercourse outside of marriage with a female under a specified age may constitute rape in the second degree, even though she has consented to the intercourse. Abduction also may in some cases be regarded as a sexual offense against the person, as when a female is forcibly carried away and detained against her will in order to be used for sexual purposes. In other words, abduction is sometimes an act preparatory to rape.

The second group includes the crimes of false pretenses committed for sexual purposes. The first is seduction under promise of marriage. The second is bigamy in most cases, for the bigamist does not usually inform the innocent party to the marriage of his or her existing spouse.

The third group includes the regulations of marriage. Marriages between persons within the prohibited degrees of consanguinity are declared void and are punished as being incestuous. Bigamy, under which term is included every form of marriage apart from monogamy, is prohibited and punished. Adultery is punished as a violation of the marriage bond. Divorce is absolutely prohibited in some places and is narrowly limited in many places. For example, it is prohibited in South Carolina and is permitted only for adultery in New York State.

The fourth group includes regulations of extra-marital sex relations. Every form of extra-marital sexual intercourse under the name of fornication is absolutely prohibited and punished in some places. In many parts of the civilized world fornication as such is not punished, though legal attempts are often made to discourage and limit it. Concubinage, or long continued fornication between the same parties, is sometimes distinguished and punished more severely than ordinary fornication. Fornication between persons within the prohibited degrees of consanguinity is also punished more severely as being incestuous. Prostitution, or fornication for profit, is punished in some places, while nearly everywhere there are regulations of prostitution with a view to discouraging and limiting it.

The fifth group includes regulations pertaining to reproduction. Abortion is prohibited and punished in most communities. The use of contraceptive measures to prevent conception is prohibited in many places. To become the parent of an illegitimate child is penalized in

[2] All the laws regulating sex in New York City have been compiled in convenient form by A. B. Spingarn, *Laws Relating to Sex Morality in New York City*, New York, 1915. This book furnishes a good picture of sex regulation from the conventional point of view in one civilized community.

some places, while in many places regulations exist for the purpose of discouraging bastardy. In some places bastards suffer from certain legal disabilities.

The sixth group includes regulations of sexual variations or aberrations. Among them are ways of satisfying the sexual impulse which are usually regarded as abnormal and which are rather vaguely comprehended under the terms sodomy and buggery. Sexual variations may arise by means of the sexual impulse becoming directed toward objects other than the normal object, such as toward individuals of the same sex (homosexuality), toward the sexually immature (pederasty), toward animals (bestiality), and toward inanimate objects (sexual fetishism).

The seventh group includes all regulations of acts and objects which are incidental to sex or suggestive of it, or which are popularly regarded as being related in some way to sex. In accordance with the conventional moral standard these acts and objects are usually called licentious, libidinous, lecherous, lustful, unchaste, indecent, obscene, lewd, lascivious, salacious, immodest, etc.

In the last group of regulations are the laws and conventions which forbid an unusual degree of exposure of the body in public. Such exposure is ordinarily regarded as immodest and indecent, because it is sexually suggestive to the conventional mind which is almost invariably highly prurient. Dancing has sometimes been prohibited because it involves close contact between the sexes. These regulations also include the prohibition of spoken references to sex in private or in public, as, for example, on the stage; written references to sex in books, journals, etc.; and artistic or other representations of matters related to sex, as in pictures, statues, etc.

The preceding conspectus of sex regulations, brief and concise though it is, is sufficient to indicate that the factors mentioned in the preceding chapter are still at work. In these regulations we can discern the influence of the magical notion of the uncleanness of sex, and religious and especially the Christian notions of asceticism and the sacramental character of marriage, the economic dependence of women, etc. These regulations represent what is usually called the Puritanical attitude toward sex.

The enlightening Kinsey Report furnishes many data with respect to the large number of acts which are or are supposed to be related to sex which are penalized in the United States and the great differences in their treatment between the different States.[3] Among these acts penalized somewhere in the United States are contraception;

[3] Alfred C. Kinsey, Wardell B. Pomeroy and Clyde E. Martin, *Sexual Behavior in the Human Male*, Philadelphia, 1948.
Summaries of this report are furnished in *American Sexual Behavior and the*

unchastity and incontinence; cunnilingus and fellatio; bastardy, inde cent exposure, exposure of the person and nudism; contracts for sex ual purposes; transportation for sexual purposes, obscene language, obscene books, letters and communications; and miscegenation. The great differences in their treatment is indicated by the facts that adul tery is no crime in four states, and is punished by fines ranging from $10 to $2,000 and/or prison sentences ranging from three months to five years in the other states; that fornication is no crime in fifteen states, and is punished by fines of from $10 to $1,000 and/or jail sent ences of from thirty days up to four years in the other states; that seduction is no crime in thirteen states, and is penalized by fines of from $100 to $5,000 and/or prison of from three months to twenty years elsewhere in the United States; and that sodomy (which is ill-defined in most state legislation and may include homosexuality, dual or mutual masturbation, oral contact, and bestiality or animal contact) is no crime in two states and the District of Columbia, and is pun ished by fines ranging from $100 to $5,000 and/or imprisonment from one year to life in the other forty-eight states.[4] Of the 48 states and the District of Columbia, 27 punished all four of these acts alleged to be criminal, 14 penalized three of them, 5 punished two of them, and 3 penalized only one of them.

While there are great variations between the acts stigmatized as immoral and penalized as criminal between different countries, as well as between different periods of time, there has perhaps never been so much variation within one country at the same time as there is in the legislation pertaining to sex in the United States at the pres ent time. It seems to indicate great confusion in the minds of the American people as to the social and ethical significance of sex.

In many libraries are restrictions upon the use of books dealing with sex. For example, in the reference division of the New York Public Library not only the books ordinarily called "sex books," but also many other works, including some of the best known psychoana lytic treatises, are segregated in one room under a close guard. These books are designated in the catalogue by a distinctive numeral, are issued only to persons approved of by the library authorities, and must be read in the "cage."

According to the director of this library, the purpose of these restrictions is to prevent "prurient" individuals from reading these books. The library authorities must indeed be endowed with super natural insight to be able to discern pruriency or its absence in the

Kinsey Report, by M. L. Ernst and D. Loth, New York, 1948; and in *About the Kinsey Report,* edited by D. P. Geddes and Enid Curie, New York, 1948.

[4] See J. R. Miller, "Sex Laws of the 48 States," in *'48,* Vol. 2, No. 2, February 1948, pp. 24-31.

minds of those who call for these books! In the library of the New York Academy of Medicine, which professes to be a scientific institution, books on sex are doled out one at a time only to approved individuals. According to the librarian, this is to prevent "morbid" persons from reading these books.[5]

There are maladies of sex just as there are maladies of the stomach, and some of those suffering from sexual disorders may be injured by perusing literature about sex. But to impose these offensive and irksome restrictions upon the public for this reason is like clubbing the dog to death in order to kill a flea. A poisoner may use a book on drugs to help him commit a murder, but that is no reason for prohibiting all books on drugs. A sadist may derive enjoyment from reading an account of a brutal act, but that does not justify the prohibition of all historical works which describe acts of cruelty.

In fact, however useful an article may be, it is possible to misuse it. The problem with regard to sex books, as with regard to everything else, is as to whether or not their abuse will exceed their use. Librarians are wont to allege that they should be used by scholars and specialists on sex, but not by the general public. They display much trepidation lest, perchance, some readers may derive enjoyment from reading these books, overlooking the fact that numerous readers derive a vast amount of sexual pleasure from reading many of the books of fiction, poetry, etc., in the libraries.

I need not point out again the importance of sex in the life of mankind. In view of its importance every human being should have some knowledge of its nature and functions. The libraries, instead of endeavoring to perpetuate the puerile traditions of taboo and ignorance, should willingly and gladly furnish literature on sex to all sexually mature persons. The libraries and schools should become centers for the dissemination of knowledge on this subject, as on every other important subject. And inasmuch as the schools at present fail almost entirely to perform this function, it is all the more essential that the libraries should do it effectively.

If this liberal and enlightened policy were followed, most of the pruriency and morbidity which the librarians fear would disappear. Pruriency arises mainly out of ignorance and repression, and by far the worst form of pruriency is that of the would-be moralists who do the repressing. If some of the readers can derive enjoyment from sex literature, so much the better. Life is dreary enough at best for most persons without destroying any more sources of pleasure.

There is another important aspect of this form of sex regulation which should not be overlooked. One of the most fundamental of

[5] I have described these restrictions in libraries in my book entitled *Personality and Conduct*, New York, 1915, pp. 130-134.

human rights is the right to the knowledge which is the common heritage of mankind. What right then have librarians and directors of libraries to withhold the sources of this knowledge from the public? Such restrictions can be justified only in the case of young children, who are easily recognizable, and of some of the mentally incompetent, such as the insane and the feebleminded whose mental disabilities are peculiarly related to sex, most of whom are already under custodial care. There is no need of a censorship in the libraries, and such a censorship is an insult to the public; while to deprive any person of the sources of knowledge is to violate the above-mentioned fundamental right. In fact, these restrictions upon the dissemination of knowledge on this subject constitute another manifestation of the age-long taboo upon sex which has arisen from the magical and religious notion that there is something evil in sex *per se.*

Like almost every other part of human nature, the sexual instincts, feelings, and sentiments require a certain amount of regulation. Such regulation is needed both in the interest of the individual and in the interest of society.

Conflict arises in man's sexual nature as in other parts of his nature. The desire for sexual gratification sometimes leads to excessive indulgence which in turn leads to a satiety which dulls the capacity for further enjoyment. Continued excessive indulgence leads to a permanent diminution or even a complete loss of virility, and may give rise to physiological and mental disorders. Careless and injudicious sexual indulgence may result in the acquisition of an injurious and troublesome disease. The gratification of a passing sexual whim may injure a permanent sexual bond which is more satisfactory in the long run. The play function and the reproductive function of sex are likely to conflict if they are not recognized and understood and adjusted to each other in an intelligent manner.

The sexual impulse is powerful and sometimes becomes ungovernable. Regulatory measures are required to protect the individual and society against genuine sex offenses. Rape and abduction for sexual purposes usually are grave crimes. All sex relations obtained under false pretenses should be punished. Sex relations between persons closely related by blood should be discouraged, not as incestuous, but as disturbing family relations. The sexually immature should be protected in their weakness and ignorance. The spread of venereal diseases should be restrained as far as is feasible.

But it is the human and social tendency to go too far in its regulation of sex as in its regulation of other parts of man's nature. Much of the sex legislation which I have noted is unwise because it is unenforceable. Such legislation gives rise to disrespect for the law, police and political corruption, and various other social evils. Even when sex legislation is enforceable, it often furnishes the opportunity for criminal conduct, such as blackmail, and leads to violations of the play function of sex, restrictions upon literature, art and science, degradation of the human body, etc.

Sex legislation is usually sumptuary in its character. The sex life belongs to the most private and intimate part of the life of the individual. While there are several ills in the sex life of mankind which it would be desirable to prevent, it is usually dangerous to attempt to do so by invading the private life of the individual. On account of their invasive character, direct regulatory measures almost invariably do more harm than good. Sexually mature persons should be left free in the main in their sex life, and dependence should be placed upon indirect measures for the prevention of ills which arise.

Most of the sex legislation and much of the regulation which arises out of custom, public opinion, and conventional moral ideas leads to an excessive and abnormal degree of sex repression. Such repression gives rise to numerous physical and mental ills which will be described presently.

The laws against fornication and adultery are rarely ever enforceable. The practice of fornication is widespread in every community. Even if only a comparatively small proportion of these offenders were detected and imprisoned, the jails and prisons would be filled many times over. In similar fashion, adultery is rarely ever punished, though it often serves as the basis for a divorce.

These invasive laws constitute grave violations of the rights of the individual to form sex relationships within or outside of marriage. The criminal laws against fornication and adultery will before long be stricken forever from the statute books. Adultery as a breach of the marriage contract will then become a tort like the breach of any other civil contract. Thus will the religious element be eliminated from marriage, because it will no longer be regarded as a sacred bond which it is a sin to break, but as a mutual agreement to be adjusted between the parties concerned. Furthermore, the abolition of the law against adultery will help to remove the idea of property right which still inheres to a considerable extent in marriage.

It is well known to every educated person that there is no innate sense of modesty. As a matter of fact, there is the highest possible degree of variation in the amount of clothing worn by human beings in different parts of the world. Clothing should be regulated by climatic, hygienic, economic, and esthetic considerations, and not by moral and religious dogmas and penal laws. There can be no justification of legal regulation of exposure of the body.

The regulation of literature and art by the law or by public opinion is almost entirely mischievous and harmful. It is the peculiar

867

function of scientists and artists to think along original lines and to give new ideas to society from which the useful ones can be selected and applied. Hence it is dangerous to place restrictions upon scientists and artists in the performance of this valuable function.

The harmful results from repression and regulation are to be witnessed on every hand. Excessive sex repression leads to both the extremes of sexual abnormality, namely, erotophobia and erotomania. The fear of sex which is likely to be aroused by the ideas and beliefs which underlie such repression leads to sexual frigidity and various psychiatric diseases, such as hysteria, psychasthenia, certain forms of insanity, etc. These erotophobic results of sex repression are perhaps more frequent among women than among men for physiological as well as social reasons, because the reproductive function of sex plays a more important part in the physiology of women.

On the other hand, excessive sex repression drives many persons to the other extreme. If unusual difficulties are placed in the way of the satisfaction of sexual desires, they may become irritated and accentuated to a high degree, and an abnormal interest in sex may be aroused. The gravest manifestations of this erotomania are in the forms of rape, abduction, seduction, various sexual deviations, etc. Its milder manifestations are in the forms of so-called pornographic art and literature, undue emphasis upon sex in literature and art, the exaggerated role played by sex upon the stage, etc. All of these pathological manifestations are indications of suppressed sexual desires struggling to express and gratify themselves. Indeed, the somewhat hectic quality of modern civilization is due in part to excessive sex repression. The ascetics, prudes, vice crusaders, and all other persons with prurient minds who are zealously engaged in trying to suppress these manifestations of sex are themselves to blame for them at least in part.[6] The only effective preventive of both erotophobic and erotomanic manifestations is a satisfactory sex life for all humans.

These psychiatric conditions inevitably give rise to physiological injury. When the repression of the sexual instincts and feelings results in insanity or a neurotic state, it is evident that a pathological condition of the nervous system has arisen. This neural pathological condition is almost certain to be accompanied by or to give rise to other physiological disturbances, such as disturbances of digestion, of

---

[6] In the last sentence I have used the adjective "prurient" advisedly, for there is plenty of psychological evidence that the persecution mania of the vice crusader arises largely if not entirely out of his own unconsciously suppressed sexual desires.

See my book entitled *Nudism in Modern Life,* fifth revised edition, 1952; in which are described attempts of several public officials to suppress my book, and is reprinted the scholarly decision, written by Justice Justin Miller, of May 14, 1940, of the United States Court of Appeals of the District of Columbia, which ranks next to the United States Supreme Court.

circulation, etc. And even when the repression of the sexual instincts and feelings results merely in mental complexes which harass the victim of the sex repression, these complexes are sure to give rise to a physiological strain which decreases at least to a slight extent the physical efficiency of the individual.

Total or long continued sexual abstinence, while it will not ordinarily make a person of average strength and health ill, or even have an appreciable harmful effect upon the sexual organs, is certain to cause at least a small amount of physical and mental injury by its disturbing influence upon the physiological state of the individual. The ideal sexual regime is a continent use of sexual intercourse without going to the extreme of incontinence, which may be harmful to every one.

There can be no universal rule as to the desirable frequency of sexual intercourse, since this depends upon the circumstances and traits of the individual. The distinction between continent and incontinent sexual intercourse is biological and mental and not legal and moral, so that the circumstance of whether or not the sexual intercourse is within or outside of marriage is immaterial and inconsequential with respect to the question of whether it is continent or not. In fact, there is far more incontinence and unchastity within than there is outside of marriage.

Among the pathological results from an excessive degree of sexual abstinence are the sexual variations or aberrations, sometimes called perversions. These aberrations usually arise by means of the sexual impulse becoming directed toward objects other than the normal object because the normal object is not available, though in some cases they arise as a result of excessive sexual indulgence. These aberrations replace or displace the normal heterosexual relation. They include homosexuality in which the sexual impulse is directed toward individuals of the same sex, pederasty in which it is directed toward the sexually immature, bestiality in which it is directed toward animals, and sexual fetishism in which it is directed toward inanimate objects. Owing to the enforced and long continued abstinence, prison life furnishes numerous examples of these sexual deviations.

Sexual abstinence results frequently in auto-erotism in the form of masturbation as a substitute for sexual intercourse. In most of these cases the degree of auto-erotism is comparatively slight and the masturbation causes little if any injury. In some cases the tendency to masturbate is indulged to an excessive extent and does harm. In a few of these cases it leads to sexual exhibitionism.

The most widespread injury from sexual abstinence is psychic sexual impotence. The ability to have normal and satisfactory sex relations diminishes, though there is not necessarily any decrease in

869

the ability to procreate. In other words, there develops *impotentia coeundi,* but not *impotentia generandi.* Sexual impotence means a decrease in the virility and therefore the vigor of mankind. It injures the play function of sex. It is the most harmful social result from sexual abstinence.

The prevailing moral ideas and forms of social control do not promote the best type of sex relationship. This relation among human beings exists to fulfill the play function of sex, which can be attained only by suitable sexual mating, and for reproduction. Religion, and especially Christianity through its ascetic influence, has by making marriage a sacrament shifted the emphasis from the sex relation as a natural union, to be judged and regulated according to the compatibility of the parties to the union for fulfilling these functions of sex, to a mystical and mythical relation. Even the secular conception of marriage has often regarded it as an artificial product of the law, instead of a biological, psychological, and social phenomenon which exists prior to law, and which is registered and officially recognized by the law like all other civil contracts.

The conventional conception of marriage has fostered the erroneous notion that there is an intrinsic difference between sexual intercourse within and outside of wedlock. Extra-matrimonial sex relations are stigmatized as lewd and incontinent as contrasted with matrimonial relations which are supposed to be pure and continent *per se.* Biologically and psychologically there could be no such intrinsic difference.

As a matter of fact, there is vastly more incontinence within marriage than there is outside of it, and the average unmarried person is far more continent than the average married person. Extramatrimonial sex relations often are purer than most matrimonial relations in the only true meaning of sex purity, namely, as a spontaneous gratification of erotic desires and expression of genuine personal feelings. It is infinitely more important for the normal and healthy sex life of mankind that such spontaneous sex relations should be encouraged than that the prevailing type of conventional marriage should be preserved.

As I have already stated in the preceding chapter, the ascetic denial of the play function of sex has enthroned the dogma of sexual intercourse solely for the purpose of reproduction, and has resulted in many countries in the legal prohibition of abortion and contraceptive measures as methods of controlling procreation. This religious dogma has been reinforced and strengthened by capitalist and militarist interests which have desired cheap labor and human fodder for cannon. It should be replaced by the humane and social doctrine that repro-

870

duction is primarily a matter of choice for the individual parents, and that unwilling or unexpected procreation is inhuman and anti-social.

It is possible that the opposition to the use of birth control methods has a slight biological basis in an unconscious desire for parenthood universal in mankind. This desire has social value and should be cultivated. In an ideal society every individual would have the opportunity to gratify this desire. Under actual conditions parenthood often is a burden, and under such conditions it is a grave injustice to the offspring to permit them to come into the world.

As soon as contraceptive methods can be used freely, unwilling and unexpected pregnancies will become rare, so that abortion will become rarely necessary. Thus will be obviated this operation which is so frequently made necessary today by the prohibition of contraceptive measures, an excellent instance of how one criminal law may be responsible for violations of another law. The disappearance of abortion will be a great boon, because this operation is physically dangerous to the woman and shocking to her maternal instincts and feelings. Furthermore, it is offensive to the deeply rooted sentiment of the supreme value of human life which is more or less widespread in society.

It would be an insult to the readers of this book to assume that they are not acquainted with the vast social importance of the problem of population.[7] Birth control measures are directed toward regulating the growth of population intelligently. To attempt to prevent the use of these measures by penal restrictions, and to repress the free discussion of such measures is an exhibition of crass stupidity which is fraught with a vast amount of injury to society.

The only social regulation of reproduction which is justifiable at the present time is the prohibition of reproduction for a few congenitally abnormal types. If the time ever comes when the world reaches absolute over-population, it may become necessary to place a general check upon reproduction. But such a time is far distant in the future, and may never come.

[7] I have discussed the problem of population at considerable length in my *Poverty and Social Progress,* New York, 1916; and in my *Farewell to Poverty,* New York, 1935.

Chapter L

The Double Standard of Sex Freedom

ONE of the most striking features of the sex life of mankind is the double standard of sex freedom. This standard discriminates against woman and in favor of man by giving man more freedom in his sex relations. In civilized society the same moral regulations with respect to sex exist in theory for both sexes. In practice transgressions of these regulations by man are usually readily condoned, while similar transgressions by woman are severely reprehended.

The existence of the double standard is generally recognized. Furthermore, it is almost invariably denounced by religionists and professional moralists. But few if any attempts have been made to explain it. So far as I am able to discover after an extensive research, no adequate analysis of the origin and causes of the double standard of sex freedom has ever been made. This is probably due to the fact that most writers have been prevented by religious prejudices and a moral bias from discussing the subject impartially. And yet it is impossible to appraise the double standard correctly without an understanding of its origin and causes.

This double standard is by no means a new feature of the life of mankind. Among many savage and barbarous peoples the male sex has had more freedom in its sex relations than the female sex. Promiscuity before marriage has often been permitted for both sexes or for the male sex alone, but has been prohibited after marriage for both sexes or for the female alone. Or promiscuity has been forbidden before marriage for both sexes or for the female alone, but has been permitted after marriage for both sexes or for the male alone. There has apparently been more freedom on the whole for the male than for the female. Rarely ever has there been more freedom for the female. This may have happened in a few cases under polyandry. But polyandry has been very rare, while polygyny has been much more frequent.

872

There is, however, an important distinction between the moral status of the double standard of sex freedom in savage and barbarous society and in civilized society. The double standard has usually been recognized and approved by savage and barbarous moral codes, while it has almost invariably been denounced by the conventional civilized codes. Consequently, the double standard has been applied more frankly and openly among savage and barbarous peoples than in civilized society.

The fundamental factor in creating the double standard of sex freedom is the physiological dissimilarity of the sexes which gives rise to the difference in the roles of the sexes in reproduction. It was to be expected that as soon as mankind discovered the connection between sexual intercourse and reproduction, sex relations would be regulated for the purpose of controlling reproduction. This obvious fact has been ignored in most discussions of this subject.

The purpose of controlling reproduction has sometimes been to restrain too rapid a growth of population, but usually to compel reproduction to take place within the forms and in the manner prescribed by society. In other words, the main purpose of such regulation has been to require reproduction to take place within marriage, thus discouraging bastardy. Inasmuch as sexual intercourse involves the risk of pregnancy for woman, and as procreation has a greater effect upon woman and is more dangerous for her than for man, these regulations would inevitably have a more drastic effect upon her than upon him.[1] Such regulation has, therefore, been partly for the protection of woman herself, as well as for the control of reproduction.

Male sexual jealousy has probably been another important factor for the double standard of sex freedom. In fact, it is possible that this factor gave rise to a double standard before the connection between sexual intercourse and reproduction was discovered by man. Some writers have believed that jealousy developed from the sense of ownership which may have originated after the discovery of the connection between sexual intercourse and reproduction.[2] However, psychology seems to indicate that sexual jealousy is a more or less powerful emotion innate in man. It probably began early in the life of mankind

[1] Sumner referred very briefly and rather vaguely to the influence of the physiological differences between the sexes in the following words:

"Woman bears an unequal share of the responsibilities and duties of sex and reproduction just as man bears an unequal share of the responsibilities and duties of property, war, and politics. The reasons are in ultimate physiological facts by virtue of which one is a woman and the other is a man." (W. G. Sumner, *Folkways*, Boston, 1907, p. 362.)

[2] Hartland expressed this view when he said that "the sense of ownership has been the seed-plot of jealousy." (E. S. Hartland, *Primitive Paternity*, London, 1910, Vol. II, pp. 102-103.)

873

to lead men to monopolize women and to restrict them from free sex relations. The sense of ownership which was gradually acquired reacted upon the primal emotion of jealousy and enhanced its strength.

Male sexual jealousy furnished man a powerful incentive for restricting woman in addition to the economic reasons for subjugating her. He was aided in attaining this end by his superior physical strength and by the helplessness of woman during child bearing and child rearing. Some writers also allege that he was aided by a mental superiority over woman. This is a moot question which we need not discuss here.

In barbaric society there developed the patriarchal system which subjected woman more or less effectually to man. Mrs. Gallichan attributed the double standard of sex freedom largely if not entirely to the subjugation of woman under the patriarchal system: "Sexual penalties for women are always found under a strict patriarchal regime. The white flower of chastity, when enforced upon one sex by the other sex, has its roots in the degradation of marriage. Men find a way to escape; women, bound in the coils, stay and waste. There is no escaping from the truth—wherever women are in subjection it is there that the idols of purity and chastity are set up for worship." [3]

The factors I have already described indicate that the double standard probably antedated the patriarchal system. The physiological differences between the sexes and male sexual jealousy brought the double standard into existence before the patriarchal system originated. The patriarchal system, however, strengthened greatly the double standard of sex freedom, because woman had now become practically a chattel of man.

While the patriarchal system has disappeared in the main from civilized society, the economic dependence of woman which formed an important part of it remains to a considerable extent. In recent times woman has gained a certain amount of economic independence. But this development has not progressed far enough to give her complete freedom in marriage. Marriage has not yet attained the ideal of a free contractual relation which existed for a time in ancient Rome and which is reappearing in modern civilization. Westermarck described this episode in Roman history as follows:

"In Rome, in ancient times, the power which the father possessed over his daughter was generally, if not always, by marriage transferred to the husband. When marrying a woman passed in *manum viri,* as a wife she was *filiae loco,* that is, in law she was her husband's daughter. . . . Gradually, however, marriage

[3] Catherine Gasquoine Hartley Gallichan, *The Truth About Woman*, London, 1913, p. 226.

874

with *manus* fell into disuse, and was, under the Empire, generally superseded by marriage without *manus,* a form of wedlock which conferred on the husband hardly any authority at all over his wife. Instead of passing into his power, she remained in the power of her father; and since the tendency of the later law, as we have seen, was to reduce the old *patria potestas* to a nullity, she became practically independent.

"This remarkable liberty granted to married women, however, was only a passing incident in the history of the family in Europe. From the very first Christianity tended to narrow it. . . . And this tendency was in a formidable degree supported by Teutonic custom and law. Among the Teutons a husband's authority over his wife was the same as a father's over his unmarried daughter. This power, which under certain circumstances gave the husband the right to kill, sell, or repudiate his wife, undoubtedly contained much more than the Church could approve of, and so far she has helped to ameliorate the condition of married women in Teutonic countries. But at the same time the Church is largely responsible for those heavy disabilities with regard to personal liberty, as well as with regard to property, from which they have suffered up to recent times."[4]

Christianity by making marriage a sacrament and by opposing divorce and birth control has endeavored to fetter women in marriage, and her economic dependence has enabled this religion to succeed in a large measure. By so doing Christianity has caused women an untold amount of unhappiness. It has also caused many men a vast amount of misery, because the bonds of marriage have often been irksome to men as well as to women.

The Christian attitude toward sex is an illustration of certain

[4] E. Westermarck, *The Origin and Development of the Moral Ideas,* London, 1906, Vol. I, pp. 652-4.

There is evidence that women attained and possessed for a time a similar freedom in Babylon and ancient Egypt, as was pointed out by Havelock Ellis in the following words: "Nothing is more certain than that the status of women in Rome rose with the rise of civilization exactly in the same way as in Babylon and in Egypt. In the case of Rome, however, the growing refinement of civilization and the expansion of the Empire were associated with the magnificent development of the system of Roman law, which in its final forms consecrated the position of women. In the last days of the Republic women already began to attain the same legal level as men, and later the great Antonine jurisconsults, guided by their theory of natural law, reached the conception of the equality of the sexes as the principle of the code of equity. The patriarchal subordination of women fell into complete discredit, and this continued until, in the days of Justinian, under the influence of Chrisianity the position of women began to suffer." (*Sex in Relation to Society,* Philadelphia, 1911, p. 395.)

magical and religious ideas with respect to sex. Sexual phenomena have always been more or less mysterious to man, especially to primitive man. Consequently, he has viewed them with mingled feelings. While sexual experiences have afforded him much pleasure, their mysterious character has inspired fear in him. This fear has furnished one of the incentives for putting restrictions upon sex.

Some features of the sexual function have aroused disgust as well as fear in man. This has been especially true of the flow of blood in woman at various crises in her life, such as the hymenal flow in connection with puberty, the menstrual flow at the times of the periodic catamenial function, and the puerperal flow at parturition. Primitive man seems at any rate to have felt fear if not disgust toward blood. So that these features of the sexual function have played an important part in giving rise to the notion which is still more or less prevalent that there is something repellent and unclean about sex, especially in woman. The sexual taboos both of the past and of the present can be attributed to a large extent to this notion.

The principal source of the Christian religion is Judaism which contains many of these magical and religious ideas with respect to sex. For example, the notion of the uncleanness of sex plays a prominent part in the Hebrew religion. A considerable portion of the Jewish law is devoted to the regulation of sex with respect to its uncleanness. The following passages from the Old Testament illustrate this part of the Jewish law.

Leviticus XV describes the uncleanness of the sexual issues of men and women and prescribes how they are to be cleansed: "And if any man's seed of copulation go out from him, then he shall wash all his flesh in water, and be unclean until the even. . . . The woman also with whom man shall lie with seed of copulation, they shall both bathe themselves in water, and be unclean until the even. And if a woman have an issue, and her issue in the flesh be blood, she shall be put apart seven days: and whosoever toucheth her shall be unclean until the even. . . . And if any man lie with her at all, and her flowers be upon him, he shall be unclean seven days; and all the bed whereon he lieth shall be unclean." This law reveals the notion of the greater sexual uncleanness of woman, and of how man may be defiled by her uncleanness.

Leviticus XII specifies how women are to be purified after childbirth: "And the Lord spake unto Moses, saying, Speak unto the children of Israel, saying, If a woman have conceived seed, and borne a man child: then she shall be unclean seven days; according to the days of the separation for her infirmity shall she be unclean. . . . But if she bear a maid child, then she shall be unclean two weeks, as in her separation: and she shall continue in the blood of her purifying

876

threescore and six days." This law reveals the inferior position of woman and the belief in the greater uncleanness of sex in woman, for it was more defiling to give birth to a female child than to give birth to a male child.

In the Christian religion these ideas imported from Judaism developed into a form of asceticism which exalted celibacy. For example, in *Revelations* XIV, 4, it is said: "These are they which were not defiled with women; for they are virgins." Throughout the New Testament the dominant theme with respect to sex is that sex is unclean; that virginity and chastity are highly meritorious; that the flesh, by which is usually meant sex, is antagonistic to the spirit; and that marriage is a grudging and questionable concession to the flesh.[5]

The Christian attitude toward sex is well stated in the Pauline epistle, *I Corinthians* VII, as will be seen from the following excerpts:

"It is good for a man not to touch a woman. Nevertheless, to avoid fornication, let every man have his own wife, and let every woman have her own husband. . . . I say therefore to the unmarried and widows, It is good for them if they abide even as I. But if they cannot contain, let them marry: for it is better to marry than to burn. . . . He that is unmarried careth for the things that belong to the Lord, how he may please the Lord: but he that is married careth for the things that are of the world, how he may please his wife. There is difference also between a wife and a virgin. The unmarried woman careth for the things of the Lord, that she may be holy both in body and in spirit: but

[5] Westermarck stated the Christian ascetic doctrine with respect to sex as follows:

"For a nation like the Jews, whose ambition was to live and to multiply, celibacy could never become an ideal; whereas the Christians, who professed the most perfect indifference to all earthly matters, found no difficulty in glorifying a state which, however opposed it was to the interests of the race and the nation, made men pre-eminently fit to approach their god. Indeed, far from being a benefit to the kingdom of God by propagating the species, sexual intercourse was on the contrary detrimental to it by being the great transmitter of the sin to our first parents. . . . Religious celibacy is, moreover, enjoined or commended as a means of self-mortification supposed to appease an angry god, or with a view to raising the spiritual nature of man by suppressing one of the strongest of all sensual appetites. Thus we find in various religions celibacy side by side with other ascetic observances practiced for similar purposes. . . . Finally, it was argued that marriage prevents a person from serving God perfectly, because it induces him to occupy himself too much with worldly things. Though not contrary to the act of charity or the love of God, says Thomas Aquinas, it is nevertheless an obstacle to it." (E. Westermarck, *op. cit.*, Vol. II, pp. 420-421.)

See also, for a discussion of asceticism in Judaism, Christianity, Mohammedanism, and other religions, W. G. Sumner, *op. cit.*, Chap. XVIII.

she that is married careth for the things of the world, how she may please her husband."

The utterances of the principal apostle of Christianity, Paul, did much to establish this anti-social and immoral doctrine in the Christian religion, and thus to carry it into Occidental civilization.

The Christian ascetic doctrine has had many harmful results. It has served as an additional factor to degrade woman, because woman is generally regarded as symbolizing sex much more than man. It is ordinarily claimed by the official representatives of Christianity that this religion has raised the position of woman through its humanitarian doctrines. But it is very doubtful if the Christian religion has benefited woman more by its amiable tenets than it has injured her by its asceticism.[6]

In theory Christianity preaches the same standard of so-called sex "morality" for both sexes. As might have been expected, it has failed utterly in practice to maintain this standard. The double standard of sex freedom is perhaps as prevalent in Christian as in non-Christian countries. The inevitable result has been a vast amount of smug hypocrisy which is one of the most discreditable features of so-called "Christian" civilization.

Several writers have commented upon the failure of the Christian religion to maintain and enforce a single standard of sex morality, and upon the hypocrisy in matters of sex which has resulted therefrom. Lecky, himself a Christian devotee, admitted rather grudgingly that the double standard is about as prevalent under Christianity as under Paganism: "At the present day, although the standard of morals is far higher than in Pagan Rome, it may be questioned whether the inequality of the censure which is bestowed upon the two sexes is not as great as in the days of Paganism, and that inequality is continually the cause of the most shameful and the most pitiable injustice. . . . The fundamental truth, that the same act can never be at once venial for a man to demand, and infamous for a woman to accord, though nobly enforced by the early Christians, has not passed into the popular sentiment of Christendom."[7]

Westermarck commented more impartially upon this failure of Christianity in the following words: "It seems to me that with regard to sexual relations between unmarried men and women Christianity has done little more than establish a standard which, though accepted

---

[6] I have discussed this question in my *Poverty and Social Progress*, New York, 1916, pp. 240-241; *Personality and Conduct*, New York, 1918, pp. 161-169; and *Oriental and Occidental Culture*, New York, 1928, pp. 161-165.

[7] W. E. H. Lecky, *History of European Morals*, New York, 1877, Vol. II, pp. 316-347.

878

perhaps in theory, is hardly recognized by the feelings of the large majority of people—or at least of men—in Christian communities, and has introduced the vice of hypocrisy, which apparently was little known in sexual matters by pagan antiquity."[8] Maxwell also criticized Christianity severely for this failure and for its hypocrisy. He pointed out that the equalizing of the sexes is counteracting the Christian influence by giving woman the same freedom as man. Maxwell went on to describe the double standard of sex freedom in non-Christian countries.[9]

The Christian single standard of sex morality has failed because it is based upon an ascetic doctrine which is diametrically opposed to the facts of human nature. The hypocrisy which has resulted inevitably from this failure is one of the most baneful of Christian influences.

The above survey of the causes of the double standard of sex freedom proves conclusively that the double standard is not due to the perversity of men, as is preached by the popular oracles of morality, nor to the weakness of character of women, as is sometimes intimated; but to factors which mankind has not as yet clearly and generally recognized, nor attempted to control.

The fundamental factor in creating this double standard is the physiological dissimilarity of the sexes which makes sexual intercourse a much more serious matter for woman than for man, since it is likely to result in pregnancy. It is therefore important that she should not take this risk unless conditions are suitable for her to bear children. The double standard is accentuated by the prohibition of measures for controlling procreation and by the punishment of reproduction outside of the narrow limits prescribed by religion, conventional morality and the law.

The double standard has been strengthened by the proprietary attitude displayed by men toward women. This attitude is due in part to an innate sexual jealousy, but is largely artificial, since it has been encouraged by economic and other social factors.

Magic and religion also have given rise to discrimination against women in matters of sex freedom. As indicated above, sex taboos have weighed more heavily upon women than upon men, because sex plays a more important part in the life of woman, and is believed to be more unclean in woman.

The double standard is inevitable under present conditions. Indeed, it may even be said that under existing conditions it has its utility, because it deters many women from sharing the fate of their hapless sisters who, because they become known to have indulged in

[8] E. Westermarck, *op. cit.*, Vol. II, p. 434.

[9] J. Maxwell, *Le concept social du crime*, Paris, 1914, pp. 287-288.

so-called illicit sexual intercourse or to have borne children outside of wedlock, fall under the condemnation of the prevailing mores.

Furthermore, by permitting more or less sex freedom for men the double standard upholds for one half of mankind an ideal of freedom which will eventually become a part of the birthright of women as well. The single standard of morality consisting of sex repression and oppressive regulation for both sexes now being striven for by the professional moral reformers is a harmful and spurious standard which can never succeed in practice, and which will prolong the discrimination against women which is inherent in the existing double standard. The agitation in favor of such a single standard is at present the principal factor for increasing hypocrisy in matters of sex, of which hypocrisy there already is altogether too much.

The double standard of sex freedom is at best a necessary evil, and should be obviated if its causes can be removed. If the risk of pregnancy could not be prevented or greatly lessened, the double standard would always be needed for the protection of women. In that case, the discrimination against woman involved in the double standard would have to be endured by her as one of the burdens caused by her child bearing function, just as man has to endure the dangers and terrible sufferings of war, exploration, and other difficult tasks which fall to his lot.

There are effective and harmless contraceptive measures whose use reduces the risk of pregnancy to almost nothing. Women should be able to use these measures to prevent conception, except when conditions for child bearing are suitable. The legal, moral, and religious restrictions upon the use of contraceptive measures should be removed in order to obviate the double standard of sex freedom. These measures are also needed as birth control measures for the regulation of the increase of population.

It is more difficult to remove the proprietary attitude of men toward women. If the artificial reinforcement of male sexual jealousy can be abolished, it will be no stronger a force for the double standard than female sexual jealousy, which is as powerful an innate trait. The problem therefore is to fortify woman's status in society so that she cannot be appropriated by man.

The principal step toward this end is to secure her economic independence. Many women have become economically independent in recent years, and many more women will become independent in the near future. But there are at least three obstacles in the way of economic independence for many women. In the first place, child bearing and rearing interfere with female labor. Second, marital unions often conflict with the mobility of female labor, since it is essential that a wife live with her husband. Third, male gallantry is

880

a check upon woman's economic activities because it impels men to support women when they might be engaged in economic production.[10]

Whether or not these obstacles will always make a sufficient number of women economically dependent to maintain the double standard of sex freedom, it is impossible to foresee. Certain it is that so long as the property right in woman persists with any degree of strength, she will retain the notion that her sex is of peculiar value and must therefore be bartered for a consideration. This idea still governs many women in their dealings with the other sex, whether they be prostitutes or married women who in their marital unions have complacently sold themselves under the sanctions of religion, the law, and conventional morality.

If these obstacles prove to be sufficiently strong to maintain the economic dependence of woman and the double standard, it will be incumbent upon society through its organized agencies to counteract these obstacles. By means of measures for subsidizing women for performing the functions of child bearing and rearing the state may be able to obviate this factor which renders her dependent upon man. It may be possible to organize industry so that married women can be provided with employment wherever they may live with their husbands.

Male gallantry cannot be abolished by law. It is mainly a vestige of medieval chivalry. Male affection and sympathy for women arise out of sex and profound human traits which have no causal relation with chivalry and gallantry. If it is not encouraged by the educational system and by the prevailing mores, it will probably not be strong enough to maintain unaided the economic dependence of woman and the double standard of sex freedom.

The economic independence of women doubtless is the greatest force for a genuine single standard of sex morality for both sexes. The problem of the double standard is, therefore, not a problem of raising the morality of men or of lowering the morality of women, as is often alleged, but of placing the sexes upon an equality in their freedom to choose their mates and to procreate. Justice can be done to women only by placing them upon the same plane with men in their freedom of choice.

Prostitution signifies the sale of sexual gratification. It is a commercial and sometimes a professional activity. But it is not the sale of the prostitute, as is often asserted. Sexual intercourse in prostitution may be and often is accompanied by repugnance and antagonism

[10] I have discussed the obstacles in the way of the economic independence of women in an article entitled "The Economic Basis of Feminism," in the *Annals of the American Academy of Political and Social Science*, November 1914, pp. 18-26.

on the part of the prostitute, so that there is no giving of the prostitute's self. To assert that prostitution involves the sale of the prostitute is to identify the personality entirely with the physical aspect of sex. This notion reflects the tendency to over-emphasize the sexual nature of woman as manifested in the double standard of sex freedom.

Prostitution has been limited almost entirely to the female sex. The fundamental reason for woman's monopoly of this profession is that a female can gratify sexual passion in numerous males, whereas a male can gratify sexual passion in few females. This is due to the physiological differences between the sexes. The result is that prostitution is a more feasible commercial and professional activity for women than it is for man. Other reasons for the great preponderance of female over male prostitution will be mentioned in the course of this chapter.[11]

Prostitution is in the main a phenomenon of civilization. In the primitive and simpler societies it has been customary for the young to mate very early. Such promiscuity as has existed before or after mating has not usually been of the sort which could be characterized as prostitution, since it has not usually had the commercial and professional features mentioned above. In exceptional cases only could the sexual freedom of the unmarried, sexual hospitality to strangers, the exchange of wives, etc., be called prostitution.

Much of the promiscuity due to magical and religious notions cannot be regarded as prostitution. Among the forms of promiscuity due to magic and religion are saturnalia, practices connected with phallic worship, etc. Even sacred prostitution, though of historical interest, can hardly be regarded as having practical importance for

[11] Attempts at definition: A prostitute is:

(1) "A woman, married or not, who permits the sexual use of her body to a man who is not her husband." (The puritan definition.)

(2) The same as one, with the addition: "With gainful intentions."

(3) The same as two, with the addition: "Making her livelihood in this way."

(4) The same as three, with the addition: "indiscriminately."

(5) The same as four, with the addition: "Soliciting customers."

(6) The same as five, with the addition: "registered with the police."

(7) The same as five, with the addition: "not registered, but tolerated by the police."

(8) The same as five, with the addition: "not tolerated, but occasionally raided by the police, and brought to justice because of immoral conduct."

(9) Various combinations of all the aforesaid.

(Fritz Wittels, *The Sex Habits of American Women*, New York, 1951, p. 168.)

The *Encyclopedia Britannica*, 1942, Vol. 18, p. 596, defines prostitution as follows: "Prostitution, a word which may best be defined as promiscuous unchastity for gain."

The *Encyclopedia Americana*, 1948, Vol. 22, p. 670, under the heading *Prostitution* refers to *Vice, Regulation of,* thus implying that it is immoral.

the evolution of prostitution.[12] Prostitution may have been stimulated a little in its early stages by the avarice of priests, but it would have attained as great proportions in the long run, even had there been no sacred prostitution, for it is due mainly to other factors.[13]

Prostitution is a feature of the complex life of civilization, especially in cities. A brief discussion of the causes of prostitution will indicate the significance of this statement. This discussion will deal, on the one hand, with the causes of the demand for prostitution, and, on the other hand, with the causes for the supply of prostitutes. While these causes are in large part the same, there are a few differences which must be noted.

The first and fundamental cause of the demand for prostitution is biological in its character, namely, the powerful sexual impulse which must seek and obtain gratification. If it cannot secure this gratification in some form of marriage or in free and spontaneous promiscuity, it will secure it in commercialized promiscuity, namely, in prostitution.[14]

The second cause of the demand for prostitution is psychological in its character, namely, the play interest in sex. Those who have not the opportunity or who fail to satisfy this interest as well as the sexual impulse in marriage or in some other form of sexual relationship must seek to satisfy it among prostitutes. This psychological factor is not recognized by many writers on this subject. And yet it plays an important part not only for the youthful tyro in matters of sex, but

[12] Regnault suggested that commercial prostitution may be traced back to sacred prostitution. (F. Regnault, *L'évolution de la prostitution*, Paris, 1906.)

[13] Historical accounts of prostitution are very numerous. A few which may be mentioned are the following: P. Dufour, *Histoire de la prostitution*, Paris, 1851-1853, 6 vols.; W. W. Sanger, *The History of Prostitution*, New York, 1859; A. P. E. Rabutaux, *De la prostitution en Europe depuis l'antiquité jusqu'a la fin du XVIe siecle*, Paris, 1869; A. Semerau, *Die Kurtisanen der Renaissance*, Berlin, 1914.

[14] The Catholic Church has conducted a long experiment extending over many centuries in attempting to enforce chastity by means of the institution of sacerdotal celibacy. This attempt has failed throughout and has always been a prolific cause of corruption and immortality. Ample evidence of this failure down to the present time is furnished by Lea, the historian of the Church. (H. C. Lea, *An Historical Sketch of Sacerdotal Celibacy in the Christian Church*, 2nd edit., Boston, 1884, *passim*.)

"If the irregular though permanent connections which everywhere prevailed had been only the result of the prohibition of marriage there might perhaps have been little practical evil flowing from it, except to the church itself and to its guilty members. When the desires of man, however, are once tempted to seek through unlawful means the relief denied them by artificial rules, it is not easy to set bounds to the unbridled passions which, irritated by the fruitless effort at repression, are no longer restrained by a law which has been broken or a conscience which has lost its power." (*Op. cit.*, p. 341.)

also for the disappointed and disillusioned spouse, and for the satiated individual.

The third cause or group of causes of the demand for prostitution is economic and social in its character. In our complex civilization with its great variations in wealth it has become impossible for many men and women to mate early in life, and for some of them to mate at all. Class, caste, and other social barriers; religious prejudices; restrictive laws; and economic and other obstacles have arisen in the way of the mating of many. In contrast to the primitive societies of the past and the simpler communities of today, in which practically every member of the group is mated soon after puberty, in civilized communities there is a large class of the sexually unmated which so long as it exists will perforce create a demand for prostitution.

The biological factor is much less important as a cause for the supply of prostitutes. We need not enter here upon a discussion of the relative strength of the sexual impulse in man and in woman. All that it is necessary to know for our purpose is that it is a powerful force in both sexes. But the woman who must have sexual gratification is usually able to secure it within or outside of marriage without herself becoming a prostitute or seeking the services of a male prostitute. So that it is only in the exceptional cases of the nymphomaniacs, whose sexual cravings are excessively great, that the sexual impulse is the sole or the principal factor in driving the woman into prostitution, for these over-sexualized women can secure complete satisfaction only through the oft repeated sexual intercourse of commercialized promiscuity.

However, the sexual impulse is one of the factors in leading many of the prostitutes, probably the great majority, into prostitution. On account of the social obloquy which almost invariably falls upon women who indulge in extra-matrimonial sex relations which become known, it is one of the factors for prostitution in many cases. So that the moralists who create this obloquy are largely responsible for the prostitution of these unfortunate women.

Psychological factors also play a part in creating a supply of prostitutes, though not in exactly the same way that they create a demand for prostitution. The play interest in sex is probably a much less potent factor for leading women into prostitution than it is for leading men to make use of prostitutes. But other psychological factors play an important part in the etiology of the prostitute. Among these are vanity, which requires for its satisfaction fine raiment and the adulation of men; and the love of excitement and adventure, which often has little opportunity for gratification in the monotony of everyday life.

The economic factors are the most important in creating a supply

884

of prostitutes, though it is difficult to estimate the relative influence of the different factors for prostitution. I have already pointed out that, on account of the economic difficulties in the way of marriage, there is a large unmated group, which furnishes a considerable part of the material for prostitution. But the immediate economic factors are in the form of the pressure which arises from the smallness of the income of the father, husband, or other person upon whom the woman is dependent, or her own meager wages.

Under such conditions the temptation may become great for the woman to supplement her meager earnings or to supplant them entirely with the rewards of prostitution. It is doubtful if there are many cases where the woman has been actually forced into prostitution by economic factors in the sense that she would have starved if she had not become a prostitute. But the temptation which arises as a result of the economic pressure described above, along with the other factors which have been mentioned, has drawn many women into prostitution.

There are several other facts to be considered with regard to the etiology of prostitutes. The above factors will act most effectively upon persons who are weak in mind and character. Weakness of character involves a low degree of resistance to the temptations named above. Feebleness of mind lessens the degree of foresight as to the ultimate consequences of a life of prostitution. It is, therefore, not surprising that among the groups of prostitutes which have been carefully examined there has been found almost invariably a relatively high percentage of feebleminded women.[15]

At the same time it must be remembered that many of the prostitutes are, to say the least, not below the average in character and intelligence, and have become prostitutes either on account of economic misfortune or because they possess traits which under other social conditions would have great value and would contribute to their success, but which under present conditions lead them into prostitution.[16] In this group are some if not many women who act

[15] It must, however, be borne in mind that the feebleminded prostitutes are the most likely to be segregated and put under restraint in such a fashion as to make possible a mental examination. It must also be remembered that many prostitutes have degenerated as a result of dissipation. Some writers on this subject have failed to make proper allowance for these facts and have, consequently, made exaggerated estimates of the extent of feeblemindedness among prostitutes. There is little reason to believe that more than a small absolute percentage of the total number of prostitutes are feebleminded.

[16] For an extended discussion of the good traits of prostitutes, see A. J. B. Parent-Duchatelet, *De la prostitution dans la ville de Paris*, Paris, 1857, Vol. I, Chap. 2.

Lecky characterizes certain types of prostitutes as follows: "The victims of

with courage and independence in response to their natural impulses, but who then find that they cannot afford to do so in society as it is now organized.

The more or less prevalent notion that sex in woman has a pecuniary value and is therefore to be bartered has its influence upon prostitution. This influence is not restricted to prostitution, for it encourages the sale of women in marriage. The marriage price may not be paid in as obvious a manner as in simpler communities in which marriage by purchase prevailed. But many marriages in modern civilized communities still retain some of the character of a commercial transaction, though the attempt is usually made to conceal the commercial features by means of euphemistic subterfuges. In prostitution the barter is frank and open, and no attempt at concealment is usually made between the parties to the transaction. The sale of women attains its most obvious form in the white slave traffic.

I have not the space to describe in detail the evolution of this notion of the pecuniary value of sex in women. Various factors have played a part in its development at one time or another, such as exogamy in primitive communities, the patriarchate, the economic value of female labor, the economic value of the offspring of the bartered woman, etc. There is reason to believe that there will continue to be more or less bartering of women both within and outside of marriage so long as women are economically dependent.

If women become economically independent and there is freedom of mating for both sexes, the bartering of women or of sex in women will disappear almost entirely. Sex relations will then become matters of choice based upon personal inclinations undisturbed by any extraneous considerations. This condition will furnish the best possible basis for the development of the play function of sex both for men and for women.

It is alleged by many vice reformers and other persons that much prostitution is due to an artificial stimulus given to it by vice enterprisers who are exploiting prostitutes for their own benefit. There is a measure of truth in this assertion. But it is an exaggeration to assert that a considerable part of prostitution is due to such exploitation. The principal causes for the demand for prostitution and for the supply of prostitutes have been stated above, and the exploiter can aggravate these causes only to a comparatively slight extent.

seduction are often led aside quite as much by the ardor of their affections, and by the vivacity of their intelligence, as by any vicious propensities. Even in the lowest grades, the most dispassionate observers have detected remains of higher feelings, which, in a different moral atmosphere, and under different moral husbandry, would have undoubtedly been developed." (W. E. H. Lecky, *History of European Morals*, New York, 1877, Vol. II, pp. 285-286.)

Many injurious acts have been committed by vice reformers owing to mistaken emphasis upon the influence of the vice enterpriser. Exploitation of prostitution would disappear immediately if the fundamental causes of prostitution were removed, so that it is a wasteful and harmful expenditure of energy to concentrate attention upon suppressing the exploiter while ignoring these fundamental causes.

The above description, brief though it has been, is sufficient to indicate that prostitution is inevitable under present conditions,[17] while there may always be an irreducible minimum of prostitution which cannot be removed under any conditions. Furthermore, this description suggests that there is a good deal of justification for prostitution under existing conditions.

---

[17] "In the presence of a majority still thinking quite differently it is absurd to preach total sexual abstinence to all unmarried young men, as certain moralists do (Tolstoi, for example). Though there are men who abstain without injury to their health, these moralists forget that the satisfaction of the sexual desires is one of the most important needs of the majority of men (the life of our day certainly increases these desires), and that present social conditions are the cause of men's considering woman their inferior. Dr. Blaschko, in his work *Die Prostitution im XIX Jahrhundert*, rightly says: 'The sexual requirement in the case of mankind as of all other beings is an entirely natural one. To be sure, it is not so strong and compelling as the necessity of food and drink; it can be suppressed in the case of any one for a time, and with many permanently, without injury to the health. But what is true of this or that person does not hold for the mass of mankind, for whom sexual intercourse is doubtless a necessity.' " (W. Bonger, *Criminality and Economic Conditions*, Boston, 1916, p. 323.)

Chapter LI

The Function of Prostitution

THE sexual organs perform their functions in one way or another. The powerful instincts and feelings based upon their processes must find expression in some fashion. The most natural manner of attaining these ends is through sexual intercourse. However, the urgent physiological sexual processes may take place apart from sexual intercourse.

The sexual glands can relieve themselves of their secretions from time to time, even though they do not receive the normal sexual stimulus. Hence it is possible that no direct physiological injury is caused by chastity. There is, however, ample evidence that total sexual abstinence is injurious psychologically and culturally, and indirectly causes a vast amount of physiological injury as well. The pathological results from sex repression have already been described in Chapter XLIX.

When the sexual instincts and feelings do not attain their normal expression in sex relations, they give rise in many cases to psychiatric conditions. This may happen whether the abstinence is by compulsion or by choice, but it is much more likely to happen when the abstinence is by compulsion. In the gravest cases some form of insanity arises. In the graver cases a neurotic condition results, as, for example, hysteria. In the milder cases mental complexes arise from the repression of the sexual instincts and feelings which give the victim of the sex repression more or less mental discomfort.

In fact, total sexual abstinence could not exist without giving rise to at least a few of these complexes. The literature of abnormal psychology, psychiatry, sex psychology, and psychoanalysis contains numerous data concerning the psychiatric phenomena resulting from sex repression. Furthermore, they are almost universal facts of human experience, for nearly every one has tested at some time or other the effects of sexual abstinence.[1]

[1] The moral prejudices and ignorance of psychiatry of most of the medical

888

The sex relation has great cultural value. This fact has already been amply demonstrated in the description of the play function of sex in Chapter XLVIII. Sex experience is an essential and important element in the development of personality. There can be no well rounded personality without this experience. Inasmuch as the development of personality is the highest aim of civilization, the Christian ideal of virginity is a barbarous ideal. It should be replaced by the civilized ideal of the sexually mature man or woman who develops to the full the play function of sex, and who is permitted by circumstances to perform the reproductive function as well.

The significance of the utility of and the need for the sex relation in the life of mankind with respect to prostitution is obvious. So long as many individuals are unmated prostitution furnishes a means of sexual gratification for some of these persons, though it is unsatisfactory in some ways. Prostitution has a limited utility under the existing disorganized state of sex relations.

In a few cases prostitution prevents rape on the part of individuals to whom it affords relief from their otherwise uncontrollable sexual passion. It prevents some of the physiological and psychological injury arising from the obstruction of the sexual impulse. It affords at least a small scope for the development of the play interest in sex for many individuals. It furnishes a means of sexual relief always ready at hand without the emotional stress often involved in love and marriage. As has been pointed out by Ellis, it adds something to the variety and gaiety of life which has its value for civilization.[2]

profession were revealed at the 68th annual session of the House of Delegates of the American Medical Association in New York City, June 4-8, 1917, which adopted the following resolution: "That sexual continence is compatible with health and is the best prevention of venereal infections." (*Proceedings*, pp. 68-69.)

[2] "There is, however, another argument in support of prostitution which scarcely receives the emphasis it deserves. I refer to its influence in adding an element, in some form or another necessary, of gayety and variety to the ordered complexity of modern life, a relief from the monotony of its mechanical routine, a distraction from its dull and respectable monotony. This is distinct from the more specific function of prostitution as an outlet for superfluous sexual energy, and may even affect those who have little or no commerce with prostitutes. This element may be said to constitute the civilizational value of prostitution." (Havelock Ellis, *Sex in Relation to Society*, Philadelphia, 1911, pp. 287-288.)

A woman writer has expressed a similar idea in the following words: "No woman can have failed to feel astonishment at the attractive force the prostitute may, and often does, exercise on cultured men of really fine character. There is some deeper cause here than mere sexual necessity. But if we accept, as we must, the existence of these imperatively driving, though usually restrained impulses, it will be readily seen that prostitution provides a channel in which this surplus of wild energy may be expended. It lightens the burden of the customary restraints. There are many men, I believe, who find it a relief just to talk with a prostitute— a woman with whom they have no need to be on guard. The prostitute fulfils that

It has also been asserted by some writers that prostitution furnishes valuable protection to monogamous marriage and to the family. The question of the influence of prostitution upon marriage and the family constitutes a complicated problem which I shall discuss presently, after the ills arising out of prostitution have been described.

Prostitution involves hardships for many of the prostitutes. Some of them, owing to their beauty or adroitness, earn more and live more comfortably than most of their so-called virtuous sisters. But the earnings of the great majority of prostitutes are comparatively small. Their earning capacity does not last very long on the average, because disease, dissipation, premature old age, etc., usually destroy the usefulness of a prostitute after a few years of professional activity.

A very small percentage of the prostitutes have been forced into prostitution by the white slave traders. The great majority of them have entered it by choice, or have drifted into it through force of circumstances. All of them suffer from the weight of moral and social condemnation and disapproval. Many of them are penniless when they reach the end of their period of usefulness as prostitutes, and have been incapacitated by their previous life for other kinds of activity. However, some of them are able to earn a comfortable living as procuresses and as employers of prostitutes, and a certain number are provided for in marriage.

The hardships of prostitutes are greatly accentuated at present by unwise attempts to suppress and stamp out prostitution entirely. Legislation which makes prostitution criminal and in other ways attempts to repress the prostitutes is sure to have this effect. The harassing and hounding which they receive from the police and the courts drive them into the arms of pimps, procurers, and other exploiters of prostitutes who stand ready to fleece them in every possible way.

This hounding also forces them into association with criminals and encourages them to become the consorts and accomplices of thieves, murderers, etc. From this stage it is an easy step for them to become thieves, receivers of stolen goods, etc., themselves. These repressive measures increase greatly the degradation of the prostitute and drive her into still lower depths of dissipation and vice.

The regulation of prostitution, even when it is not governed by the object of suppressing prostitution immediately or ever, is also in danger of increasing the hardships of the prostitutes. This danger

need that may arise in even the most civilized man for something primitive and strong: a need, as has been said by a male writer, better than I can express it, 'for a woman in herself, not woman with the thousand and one tricks and whimsies of wives, mothers and daughters.'" (Catherine Hartley Gallichan, *The Truth About Woman*, London, 1913, pp. 372-373.)

can be avoided in large part if not entirely if the regulating is done wisely. Every regulation which is enforced should be adopted only after a broad survey of the interests both of society at large and of the prostitutes. Thus only can justice be done to the prostitutes.

Prostitution encourages a low grade of play interest in sex. In fact, so far as the prostitutes themselves are concerned, the constant repetition of sexual intercourse and the indiscriminate promiscuity involved tend to stamp out the play interest entirely, so that the sexually hardened prostitute may have no more of it than the sexually desiccated old spinster and virgin.

This is one of the most deplorable effects of prostitution. It destroys to a large extent the play function of sex for the prostitutes, and tends to develop sexual frigidity in them. It may indeed be true, as is believed by some of the students of prostitution, that many of them are sexually frigid before they become prostitutes, and that their sexual frigidity has encouraged them to enter prostitution because their lack of passion leads them to look upon sexual intercourse as an inconsequential matter not to be esteemed highly. But whether their frigidity exists before they become prostitutes or develops as a result of prostitution, their play interest in sex is rarely ever stimulated by their commercialized promiscuity.

So far as their customers are concerned, also, prostitution tends to develop a low grade of play interest in sex. This is not necessarily because it is promiscuous, for a high degree of play interest may exist even in promiscuity so long as it is free and spontaneous. But in commercialized promiscuity there is little or no response from the woman. Furthermore, the sexual intercourse is not usually accompanied with and followed by a period of association long enough to develop a close acquaintance with personal traits, though intimacy may develop rapidly while it lasts on account of the absence of conventional restraints.

The value of prostitution for the customer from the point of view of the play function of sex depends, therefore, upon whether or not it is the best he can do under the circumstances. For many men no other sex relation is available, so that the commercialized form is better than none at all. If a man is able to secure an uncommercialized relation, it is almost invariably superior to the commercialized form.

The most harmful result from prostitution at present is its effect in spreading the venereal diseases, namely, gonorrhoea and syphilis. This is due to the promiscuity involved and has nothing to do with the moral aspect of prostitution. Furthermore, this effect is accentuated in the commercialized promiscuity of prostitution for the prostitutes themselves. Their promiscuity is concentrated in a comparatively small group of women who become the depositories, so to speak, of

891

the germs of these diseases and from whom these germs are communicated to their numerous male customers.

These men in turn pass these germs on to many women who are not prostitutes and thus the diseases become widely disseminated in society at large. Uncommercialized promiscuity does not have as dire results because it is more widely diffused in society at large and is not so highly concentrated among the women who indulge in it. These women probably exercise more care, so that they do not become the depositories of these germs to the same extent as prostitutes. It is unnecessary to dwell upon the vast amount of suffering and social injury caused by the venereal diseases. The problem of their prevention is a sanitary and prophylactic problem, and not a moral problem as is often asserted.

It is alleged that prostitution tends to check mating in marriage. For this as well as for other reasons, it is said to endanger monogamy and the family. It is also said to promote the double standard of sex morality. As has been noted above, prostitution is, on the contrary, alleged by some writers to be a valuable protection for monogamous marriage and the family. It is impossible to solve this problem without a preliminary discussion of the evolutionary relation between prostitution and marriage.

It is suggested by some writers that prostitution and marriage, or at least monogamic marriage, have a common origin or that prostitution resulted from monogamic marriage.[3] In a general sense it is true that prostitution and marriage have a common origin, inasmuch as both of them are due to the sexual impulse. Speaking more strictly, they cannot be said to have a common origin.

Marriage, by which I mean mating of considerable duration, has existed for a long time. It is found among some of the animal species other than man, and is found among the most primitive men. Prostitution, on the contrary, does not exist among animals, and seems to be a comparatively late development in human social evolution, so far as we can judge from anthropological and historical evidence. So that prostitution must be due to comparatively recent social conditions and factors which did not play a part in giving rise to marriage.

Monogamic marriage also is very ancient, for it is found among some animals and among primitive men. So that monogamy in gen-

[3] For example, Mrs. Gallichan suggests that prostitution may have resulted from monogamic marriage: "Every attempt hitherto to grapple with prostitution has been a failure. Women have to remember that it has existed as an institution in nearly all historic times and among nearly all races of men. It is as old as monogamic marriage, and may be the result of that form of sexual relationship, and not, as some have held, a survival of primitive sexual licence." (*The Truth About Woman,* p. 362.)

eral can scarcely be regarded as the origin of prostitution, for if that were the case prostitution would have originated much earlier than it did. It is possible, however, that prostitution originated from and is encouraged by a certain form or certain forms of monogamy. We must, therefore, consider what forms of monogamy are accompanied by prostitution in order to determine whether or not there is a causal relation.

I have already noted the fact that the pecuniary valuation of sex in women influences not only prostitution but also modern marriage.[4] This fact suggests a close relation between the two and indicates that to this extent at least they have a common origin. At the same time other factors have played a part in the origin of both of these institutions, as, for example, the influence of religion in giving rise to prostitution.

Monogamy as a sacred dogma makes the dissolution of marriage by divorce difficult, and thus creates a potent force for prostitution. Many of the married men who indulge in prostitution would not do so if they were happily married, and free divorce would lessen the number of unsuccessful matings and would increase the number of happy unions. To the religious obstacles must be added the serious economic obstacles already mentioned in the way of spontaneous early matings which would furnish a satisfactory sex life for all.

Thus we see that, while prostitution is not a necessary accompaniment of marriage and of monogamy, it is a result from, or, to say the least, an inevitable concomitant of the existing form of marriage. This fact makes the discussion of the influence of prostitution upon marriage of somewhat academic importance. However, it may be worth while to discuss whether, as is alleged by some persons, prostitution is a protection to monogamy and the family, or, as is alleged by others, prostitution is dangerous to those institutions.

It is asserted by the upholders of the first theory that prostitution prevents a certain amount of seduction and rape which would take place if an outlet for male passions was not furnished by prostitutes. Thus the daughters, wives, and prospective wives of the monogamously married males are saved to that extent from the menace of violation, and monogamy and the family are protected.[5]

---

[4] Mrs. Gallichan characterizes marriage as follows: "Marriage is itself in many cases a legalized form of prostitution. From the standpoint of morals, the woman who sells herself in marriage is on the same level as the one who sells herself for a night, the only difference is in the price paid and the duration of the contract. Nay, it is probably fair to say that at the lowest such sale-marriage results in the greater evil, for the prostitute does not bear children. If she has a child it has, as a rule, been born first; such is our morality that motherhood often drives her on to the streets." (*The Truth About Woman*, p. 342.)

[5] This appears to be the meaning of Lecky in the following melodramatic pas-

It is sometimes added in support of this theory that prostitution also affords an outlet for the passions of married men when it is desirable that their wives shall not be compelled to experience sexual intercourse, as, for example, toward the end of pregnancy. According to this theory, therefore, in the economy of the sexual division of labor the prostitutes constitute a relatively small group of women who possess the specialized professional activity of drafting off male sexual energy at times when this energy endangers monogamously married females.

It is impossible to measure the extent to which prostitution serves as a preventive of rape and seduction. To the extent that it performs

sage, which has often been quoted:

"The family is the center and the archetype of the State, and the happiness and goodness of society are always in a very great degree dependent upon the purity of domestic life. The essentially exclusive nature of marital affection, and the natural desire of every man to be certain of the paternity of the child he supports, render the incursions of irregular passions within the domestic circle a cause of extreme suffering. Yet it would appear as if the excessive force of these passions would render such incursions both frequent and inevitable.

"Under these circumstances, there has arisen in society a figure which is certainly the most mournful, and in some respects the most awful, upon which the eye of the moralist can dwell. That unhappy being whose very name is a shame to speak; who counterfeits with a cold heart the transports of affection, and submits herself as the passive instrument of lust; who is scorned and insulted as the vilest of her sex, and doomed, for the most part, to disease and abject wretchedness and an early death, appears in every age as the perpetual symbol of the degradation and the sinfulness of man. Herself the supreme type of vice, she is ultimately the most efficient guardian of virtue. But for her, the unchallenged purity of countless happy homes would be polluted, and not a few who, in the pride of their untempted chastity, think of her with an indignant shudder, would have known the agony of remorse and despair. On that one degraded and ignoble form are concentrated the passions that might have filled the world with shame. She remains, while creeds and civilizations rise and fall, the eternal priestess of humanity, blasted for the sins of the people." (W. E. H. Lecky, *History of European Morals*, New York, 1877, Vol. II, pp. 282-283.)

Mrs. Gallichan expresses a similar idea, but with a broader and more liberal outlook than Lecky she recognizes that the present utility of prostitution is largely due to the defects of the existing form of marriage:

"Our marriage system is buttressed with prostitution, which thus makes our moral attitude one of intolerable deception, and our efforts at reform not only ineffective, but absurd. Without the assistance of the prostitution of one class of women and the enforced celibacy of another class our marriage in its present form could not stand. It is no use shirking it; if marriage cannot be made more moral—and by this I mean more able to meet the sex needs of all men and all women—then we must accept prostitution. No sentimentalism can save us; we must give our consent to this sacrifice of women as necessary to the welfare and stability of society." (*The Truth About Woman*, p. 341.)

"The time is not far distant when the mothers of the community, the sheltered wives of respectable homes, must come to understand that their own position of moral safety is maintained at the expense of a traffic whose very name they will not mention." (*Op. cit.*, p. 361.)

894

this service it may serve as a protection of monogamy and the family. But it performs this service for women in general, and not merely, as seems to be implied in the moralistic and grandiloquent phrases of Lecky, for the sacred ark of the monogamous family of today. Furthermore, the dangers of rape and seduction are due in large part to the existing type of marriage, so that prostitution is alleged to protect marriage from the dangers which marriage itself creates in the main.

On the other hand, it is alleged that prostitution does injury to monogamy by acting as a check upon mating. It is impossible to ascertain the number of instances in which men are turned away from mating by prostitution. It is probable that the number is small, for there are few men who would not prefer a satisfactory sexual mating to the commercialized promiscuity of prostitution.

In any case, this argument is putting the cart before the horse. Prostitution is due in large part to the failure of marriage, so that this failure could not be due to any great extent to prostitution. Furthermore, prostitution leads to a certain amount of mating, either within or outside of marriage.[6]

It is also alleged that prostitution gives rise to and perpetuates the double standard of sex morality, and thus menaces monogamy and the family. I have described the causes of the double standard in the preceding chapter. In the light of that discussion this argument is manifestly absurd. Prostitution and the double standard are due in the main to common causes, so that the only way to abolish either or both of them is to remove these common causes.

It is alleged, in the third place, that prostitution menaces monogamy and the family by disseminating venereal diseases. Even though this is true, prostitution menaces in this respect not merely the sacred ark of the monogamous family, but all women and all men as well. So that this objection to prostitution should be used, not in behalf of monogamy in particular, but in behalf of society as a whole. However valuable and permanent the monogamous family may be, it is not justifiable to subordinate everything else to it.

Inasmuch as prostitution is a result of, or, to say the least, an inevitable correlative or concomitant of, the existing type of marriage, it is a waste of time to discuss whether or not the effect of prostitution upon marriage and the family be beneficial or harmful. The question of practical importance is the reform of marriage which will obviate prostitution entirely or in large part.

Such a reform will come about only when marriage affords an opportunity for a normal sex life for practically every adult member of society. Unless marriage can be reformed in this fashion, prostitu-

6 See, for example, W. Acton, *Prostitution*, London, 1870, pp. 39-49.

tion will persist as a remedy for the defects of marriage. In that case it will perforce become respectable, as has been pointed out by the French sociologist, Gabriel Tarde.[7]

And yet it is doubtful if prostitution can ever be permanently satisfactory as a solution of the sex problem. While the *hetairae* in ancient Greece and elsewhere played an important and valuable role, and while prostitution is inevitable in the existing civilization, commercialized sex relations can never adequately meet the requirements of both the play and the reproductive functions, and will always conflict in a measure with the feelings and instincts connected with those functions of sex.

Deplorable indeed is the present situation in the organization of the sex relations of mankind. On the one hand is the vast mass of men and women who are not sexually mated or who are unsatisfactorily mated, and who, therefore, are unable to live a normal sex life. This is the greatest defect in the present situation, for it does injury to the largest number of persons. And yet it is usually overlooked in the discussion of this subject. On the other hand is the relatively small group of women who are, in a sense, sacrificed to meet these sexual needs, and whose sacrifice constitutes the lesser of the two defects in the present situation. Could there be two better reasons for re-organizing marriage and the other institutions connected with sex?

At the same time, it is erroneous and misleading to call prostitution "the social evil," as is the custom of conventional vice reformers. Prostitution is primarily one of the sexual ills. It is no more of a

[7] G. Tarde, "La morale sexuelle," in the *Archives d'anthropologie criminelle*, Vol. XXII, January 1907, pp. 39-40.

Isaacson proposed a scheme which, he thinks, will, among other things, prevent prostitution by obviating the need for it. (E. Isaacson, *The Malthusian Limit*, London, 1912.) He proposed to organize sex relations by means of a two-class system. The first will be a relatively small "fecund" class made up of the men and women who are physically best fitted to procreate and whose chief function will be to reproduce the race. The second will be a relatively large "surplus" class made up of the remainder of society who will refrain from procreating but will be free to mate as they choose, the women being economically independent and upon the same status as the men of the same class. Thus a sex life will be furnished for practically every person in society and the sexual need for prostitution will be obviated. (Compare the three classes of population discussed by Georg Hansen, *Die drei Bevolkerungsstufen*, Munich, 1889.)

Isaacson's scheme will, in my opinion, never be feasible because the desire for parenthood is too widespread to make it possible or desirable to limit the right to have children to a small class. But he is entirely justified in emphasizing in this connection the importance of the pressure of population, and in asserting that it is the fear of reproduction under conditions which make it undesirable which determines to a large extent the existing standard of sex morality. (For a discussion of the problems of population see my *Poverty and Social Progress*, New York, 1916, especially Chaps. XII and XIII; and *Farewell to Poverty*, New York, 1935, Chap. XXIX.)

social evil than many other evils in society, and is not so great a social evil as some of them, such as poverty, war, crime, and intemperance. The emphasis placed upon prostitution as *the* social evil by vice crusaders often is in reality an attempt to draw a red herring across the pathway of the reform and abolition of some of the greater of the social shortcomings.

The sexual impulse is one of the most useful factors in the life of mankind. No manifestation of this impulse *per se* can be regarded as unhealthy, abnormal, or vicious. It is only when the expression of the sexual impulse is misguided, is carried to an excess, or is misused in some way, that it can be regarded as vicious.

The two fundamental misfortunes arising out of prostitution have been described. Prostitution violates the play function of sex, and disseminates venereal diseases. Other injuries are alleged on religious and pseudo-moral grounds which have no basis in fact. Of the two genuine ills of prostitution, the second can be obviated in large part if not entirely by means of prophylactic measures. The first will persist as an inevitable accompaniment of prostitution.

The dissemination of disease is the principal misfortune arising out of prostitution at present. But the violation of the play function is its permanent ill, and, therefore, the most serious in the long run. The pecuniary valuation of sex inherent in prostitution diminishes somewhat the spontaneity of the sex relation which is essential for the highest development of the play function.

On account of these defects of prostitution it would be desirable if feasible to abolish it entirely. This has been attempted many times in the past. Christianity, owing to its hostility to sex, has encouraged many of these attempts. Some of them have been due to the desire to prevent disease, to safeguard marriage and the family, etc.

These attempts to abolish prostitution have failed.[8] This is

---

[8] "From the time when Christianity gained full political power, prostitution has again and again been prohibited, under the severest penalties, but always in vain. The mightiest emperors—Theodosius, Valentinian, Justinian, Karl the Great, St. Louis, Frederick Barbarossa—all had occasion to discover that might was here in vain, that they could not always obey their own moral ordinances, still less coerce their subjects into doing so, and that even so far as, on the surface, they were successful they produced results more pernicious than the evils they sought to suppress. The best known and one of the most vigorous of these attempts was that of the Empress Maria Theresa in Vienna; but all the cruelty and injustice of that energetic effort, and all the stringent, ridiculous, and brutal regulations it involved —its prohibition of short dresses, its inspection of billiard-rooms, its handcuffing of waitresses, its whippings and its tortures—proved useless, and were soon quietly dropped. No more fortunate were more recent municipal attempts in England and America (Portsmouth, Pittsburgh, New York, etc.) to suppress prostitution offhand; for the most part they collapsed even in a few days." (H. Ellis, *The Task of Social Hygiene*, London, 1912, pp. 285-286.)

proved, in the first place, by the fact that prostitution is widespread today. Indeed, owing mainly to the rapid development of cities in modern times, it may be more widespread than ever before.[9]

In any case prostitution is inevitable so long as the sexual impulse does not have adequate opportunity for expression in other ways. Attempts at suppressing it absolutely must be hopeless of success, and are likely to cause much injury. The wise measures against prostitution, therefore, are those that are directed toward providing greater opportunities for the better types of sexual expression. By these measures prostitution can be greatly lessened, though it is doubtful if it can ever be abolished entirely.

The harmful results from the stupid policy of attempting complete suppression of prostitution under present conditions have been illustrated over and over again in the United States. Every time that a segregated district has been closed by the police, or any other sort of drastic suppression has been attempted, the prostitutes have been scattered among the tenement houses and in the residential districts in general, and have hidden themselves in massage parlors, manicure parlors, and in many other kinds of resorts. Thus clandestine prostitution has been encouraged, and the harmful influence of prostitution has been made more insidious if not more widespread. It is impossible to measure the extent of clandestine prostitution. Owing to its insidious nature it is more harmful than open prostitution, and more difficult to regulate.

The injunction and abatement laws which have been enacted in several states illustrate the extreme to which the vice reformers go in their attempts to stamp out prostitution, and the injustice which results from extreme measures. Such a law usually ordains that a house cannot be used for any purpose whatsoever for one year after it has been proved that it has been used for purposes of prostitution. If prostitution is inevitable at present, and therefore it is better to tolerate it than to try to suppress it entirely, it is also inevitable that houses should be used for this purpose. It is, therefore, inconsistent, as well as unjust, to penalize the owners of these houses for permitting something that is inevitable. The most that can be fairly required of these owners is that they shall not tolerate any criminal practices, such as rape or white slavery, in connection with prostitution in their houses.

The same point may be illustrated with respect to the laws

9 According to the Federal Census there were in 1940 in the rural communities 36.4% single males 15 years of age and over, and in the urban communities 32.6% single males of the same age period. In the rural communities there were 24.3% single females 15 years of age and over, and in the urban communities 27.4% single females of the same age period. (*Statistical Abstract of the United States,* 1950, p. 21.)

898

against procuration. Any man or woman who makes a girl or woman a prostitute by force or by fraud and deception should be punished. The procurers who use these criminal methods should be relentlessly pursued and prosecuted, for few crimes could be worse than forcing a woman involuntarily into prostitution. To this extent the laws and the international agreements against the white slave traffic are necessary and desirable.

On the other hand, so long as prostitution is inevitable, it is inevitable that there are madames of houses of prostitution, go-betweens, and other promoters and exploiters of prostitution. As a profession for pecuniary profit, prostitution must have its commercial aspect. It is inconsistent to penalize those who traffic in prostitution so long as they indulge in no criminal practices. It is a misuse of words to call it the white slave traffic, unless force and deception are used, because no prostitute is a white slave unless she has been forced into and is held in this profession by coercion.

In the United States the attempt has often been made to prohibit all forms of trafficking in prostitution, the non-criminal as well as the criminal.[10] This is impossible since prostitution is in itself a commercial activity and as such requires its enterprisers, organizers, promoters, and exploiters like every other form of commercial activity.

The worst example of unwise legislation against procuration is the Federal White Slave Traffic Act enacted in 1910. This vicious law penalizes not only persons trafficking in prostitution but many others who have nothing whatsoever to do with this traffic, but who, in their private lives, have committed acts which are alleged to be immoral by prejudiced and narrow-minded legislators.[11]

As was to be expected when it was enacted, this law has given rise to an enormous amount of blackmail, and has caused injury, suffering, and gross injustice to many innocent persons. Its enactment was due largely to sensational and grossly exaggerated reports about the white slave traffic which circulated in the popular press and literature of the day, and which were well calculated to lead to hysterical and ill-advised legislation.

The injunction and abatement laws and the laws against procuration indicate that many of the laws against prostitution are neither

[10] For example, the New York law reads in part as follows: "Whosoever shall keep or maintain a house of ill-fame or assignation of any description or a place for the encouragement or practice by persons of lewdness, fornication, unlawful sexual intercourse or for any other indecent or disorderly act or obscene purpose therein or any place of public resort at which the decency, peace or comfort of a neighborhood is disturbed shall be guilty of a misdemeanor." (*New York State Penal Code*, 1944, Section 1146.)

[11] *U.S. Code Annotated*, Title 18, Crimes and Criminal Procedure, 1951, Chapter 117, paragraphs 2421-2424.

scientific nor practical, because they cannot possibly attain the object toward which they are directed, namely, the abolition of prostitution. This social ill can be prevented only to the extent that the normal sex life is posssible for mankind. In spite of this fact, the numerous religionists, professional moralists, sentimentalists, philanthropists, reformers, prigs, prudes, etc., who are trying to suppress prostitution, not only are not trying to provide the normal sexual life for all, but many of them are trying to deprive as many persons as possible of this life.

Since the abolition of prostitution is impossible at present, the practical question is as to whether or not regulation is possible, and what kind of regulation is desirable. The primary cause of prostitution is the sexual impulse, which is one of the most powerful and most useful dynamic forces in human nature. Prostitution must be regulated with the utmost caution in order not to diminish the utility of sex in the life of mankind. So long as prostitution persists society must take cognizance of it and decide how to deal with it. The difference of opinion with respect to this question ranges all the way from the opinions of those who think that prostitution should not be regulated at all to the opinions of those who think that it should be strictly regulated. The discussion of this subject involves the study of the administration of police measures, the treatment of the procurer and the pimp, and various sanitary measures.

Prostitution has been regulated by the law at many times and places. In recent years it has been customary to regulate it in most of the European countries. The principal objects of such regulation have been to rob prostitution of needless publicity, to limit its scope as far as is feasible, to lessen as far as possible its influence as a factor for disease, and to aid in the detection of criminals.

Among the principal measures used to attain these ends have been the prohibition of soliciting in the streets and other public places, the segregation of houses of prostitution, the registration of the prostitutes, the periodical medical examination of the prostitutes, and the establishment of a special morals police for the supervision of prostitution and for the enforcement of these regulations.[12]

[12] The legal and police regulation of prostitution has been described by many writers, among whom may be mentioned the following: A. J. B. Parent-Duchatelet, *De la prostitution dans la ville de Paris*, 1857, 2 vols.; W. W. Sanger, *The History of Prostitution*, New York, 1859; W. Acton, *Prostitution Considered in Its Moral, Social and Sanitary Aspects*, London, 1907; S. Amos, *A Comparative Survey of Laws in Force for the Prohibition, Regulation, and Licensing of Vice in England and Other Countries*, London, 1877; Y. Guyot, *Prostitution under the Regulation System*, London, 1884; F. Regnault, *L'evolution de la prostitution*, Paris, 1906. Also the following articles in the *Archives d'anthropologie criminelle*: V. Augagneur, La prostitution des filles mineures," Vol. III, 1888, pp. 209-28; Wahl, "Peut-on

Such regulation has encountered violent opposition from various sources. Many persons, especially in the United States and in Great Britain, have denounced the official recognition of prostitution by the state. They have advocated the ostrich-like attitude of ignoring its existence, either because they indulge vain hopes of being able to exterminate it entirely, or because this is the easiest policy.

This is the point of view ordinarily assumed by the religionist and the professional moralist. Some individuals, especially in England, have opposed regulation from the individualistic point of view, on the ground that it is an unjustifiable invasion of the rights of the prostitutes and of any other persons concerned. Other individuals have opposed it on the ground that regulatory measures have failed in practice.

In view of what has been said it is obvious that the first point of view is wholly untenable. Inasmuch as it is hopeless to exterminate prostitution, it is harmful to ignore its existence and to refuse to face the problems it presents. The second point of view has some justification, since prostitutes and others concerned have often been mistreated by regulatory measures. On the other hand, certain social interests are involved which must be safeguarded. It is also true that regulatory measures have often failed in practice, either because they were not feasible measures or because they have not been administered efficiently. But this is not conclusive proof against regulation, so that the third point of view cannot be justified.

It is impossible to describe here all of the regulatory measures which may be used. But the principles upon which they should be based can be stated briefly. To began with, prostitution as such should not be stigmatized as criminal for reasons which have already been adequately stated. The regulation of prostitution should have the same status as the regulation of many other professions in the behalf of the public welfare, such as medicine and pharmacy.

The publicity of prostitution should be restricted by law as much as is feasible. The principal reason for this restriction is the protection of the young. It is needless and often harmful for the sexually immature to come in contact with this profession. It is desirable also in order to avoid unnecessary stimulation of the sexual impulse in the sexually mature as well. This impulse is usually strong enough to manifest itself so far as is useful without any artificial stimulation.

supprimer la prostitution?" Vol. XIX, 1904, pp. 475-83; J. J. Matignon, "La prostitution au Japon, le quartier du 'Yoshiwara' de Tokio," Vol. XXI, 1906, pp. 697-715; E. Pachot, "Le regime actuel des moeurs en France, sa reforme," Vol. XXIII, 1908, pp. 697-721.

Flexner has given a description of regulation in Europe which is much prejudiced against regulation. (A. Flexner, *Prostitution in Europe*, New York, 1914.)

Inasmuch as sex relations are essentially private and intimate in their nature, they should not be degraded by giving them needless publicity. By this I do not mean a prudish concealment of the facts of sex, but a judicious restraint upon publicizing the activities of a profession whose function is the gratifying of sexual passions.

Such public advertising and exploitation of sex shocks the feelings and sentiments of many persons. It is liable to hinder the efflorescence of the play function of sex in its more complex forms. In this respect prostitution is no more indecent than weddings and conventional marriage in general are indecent in the vulgar publicity which they give to intimate personal relations between individuals of the opposite sexes. But weddings and marriage have the sanction of the church and the state, while the unfortunate prostitutes are trod into the mud of social scorn and degradation.

Various methods may be used to restrict the publicity of prostitution. Open soliciting on the streets, in theaters, and in other public places should be prohibited. But the police should not be permitted to hound the prostitutes by arresting them every time they appear in the streets. The courts should require incontrovertible proof of public solicitation before convicting.

Ordinarily prostitutes should be prohibited from residing, or, to say the least, from plying their trade in certain sections of the city. As a general rule, they should be barred from carrying on their professional activities in the residential sections. They should be limited in this respect to the outskirts or other isolated parts of the city, or to the business districts.

Whether or not it is desirable to have a definite segregated district depends upon local conditions. In Japan and elsewhere this method has been successful. It has the advantage of making possible a close supervision over the prostitutes. It is probably the best method in great commercial centers and wherever there is a large transient population. In smaller and quieter communities with a more stable population it may not be desirable. In all cases the sale of alcoholic beverages should be prohibited in houses of prostitution because of the disorder which results from it, and advertising by prostitutes should be narrowly limited.

Enforced medical examination of prostitutes has often been more or less of a failure because it has been carried out inefficiently. But the venereal diseases constitute so grave a social danger that medical inspection should be rigorously enforced wherever possible. In the places where this had been done the venereal morbidity has been greatly diminished. The prostitutes are the principal centers of venereal infection and every possible measure should be taken to lessen their dangerousness.[13] Persons who, owing to ethical prepossessions and religious prejudices, oppose these measures on the ground that they constitute official recognition of an immoral profession are among the worst enemies of the health and welfare of mankind.

The medical inspection of prostitutes should be supplemented with the spreading of knowledge among the public at large of prophylactic measures. Every sexually mature person should be adequately instructed in sexual hygiene and in the control of procreation. Not otherwise can human beings regulate wisely this important aspect of their lives. Ample clinical and hospital facilities should be provided for the treatment of all venereally infected persons, and no invidious distinctions should be made between these patients and those who are afflicted with other diseases. In course of time medical examination may be required of all persons and treatment may be made compulsory for all ailments. When that time comes there will be no longer any invidious discriminations against prostitutes in these respects.

We come now to the perplexing question of the registration of habitual prostitutes. Such registration is customary in many parts of Europe and has been tried in some American cities. It has been denounced as an official recognition of prostitution and as stigmatizing the prostitutes unnecessarily and putting them in the power of the police. But it helps greatly in carrying out regulatory measures, especially with respect to limiting the scope of prostitution, medical inspection, and the detection of criminals. If prostitution is not made a crime and the regulation is not too drastic, the power of registering prostitutes is not likely to be abused by the police. The desirability of a so-called "morals" police depends largely upon local police conditions. When properly organized and controlled, such a body is likely to be useful in large cities. But in smaller places there is usually no need of it.[14]

Regulatory measures can never be applied to all of the prostitution that exists, for there will always be some clandestine prostitution. Such regulation can reach only the habitual prostitutes and not all of them, but cannot reach the large number of women who prostitute themselves occasionally. Furthermore, it is only fair to the prostitutes to recognize that in the broadest sense of the word any pecuniary remuneration for sexual gratification constitutes prostitution. A vast

13 See Harry Elmer Barnes, "A Realistic Approach to Venereal Disease," in *The American Sociologist*, August 1944, Vol. VI, No. 6.

14 For an exhaustive discussion of the problems connected with the "morals" police, see the following report of a French extra-parliamentary commission: L. Fiaux, *La police des moeurs*, Paris, 1907-1910, 3 vols.

number of idle wives and "kept" women contribute to the sum total of prostitution. These quasi-prostitutes cannot be reached by the above-mentioned regulatory measures, but there is not the same social need for their regulation that there is for the regulation of the highly promiscuous habitual prostitutes.

There will always be at least a small amount of corruption in the administration of these regulations, just as there is in every branch of police activity. The best guarantee of the effectiveness of these regulations and the best preventive of corruption is to avoid making these measures too drastic. Whenever the authorities stigmatize prostitution as criminal and endeavor to stamp it out entirely, regulations become ineffective and corruption becomes rife, thus demoralizing the police and endangering the lives and property of the public. If the policy of recognizing and permitting the irreducible minimum of prostitution is adopted, regulatory measures will have a fair prospect of success.

In this connection may be mentioned the treatment of the pimp by the law. The pimp is a character who merits more or less the obloquy cast upon him by society. But he scarcely deserves the drastic treatment meted out to him by the law,[15] because several things may be said in extenuation of the pimp.

In the first place, the existence of the pimp is due in many cases to the natural and normal desire of the prostitute for a more or less permanent relationship with a man. This relation gives her relief from the ordinary sexual promiscuity of her life, and furnishes her an object for what is often a genuine love and devotion. In these cases the pimp is for her the mate craved by every normal human being, and it is even conceivable that in some cases this feeling is reciprocated by the pimp. The pimp is sure to exist as long as prostitution, and it is fatuous to expect to destroy him by the law.

In the second place, the pimp is often useful to the prostitute. Sometimes he protects her from physical violence on the streets and elsewhere. But more frequently he assists her in her conflicts with the law. He furnishes this assistance by securing bail for her when she is arrested, by engaging counsel for her defense, by keeping in touch with her when she is committed to a prison or a hospital, and by aiding her to reestablish herself when she returns to the practice of her profession. In many cases it would be impossible for her to main-

[15] The New York State law reads as follows: "Every male person who lives wholly or in part on the earnings of prostitution, or who in any public place solicits for immoral purposes, is guilty of a misdemeanor. A male person who lives with or is habitually in the company of a prostitute and has no visible means of support, shall be presumed to be living on the earnings of prostitution." (*N. Y. State Penal Code*, 1944, Section 1148.)

tain herself without his assistance, and he becomes in effect a partner with her in her profession.

It may appear as if the law should try to suppress the pimp because of the assistance which he furnishes to her. But she needs this aid largely on account of the harsh and drastic treatment which she often receives from the law and the police. She is usually too weak and ignorant to obtain even the barest justice in the courts without this aid, and she would become to an even greater extent the prey of the police, bondsmen, lawyers, etc. The actual situation in a vast number of cases is that the prostitute is driven unwillingly into the arms of the pimp by the persecution and hounding she receives at the hands of the police, the courts, etc. However much he may maltreat her and deprive her of her earnings, she is under many circumstances better off with him than she would be alone. The prevention of the pimp depends more upon the reform of the law in the direction of a more just and lenient treatment of the prostitute than it does upon the legal prohibition of the pimp. This is one of the worst features of the present situation that the law itself puts the prostitute so often at the mercy of the pimp.

In the last place, it may be said in extenuation of the pimp that he should be classified with the other parasitic classes in society, such as the idle wives and the leisure class of men and women in general. The pimp may seem to display rather less delicacy of taste as to the manner in which his income is acquired. And yet who shall say that it is any worse than the taste of the wealthy men and women whose income is derived from the suffering and sacrifice of millions of men, women, and children who are sweated in the factories, fields and elsewhere; or the taste of the many women who have bartered themselves in the "holy" bonds of matrimony for the pecuniary consideration of a life of indolent luxury. With the wealthy should be included their retainers and henchmen, such as priests, lawyers, bankers, journalists, and other professions which profit by sharing the ill-gotten wealth of the plutocratic class in return for their services. If the pimp is to be penalized, it would be only just to him to penalize these other parasites as well.

At the same time, as has already been said with regard to procuration, any man who forces a woman into prostitution and keeps her in it against her will should be punished. The prostitute should be given ample recourse at law and effective protection against the man who coerces her or who terrorizes her into giving to him her earnings. Among the criminal procurers and pimps are to be found some of the vilest men and women in existence. They seem to be destitute of most of the kindly feelings and are responsible for a form of human slavery almost as hideous as any which has ever existed.

Another example of unwise legislation due to the hysterical agitation against prostitution and alleged sexual immorality is with respect to the "age of consent" for females. In many places the penal law now prescribes that sexual intercourse with a female under eighteen years of age to whom the culprit is not married constitutes rape.[16] In some places the age of consent is even higher and many anti-vice societies and other religious, ethical and reform organizations are constantly endeavoring to push the age limit up as high as possible, even as high as twenty-one years.

The human female attains sexual maturity considerably earlier than any of these ages, usually as young as fourteen or fifteen years of age. It is possible for the female of fourteen or fifteen to be morally and sexually, so to speak, responsible for sexual intercourse. In other words, she may be the seducer herself, instead of having been seduced or raped, and, as a matter of fact, this is the actual situation in many cases. It is conceivable that she may be morally responsible even before she has attained sexual maturity, for curiosity or some other motive may lead her to induce a boy or man to have intercourse with her. It would be the grossest injustice in any one of these cases to punish the male.

Furthermore, it is an insult to the female of twenty, or eighteen, or sixteen, or even fifteen or fourteen, to assume that she is totally lacking in intelligence and discretion, and that her part in sexual intercourse could be nothing more than that of an automaton. What is much worse is that it is anti-social and therefore immoral to regard as morally irresponsible a person who can be and is responsible, for by so doing such persons will escape the consequences of their acts. One of the greatest achievements in the evolution of criminal law has been the gradual recognition of the moral responsibility of the individual, so that the legislation with respect to the age of consent for females is a step backward in the history of law.

For all of the above reasons there can be no excuse whatsoever for an arbitrary age of consent for females. The existing laws against seduction and rape are amply sufficient to cover all of the cases of enforced and involuntary sexual intercourse for all females of any age whatsoever. The usual legal criteria of responsibility can be applied in these cases as in all other cases where extreme youth raises a question as to the moral responsibility of the individual.

[16] For example, the New York law reads as follows: "A person who perpetrates an act of sexual intercourse with a female, not his wife, under the age of eighteen years, under circumstances not amounting to rape in the first degree, is guilty of rape in the second degree, and punishable with imprisonment for not more than ten years." (*N. Y. State Penal Code*, 1944, Section 2010.)

Rape in the first degree takes place when there has been resistance, or when resistance has been impossible.

This is not all that can be said against these laws. Such legislation has failed almost entirely of its intended effect because judges and juries are naturally slow to inflict the penalty when there is more or less probability that the female is as responsible or even more responsible than the male. There is little question that some genuine crimes of rape have escaped punishment when prosecuted under such a law because the courts have been fearful of punishing innocent persons.

What is worse is that such legislation renders still more facile the bringing of false accusations against innocent men. This is sometimes done by hysterical or insane females who do not realize the falsity of their accusations. Or it is done for purposes of blackmail by clandestine prostitutes or by immoral and criminal females. While these accusations are not necessarily successful when prosecuted, or may not even be prosecuted, they are almost certain to do a vast amount of injury to their innocent victims, and thus cause much injustice. It is easy enough to make false accusations under the existing laws against seduction and rape. It is easier to do so under the "age of consent" law, because less evidence is needed for conviction under this law.[17]

[17] I have discussed all of these matters relating to prostitution in several chapters of my book entitled *Personality and Conduct*, New York, 1918.

Chapter LII

Free Contractual Marriage

THE young need education with respect to sex as well as every other important aspect of life. Prior to puberty there is comparatively little sexual feeling and desire, so that there is slight need of parental direction. During this early period the child should be given scientific information as to the aspects of sex which it is capable of understanding, in order to prepare it for the time when matters of sex will be of vital importance for it.

Every intelligent child has its curiosity aroused with respect to the origin of humans, its relations to its parents, and the relation of its parents to each other. Rather than to keep it in ignorance with regard to these important facts or to permit it to acquire misinformation from other sources, it should be taught the elementary facts with respect to reproduction and the family organization by its parents or other adults who have care of the child.

This teaching should include the essential facts with regard to the fertilizing of the mother by the father, the growth of the child within the mother and its delivery from the mother, the love of parents for their children and their duty to care for them, and the biparental family as the natural unit for the rearing of children. Children can be taught these facts and should know them prior to puberty. This teaching can be made more interesting and more concrete by illustrations from animal and plant species which will indicate to the child its relation to the organic world. But this will not take the place of information about the human species.

The child is incapable of understanding many of the features of the sexual life of man until it experiences the sexual instincts and emotions. These instincts and emotions do not mature until after puberty is reached. Psychological research has, however, proved that even prior to puberty the child may experience sexual impulses and

908

feelings.[1] The sexual organs and the erogenous zones are peculiarly sensitive to stimulation from the time they first develop, so that parents should guard their children from such stimulation from the earliest infancy.

Puberty takes place for boys usually from thirteen to fifteen years of age, and for girls usually from eleven to fifteen years of age. This is the age at which the sexual organs attain maturity and the physiological processes connected with sex commence. During puberty also develop the secondary sex traits, such as the beard and the bass or tenor voice in the boy, and the well-rounded breasts and pubic hair in the girl. Furthermore, at this age there take place certain psychological changes which are of great importance. Puberty is also a period of rapid growth for the young.

There are individual differences between children in their sexual traits as in all their traits. The age at which puberty is reached is not the same for all. The rapidity with which the sexual organs mature, and the length of duration of the period of puberty and adolescence, varies considerably from one person to another. The physical changes caused by puberty have a varying effect upon the mental states of the boy or girl.

At puberty the sexual glands begin to secrete their characteristic fluids. These fluids contain the germ cells which when fertilized develop into new human beings. But the secretions of the sexual glands, like those of several other glands in the body, also send stimuli to all parts of the body and thus have a constitutional effect. This stimulation apparently takes place by the absorption of some of the fluid secreted by the sexual glands into the blood, which is then carried through the vascular system and excites the nerve centers in many parts of the body.

This stimulation is a new experience and a new factor in the life of the adolescent. It has a marked effect upon the mental states of the individual. It is the principal cause in the adolescent of the restlessness, the excitability, the variability of mood, the awakening of ambition, the shyness and reticence, and the new romantic and erotic interest in the opposite sex which characterizes adolescence. It is an indication of the maturing of the sexual instincts and emotions which will thereafter play an important part in the life of the individual.

This physical and mental condition puts the adolescent under great strain, and not the least trying feature of this condition is the ignorance of the adolescent as to its causes. It is therefore most important that as rapidly as is feasible this information should be imparted

[1] For example, the literature of psychoanalysis furnishes evidence of sexuality in infancy and childhood.

to the adolescent. The way in which it is given must be adjusted to the previous education, the intelligence, and the temperament of the individual adolescent. It demands the best judgment and the utmost sympathy and tactfulness on the part of the parent or teacher.

On account of the extent of the changes of puberty and adolescence and their great significance for the after life of the individual, parents should watch their children for the first signs of puberty. If they are not sure of being able to detect these signs, it may be well to use medical assistance for this purpose. They should then be prepared to give their children the physical care, the training, and the instruction which their condition demands.

Owing to the strain caused by rapid growth and the changes which have been described, adolescents should be under the best possible physical conditions. They should have plenty of wholesome food, restful sleep, and opportunity to play, and should not be required to work very hard. Furthermore, this is an important period for the training of character, during which the will, the judgment, and the sympathetic nature of the adolescent should be developed. In these respects the period of puberty and adolescence does not differ greatly from the earlier period of the life of the young, for during early childhood also the physical environment should be healthful and the character should be trained. But with puberty come the physiological processes connected with sex and their mental consequences. These changes mark this period off from the previous life of the individual and call for several changes in the education of the adolescent.

The significant differences, therefore, between adolescence and the pre-adolescent period is that with the arrival of puberty come impulses and feelings which give rise to new mental states and may lead to new kinds of conduct. While the information given to the pre-adolescent is largely in response to an intellectual curiosity with respect to the facts of reproduction, the information now given should be for the purpose of influencing the mental condition and directing the conduct during the period of mental and physical stress incident upon the changes of puberty and adolescence. Pre-adolescent experiences do not furnish an adequate basis for comprehending the relations between men and women, so that this comprehension can be attained only after puberty is reached, and it should be the purpose of the sex education of adolescents to give them this comprehension.

As much as possible of this instruction for adolescents, as well as for the younger children, should be in a general scheme of scientific education to be carried out in the schools. In such a scheme the facts with regard to reproduction would be taught at the proper point in the study of the organic world. They should be taught by teachers who are well equipped for the task and who will point out the relation

910

between these facts and the other facts of nature. Thus the child and adolescent would learn many of the essential facts concerning sex without any undue emphasis which would arouse an abnormal interest in them. This teaching should be as impersonal as possible. Few if any schools as yet furnish adequate instruction on this subject, and many of them offer none at all. It is at present incumbent upon most parents to furnish all or most of this instruction to their children. Even if the schools generally offered adequate instruction concerning sex, it would still be necessary for parents to play an important part in the sex education of their children.

The school teacher cannot be well acquainted with the individual peculiarities of his or her pupils. In fact, the teacher should ordinarily deal impersonally with these matters so far as the pupils are concerned. On the other hand, the parents are the natural advisers and confidants of their children in such matters. They can and should acquaint themselves with the individual peculiarities of their children, and should try to attain a footing of sympathetic intimacy with them. Parents must prepare themselves for this task. They should recollect as vividly as possible their own experiences during puberty and adolescence in order to be able to sympathize with the corresponding experiences of their children. They should acquaint themselves with the anatomy and physiology of the sexual organs and the changes which take place during puberty and adolescence, and also with the psychology of puberty and adolescence and of sex in general.

The best source of information concerning the anatomy and physiology of sex is in the standard general treatises on anatomy and physiology. From these works available in the libraries the parent, though a layman in science, can glean enough information for the sex instruction of the adolescent. Many popular books for adolescents and for the parents of adolescents have been written. Most of these books are not scientifically reliable, because they have been written by religionists and professional moralists with a religious and moral bias or by other equally incompetent persons. In any case, the standard works furnish the best source of information. In addition to this information the marital and parental experiences of the parents should aid them greatly in determining what kind of training and instruction are needed by their children to prepare them for similar experiences when they have attained maturity.

With this preparation parents should be able to make their offspring comprehend the functions of sex. In all of the species characterized by sex the first function of sex is the reproduction and the perpetuation of the species. In the higher animals sex has attained another function which in man has acquired great cultural value. In order to bring the sexes together for purposes of reproduction and to provide for the care of the young, powerful instincts and emotions have evolved in the higher animals, and especially in man, which attract the sexes to each other and hold together those who have mated in order to form the family group in which the young can be reared.

This secondary function of sex, which I have named the play function, has played an important part in social and cultural evolution both because it has aided the evolution of the family, and because these sexual instincts and emotions have caused much of human achievement. Many military, political, and economic exploits have been due to male gallantry in behalf of women and sexual rivalry among men, while the tender devotion of woman for man has enriched human life greatly. Even more important are the human achievements in science, invention, technology, both the industrial and the fine arts, music, and literature. The wasteful and noxious by-products of sex have been in the fields of religion, magic, theology, metaphysics, ethics, war, exploitation, genocide; in other words, the more irrational, hateful, and predatory of human activities.

The instruction in each case must be adjusted, according to the best judgment of the parents, to the peculiarities and circumstances of the individual adolescent. The age at which and the extent to which curiosity is aroused with respect to sex varies considerably from individual to individual, and is influenced somewhat by the environment. If there has been no school instruction in sex and no parental instruction during early childhood, the instruction must begin with the elementary facts concerning sex. In doing so the parents should endeavor to ascertain whether or not the child has already acquired any misinformation on the subject, and try to counteract the effects of such misinformation.

If the child has already received school or parental instruction, the endeavor of the parent should be to supplement the knowledge already received so as to make it more adequate with respect to the functions and significance of sex. If there is school instruction, but the child is intellectually precocious, or puberty comes unusually early, it may be well for the parent to anticipate the school instruction by furnishing the desired information. In some cases it may be possible to quiet the child's questionings until such time as it receives the information in school. As a rule it is better to give the information as soon as curiosity has been aroused.

There is perhaps no period of life during which a sympathetic understanding of his or her condition is more needed than by the adolescent. For this reason it is as a rule preferable that the male adolescent shall receive his less sex instruction from his father and the female adolescent shall receive her instruction from her mother. The father can understand more sympathetically the condition of the son because of his own experience with male adolescence, and the mother can understand more sympathetically the condition of the daughter because of her own experience with female adolescence. At times the adolescent should discuss these matters with both parents in order to realize more fully than would otherwise be possible the mutuality of the parenthood of the parents and their cooperation in the rearing of their offspring.

The education of the child concerning the reproductive process may now be completed in connection with the explanation of the physiological processes which begin at puberty. The significance of the periodic menstruation for reproduction should be explained to the girl and the corresponding significance of the seminal flow should be explained to the boy. At the same time or as soon after as seems advisable the adolescent of each sex should be told of the related physiological process in the opposite sex. The adolescent will now have an adequate conception of the function of sex in parenthood and of the mutual character of parenthood. In this connection, it may also be well to describe briefly the nature of the parental instincts and emotions which are already awakening, and which will attain their full expression later when the adolescent experiences parenthood.

The adolescent should now be taught the significance of the relations between the sexes apart from and in addition to reproduction. The main object of this instruction should be to make the adolescent realize that, in addition to resulting in reproduction and all that parenthood implies, the sex relation is an important and necessary part of a satisfactory life throughout maturity. It should therefore be impressed upon the adolescent that it is his or her duty and interest to prepare for a sex relation which will add greatly to the happiness and richness of life. The chief requisite to attain this end is the choice of a suitable mate both for mutual parenthood and as a life companion.

The instruction with respect to the second or play function of sex should be commenced during adolescence. It need not be completed until after that age is passed, and should be continued until the adolescent has attained maturity and is prepared in every respect to contract a sex relation. This part of the sex education should be connected with a discussion of the larger aspect of sex as a powerful force in social and cultural evolution. The time for commencing the second part of sex education must depend upon the individual peculiarities of the adolescent. If puberty is tardy or the intelligence is sluggish, it may be necessary to postpone most of this part of the education until after adolescence.

The fundamental note of all sex education should be positive with a view to preparing the young for a sex life which will be normal in every respect during maturity. But it is also necessary to touch more lightly upon the negative side of sex in order to guard the young against the dangers incident to sex. The extent to which it is necessary for the parent to discuss these matters with the adolescent depends upon the environment and traits of the individual. If the environment furnishes many temptations and the adolescent is temperamentally prone to succumb to such temptations, it may be necessary to discuss these dangers at length and in detail in order to impress the adolescent with the importance of avoiding them. Otherwise it is preferable to delay the discussion of these matters until later, perhaps until after adolescence is passed, in order to put the emphasis on the positive aspect of sex.

In all discussion of these dangers the utmost care should be taken to avoid shocking and alarming the boy or girl in such a way as to cause a shrinking and fearful attitude toward sex which will interfere with a normal sex life during maturity. In fact, such a shrinking and fearful attitude is in itself a serious danger, because it may lead to frigidity or psychic impotence. The principal dangers to be mentioned are those of disease, so-called "self-abuse," and premature parenthood. The diseases connected with sexual organs and communicated by sexual relations which are called the venereal diseases are, like all other diseases, disagreeable and distasteful to contemplate. They are especially offensive in their nature because they are connected with organs and processes which have a peculiar value and significance for the individual and for the race. For this reason it is desirable to keep the knowledge of the existence of these diseases from the young so long as it is safe to do so, in order to avoid the possibility of marring the beauty of their first impressions of sex with a repugnant association.

If their environment puts them in danger of these diseases, they should be informed fully and frankly as to the nature of these diseases as soon as seems necessary. They should be fully impressed with the seriousness of these diseases, but these dangers should not be exaggerated, because such exaggeration may cause a reaction against sex which will interfere seriously with the normal sexual activity of the individual throughout maturity.

Adolescents, and especially boys, may acquire the habit of masturbation. Parents should watch their children with a view to ascertaining whether or not this habit is becoming established. They should explain to the boy or girl that such a habit, while not harmful in moderation, is a strain upon the body and mind in excess. Along with such instruction the parents should take prophylactic measures, the

914

most important of which is to furnish the adolescent with plenty of opportunity for vigorous out-of-door exercise.

From the humane point of view no form of parenthood is offensive. But it should be impressed upon adolescents that it is not desirable to become a parent until sufficient maturity has been attained to fit a person for the rearing of children and until a suitable mate has been found. Premature parenthood is unfair to the offspring. The girl especially should be taught the dangers of premature pregnancy and motherhood. The boy should be brought to realize the seriousness of causing pregnancy in a woman and of becoming a father himself.

Adolescents of both sexes should be made to feel that for biological, economic, and social reasons they are not yet fitted for parenthood but should be preparing for it. They should be taught contraceptive measures so as to be able to use them when they begin to have sexual relations. They should also be given some knowledge of eugenics to aid them in choosing a suitable mate for mutual parenthood. They should feel that not until a suitable mate has been found are they ready for successful bi-parental rearing of offspring.

The sex education of the young should be extended by pre-pubertal observation of sex relations between their parents or other elders, and by adolescent instruction in an *Amatorium,* an institution of the future which I propose and describe in my book on the play function of sex.[2] By such measures it will be possible to obviate the more sordid forms of sex expression, to rear the young in a normal and healthy attitude toward sex, and to give to sex the recognition which it should receive in the life of mankind.

The preceding four chapters furnish a brief survey of man's attempts to organize and regulate one of the most important aspects of his life, namely, his sex life. This survey reveals a long series of blunders and failures which have caused a vast amount of unhappiness and misery for mankind. It is only necessary to mention asceticism, the double standard of sex freedom, prostitution, bastardy, indissoluble marriage, the venereal diseases, the sexual aberrations, frigidity, psychic impotence, the mismated and the unmated to indicate the extent of this misery.

The sex problem was much simpler for primitive men. We are probably justified in surmising that under the influence of the sexual urge early men took their sexual gratification as they could find it. The males appropriated the females for this purpose, and the females probably did not usually resist because it was a source of gratification

[2] In my *The Play Function of Sex,* 1960, I have described how the *Amatorium* can aid in the sex education of the child and the sexual initiation of the adolescent.

915

for them also. Perhaps the only sufferers were the weaker men who were unable to secure mates.

As time went by many restrictions arose, some of which have been described in the three preceding chapters. The discovery of the causal relation between sexual intercourse and reproduction led to many of these restrictions. Magical and religious beliefs gave rise to numerous restrictions. Among primitive peoples totemic and exogamous relations of sex played an important part. These regulations have disappeared almost entirely among civilized peoples. The evolution of more or less permanent forms of economic and social organization led to more or less fixed types of sex relationship. Various forms of marriage thus arose, including group marriage, polygyny, polyandry, and monogamy.

Monogamy has become the conventional type of marriage among most civilized peoples, and is recognized and enforced by the law. This type of marriage is supported in part by the prevalent theory that mankind is by nature monogamous and not promiscuous. This theory is not necessarily proved by the available facts. Monogamous marriage is maintained in large part by artificial institutions and conventions which may or may not be in accordance with human innate tendencies. There was doubtless a great deal of promiscuity among early men, while there is still much promiscuity outside of the conventional bonds of marriage despite the powerful forces of law, religion, and conventional morality.

The truth probably is that while there are certain strong forces for monogamy, which I will mention presently, human sexual impulses and desires are more or less wayward according to the nature of the education and training received and the exigencies of the environment. In other words, it is impossible to characterize mankind categorically as either monogamous or promiscuous. Both of these tendencies must be recognized in human nature. This fact should be remembered in any attempt to organize sex relations.

It is customary nowadays to regard so-called "purity" in sex relations as limited to the conventional monogamic relation. Monogamy is characterized as "chaste" and "continent" as contrasted with all other relations which are by implication "unchaste" and "incontinent." This notion is especially pronounced as applied to woman. Virtue in woman is restricted almost entirely to her conformity to the prevailing sex mores. These terms are grossly misused. Purity and virtue are concerned with the whole life of man, and not with the sex life alone. Chastity is sexual abstinence, which usually is unhealthy and harmful. Continence is self restraint in sexual indulgence. Monogamic marriage is far more unchaste and incontinent than other forms of sexual indulgence, because it has the advantage over these other forms of possessing the sanctions of law, religion, and conventional morality, and of permitting continuous accessibility.

An excessive degree of reticence prevails at present with respect to the discussion of sex. It is due in part to the strong emotional content of sex which makes it difficult for men and women to discuss matters of sex calmly and impersonally. This reticence has been exacerbated into an unnatural and almost morbid attitude by sex repression arising out of magical and religious notions with respect to the uncleanness of sex, and the conventional ideas with respect to the impurity of sex manifestations outside of the orthodox monogamic bond. An intelligent discussion and solution of the sex problems of the day demand a frank and natural intellectual and emotional attitude toward sex. It is one of the most important aspects of human life, and the gratification of the sexual impulse is an imperative need second only to hunger. The prevailing sex taboo, on the contrary, gives rise to an unhealthy and ugly pruriency.

On the other hand, as soon as the sex problem is faced and solved, sex will no longer occupy an exaggerated place in the consciousness of mankind, as is the danger under existing conditions of sex repression. Under such repression sex tends to break out at many points and to color human activities unduly, thus giving modern civilization a misleading appearance of being over-sexed. Furthermore, when sex is repressed it is very likely to manifest itself in pathological forms, as, for example, sexual aberrations, such as homosexuality, sexual fetishism, sadism, masochism, etc., some of which are relatively innocuous but others cause a good deal of harm. If sex were given its proper scope, it would not invade other spheres of human thought, feeling, and activity.

The starting point for an intelligent discussion and solution of the sex problem is sex education and training. Such a system of education as has been described in this chapter would develop a natural and frank attitude toward sex on the part of the young. It would furnish each adolescent an intelligent comprehension of all the interests involved in the sex relation, namely, the interests of the opposite sex and of possible offspring, as well as his or her own interests. Thus the adolescent would be enabled to estimate fairly accurately the extent to which sexual indulgence is desirable and justifiable, and what degree of self restraint is demanded by the interests of others. Such restraint will be far more effective and beneficial in the long run than the artificial restrictions which arise out of secrecy, beliefs contrary to the patent facts of human nature, and the coercion which arises therefrom. It will give rise to a genuine continence in the place of the spurious continence of the conventional marriage of today. It will supply most of the check which is needed upon the sex passion.

It is believed by many persons that the sex impulse is so powerful that society should place heavy restrictions upon it. Incontinence is bad for all, especially for men, since the male capacity for sexual intercourse is far more limited than the female capacity. The popular notion is that marriage furnishes most of the necessary restraint, but this notion is false. As a matter of fact, there is much more incontinence within the bonds of matrimony than there is outside of wedlock. Many a man has had his career ruined because of the excessive drain upon his strength in endeavoring to satisfy the cravings of a highly sexed wife. There is no feasible legal method of preventing incontinence. The best preventives are the system of discipline and education briefly outlined above, and the public opinion with respect to a healthy and normal sex life for all which would develop as a result of this system.

With the knowledge and discipline derived from this system of sex education and training the adolescent would be adequately prepared to begin the sex life. He or she would then begin a sex relation with the intention of developing the play aspect of sex to the highest possible degree, at the same time using contraceptive measures to prevent the relation from resulting in reproduction until it became fairly certain that the play function was developing in a full and permanent form. Thus would be prevented the deplorable condition, harmful both to parents and offspring, of a more or less permanent mating and reproduction without a development of the play function. This is a frequent result from the marriage of today, which is based upon no adequate testing of the fitness and the compatibility of the spouses for mating.

As soon as puberty and adolescence are passed, the young adult should begin a sex relation. The exact age at which this point is reached cannot be stated, since it varies according to climatic conditions, racial traits, and individual peculiarities. Until this time the parents or other natural guardians can in most cases furnish all of the restraint that is necessary. In some of the simpler communities of today and in many communities of the past this state of affairs has prevailed. It is one of the deplorable concomitants of complex modern civilization, due usually to economic conditions, that the usual age for sexual mating has been delayed far beyond the natural age.

The first sexual union for the young adult should not be in the bond of an indissoluble marriage. It should be in the nature of a preliminary or trial marriage with a partner who gives promise of becoming a suitable mate for a permanent union. In view of the uncertainty of the outcome of this trial union it would be advisable ordinarily for the young couple not to become entirely independent of their parents until the union gives indications of becoming permanent. Further-

918

more, as I have already asserted, contraceptive measures should be used to prevent reproduction until the play function develops in a strong and apparently lasting form. Begun under such favorable auspices most of the trial unions would in all probability turn out successfully. Even those that fail would furnish their participants knowledge and experience which will aid them in attaining success in the second or later trials. Thus the trial union would serve as a sort of preparation or novitiate for permanent marriage.[3]

As I have already pointed out, promiscuity possesses a certain charm for mankind, owing to the novelty of the pleasurable sensations derived therefrom. The tendency to promiscuity has at all times manifested itself in extra-matrimonial relations, and sometimes to a smaller degree in group marriage. The male sex manifests it occasionally in polygyny, and the female sex more rarely in polyandry. In spite of this promiscuous tendency and these other forms of marriage, there are at least four reasons for thinking that monogamy will remain the prevailing form of permanent sex relation. The approximate numerical equality of the sexes will always be a strong force for monogamy. In a society organized upon a democratic basis it will become more and more difficult for an individual to monopolize more than one member of the opposite sex. Polygyny and polyandry can be prevalent only when the sexes are for any reason not equal numerically, or when a favored class can enforce monopolistic rights.

In the second place, as I have already pointed out in Chapter XLVIII sexual jealousy is likely to be a powerful force for monogamy. Whenever a sex relation is based upon a strong affection, neither party to the union is likely to look with favor or to tolerate another sex relation for his or her mate. As I have also pointed out in Chapter XLVIII, the rearing of the young requires more or less permanent unions. Mutual parenthood is likely to make such a union monogamous. This is because mutual parenthood usually draws the parents closer together and reinforces the play function of sex, thus decreasing the desire for and excluding to a large extent the feasibility of another sex relation for either parent.

The desire for companionship in old age is in some cases a factor for monogamy. In order to secure such companionship it is essential to form a strong union which is not likely to be broken before death. Such a union cannot be obtained through promiscuity. It is not likely to be so strong in polygynous or polyandrous marriage. These considerations do not have much influence in the flush of early youth. They acquire greater weight with advancing years. As human fore-

[3] Trial marriage has existed at many times and places in the past. Several of these instances are described by H. Ellis, *Sex in Relation to Society*, Philadelphia, 1910, Chap. IX.

sight increases, these considerations will have more and more influence upon sexual matings. While these four reasons for monogamy exist, it is not to be assumed that monogamy should be imposed and enforced by law, conventional morality, and religion. It is such compulsion in marriage that has caused a vast amount of unhappiness in the past. It will do the same in the future, and will defeat its own ends even more than in the past.

When the young have been adequately educated and trained, and when women as well as men are economically independent, so that the sexes are on an equality in their freedom of choice, it will be safe to leave sexually mature adults free to choose any form of sex relation which they desire. A few will elect to remain promiscuous always in their sex life. The majority will probably desire and seek a permanent relation, though this will depend in part upon the extent to which the domestic and household economy is collectivized, providing for the care of the children, and rendering possible a somewhat communal form of sex relation from which jealousy has largely disappeared, because all men and women would regard each other as potential mates.

The marital relation should become a genuinely free contract for those who desire to enter it.[4] Thus the contract should specify the length of time the relation is to endure, that is to say, as to whether it is to be permanent or for a definite or indefinite term. It should specify whether or not the marriage is to be exclusive, that is to say, monogamous. For the reasons stated above the majority of individuals may choose to make their marriages monogamous and permanent.

The law should permit other forms of marital relationship for the persons who desire them. Thus the marriage contract may specify that one or both parties to the union may have extra-matrimonial sexual relations. It may specify that one or both parties may form other marital relations, thus becoming polyandrous or polygynous, as the case may be. Beside the prevailing monogamic type of marriage would arise a few polyandrous and polygynous unions, but these unions would doubtless remain in a small minority.

The contract could also specify as to whether or not reproduction is an object of a marital union, and as to what provision is to be made for the care and rearing of the offspring. The law would be justified at this point in insisting, in the interests of society, that adequate pro-

[4] Free contractual marriage was first described and advocated in my *Personality and Conduct*, New York, 1918, pp. 261-266.

Judge Lindsey seems to have had a somewhat similar conception of trial marriage in his *The Companionate Marriage*, by Ben B. Lindsey and Wainwright Evans, New York, 1929. However, Lindsey failed to grasp the concept of free contractual marriage as I had already developed it eleven years before him.

vision be made for the young, if not provided by the collective commonwealth. Parental responsibility for offspring should be enforced. But no distinction should be made in this respect between intra- and extra-matrimonial offspring. In other words, the distinction between legitimacy and illegitimacy should be abolished, so that bastardy, with all of the odious stigma which is attached to it, would disappear from the face of the earth. Owing to the development of the play function and the use of contraceptive measures, there would be few births which were not desired and which did not come to parents who were permanently mated, so that the majority of children would receive biparental rearing and few would be left entirely to the care of the state.

The marital contract could also specify as to the distribution of property and income between the contracting parties. As it becomes more and more customary for women to earn their own living, economic dependency in marriage will diminish. It would be foolish to prophesy as to whether or not the time will come when it will be justifiable to forbid economic dependency in marriage when it is acceptable to the parties concerned. Under some form of collectivism every person may be obligated to earn his or her own living, so that there will be no parasitism of any sort. Until that time comes it will be possible for a man to agree to support a woman or for a woman to agree to support a man, when they desire to do so.

In fact, it should be possible for men and women to come to any agreement they choose in a marital contract, provided it is not contrary to the interests of society. When a contract is violated, it should be possible for the injured party to secure redress in the civil courts. If support is provided in the contract, there can be suit for non-support, but not otherwise. Sexual intercourse outside of marriage would be adulterous only when in violation of the marital contract, but not otherwise. Adultery would not be penalized or even stigmatized as wrongful, but should be sufficient cause for abrogating the contract when the non-adulterous party desires it in accordance with the terms of the contract. This arrangement would solve the problem of divorce. A marital contract would be dissolved whenever both of the contracting parties agreed to such dissolution, or when one of the parties had violated it to such an extent as to give the other party sufficient grounds for abrogating it. Divorce would thus come about more or less automatically as the result of the termination of marital contracts.

In such an organization of sex relations as I have described, marriage would become a genuine free contractual relation. All persons entering upon this relation would fix for themselves the terms of their contract. This fact would increase greatly their sense of responsibility. They would no longer be able to blame coercive laws if their marital

921

ventures failed. They would be compelled to realize that their success in marriage depended largely if not entirely upon themselves. They would be much more careful to know each other well before entering upon a binding contract. The preliminary or trial marriage would furnish them a means of acquiring this knowledge concerning each other.

To some persons it may appear that such an organization of sex relations will furnish a license for a sexual orgy. This would be impossible in any enlightened community, because the lasting interests of suitable mating and reproduction would far outweigh for most individuals the ephemeral attraction of a temporary promiscuity. Even if some varietism resulted from this organization of sex relations, it could not do as much injury to society as the sordid and degrading promiscuity of today. The sexual license which would arise from this future organization would have a frankness and spontaneity which would place it upon a far higher mental and social plane than the prostitution and much of the extra-matrimonial promiscuity of the present.

On the other hand, the organization of sex relations I have described would banish much of the misery of the vast number of mismated and unmated persons in modern civilization. The unobservant person may be deceived by the artificial smile of frozen respectability which maintains a smooth surface most of the time over the marital institutions of today. But to the observer with mental and moral insight who has looked into many lives and homes it is obvious that many millions of men and women are being marched annually to the hollow sound of the wedding bells and the unctuous tones of the meddlesome priest and parson into an indissoluble or almost indissoluble wedlock, there to lie upon a Procrustean bed of discomfort and often of torture. When men and women come to know themselves and each other, most of the mismatings can be obviated, while many of the numerous unmated can secure suitable mates.

What criminal offenses relating to sex would remain if the social institutions relating to sex were reorganized in the manner described? Attempts to force any one into a sex relation should be penalized. Thus rape, forcible abduction, and attempts to force any one into acts of sexual deviation would be crimes. It would also be well to penalize attempts to incite a minor to deviant or aberrant acts. Any attempt to secure a sexual relation on false pretenses should be penalized. Thus seduction, and bigamy, where the innocent party had not been informed of an already existing marital relation of the offender, would be crimes. It may also be advisable to make criminal the concealment of a grave contagious disease which may be readily transmitted in the sex relation.

922

Sexual relations between persons closely related by blood probably should be discouraged. Not that there is anything biologically harmful necessarily in incestuous intercourse, but because it is socially desirable that close blood relationships (such as parent and child, brother and sister) should not be confused with sexual relationships.

While the normal hetero-sexual relation may be the most desirable, it is wholly indefensible to penalize homosexuality, sexual fetishism, and other variations from the normal. The persons characterized by these sexual deviations are not usually able to avoid them, and often are useful members of society. They should not be molested by the law, unless they attempt to force their practices upon others. Sex is polymorphic in its forms of expression because much of the human body is erogenic. Many buccal and bodily contacts, in addition to the usual ones, enrich the range of sexual satisfaction and should not be prohibited by laws and moral ideas inherited from barbaric times when sex relations were sanctified only by the scriptural injunction to breed and multiply. Such sexual contacts are already widely used in marital as well as extra-marital relations.[5]

The use of contraceptive measures should not be penalized but should be encouraged by the government, as is already done in a few civilized countries. Abortion should not be penalized in most cases today, for it is almost invariably caused by the law in forbidding the use of contraceptive measures and is not the fault of the individual. When contraceptive measures are freely permitted, it may become justifiable to penalize abortion where it is due to inexcusable negligence in failing to use contraceptive measures. However, this is a question which will have to be decided in the future.

Bigamy, adultery, fornication, concubinage, and prostitution will disappear as criminal offenses. Divorce will become free and there will no longer be any legal stigma upon bastardy. When a strong public opinion with respect to a normal sex life for all has developed, pruriency of mind will disappear, and along with it the crimes incidental to sex. Thus indecency, immodesty, obscenity, etc., will be wiped out of the penal code.

This new organization of sex relations cannot come into being in a day, nor can all of its details be determined upon at present. Before it can be fully developed many other important social changes will have to take place. The principal changes are the economic changes which will obviate late marriages. I have, nevertheless, considered it worth while to outline it here as an ideal, because it is of

[5] The *Kinsey Report* of 1948 revealed that cunnilinctus and fellatio are so widespread in the United States as to be a usual and normal mode of sex expression, and not as ethically wrong or as psychologically abnormal.

assistance in securing a true perspective for the study and criticism of the existing system of sex relations.

The terms of the marital contract, freely assumed by all the parties to it will cover:

(1) The duration of the contract, which may be definite or indefinite.

(2) Its degree of exclusiveness, which may exclude one or both or all of the parties from extra-marital relations or admit one or both or all of them to such relations.

(3) The economic obligations assumed and the rights and privileges acquired by any party to it.

(4) To what extent reproduction is an objective and how many children are to be procreated.

(5) The financial provisions made for the care of prospective offspring.

(6) The agreements as to the bi-parental rearing of children.

(7) Any other terms not contrary to public policy, such as the frequency and form of the sexual unions desired, and the degree of commensalism to be practiced.

As already indicated, the future course of social evolution will have a material bearing on several of these aspects of the free marital contract, as, for example, the economic obligations and privileges such as rights of inheritance involved, the support and rearing of children, parental authority over offspring, and the degree and form of commensalism. The extent to which society becomes collectivized will have a decisive effect upon some of these relations between the sexes.[6]

---

[6] In my *Play Function of Sex* I have proposed the *"Amatorium."* This social institution would aid the sex education of the young, the preparation for mating of young adults, and would furnish facilities for sex expression for any and all adults. The *Amatorium* would also obviate most of prostitution, would decrease venereal disease, and would facilitate the regulation of population by contraceptive means. It would provide facilities for satisfactory sex expression lacking in the conventional marriage of today.

In that book I have discussed free contractual marriage at length and in detail. See especially Chapters VIII and IX, "Sex Freedom and Integral Man and Woman," and "The Future of Sex Relations—Free Contractual Marriage."

Chapter LIII

Reproduction and Population

IN a voluminous treatise on "the science of anthropology," comprising 678 pages and about 450,000 words, the index of 37 pages, containing many hundreds of entries and thousands of references, mentions sex seven times, marriage twice, and women only once. The family is mentioned thirteen times, presumably because it plays an important part in social organization and is the result of the reproductive function of sex. Apparently not more than four percent of this book deals with sex whereas lengthy chapters are devoted to physical type, culture areas, technology, economics, education, religion, art, language, and the like.[1] And yet sex is no more physiological and psychological than all other cultural phenomena, such as economic, political, esthetic, and linguistic phenomena. Hence it belongs just as much in a treatise on cultural evolution. It is indeed a curious question as to why sex is almost completely ignored in history and the social sciences and in biography, and is treated only gingerly and unrealistically in belles lettres in which there is much evasion and double talk. An inhibiting taboo represses the discussion of this important subject in most of literate society, though the taboo is not so widespread in non-literate society.

In the preceding five chapters has been given some indication as to how magic, religion, and social institutions, such as marriage and the family, have played a part in giving rise to this taboo. In its most extreme form it denies the existence of the play function of sex. For example, the Roman Catholic Church recognizes only its reproductive

---

[1] Melville J. Herskovits, *Man and His Works, The Science of Cultural Anthropology*, New York, 1948, XVIII, 678, XXVII. However, this anthropologist in comparing nonliterate with literate marriage recognizes the taboo on sex prevalent in literate society: "Those who enter on marriage are thus not exposed to the psychological hazards, manifest in the frequency of frigidity in women and impotence in men found by modern psychopathology in our own society, where matters of sex must be spoken of secretively, are often considered as partially evil, and for which the young person is prepared in a haphazard manner." (P. 321.)

function. Nevertheless, the play function is the first to operate in the life of the individual and continues as a dynamic factor throughout his life. Procreation is, as it were, an accidental and inadvertent by-product of the play activity of sex. But the human population which results from it is of so much economic, social and political significance that it has compelled discussion despite the prevalent taboo on sex.

A certain minimum density of population is indispensable in order to produce a civilization. If mankind had remained as sparsely distributed as the Australian aborigines or the Arctic Eskimos, no civilization could have developed. Civilization first made its appearance in fertile river valleys, such as those of the Nile and the Euphrates, the Indus and the Ganges, the Hwang Ho and the Yangtze Kiang. In these valleys and similar regions nature could easily support a relatively dense population without a highly developed mechanism of production. Enough could be produced to amass the surplus wealth necessary for the physical basis of civilization. In the human agglomerations in the towns and cities could arise those more complex relationships which form the social structure of civilization. A density of population sufficiently great to permit of civilization now exists in about 62 percent of the land surface of the world, while 38 percent consists of unproductive tundra, desert, arctic and antarctic regions which have less than one inhabitant per square mile.[2]

The maximum limit is a population too great to be supported by the aggregate resources of the world. The world's population is still far from this limit. Although it is of little practical importance today, it should not be entirely ignored as a possibility for the future. Whether or not there is relative over-population, that is to say, a population too great for such natural resources as have so far been utilized, is at times an important question.

There are no *a priori* reasons for a higher or lower density of population. It depends upon the relation between population and production with respect to the distribution of wealth in such a fashion as to bring about the largest amount of human happiness. Nevertheless, many arguments have been used on both sides of this question which are largely or entirely *a priori*.

This has been most true of those who have advocated the increase of population. One of the most superficial of these arguments arises out of the patriotic and nationalistic desire for a large population merely for the sake of size, especially if it outstrips every other country. In the United States chauvinists have gloried in the prospect that the population will presumably increase to two hundred, three hun-

[2] See Maurice Parmelee, *Geo-Economic Regionalism and World Federation*, New York, 1949, pp. 104-105. Of a total area of 55,900,000 square miles about 21,000,000 are relatively uninhabitable.

926

dred, four hundred millions of inhabitants, and so on up to many more hundreds of millions.

So long as the national state persists, the concept of national sovereignty will dominate. Under its influence the state becomes an abstract entity whose honor must be upheld at all costs, and to which the individual is subordinated and often sacrificed. The national state, or rather the hidden capitalist power which controls it, often desires more territory for its expanding population, or in order to secure more markets for its surplus products, or to exploit labor which costs less than at home thus giving the capitalists a larger margin of profit. Even when it seeks no territorial expansion, it almost always desires more citizens. A larger population enhances the prestige and the military and economic power of the state. Demographic policies have hitherto been governed more by the interests of the artificial state than by the natural biological and economic interests of mankind. A scientific demographic policy in the interests of mankind as a whole cannot be adopted until the national state has disappeared.

This explains in part why fascism and bolshevism, so unlike in other respects, are somewhat akin in their theories of population. Each seeks the aggrandizement of its respective state. Bolshevism is negatively and fascism positively anti-Malthusian. Birth control is tolerated in Soviet Russia and prohibited in Italy with the encouragement and support of the Catholic church. Neither bolshevism nor fascism has faced the problem of population and studied it scientifically. Bolshevism is misled by Marxian errors with regard to the law of population, and fascism by vain nationalistic aspirations. The fascist delusion of a highly industrialized Italy and dream of extensive colonies seem to justify a much greater population. Both countries have a relatively low standard of living, and Italy a vast amount of poverty. Neither country can escape ultimately from the inexorable operation of biological and economic forces. Nazi Germany followed the Italian example, but with somewhat more discrimination. It was trying to secure a selective birth-rate by eliminating the hereditarily diseased lines of descent.

There is little hope of a higher standard of living for a much larger population in Italy and Germany. In such countries an increase of population can only mean accentuated misery and more "Kanonen-Futter." Russia is a vast and thinly populated country with a rapidly rising productive capacity. For a time it can assimilate an increasing population with a rising standard of living. Every country and geographical region reaches its optimum population determined by its natural resources and technical equipment. Beyond this point an increase of population causes a relative decrease of productive capacity and a lower standard of living.

927

Marx contended that Malthus taught that mankind increases more rapidly than the means of subsistence and that starvation is a law of nature, thereby soothing the conscience of the ruling class. He himself asserted that each historical period has its own law of population. This has encouraged the socialists and communists to assert that a low standard of living has been due solely to exploitation by the ruling class, and that under a socialized system there will be an abundance of wealth for an unlimited population. There is much truth in Marx's demographic teachings. But natural resources are not unlimited, and may eventually be exhausted in large part if not entirely. Even in the early stages of the evolution of a socialized system of production, this should be remembered. With the coming of an international political organization the nationalistic, militaristic, and propagandistic motives for increase of population will disappear. It will then be possible to adopt a worldwide scientific policy with regard to population.

Certain religious doctrines have served as arguments for the increase of population. Some of them have been used, not so much to stimulate the growth of population directly, as to forbid the efforts to check this growth. These doctrines allege that such efforts interfere with the intentions and purposes of divine beings, or do violence to spiritual beings in the form of souls and frustrate their intentions and desires to have a mundane existence in a corporeal investiture. All this and more besides may be found set forth with ponderous solemnity in portly tomes of ecclesiastical provenance. These arguments are based upon theological beliefs and dogmas which are wholly *a priori* so far as a scientific discussion is concerned.

There are sentimentalists who advocate rapid increase of population in order to have numerous progeny in each family. This notion has a biological foundation in the parental instincts and emotions to be mentioned presently. The sentimentalist usually fails to comprehend the biological justification for philoprogenitiveness.

Aprioristic arguments have been less used by those who favor restriction of population. Some writers have argued that such restriction alone would cure numerous human and social ills. In particular has this been argued with respect to the evil of poverty. One writer has revealed complete ignorance of the social causes of poverty by asserting that "over-propagation in under-endowed classes is the source of modern poverty."[3] A Harvard University professor has displayed an equally one-sided understanding of the problem: "If the human race really desires a continued progress, a fair chance, a longer and happier life for every individual, the birthrate must come down

[3] E. Bowen, *An Hypothesis of Population Growth*, New York, 1931, p. 221.

928

faster and faster. . . . Half the people in the world lack sufficient brains to cope with the intricate system of social life the industrial age has brought about. Half the remainder are without the proper training; they lack the power of knowledge."[4] Whether or not the birth rate should come down, to attribute poverty entirely or even in considerable part to the size of the population or to the intelligence of its individual constituents is to misunderstand almost entirely the causes of poverty which is due mainly to exploitation by the master class.

During the nineteenth century, population increased greatly in almost every part of the world so that mankind nearly tripled since 1800. Since the commencement of the twentieth century the rate of increase has fallen in most Occidental countries. This is strikingly illustrated by the population of the United States which increased more than 35 percent in each decade from 1790 to 1860. It increased more than 10,000,000 in each decade from 1870 to 1930. The percentage of increase fell from 26.0 from 1870 to 1880 to 21.0 from 1900 to 1910, and 14.9 from 1910 to 1920. It fell to 7.2 between 1930 and 1940, but rose to 14.5 between 1940 to 1950 mainly due to the large number of marriages caused by the war of 1939 to 1945. From 1850 to 1950 the population of the United States increased from 23,191,876 to 150,697,361 or 6½ times. From 1851 to 1951 the population of Great Britain (England, Scotland and Wales) increased from 20,816,-000 to 48,841,000 or 2⅖ times.

While the death rate has been falling, the birth rate has been falling even faster. The vital statistics per 1,000 of population in the birth registration area in the United States in recent years are as follows:[5]

	1915	1920	1925	1930	1940	1950
Births	25.0	23.7	21.3	18.9	17.9	23.5
Deaths	13.2	13.0	11.7	11.3	10.7	9.7
Excess	11.8	10.7	9.6	7.6	7.2	13.8

On the other hand, the percentage of married persons has been increasing in the United States. "Two out of every three persons in the civilian population 14 years old and over in March 1950, were reported as married. Sixty years ago when the Census Bureau first published statistics on marital status, only 53 percent of the population 14 years old and over were married, as compared with 60 percent in 1940 and 67 percent in 1950."

Various estimates have been made as to the population capacity

[4] E. M. East, *Mankind at the Crossroads*, New York, 1923, p. 350.

[5] All these statistics of American population are derived from the publications of the U.S. Bureau of the Census. The increased excess in 1950 was due mainly to the high marriage rate during 1940 to 1950.

of the land area of the world. Thompson calculated that there are about 10,000,000,000 acres, or 15,625,000 square miles, of reasonably good agricultural land available. If cultivated and the products consumed according to American standards, this area should support "about 3,000,000,000 to 3,500,000,000 people, or 60 to 100 percent more than are now here.[6] If cultivated according to European standards they should support 4,000,000,000 to 5,000,000,000 people. Smith and Penck made somewhat higher estimates: "If we sum up all these regions, we have a grand total of 5,666,000,000 as against 2,024,286,000 present world estimated population. Penck's total estimated possible world population is 7,689,000,000."[7]

The question of practical importance is what density of population between the minimum and maximum limits is most desirable. This norm would indicate what constitutes relative under-population and what is relative over-population. The determination of the most desirable density depends upon the criterion used. This criterion might be the largest possible amount of economic goods. For this purpose the largest possible population, namely, a population on the verge of absolute over-population, would be the most suitable. A population on the outer limit of the means of subsistence is not likely to be so efficient a labor force as a smaller population whose means of subsistence are relatively more abundant. The capital equipment might not be sufficient to employ all the labor force furnished by so large a population. Some of it would be unproductive and would hamper the productive part of the population. In order to produce the largest possible amount of goods, the population would have to be somewhat below the maximum.

The foregoing criterion is not suitable from the point of view of the elimination of poverty, and the attainment and maintenance of the highest standard of social welfare. Even though the largest possible amount was produced, if a small number of persons received a large part of the product, there would still be as much as or a proportionally larger amount of poverty than at present. If the per capita production is accepted as the criterion, it is impossible to determine a priori how dense a population would produce the largest per capita yield. It would be the population so well adjusted to the means of production as to work with the highest degree of efficiency. As I said many years ago: "Even though the per capita production was the highest, if a small number of persons received a large part of what was produced, there might still be as much poverty as at present. If distribution was equal or much nearer equality than is the case now, the per capita

[6] W. S. Thompson, *Population Problems*, New York, 1930, p. 251.

[7] Warren D. Smith, "World Population," in the *Scientific Monthly*, New York, January 1935, p. 41.

production would be the correct one, for under those conditions society as a whole would be most prosperous."[8]

Many writers have accepted the economic criterion of the optimum population. Most of them have assumed the capitalist system more or less as it now exists. Wolfe has said that "productivity is to be measured by the per capita income of ultimate consumers' goods. This ratio is called the *optimum*, and a population of this most efficient size the *optimum* population."[9] Fairchild has stated the criterion more broadly in terms of the standard of living: "The question of optimum population is a question of how varying sizes of population, given certain conditions of land and the stage of the arts, will affect the standard of living. . . . The only objective, and therefore scientific, conception (of the standard of living) is that of an existing condition (material, tangible goods)."[10] Mukerjee has broadened the economic criterion by adding the conception of longevity: "As populations, whether animal or human, overstep a suitable density, the average duration of life decreases, and sometimes the birthrate falls. Optimum density can be maintained only with a high average length of life and a moderate reproduction. Thus both ecological theory as well as demography indicate the highest average longevity of a living community as the suitable criterion of welfare. It includes the economic criteria of highest average productivity or income of consumers' goods, for high average length of life is an indication of economic prosperity, but it is an indication of something more—wise distribution of wealth, sane expenditure, rational use of leisure, 'good morals, enlightenment and social peace.' "[11]

Briefly stated, it may be said that the density of population at any given time and place is a function of natural resources, progress of the arts and sciences, capital equipment, standard of living in effect or desired, and span of life in existence or desired. The problem of the optimum population assumes a very different aspect in a socialized system from the form it takes in a capitalist system. The incidence of most of the physical, economic, social, and cultural factors involved changes radically when the transition is made from capitalism to collectivism. It is scientifically unwise and practically misleading to

---

[8] Maurice Parmelee, *Poverty and Social Progress*, New York, 1916, p. 170. See also my *Farewell to Poverty*, New York, 1935, especially Chapter *XXIX*, "Population and Geo-Economic Regionalism."

[9] A. B. Wolfe, "The Optimum Size of Population," in papers presented at the eighty-sixth annual meeting of the American Statistical Association, December 1924, Boston, 1926, p. 68.

[10] H. P. Fairchild, in the *Proceedings of the World Population Conference*, London, 1927, p. 75.

[11] Radhakamal Mukerjee, "On the Criterion of Optimum Population," in the *American Journal of Sociology*, Chicago, November 1934, p. 348.

attempt to predict the future movement of population when the incidence of these factors can be so little foreseen.

Like all animal and plant species mankind has ecological relations with nature which are of profound significance with respect to population. Unlike every other species mankind can influence and to a considerable extent control these relations so as to expand greatly the maximum limit of population. The basic sciences of physics, chemistry, and biology furnish man the conceptual means to exercise this control. He can limit or exterminate the species which do him injury. He can stimulate the reproduction of the species which benefit him and improve them by artificial selection. He can increase the production of plant food by applying the principles of agrobiology. He can extract the mineral resources of the earth and create usable substitutes of some of them. He can convert to his own productive use manifold sources of power extraneous to himself.

Human control of the natural environment has gone on apace since the early days of cultural evolution. The tempo of this advance has increased greatly during the past century or two. It is now known that human utilization of natural resources is susceptible of indefinite expansion. Capitalism, however, places narrow artificial limitations upon this expansion. Production is governed by profit-making rather than by human and social needs and wants. Crops are planted with a view to salability in the market. Food and domestic animals may even be destroyed in order to accentuate the market demand and enhance prices. Power already available for use is wasted or not utilized. These capitalist limitations lower greatly the maximum limit of population.

In a socialized system all these artificial limitations disappear. The sciences are no longer frustrated and the arts can be applied without restraint. The ecological and biological possibilities of population are expanded to their outermost limits. How far those possibilities are realized can then be determined by purely human and social considerations.[12]

In each geo-economic region the original factors which determine the outermost limits of population are the fertility of the soil, the mineral resources, and the sources of power. On the basis of these factors a capital equipment can be constructed and a certain density of population maintained according to the standard of living desired and the span of life sought. The geo-economic regions vary greatly in these original factors. With the application of agrobiological prin-

[12] Enid Charles, *The Twilight of Parenthood*, New York, 1934.
Mrs. Charles has graphically outlined a "rationally planned ecology of mankind" and a "biologically planned universe." She is inclined to postulate a large population as desirable *per se* without sufficient regard for all the human and social considerations involved.

ciples many, probably the great majority, of these regions can be made sufficiently fertile to maintain a high density of population. Mineral resources are much more unevenly distributed. The less bulky of these raw materials can be transported long distances and regional deficiencies thereby supplied. In order to import these raw materials a region must be able to exchange them with its own products which are needed and desired by other regions. Otherwise it will be unable to import these necessary raw materials and this deficiency will act as a restriction upon its density of population.

The sources of power vary greatly in different parts of the world and power cannot readily be transported over long distances. Water power is available only where it is located. Coal is very bulky and heavy, and oil only somewhat less so. Though an electric charge can be sent around the world, the high-power transmission of electricity is not effective beyond the range of a few hundred miles. The supply of power, therefore, is most likely to be the decisive factor in determining the density of population in a region where a high standard of living prevails. Abundant power for mass production of goods and labor-saving devices is necessary to maintain such a standard. Atomic power may meet this need.

The North American continent is richly endowed with all these natural factors. The regions which lack soil fertility, raw materials, power—one, two, or all three of these factors—cannot maintain so dense a population with as high a standard of living as is possible on this continent. With a low standard of living, soil fertility alone has often maintained a dense population, as in parts of India and China. When the same or approximately the same high standard becomes prevalent the world over, demographic adjustments to geo-economic conditions will have to take place temporarily by migrations of surplus populations and permanently by differential regional birth rates.

Within these limits set for each region by its geo-economic conditions the density of population can be determined by human and social considerations. In a socialized system procreation will not be influenced by the economic status and interests of individuals. In other words, people will not refrain from having children because they are a financial burden. On the other hand, numerous progeny will not be procreated in order to support the parents in their old age. In similar fashion the aged will no longer be an economic burden upon their children, other relatives, or any other individuals. In a society which guarantees economic security to all its members throughout life, procreation can be completely divorced from individual pecuniary, financial, and economic considerations. Each individual on the average will pay for the social support he receives by means of his

933

contribution of work during his period of service. He will receive it throughout the span of his life, regardless of his longevity. There will be no dependents and paupers. The only persons who will receive this support without making a contribution will be the very small number who for any reason are incapacitated from work, such as the mentally deficient and the crippled.

Under these conditions the parental instincts and emotions can for the first time in history express themselves in their most genuine form. They will be subjected to no repression, distortion, or undue stimulus. How this new cultural situation will affect the birth rate remains to be seen. There will be no ethical or social reason for an increase or decrease of population *per se*. The only exception will be the extreme case, which will arise rarely if ever, in a society with a highly developed technique of production, when the outermost limit of population established by geo-economic conditions is reached or approached.

Some phases of this situation with regard to parentage and reproduction are already adumbrated in Soviet Russia, where there are many institutions for the care of children. Such institutions are necessary for the attainment of communistic ends. If the women are to be economically independent and each woman is to have her own job in agriculture or industry or education or administration, it will no longer be possible for each woman to devote so much of her life to the rearing as well as the bearing of children as she does under the family system. Hence the numerous crèches, nurseries, and kindergartens in Russia. Nearly every factory and farm of any size has its nursery where the women can leave their children while at work.

In order to enable women to bear children, a leave of absence with full pay is given. Ordinarily a woman engaged in physical labor is given two months before and two months after childbirth, or three to four months in all. A woman employed in an office is given six weeks before and six weeks after childbirth, or three months in all. After reaching the fifth month of pregnancy a woman cannot be sent on commissions at a distance from her usual place of residence. During the period of lactation a woman is given in addition to the usual meal periods half an hour every three and a half hours to feed her infant.

Under the family system the rearing of the young is almost exclusively in the hands of the family. Under the Occidental capitalist system the state is not much more concerned with it. Compulsory public education exists in a good many countries. Almost all the moral training, and much of the mental education as well, are left in the hands of the parents. There are several classes in society. The rearing of each person is supposed to fit him for the social and economic status

934

for which he is more or less inexorably predestined. The vast majority remain poor and relatively uneducated.

Under communism the state prepares the young so that they will fit into the collective commonwealth. Their individualities must be moulded accordingly. This is to a certain extent necessary in every society, because undisciplined individualities are unsuitable for any sort of social life, but it is exceptionally important in the communistic society. This, however, does not mean that the development of personality will not be encouraged under communism.

This situation decreases parental authority. Under bolshevism filial obedience is no longer a prime virtue. Even the very youthful individual is rapidly becoming more integrated in the communistic society than in the family organism. Parental authority is sustained to the extent that it has " pedagogical" value, that is to say, is beneficial to the child from a communistic point of view. Upon attaining his majority, the age of eighteen, all parental authority over the child ceases. He then has the right to change his name, if he so desires.[13]

Life under capitalism is singularly barren of broad social relationships for the vast majority. Power is concentrated in the hands of a privileged few who usurp and monopolize most of the available material and cultural advantages from which they can derive a rich social life. Persons without marital and familial relations are usually condemned to an existence of dismal loneliness. The happiness of many individuals depends almost exclusively upon the slender thread of the life of one person—a spouse, a child, a parent, a lover. Those possessing families are harassed by the responsibilities and risks arising out of the economic insecurity of capitalist civilization, which poison family life to a large extent.

In a collectivist society there are no economic obstacles in the way of mating. Freedom in sex relations renders possible the personal adjustments which lead to congenial and satisfactory mates. The begetting of children and parental and filial relations can be enjoyed without the dread menace of hunger and starvation. A high standard of living and many cultural facilities give rise to numerous social relationships shared by all. Death thereby loses some of its terror. Few of the survivors are threatened by utter loneliness. The average length of life is extended. The heightened vitality and virility postpone old age and senility. Most of human existence is enjoyed in a state of health and of youthful strength. All these features of a socialized system augment greatly the happiness derived from mating and reproduction. Human beings come into their own at all stages and

[13] See my *Bolshevism, Fascism and the Liberal-Democratic State*, New York. 1934, Chapters VI entitled "The Transformation of Marriage and of the Family," and VII entitled "Communistic Education."

in all phases of life, namely, as children, lovers, mates, parents, workers, and in old age. The play and reproductive functions of sex become harmonized and integrated with each other.

In his inaugural address of January 20, 1949, President Harry S. Truman of the United States recognized the misery which is widespread in the world: "More than half the people of the world are living in conditions approaching misery. Their food is inadequate. Their economic life is primitive and stagnant." But he failed to recognize that this misery is due mainly to the predatory economic system which he represented and to the destructive and murderous warfare which he and his complotters incite and instigate. The same is even more true of his successor, General Dwight D. Eisenhower.

PART III

GEOGRAPHICAL AND FUNCTIONAL FACTORS

Chapter LIV

The Oriental and Occidental Cultural Zones

ORIENTAL culture is mainly tropical in its provenance, while Occidental culture has evolved almost entirely in the temperate zone. The latter originated and has had its principal development in the Mediterranean basin. It has spread over the whole of Europe and America, and has been carried wherever men of European origin have established colonies or centers of exploitation. The former is represented chiefly in the Indian and Chinese cultures, which are so distinctive that it is hardly possible to speak of a single and identical Oriental culture.

The East is less unified than the West, both culturally and geographically. Just as the Himalaya mountain range thrusts its physical bulk between India and China, so are they separated from each other culturally. The West has had its own continuous, more or less uniform, and recent rapid development. The East has had several coeval lines of development and in modern times has remained comparatively unchanged. The West has had its urban centers of decisive cultural significance for the whole of the Occidental world. The East has had no Athens or Rome, no Paris, London, or New York.

As to whether the Chinese or the Indian is the most characteristic Oriental culture, it would be difficult to say. Each has dominated a vast area in the Eastern world. Japan is culturally the disciple of China. In modern times it has outstripped its ancient tutor in its imitation of the technology of the West. It now stands at the crossways between Oriental and Occidental civilization. China and India have not yet reached this point, at least in so far as technology is concerned. Whether or not the East influenced the West more than the West influenced the East in the past, it is impossible to say. The West is influencing the East greatly at present. Indeed, for the East the situation is very critical, because it may mean an extensive transformation of its culture. For the West the situation is not so critical nor of such immediate importance. But whatever happens in the East cannot fail to react in the long run upon the West. For both of these two great divisions of mankind it is a process of cultural contact and assimilation.

Between the Orient and the Occident lies an indeterminate zone including Asia Minor, Persia, the Arabian peninsula, Egypt, and the North African littoral. Westerners usually classify this region with the East, and Asia Minor is often called the Near East. Much of this culture arose in the Mediterranean area, and it is questionable whether it belongs to the East more than to the West. The Orient is divided into two great cultural zones, the Chinese and the Indian, with several minor cultural systems each of which is more or less closely related to one or the other of the two principal cultures. Which of these two is the most characteristic of the East it is needless to discuss here, and would in any case be more or less futile.

It is often alleged that Oriental is much older than Occidental culture. The principal reason for this widespread notion is the fact that within the historical period the East has remained relatively unchanged in comparison with the West. China is usually cited as possessing the oldest civilization in the world. Inasmuch as the essential features of Chinese culture took shape during the Chou dynasty (1122-249 B.C.). and have diplayed a remarkable degree of permanence and stability for more than 2,500 years, it appears very ancient in contrast to the rapidly changing West.

Another reason for this notion is the popular hypothesis that mankind and culture originated in Asia. A necessary corollary is that the West derived its culture from the East. This hypothesis raises the problem of the place of origin of man, and of the location and date of commencement of the main course of cultural evolution. The expeditions of the American Museum of Natural History and similar enterprises by other scientific institutions have focused attention upon central Asia. But the available data are still inadequate to answer these questions. Indeed, so far as climate is concerned, it is doubtful if central Asia was at any time since human origins warm enough to furnish a cradle for mankind. Man apparently evolved from an anthropoid stock adapted to life only in the tropics. Not until he had acquired a certain amount of material culture in the way of tools, clothing, and fire could he venture into this relatively inhospitable region. So that if he is Asiatic in origin, it may have taken place in the southern peninsulas of that great continent.

Even if man originated in Asia, this does not mean necessarily that the decisive steps in the earlier stages of cultural evolution took place there. Human groups in many parts of the world have attained a certain stage of culture, and then died out, leaving no heritage behind. It is only the advances which are preserved and transmitted

940

permanently that count. Where and when most of the early additions to culture took place it is not even possible to surmise.

The most complete picture of cultural evolution has been obtained for the European and Mediterranean area. This is because the science of anthropology was first developed in Europe, so that there were anthropologists at hand to recognize the significance of finds. Beginning with the Eolithic and the early Paleolithic culture of Heidelberg man, the early and middle Paleolithic culture of Neanderthal man, the later Paleolithic of Aurignacian man, and so on down through the Neolithic to the metal ages, can be traced the pre-historic stages of cultural evolution. At several sites in the classical region of European anthropology, the Dordogne Valley in southern France, there is scarcely a break between the layers representing these cultural horizons. While inspecting the sections exposed at Laugerie Basse, Laugerie Haute, and Le Moustier, in 1926, I was particularly impressed by this fact.

And yet this would not necessarily mean that all of this evolution was indigenous. Climatic changes doubtless gave rise to some of the cultural transformations, as when a late ice age produced the Magdalenian culture. But the intrusion of alien races may have brought cultural elements. Aurignacian man appeared with comparative suddenness after Neanderthal man. Indeed, it is possible that all of the racial types in European anthropology originated elsewhere, and migrated into the European and Mediterranean area.

For the later stages we have to turn to Asia Minor and in particular to Egypt, where was more than anywhere else the cradle of Western civilization. Then crossing the Mediterranean by way of Crete, it reached the historical stage and its efflorescence in the Greek and Italian peninsulas. Concerning all of these stages there is available a rich mass of data.

When we turn to Asia proper, the data become very scanty. Few anthropologists have so far devoted attention to this continent. Most of its vast area is thinly populated in comparison with Europe. Much valuable material which has been found by accident has doubtless been destroyed because no one capable of recognizing its significance was present. Within recent years, however, a few important discoveries of prehistoric remains have been made in eastern Asia.

These sites were in and below the eolian loess, and were accompanied by a fauna of middle Pleistocene appearance. The implements resemble in the main Mousterian and to a certain extent Aurignacian and Magdalenian paleoliths of the European stages. Surface indications of a similar Paleolithic industry were found about 1920 by the third Asiatic expedition of the American Museum of Natural History about 700 miles away from China in western Mongolia. In no one of

941

these sites was a continuous series found. In each case the culture appeared and disappeared suddenly. Moreover, no human remains were found. So that as yet nothing can be said as to the place of origin of this culture, or its relation to the Paleolithic periods in other parts of the world. But these finds prove conclusively the existence of Paleolithic man at a relatively early period in China and Mongolia.

The significant fact about these Paleolithic and Neolithic sites is that nowhere has been discovered a continuous series throughout the Paleolithic stages, from the Paleolithic to the Neolithic, and throughout the Neolithic stages. The connection between the Neolithic and the metal ages and historical times is more apparent. Whether this means that there were actual breaks in the cultural sequence, or that evidence of the sequence has yet to be found, it is impossible to say. It is not improbable that the sequence was continuous, at any rate throughout the Neolithic period, but that influences from the west, from the south, and possibly also from the north, from time to time gave the appearance of a new start. It is even more difficult to make assertions as to the influences from the east to the west during pre-historic times.

So far as we can judge from the scanty data available, the Chinese culture was partly indigenous in its origin and partly derived from elsewhere. It apparently assumed its characteristic form in the middle and lower courses of the Yellow River, and spread eastward into what are now the Chihli and Shantung provinces and southward toward the Yangtse. If linguistic relations furnish any guide, Annam, Siam, Burma, and Tibet belong to the same culture complex, because the languages of those countries belong to the same family as the Chinese tongue. The Chinese appear never to have been pastoral, but always have been agriculturists and village and town dwellers. Such a civilization could readily develop in the fertile valleys of the Hoang-ho (Yellow River) and Yang-tse-Kiang, especially the former.

For the historical period, China has, with the exception of a few doubtful tombs, only literary evidence of the antiquity of its culture. The first more or less authentic dynasty was the Hsia (2205-1766 B.C.), followed by the Shan or Yin dynasty (1766-1122 B.C.). Up to this time what now constitutes China consisted of several independent kingdoms and regions inhabited by unconquered savage and barbarous peoples.

During the long-lived Chou or Chow dynasty (1122-249 B.C.) China became a federation of states ruled by feudal lords owing a loose allegiance to the emperor. Many wars took place between the different states, and the efforts to unify China have continued without entire success down to the present day. For the first two thirds of this dynasty we have the historical record compiled by Confucius (born 551 B.C.) in the Shu-king. While wars and political dissensions were rife, it was

942

nevertheless the classical and constitutional period during which Chinese culture took its characteristic form which served as a unifying bond, and eventually spread to Japan, Korea, and other contiguous countries.

The Chou-li (*circa* 1100 B.C.), a code compiled near the beginning of this dynasty, provided for the ministries of the government, established the different classes, prescribed the order of precedence, and in many other ways regulated Chinese life. In its essential features it was followed down to the present century. It has perhaps had more influence upon a larger number of people over a longer period of time than any other book. During this dynasty also the Chinese classics were edited and compiled, in part by Confucius, which have guided the footsteps of the Chinese people down to the present day.

These classics include, first, the Wu-king or "Five Canons": 1. The Yi-king, or Book of Changes, which is philosophic, containing the Eight Diagrams, and was pre-Confucian. 2. The Shu-king, or Book of History, collected and edited by Confucius. 3. The Shih-king, or Book of Odes, selected by Confucius. 4. The Li-ki, or Book of Rites, which was post-Confucian. 5. The Hsiao-king, or Book of Filial Piety. The Ch'un-ts'iu, or Spring and Autumn Annals (722-481 B.C.) of the State of Lu, which is usually not considered a canonical work, was written probably by Confucius with Tso Chuan's Commentary. The classics include, second, the Ssi-shu or "Four Books": 1. The Lun-yu, or Discourses or Analects of Confucius concerning filial piety. 2. The Ta-hsio, or Great Learning for adults, a short politico-ethical treatise from the Li-ki, or Book of Rites. 3. The Chung-yung, or Doctrine of the Mean, from the Book of Rites. 4. Mencius (372-289 B.C.) expounder of Confucius.

It will be noted that the four books were in part excerpts from, elaborations of, and commentaries on the five canons. These classics and the Chou-li probably constitute the oldest classical literature extant, the only possible exception being the Indian Vedas, which will be discussed later. Fragments only survive of the older Egyptian literature and of the literatures of the ancient civilizations of the Mesopotamian Valley.[1]

During the short-lived Tsin dynasty (249-206 B.C.) reigned the Emperor Shih Huang Ti, who wished to establish a new regime and therefore tried to destroy all of the classical literature. The most important event of his reign was the completion of the Great Wall by joining together existing walls, in order to keep out the nomad Tartars from the north. For many centuries this wall was symbolic of the

---

[1] The Theban Recension of the Egyptian *Book of the Dead* is said to date from 1700-1200 B.C. (E. A. Wallis Budge, *The Gods of the Egyptians*, London, 1904, Vol. I.)

long period of isolation from which China has only recently emerged. He also suppressed feudalism, which, however, was revived from time to time whenever the central government was unusually weak.

During the Han dynasty (206 B.C.-A.D. 221) the imperial form of government was developed and the boundaries extended as far south as the provinces of Kwangsi and Kwangtung. The Chinese, with the exception of the Cantonese, often call themselves the Sons of Han. During this dynasty China had relations with India, whence came Buddhism, Asia Minor, and the Roman Empire.

Owing to civil war, after the Han dynasty ended in 221 A.D., China was for a time divided into the three kingdoms of Wu in the south, Shu in the west, and Wei in the north. Then followed a long period of disunion, until China was consolidated again at the commencement of the T'ang dynasty (A.D. 618-907). During this dynasty the empire was extended southward to Annam and westward to the Caspian Sea. The latter extension brought China into renewed touch with western Asia. As a result of the assimilation of the south, the Cantonese often call themselves the Men of T'ang. It was a period of creative activity in literature and art and in invention. Printing was probably discovered during this period.

The T'ang dynasty was followed by a period of disorder known as the Five Dynasties (A.D. 907-960). Owing to the civil war, the Tartar tribes, especially the Kin tribe, overran the north. The Sung dynasty (A.D. 960-1280), unable to drive out the Kins, was forced to move its capital southward to Nanking and then to Hangchow. Later the Kins were defeated by another Tartar tribe, the Mongols.

In the year 1213 the Mongol chieftain Jenghiz Khan (born A.D. 1162) conquered northern China. Then turning westward he invaded western Asia and Russia. His son Ogatai penetrated Europe as far westward as Hungary and Poland. His grandson Kublai Khan completed the conquest of China and established the Yuan dynasty (A.D. 1260-1368). The Mongols also conquered Korea, Burma, and Annam, but did not succeed in conquering Japan. Their empire extended from the Black Sea to the Yellow Sea, and from northern Mongolia to the Himalayas and Indo-China.

After a century the Mongols were driven out and a Chinese dynasty, the Ming (A.D. 1368-1644), was established, first at Nanking and then at Peking. Under this dynasty the old regime was restored, the civil-service examinations were reorganized, and the government assumed the form which it retained until the establishment of the republic. After nearly three centuries, a Tartar tribe, the Manchus, invaded China and established the Tsing dynasty (A.D. 1644-1911), which lasted until the revolution of 1911 and the Chinese Republic.

During the 4,000 years which have passed since more or less

authentic Chinese history began to be recorded, owing mainly to its geographical position, China has been largely isolated from the rest of the world. While at no time has it been entirely cut off, yet vast distances, lofty mountain ranges, such as the Altai, the Tien-shan, and above all the Himalayas and the Tibetan plateau, and long stretches of arid desert have prevented it from maintaining frequent and close relations with the West or with India. Since the beginning of the sixteenth century, when the first Portuguese traders arrived by way of the sea, these relations have been steadily increasing, so that now China is more exposed to influence from outside than at any time in its history.

When we turn to India we are in what may have been the region of the origin of man. The discovery of the Siwalik fossils suggests that the primates were differentiating rapidly in that region during Miocene time, and that the anthropoid stock may have diverged from the simian during that period. The *Pithecanthropus erectus* found in Java and belonging to the Pliocene may have inhabited India also, because Java was at that time connected with the mainland.

Whatever may have been true as to the origin of man, in India are to be seen numerous cultural remains of prehistoric times. In the Indian Museum in Calcutta and the Madras Museum, in 1926 and again in 1953-4, I inspected large collections of Paleolithic and Neolithic implements, and smaller collections in the Prince of Wales Museum in Bombay and elsewhere. They furnish valuable material for the study of prehistoric man in Southern Asia. They have been little studied by anthropologists, so that their significance is not yet fully known.

Rough stone implements, possibly eoliths, have been reported from the upper Miocene in Burma at Yenangyaung in the valley of the Irrawaddy. Paleoliths of a pre-Chellean type have been found in the Pliocene in the valley of the Godavari River, which flows into the Bay of Bengal on the central east coast of India, and in the valley of the Narbada River, which flows into the Indian Ocean on the West coast from the Central Provinces. All of these finds were associated with extinct animals. If the geological horizons of these implements have been correctly designated, they indicate the extreme antiquity of man in southern Asia, probably greater than in Europe or in central and eastern Asia. Paleoliths of various types have been found at numerous other sites, as, for example, in Madras, in the Deccan in central India, in Rajputana in the north, and in eastern India.

Neolithic implements have been found in great abundance in almost every part of India. No continuous series from the Paleolithic to the Neolithic periods has been discovered. In fact, so far as the existing record goes, there seems to be a large interval of time between the two stone ages. This may well be due to lack of sufficient material and inadequate study of the sites already discovered. It is hard to believe that India has not been continuously inhabited since the beginning of cultural evolution.

In northern and central India the Neolithic was followed by a copper age, but little trace has been found of a bronze age. Important remains of copper have recently been discovered at two sites, Harappa in the Punjab southwest of Lahore in the old bed of the Ravi, a tributary of the Indus, and Mohen-jo-daro in Sind, south of Larkana, in the old bed of the Indus. Both of them appear to be the sites of what were once large cities.

The most significant objects found are stamp-seals, painted pottery, and copper coins. On the seals are as many as sixteen characters which resemble characters in the Sumerian syllabary dating from about 3000 B.C. These include most of the characters on these seals. In the earliest stratum at Mohenjo-daro were found the pottery and copper coins with pictographic signs. The pottery resembles a painted pottery found at Susa in Elam, which has been assigned to the fifth millennium B.C. The earliest of the coins are unlike coins found anywhere else, but some of them bear pictographs which suggest Iranian affinities.

These remains indicate that there was a well-advanced culture in the Indus Valley at a relatively early age. The resemblance between the stone objects, brick work, funeral pottery, and pictographs discovered at Harappa and Mohenjo-daro and Sumerian remains found in Mesopotamia has suggested either that the Indus culture was derived from Mesopotamia, or that the Sumerian culture originated in India. Inasmuch as the Sumerian bears no resemblance to the so-called "Aryan" culture which later dominated northern India, it has also been suggested that the former was Dravidian in origin, that is to say, from southern India. But phases of the Sumerian culture have been found at Susa in Persia and at Anau in Russian Turkestan, and at both of these sites the cultural series goes back continuously to Neolithic strata. So that it seems not unlikely that the Sumerian culture originated in central Asia, and reached India by way of Mesopotamia.

Another feature of Indian prehistory which suggests cultural relations with other parts of the world is furnished by the megalithic monuments. These consist largely of numerous dolmens found in most parts of India from the Narbada River to Cape Comorin. They are very numerous in the Deccan in central India. There are said to be over two thousand in the Bellary district alone. These monuments are used mainly for funerary purposes. Hence they were constructed by peoples who practiced burial. During the iron age, when most of these monuments were erected, burial and cremation were practiced

946

sometimes side by side in central and southern India. Since that time the Hindu custom of cremation has prevailed. Megalithic monuments have been traced all the way from India along the north coast of Africa and the west coast of Europe to Scandinavia. They have also appeared in remote parts of the earth, such as Japan, America, and the South Seas. These facts have given rise to the hypothesis of a single megalithic race which originated this custom. It has also been suggested that it may have originated in India, possibly with the Dravidians of southern India. This is too extensive and complicated a question to decide without more data, and it is sufficient for our purpose to call attention to this cultural relation.

The historical period in India presents a serious difficulty of chronology. We have seen that Chinese chronology goes back four thousand years or more with a good deal of accuracy. Egyptian chronology goes back five thousand years or more. Even as far back as two thousand years, Indian chronology becomes very vague. This appears strange, because a relatively advanced culture doubtless existed there long before that time. It has usually been explained by the fact that the Hindus believe in nirvana or a future state of peace and bliss, when the consciousness of the individual will be obliterated so that time becomes meaningless. Hence time relations in the present existence seem to them to be of little significance.

The lack of a chronology was probably due in part to political conditions. India has at no time been united under a single strong central government. There was no dynasty desirous of keeping a record of events in order to enhance its renown, like the dynasties of China and Egypt. Such records as were kept by local rulers were intermittent and did not give an unbroken chronology.

Other factors which interfered with the keeping of a chronology were the widespread practice of cremation, the limited use of writing, and the character of the Indian classics. Cremation destroys effectually the records of individual lives often found on funerary monuments, which have in Egypt and in many other countries furnished valuable historical data. It discourages the remembrance of the dead or soon turns these memories into myths, unless convenient methods of keeping a written record exist, which was not the case until the era of printing and of books arrived.

Long after writing was introduced, texts were handed down verbally, partly because of the lack of suitable writing materials. The palm leaf is not durable in contrast to papyrus, which made possible permanent written records in Egypt. The principal texts are the Vedas or "Books of Knowledge," consisting mainly of sacred lore, and the two great epics, the Ramayana and the Mahabharata, consisting mainly of myth. All of the Indian literature is permeated with re-

947

ligion and largely mythological, so that there is little room for a historical record.

I have already mentioned the ancient sites at Harappa and Mohen-jo-daro in northwestern India, where cities existed perhaps as long ago as 3000 B.C. North of Harappa is the ancient site of Taxila (at Sarai Kala, near Rawal Pindi), where a city existed probably as early as 2000 B.C. As has been pointed out, the first two cities, and perhaps the third also, represented a culture which may have been derived from Mesopotamia. While it doubtless left its mark on Indian civilization, it seems to have in large part disappeared from this region, or at any rate to have become merged in the culture which became dominant.

About the year 2000 B.C. there began to penetrate into India, probably from the north, the so-called "Aryan" culture. It is often assumed that it was brought into India by an "Aryan" people. This raises the much-debated "Aryan" question. Suffice it to say that there gradually developed the social system now known as Hinduism. It was probably due in part to external forces and in part to indigenous elements. At first it was dominant in the Punjab and in the valleys of the Jumna and the Ganges. Then it slowly worked its way southward. When the Manava-dharma-shastra or Manu-smriti (Code of Manu) took its present shape (between 200 B.C. and A.D. 200), Hinduism was dominant from the Himalayas to the Vindhya range in central India. Eventually it spread over the whole of the Dravidian south, though absorbing some of the Dravidian culture.[2]

In default of an orderly record, a few important events of the four thousand years or so since "Aryan" culture entered India may be noted. The first thousand years and more are shrouded in darkness. During this period the Vedic literature was taking shape, probably from 1500 B.C. onward. The Ramayana and the Mahabharata were probably evolving from 500 B.C. Gautama Buddha was born about 563 B.C. Alexander the Great invaded northern India from 327 to 324 B.C., leaving several Greek garrisons behind. This invasion had considerable cultural significance in bringing Indian in contact with Western culture. Chandragupta Maurya conquered Magadha in 322 B.C., and established the Mauryan dynasty. His grandson Ashoka, who reigned from 274 to 237 B.C., embraced and propagated Buddhism with great zeal. His dominion extended from the Hindu Kush Mountains to approximately Lat. 15°N.

Various foreign dynasties have ruled over different parts of India, such as the Indo-Greek and Indo-Parthian dynasties from 250 B.C. to A.D. 60, the Indo-Bactrian kings from 100 B.C. to A.D. 300, and the

[2] See G. Slater, *The Dravidian Element in Indian Culture*, London, 1924. Dr. Slater lived in Madras from 1915 to 1922.

Kushan or Indo-Scythian dynasty from A.D. 45 to 225. Mohammedan invasions commenced shortly after the origin of Islam (*circa* 600 A.D.). The first Moslem dynasty began in A.D. 1206. Timur, or Tamerlane, the Mughal Tartar, sacked Delhi in 1398. The six great Mughal emperors (Baber, Humayun, Akbar, Jahangir, Shah Jehan, and Aurung-Zeb) reigned from 1526 to 1707. Various European nations began to establish colonies in the sixteenth century, the first being the Portuguese at Goa on the west coast in 1510. England extended its suzerainty over the whole of India during the eighteenth and nineteenth centuries.

The preceding survey indicates clearly that sufficient data are not yet available to weigh with any degree of precision the relative influence upon each other of Eastern and Western culture during the prehistoric and early historical periods. Two regions stand out with peculiar prominence because of the antiquity and the continuity of the cultural series there exposed. In Egypt a relatively high culture existed more than five thousand years ago and was preceded by a well marked Neolithic culture. There are also numerous Paleolithic sites which may or may not have been connected with the Neolithic. At Anau on the eastern border of the Iranian plateau, the cultural series goes back through agricultural and pastoral stages to the Neolithic, the lowest strata perhaps dating as far back as 6000 B.C. It has sometimes been suggested that the domestication of animals and agriculture originated in this region. There is also some evidence that agriculture originated in Egypt. It is not impossible that it developed independently in both regions.

These two regions lie to the west of the greatest natural barrier in the world—namely, the Hindu Kush, the Pamirs, the Kwenlun, the Karakoram, and the Himalaya ranges forming a continuous mountainous wall, while the Tien-shan and Altai ranges extend to the northeastward. The barrier is reinforced with the aid of the deserts of eastern and southern Persia, Baluchistan, Turkestan, and Mongolia. This great barrier more or less effectually separated India and eastern Asia from the West, and India from eastern Asia.

This is why I have already asserted that the frontier between Oriental and Occidental civilization lies considerably farther to the east than is usually assumed. Asia Minor, Mesopotamia, Arabia, Egypt, and Persia belong to the cultural series represented in its later stages by the Mediterranean culture. While the cultural area represented by Anau lies to the west of the great barrier, it apparently exercised a good deal of influence in both directions.

China has influenced the West very little. Its culture may have been derived in the first instance from a type of culture developed in northern or central Asia eastward of the great barrier. A peculiar feature of this culture was an aversion to milk as a food, which is still characteristic of eastern Asia, whereas it is eaten by Indo-Europeans, Semites, Scythians, Turks, etc. As we have seen, it was subjected to occasional influences from the West. The Chinese culture has developed along the line of a powerful family organization based on ancestor worship, the sacredness of the family, filial devotion, and marriage enjoined upon every one as a duty to the ancestors. The resulting subjection of the individual to the family, and to a much less degree to the state, accounts in large part for the racial and national continuity of the Chinese and the tenacity of their culture. This culture has become dominant throughout the world of the so-called Mongoloid or yellow peoples.

The only phase of the "Aryan" culture of which we can be certain is linguistic. Indeed, this is probably the only sense in which the term has any meaning, so that it is as well to abandon the word "Aryan" entirely. Northern India is linguistically Indo-European, whereas there is no such linguistic connection between China and the West. Ethnically also it is closely related to the white race in features, hair, etc. The only outstanding difference is a darker skin color. But the culture which now dominates the whole of India was in all probability developed at home. Its religion permeates its culture to a degree unequaled by any other religion, and its social organization is based upon the amazing caste system, the like of which has never existed at any other time or place.

Let us say, then, that the dividing line throughout prehistoric and historical times down to the present between Oriental and Occidental culture has run, roughly speaking, northward from the Gulf of Oman along the eastern Persian frontier, and then northeastward along what are now the western frontiers of Chinese Turkestan and Mongolia. They are separated by a wide indeterminate zone where the cultures mingle, so that it is often difficult to say which is predominant. As it is impossible to decide which of these two great divisions of mankind influenced the other the most in the past, each should maintain a becoming modesty on this point. Unlike the West, the East is divided into two great cultural spheres of influence, the Chinese in eastern and the Indian in southern Asia.[3]

[3] This chapter is derived mainly from the first few chapters of my *Oriental and Occidental Culture, An Interpretation*, New York, 1928.

Chapter LV

The Religious East

WHILE the sacred cow of the Hindus is a characteristic feature of their religion which seems like an obsolete superstition to all non-Hindus, Hinduism displays a wide range of belief and practice, more so probably than any other religion. The Hindus trace their religion to the Vedas (Books of Knowledge) of which there are a hundred or more. The most important are the Rig Veda, containing 1,028 psalms, or hymns praising the gods; the Yajur Veda, consisting of sacred formulas; the Sama Veda, containing selections from the Rig Veda in the form of chants; and the Atharva Veda, consisting of charms and other magical devices. They were followed by the Brahmanas (1000-800 B.C.), which are priestly treatises laying special emphasis on the sacrifices to the gods.

The religion of the Vedas was mostly nature worship derived from a primitive form of animism. The Rig Veda contains prayers and praises to some forty-two objects of worship, such as the sun, moon, sky, wind, rain, air, fire, dawn, earth, etc. The prayers are for long life, sons, good crops, freedom from disease, cattle, success over enemies, worldly prosperity in general, etc. Among the so-called "Aryan" gods, personifying forces of nature, which have played a part in Vedic religion, were Indra (wind and rain), Dyaus Pitar (Heaven- or Sky-Father. Compare Zeus), Prithivi Matar (Earth-Mother), Agni (fire), Mithra (sun), Soma (intoxication), etc.

The Hindus allege that theirs is the oldest religion, and often attribute an incredible antiquity to it, sometimes going back hundreds of thousands and even millions of years. Professor Max Muller estimated that the Vedic literature, which during its earlier stages was transmitted mainly or entirely by word of mouth, was taking shape from 1500 to 500 B.C. It is likely that the Vedic religion was developing from about 2000 B.C. onward, first in the valley of the Indus and later in the valleys of the Jumna and the Ganges. The caste system, which constitutes an integral part of the Hindu religion, probably

951

developed during the latter part of this period. As has already been indicated, the Vedic religion incorporated a considerable part of the Indo-European ("Aryan") mythology. But in its own peculiar form Hindu religion is an indigenous product.

Two lines of development from the Vedic religion may be distinguished, the more philosophic and esoteric, and the popular. The Upanishads are philosophic treatises, prepared about 800-600 B.C., which deal with Brahma the Absolute as the only reality. Three schools of Brahmanic thought and philosophy were founded more than twenty-five centuries ago. The Sankhya school is materialistic, but is dualistic because it teaches that individual souls exist. It believes in no Divine Being, is therefore atheistic, and advocates action. The Vedanta school is monistic and pantheistic. The Yoga school prescribes the attainment of nirvana by means of renunciation, self-effacement, and asceticism. Its methods are used in varying degrees by most of the Hindu sects and by Buddhism as well.

Popular Hinduism is polytheistic, its pantheon containing numerous gods and goddesses, most of whom are in conjugal relations with each other, and have offspring. Early in its evolution three gods acquired the ascendancy and form the Hindu trinity. They are Brahma the Creator, Vishnu the Preserver, and Shiva the Destroyer and Reproducer. The two latter are probably derived from nature-gods. Philosophic Hinduism regards them as personal manifestations of Brahma the only reality, and interprets polytheism and its worship as symbolic of spiritual truth. Popular Hinduism has no enthusiasm for the worship of Brahma, who is too remote and impersonal to come within the ken of the common people. But Vishnu and Shiva are very human deities who are ardently worshiped in the forms of their idols and their symbols. The literature of popular Hinduism includes the Puranas or religious tales, and particularly the two great epics, the Mahabharata or "Great Bharata War," and the Ramayana or "Career of the god-hero Rama."

Vishnu typifies the universal belief in transmigration and reincarnation taught by philosophic and popular Hinduism alike. He has come down to earth nine times already and is expected a tenth time. The last three of his mundane incarnations were as Rama, the hero of the Ramayana; Krishna, whose biography is related in the Mahabharata; and Buddha. The latter incarnation resulted from a compromise with Buddhism, and helped to absorb Indian Buddhism into the Hinduism whence it had sprung. The worship of Vishnu as Rama the model man, and as Krishna the savior, is very popular throughout India.

Shiva, known also as Mahadeva, the great god, has innumerable temples dedicated to his worship, and also to his wife Parvati, who has several characters. As reproducer, he is worshiped in the form of an appropriate symbol, the lingamyoni, or union of the external sex organs. His destructive functions are more particularly associated with his wife in one of her characters, Durga or Kali the terrible.

In addition to idolatry, there is a great deal of fetishism or the worship of natural objects. Not only the cow but to a lesser degree the monkey and certain other animals are treated with reverence, if not worshiped. In its most extreme form, as in the Jain religion, this zoophilism is carried to the point of revering all animals and of refraining from killing any of them, even those dangerous to man. Belief in transmigration of souls encourages this practice in a measure, because any animal or plant may be an ancestor, a holy person, or even a god. Places which have been inhabited by gods, saints, and other holy personages acquire sanctity thereby.

The doctrine of metempsychosis, or transmigration of souls, is universally accepted. But it is not wholly satisfactory, because it involves effort if the individual is to attain to higher incarnations. Consequently, we find a doctrine of salvation by faith creeping into Hinduism, just as it has into many another religion, because it promises an easy way of attaining eternal bliss. The Bhagavad-Gita, or "Song of the Adorable One," is incorporated in the Mahabharata, but was probably composed after the beginning of the Christian era, rather late in the development of Hinduism. It is ostensibly a treatise on Yoga, and expresses many of the characteristic Hindu beliefs. It manifests fear of the mingling of castes, and asserts the indestructibility of the soul as a part of the World Soul. It stigmatizes conscious existence as an evil and proclaims the extinction of individual consciousness as desirable. It derogates work as evil, and characterizes absorption in the Supreme Being and emancipation from rebirths as the highest good. This may be attained by knowledge, which is subjugation of the senses. The Yoga system is one method of attaining this end. But in the eighteenth or last discourse faith in the Lord Krishna is exalted as the best method. Thus speaks the Lord to his faithful disciple Arjuna: "Abandoning all duties come unto Me alone for shelter; sorrow not, I will liberate thee from all sins."

The contrast between popular and philosophic Hinduism is in some respects very great. Indian religious thought ranges all the way from the different forms of theism through monism and pantheism to skepticism, materialism, and atheism. Though the three latter cannot be regarded as religion, Hinduism displays a remarkable degree of catholicity in tolerating them. Their ablest representatives often assert that all religions can be incorporated in their own, as contrasted with the mutually exclusive religions of the West.

Another religion originated in India and has spread over a large part of Asia, though it has for many centuries had little influence in the land of its origin. The Brahman or priestly caste early gained a prestige and ascendancy which it has retained to the present day. Some twenty-five centuries or so ago there took place a struggle between the Rajputs of northern India, who belong to the warrior or Kshatriya caste, and the Brahmans, whose domination they resented. About the year 536 B.C. was born a Rajput prince, Siddhartha Gautama, the son of Suddhodana, ruler of the Sakya clan, who later became known as Buddha (the Enlightened) or Sakyamuni (sage of the Sakyas). The accounts of his life in the Buddhist sacred literature are mostly legendary. It is alleged that early in his career he became disgusted with the arrogance of the Brahmans, shocked at the injustice of the caste system, and appalled at the poverty and degradation of the lower castes. Accordingly, he renounced his princely rank, left his family, and devoted a long life (ca. 563-483 B.C.) to meditation and teaching.

To what extent Buddha himself created the Buddhistic system of thought and of practice it is difficult to say. Back of it lies the Sankhya philosophy of materialism and atheism alluded to above, while the rivalry of the Rajputs and the Brahmans doubtless had its influence. The original Buddhism rejected belief in god and in the soul. With respect to the solution of the ultimate problems of philosophy, Buddha is reputed to have been as skeptical as the modern scientist. At its inception, therefore, Buddhism was not a religion, because it did not contain animistic beliefs in the supernatural which are essential in order to constitute a religion. It was a movement of reform against the social evils which then existed, and a system of ethical teaching.

As might be expected of a non-religious system, primitive Buddhism laid emphasis upon conduct in this life. Buddha taught the middle course between indulgence and asceticism, and outlined the eightfold path of right belief, resolve, speech, action, livelihood, effort, thought, and meditation. At the same time it incorporated the characteristic Indian belief in nirvana, or a state of bliss in which all desire has disappeared so that perfection is attained.

For the first two or three centuries Buddhism made little headway. Then Ashoka, the third Mauryan king of Magadha, who reigned over a large part of India from 274 to 237 B.C., became an ardent convert. By means of edicts embodying the moral principles of Buddhism, by collecting the sacred books, aiding the monasteries, building stupas (temples), and in other ways he spread it over his country. By means of missionaries, he propagated it in other countries. Partly as a result of the impetus given by him, Buddhism became the predominant religion from the third century B.C. to the fourth century A.D. But the popular Hindu religion had not died during this period, and

954

it was manifestly to the interest of the Brahmans to revive it. Gradually it won its way back, so that at the end of a thousand years or so Buddhism had disappeared almost entirely from India.

Hardly had Buddha passed away before his followers began to exalt him, first as the perfect man, then as a god. Thus the erstwhile prince Gautama and humanitarian sage, contemptuous of gods and supernaturalism, became the Supreme Being. Then there arose a belief in recurrent incarnations of Buddha as Bodhisattvas (living buddhas), who intercede with him in behalf of men. About the second or third century A.D. in northern India these beliefs assumed the form of Mahayana (greater vehicle) Buddhism, with numerous temples and monasteries, an elaborate ritual, and incorporating many gods and demons in addition to Buddha and his incarnations. This form of Buddhism, so different from the original, eventually spread to Tibet, China and Japan. In Tibet it developed into a highly ritualistic cult with a complicated hierarchy of spiritual potentates known as Lamaism, which is widespread also in Mongolia, to a lesser extent in Manchuria, and to a small extent in northern China. In recent years Mahayana Buddhism has been most alive in Japan, where it is developing along its own lines. The earlier or Hinayana (lesser vehicle) Buddhism has persisted in name in Ceylon, Burma, and Thailand (Siam). But the animistic beliefs and magical practices which characterize it in these countries bear little resemblance to the conceptions of its founder.

A Chinese funeral is symbolic of the religious situation in China. First come ill-clad men and boys carrying banners, followed by the band. Then come the priests, Taoist, Buddhist, Lamaist, and if there were Confucian priests, they would be there too. The bier and the mourners follow. If the deceased is the father of the family, perhaps the eldest son will be walking barefoot behind the bier, clad in white rags and supported on either side by friends.

The canny Chinaman summons the official representatives of all the cults, for is it not safest to propitiate all of the gods which are said to exist in behalf of the departed relative whose spirit is now wandering in the other world? To the Westerner accustomed to monotheistic religions which are bitterly opposed to each other, and which often persecute each other's adherents, it is a strange sight. Is it an indication of religious decadence or of a remarkable degree of tolerance?

In eastern Asia as elsewhere religions arose out of a primitive animism which personified the spirits of the forces of nature. These spirits play an important part in popular religion. Probably owing to the central position occupied by the clan and the family in Chinese social organization, the worship of the dead early became the chief

955

feature of the religion of China. The Confucian literature gave the classical expression of this worship. In other respects it is not a religious literature. The Li-ki, or Book of Rites, describes this worship, and the Hsiao-king and Lun-yu, or Analects of Confucius, are discourses on filial piety. Thus the cult of the ancestors became the principal organized religion. What corresponded to atheism was refusal to worship one's ancestors. In so far as religion served as a means of social cohesion, it was filial piety which bound together the clan and the family, and to a less degree the nation.

Confucianism is, therefore, mainly a domestic religion. Whenever an individual dies, a wooden tablet bearing his or her name and title is put up in the home or in the temple of the clan or greater-family. From time to time offerings are made to the deceased ancestors. There is little opportunity for personal religion, because the family or clan and not the individual is the unit, and prayer is little used. Modeled after the domestic, there developed an official religion. The emperor was the Son of Heaven, and at stated intervals made offerings to heaven and also to the earth. With the establishment of the republic in 1911, the official religion disappeared. But ancestor worship is still the most widespread form of religion in China.

Shortly before Confucius (551-478 B.C.) came Lao-tze (born *circa* 604 B.C.), a philosopher concerning whom little is known. He taught a mystical doctrine contained in the *Tao-teh-king*. This book is attributed to him, but (probably compiled in the 3rd century B.C.) contains only a few of his sayings and consists largely of meaningless padding. His doctrine is suggested in the following excerpts: "The self-controlled man makes it his business to dwell in the Inner Life; he teaches, not by words, but by actions." "Many men have superfluous possessions. I have nothing that I value; I desire that my heart be completely subdued, emptied to emptiness." "Tao gives Life to all beings. Teh nourishes them. It gives to each being its form. It gives the inward urge towards perfectness." [1]

The Taoist religion, which is traced back to Lao-tze, contains little of his teachings. It has incorporated many of the popular beliefs with respect to good and bad spirits which are supposed to influence the life and well-being of mankind, and is mainly a system of magic to coerce these spirits. The Taoist priest is a prayermonger and diviner for rain. He practises geomancy and necromancy, and seeks to protect against evil spirits and illness by magical means. The Taoist cult searches for immortality and is the spiritualism and witchcraft of China. Thus the popular Taoism is on a much lower intellectual level than Confucianism, which includes many ethical and social

---

[1] These excerpts are taken from Chapters II, XX, and LI of the translation by Isabella Mears, Theosophical Publishing House, London, 1922.

teachings. Whether Taoism as a personal religion of mysticism still survives and is practised by a few, it is difficult to ascertain.

The missionary zeal of Buddhism reached China at an early date. It is said that in 217 B.C. eighteen missionaries arrived. About the year A.D. 65 there returned with Buddhist missionaries a delegation of Chinese who had been sent to India by the emperor to investigate this religion. In A.D. 399-414 Fa-hien went to India for the same purpose. Bodhidharma, one of the living buddhas, came to China in A.D. 520. Huien-tsiang (Yuan Chwang) went on his journey to India, of which he wrote a detailed account, in A.D. 629-45, and I-tsing in 671-95.

Through such contacts Buddhism, in its later Mahayana form, became permanently established in China, though it experienced at times persecutions and attempts to expel it. Mahayanism had certain advantages which aided it in gaining a foothold. While belief in a chief god—namely, Shang-ti the Over-Ruler—already existed, the Lord Buddha furnished a more human and attractive personality to worship. The Bodhisattvas, who deny themselves nirvana in order to save mankind, offered an easy way of attaining salvation. The living buddha Amitabha is especially loved and revered, also an Indian goddess (Avalokiteshvara), who became the goddess of mercy and pity in the Mahayanist pantheon and is known in China as Kuan-yin. This religion taught an attractive doctrine of a paradise in the west to which the saved will go for an eternity of bliss. Prayer and invocation are much used, and furnish a ready means always at hand of trying to influence the divine beings who decide the destinies of men. Last, but perhaps not least, a numerous clergy of priests and monks were at hand to propagate this religion. Mahayanism furnishes a more personal religion than either Taoism or Confucianism.

China presents the extraordinary spectacle of three religions side by side, all of which may be professed by the same people at the same time. In the Hall of the Three Religions the images of Confucius, Lao-tze, and Buddha stand on the same platform, but the Indian sage who attained godhood occupies the place of honor in the center. In the temple of all the gods are to be found the images not only of the gods of the three great religions, but also local gods, nature gods, family gods, and any other gods whose renown has reached the community, so catholic is the Chinese sentiment in matters of religion. Confucius himself was raised to the highest divine rank by the Imperial Government as recently as 1906, probably in order to make him equal to Jesus Christ.

Confucianism, in the form of ancestor worship, ranked highest officially under the empire, and probably does still among the upper classes. Taoism is often resorted to by the common people for aid in meeting the problems of daily life. It is said that Mahayanism appeals more strongly to the women than to the men.[2] The two latter have become chiefly forms of ritual. In practice the three religions are much mingled. Chinese religion is largely a belief in good and evil spirits which must be exorcised or propitiated by magical or by religious means. The general result from this situation is that there is a high degree of tolerance in religious matters, and that a large part of Chinese life is secularized because no one religion has succeeded in dominating it completely.

While visiting many Buddhist temples throughout Japan, several times I saw a group of women (the men were conspicuous by their absence) being addressed by a priest, who was apparently imparting religious and moral instruction. The image of Amidha Buddha (known in China as Amitabha) appears often, and there are a number of temples dedicated to the goddess Kwannon (known in China as Kuan-yin).

These incidents illustrate various phases of the religious situation in Japan. Mahayana Buddhism was introduced from Korea in A.D. 552.[3] Up to that time writing was little used, and Japan had only in part imbibed the civilization of China. Along with the religion came a good deal of this civilization. Mahayanism rapidly superseded the earlier Shinto religion, because it was better organized, carried along with it an ethical code which met some of the needs of the people, advocated the contemplative life which appealed to a certain number, and had a highly developed art.

In course of time several sects were introduced from China, and new ones developed at home, so that sectarianism is now almost as prevalent in Japanese Buddhism as it is in Christianity. According to the Department of Education, in 1919 there were 71,626 temples and 52,894 priests. Most of the temples belonged to the six leading sects, of which the Shin sect had nearly twenty thousand temples and the Nichiren sect about five thousand. In Kyoto, Koyasan, and elsewhere I talked with representatives of several of the sects, and found that their theological differences resemble in some respects the differences between the Christian sects, though in no case so great as the schism between Protestant and Catholic Christianity.

Ritualism has characterized Mahayanism for many centuries. While prominent in Japan, it has not become as formalistic and sterile as

[2] See, for example, W. E. Soothill, *The Three Religions of China*, London, 1913.

[3] Some of the principal Mahayana sects in Japan with dates of origin are Tendai, 805 A.D.; Shingon, 806 A.D.; Jodo (Pure Land), 1175 A.D.; Zen (Meditation), 1191, 1227 A.D.; Shin (True Pure Land), 1224 A.D.; Nichiren, 1253 A.D.

in Lamaism. It has retained the characteristics of a personal religion. During the last few decades it has been influenced by Western humanitarian ideas, and is now engaged in many works of amelioration and of social reform. On the whole, it resembles the highly organized Western church more than any other Eastern religion, having congregational worship and singing, schools for religious instruction, a young men's association, and women's societies. It has imbibed something of the same "punch" which Japan has borrowed from the West in many phases of its recent life.

Another Japanese religion was revived or given a new form after the restoration to power of the Mikado in 1867. This is Kami-no Michi, or "The Way of the Gods," translated into Chinese as Shin-tao and usually called Shinto. At Yamada in the Ise peninsula in 1925 I stood in a somber grove of cryptomeria trees beside the holiest Shinto shrine. It is an austerely simple wooden structure with a white screen at the entrance, beyond which nothing can be seen. A large class of school-boys marched up under the guidance of their teachers and bowed low before the screen. Then came a similar class of school-girls. At frequent intervals arrived groups of adults or single individuals. From a neighboring squadron of warships came a large company of sailors, parading under the command of their officers, to make their obeisances before the sacred shrine. What did it all mean?

The Japanese race came largely from northern Asia by way of Korea in successive immigrations, with occasional Malay infusions from the south. Sun worship was an important feature of Tartar religion. The worship of the sun goddess and of the goddess of agricultural or food goddess, joined with more primitive forms of nature worship, became the early religion of Japan, known as Shinto, the way of the gods. As already indicated, Buddhism displayed it to a large extent, and some attempts were made to combine the two. But the belief still persisted that the mikado was descended from Amaterasu Omikami, the sun goddess, in a direct line, and that the Japanese people is in some way related to her. The constitution, promulgated in 1889, states that the imperial line is "unbroken for ages eternal," and that "the emperor is sacred and inviolable."

When the restoration took place in 1867, an almost religious worship of the mikado commenced though the earlier mikados had not been deified. In the outburst of nationalism which followed, the Japanese Government saw fit to revive and foster the old religion as a means of intensifying this nationalism. Numerous shrines were constructed and put under the charge of the Department of Home Affairs. In 1920 there were 115,509 shrines, many of them very small, and about 15,000 priests. The mikado was the chief Shinto priest. Shinto rites were used at state ceremonies.[4] The right of officiating at funerals and at marriages was given to the priests, though formerly marriage had been a civil contract. In addition to and in a measure apart from the official religion, there are several Shinto sects with their own priests which carry on propaganda for the ancient religion, and preach reverence for the deities and obedience to the precepts handed down by the "divine" ancestors.

What comparisons and contrasts can we discern between the religious situation in the East and in the West? In the so-called Near East, which belongs to the Western cultural sphere more than to the Eastern, originated two Semitic religions, Christianity and Islam. The one dominates the West. The other dominates the borderland between the West and the East, with encroachments upon the former and incursions into the latter. Both are belligerently monotheistic, and therefore intolerant of strange gods. Both are based upon sacred books which profess to contain the revelations of God to mankind, and therefore to be infallible. Both are animated by a missionary zeal to convert mankind to the only "true" god and religion. Consequently, both are intolerant to a degree which has resulted in an untold number of persecutions, religious wars, and the like. Indeed, this spirit of intolerance goes so far as often to result in conflicts between the different sects of the same religion. This is particularly true of Christianity, because sectarianism is most rife in that religion, and the gulf between Catholic and Protestant Christianity is extraordinarily great.

We have seen that in China it is possible to profess at least three religions at the same time, and in Japan two. Throughout the East monotheism is the exception rather than the rule. Polytheism is usually conducive to a certain degree of receptiveness toward strange gods, for—who can tell?—the gods of the foreigners may not be wholly devoid of power, and therefore worthy of propitiation. Among its more intelligent adherents, there is a tendency to regard Hinduism as a synthesis of religions, and therefore to welcome strange and new religions to a place in the synthesis. On the other hand, the orthodox Hindus regard Hinduism as acquired only by birth, so that their attitude toward other religions is one of indifference rather than either of acceptance or of rejection. While religious fanaticism and bigotry are widespread in the East, especially in India, which is intoxicated

---

[4] Professor Chamberlain, who taught for many years in Japan, asserted that mikado and Japan worship was invented since 1888, and was grafted on to Shinto, a primitive nature cult, while the common people clung to Buddhism. He asserted also that the moral ideals, especially loyalty and filial piety, now attributed to imperial ancestors, were derived from the Chinese sages during the period when Chinese culture was influencing Japan greatly. Shinto has no sacred book, but important imperial rescripts may eventually form one. (B. H. Chamberlain, *The Invention of a New Religion*, London, 1918.)

with religion, the factors cited discourage an aggressive intolerance toward other religions, except when they interfere with their own practices, as through missionary endeavor or through conquest. Even Mahayana Buddhism, the only missionary religion of the East, probably because its Supreme Being was derived from the humanitarian Indian sage, is gentler and less aggressive in its missionary enterprises than the religions whose Supreme Being was derived from a ferocious Semitic tribal deity. But in the East, as in the West, every religion is intolerant of all others in the sense that it is contemptuous of them. And it is inevitable that it should be so, because each religion professes to teach the absolute truth, than which there can be no other.

Religion is much more institutionalized in the West than in the East. The extreme form is Roman Catholicism with its elaborate hierarchy ranging from the Pope and his College of Cardinals down to the lower clergy. Protestant Christianity also is highly institutionalized, though not always hierarchically, each church being a distinct entity, often politically and legally recognized. Furthermore, there is almost invariably a professional priesthood under whatever name (priest, deacon, pastor, parson, minister, preacher, clergyman, canon, bishop, archbishop, *et al.*) Services are held at stated intervals before congregations which attend regularly. The church thus becomes a social gathering-place. The priesthood exhorts and preaches. Individuals are admitted to membership by means of prescribed ceremonies (baptism, confirmation, etc.).

Islam also is somewhat institutionalized, though less than Christianity. The larger part of the Mohammedan world looks up to the calif as its spiritual head. Since the overthrow of the Turkish sultanate in 1923, the califate is in a state of confusion. This may be temporary, for the Moslems, even in distant countries like Pakistan, desire a new califate. There is a professional priesthood, through not so well defined as in Christianity. There are regular times for prayer observed by Mohammedans the world over. There are services in the mosques at stated intervals often attended by large congregations, and sometimes including exhortations by mullahs. But Islam adjusts itself readily to local conditions, much more so than Christianity, when it is propagated among so-called "backward" peoples. Then only a profession of belief in Allah and in Mohammed his prophet may be required, and Islam as an institution hardly exists at all. For example, most of the Javanese profess Islam. And yet in Java in 1925 I saw no mosque or mullah, though many wear the cap which indicates that they have made the *hadj* (pilgrimage) to Mecca in order to acquire merit thereby. Because Islam is little exacting, many of their Malay and African converts retain most of their primitive animistic beliefs.

In the East the fane is a shrine rather than a church. To it come the devotees at any and all times, when it is convenient and when they are in need, to genuflect and to pull a rope which rings a bell, to light a candle and to leave offerings, to utter a prayer or to mutter an incantation. Ceremonies are held at times, but usually not at frequent and stated intervals. The hebdomadal sacred day of Semitic origin, which encourages regular ceremonies, does not exist, except to the slight extent that it has been introduced from the West.[5] Aside from unimportant cases like Tibetan Buddhism, no Eastern religion has an elaborate hierarchy. Confucianism has no priesthood. The Taoist priests are in the main magicians. The Brahmans wield a powerful influence and have an enormous prestige. But they form a caste in the social organization, and, in theory at least, perform important social functions. The Mahayanist priesthood and monkhood are perhaps most similar to the Western clergy. Though Eastern religion is not so highly institutionalized, the shrine is nevertheless an important social center. Markets and places of amusement gather around it, so that it becomes a center both for trade and for recreation.

This brief comparison is not concerned with the question as to whether any particular religion, or religion in general, is true or untrue, right or wrong. Such questions are irrelevant for the immediate purposes of this treatise. Moreover, the comparisons and contrasts suggested are relative and not absolute. For example, I have said that Western religion is monotheistic. And yet Christianity, for all its boasted monotheism, has an inexplicable doctrine of a divine trinity in which, by means of a mysterious mathematics, three are one and one god becomes three. The Christian God has a son who himself ranks high as a deity. The angels and demons derived from Zoroastrianism and Judaism, especially Satan the archdevil, form a host of minor deities, while human beings themselves with their immortal souls are godlike in comparison with the dumb beasts. Islam also has its complement of angels and good and bad jinns or genii midway between men and angels, while Mohammed and some of the saints (*e.g.,* Ali and his sons Hassan and Husein, all of whom were martyrs) waver on the brink of godhood. In fact, no religion ever has been entirely monotheistic, and no religion can become so, because when it reaches that stage it passes over into a form of monism which is a philosophy rather than a religion.

Throughout such a comparison arise many likenesses and points of contact. Prayer is used in the East as in the West in an endeavor to secure the many things which mankind craves. Heaven in some form usually exists to reward the faithful, and sometimes a hell for the unfaithful. Jesus, Krishna, and Amidha Buddha alike intercede with the chief god, whatever his name may be, to save men from the evil consequences of their conduct. It is often asserted that these

[5] See, for example, Hutton Webster, *Rest Days*, New York, 1916.

likenesses are due to imitation, that Jesus was derived from Krishna, and that Buddhism became a religion of salvation by mediation through intercourse with Christianity in the region of northwestern India, Kashmir, and Afghanistan. Even though a certain amount of borrowing may have taken place, these likenesses indicate fundamental similarities of human nature.

Whether the East or the West is the more religious is a complicated question. India is the most religious country in the world. Mysticism is prevalent in the East. Astrology, geomancy, necromancy, and other forms of magical belief and practice, which are closely allied and mingled with religion, are widespread in the East, whereas science has checked them to some extent in the West. Science has also secularized many phases of Western life. All of these facts suggest that the East is more religious than the West. They raise various psychological questions as to habits of thinking and ways of acquiring knowledge which will be discussed in later chapters.[6]

[6] It should be noted that the defeat of Japan in 1945, and the coming of communism to China in 1949, have caused marked changes in the Oriental religious situation, as well as in many other phases of Oriental life.

Chapter LVI

Eastern Mysticism and Western Science

IN another work I have said that "all knowledge is subjective because it comes to us through our senses in the form of sensations, and we cannot be absolutely certain that these sensations represent to us truly the nature of the world which is exterior to us. For scientific purposes, however, we need to practise what is sometimes called 'naive realism' and assume that things in the exterior world are actually as our senses represent them to be."[1] By exploring the universe within our reach, by comparing our sensations at different times and places and with the sensations of others, by observing the behavior of our fellow-creatures, by undertaking experiments to ascertain how things take place—by these and various other methods we arrive at knowledge which is objective, because tests have been applied to it other than those of our own senses at any one time or place. The sum of this knowledge constitutes science.

The Western world has by such means acquired in considerable measure the scientific point of view and attitude of mind. In the East, on the contrary, knowledge is still largely subjective in its origin, because impressions received through the senses are not submitted to these external tests. Many believe that they have attained absolute knowledge by means of contemplation, meditation, or physical exercises. These methods are most fully exemplified in the yoga systems of reaching union, equilibrium, or harmony with the divine will or world soul. The Bhagavad-Gita (early A.D.), or Hindu "New Testament," which is very eclectic, in its eighteen sections discusses seventeen of these systems, including yoga by the Sankhya philosophy of evolution, yoga of action, of wisdom, of the renunciation of action, of self-subdual, of discriminative knowledge, of the vision of the universal form, of devotion, etc., not all of which are consistent with each other.

Yoga methods have been advocated by all systems of Indian phi-

[1] *The Science of Human Behavior*, New York, 1913, p. 4.

964

losophy, and used by every Indian religion. Buddhism has carried them into other parts of Asia, and rumors of them have reached Europe and America through yellow-robed swamis and Western devotees returned from the Orient. Yoga is supposed to illustrate an interest in the absolute which is universal in the East as contrasted with the West. As we shall see, this contrast exists only in part.

A description of some of the yoga methods, both physical and mental, will indicate what sort of knowledge is supposed to be acquired. An erect sitting posture is assumed with head, neck and chest in a straight line. Breathing exercises are used, as inhaling through one nostril and exhaling out of the other, and then alternating. Thus "purity of nerves" is said to be attained. A bodily rhythm is developed, and, through the respiratory center, control of other centers is acquired. Muscular control plays an important part in yoga. It is alleged that adepts gain control of almost every muscle, and that some of them can control the lungs to such a degree that they can be buried for months and yet live without breathing. An abstemious diet is recommended, as, for example, of milk and cereals.[2]

The mental exercises commence with a state of revery in which the mind is allowed to run on without restraint. At first many thoughts will pass through. They will gradually decrease in number, so that eventually, perhaps after months of practice, they become very few. Then concentration is begun. The effort is made to feel certain parts of the body to the exclusion of other parts. The eyes are focused on the tip of the nose, or the attention is fixed on the "lotus" of the heart or on the center of the head. It is alleged that by such concentration the intellect and reason are eventually surpassed and a higher plane of super-consciousness is attained. On this plane, facts are learned which cannot be acquired through instinct and reason.

Whenever possible, these exercises are performed in a place with "holy" associations and atmosphere. "Unholy" persons are not admitted to pollute it. A species of mental telepathy is used. "Holy" thoughts are sent in all directions, as for example, by repeating, "Let all beings be peaceful; let all beings be blissful." These projected thoughts are supposed to benefit not only the sender but also those who are said to receive them.

The physical consequences from these practices are described in the second chapter of the Svetasvatara Upanishad as follows: "The first signs of entering yoga are lightness of body, health, thirstlessness of mind, clearness of complexion, a beautiful voice, an agreeable odor in the body and scantiness of excretions." In the third book of the Sankhya philosophy, it is alleged that "by intensity of meditation,

[2] In Bombay in 1953 I visited a yoga school in which these methods are taught. Swami missionaries teach them in a few European and American cities.

all things come to the pure-minded yogi." A modern Vedantist practitioner and preacher avers that the adept, or yogi, acquires infinite and transcendental knowledge. "No more, then, will they need to go to books for knowledge; for their own minds will have become filled with infinite knowledge. . . . The knowledge that comes to such a mind is real metaphysical knowledge and is beyond all physical knowledge. Metaphysical or transcendental knowledge thus comes to man."[3]

The yoga systems, though conflicting to a certain extent as to method, are all based on the notion of a cosmic intelligence or consciousness, which can be tapped, so to speak, by the individual. Often a religious and theological turn is given to the characterization of this cosmic something or other.[4] Sometimes it is expressed in such a fashion as to imply solipsism. It is suggested that the individual includes the cosmos. In moments of exaltation due to the feeling of an infinitely extended ego, it is asserted in such declarations as the following: "Thus, Him, Whom men ignorantly worship under various names, through fear and tribulation, the Yogi declares unto the world to be the living Power that is lying coiled up in every being, the Giver of eternal happiness."[5]

Such beliefs furnish a basis for mysticism. The mystic believes that he stands in a peculiarly intimate and personal relationship with the world spirit, whatever it may be called. He alleges that he has become one with this spirit, or that it is in some mysterious fashion in him. Mystics appear the world over, and are likely to belong to the introvert type which turns its imagination inward and creates a world of its own. They are unwilling or reluctant to face frankly and grapple with the difficult problems of the world into which we have been unwittingly pitchforked, or perhaps they are incapable of doing so. They seek escape in a world of their own creation. Whether yoga is responsible for the prevalence of mysticism in the East, or *vice versa,* it is difficult to say. They have probably acted and reacted upon each other. It is not necessary to assume that there is a preponderance of persons of the mystical type in the East, but climate may have had an influence, as we shall see presently.

Yoga resembles certain notions and practices known in the West, such as faith-healing, mental-healing, Christian Science, spiritualism, telepathy, etc. They are alike in assuming the existence of a mind, or "soul," which stands apart from the body as a distinct entity,

---

[3] Swami Vivekananda, *Raja Yoga*, Calcutta, 1923.

[4] "In its essence this cosmic energy known as matter, or thought, or force, or intelligence, or whatever name you choose to give it, is simply the manifestation of that cosmic intelligence, or, as we shall call Him henceforth, the Supreme Lord." Swami Vivekananda, *Jnana Yoga*, Calcutta, 1923, p. 165.)

[5] Swami Vivekananda, *Raja Yoga*, p. 55.

though this is less true of the yoga based on the Sankhya philosophy than it is of the more religious systems. The method of revery with which it commences its mental exercises is similar to the basic method of psychoanalysis. By this method the psychoanalyst seeks to delve into the unconscious and subconscious of the patient. By means of revery and concentration the yogi believes that he reaches the height of *"samadhi"* or super-consciousness, whatever that may be. It is not unlikely that he is actually plumbing the depths of the unconscious and subconscious.

The theory and practice of yoga are based largely upon psychological errors and delusions as to the constitution of the universe. Instinct is regarded as the lowest means of acquiring knowledge, as if it were an unconscious mode of thinking. In the course of instinctive behavior the organism learns a great deal. But instinct is not in itself a process of thought but an innate tendency to certain specific modes of action. While intellect is recognized as a mode of thinking, the essential doctrine of yoga is that there is a kind of knowledge beyond the intellectual to which man can attain. This doctrine is based upon the postulate of a universal consciousness, for which there is no evidence whatsoever. So far as we know, consciousness is limited to mankind and the higher animal organisms—in any case, to the organic world. To postulate a cosmic consciousness is a wholly untenable and gratuitous assumption, and therefore a delusion.

Through the yoga the yogi thinks he attains to this higher knowledge. The above description indicates clearly that he actually renders his consciousness a blank, so that in reality he reaches a condition of nescience. His methods deprive him of whatever he may have succeeded in learning through his intellect. However unintentional on his own part it may be, he is manifestly the victim of self-hypnosis, or at least of self-deception. To believe that he has passed beyond the bounds of time, space, and causation, and has attained the absolute is the most egregious delusion of all. It gives rise to the presumptuous claim that he belongs to a class apart from and superior to common mortals who have not attained the absolute, in which respect he is like mystics and religious fanatics the world over.

And yet, however exaggerated and often ridiculous are the pretensions of the yogi, the yoga methods should be considered on their own merit, and may possess something of value. The physical exercises probably are beneficial, though very one-sided. Exercises which bring the whole body into action are extremely important as well as posture and breathing. Rhythmic bodily movements are more valuable than the comparatively limited rhythm arising out of respiration. Many of them are much more interesting and enjoyable when performed with a specific object, as in work and play, than when imposed as a task, as in yoga. An abstemious diet is often beneficial. But the yoga dietetic ideas are not based upon a broad and scientific knowledge of physiology, so as to constitute a well-rounded dietetic system.

A state of revery may be useful for several purposes. It often serves for rest and relaxation, especially after intense mental application. In the course of it, stimulating ideas may, so to speak, come to the surface. Unperceived relations between facts and ideas may unexpectedly reveal themselves. Concentration is useful when intelligently directed. The attention should be centered on facts and ideas which are of interest and importance. This may necessitate the temporary exclusion of other facts and ideas. But the excluding is not for its own sake, because the latter facts and ideas may be useful on other occasions.

Generally speaking, the richer the mental life, the more numerous are the facts and ideas entertained and concentrated upon. Needless to say, most of this food for the mind must come from without, for no mind can contain *ab initio,* or at any time, all of the vast store of knowledge available. Furthermore, alternation between the sort of meditation and contemplation induced by a state of revery and the kind of meditation involved in concentration is necessary for the most effective functioning of the mental processes.

How barren is the yoga procedure as compared with the one just outlined! Instead of resulting in a higher form of knowledge, it signifies a progressive denudation and deadening of the mind. As a means of escape from the problems which beset every live and active mind by simulating the new-born infant and idiot, it may have utility. But instead of attaining to a super-consciousness, it has the diametrically opposite effect of stifling the consciousness in so far as it expresses itself in intelligence and personality.

In another work I have described at length the nature of intelligence, consciousness, mind, and personality, and have demonstrated that "consciousness is a complex process made up of feelings and ideas which are unified by the sense of personality which may begin as a vague feeling, but which becomes in course of time a clear-cut idea."[6]

---

[6] *The Science of Human Behavior,* p. 321. See especially Chapters XIV, XV, and XVI. My book shows that the mental processes which we call intelligence, feeling, consciousness, etc., have arisen in the higher animals on the basis of sensation. "In an animal with a well developed central nervous system which has acquired a large and varied store of memories, the behavior which results from a certain stimulus may be vastly different from the purely inherited reaction which would respond to that stimulus if these memories were not present to vary and complicate the behavior. Such behavior is intelligent, and the capacity for such variations in behavior constitutes intelligence." (P. 265.)

Man's superior intelligence "is due in part to the superiority of certain of his senses, which are of peculiar value in acquainting him with his environment,

This disproves conclusively the fallacy of the yoga theory of consciousness.

I have briefly described and criticized yoga because it illustrates concretely and graphically several of the differences between Eastern and Western modes of thought and ideals. To generalize with regard to them is likely to give rise to misunderstanding. I shall nevertheless state some of these differences as generalizations, with the proviso that each generalization is subject to many exceptions and qualifications. All of the characteristics to be mentioned apply to a certain extent to both East and West. Moreover, they apply in varying degrees to the different parts of the East, which is much less unified than the West, and more to India than elsewhere. They indicate norms set up by thinkers and leaders who influence the common people in a measure. The life of the masses the world over is much the same in that they are primarily concerned with satisfying the fundamental human wants.

The West emphasizes action, work, and accomplishment; the East, meditation and contemplation. The West is intensely interested in the present mundane existence. The East yearns after a nirvana of non-existence. The West is principally concerned with the relative. The East is preoccupied with the idea of the absolute. The West deals with the particular; the East with the ultimate and the universal. The West is turning more and more to science for guidance. The East still clings to religion and metaphysics.

The West is endeavoring to control nature. The East resigns itself to natural forces. Western control of nature dissipates fear of natural forces through science, invention, and industry, which are rapidly supplanting magic and religion. The East deadens this fear by means of resignation, inaction, and anticipated personal extinction through mergence with the infinite. The West recognizes no past existence, and pays less and less attention to a future one in which it professes to believe. The East believes in a past existence and anticipates a series of future ones.

The East tends to regard the world of phenomena as illusory, and confuses the natural and the supernatural, even though it usually recognizes the distinction between them. The West distinguishes sharply between the two, when it recognizes the supernatural at all, and considers this world as very real. The East is still swayed by a static philosophy of changelessness and fixity. The West is dominated

inasmuch as they are the functions of distance-receptors. It is due in part to his action-system, which enables him to go through an unusually varied number of movements. It is due in the last place to his extended association areas, which furnish the basis for an unusually extensive and complicated system of connections between sensations, images, and movements." (P. 280.)

by a dynamic, pragmatic, instrumental philosophy of change. The East believes in a periodic law of cyclism, of eternal rhythm, which makes it fatalistic. The West is enamored with the idea of evolution and progress toward some goal, whatever it may be, which makes it self-confident and hopeful.

The Easterners are said to be less individualized, because they look forward to ultimate extinction. The West lays great emphasis on individuality and the development of personality. The Eastern doctrine of reincarnation is said to encourage inaction, and perhaps indolence, because its believers think they have many existences to live through automatically. Christianity and Islam teach that there is only one life, the future life being of an entirely different order, so that Westerners live the present life more intensely, endeavoring to get all they can out of it, and leave it reluctantly. The East preaches a gospel of renunciation; the West one of fulfilment. The East is prepossessed with the divine; the West with the human.

These categorical generalizations, which, like every summary statement, are only partially true, apply most of all to India, because certain theological and metaphysical doctrines originated or, to say the least, have been pushed to their logical (or illogical) extreme there. Thence they have spread to other parts of the East, but have had much less influence upon the West. These are the doctrines of maya, or the illusory character of the world in which we live, of metempsychosis resulting in nirvana or extinction by mergence in the infinite, and of Karma or fate.[7]

It is not easy to explain the origin and development of this complex of ideas, which arose perhaps as much as three thousand years ago. It has been suggested that the maya doctrine is appropriate to the tropics, where man does not have to struggle for his existence with nature to the same extent as in the temperate zone, so that the world never becomes so real a thing for him. It is also possible that a temperate and cold climate stimulates keener sensations and therefore a more vivid impression of the exterior world. While these explanations sound plausible and probably deserve some weight, I know of no other tropical people which has developed a similar doctrine. However, it is not improbable that a hot climate fosters day-dreaming and revery which distract attention from the environment.

The doctrine of metempsychosis, in some form or other, has been held by many primitive as well as civilized peoples. It has probably arisen spontaneously many times out of primitive animistic ideas which have made men feel a close kinship with animals and plants and even with inanimate objects. In India it takes the form of a cycle of

[7] Such words as maya, nirvana, and karma are translated in different ways. I have tried to give them their most significant meaning.

existences whose ultimate goal is nirvana, or extinction through mergence with the infinite and absolute. This doctrine is akin to the maya doctrine, because it implies that this world is unreal, and its origin can perhaps be explained on similar grounds. While in India I was often impressed with the strength of the hold which the idea of metempsychosis has upon the Indians. It happened several times that while conversing with Hindus trained in Western science, I discovered that a firm belief in reincarnation persisted back of their scientific ideas. This is a fact which must always be remembered when endeavoring to understand the Indian mind.

The doctrines of maya, metempsychosis, and nirvana lead naturally and inevitably to fatalism, because human destiny is preordained by whatever power or powers are conceived to preside over it. But fatalism is a doctrine which can never be wholly acceptable to human nature, which craves certain things too strongly to refrain entirely from trying to secure them. Thus we have seen that yoga is an attempt to arrive at nirvana more speedily by skipping some of the reincarnations which may otherwise be necessary. The intercessionary religions of Krishna and Amidha Buddha adopt the easier methods of salvation through the mediation of these powerful deities. Mahayana Buddhism preaches a paradise of the west (sunset) with pleasures much more sensual than the eternal peace and bliss of nirvana. Popular Hinduism has a heaven of very earthly delights.

A consideration of this complex of ideas indicates that during a period of perhaps three thousand to twenty-five hundred years ago there took place in India a remarkable episode in the development of human thought. This was the period when the Upanishads were composed, the Sankhya philosophy took shape, and various attempts to place religion on a monistic basis occurred. It closed with the life of Gautama Sakyamuni, who was more of a reformer than a philosopher, though he was probably influenced by these philosophers.

During this period there were apparently numerous ascetics and sages who devoted themselves to a consideration of the problems of the universe and of man's destiny. The results were the subtlest and in some respects the soundest hypotheses and theories which mankind evolved prior to the development of modern science. Through the hazy mists of twenty-five centuries we can dimly discern the human mind striving to find a basic unity and a universal law. Thus the paramatman or primeval world-soul and cyclic periodicity of these sages of old faintly foreshadowed the energistic concepts and evolutionary and involutionary processes of the modern scientists. However bizarre may have been some of the notions developed, this episode deserves a place in the history of human thought.

It is difficult to account for this noteworthy episode. Climate may have had something to do with it. The abstention from animal food and alcohol, which became a tenet of the Vedic religion during its later development, may have converted the aggressive and turbulent "Aryan" into the mild and contemplative Hindu. The Indian writers, with their lack of a historical sense, have left us no record by which we can confirm these suggestions. Whatever the causes may have been, the Vedic religion was succeeded by an efflorescence of thinking which surpassed its simple nature worship, and which has colored Indian thought ever since.

The Vedanta philosophy, perhaps the earliest of the Indian systems of thought, is supposed to have been based upon the Veda, was formulated in part in the Upanishads, and became the philosophy of orthodox Brahmanism. It teaches *advaita* or an unscientific and somewhat spurious kind of monism. The phenomenal world with which we become acquainted through our senses is maya or an illusion. The only reality is Brahma or the world soul. This philosophy was restated by Shankara in about the eighth century of the Christian era. In a modernized form it is taught by certain Indian philosophers and religionists who reject much of popular Hinduism, including the caste system, which is an integral part of orthodox Brahmanism. This was true of Ram Krishna Parahamsa, a saint who lived during the nineteenth century, and his disciple Vivekananda. Unlike the orthodox Hindus, these modern Vedantists regard their philosophy and religion as universal and are trying to teach it to mankind. They combine with it the yoga methods I have described, by means of which they expect to free themselves from maya and to attain nirvana by absorption or extinction in the world soul.

The Sankhya philosophy probably came into being between 800 and 550 B.C. This philosophy rejects Brahma and the world soul. Matter is real. Primeval matter (*prakriti*) consists of three constituent elements known as *gunas*—namely, energy, inertia, and existence (conditioned being). While it is a philosophy of realism, it teaches the existence of an infinite plurality of individual souls. Consequently it is dualistic, in contrast to the monistic Vedanta philosophy. As I have already indicated, Gautama apparently was reared in the atmosphere of Sankhya thought and based his teachings upon it, so that Buddhism has been much influenced by this philosophy.

While journeying in Asia, I found the Indians ever ready to expound their views on life and the universe. The Chinese and Japanese are more reserved, and have apparently devoted less thought to these religious and metaphysical problems, being preoccupied with more mundane matters. There is no evidence of an episode similar to the one in India which has been described. Lao-tze (*ca.* 6th century B.C.) was apparently a mystic who taught a doctrine of quietism,

972

and his principal disciple, Chuang-tze (*circa* 330 B.C.), who came several centuries later, was almost nihilistic in his point of view. Taoism degenerated into little more than witchcraft. Confucius (B.C. 551-478) was a traditionalist principally concerned with human relations. Then there were Yang Chu (fourth century B.C.), the pessimistic philosopher, and Mo Ti (fifth and fourth centuries B.C.), the revolutionary altruist, whose philosophy seems to have been pragmatic and therefore more Western than Eastern in its character.

It is said that eighteen Buddhist missionaries reached China in the third century B.C., but Buddhism was not formally introduced until A.D. 65 As we have seen, it was Mahayanism which took root in China and later went in to Japan, and this religion had diverged greatly from the original Buddhism. In China it was influenced by the practical spirit of Confucianism. In Japan it became to a considerable extent a religion of soldiers, which was indeed a far cry from the spirit of the gentle Indian sage. There is no evidence that philosophy ever flourished in Japan.

In fact, with reference to these matters, almost as sharp a distinction must be drawn between India and the eastern Asiatic peoples as between India and the West. The mystery of the universe may present itself more forcibly to the Asiatic than to the Western mind. But neither China nor Japan is as deeply interested in metaphysics, theology, and religion as is India.[8]

It is sometimes alleged that there is a likeness between Oriental mysticism and that of the European Middle Ages. I have shown that contemplation and meditation for the Indian mystic is a process of gradually eliminating everything from the mind, thus attaining to so-called "*samadhi*" or super-consciousness, and eventually to nirvana or union with the universal consciousness or world soul. It is therefore an essentially impersonal form of mysticism. The Christian mystic, on the contrary, seeks an intimate relation to and union with God and his incarnation upon this earth, Jesus. Christian mysticism is therefore intensely personal. It contains little contemplation in the Indian sense. It is very sensual and more often erotic than in the East.

This contrast is due primarily to the difference between the more philosophic character of the Oriental religion upon which Eastern mysticism is based and the narrowly personal character of Christianity, which centers around a highly anthropomorphic god and his still more

[8] Dickinson, one of the most impartial observers of the East, said that the dominant note of India is religion; of China, humanity (by which he apparently meant interest in human affairs rather than love of mankind); and of Japan, chivalry. He said that in India religion is life, matter is unreal, human misery illusory, and time has no meaning. (G. Lowes Dickinson, *An Essay on the Civilisations of India, China and Japan*, London, 1914.)

anthropomorphic son.[9] It is also due to the fact that mediaeval mysticism was almost entirely monastic, whereas in the Orient mystics are found in many walks of life. Indeed, in India it is expected that the aspirant to yogihood should already have been a householder, parent, and head of a family, and many mystics retain a close touch with the world at large. Thus their senses, and in particular their sexual impulses, have not been repressed in the narrow confines of celibate monastic life. In the latter it is to be expected that the sensual passions, deprived of their natural and normal expression, will manifest themselves in neural and emotional disturbances, in visions and hallucinations, in strange cravings and abnormal practices, in erotic dreams and amorous utterances which are supposed to state Christian doctrines and beliefs in a symbolical manner.

St. Bernard (1090-1153), abbot of Clairvaux (Clara Vallis), who promoted the Second Crusade, was perhaps the most notorious of mediaeval mystics. In his *De Consideratione* he characterized contemplation as follows: "*Contemplatio* may be defined as the true and certain intuition of the mind (*intuitus animi*) regarding anything, or the sure apprehension of the true: while *consideratio* is thought intently searching, or the mind's endeavor to track out the true." (*Lib.*

[9] In interesting contrast with the Oriental mysticism which I have described is the following statement regarding mysticism according to Christian theology, by a devout and pietistic Christian writer of today, which illustrates the intensely personal character of Christian mysticism:

"By the grace of God, supremely manifested in the Incarnation, the man is humbled, and his heart is touched and drawn to love the power of the divine pity and humility. The lesson of the Incarnation and its guiding grace, emboldens the heart and enlightens the mind; and the man's faculties are strengthened and uplifted to the contemplation of God, wherein the mind is satisfied and the heart at rest. . . . [Mysticism] includes a sense of the supreme, a sense of God, who is too great for human reason to comprehend, and therefore a mystery. And it includes a yearning toward God, the desire of him, and the feeling of love. . . . The final goal attainable by this mystic love is, even as the goal of other love, union with the Beloved. The mystic spirit is an essential part of all piety or religion, which relates always and forever to the rationally unknown and therefore mysterious. Without a consciousness of mystery, there can be neither piety nor religion. Nor can there be piety without some devotion to God, nor the deepest and most ardent forms of piety, without fervent love of God." (H. O. Taylor, *The Mediaeval Mind*, London, 1925, fourth edition, 2 vols., Vol. II, pp. 392-3.)

Taylor furnished an abundance of data concerning monastic mysticism. But the Christian propaganda which he avowed in his Preface rendered him incapable of subjecting them to an unbiased, critical, and scientific analysis and interpretation.

A modern European mystic gave a somewhat broader and less personal definition of mysticism:

"Mysticism is the art of union with Reality. The mystic is a person who has attained that union in greater or less degree; or who aims at and believes in such attainment." (Evelyn Underhill, *Practical Mysticism*, New York, 1915, p. 3.)

974

II, *cap.* 2.) This is the claim to an esoteric and super-rational source of knowledge and mode of attaining the truth characteristic of all mystics. In Bernard's case the expression of mysticism often took an ecstatic form, as when he cried in his yearning for Jesus: *"Ipse, ipse me osculetur"* ("He himself, let him kiss me."). His sermons were devoted largely to love of Christ and of God. He utilized the sensual and carnal language of the flesh, his texts often being taken from the amorous Canticle or Song of Solomon. "O love (amor), headlong, vehement, burning, impetuous, that canst think of nothing beyond thyself, detesting all else, despising all else, satisfied with thyself! . . . Everything which the soul-bride utters resounds of thee and nothing else; so hast thou possessed her heart and tongue." (*Sermo* LXXXIX in *Cantica.*)

Many nuns experienced visions, hallucinations, morbid delusions, trances, and the like, which often were deeply tinged with eroticism centering around visual images of the body of Christ and sometimes involving a visualization of the Almighty Himself. One of the most revered was Ste. Mary of Ognies (*circa* 1177-1213), who had a trance lasting thirty-five days in communion with Jesus, only occasionally saying: "I desire the body of the Lord Jesus Christ" (the Eucharist). Sister Mechthild (*circa* 1212-1277) described her experiences of divine love in a book entitled *The Flowing Light of God,* which is passionately sensual in its style. "To God I go, who is my Father by nature, my Brother through his humility, my Bridegroom through love, and I am His forever." (*Das fliessende Licht,* etc., I, 38-44.) Numerous instances could be cited of the hypersensual mysticism of the mediaeval monks and nuns as contrasted with the relatively calm and quietistic mysticism of the East.

The outstanding intellectual difference between the East and the West is with respect to the scientific point of view and attitude of mind. During the past three centuries science has made greater strides in the West than during all preceding time. It has transformed Occidental culture not only materially but mentally as well. Most of the intellectual leaders of the West have a scientific point of view. Few of the masses possess it consciously. But in their daily life they are applying it constantly. In the factories the workers are continually using machinery and methods which are due almost entirely to science. The use of steam and electricity, the engine, steamship, railroad, telegraph, telephone, aeroplane, automobile, and many other everyday appliances would not be in existence were it not for science. Even the conservative agricultural class is applying science more and more in the fertilization of the soil, the rotation of crops, and in the use of machinery.

The contrast with the Orient in these matters is very great. How

975

much the East accomplished in the scientific world prior to modern times is a moot question. It has played almost no part in the modern development of science, which constitutes much the larger part of it. Even the scientific studies of Oriental countries have been made by Western scientists. The anthropology, history, sociology, geology, biology, and psychology of the East has been a Western study, with a few slight exceptions. The scholars of the Orient find themselves confronted with an already extensive body of data to which they must adjust their ancient lore and adapt their methods. Many of their prepossessions must be swept away before they can begin to acquire a scientific point of view.

As for the Oriental masses, the material culture which has resulted from modern science has not yet been introduced into the East to a sufficient degree to give them the feeling of the regularity and recurrence of natural phenomena which is already somewhat prevalent among the common people of the Occident. The use of supernatural devices to influence natural processes is widespread. In India and many other parts of the Orient religion plays a more important and intimate part in the daily life than in the West. Magic in the form of astrology, geomancy, necromancy, and the like is widely used. This contrast is so striking and so far-reaching in its consequences that it is worth while to consider why the Orient failed to reach the scientific stage of its own accord. Indeed, there is reason to believe that without the leadership of the Occident the East would not have attained this stage for a long time.

It is often alleged by Hindus that India in ancient times discovered almost all of the data and principles of modern science. This claim has been made among other sciences with respect to physics, chemistry, biology, and the theory of evolution. Ancient India made some contributions to mathematics, astronomy, probably to biology, and possibly to a few other sciences. There is no evidence that Western science was anticipated. In the first place, there is not a trace of modern science in the ancient literature. This claim is based on a misinterpretation of the texts by reading into them many modern ideas of which their writers never dreamed. This is an error easy to commit, because the Indian sages were given to developing cosmological ideas and systems. They often made general statements which might mean almost anything or nothing at all. Their method was not inductive, and they had none of the vast mass of carefully and laboriously gathered data upon which Western science is based.

Second, if India had anticipated most or all of Western science, it is inconceivable that Indian culture would be as it now is. Its material culture would have been greatly modified by the application of these scientific facts and ideas in the arts. The belief in the super-

976

natural could not have so strong a hold upon the minds not only of the masses but of the intellectual leaders as well. The modes of thought would be very different. Indian philosophy is not based upon a rigorous use of inductive and deductive methods. It arises largely out of meditation over phrases in which the thinker tries to immerse himself until it takes complete possession of his mind. Out of such meditation arise the rather monotonous and often repetitious generalizations of Indian metaphysics. The Indian mother teaches her child the art of meditation as the submission of the will into the highest mental state which it can conceive. Such methods tend to emasculate the mind, and to divorce it from dealing effectively with the only world with which we can be acquainted—namely, the world of phenomena which we know through our senses.

The signs of this situation are visible on every hand in India. Many of the Hindus bear painted on the brow the insignia of their sects. Thus it is possible to ascertain at first sight whether such a Hindu is a follower of Shiva or of Vishnu. In most matters of common interest the lines are drawn according to the religious cult. The term "community" invariably means a religious group. While religious factors enter at times into politics, sport, etc., in Europe and America, most matters of common interest have become secularized and the religious differences are ignored.

The medical lore of India is contained in the Ayurveda. Based upon it is the ayurvedic system of medicine which is still widely used by the Hindus. Its central theory is that illness is due to disorder in one of the four humors. Its therapeutic measures consist largely in the prescription of potions made from herbs, supplemented in many cases by the repetition of mantras or charms. Its acquaintance with anatomy and physiology is very slight, because it is not based upon dissection. Of the zymotic causes of disease it knows nothing, because it has not had the use of high-power microscopes with which to isolate the germs which give rise to many diseases. Before me lies the calendar (dated 1923) of the government Ayurvedic College of the State of Mysore, which I have visited. The requirements for admission are that "candidates must possess a fair knowledge of Sanskrit" and that "a knowledge of English will be a necessary qualification." The four years' course is devoted to the ayurvedic methods with the exception of Western anatomy taught in the first year, Western physiology in the second year, and Western hygiene in the third year.

Lacking a basis in experimental science, the ayurvedic, unani, and other Asiatic systems of medicine have been wholly unable to cope with epidemics. With little knowledge of anatomy and physiology, and ignorant of the causes of infectious diseases, the gaunt figure of disease aided by frequent famines could stalk unchecked and reap its

977

annual harvest of deaths. Not until Western medicine and sanitation were introduced did the mortality and morbidity rates begin to fall in India, Java, the Philippines, and elsewhere where Western nations had assumed control. By preventing disease and famines, as well as in many other ways, Occidental science has already improved the material welfare of the Orient greatly.

The failure of China to develop science is to be explained on somewhat different grounds from the case of India. China possessed a relatively high material culture as much as three thousand years ago, which has persisted to the present day. The Great Wall, which is more than fifteen hundred miles in length, was completed over twenty-one centuries ago. The irrigation system of the Chengtu plain in western China is nearly as old, and is still in use. The Grand Canal, extending for a thousand miles from Hangchow to Tientsin, was reconstructed about six centuries ago. The diking of the turbid and unruly waters of the Yellow River has repeatedly necessitated vast engineering enterprises.

The magnetic needle was in use very early for geomantic purposes, but was not utilized as the mariner's compass until it was seen applied to navigation by Arab traders who came to Canton perhaps as early as A.D. 300. Explosive powder was discovered probably very early, but was used only for fireworks until its application to firearms was learned from the Europeans.

The Chinese are not very religious and to that extent they are tolerant. Their social and cultural institutions have in the main been secular in character. They are rational in the sense of trying to adjust their human and social relationships in a reasonable fashion, though they have displayed little of the higher types of reasoning involved in philosophical and scientific thought. Their art and literature contain comparatively few references to the supernatural, and are simple in the sense of not being bizarre and grotesque or unduly ornate. Poetry is extant from 1100 B.C. and even earlier which is realistic even when intended to be suggestive. There is no epic literature, and the drama and novel were introduced under the Mongol dynasty (A.D. 1260-1368).[10]

China played an important part in four inventions which have had a large share in the making of modern civilization—namely, paper, printing, gunpowder, and the compass. The two latter I have already mentioned. The two former are closely connected in their use and significance.

Seals have been found dating as far back as 255 B.C., just as they had been used much earlier in Babylonia and Egypt. Genuine paper,

[10] See H. A. Giles, *A History of Chinese Literature*, New York, 1901, p. 256.

that is to say, paper made from rags, was apparently invented early in the Christian era, probably about A.D. 100. The earliest extant block prints date from A.D. 770. Printing was apparently encouraged by the Buddhists to aid in the dissemination of Buddhistic literature. The earliest printed book which has so far been discovered is the Diamond Sutra, dating from A.D. 868. Movable type was invented in the eleventh century. It was first wooden, then metal. The first metal type was cast in a foundry in Korea, and the earliest extant book printed from movable metal type was in Korea in 1409.

These inventions slowly made their way westward across Asia and eventually reached Europe. First came paper, which was an essential preliminary to printing. Then came the various forms of printing. So that Gutenberg's discovery (Johannes Gutenberg, 1397?-1468 A.D., German reputed inventor of printing) may not have been wholly or even in large part original, since it may have been inspired by these products from the Far East.[11]

The technical and inventive skill of the Chinese, their tolerance, the secular character of their institutions, the rationalism displayed in their everyday life, the orderliness of their social organization, and various other traits seem to indicate that they should have developed science. And yet they have failed to do so as completely as the Indians. While this is not easy to explain, a few facts may be cited which throw some light on the situation.

Chinese scholarship is extensive, and some of it of excellent quality. The Chinese, unlike the Indians, have a strong historical sense. Their histories are numerous, and with a more or less exact chronology. But they are rarely ever illuminating as to the causes of historical

[11] A full account of these matters is given in Thomas F. Carter, *The Invention of Printing in China and Its Spread Westward*, New York, 1925.

"Of all the world's great inventions, that of printing is the most cosmopolitan and international. China invented paper and first experimented with block printing and movable type. Japan produced the earliest block prints that are now extant. Korea first printed with type of metal cast from a mould. India furnished the language and the religion of the earliest block prints. People of Turkish race were among the most important agents in carrying block printing across Asia, and the earliest extant type are in a Turkish tongue. Persia and Egypt are the two lands of the Near East where block printing is known to have been done before it began in Europe. The Arabs were the agents who prepared the way by carrying the making of paper from China to Europe. Paper making actually entered Europe through Spain, though imported paper had already come in through the Greek Empire at Constantinople. France and Italy were the first countries in Christendom to manufacture paper. As for block printing and its advent into Europe, Russia's claim to have been the channel rests on the oldest authority, though Italy's claim is equally strong. Germany, Italy and the Netherlands were the earliest centers of the block printing art. Holland and France, as well as Germany, claim first to have experimented with typography. Germany perfected the invention, and from Germany it spread to all the world." (P. 185.)

events. Many dictionaries have been compiled and several encylo-pedias, the principal one being in many volumes. The essay has been a favorite type of writing. There are works on medical jurisprudence which are extremely inaccurate in their knowledge of human anatomy and physiology. Chinese scholars have displayed great industry in amassing numerous facts, but have done little to interpret them. Most of their works have been commentaries on the classics, the Confucian classics in particular. Generally speaking and with certain exceptions and qualifications, the Chinese mind as revealed in their scholarship is traditionalist, uncreative, lacking in imagination and the spirit of adventure, unsystematic, unconstructive, and too much given to detail to be synthetic and to arrive at broad generalizations.

Ancestor worship is well calculated to encourage conservatism and traditionalism. The highest morality is to follow the example of the dead, which is not conducive to change and progress. It led in China to excessive emphasis on the classics, especially the Confucian classics, because they contain the teachings of the venerated forefathers. Chinese education has consisted largely of memorizing the classics, which does not develop the logical and reasoning faculties. The colossal example of this was the examination system, in which the chief requisite for success was ability to memorize. Such training could not prepare the Chinese mind for the individual initiative, intellectual curiosity, freedom from hard and fast notions, desire to gather new data, and ability to analyze and generalize which are necessary for scientific research.

The Chinese language and script have been serious hindrances. The nouns are apparently indeclinable and have no gender and case. The adjectives have no degrees of comparison. The verbs have no voice, mode, tense, number, and person. There is no recognizable distinction between nouns, adjectives, and verbs, for any character may be used in each of these capacities. Such a language invites "intellectual turbidity," because it is difficult to express in it clear and precise ideas. The script is clumsy beyond measure, and requires years of laborious effort to master. The standard dictionary, compiled during the Kang-h'si period (seventeenth century A.D.), is said to contain 44,449 characters. Inasmuch as until recently, all writing was in the classical language and script comprehensible only to the literati, the vast majority were entirely excluded from scholarly work.

For many centuries China was surrounded by countries much inferior to it in their culture. The vanity of the Chinese was flattered, and a contempt for foreigners inspired which was directed against their dress, ignorance of the Chinese language and customs, failure to conform to Chinese ideals of ceremony (which assume great importance in their eyes), and freedom between the sexes in the case of Europeans. This attitude toward foreigners exists to a certain extent in every country, but was emphasized in China by centuries of comparative isolation. The literati, or scholars, have been the chief enemies of foreigners when they have seen their prerogatives menaced by a new literature and different standards introduced from outside. This happened toward the Buddhist missionaries, and led in several cases to persecution. It has also happened in their attitude toward Westerners.

Inasmuch as science failed to develop, magic persisted to a degree which is astonishing in view of the high plane attained by Chinese culture in other respects. Perhaps the most prevalent form is *feng-shui* (wind-water), which is a complicated system of geomancy by means of which the good luck of sites and buildings is determined. It seems to have developed out of the older *yin-yang* idea. *Yin* means evil spirits, and also moon, darkness and female. *Yang* means good spirits, and also sun, light, and male. While Taoism specializes in magic, geomancy is so widespread that there are Confucian and Buddhist as well as Taoist *feng-shui* specialists. *Feng-shui* has often hindered mining operations, irrigation schemes, construction works, railway projects, and the like. On the other hand, it has led to the building of many pagodas to appease evil spirits. Necromancy also is prevalent. Unburied coffins often wait some time for the choice of lucky graves by necromancers. [12]

It is difficult enough to explain why events take place in cultural evolution. It is often even more difficult to explain why they do not happen. A complete and conclusive explanation as to why science did not develop in the East is out of the question. We have seen that in India an ardent interest in religion, a strong tendency toward cosmological and metaphysical speculation, and an intense desire to transform the personality by methods which encourage introspective rather than objective habits of thinking were antithetical to the inductive and experimental methods which are essential for science. In China ancestor worship early acquired a firm grip and promoted the stability of the Chinese culture. But the filial reverence which it inspired gave rise to a conservatism and self-satisfaction which effectually prevented the radical departure which science and its application require.

It must not be forgotten that science as a dynamic cultural factor is comparatively recent in the Western world, and might very easily have failed to develop at all. The Greeks in Asia Minor and the Hellenic peninsula, influenced from Indian, Mesopotamian, and

[12] See W. E. Soothill, *The Three Religions of China*, London, 1913. Soothill was for many years an English missionary in China.

Egyptian sources, made a small beginning, and then came a long interlude. The Roman Empire, somewhat like its great contemporary the Chinese Empire, spread a political and military order throughout the West. Its authority was highly centralized, so that it did not foster a spirit of free research and investigation.

It was succeeded by the Roman church, which was and is the most centralized and institutionalized religion in the world. Under its hierarchical rule there was little freedom for independent thinking. It was largely responsible for the gloomy centuries of the Dark and Middle Ages. Monastic ideals and a static philosophy prevailed, and the universities existed largely for the training of monks. The sort of contemplation and meditation encouraged was hardly more fruitful than that of the Indian yoga systems. For nearly two thousand years science was at a standstill, almost the only exceptions being a few contributions from the Arabic culture, which were by-products, so to speak, of the sudden and rapid spread of Islam. But no more than Christianity did Islam contain the possibility of stimulating science to develop to its full fruition.

Then came a concatenation of events which played their part in preparing the way for the coming of science, such as exploration leading to the discovery of America and the routes to the East, the invention of printing, the renaissance of learning, the discovery of the ancient classics, the revolt against the church, the increase of wealth and leisure. These and many other factors aroused men's minds and broadened their outlook. The Greek tradition of questioning and investigating was awakened. Unlike the speculative cosmologies and metaphysics of the East and of the mediaeval philosophers, the scientists sought first the pertinent data and then based their theories thereon.

The empirical method led to an inductive logic, which in turn gave rise to habits of thinking and reasoning markedly different from those of the Orient. While India dreamed in its mental seclusion and China plodded along its well-worn path in its geographical isolation, men of the West were beginning to realize that religious dogmas, metaphysical hypotheses, human desires and fantasies, ethical doctrines, political theories, and social and economic systems must bow their heads before what William James called "the irreducible and stubborn facts" of science.

Science is derived in part from intellectual curiosity as to the nature of observable phenomena and whatever may lie back of them, and in part from attempts to attain practical ends, which, however blundering and ineffective they may be, result in accidentally bringing to light new data. Thus astrology aided the development of

982

astronomy, alchemy of chemistry. Science is in turn applied to the attainment of these ends. The application of modern science has encouraged more and more the hope of controlling nature in the interest of mankind as far as possible. When such control is or appears to be out of the question, it is supplemented or replaced by adaptation to nature. Thus the ideas of control and of adaptation are increasingly influencing the Western world under the guidance of science. They encourage a mental flexibility, an open-mindedness toward change and progress such as has never before existed to the same degree in the world.

In the East man still retains in the main an attitude of resignation toward the natural forces which he knows no way to control, though he tries to influence them by means of religion and magic. Droughts, floods, famine, disease, an excessive birth-rate, and like ills are fatalistically accepted instead of striven against as in the West. Since nothing can be done with nature, the attainment of perfection becomes the ideal, rather than adaptation to the environment. In India the ideal is to acquire holiness, saintliness, and divinity. Consequently, this vast peninsula is overrun with sadhus, sannyasins and yogis. Some of the methods used by the yoga systems have been described.

In China the craving for holiness is much less prevalent than in India. Indeed, it may be said to exist only to the extent that Buddhism has succeeded in introducing it. But another ideal of perfection wields a powerful influence. Instead of the gods, the revered ancestors constitute an archetype to be copied. Traditionalism and formalism expressed in elaborate ceremonies, a code of formal courtesy which is a ritual of technicalities, the observing of "face" and of "good" form which constitutes "propriety," play an important part in the make-up of the Chinese gentleman and "moral" person.

While these traits exist everywhere, in the West there is greater latitude and more opportunity for adaptation and adjustment on the part of the individual. The Chinese moral code has played a large part in the perpetuation of Chinese civilization. But its ideal of perfection is too narrow to afford much opportunity for the development of individual types. And yet, as we shall see in the following chapter, the greater flexibility and adaptability of the West have in some respects socialized its ethics more than has taken place in the East.

One of the outstanding contrasts between the East and the West is with respect to standards of precision and accuracy. Every European and American country accumulates a large mass of statistics concerning many matters of scientific and social significance. While traveling in the Orient, I was often hampered by the dearth of accurate statistical information. In China there were only vague and widely varying estimates of population. Japan has already copied the Occident with characteristic thoroughness. In that country I was deluged with statistics by governmental departments, scientific organizations, and the like. I have already commented on the Indian lack of interest. The principal source of precise and reliable information was the census of India, which was entirely due to the British administration.

This indifference to measurement and size is another indication of the absence of a scientific attitude of mind in the East. This does not mean that the Orient is not alive to some qualitative distinctions whose significance is perhaps not fully appreciated in the Occident. The concept of evolution now has much influence over the Western mind. But to it is often given a teleological interpretation which colors the prevalent ideas of social and cultural progress. Even certain religious sects have accepted the theory of evolution in its erroneous teleological misinterpretation.

So far as science is concerned, evolution is merely a name for a process of change. Its first great exponent, Herbert Spencer, recognized this fact and indicated clearly that evolution is correlated with and balanced by involution. This fact was dimly perceived by Indian sages two or three thousand years ago, though they failed to describe this process of change accurately and in detail, as has been accomplished to a considerable extent by Western scientists. But these sages of old and scientists of today are at one in realizing that there can be no purpose or end in this infinite and universal process of change.

The West is obsessed with an idea of progress which is largely dominated by a quantitative ideal of magnitude. In another book I have said that this ideal of Occidental civilization "includes a large population, much of which is crowded into monstrous cities, the production of huge quantities of material goods, the intensive exploitation of natural resources and of human labor, the extensive use of physical force in industry and warlike activities, and the employment of science and invention mainly for these purposes. In this crudely materialistic welter the principal criterion is quantity rather than quality, while the promotion of human happiness, the development of personality, and man's intimate relation with nature are almost entirely ignored and forgotten." [13]

When Eastern thinkers see the hustle and bustle, the struggle and strife of the West, its murderous wars and insensate rivalry, it is

[13] *The New Gymnosophy*, New York, 1927, pp. 256-7. Later entitled *Nudism in Modern Life*, 5th revised edition, 1952.

not surprising that they raise the pertinent question as to the purpose of all this noise and effort. But the Orient also has failed lamentably in solving the difficult problem of the art of living. Hence it is a joint undertaking for East and West to attempt to solve, with the aid of science, this problem which is of supreme importance, not to a universe coldly and sublimely oblivious of human welfare, but to mankind alone.

Chapter LVII

Oriental Familism and Occidental Individualism

IT is often said that the individual is the unit of society in the West, the family in the East. While this is too categorical a statement to be entirely true, it raises several interesting questions. Is individuality suppressed, causing greater uniformity of personality in the Orient? Is there greater differentiation of personality and more freedom for genius in the Occident? Is morality more socialized in the East? Is there more democracy in the West? Is there more formal courtesy in the Orient? What effects do these partly contrasted systems have upon human relations, such as between husband and wife, parent and child, master and servant, employer and employee? Does Eastern family life stand in the way of a broader social life?

In China what is called the family is usually the greater-family or clan.[1] According to Confucian doctrine a newly married pair is not a distinct entity, as it is in the Occident. Usually it becomes a part of the husband's household under the rule of his father, the bride coming largely under the domination of her mother-in-law. When a household breaks up on account of the death of the father, or because it has become too unwieldy, or for any other reason, the kinship relations with the greater-family are retained. The family is ruled by the father, the clan by a board of elders, which is a more democratic arrangement.

The family and clan organization is said to be stronger in southern China, where life is more settled than in the north. This type of social organization cannot maintain itself in a migratory population.

---

[1] "The Chinese family is seldom an independent unit, but a member of the greater-family. In the Chinese village, families bearing the same surname live together. The members of the greater-family generally number hundreds and sometimes thousands. They have a common ancestral temple which is the center of their social and religious life." (Ching-chao Wu, "The Chinese Family: Organization, Names, and Kinship Terms,' in the *American Anthropologist*, July-September, 1927, Vol. XXIX, No. 3, p. 316.)

The strong desire of the Chinese to be buried at home due to their family feeling causes unequal distribution of population, because it is difficult to induce the inhabitants of the densely populated provinces to migrate to the thinly settled regions, such as Manchuria and Mongolia. Recent attempts at colonization have been hampered by this sentiment in favor of home burial.

The life of the clan centers around its temple, where a tablet of wood is placed for every member who dies. Ancestor worship takes place on certain festivals and family anniversaries. Owing to the overwhelming importance of ancestor worship, domestic religion is much stronger than personal religion. This accounts in part for the tolerance and catholicity of the Chinese in matters of religion and their secular attitude toward many phases of life. Mysticism is not likely to proliferate under such conditions.

The board of elders manages the affairs of the temple and administers the funds of the clan. It has a certain amount of judicial authority to settle disputes between family households within the clan, and to impose punishments, such as reproof and expulsion from the ancestral temple, and sometimes more drastic penalties.

Owing to the great importance of family relationships and the varying significance of relationship to older and younger relatives and through male and female ascendants, there are many more kinship terms in Chinese than in European languages. For example, there are five terms for uncle—namely, father's older brother, father's younger brother, husband of father's sister, mother's brother, and husband of mother's sister. The importance of the family is emphasized also by placing the family name before the personal name, in contrast to the European custom of placing the surname last.

Throughout mankind the older is likely to be more influential than the younger generation, because of its superior knowledge and experience, and because it has a long start over the younger. The power of the ascendants over their descendants is greatly emphasized where the clan or family system prevails, especially if accompanied by ancestor worship. The patriarchal authority tends also to increase the power of the males over the females. Marriage is enjoined upon every one as a duty in order to perpetuate the family and to breed descendants to worship at the shrine of the venerated ancestors. Polygyny may be encouraged when the wife is childless by taking another wife or a concubine in order to secure offspring. Overpopulation may also result from the inordinate desire for children.

The family situation in China until the Communist revolution of 1949 was revealed by the legal status of the family and marriage. According to Chinese jurisprudence as reflected in the decisions of the supreme court, a man could not share in the wealth of his family or

987

set up a separate establishment without the consent of all of his surviving parents and grandparents. The consent of parents and grandparents was also required to invalidate a marriage. More or less elaborate betrothal and marriage ceremonies were prescribed. The institution of concubinage or of having secondary wives was recognized by the law. In case of destitution the duty of support existed between father and son, grandfather and grandson, brothers, and husband and wife. The cult of the worship of the ancestors, and the inheritance of most of the family wealth, were transmitted through the male descendants.

Divorce might take place by mutual consent, but the civil code under the Republic provided that if the husband was under thirty or the wife under twenty-five, the consent of his or her parents, as the case might be, was also required. The seven ancient causes for the repudiation of a wife were recognized—namely, childlessness, wanton conduct, neglect of duty toward her husband's parents, loquacity, thievishness, jealousy, a grave disease. Exceptions were made when the wife had mourned for three years for the parents of her husband, when her husband had risen from poverty to riches, and when the wife no longer had a family to which she could return. However, divorce was said to be not very common. Adultery on the part of the wife was probably the most frequent cause, because it is most fatal to the existence of the family.

Prior to the modernization after 1867, Japan was divided into 262 fiefs ruled by the daimyos or feudal lords, exclusive of the land belonging to the shogun. These feudal clans were unlike the Chinese greater-family or clan, which has at no time been feudal or military. Ancestor worship has not existed, except to the slight extent that it has been imitated from China. Shinto, as we have seen, is ancestor worship only to the extent of worshiping the sun goddess as the ancestress of the imperial family. The family as an institution has, nevertheless, been powerful. The authority of the father is great, and the family ideal is to have many children to honor their parents and work for them. This is the chief cause of overpopulation in Nippon.

Indian social organization has been dominated by the caste system. Within the barriers of caste the family plays a very important part. The greater-family or clan is not formally organized as in China. But households often contain several related families and generations. A joint family system is widespread which assumes responsibility for the welfare of every member. It may also encourage idleness on the part of the more indolent, and sometimes leads to family dissension.

The home is a religious center in India to a greater degree than in any other country. Even the building of the house is governed by religious rules. The preparation of the food and much of the house-

988

hold work is often accompanied by a ritual. The morning and evening prayers are more or less obligatory and elaborate ceremonies required. Hindu religion, which embraces the whole of life and is strongly personal as well as domestic, makes of the home a veritable sanctuary. While the Chinese home contains a shrine to the ancestors, no one of the religions of China has the personal and all-pervasive character of Indian religion.

The influence of the woman in the Indian home is said to be very great. The same is probably true in China and in other Oriental countries. Whether or not it is greater than in the Occident, it is difficult to determine. Suffice it to say that her career is restricted to the home much more than that of her Western sister. Her devotion to her husband is also said to be great. It was symbolized in the past by the practice of suttee (cremation of the widow on her husband's funeral pyre), and at present by the degradation of the widow.

Certain Western observers have commented on the unusual degree of intimacy of Indian home life. Indians have sometimes asserted that this is due to child marriage. The bond established very early in life, though not necessarily consummated physically until later, and the courtship which comes after marriage, if at all, may have something to do with it. Home life is unusually important in India, partly because there are comparatively few distractions outside of the home. Recreation and a common social life are less organized than in the Occident. Several Western observers have asserted that Easterners are less individualized than Westerners. It is also asserted that there is greater difference in the Occident between the common herd and persons of ability—in other words, that there is more genius, and of a higher order, in the West than in the East. It is therefore assumed that the Orient is less advanced, its rate of progress less rapid, and its individual members more alike in character, that is to say, more homogeneous.

The facts which have been cited concerning the Oriental family lend plausibility to these assertions. The Easterner is forced by custom and public opinion, and sometimes by law, to give more heed than in the West to the wishes of his family, and to be guided by its head long after adulthood is attained. He may be forced or coerced often to sacrifice his own interests to those of his family. He is more likely to have to enter an occupation in accordance with the traditions and status of his family. In the West there is greater freedom of choice, and several occupations are often represented in the same family. The right of women to careers of their own is becoming more and more recognized, and they are no longer regarded as animals for breeding purposes only. Under the Oriental family system there is a greater tendency for the individual career to be hampered by group interests, for the younger to be repressed by the older generation, and for women to be devoted exclusively to the rearing of children and the care of the home.

There is no reason to believe that there is less innate ability in the East than in the West. Its manifestation everywhere depends to a considerable extent upon the social environment. The relative freedom from family restrictions in the Occident, permitting greater differentiation of personality, furnishes more scope for the expression of ability and genius. The broader social life, especially in Western cities, also serves as a stimulus. It is therefore not surprising that a survey of the past as well as of the present reveals a larger number of outstanding personalities in most fields of human effort. Individual initiative and leadership have on the whole been more characteristic of the Occident than of the Orient.

Every form of social organization has its characteristic ethical ideas and ideals. To say that one social system is more moral than another is futile and meaningless. Each is moral in the manner which is essential to its own maintenance, and usually somewhat more so. It has been asserted that Eastern civilization moralizes the individual more than Western civilization. This may be true in the sense that group morality is intensified in the Orient so that the responsibility of the small group, such as the family or the clan, for its members is great, and the duties of the member toward his group are rigorous. On the other hand, in the Occident the law and justice for the individual are more developed. His obligations toward society as a whole also are often more clearly defined. So that it is perhaps not inaccurate to say that, in contrast to the group morality of the East, there is a more socialized system of ethics in the broadest sense of the term in the West.

This brings us to the question as to the comparative degree of democracy in East and West. Of political democracy there is more in the West, partly because the Orient has not yet fully outgrown the tradition of autocracy. But democracy is much more extensive than political organization alone. In its broadest sense it signifies equality of opportunity and freedom for every one. This has its economic and social as well as political aspects. In the Occident the economic organization is at present dominated by the capitalist system. The means of production are owned in the main by the capitalists, and to them goes a large and wholly disproportionate share of the total income in the form of profits, interest, and rent. Upon this economic basis has developed a class organization in which the breach between the capitalist and the proletarian classes is ever becoming wider, and the disproportion in the distribution of wealth greater. Under such a

990

system there is little equality of opportunity for the vast majority of the workers.

The application of many scientific discoveries along with and in part by capitalism has resulted in a large scale machine and factory method of production which has subordinated the individual worker to the position of a cog in the wheel. The bourgeois standard of morality regulates the conduct of the individual in many respects which are not of public and social concern, and often suppresses freedom of speech and of publication. So that while the Westerner has succeeded in freeing himself to a large extent from the narrow bonds of the group morality of the family and the clan, and from the domination of the church, he has lost much of his freedom by becoming subjected to the crushing power of the capitalist state.

The proletarian class is organizing and is gaining more and more power in its fight against the capitalist class. Whether or not domination by the proletariat will mean greater freedom for the individual it is impossible to foresee. It is too soon to judge from the experience of Russia. So far the soviet state has curtailed appreciably the freedom of the individual. The Bolshevist leaders assert that this is a temporary condition which will persist only until the rule of the proletariat is firmly established. One of the crucial problems for mankind to solve in the future is how to carry on large collective enterprises with all the saving due to the use of machinery, specialization, and a detailed division of labor, without crippling the personality and destroying the happiness of the individual by means of unnecessary restrictions upon his freedom. It is the tendency of every social system to regulate its members more than is essential for its own survival. The mores or folkways carry along much obsolete baggage in the form of outworn ethical ideas and ideals which are useless and often harmful. This is especially true wherever institutionalized religion is influential, for it is always archaic in its outlook. It is therefore a hopeful sign for the future that religion is declining in its power.

The situation in the Orient with regard to economic and social democracy cannot be summed up in a word, for there are great variations.

With astonishing speed Japan jumped almost without any transition from feudalism into capitalism. As it has comparatively little arable land, it could not become a great agricultural country. Consequently, its transformation has taken the form of the development of commerce and industry, especially the latter. Its cities are rapidly becoming forests of factory chimneys. Its capitalism is of a rather paternalistic type, which is not surprising in view of the feudalistic background. There is not much room for democracy in such a system.

While there is a parliamentary system, the centralized and bureaucratic form of government reduces greatly the power and influence of the Diet. As late as 1925 the elected chamber of the Diet was chosen by less than 3,000,000 voters. What effect the American military occupation of 1945 to 1952 will have remains to be seen.

China has had the reputation of being a democratic country in its economic and social organization. The Chou-li (*circa* 1100 B.C.), or ancient code, established the following order of precedence among the workers: 1. Farmers; 2. Gardeners; 3. Woodworkers; 4. Cattle-raisers; 5. Artisans; 6. Merchants; 7. Female textile-workers; 8. Servants; 9. Vagabonds. This indicated the high esteem in which agriculture was held, owing to the fact that China is primarily an agricultural country. The Chinese were in the habit of classifying themselves as scholars, farmers, workmen, and merchants. Scholarship had a high place in the popular esteem.

For more than two thousand years China has had no theocracy, aristocracy, or feudalism. While for most of that time it has been a monarchy or empire, the central government has never been very powerful, and there has been a large measure of local autonomy. Under the system of state examination, any one could compete and work his way up to the highest official positions. In this sense the government was democratic, though there was little representative and no parliamentary govenment until the establishment of the republic in 1912.

During these two thousand years and more the industrial life was organized in the form of guilds. Every trade had a guild which included both employers and employees. The guilds regulated prices, wages, and terms of apprenticeship, and were democratic in character. Competition was not adapted to the Chinese system of industry, and these guilds furnished the necessary regulation without competition. The guilds could deal better with the government than isolated employers and employees, and they administered justice to a certain extent. There were also chambers of commerce including many kinds of business. But the factory system which is spreading has been breaking down the guilds, because the interests of capitalists and of wage-earners are too divided to permit of so democratic a form of cooperation. So far as the employees are concerned, their place is being taken by labor unions, and since 1949 by the Communist state which has supplanted capitalism.

A form of individualism often displayed in China is manifested in the absence of public spirit and in a lack of appreciation as to what is to the best interest of all concerned. A classic example is the condition of the roads. In many cases roads which are for public use pass over private property. The proprietors assume no responsibility for

992

them, so that usually they are very bad, much to the discomfort of themselves and of all others who use them. Peddlers preempt positions in narrow streets where they obstruct the traffic and seriously inconvenience passers-by. In Peiping I often passed through one of the principal streets where for a long distance the sidewalk was cluttered up with itinerant barbers, knife-grinders, and the like. The phase of such a situation which strikes a Westerner as most curious is not their indifference to the public interest but the meek tolerance of those who are inconvenienced. It is perhaps another indication that ethics are not as socialized in the East as in the West. The Chinese are naturally law-abiding and orderly. They have as yet very little of the so-called "social" legislation which is common in the West. This sort of individualism does not in the long run promote the freedom and welfare of the individual, because all the individuals who constitute the community suffer from it. However, it may indicate a certain independence on the part of the individual which has persisted despite the domination of the family.

The preceding discussion indicates that it is well-nigh impossible to give a categorical answer to most of the questions which have been raised, so imponderable are many of the factors involved. The family is much more powerful in the Orient. It hampers the career of the individual by limiting the choice of occupation and of spouse, by restricting freedom of movement, and by accentuating paternal authority. It also stands in the way of a broader social life. In the West the individual usually belongs to several social and cultural circles, and the women share this life with the men. The seclusion in the home of the Oriental woman cuts her off almost entirely from this broader social life. The predominant position of the family as the central unit of society narrows the outlook of the man, so that he is less likely to be interested in political, national, and world affairs. There are fewer cultural organizations to which he can belong.

On the other hand, Occidental life creates many petty social duties, and arouses new wants which incite the individual to struggle and strive in a manner which may or may not be worth while. At any rate, it creates a form of bondage of its own. While the West often professes to be democratic, we have seen that its democracy is in certain respects narrowly limited. The East makes fewer professions of this sort. But it has a good deal of freedom in the sense that if the fundamental interests of the family are conserved, and sometimes of religion, and certain external formalities are observed, the individual is usually left free to do as he pleases without suffering from the social and moral opprobrium often wreaked upon his head in the Occident for conduct which is not of public concern.

Oriental life is exempt from many of the worries of the Westerner due to a more complicated social life. It has even a certain equality in inequality which promotes human intercourse to a degree which is almost democratic. For example, the Indian caste system was fundamentally undemocratic in that it denied equality of opportunity, and was antisocial in many other respects. But it fixed the social status of the individual for life, so that he need never devote thought or effort to trying to better it. Moreover, it determined the relations not only of members of the same caste but of different castes, so that these relations could go on with an assurance which is not always present in the Occident.

The seclusion of women in the home has existed in varying degrees at many times and places, in the Occident as well as in the Orient. It is far more characteristic of the East than of the West. It must, however, be remembered that at all times and places where it has existed it has been primarily and mainly true of the women of the upper classes. The women of the lower classes usually have to work with the men in the fields and elsewhere. Their homes are too small to render possible the segregation of the sexes which a thoroughgoing seclusion of women requires. Like polygyny wherever it has existed, the complete seclusion of women is largely a luxury of the men of the upper classes.

We have seen that the family system, which is almost always based upon patriarchal authority, enhances the power of the males over the females. It devotes the women specially to purposes of breeding, and cuts them off to a considerable extent from a broader social life. A complete seclusion of women is rare. But the family system in the Orient renders the life of the women much more secluded than that of the men.

According to the civil code of Japan, men and women are in theory upon an equality. But a married woman cannot perform many important legal acts without the consent of her husband, and she has fewer causes for divorce than he. Male heirs have superior rights over female heirs. Until 1922, women were forbidden by law to promote or attend any political meetings whatsoever. They have been given the suffrage since the American military occupation of 1945 to 1952.

The position of women in Japan is similar to many other phases of the situation in that country. The rapid adoption of the Western economic system has created a demand for female labor in industry, especially in the textile factories, and as stenographers, clerks, and the like, in commerce and business in general. These changes have not as yet had much influence upon public opinion as to woman's status and functions. As we have already seen, the family system still dominates with its concomitant idea of rearing many children, as indicated by the rapid increase of population and opposition to birth control. Militarism may also have its influence, for it requires a sharp differentiation between the functions of men and women. Woman still is regarded as primarily and principally a breeder of children and housekeeper. While the external form has changed in part, the spirit remains largely as of old.

The position of the Japanese woman seems free as compared with her sisters in most Oriental countries. Until recently Korean upper-class women were almost completely secluded in their homes. In Songdo, an old-fashioned Korean city, I saw many women wearing the white national costume with a long piece of cloth which formerly covered the face but which is now thrown back over the head. The Japanese administration of Korea since 1910 furnished educational facilities for the Korean girls. The missionaries have probably had more influence in Korea than in any other Oriental country, largely because of the decadence of Korean culture. Through missionary influence many young Koreans have gone to the United States to study. All of these influences signify a wider and more independent life for Korean women in the near future. They have not yet had sufficient time to change materially the life of these women behind the stone walls which inclose the Korean home.

The bound feet of the Chinese women constituted a striking symbol of their seclusion. While this practice was forbidden by law shortly before the establishment of the republic, its victims still hobble along city streets and country roads. As late as 1925 I saw many who had not yet lost their youthful appearance. The origin of this custom is obscure, but must have been closely related to the seclusion of women. Few measures are better adapted to restrict their freedom of movement. Esthetic considerations were probably an after-thought. Only within the last few decades have upper-class Chinese women begun to appear in public. But foot-binding was prevalent among the proletarian and peasant classes as well.

How early the doctrine of the seclusion and subjection of women became a part of Chinese culture it is impossible to determine. That it was firmly established in Confucian times is clearly indicated in Li-ki, the Book of Rites or Ceremonies. "The woman follows the man. In her youth she follows her father and elder brother; when married, she follows her husband; when her husband is dead, she follows her son." (Book IX, 10.) Drastic separation between the sexes is maintained. "The Master said: 'The ceremonial usages serve as dykes for the people against evil excesses. They exemplify the separation between the sexes which should be maintained, that there may be no ground for suspicion and human relations may be clearly defined.'" (Book XXVII, 33.) The importance of propriety in the most important relation between the sexes is emphasized. "The observance of propriety commences with careful attention to the relations between husband and wife." (Book X, sec. ii, 13.) The separation between the sexes is extended to domestic and extramural affairs. "The men should not speak of what belongs to the inside of the house, nor the women of what belongs to the outside." (Book X, sec. i, 12.) "Outside affairs should not be talked of inside the home, nor inside affairs outside of it." (Book I, sec. i, pt. iii, c. vi, v. 33.) In view of the overwhelming influence of Chinese civilization in eastern Asia, it is not surprising that this doctrine was adopted in an extreme form by Korea and eventually in a milder form by Japan.

As China is the classic land of the family system, the position of the women has been determined largely by this system. Its patriarchal character made boys more valuable than girls. When the pressure of population on the means of subsistence encouraged infanticide in the congested regions, it was female and not male infanticide which took place. Marriages were made by the parents, usually at a comparatively early age, sometimes through middlemen, and presumably in the interest of the family. The parties often did not see each other until it was consummated. Woman was not regarded as the companion of man but as the mother of his children and his housekeeper.

According to Confucian theory the wife has no rights which the husband must respect. The woman, nevertheless, has a great deal of influence and authority within the home. During the first years of married life she is under the autocratic rule of her mother-in-law. After she has become a mother, especially if she bears male offspring, her influence increases until she in turn becomes the head of the internal economy of a household. Barrenness, on the other hand, may result in her being supplanted by another wife. Mencius uttered the dictim that to leave no posterity is the worst of three lines of unfilial conduct. In ignorance of the biological laws of heredity, the wife alone is held responsible for sterility.

In the cities the life of the women goes on largely behind the high stone walls of the Chinese house. While her physical seclusion is less, the mental seclusion of the peasant woman is as great as if not greater than that of her urban sister. For women as well as for men this mental seclusion can be broken only by means of the education which comes through the use of books, travel, and taking part in the broader social life outside of the home. This is as true in the Orient as it is in the Occident, whatever claims may be made as to esoteric and recondite sources of knowledge.

Partly owing to the lack of an alphabet and the extreme difficulty of learning to read, the standard of literacy has always been low in China. It was, in fact, practically a monopoly of the literati, who studied mainly for the purpose of taking the state examinations. Until recently there was no female literacy and no organized education for girls. There were a number of books on the duties of womanhood which were presumably read to them, but no other formal education. In this regard, to be sure, they were no worse off than in most Oriental countries, or, for that matter, in many Occidental countries until comparatively recently.

In the picturesque Indian scene perhaps the most striking note is furnished by the women. The colorful *sari* flows gracefully from head to foot, and is drawn tightly into many folds at the waist. Its color is often set off by a breastband of another hue, while between it and the waist gleams an expanse of the woman's bronzed skin. She is profusely decorated with a nose-ring, ear-rings, finger-rings, toe-rings, necklaces, bracelets, armlets, and anklets. Especially in southern India the woman becomes the treasure house of the family. On her forehead is the insignia of the Hindu and her fingers and toes are stained with henna. Far more impressive than all of this external and often excessive ornamentation is her magnificent carriage. With head erect, straight figure, and undulating body, she moves smoothly, gracefully and often swiftly over the ground. Here, to all appearances, must be a free creature.

Unfortunately, however, appearances often are deceptive. Her splendidly independent carriage is not due to freedom of thought and action on her part, but to the custom of carrying pots of water and other weights upon the head and to the barefoot tread, for unlike many of the men she has not yet succumbed to the Western habit of footwear. Her husband is chosen by her parents, sometimes before she is born, and she is married at an early age, often before puberty. As in China, she passes under the rule of her mother-in-law, and only gradually acquires influence and authority in the home. Usually she becomes the mother of numerous children and has little opportunity for social life and recreation outside of the *zenana* (women's quarters). If she has the misfortune to become a widow, she is in many castes forbidden to remarry, even though she is still a virgin, and the remainder of her life is passed in seclusion and drudgery.

The position of woman varies in different parts of India. The cultural situation is less uniform than in Japan or China. There have been several indigenous cultures, and others which have been imported and have met and mingled there. In fact, India is to a large extent a cultural and anthropological museum. The numerous castes vary considerably in their treatment of women. So that the situation is complicated, and only a few outstanding facts can be stated.

The majority of the Indian Moslems dwell in what since 1949 is Pakistan. Among them the custom of the "*purdah*" (curtain or screen) or physical seclusion of women is strong. Hindus have asserted to me

997

that Islam introduced the *purdah* into India, and that in ancient times the Indian woman was free. This belief is manifestly erroneous, and is fostered by Hindus who dislike Western criticism of the position of their women. There is evidence in the ancient literature as well as historical evidence that in certain parts of India woman led a very secluded existence long before the advent of Islam. It is, however, probable that Islam has encouraged the custom and caused it to persist in an accentuated form even among the Hindus. Thus in the Punjab and United Provinces *purdah* carts and palanquins containing women are often to be seen. But even in northern and central India the majority of the Hindu women, at any rate the lower-class women, are free from the *purdah* so far as appearing in public with faces uncovered is concerned.

In southern India there has never been any trace of the *purdah*. The women move about freely and with no attempt at concealment. Whether or not this was characteristic of the indigenous Dravidian culture, it is difficult to determine. On the southwest coast there still survive traces of matriarchal institutions from an early date. But in southern as well as in other parts of India, Hindu culture restricts woman's interests and activities mainly to the home, where her mental seclusion is as great as in most Oriental countries. Until the independent state of India was established in 1947, Indian marriage was religious and sacramental and regarded as indissoluble, all family property was owned jointly by the male members of the family, the head of the family cared for the daughters until their marriage, and the wife was largely under the domination of her husband. The Indian Parliament has been enacting legislation to make marriage civil and secular, to grant women as well as men the right of divorce, and to give women a share in the joint family property.

Many of the peoples of the Malay States and of the East Indies are Mohammedan. Islam rests lightly on the Malay folk, whom it has not succeeded in completely subduing. Consequently, the physical seclusion of women is not prevalent among them. In Java I saw no signs of it at all. In that beautiful island the gay and laughing Javanese women in their colorful garb move about freely in public. But that does not mean that their activities are not almost entirely restricted to the home, and that their mental seclusion is not as great as in other Oriental countries.

In Burma I have watched the smiling women, often puffing huge cigars, buying and selling in the markets and shops. Almost one is persuaded that they rather than the men conduct the business of this land of many stupas. To what extent this is true I do not know. Property is retained by each spouse, and what is earned during marriage is divided in case the conjugal tie is broken. Hinayana Buddhism

998

has long held sway in Burma, and its gentle and humanitarian doctrines may account in part for the relatively high position of the Burmese woman. There are doubtless other cultural factors which are not obvious on the surface.

As the breeder of children and the physically weaker sex, woman has with few exceptions been more closely associated with the home than man. Temperamentally also she may crave home life more than man. If this be true, the seclusion of Oriental women is not as great a hardship as it appears to be to Western eyes.

However that may be, in the course of social evolution there has been considerable variation in the extent to which she has engaged in pursuits outside of the home. It is not improbable that she played an important part in the development of agriculture and certain of the early industries, while man was engaged in hunting, fishing, and fighting. In primitive society the basket makers, potters, weavers, embroiderers, leather-workers, etc., were to a large extent craftswomen, and these trades were in part household industries.[2] In certain societies militarism was developed to such an excessive degree that man devoted himself almost exclusively to military pursuits, while woman took over practically all of the economic activities. A few such barbarous communities still survive in remote corners of the world.

As industry was removed more and more from the home, in the Occident as well as in the Orient these economic activities have usually been carried on by the men. The industrial revolution, however, has again furnished woman with many opportunities for work outside of the home, though the direction and control of industry and commerce still remain largely in the hands of the men, and the same is true of political activities. The Orient has as yet been only slightly touched by this great revolution, but it will doubtless materially influence the position of the women within the near future.[3]

[2] See O. T. Mason, *Woman's Share in Primitive Culture*, New York, 1894.

[3] The Orient is not only subject to pressure from the Occident, but is under the violent impact of an Occident which is rent into two hostile camps, while an imperialist United States is trying to dominate the world. (See Chapter XXXIV entitled "The Rise of American Imperialism in the Twentieth Century.")

Whether the Orient will be conquered by capitalism or communism, or will form some sort of compromise between collectivism and so-called "free" private enterprise, remains to be seen.

Chapter LVIII

The Recognition of Sex in the Orient

ON the banks of the holy Ganges in the city of Benares, sanctified by the spiritual emanations of many saints, stands a small temple whose pillars are carved with numerous human forms entwined in various sexual attitudes. This Hindu temple I visited while in India in 1925-26 and 1953-54. To the casual visitor from the Occident erotic art and symbolism in association with religion seem not only indecent but blasphemous. The lingam-yoni, or united external genital organs of the sexes, as the symbol of the worship of Shiva the Reproducer, is the most notable illustration. The nahman, or union of the virile and menstrual fluids, is a similar symbol. In the Tantric mysteries, in which is worshiped Parvati, the wife of Shiva, sex plays an important part.[1] While it may have a baser side in orgies which may or may not have utility, the recognition of sex in connection with what is regarded as most sacred lends to it a dignity and importance which it deserves, and which usually are not adequately recognized in Europe and America.

The significance of sex is often exaggerated by extending it far beyond the organic world to which it is restricted. The deities are regarded as sexed, often highly sexed, and mated. Shiva and his wife Parvati form a licentious pair. Vishnu's spouse is Lakshmi, and even the great god Brahma has his consort Sarasvati. The gods procreate and some of them, as Krishna the prolific warrior, have numerous offspring. Kama is the god of ove or sensual pleasure. All of these notions are due to the anthropomorphic tendency of the human mind everywhere. The deities of ancient Egypt, Greece, and Rome also were mated. The Jehovah of the Jews, the God of Christianity, and the Allah of Islam are alike male. Mariolatry furnishes to a large part of Christendom an opportunity to worship the female. Theologians

---

[1] "Tantricism owes its origin to the esoteric and erotic practices associated with Vedic mysticism." (*Indian Culture*, edited by Motilal Das, Calcutta, 1951, p. 293.)

1000

have devoted much thought and ink to the portentous question as to whether angels are male or female.

Some idea of the Oriental recognition of sex can be derived from its erotic literature. The Indian science of love (*kamashastra*) is closely related, on the one hand, to *arthashastra* (science of practical life), and, on the other hand, to *ayurveda* (medical science). The principal works of the Indian literature are the "Kama Sutra," or aphorisms concerning love, and the "Kama Shastra," or principles or doctrine of love, which incorporate ancient lore on this subject. The "Kama Sutra" was compiled by Mallanaga Vatsyayana probably in the fifth century of the Christian era, and belonged to the period of the Brahman renaissance against Buddhism. As might be expected of an Indian work, the author avows a religious motive for his treatise: "This work has not been prepared to serve simply as an instrument for the satisfaction of our desires. Anyone who, grasping the true principles of this science, cultivates with care his *dharma* (religious merit), his *artha* (temporal wealth), and his *kama* (sensual pleasure), and takes into consideration the practices of our people, is sure to arrive at a mastery of his senses." In other words, his ultimate object is somewhat similar to that of the yoga philosophy and practices which I have discussed in Chapter LVI.

The "Kama Sutra" is primarily a manual of love, but also discusses the acquisition of wealth, the management of a household, civic and family life, etc. It describes various ways of stimulating sexual feeling and forms of sexual intercourse, and the different physical and psychological types, both male and female, with respect to love. A considerable portion consists of advice to courtesans how to succeed in their profession. Vatsyayana tells us that his science of love is based upon the ancient texts, and that while preparing his work he was leading the life of a religious student and was totally absorbed in the contemplation of divinity. He does not tell us how he was able to consider at the same time the more mundane matters of love.[2]

The "Kama Shastra" was written more than a millennium later, in the sixteenth century, by the Brahman poet Kalyana Malla, and was prepared for the sex education of the son of a ruler of the Gujarat region in western India. The author commences in the usual religious manner: "Of a truth, no joy in this world of mortals can compare with that caused by a knowledge of the Creator. But immediately after, and ceding only to that joy, come the satisfaction and pleasure resulting from the possession of a beautiful woman." He then expounds the importance of the art of love.

This treatise deals in particular with conjugal love, little or

[2] A detailed commentary on the "Kama Sutra" entitled "Jayamangala" was written by Yasodhara Indrapada in the thirteenth century.

nothing being said about courtezanship. With the aid of tables are described in great detail the different physical types of both sexes and their compatibility with each other, arriving at the following eminently practical conclusion: "From a consideration of these tables it is entirely evident that the greatest happiness consists in the correspondence of the dimensions (of the sex organs), and that discontent increases in proportion to the lack of accord." In similar fashion are described in detail the forms of sexual intercourse. Concerning the one in the posture of the "sacred cow," the author piously ejaculates: "There is in this form great religious merit." He also discusses sexual intercourse in relation to the days of the lunar fortnight and the hours of each day. We may well be skeptical as to whether the moon has as much influence as he alleges.

Both of these compilations furnish many love philters, charms, and other prescriptions for making the sexes more attractive to each other. The efficacy of some of these measures may be questioned, as, for example, the following taken from the "Kama Sutra":

"Sweetened milk, wherein has been boiled a ram's or goat's testicle, produces (sexual) vigor."

"If a man, having mixed the powder of the milky hedge plant and of the kantala plant with the excrements of a monkey and the ground-up root of the lanjalika plant, throws this mixture upon a woman, she will no longer love any other person."

"To drink the milk of a white cow which has a calf with white feet, is of good augury, gives a good reputation, and preserves life. The propitiatory benedictions of venerable Brahmins have the same effect."

The "Kama Shastra" gives the following dubious recipes for fertility and sterility:

"The woman who will drink habitually in cow's milk equal parts of dry powdered ginger, pepper, long pepper, thorny solanum (*Solanum Jacquini*), and cassia buds, will conceive and bear a son, however long she may have been sterile." [3]

"The woman who will eat each day for a fortnight forty mashas of molasses (*jagri*) which is three years old, will remain sterile all of the remainder of her life."

The following charm is said to assure an easy travail and the happy delivery of a child:

[3] The fondness of the Hindus for aphrodisiacs may be due in part to the fact that most of them are vegetarians, eschew alcoholic beverages, and drink only water. This may explain their faith in curry, ginger, pepper, cinnamon, cloves, and other spices, which they call hot condiments (*garm masala*), and which are reputed to be aphrodisiac.

1002

"Let a holy man recite over water a mantra or charm whose power he knows, and then give it to the woman."

The "Kuttanimata," or lessons of a go-between, is a lyric poem composed in the eighth century A.D. by Damodaragupta, prime minister of the king of Kashmir, and based on ancient texts. It relates how a beautiful young girl who wishes to become a courtezan goes for instruction to an old woman who is a skilful go-between or procuress. The spirit of the work is indicated in the following passage: "For love, anger, craftiness, pretty ways, childish manners, modesty (or shame), all of these constitute, for these women, the very woof of life. Like unto a miserable wisp of straw is the life of a courtezan whose heart is subjugated by a high and powerful love and who cannot think of seeing herself separated from her well-beloved."

The "Samayamatrika," or breviary of the courtezan, is a similar poem composed by Kshemendra Vyasadasa, a versatile and prolific writer of Kashmir who lived in the eleventh century, and perhaps imitated the preceding work, though on a broader scale. A beautiful courtezan receives lessons from an old go-between, who characterizes the profession as follows: "The prostitute who, for those who attach themselves to her is an intoxicating beverage, for those who can command money, a goddess of beauty and happiness, for wealthy men, a nectar, for those whose wealth has disappeared, a poison, dazzles, O courtezan with the beautiful eyebrows, the very gods themselves."

In the twelfth century Jayadeva wrote his voluptuous pastoral poem entitled "Gita Govinda," or cowherd in song, in which appear the amorous god Krishna as a youthful cowherd and the beautiful *gopi* (milkmaid or cowherdess) Rahda. In his description of the delight of voluptuousness is the following characteristic passage: "For some moments voluptuous tremors put an obstacle to close embraces, the winking of the eyes to the longing looks cast upon the play of love, entertaining remarks to the pleasure of drinking the honey of the lips, the overflow of felicity to the struggle in the art of Kama; and this marvellous prelude to their hymeneal union became a ravishing thing." [4]

[4] Numerous poets have written of the love of Rahda and Krishna, such as Vidyapati Thakur in the fifteenth century. There are many other poetic and dramatic works in the Indian erotic literature. In the fourth or fifth century A.D. the famous dramatist Kalidasa wrote several amorous poems, and in the seventh century Bhartrihari made a collection of stanzas entitled "Shringara-shataka," or hundred stanzas of love. Later came the "Panchasayaka," or five arrows of love, of Jyotirisvara; the "Anaru-shataka," or hundred stanzas of Amaru; the "Ratirahasya," or secret of love, by Kokkoka (probably in the twelfth century); the "Ananga-ranga," or stage of Cupid, by Kalyana Malla, in the sixteenth century; etc., etc.

1003

In the dark obscurity of Indian history it is not easy to explain the efflorescence of this erotic literature. I have already referred to the struggle for domination which took place between the Brahmans and Kshatryas. When the Kshatrya Rajput, Prince Gautama, founded Buddhism in the sixth century before Christ, this struggle became identified with the contest for supremacy between Brahmanism and Buddhism. The humanitarian tenets of the latter religion attracted to it the lower castes and outcastes who had been downtrodden by the Brahmans. But it also exalted celibacy, which can never make a wide appeal. There is some reason to believe that in order to oppose their rivals effectively the Brahmans exalted the sexual instinct, placing it and procreation on a divine plane, thus encouraging lust in order to allure the populace. This may have disseminated the cult of Shiva, the worship of the amorous god Krishna, and other more or less erotic cults. To this day Shivaism dominates at Benares, and Shiva and Krishna are the most popular of the Hindu gods. The cult of Krishna is often identified with that of Kama, the god of sensual pleasure.

This may explain why, not only in the literature of love which has been described, but in the religious literature, such as the Puranas, the Sutras, and the Tantras, and also in the epic poems, there is much of an erotic character. It is a notable fact that much of the erotic literature arose during the aforesaid struggle between Brahmanism and Buddhism. After the invention and adoption of Sanskrit writing, it had a renaissance in Hindu poetry during the period of approximately from the eighth to the sixteenth century. Much of this was in the form of didactic poems which were inspired by the ancient erotic works and repeated them in effect.

Most of this literature clearly indicates the high rank assigned to the courtezan. This is to be expected wherever sex and sensual pleasure are exalted by religion. The courtezan has often been invoked as the priestess of Kama. To this day they are sometimes attached to the larger temples in an almost sacerdotal position. This has had an effect upon their social standing and functions. On the other hand, the woman as wife, and still more so as mother, plays a minor part in this literature, which is also a significant fact.

It has been thought that the phallic cult of Priapus in ancient Greece and Rome was derived from the cult of Shiva by way of Assyria, Phenicia, Cyprus, and Asia Minor. This is not necessarily the case, because phallicism has probably arisen spontaneously more than once. However this may be, the Indian erotic literature doubtless has had an influence upon the literature of the countries of the Near East, such as Persia, Arabia, Egypt, and Turkey. This was per-

1004

haps most true of Arabia, whose culture, after the rise of Islam, dominated for many centuries the southern part of Asia Minor, northern Africa, and penetrated into the Iberian peninsula, thus carrying its influence into Europe.

The "Perfumed Garden" was written at Tunis in about the year A.D. 1520 by an Arabian sheik. It has since been amplified by additions from ancient texts and Indian works and is obviously modeled after the "Kama Sutra" and "Kama Shastra." Like them, it commences with a pious ejaculation: "Praise be to God, who has put the greatest pleasure of men in the genital parts of women and the greatest joy of women in the sexual parts of men." The Koran is quoted as saying: "Women are your field, go to your field whenever you wish." (Chapter II, verse 223.) The traits which render the sexes attractive to each other are described. It is asserted that "woman loves man only for coition," hence he should be richly endowed as to his sex organs. The woman should be in embonpoint and have a large bust and abdomen.

The author asserts that erotic literature is useful to stimulate waning sexual vigor, and truthfully states that the whole world has "a taste for this kind of books which may be compared with the philosopher's stone which transmutes common metals into gold." Thirty-nine names for the virile organ and forty-three names for the female genital organs and the reasons therefor are stated. Numerous methods of sexual intercourse are described in detail. There is a section on aberrant forms of sexual indulgence. Some of the prescriptions for stimulating sexual feeling are no more reliable than the corresponding Indian ones, the hardy ass taking the place of the cow, as the following will indicate:

"The virile member rubbed with ass's milk acquires an unparalleled vigor and energy."

"Cook the male organ of an ass with onions and wheat, then feed this mixture to hens which must eventually be eaten."

The Arabian manual is less religious in tone than the Indian manuals of love, and therefore more frankly carnal in its nature. It rejects some of the Indian methods as causing more trouble than pleasure, and adds the following truthful observation: "The things which are preferable in coition, and which cap the climax to its enjoyment, are the embrace, the kisses and the sucking of the lips, thus is human coition distinguished from that of the animals." The Arab accepts without question sexual pleasure as the free gift of God. The Indian regards it as preliminary to and preparation for the more important matters of religion and as a lower stage in the eternal transmigration of souls, as the "Kama Shastra" puts it: "In the meas-

1005

ure that a man advances in age and moderates his passions, he is free to think of his Creator, to study religious subjects and to acquire the divine science."

The Arabian literature contains many amorous poems. The Arabian women are reputed to be beautiful, and in early youth wear little or no clothing. This may explain the frequent description of their physical charms as illustrated in the following passage from the "Moallaka" of Nabigha al Dhubyani, written in the sixth century: "The amber of her skin clothes her like a robe of silk, a perfect creature, she has the suppleness of a bending branch. Her abdomen is sleek and pleasing, very firm breasts swell out of her bosom."

The "Thousand and One Nights," often called the "Arabian Nights," is largely made up of tales of amorous intrigues which were collected principally in the eighteenth century. The scene is usually laid in Bagdad or its vicinity. Many of these tales have come from elsewhere, being borrowed from Persian, Indian, and Chinese as well as Arabian sources. The tales, exaggerated though they may be as a realistic picture, seem to indicate that the desire for adventures of love succeeds at times in breaking through the strictest seclusion imposed upon the women of the Orient, in which respect they are not unlike their sisters elsewhere.

Many other examples of Near Eastern erotic literature might be mentioned, such as the voluptuous Jewish "Song of Songs," attributed to King Solomon, but which is probably a collection of Hebrew amorous lyric poems, to be found somewhat bowdlerized in the King James version of the Old Testament; Persian, Turkish, Egyptian, and Afghan amorous poetry. In the "Song of Songs," which probably began to accumulate, about 1000 B.C., and which after receiving an allegorical religious interpretation (the "bride" is the Church) was included by the rabbis in the scriptural canon about 100 A.D. appear several descriptions full of imagery:

"The joints of thy thighs are like jewels, the work of the hands of a cunning workman. Thy navel is like a round goblet, which wanteth not liquor. Thy belly is like a heap of wheat set about with lilies. Thy two breasts are like two young roes that are twins. Thy neck is as a tower of ivory; thine eyes like the fishpools in Heshbon. . . . How fair and pleasant art thou, O love, for delights! This thy stature is like to a palm tree, and thy breasts to clusters of grapes." (Chapter VII.)

The following is a stanza from a ballad by a modern Afghan poet, Mirza Rahchan Kayil (A.D. 1855-1901):

Oh! this odor which floats over thy nape, thy throat and thy arms,
Which hovers around thy loins and thy golden-hued belly,

This odor which is fed without ceasing as by two inexhaustible
vials
From the tufted fleeces which shadow thy humid arm-pits.
I carry with me the scent of thy body.

In modern times the Occident has begun to influence this literature. This is illustrated in the work of the Turkish poet Djenab
Chehaboudin, born at Constantinople in 1870, who studied in Paris.
He terminated a lyric entitled "Poem of Love" with the following
words:

Unbutton your vest, that these eyes may see your body of silver.
Remember the old proverb: too much coquetry tires the lover.

I do not know to what extent this erotic literature has been and
is read in India and its neighboring regions, and how widespread is
its direct influence.[5] The fact that it exists and is honored and sometimes regarded as sacred is of great significance. When it attempts to
be scientific, it is often pseudo-scientific and therefore provocative of
mirth. The practical experience in the art of love which it embodies
is of greater value. Much of it represents a serious attempt to deal
frankly and openly with one of the most important aspects of human
life.

In the Occident, on the contrary, such literature has usually been
regarded as obscene and pornographic, and when tolerated at all only
under narrow restrictions. This pernicious and almost inhuman attitude has placed great difficulties in the way of its serious students and
creators. Indeed, it may be said that love as one of the greatest of
human arts and the scientific facts upon which it should be based are
scarcely recognized at all in the Anglo-Saxon and north European
countries. This situation has encouraged incompetent persons to try
to meet this universal human craving by producing and distributing
by devious methods a scabrous literature unworthy of the name of
either art or science. The most notable exception has been France,
whose glory it is that it has maintained a greater freedom in these
matters. As a consequence, not only has its own erotic literature developed more fully, but the literature of the Orient has circulated
there more freely.[6] When the science of the West can join and cooper-

[5] A Hindu writer comments as follows: "Sex has been a principal motif of
Hindu literature and art. Sex has ever occupied a powerful position in the formation of religions, precepts, and practices. And the sex idea has been prominent also
in domestic life and social institutions." (B. K. Sarkar, *Love in Hindu Literature*,
Tokio, 1916, pp. 66-67.)

[6] To any one who is acquainted with the erotic customs and literature of the
East as well as of the West, it is amusing to note that certain practices are stigmatized as French which were known in the Orient long before the French nation
came into existence.

ate with the joyous zest in the practice of love of the East, then can a genuine science and art of love develop which will benefit the whole of mankind.

Certain traits of this Oriental literature which has been reviewed should be mentioned. There is little in the nature of sex education for the young. The "Kama Shastra" was, to be sure, written for a young prince. But like the other manuals, its style is more adapted for adults than for children, who should be introduced to the subject in simple language and by degrees. All of these works assume a previous sex experience on the part of the reader.

Three types of sex relations are indicated—namely, marriage of a cut-and-dried sort, prostitution, and to a much less extent amorous intrigues often on the part of married women. With respect to conjugal relations, the intention of the manuals is to serve the useful purpose of making them in their sexual aspect as satisfactory as possible for both spouses. There is little indication of what is known in the West as romantic love, and still less of the play function of sex.

The erotic literature of the east Asiatic countries seems meager compared with that of India and the Near East. The students of the Chinese classics say that they contain no indecencies, by which I suppose they mean that they do not discuss sex.[7] The literature of China, which is very voluminous, is still to a large extent a *terra incognita* to Western students, and it may contain erotic works which are as yet unknown. There are said to be many works of fiction. Chinese poetry is singularly free from amorous characteristics, and is devoted largely to the exaltation of friendship between men. While Europeans and Americans cast an air of romance and mystery around sex relations, as is often illustrated in Occidental poetry and fiction which are preoccupied with love, the Chinese apparently regard these relations as obvious, a necessity for the body but not a satisfaction for the emotions. This satisfaction is derived through friendship.[8]

The early Shinto religion of Japan is said to have contained phallic elements, traces of which linger in the popular customs.[9] This may account in part for the erotic features of Japanese literature. There are many amorous poems which express the finer shades and external forms of love. More sensual are the romances. The first in order of time which we know is "Genji" by Murasaki no Shikibu, a lady of the court, written about A.D. 1000. It relates the love adven-

[7] See, for example, A. H. Smith, *Chinese Characteristics*, New York, 1894, fifth edition; W. E. Soothill, *The Three Religions of China*, London, 1913. Both of these authors were missionaries in China.

[8] Arthur Waley, who has translated many Chinese poems, has discussed this in the introduction to his *170 Chinese Poems*, London, 1918. He says that the poetesses usually write of the "rejected wife."

[9] See W. G. Aston, *Shinto (The way of the gods)*, London, 1905.

tures of Genji, a son of the mikado and a concubine, and gives a picture of certain aspects of the morals of the time. Still more interesting in this connection are the works of Ibara Saikaku, who was the leader of the school of popular realism in the seventeenth century. He pictures the customs of the bordels, which constitute an important feature of the life of Japanese cities.[10] Japanese painting also is said to contain many erotic works.[11]

The recognition of sex reflected in this Oriental literature is expressed in a measure by the custom of early marriage. This custom is due in large part to the family system which demands numerous progeny, and the parental authority which arranges the marriages and wishes to have them consummated before the children grow old enough to rebel and choose for themselves. A recognition of the sexual need, which arises when puberty is attained and should be satisfied before long in both sexes if a normal life is to be led, has also had its influence.

The most striking and exaggerated example of all of these factors for early marriage is to be found in the Brahman marriage customs. Among most of the Brahmans and some of the higher castes, especially in southern India, pre-puberty marriage is the rule and post-puberty marriage is regarded as sinful, especially for the girls. This custom is based on the Hindu ideals that marriage is a *"samskara"* (religious duty), and that by placing an age limit all will be forced to marry; that the girls should love those whom they marry and not marry those whom they love; that early marriage not only makes the girl a partner in the life of her husband but also a member of his joint family before her character is formed, so that she becomes thoroughly assimilated to it; and that it monopolizes the women for the lust of their husbands and insures the paternity of the children, so that the sacred blood of the Brahmans will not be tainted by an infusion of common blood. Several of these arguments for early marriage imply the sexual need, because they recognize that all should have sex relations, though it is sometimes alleged by Hindus as by many Christians that the purpose of sexual intercourse should not be pleasure.

Under British rule the authorities, wishing to maintain neutrality in matters of religion, recognized the pre-puberty marriages of the Brahman and other castes which practice it, and made post-puberty marriages among these castes illegal. Since Indian inde-

---

[10] See W. G. Aston, *A History of Japanese Literature*, New York, 1899. Aston, who was very religious and prudish, denounced "the pornographic school of popular fiction which disgraced Japan in the eighteenth and nineteenth centuries." (P. 56.)

[11] See the works of the brothers Goncourt on Japanese art.

pendence in 1947 social-reform ideas derived principally from the Occident have led some of the more progressive and heterodox Hindus to try to secure legislation prohibiting pre-puberty marriage. The obvious arguments against it are that it causes physical injury to the girls through premature sex relations and maternity; that it forces wifehood upon cripples, deaf-mutes, lepers, the blind, and others who are unfit for it; that it gives rise to infant and child widows who are often prohibited from marrying again even though they are still virgin; and that it is an impediment to female education. On the other hand, late marriage is becoming more and more a curse of the Occident, and compares in its harmful effects with the child marriages of India and certain other parts of the Orient.

The attitude toward prostitution in the Orient is perhaps a better illustration than early marriage of the recognition of the sexual need, at any rate for men. Figures are not available to compare accurately the extent of prostitution in the East with the West. A survey of the situation indicates that this ancient institution is more frankly and openly recognized in the Orient, and that prostitutes are not degraded and debased to the same degree by social scorn and contumely and by legal persecution. The effect upon the prostitute is to maintain or enhance her self-respect and to preserve if not to elevate her character by making her feel that she is performing a useful and therefore legitimate social function. In the Occident, on the contrary, the degrading and repressive treatment accorded her often drives her into the arms of the baser elements, to become the accomplice and consort of criminals.

Asceticism has a long history and has existed to a certain extent among all peoples and in connection with nearly every religion. At certain times and places it has exercised an exceptional degree of influence, usually owing to the peculiar tenets of a particular religion. At least three principal factors have played their part in giving rise to asceticism. The first is the magical notion of the uncleanness of sex, whose origin I have described in another work.[12] The second factor is the attempt to propitiate deities by foregoing sexual pleasure in

[12] "Some features of the sexual function have aroused disgust as well as fear in man. This has been especially true of the flow of blood in woman at various crises of her life, such as the hymeneal flow in connection with puberty, the menstrual flow at the times of the periodic catamenial function, and the puerperal flow at parturition. Primitive man seems at any rate to have felt fear if not disgust toward blood. So that these features of the sexual function have played an important part in giving rise to the notion which is still more or less prevalent that there is something repellent and unclean about sex, especially in woman. The sexual taboos both of the past and of the present can be attributed to a large extent to this notion." (Maurice Parmelee, *Personality and Conduct*, New York, 1918, p. 162.)

order to expiate sin and attain purification. The third is the desire to conserve sexual vigor in order to concentrate all energy upon a single pursuit, usually religion, more rarely intellectual or other pursuits. Thus has arisen the ideal of monasticism and of a celibate priesthood. In the Roman Catholic church, however, celibacy was enjoined upon the clergy in order to prevent church property from being partitioned among the children and legal heirs of the priests, monks, and nuns.

In the Occident ascetic ideas have had much influence, principally through the medium of Christianity. In this religion the magical notion of the uncleanness of sex has combined with the desire to propitiate the deity by expiation and purification through chastity. The monastic ideal and a celibate clergy have characterized many Christian sects. Thus the ascetic ideal has played a prominent part in Christianity and has influenced the regulation of sex down to the present day. Islam, on the contrary, has scarcely been touched by these ideas, probably owing to the character of its founder, and has never encouraged monasticism.

Asceticism has probably had less influence in the East, though its Oriental form is often very intense. The East Asiatic religions have apparently never been permeated with ascetic ideals. There is a good deal of austerity and some self-denial in the teachings of Confucius, in the older Taoism, and in the Japanese morality exemplified in bushido or the feudalistic chivalry of the Samurai military caste. The austere mysticism of Lao-tze is expressed in the following passage from the Tao-teh-King: "The riches of the self-controlled man are in the Inner Life. When he spends for others, he has more for himself. When he gives to others, he has much more for himself." Rarely is there in these moral and religious teachings any suggestion of the suppression of sex which is the essential feature of asceticism. In so far as asceticism has influenced eastern Asia, it has done so mainly through Mahayana Buddhism, which introduced monasticism.

Hinduism recognizes sex frankly and openly as a necessity and even a duty for the great majority. But it regards it as characteristic of a lower stage in the process of transmigration, which it visualizes in a very anthropomorphic fashion, so that in later reincarnations sexual desire should be overcome and surpassed. Both Hinayana and Mahayana Buddhism have exalted the monastic ideal, so that many parts of the Orient are overrun with monks who are or are supposed to be celibate. Owing to the inferior position of woman, religion is regarded less as a vocation for her than for man, her place being in the home. Consequently, there are fewer nunneries in the East than in the West.

In the Orient asceticism is usually regarded as a means of acquiring religious merit by those peculiarly fitted for the religious vocation,

1011

but not as a discipline to be forced upon others, as is often the case in the Occident. Christian asceticism, on the contrary, has succeeded in attaching a certain amount of stigma to the sex relation *per se*, so that its legitimacy is usually admitted by the conventional standard of morality rather grudgingly only for purposes of reproduction, and not always even for that purpose. The principal founder and apostle of Christianity, the misogynist Paul, was largely responsible for this attitude toward sex.[13]

It is more difficult to decide whether there has been more prudery in the West or in the East. The frank recognition of sex would seem to indicate less prudery in the Orient. But the separation of the sexes and the seclusion of women render many forms of intercourse between men and women indecent which are not so regarded in the Occident. The close bodily contact between the sexes in Occidental social dancing is generally regarded as immoral in the Orient. And it doubtless is inconsistent with Western prudery and asceticism. But in the long run, for those accustomed to it, the waltz, the two-step, the one-step, the fox-trot, the tango, and the like, serve in a measure to subdue as well as to stimulate sexually. They bring the sexes together in rhythmic movements which promote an esthetic harmony between them. This form of intimacy can be enjoyed with many individuals of the opposite sex, and enlarges considerably the field of association between the sexes. In the East, on the contrary, almost the only intimate relation between them, outside of the conjugal relation, is coition. Oriental men may readily be sexually stimulated by association with Occidental women, because they are not accustomed to so much freedom of intercourse. They are therefore easily led to believe that such freedom necessarily gives rise to promiscuous and illicit sex relations.

The freedom with which men and women in Europe and America are seen together in public, meet in social gatherings, and mingle in their work and play seems indecent to the Oriental. Especially true is this of the mingling of the youths and maidens and the courtship and freedom of choice which ensue. The Orient assumes a prudish attitude toward many forms of association between the sexes which are regarded as innocent in the Occident. This is matched by Western prudery with respect to the degree of bodily exposure practised in

---

[13] See the Pauline epistle, I Corinthians, VII, 1, 2, 32, 33, for a statement of the Christian attitude toward sex:

"It is good for a man not to touch a woman. Nevertheless, to avoid fornication, let every man have his own wife, and let every woman have her own husband. . . . He that is unmarried careth for the things that belong to the Lord, how he may please the Lord: but he that is married careth for the things that are of the world, how he may please his wife."

many Oriental countries, erotic literature, sexual symbolism in religion, and the like.

With respect to the double standard of sex morality, there can be little question that it is more frankly recognized in the Orient, and that consequently there is less hypocrisy in this connection than there is in the Occident. This is due primarily to the patriarchal system dominant in the East. The double standard has arisen out of the anatomical and physiological differences between the sexes with respect to reproduction, male sexual jealousy, and the economic dependence of women.[14] Under the patriarchal regime women are subjugated to an excessive degree, and the difference in the amount of freedom accorded to the sexes is accentuated. Thus men acquire more and women less sexual liberty than in the West.

Christianity has preached a sort of single standard of sex morality for both sexes based on asceticism. In other words, it has endeavored to equalize the freedom of the sexes by restricting the male as narrowly as the female. This has been accepted in theory in a considerable part of Christendom. Inasmuch as it is based upon an ascetic doctrine contrary to the facts of human nature, it has failed in practice. The inevitable result from this divergence between theory and practice has been an enormous amount of hypocrisy. Islam has not fallen into this discrepancy. In Mohammedan countries the women who violate the narrow code of morality prescribed for them are severely punished, while the men are allowed a large measure of freedom.

In so far as woman has acquired greater freedom in the West, it has been due not to Christianity but to social and intellectual evolution. The economic changes of the last century or two have increased her independence greatly. Science has discovered effective contraceptive measures which enable her to control procreation and thus to eliminate the danger of unwanted pregnancies. By such means is a single standard of sex freedom being gradually approximated in the Occident, and only in a similar fashion can it be attained in the Orient

[14] "The fundamental factor in creating this double standard is the physiological dissimilarity of the sexes which makes sexual intercourse a much more serious matter for woman than for man, since it is very likely to result in pregnancy. It is therefore very important that she should not take this risk unless conditions are suitable for her to bear children. . . . The double standard has been greatly strengthened by the proprietary attitude displayed by men towards women. This attitude is due in part to an innate sexual jealousy, but is largely artificial, since it has been encouraged by economic and other social factors." (Maurice Parmelee, *Personality and Conduct*, New York, 1918, pp. 169-70.)

The influence of economic conditions, and of the right of private property in particular, upon standards of sex morality is discussed at length in the following work: R. Briffault, *The Mothers: A study of the origin of sentiments and institutions*, New York, 1927, 3 vols.

as well. Until that time comes the double standard will be openly recognized and applied.

The foregoing survey indicates clearly that neither in the East nor in the West is sex recognized in a complete and thoroughgoing manner. The Orient recognizes the sexual need for men fully, but not adequately for women except in connection with reproduction. In the Occident it is not adequately recognized for either sex. While the East recognizes the physical aspects of sex more frankly, the West recognizes and puts into practice a much wider range of relations between the sexes, including a degree of comradeship which is impossible in the Orient owing to the seclusion of women.

In the East there is little of the so-called romantic love which bulks large in the West. As a consequence, woman figures much less in Eastern than in Western literature, and there is much less of gallantry and chivalry toward women in the East. This lack is not resented by Oriental women, so that apparently these traits do not respond to an innate need, as is often alleged in Europe and America. The women receive their share of recognition as mothers and as the dominant factors in the home. Indeed, in certain parts of the Occident, as in America, gallantry and chivalry are carried to such an extreme that women acquire more rights and privileges than men, and many men slave at their work to maintain their women in idleness and luxury.

Far surpassing romantic love in importance stands what I have called the play function of sex, which is as yet scarcely recognized in the West and still less in the East.[15] Under this name may be subsumed the part played by sex in human life aside from its reproductive function, which is fully recognized everywhere. The play function includes not only the purely physical aspects of sex but its psychological aspects as well—namely, its effects upon the affective and intellectual life. Mankind stands as yet only upon the threshold of the recognition and understanding of this important function of sex. Not until its far-reaching ramifications have been thoroughly studied and the results of this research have been embodied in the education of the young can the recognition and comprehension of sex attain their complete fruition in the life of both the Orient and the Occident.[16]

---

[15] I proposed this name in my *Poverty and Social Progress*, New York, 1916, pp. 310-17; and described this function of sex at length in my *Personality and Conduct*, Chapter IX, entitled "The Play Function of Sex." I have also discussed certain aspects of this subject in my book entitled *The New Gymnosophy*, New York, 1927; and in my *Oriental and Occidental Culture, An Interpretation*, New York, 1928.

[16] In my book entitled *The Play Function of Sex*, 1960, I have described this aspect of sex fully and in detail.

Chapter LIX

Recreation in Orient and Occident

WHILE India is especially barren in public recreational facilities, the Orient in general has less public recreation and social life than the Occident. One of the principal reasons for this difference is the seclusion of women. This institution excludes the larger part of one sex from most public forms of recreation. Social life is necessarily more private in its nature, being restricted largely to the home. This is true even of much of the social life outside of the home. For example, there is little in the way of public eating in the Orient. Hotels and inns do not as a rule have dining-rooms, but the meals are served to the guests in their own rooms. Restaurants are divided up into small rooms and have screens and curtains by which to separate each party from the others. In fact, the visitor from the West comes to feel that it is almost improper if not indecent to eat in public.

What I have said with regard to the privacy of social life applies more particularly to the upper classes. The poor people usually have to live in narrow quarters where many persons are huddled together under conditions which render much privacy out of the question, and to eat whenever and wherever they can regardless of the proprieties. It applies more to city than to village life, because the seclusion of women is carried out most fully in the upper classes and in the cities.

The absence of a periodical day of rest affects considerably recreation and social life in the Orient. The hebdomadal week has existed at various times and places in different parts of the world.[1] But the Hebrew Sabbath, which through the spread of Christianity was universally adopted throughout the Occident, has not existed in the Orient, except to the extent to which it has recently been introduced from the West. This is true principally in Oriental ports where there is the closest contact with the West, and in Japan where it has to a certain extent been adopted. In the cities in the interior and in

[1] See Hutton Webster, *Rest Days*, New York, 1916.

the rural regions throughout the East the Occidental Sunday is almost unknown. There are, however, more or less frequent festivals which correspond to the European and American holidays.

In China the half moon from the Chinese New Year to the Feast of Lanterns is a national vacation period, and there are a few other festival days. In Japan there are a number of religious, patriotic, household, and seasonal festival days. In India the diversity of religions gives rise to several schedules of festivals. Some of the Hindu festivals are in honor of the gods Shiva, Vishnu, Krishna, and Ganesh, the goddesses Durga (Parvati) and Lakshmi, and the beginning of spring and the vernal equinox. Among the Mohammedan festivals are those in honor of Mohammed, Husain, and Abraham, and at the close of the fast of Ramazan. The Parsees celebrate in honor of Zoroaster and at the new year. In Buddhist countries are festivals in honor of the last birth of Gautama, and at the new year. In Ceylon the coming of Buddha to the island is celebrated. Many other festivals in these and other Oriental countries could be mentioned.

It would be difficult to state how many festival days there are on the average throughout the Orient. It is probably considerably less than the fifty-two Sundays plus the national holidays of the Occident. To what extent this difference is compensated for by shorter hours and a more leisurely mode of work it would be impossible to estimate. This may also be due to a weaker sense of the value of time. Many Western observers are of the opinion that Orientals labor less strenuously than Occidentals. However this may be, the lack of a periodical and uniformly observed rest day hampers in a measure the organization of means of recreation for the public at large.

So far as my observation goes, the theater is more varied and highly developed in Japan than elsewhere in the Orient. An excellent sense of comedy, especially of the grotesque, is displayed, and there is usually comic relief in connection with tragedy. Music and dancing are often utilized in connection with drama. Historical plays are much used. Mediaevalism is even more prominent in the theater than in daily life. The knightly (Samurai) virtues of courage, loyalty, patriotism, *hara-kiri* (suicide by disembowelment), are extolled. The *No* drama, which was developed by the Samurai caste and is somewhat operatic in character, is still played occasionally with its simple scenery. The kabuki style of drama, which was plebeian in its origin, is much more used.[2] It includes both historical and domestic pieces. There is not much treatment of present-day problems in the Western style—namely, in a critical and introspective manner. But Occidental influence is beginning to manifest itself in other ways. Actresses now

[2] Zoe Kincaid, *Kabuki, the Popular Stage of Japan*, London, 1925.

1016

appear on the stage where formerly feminine roles were impersonated by actors.

The drama is said to have been introduced into China under Mongol rule in the thirteenth century and to have come probably from Tartar sources.[3] The Chinese theater is so remote from anything Occidental that it is difficult to judge it. The drama is usually played with practically no scenery and no curtain. The musicians sit on the stage and the attendants move about freely under the eyes of the audience. The players approach the front of the stage as their turn comes. Their elaborate and often grotesque dress and appearance usually render their roles inexplicable to the foreigner. The absence of scenery often necessitates pantomime which is sometimes very realistic. The Chinese drama is said to cover a wide range of topics. A strong sense of the comic is often displayed. Until 1912 there were no actresses. In the audience the sexes sit on opposite sides of the theater, but this division is beginning to disappear. In the rural districts there are itinerant companies.

In India the hand of religion weighs heavily upon the theater as upon almost every phase of life. In Calcutta in 1925 I was invited to the leading Hindu theater by a well-known solicitor. The play was the story of the Ramayana epic slightly modernized by a dramatist whom I met at the theater. It was so sentimental that it would have been laughed off the stage in New York or London, Paris or Berlin. But the audience followed its every line with rapt attention. My host told me that he had seen it over thirty times and was not yet tired of it. The play depicted the adventures of the heroic Rama, the seventh avatar of Vishnu, and of his devoted wife Shita. There was little or no comedy, but many beautiful costumes and a nautch dance to relieve the eye.

The Indian theater is romantic and sentimental to an excessive degree. Only the religious sentiment deeply rooted early in life could render tolerable the constant reiteration of these tales of gods and goddesses. Were it not for the *naïveté* promoted by their religion's feeble sense of humor, they would not be acceptable even as fairy tales. The excessive interest in the two great epics, the Mahabharata and the Ramayana, has had a deadening and restricting influence upon almost all branches of Indian literature. The sacred literature—namely, the Vedas, Puranas Shastras, Sutras, Smitris, etc—have had a similar influence upon science and philosophy as well as upon literature, like the deadly effect of the Hebrew-Christian Bible upon Occidental culture. The contrast between the infantile drama of India and the more highly evolved drama of China and Japan illus-

3 H. A. Giles, *A History of Chinese Literature*, New York, 1901.

trates the fact often forced upon the mind of the traveler that the Mongolian has a more rounded personality than the somewhat one-sided Indian. While India has had famous dramatists in the past, the Indian stage of today does not give even the simple picture of the life of the people which it is the peculiar function of the theater to mirror.

Pantomime, both by animate and inanimate actors, plays an important part in Oriental drama. At Djokjakarta in central Java I witnessed a shadow show in which grotesque figures with huge beak-like noses were thrown on a screen. In the open air at Pegu in Burma on a moonlight night I was present at a *pwe*, the national amusement of the Burmans. In addition to music and dancing by both men and women, there were pantomimic clowning and a marionette show. The unspoken drama, in the forms of pantomime and mimicry, is often very expressive and can be developed to a high degree of skill. But it is not as highly evolved as the spoken drama which can express more feeling and especially ideas than the unspoken.

This use of pantomime is one of many indications that the Oriental theater is not so extensive and diversified as the Occidental. Practically every dramatic form used in the East is also represented in the West. In addition the Western stage presents a more detailed and realistic picture of life. This is partly due to its material equipment, which is richer than that of the Eastern stage. It is more due to intellectual differences. The Western drama in its higher forms includes introspection into human nature, analysis of the causes of social phenomena, and criticism of the conditions under which mankind lives. The recent development of science is largely responsible for this type of drama, because it has freed the minds of some men and women to think about these human and social phenomena and to express themselves concerning them. Since this mental attitude is as yet little prevalent in the Orient, it has not found expression in a psychological and social drama.

In recent years the West has sent a new form of entertainment to the East which bids fair to become as popular as it already is in its place of origin. The cinematograph is inexpensive and easy to transport. It reveals to the eyes of the Orientals the strange and wondrous Occident and furnishes them endless amusement. There are already numerous cinema theaters in every large Oriental city, and they are rapidly spreading not only to the smaller cities and towns but even to the villages. In fact, it is not unlikely that the moving picture which came out of the West will do more than any other agency to accustom the Orient to public forms of recreation. It has already had a little influence in breaking down the seclusion of women, for its fascination attracts many women as well as men to seek an unwonted amusement and entertainment outside of the home.

The cinematograph is an admirable means of acquainting the Orient and the Occident with each other, and might serve as an excellent educational agency. But the imported and particularly the American films are giving Eastern peoples an almost wholly distorted view of Western life. Most of these films are either luridly sensational or sickeningly sentimental, many being scenes of violence so that they do not furnish a true picture of life as it is ordinarily led anywhere in the universe. The comic pictures are the most innocuous, for they are bringing amusement and entertainment into many barren and monotonous lives, and can do little injury through being misunderstood, because the appreciation of humor is universal. When both the East and the West produce and exchange pictures which depict truly their manners, customs, institutions, and the conditions under which they live, the cinematograph will be a powerful factor for promoting understanding and sympathy between these two great divisions of mankind. The same may be true of radio and television.

The Orient is beginning to make its own films. Japan already manufactures much of what it uses. In Kyoto I saw an excellent Japanese film which depicted graphically and with much humor the adventures of a country lad who goes to the city. While it was being exhibited a reader recited its story to the audience. The first Chinese films were being manufactured while I was in China in 1925. In Rangoon in 1925 I saw a very badly made Indian film filled with gods and goddesses and their impossible exploits. Unless they can forget their deities for a time, the Indians are not likely to make good films. In India from 1953 to 1954, I saw well made historical films, and in Burma an entertaining operetta.

In Peiping there was no public park until recently when a part of the grounds of the Imperial Palace was opened to the public. Temple precincts have sometimes furnished urban dwellers breathing spaces. As a rule, gardens and other open spots in Oriental cities have been inclosed for the exclusive use of king and prince, nobleman and rich man. The cities have usually not been planned, but even when planned no space has usually been allotted for the rest and recreation of the populace. Most of the parks now in existence are due to Western domination or imitation of the Occident.

In eastern Asia the American amusement park has been copied. Asakusa Park, the "Coney Island" of Tokio, contains in addition to the popular Kwannon Temple many movies, variety theaters, peep shows, restaurants, and various mechanical devices for the entertainment of the plebeian and proletarian masses. The "New World" in

Peiping is a similar innovation, with pool- and billiard-rooms, movies, recitals by sing-song girls, cafés, peep shows, and the like. In 1925 I visited a "New World" also in Shanghai, Canton, and Singapore, where there are many Chinese residents, and a similar amusement park in Weltevreden (Batavia now Jakarta), Java. This American influence has not yet reached India, where the populace is not sufficiently mirth-loving to appreciate it. In Hyderabad, in central India, a traveling circus camped for a night or two in the front yard of my hotel. In Tokio I visited a circus in a large and lofty tent with a full equipment of trained animals, acrobats, and clowns. I am not sufficiently acquainted with the history of circuses to be able to state whether their origin is Eastern, Western, or both.

In sport and athletics the contrast between the Orient and the Occident is great. In the Butokuden (Hall of Martial Valor) in Kyoto I watched some of the historic Japanese sports. The *Kenjitsu* (fencing) practice was about to begin. A large group of fencers wearing masks, gloves, short tunics, and with bare feet, filed in. Kneeling down they prostrated themselves on the polished floor before the shrine at the side of the hall. Then they squatted while waiting their turns. One by one a fencer would bow formally before another, thus inviting him to a bout, until several pairs were at work. The foil was of split bamboo, about four feet in length, with a hilt twelve inches long for a double grasp. They banged each other over the heads until the hall was filled with a terrific din of noise. There was a solitary little woman fencer who bowed before a man with a much longer reach from whom she was apparently taking lessons.

In another part of the hall several men were practicing *judo* or *jujitsu*, the Japanese art of self-defense. They wore strong coats with a band around the waist. The edge of the coat is firmly grasped and by means of jerks, twists, and turns, which sometimes break bones, the opponent is violently thrown to the ground or mat. In an adjoining covered gallery archery was going on at the same time. All of this was reminiscent of the mediaeval and martial sports of the Samurai caste.

Sumo or wrestling has become professionalized to a considerable degree. It is an ancient sport which was encouraged by feudalism. Thus we see that the national sports were martial in their origin and consisted largely of combats between individual fighters. I know of no organized game played by teams which was indigenous to Japan. But American baseball has become quite popular.

The Chinese recognized six arts—namely, ceremonial, music, archery, charioteering, writing, and mathematics. Of these arts archery and charioteering may be regarded as sports, and were presumably

1020

military in origin. China was never as martial as Japan and probably for that reason has devoted less attention to sport.

Polo is said to have come to the West from India. It was not necessarily indigenous to that country, as it may have been imported or invented by some of its foreign conquerors. The pacific, pietistic, and somewhat inert Indian is not given to the rivalry and exertion involved in sport. Indeed, it is probably safe to say that Orientals in general are less disposed to engage in activity for its own sake than Occidentals.

It would be superfluous to describe the important part played by sport in the Occident, especially among the peoples of North European descent. Its origin there as elsewhere doubtless was largely military. Sport was and to a certain extent still is mimicry of and preparation for warfare. It has developed largely in the form of games in which numerous players organized as teams oppose each other. In recent times its military aspect has to a considerable extent been superseded by a recognition of its value for health and also for the discipline of character. The West may, indeed, be said to be possessed by an athletic complex as compared with the East.

Western sports are now being introduced into the Orient. At Waseda University in Tokio I saw an excellent baseball diamond and many enthusiastic players. In Hibiya Park I witnessed a scratch game in which some of the players were seriously impeded in their running by the national costume. In Kyoto and elsewhere I saw games after the American model. While baseball is far in the lead in popularity, many other sports have been introduced, including track and field athletics, football, tennis, golf, rowing, basketball, volley-ball, skating, skiing, and boxing. Some of them are being taken up by the women. The Japan Amateur Athletic Association is the central body which is trying to develop these sports and to establish standards of sportsmanship. Physical culture in the form of gymnastics and calisthenics has been introduced into many of the schools both for boys and for girls.

China has as yet adopted these sports much less than Japan. They exist principally in schools of Western origin. The American occupation of the Philippine Islands has introduced these sports on an extensive scale. In 1913 was held the first Far Eastern Olympiad, which takes place every two years and includes Japan, China, and the Philippines. So far Japan and the Philippines have surpassed China in their exploits at these international games.

British rule has introduced cricket into India, where, it is said, the Parsees were the first to adopt it, because they were in closest touch with their conquerors. In Bombay I attended championship matches between Hindu, Moslem, Parsee, and British teams. Thousands of

1021

enthusiastic and excited spectators were present, and the newspapers devoted long accounts to the games. Tennis also is played to a certain extent. India has not as yet displayed as much interest in Western sports as some of the Far Eastern countries, perhaps due partly to its tropical climate, but probably more on account of the psychological factors mentioned above. The Nationalist movement also may impede somewhat their introduction. So far it has been almost impossible to popularize them among the girls and women.

In the Occident social dancing constitutes one of the most popular forms of indoor recreation and an important aspect of social life. In Chapter LVII I have described how the seclusion of women and the relations between the sexes render it almost impossible in the Orient. Until the status of women changes and the relations between the sexes become much more free, it cannot take its place as a recreation and a form of social life. Indeed, even exhibition dancing is not practised to the same extent and has not been developed in so great a variety of forms as in the Occident. It plays a small part in the Oriental theater. It is also used for the private entertainment of guests in some Eastern countries.

A prominent banker in Osaka invited me to dine and to meet some of his colleagues. We gathered in a beautiful restaurant and were ushered into the rooms reserved for us, where we seated ourselves upon mats. Several women entered bearing small, low tables which were placed before us. Then they brought a long succession of Japanese dishes. While the food was being eaten they chatted and laughed with my host and his guests. As no one of the women could speak a European language, I was almost entirely excluded from the conversation. About half-way through the meal they appeared with a *samisen* (three-stringed guitar), a *koto* (thirteen-stringed lyre), other musical instruments, and fans and parasols, and sang and danced. At the close of the meal they continued this performance. These were geisha girls who furnish entertainment at every social function of any degree of distinction in Japan. While their ministrations were interesting and enjoyable, they effectually destroyed the serious conversation which I had hoped to have with these important bankers and business men.

In Seoul in 1925 a group of Korean journalists invited me to dinner at a restaurant. Soon after we arrived several young girls appeared and sang and danced. When we seated ourselves at a long, low table heavily laden with food, all of the courses being served at once, they joined with us in partaking of the rich viands. Later they left us alone to discuss matters of mutual interest.

At Chinese social functions it is customary for sing-song girls to be present to furnish music and take part in the conversation. China, the most populous country in the world, presents the extraordinary

1022

spectacle of a land where not only social but also exhibition dancing is almost non-existent. Whether or not this has always been the case, I do not know. The custom of foot-binding for the women was doubtless largely responsible for preventing the development of this art and means of entertainment and recreation.

The sacred dance is still used to a slight extent in the Orient. At Nikko is the most beautiful Shinto shrine in Japan, built as a mausoleum for Ieyasu, the founder of the Tokugawa shogunate in the seventeenth century, and Iemitsu, his grandson. At the annual festival in June 1925, a long procession passed down the broad avenue lined with stately cryptomeria trees. In addition to the priests and state dignitaries, musicians and dancers, the procession included several hundred men clad as spearmen, bowmen, lancers, etc., representing the defunct Samurai caste and their retainers, thus making it a historical pageant as well as a religious ceremony. Just before it started, I saw in a pavilion before the Futawara temple a dancer with a grotesque mask performing the *kochiki odori*, a sacred dance said to be many centuries old. When the procession reached its destination at the Odabicho shrine, several male dancers performed the *azuma* dance in the presence of the imperial envoy. The *kagura* is danced at the most holy Shinto fanes, the Naigu and Gegu shrines at Yamada in the Ise peninsula.[4] At the Kasuga shrine in the great park in Nara several young girls attired in beautiful costumes are prepared to perform sacred dances for a financial consideration, thus very conveniently combining piety with business, as is often the case the world over. In another temple in 1954 I witnessed a dance by priests.

One evening in Madura I watched a procession in honor of a god file out of the gloomy recesses of the great temple. It included Brahmans, elephants, musicians, torches, monkeys, portable shrines, and other paraphernalia of an Indian religious festival. After passing through several streets it halted, and a nautch girl attached to the temple danced before the shrine of the god while the bracelets on her arms, the bangles on her legs, and the bells on her toes jingled and tinkled. As the only foreigner present, I had been accorded a position in the front row of spectators. While her sinuous body went through the voluptuous movements of the dance in honor of her divine master, she smiled and cast friendly glances toward me for reasons which I will not attempt to conjecture.

These are random memories of scenes witnessed. They are similar to the reminiscences which an Oriental who visits the Occident

4 "Like the ancient Greek tragedies and the mystery plays of the Middle Ages, the drama in Japan was in its beginnings closely associated with religion. Its immediate parent was the Kagura, a pantomimic dance." (W. G. Aston, *A History of Japanese Literature*, New York, 1899, p. 197.)

takes back with him of altars, pulpits, priestly raiment, choirs, pipe-organs, chanting, chimes, so-called "holy" water, and the like. Whatever significance the dance may still have in Oriental religion, the sacred dance contributes very little to recreation and social life.

It is impossible to determine whether or not indoor games are played as much in the East as in the West. They are prevalent in China and to a slightly less extent in Japan. Ma Chiang, or the sparrow game, which is said to be the most popular, has recently been introduced into the West. Chess is supposed to have originated in China, but is played differently in that country and Japan from its Western form. Gobang is a somewhat similar Chinese game which is also played in Japan. Card games are popular in China, probably because the Chinese are fond of gambling, which, indeed, seems to be their favorite form of amusement. So far as my observation goes, indoor games are much more prevalent in China and Japan than they are in India. Needless to say, children have their indoor as well as outdoor games everywhere.

The preceding survey clearly indicates that organized means of recreation and social life in public are much more limited in the Orient than they are in the Occident. This is due partly to the seclusion of women and partly to a less complicated scheme of life. Whether or not this lack is fully compensated by Eastern home life it would be impossible to say without an intimate knowledge of the Oriental home, which it is difficult for the stranger to acquire. Such a question involves the consideration of psychological and social phenomena too intangible and imponderable in their character to be accurately measured. Whether or not a less complicated life enables the Oriental to retain a closer touch with nature is another difficult question which I shall discuss in the following chapter.[5]

---

[5] During my sojourn in the Far East in 1953 to 1954, I noted that the influence of the West was greater than I had observed in 1925 to 1926.

Chapter LX

Nature and Artificial Life in East and West

THE past two centuries of invention have caused a tremendous change in the material aspects of Occidental life. Most of the things now produced are manufactured by machinery run by steam, gas, electricity, atomic, or other form of power not directly resulting from human labor. Hence the volume of products has enormously increased. The railway, steamship, and aeroplane have greatly accelerated transportation, while the telegraph, telephone, and wireless have rendered possible instantaneous communication over long distances. Almost every phase of the domestic life of nearly every Occidental people is carried on with the aid of a vast number of appliances which were unknown a century or two ago. These changes have resulted in increasing greatly the population of the West and of concentrating a much larger proportion of it in cities. This population has been almost entirely separated from natural surroundings and its existence rendered much more artificial in the sense that its life is conditioned and controlled by a multiplicity of things which do not exist in nature but which have been made by man.

While the Occident has been passing through this sudden transformation the Orient has remained unchanged, except to the comparatively small degree that it has been influenced by the West. At first sight, therefore, it would appear that the East must be in closer touch with nature and its life less artificial than that of the West. Climatic conditions also lend plausibility to this view. The warmer regions are more conducive to a life close to nature and less artificial than are the colder regions. Occidental culture originated in the Mediterranean area, which is only partly subtropical, and developed in Europe and North America entirely in the temperate and cold zones. Indian culture evolved in large part in the temperate zone, but southern China is subtropical and tropical. Japan is entirely in the temperate zone, but its culture bears internal evidence of being partly tropical in its origin.

This question is not so simple as it appears at the outset. Several aspects of life have to be considered before an answer can be hazarded, and even then it can be only tentative and not categorical. A cursory survey alone is sufficient to indicate that the attitude of men and women toward nature and the extent to which their life becomes artificial are determined not only by the material conditions under which they live but also by their ideas, beliefs, customs, manners, and institutions. These psychological and social factors, intangible and yet powerful, may render the life even of a so-called primitive folk artificial in the sense that it is far removed from that of mankind in a state of nature—namely, where its behavior is determined entirely by its original traits uninfluenced by culture.

In attempting this comparison between the East and the West I shall discuss clothing and the exposure of the body, certain of the fine arts, religious beliefs with respect to the supernatural, philosophic and scientific ideas concerning man's place in nature, the relation to the animal world, diet and temperance, housefurnishings, the attitude toward work and leisure, and formal courtesy.

Man is not only an unclothed animal but lacks a hairy pelt, so that in all probability he was originally a denizen of a warm region where fur was unnecessary. Owing to migration or climatic changes he became a dweller in colder regions where clothing is necessary as an artificial adjustment to the environment. The great variability of dress proves conclusively that modesty with respect to nudity is artificial, for if there were an instinct of modesty it would manifest itself more or less consistently in covering the same parts of the body always and everywhere. On the contrary, modesty applies to diverse parts of the body among different peoples and at different times. It has applied to the face, the back of the head, the top of the head, the breasts, the navel, the genital region, the buttocks, and the feet. It may be concentrated upon one part of the body only or be distributed with varying degrees of strength over several parts. In the same community and during the same period of time it may apply under certain conditions, and under other conditions disappear to such a degree that even complete nudity is not regarded as immodest.

There is a widespread belief that in one Oriental country there is, or until recently was, no artificial modesty with respect to nudity. This belief is based upon numerous accounts by travelers since the opening of Japan to foreigners a century ago. According to these reports it was customary for the sexes to bathe together in the public bath-houses and also to bathe in each other's presence at home.[1] There

---

[1] Finck described mixed nude bathing in the cities and more or less nudity in the villages at the time of his visit. (H. T. Finck, *Lotos-Time in Japan*, New

is no evidence that there has ever been the habitual practice of nudity. On the contrary, Japan presents an example of its toleration under certain circumstances, but of the strict requirement of dress at all other times. It is similar to the mixed bathing in certain parts of Europe in the Middle Ages, and the male nudity in athletics in ancient Greece.

According to Japanese convention, the body should ordinarily not only be fully clothed but even the lines of the figure should be concealed. The Japanese often consider Occidental dress indecent; especially decolletée feminine garments which reveal the lines of the bust and hips. Contact with the West, resulting in imitation of Occidental manners and morals, is gradually stamping out mixed nude bathing, just as it has influenced Japan in many other ways.[2] While traveling about the Island Kingdom in 1925 and 1954, I observed great variability as to the strength of this custom.

These bathing customs are to be explained in part by the fact that the Japanese culture is of tropical origin transplanted into a temperate climate and only partially adapted to that climate. The houses are flimsy structures of wood and paper ill fitted to keep out the cold of winter. One of the methods of keeping warm is to soak the body in hot water, thus accumulating enough heat to repel the cold for a time. As the means for heating water are scanty in most dwellings, and hot water is expensive, the same water is used by numerous individuals, after a preliminary soaping, both in the private houses and in the public baths. As the houses are small and the space limited, privacy is difficult and not rigorously enforced with respect to bathing. These conditions have encouraged the persistence of bathing customs which probably arose originally among the aboriginal inhabitants in connection with the numerous hot springs. Thus the love for hot baths early acquired has carried along with it the custom of mixed nude bathing.

The same is true of the robe or kimono which is the characteristic feature of both masculine and feminine dress. This is of tropical provenance, since the typical costume of cold regions consists of coat and trousers. The concealment of the lines of the body has probably

York, 1895, chapter entitled "Nudity and Bathing," pp. 286-97.)

Stratz visited Japan in 1892, and stated that he saw no public baths in the street, but that the sexes mingled nude in the public bath-houses and when bathing at home. He described a disrobing dance performed by four girls, one of whom was the daughter of his host. (C. H. Stratz, *Die Körperformen in Kunst und Leben der Japaner*, Stuttgart, 1902.)

[2] According to Black, an early visitor, as a result of criticisms by foreigners a general law against nudity was enacted as far back as 1872. (Cited by Finck from Black's *Young Japan.*) I have been unable to verify this statement.

1027

accentuated the lack of appreciation of the human form displayed by the Japanese. This is particularly true of the feminine garb, which not only conceals but distorts the appearance of the body.

The feminine girdle or obi is much wider and of heavier material than the masculine, and is worn with a complicated knot behind. This spoils the line by creating a hump in the small of the back. It is most distorting in cold or rainy weather when mantles are worn, for then every woman looks like a hunchback. It is hot and uncomfortably heavy, and the heat is concentrated in the back instead of in front where it is more needed. While it may not cause as much injury as the corset, it deforms the appearance even more than the most objectionable features of Western dress.

Other grotesque habits of Japanese women are the coiffure and use of grease and paint. The hair is liberally greased, and with the aid of combs and pins is distended in every direction, thus giving a macrocephalic appearance to the head and minimizing unduly the significance of the features. The face and neck are greased, painted, and powdered. Anything coming into contact with neck, face, and head is soiled by this filthy mixture. At night the back of the neck is placed on a wooden head-rest in order to avoid disturbing the elaborate coiffure and soiling a pillow, thus giving the woman a posture not conducive to the most restful slumber.

While artificially induced deformations are common among primitive folk, I know of no civilized people whose women deliberately disfigure themselves by means of their apparel so much as the Japanese. It is all the more singular to contemplate when one remembers that the Japanese display a delicate appreciation of certain aspects of nature. However, the women are rapidly abandoning their coiffure and grease-paint, and are adopting what are in this regard the saner Western customs.[3]

The fact that the nude figure is almost non-existent in Japanese art indicates that they have little or no perception of the esthetic significance of the human body. Finck said that religion may be partly responsible, because Buddhism inculcates contempt for the body. He thought that it is due principally to "the traditional eagerness of these artists to paint the kaleidoscopic patterns and colors of the kimonos—the gorgeous dresses of their women—which afforded them an endless variety of patterns and tints."[4] While he may have exaggerated this factor, it illustrates the excessive artificiality of Japanese art which can occupy itself with dress, however beautiful in itself,

[3] The coiffure and grease-paint are now most used by two professions—namely, actresses and prostitutes, for whom an artificially made up appearance and expression often have utility.

[4] H. T. Finck, *op. cit.*, p. 296.

and yet ignore the human features and body.[5] Greek art was incomparably superior in its natural presentation of the body, and the same can be said of some of the Renaissance and modern Occidental art. In the Imperial Museum at Kyoto and elsewhere I saw ancient wooden statues of deities whose faces have a grotesque and terrifying aspect. In the carving of their bodies human anatomy has often been depicted with skill and fidelity. This indicates that when they choose to do so the Japanese can observe accurately and give lifelike representations.

The Japanese artists are beginning to be influenced by Western art. In the spring of 1925 and again in 1954 I saw at Ueno Park, Tokio, an exhibit of contemporary art which showed this influence unmistakably. There were several nude statues, both male and female, and a few paintings of the nude. One of the sculptures was of a male and female figure in an embrace. This would have been both unesthetic and indecent according to the older canons.

The Japanese have an excellent opportunity to combine the best features of their dress with those of European dress. Combinations are often to be seen, but they usually display no intelligent discrimination. For example, the flowing kimono hampers the freedom of the lower limbs. And yet the lower part of the native garb in the form of a skirt is often combined with the upper portion of Western dress, as in the costume worn by many of the school-boys.

A Japanese lady, who at the moment was in her native garb, was saying that she preferred European dress, and was criticizing her costume on account of the weight and excessive warmth of the obi. I agreed with her concerning the obi, but pointed out the obvious fact that she had already deformed her feet almost as much as white women by the use of European boots and shoes.

This situation is due in part to certain psychological factors. Even more than most peoples the mind of the Japanese is mechanical and unyielding in its devotion to convention. When they imitate anything, they usually do so "lock, stock, and barrel," and swallow along with it all of its conventions and other encumbrances. Thus the Tokio police have been known to occupy themselves with the degree of decolletage permissible when Japanese women wear European dress—not unlike the police in certain American and European countries.

These traits also lead to an extreme degree of regimentation and suppression of individuality, though perhaps not more so than in certain Occidental countries. In view of these mental traits, the Japanese are not likely to develop a society in which there would be

[5] Stratz thought that the Japanese, like all Mongols, lack an esthetic appreciation of the beauty of the human body. (C. H. Stratz, *Die Rassenschönheit des Weibes*, Stuttgart, 1903, third edition, pp. 86-87.)

freedom to practise nudity and to vary widely in matters of dress. In spite of their fondness for bathing indoors, the Japanese have scarcely used their lengthy coast for sea-bathing, perhaps because sea-water feels cold in comparison with the hot water used indoors. Sea-bathing has been introduced recently, mainly in imitation of Europeans. Here was an excellent opportunity to practise nudity under the most natural conditions. But the opportunity was wasted, for along with the sea-bathing came the European bathing costume.

There is a movement in a few Western countries which indicates that the practice of social nudity has great value for health and comfort, for communion with nature, for normal and satisfactory relations between the sexes, for the education of the young, for esthetic enjoyment, and for the evolution of a democratic and humanitarian social organization.[6] Even though the Japanese tolerate nudity in connection with bathing, they ignore its value for these important purposes. They are losing a remarkable and almost unique opportunity to combine the best that there is in Oriental and Occidental culture. Otherwise, their bathing customs might furnish the germ for one such combination.

In China and Korea the seclusion of women has broken down in a measure only within the twentieth century. It still persists in the home life, though women appear unveiled and move about more or less freely in public. Under conditions of seclusion no such bathing customs could arise as in Japan, where women have never been secluded to the same degree.

The Korean women wear a bodice similar to the Indian, thus revealing a portion of the upper part of the body. The Chinese men and women reverse the Western style, the women often wearing trousers and the men long robes. The Chinese woman of the upper class uses cosmetics on her face, more than European women, but less than her Japanese sister. On the other hand, the bound feet, now disappearing, constitute the most horrible deformation ever practised extensively by a civilized people. In the villages I caught a glimpse occasionally of a woman at work naked to the waist. As a general rule the Chinese woman is fully clad. The Chinese coolie wears little more than a loin cloth in hot weather. Many small shopkeepers and others belonging to the lower middle class often sit in their shops and offices unclad to the waist, with the ubiquitous fan in hand.

Like their Japanese brethren, the Chinese show no esthetic ap-

---

[6] Maurice Parmelee, *The New Gymnosophy: The Philosophy of Nudity as Applied in Modern Life*, New York, 1927. I have described and discussed the above-mentioned movement in this book, later entitled *Nudism in Modern Life*, 5th revized edition, 1952. Three editions of this book have appeared in England and a German translation in Germany.

preciation of the human body. It rarely ever appears in the nude in their art, and then almost invariably in a grotesque and fantastic form. While much of their art is grotesque and unrealistic, this is peculiarly true of their treatment of the human figure.

The body is exposed in public to a greater degree in India than in any other civilized country. The men of the laboring and peasant classes usually wear no more than a loin cloth or *dhoty,* which is a long cotton cloth wrapped around the waist and then passed between the legs. Even in the upper classes the men are often naked to the waist. This may be due in part to vanity, because they wish to display the "sacred" thread worn over the shoulder and across the chest by the three upper castes who are "twice-born." This thread is alleged to protect its wearer against evil influences, because it has been sanctified by the blessings of Brahmans and the reading of sacred texts over it.

The bodice of the Indian woman is often very exiguous and barely covers the breasts. The *sari* is a sheetlike mantle which covers the lower half of the body and, if a bodice is worn, usually comes up over the head. Among the lower classes the bodice is often omitted. Then the *sari* constitutes the only garment of the wearer, and a corner of it is pulled over the shoulder but usually hides very little of the breasts. In the villages she is often naked to the waist. Both sexes usually go barefoot, especially the women. The Indian woman, especially in the south, is much addicted to jewelry. In fact, she is often the peripatetic treasure house of her family. Toe-rings, anklets, bells, bracelets, ear-rings, and nose-rings are some of the ornaments she affects. The most unsightly are the jewels, often of considerable size, fastened to the nose, which seriously mar the appearance of her face.

Ritual bathing, which is one of the characteristic features of Hindu religion, has probably influenced the dress of both sexes to a certain extent. Rivers and springs are supposed to be inhabited by spirits which are usually benignant. By bathing in them moral if not physical cleanliness is acquired. The Hindus, especially the men, try to bathe every day in flowing water in the open. While this is not usually done in complete nudity, it causes a good deal of familiarity with the appearance of the body. It is not considered so essential that clothing should cover the whole body.

Until nudity in public was prohibited by British law, various kinds of ascetics and other religious devotees lived habitually naked. Nudity has always been regarded in India as a sign of peculiar sanctity. About the year A.D. 80 there took place in the Jain sect a schism between the Svetambaras (white-clad) and the Digambaras (sky-clad or naked). Whether the Digambaras still practise nudity I do not know. Nudity has also been used in India, as in many other countries,

1031

in connection with various magical rites, such as rain-making. One form of this rite in northern India is for the women to go into the fields at night, remove all of their clothing, and plow for a time while invoking the rain god to send rain and permit the seasonal plowing to continue.

Most of what has so far been said applies in particular to the Hindus. The Moslems of India, however, owing in part to the Semitic origin of their religion, cover the body much more fully. While many of the Mohammedan laborers and peasants in Pakistan as well as India wear no more than their Hindu fellows, the Moslems of the upper classes usually wear trousers and coat. Inasmuch as most of the Mohammedan women are secluded behind the *purdah,* there can be no question of exposure on their part. In certain parts of northern India the Hindu women also live behind the *purdah,* but this does not apply to the majority of Hindu women. As I have already pointed out, wherever the *purdah* exists it applies in particular to the women of the aristocratic and upper classes, but to a much less extent to the women of the lower classes.

In Burma, where the Mongolian influence is strong, both sexes are fully clad in the cities. As in other countries, there is more exposure of the body in the rural districts. The contrast between India and Burma in this regard is strikingly manifest in Rangoon, where there are many Indian immigrants.

Most of the inhabitants of the Malay States and of the East Indies are Moslem. Islam rests lightly on the Malay peoples, whom it has only partially conquered. The seclusion of women has not been prevalent among them. In Java the men as well as the women are usually fully clad in the cities. In the villages it is not uncommon for the women as well as the men to be naked to the waist.

In all of these Oriental and tropical countries there is a serious obstacle in the way of the observation of these conditions, especially in the rural districts. When they see white folk approaching, the native women will often hastily cover exposed portions of the body. This is due in part to the fact that they have discovered that the whites consider the human body indecent. It may also be due to magical notions as to evil influences emanating from these alien and perhaps hostile folk, against which clothing may furnish some protection. In India the women will sometimes go so far as to shield the face from the foreigner. This is most likely to happen in the regions where the institution of the *purdah* still has influence. It is probably due in part to fear of the "evil eye" which the stranger may possess.

This survey indicates that, in view of the changes now taking place in the Japanese bathing customs, India is the Oriental country which is most likely to carry on the tradition of the free exposure of the body, thus opposing the prudish and artificial standard of modesty being instilled into many Orientals by missionaries and other Westerners. The more natural and healthy attitude toward the body in the Orient is in danger of disappearing.

With respect to fashion, the contrast between East and West is extraordinarily marked. A style decreed in Paris is within a few weeks seen on the streets of San Francisco and Sydney, of Cape Town and Copenhagen. Not so in the Orient, where each country has its own distinctive costume or costumes which change slowly, so that fashion can hardly be said to exist. As all Western countries have the same cultural origin, they are dominated by uniformity, but with constant change especially in feminine dress. The East, on the contrary, with its varied cultural origins, is characterized by a diversity of national costumes which are stable. In neither region is there much latitude for individual variation.

If Occidental fashions were determined by health, comfort, and beauty, they could not change with lightning speed. As they are governed largely by the commercial greed of dressmakers and tailors and the whims of the leaders of fashionable society, they are artificial in the most harmful sense of the term, and cannot be adjusted to the great variety of climatic conditions under which they are worn. The national costumes of the Orient came into existence more naturally, and are more or less adjusted to climate. But they also often violate hygienic and esthetic canons. The elaborate headdress of the Manchu woman and the absurd hat of the Korean man have neither beauty nor utility. The Indian woman winds her *sari* so tightly around her abdomen as to cause a deep stricture. Both in the East and in the West clothing is constantly worn when the temperature does not require it, thus putting an unnecessary artificial barrier between the human body and the beneficent forces of the air, light, and sun. This is one of the most striking illustrations of the fact that nowhere has mankind fully realized that it is a part of nature. The same fact is demonstrated in the fine arts.

In its origin Japanese art was Buddhistic and Korean, which in turn came from China under the Han dynasty (206 B.C.-A.D. 251). China was at that time under the influence of Indo-Grecian art through Mahayana Buddhism, so that Japanese art represents in a measure a blending of the principal factors in Oriental art. Hoshin Kuroda, an authority on its history, has made the following comparison between the fundamental traits of Japanese and Occidental art:[7]

1. Its materials are of vegetable much more than of animal or

[7] *Dai Nippon Bijutsu-shi* (*History of Japanese Art*), 1922.

mineral origin. In architecture and sculpture wood is used almost exclusively. Hence Japanese houses and statues are characterized by a grace and delicacy which are more difficult to attain when stone or metal is used. The art of decoration by lacquer is also characteristic of Japan.

2. The subjects are taken from nature rather than being human objects. Japanese pictures are usually of landscapes, flowers, and birds.

3. Japanese artists emphasize line rather than perspective or light and shade, so that their style is idealistic rather than realistic.

4. The idealistic style gives rise to symbolism and a conventional rather than an individualistic manner of treatment.

5. Japanese art has great external beauty but little internal depth. It is highly decorative but has little utility. The decorative art is carried to a high pitch in lacquer, cloisonné, inlaid objects, and in picture scrolls.

As I have already indicated, the West is influencing Japanese art considerably. This influence began through the Dutch traders who brought some paintings in the seventeenth century. Since the opening of Japan to foreigners, many artists have visited Europe and America or have studied Occidental methods at home. They have found this study an excellent training even when they have reverted to the native style, because Western art requires a knowledge of human anatomy and an accuracy of depiction of objects in nature which exceeds anything in Oriental art. But the native art stands higher than Occidental art in popularity and in the public esteem.

Like most Oriental music, Japanese music is very simple compared with its Western counterpart. A thousand years or more ago was introduced from China and India the *gagaku* or so-called elegant music, which was complicated and played by large orchestras. This has disappeared and is played only as classical ceremonial music at the imperial court. The *utai* is a somewhat monotonous vocal music which accompanies the *No* dance and is used among the upper classes. The *zokugaku* or people's music is widely used. Its most common form is vocal accompanied by the samisen or three-stringed guitar. One of my most vivid memories of Japan is of the silvery-toned, slowly played samisen often heard in the evening. Other musical instruments are the *koto* or lyre, the *shakuhachi* or bamboo oboe, and the *biwa*, or lute. In the Orient there are no such elaborate instruments as the piano and the pipe organ on which complicated music can be played.

Most of what has been said of Japanese art applies also to Chinese art. There is greater use of stone in architecture and sculpture. There is more that is grotesque and less that is decorative in Chinese art. But in their idealism, symbolism, indifference to the human figure, and preference for objects taken from nature, the two national systems

1034

of art are much alike. The conventionality of Chinese art is perhaps even more pronounced. The high place given to calligraphy as an art is an excellent illustration. In both China and Japan I have often seen specimens of fine writing hung upon the walls of rooms for purposes of decoration. In fact, in the six arts recognized by the Chinese —namely, ceremonial, music, archery, charioteering, writing, and mathematics—painting and sculpture are included under writing. This is reminiscent of the fact that the written characters were derived more or less directly from pictographs.

I have already indicated that love seldom appears in Chinese poetry, partly because of the subordinate position of women, and the same is true to a lesser extent of Japanese poetry, while friendship is often extolled. Much of this poetry is devoted to a description of nature. As an American critic has said: "Art is to the Chinese and the Japanese artist something two-dimensional. It is a beautifully colored, or a beautifully woven surface. And as the artist will have nothing to do with a third dimension, so the poet will not hear of a fourth dimension."[8]

The upshot of this brief survey is that no sweeping generalization can be made as to the attitude toward nature displayed by Far Eastern as compared with Occidental art. While objects from nature play a prominent part in this Asiatic art, man is in the main ignored. And yet mankind also is a part of nature, and the human body is the natural object closet to and of the greatest importance for mankind. This is a singular omission indeed. Even the features of the face, the most obvious and expressive portion of the body, are largely ignored. When expression is given to the face, characteristic features are usually so accentuated as to constitute a caricature. No Oriental country has as yet produced a Rembrandt or a Rodin.

Every art at all times and places has a tendency to become conventionalized except when under the impetus of forces which are producing new forms. Its idealism and symbolism tend to emphasize the conventionality of Oriental art and to rob each of its products of an individuality of its own.[9] While nature in many of its varied

[8] P. A. Hutchison, in *The New York Times*, June 12, 1927.

[9] Many writers have commented on the conventionality of Oriental art, from whom I will cite the following:

"Oriental art is highly conventionalized and does not strive to be realistic, while Occidental art approaches exactness in reproduction." (C. Wissler, *Man and Culture*, New York, 1923, p. 233.)

"Chinese painting as we know it shows not an evolution but an up-and-down of fashions for more than a thousand years on end; and this unsteadiness must have set in as early as the Han period. The final result is that endless industrious repetition of a stock of fixed forms which we see today in Indian, Chinese, and Arabian-Persian art." (O. Spengler, *The Decline of the West, Form and Actuality*, New York, 1926, p. 295, translated from the German.)

moods appeals to Oriental artists, they do not reproduce it and bring it home to their public with the skill of their Western colleagues. It is therefore difficult to determine whether or not Oriental art reveals a greater or deeper appreciation of nature. Perhaps the most that can be said is that Occidental art displays a wider range in its treatment of objects taken from nature.

Indian art is, as one of its students has written, "a by-product of religious emotion." The poetess, the late Mrs. Sarojini Naidu, said to me in Bombay in 1925 that the Hindus are not esthetic because they are very religious and ascetic. This judgment, by one of their most distinguished representatives, is perhaps too severe. But their art, like most phases of their culture, is deeply tinged with religion. Its history began in the main with the Mauryan Emperior Ashoka (274-237 B.C.), the ardent patron and propagandist of Buddhism, so that in its early stages it was largely Buddhistic. It was also affected considerably by Persian and Hellenic influences. Several styles of architecture were developed and there was a good deal of sculpture in stone. After the defeat of Buddhism, there was a period of decay until Indo-Mohammedan art began about A.D. 1200. Thus each phase has been more or less closely related to a religious cult.

Some of the decorative arts have been developed to a high degree, such as metal work, pottery, carving, jewelry, weaving, embroidery, and dyeing. The artistic skill of the craftsman is largely due to the hereditary character of his trade. Most of these crafts are monopolized by castes, so that the son must follow the occupation of his father, and custom and to a certain extent religion impel him to imitate his father's work. While great technical skill in displayed, there is less creative ability.

In architecture also tradition has been closely followed. A part of this tradition has been to decorate profusely the outer surfaces of buildings, especially the temples. This has permitted a more or less free play of imagination in carving and engraving. Many subjects are taken from nature, but the human figure also appears frequently. The depiction of events from the Indian epics and religious scenes has introduced many human and social themes as contrasted with eastern Asiatic art. Sculpture also in stone, metal, and wood has portrayed the human figure, often in grotesque representations of the gods and goddesses.

There seems to have been an early Indian art of painting which began prior to the Western influences and continued until about the time of the disappearance of Buddhism. In fact, India under Brahmanism has on the whole not been favorable to artistic activity. During the Mohammedan period the art of painting portraits, especially in miniature form, was highly developed. So far as my observa-

1036

tion goes, Indian painting is childish and immature in its technique as compared with the highly finished products of Chinese and Japanese art. But it is more realistic in its style and more human in its subjects than the Far Eastern art.

Man's attitude toward nature is considerably influenced by his notions concerning a hypothetical supernatural world. Belief in the supernatural is widespread the world over, all religions being based upon this as their fundamental tenet. In the Occident the tendency is to distinguish sharply between the natural and the supernatural. It is not generally believed that the supernatural has much influence in the natural world, but while recognized and respected it is related to a remote region of its own to which the souls of the dead depart. Western religion is highly institutionalized in the organization of the church with priests, formal ceremonies at stated intervals, preaching, praying and the like. God is worshiped on Sunday with due decorum, and then forgotten during the rest of the week by the vast majority, who are preoccupied with the much more interesting and engrossing affairs of this world.

As I have indicated in Chapter LV religion is less institutionalized in the Orient. The church organization is not so highly developed. There is no Sabbath specially dedicated to religion which would leave other days conveniently free for temporal matters. While a priesthood exists in most Oriental countries, and is often specialized, religious duties weigh more or less heavily upon the layman as well. Eastern religions are closer to the earlier nature cults out of which all extant religions have directly or indirectly arisen. They are avowedly polytheistic, with a multitude of gods and goddesses, many of whom are very human and therefore not so exalted and remote as the Hebrew Jehovah, the Christian God, or the Mohammedan Allah, all of whom, like Brahma, are almost beyond the ken of the ordinary man and woman.

Most of these things are especially true of India. I have already commented several times upon the overweening influence of religion and the extent to which the idea of the supernatural pervades thought in that country. As an Indian writer has expressed it, for the Indians the natural is a projection of the supernatural and the supernatural a continuation of the natural.[10] The distinction between the natural and the supernatural, between the objective and the subjective, is not so sharply drawn as in the West, as I have pointed out in discussing the yoga philosophy in Chapter LVI. According to the mava doctrine, the world in which we live is unreal and illusory and fades into another world. Such beliefs promote mysticism and a rather hazy conception of the natural universe.

[10] D. G. Mukerji, *My Brother's Face*, New York, 1924.

The belief in metempsychosis tends to break down the barrier between man and the remainder of the natural world. If the souls inhabiting human bodies also dwell at various stages in their careers in beasts, plants, and even inanimate objects, man may well have a feeling of close kinship with his organic and inorganic surroundings. It sometimes leads to an exaggerated form of zoophilism. Some of the Buddhist sects kill no animals whatsoever. In Ahmedabad I visited a Jain *prinjrapole* where animals ranging in size from small insects to oxen were being fed by the donations of the devout. There are many *gaushalas* (cow asylums) in India. This signifies little more than a pious gesture, for animals in general are probably treated as badly in the East as in the West. In accordance with the Indian doctrine of *ahimsa* (non-violence) many animals are not killed, but they are often left to starve to death. There are probably fewer animal pets in the Orient, though in some countries this is due in part to scarcity of food. In Japan the rarity of dogs and cats is noticeable and is due to the limited supply of meat. Adjoining the Willow Tree Pattern Tea House in Shanghai and elsewhere in China I watched Chinese gentlemen airing their birds in their cages. This is a sort of esthetic cult, and cruelty to animals is often to be seen in China.

These Oriental doctrines have led certain writers to opine that the East more than the West regards man as a component part of nature, and that the doctrine of the transmigration of souls encourages a feeling of unity with nature. Belief in the supernatural is even more widespread in the Orient, and anthropomorphism as prominent there as in the Occident. But the natural and the supernatural tend to be confused and to become merged into one another. In this sense the East has a feeling of an all-inclusive unity of the natural and the supernatural, of man and of nature. In this union the Oriental assumes in the main a fatalistic attitude of resignation toward these natural-supernatural powers which he little understands and has less hope of controlling. Among the common people these powers are usually personified, owing to the strong anthropomorphic tendency of the human mind everywhere, and gods and goddesses, fairies and hobgoblins abound throughout the Orient. In the intellectual class, however, especially in eastern Asia, belief in a personal deity is perhaps less strong than it is in the Occident, where the Jehovah-God-Allah deity of Semitic origin, having vanquished other tribal gods, jealously maintains his putative monotheistic supremacy and monopoly.

In the West, on the other hand, science has been developing a new attitude toward nature. Based upon a much more extensive and accurate knowledge of natural phenomena has arisen a concept of a fundamental unity between man and nature which eliminates the

supernatural by bringing all phenomena, human and non-human, animate and inanimate, under the same realm of law and order. Through
an understanding of natural law man in the West has acquired a certain measure of control of the field of nature within his puny grasp and
to this extent feels himself its master. To whatever he cannot control
he endeavors to adapt himself, provided he does not become drunk
with power and arrogant in his attitude toward nature. The latter is
perhaps exemplified in the cities of the Occident, monstrous creations
by means of which mankind has been cut off almost entirely from
nature, much to its injury. With this arrogance may be contrasted the
supine yielding of the Orient to the forces of nature. The happy medium is somewhere between these two courses.[11]

The foregoing survey indicates that the situation is conflicting
and that no categorical conclusion can be reached as to the attitude
toward nature. The Orient may have a somewhat more intimate
feeling for nature. But the Occident has a more accurate comprehension of man's place in nature and more power and skill in utilizing
natural forces. Westerners have nevertheless not succeeded as well in
adapting themselves to tropical conditions as Easterners. It is commonly believed that the tropics are unfit for the white race. This fallacious notion has arisen out of the manner in which the great majority
of white men live in tropical countries in the Eastern Hemisphere.[12]

Until the war of 1939 to 1945 most of these countries were ruled
by Europeans, so that it was to the interest of these alien rulers to
maintain as vast a difference as possible between their manner of life
and that of their native subjects. This consideration, which influenced
them even when they were not conscious of it, their ignorance and
lack of appreciation of non-European culture, and contempt for the
darker races led them to introduce most of the features of their European mode of life, in spite of its unsuitability for tropical conditions,
and to ignore the ways in which the natives have adapted themselves
to the climate. Their diet usually included much meat and other rich
foods, which render it too heavy even for a cold climate. Very often it

[11] Tagore has asserted that Western civilization is city-bred and assumes an
aggressive attitude toward its natural environment, while Indian civilization is
forest-bred and has a more tolerant attitude of reconciliation with its environment.
The West tries to dominate nature, and the East to cooperate with it. He averred
that the West believes there is a decisive gulf between mankind and animals, while
Eastern thinkers have urged men to recognize a close relation between themselves
and the objects in their natural environment and to harmonize themselves with it.

In view of the above discussion and of the biological doctrine of evolution, the
West is not as unreconciled to the animal world and to nature in general as
Tagore intimated. (See Rabindranath Tagore, *Sadhana, the Realisation of Life*,
New York, 1914.)

[12] The following paragraphs are paraphrased from my book entitled *The New
Gymnosophy*, whose central theme is man's relation to nature.

was generously diluted with alcoholic liquors, which are less used in Oriental countries than in countries which boast of European culture. The habit of alcoholic drinking is being spread in the Orient by the Occident. While the heat compelled them to adopt clothing lighter than at home, it was heavier than the open and scanty dress of the natives.

In tropical countries labor is usually cheap and plentiful. The indolence encouraged by the unaccustomed heat, and the desire to maintain his prestige as a sort of superhuman or semi-divine personage, soon led the European rulers to cease almost entirely from physical exertion. The effect upon their women was even worse, for they spent most of their time in mental as well as physical idleness. Combined with their immoderate eating and often drinking, this had the most dire consequences for their health. While a few kept up for a time their sports and athletics, they succumbed almost invariably to the enervating effect of their social as well as their climatic environment.

If Europeans and Americans will reduce their clothing, adopt a light diet, eliminate alcoholic beverages, take plenty of exercise, and accustom themselves to the sun's rays, from which they always flee, there is no reason why they should not live and work successfully and happily in the tropics. The same applies as much to their children, who, if reared naturally, probably have as much chance for survival in tropical countries as elsewhere.[13]

As a matter of fact, white peoples have in the past developed great civilizations under tropical conditions. European culture was evolved in part under such conditions. Many of the inhabitants of hot and semi-tropical countries today are closely related by blood with the peoples of Europe and America. This is true of the peoples of northern Africa, of Arabia and Persia, and of the so-called "Aryan" peoples of India. Hence it is that in learning from tropical peoples, Europeans and Americans will be recovering some of the ancient lore of their ancestors.

The ordinary methods of cooking are bad everywhere, in many places they are worse. Mankind displays an almost diabolical skill in spoiling good food by frying, and in other ways rendering it indigestible by combining aliments which are not dietetically congruous, and in many other ways creating havoc in the digestive processes. In this unwholesome and unnatural rivalry East and West vie with each other, and it is difficult to decide which does the worst. The West proclaims the French culinary art the best, the East the Chinese. While both

[13] Davids said that the baneful influence of the Indian climate has been exaggerated and that it is not bad for both physical and intellectual energy and work, for Europeans as well as for the natives. (T. W. Rhys Davids, *Buddhist India*, London. 1903.)

tickle the palate, they violate dietetic principles as heedlessly as the most unpalatable cuisines.

Much of the Orient is in a tropical environment, and it is poorer and less developed economically, so that its diet is comparatively simple though usually ill prepared. Meat is less used. A colder climate and greater wealth encourage richer and heavier foods in the Occident. While there is much eating to excess in the West, the East is on the whole under-fed, which is one reason for the lower efficiency of the Oriental worker. The only hope for mankind in this matter of fundamental importance is through science which is beginning to discern the most elementary of dietetic principles, which have as yet had little influence upon the culinary art.

Religion and poverty discourage the use of alcoholic beverages in the Orient, while a large proportion of the inhabitants of the Occident imbibe these noxious beverages daily, thus subjecting themselves to a gradual process of poisoning.[14] In like fashion is tobacco more widely used. While coffee is of tropical provenance, it is imbibed much more in the West. The same may be true of tea in spite of the fact that it is used in Japan and China. Recently tea-drinking has been introduced into India. The sedative drugs such as morphine and cocaine are probably more widely used in the West, and the same may be true of opium. Western addiction to stimulants and sedatives is largely due to the more hurried and nerve-racking life of the Occident.

Housefurnishings, such as chairs and tables, are much less used in the East. In fact, it may be said that the material equipment of Oriental life is on the whole much simpler.[15]

Much of the work of the West is artificial in the sense that it does not exist in a state of nature. This is true of most of the intellectual labor and all work with machines and other complicated tools. Most of this work is done under great pressure of time and nervous strain. There is less of such work in the East, and Oriental life is more leisurely.

Genuine courtesy is more or less evenly distributed the world over, for it arises out of individual traits universal to mankind. Formal courtesy varies greatly in extent and character according to the relations between castes and classes, and traditional and customary

[14] Few statistics of the use of alcohol in the Orient are available. From 1906 to 1910 the consumption of potable alcohol in Japan was about one tenth that in France, which consumed the most of any nation, one fourth that in Great Britain, and one third that in the United States, during the same period. (See my *Personality and Conduct*, New York, 1918, pp. 21-24.)

[15] For a discussion of simplicity see my *New Gymnosophy*, Chapter XIV, entitled "The Simplication of Life."

observances. The Indian mode of salutation, the palms meeting in front of the breast without physical contact between the persons greeting each other, is simpler and more pleasing than the Western modes of hand-shaking, kissing, etc. Indeed, there is less physical contact in Oriental than in Occidental courtesy, which is as it should be, for such contact should be reserved for more intimate personal relations. The Japanese mode of salutation is excessively formal and elaborate, with many low bows and genuflections and the use of numerous honorific terms. The more leisurely life of the Orient perhaps encourages more formal courtesy than in the West, thus introducing an unnecessary degree of artificiality and a good deal of hypocrisy into human relations.

Chapter LXI

The Military and Missionary Invasion of the East

THE first important attempt at domination of the Orient by the West was Alexander's vainglorious invasion of India in the fourth century before Christ. While it failed as a permanent conquest and the Greek garrisons eventually withdrew, it established a cultural contact with the Occident which had far-reaching consequences not only for India but also for China and other Oriental countries, because India influenced China in religion, art, science (mathematics in particular), and philosophy. Overland trade between the East and the West continued. The Romans traded with China through the Parthians, and there were other commercial relations.

The attempt at domination of special significance commenced at the outset of the sixteenth century, with the Portuguese in the lead. The navigator Vasco da Gama rounded the Cape of Good Hope and reached Calicut in 1498. The viceroy Albuquerque came in 1503 and in 1510 established the first European colony at Goa. The Philippine Islands were visited by Magellan in 1520, and occupied by the Spanish in the sixteenth century. The Portuguese acquired extensive territories in India until the Dutch arrived in 1595 and competed successfully with them. The French came at the beginning of the seventeenth century, and later conquered extensive territories until defeated by the English at Plassey in 1757, after which their power rapidly dwindled. Dutch, French, and British East India companies were formed to carry on trade. The English began to come early in the seventeenth century, and eventually acquired suzerainty over the whole of India with the exception of the small Portuguese colony at Goa and five French colonies comprising less than two hundred square miles.

Oversea commerce with China began at Canton about A.D. 300. For centuries it was controlled principally by Arabs, though it included some Hindu traders. The Portuguese reached China in 1516 and Japan in 1541. The Dutch reached China in 1604, the British in 1607, and the Americans in 1784. The Russians were in communication with China overland, and the first treaty between China and a European power was concluded with Russia in 1689.

Seafaring trade brought the West to the East in a decisive fashion. Western seafarers and merchants were seeking for raw materials which could be secured only in the Orient, markets for finished products, and cheap labor with which to manufacture goods. These were in the main legitimate ends. They sometimes met opposition and contempt. This was particularly true of China. The Chinese had conquered all of their neighbors and for many centuries were almost entirely isolated from the rest of the world. This situation had developed in them an arrogant attitude which has rarely if ever been surpassed. Their emperor considered himself the ruler of the whole world. When George III sent Lord Macartney in 1792 to negotiate a commercial treaty, and demanded treatment as an equal, the Emperor Chien Lung despatched the following message to the English monarch: "It behooves you, O King, to respect our wishes and by perpetual submission to our Throne in the future to bring prosperity and peace to your people. Tremble and obey."

Whatever arrogance the East displayed was more than matched by the aggressiveness of the Westerners. They were usually better armed than the Orientals and possessed a power on the sea unequaled by any Eastern nation. Their firearms were of larger caliber and longer range and their ships of greater burden. The peaceful pursuit of trade soon developed into invasion and conquest, often aided and abetted by a Christian zeal which regarded all Oriental religions as false and evil. In the course of four centuries a large part of the Orient passed under Occidental domination. Until the twentieth century India, Burma, the Malay States, northern Borneo, eastern New Guinea, and minor possessions elsewhere were under British sway, with British influence strong in Nepal, Bhutan, and Siam, and menacing in Tibet. France ruled Indo-China and minor possessions elsewhere. Holland possessed most of the East Indies. The United States ruled the Philippine Islands. Russia still dominates all of northern Asia from the Urals to the Pacific. In fact, nearly three fifths of the area of Asia and one half or more of its population were under Occidental suzerainty.

Even where suzerainty had not actually been declared, a certain measure of domination was secured. China, in addition to losing several important ports, was for a time divided up into several "spheres of influence" by the leading Western powers, and its political integrity was not free from danger until the successful issue of the revolution in 1949. Extra territorial rights for foreigners and regulation of the customs duties were imposed upon Japan, China, and several other Oriental countries. Western capital invested in Eastern railways, factories, etc., levied a heavy tribute and often interfered with the political

1044

affairs of these countries. The only country which succeeded in freeing itself entirely from these restrictions was Japan. It did so by imitating the material aspects of Occidental civilization—in other words, by equaling and sometimes beating the West at its own game of force and aggression. Thus did Western empire, political and economic, spread over practically the whole of the East, and presented the most extensive display of imperialism in the history of mankind. Not even Rome in its palmiest days could equal it.

This extraordinary situation did not come into being wholly intentionally. The West did not by a premeditated and concerted design conquer the East. It came about partly through the frequent resistance of the East to Western advances, and its unwillingness to adjust itself to the sort of international finance, trade, and industry which was developing under the rapid scientific and technical progress of the West. In many Oriental countries the laws were of such a nature that foreigners could not live and do business under them, thus giving rise to the demand for extraterritorial rights. Sometimes these countries isolated themselves entirely or gave only very limited rights of residence to foreigners. For more than two centuries Japan excluded all foreigners, with the exception of a few Dutch merchants who were permitted to live on a small island in Nagasaki harbor. In Canton the foreigners were banished to a mudbank in the Pearl River, which they filled in and built the city of Shameen. At Shanghai they were assigned the swampy strand of the Whangpoo River, where stands the former International Settlement.

Balked and irritated by such discriminations against them, by the indifference and somnolence of the Orient, and its inefficiency according to Occidental standards, Western powers often went on to conquer where it was at first intended only to trade. But this imperialism was due even more to Western greed and aggressiveness, which could not be restrained from exploiting by force the physically weaker East.

Whether or not this imperialistic outcome could have been avoided it would be useless to discuss. Its dangerousness is too obvious to require proof or extended comment. Occidental historians and other writers, with characteristic arrogance, usually call the European War of 1914 to 1918 the "World" War. It was a war which originated solely in Europe between rival groups of European powers and should have been settled by them alone. With the exception of Japan, which had already entered the European game of balance of power, the Oriental nations which became involved were dragooned into it by Western imperialism. It concerned them only indirectly—namely, in so far as they were the pawns and spoils over which their alien rulers were quarreling and fighting. To call such a war the World War is a

1045

misleading piece of inaccuracy. Only a myopic view of the world which regards the Orient as a caudal appendage of the Occident could be guilty of this egregious error, so insulting to the East.[1]

The European War prepared the way for a genuine world war. It taught the Orientals that the Occident is not united, is capable of fighting over the spoils, some of which are in the East, and is divided between capitalism and collectivism. It showed them the way to independence and power by means of land, naval, and aerial armaments. The war of 1939 to 1945 freed most of the East from Western rule by breaking the yoke of colonialism. African peoples are following its example.

In this book I am concerned with the broadly cultural rather than the specifically political and economic aspects of this attempt at domination by the West. It has served to bring a considerable measure of Occidental culture to the Orient. Indeed, had it not been for the commercial enterprise of the seafaring peoples of Europe in the sixteenth century and later, the East would probably still be almost wholly ignorant of and indifferent to Western culture. But it has been largely through coercion and by imposition from above that this culture has come to the Orient. As the Occident has not been subjected to a similar coercion, it is still indifferent to Oriental culture, and largely ignorant of it.

The manner of contact between the two cultures has therefore not been of such a nature as to promote assimilation and interpenetration. The Westerners, coming as conquerors and exploiters, assumed a supercilious and contemptuous attitude toward Oriental culture. The Easterners usually assumed a subservient or at least deferential manner toward these alien rulers and exploiters. While this manner may be due in part to Oriental politeness, it arose mainly out of fear of Occidental might and belligerence. But it concealed a contempt and hatred for the West which fully equalled the feelings of the Western imperialists toward the East.

This situation is aggravated by racial prejudices and antagonisms. Orientals are on the whole of a darker color than Occidentals. The dominant Western powers in Asia were British and American. For about two centuries Great Britain ruled India and other extensive territories. In recent years the United States has been England's principal rival in eastern Asia, not by conquest but by the more subtle method of heavy investments of capital in Oriental enterprises.

[1] My books entitled *Blockade and Sea Power*, New York, 1924, *Oriental and Occidental Culture*, New York, 1928, etc., are among the very few books concerning this war which do not commit this error. I have invariably called it the "European" War.

1046

The Anglo-Saxon influence was the most powerful throughout the world. Anglo-Saxon peoples are predominantly or, at any rate, traditionally of the lightest-colored race, the so-called Nordic. The "Nordics" have been for the moment on top, and can display to the full their dislike for the dark-skinned peoples who constitute the vast majority of mankind.

Anglo-Saxon antipathy toward the dark races is exemplified in the laws to exclude Oriental immigrants enacted by the United States, Canada, Australia, New Zealand, South Africa, etc. While these laws are intended primarily to keep out cheap labor, racial prejudice also plays its part. This was strikingly illustrated in the clause excluding the Japanese in the Immigration Law passed by the American Congress on the twelfth of April, 1924. The Japanese Government had displayed its willingness to recognize the economic reasons for restricting immigration. In accordance with the "gentlemen's agreement" of 1907, the Japanese Government prevented laborers from going to the United States. As a consequence, the excess of incoming over outgoing Japanese during the years 1908 to 1923 was only 8681, and this number included merchants, students, tourists, government officials, and others who are permitted to enter. Under the Immigration Restriction Act the annual quota for Japanese immigrants would have been only a little over one hundred. It was therefore a wholly gratuitous insult to discriminate against the Japanese nation by specifically excluding its nationals.

Physical and mental racial differences have not yet been sufficiently studied to warrant definite conclusions. Most of the assertions made with regard to the alleged inferiority or superiority of various races have no scientific justification whatsoever, and are based on preconceived notions, casual observations, misinterpreted anecdotes, mistaken assumptions as to the causes of cultural differences, and racial and national prejudices. An extensive investigation of a rigorously scientific nature is necessary before reliable conclusions can be reached.

Many of these allegations of racial inferiority have been made concerning the negroes, and because some of the Oriental peoples also are dark-colored, it has been assumed that the same could be extended to them. Whether or not such allegations against the negroes are justified is very debatable. Inasmuch as negro blood is no more prevalent in the East than it is in the West, this question is of no more significance for the Orient than it is for the Occident. There are many dark-skinned peoples which are not negroid. Many egregious errors are made in this connection.

I have discussed this back-thrust of imperialism with educated

1047

and cultured representatives of several Oriental countries who are humiliated and alarmed by this outburst of race prejudice and discrimination against their peoples. They fully realize that it indicates a belief prevalent in the Occident that they are racially and culturally inferior. The feeling of resentment thus aroused does not encourage them to welcome and to try to assimilate the best that there is in Occidental culture, but turns them back toward their own culture, thus aggravating the cultural dissimilarity and antipathy between the East and the West.

This contemptuous attitude toward the Orient is manifested at its worst by the European and American residents in the East, most of whom are imperialist. Their ignorance of and indifference toward the culture of the peoples among whom they live are almost complete. The term "native" as used by them is often intentionally insulting, and the phrase "going native," as applied to Westerners who adopt Oriental customs is always intended as a criticism and condemnation. Contempt for strangers is common the world over, but the Occidental foreigners in the Orient succeed in surpassing it in their contempt for the natives. This is due not only to provincialism and prejudice but also to a desire to dominate the peoples whom they are trying to rule and exploit by setting themselves as far apart from them as possible. A foreigner who does not follow this policy is therefore a traitor to their cause. And yet an Oriental who carries with him to the Occident his own dress, manners, and customs, is likely to suffer from chauvinism and intolerance, though Westerners are constantly doing the same with impunity in the Orient.

The foreign communities in China furnished characteristic illustrations of all of these points, as I had ample opportunity to observe in Tientsin, Hankow, Shanghai, Canton, Hongkong, and elsewhere. Huddled together in their concessions and settlements, these aliens from the Occident secluded themselves as much as possible from the Chinese. Their only interest in the country was to make as much money as possible out of its people. The information of the "old China hand" concerning the country in which he had resided for decades often was extraordinarily limited. Their lack of a sympathetic interest established a barrier between them and the natives, in spite of the fact that their economic activities often were to the mutual benefit of both foreigners and natives.

This tension is accentuated by the belief prevalent among imperialists that they are performing an altruistic mission in ruling or attempting to rule the Orient. This notion is based upon the postulate that they are morally as well as intellectually superior to the Orientals. As the raucously imperialist poet Rudyard Kipling vulgarly and insultingly expressed it:

Ship me somewheres east of Suez where the best is like the worst,
Where there ain't no Ten Commandments, an' a man can raise a
thirst.

This belief was more elegantly phrased when Lord Rosebery, a
former Liberal prime minister (1894-1895), asserted that the British
Empire is "the greatest secular agency for good known to the world."
Certain benefits derived from British and other colonial rule are not
to be denied, but they are benefits which are forced upon and not
solicited by these peoples. It is not surprising that the officials and
other imperialists are irritated and angered by the obvious lack of
appreciation of this alien rule displayed by its unwilling recipients,
nor is this lack of appreciation any more surprising. The best commentary on the self-assumed "white man's burden" has been furnished
by the eminent English economist, John A. Hobson:

"Imperialism is a depraved choice of national life, imposed by
self-seeking interests which appeal to the lusts of quantitative acquisitiveness and of forceful domination surviving in a nation from early
centuries of animal struggle for existence. Its adoption as a policy
implies a deliberate renunciation of that cultivation of the higher
inner qualities which for a nation as for an individual constitutes the
ascendancy of reason over brute impulse. It is the besetting sin of all
successful States, and its penalty is unalterable in the order of nature."[2]

Until the Occident ceases its attempt at domination, accompanied
by unctuous professions of doing good or by more frank and truthful
assertions of pecuniary gain and political power as its motives, it will
not be possible for the East and the West to profit by an entirely free
and mutually helpful exchange of their cultures.

It is impossible to state accurately the number of adherents of
most of the religions of the world. In China Confucianism, Taoism,
and Buddhism overlap because many individuals profess more than
one religion and practice all three to a certain extent, and a similar
situation exists in Japan with respect to Buddhism and Shinto. Statistics of all four of these religions are of dubious value. It is customary
to credit all of the population of Europe and of North and South
America to Christianity. But not all of the aboriginal inhabitants of
the Western Hemisphere have been Christianized, while a considerable
portion of the civilized population, including a much larger proportion of its intellectual classes, professes no religion whatsoever.

It is nevertheless certain that Christianity is the strongest numerically, and includes about one-third of mankind. What is more important, it is the dominant religion of the Occident. Inasmuch as the
Occident, though numerically weaker, is politically and economically

2 *Imperialism*, revised edition, 1938, London, p. 368.

stronger than the Orient, Christianity acquires thereby an enormous social and material prestige. Leaving aside the question as to the relative merits of the different religions, if any religion is advantageously situated to become the dominant or universal religion, it is Christianity. The following estimate gives some indication of the numerical strength of the leading religions:[3]

Principal Religions of the World, 1954

		Millions
Christian—total		742
Roman Catholic	421	
Eastern Orthodox	128	
Protestant	193	
Mohammedan		316
Confucian		300
Hindu		256
Buddhist		150
Primitive		121
Taoist		50
Shinto		25
Jewish		11
Zoroastrian		0.1
Others or none		247
Grand total		2,218

Missionaries have been at work in the Orient since early in the Christian era. After the condemnation of the Nestorian heresy by the Council of Ephesus in A.D. 431, Syrians came to the Malabar or west coast of India and founded colonies which still flourish, especially in the southern states of Cochin and Travancore. The Nestorians are said to have reached China in A.D. 505. The Nestorian stone tablet at Sian-fu dates from the seventh or eighth century. Roman Catholic missionaries are said to have arrived in Peking in 1293, just after the departure of Marco Polo. Francisco de Xavier reached India in 1542, Japan in 1549, and died in China in 1552. The Jesuit Matteo Ricci arrived in China in 1582. The Roman Catholics are said to have entered Korea about the year 1600. Russian Orthodox missionaries reached Peking in 1685. Protestant mission work began in India in the early part of the eighteenth century, in China at the beginning of the nineteenth century, and in Japan in 1859.

[3] *Information Please Almanac*, 1954, p. 485, compiled from the *Encyclopedia Britannica*.

According to the census of India, in 1921 the Christians numbered 4,753,174, being about 1½ per cent, of the total population of India and Burma. This figure included 4,464,396 Indians, 113,041 Anglo-Indians—namely, Eurasians—and 175,737 Europeans and other Westerners. There were 1,823,079 Roman Catholics, 1,803,964 Protestants of the principal sects, and 676,957 members of the Syrian church, the remainder being distributed among the smaller sects. In Ceylon in 1921 there were 443,400 Christians, or nearly 10 per cent. of the total population of 4,498,605, of whom 368,499 were Roman Catholics.

In Japan in 1925 there were 219,862 Christians, including 77,191 Roman Catholics, and 14,206 of the Russian Orthodox church. This was barely one third of 1 per cent. of the total population. In Korea in 1924 there were 349,375 Christians, of whom about 80,000 were Roman Catholics. This was barely 1½ per cent. of the total population.

Chinese statistics are notoriously scarce and inaccurate. The China Year Book, 1928, estimated that there were 700,000 Protestants, of whom 350,000 are communicants, and 2,300,000 Roman Catholics in China. But the Catholic Encyclopedia, published in 1911, claimed barely one million adherents in China and its dependencies. In all probability considerably less than 1 per cent. of the Chinese are Christian. The Catholic Encyclopedia claimed about one million adherents in Indo-China and its neighboring countries. Owing to the long Spanish occupation, there are said to be six or seven million Catholics in the Philippine Islands, or about one-third of the total population.

These figures indicate that, even though numerous missionaries have been sent and much money has been expended, Christianity has made little impression upon the Orient so far as the number of conversions is an indication. The Blue Book of Missions, published in 1907, estimated that Protestant missionary work in the entire world had resulted in only 1,817,450 communicants and 4,361,138 adherents. In spite of the fact that Islam, the other great Semitic religion, came into existence more than half a millennium later, it has been much more successful. According to the census of 1921 there were more than 68,000,000 Moslems in India, or about 22 per cent. of the total population. According to the China Year Book, 1925-26, there were fifteen to twenty millions of Moslems in China, or perhaps 4 to 5 per cent. of the population. Islam is the dominant religion in a large part of Malaysia and the East Indies.

In spite of its social and political prestige, and its close association with Occidental imperialism, Christianity has had little success in the Orient. Leaving aside the case of the Philippines, where Roman Catholicism was forced upon a primitive people by a despotic European government, Ceylon, a small country where a hybrid mixture of Asiatic and European culture prevails, is the only place where the proportion of Christians approaches 10 per cent. Next comes Korea with less than 2 per cent. Korea has no vital religion of its own, the upper classes favoring Confucianism and the lower classes Buddhism. The almost complete failure of the Christian offensive on the Orient is a striking fact worthy of careful consideration.

The missionary spirit is much stronger in the Occident than in the Orient, and is correlated with the more aggressive spirit of the West. both Christianity and Islam are proselytizing religions, partly because each is monotheistic and professes that its god should dominate the whole world, but also owing to other tenets soon to be mentioned. The contrast between the Occidental and Oriental religions with regard to their proselytizing zeal is of considerable significance in relation to their respective cultures and their contact with each other.

Three great religions profess to be universal—namely, Buddhism, Christianity, and Islam. Judaism at one time entertained the hope that its Jehovah would some time rule the world. But Jehovah never became much more than a tribal god. The Jews persisted in considering themselves a people chosen by divine preference over other peoples, and to whom the deity was to send a messenger, the Messiah. With such a narrow and exclusive outlook Judaism could never become a great missionary religion.

Christianity derived its deity from Judaism. While both Jehovah and God are monarchs, wielders of brute force and avid for power, God is the greater king who contemplates dominion over the whole earth in a not too remote future, whereas Jehovah was never quite so ambitious. In one of its principal aspects Christianity is as monarchical, militarist, bombastic, and domineering as Judaism. The phrase "kingdom of God," with its variant "kingdom of Heaven" in the gospel of Matthew, appears more often than any other phrase in the four gospels.

> Let thrones and powers and kingdoms be
> Obedient, mighty God, to Thee!
> And, over land and stream and main,
> Wave Thou the scepter of Thy reign!

On the other hand, Christianity has also professed the doctrine that God is a father as well as king. He is called the "Father" three hundred times in the New Testament. Inasmuch as Christians believe that the Messianic hope has been fulfilled, they are willing to extend the fatherhood of God and the ministrations of his son to the rest of

1052

mankind. The mythical character of Jesus furnishes a concrete object toward which to direct personal loyalty, more so than in most religions. Thus Jesus also becomes king and martial leader to be followed into battle like God himself.

> Great God! whose universal sway
> The known and unknown worlds obey;
> Now give the kingdom to Thy Son;
> Extend His power, exalt His throne.
> The Son of God goes forth to war,
> A kingly crown to gain;
> His blood-red banner streams afar!
> Who follows in His train?

Christian hymnology, derived mainly from the Psalms and the New Testament, furnishes abundant evidence of the belligerent character of this religion. While some of the hymns reflect its more amiable tenets, speak of God as love, and dwell upon a peaceful though rarely if ever upon a contemplative or thoughtful life, a large proportion of them are filled with the dust and din, the boasting and bellicosity of war. The Christian is repeatedly characterized as a warrior.

> The Christian warrior, see him stand,
> In the whole armor of his God.
> Soldiers of Christ, arise,
> And put your armor on.
> Gird thy heavenly armor on,
> Wear it ever night and day;
> Ambushed lies the evil one:
> Watch and pray.

The bellicose spirit of Christianity is to be explained in part, if not entirely, by its strong sense of evil and sin in the world. This it derived from Zoroastrianism and Judaism, but has considerably intensified and amplified it. In the cruder forms of this doctrine, evil is personified in numerous hobgoblins, genii, demons, and the like, whose weaker magic is pitted against the superior magic of God and his followers, as is illustrated in this characteristic bit of sacred doggerel.

> And though this world, with devils filled,
> Should threaten to undo us,
> We will not fear, for God hath willed
> His truth to triumph through us.

1053

In Martin Luther's famous hymn, which describes God as a "mighty fortress," the arch-fiend Satan is depicted in the most uncomplimentary terms.

> For still our ancient foe
> Doth seek to work us woe;
> His craft and power are great,
> And, armed with cruel hate,
> On earth is not his equal.

The battle hymn of Christianity presents this religion arrayed in the full panoply of pomp and power against the evil one.

> Onward, Christian soldiers!
> Marching as to war,
> With the Cross of Jesus
> Going on before.
> Christ the Royal Master
> Leads against the foe;
> Forward into battle,
> See, His banners go!

These hymns mirror those features of Christianity which have made it a belligerent religion, for the sacred poetry and music of a religion reflect its most dynamic traits. Sung by myriads of Protestant believers, they have spurred them on to renewed efforts to fight the devil and convert the benighted heathen from their wicked ways.

Christians usually believe that Christianity is a missionary religion because Jesus is reputed to have said to his disciples: "Go ye therefore, and teach all nations, baptizing them in the name of the Father, and of the Son, and of the Holy Ghost." (Matthew XXVIII, 19.) "Go ye into all the world, and preach the gospel to every creature. He that believeth, and is baptized, shall be saved; but he that believeth not, shall be damned." (Mark XVI, 15, 16.) Here, then, is a formula for salvation through belief and the ceremony of baptism held forth to all mankind, but short shrift for the recalcitrants who refuse to be saved.

The foregoing exposition, however, indicates clearly the important part played in Christian theology by the dogma of the dualism of good and evil in the universe. Hence the Christian life must be a constant struggle against evil under the command and leadership of God the incarnation of good. A hymn written for the convocation of missionaries, therefore, begins appropriately as follows:

1054

Assembled at Thy great command,
Before Thy face, dread King, we stand;
The voice that marshaled every star,
Has called Thy people from afar.

This ethical dualism permits of no shading. Good is light and evil is darkness. The heathen incarnate evil, or, at any rate, are dominated by it. They must be fought and, if possible, saved, whether they wish it or not, partly for their own sake but much more for the glorification of God the inexorable king. The self-righteous Christian, therefore, goes forth to struggle against but also for the wicked heathen.

Scatter the gloom of heathen night,
And bid all nations hail the light.
The heathen in his blindness,
  Bows down to wood and stone!
Shall we, whose souls are lighted
  With wisdom from on high,—
Shall we, to men benighted,
  The lamp of life deny?

The preceding description reveals the attributes of Christianity which have rendered it one of the most aggressive, intolerant, and domineering of religions, and which explain its long history of persecuting unbelievers, its religious wars, its Inquisition and its Crusades, and its extensive proselytizing activities, some of which have been carried on with the aid of the mailed fist. These attributes are its jealous and ambitious deity, its belief in a peculiarly Christian character which is superior to human nature in general and which is incarnated in the mythical figure of Jesus, its cut-and-dried formula for salvation than which there is no other way to be saved, and its grotesque and wholly unscientific doctrine of evil. Every religion grows out and is a part of a complex of economic, political, and social factors and conditions. The intrinsic character of Christianity has harmonized well with the commercial greed and the political imperialism of the Occident.

Needless to say, there have been and are other aspects of Christianity which some of its apologists eagerly push to the fore in order to cover up what has been described. The Christian mystic, like all mystics, is absorbed in his autosuggestively and hypnotically induced inner vision. The gentler and less aggressive believer is attracted by its more amiable tenets and engages in charitable deeds. The more thoughtful adherent is appalled and shocked by the inconsistency of its ethical dualism and tries to smooth it away, often by means of

1055

casuistry. Thus it is argued that while God is responsible for the possibility of evil, he has given man free will so that the individual is responsible for choosing evil rather than good. But these phases of Christianity have had little influence upon missionary work, which is due almost entirely to the attributes described above. These belligerent attributes constitute the main body of historical Christianity and have had the most influence in the affairs of mankind.

Mohammedanism was derived in part from Judaism and Christianity. Its formula for salvation consists in submission (*islam* in Arabic) to Allah the one god. All human beings who submit and fight for this religion can be saved, thus making it universal in its appeal. Those who do not submit may be exterminated by the faithful, who attain religious merit thereby. Moslems who secure converts increase their chances of going to Paradise. All of these traits and its simplicity render Islam even more aggressive than Christianity. The Moslem is rarely ever troubled by philosophic doubts, which makes him very sure of himself. During the first millennium of its existence —namely, from the seventh to the seventeenth century—proselytizing zeal aided by the force of arms and an efflorescence of Arabic culture carried it throughout northern Africa, into southern Europe, over most of Asia Minor, and into central Asia. The conquest of a considerable part of India and several centuries of Moslem rule firmly established it there, so that it has a larger following in Pakistan than in any other country. As it carries with it a smaller cultural content than Christianity, it is readily accepted by peoples of a simpler culture without affecting materially their own culture. This explains in large part its success in Malaysia and the East Indies.

Orthodox Hinduism is based on the theory that only those belonging to the caste system can profess this religion, and that membership in a caste is acquired by birth. As a matter of fact, many tribes have been taken into Hinduism in the course of its spread over the peninsula. But this theory has tended to make the Brahmanic religion exclusive. The Arya Samaj, a heterodox Vedic sect, and various Vedantist organizations, such as the Ram Krishna mission, have undertaken to proselytize abroad as well as at home. This outbreak of the missionary spirit has taken place largely in opposition to Christian and the successful Mohammedan proselytizing activity, which has been attracting converts largely from the outcastes and lower castes.

Even if the caste system did not exist, it is doubtful if Brahmanism would be a missionary religion. *Moksha* or nirvana is the ideal of Hinduism. This goal may be reached after passing through a series of incarnations. The individual may succeed in accelerating this process by practising various forms of yoga and in other ways. There is no ready-made salvation at hand, as by submission to Allah, faith in God,

1056

or following Jesus or any other mythical or real person. Only through prolonged effort can the individual hope to influence his destiny. This world is maya or an illusion. There is no sin or evil in the absolute sense, but only ignorance and errors. All of this disappears when the individual is merged in Brahma, the impersonal world-soul, or universal consciousness, or whatever it may be called, in which distinctions of good and bad have no significance. Hence Brahmanism in its more philosophic aspect is more complicated and profound in its thought than the naive and often childishly simple Christian and Mohammedan theology.

Buddhism in its original form as a religion was as quiescent as and even more impersonal than Brahmanism. It also regards nirvana as its goal, and recognizes no absolute evil in the world. But the desire of its founder, Gautama, to cure certain social ills gave to it a reforming tendency at the outset. The enthusiasm of King Ashoka about two and a half centuries later started it on a missionary career. It was in no way restricted as to race, nation, or class. In course of time Gautama became deified. Its northern or Mahayana branch acquired a doctrine of salvation and a mediator or redeemer in the legendary person of Amidha Buddha. Thus it spread over a large part of eastern Asia, though driven out of India by the reviving Brahmanism and the incoming Islam. For several centuries it has been quiescent. Since the awakening of Japan, Mahayanism has again become propagandistic. In that country it has developed into a highly institutionalized church and has split up into numerous sects which are vying with each other, thus paralleling the situation in Christendom.

Confucianism as a religion professes belief in a remote deity, Shang-ti or the Supreme Being, and in Tien or Heaven the moral order of the universe. As a popular religious cult it consists of the worship of the spirits of the venerated ancestors. But Confucianism is mainly a system of ethics. Its central theme is the "superior man" as the ideal. This can be attained only through the effort of the individual himself. As Confucius is reported to have said: "From the highest to the lowest, self-development must be deemed the root of all, by every man." ("Ta-hsio"; or, The Great Learning, V, 6.) Among the traits attributed to the superior man are will power, purpose, poise, fortitude, self-control, self-sufficiency, earnestness, thoroughness, sincerity, truthfulness, purity of thought and action, love of truth, mental hospitality, rectitude, prudence, composure, fearlessness, ease and dignity, firmness, humility, avoidance of sycophancy, growth, capacity, openness, benevolence, broad-mindedness, charity, moderation, reserve power, and reciprocity (similar to the "Golden Rule").

Confucianism offers, therefore, no ready-made scheme of salvation or short cut to virtue through faith or magical ceremonies such as baptism or circumcision, but an austere discipline of the self by one's self. In its emphasis upon the human will it resembles the Stoicism of classical Greece and Rome. In the classics the Chinese sage, as reported by his disciples, expounds man's relations to his fellows, to the members of his household, and to the state which he regards as a larger household. The doctrine of the mean or path of moderation is taught throughout. The man capable of following this pathway is described in glowing terms. "It is only he, possessed of all sagely qualities that can exist under Heaven, who shows himself quick in apprehension, clear in discernment, of far-reaching intelligence and all-embracing knowledge, fitted to exercise rule; magnanimous, generous, benign and mild, fitted to exercise forbearance; impulsive, energetic, firm and enduring, fitted to maintain a firm grasp; self-adjusted, grave, never swerving from the mean and correct, fitted to command reverence; accomplished, distinctive, concentrative and searching, fitted to exercise discrimination; all-embracing is he, and vast, deep, and active as a fountain, sending forth, in their due seasons, his virtues." ("Chung-yung"; or, The Doctrine of the Mean, c. XXXI, V. 1, 2.) Such a system of thought and belief does not lend itself to evangelical fervor or to religious intolerance, and has, so far as I know, never been propagated by missionary methods. It was studied and to a certain extent borrowed on its intrinsic merits by the Koreans and Japanese.

Taoism in its more philosophic aspect teaches only a shadowy and impersonal Supreme Being. It is mainly a quiescent and mystical doctrine which deprecates much concern with the affairs of this world. "The sage keeps his mind in a state of indifference to all." (Tao-teh-king," XLIX, 3.) In its popular form it has degenerated into a system of magic. In neither form has it had any missionary activity and few reformers.

China has presented the most stupendous example of religious toleration in the history of mankind. For two millennia the San-chiao or Three Religions—namely, Confucianism, Taoism, and Buddhism—have existed side by side with almost no persecution. A large proportion of the Chinese take part in all three religions. Here is no fertile field for the growth of missionary zeal.

A similar situation exists in Japan. Shinto is a chauvinistic religion which can have no significance for any other country. It has never persecuted or proselytized but has only required loyalty to the nation. It has been tolerant toward Confucianism, Taoism, and Christianity, and now shares the field with Buddhism with equanimity.

The preceding comparison indicates that there is a greater modicum of thought in Brahmanism, Buddhism, and Confucianism than in Christianity or Mohammedanism. This is largely due to the

1058

fact that Oriental religion includes practically all of the philosophy and most of the very little science which the Orient has developed. Most of this is contained in the Upanishads of Brahmanism, the Buddhist Tripitaka, especially the third or Abhidhamma Pitaka, and the Yi-king or Book of Changes, the most philosophic of the Confucian classics. The eastern Asiatic peoples have displayed less interest in philosophic problems. The Yi-king contains occasional observations more or less scientific in their character, such as that "the successive interaction of the passive and active forces constitutes what is called the flow of phenomena." But this book has been used in the main for purposes of divination.

The contemplative life fostered by some of the Oriental religions has also had its influence. In one of the Upanishads it is said: "Only those of tranquil minds, and none else, can attain abiding joy, by realizing within their souls that Being who manifests one essence in a multiplicity of forms." The Indian rishis or sages of old "were they who having reached the supreme God from all sides had found abiding peace, had become united with all, had entered into the life of the Universe." The kind of thought inspired by such a life could not result in science. In India an ardent interest in religion, a strong tendency toward cosmological and metaphysical speculation, and an intense desire to transform the personality by methods which encourage introspective rather than objective habits of thinking were antithetical to the inductive and experimental methods which are essential for science. In China ancestor worship and filial reverence gave rise to a conservatism and self-satisfaction which effectually prevented the radical departure which science and its application require.

The sacred scriptures of every religion contain its theology, ethics, and ritual, mingled with a good deal of myth and alleged history. The Bible and especially the Koran contain less philosophic reasoning and speculation than the above-mentioned Oriental scriptures. Christianity and Islam attach little significance to the contemplative life, because faith and action rather than thought and meditation are emphasized and lauded.[4] Ecclesiastes is perhaps the most philosophic book in the Hebrew and Christian scriptures, and yet it ends in a theological vein:

[4] The second Sura of the Koran begins as follows: "There is no doubt in this book; it is a direction to the pious, who believe in the mysteries of the faith, who observe the appointed times of prayer, and distribute alms out of what we have bestowed on them, and who believe in that revelation, which hath been sent down unto thee and that which hath been sent down unto the prophets before thee, and have firm assurance of the life to come: these are directed by their Lord, and they shall prosper. As for the unbelievers, it will be equal to them whether thou admonish them, or do not admonish them; they will not believe. Allah hath sealed up their hearts and their hearing; a dimness covereth their sight, and they shall suffer a grievous punishment."

"Let us hear the conclusion of the whole matter: Fear God, and keep his commandments: for this is the whole duty of man. For God shall bring every work into judgment, with every secret thing, whether it be good, or whether it be evil."

Partly owing to these characteristics of the Christian scriptures science developed almost entirely independent of religion, and philosophy has gradually freed itself from its early connection with theology. The development of science gave rise to the empirical method and inductive logic, which in turn led to habits of thinking and reasoning markedly different from those of the Orient. Religion, theology, and the church have slowly and grudgingly yielded ground to the onward sweep of science in the Occident. The significance of this situation is that Western religion cannot bring to the Orient what is peculiarly lacking there—namely, science and a secular philosophy. Of religion itself the East has even more than the West.

It is usually assumed by missionaries and their supporters and sympathizers that the extent to which the Orient has adopted Occidental civilization is to be credited entirely to Christianity. This fantastic notion is due to the egregious error made by many Christians that civilization and Christianity are identical, and that all of the credit for the social change which has resulted in civilization should be given to the religion. Japan alone furnishes ample disproof of this mistake on the part of the missionaries, for while it has adopted a good deal of Western culture, especially on its material side, Japan has repudiated Christianity. The situation in this regard cannot be understood until it is recognized that no cultural system can be attributed to any one religion, because every culture is derived from many and diverse sources. In its relation to Christianity this is more true of Occidental culture, which had a complex origin in Rome, Greece, Egypt, and other parts of the Mediterranean area, than it is of the Hindu culture, which originated to a greater degree from the Brahmanic religion, and of the Chinese culture, which was formulated to a considerable degree by the Confucian ethics and religion. And yet a missionary propagandist has asserted that "the peoples of the West have derived their ideals of justice, freedom, opportunity, cooperation, and progress from no other religion than that of Jesus Christ." [5] The prevalence of this erroneous belief tends to increase the aggressiveness of the missionary attack upon the Orient and other non-Christian parts of the world.

An Indian critic of missions has said that the Orient concludes that the Western political method is first to send missionaries, second

[5] R. E. Hume, *The World's Living Religions*, New York, 1924, p. 234.

traders, and third gunboats.[6] While this method has not usually been followed consciously and intentionally, it has nevertheless often worked out in this fashion. Missionary work has been both the forerunner and the follower of Occidental imperialism. The establishment of political power has usually resulted in a large influx of missionaries. This cycle is well illustrated in India. The acquisition of power by Catholic countries—namely, Portugal and France—brought numerous Romanist missionaries. The establishment of British rule brought many Protestant missionaries. If the Orient should attempt successfully to acquire political power in the Occident, it is not impossible that such an outbreak of imperialism would incite a proselytizing spirit even in the non-missionary religions of the East.

The presence of missionaries and the establishment of missionary institutions, such as churches, schools, hospitals, and the like, have often furnished excuses for aggressive measures to secure more power. This was graphically illustrated in the case of British missions in China. Protection for these missions as well as for trade interests was one of the reasons for demands for extraterritorial rights, spheres of influence, and the like, and the British Government was ready on the slightest provocation to send gunboats for the protection of its missionaries and their institutions. The United States Government was less aggressive in China, never claimed a sphere of influence, and advocated an open-door policy. But the American missionary investment was larger than the British, and was even larger than the American commercial investment.[7] So that American missionary interests influenced its diplomatic policy greatly. The Catholic missionary investment in China was larger than the Protestant, and as much of it was French, the French Government was active in demanding diplomatic protection for Catholic missions.

The missionaries reciprocated, perhaps unconsciously, by being chauvinistic, and often endeavoring indirectly when not directly to instil into the minds of their neophytes the benefits of Western rule as well as religion and culture. With comparatively few exceptions their influence has been against nationalist movements, even when these movements were not directed against their own or other Christian governments. In Turkey the missionaries always opposed the nationalist movements of the Armenians and other subject races. In India this

[6] J. J. Cornelius, "An Oriental Looks at Christian Missions," in *Harper's Magazine*, April, 1927.

[7] Information Service Foreign Policy Association, New York, Vol. II, No. 25, February 16, 1927. According to this bulletin, the American investment in China was approximately $70,000,000 in commercial undertakings, and $80,000,000 in missionary enterprises, schools, hospitals, etc.

attitude was imposed upon the missionaries, whether they wished it or not. A missionary society, in order to secure permission from the British Government to carry on its work, had to sign a declaration "that all due obedience and respect should be given to the lawfully constituted Government, and that while carefully abstaining from political affairs, it is its desire and purpose that its influence, in so far as it may be properly exerted, should be so exerted in loyal co-operation with the Government of the country concerned, and that it will only employ agents who will work in this spirit." (British Memorandum A, Article 5: iii.) Individual missionaries also were required to sign this declaration.

Religious proselytizing is as legitimate as political propaganda, and missionaries are entitled to protection as much as traders, tourists, and other foreigners. But the correlation between missions and imperialism and their interaction upon each other are significant facts for cultural relations. They have resulted in a so-called "missionary statesmanship" in which missions and imperialism have specifically and more or less openly worked hand-in-glove for the joint spread of Christianity and political power. This is a conscious recognition of the subtle influence which is always at work, for the missionaries cannot help but recognize that the success of Christianity in the Orient depends entirely upon political power. Even where Western rule prevails, it is not likely to succeed. Lacking such power it is certain to fail. This is strikingly illustrated in Japan, where under national independence Christianity is a dead issue. Hence it is not surprising that Orientals come to regard missions as the vanguard and accomplice of imperialism. In China the nationalist movement turned against or at least its back upon the missionaries and their religion, and the same is true to a smaller degree of the nationalist movements in other Eastern countries. Thus the cooperation between missions and imperialism has proved to be fatal for Christianity, though it is doubtful if it could in any case have conquered the Orient.

In spite of its unhappy alliance with imperialism and the paucity of its cultural content, has missionary work introduced any Occidental culture to the Orient? Its educational institutions and methods, while strongly permeated with Christian doctrines, nevertheless brought some knowledge of Western language, literature, and even a little science. Its medical work disseminated some information as to sanitation. It encouraged a certain number of Orientals to go to Europe or America to study. Thus the missionaries, whose purpose is not cultural, almost unwittingly introduced a little culture. In this respect they are like the traders, whose purpose also is not cultural. But most of the imperialistic governments and some of the native governments have done vastly more than either the missionaries or the traders. The

1062

British Government of India accomplished far more in educational and sanitary lines than all of the missionaries put together. The Japanese Government sent numerous young men and women abroad to study. Systematically and on a large scale it introduced educational, sanitary, scientific, and industrial methods. The Chinese Government has done the same to a considerably smaller degree. Most if not all of this would have happened even if no Christian missionary had invaded the Orient.

Even when the missionaries disseminated a little culture, they have done so usually in a harmful manner. Western education was introduced at the expense of Oriental culture and caused a certain amount of intellectual deterioration and social disintegration. The mission schools in China neglected to recognize and emphasize Chinese literature, art, and social institutions. In India the missionaries were shocked by features of Indian religion and customs which are immoral according to Occidental standards, and, therefore, with few exceptions assumed a distinctly hostile attitude toward Indian culture. Their tendency was to picture the West in glowing colors to the East, but to report only the unfavorable aspects of the East to their Western constituents. Otherwise they are not so likely to secure the financial support which their work requires. For all of these reasons an adjustment and harmonizing of Oriental and Occidental culture is not likely to be attained through missionary methods and activities.

This situation is due partly to the intrinsic character of Christianity, and partly to the traits inherent in the missionaries themselves. As a general rule, they are sincere but narrow-minded folk, with a strong tendency toward bigotry and fanaticism. Otherwise they would not enter this occupation. They are usually very patriotic and believe that they represent not only the sole "true" religion but also a superior culture. Their attitude toward the natives of the countries to which they are sent is usually one of supercilious condescension, which renders it all the more difficult for them to become acquainted with and appreciate the indigenous culture. These traits are intensified by isolation from the home country where they might be subjected to liberalizing influences. The broadening effect of travel is lost upon them because of the prejudices and preconceptions with which they leave home. Mission societies are paternalistic in their organization, and missionaries are sure of their positions for life. They are shielded from competition and lack the stimulus of the keen rivalry which obtains in most professions and occupations. This situation encourages inefficiency, sloth, and intellectual lethargy.

The remuneration of missionaries is considerably smaller than the average income of the foreign merchants and officials. Partly for this reason they live closer to the people, this probably being even

1063

more true of the Catholic than of the Protestant missionaries. Though they rarely ever adopt the native manner of life *in toto,* they invariably learn the language and become acquainted with the local customs. Despite these advantages, their religious and moral biases are so great that it is doubtful if they come any closer to the real thought and inner life of the people than the foreign merchants and officials. In fact, it is humanly impossible for any one with so narrow and unilateral a point of view as the average missionary to understand and appreciate another viewpoint. A few missionaries have furnished some information in their writings, such as S. W. Williams on Chinese history, J. Legge in translations of the Chinese classics, A. H. Smith on Chinese life, W. E. Soothill on Chinese religion, W. G. Aston on Japanese religion, and J. P. Jones on Indian life and religion. But the missionary bias is consistently revealed throughout their works, thus diminishing their value considerably.

Changes are nevertheless taking place in the field of missionary activities, though they are being forced upon the missionaries from the outside. Missionary "statesmanship" has been occupied with a grandiose scheme for the "evangelization of the world in one generation," and was confidently talking of the "conquest of the world for Christ." The passing of the years has revealed the obdurate indifference of the Orient to these facile schemes. The rapidly growing strength of the nationalist movements is arousing a renewed interest in the native cultures and an active resistance to the religion as well as other phases of the culture of the Occident.

The effect has been to decrease the emphasis on preaching, evangelizing, and proselytizing, and to increase the scope of the other activities of missionaries. Indeed, missionary work is being driven under the ground more and more by Oriental nationalism and is becoming cloaked under the guise of education, medical work, social amelioration, sport and athletics, etc. The Y. M. C. A. and to a less extent the Y. W. C. A. have been extending their activities. In Tokyo, Peiping, Shanghai, Canton, Seoul, Bombay, Madras, Colombo, and elsewhere I have visited large and stately Y. M. C. A. buildings which offer the usual facilities for instruction, recreation, physical development, and the like, with a minor emphasis upon proselytizing.

The point has already been reached where missionaries can hope to have much success only among groups which expect to gain material advantages by changing their religion. Today this is chiefly true among the lower castes and outcastes of India who can improve their social status thereby. Christianity and Islam are now vying with each other to win neophytes from these lower social strata. Many of these "rice" Christians and Moslems have embraced these religions in village groups to escape their social disabilities and not on account of a change in their religious beliefs.

The death-knell of a successful missionary enterprise in the Orient has already sounded. The missionaries and their supporters and sympathizers often aver that their new activities are as truly missionary as the old. But education is due to scholarship, medicine to science, and sport and athletics are derived from the traditions of pagan Greece, imperialist Rome, and our barbarous Teutonic ancestors. Social work is inspired by the modern humanitarian movement which is due mainly to factors other than Christianity. The elevation of the position of women is due to the same movement. In fact, while engaged in such work missionaries are conveying various features of Occidental culture in general and not its religion in particular.

There are attempts to combine Oriental and Occidental religion, or to create a sort of higher harmony through super-religions to which the devotees of any religion may belong. Theosophy, Bahaism, and the like, probably are too artificial ways of attaining such a harmony, which, if it comes at all, will have to be attained through a very extensive mingling and assimilation of peoples and cultures.[8]

To conjecture in detail as to the future is beyond the scope of this book and to prophesy with assurance is futile.[9] Nevertheless, I venture to surmise that the Orient will not become Christian, and that in so far as Christianity persists as a minor religion in the East, it will be considerably modified. As the contact between East and West increases, Oriental religion will influence Occidental religion per-

[8] At the beginning of the twentieth century Davids suggested that the meeting of Buddhist and Occidental thought may cause a new movement of ideas during the twentieth century. He apparently had in mind a scientific and philosophic rather than a religious movement. There is little indication as yet of such a movement. (T. W. Rhys Davids, in *Great Religions of the World*, New York, 1901, written by several writers.)

[9] An estimate in millions of world religions in 1950 of "the spheres of influence of the respective churches rather than the religious convictions of individuals," in which the Roman Catholics include all baptized Catholics, and Protestants include only individuals who "join" the church is as follows: Roman Catholic—380; Eastern Churches (Greek-Orthodox, Armenian, Coptic) —100; Protestant—300; Total Christian—780.

Buddhism usually combined with Confucianism, Taoism, Shintoism, etc.—645; Hinduism—400; Islam—322; Tribal Religions—115; Judaism—12; Unknown (U.S.S.R.) —126; Grand Total—2,400, millions.

(W. S. and E. S. Woytinsky, *World Population and Production, Trends and Outlook*; Twentieth Century Fund, New York, 1953, p. 55.)

This tabulation probably underestimates the number of persons who have no religious beliefs.

According to the two tabulations in this chapter, the Christians include about one-third of the total world population.

haps more than Christianity will influence the East, for the contemplative and quiescent features of Oriental religion are as yet little known in the West. Its tendency toward mysticism is not likely to have much influence because of the counteracting effect of science. In fact, science and the secular philosophy which is developing from science will be the most powerful influences upon religion the world over.

Chapter LXII

Oriental Nationalism and Imperialism

HERETOFORE nationalism has been weaker in the East than in the West. Powerful Oriental states have usually been based upon despotism and not upon national unity. Japan has been almost the only exception. China has not had a strong central government, though possessing much cultural unity. India was a congeries of states and peoples with different languages and customs, and is just beginning a national existence. Recognition of Western exploitation is strengthening national feeling. The European War of 1914 to 1918 and the World War of 1939 to 1945 disillusionized the Orient as to Occidental superiority and unity. The East is learning political nationalism and militarism of the modern type from the West. In India the chief obstacle is the religious stumbling-block—namely, the conflict between the Hindus and the Moslems. If these religious communities had composed their differences and quelled their hatred for each other, India might have presented a united front against Western exploitation. Diversity of language is another obstacle.

The outcome of this situation may be unification of the Orient against the Occident. Although modern Japan has often found it profitable to cooperate with Western powers, in the long run it will probably cast its lot with the Orient. There is danger of an Oriental race prejudice developing against the white peoples. Already the prejudice against the dark peoples is arousing a hostile reaction on the part of educated Easterners, who would otherwise like to retain close cultural relations with the Occident. All of these factors are hindrances in the way of the interpenetration and mutual assimilation of culture.

Imperialism also has arisen among Oriental peoples in modern times. The most notorious example was Japanese imperialism in China and Korea which was terminated by the war of 1939 to 1945 in which Japan was driven from those countries by rival Occidental imperialisms. As will be shown presently, the role of industrialization in Oriental imperialism is already making itself manifest.

For many generations the Koreans did not have the opportunity to govern themselves, partly owing to their kings and nobles and partly because of the imperialism of China, Russia, and Japan. Korea furnished the occasion for the Sino-Japanese War of 1894-95, and the Russo-Japanese War of 1904-5. When President Woodrow Wilson was preaching his gospel of self-determination, many Koreans thought that their time had come. This was one of the reasons for the unsuccessful revolutionary outbreaks in 1919. In 1945 it was split into two parts and, beginning with 1950, was fought over by the United States, professedly acting for the United Nations, and China and Soviet Russia on the other side. Korea, like many nations in the past, may be fated for national extinction, perhaps by assimilation into China.

Japan has had its imperialist adventures in the past. For a time during its early history it ruled Korea, which was said to have been conquered by the legendary Empress Jingo. Later it conquered the island of Hokkaido to the north, and made conquests in northern Manchuria. In 1592 the Japanese general Hideyoshi undertook to conquer China as well as Korea, but died in 1598 before he could attain his object.

At present Japan is the only Oriental power strong enough to follow an imperialist policy. It is incited to do so by its excessive and growing population, its rapidly developing capitalism, which is seeking markets for its goods, and by the example of Western imperialism. Korea is the most striking example of its imperialism. It has also been notably imperialist in its policy toward China, having taken Formosa and the Pescadores after the Sino-Japanese War of 1894-5, and territories in the province of Shantung and in southern Manchuria a few years later. This phase culminated in the notorious twenty-one demands of 1915 when the European War had distracted the attention of the Western powers away from China.

While Japan is the most prominent exponent of modern Oriental imperialism, China was one of the most imperialist of nations in the past. Much of the territorial growth of China proper was by force of arms. Tongking and Cochin-China were conquered about 214 B.C. Chinese armies marched as far west as the Caspian Sea during the Han dynasty (206 B.C.-A.D. 221), and conquered a considerable part of central Asia. They entered northern India, and as one result Buddhism came to China. Korea was conquered during the T'ang dynasty (A.D. 618-907). Burma was invaded about A.D. 224 and again by Kublai Khan about the year 1280. In 1766 began a war which made Burma a tributary state until Great Britain acquired complete suzerainty. French imperialism in Indo-China and British imperialism in India

1068

and Burma were the successors of Chinese imperialism. Within the 20th century Chinese punitive expeditions have vied with similar British expeditions into Tibet, which each would like to make its vassal state.

Indian states and other Oriental countries also have had imperialist adventures. Indeed, any nation which acquires great military strength is likely to become imperialist. If the nationalist movement brings militarism in its train, it may give rise to a recrudescence of imperialism which will gravely menace the West, for the East has the advantage of numbers. In any case, it will seriously interfere with their cultural relations.

The development of science in Europe and America has resulted in a sense of power over nature, as contrasted with the more passive attitude of the Orient toward nature. Machinery and large-scale methods have caused an enormous increase in the amount produced, and a great saving of labor. However, they have also resulted in grave economic and social problems, such as the tremendous inequality in the distribution of wealth, the uncertainty of employment and income for the proletarian class, the instability of economic conditions for all classes, the concentration of population in monstrous urban centers, etc. While all of these ills exist in a measure in the Orient, they have been greatly accentuated in the Occident. Whether or not the social and economic problems of the East are more serious than those of the West we need not discuss here. Even granting that the Occident has reached a higher plane, the pathway of wisdom for the Orient is to avoid imitating Western ills but to copy its advantageous features.

The imminent danger is that the East will be overwhelmed and will have to pass through the same stages as the West. The more independent and radical thinkers and movements of the Occident are seeking a solution of the handicaps of capitalism in some form of socialism or collectivism which will retain the benefits of science, machinery, the division of labor, and large-scale production. Soviet Russia is the chief protagonist of this point of view and is trying to jump some of the stages of capitalist evolution on its way to communism. Whether or not it succeeds remains to be seen. In any case, it is influencing Asiatic peoples in a measure in solving this problem for themselves. The Russian experiment is of great signficance not only for Europe and America but also for Asia as demonstrated in the Chinese revolution of 1949.

During the European War of 1914 to 1918 and the World War of 1939 to 1945 it was customary to attribute every untoward event to the malevolent activities of the Germans. Now that a defeated Germany can no longer serve as a scapegoat, Russia has taken its place. Whether

1069

there be trouble in northern Africa or India, in the Balkans or in Korea, it is always alleged that the red hand of the Soviet Government is to be seen.

The capitalist press and governments talk as if propaganda is reprehensible in itself and imply that they are free from its taint. Whether propaganda be good or bad, their second allegation is preposterous. Most of the newspapers in the world are carrying on, editorially and otherwise, an anti-socialist pro-capitalist and anti-communist propaganda. Some of these journals are unofficially but more or less directly the mouthpieces of the foreign offices in their countries, which are controlled by capitalists.

All governments carry on more or less propaganda. In addition to actively promoting and aiding capitalist enterprises, which may be legitimate so long as the peoples of these countries accept capitalism, these foreign offices often utter denunciations of other economic systems in statements issued to the public or in instructions to their representatives which are not published. Such denunciations are contrary to the spirit of free institutions. In every country which professes to be democratic the people have the right to choose whichever system they prefer and to change it if they see fit. Hence it is improper for a foreign office to assume an irreconcilable and intransigent attitude toward any system whatsoever.

The chief bugaboo of the Occident in its relation to the Orient is its fear of Oriental immigrants. It is alleged that the "yellow peril" is the vast horde of dark-colored people eager to migrate to Western countries, where they will lower the wages of the native workers, contaminate the purity of the superior blood of the white race, introduce their heathen religions in opposition to the only true religion—namely, Christianity—practise their immoral ideas, bring along their alien manners and customs, and procreate their numerous progeny. So runs the argument, especially in English-speaking countries, where it is widely believed that Western culture is seriously threatened by a wave of migrants from the East whose culture is held to be much inferior. All of these fears strengthen the prejudice against the darker races.

Europe is twice as densely populated as Asia. This comparison is not as significant as it appears to be, because vast regions in Asia covered by deserts and mountain ranges are almost uninhabitable. Even after allowance is made for these uninhabitable areas, Europe is more densely populated than Asia. On the other hand, the density of population of North America is less than one third, and that of Africa and of South America is less than one fifth that of Asia. If, therefore, there is danger of an overwhelming wave of Asiatic immigration, the

1070

Western Hemisphere, Australia, and Africa rather than Europe are threatened. Hence the exclusion laws against Oriental immigrants which have been enacted by the United States, Canada, Australia, New Zealand, and the British colonies in Africa.

It is generally believed that China is very densely populated because it has the largest population of any one country. According to a census of 1948, the population of China proper is 463,492,418, and its density of population 203 per square mile, as compared with a density of a little over one hundred for Europe. In that case its density is less than one third that of Belgium and of Holland, less than one half that of the United Kingdom, and of Germany, and less than three fifths that of Italy.

According to a government estimate of 1949 the population of India is 342,105,000 and its density of population is 275 per square mile. These figures for the two most populous countries of Asia and of the world indicate that the density of population of China and India is not excessive as compared with European countries, but is much greater than that of the countries of the Western Hemisphere, the density of the United States being about one fourth that of China and less than one fifth that of India.

In Japan the situation is very different and is of great significance because Japan is more industrialized than any other Asiatic country, and indicates what may happen in other countries. Prior to 1920 the Japanese population was counted by means of the police registration. According to the first census, the population in 1920 was approximately 56,000,000. According to an official estimate, on July 1, 1951, the population of Japan was 84,3000,000, and its density of population was 570 per square mile. In 1951 Holland had a density of population of 766 per square mile.

Japan is already more densely populated than any European country with the exception of Belgium and of Holland. On the basis of inhabitable area, it is still more densely populated, because in Japan only 19 per cent is habitable, whereas in Belgium the percentage is 74, in England and Wales 73, and in Holland 67. Inasmuch as Japan is predominantly an agricultural country, this fact is of greater significance than it is in industrial countries such as Belgium and England. The tillage area is what counts, and this is greatly reduced by the mountainous character of the country.

Emigration is the first remedy usually suggested. In 1925 there were 617,929 Japanese residing abroad. During that year the number of emigrants was about 10,000. Emigration is doing little to relieve the situation. The Japanese are excluded from all English-speaking countries bordering on the Pacific. The Latin-American countries are open to them. Most of these countries are climatically well fitted for the Japanese. But they are far away and will probably not be used to any great extent for some time to come.

To the west lie Manchuria and Siberia, vast areas which are as yet little populated. They belong to the colder latitudes, while the Japanese culture is mainly adapted to a more genial climate. So that the Japanese will have to learn to adjust themselves to a colder climate if they are to make use of these regions. Political obstacles now stand in the way. The Japanese Government does not feel inclined to encourage emigration to northeastern Asia until it is able to assure protection of private property rights to its nationals.

For the present the Government is concentrating attention upon a better distribution of population within Japan itself. The northern island, Hokkaido, is only one sixth as densely populated as the whole of Japan proper. The northern provinces of the principal island, Honshu, also are less densely populated than the average. Most of Hokkaido lies between 42 and 46 degrees of north latitude and is subject to severe winters, so that adjustment to climatic conditions is necessary.

This is the first measure used by the Government in dealing with this problem. It is only a temporary palliative and cannot solve the fundamental problem of the rapid increase of population. The next method which suggests itself is agricultural and industrial development. Every one who has traveled in the densely populated regions of Japan knows the painful care with which each bit of fertile soil on hill and mountain-side as well as in the valleys and on the plains is utilized. The ground is terraced and water is brought to it by means of irrigation or otherwise. It is not likely that in the thickly inhabited regions much more can be done in the way of agricultural expansion. It is true that the methods used are still very primitive. The shocks of grain, cut and gathered by hand, are beaten upon a wooden bench in order to loosen the heads and kernels, which fall upon mats spread on the ground. These mats are beaten with large wooden flails. The grain is then put into a sieve which is pushed back and forth in grooves. The final stage is reached when the grain is poured on the mats from a height of six to eight feet while a large fan vigorously wielded blows away the small chaff and dust. All of this work is done by hand.

Geographical conditions preclude the extensive use of machinery in Japanese agriculture. There are none of the vast prairies of America or the broad plains of Europe and continental Asia. Tractors and harvesters cannot be used on steep hill and mountain-side. Intensive methods of agriculture can be somewhat improved. Recent industrial

1072

development has caused a movement from country to city. Agriculture cannot keep the pace with a rapidly growing population.

It is estimated that Japan proper has 16,407,200,000 tons of coal. Most of it is bituminous and lignite, little of it being anthracite. There is very little iron in Japan proper, the supply being estimated at 50,000,000 tons. In Korea and Formosa there are about 50,000,000 tons. It is estimated that China, so far as it has been explored, has at least 7,000,000,000 tons and probably much more. Under these circumstances there can be little hope for the development of a large iron and steel industry in Japan. The same can be said to a greater or less extent of almost every other manufacturing industry.

With comparatively limited natural resources and the competition of cheaper labor in China and elsewhere is Asia, Japan cannot expect a great industrial development. This is not entirely a misfortune, for the industrial system has brought its drawbacks as well as its benefits to Japan. During the European War of 1914 to 1918 it experienced a great business and industrial boom and prices rose very high. Since 1920 it has shared with Occidental nations the post-war depression with all of its attendant drawbacks. While the population is much more rural than in most Western countries, there is a distinct movement toward the cities.

All of these are characteristic features of the modern industrial system. They indicate that this system is not in every respect to be desired. Would it not be preferable to try to produce food enough to sustain the country and then manufacture only as much as is needed to pay for necessary imports? This would obviate an expensive and dangerous commercial as well as military and naval competition with highly industrialized countries. Japan may have to come to this policy eventually. It might therefore be wiser to adopt it at once, and thus save the waste involved in an attempt to compete with the strong industrial nations which is doomed to fail.

If this policy is followed, the population will have to be stabilized at a figure not much above the present number. In order to accomplish such stabilization, either an outlet will have to be found for the excess population, the difficulties in the way of which are indicated above, or else the increase of population must cease. Both the birth- and death-rates are above the usual European and American rates. The death-rate is certain to fall owing to improved sanitation. The birth-rate will have to fall still more in order to check the increase of population.

Like all Occidental nations, Japan faces the necessity of exercising birth-control. This idea is not in accord with the family ideal which still prevails, and which demands as many children as possible

1073

to honor and work for their parents. Until recently the advocacy of birth-control was rigorously repressed by the police. However, in this regard Japan lags only a few years behind the United States. There are still legal restrictions upon the dissemination of information with regard to contraceptive measures in the United States.

Java and Madura have the highest density of population in the world. It is estimated that they had about 5,000,000 inhabitants at the beginning of the nineteenth century, and now have about 50,000,0000, or a density of about 1000 per square mile. This tenfold increase is due mainly to the sanitation and intensive methods of cultivation which have been introduced by the Dutch. Apart from Japan and Java, Oriental countries are not more densely populated than European countries in general, while their rate of increase at present is probably smaller than that of some American countries.

There are, nevertheless, disquieting features which create a serious Oriental problem of population. The family system which is prevalent encourages the procreation of as many children as possible. Early marriage, which is characteristic of this system, brings the generations closer together than in the Occident. Contraceptive methods are almost unknown, and the family ideal and various religious beliefs and moral ideas arouse strong prejudices against birth-control.

Industrialization will doubtless result in the urbanization of the Orient. At present there are comparatively few large cities. The largest Asiatic cities are Tokio and Shanghai with perhaps seven millions each. Calcutta may have six millions.[1] Osaka, Bombay and Jakarta have about two and a half millions each; and Chungking and Tientsin about two millions each. The United States alone has at least ten cities or urban districts containing over a million inhabitants each, though it has a total population of perhaps not much more than one third as great as that of China proper.

Large cities have played an important part in the economic and cultural evolution of the Occident. They have also given rise to great ills by making life excessively complicated and artificial, and by cutting off a large part of mankind from an intimate contact and relation with nature. Industrialization and its consequent urbanization may bring the same benefits, but will certainly bring the same ills in their train to the Orient. The benefits may not outweigh the disadvantages.

So long as the Oriental standard of living is far below that of the Occident, Western labor is justified in wishing protection against cheap competition. A world-wide industrialization under capitalism will gradually equalize the standard of living. It will be a long and

[1] In 1954 in Tokio and Calcutta I was told that each city numbers over 7,000,000 population, the latter because of the sudden influx of refugees from East Bengal, now a part of Pakistan.

slow process. While it is going on, Western exclusion of Eastern labor will be a constant source of friction and irritation and will seriously disturb harmonious and mutually helpful cultural relations. International socialism would obviate this difficulty because the remuneration of labor the world over would then be based upon productivity instead of the more or less artificial national standards which now prevail, and the economy of scarcity which is inherent in capitalism, and goods would move freely to wherever they are needed unchecked by tariffs and other national barriers.

The special monopolistic interests and privileges of the owners of capital and of land reduce in varying degrees in different parts of the world the remuneration of labor as measured by productivity, and also interfere materially with the free movement of goods. Under the capitalist system the fundamental economic laws of supply and demand, of production and consumption, and of the competition of laborers according to their respective abilities and of goods according to their respective utilities, cannot work out freely on a world-wide scale. At present capitalism is so strongly entrenched, that there is no immediate prospect of international socialism, and of a world-wide economic and political organization which could solve these basic problems of the production and distribution of wealth, and of the growth and migration of population.

While there remain large areas with rich natural resources which are comparatively untouched, a premium is placed upon the continuance of the capitalist system. When efficiently exploited, these resources yield large returns to the application of capital, and also usually high wages to labor. The United States has been the favored land in this regard during the past two centuries. The capitalists will exploit the natural resources of Africa and South America as well as of Europe and North America. At the cost of continuous cold or hot war, they will try to overthrow collectivism in China, and the Soviet Union, so as to exploit their huge resources.

So long as widely differential returns from the application of capital and labor persist, capitalism may not be eliminated. Until an equilibrium between natural advantages and density of population the world over, resulting in a comparatively uniform standard of living, has been attained, it is not likely that a world-wide collectivist system will come into being. The demotic fate of the Orient is therefore bound up with the future political and economic organization of mankind.

The significance of density of population must be interpreted in terms of the relative availability for a given territory of the supply of energy for productive purposes, as well as of the area and fertility of the arable soil, and the extent of the mineral resources. The accompanying table indicates the resources of mechanical energy derived from coal, petroleum and water power in the different parts of the world in so far as they have been surveyed up to the middle of the 20th century. Of the energy resources for the world included in this table, 83.6 percent are derived from coal, 15.8 percent from water power, and only 0.6 percent from petroleum.[2] While the latter bulks large at present in transportation, warfare, and heating and lighting, it cannot be an important factor for production in the more distant future. Atomic energy and other forms of energy which have not yet been utilized in production may change considerably the picture presented by this table.

According to this table Europe outside of Soviet Russia has the largest supply of mechanical energy in relation to its territory. North America with its much greater area is a close second. Asia, excluding the U.S.S.R., has about two-thirds as much as Europe, while Soviet Russia as a continental area has less than half as much as North America. The other continental areas are far more poorly endowed with sources of mechanical energy.

Of the selected countries Germany has the largest supply of mechanical energy per square kilometer with the British Isles a fairly close second. The United States has about half as much per square kilometer as Germany for its much greater area. In Asia China proper has more than twice as much per square kilometer as Japan proper and more than ten times as much as India.

The continental areas and countries lacking in resources of mechanical energy will be handicapped unless this lack is compensated for by mineral resources or fertile soil. The manufactured products of the industrial regions can be exchanged for the mineral products of the mining regions and the cultivated products of the agricultural regions. This will furnish the only sound and stable basis for a given density of population at a high standard of living. It can be calculated only by the planning agencies of a world federation of geo-economic regions such as has been described in Chapters XLV to XLVII.

The most fortunate regions are those with large mineral and energy resources as well as much arable soil. They are the regions which can support the most dense population. With the free operation of the economic laws of supply and demand, which can be assured by

2 According to a survey of the visible reserves of fuel and power in the world in 1937 by the U.S. Department of State, coal, lignite, peat and fuelwood constituted 73.2 per cent, water power 26.7 per cent and petroleum 0.1 per cent. (*Energy Resources of the World*, Washington, 1949, p. 120.)

Of the 405,000 million kilowatt-hours of electricity available in the world in 1937, the State Department estimated that three-fifths were consumed in industry and one-fifth in domestic, commercial and public establishments. (P. 11.)

a world government which prohibits discriminatory measures by national governments, an equilibrium between population and natural resources and soil fertility will be attained.

World Resources of Mechanical Energy in Terms of Millions of Tons of Bituminous Coal *

(Sources of energy included are coal, petroleum, and water power which is taken as 1000 times the annual coal equivalent because it is inexhaustible.)

	Total in million tons	Tons per square kilometer
The world	8,670,285.8	65,505.3
Continental areas		
Europe (excluding U.S.S.R.)	799,548.8	147,382.3
North America	3,087,143.6	137,927.9
Asia (excluding U.S.S.R.)	2,347,544.1	96,440.1
U.S.S.R.	1,313,685.3	62,033.6
Africa	765,005.3	25,559.8
Australia	141,158.0	18,563.7
Oceania	190,477.7	17,064.1
South America	166,881.0	9,199.1
Selected countries		
Germany	308,170.5	655,681.9
British Isles	177,047.5	565,647.0
United States	2,513,693.4	320,665.1
Poland	97,380.5	250,980.7
China (18 provinces)	2,158,840.0	246,583.6
Czechoslovakia	32,932.1	235,229.3
Union of South Africa	210,370.0	172,152.2
Japan (proper)	41,658.2	109,053.4
France	33,472.0	60,747.7
Yugoslavia	11,359.0	45,802.4
Italy	11,320.4	36,517.4
Spain	17,220.0	34,234.6
India	99,754.6	21,296.8
Rumania	6,142.5	20,822.0
Manchukuo	4,804.0	3,400.0

*Abridged and adapted from A. P. Usher, "The Steam and Steel Complex," in *Technology and International Relations*, edited by W. F. Ogburn, Chicago, 1949, p. 69.

See also U.S. Department of State, *Energy Resources of the World*, Washington, 1949.

Chapter LXIII

The Interpenetration of Culture Between East and West

AS I have already indicated in Chapter LIV, the Orient and the Occident are separated from each other by the greatest natural barrier in the world—namely, the Hindu Kush, the Pamirs, the Kwenlun, the Karakoram, and the Himalaya ranges, with the Tienshan and Altai ranges extending to the northeastward. It is reinforced by the deserts of eastern and southern Persia, Baluchistan, Turkestan, and Mongolia. Between this lofty barrier and the West lies an indeterminate zone comprising the Arabian peninsula, Mesopotamia, Persia, Asia Minor, Egypt, and the north African littoral, which belong to the Mediterranean area but have been considerably influenced by Oriental culture. Until recently they have not followed the lead of European cultural evolution, but are doing so now to an increasing degree.

The West and the East actually meet geographically very little. The chief point of physical contact is in northeastern Asia, in Manchuria and Korea where complicated and conflicting economic, political and cultural forces are at work. For several centuries the Russians have been pushing their way across northern Asia until they reached the Pacific Ocean. Including the Asiatic states over which the Soviet Government exercises a protectorate, Russia now holds political sway over more than one third of Asia. Siberia alone is considerably more than one fourth of Asia and much larger than the whole of Europe. While the northern section is within the polar circle, much of Siberia is capable of agricultural and industrial development, so that it will eventually support a fairly large population.[1] If Mongolia and Sinkiang or Chinese Turkestan, whose combined area is greater than that of China proper, can be irrigated, they also may become thickly

[1] See Maurice Parmelee, *Geo-Economic Regionalism and World Federation* New York, 1949, p. 10.

1078

inhabited. Assuming that the Siberian population will be predominantly white and that of Mongolia and Sinkiang yellow, there will then be compact masses of Easterners and Westerners adjoining each other whose cultural contact will doubtless have far-reaching results. In any case, the construction of railroads and establishment of aviation routes across Asia will bring the East and the West much closer together.

Western education was introduced by missionaries and Western governments which had made conquests in the Orient. European settlements, such as the cantonments in India and the foreign concessions in China, furnished examples of Western modes of living. Many Easterners were encouraged to go to Europe and America to study. The Japanese and Chinese went mainly to the United States, which was at first more accessible. The Indians went chiefly to Great Britain. The Western education which the Orient has received has been largely of an Anglo-Saxon character, and English is the best-known European language in the East.

The missionary influence is decreasing, and Western domination will be eliminated eventually. But Oriental governments and institutions will probably continue to imitate Occidental educational methods. Modern Oriental journalism was derived entirely from America and Europe. If the transformation of the East goes on at its present or an accelerated rate, it will result in the greatest cultural change which has ever taken place in so short a space of time.

The feature of Occidental culture which the Orient needs most of all is its science. Of religion it has plenty and to spare of its own. Its ethical standards are probably better suited to itself than those of the Occident. It has already borrowed the applications of science to a certain extent, but has only partially acquired its spirit and theory. It is imitating Western industrial methods and to a smaller degree imbibing the economic ideas which underlie those methods. It has borrowed much of Occidental law and some of its political institutions, and is in imminent danger of embracing the baneful effects of Western nationalism, patriotism, militarism, and imperialism.

The Orient has as yet taken little of the philosophy, art, and literature of the Occident. In its business buildings and factories Western architecture has been imitated because it is better adapted to these purposes, but much less in its domiciles, temples, and other structures. The upper classes are imitating Western modes of living to a certain extent in dress (more by the men than by the women), diet, furniture, and in a common social life for men and women. But for the great masses of the East the marital and family life and the position of woman remain much the same.

The nationalist movement may hinder this process of Westerni-

1079

zation to a certain extent. Such events as the victory of the Japanese over the Russians in 1905, the European War of 1914 to 1918, the Amritsar massacre of Indians by British soldiers in 1919, the Shanghai, Hankow, and Canton riots in 1925, the outbreak between 1920 and 1940 of European dictatorships contradicting Occidental professions of democracy, and the war of 1939 to 1945 with its aftermath of rampant militarism instigated largely by the United States which had professed heretofore to be the disinterested friend of Oriental countries, and yet was trying to force the Orient into the conflict between capitalism and communism, have injured Western prestige greatly. But whether for good or for ill, the economic factors may prove to be the strongest, and may sweep the Orient into the same course of industrial and political development as has characterized the Occident during the past two or three centuries. How much of a distinctively Eastern culture will survive when this overwhelming wave has passed over the Orient it is impossible to surmise.

European languages became known in the Orient in the order that traders, conquerors, and missionaries came from the West— namely, Portuguese, Spanish, Dutch, French, English, and German. Portuguese has disappeared except in the few small Portuguese colonies. Spanish persists in the Philippine Islands, but is being supplanted by English. Dutch is used in the East Indies, and French in Indo-China. The Germans came too late to acquire extensive possessions, and have lost their colonies since the European War of 1914 to 1918. Prior to this war German had a certain vogue in Japan owing to Japanese admiration for the German economic, political, and military system. But the Japanese have forsaken German for English, whose greater commercial value they recognize.

Most of the Japanese, Chinese, and Indian students who have gone to the West have studied in Great Britain or the United States and have returned with a knowledge of English. The British conquest of India and other Oriental countries, and the American occupation of the Philippines, introduced English into many of the educational institutions of those countries. The British and American missionaries have done the same in most of their schools throughout the East. To a certain extent this was inevitable, because text-books, a general literature of, and a vocabulary for many of the subjects taught did not exist in the Oriental languages.

The foreign-language press in the Orient is principally in the English language and has helped to make English known. It has also had a vast influence upon Oriental journalism. In view of the very small number of Westerners who reside and travel in the East, the large number of these foreign-language journals is at first sight surprising. Many of the educated natives, especially in China, have

1080

depended largely upon the foreign press for their news of the world. Many special interests considered it advisable to have organs of their own. In China this was true not only of the foreign interests, such as the British, American, and Japanese, but also of various Chinese political, commercial, and militarist groups, and a similar situation, but to a less extent, exists in Japan and several other Oriental countries.

Journalism in its modern form has been learned by the Orient entirely from the Occident. In Japan the daily press began in Yokohama in 1871 and is modeled chiefly after the American pattern. The Japanese papers rival the American in their circulation, owing to the high degree of literacy due to the compulsory elementary school system for both sexes. According to the Japan Year Book, 1927, the total daily circulation was estimated at about 5,000,000, or one to every eleven or twelve of the population. The Osaka "Mainichi" and "Asahi" claimed a circulation of about 700,000 each.

The first English-language newspaper in China was the "Canton Register," founded in 1827. The Chinese press made a very small beginning about the middle of the nineteenth century, at first copying most of its contents from the foreign-language press. There are now said to be more than one thousand Chinese dailies, weeklies, and monthlies. Shanghai is the principal journalistic center. Two of the Shanghai dailies, the "Shun Pao" and the "Sin Wan Pao," probably had a circulation of about 50,000 each. Like the Japanese press, Chinese journalism is modeled after the American pattern. Owing to the small amount of literacy, the total circulation is below that of Japan.[2]

In India were many British newspapers, some of the principal ones being the "Statesman" and "Englishman" of Calcutta, the "Times of India" of Bombay, the "Pioneer" of Allahabad, and the "Mail" of Madras. There is a larger number of Indian newspapers published in the English language. Among the principal ones are the "Forward," "Bengalee" and "Amrita Bazaar Patrika" of Calcutta, the "Evening News of India" and "Indian Daily Mail" of Bombay, the "Hindustan Times" of Delhi, and the "Hindu" of Madras.[3] As the literacy in the

[2] See Y. P. Wang, *The Rise of the Native Press in China*, Columbia University, New York, 1924.

"While China can justly claim the most ancient of the world's magazines and the oldest of newspapers in point of continuous publication, the daily press as it exists today in China, is, as the history of the European press in China shows, the result of the efforts of the Americans and British at Canton and Hongkong in this direction." (P. 16.)

[3] The Indian Year Book, 1927, stated that in 1923-24 there were 1363 newspapers in India, but does not indicate how many of them were in the English language.

native languages in 1921 was 22,600,000, or barely 7 per cent, and the literacy in English was only 2,500,000, the total circulation of these journals in proportion to the population was very small.

The explanation for these Indian papers in the English language is the great diversity of tongues, of which 222 were reported by the British census of 1921. This also explains why the transactions of the Indian National Congress and of many other congresses are conducted chiefly in English. In Bombay in 1925 I was present at a *mahasabha* (great meeting) attended by many leaders from all parts of India, at which most of the speeches were in English. In Western India the Bengalee language is as little known as Russian in England. In New Delhi in 1954, I attended a session of the House of the People at which Prime Minister Nehru and other members spoke in English.

In fact, English has become the principal medium of communication for the educated Indians, and the language most used in the higher educational institutions. The following statistics of the principal languages are compiled from the census of 1921:

Western Hindi	96,714,000
Bengalee	49,294,000
Telegu (Dravidian)	23,601,000
Marathi	18,798,000
Tamil (Dravidian)	18,780,000
Panjabi	16,234,000
Rajasthani	12,681,000
Kanarese (Dravidian)	10,374,000
Oriya	10,143,000
Gujarati	9,552,000
Burmese (Mongolian)	8,423,000
Malayalam (Dravidian)	7,498,000
Lahnda or Western Panjabi	5,652,000

All of the above-mentioned languages, unless otherwise indicated, are Indo-European. The Indo-European languages, based upon Sanskrit, were spoken in 1921 by 232,846,000. They are written mostly in the Deva-nagari or Sanskrit characters. Urdu, called Hindustani by the British, is a form of Hindi with a considerable admixture of Persian and Arabic, and is written in Persi-Arabic characters. It originated during the Mohammedan domination and is spoken largely in the northwest and by many of the Moslems. It was generally recognized as the native official language. It is the official language of Pakistan.

The Dravidian tongues of the south belong to an entirely differ-ent linguistic family from the Indo-European. They were spoken in 1921 by 64,128,000. The principal Dravidian languages are Telugu, Tamil, Kanarese, and Malayalam.

The Tibeto-Chinese tongues of the north of India were spoken in 1921 by 12,885,000, and with Burmese belong to the Mongolian linguistic group. Compared with the Indo-European and Dravidian languages they have played a very small part in Indian culture.

The factors which have been described—namely, conquests by Occidental powers, missionary activities, the influence of Western education and the foreign language press—have established English as the predominant European language in the Orient. To these factors must be added the tremendous economic, political, military and cultural prestige of Great Britain and the United States in the present era. In fact, while traveling in the Orient it seemed to me that its predominance there might turn the scales in its favor as against its rival European tongues and make it the universal medium of com-munication the world over. In any case, it is not likely now that Pidgin-English will become a universal lingua franca. While it is a picturesque and, to English-speaking peoples, amusing jargon, it is not sufficiently developed to serve as a cultural or even as an adequate commercial medium of communication.[4]

There is much to be said in favor of English as a universal lan-guage. It is the mother tongue of more people than any other language except Chinese; and Chinese is divided into several dialects which are not mutually comprehensible, so that it is a question whether it is a single language or a family of languages. English, on the contrary, is so much alike the world over that it is mutually comprehensible to all English-speaking peoples. It is by far the most widely diffused language. It has a tremendous commercial, political, and cultural prestige. It contains by far the most extensive literature both in the original and through translations. English is the key to more doors than any other tongue.

English has a rich vocabulary adequate for every need. Its gram-mar is simple, with little unnecessary elaboration of declension and conjugation. Its construction is fairly straightforward and logical. It does not contain the imbecility of sex attributed to inanimate things, except in so far as the poets have introduced this pernicious practice. It is capable of expressing many fine shades of meaning. In fact, there

---

[4] This is an intermixture of English with Chinese, Hindustani, Portuguese, French, etc., used from Japan to India and in Oceania. In Pidgin missionary is "number-one-go-to-heaven-man," God is "big masta fella," and to read is "look book."

is almost a redundancy of ways of expressing the same or similar things.

English has, however, several grave defects.[5] It contains many irregularities in its verbs and plural nouns which are peculiarly difficult to master. It is much inferior as a spoken language to its character as a written language. Its accentuation often is uncertain and wavering. It contains a good many homonyms, that is to say, words with the same or very similar pronunciation but with different spellings and meanings. Its greatest defect is its orthography, which is largely unphonetic. In this undesirable trait it is surpassed only by the classical Chinese, which does not even pretend to be phonetic.

For the hapless foreigner who is trying to learn to speak English, its orthography is a bewildering and time-destroying obstacle. It is an enormous waste for the English-speaking peoples as well, each generation of which has to sacrifice much valuable time to master this stupid system. The Americans have taken a few steps toward reforming their spelling. They are held back by the British, most of whom regard this grotesque anachronism, as well as their equally grotesque currency and weights and measures, with the same blind veneration that the Chinese literati display toward their preposterous syllabary. The British ought to cooperate with their American brethren in removing this blot from the fair name of their common language.[6]

French has graver defects than English in its more complicated grammar, with many irregularities and two genders attributed to inanimate objects. German is even worse, with a still more complicated grammar with numerous irregularities and three genders attributed to inanimate objects, thus making confusion worse confounded. That the latter trait does not even arise out of a universally consistent tendency to sexualize natural objects is indicated by the fact that in French "*soleil*" is masculine and "*lune*" feminine, whereas in German "*sonne*" is feminine and "*mond*" is masculine. If any living language is to become a universal medium of communication, Spanish is perhaps the best fitted for this purpose. Its grammar is comparatively simple and regular. Its orthography is consistently phonetic. Its pronunciation is easy and euphonious. It is the mother tongue of many nations. But it has little commercial, political, and cultural prestige at present. If a dead language is chosen, the Occident would doubtless favor Latin, which is a logically constructed and compact language, while the

---

[5] Havelock Ellis has given an excellent discussion of the faults of the English language in his *Task of Social Hygiene*, London, 1912, Chapter XI, "The Problem of an International Language."

[6] The most notorious instance of unphoneticism in the English orthography is the following: plough (ow), though (owe), through (oo), cough (off), rough (uff), hiccough (up), lough (ock).

Indians would perhaps advocate Sanskrit, which is the origin of many of their languages and one of the oldest of the Indo-European linguistic family. The Indian Constitution of 1949 prescribes Hindi in Deva—nagari script as official, and the English also as official for 15 years from 1949.

If English fails to establish itself as the world's common medium of communication, an artificial language seems to be the most feasible solution for this serious problem. Three such languages have received some publicity—namely, Volapuk, Esperanto, and Ido. The first failed and has disappeared entirely. The third professes to be an improvement on Esperanto, but has not yet succeeded in supplanting it. Esperanto is at the present time the most in vogue.

An artificial language possesses certain great advantages. It is entirely regular, so that after learning a rule it is not necessary to unlearn it in the case of many exceptions. It is derived in large part from roots contained in many living languages. The words are built up from the roots in a logical fashion by means of the addition of affixes which have definite and fixed meanings. The grammar is sufficiently flexible to express any meaning without being unnecessarily complicated and elaborate. It can grow and expand to meet new needs by combining roots and affixes in novel combinations. It does not encounter the rivalry of living languages each of which resents ascendancy by any other. It is not cluttered up with a lot of etymological odds and ends, survivals from the past, such as obsolete and obsolescent expressions, redundant words and phrases derived from two or more linguistic sources, local idioms, dialects, and the like. It is in reality a living language pruned and cured of its worst faults.

It may be alleged that an artificial language cannot attain the graphic vividness of a living language which grows through slang, local variations, etc. Even if this be so, the purpose of an artificial language is to serve as an auxiliary and not necessarily to supplant any living languages. By means of a world-wide organization with a centralized control it can be held to norms of vocabulary, syntax, orthography, and pronunciation which will be equally useful the world over. Moreover, it may influence the various linguistic groups to hold their own mother tongues to similar norms. Like every other human institution which evolves spontaneously, language is clumsy, wasteful, and ill-adapted to attain its purpose. Conscious effort and forethought cannot fail to improve it considerably. Such a world-wide linguistic organization would also be a powerful force for developing an international spirit and promoting international peace.[7]

[7] For an excellent survey of this subject see A. L. Guerard, *A Short History of the International Language Movement*, London, 1922.

Dodd asserts that an international auxiliary language should be idiomless,

Esperanto is more or less widely diffused in many countries of Continental Europe, to a small extent in Latin-American countries, and to a very slight extent in English-speaking countries. It has a central organization, with its headquarters in Switzerland, which is endeavoring to promote more friendly international relations. To what extent an artificial language may serve as a means of communication between the Occident and the Orient remains to be seen. Esperanto may well appeal to the Indo-European languages of India, Persia, and Asia Minor. It cannot make as strong an appeal to the Mongolian, Dravidian, Malay, and other "non-Aryan" languages. Inasmuch as the largest of these linguistic groups, the Mongolian, is less diffused than the Indo-European, no one of them can with justice demand an artificial language based upon itself.

In Japan there is a small so-called "Romanic" movement whose purpose it is to write Japanese in the Roman characters. Short of a predominant living language or an auxiliary artificial language, a common script would be useful in aiding the peoples of the world to learn one another's languages. It might be difficult, however, for some languages, such as Chinese, with its peculiar tonal values, to be written in such a common script.

The Oriental nationalist movement may cause a reaction for a time against the use of European languages. In Hyderabad in 1926 the minister of finance, who had been minister of education, described to me with great pride how he had changed the language of instruction in Osmania University, the highest educational institution of the state, from English to Urdu. The proponents of this change claimed that the students could learn better in their mother tongue, which is true. In this instance, however, this was not a wholly effective argument, because the great majority of the inhabitants of this state are Hindu, and most of the Hindus do not speak Urdu, which was then the official language of the autocratic Moslem government of Hyderabad. So far as I am aware, no other Indian institution of learning which uses English has followed suit by changing to a native language.

In theory there is no more reason why the Orient should use a European language than there is for the Occident to use an Asiatic language. But for some time to come the Orient must learn a great deal from the science and literature of the West. In some ways it can do so more economically through a European language, though this need not always be the case. In the long run the interpenetration and

uninflected, without synonyms and homonyms, phonetic in spelling, uniform in pronunciation everywhere (no dialects), with every letter unique in shape and sound, and have the order of the words obey rules without exception. (S. C. Dodd, "On Measuring Languages," *Jour. of Am. Statistical Assn.*, March 1949, pp. 77-88.)

assimilation of culture between East and West will be greatly accelerated by a common medium of communication, whether that be English, another living language, or an artificial language.

Europeans and Americans usually assume that their culture is superior to that of the Orient. Whether or not this assumption is correct, it renders the West more or less immune to Eastern influence. The great majority of Westerners who have resided in the East have carried their own manners and customs with them to such a degree that they have learned little of the life and culture of the Orient. Even those who have written books about the East have usually displayed little genuine knowledge and no appreciation of Oriental culture. This was true of the earliest and most famous of them all.[8]

Marco Polo was a matter-of-fact merchant who learned very little about the culture of the Asiatic countries he visited and almost nothing about the intimate life of the people. Most of the information in his book is about material things, and being rather credulous even for his time he reported many impossible marvels. His estimates of distances were usually extraordinarily inaccurate. Though apparently loyal to Kublai Khan, who employed him during his long residence in China, he was very Christian and therefore could give no accurate information about the religions of the Chinese, whom he regarded as "idolaters." He was little concerned with moral questions, but when making moral judgments he invariably applied the European ethical code.

The missionary writers have been largely influenced by their religious bias, the imperialists have endeavored to justify their attempts to dominate the Orient, and the tourists have given very superficial and often condescending descriptions. Many of those who have devoted some effort to study the East have been one-sided in their criticisms. Perhaps the best work has been done in the works on Oriental art by writers who were desirous of finding forms of art which are unknown in the Occident.

On the other hand, there have been a few writers who have conceived an uncritical and almost unbounded admiration for Oriental culture, which, while more amiable, is perhaps almost as egregious an error as that of those who can see little or no good in it. During the latter part of his life Lafcadio Hearn adopted the Japanese mode of living with his Japanese wife. Enamored by the beauty of Japanese art and the esthetic feeling displayed by the Japanese in many phases of their life, he ignored almost entirely the uglier aspects of that life.

[8] *The Travels of Marco Polo (The Venetian)*.
Polo was born in 1254, was traveling from 1271 to 1295, wrote his book in 1299, and died in 1324.

Sister Nivedita (Miss Margaret Noble) [9] became an ardent devotee to Hindu religion before going to India. While working with and for Hindu women she acquired an intimate knowledge of the Indian home which she portrayed in her writings. But with the zeal of the neophyte she attempted to justify and idealize almost every phase of Hindu life and religion.

H. Fielding Hall, [10] though a British official, conceived a great admiration for Buddhism and the Burmese manner of living, which he described in a somewhat romantic and rather uncritical fashion. Another British official, Sir John Woodruffe, became an ardent convert to Tantrism, which phase of Hindu religion he zealously expounded. H. Keyserling, [11] with chameleon-like facility, embraced in turn every Oriental religion and philosophy. However, the Orient, like the rest of the universe, served him primarily as a background for his own exaggerated ego.

Reacting hostilely against Western capitalism and the Bolshevist dictatorship in Russia, Bertrand Russell was caught on the rebound by China, where he received a flattering reception from the modern Chinese intelligentsia. While more critical than some of the above-mentioned writers, he often displayed an excessive admiration for Chinese culture. [12] Much more judicious was G. Lowes Dickinson, whose attitude toward the Orient was not unfriendly, but who did not hesitate to criticize severely and usually with acumen. [13]

The Eastern literature concerning the West may be no better than the Western literature concerning the East. But most of the Orientals who have visited the Occident have come with the desire and intention to learn, and have taken back with them much information which has already had a marked effect upon the East. Western criticism of the East is, through its literature, more or less widely known and is having a considerable influence in the Orient. Oriental criticism of the Occident is almost unknown in the West. Few Orien-

---

9 *The Web of Indian Life*, New York, 1904.

10 *The Soul of a People*, London, 1898.

11 *The Travel Diary of a Philosopher*, New York, 1925, trans. from the German.

12 Bertand Russell, *The Problem of China*, New York, 1922.

No people could attain to so high a degree of superiority as Russell attributed to the Chinese. "The Chinese are gentle, urbane, seeking only justice and freedom. They have a civilization superior to ours in all that makes for human happiness." (P. 175.)

He was nearer the truth when he said: "In art they aim at being exquisite, and in life at being reasonable. There is no admiration for the ruthless strong man, or for the unrestrained expression of passion." (P. 200.)

The following assertion is entirely correct: "We must make room for Asia in our thoughts, if we are not to arouse Asia to a fury of self-assertion." (P. 23.)

13 G. L. Dickinson, *An Essay on the Civilisations of India, China and Japan*, London, 1914.

tal books are translated, so that the benefit of such criticism is lost.

During the Dark and Middle Ages the Greco-Roman culture was almost entirely submerged, and the Roman Catholic church throttled the European mind. While the West was passing through this period of barbarism, China was maintaining a much higher level of civilization, and the same was probably true of India. Then came the renascence of learning, the development of science, geographical discoveries, numerous inventions, and the like, which enabled the Occident to forge rapidly ahead of the Orient. The East has many tangible and definite things to learn from the West in the way of science and its applications, political and economic theories, forms of social organization, and the like. What the West has to learn from the Orient is more intangible and therefore not so easy to define and describe.

Many of the Westerners who are favorably disposed toward the East believe that the Occident has much to learn from Oriental religion. In its popular form religion is perhaps even more degraded in the East than in the West. In its more esoteric phases Oriental religion is more philosophic and less militant. While there is no evidence whatsoever for life other than our present mundane existence, if such a life is postulated the Oriental conception of it is on the whole more logical and humane. Christianity and Islam each professes belief in a deity who is responsible for both good and evil in the universe and who creates both good and bad souls. God and Allah each is to blame for the illogical and unjust fate of the bad soul which the deity has created.

The Oriental religions have not attained to the same grotesque extreme of ethical dualism. The Indian religions teach the doctrine of reincarnation, and through the spread of Buddhism this belief has reached eastern Asia. According to this doctrine the individual soul is eternal, and must attain its own salvation by working its way up from a lower to a higher plane. While Confucianism does not include a belief in reincarnation, its central doctrine of the self-development of the superior man is somewhat akin to this phase of the doctrine of reincarnation and encourages self-reliance and an austere self-discipline. From a scientific point of view the eternal soul of the doctrine of reincarnation is no more plausible than the immortal soul created by a Semitic deity. But Oriental religion may be able to temper somewhat the harshness and crudity of Christian and Moslem theology and render it a more satisfactory sedative for the many who are not yet prepared in mind and character to accept the scientific conception of the universe.

There are other things of greater value than religion to be learned from the East. The Chinese family system and the Indian caste system represent lower forms of social organization to which the West cannot and will not revert. The political state furnishes a broader form of social organization capable of accomplishing more for mankind when directed toward that end. But the state and patriotism are in at least one respect more dangerous than the family and filial piety, because they direct loyalty toward what may be and usually is made into a large and effective fighting body and thus render war more destructive and devastating.

The Western economic system is more efficient and productive than the comparatively primitive economic system of the East. But it furnishes fewer guarantees of a permanent livelihood to the individual. The West cannot and should not pattern itself politically and economically after the East. But Oriental life affords the individual a certain measure of stability and security which the Occident should endeavor to introduce into its more progressive and complicated but less stable social organization.

Sex is the same everywhere, but its recognition and expression are considerably influenced by cultural factors. The art of love is perhaps most highly developed in India, where the worship of sex is sometimes carried to a ludicrous and grotesque extreme. At any rate, this worship shows that the Hindus recognize the importance and significance of sex.[14] In eastern Asia also sex is frankly recognized but not worshiped and given a symbolic significance as in India.[15]

The early age at marriage characteristic of Oriental countries is due largely to the family system. The youth of both sexes are expected to accept the spouses chosen for them by their elders in the interest of their families, and to sacrifice any personal preferences which they may have. But early marriage is probably due in part to a recognition of the sexual need which arises as soon as puberty is reached.

In the Occident economic conditions, religious beliefs, and the prevalent ethical ideas have postponed the average age at marriage to several years beyond the time when this need arises. To that extent life is rendered unnatural and contrary to the biological and psycho-

[14] "The Hindu has never believed in the atrophy of any sense or sense-organ. He has therefore idealized and deified every human passion and every phase of human beauty. Sex with all its functions has thus its own apotheosis in the Hindu system of life and thought; and *Kama-shastra* or erotics is one of the oldest Indian sciences. The joys and griefs of amorous life are, therefore, as sacred as the joys and griefs of life in other spheres." (B. K. Sarkar, *Love in Hindu Literature*, Tokio, 1916, p. 70.)

[15] "Eroticism has never been looked upon in China as debasing or sinful. Sex passion as such is appreciated without constraint as a natural instinct, just as the other instincts are. On the other hand, it is not given a mysterious and sacred meaning, nor is it looked upon as something to be worshipped." (Richard Wilhelm, "The Chinese Conception of Marriage, in *The Book of Marriage*, edited by H. Keyserling, New York, 1926.)

logical demands of human nature.[16] Without borrowing the sacrifice of the individual to the family system, the Occident may learn from the Orient a franker recognition of sex and a more adequate means of satisfying the sexual need. Western writers usually denounce early Oriental marriage for the drawbacks often associated with it, but ignore the graver ill of belated Occidental marriage. A good deal of Occidental legislation is directed toward the postponement of mating, such as the laws placing the age of consent at sixteen years or higher, some of the laws concerning seduction and rape, etc. The West should, on the contrary, endeavor to facilitate normal mating at an early age by encouraging the economic independence of women as well as of men, and the free use of contraceptive measures.[17]

The very interesting and significant erotic literature of the Orient is almost entirely ignored by Western writers. The most voluminous treatise on Indian literature gives only five pages to its erotic section, and another voluminous German treatise gives only two or three pages.[18] The works in the English language characteristically ignore it completely, except a book which plagiarizes a page and a half from Winternitz.

The life of the masses the world over is much the same in that they are primarily concerned with satisfying the elementary human wants. There are, nevertheless, many striking differences between Eastern and Western modes of thought and ideals which indicate norms established by thinkers and leaders who influence the common people in a measure.

The Occident exalts work, activity, and accomplishment, while the Orient appreciates leisure. The West values change, progress, and efficiency without clearly recognizing toward what goal. In the East

[16] A British sexologist, Dr. Norman Haire, commented upon the age for normal matings as follows: "This brief outline of a rational sex-education leads us to the age of sexual maturity, which in temperate climates is complete, physically, at about sixteen years of age. At this age normal youths and maidens are ripe for mating. Puberty has ensued as a direct result of the increased activity of the gonads—the boy or girl is now an adult. Mating should occur without further delay. Long postponement of normal sexual activity may lead to physical and mental ill-health, to a continuance of auto-erotic activity (which in the adult is an unsatisfactory substitute for normal sexual intercourse, and which, if persisted in too long, may even lessen the person's fitness for normal mating), or to various forms of sexual aberration." (*Hymen or the Future of Marriage*, London, 1927, pp. 51-52.)

[17] I have discussed these subjects at length in my *Personality and Conduct*, New York, 1918; and in my book entitled *The Play Function of Sex*, 1960.

[18] M. Winternitz, *Geschichte der indischen Literatur*, Leipzig, 1905-20, 4 vols.; L. von Schroeder, *Indiens Literatur und Kultur*, Leipzig, 1887.

I have not seen the following German work: R. Schmidt, *Beiträge zur indischen Erotik*, Leipzig, 1902, second edition, Berlin, 1911.

is prevalent a belief in an eternal rhythm which renders no end possible. Recognizing the finitude of human endeavor in the face of cosmic infinity, the Orient inclines toward meditation and contemplation of a rather passive sort, and is willing to renounce what apparently or in fact cannot be attained.

Partly owing to these differences of thought and ideal, Eastern life is simpler and more tranquil. Oriental society is stable rather than progressive. These phases of its life include features which the Occident may well emulate. The nerve-racking rush of Western life might be tempered by an appreciation of leisure as such, by an enjoyment of life for its own sake.

Oriental dress is not so capricious as to fashion and yet often more colorful. It is on the whole better adapted to climate, and usually does not cover and conceal the body as much as clothing in the Occident. A lighter and more temperate diet should take the place of the heavy food, often drenched with alcohol, of Europe and America.[19]

Oriental art is beginning to receive the recognition and attention which it deserves. Whether it be Chinese poetry or engraving, Japanese music or drawing, Indian painting or architecture, as to line, color, or appreciation of nature, the Occident has much to learn.

These are suggestions of what the West can learn from the East. The Orient is divided into two great cultural zones, the Chinese and the Indian, with several minor cultural systems each of which is more or less closely related to one or the other of the two principal cultures. Which of these two is the most characteristic of the East it is needless to discuss here, and would in any case be more or less futile. Each has its lessons to teach which the Occident can learn if it will overcome its contempt for the Orient and egocentric self-satisfaction. The cultural diversity of the East renders it a richer field for the West to study.

This survey and comparison of Oriental and Occidental culture emphasizes again the essential likeness and fundamental unity of mankind. Owing to this unity, culture is inevitably devoted to similar ends the world over, for it has developed by a process of natural selection for the purpose of fulfilling the basic human needs and desires. Lofty mountain ranges, vast stretches of water, and other natural barriers have hitherto kept the Orient and Occident apart, and have given rise to noteworthy differences and contrasts in their manners, customs, and institutions—in other words, in their methods of attaining the fulfilment of these needs and desires.

While these differences may never disappear entirely, each of these two great divisions of mankind will profit greatly by availing

[19] The high incidence of heart disease in the Occident is now attributed in the main to a rich diet containing much fat, such as cholesterol.

1092

itself of the best features of the other's culture. The natural barriers are rapidly being overcome, so that knowledge and mutual sympathy will take the place of ignorance and isolation. The Orient is already learning many things from Europe and America. It remains for the Occident to follow suit, and to play its part in developing a world-wide civilization shared by the whole of mankind.

Chapter LXIV

Clothing—The Utility and Disutility of Culture

IT has been amply demonstrated in preceding chapters that the evolution of culture has produced numerous practices, customs, ideas, beliefs, and material devices which are injurious to mankind, as well as many which are beneficial. For example, tools have caused an enormous saving of labor and have rendered possible the production of a vast abundance of commodities. But they have also occasioned a high degree of industrialization which has given rise to many ugly consequences, such as monstrous cities. Clothing is a significant illustration both of the utility and of the disutility of culture.

Among the earliest forms of clothing were the girdle, apron, loin cloth passing between the thighs, breast band, and mantle. These garments were not sewn, and were used mainly for decoration and in connection with the sexual functions. As the colder areas were occupied, warmer sewn garments were required, and there evolved the trousers from the loin cloth, the skirt from the apron, the coat from the breast band and mantle. Racial, national and class costumes the world over are derived from these fundamental types and their various combinations.[1]

Clothing should be warm enough to protect the body against cold, for chilliness and shivering are not only uncomfortable, but diminish vitality and may result in serious illnesses. Often more is worn than is called for by the temperature. This is specially true in summer, when artificial modesty and fashion combine to torture the long-suffering body with many garments, when little or nothing is needed. The amount of clothing is often adjusted, especially in winter, to the coldest temperature likely to be experienced during the day or season, and is not diminished to a commensurate degree when the weather becomes milder, or when one goes from out-of-doors to the warmth

[1] The evolution of feminine clothing is discussed by C. H. Stratz, *Die Frauenkleidung*, Stuttgart, 1900; and F. von Reitzenstein, *Das Weib bei den Naturvoelkern*, Berlin, 1923.

1094

of heated houses. The garments should be so constructed and adapted to each other that they can be readily thrown off or put on, according as the wearer is passing from sunshine to shade, from a shielded spot into the wind, from out-of-doors into a house, from exercize to repose, and as the temperature rises or falls with changes in the weather.

In most styles of dress, the warmth is not properly distributed over the different parts of the body. The head, which requires warmth only in extreme cold, is almost always covered out-of-doors, and sometimes indoors as well. The neck, which can be left bare in ordinary temperatures, is almost always clothed in masculine garb, and sometimes in feminine dress. The arms are almost invariably clothed in masculine attire, and often in feminine apparel, and the legs of both sexes are habitually clothed. Ordinarily neither the upper nor the lower limbs suffer when exposed. On the other hand, the abdominal region should be well protected from the cold on account of the viscera underneath. It is often unduly clothed by masculine dress, because the underclothing, trousers, waistcoat and coat overlap at this point, but is not always adequately protected in cold weather by feminine attire. The breast requires a moderate amount of protection, though considerably less than the abdomen. Women require less protection for the upper part of the breast and the shoulders than men, because they have more fat in these regions. There is considerable variation between individuals as to the amount of covering required by the back. The rump and thighs require comparatively little protection, because they are covered with more or less fat. In repose the feet sometimes require covering, because the circulation is not active in the extremities. When walking or running it is rarely ever necessary, unless for protection from rough ground or vegetation.

There are great variations between individuals with respect to all parts of the body, these variations being due mainly to differences in the amount and distribution of fat and in the circulation of the blood. The practice of nudity, especially if begun in infancy, usually serves to harden the individual, thus diminishing the amount of clothing required. Inasmuch as very few are accustomed to this practice, on the average more is worn than is physiologically and hygienically necessary or desirable.

In a few occupations the body needs protection from occupational risks. The blacksmith and the iron molder sometimes must wear a leather apron to keep off the sparks. In most occupations no protection is necessary, so that nudity is entirely feasible so far as the occupation is concerned. Because the skin is habitually covered by clothing, it is generally believed to be more delicate than it actually is. The skin is in reality a relatively tough integument, and will resist ordinary pressures, rubs, scrapes, etc. I have seen a good deal of work, such as digging and carpentering, done unclothed, and have never witnessed a serious injury therefrom. The laborer soon becomes accustomed to adjust the exposed body to the conditions of his occupation. And for at least several months in the year, the freedom from clothing is a blessed relief to the worker and increases considerably his efficiency.

In view of these facts, it is pitiful to observe that manual workers are usually excessively clothed. I have been employed in factories, construction work, on farms, and the like, where this was almost invariably true of my fellow laborers. During the winter I worked in a carpentering and cabinetmaking shop. Though it was heated to a high temperature, so that I could wear with comfort little more than a cotton shirt and a pair of overalls, my comrades wore woolen shirts, sweaters, heavy trousers, and the like. Even in warm weather and out-of-doors, laborers burden themselves with similar garments. Thus the convention of artificial modesty and a low standard of hygiene diminish the efficiency of the workers, and render them unnecessarily miserable.

In certain regions protection is sometimes needed against thorns, brambles and thistles, and noxious vegetation such as poison ivy, and against insects such as mosquitoes, flies and ants, and poisonous animals such as snakes. When tramping through woods and wherever vegetation is dense, it is usually desirable to wear boots and hose or puttees to protect the legs. Many primitive peoples daub the body with clay, ocher or some other earth as protection against insects. Civilized peoples would not care to imitate this example, but use perfumes and ointments for the same purpose. Man's principal task is to adjust himself to his environment, or rather to adapt the natural environment to himself whenever possible. In course of time injurious vegetation will disappear from all inhabited regions, and noxious animals such as scorpions, centipedes, mosquitoes and snakes will vanish entirely from the face of the earth.

In addition to health and safety, comfort is of great importance in designing and manufacturing clothing, for health and comfort promote each other. Garments worn next to the skin should be of a texture so smooth as to cause the slightest possible irritation to the skin. Fine silk and cotton, and synthetic textures such as rayon, nylon and orlon, are most suitable for this purpose. Wool, even of the finest quality, is somewhat irritating and should preferably be worn outside of the garments which are contiguous to the skin. Paper sufficiently soft, smooth and pliable to be worn comfortably next to the skin will be invented. It will then be possible to wear paper garments which can be discarded after use, thus promoting personal cleanliness and saving the vast amount of labor expended in laundering.

Clothing should exert pressure nowhere upon the body. No

1096

garments should be tightfitting. The underclothing may fit closely, but should be sufficiently pliable and elastic to adjust itself to every movement of the body. All the implements of torture with which mankind voluntarily adorns itself, or rather in which it incases itself, as if in strait jackets in prisons and asylums, should be discarded. This means the collar, and especially that abomination of masculine attire, the stiff collar, which binds and chokes the neck as if man were a dog to be chained to its kennel, or a monkey to be tied to a stick. It means that much greater abomination of feminine attire, the corset. It includes belts, and to a less extent garters, which cause discomfort, interfere with the digestive processes, and impede the circulation of the blood. It means above all those instruments of torture, boots and shoes. In no other way has mankind deliberately caused itself more misery than by the use of these agencies of deformation. It is not necessary to go so far afield as the footbinding of Chinese women, and the deformities created thereby, for illustrations. The narrow toes and high heels of the footwear of Occidental women result in a vision of toes jammed together and weakened arches, a nightmare to any one with esthetic sensibilities.

The corset furnishes a repulsive example of the manner in which human beings will deliberately torture and deform themselves, in this instance in the alleged interests of beauty. The chief purpose of the corset is to accentuate some of women's secondary sexual characters. It diminishes the size of the waist, thus making the pelvic and thoracic regions appear to be broader than they really are. It supports the breasts and thus emphasizes their firmness and exaggerates the size of the bust. It causes thoracic breathing, which is regarded as more alluring than abdominal breathing because the rise and fall of the breasts calls attention constantly to these prominent secondary sexual traits.[2] The primary object of the corset is to increase the physical sexual appeal of the human female. In a leisure class it may acquire the secondary purpose of emphasizing her uselessness, and rendering her a symbol of conspicuous waste.[3]

The corset weakens the spine by pushing it forward, and decreases the height. If worn from early youth and tightly laced, it diminishes the size of the pelvic basin, thus lessening the wearer's fitness for childbearing. It forces fat on to the thighs and buttocks, and causes creases

[2] "The tightening of the waist does not merely emphasize the pelvic sexual characters; it also emphasizes the not less important thoracic sexual characters." (Havelock Ellis, *Man and Woman*, London, 1914, 5th edition, p. 285.

[3] "The corset is, in economic theory, substantially a mutilation, undergone for the purpose of lowering the subject's vitality and rendering her permanently and obviously unfitted for work." (Thorstein Veblen, *The Theory of the Leisure Class*, New York, 1899, p. 172.)

1097

and folds in the skin around the waist and under the breasts. It weakens the ability of the breasts to support themselves. It interferes with the digestion and the circulation of the blood, thus darkening the skin around the waist and rendering the face pale. If worn during the latter part of pregnancy, it may do the offspring grave injury. In every respect it is opposed to the development of a strong and well-formed body.[4]

During the twentieth century the harm done by the corset has been mitigated to a considerable extent. Hygienic considerations have diminished the degree of tight lacing. Some of the corsets now worn are designed to equalize the width of the waist and of the hips rather than to exaggerate their differences. These corsets terminate below the breasts, which are supported and covered by brassieres, which minimize rather than accentuate their size and prominence. Over these garments is often worn a one-piece gown in which a waist line is somewhat faintly marked, and which wanders up and down between breasts and hips in obedience to fashions regardless of anatomical considerations. While this garb eliminates the violent stricture at the waist, there still remains a good deal of pressure upon the hips and breasts.[5]

If the straight line in the feminine figure is merely a vagary of fashion, the old-fashioned corset may come back into vogue, because the dictators of fashion have a propensity to revive obsolete fashions, however harmful they may be, as the pendulum swings to and fro. But sport, industrial and business occupations, and the feminist movement are powerful factors for freeing woman from the corset, as from long and clumsy skirts, highheeled and tight shoes, long hair, and the like. Women are becoming more and more the comrades, lovers and mates of men and not so much their dolls, housekeepers and paramours. Rational birth control is gradually taking the place of unrestrained and undirected procreation. Sex in woman is not so likely to be emphasized by artificial means, and the dress of the sexes will not be so sharply differentiated as in the past.

The belt is as harmful as the corset in so far as it constricts the waist, presses against the spine, impedes the circulation of blood, and interferes with the digestion. The one-piece gown, by eliminating the waist band, has diminished this injury for women. But the men have

---

[4] The following book describes the disadvantages of the corset and also of feminine footwear: P. Schultze-Naumburg, *Die Kultur des weiblichen Korpers als Grundlage der Frauenkleidung*, Jena, 1922, first published in 1901.

[5] Kroeber studied the cycle of change in fashion since the middle of the 19th century: "The major proportions of dress change with a slow majesty, in periods often exceeding the duration of human life, and at least sometimes with the even regularity of the swing of an enormous pendulum.' (A. L. Kroeber, "On the Principle of Order in Civilization as Exemplified by Changes of Fashion," in the *American Anthropologist*, New Series 21, July-September 1919, pp. 235-263.)

adopted the belt, especially in summer time when it is used to support the trousers in the place of suspenders. A lightweight and beautiful style of braces for summer wear should be designed, to use so long as men persist in wearing the ugly and uncomfortable trousers. The Bavarian and Tyrolean mountaineer and peasant costume furnishes a graceful pattern.

Boots and shoes cause for men as well as for women not only deformations of the bony structure, such as flat feet due to broken arches, which destroy the form and shape of the feet, but also corns, bunions, callouses, blisters, itches, cracks in the skin between the toes, scaling flesh, ingrowing toenails, excessive sweating and an offensive odor therefrom, and many other discomforts and hygienic ills. Barefoot peoples suffer from no one of these troubles which harass and torture all civilized peoples. During the European War the United States Government drafted into its army in 1917 and 1918 four million men, of whom 85 per cent had specific and well-marked foot troubles. This is not surprising in view of the fact that 65 per cent of American school children already have stiff or spastic feet, because from infancy their feet have been squeezed into ill-shaped shoes. Corns, bunions, and callouses have no roots, as is commonly believed, but are solely due to ill-fitting shoes and stockings. If no footwear whatsoever were used from infancy, all of these troubles would be avoided, while if the footwear fitted well, many of them would be obviated.

Going barefoot is at first difficult for those not brought up to it. The skin of the soles is tender. Footwear has jammed the toes together so that they are not prehensile, and do not furnish a broad and muscular base for the body. The bodily and mental adjustments necessary to save the feet from accidents are lacking. We have developed a footwear physique and psychology, namely, to tread heavily, and not to beware of sharp things and obstructions. We blunder along knowing that our heavy thick-soled shoes will prevent injury from thorns, nails, pointed stones, from stubbing our toes against rocks, from falling objects, and the like. The barefoot pedestrian learns to step lightly, bringing the weight down not only on the heel, which is protected by its thick skin, but also on the ball of the foot. The feet are kept fairly parallel with each other, and there is less likelihood of toeing in or out excessively. They react instantaneously from injurious objects, and the habitually barefoot person learns to place the feet where they are not menaced by falling or moving things. The barefoot pedestrian develops a light and springy tread, which is beneficial for the spine and the whole system, and is much more hygienic than pounding along on the heels of shoes which, even when made of rubber, are not as springy as the heels of the feet themselves. Under ordinary circumstances the barefoot tread is much more comfortable for persons of all ages who are accustomed to it, because of the feeling of ease experienced by the free heel, ball and toes.[6]

The problem of dress is to devise garments and costumes which will promote health, comfort, utility, and beauty. A new style of dress should cover the body no more than is absolutely necessary for warmth or protection, and should be easily removable when no longer needed, as when the sun comes out, the house is heated, or exercise is taken. The garments should be as open and airy as possible, and should not press the body anywhere, except on the shoulders, from which the weight of all of the garments should be suspended.

Experimentation will be necessary before the most suitable types of clothing can be designed. A number of garments now in existence furnish suggestions. On cool summer days and on summer nights a close-fitting sleeveless jersey of cotton or silk knit material covering the breast and abdomen, but not extending under or below the crotch, would ordinarily be sufficient for both sexes. If a little more warmth is needed, a tunic with half length sleeves and extending to the middle of the thigh can be worn. In order to permit the axillary perspiration to evaporate rapidly, sleeves should always be cut out under the arm pits, or at least made loose at that point. A cape with holes for the arms, thus making a sort of sleeveless cloak, and extending to the middle of the thigh or to the knee, is useful, since it can be put on quickly and easily thrown off. It should have a soft and smooth texture which will not irritate the skin. With the addition of a hood, it furnishes excellent protection against rain. It can be readily carried suspended from the neck and hanging behind. With the addition of pockets, it solves the problem of carrying money and other necessary articles. It is a useful garment, in weather when no clothing is ordinarily needed, to carry as a safeguard against a sudden drop in temperature. The Central and South American poncho, which consists of a rectangular piece of cloth with a round hole in the center through which the head is passed, is a useful garment in rainy weather. A hood may be attached to the poncho to protect the head.

A garment resembling the Scottish kilt furnishes excellent protection for the abdomen in cold weather. The kilt is pleated with numerous folds, thus furnishing the warmth of several layers of cloth, and is at the same time very pliable and elastic. It fits closely around the abdomen, and then flares out somewhat and extends to a point a little above the knee. The genuine Scotchman wears nothing under the kilt, which is as it should be, since the air should enter freely

---

[6] "Like Waterton I have found that the feet take very kindly to the earth, however hot or cold or rough it may be, and that shoes, after being left off for a time, seem as uncomfortable as a mask." (W. H. Hudson, *Idle Days in Patagonia*, New York, 1917, p. 218.) See also H. G. Wells' essay entitled "The Misery of Boots."

1100

up to the crotch. If the texture of the kilt is irritating to the skin, it should be lined with a soft material extending to the crotch, or a lightweight shift should be worn not extending below the crotch. The kilt should not be suspended from the waist around which it should fit snugly. It should be fastened to the garment covering the breast, or, if the breast is bare, to straps passing over the shoulders. The upper garment should be in the nature of a shirt, doublet, or blouse with half sleeves. The weight of the material should be adjusted to the season.

The cummerbund or cholera belt, much used in the Orient, also furnishes protection for the abdomen. In its simplest form it is a band of flannel, a foot or so in width, passed around the body and over-lapping in front, and fastened with two or three safety-pins. It gives the abdomen twice as much warmth as the back. It should reach from the breast-bone to a point just above the crotch, thus covering one of the most vital regions of the body. This region is also one of the least protected from an anatomical point of view. With it well covered, it is possible to clothe the rest of the body more lightly.

No garment should pass under the crotch, if it can possibly be avoided. In this region as under the arm pits there is much perspiration, and the air should be permitted to enter freely to evaporate the sweat. Otherwise various forms of skin eruptions and itches are likely to appear. Furthermore, clothing at this point irritates the external genitals constantly, and causes at least slight sexual disturbances in both sexes. This is another of the numerous reasons why clothing should be discarded whenever feasible.

The feet are liable to injury from stubbing the toes, through bruising, cutting, spraining, and from noxious plants and poisonous insects. Among civilized peoples they require protection more than any other part of the body, unless much hardened with usage. Going barefoot should be practised whenever possible. It strengthens the arches, makes the feet agile, and the toes prehensile. Peoples who go barefoot habitually and climb trees have toes which are almost as prehensile as fingers.[7] If the soles are sensitive or the ground rough, light and flexible sandals, which are roomy but fairly rigid around

---

[7] The toes of the Marquesas Islanders, who climb cocoanut and bread-fruit trees a great deal, have been described as follows: "Each brown toe clasped the boughs like a finger, nimble and independent of its fellows through long use in grasping limbs and rocks. This is remarkable of the Marquesans; each toe in the old and industrious is often separated a half inch from the others, and I have seen the big toe opposed from the other four like a thumb. My neighbors picked up small things easily with their toes, and bent them back out of sight, like a fist, when squatting." (F. O'Brien, *White Shadows in the South Seas*, New York, 1920, p. 115.)

the toes, and fit snugly around the heels, can be worn, in which the feet have almost as much exercise as when going barefoot.

Cold, rain, snow, ice, rough ground, thick vegetation, mountain climbing, and various other conditions sometimes require the wearing of shoes or boots. These should be constructed to fit the feet, instead of forcing the feet to fit them, as is usually the case nowadays. They should be straight on the inside line, and rounded instead of coming to a point. They should furnish plenty of room for the free play of the toes, and should have very low heels or none whatsoever, in order to make the gait as nearly as possible like going barefoot. They should be made of very pliable leather, and should be so flexible as to become adjusted readily to the form and the movement of the feet. They should fit closely around the instep, and their weight be borne mainly by the upper side of the instep. The moccasins of the North American Indians furnish an excellent model for shoes, because they are broad-toed, heelless, pliable, light-weight, and more or less watertight. Soles can be added to them for use on rough ground.

Whenever possible shoes should not extend above the ankle. For rough work, in stormy weather, and in wild country, high shoes and boots are often necessary. Boots and shoes are usually not sufficiently smooth on the inside to be worn on the bare feet. Consequently, socks or stockings must be worn, which absorb the perspiration as well as protect the feet from calluses and abrasions.[8] Socks and stockings may be of cotton, silk, wool or synthetic textures. The woolen ones protect the feet and absorb more perspiration, but they are usually too warm and irritate the skin. Boots and shoes should be made as much as possible without the use of nails, because these are almost certain to work their way through and tear the socks to pieces and injure the feet.

Whenever possible boots and shoes should be ventilated, because many foot troubles arise from lack of ventilation. However, ventilation would also admit dampness and cold, so that it has to be dispensed with in footwear which must be watertight. Boots and shoes should be removed upon entering the house, as in Japan and other Oriental countries. By going barefoot, in stocking feet, or in light slippers, the feet receive some ventilation, and the house is kept much cleaner.

[8] The following citation indicates why there is copious perspiration of the feet, under the armpits and in the vicinity of the crotch: "Sweat glands are distributed over the entire skin except that of the glands and the inner layer of the praeputium penis. They are most numerous in the palms and soles. In the axilla there are large forms with 30 mm. of coiled tube. They acquire their large size at puberty and have been considered as sexual 'odoriferous' glands. In the vicinity of the anus there are branched sweat glands, and the large unbranched 'circumanal glands' together with other modified forms." (F. T. Lewis, Stohr's Histology, Philadelphia, 1906, p. 326.)

The Japanese wear, when not imitating injurious Occidental customs, socks with the big toe separated from the other toes, or no socks at all. Sandals are worn in the street, and clogs and buskins in rainy weather. Both sandals and clogs are usually retained on the feet by means of a strap passing between the big toe and its neighbor. Thus the feet and especially the toes receive full play, and are much more agile and prehensile than the feet of Occidentals squeezed into tight and stiff boots and shoes. However, the Japanese sandals, and, to a less extent, clogs, develop in their wearers the habit of toeing in. This is no worse than and possibly not as bad as the Western habit of toeing out. It is preferable to keep the feet as nearly as possible parallel to each other. Loose sandals and slippers encourage the habit of shuffling along the ground, which is not as graceful or as hygienic as a firm, cleancut step. When wearing clogs, the body is part of the time balanced on the forward cleat of the clog, and is, so to speak, falling forward as in running. While wearing the native garb in Japan, I discovered that it is surprisingly easy to walk and even to run on clogs, at any rate on smooth ground, and that the gait is pleasing and graceful. The clattering of numerous *geta* (clogs), however, sometimes adds too much to the city noises.

The habit of kneeling and squatting develops the muscles of the legs and hips, and is said to have rendered arteriosclerosis less prevalent in Japan than in Europe. But it diminishes the stature slightly, and may have encouraged a rounded back.

In Asia Minor and the Balkans I have seen the peasants wearing sandals similar to the North American Indian moccasins, but without giving the feet so much protection. In Turkey I have often seen clogs used in rainy weather. But in countries of Occidental culture tight and rigid footwear usually prevent the feet and toes from receiving adequate exercise. In default of better opportunity, they can be given a little exercise for a few minutes in bed at night.

Light garments which can be quickly put on or off, and readily carried when not being worn, are greatly needed. In gymnosophic recreation and holiday centers, when clouds or the approach of evening chills the air, it is customary to put on a little clothing. Under garments are ugly, and outer garments are not only ugly but often uncomfortable to the skin. The light cape or cloak described above ordinarily furnishes sufficient warmth, and can be cut with graceful lines. Other garments may also be devised which are beautiful, and do not suggest the ordinary dress of a society where artificial modesty prohibits the exposure not only of the body but also of under clothing. The use of the latter may be objectionable because under garments are usually though not necessarily ugly and often unclean.

During menstruation concealment of the mons veneris may be

1103

considered desirable. At present the feminine wardrobe furnishes the chemise, skirt, bloomer, bathing suit or trunks for this purpose. But these garments are unsuitable in themselves, and suggest the ordinary dress of today. Moreover, they all cover more of the body than is necessary. A loin or breech cloth furnishes sufficient cover. Or a small sanitary napkin of highly absorbent cotton may be worn internally. During the later stages of pregnancy a lightweight short skirt or apron suspended by straps from the shoulders may be worn, though ordinarily there is no occasion for concealment.

Much can be learned with respect to dress from the past as well as from the present. In many great cities and capitals are museums containing numerous costumes of the past, some of which furnish suggestions. Clothing in the past as in the present has usually been too plentiful and complicated, partly on account of artificial modesty and partly due to the vagaries of fashion. Hygienic dress is entirely free from bondage to the convention of artificial modesty, and covers the body only when necessary. It is uninfluenced by fashion, and is governed solely by utility and beauty. The garments worn are as few and as scanty as is compatible with the rigor of the weather and the necessity for bodily protection. Furthermore, conventional dress usually distinguishes sharply between the sexes, in order to accentuate sexual differences. Gymnosophic dress needs to distinguish little if at all between the sexes, because gymnosophists are well acquainted with the actual and genuine sex differences and do not need to have them emphasized by artificial means. The only sex differences called for are those due to slight differences in the distribution of artificial warmth due to variations in the distribution of fat, and occupational differences.

I have already mentioned several features of the conventional dress of today. The feminine attire is in certain respects preferable to the masculine. The neck and arms are often left bare or lightly clothed. Thin stockings or none at all and lightweight shoes are usually worn. Many women even in winter wear cotton, linen, rayon, nylon or silk chemises and drawers and light-weight clothing over them, so that the air can come up more or less freely under the drawers and between the thighs, and the region of the crotch is left comparatively free. While the preposterous goddess of fashion creates many hideous monstrosities, she also blunders now and again upon beautiful effects. On the other hand, feminine apparel does not always sufficiently protect the sensitive abdominal region. Corsets and highheeled and narrow-toed shoes are among the most diabolical of the many abominations invented by perverted human ingenuity. Tight bodices and skirts often restrict freedom of bodily movement. It can perhaps be said that the feminine attire is, on the whole, cooler, more airy and more beauti-

1104

ful than the masculine. But the latter attire is, on the whole, better suited for exercise, for out-of-doors, and for cold weather.

So far I have spoken only of day clothing. The god of prudery has decreed that even in the secret places of the night, the privacy of the sleeping compartment, and the intimacy of one's own bed, a garb must be worn. Since human eyes cannot pierce the darkness, night clothing is presumably intended to protect the shamed eyes of prudish deities and spirits which, like bats and owls, can see in the dark and haunt the nocturnal spaces. Some time ago there was imported from the Orient a costume known as pajamas, which is in its original habitat a day costume. In the Occident it has become a widely used nocturnal garb, and graces the forms of bashful maidens and callow youths, of buxom matrons and portly gentlemen. It consists of an upper garment resembling a lady's bodice, often more or less ornately decorated, and a pair of long trousers fastened at the waist. In other words, it is a costume sufficiently elaborate to be suitable for street-wear in the most prudish and conventional community, and is, in fact, used for this purpose in certain Oriental countries and other parts of the world. It causes stricture around the waist, which is always harmful, especially at night when all muscles should relax and the circulation of the blood should be entirely free from pressure. The trousers come up into the crotch which is always undesirable, and cover the inner sides of the thighs which is entirely unnecessary.[9] The only thing that can be said for the pajamas is that they furnish a certain amount of warmth, which may be needed in cold weather.

If the human body, unlike that of every other living being, is so indecent that it should not be seen even by one's legally and ecclesiastically wedded spouse in the virtuous intimacy of the connubial chamber, or by one's self in the isolation of one's own room, then the old-fashioned night shirt furnishes ample concealment to satisfy the most exacting demands of Mrs. Grundy and her followers. The night shirt is not tight at any point, does not come up into the crotch, and is more comfortable than the pajamas. It is by far the most hygienic night garment and much more reposeful than pajamas.

It is unnecessary even for those who worship artificial modesty to use night clothing. When asleep one is habitually alone, or with persons with whom mutual nudity is permissible even according to relatively prudish standards. To appear in public in night clothing, though it covers the whole body, is considered almost as immodest as appearing nude, so that nudity might as well be adopted as the *costume*

---

[9] "Leigh Hunt wrote an amusing paper on the pleasures of going to bed, when the legs, long separated by unnatural clothing, delightedly rub against and renew their acquaintance with one another. Everyone knows the feeling." (W. H. Hudson, *op. cit.*, p. 219.)

de nuit.[10] Sleeping unclothed is more restful for the skin, because there is less texture in contact with it, and the skin receives more air. Then there is the joy of being free from clothing at least a part of the time As bed covering, down quilts are preferable to blankets, especially in cool or cold weather, because they are softer and lighter and can be drawn closely around the neck, thus keeping the body warm. In excessively cold weather, a long, loose flannel night shirt may be used, but otherwise no garment whatsoever is necessary.

Clothing illustrates the disutility of culture not only in that it is often used when superfluous or harmful, but also in that it is due to the vulgar superstition that the human body as a whole or in part is obscene. It is, indeed, an incongruous phase of cultural ideology that decrees that the object of the greatest interest and value in the universe for mankind is regarded as indecent and therefore to be hidden from human eyes. Many so-called primitive peoples have been more fortunate in that they have not developed this deleterious phase of cultural ideology.

[10] Until about the close of the Middle Ages night clothing was unknown in Europe, and many peoples in Asia and elsewhere still do not use it.

Chapter LXV

Human Esthetics

THE new gymnosophy is a philosophy both of nature and of cultural evolution. It embodies the enjoyment of all of the beneficent aspects of nature, of which mankind is in large part deprived, and also the utilization of every beneficial product of culture. While it involves the simplification of life in many respects, it does not require a "return to nature" in the sense that everything artificial is to be discarded. It faces the two fundamental human problems, namely, man's relation to nature and to his fellow men.

The new gymnosophy endeavors to regain what mankind has lost through civilization, without rejecting anything of human, social, and cultural value. Mankind has become largely cut off from nature, much to the detriment of its health and happiness. Man can, therefore, little know and understand himself, his fellows, and his natural environment. This ignorance causes much of the stress and strain of human existence. This situation is strikingly exemplified in the concealment of the body, which hampers and distorts the rearing of the young, gives rise to unhealthy mental complexes, and creates abnormal relations between the sexes which do not promote the play function of sex.

Nudity aids materially in bringing mankind closer to nature, in promoting more genuine and sincere relations between the sexes, and in the normal rearing of the young. Nudism is symbolical of a life healthier and saner than the present hectic existence of mankind. Such a life would be possible in a more humane and democratic society which has not yet existed.

Gymnosophy, by the logical outcome of its philosophy, signifies the simplification of life not merely in dress, but also in almost every other respect. The universal or widespread practice of nudity would involve the obliteration to a large extent of class and caste distinctions. It would mean more democracy and individual freedom through the disappearance of many oppressive conventional, moral and legal restrictions. It would restore to the body the importance and dignity

1107

to which it is entitled. Thus could the spirit of youth play a more important part in the life of mankind, not only the youth of the individual, but also the youth of the race.

The basic features of cultural evolution are the utilization of the natural environment for the benefit of mankind, and the social organization of human beings for their mutual welfare. The invention and use of clothing illustrate one aspect of the utilization of the natural environment, because clothes are manufactured from such natural products as fur, wool, and vegetable fibers. But clothing is constantly used when it does harm, by preventing the body from receiving the beneficent effects of the air and sun, thus diminishing the utilization of the most valuable features of the natural environment. It is wise to utilize dress when it is needed, and not to misuse it when more can be gained by going without.

The new gymnosophy promotes not only the practice of nudity whenever feasible, but also the utilization and enjoyment of every beneficent aspect of nature. Gymnosophy stands for simplicity and temperance in every phase of life. It is useful in the rearing of the young, in the relations between the sexes, and in promoting a democratic and humane organization of society. Its implications extend far beyond the practice of nudity alone, for it connotes a thoroughgoing transformation in the outlook upon and mode of life. In this chapter I shall deal with the esthetics of the human body.[1]

Many tomes have been devoted to the subject of beauty, most of which are as futile as theological writings, because based on the postulate of absolute beauty.[2] Such beauty exists no more than absolute right and wrong, or absolute good and evil. Our concept of beauty arises out of sensations which are pleasing to us for various reasons. A symmetrical design is apprehended by the eye and visual nerve centers with little effort. It is, therefore, reposeful, and conveys the impression of harmony. Certain rhythms in sound give a pleasing stimulus to the auditory nerve centers. Many nerve stimuli are regarded as beautiful because they arouse instincts and their correlated emotions which are pleasant. The odor of food is beautiful to the hungry person. The infant, however ugly it may appear to others, is beautiful

---

[1] See Maurice Parmelee, *The New Gymnosophy*, New York, 1927. Fifth revised edition under the title of *Nudism in Modern Life*, 1951. In this book I have treated at length every phase of gymnosophy.

The ancient gymnosophists were Hindu philosophers who lived an ascetic life, wearing little or no clothing, and rejecting the pleasures of life. Modern gymnosophy is not ascetic. But it resembles the gymnosophy of old in trying to simplify life by dispensing with dress as much as is feasible.

[2] See, for example, D. R. Hay, *The Natural Principles of Beauty as Developed in the Human Figure*, Edinburgh and London, 1852. This author attempts to demonstrate the absolute beauty of the human figure, attributing it to God.

1108

to its mother, because it gratifies the powerful maternal instincts and emotions. The sight and touch of the loved one are beautiful, because they arouse pleasing sexual instincts and emotions.

Many objects acquire a sort of subsidiary beauty by association, because they suggest pleasant experiences. This is true of many objects and sounds in nature which would not on other grounds be accounted beautiful. On the other hand, objects which suggest unpleasant experiences acquire a sort of subsidiary ugliness. Customary objects tend to acquire beauty, because they can be apprehended with little effort. Unaccustomed objects are likely to be regarded as ugly, because of the nervous strain entailed in apprehending them. In moods of ennui and boredom, however, the customary may become ugly, and the novel, beautiful.

The concept of beauty has grown out of these and other simple factors which are combined in endless complicated ways, so that it is often difficult to explain how and why beauty is apprehended in a given case. Enough has been said to indicate that beauty is subjective, and its perception is related to and determined by the inborn and acquired traits and the experience of the individual. This accounts for the differences, often contradictory in their character, between esthetic standards, both of individuals and of large groups, such as peoples, nations and races. Similar differences doubtless exist between humans and animals who, though they have never formulated concepts of beauty and esthetic standards, experience pleasant and unpleasant sensations, and probably contemplate objects in a manner somewhat akin to human appreciation of beauty.[3]

I shall not discuss the esthetics of the human body dogmatically, for I am fully aware of the variability of appreciation due to personal, class, national, and racial differences, which I have had ample opportunities to observe the world over. The esthetic judgments uttered will be governed by my own esthetic taste, which has been determined by my personal traits influenced by the race and culture to which I belong, namely, the white race and Occidental culture. My taste does not conform to any illusory divine or absolute standard, and I do not profess that it is necessarily superior to many other equally relative standards. Over a period of years I have been able to observe almost daily many men, women and children of the white race and culture in a state of nudity. In the aggregate I have witnessed many thousand, working and playing, eating and sleeping, talking and writing, indoors and out-of-doors. Inasmuch as I have been one of them and not a

[3] Santayana said that beauty "is value positive, intrinsic, and objectified" or "pleasure regarded as the quality of a thing." (George Santayana, *The Sense of Beauty*, New York, 1896, p. 49.)

hostile or unsympathetic observer, our relations have been of the most natural and spontaneous character. Out of this extensive experience of considerable cultural significance has arisen the following description and discussion.

The vast majority of humans are accustomed solely to a clothed mankind. To many of them nudity seems ridiculous, comical, and sometimes even ugly and grotesque, because it is strange and unaccustomed. In the case of prurient minds, its fancied ridiculousness and ugliness may be due to an unconscious attempt to suppress sex feelings aroused by nudity. This also is due to its strangeness, for nudity *per se* cannot be sexually suggestive when it is habitual and customary.

When the practice of nudity becomes customary, it will no longer be regarded as ridiculous or ugly, and esthetic standards concerning the human body will change and develop. Personal beauty will no longer be judged almost solely by the face, but by the body as a whole. The body below the head will become esthetically more important than the face, and this is as it should be, because the body is far more extensive than the face. Healthier and more robust ideals of beauty will develop as a result of bringing the body into view. Artificial deformations will become repugnant instead of being deliberately created, as is often true in clothed society, especially among the women. All of these things I have observed in gymnosophic circles. They will become true of society at large when the practice of nudity becomes widespread and universal.

A symmetrical design is more readily apprehended, and is, therefore, other things being equal, more pleasing, than an unsymmetrical design. The symmetry which characterizes most organic forms plays an important part in rendering plants and animals beautiful in our eyes.[4] Owing to his upright position, this symmetry is revealed with exceptional distinctness in man. In full face are clearly exhibited—in the head the corresponding eyes, cheeks, ears, etc.; in the torso, the shoulders, the breasts, and the faint outlines of the skeletal box; and the evenly balanced limbs, conveying a fine sense of graceful harmony. A faint line is drawn between the two sides by the nose, neck, hollow

---

[4] In another work I have described organic symmetry as follows: "Symmetry is an almost universal phenomenon in the organic world. Three main types of symmetry may be distinguished—linear, bilateral, and radial symmetry. In linear symmetry parts are repeated in consecutive order, as, for example, in the case of the rings of a worm or snake or of vertebrae in a vertebrate. In bilateral symmetry a part is repeated once in a corresponding position, as in the case of the arms and the legs of a vertebrate. In radial symmetry parts are repeated, branching out from a central point, as in the tentacles of a starfish or the petals of a flower." (Maurice Parmelee, *The Science of Human Behavior*, New York, 1913, p. 47.)

1110

between the breasts, navel and crotch.[5] Clothing blots out or obscures this symmetrical design to a large degree, so that it can be fully appreciated only in the nude. The symmetry of quadrupedal forms, while often beautiful, is somewhat obscured by their position. It is impossible to see all four limbs at once, and the head and torso are turned toward the ground.

The human form is based upon the bony structure of the body, covered with layers of muscle, fat and skin. No line of the surface is entirely straight. While the general outline of the skeletal conformation should be revealed, the structure should be sufficiently covered to give a fairly smooth and even surface. If the covering is not adequate, the form is too angular, as at the shoulders, and the smoothness of the contour is broken at too many points, as when the ribs show through plainly. On the other hand, excessive covering unduly conceals the skeletal outline. If the superfluous covering, usually composed of fat, is unevenly distributed, it creates an impression of distortion, which is esthetically unpleasant.

The massive muscles in motion under the skin suggest strength and vitality, and acquire a secondary beauty in addition to whatever beauty of symmetry, line, and surface they may already possess. Partly for this reason, but also because the limbs are completely revealed, nude bodies are much more expressive in motion than clothed bodies. In fact, I know of no more beautiful sight than a group of nude persons dancing, playing a game, running, or engaged in some other activity involving the whole body.

The female form is more curved than the male, swelling out at the breasts, curving in at the waist, and swelling out again at the hips. These sex differences are due partly to differences in skeletal conformation, but also to differences in the superficial layers. The female form has more fat distributed over it than the male, but less muscle.[6]

---

[5] No organic form is absolutely symmetrical, and in some individuals the asymmetry is sufficiently great as to be noticeable.

"This inequality can generally be recognized in the skull of the living man by the prominent part of the back of the head. The whole skull, however, is marked by asymmetry; indeed, it is quite generally found in the face, and to such an extent that a human face with the two halves perfectly equal would seem to us unnatural." (Hermann Klaatsch, *The Evolution and Progress of Mankind*, London, 1923, p. 141, translated from the German.)

"The two sides of the head are symmetrical structurally. This is theoretically true of the details as well as the larger forms; but in actual character there are many deviations from the regular." (J. H. Vanderpoel, *The Human Figure*, Chicago, 1922, pp. 54-7.)

[6] Woman's tendency to put on fat is closely related to her reproductive functions. "She accumulates in her system incompletely oxidized material ready for impregnation or lactation, and when not otherwise utilized or integrated it forms adipose tissue. This tendency, while it is chiefly responsible for the charm and

Consequently, the female form is more rounded and billowy, the male is straighter and more angular. While individuals of each sex vary from the ideal sex types in both directions, more of the male variations are in the direction of too great angularity, and more of the female in the direction of too much curvature due to excessive fat. In other words, while there is no adequate statistical evidence on this point, taking mankind in the aggregate, there are probably more lean men and more fat women.

Infants are usually chubby and relatively formless, because more or less covered with fat. The limbs have not yet straightened out from the prenatal curvature, and therefore lack graceful lines. As they grow older, they become leaner and more straight, but are still characterized by a good deal of formlessness, because of the rapid growth and changes which are taking place. The abdomen usually protrudes somewhat during childhood. They still lack the bodily strength and stability necessary for a well defined form. The body is often not held sufficiently erect, and may be lopsided. They gradually attain the upright form, which is one of the beauties of the human body. The navel is usually shallow and often displays a button, thus indicating the recent separation from the mother.

During infancy and childhood the sexes are more or less alike, with the exception of the sex organs. In other words, there are few secondary sex differences. The breasts are rudimentary in both sexes, and the body is only thinly covered with fine hair. It has seemed to me that the abdomen is somewhat more protuberant in the female child, but I have no statistical evidence on this point. With the coming of puberty the breasts begin to develop, and the coarse and thick pubic hair to appear. The girl changes much more than the boy. The rapid swelling of the breasts is the first noticeable change. A little later the hips begin to broaden, and the thighs to display the inflare characteristic of the female form, so that the waist makes its appearance.

These facts indicate that children are on the whole less beautiful than adults, so far as symmetry and lines are concerned. Infants usually appear beautiful only to their parents. As they grow older, children are awkward and ungainly. But they acquire a secondary beauty in the appeal they make to the parental feelings implanted in every normal adult. Their early helplessness arouses the impulse to protect them against harm, and their later growth the desire to see

softness of the smoothly rounded feminine form, results in women possessing a larger amount than men of comparatively non-vital tissue, and makes them appear larger than they really are." (Havelock Ellis, *Man and Woman*, London, 1914, 5th edition, p. 49.)

1112

them fulfil the promise of their youth. One of the most exquisite delights of life in gymnosophic circles is to be able to watch the young attain manhood and womanhood under the most natural and healthy conditions, whereas in clothed society this development is largely obscured from view by ugly and often injurious garments. The union between man, woman and child is much closer when they have passed through these universal human experiences together.

Our standards and ideals of human beauty are determined largely by the fundamental human type, by the racial type to which we belong, and for each sex by the sex type. With respect to the beauty of these types there can be no argument, for they are the types to which we are accustomed, and which are natural and normal for us. Such statues as the Aphrodite of Melos and the Doryphorus of Polycleitus (ca. B.C. 430), commonly known in ancient times as "the Canon," are generally regarded as beautiful because they conform or are supposed to conform to the "perfect," that is to say, normal human type. However, as I have pointed out, certain considerations of symmetry, proportion and line may nevertheless be applied to the different parts of the body, because they are of significance with respect to the ease with which these parts may be apprehended by our sense organs, in particular the visual sense. Furthermore, each part should be considered in relation to its adjoining parts and the whole form, because the ease with which the ensemble can be perceived depends upon the relationship between the parts. Generally speaking, there should not be too sudden changes and violent breaks, but at the same time there should be sufficient variety to avoid the impression of monotony.

The neck is of principal significance with respect to the relation between the head and the torso. It should be long enough to give the head the prominence it deserves, but not so long as to make the head appear too much detached from the torso. When lean and scrawny the neck appears too long, and when thick and fat it appears too short. While neither is desirable, the former is the most objectionable from an esthetic point of view. The neck should curve gracefully into the shoulders. The shoulders should be somewhat sloping and not too square. The collarbones should be only faintly visible. The arms should taper gradually from the shoulders. The upper arms of many persons, owing to deficient muscular development, especially among women, are too thin. This causes too sudden a change from the body, and renders the corners of the shoulders unduly peaked.

The shoulders should be broad and the chest deep, for the upper part of the torso should be the most massive part of the body. It is, so to speak, the axis about which the rest of the body turns, or the fulcrum from which neck, arms, lower torso and lower limbs secure their leverage. The breasts in men should be only slightly prominent, so as to cause not more than a faint line beneath them. In women they should be saucer or cup shaped, and so firm that they vibrate only slightly when the body is in motion. Female breasts are among the most variable of physical traits. Sometimes they are little developed and flat, and, therefore manlike. Hence they do not conform to our ideal of the sex type. Sometimes they are skinny. Much oftener they are fat and pendulous, sometimes tubular in shape. This is frequently due to maternity, though it could usually be prevented if proper care were taken.[7] It is also true of many women who have borne no children. While from a purely esthetic point of view large and overhanging breasts are not beautiful, because they overshadow the region below and quiver too much, they are not offensive, and may even acquire secondary beauty because they are associated with the supremely important function of nourishing the young.[8]

The hips in men should be slightly narrower than the chest, so that the side lines from chest to hips are almost straight and vertical. In women the hips must proportionally be somewhat broader, in order to furnish room for the womb. The indentation at the waist is not so great in the normal woman as is commonly supposed in clothed society, where corsets, belts, skirtbands, and other forms of constrictive and deceptive clothing often exaggerate the smallness of the waist.[9]

The abdomen in the normally formed individual is comparatively flat, curving toward the sides and crotch and to a smaller degree

[7] "Das Lebensalter hat wenig mit der Schönheit der Brust zu tun. . . . Bei richtiger Pflege und als Vorbedingung elastischer Haut können auch Geburten und Wochenbetten spurlos an der weiblichen Brust vorübergehen." (C. H. Stratz, *Die Schönheit des weiblichen Körpers*, Stuttgart, 1920, 28th edition, p. 243.) Freely translated: "The age of the woman has little to do with the beauty of the breast. With proper care and an elastic skin to start with pregnancy and delivery can take place without leaving any trace upon the female breast."

[8] "Die schönste Form der Brüste ist zweifellos die vollkommen gleichmässig gerundete, die ebenmässig in den Körper verläuft, ohne unter oder gar über oder zwischen ihnen eine Falte aufkommen zu lassen." (Paul Schultze-Naumburg, *Die Kultur des weiblichen Körpers als Grundlage der Frauenkleidung*, Jena, 1922, first published in 1901, p. 4.) Freely translated: "The most beautifully formed breasts are fully and symmetrically rounded and shade evenly into the body without a crease under, above or between them."

The following classification of the development and types of the female breast is given by von Reitzenstein: (1) puerile, (2) button, (3) budding, (4) nature, (5) cup shaped, (6) semi-spherical, (7) conical, (8) lemon or udder shaped, (9) pendulous, (10) withered. (F. von Reitzenstein, *Das Weib bei den Naturvölkern*, Berlin, 1923.)

[9] The length of the trunk is approximately the same in man and woman, the difference in height being due mainly to the longer lower extremities in man.

The following tables indicate the comparative proportions of the sexes, based upon the measurement of a considerable number of individuals:

1114

toward the hips, there forming a faint line. In very young adults the level of the abdominal wall may be somewhat deeper than the thorax and chest, thus forming a shallow concavity in the abdominal region. The distance between the navel and the pubes is greater in women than in men, a large abdomen being a female as well as an infantile and primitive trait. Partly for this reason, in normal woman the abdomen is more protuberant than in normal man. The abdominal wall is composed of a network of massive muscles, which should have only a thin layer of fat on the outside. But the abdominal region is the ugliest portion of the human form in a vast number of individuals, probably in the majority of mankind. The usual cause is obesity. Some persons are born with a constitutional tendency to corpulence, which it is difficult to overcome. Childbearing loosens the abdominal walls, so that mothers are likely to have protuberant abdomens, though this can be largely averted in healthy women by proper care.

In the great majority of cases in both sexes, the ugly, protuberant abdomen is due to overeating, lack of exercise and other unhygienic modes of life. It is the most unsightly mark left upon the body by the unhealthy and unnatural life created by our civilization. While the fat belly is altogether too common among both sexes, it is more characteristic of women, not only because the female body has proportionally more fat, but also because women lead on the whole more sedentary

Comparative Measurements of the Sexes

	Male	Female
	Centimeters	
Height	165.5	158
Width of shoulders	47	37
Width of waist	25	23
Width of hips	32.5	34

(From F. Merkel, *Handbuch der topographischen Anatomie*, Vieweg, 1896, Vol. II, pp. 182 and 256.)

Relative Proportions of the Sexes in Head-Lengths (Skull-Lengths).

	Male	Female
	Head-Lengths	
Height	8	7½
Width between shoulders	2	1¾
Width between hips	1½	1¾
Width between nipples	1	variable

(From George McClellan, *Anatomy in Its Relation to Art*, Philadelphia, 1900.)

lives than men. This unwieldy mass of flesh, sometimes containing folds and creases, and quivering jellylike with the motion of the body, is one of the most unpleasant sights in gymnosophic circles. Here its ugliness is not concealed by clothing, so that gymnosophy is the most effective measure for eliminating this monstrous distortion by spreading an ideal of human beauty and shaming those who fall so far short of it.

The navel, reminiscent of our early intimate relation with our mothers, is an agreeable resting place for the eye in the broad oval expanse below the chest. This lightly shaded spot furnishes relief from the smooth surface of thorax and abdomen. It is most beautiful when round and hollowed, but is rather ugly when irregularly shaped, flat, and with the button visible.

The nipples bring out effectively the points of the breasts, whose shape would not otherwise be so easy to perceive. In men they are rarely ever too obtrusive. In some women they are so large and long as to interfere with the appreciation of the breasts. In a few women the pigmented spots surrounding the nipples are so broad and dark as to obscure the breasts. The nipples, the faint lines under the breasts, and the navel serve to accentuate the symmetry of the torso.

The thighs taper from the hips to the knees, thus causing a sort of inflare, especially in women because of the breadth of their hips. The thighs are lightly separated in men, but come close together in women, giving them a slightly knockkneed appearance. In both sexes the most graceful lines are produced by a gradual tapering effect from the shoulders to the feet. In many individuals of both sexes, there is variation from the ideal in both directions. Sometimes the thighs are too thin, thus causing too violent a break from the broad torso. More often the thighs are too thick, especially in the upper part. This is true of many women, whose tendency to accumulate fat shows itself here as in the abdominal region and the breasts.

The legs turn out slightly from the knees, especially in women. If this outflare is exaggerated, it produces bowlegs, which is ungraceful because it causes a break in the approximately straight line which runs from the top of the head through the neck, torso and knees to the feet. The calves give rise to a moderate swelling below the knees. If this is exaggerated, as is often the case due to fat caused ordinarily by too sedentary a life, it gives the legs too much prominence in the general outline, and interferes with the tapering effect. Less frequently the legs are too thin, thus causing a break in the tapering effect from the hips to the ankles, and conveying an impression of topheavy weakness.

Feet vary considerably in size in relation to the remainder of the

1116

body. While excessive variations in length or width may not appear beautiful, the shape of the foot is of most importance from an esthetic point of view. In a well-formed foot the ankle should be narrow, and the upper part of the heel thin. The arch should be comparatively high, giving an impression of springiness and flexibility to the whole body. The inner side of the foot should be straight from the heel to the end of the big toe. An appreciable space should separate the big toe from the adjoining one. The other four toes should lie parallel with each other and closer together, but not pressing against each other. The tips of the toes should make a fairly straight line running diagonally backward. In some individuals the four smaller toes are abnormally long, so that the second toe extends beyond the big toe, thus distorting the line of the tips of the toes. In such abnormally long toes the joints are usually very prominent, and their movements almost painfully visible.

The feet are artificially deformed more often than any other portion of the body. To any one who has an ideal of a beautifully formed body, the feet are eyesores, not only in gymnosophic circles, but also at bathing beaches and wherever men and women uncover their feet. The most frequent and hideous cases are among women. It is one of the ludicrous anomalies of human nature that the sex which is most avid for physical beauty destroys with the utmost deliberation the beauty of an important part of the anatomy. This distorted and perverse conception of beauty has arisen in a clothed society where the body is always or usually concealed. While many primitive peoples that are habitually unclothed deform the lips, nose, ears, external sex organs, and less frequently the shape of the head, for esthetic or magical reasons, I know of no primitive people which deliberately deforms the feet.

I shall not attempt to trace the origin and development of the ideal of the small female foot. Various factors have played a part, as, for example, the desire to make woman partially or entirely helpless, to distinguish aristocratic leisure class from working women, and the like. The ideal has been carried to its most horrible though logical extreme in China, where the feet of the female children were bound so that they could not grow, thus rendering them almost helpless.[10]

In Occidental society the highheeled and pointed shoe has been used for several centuries to make the foot appear smaller. In the Musée de Cluny in Paris are highheeled shoes dating from the six-

[10] In 1925 I saw many young women with bound feet in China. The custom is rapidly dying out, owing to prohibitory legislation and an increasingly enlightened public opinion, since the Republic of 1911-1912, and especially since the Revolution of 1949 which established the Chinese People's Republic.

1117

teenth century. The purpose of the high heels is to make the foot appear shorter by forcing some of its length into the height, making the body appear taller, and to thrust the breasts forward, thus making them more prominent. This brings some of the weight of the body upon the tips of the toes, pressing them back and doubling them under to a certain extent. The pointed shoe makes the fore part of the foot appear smaller. The big toe is forced over against the second toe, destroying the straight line of the inner side of the foot and obliterating the space between these toes. The four smaller toes are jammed together, and in many cases forced under and over each other. The nails as well as the toes are distorted, and their healthy growth is prevented.

Men have more beautiful and stronger feet than women because they have not been so much addicted to high heels and pointed shoes. But clumsy, awkward, ill-shaped footwear, manufactured from stiff and inflexible leather, has had its deforming effect upon the feet of the great majority of men. Very often fashion has decreed boots and shoes which are not sufficiently broad for men as well as for women, so that the big toe is forced over and the smaller toes jammed together. However, men are much less likely than women to have broken arches and flat feet, which are often caused by high heels.

Footwear, especially for women, is peculiarly subject to the whim of the goddess of fashion. Sometimes the prevailing mode becomes temporarily better. In the Musée de Cluny in Paris are low-heeled and broad-toed shoes worn by women under the Consulate and First Empire in France at the beginning of the nineteenth century. Whether this was an indication of a desire for a simpler and more hygienic dress, or merely a vagary of fashion, I do not know. It is alleged that feminine apparel was unusually scanty during that period. It is possible that the revolutionary spirit gave rise to a back to nature movement, albeit very weak and temporary, which caused saner styles in feminine attire. Ordinarily fashion rules, and only by chance produces genuine improvements. Many women have been wearing light sandal-like slippers, cut down to the sole over the instep, which are cool and airy, and often without stockings in warm weather. But they are perched on high heels, and have pointed toes. Only the gymnosophic ideal can make footwear as well as other articles of dress both hygienic and beautiful, for they will then be adjusted both anatomically and esthetically to the human body.

The upper part of the back should be fairly flat, curving gently into the shoulders. Many persons do not stand erect, so that the upper back is too curved, and some of it merges into the shoulders. Under such conditions the shoulder blades are likely to stick out

1118

unduly, thus breaking the smooth contour of the back. The middle of the back should curve in gently, and then out into the rump, which should be well rounded but firm. Persons with corpulent abdomens are likely to have an adipose rump. This happens more often among women than men, and is always an unpleasant sight, especially when the body is in motion. The gait of corpulent persons, even when swift, resembles a waddle. Much of the surface of the body is covered with a wadded quilt of adipose tissue, which moves with every movement of the legs, and conveys an impression of strain and painful effort at every step. When the body is firm and well-knit, it is carried along by the legs, only the movement of some of the body muscles being faintly visible, and an impression of ease and agility is given.

The general proportions have some influence upon the esthetic appearance of the body, though not so much as the formation of the parts, except in very abnormal cases. The height is of little importance if the body is well proportioned. The trunk is about the same in both sexes, man's greater stature being mainly due to his longer limbs. Sometimes the torso appears too long in proportion to the limbs, more often in women, and sometimes the limbs appear too long, more often in men.[11] Neither is seriously objectionable if the parts are well formed. Too great length of limb is perhaps the least pleasing because it makes the torso appear weak, while there is a slightly ludicrous resemblance to certain insects with long legs. When the torso is too long, the gait appears too short, as if mincing.

The skin should be smooth and clear, and feel pliable yet firm. Friction or other hard usage may render it rough, and in some persons it is covered with pinpoints giving it the appearance of gooseflesh. Numerous maladies of the skin, blood, digestion, etc., produce red points, spots and blotches which are unsightly. In gymnosophic circles I have observed that the skin of some of the novices is an unhealthy bluish white, due probably to poor circulation of the blood, or to interference with the circulation by corsets, belts, garters, and other forms of constrictive clothing. This appearance soon vanishes with continual exposure to the air and sun. In the very aged the skin becomes lined and wrinkled. In corpulent persons numerous folds and creases appear.

The esthetic ideal for the color of the human skin is determined mainly by racial traits, but may be influenced by culture. The white poet sings of the ivory skin of his loved one, the black poet of an ebony skin, and the yellow poet of an amber skin. If there were blue

[11] "Speaking generally, it may be said that relatively to the total height, in women the head is longer than in men, the neck shorter, the trunk longer, and the legs and arms shorter." (Havelock Ellis, *op. cit.*, pp. 49-50.)

and green colored races, the peacock's feathers and jade would appear as metaphors. Perhaps the most that can be said is that the skin color should be uniform, though many primitive peoples have found a particolored skin pleasing, and modern woman persists in using rouge pot, lip stick, nail polish, and powder puff.

Gymnosophists are able to emancipate themselves in a measure from the bondage to the racial color. They watch the sun paint a rich brown, not only over face and hands, but chest and abdomen, back, rump and thighs, thus producing the satinlike sheen of a completely tanned body. And inasmuch as brown is not necessarily less beautiful than white, and is closely associated with the joy and healthful activities of life in gymnosophic circles, it acquires a charm of its own. The unnatural pallor of a white skin then becomes less pleasing, because it suggests ugly, uncomfortable and unhealthy clothing, and an existence remote from the sun and out-of-door nature. Very unpleasing is the appearance of persons who, owing to artificial modesty, cover part of the body when bathing in the open air. The body then becomes demarkated by the bathing suit into sharply defined areas of white and of brown. The outline of the suit is sketched in the most ludicrous fashion upon the surface of the body. In the uniformly tanned body there is an evenness of shading which is very attractive.

In the foregoing description of the human body from an esthetic point of view, I have, for the sake of brevity, been more dogmatic in my manner than has been my meaning. As I have already pointed out, esthetic standards are in the last analysis determined by custom and taste, which vary greatly. This should be borne in mind when comparing groups.

To compare the sexes esthetically is not only invidious, but in the main futile. Each sex is beautiful according to its own norm and in the eyes of the opposite sex. Male traits in a woman and female traits in a man impress most persons as unpleasant and ugly.[12] It is an exaggeration of this natural tendency to vary from each other which leads to excessive emphasis upon sex differences by means of dress and other artificial devices.

A beautiful individual of either sex is admired by all, but is specially attractive to normal persons of the opposite sex, because of

[12] "Unschön sind Weiber, deren Erscheinung männliche Zuge trägt, deshalb, weil darin eine Vereinung des weiblichen Wesens liegt." (F. von Reitzenstein, *Das Weib bei den Naturvölkern*, Berlin, 1923.) Freely translated: "Women whose appearance displays male traits are not beautiful, because these traits deny their female character."

This writer pointed out that among some primitive peoples mannish women are favored, because they are more useful for hard physical labor. In these cases an economic consideration may influence the esthetic judgment.

the subtle appeal of sex which suffuses all relations between the sexes. Each sex is, therefore, more beautiful to the other. To put it more concretely, to men women are usually more beautiful than men, and to women men are usually more beautiful than women. Each sex looks at the other with eyes which are in a measure colored by the emotions associated with sex, and this is a useful adaptation for the fulfilment of the two functions of sex, namely, the reproductive and the play functions.

At the same time both sexes conform to the fundamental human type, and are more alike than they are different. Clothing is misleading and deceptive, because it conceals some of the genuine sex differences and exaggerates other differences, while it hides in part the fundamental likeness of the sexes. Thus the habitual use of skirts by women conveys the impression of a sex without lower limbs. A precise appreciation of the similarities and dissimilarities between the sexes can be acquired only through the habitual or frequent practice of nudity. Not otherwise can men and women know and enjoy each other fully.

Men are more bony and angular, and women fatter and more rounded in contour. Women show more graceful curves. Men convey a greater impression of strength, partly because the male body displays more muscle. In motion, especially in swift motion, such as running and jumping, men have much the advantage. The inflaring thighs, knockknees, and outflaring legs of women convey an impression of clumsiness. The vibration of adipose tissue in various parts of the body, especially noticeable in the older women, distracts attention from the movements of the limbs and the general motion of the body. The female form is, on the whole, more beautiful when stretched out than when bent. When reaching upward the creases and folds of fat are largely or entirely wiped out, the breasts stand out more firmly, the abdomen does not sag, and the contour of the body is clearly to be seen.

The female genital region is little noticeable, being usually covered by the pubic hair. In both sexes the hair at the crotch furnishes a touch of pleasing color which accentuates the middle line and, with the navel and nipples, the symmetry of the body. The male genital region may be regarded by some persons as a little too prominent from a purely esthetic point of view, but is through habituation inconspicuous to gymnosophists. Hair elsewhere on the body is natural and therefore not offensive upon men, and also not upon women, when not too heavy.

Generally speaking, the male body conveys more of the tapering effect from the shoulders to the feet. The lines of the female body are broken by the indented waist, flaring hips, and protruding breasts. However, beautiful specimens of both sexes are more nearly alike than ugly specimens. Gymnosophy will increase this likeness, because it will promote health and beauty. Hence it is that, whatever may be thought of the relative beauty of the sexes at present, this question will largely lose its significance in the gymnosophic society, where healthy and beautiful individuals of both sexes will predominate.[13]

The aged are likely to lose much of their fat, and to acquire a wrinkled skin. And yet a healthy life results in an aged body which is far from ugly. A septuagenarian has come to our recreation center regularly for over twenty years. Each day with obvious enjoyment he plays ball vigorously and skilfully. He always speaks of the benefit he derives, even in cold weather. His tall figure is erect, and his skin only slightly wrinkled, while his muscles are hard and firm. He is still a fine specimen of a man, and this is not a little due to his long continued exposure to sun and air. I have seen fewer cases of well-preserved age among women.

When we come to the differences between the races, nothing could be more true than the saying "de gustibus non disputandum." The esthetic standard of each race is determined largely by its racial color, bodily conformation, and the like. The preceding discussion was from the point of view of the white race, and much that I have said conflicts with the esthetic canons of other races. It would be futile

[13] After a judicial examination of the question, Ellis arrived at the conclusion that the male sex is the more beautiful from a purely esthetic standpoint: "It is mainly because the unesthetic character of a woman's sexual region is almost imperceptible in any ordinary and normal position of the nude body that the feminine form is a more esthetically beautiful object of contemplation than the masculine. Apart from this character we are probably bound, from a strictly esthetic point of view, to regard the male form as more esthetically beautiful. The female form, moreover, usually overpasses very swiftly the period of the climax of its beauty, often only retaining it during a few weeks." (Havelock Ellis, *Studies in the Psychology of Sex*, Vol. IV, *Sexual Selection in Man*, Philadelphia, 1905, p. 162.)

Schopenhauer (1788-1860) asserted very emphatically that the female sex is not beautiful, but he was influenced by misogynist prejudices: "It is only the man whose intellect is clouded by his sexual impulses that could give the name of the fair sex to the undersized, narrow-shouldered, broad-hipped, and short-legged race; for the whole beauty of the sex is bound up with this impulse. Instead of calling them beautiful, there would be more warrant for describing women as the unesthetic sex. Neither for music, nor for poetry, nor for fine art, have they really and truly any sense or susceptibiilty; it is a mere mockery if they make a pretence of it in order to assist their endeavor to please." (Arthur Schopenhauer, *Essay on Women*.)

Another misogynist, who was a disciple of Schopenhauer, Otto Weininger in his *Sex and Character* stigmatized woman still more emphatically as ugly. "A nude woman may be beautiful in details, but the general effect is not beautiful. . . . But even in the details of her body a woman is not wholly beautiful."

to try to assimilate and harmonize these partially incompatible ideals. Nevertheless it is of the utmost importance to recognize that these different ideals exist, and that each race has a beauty of its own. Dislike of the physical traits of other races is one of the principal causes of racial prejudice, and should be overcome at least to the point where the different races can mingle together clothed or unclothed without being mutually objectionable. However difficult it may be to enjoy the beauty of other races, an earnest effort should be made to comprehend at least to the point of sympathetic appreciation.[14]

Clothes conceal much that is ugly as well as much that is beautiful. Some persons look better nude, others clothed. The face is most important when clothed, but when nude the figure is of greater importance. Other things being equal, slender persons look better nude than corpulent persons. Clothes conceal the unsightly layers of fat. Many women have hesitated to enter gymnosophic circles because they have feared that they would not look so well nude as clothed, but such instances are much fewer among men. Some of the deformations and defacements caused by dress are due to attempts to correct or conceal real or imagined defects of the figure. Feminine fashions are designed in part with this end in view.[15]

I am inclined to think that the practice of nudity discloses more beauty than ugliness. Whatever may be true of the present generation, through sexual selection gymnosophy will eventually produce a more

[14] An American woman who had travelled and lived in Japan has described in detail the differences between the Japanese and our ideals of female beauty. She stated that the Japanese esthetic standard requires that the face be long and narrow, the eyes long and narrow and slanting upwards at the outer corners, the hair black and perfectly straight, the nose with a low bridge, no color in the face but full and red lips, the neck long and slender, the waist long but not especially small, and the hips narrow. (Alice Mabel Bacon, *Japanese Girls and Women*, Boston, 1891, pp. 58-60.) This ideal conforms in the main to the Japanese racial traits and makes a vivid contrast with the blond, red-cheeked, full-bosomed, broad-hipped and buxom North European type, which appears coarse and unlovely to the Japanese eye.

Stratz has described at length racial, especially the Japanese, ideals of beauty. (C. H. Stratz, *Die Rassenschönheit des Weibes*, Stuttgart, 1903, 3rd edition; *Die Körperformen in Kunst und Leben der Japaner*, Stuttgart, 1902.)

Ellis well characterized racial ideals of beauty: "To the average man of every race the woman who most completely embodies the type of his race is usually the most beautiful, and even mutilations and deformations often have their origin, as Humboldt long since pointed out, in the effort to accentuate the racial type." (Havelock Ellis, *Sexual Selection in Man*, p. 175.)

[15] In a fashion review is the following rather incoherent statement which probably exaggerates this purpose: "Fashion has taken upon itself the role of philanthropist, beauty specialist—call it what you will. Styles are designed not nearly so much for the enhancement of beauty and certainly far less for the merely mundane purpose of clothing, as for the exalted mission of concealing defects."

1123

beautiful mankind. Gymnosophists have every incentive to avoid deformations of the body, and to strive by means of a healthy and natural life for a well developed form, because deformities and malformations are all too apparent in a state of nudity. When gymnosophy becomes widespread, pretty faces and a pearly-white skin can no longer be predominant factors in mating. Women will not hesitate to become brown in the sun, because they think a white skin is more seductive. On the contrary, a healthy tan will signify sport or work, and companionship with men in the open. Men and women will then look upon each other's bodies and into each other's eyes without fear and without shame. They will choose each other, so far as physical traits determine the choice, according to the beauty of the body as a whole, and not merely of a small portion. They will then be genuine comrades and mates, and fit parents for the more beautiful mankind of the future.

The objection may be raised that gymnosophy deprives life of some of its romance. Does not the mystery of the draped body heighten the interest of courting and mating? Will not gymnosophy decrease sex enjoyment by diminishing the visual stimulus? Would not the play function of sex be limited and minimized in a gymnosophic society? Do not changes of costume introduce a welcome variety into life? Would not customary nudity give rise to bacchanalian orgies of dress?

It is true that concealment of the body accentuates lust by aggravating curiosity, and thus heightens sexual enjoyment. But the effects of such stimulation can be only temporary, and are very likely to be followed by disillusionment and disappointment when the concealment is removed. Such disappointment is likely to give rise to a nervous and mental shock, and to a revulsion of feeling which may result in a morbid state. The normal expression of the sex instinct and emotion is to a certain extent repressed and inhibited, and the development of the play function of sex is seriously hampered. So that a heavy price is paid for the momentary pleasure derived from an accelerated pursuit on the part of the male, and from coquetry on the part of the female.

Inasmuch as in a clothed society the sight of the body usually gives rise to sex feelings, the question may be raised as to whether the habitual practice of nudity would not diminish the total stimulus to sex feeling, or, on the contrary, would the stimuli received through the tactile, olfactory, auditory, and gustatory senses be commensurately increased. In the first place, it is not suggested that gymnosophy destroys the gratification derived from the sight of the opposite sex. While this gratification is less acute than what may be furnished under present conditions by the sight of unaccustomed nudity, it is diffused throughout the more or less continuous association of the sexes. As in all relations between the sexes, it is permeated with a certain degree of sex feeling. In the second place, the diminution of the visual sex stimulus would be compensated at least in part by an accentuation of the stimuli through the other senses. The tactile sense is the most important in sex feeling.[16] A slight increase in tactile sex stimulus would compensate for the loss in the visual sex stimulus, and such changes are feasible either spontaneously or through training in the art of love.

In view of these considerations it is unlikely that gymnosophy can injure or diminish the play function of sex. It is possible that it will render it a little slower to commence, because the artificial stimulus of the curiosity-provoking concealment will no longer whip the sexual urge to white heat. In other words, men and women, and especially young men and women, will not so often be precipitated into sex relations through curiosity, mystery, and sham modesty, and ignorance of sexual facts will not so often give rise to psychic impotency and phobias. On the other hand, when the practice of nudity is customary, men and women will know each other better, so that the sex relation when once begun will develop the play function in a stronger and more enduring form.

Gymnosophy is no panacea for social ills, and will not render mankind ideal and perfect. But it can ameliorate certain of these ills, and can render the relations between the sexes much happier and more beautiful. If the practice of nudity were customary, some individuals might indulge in bacchanalian orgies of dress. However, such orgies could not be more sordid and ugly than many orgies of a different nature which take place constantly in clothed society.

Clothing will always be needed at times as a protection against the weather and other natural forces. It should then be used to introduce color and variety into human existence. It fails in the main to do so now, because esthetic considerations have comparatively little influence upon fashions and style in dress. When the cold renders clothing necessary, it should beautify as well as protect. At present it is attempted to make only feminine clothing beautiful, not always successfully, while masculine apparel is ill formed, drab and ugly. In

---

[16] There are no adequate experimental and laboratory data on the sex stimuli received through the different senses, and the relations between them. Among the books which discuss these problems are the following: Albert Moll, *Untersuchungen über die Libido Sexualis*, Berlin, 1897-8; Havelock Ellis, *Studies in the Psychology of Sex*, Philadelphia, Vol. III, *Analysis of the Sexual Impulse*, 1903, Vol. IV, *Sexual Selection in Man*, 1905; J. S. Van Teslaar, *Sex and the Senses*, Boston, 1922.

gymnosophic society there will be little if any occasion to distinguish between the sexes in dress. Clothing will no longer be used to conceal and to deceive, though it may still be used by some persons to seduce and to gratify vanity. Dress will then probably conform more to individual than to sex traits, thus rendering the garb much more expressive and more colorful and varied than heretofore.

In the foregoing discussion of the esthetics of the human body, I have said nothing of the head and face because they are always visible, and I wished to describe parts of the body which are rarely ever seen under the existing prudish and prurient regime. The face is the most expressive portion of the body. From the eyes and mouth in particular much can be learned with regard to the temperament and character of the individual. But the torso and limbs are also more or less expressive, especially when the body is in motion. Clothing obscures the movements of muscles and limbs, and thus conceals the expression. It is peculiarly obnoxious in dancing, for the body is never more expressive than when in the rhythmic movements of the dance the dancer can give full and free expression to his feelings, and to a certain extent suggest thoughts and ideas.

Gymnosophy will contribute greatly to the beauty of human existence, especially when its influence through sexual selection results in a more beautiful species. But it should never be forgotten that the practice of nudity is beneficial not only for esthetic reasons, but also because it promotes health, comfort and efficiency, and gratifies a profound desire to see and know the body. I mention this because I have observed in certain gymnosophic groups a tendency to develop a sort of cult of beauty, which overshadows the other aspects of gymnosophy. In some of these groups ill-formed, deformed and mutilated persons are excluded. While extreme cases of deformity and mutilation can be so distressing and painful to view that there may be some justification for such exclusion, it is of supreme importance that the gymnosophic movement be maintained on a humanitarian plane. Gymnosophists should never forget that the sun and air, nature and the planet upon which we live exist for mankind as a whole, and not principally for the beautiful and more favored of its sons and daughters.

Chapter LXVI

The Gymnosophic Society

IT may not be amiss to sketch in outline the effect which the general acceptance of gymnosophic ideas may have upon society, thus furnishing a basis for comparison with the past. It would be characterized by simplicity not only in dress, but in many other respects as well. A large part of the things invented and manufactured are useless and often harmful. Among them are unnecessary and unhealthy clothing, useless structures built largely for show, ugly and uncomfortable furniture, much bric-a-brac intended for decoration, and many superfluous and injurious kinds of food and drink. Some of these are due to abnormal and artificial appetites which have been acquired by mankind, as for many indigestible foods and poisonous drinks, such as alcoholic beverages, and for opium, morphine, tobacco, and other stimulants and sedatives. Much of the expenditure of persons whose incomes are above a subsistence minimum is for the purpose of displaying their purchasing power, and thereby their economic and social status, and is, therefore, conspicuous waste. Whatever satisfaction may thus be gained in the form of prestige, adulation, and power in our present society, ostentatious expenditure would be pointless and futile in the democracy of a gymnosophic society.

A few articles of clothing would be needed for cold weather, and for protection in certain occupations, but the wardrobe of every individual would be comparatively small. All clothing would, however, be comfortable and beautiful, so that any garment, unlike the undergarments of the present could be seen without embarrassment to the wearer. The garments would be so constructed and adjusted to each other that they could be put on or taken off one after another in accordance with changes in temperature. In order to carry and conceal such things as money and keys, a substitute for pockets would be required. This could be a pouch attached to a girdle at the waist, or to a shoulder strap, or suspended around the neck, or attached to the arm or wrist, or carried in the hand as women do at present, according to the size and weight of the pouch. While human nature will not change inherently under gymnosophy, in a democratic society with equality of opportunity for all there will be less temptation to dishonesty, so that the lack of pockets will not be a serious drawback. Wherever life is relatively simple, and everybody is assured of a comfortable existence, few persons are likely to crave the personal property of others.

Under gymnosophy, individual, conjugal and family privacy will be respected as much as at present. Dwellinghouses will be so constructed as to furnish this privacy to every one for work, meditation, and rest, as well as for the intimate details of the care of the body. Each person will be assured of a room to himself, including adequate bathing facilities, with communication between rooms in the case of conjugal couples or others who wish to be in close touch with each other. The disappearance of the tradition of artificial modesty will bring the sexes closer together in their common life. Convent and monastery, harem and military barrack, clubs and schools exclusively for each sex will disappear, and the sexes will live a more normal and happier life together. Hence much duplication of buildings, which is inevitable when the life of the sexes is largely separated, can be avoided. Furthermore, gymnosophists pass as much of their lives as possible out-of-doors, and in the gymnosophic democracy there will be no occasion for luxurious waste solely for purposes of display. While there will be great economy in these respects, the standard of comfort will be considerably higher. Dwelling-houses, offices, factories, public meeting-places, etc., will be so constructed as to be well ventilated at all times, comfortably warm in cold weather, and airy and relatively cool in hot weather. They will have extensive window space to admit as much sunlight as possible, sleeping porches, swimming pools and gymnasiums in the basements, and solaria upon the roofs to use in winter.

In similar fashion there will be great economy in furniture and decorations, through the elimination of unnecessary duplication and luxurious waste for display. But the household equipment will be more comfortable and more beautiful. Chairs and benches will be covered with a material which is not too hard and chilly for the skin. All of the furniture will be designed so that, both as to line and color, it will furnish a suitable background for the human figure. The walls should be decorated simply, and so as to suggest objects from nature, because gymnosophists retire into houses only when the weather and the exigencies of their work compel them to do so. Architecture, interior decoration, and the designing of furniture, utensils, tools, etc., will furnish useful tasks for the artists of the gymnosophic society.

An unhealthy phase of the evolution of culture has been the invention of numerous edible concoctions, most of which are indigestible. Thus has been created a great diversity of artificially prepared dishes which tempt the appetite unduly, and often lead to overeating. Many of these dishes are concocted from nutriments which, however good by themselves, do not harmonize well, and cause havoc in the digestive processes. The simplification of food and its preparation in accordance with scientific dietetic principles are of the utmost importance for the health of mankind. The simplification of life encouraged by gymnosophy will aid greatly in bringing about these dietetic changes. The taste for these complicated and unhygienic dishes is created largely by the abnormal and unhealthy conditions of modern life. A life free from clothing, and spent largely in healthful activity in the open, will spontaneously and without forethought stimulate an appetite for a simpler and better balanced diet. While gymnosophy should not be attached to any particular dietetic reform, such as a vegetarian or a raw food diet, it will inevitably lead to a more hygienic dietary. It will destroy the craving for stimulants and sedatives caused by the nerve-racking life of civilization.

It may be objected that this simplification of life will result in the absence of an agreeable and entertaining diversity, so that human existence will become monotonous and boresome. But gymnosophy means much greater enjoyment of nature than is at present feasible for most humans. It signifies more intimate and satisfactory relations between the sexes, and much less of the unhealthy and abnormal sex-starvation which now prevails. It includes an abundance of recreation in the form of games, sport and dancing, which are much more gratifying to healthy and normal individuals than many of the amusements of both the urban and rural communities of today.

It may be alleged that ceremonial and symbolic observances are required by mankind, and that these observances must be somewhat ornate in their character in order to be duly impressive. Both primitive and civilized peoples display a tendency to make a ceremony of the repast. Savages often accompany it with magical observances. Many civilized persons assume a distinctive garb before dining, sometimes prelude the meal with prayer, and occasionally postlude it with oratory. The church is largely a ceremonial institution, wtih a strong emotional appeal with its ritual, sacraments, ecclesiastical vestments, lights, colors, odors, music, chanting, and intoning.[1] The state organizes many ceremonial spectacles with the aid of official and military uniforms, army and navy reviews, martial music, and the pomp of

[1] In New York I attended a midnight mass in which all of these ceremonial elements were exemplified. In Istanbul I attended the great prayer on Friday in Aghia Sofia where most of these elements were present, though the Mohammedan ritual is simpler than the Christian.

royal progresses and patriotic processions. The stage contributes its large and colorful share to ceremonial and symbolic observances. Even the universities, though professedly institutions of learning and of scientific research, add their touch with the aid of ornate and ofttimes gaudy doctoral gowns decorously trailed through solemn and sedate academic processions.[2]

Whether or not mankind will ever develop beyond the point where ceremonial and symbolic observances are required is yet to be seen. When men and women arrive at a better comprehension of the universe in which they live, and of the conditions to which they must adjust their lives, it is possible that they will no longer need ceremony and symbolism to impress upon their minds the things which are or are supposed to be of importance. They will be better able to appraise and appreciate relative and intrinsic values, when mankind has passed beyond its present infantile stage.

In any case, if ceremony and symbolism are still required in the gymnosophic society, they can be supplied without the aid of dress. To diversified architecture, furniture and decorations can be assigned a symbolic significance. Dramatic spectacles, exhibitions of dancing, and music can furnish ceremonial observances, so that gymnosophy constitutes no obstacle in the way of whatever of a ceremonial and symbolic character may be demanded. But the influence of gymnosophic living will diminish greatly the demand for the ceremonial and symbolic, which is now largely due to the hollowness and futility of human existence.

The spread of gymnosophy would be aided and hastened by the establishment of gymnosophic colonies in a suitable environment, where a simple manner of life might be adopted and pursued from the outset, and not gradually and slowly introduced. These colonies might be agricultural and industrial in their character, and, therefore, self-sustaining. They should not be located in cold regions, but either in the tropics or in the temperate zones. They might be located in thinly populated regions of civilized countries, such as Soviet China and Russia. In those countries the peasantry would perhaps offer less op-

---

[2] While a teacher in various universities, I felt the pressure, placed upon members of the academic profession by the potentates of the university hierarchy to don these garments which are utterly incongruous with the spirit and character of their profession, which they call learned. In this connection the following quotation is of interest: "It is significant, not only as an evidence of their close affiliation with the priestly craft, but also as indicating that their activity to a great extent falls under that category of conspicuous leisure known as manners and breeding, that the learned class in all primitive communities are great sticklers for form, precedent, gradations of rank, ritual, ceremonial vestments, and learned paraphernalia generally." (T. Veblen, *The Theory of the Leisure Class*, New, York, 1899, p. 367.)

position than the rural population in most countries. Traces of the primitive practice of nudity may still linger in the home life and bathing customs of the Russian peasants, so that it might be feasible to propagate gymnosophy among them.[3] In tropical regions it might be possible to establish colonies in the vicinity of peoples who still retain their primordial nudity. Care would have to be taken to avoid regions where diseases such as malaria abound, and which are infested by venomous and pestiferous insects to which civilized peoples are not adapted.

In many parts of the world unwise and injudicious persons, such as missionaries, colonial officials, etc., have imposed clothing upon the aboriginal inhabitants. This is true of most of the South Pacific islands which in many respects are admirably fitted for gymnosophic purposes.[4] The native inhabitants now have much to unlearn as a result of the meddlesome activities of their self-appointed tutors. Where primitive peoples are still untouched by outside influences, they can cooperate with gymnosophists to bring into being a healthier, saner and simpler mode of life. Thus can the best features of primitive and civilized culture be combined. Not only can these peoples learn what is useful in civilization, but the proud and haughty civilized peoples, putting aside their arrogant disdain, can learn valuable lessons in simplicity from primitive culture. Many primitive peoples, however, have already acquired a code of artificial modesty, which is an obstacle to gymnosophy among them as it is among civilized folk.

While gymnosophists are not necessarily socialists or communists, these colonies furnish excellent opportunities for experiments along collectivist lines, some of which may be successful and very instructive to mankind. To say the least, these colonies would be democratic in their character. Customary nudity is impossible under the existing undemocratic social, economic, and political organization. Distinctions, external and visible, must be made between king and subject,

[3] In Moscow in 1928 I asked the director of the school for training gymnasium instructors whether there is any nudism in Soviet Russia. He replied that the Russians are not yet cultured enough for gymnosophy thereby indicating his recognition of its value for mankind.

[4] "We remarked that while we plunged into the sea bare, Tahitians never went completely nude, and they were more modest in hiding their nakedness than any white people we had ever met." (F. O'Brien, *Mystic Isles of the South Seas*, New York, 1921, p. 412.) It is possible that the Tahitians had already been corrupted by the whites. O'Brien is speaking of himself and the late English poet, Rupert Brooke, who visited the South Pacific in 1913 and 1914, and was very fond of swimming. If the European War had not caused Brooke's untimely death, he might have become a gymnosophist, for there is something akin to the spirit of gymnosophy in his poetry.

nobleman and commoner, officer and private, ecclesiastic and layman, owner and slave or serf, master and servant, employer and employee, rich and poor. Dress is one of the principal means of making these distinctions, and can scarcely be dispensed with so long as artificial classes and castes, orders and ranks, hierarchical and titular gradations, persist.

In a state of nudity, man is without trappings and distinctions, and all external and artificial signs of rank, class and caste, disappear. But nudity does not abolish distinctions of intelligence and of character, of strength and of beauty. These genuine and intrinsic mental and physical traits can be read from the face and the body, from the features and the form, from the voice and the gestures. When clothes are absent, there is nothing to disturb and mislead the judgment. I have made the acquaintance of many hundreds of men and women while unclothed, and have found that I could judge their intelligence and character at least as well as and often better than if they were clothed, though I could determine little or nothing as to their rank and economic status, except by inference from their range of knowledge and maner of speech.

This feature of the practice of nudity makes gymnosophy and democracy very congenial to each other. Indeed, it is hardly possible to conceive of a genuine democracy which is not also gymnosophic, while, on the other hand, dress is essential in an undemocratic society. This is a fact so obvious that it has been perceived and noted even by writers who knew nothing of gymnosophy. For example, Thomas Carlyle, who was very conventional and conservative, pointed out this fact in satirical language: "Lives the man that can figure a naked Duke of Windlestraw addressing a naked House of Lords? Imagination, choked as in mephitic air, recoils on itself, and will not forward with the picture. The Woolsack, the Ministerial, the Opposition Benches—*infandum! infandum!* And yet why is the thing impossible? Was not every soul, or rather every body of these Guardians of our Liberties, naked, or nearly so, last night; 'a forked Radish with a head fantastically carved'? And might he not, did our stern fate so order it, walk out to St. Stephen's as well as into bed, in that no-fashion; and there, with other similar Radishes, hold a Bed of Justice?"[5] Thoreau said in simpler language: "It is an interesting question how far men would retain their relative rank if they were divested of their clothes. Could you, in such a case, tell surely of any company of civilized men, which belonged to the most respected class?"[6]

Dress is needed to inspire awe in serf and slave, servant and wage-

[5] T. Carlyle, *Sartor Resartus,* Boston, 1835, Book I, Chapter IX.
[6] Henry D. Thoreau, *Walden,* Boston, 1854, p. 26.

earner. It is useful in the decoration of women as a display of wealth, and in other forms of luxurious waste. Hence the universal practice of nudity cannot come until a genuine democracy is established, and great differences of wealth are abolished. The fate of democracy and gymnosophy is much the same. They must go hand in hand and aid each other, for neither can hope to be more than partially successful without the other. I do not mean to imply, however, that nudity is the only factor for democracy. Much more than the practice of nudity is necessary for a thoroughgoing democracy. In like fashion, democracy is not the sole factor for gymnosophy. I have described many other factors, such as the hygienic and the esthetic factors. Many persons who profess to be democrats fail to see the democratic significance of gymnosophy, while some of the gymnosophists are inconsistent in displaying undemocratic racial and social prejudices.

Gymnosophy is a decided humanitarian influence. One of its most important achievements is in bringing the sexes together on the same plane. They enjoy the air, sun, and water together, and to a large extent their sport, thus spending practically all of their leisure time together. Each sex has a humanizing effect upon the other, promoting a greater spirit of gentleness between the sexes. Furthermore, nudism promotes gentleness within each sex. The men are not so prone to be rough with each other. The absence of clothes renders the body less protected against aggression, so that caution develops in handling the body. Gymnosophy has an ameliorating effect upon games. Rough games are not popular among gymnosophists, because they endanger the skin. The playing of games by the sexes together also humanizes games.

The gymnosophic movement should, indeed, be entirely humanitarian. It should be divorced from economic, political, religious, and social biases, prejudices, and propaganda, and should include men and women as human beings regardless of race, religion, class, caste, or sex. It is impossible to eliminate undemocratic influences entirely at present. In spite of the disappearance of clothes, removing all artificial distinctions, social distinctions manifest themselves at times. One of the German societies to which I belonged was controlled by the "white collar" crowd, who were trying to make it socially exclusive. These gentry also had political ideas which they were trying to propagate. Furthermore, race prejudice made its appearance. In this society the notion was prevalent that the nordic blond type is much better adapted for gymnosophy than the Mediterranean brunette type. When the persons sharing this notion gained control, they promulgated an edict that representatives of the south European races would not be admitted to membership. It is almost superfluous to add that these race bigots were bitterly antisemitic, and would under no circumstances admit a Jew. In fact, they were among the fore-runners of the Nazis.

Race prejudice is, indeed, somewhat of a problem for gymno-sophy. It raises the question as to whether or not this form of preju-dice arises out of inherent physical antipathy, which is inextirpable and is accentuated by exposure of the whole body, or is acquired, and can, therefore, be eliminated by appropriate training and education. Certain facts lend some plausibility to the former assumption. The whites think they detect a characteristic odor of the negroes, and a less pronounced odor of the mongolian peoples. I presume that, in similar fashion, the negroes and mongols think they detect an odor of the whites. External racial traits, such as color and shape of the features, are usually regarded as ugly and sometimes as grotesque by other races.

Gymnosophic practices may sometimes intensify race prejudice in a person who had such prejudices at the start. That is to say, such a person will be even less inclined when nude to associate with repre-sentatives of the races toward which his prejudices are directed. This is because the racial differences are more apparent. However, race prejudices are sometimes based upon more or less factitious differences. I have observed anti-semitism, even among the more liberal-minded gymnosophists. And yet there is no striking difference between Jews and Gentiles, both of whom belong to the white race, so that this can-not be the actual reason why these gymnosophists refuse to associate with Jews. It is due to the fact that until gymnosophy becomes more or less wide-spread, the mutual practice of nudity implies a degree of trust and confidence which anti-semites do not like to extend to Jews, against whom they have preconceived and unfounded prejudices.

Racial differences may always keep the races somewhat segregated. That is to say, it is not likely that the white, negro, and mongolian races will ever become entirely assimilated to each other, at any rate, not within a long period of time. But they already mingle together a good deal, and will do so to a greater extent in the future. There is no reason why they cannot become accustomed to seeing each other nude as well as clothed. The racial traits which may at first seem offensive and ugly will soon be ignored under gymnosophic usage. So that race prejudice should not militate against gymnosophy in partic-ular. Such prejudices are serious obstacles in the way of democracy and humanitarianism, and in this fashion stand in the way of the coming of a gymnosophic society. It is of great importance for gym-nosophy that race prejudice disappear entirely, or be reduced to the lowest possible minimum.

A powerful factor for race prejudice and serious obstacle in the way of gymnosophy is the prevalent belief that the tropics are unfit for the white race. It is easy to understand how this fallacious notion has arisen when one observes the manner in which the great majority of white men live in tropical countries in the eastern hemisphere.

Some of these countries are ruled by the whites. It is to the interest of these alien rulers to maintain as vast a difference as possible between their manner of life and that of their native subjects. This consideration, which influences them even when they are not conscious of it, their ignorance and lack of appreciation of non-European culture, and contempt for the darker races, lead them to introduce most of the features of their European manner of life, in spite of its unsuitability for tropical conditions, and to ignore the ways in which the natives have adapted themselves to the climate. Their diet usually includes much meat and other rich foods, which would render it too heavy even for a cold climate. Very often it is generously diluted with alcoholic liquors, which, be it said to their credit, are much less used in Oriental countries than in countries which boast of European culture. While the heat forces them into cooler clothing than at home, yet it is much heavier than the open and scanty dress of the natives.

In one important respect, however, the white man changes his manner of life considerably, and very much for the worse. In tropical countries labor is usually cheap and plentiful. The indolence encouraged by the unaccustomed heat, and the desire to maintain his prestige as a sort of superhuman or semi-divine personage, soon lead the white man to cease from practically all physical exertion, and the effect upon the white women is even worse. Combined with his immoderate eating and often drinking, this has the most dire consequences for his health. While a few may keep up for a time their sports and athletics, they succumb almost invariably to the enervating effect of their social as well as their climatic environment.

This I found to be one of the most distressing features of my travels in tropical and Oriental countries. It was impossible to emerge from my hotel without being besieged by rickshaw coolies, cabmen, donkey drivers, chair carriers, or whatever the local conveyances happened to be. It was inconceivable to these servitors that a "Sahib" would want to go a step on his own legs. The lack of exercise, combined with the heavy and unsuitable food served to Europeans in the hotels, soon had an effect upon my health.

If white men and women will reduce their clothing, adopt a light diet, eliminate alcoholic beverages, take plenty of exercise, and accustom themselves to the sun's rays, from which they always flee, there is no reason why they should not live and work successfully and happily in the tropics. The same applies just as much to their children who, if reared naturally, probably have as much chance for survival in tropical countries as elsewhere.

1135

As a matter of fact, white peoples have in the past developed great civilizations under tropical conditions. European culture was evolved in part under such conditions. Many of the inhabitants of hot and semi-tropical countries today are closely related by blood with white peoples of Europe and America. This is true of the peoples of northern Africa, of Arabia and Persia, and of the so-called "Aryan" peoples of India.

Occidental life has become too artificial and complicated, especially in the cities. Mankind has been cut off from nature to a large extent. Our manner of life is not only unnatural, but harmful to a high degree, and is rapidly developing a degenerate and degraded human breed.

Whether or not the Orient appreciates nature more than the Occident, I do not know.[7] Life on its material side has not yet become so complicated in Eastern and tropical countries as it is in the West. The value of simplicity with respect to clothing, food, and certain other aspects of life may be learned from the East by the West. At the same time, the East can learn valuable lessons concerning political democracy, science, labor-saving devices, and sanitation, from the West. By such mutual tuition the two great divisions of mankind can be brought into closer contact and harmony with each other, and strengthen the humanitarian spirit which is an essential feature of gymnosophy.

As regards the ultimate course of social evolution, one of the most important results from the universal adoption of gymnosophy would be to encourage a tendency to move away from the cold regions into the temperate and tropical zones. This would be in accordance with man's biological nature, because he is an animal adapted to a warm climate. No mammal without a thick fur is well adapted to a cold climate, and man with his bare skin is the least adapted of all.

Mankind can survive in cold regions only with the aid of clothing. While this is a necessary and useful protection against cold, it is injurious in many ways which I have described. The sensible thing for man to do is to retire from the frigid zones to the warmer regions, where he can lead a more comfortable and happier existence. Here not only is nudity feasible most of the time, but it is much easier to procure the necessaries of life, so that labor is greatly decreased. Furthermore, it is possible to live in close contact with nature practically all the time, whereas in the frigid north and south the vast majority of persons are almost entirely cut off from nature for many months of the year. It is egregious folly on the part of mankind to persist in

[7] See my *Oriental and Occidental Culture, An Interpretation*, New York, 1928, Chapter XI entitled "Attitude toward Nature and the Artificial Life."

dwelling in those portions of the earth where the cold and gloomy winter destroys much of the joy of living for more than half of the year.

The human species doubtless originated in the warmer regions of the earth. The pressure of population upon the means of subsistence compelled mankind to migrate into the colder regions, where the conditions of life are much harder. The abandonment of the frigid zones and of the colder portions of the temperate zones would necessitate the restriction of population. This has already become necessary in order to maintain the standard of living, and birth control will become more essential as the density of population increases.[8] The cold regions could be visited during the warm months for a change and recreation, and also to secure useful mineral, animal and plant products, but should be deserted during the dark and inhospitable winter months.

The area of permanent and continuous human habitation should be determined by the isothermal lines. The isotherms of 20° Centigrade (68° Fahrenheit) in the northern and southern hemispheres include almost all of Africa and Australia, most of South America, and the southern parts of North America and of Asia.[9] This comprises more than half of the land surface of the world. The Antarctic continent, which is entirely uninhabited, constitutes one-tenth of the total land surface, and to this should be added the Arctic region and extensive sub-Arctic areas in Asia and North America which are almost uninhabited. If these regions, which can never become densely populated, are deducted, about one-fourth of the total land surface is eliminated from the habitable area. The excluded area is very thinly populated in comparison with the densely populated regions. The density of population per square mile in Africa (14) is scarcely one-tenth the density in Europe (145), though its area is three and one-third times as great, and one-fifth the density in Asia (71). The density of population in South America (15) is only 10 per cent of the density in Europe, though its area is nearly twice as great, and 21 per cent of the density in Asia.[10] So that the habitable area furnishes plenty of space for the population of the excluded area.

In creating the gymnosophic society, there also is a problem of

[8] I have discussed the subject of population at length in my *Poverty and Social Progress*, New York, 1916, especially in Chapter XII and XIII, entitled "The Growth of Population and the Increase of Wealth" and "Population and Poverty"; and in my *Farewell to Poverty*, New York, 1935, Chapter XXIX, entitled "Population and Geo-Economic Regionalism.' Here will be found ample evidence of the necessity for controlling the increase of population.

[9] The average annual temperature of Mediterranean Europe is 15°-19° Centigrade (59°-66° Fahrenheit).

[10] *The World Almanac*, New York, 1950, p. 218.

the distribution of population between city and country, as well as of its density. The concentration of population in urban centers was necessary for the evolution of the higher culture, as I have pointed out in another work.[11] The cities have, however, become hideous monstrosities, which blight the lives and happiness of a large part of mankind. In the United States in 1940, 40.1 per cent of the population lived in towns and cities with 25,000 or more inhabitants and 28.9 per cent in cities having 100,000 or more inhabitants. In 1790 only 5.1 per cent of the population were in towns of 2,500 or more inhabitants, and in 1950 59 percent were in towns and cities of 2,500 or more inhabitants.[12] A similar situation exists throughout the civilized world.

The principal cause for the rapid increase of urban population has been the development of the factory system, which has necessitated the concentration of population in urban centers.[13] Machine and factory, namely, large scale methods of production having increased enormously the amount produced, have made possible a much larger population. Most of the fertile land in civilized countries has been settled upon and cultivated. Hence the tendency of population is to flow from the country to the city. Thus are aggravated the concentraion and congestion in towns and cities, which now consist mainly of unsanitary factories, crowded office buildings, and tenement and apartment houses in which humans swarm and procreate like rabbits in their hutches. Through it all roars the ear-splitting din, nerve-racking rush, and insensate turmoil of urban existence. Under such conditions mankind is cut off from the spaciousness, the tranquillity and the beauty of nature, and is deprived largely of the open air, fresh food, and sufficient physical exercise.

The simplification of life brought about by gymnosophy will lessen the demand not only for clothes, but also for many other useless and harmful objects. It will be all the easier to discard these objects when mankind has retired from the cold regions, and is segregated in the warmer zones, where a life close to nature is easy and comfortable. This simplification will, therefore, decrease the number of factories, warehouses, docks, ships, railways, airplanes, offices, automobiles, shops, etc., necessary to supply human wants. The progress of science will constantly render it easier to manufacture whatever machine products are needed. Work will become mainly that of raising the food, which a genial climate will readily supply, combined with handicrafts carried on in the home, by means of which some of

11 *Farewell to Poverty*, p. 437.

12 *16th Census of the United States: 1940*, Population, Volume I, Washington, 1942. *17th Census of the U.S.: 1950*, Population, Volume II, Part I.

13 See my *Poverty and Social Progress*, pp. 164-7.

the simple objects required can be produced. This will restore to the hands and muscles the training and skill of which they have been deprived by the present machine age. Consequently, the cities will become smaller and the population can spread itself over the land, in order to cultivate it and to enjoy a life in close contact with it.

This description of the future course of social evolution will doubtless seem to many readers as no better than a utopian dream. But it involves changes no greater than those which have taken place within the historic period, to say nothing of prehistoric times. It conflicts with many social ideals which have had a vast influence in human affairis. Hitherto it has been deemed a laudable and desirable end to increase the population of the world, and to render as much as possible of the earth's surface habitable. This motive has played an important part in exploration, migration, colonization, and the production of wealth. Too much cannot be said in praise of the bravery and fortitude of explorers, who have gratified human curiosity and have contributed to the advancement of science by exploring the frigid and icy masses of the polar regions, the sandy wastes of the arid deserts, the torrid jungles inhabited by dangerous beasts of the tropical forests, the watery expanses and the islands of the uncharted seas, the tortuous windings of unknown rivers, and the precipices and high altitudes of the mountain ranges. They and the pioneers who first settled uninhabited areas have endured untold dangers and tribulations, which render them heroes in the human epic upon this planet. Mankind can never adequately thank and recompense them for their sufferings and their valor.

While the day of the explorer and the pioneer is not entirely past, the time has come for mankind to consolidate its achievements and its resources, and to organize its life for the promotion of human happiness. The ideal of mere magnitude in the size of population and in the extent of territory inhabited too often conflicts with the ideal of the greatest possible happiness. The ideal of magnitude has been encouraged by patriotic and nationalist delusions, which have led chauvinists to crave numerous inhabitants and extensive territories for their countries, and by certain religious doctrines which have encouraged procreation, or, to say the least, have opposed birth control on the ground that such measures are contrary to divine purposes.

When mankind has gathered voluntarily in the regions of a genial climate, and the conditions of existence have been simplified, the normal life in accord with the natural environment and fundamental human traits will commence. Then will be more feasible the free and spontaneous expression of human nature, limited only by the restrictions upon the individual in recognition of the rights and interests of other individuals, which are inevitable in every community.[14] Here will be ample opportunity for adventure and experimentation in ways of living as interesting and exciting as the era of exploration and pioneering. The environment is sufficiently diversified, with its highlands furnishing a bracing and rarefied atmosphere, and its lowlands in close proximity to seas, lakes, and rivers, thus furnishing all kinds of topography and of flora and fauna.

In the inhabited region are mountain ranges, such as the Sierras and Andes of the Western Hemisphere, the Iberian Sierras, the Italian Apennines, the classical mountains of Greece, the Atlas and other ranges of Africa. The average altitude of the African continent is 650 meters (2100 feet), as contrasted with an average altitude of only 300 meters (1000 feet) in Europe. The average altitude of South America is 650 meters (2100 feet), only slightly less than the average altitude of 700 meters (2300 feet) in North America. The average altitude of Australasia and Oceania is 350 meters (1150) feet. The principal loss, so far as altitude is concerned, will be Asia, whose average altitude is 950 meters (3100 feet). But a large part of the Asiatic highlands could under no circumstances be thickly populated.

To many readers the changes which I have outlined may seem a regression to a more primitive state. It will be rather a sloughing off of cultural institutions which are demonstrably injurious to mankind, and their replacement by a culture better adapted to man's original and fundamental traits. The gymnosophic culture will not be perfect at the outset, or at any time, because perfection can never be attained in human affairs. The new culture can come into being only slowly, in the course of many generations, perhaps of many centuries. Most men and women are unprepared and unfitted for it, and would not like it if it were forced upon them. They have been reared under the existing culture, and have acquired the tastes and ideals which dominate it. These tastes and ideals are artificial, and can and will be transformed when the young are reared in a more natural manner. The hope of gymnosophy, like that of every great and far-reaching reform, is in the education and training of the youth. When a generation free from artificial modesty, and fond of a life close to nature, has arisen, then will the gymnosophic society blossom forth into its fruition.

The view which I have presented is fundamentally different from the views which are usually held and stated with regard to the human habitation of the world. Numerous writers have pointed out that it

[14] I have defined the normal life in my *Poverty and Social Progress*, New York, 1916; the spontaneous expression of human nature in my *Personality and Conduct*, New York, 1918; and have described the degree of social control of the individual which will always be necessary in my *Criminology*, New York, 1918.

has been the tendency of civilization to move from the warm to the colder regions.[15] The leadership in cultural evolution has passed from Sumeria, Akkadia, Babylonia, and Egypt over Crete to Greece, to Rome, and so on northward to Paris, London, and Berlin. This has been interpreted to mean that the temperate zone, and especially the colder portions of this zone, are best adapted for the higher civilization. The two principal reasons adduced are that cold is more bracing than warmth, and that the high degree of variation between the winter and summer temperatures is stimulating both physically and mentally.

A writer on climate has expressed this view as follows: "The monotonous heat of the tropics and the continued cold of the polar zones are both depressing. Their tendency is to operate against man's highest development. The seasonal changes of the temperate zones stimulate man to activity. They develop him physically and mentally. They encourage higher civilization."[16] An Arctic explorer has expressed it thus: "Man, as an animal, is indeed, a tropical animal. But man, as distinguished from animals, is not at his best in the tropics or very near them. His fight upward in civilization has coincided in part at least with his march northward over the earth into a cooler, clearer, more bracing air."[17] Another climatologist has endeavored to describe the ideal climate in the following words: "On the basis of our factory operatives and students, the best climate would apparently be one in which the mean temperature never falls below the mental optimum of 38° (Fahrenheit), or rises above the physical optimum of 60° or possible 65°. From this point of view the most ideal conditions would seem at first thought to be found where the temperature at all seasons averages not far from 50°, but this conclusion needs modification as will shortly appear."[18]

These and other writers are enthusiastic about the "northward course of empire,"[19] because it signifies a greater human population, the exploitation of new natural resources, the production of more wealth, and the spread of a culture with the material and artificial features of our existing civilization. Some of them are much concerned to prove that civilization can and should push farther northward. An

---

[15] See, for example, Benjamin Kidd, *The Control of the Tropics*, New York, 1898; Robert De Courcy Ward, *Climate considered especially in Relation to Man*, New York, 1908; Ellsworth Huntington, *Civilization and Climate*, New Haven, 1915; S. C. Gilfillan, "The Coldward Course of Progress," in the *Political Science Quarterly*, Vol. XXXV, No. 3, September 1920, pp. 393-410; Vilhjalmur Stefansson, *The Northward Course of Empire*, New York, 1922.

[16] R. D. Ward, *op. cit.*, p. 273

[17] V. Stefansson, *op. cit.*, p. 1.

[18] E. Huntington, *op. cit.*, p. 129.

[19] The "southward march of empire" is narrowly limited by the scarcity of land in the southern hemisphere.

1141

Arctic explorer has written voluminously to demonstrate that the Arctic regions are not so cold as is usually supposed, that reindeer, ovibos (musk ox), and the like, can be raised on the grass lands, and that there is an abundance of fish in the Arctic waters, so that a large population can dwell in these regions, and that this population will be superior to the population of the warmer regions.[20]

Many of the facts adduced by these writers are true. It is undeniable that with the movement northward the human population has greatly increased. It is indisputable that the centers of what is commonly called "civilization" have gradually moved northward during the past three or four thousand years. It is probable that the cold climate has stimulated a good deal of exertion. This has been devoted to exploiting many natural resources, building the largest cities ever known, producing an enormous amount of material wealth, creating huge armies and navies, waging vast and destructive wars, and also to numerous inventions of new appliances, and to the advancement of science. A considerable population with the aid of warm clothes, houses and fuel, could inhabit the frigid regions and produce more or less material wealth.[21] However, some of their interpretations of fact are subject to qualification.

European civilization evolved in the Mediterranean area in a

---

[20] V. Stefannsson, *The Friendly Arctic,* New York, 1921; *The Northward Course of Empire,* New York, 1922. "So long as we have competitive civilization and so long as public opinion continues to allow the energetic and the powerful to take whatever they wish from the lethargic and the weak, so long will the North continue to dominate the South as it is doing today, for it produces the one crop that matters— men of unsleeping energy and restless ambition." (P.84.)

[21] Stefansson himself admitted that the North will not become densely populated, at least in the near future: "We look upon the immediate development of the North as consisting mainly in great stock ranches where a few people will be all that are needed to look after thousands of animals and tens or hundreds of square miles of grazing land." (*The Northward Course of Empire,* p. 227.)

In a review of Stefansson's book, Huntington commented upon this point as follows: "In Stefansson's northland the population, except in the mining centers, must apparently always be sparse. How sparse, even the author of 'The Northward Course of Empire' does not seem fully to realize. According to his own statement thirty reindeer or an equivalent number of ovibos can be supported on an average square mile of the tundras. One Eskimo is needed to care for about 1500 reindeer. But 1500 reindeer require fifty square miles of pasturage. One family, then, in the reindeer country would be all that would be needed to develop the grazing possibilities of an area five miles by ten, and the conditions where ovibos are raised would be similar. . . . That Stefansson's dream of a northland which supplies southern regions with great quantities of meat will come true seems highly probable. But that the northern regions will ever be more than an outpost of civilization, a ragged fringe upon the borders of the main centers, seems doubtful." (E. Huntington, *Yale Review,* January 1924, p. 390.)

The population of Alaska decreased from 64,356 inhabitants in 1910 to 55,036 in 1920, and then increased to 72,524 in 1939, when the density of population in

genial climate. It moved northward not solely or even mainly owing to climatic factors. The desert region stretching across northern Africa and Arabia, and connecting with other natural obstacles to the east in the form of mountain ranges, deserts, and seas, formed an effective barrier against its spread southward and eastward. During the past five thousand years the region to the east of Palestine has been growing more arid, aiding in the extinction of the ancient civilizations of Mesopotamia, and strengthening the barrier toward the east.[22] The deserts of Arabia and Mesopotamia, the mountain ranges of Central and Eastern Asia Minor, the Caucasus, the Black and Caspian seas, form this barrier. Hence it was to be expected that these topographical factors would cause the cultural movement originating in the Nile valley and the eastern Mediterranean littoral to expand northward and westward.

It must also be remembered that the ancient civilizations of India and of China served to a certain extent as a cultural barrier. These civilizations originated and were located in part in warm regions. It is an error to assume that a highly developed civilization is possible only in a cold climate.

These writers are dominated by the ideal of Occidental civilization, which includes a large population, much of which is crowded into monstrous cities, the production of huge quantities of material goods, the extensive exploitation of natural resources and of human labor, the extensive use of physical force in industry and warlike activities, and the employment of science and invention mainly for these purposes. In this crudely materialistic welter the principal criterion is quantity rather than quality, while the promotion of human happiness, the development of personality, and man's intimate relation with nature are almost entirely ignored and forgotten.

In contrast to the above is an ideal whose criterion is quality rather than quantity. According to this ideal, a happy mankind is more important than a vast population, life in a close relation to nature is preferable to huge cities, and the development of personality is more valuable than the expenditure of an enormous amount of physical force. The obstacles in its way are great, and may prove to be insuperable. It is nevertheless worth while to state the ideal.

continental United States was 348 times as great as in Alaska. (*16th Census of the United States: 1940*, Population, Volume I, Washington, 1942.)

Most of Alaska lies between Lat. 60° and 71° N. The war of 1939 to 1945 and its aftermath caused some artificial and partly temporary increase of population due to the military operations in Alaska. According to the census of 1950 it was 126,661. (*Congressional Record*, November 29, 1950, p. 16103.)

22 E. Huntington, *Palestine and Its Transformations*, Boston, 1911. According to Huntington, Palestine and the region to the east have been growing arid since 3000 B.C.

1143

During the past ten thousand years has arisen our civilization, which has become in the main urban. Man himself has changed very little during that period. The remains of the Aurignacian and the Cro-magnon men, who lived in Europe twenty-five thousand or more years ago, indicate a type substantially the same as the human type of today. While his artificial environment and mode of life have changed greatly, man's physical traits have remained essentially the same. Hence has arisen the acute maladjustment between man the air and light animal, and his civilized and urbanized existence. By giving to the human body its proper dignity, gymnosophy will aid greatly in restoring mankind to a more natural existence, and it implies and connotes many other important and beneficent changes for the individual and for society.[23]

In imagination we can foresee the city of the future where gymnosophy prevails. It will be far more spacious than our warrens and sties in which human animals breed and huddle together like rabbits and swine. It will be flooded with air and light. Possessing an abundance of foliage, it will combine the advantages of city and country. The rural folk also will be leading a more natural and healthy existence. While they are surrounded by nature today, they cut themselves off largely from its beneficent influence by their clothing and manner of life. Thus will gymnosophy assist mankind not only to develop and enrich all that is of value in existing culture, but also to recover much that we have lost through artificial civilization.

The foregoing surmise as to what lies ahead may seem rather visionary. And it would indeed be foolish to attempt to prophesy with too much assurance what path will be taken by cultural evolution in the far distant future. But this tentative glimpse may be helpful.

It is only human to dream of a saner world in which mankind will not be largely deprived of contact with nature, and where under its beneficent influences children will grow up into healthy and happy adults; a world in which equality between the sexes will encourage harmonious relations between men and women; and where races and nations will dwell together in perpetual peace, prosperity and with mutual respect in a federation which will furnish world citizenship to the whole of mankind.[24] No free and frank discussion as to how these ends may be attained can wholly fail to aid in promoting, in however small a measure, the health and happiness of mankind.

[23] Much of this chapter has been paraphrased and brought up to date from my book entitled *The New Gymnosophy*, New York, 1927; later published under the title *Nudism in Modern Life*, 5th revised edition, 1952.

[24] See my book entitled *Geo-Economic Regionalism and World Federation*, New York, 1950, pp. 52-53.

Chapter LXVII

The Role of the Fine Arts

THE fine arts are not indispensable and are much less important than the industrial arts, technology, invention, and science. However, they cater to human esthetic senses and are sufficiently influential to deserve some attention. Especially significant is the relation of these esthetic arts to man's contact with and appreciation of nature. In a sense they are fringent or incidental to the main course of cultural evolution. At any rate, they could disappear or diminish very greatly in extent without having a serious effect upon cultural evolution, whereas no one of the above dynamic factors could diminish greatly or disappear without having a very disastrous if not mortal effect upon culture.

Life is an end in itself—it is, indeed, the supreme end of the organic world. The enjoyment of nature in its manifold variety also is an end in itself, for it gratifies the senses and such gratification is essential for the most complete realization of the life of the human organism in all of its phases and activities. Art is at most a means to an end, endeavoring by artificial means to gratify the senses, human desires and impulses. At times a useful complement, it can never fully take the place or supersede the direct appreciation and enjoyment of nature.

In its broadest and most philosophic meaning, everything in the universe is a part of nature and is natural. I am using the term "nature" in its narrower anthropocentric sense by which mankind distinguishes itself and its works from the remainder of the universe. By "artificial" I mean whatever is created by man, not only artifacts such as tools, machines, boats, houses, etc., but also science, philosophy, technology, religion, art, etc. These human products are fashioned out of materials furnished by nature. But these objects would not have their present form were it not for human thought, feeling and effort. Whatever is artificial is not unnatural, but is that part of nature which has been modified and sometimes transformed by man.

In the following discussion it is not my intention to oppose art to nature or even to compare them, for they are not usually comparable. As a substitute for nature, art is not effective or desirable. When viewed from this standpoint, a portrait or statue is lifeless compared with the animation of the living form. Nevertheless the industrial and some of the fine arts create many things which do not exist in nature, and the physical basis for man's culture is furnished in large part by these arts. It is in the development of these arts and of science that man is chiefly distinguished from other animals. While nature cannot be surpassed in its own field, art has produced many things of utility and value. It is futile to make either art or nature a fetish, for both can be utilized for the benefit of mankind.[1]

At certain times and places has been manifested a tendency to rank art above nature. This has usually happened during a period of decadence accompanying or following the culmination of a cultural movement. It is similar to the tendency to place institutions above the interests they subserve, such as the state above society, society itself above the individuals of which it is composed, the nation and patriotism above human life and happiness, the family above the personality of the individual, the increase of population above the satisfaction of the parental instincts and emotions, and marriage above the play function of sex.[2]

[1] In his last book a literary artist expressed the opinion that nature is paramount to art: "Looking at art from the outside, we may say that it is insignificant 'n relation to the realities of life. To the artist, particularly when he contemplates the immortal works, as he deems them, of the foremost geniuses, it no doubt seems a very great thing—the highest achievement of man. To the mass of humanity it is something unimportant, negligible. The reason is that in the works of art the universal sense of beauty, the fiery principle, a sweetener of life and joy forever, can never find its fullest, freest and its final expression. The artist himself in spite of his delusion will sometimes confess it." (W. H. Hudson, *A Hind in Richmond Park*, New York, 1923, pp. 285-6.)

The same may be said as to sex. The authors of the *Kinsey Report* assert that sexual sublimation is almost impossible: " A great many persons have tried to establish their sexual lives on the assumption that sublimation is possible and the outcome desirable. . . . If one removes those who are physically incapacitated, natively low in sexual drive, sexually unawakened in their younger years, separated from their usual sources of sexual stimulation, or timid and upset by their repressions, there are simply no cases which remain as clear cut examples of sublimation." (A. C. Kinsey, W. P. Pomeroy, and C. E. Martin, *Sexual Behavior in the Human Male*, Philadelphia, 1948.)

[2] I have named the part played by sex in human life, apart from and in addition to the reproductive function, its play function. See my *Personality and Conduct*, New York, 1918, Chapter IX. "This second function is due to an efflorescence of the sexual impulse, largely through the affective traits of the warm-blooded animals." (pp. 102-03.)

See also Havelock Ellis, *Little Essays of Love and Virtue*, New York, 1921, Chapter VI, in which he gave me credit for originating this concept in my *Poverty and*

The most powerful modern enemy of the play function of sex is the Roman Catholic Church. On December 31, 1930, Pope Pius XI issued the papal encyclical "Casti Connubii" (Chaste Spouses) which forbade contraception. On October 29, 1951, Pope Pius XII declared that "This prescription is in full force because it is not a simple precept of human right but the expression of a natural and divine law." He inveighed against the "cult of pleasure," and denounced books and articles which teach that "happiness in marriage is in direct proportion to reciprocal pleasure in conjugal relations." Thus does the frustrated and emasculated personality of an ostensible celibate, erroneously dubbed a "father," usurp authority over hundreds of millions of human beings in matters of vast import for their lives and happiness. This is one of the many instances of the irreparable injury done to mankind by religion.

Mankind needs again and again to save itself from the overdevelopment and misdirection of culture which render it the slave of its institutions. While man has in many ways profited greatly from the evolution of civilization, he must endeavor to recover a good deal that he has lost thereby, namely, the complete expression of his original nature so far as that is compatible with a life in common with his fellows.

In highly industrialized and urbanized civilization the artificial often encroaches unduly upon the natural mode of existence, various forms of art supplanting the spontaneous expression of many of the most profound human impulses. This is life at secondhand, and a readjustment between the artificial and the natural is imperative if human personality is to attain complete development. The American poet Masters has expressed the inadequacy of art as well as religion:

> "Art does not suffice—
> Religion is not life, but life is living.
> And painted cherries to the hungry thrush.
> Is art to life. The artist lived his work.
> You cannot live his life who love his work.
> You are the thrush that pecks at painted cherries
> Who hope to live through art." [3]

Social Progress, New York, 1916, Chapter XXI entitled "Eugenic Measures and the Human Breed," in which I discuss harmonizing the two functions instead of suppressing the play function by the reproductive function. In my book entitled *The Play Function of Sex*, I have described in detail this important phase of sex.

[3] Edgar Lee Masters, "Victor Rafolski on Art," in *Toward the Gulf*, New York, 1918, p. 83. A psychoanalyist has expressed a similar thought. "It is certainly not, however, merely the outward deprivation (that is, the pressure of the mechanical age) that obstructs the artistic development of modern individuals, but the strong impulse

Art, like science and philosophy, invention and industry, magic and religion, is one of the cultural forms in which mankind expresses itself. No hard and fast lines can be drawn between these different forms of expression. Like the varied types of human nature they merge into each other and are inextricably interwoven in the effort to attain expression. Though science and religion are opposed to each other in the conclusions at which they have arrived, both have arisen out of attempts on the part of man to explain the universe in which he lives. Though magic and inventive technology are based on fundamentally contradictory ideas and theories, both are attempts to utilize and control the forces of nature for the benefit of mankind.

Art has instinctive, intellectual and emotional origins. Every organism must expend a certain amount of energy in order to maintain the vital processes because complete inanition would soon result in death. Human energy is expended in work and play, in imitation and in invention, in science and in industry, in art and in religion. When producing something, human energy is creative. All human activities, whether creative or not, are determined by instincts, feelings and intelligence. Instincts are inherited tendencies toward more or less definite modes of action. Feelings are affective sensations, that is to say, sensations with a pleasurable or a painful content. Intelligence is the capacity for varying inherited forms of behavior, such as reflexes and instincts, and is due to memory and experience. The initial impulses arise from the instincts and general innate tendencies, but they are influenced and in part directed by the feelings and the intellect.[4]

The artist endeavors to express sensations which he has experienced and which have interested him, given him pleasure or relieved his pain and discomfort. These sensations having been caused by forms, colors, sounds and the like, in order to experience them again, to intensify their effect, or to give concrete expression to emotions which need an outlet, the artist produces drawings, engravings, paintings, carvings, statues, musical compositions, dramatic and literary representations, etc. These works of art are representational or symbolical, though not in photographic detail. By combining and rearranging his sense impressions and by diminishing or eliminating what are insignificant and non-essential details for him, the artist reveals and emphasizes whatever apeals to him as important and significant

towards life which goes hand in hand with personality-development and makes the creative will of the individual feel that artistic creation is an *unsatisfactory substitute* for real life." (Otto Rank, *Art and Artist, Creative Urge and Personality Development*, New York, 1932, translated from the German, p. 428.)

[4] I have described instinct, feeling and intelligence at length in my *Science of Human Behavior*, New York, 1913.

and whatever appears to him to have value and which he would like to preserve. This is determined in part by his own feelings and ideas, but also in large part by those of his social environment.

The artist is the child of his environment. He is a conscious or unconscious exponent of the feelings and sentiments and, to a much less degree, of the ideas of his time. He holds up a mirror to society and expresses its dreams and desires which he shares with and often feels more intensely than most individuals. Because he has acquired facility in some form of art, he expresses these dreams and desires through this medium. If he possesses exceptional ability and original-ity, he may modify his art medium or may develop new forms. He may also acquire ideas at variance from the prevailing ideas of his time, and give expression to them. But this is exceptional because the artist is emotional rather than intellectual by temperament, and ac-quires such ideas as he may possess by imitation rather than by origi-nal thinking.

The artistic method, utilizing the principles of proportion, rhythm, harmony, and unity, achieves economy of effort on the part of the recipient in grasping the essential, and in apprehending much with little exertion. In this respect any creative work and all modes of human expression are artistic to the extent that they approach or attain perfection of expression. The pleasure derived from this econ-omy of effort contributes to and is a part of the sense of beauty, and is to this degree esthetic.

The artist is, therefore, a creator in his field, just as the scientist and philosopher and sometimes the inventor are in the world of thought and ideas, and the technician in the realm of material ob-jects. Artistic activity gratifies the creative impulses in human nature. The preliterate man who daubs colored earth on the side of a cave and carves rocks and bones, and the child who draws an animal or human profile in the dirt or sand, are trying however unconsciously to imitate the creative forces of nature.

While art is useful for the attainment of certain intellectual ends, such as the communication of information, and is used in magic and religion, the principal utility of art is emotional both for the artist himself and for the spectator. Its purpose usually is to stimulate pleasurable or to subdue painful feelings. By producing his work of art the artist stimulates specific feelings directly and immediately in himself, and by extending and communicating the desired feeling to others he is able to accentuate it in himself. As Hirn has expressed it: "Like him (Dionysus, the god of music) art moves among men, ennobling their joy and blunting the edge of their sufferings." [5]

5Y. Hirn, *The Origins of Art*, London, 1900, p. 110. "Every man seeks automati-cally to heighten his feelings of pleasure and to relieve his feelings of pain. The

The kind of art whose goal is beauty is exemplified in the fine arts. The industrial arts are devoted to the production of useful articles, the fine arts to the creation of objects of beauty tangible or intangible, such as beautiful sounds. This distinction is not absolute, for the fine arts cooperate with the industrial arts in making useful articles beautiful, while objects of beauty may justly be regarded as useful because they gratify human desires.[6]

Artistic expression is the individualistic phase and esthetic appreciation the social aspect of art. The artistic expression is that of the artist himself. The esthetic appreciation which is furnished by his public renders art a medium for social expression. This appreciation comprises a sympathetic appreciation of the beauty of the art stimulated by the appeal it makes to the senses, and an intellectual comprehension of the ideas which it sometimes endeavors to convey.

Esthetic standards are not absolute but relative, and vary according to personal traits and social environment. In Oriental countries I have often heard music which sounded to my Occidental ears like a cacophony, but which was enjoyed by the native auditors who were trained and accustomed to appreciate its form and harmony. Artistic expression varies greatly in the forms which it assumes in different parts of the world, but is nevertheless due to a similar artistic impulse and to more or less similar social factors.

The evolution of the fine arts, as revealed by anthropology, sociology and history, indicates the existence of many factors which have led to artistic expression. Magic and religion gave rise probably early in cultural evolution to works of art, though these were not necessarily the first produced. Sympathetic magic often requires images of the objects upon which it is supposed to work its spell, of the animals hunted in hunting, of the enemy in warfare, etc. Paleolithic carvings and engravings of animals and of human beings were often for purposes of sympathetic magic. Totemism has led to images of the totemic animal. As deities, which are always anthropomorphic, were evolved,

artist is the man who finds that he can gain such enhancement or relief, not only by the direct action of giving expression to his feeling, but also by arousing a kindred feeling in others." (p. 302.)

Croce has expressed a similar thought: "By elaborating his impressions, man frees himself from them. By objectifying them, he removes them from him and makes himself their superior. The liberating and purifying function of art is another aspect and another formula of its character as activity. Activity is the deliverer, just as it drives away passivity." (Benedetto Croce, *Aesthetic as Science of Expression and General Linguistic*, London, 1922, translated from the Italian, p. 21.)

[6] "By an aesthetic or artistic activity we mean one which in its course or in its direct result possesses an immediate emotional factor—in art it is usually a pleasurable one." Ernst Grosse, *The Beginnings of Art*, New York, 1897, translated from the German, p. 48.)

images of them were prepared, to render them more concrete to the minds of their devotees, and sometimes were worshiped as if they were the deities themselves. Thus art is utilized to assist magical and religious practices whose purpose it is to satisfy many human desires. Sometimes it is used to depict graphically an ideal of character and temperament, often embodied in a deity, to which man aspires. Art will remain in the service of magic and religion so long as these two forms of human belief persist.

Personal adornment was one of the earliest purposes of art, either by painting, tattooing or deforming the body itself, or by suspending works of art thereon. Probably the most important end of personal adornment was and is to attract the opposite sex. Another important end of adornment is to appear to attain to a standard of beauty which the individual craves but does not actually possess.

Other purposes of art have been and are to impress one's fellows and to frighten the enemy. Along with and in addition to these ends, it has served to gratify personal vanity and to strengthen and extend one's ego. Art has often been used as a means of social control.[7] Rulers have almost invariably used art to awe their subjects, and to inculcate obedience.

The earliest methods of communicating information by manual delineation were pictographic. Written language with its conventionalized alphabets has evolved from these pictographic methods. Drawings and engravings are still often used to depict more graphically than words can describe. In modern times especially art has been used extensively as a means of propagating ideas and programs of social reform.

There is a demand for artistic forms and decoration in the objects of daily use such as buildings, furniture, utensils, tools, etc. The sheer ugliness of ordinary life, and the surroundings in which it must be passed, creates a demand for adornment and decoration. This is specially true in cities whose inhabitants are almost entirely deprived of the opportunity to enjoy the beauties of nature. In civilized society art has attained a conventional significance as a mark of refinement and culture, so that many persons of wealth demand works of art which they are capable of appreciating very little or not at all.

These and other factors which have not been mentioned create a demand for works of art which furnishes a pecuniary motive to the artist to produce.[8] But the forces which impel the artist are often not

[7] Cf. E. A. Ross, *Social Control*, New York, 1901, Chapter XX.

[8] Haddon has given a fourfold classification of the factors for artistic expression which is not adequate. "There are certain needs of man which appear to have constrained him to artistic effort; these may be conveniently grouped under the four terms of Art, Information, Wealth, and Religion." (A. C. Haddon, *Evolution*

wholly or even at all commercial in their nature. As the preceding psychological analysis has shown, the urge for self expression becomes an artistic impulse *per se* which is a factor for artistic expression. This impulse is similar to the psychological factors involved in the creation of the demand for works of art. Some of the fine arts, such as music and dancing, appeal to fundamental traits, such as the sense of rhythm. Other arts attempt to furnish substitutes, however unsatisfactory, for things craved by human nature but which are lacking in the ordinary life of today. Sometimes they merely give expression to desires and longings without furnishing anything for their satisfaction, except to the extent that giving them expression brings relief. Often the arts aid or are supposed to aid in attaining the ends for which men and women strive.

A landscape painting, though filled with color and all that an artist can depict and express, is colorless and lifeless as compared with the mountains and the seas, the forests and the rivers. It cannot be a substitute for nature, but can merely bring a touch of color and a faint reflection of nature into the drab lives of urban dwellers who are cut off from it. While the artist has derived more or less gratification from producing this painting, this gratification cannot be transmitted to the spectator. It may arouse sensations distantly related to those aroused by the original scene, but only as viewed through the artist's eyes and as depicted by him.

Much of literature is devoted to love and the relations between the sexes. By stimulating the imaginations of the readers it furnishes an anemic substitute for the love life to a vast number of persons whose cravings for love is wholly thwarted or only partially satisfied. Sometimes it leads to the elaboration and acceptance of ideals which cannot actually be realized. While it may be better than nothing for some persons, it often encroaches unduly upon real life and replaces it in phantasy with a life of romance and of adventure which is artificial to an excessive degree. A considerable part of literature, especially in the form of poetry, expresses human aspirations and longings which have been balked and baffled without offering any satisfaction, but the expression of these feelings creates a sympathetic understanding which affords some relief to the poet and his readers. It is sometimes the "poetic cure" for pain, distress, and mental disturbance.

By arousing a similar feeling in those who come in contact with it, the emotions stimulated by art afford a kind of vicarious experience of life as seen through the artist, whose feelings are more intense and perceptions keener than those of his public. His function often is to express for himself and for others desires, longings and

in Art as Illustrated by the Life-Histories of Designs, London, 1895, p. 4.) By "Art" Haddon means art for art's sake as it is defined and treated in esthetics.

impulses which in some cases are unattainable, but often are unfulfilled because of repression by the self or by society. Hence artistic expression may take the form of sublimation by turning unfulfilled desires and impulses into different channels, thus serving as a sort of cathartic by furnishing a measure of relief from the suppressed impulses.[9]

Drawings, paintings and statues of the human figure are pale adumbrations of the object in which men and women are most interested. This lifeless art is inadequate as a substitute for the living reality. While walking through the art galleries of the world, I have often been conscious of the discrepancy between nudity in art, even when portrayed by the greatest artists, and nudity under natural conditions. Not only is their art lifeless, but when obviously striving for beauty, they rarely ever attain a close approximation to the beautiful form, and never communicate natural nudity.

Many of their figures are partially clothed, that is to say, not clothed as much as is required by convention, and yet not entirely nude. The loins are usually covered. Sometimes one breast is bare, the other is covered. A more or less transparent veil may cover part or all of the body. Clothed and unclothed persons appear in the same group in a way which is incongruous according to existing conventions, as in many mythological scenes. Even when the figures are nude, clothes are usually seen or suggested. How many paintings there are of Susanna in her bath surprised by the elders, and of Rubens' plump and fleshy women with their draperies nearly discarded. By all these means the appetite of the clothed onlooker is whetted. Disrobing scenes connected with the bath or the bed aggravate this effect.

These figures almost invariably reveal that they are unclothed rather than nude by their pose, which suggests turning away or shrinking, by their gestures, or by a self-conscious smirk on their faces. In the Louvre in Paris hangs Manet's "Olympia'" (dated 1863). An un-

---

[9] "By its character as a palpable, objective reality, the work of art may diminish the subjective disturbance in which it originates." (Y. Hirn, *op. cit.*, p. 105.)

The psychoanalysts have attempted to analyze and interpret art as a form of sublimation of unfulfilled desires and repressed impulses. Freud has done so in his study of Leonardo da Vinci, but not with complete success, as he himself seemed to recognize. "The tendency to repression, as well as the ability to sublimate, must be traced back to the organic bases of the character, upon which alone the psychic structure springs up. As artistic talent and productive ability are intimately connected with sublimation, we have to admit that also the nature of artistic attainment is psychoanalytically inaccessible to us." (S. Freud, *Leonardo da Vinci, A psychosexual study of an infantile reminiscence*, New York, 1916, translated from the German, pp. 127-8.)

A more fundamental psychological analysis than is possible by the psychoanalytic method is necessary for this purpose. As I have indicated above, it must be based upon a knowledge and study of the instincts, feelings and intelligence.

clothed woman lies on a couch with one bath slipper on. She wears earrings, a black cord and bangle around the neck, and a bracelet with bangle attached on her right wrist. A black maid is in the background holding a bouquet of flowers wrapped in paper, and a black cat emphasizes the pallor of her skin. The bold eyes of the courtezan look at the spectator and proclaim the fact that she is unclothed for professional ends. Her left hand lies significantly over the pubes. However great may be the technical excellence of this work of art, and however realistic its depiction of certain aspects of modern life, it is a painting of the unclothed rather than of the nude, a subjective distinction which it is psychologically justifiable to make with regard to almost all paintings, engravings, carvings, drawings, and statues.

Works of art almost invariably suggest that nudity is not natural and permissible in ordinary life, many artistic portrayals of the nude being mythological or religious scenes and personalities. By imparting such a character to their work, the artists remove nudity from the sphere of everyday life. Their nymphs, fauns, mermaids, gods, goddesses, and saints, often only remotely resemble the human body in its beauty and strength, its ugliness and weakness. The more realistic portrayals of the nude often are placed in exotic surroundings, as in Oriental scenes, in the South Seas, or elsewhere. In this regard Edouard Manet (1833-1883) was superior to most artists, for he had the honesty frankly to portray nudity in the limited and unsatisfactory fashion in which it exists in Occidental society, and it was for this peculiar excellence that he was denounced and condemned by a hypocritical generation.

Among the many thousands of works of art which I have seen, very few portray nudity without the suggestion that it is unclothed. As the artists observe the nude only under the temporary and exceptional conditions of their studios, this situation would be different if they were accustomed to see the human body as a natural and habitual object. The technical excellence of their work would be much greater because they would be able to observe many nude persons of both sexes, of all ages, and of all manner of physical traits, both in action and in repose.[10]

Artists being steeped in the ideas and ideals of a prudish civilization, the human figure for them as for almost every one is unclothed rather than nude, and it is inevitable that consciously or unconsciously they communicate this impression to their products. They see

[10] Both ancient and modern sculptors have chosen their subjects and their poses from a limited number, often imitating famous statues. Gymnosophic experience should increase greatly the number of subjects and poses and emphasize the anatomical realism of statuary.

their models usually only in poses artificially taken.[11] The models being unclothed for commercial reasons have no conception of nudity as a natural and normal state, and are incapable of expressing it. Comparatively few models have beautiful bodies since they usually come from the poor and badly nourished classes, and like most persons in a clothed society, are disfigured and deformed by belts, corsets, footwear, garters, skirts, trousers, and the like. Very few have feet which are not deformed by ill-fitting foot-gear. The public which demands these works of art, being ignorant of natural nudity, innocently and somewhat shamefacedly calls for the unclothed rather than the nude.

Mankind strives through art, as through magic and religion, to secure the things it craves. Some of these things are unattainable, but others might be attained were it not for harmful beliefs, ideas, and institutions. I have said in another work that "an excessive degree of uniformity is imposed upon human nature by fashion, needless customs, conventional morality, formal courtesy, and institutionalized religion. By means of these fetters, which it has blindly forged for itself, mankind has checked the spontaneous expression of human nature and has retarded the development of personality."[12] The problem is to what extent human nature can free itself from this artificial bondage and can satisfy the instincts, feelings and intelligence more fully and spontaneously than is possible through art. Generally speaking, artistic expression exists in inverse ratio to the extent to which human desires are fulfilled and impulses are satisfied. But this statement requires certain qualifications which will be indicated presently.

The few specimens of gymnosophic art and literature in existence in the way of stories, poems, dances, and dramas indicate that nudity in everyday life would eliminate much art and literature which is popularly regarded as sensual because it treats of the human body, but which is objectionable not on account of its sensuality but owing to its artficiality. If nudity ever becomes customary, it will create an art and literature which will replace in part what will be eliminated. While it is futile to attempt to predict in detail the features of a gymnosophic art and literature, it will certainly not be preoccupied with nudity as an exotic or erotic thing because the body will take its place as a familiar and obvious feature of life.

As gymnosophy implies a life closer to nature and less artificial

---

[11] A famous French sculptor, Auguste Rodin (1840-1917), is reputed to have observed several nude persons of both sexes moving freely about his studio before beginning to model a statue of the nude. He would have done better had he taken part in gymnosophic activities.

[12] *Personality and Conduct*, New York, 1918, pp. 269-70.

than that of clothed society, the field and functions of the fine arts would be considerably different in a gymnosophic society. Gymnosophy will not only check the flood of art and literature which exploits the human body in an artificial manner, but will probably diminish the volume of art and belles-lettres in general. The educational, political and economic changes implied by gymnosophy will furnish an ampler opportunity for the formation of all natural and normal relationships, such as the sexual and the parental. Other desires, such as the gratification of the senses, the impulse to play and to indulge in physical activity, the love of nature, etc., will be satisfied more fully than is now possible. Social organization for human happiness instead of for bloody and destructive warfare will afford additional means for self expression and more precise means for social expression.[13] The need for many forms of artistic expression will decrease, for they will be replaced by the direct and spontaneous expression of human nature.

The different fine arts will be influenced in varying degrees. A more adequate satisfaction of human wants will diminish the arts which are devoted mainly to furnishing substitutes and other forms of relief for unfulfilled desires and impulses, but will encourage the arts which beautify the environment and minister to the gratification of fundamental traits such as the sense of rhythm.

The accumulation and greater diffusion of knowledge, aiding man to understand the true character of his wants, will increase comprehension of his environment, both physical and social, thus enabling him to realize under what conditions his desires and impulses can be fulfilled. Better comprehension of human nature and its environment will result in a higher degree of self direction and self control, and in the recognition of the relative importance of impulses and the subordination of the smaller to the greater when conflicts arise. Work being so adjusted as to constitute a form of self expression, will satisfy many desires. The economics effected by the elimination of useless luxuries and unnecessary wastes will furnish more leisure in which to gratify impulses not satisfied in work, and an ample supply of material goods to serve as instruments for the satisfaction of desires.[14]

Ignorance and social restrictions, however, always give rise to some artistic and symbolic expression in children and adolescents,

[13] I have outlined a program for these changes, especially on the economic side, in my *Poverty and Social Progress*, New York, 1916; and *Farewell to Poverty*, New York, 1935; and for the prevention of war in my *Geo-Economic Regionalism and World Federation*, New York, 1949.

[14] I have discussed the simplification of life in *The New Gymnosophy*, New York, 1927, published in England under the title *Nudity in Modern Life*, London, 1929, Chapter XIV. Revised edition under the title *Nudism in Modern Life*, New York, 1931; and London, 1933. Revised edition in 1941 and in 1951.

1156

who have not yet acquired knowledge of themselves and of their environment, and in abnormal types such as the feebleminded and the insane who experience difficulty in adjusting themselves. Temperamental incompatibility, unreciprocated love, jealousy, and frustrated ambition lead to disappointment and dissatisfaction. Accidents, disease, and old age never cease to cause pain and misery. Inexorable death forever separates parents and children, lovers and friends, bringing grief and sadness. From these inevitable ills men and women will continue to turn for relief among other things to art, as they have in the past to religion and magic.

Artistic expression assumes the following forms:

1. Design, depiction, delineation or description.
2. Comedy.
3. Tragedy.

Design is used in all kinds of art, such as drawing, engraving, sculpture, carving, literature, music, etc., for all art, even the most informal or the most imaginative, must have a minimum of form in order to convey a definite impression. Otherwise there would be a chaotic welter of impressions which would be meaningless, and often disharmonious, and therefore unpleasant. Comedy portrays the comic element, and tragedy the tragic element in life. These three aspects are obviously not mutually exclusive because depiction is used constantly in both comedy and tragedy, and the comic and the tragic are intermingled in many works of art.

Often we have to eat with ugly utensils, sit and lie upon clumsy and uncomfortable furniture, and dwell in hideous houses. This is partly due to the fact that we live in a machine age in which craftsmanship is almost entirely ignored, and the products manufactured have lost not only the touch of the hand but also that of nature. We cannot dispense with machines for they are labor-saving devices which increase the quantity of material goods produced and make possible more leisure. The arts of design, the graphic and plastic arts, will always be necessary in the making of tools, utensils, implements, furniture, pottery, textiles, buildings, boats, and all other useful articles. By cooperating with the industrial arts in making machine-made goods as beautiful as possible, important work is provided for drawing, engraving, painting, carving and molding.

Architecture would continue to be one of the principal fine arts. The structures in which we live, and by which we are surrounded, constitute the largest and most permanent feature of our artificial environment. In designing them architects would endeavor not only to make them beautiful in themselves, but to harmonize them with

1157

their natural environment so as to deprive them of as much of their artificial character as possible.

The arts of painting and sculpture may be expected to diminish, for they would be replaced in large part by the enjoyment of beauty in nature and in mankind. Landscape scenes and paintings of trees, flowers and fruits, and of animal life, will be less needed when mankind lives close to the soil and the sky, to the forests and the water, to plant and animal life. When mankind escapes from the hard pavements and the obscured sky of monstrous cities, and can see the fertile earth and the starry heavens, and can rear their offspring in these surroundings, colored canvases will seem like very inferior and weak imitations. When men and women can see each other as they really are, statues will more than ever appear like cold and lifeless images, travesties of the warm and sensient body. In similar fashion will sculptured animals be totally inadequate and superfluous when surrounded by dogs, horses, cats, birds and all the animals that run and fly and swim. To persons living close to the earth painting and sculpture can no longer be a substitute for reality, but at best can only supplement it.

Painting will always be needed to add color to furniture and utensils and for mural decoration. Sculpture may still be used to a slight extent in making statues commemorating great men and women in public buildings and places and in friezes depicting historical scenes, though this custom is likely to decrease. The natural simplicity of architecture in the future will probably require very little carving in wood and stone.

While the arts of spatial design are sensual arts appealing to the sense of vision, their products are inadequate substitutes for what already exists in nature. Music, on the contrary, is a sensual art which can never be replaced and which appeals to profound human traits. While there are sounds in nature which are musical, such as the songs of birds and sounds made by wind and water, the art of music has developed many complicated combinations of sounds which are not found in nature. In most persons music makes a strong appeal to the so-called sense of rhythm and arouses many of the affective states. Most feelings and emotions can be aroused by appropriate music. It stimulates some of the instincts and is sometimes conducive to intellectual activity. Closely related to music is dancing which gratifies the desire for rhythmic activity which is usually not satisfied in work. Whether music or dancing was the earlier art is partly a question of definition. They are two of the original and fundamental arts and their essence is rhythm.[15]

[15] Ellis was of the opinion that dancing is one of the two primary and the earliest of all arts: "Dancing and building are the two primary and essential arts.

In its broadest sense, rhythm is repetition, and is found in all forms of art. Symmetry is based usually, if not always, upon rhythmic repetition.[16] Hence rhythm is one of the fundamental elements of art and much of artistic activity consists of the creation of rhythm. In the arts of design the tendency always is toward a geometrical form in which lines and figures are rhythmically repeated so as to constitute a symmetrical arrangement of the whole. In literature and in poetry in particular rhythm appears in the repetition of a given number of syllables to a line, in rime, and sometimes in alliteration. The rhythmic arts *par excellence* are music and dancing. In music takes place a grouping of sounds with an accentuated beat at uniform intervals. In dancing, movements of the body are repeated within regular intervals of time as in music.

The esthetic appeal of symmetry is due in part to the fact that there is an economy of effort in apprehending a symmetrical arrangement of sense stimuli as compared with an asymmetrical arrangement. The simplest form of symmetry is the repetition at regular intervals of a single element, as in a series of dots, lines or circles, or a succession of sounds of the same pitch. The economy of effort in apprehension is apparent, for the eye or the ear "grasps" a regular arrangement more readily than an irregularly spaced series. But the esthetic appeal of so simple a symmetry is very slight, for it soon grows monotonous to the sense apprehending it and is, therefore, no longer pleasurable and may become painful. It has, indeed, been used as a means of torture, and our senses try to break up a uniform series of sensations and make it rhythmic. Variety must, therefore, be introduced into the symmetry in order to render it pleasurable. If the elements utilized are so grouped that a more striking effect comes at regular intervals, such as the accentuated beat in music, a rhythm has been created.

Rhythm appeals to profound organic traits, but it is not easy to explain this appeal. Various philosophical writers and mystics allege that there is a universal rhythm. No evidence of such a rhythm is available and our knowledge of the universe is too limited to enable us to demonstrate a universal rhythm. Even if we had proof of its existence, it would be too far-fetched to assume that it explains the

The art of dancing stands at the source of all the arts that express themselves first in the human person. The art of building, or architecture, is the beginning of all the arts that lie outside the person; and in the end they unite. Music, acting, poetry proceed in one mighty stream; sculpture, painting, all the arts of design, in the other. There is no primary art outside these two arts, for their origin is far earlier than man himself; and dancing came first." (Havelock Ellis, *The Dance of Life,* Boston, 1923, p. 36.)

[16] *Cf.* George Santayana, *The Sense of Beauty,* New York, 1896, "Symmetry is evidently a kind of unity in variety, where a whole is determined by the rhythmic repetition of similars." (P. 95.)

esthetic appeal of rhythm. This appeal probably is in some way related to the repetitive character of the physiological functions, such as the pulse of the heart, and the respiration of the lungs. Certain it is that the so-called sense of rhythm is largely if not entirely kinesthetic, that is to say, it arouses sensations of movement. This is peculiarly true of dancing which in itself consists of bodily movements. It is also true of music which displays a strong propensity to set us in motion, as is often manifested by swaying of the body, the tapping of the hand or foot, etc. The effect of poetry is largely due to the fact that we unconsciously hum or sing the words to ourselves, thus feeling the kinesthetic sensations derived from music. It is more difficult to explain the appeal of rhythm in the arts of design. But here also the visual sensations received often suggest gliding, rolling, leaping, waving, and the like, which in turn stimulate kinesthetic sensations. The effect of rhythm apprehended through any of the senses is in the last analysis to stimulate all or most of the vital processes and thus to heighten the massive organic feelings of well-being. The successful use of rhythm in many branches of industry corroborates this theory, and explains its value in work and in play.[17]

As to the origin of music, Darwin believed that it originated as a factor in sexual selection, and Spencer thought that it developed out of speech.[18] Various writers have asserted that it evolved out of rhythmic sounds. Rhythm has always played an important part in music. Primitive music consisted almost entirely of rhythmic sounds, there being little or no melody.[19] Music and dancing were almost invariably connected, the association between music and poetry apparently having arisen later. We cannot know when rhythmic sounds were first used in connection with work, but singing has accompanied work among many peoples and in many occupations. The rhythm in music stimulates and aids activity in work as it does in dancing.[20]

[17] In another book I have discussed at length symmetry as a factor in organic evolution: "Symmetry is an almost universal phenomenon in the organic world. Three main types may be distinguished—linear, bilateral, and radial symmetry." (Maurice Parmelee, *The Science of Human Behavior, Biological and Psychological Foundations*, New York, 1913, p. 47.)

[18] *Cf.* C. Stumpf, *Die Anfänge der Musik*, Leipzig, 1911.

[19] "From the character of primitive music, . . . I venture to conclude that the origin of music is to be sought in a general desire for rhythmical exercise, and that the 'time-sense' is the psychical source from which it arises. The rhythm through itself leads us to certain tones (and consequently tunes) by which rhythmical periods are better marked, and the whole movement becomes more distinct." (R. Wallaschek, *Primitive Music*, London, 1893, p. 294.)

[20] For description of many work songs, see Karl Buecher, *Arbeit und Rhythmus*, Leipzig, 1899, 2nd edition.

"La conscience plus ou moins claire de l'activité facile étant à la base du plaisir, on comprend l'agrement du rythme qui se manifeste dans toutes les condi-

1160

In a gymnosophic society music and dancing, the principal arts of rhythm, would doubtless play an ever increasing role. From the earliest age the young would be trained to dance both alone and in unison with each other, and the frequent practice of dancing would provide a constant outlet for many fundamental impulses. Dancing is also incomparably the best of all the fine arts for the health and for the development of a beautiful form, bringing into play every part of the body. It is superior to most of the arts because the dancer is himself the creative artist when dancing. While exhibition dancing by exceptionally skilful dancers will always have its place, it is dancing by the individual himself or in unison with others which has the greatest value. Dancing furnishes the best artistic medium for the spontaneous expression of human nature both in its physical and its psychical aspects. Almost every individual is capable of acquiring the ability to produce some form of music. As music requires a good deal of technical skill, few persons can become skilful musicians. But every one could hear good music more frequently than is the case now. Whenever feasible the auditors could dance in accompaniment with the music so as to enjoy both arts at the same time.

In a natural and healthy existence the tactile, olfactory and gustatory senses receive abundant gratification without the aid of special fine arts. In a life close to nature, spent in healthful activity, and so far as possible free from clothes, the body derives much gratification from contact with the soil and vegetation and from the air and the genial warmth of the sun.

An outdoor life, free from catarrhs, colds and chills, increases greatly the acuteness of the sense of smell. There are many pleasing odors in nature and the cultivation of flowers and of other sweet smelling plants provides a rich gratification to this sense. Under civilized conditions the human olfactory sense has become weak, or, at any rate, largely dormant. As a field naturalist has said: "The more civilized man becomes, or the more he secures himself against the forces of nature by improving his conditions, the less important to his welfare does this sense become. The dangers he is warned against by smell in a state of nature have been removed artificially; in an environment in which the function of the olfactories has been superseded, the inevitable result is their decay."[21]

Fruits and vegetables unspoiled by unhygienic cooking afford much satifaction to the sense of taste when eaten with a healthy appetite and normal digestion. But the culinary art as it is usually

tions où le rythme procure une plus grande facilité du travail." C. Féré, "L'influence du rythme sur le travail,' in *L'année psychologique*, Vol. VIII, 1901, pp. 49-106.)

[21] W. H. Hudson, *A Hind in Richmond Park*, New York, 1923, p. 53.

practiced falls far short of being a fine as well as a useful art, and injures greatly the natural flavor of many foods by the manner of cooking, by jumbling together inharmonious combinations of food in itself nutritious and palatable, and by the excessive use of condiments which conceal the original flavors. These culinary methods not only render food unpalatable but also often make it dietetically injurious or reduce greatly its nutritious value. The conventionally good cooking is often the worst in committing these dietetic and esthetic errors.

A more natural life is likely to diminish greatly artistic expression in the non-sensual or ideational arts. The drama will probably decrease because life will become more varied and the dramatic in life will be better appreciated. People go to the theater largely because life is monotonous and they are bored. There they find romance and adventure. The dramatist has epitomized life and the actors give to it a semblance of flesh and blood reality. At its best drama depicts succinctly and symbolizes the comedy and the tragedy of life, and is both instructive and entertaining. But if men and women could have plenty of romance and adventure in their work and in their play, in travel and in sport, in their love life and in their friendships, they would no longer need the substitute for the reality which the drama offers to them.

The same may be said of literature, both in prose and in poetry. While at its best it gives a more or less faithful and moving picture of life, it is and can be only a picture. With the expansion of knowledge and the improvement of education, life and character will be better understood at firsthand. The comic and the tragic will be expressed more directly and simply in life itself, so that there will not be so much need for explanation and interpretation in literature. The current deluge of stories and novels, poems and plays, essays and reviews, is in part an indication of a genuine and earnest effort to understand and interpret as well as to entertain and amuse. Its fictional and imaginative portion will begin to ebb when mankind becomes better acquainted with human nature, and finds life itself more enjoyable and absorbing.

The diminution of artistic expression in the non-sensual or ideational arts and in some of the sensual arts as a means of substitution, would release a considerable amount of creative energy. Part of this energy would doubtless be expended in play and in the enjoyment of life. The remainder would be available for intellectual pursuits resulting in the increase of knowledge and the advancement of science, inventive pursuits, and industry.

The preceding discussion suggests that a large part of that art which is life at secondhand would be supplanted by a life closer to

1162

nature and furnishing more adequate opportunities for gratifying all phases of personality. While some of the sensual arts, such as music and dancing, would be extended, and while the fine arts would still be used to beautify the material environment, the direct and spontaneous expression of human nature would then take the place of its indirect artistic expression.

Chapter LXVIII

Radicalism and Conservatism—Revolution and Permanence

THERE has been a multiplicity of causes for change in modern times. Among the most obvious have been the Renaissance of thought and learning, the Reformation which liberated religious thought and belief in a limited measure, the development of science which has added greatly to the knowledge and ideas of mankind, and many inventions due partly to technology arising from scientific discoveries. The discovery of America and of other parts of the world which has caused an immense increase of the population of the world and many migrations in that population, and the industrial revolution which has increased wealth enormously and has transformed the economic organization of society, were other important factors.

Modern even more than ancient history, therefore, furnishes numerous illustrations of the fact of change. At the same time many features of human life remain unchanged. The fundamental traits of mankind have changed very little during the historical period. So that the basic human relations, such as the parental, filial, and sexual relations, remain the same in their essential features.

In this chapter I shall describe the human forces for change and for permanence. On the one hand are the relatively immutable human traits which give rise to permanence and stability in behavior. On the other hand are the variable elements in human nature which lead to variation and flexibility in behavior. These contrasted traits furnish the basis for two somewhat distinct mental attitudes, usually called radical and conservative.

Radicalism is primarily openmindedness toward the possibility of change, and usually involves belief in the desirability of certain changes. When such a belief results in action it is determined not by absolute standards or conventional considerations, and is directed toward bringing into being a more or less different state of society.

Such changes are sought either in the interests of the individual or of the group, but usually for both individual and social reasons.

Men and women become radical owing to a process of thinking; or because they have, in an effort to attain better circumstances, come into conflict with the prevailing standards and institutions; or as a result of disillusionment with respect to things they have regarded as certain; or owing to a shock, usually painful in its nature; or because they have been reared as radicals. The reaction in each case is rational, emotional, sentimental, egoistic, humanitarian, violent, peaceable, etc., according to the experience and idiosyncracies of the individual. So that there are several types of radicals and of radical behavior which vary more or less from each other.

Conservatism is primarily a belief, usually vaguely but sometimes definitely formulated, in a residuum or substratum of things or of principles which are permanent. This belief may have a philosophic basis in a metaphysical theory of the immutable, but in most cases has no more of a rational basis than the apparent permanence of certain things in the universe. It may lead to effort to preserve the established order of ideas and institutions in opposition to the forces for change, but usually merely sanctions behavior which is mainly in conformity with the established order without any special effort to preserve the existing order unless it is threatened.

Persons are conservative partly owing to congenital traits, and partly on account of education, experience, and especially circumstances of life. Conservatism is often due to mental inertia which shrinks from the thought of change, and which is strongly reinforced by habit, custom and tradition. Closely connected with this inertia is the desire shared by many persons to believe in at least a few permanent and sure things. Social conventions and customs and education in traditional beliefs, such as religious dogmas and absolute moral standards, influence most persons to be conservative. A small minority is made up of a few individuals who profit greatly by things as they are, and consequently are actively interested in preserving the established order. They use many devices to induce or coerce the majority to aid them in maintaining this order and in preventing or overthrowing a revolutionary change.

Conservative behavior is rational, emotional, sentimental, egoistic, humanitarian, violent, peaceable, etc., according to the experience and idiosyncracies of the individual, and may be directed toward economic, political, moral, religious or other ends. It is usually in accordance with prevailing traditional, conventional, religious, ethical, political, economic, and customary beliefs and standards.

Men and women can be classified roughly as radicals or conservatives according to the extent to which they approximate the radical or the conservative mental attitude. There are, however, no ideal radicals or conservatives, because elements of radicalism and of conservatism are to be found in all human beings.

It is impossible to understand radical and conservative behavior without comprehending the fundamental factors in human behavior in general. The earlier philosophical psychologists recognized three aspects to man's mental makeup, namely, the conative, the affective, and the cognitive. The conative factors were supposed to make man will and and act, the affective factors to make him feel, and the cognitive factors to make him think.

Modern scientific psychology also recognizes three aspects to man's mental makeup which correspond in a measure to the conative, the affective, and the cognitive. The tropisms, reflex actions and instincts are the congenital impulses to action which are the fundamental dynamic forces in human nature. The feelings and emotions, in the form of painful and pleasurable sensations, influence behavior considerably, and thereby determine to a large extent the well-being of the individual. The intelligence enables man to think and to reason. Psychology also recognizes that these three mental aspects are closely related to each other. They act and react upon each other to so great a degree as to form one intricate, complex whole which it is not easy to analyze. In fact, in many cases it is impossible to distinguish the mental elements from each other.

What is the significance of these mental elements for radicalism and conservatism? It is sometimes alleged that instinct is conservative because it is supposed to be unchangeable, and conservatism is said to originate from the instincts. In similar fashion it is asserted that the intellect is radical because it conceives of and leads to change, and radicalism is said to originate from intelligence.

There is a measure of truth in these notions. Instincts are relatively permanent and respond always in much the same way. There could be little variation in purely instinctive behavior. On the other hand, the instincts furnish most of the dynamic impulse to all action. They provide the muscular innervation which is attributed by some writers and schools to the will to power, the motive force, the vital urge (*élan vital*), the libido, etc. They furnish the energy for radical as well as conservative behavior. In fact, any instinct may under the appropriate circumstances lead to radical behavior. Certain instincts are more or less likely to lead to such behavior. If there is a constructive instinct, it is likely to give rise to inventions. If there is an instinct of curiosity, it is sure to stimulate the acquisition of new ideas. The parental instincts may lead to humanitarian radicalism, such as altruistic acts.

The intellect is the immediate cause of genuine radicalism in the

1166

sense that it makes possible the conception of change, and a conscious striving toward change. It is in a sense the immediate cause of genuine conservatism as well, for it renders possible the conservative point of view and philosophy. However, the intellect is a more effective factor for radicalism than it is for conservatism. Changes take place much more rapidly under the influence and guidance of the intellect, whereas when the intellect is absent or quiescent things are likely to remain in the *status quo*. In any case, little is to be gained by attempting to classify the mental elements with respect to radicalism and conservatism. The task of importance is to analyze these elements in their almost infinite complexity in order to ascertain as far as possible how radical and conservative ideas and actions come into being.

The French philosopher and mathematician, Descartes (1596-1650 A.D.), is sometimes called the father of modern philosophy. He stated the first principle of his philosophy as follows: "Je pense, donc je suis," or, in Latin, "Cogito, ergo sum" (I think, hence I am), to demonstrate the verity of personal existence.[1] This statement suggested the subjective and introspective character of the earlier psychology which was much influenced by philosophy. It indicated the tendency of the earlier psychologists to seek for their data by looking within themselves, and often led to solipsism. When the introspective method is used too much, the personal equation acquires an excessive influence, and is likely to vitiate the accuracy of the results.

With the rise of modern science, and especially of biology, an objective psychology has developed. This psychology does not repudiate introspection entirely. But it regards it as subsidiary and supplementary to the observation of behavior and of the physiological processes which condition the mental processes. The use of the objective method in experimental psychology, comparative psychology, and in the study of behavior, has furnished a much better understanding of human nature and behavior.

Behavior is due, in the last analysis, to the mobile and plastic character of organic matter. These traits arise from certain peculiarities of organic matter which have made organic, mental and social evolution possible. In the first place, the principal elements in organic matter are characterized by *allotropism*. This is the capacity of an element to assume different forms, as, for example, when carbon appears as diamond, graphite, or amorphous carbon, or when oxygen appears as ozone. These allotropic forms are apparently due to a varying arrangement of the atoms within the molecules of the element.

In the second place, *isomerism* in many organic compounds is analogous to allotropism in the elements. The isomeric compounds

[1] René Descartes, *Discours de la methode,* Leyden, 1637; *Les principes de la philosophie,* Amsterdam, 1644.

assume different forms, apparently owing to a varying arrangement of the molecules of the elements within the molecules of the compound. Allotropism and isomerism make organic matter less stable and subject to change than inorganic matter.

There are other traits and forces which promote the mobility and instability of organic matter. Three of the four principal organic elements, namely, oxygen, hydrogen, and nitrogen, are almost invariably gases, while carbon is usually a solid. The mobility of the gaseous elements promotes the mobility of organic matter. Furthermore, there are great dissimilarities between the organic elements which accentuate the instability of organic matter. Oxygen has great chemical energy, while nitrogen is very inert. Carbon displays a high degree of atomic cohesion, while oxygen, hydrogen, and nitrogen have little atomic cohesion. These differences render organic matter unstable because these elements are readily separable by external forces. This instability furnishes the basis for the process of differentiation and integration which constitutes organic evolution.

From these carbon compounds originated the primordial protoplasm which forms the basis of all life. The mobility of organic matter has made it responsive to its environment, and through a process of constant adjustment and adaptation all of the organic types from the lowest unicellular to the highest multicellular have evolved. At the same time the atomic cohesion of carbon and the inertia of the relatively large molecules of the complex organic compounds furnishes a sufficient degree of stability to the structure of the organism to keep it intact and to save it from dissolution in the course of the metabolic and excretory processes.

Metabolism is the fundamental physiological process by means of which nutritive matter is transformed into a part of the organism. Respiration is the process by which waste matter is oxidized and prepared for excretion from the organism. Circulation is the process by which water flows into the organism, bringing in nutritive ingredients, and flows out carrying with it the waste matter.

Reproduction is the process by which the life of the organic world and of its species is perpetuated from generation to generation. Beginning with the simple fission of the unicellular species, there have developed in the multicellular forms specialized germ cells for reproductive purposes. Furthermore, there developed two types of germ cells, the spermatozoan and the ovum, which have given rise to the distinction between the sexes, and complicated reproductive organs. In the course of reproduction the forces of inheritance enable many traits to persist, while the forces of variation are constantly bringing about change.

On the foregoing physico-chemical, anatomical, and physiological

1168

basis have arisen mental phenomena and the forms of behavior. The sensitiveness or irritability of organic matter is of most significance in this connection. Owing to its instability and mobility organic matter is affected more readily than inorganic matter by the molecular and molar forces which act upon it.

The direct reaction of an organic cell or of a simple organism to an external force is usually called a *tropism*. The external forces which act upon organisms are gravity, electricity, light, heat, water, density of the medium, chemical substances, and molar agents. By their mechanical and chemical effects upon the sensitive substance of the organism they give rise to motions which constitute the behavior of the organism. Among the tropisms which have been distinguished and described are phototropism (heliotropism) or reaction to light, chromotropism or reaction to color, geotropism or reaction to gravity, chemotropism or reaction to chemical substances, electrotropism (galvanotropism) or reaction to electricity, stereotropism (thigmotropism, also barotaxis) or contact irritability, rheotropism or reaction to a current of water, anemotropism or reaction to a current of air, thermotropism or reaction to heat, hydrotropism or reaction to variations in humidity, tonotropism or reaction to variations in the density of the surrounding medium, etc.

The motions of which an organism is capable depend upon its structure. Its movements depend upon its locomotor organs. An animal without feet cannot walk, and an animal without wings cannot fly. The whole set of the simple movements and of the combinations of simple movements of an organism has sometimes been called its *action system*. Repetition of a movement causes greater facility in its performance and furnishes the physiological basis for habit, memory, and learning.

As the more complex animal organisms evolved there was a progressive increase in the self-determination of behavior. This increase was due largely to the evolution of the nervous system. Nerve substance is more sensitive and irritable than organic matter in general, and is affected by mechanical and chemical forces even more readily than other forms of organic matter. In course of time there evolved an elaborate system of nerve fibers running to all parts of the organism. Along these fibers are carried stimuli to and from the surface of the organism and within the organism. There also evolved the central nervous system composed of the spinal cord and brain to which most of the sensory stimuli coming from outside are carried, and from which most of the motor impulses are sent. The central nervous system directs and controls the behavior of the organism to a high degree, and makes possible a large amount of self-determination.

The fundamental type of reaction caused by the nervous system is the reflex action, which is the reaction of a muscle or gland or other effector organ caused by a nervous stimulus. As the central nervous system evolved, the simple reflexes were combined in compound reflexes, some of which are very complicated in their character. These reflexes are usually known as instincts. In another work I have defined instinct as follows:[2]

> "*An instinct is an inherited combination of reflexes which have been integrated by the central nervous system so as to cause an external activity of the organism which usually characterizes a whole species and is usually adaptive.*"

Human behavior is not determined solely by reflexes and instincts. Feeling and the intellect have a marked influence upon behavior. Feeling is the most intangible aspect of the mind. While it is possible to define and illustrate reflexes and instincts in terms of movements and actions, and while it is possible to define and illustrate intellect in terms of images and ideas, it is impossible to define and illustrate feeling in terms of anything else. Perhaps the most that we can do is to say that feelings are sensations with a strong affective aspect, though this adds nothing in the way of definition.

While we may be unable to define and describe feeling, we have nevertheless incontestable evidence of its existence in ourselves. In fact, feeling is perhaps the most pervasive element in consciousness. Through its characteristic expressions we can readily infer its presence in our fellow-beings. Furthermore, it accompanies many forms of behavior, though it is difficult to say to what extent it is the cause of that behavior.

The stimulation of the emotions, which are strong states of feeling more or less constitutional in extent, is followed by the display of much energy by the organism, as, for example, when fear, anger, sexual passion, etc., are aroused. A theory was formulated by James and Lange to the effect that the emotions are not the causes of these organic reactions, but that they are due to the visceral or vascular processes which lead up to these displays of energy.[3] That is to say, a stimulus from an appropriate object, such as a feared or a hated object, will arouse an instinctive reaction, and the visceral or vascular processes necessary to produce the reaction will affect the nerves

[2] Maurice Parmelee, *The Science of Human Behavior, Biological and Psychological Foundations,* New York, 1913, p. 226. In this book is contained a more or less detailed description of the evolution of the tropisms, reflex actions, instincts, etc.

[3] William James, *Principles of Psychology,* New York, 1896, 2 vols. C. Lange and W. James, *The Emotions,* reprinted from their original works in "Psychological Classics," Baltimore, 1922.

associated with these organs in such a manner as to give rise to an emotional state. It is partly for this reason that the thoracico-lumbar system of nerves is often called the "sympathetic" system.

More recently some investigators have been inclined to believe that emotion is a genuine cause of behavior. Sherrington seemed to be of this opinion as a result of experiments in decerebration and spinal and vagal transection by himself and by Goltz. This opinion was implied in the following statement: "There is a strong bond of union between emotion and muscular action. Emotion 'moves' us, hence the word itself. If developed in intensity, it impels toward vigorous movement."[4]

Cannon seemed to be of the same opinion as a result of his study of visceral conditions and of glandular processes, especially of the adrenal glands, during emotional states. Speaking of his researches he said that they "have revealed a number of unsuspected ways in which muscular action is made more efficient because of emotional disturbances of the viscera. Every one of the visceral changes that have been noted—the cessation of processes in the alimentary canal (thus freeing the energy supply for other parts); the shifting of blood from the abdominal organs, whose activities are deferable, to the organs immediately essential to muscular exertion (the lungs, the heart, the central nervous system); the increased vigor of contraction of the heart; the quick abolition of the effects of muscular fatigue; the mobilizing of energy-giving sugar in the circulation—every one of these visceral changes is *directly serviceable in making the organism more effective in the violent display of energy which fear or rage or pain may involve*."[5]

Cannon spoke still more emphatically in the following passage: "If various strong emotions can thus be expressed in the diffused activities of a single division of the autonomic—the division which accelerates the heart, inhibits the movements of the stomach and intestines, contracts the blood vessels, erects the hairs, liberates sugar, and discharges adrenin—it would appear that the bodily conditions which have been assumed, by some psychologists, to distinguish emotions from one another must be sought for elsewhere than in the viscera. We do not 'feel sorry because we cry,' as James contended, but we cry because we are sorry or overjoyed or violently angry or full of tender affection—when any one of these diverse emotional states is

[4] C. S. Sherrington, *The Integrative Action of the Nervous System*, New York, 1906, p. 265. The experiments by Goltz were reported in the following article: F. Goltz, "Der Hund ohne Grosshirn," in *Pfluger's Archiv*, Vol. LI, 1892.

[5] W. B. Cannon, *Bodily Changes in Pain, Hunger, Fear, and Rage*, New York, 1915, pp. 215-16.

present—there are nervous discharges by sympathetic channels to various viscera, including the lachrymal glands."[6]

Sherrington asserted that "emotion is primarily a cerebral reaction," and Cannon agreed with him. In other words, these investigators denied that emotions are visceral in their origin. On the contrary, they insisted that emotional impulses from the brain stimulate the visceral processes which energize the muscles to unusual efforts.

These differences of opinion are, I believe, due in part to differences of terminology. The actual course of events, so far as we can make out, takes place as follows. The feared object, or hated object, or sex object, or edible object gives rise to a stimulus which passes to the central nervous system and usually to the cerebrum. From thence starts the stimulus for the appropriate reaction toward this object. This stimulus passing out from the central nervous system along nerve fibers arouses glands, visceral organs, etc., to energize the muscles by furnishing sugar to the blood and in other ways.

The mechanism by means of which this process takes place has been named by Crile the "kinetic system." He said that this system "is specifically adapted to transform potential into kinetic energy for the production of heat and motion. The principal organs comprising the kinetic system are the brain, the thyroid, the adrenals, the liver and the muscles. The brain is the great central battery which drives the body; the thyroid governs the conditions favoring tissue oxidation; the adrenals govern immediate oxidation processes; the liver fabricates and stores glycogen, and is the great neutralizer of the acid products of energy transformation; and the muscles are the final converters of latent energy into motion and heat. While the kinetic system does not directly circulate the blood, exchange oxygen and carbon dioxide, perform the functions of digestion, urinary elimination or procreation, it does play an important role in each of these processes. In turn, digestion, elimination, procreation, etc., may be regarded as aiding materially, though indirectly, in the function of the kinetic system."[7]

[6] *Op. cit.,* pp. 279-80.

[7] G. W. Crile, *Man—An Adaptive Mechanism,* New York, 1916, pp. 158-9. Elsewhere in the same book Crile described the kinetic system as follows: "The *brain* is the initiator of response, being activated by the environment within or without the body; acting like a storage battery, it contributes the initial spark and impulse which drives the mechanism. The *adrenals* act as oxidizers, making possible the transformation of energy and the neutralization of the resulting acid products. The *liver* is the chief fabricator and storehouse of the carbohydrate fuel by which muscular action and heat are produced. The liver also plays a large role in the neutralization of the acid products of the transformation of energy. The *muscles* are the engine or motor in which is consummated the final step in the transformation of energy into heat or motion. The *thyroid* by supplying a secretion which

This highly adaptive series of reflexes and reactions is thoroughly integrated and leads to forms of behavior which are ordinarily called instinctive. I believe, therefore, in accordance with my definition of instinct, that it is better to call the cerebral impulse which arouses these visceral and vascular processes instinctive rather than emotional. To call this impulse emotional is to violate the unity of the instinctive mechanism.

If we follow this usage the emotion is the state of feeling which is aroused by this series of instinctive reflexes and reactions and which accompanies them. Whether or not the emotion exists and is felt in the brain depends upon whether or not the brain is cenesthetic. It has been commonly believed that the brain is anesthetic and analgesic, that is to say, incapable of sensation. If this is true an emotion could not be felt in the brain, because a feeling is primarily a sensation. But if the brain is capable of sensations, an emotion may be felt in the brain as in other parts of the nervous system. In that case an emotion would be cerebral in the sense that it would be felt in the brain, but not in the sense that the cerebral impulse is the emotion or a part of the emotion.[8]

Even if we assume that the cerebral impulse is not a part of the emotion, we are not forced to assume that emotions have no influence upon behavior. On the contrary, there is every reason to believe that the emotions and the feelings in general influence behavior greatly. This is due to the fact that all feelings are pleasurable or painful, or, to say the least, pleasant or unpleasant. Memories of feelings cause variations in the manifestations of the instinctive tendencies to action. That is to say, the memory of a painful or unpleasant feeling will serve to inhibit the act which gave rise to that feeling. In similar

facilitates the passage of ions would seem to be the organ of speed control, governing the rate at which the transformation of energy is effected." (Pp. 9-10.)

The same subject is discussed also in his book entitled *The Origin and Nature of the Emotions*, Philadelphia, 1915.

[8] Sollier argued at length that the brain is cenesthetic, that is to say, capable of sensations. But he also seemed to be of the opinion that the cerebral impulse is the emotion or a part of the emotion. He argued that the brain is characterized by "emotivity" by which he seemed to mean the capacity for initiating these impulses:

"C'est à une théorie purement cérébrale qu'on se trouve conduit, si l'on veut tenir compte des aspects si divers, et des particularités si nombreuses que presente le phénomène de l'émotion. Elle repose sur la propriété même du cerveau de réagir d'un façon plus ou moins diffuse aux excitations—émotivité—; sur les conditions de conservation, de libération et de diffusion de l'ènergie cérébrale,—mécanisme et dynamisme, émotion proprement dite—, sur la possibilité, enfin, pour le sujet de percevoir les modifications fonctionelles produites dans le cerveau par l'énergie cérébrale mise en liberté,—cenesthesie cérébrale. L'émotivité conditionne l'émotion, et l'émotion entraine les reactions connues sous le nom d'expression des émotions." (P. Sollier, *Le mécanisme des émotions*, Paris, 1905, p. 303.)

fashion, the memory of a pleasurable or pleasant feeling will reinforce the act which gave rise to that feeling. In other words, feelings exercise this influence indirectly through the intelligence.

The intellect arises from memory. In the cerebrum of the higher animals are the association areas which make possible numerous memories, which in turn make possible the establishment of many associations between instinctive reactions. In another treatise I have stated the influence of the intellect upon behavior in the following words: "*So it is that in an animal with a well-developed central nervous system which has acquired a large and varied store of memories, the behavior which results from a certain stimulus may be vastly different from the purely inherited reaction which would respond to that stimulus if these memories were not present to vary and complicate the behavior. Such behavior is intelligent, and the capacity for such variations in behavior constitutes intelligence.*"[9]

The preceding brief description of the mental elements, namely, instinct, feeling, and intelligence, indicates their significance for radicalism and conservatism. The evolution of the intellect increases greatly the complexity of the mind and the variability of behavior.[10] Memories become associated and form more or less complex ideas. An orderly succession of these ideas constitutes a process of thinking. The highest form of thinking consists in abstracting general ideas from concrete images and ideas and formulating concepts.

Thus were derived the concept of the possibility and desirability of change, and the concept of the possibility and desirability of permanence. It is doubtful if any intellect other than the human intellect is capable of abstract thinking, or only in a rudimentary form. No animals other than man can be said to be truly radical or truly conservative in the sense that they conceive of change or of permanence as an end toward which they consciously strive.

The feelings furnish the hedonistic basis for all behavior. Much if not all of radical and conservative behavior is conscious or unconscious pursuit of pleasurable ends. Feelings may become associated with either radical or conservative ideas and modes of behavior in sentiments, etc., and influence radical and conservative manifestations considerably. The affective element is especially strong in several radical and conservative types.

[9] *The Science of Human Behavior*, New York, 1913, p. 265.

[10] Crile correlates the complexity of the mind with the complexity of the "action pattern": "*Action patterns*, as may be seen, are synonymous with 'associative memory,' with 'mind,' with 'intelligence,' with 'individuality.' The single action pattern of Venus fly-trap makes up its limited life and constitutes all it has of 'mind.' The multitudinous *action patterns* of man, representing every phase and degree of animal existence, constitute man's life and man's 'mind.'" (G. W. Crile, *Man—An Adaptive Mechanism*, New York, 1916, p. 59.)

As pointed out above, the instability of organic matter makes it easily affected by the forces which act upon it. This furnishes the basis for the irritability of organic matter, which in turn makes possible the sentience of living organisms. Furthermore, it makes possible memory, which leads, on the one hand, to habit, and, on the other hand, to learning.

An action will as a rule leave its mark which makes its repetition more easily performed. The neural pathways become more sensitized and respond more readily to stimuli, mental associations are established, the muscles become stronger, etc. Thus arise habits which may become powerful and influence greatly the behavior of the organism. On the other hand, in the higher animals the memory of an experience often influences behavior by changing the usual form of reaction, thus giving rise to learning. Habits are forces for permanence in behavior, while learning is a factor for change.

Many habitual acts are instinctive or mainly instinctive actions. In these cases the habits reinforce the instinctive impulses, and have therefore sometimes been called "habit-instincts." Habits are also likely to be accompanied by characteristic states of feeling which are sometimes called habitual.

Imitation leads both to change and permanence in behavior. An individual often acquires a form of behavior which is new for him by imitating another person. Thus imitation is a method of learning for the individual. On the other hand, if imitation is the only method of learning, no new forms of behavior will be created for society. If a certain form of behavior is imitated by all persons, it becomes the habitual and customary mode of behavior, which usually is difficult to change.

Sentiments are combinations of ideas and feelings which may influence behavior greatly.[11] A sentiment arises as a result of a mental association becoming established between the image or idea of an object, such as a person or a thing, and a state of feeling. The mental association is due to juxtaposition in space or in time, or to a more indirect relationship. Every image and idea has its own "affective tone," and when this affective element is more or less permanent and well organized a sentiment comes into being. In this fashion feelings and emotions determine in a measure the influence of images and ideas. The sentiment is pleasant or unpleasant according to whether its emotional content is pleasurable or painful. A sentiment may lead to change or permanence. This depends upon its own character and the nature of the circumstances under which it manifests itself.

[11] By some psychologists the term "emotional complex" is used to signify much the same thing as "sentiment." (See, for example, Morton Prince, *The Unconscious*, New York, 1914, pp. 265 *ff*.

1175

Up to this point I have not attempted to distinguish between the conscious and the unconscious elements in these human factors for change and permanence. In my treatise on human behavior I have discussed the subject of consciousness at considerable length.[12] In that book I have pointed out the difference between the conscious and the unconscious, and also the distinction between the conscious and the sub-conscious.

Consciousness consists of ideas and feelings. So that all of the plants and the lower animals which are incapable of experiencing ideas and feelings are lacking in consciousness. In the higher animals the reflex and instinctive processes which do not arouse ideas and feelings are said to be unconscious. However, in man there are few if any instinctive acts which are entirely unconscious, because most instinctive acts stimulate ideas and feelings. But many of the reflex physiological processes are unconscious.

The distinction between the conscious and the subconscious is largely one of degree. Ideas and feelings are involved in both of these mental states. In the subconscious these ideas and feelings are not in the center of attention. The human mind and personality cannot attend to more than a few ideas and feelings at the same time. At any time the great majority of ideas and feelings are subconscious, while many ideas and feelings always remain in the subconsciousness. Much of human behavior is to be explained by these subconscious processes which are not recognized and known by the person experiencing them.

Consciousness is sometimes called metaphorically a stream with fringes. Whatever idea or feeling swims into the center of the stream upon which the attention is concentrated, so to speak, becomes conscious. All of the forces of heredity and environment play a part in determining which ideas and feelings are to become conscious. Along the edges are extensive twilight areas of subconscious ideas and feelings. From these areas some ideas and feelings emerge into the full light of consciousness, while others manifest themselves in dreams, somnambulistic and hypnotic states, in dissociation of personality, etc.[13]

We can now form some conception of the ontogenesis of the individual who is to become a radical or a conservative. Each individual is born with the capacity for numerous reflex and instinctive reactions

12 *The Science of Human Behavior*, New York, 1913, Chapters XV and XVI entitled "Consciousness: Sensation, Attention, Feeling, Pleasure, Pain, and Emotion as Conscious Elements," and "Personality, Intelligence, Consciousness, and the Nature of Mind."

13 Prince defined the subconscious, and unconscious as follows: "I have, accordingly, divided the subconscious into two classes, namely (1) the *unconscious*, or neural dispositions and processes, and (2) the coconscious, or actual subconscious ideas which do not enter the content of conscious awareness. An unconscious pro-

to external stimuli. Most of these reactions have not had an opportunity to manifest themselves in the narrowly limited intra-uterine environment. The pre-natal life is largely affective in its character. Memories of the feelings experienced during the life in the womb may influence the post-natal life to a certain extent. These feelings are both pleasurable and painful.

After birth the child soon has opportunity to manifest many of its congenital tendencies to react in eating, crying, moving its limbs, etc.[14] But it encounters resistances and obstacles in the way of some of its acts which force it to vary them, and in some cases to suppress them entirely. Thus the individual learns, acquires habits, and represses some parts of its nature. All of these processes form a part of its adaptation to its environment.

The basic determinants of human behavior have been described in the present treatise in Chapters IV to VI entitled "The Dynamics of Behavior," "The Directives of Behavior," and "The Integration of Behavior." They have been briefly summarized in the present chapter with respect to the human traits for change and permanence. They are present in varying degrees in every other phase of human life and activity so that this chapter epitomizes the psychological factors in human behavior. Among these phases are professional and sexual choice,

cess and a coconscious process are both therefore *subconscious* processes but particular types thereof—the one being purely neural or phyical and the other psychological or ideational.' (*The Unconscious*, p. x.)

He defined the unconscious also in the following words: "*The unconscious is the great storehouse of neurograms which are the physiological records of our mental lives.*" (*Op. cit.*, p. 149.) He subsumed the unconscious as well as the subconscious under the term "subconscious," and applied the term "coconscious to what I call the subconscious."

[14] Thorndike attempted to describe these congenital reactions. (E. L. Thorndike, *The Original Nature of Man*, New York, 1913.) Some of the traits he mentioned, however, are too complex to be entirely congenital and include some acquired elements. Among the traits he enumerated are the following: Responses resulting in sensitivities, attention, gross bodily control, food getting (eating, reaching, grasping and putting into the mouth, acquisition and possession, hunting, collecting and hoarding, avoidance and repulsion, rivalry and cooperation), habitation (responses to confinement, migration and domesticity), fear (unpleasant expectation and dread, anxiety and worry, dislike and avoidance, shock, flight, paralysis and other forms of behavior), fighting, anger. (Pp. 43 *ff.*) Responses to the behavior of other human beings include motherly behavior, responses to the presence, approval and scorn of men, (gregariousness, attention to human beings, attention-getting, responses to approving and to scornful behavior, responses by approving and scornful behavior), mastering and submissive behavior (display, "self-conscious" behavior), sex behavior, secretiveness, rivalry, cooperation, suggestibility and opposition, envious and jealous behavior, greed (complex of acquisition, fighting to retain, etc.), ownership (acquisition, etc.) kindliness (complex of sympathy, motherly behavior, etc.), teasing, tormenting and bullying (complex of manipulation, curiosity, hunting, scorn, mastery), imitation. (Pp. 81 *ff.*)

occupational and sexual activity, agricultural and industrial activity, political and esthetic activity, etc. Human nature expresses itself in all forms of behavior. There is, however, some variation of emphasis in accordance with the extent to which the conative, the affective and the cognitive traits are operative. These differences may be detected as between copulation and parturition, parental and filial relations, master and servant, upper and lower class conflicts, science and technology, invention and imitation, art and religion, etc. In all these relationships and forms of behavior mankind acts and feels and thinks as it expresses itself both individually or collectively in group and mass movements. Political, economic, and social revolutions often call forth these traits in an exceptionally accentuated form.

A revolutionary situation exists when a society is torn by the antagonism between the upper and the lower classes. A revolution is heralded by the restlessness of the masses and outbursts of violence. These outbursts are rigorously suppressed by the upper class so long as it can maintain the upper hand. If a revolution breaks out and gains some momentum, it may encounter little internal opposition. It may unite the people in a common revolutionary action and feeling. The psychological influences of suggestion, imitation, and fear play some part in creating an appropriate emotional atmosphere. The primary and fundamental factor is the inability of the old regime to function in the revolutionary situation. Hence prolonged fighting and much loss of blood are rarely ever necessary after an overt revolution has commenced.

Lenin said that "a revolution occurs when the upper class cannot and the lower class will not continue the old system." [15] A Danish sociologist has expressed a similar idea in saying that "a great revolution occurs only when the disintegration of the dominant social system has reached an advanced stage and its stultifying effect upon progressive forces has become intolerable." [16] Such a revolution destroys the dominance of the upper class and frees the lower class from the exploitation against which it has been struggling. An American Marxist has said that "as the ruling class fails to 'deliver the goods', mass faith in the old order breaks down and provides the revolutionary class with the opportunity to strike for the conquest of political power." [17]

[15] V. I. Ulianov (Nicolai Lenin), *The State and Revolution, Marxist Teaching on the State and the Task of the Proletariat in the Revolution,* Chicago, 1924, first published in Russian in 1917.

[16] Alfred Meusel, article on "Revolution and Counter-Revolution," in the *Encyclopaedia of the Social Sciences,* Vol. 13, New York, 1934.

[17] Lewis Corey, *The Decline of American Capitalism,* New York, 1934, p. 544. Corey has described the revolutionary factors as follows: "The long-time factors of revolution—the accumulation of economic, cultural, and political changes arising

1178

Trotzky has described the first stages of a revolution: "At those crucial moments when the old order becomes no longer endurable to the masses, they break over the barriers excluding them from the political arena, sweep aside their traditional representatives, and create by their own interference the initial groundwork for a new regime." "A revolution breaks out when all the antagonisms of a society have reached their highest tension." "A revolution takes place only when there is no other way out. And the insurrection, which rises above a revolution like a peak in the mountain chain of its events, can no more be evoked at will than the revolution as a whole." [18]

The bourgeois revolutions of the seventeenth and eighteenth centuries expressed the growing power at first of the merchants and then of the industrialists as well, against the vested rights of the feudal nobility and against monarchical authority. The English Rebellion of 1640 and Revolution of 1688 gave the middle class much power. The invention of the steam engine in the eighteenth century rendered possible large-scale production and enriched greatly the manufacturers and industrialists. The industrial revolution, which commenced in England, gave the final and decisive blow to feudalism. The French Revolution freed the bourgeoisie politically, and removed the last remaining restrictions upon capitalist enterprise. The American War of Independence made the middle class supreme in the North. The Civil War of 1861 to 1865 destroyed the feudalism of chattel slavery, and of the plantation system in the South. Feudalism was now suppressed throughout most of the Occident. Agriculture, industry, and commerce, were ostensibly liberated. It became possible to produce anything in any quantity, except in so far as the intrinsic nature of capitalism imposes restrictions.

The middle class was formerly the mercantile class with an economic and social status between the feudal lords and their serfs. It now became merged with the capitalists. The latter became the heirs of the feudal monopolists and established their own monopolies. Capitalism is essentially and inevitably monopolistic because a privileged few own the means of production. Economic power leads in turn

out of the development of new forms and relations of production, a new social order, within the shell of the old; this increasingly saps the foundations of the old order and prepares the objective, or class-economic, and the subjective, or class-ideological, conditions for a revolutionary overthrow. The short-time factors of revolution—the accumulation of economic, ideological, and political changes, which aggravate contradictions and antagonisms arising out of an intensified clash between the old and new forms and relations of production; this results in decline and decay." (P. 544.)

[18] Leon Trotzky, *The History of the Russian Revolution*, New York, 1932, 3 vols., translated from the Russian, Vol. I, xvii, 76, Vol. III, 167.

to a preponderant political influence. The capitalist class is now able to exploit the proletarian class almost without restraint. The workers, nominally free, are actually at the mercy of the capitalists because they own the tools of production even less than under feudalism.

The stage is set for a worldwide proletarian revolution probably in the latter half of the 20th century. On the one hand, the proletariat is becoming more class conscious and aware of its power. On the other hand, the ownership of wealth and the control of production are becoming more and more concentrated in the hands of a few. The crisis of capitalism is becoming more acute. The profit system is incapable of utilizing science and technology in large part, and is maintaining a highly artificial state of scarcity. The burden of suffering for the inefficiency and malfunctioning of capitalism falls mainly upon the workers, to whom are granted in very limited quantities purchasing power and employment as the only means of securing a miserable existence.

The proletarian revolution greatly transcends the bourgeois revolution in importance. The transition from the capitalist to the classless society is far more radical than from the feudal to the bourgeois system. In the latter case the exploitation of one class by another persisted and merely changed its form somewhat; in the former case it will disappear entirely. Capitalism required little more economic and political organization than feudalism, though the form of organization changed somewhat. A socialized system calls for a planned society, whereas capitalism is in the main anarchic, chaotic, and disorganized.

If a revolution is more or less successful in its initial stage, it may collapse into a compromise in which only a part of its objectives are attained. For this reason it may sometimes be expedient that a revolution at first aggravate rather than mitigate economic difficulties and the privations of the exploited class. The disturbances thereby stimulated may release additional revolutionary forces. The moderate group, often composed of the so-called liberals, which is prone to compromise, is weakened. The conflict between the reactionary and radical extremes is intensified. Monopoly, capitalism and fascism are accentuating this conflict at present.

The lower class is at first hampered by the fact that it is not accustomed to authority. It has a slave psychology which may lead it unwittingly to succumb to the prestige of the upper class. It requires a strong and militant radical organization to uphold its morale as a conquering class. It is this need which gave rise to the Committee of Public Safety in the French Revolution and the Tcheka-OGPU in the Russian Revolution.[19] A revolutionary army may also be necessary to defend the revolution against foreign intervention and aggression on

[19] The OGPU was abolished and the Soviet Commissariat of Internal Affairs established on July 10, 1934. It is the Narkomvnudel, known as the N.K.V.D.

the part of the class interests endangered by it. While this army may absorb part of the army maintained by the erstwhile dominant upper class, it must be organized in a more democratic fashion and imbued with the revolutionary ideology.

During the French Revolution Robespierre declared that "the despotism of liberty against tyranny" must precede the free egalitarian society. This doctrine resembles the Marxist-Leninist theory of the "dictatorship of the proletariat" during the transition period before a classless society can be attained. A dictatorship is likely to follow a revolution. It may be a dictatorship of the right or of the left. The French Revolution was succeeded by the reactionary dictatorship of the Napoleonic empire. A reactionary dictatorship is intended to be permanent. It may be the personal and oligarchical dictatorship of fascism under which the individual is sacrificed to the alleged interests of a mythical entity called the nation or the state. In recent times it has become more or less essential for a reactionary dictatorship to wear a plebeian mask in order to succeed even temporarily. In Germany national socialism appealed to the lower middle class, the peasants, and even to a portion of the industrial proletariat. It pretended to promote collaboration and fraternal relations between the classes.

A dictatorship of the left is by its very nature temporary. It is intended to last only so long as class distinctions are not yet entirely obliterated.[20] When this point is reached there can no longer be exploitation of one class or group by another class or group, and the democratic society ensues. If a new class alignment arises leading to a new form of exploitation, the revolution has failed. Or the new revolutionary government may be overthrown by internal or external opposition, and supplanted by a reactionary dictatorship. This in turn may prove to be temporary, like the Napoleonic dictatorship. The revolution may then be resumed and its objectives attained in part, as in some of the European revolutions of 1848.

Although certain fundamental conditions of revolution remain the same, revolutionary tactics, programs, and techniques must depend in part upon the situation at a given time and place. In Europe the industrial proletariat has developed a good deal of class feeling and consciousness of the class struggle. A revolutionary situation is at least in part in existence. During the 20th century there have been abortive attempts at a proletarian revolution in several European countries. The fascist domination over central and southeastern Europe during some of this century was largely due to a reaction against these revo-

20 See my *Bolshevism, Fascism and the Liberal-Democratic State*, New York, 1934, Chapter II entitled "Bolshevist Party Dictatorship and the Soviet Government."

lutionary forces. These forces in western and southern Europe, now dormant under rigorous suppression by capitalism, may manifest themselves whenever a favorable opportunity arises. The next great war may furnish this opportunity. This event would release revolutionary energies throughout the continent, so that before long the whole of Europe may belong to the Soviet Union. A large part of the French, German, English, and Italian proletariat is ripe for such a revolution.

The American proletariat has as yet developed little consciousness of class. The fallacious notion that a new country furnishes everyone a good chance to amass a fortune has until very recently wooed the workers with its false appeal. The labor movement is excessively conservative. Every attempt to establish industrial unionism has failed. The American Federation of Labor-CIO is a reactionary organization of craft unions. Their leaders are as capitalist in their principles as the capitalists themselves. No radical political party has as yet succeeded in acquiring a large following or polling any considerable proportion of the votes.

In the United States there is no political party with mass support which advocates any far-reaching change in the economic system. The American labor movement has always supported free private enterprise. At their annual meetings in 1946 the two great labor organizations,[21] namely, the American Federation of Labor and the Congress of Industrial Organizations, united in 1955, reiterated their firm belief in this system. The latter through its President, the late Philip Murray, issued in 1947 a "national economic program" which contained not a single far-reaching change. The American labor movement has never advocated economic planning with a view to producing a vastly greater volume of goods, and then distributing them much more equitably in order to give every citizen and consumer a high standard of living. It has been limited almost exclusively to attempting to secure, by means of collective bargaining or more aggressive measures, a larger share in the partition of the wealth actually being produced. Indeed, it has at times endeavored to limit production in the interest of the members of its craft unions.

These features of the American labor movement are survivals from the early history of the United States. While there was ample free land and a rapidly expanding economy, there was a very little

[21] *The World Almanac,* 1951, p. 260.

According to figures obtained by the United States Department of Labor from union sources revised to June 30, 1950, the total of organized workers ranged from 14,000,000 to 16,000,000 of which the A.F. of L. had about 8,000,000, the C.I.O. from 5,000,000 to 6,000,000, and the independent unions from 2,400,000 to 2,800,000.

opportunity for the common man, by shrewdness or by luck, by hook or by crook, to amass a fortune. A relatively small number of proletarians were thereby raised into the capitalist class. This day is almost past. As an American journalist with European experience has said: "Until some years ago, the United States urban or rural proletarian looked on himself, not as such, but as a millionaire *manqué*. . . . This illusion is now disappearing. That is the profound meaning of the halting but continuing steps toward the creation of parties along class lines, as in Europe."[22] In the meantime, American liberals and progressives are in utter confusion with their monetary and other legislative nostrums to save capitalism from its contradictions.

The present outlook is that the United States may continue in its present course for another two or three business cycles. Beyond that point it would be too hazardous to prophesy. It seems probable that it will be the last important capitalist country. Its great natural resources, rich capital equipment, and relatively high standard of living of its population may enable it to pursue this course for a generation or two without precipitating any revolutionary economic and political changes. But it must sooner or later face the grave problem of adjusting its economic and political organization to the far-reaching changes caused by science and technology, especially in the emergent atomic age with its tremendous constructive as well as destructive possibilities.

The notable absence of a revolutionary movement is all the more striking in comparison with the rapid tempo of capitalism on the North American continent. In its technical equipment, in the efflorescence of its monopolistic phases, in the concentration of wealth and disparity of incomes, in the accumulation of surplus capital and of debt obligations, in the acuteness of the crisis as exemplified by the wide divergence between productive capacity and purchasing power, and in the excessively high percentage of unemployment, capitalism has gone farther toward its ultimate dissolution in the United States than in any other country. In some respects this country, which has been the richest and most favored of all capitalist countries, seems already to have reached the final stage of a permanent major crisis and state of depression.[23]

The lack of a revolutionary movement may be due principally to the fact that the workers have profited by the rapid development of a new country and have received the highest real wages in the world. What the effect of a prolonged depression will be upon the ideology of the American workers remains to be seen. It is certain to make them more hopeless of better conditions under the present system.

[22] Sherry Mangan, *Fortune Magazine*, November 1943.
[23] *Cf.* John Strachey, *The Nature of Capitalist Crisis*, New York, 1935.

Furthermore, monopoly capitalism is rapidly proletarizing the lower middle class and is thereby creating a new factor for a revolutionary situation. The professional class also is becoming in part proletarianized. The intellectual class in general is drifting toward the left.[24] But without a revolutionary proletariat the intellectuals cannot bring about a revolution.

In view of the internal difficulties capitalism is now experiencing, the possibility of a breakdown of the present system may seem imminent. If this should happen, some sort of an improvised system would have to take its place, even though a revolutionary movement was not prepared to meet the emergency. However, it is unlikely that capitalism will disappear of its own accord and if not overthrown. The capitalists will continue to squeeze their profits out of the system as long as possible, however badly it may be functioning. The difficulties of capitalism will be resolved temporarily, so far as they can be resolved at all, by stabilization at a depression basis. The capitalists will have to accept a lower rate of profits but will acquire greater security and stability for the time being until the revolutionary forces become sufficiently strong to overthrow the system.

It has been widely believed that a new economic and social system may come into being through a process of "gradualism." According to this program, the government would gradually collectivize the system by choosing certain industries or forms of economic activity from time to time for socialization. It is usually assumed that the so-called "key" industries and economic activities would be the first to be socialized. Among them are banking, transportation, power, the extractive industries, the iron and steel industry, etc. In course of time, all the capital goods industries would be socialized. Industries which have a tendency toward monopoly control would also be socialized.

The proponents of "gradualism" usually advocate heavy taxes upon the rich which would yield a large revenue which could be used

[24] Cf. George Soule, The Coming American Revolution, New York, 1934. Soule said that a social revolution requires (1) basic changes in ways of conducting affairs (invention and technique); (2) a new alignment of social classes; (3) activity of intellectuals and ferment of ideas; (4) reforms which strengthen new classes; (5) a revolutionary crisis when the old ruling classes can no longer carry on and the rising classes have already acquired substantial power.

His final conclusion was that "just as feudalism was compelled in the end to give way to the rise of the middle classes and capitalism, so capitalism must in the end give way to the rise of the working classes and socialism." (P. 283.)

An American bourgeois sociologist has acknowledged that "this country, in common with all others in which the industrial revolution has developed, is destined to evolve through capitalism into some sort of social control of industry." "The laboring man seems destined to be the ruler of the future." (L. P. Edwards, The Natural History of Revolution, New York, 1927, pp. 6, 211.)

in improving the condition of the poor. This is a clumsy and wasteful method of trying to remedy the excessive inequality in the distribution of wealth. It would be much simpler and more effective to deprive the capitalists in the first instance of the privilege of exploiting their fellow men. Furthermore, heavy taxation interferes seriously with the functioning of the capitalist system. It deranges market relations, disturbs the competitive fixation of prices, and decreases profits, thereby diminishing the incentive to business enterprise. If capitalism is to be retained at all, it should be permitted to function at its best, however ineffective that may be.

Some of the advocates of gradualism believe that the socialization of the economic world should eventually be complete. Others think that it will be sufficient to socialize the key industries. Most or all of the consumption goods industries would then be left to private enterprise. In the first case, semi-collectivism would prevail for a considerable period of time. In the second case, semi-collectivism would be permanent. This would create all the contradictions of socialized and unsocialized economic activities trying to function side by side. It is doubtful if such an inharmonious situation could continue very long. It is almost certain that one would soon drive the other out.

Capitalism as an economic system has been described in Chapters XXXVI to XLII of this treatise.[25] It has been shown that capitalism is a scarcity economy, even though abundance is feasible and readily attainable, because production is subordinated to private profits for which scarcity is essential. The inadequacy of purchasing power distributed to the masses to absorb all of the volume of commodities produced gives rise to the recurrent periods of depression typical of capitalism. War and preparation for war, and boondoggling in peacetime, are the only remedies for depression possible under capitalism. But the deliberate and calculated waste and destruction of wealth, namely, sabotage by the capitalists, is no cure for the business cycle.

It may be added that under capitalism there is no economic security for any class, even the most wealthy. In several important respects capitalism and technology are antagonistic. Capitalism is ambivalent in that both competition and monopoly flourish under it, with the odds perhaps in favor of the latter. Last but not least, economic planning is not feasible, so that an orderly and well organized economy is impossible under capitalism.

These considerations suggest that the time may soon be ripe for a revolution in the capitalist world. Earlier in this chapter I have stated the psychological reasons arising out of habit and custom why

25 I have described capitalism at greater length in my *Farewell to Poverty*, New York, 1935; and *Poverty and Social Progress*, New York, 1916.

mankind is reluctant to bring about a revolution. The American Declaration of Independence of July 4, 1776, recognized this hesitancy when it said that "all experience hath shown, that mankind are more disposed to suffer, while evils are sufferable, than to right themselves by abolishing the forms to which they are accustomed." However, this document, written mainly by Thomas Jefferson, and impelled partly by Thomas Paine's *Common Sense*, went on immediately to say: "But when a long train of abuses and usurpations, pursuing invariably the same Object, evinces a design to reduce them under absolute Despotism, it is their right, it is their duty, to throw off such Government, and to provide new Guards for their future security."

Chapter LXIX

The Division of Labor and Technological Change

THE next few chapters of this treatise will deal with conditions and factors of change and of stability, of likeness and of dissimilarity, of evolution and of devolution. The intricate interaction between human nature and environment, out of which all cultural phenomena have arisen, will be illustrated thereby. These processes have been discussed in earlier chapters and described at least in part. The following chapters will analyze these processes insofar as the available data permit. They may even arrive at a few tentative theoretical conclusions, which will, however, not be of the ideological and speculative nature characteristic of former philosophers of history and of culture.

In the immediate present bulks largest the current struggle between bolshevism, fascism and liberal democracy. However much this struggle may change its form in the near or more distant future, it includes phases which have been perennial problems for human society. Among them are the problems of personal freedom or the relation between the individual and the group, the relation between youth and adulthood, and the relations of the sexes to each other.

One of the gravest problems has been as to the degree and manner of using force. In Chapter XXI and elsewhere we have seen that the state heretofore has been an agency of power usually of a violent and brutal character. This power has often been seized by an individual, the "man on horseback," who has sometimes had an alleged charismatic aura which has seduced the public. The most seductive has been the military hero combined with "charisma." The butcher of humans acquires a romantic glamor in the eyes of the unthinking multitude.[1] This personal authority and leadership have ordinarily

[1] Political freedom is one of the civil rights, including the right to vote. Of 33 United States presidents from 1789 to 1959, 29 were elected president, 4 being vice-presidents who succeeded to the presidency upon the death of a president. Of these 29, 6 were commanding generals in a war and were elected as military

been used for ends destructive of the lives, property and welfare of the public. The authority exercised has in fact usually been that of a small group, so that the rule and dictatorship has ordinarily been more oligarchical than monocratic.

In recent times this oligarchical rule has usually called itself a monolithic party rule, thereby borrowing the terminology of the parliamentarism which it has cast aside or rendered meaningless. This has been true not only of totalitarian fascist and communist parties, but also of capitalist political parties. For example, in the most capitalist country, the United States, the Republican-Democratic party is as much the capitalist totalitarian party as was the Fascist party in Italy from 1922 to 1943, and the National Socialist (Nazi) party in Germany from 1933 to 1945. Since the war of 1939 to 1945 it has practically suppressed every other political party in the United States because of its fear of communism.[2]

Underlying oligarchical rule over the masses is the pervasive covert or overt conflict of the classes. Its solution is perhaps the gravest problem which confronts society. So long as society is dominated by a small upper class, social control will be largely class control. Until this class control is abolished, society cannot regulate itself in its own interest. In fact, in Chapters XVIII and XIX , I have demonstrated that little genuine and authentic social control has existed up to the present time. It is doubtful if a genuine collective authority has ever existed. In like fashion, genuine democracy has never existed, because there has never been equality of opportunity for every one.

Alongside of the class conflict runs the conflict between science and religion, or more broadly speaking, animism. Science has often been used by the dominant class in its own interest and to a certain extent in the interest of the public. In spite of the incongruity and contradiction between science and religion, the dominant class has retained, supported, and propagated religion in order to maintain its control, as has been described in Chapter XV and elsewhere in this treatise.

At the heart of the human and social problem of existence and perpetuation lies the almost completely misunderstood subject of economic organization. It has at least four major aspects. First, there should be a productive process so organized as to produce an abun-

heroes. They were Washington, Jackson, W. H. Harrison, Taylor, Grant, and Eisenhower. Of the others, at least 9 had been army officers in a war and were elected in part because of military service.

[2] An assistant attorney general, commenting on the exclusion from the Illinois ballot in 1952 of the Socialist Workers Party, said: "The right to have one's name printed on the ballot is not a part of freedom of speech, freedom of assembly, or freedom to petition for redress of grievances." (*Chicago Sun-Times*, May, 1952.)

dance for a given society. Second, the routine work should be so arranged as to produce an abundance with a minimum of labor and a maximum of leisure. Third, the distributive process should be so organized as to furnish every citizen an ample supply of goods. Fourth, consumption should be rationalized so that the wasteful and deleterious methods often used by consumers will be largely eliminated. No one of these four fundamental aspects of economic organization is adequately treated in the numerous treatises which daily pour from the printing presses. I have attempted to do so in two earlier books and in Chapters XXXV to XLII inclusive of the present treatise.[3]

The political organization of a planned economy implies a state very different from the power state of an exploitative society. It will be much less an agency of power and much more a political and economic organization. This will mean in turn that the role of compulsory social organization will diminish and that of voluntary organization will be enhanced. While this politico-economic development is already commencing in certain countries, it cannot be restrained within national boundaries. As it becomes international and world-wide in its scope, it will be compelled by geographical factors to take the form of geo-economic regionalism as described in Chapters XLV to XLVII inclusive.

The relations between the Occidental and Oriental cultural zones as described in Chapters LIV through LXIII do not necessarily create and present problems. They do, however, illustrate the great diversity of cultural forms and of the consequences of their contact and assimilation. We are now approaching the massive impact of the Orient upon the Occident which has so far been almost entirely heedless of the Orient's existence. The Orient has already been feeling the impact of the West for more than a century.

Last but not least, we come to the problem of war and peace which now threatens for the first time in human history to become global and total. It places in glaring contrast the destructive effects of war with the productive technology of peace. It also arouses the fateful question as to what kind of an animal man is. An English writer has said: "Man is naturally a solitary, suspicious, quarrelsome animal."[4] To this view may be contrasted the description of man as a cooperative animal presented by a distinguished Russian scientist and anarchist.[5]

[3] See Maurice Parmelee, *Poverty and Social Progress*, New York, 1916; and *Farewell to Poverty*, New York, 1935.
[4] H. Stafford Hatfield, *The Inventor and His World*, London, 1949, p. 215.
[5] P. A. Kropotkin, *Mutual Aid A Factor of Evolution*, New York, 1903.
"In the practice of mutual aid, which we can trace to the earliest beginnings

There is almost no social division of labor or cooperation or mutual aid among animals, as we have seen in Chapter XII. Such insect societies as the ants and the bees are in reality reproductive groups and therefore biologically and not socially determined. In like fashion, the sex division of labor characteristic of many animals and of mankind from its lowest stage is biological and destined for reproductive and not social purposes.

The division of labor has at least two far-reaching economic and social consequences. On the one hand, it implies and requires the exchange of goods for otherwise it would have no utility. Here is the starting point and fountainhead of the vast development of trade and commerce which has played so important a part in cultural evolution. On the other hand, it has created occupational groups which have often hardened into status.

A French sociologist asserted that mechanical solidarity is attained owing to the likeness between the individual members of a society. This solidarity leads to repressive legal measures in the form of penal law in order to enforce uniformity among these individuals. He contended that organic solidarity is due to the social division of labor. This often leads to contractual solidarity. Whatever we may think of the detailed exposition of his theory, it suggests the far-reaching effects of the division of labor upon the ideas and forms which constitute much of culture.[6]

The biological sex division of labor is supplemented in non-literate and pre-literate societies by the social division of labor among the various crafts. In the earliest societies these include hunting, fishing, and tool-making. Thus arrives the industrial division of labor. This, however, does not at first involve the intra-industrial division of labor as in the later machine cultures. Nor does it include the inter-communal division of labor which gives rise to the geographic division of labor.

The most obvious and logical basis for the division of labor is native aptitude for and skill at performing the task required. However, to choose the individuals fitted by skill for the various occupations requires a mechanism of testing and examination not yet attained for many positions in modern society. What happened in pre-literate society we can hardly more than conjecture. It may be that some

of evolution, we thus find the positive and undoubted origin of our ethical conceptions; and we can affirm that in the ethical progress of man, mutual support— not mutual struggle—has had the leading part. In its wide extension, even at the present time, we also see the best guarantee of a still loftier evolution of our race." (P. 300.)

[6] Emile Durkheim, *The Division of Labor in Society*, New York, 1933. Translated from the French.

occupations were transmitted by social inheritance from one generation to another. This would depend in part upon whether or not the group in question was a family group or a horde made up of several families. After a rigid caste system had come into existence, the hereditary transmission of occupations became predominant thereby ignoring the criterion of aptitude and skill.

In dealing with this problem as with so many other cultural origins, we confront a dark prehistoric past which yields us very few data. The anthropologists and cultural historians have studied the few remaining pre-literate peoples, and have often assumed that their customs and institutions characterized the past of all mankind. This, however, is not a safe assumption to make. The extant pre-literate peoples have had as long a past as the literate peoples and have presumably experienced a long and varied cultural evolution. Only a few of these assumptions may be noted as reasonably probable.

In Chapter XVIII we have discussed the evidences of sex and age dominance in the past, remnants of which persist down to the present day. In Chapter XIX we have characterized classes as a basis for the division of labor; and in Chapters XXV to XXVII, inclusive, of the same volume we have described the origin of the social classes and the rise of class dominance and of stratification according to class constituting status.

Our survey of the past has indicated that the division of labor has been determined largely by the caste or corporate organization of occupations. The rigidity of this sort of organization has been indicated by the symbolical designation of occupation and of rank in society, most of all by clothing. As an American anthropologist has said: "Wherever clothing is worn, the sexes are distinguished by their garments. . . . Where class differences exist, clothing marks off the individual who commands position and means from those of inferior status."[7]

In Chapter XXVIII we have described the gradual transition from rigid status to class mobility which has been only partly achieved. Prior to the modern evolution of large-scale machine production, the worker often owned his tools of production and therefore did not become a commodity to be bought and sold in a labor market, as under the capitalist system, unless he was still in the rigid and immutable status of a slave or a serf. The modern so-called free laborer who has attained the apparent mobility of a fluid class system is nevertheless more bound to his class and to his occupation than is apparent on the surface. While he is ostensibly free to go and come where he pleases, and to choose the kind of occupation he desires,

[7] M. J. Herskovits, *Man and His Works*, New York, 1948, p. 260. See also his *The Economic Life of Primitive Peoples*, New York, 1940.

when the factories in which he seeks employment shut down he is unable for lack of tools to continue to produce. Furthermore, when a job is offered to him it is usually in the occupation in which he has had experience because the employer does not want the expense of training an inexperienced worker. When unemployed he loses even his only means of subsistence. The freedom of the so-called free labor market is very limited both as to choice of occupation and as to the time and place of employment.

As we have seen in Chapters XVIII and XXVI, class dominance arose from the division of labor buttressed by the concentration of wealth. Language and the division of labor have been and are the most important cultural phases or factors, but the concentration of wealth has been an ever disturbing factor. While aptitude and skill constitute the only logical and rational test or criterion for the choice and designation of persons in the division of labor, we have seen that at different times and places brute strength or sex or age or kinship has served as the decisive test. Last but not least and down to the present day, wealth and social status usually based upon wealth have been the most decisive criteria.

The artificial right of inheritance of property which arose and has persisted in a predatory society perpetuates class status from generation to generation. Modern industrial technique cannot tolerate the rigidity of a caste system because it requires a certain amount of flexibility in the labor force. In India, for example, the factory system and the railroads have threatened to break down the organization of the castes. The modern class system has had sufficient mobility to adjust itself to modern industry with, however, a good deal of loss of labor and diminution of production. In a socialized economy there should be much labor saved over a predatory economy such as capitalism. Under collectivism the individual would be judged by his personal traits and not assigned to his function in the industrial economy by his racial or national origin or his property status or his class status.

The so-called division of labor of most importance, or at least of the greatest prominence at present, is that between landowner, manufacturer, merchant, laborer, and capitalist entrepreneur or financier. The relationship between these economic groups is, however, not one of skills but a predatory and exploitative relation. Each is trying to secure the largest possible share in the partition of wealth at the cost of its rivals. This has even become true in recent times of the labor group through their trade organizations. With this sort of a competitive goal the largest possible production of wealth cannot be attained. The sort of competitive effort characteristic of such a society is wasteful and spurious insofar as the attainment of the legitimate purpose

1192

of a social economy is concerned, namely, the production and equitable distribution of wealth.

The preceding paragraph indicates clearly that capitalism, or any exploitative economic system, places a narrow limitation upon the most genuine form of competition, namely, competition between individuals as the most efficient producers of goods or of services. The landowner usually renders no service whatsoever insofar as the ownership of his land is concerned, though he may also be an agriculturist. The capitalist usually produces nothing insofar as the ownership of his capital is concerned, though he may also be an industrialist. The manufacturer may increase production somewhat by organizing the factors in the productive process. The merchant may contribute some place and time value to the goods which he buys and sells. The laborer, both agricultural and industrial, is the only person in this largely spurious division of labor who produces goods or renders services of intrinsic and genuine value to society.

The mechanization and automatization of the productive process may result in a return to the generalized worker in the place of the somewhat specialized worker who now characterizes the productive process in the highly industrialized countries. This will not mean the complete abolition of the division of labor. Different skills will always be needed and will play their differentiated roles in the productive process. The recrudescence of the more generalized type of worker may constitute a step nearer to the time when every human will be primarily and fundamentally a member of the human species and a citizen of the world.

As indicated above, the division of labor would have no utility were it not for the exchange of goods produced by the various participants in this division. Presumably, this exchange took place at first in the simplest form of barter. It may at times have assumed the form of gifts which were only a concealed form of barter. Later in cultural evolution arose the money economy in which a common medium of exchange served as an intermediary between various goods to be exchanged. Exchange led in turn to inter-communal division of labor which in course of time became a geographical division of labor. This was accomplished by the merchant transporting his goods far and wide through commerce. The exchange of goods through trade therefore consummated and rendered socially valuable the division of labor among the genuine factors of production.

Technology arose almost entirely out of the division of labor. Presumably, its origin was in the instinctive endowment of mankind and of the process of trial and error which resulted in the establishment of certain habits. But technology could not develop very far on this basis alone. The division of labor produced workers with specialized skills and knowledge who had considerable incentive to enlarge and improve the techniques of their various crafts. Here may have originated the social process of invention which created a good deal of technology as will be discussed in the following chapter. Much later came the evolution of science, as described in Chapters XXIV and XXXI, which has created or furnished the basis for most of modern technology.

The development of technology has, however, been much hampered by many cultural survivals, such as magic and religion, and certain forms of social organization, such as theocracy, feudalism, and capitalism. As has been pointed out repeatedly in this treatise, technology has been hampered perhaps most of all by the contempt for labor due to class dominance which has persisted to the present day. This debasement of labor has frustrated not only technology, but also science from which much of technology has arisen. So long as the economic activities of mankind were largely directed by magic and religion, science had little opportunity for development.

Science has a logic of its own which is deadly to magic and religion. Science and technology, which is its offspring and disciple, assume a universe of natural law and energy not dominated or even influenced by irresponsible mythical deities. In a large part of the world the methods of physical and material production have become so secularized that religion is ignored in practice, though it may be given lip service in theory. While this may be true of the technology of physical production, it is scarcely at all true of social technology which may indeed be said hardly to exist. And yet because the various phases of technology are closely related to each other, the absence of a social technology has its restraining effects upon physical technology. In fact, it is one of the principal reasons why there is not yet a genuine social economy in which technology of every type can fully develop.

As has been amply demonstrated in this treatise, social and technological changes are closely interrelated. The latter changes often give rise to economic factors which result in cultural changes which may be for better or for worse according to the dominant social system. Capitalism ordinarily has the outward appearance of peace and order. But it is the peace of an armed truce. The dominant classes are always under the potential threat of the depressed classes. The right of private property, and the inheritance of wealth basic to capitalism, curtail the freedom of competition and rivalry between individuals as human beings. This is because under these conditions there is no equality of opportunity, and there is discrimination against the vast majority.

This situation constitutes an ever present danger of revolution.
1194

Up to the twentieth century this danger had hardly manifested itself. The preceding revolutions, such as the French Revolution of 1789, and the American Revolution of 1776, were struggles between two or more exploiting classes rather than struggles between exploiting and exploited classes. The Russian Revolution of 1917, and the Chinese Revolution of 1949, were the first far-reaching and more or less successful revolutions of the exploited classes, or at least in their behalf. While they have created for the time being discriminations peculiar to themselves, they may be harbingers of a world-wide uprising of the exploited classes. This will have far-reaching effects upon physical technology which will create a social technology and which will bring into being a genuine social economy.

Chapter LXX

Invention and Diffusion

AN INVENTION may be defined as a combination of psychological or physical cultural elements in new forms. It is sometimes identified with a discovery but the two terms are not synonymous. A discovery is the finding of something already in existence, whereas an invention is the creation of something new.

The question may now be raised as to whether science is an invention or a form of discovery. So far as we know, the facts which constitute science have existed throughout eternity so that they could not be invented and can only be discovered. A writer on invention has asserted that the atomic bomb was not an invention but an application of science: "The bomb was not an invention in the sense of this book. It was the obvious corollary of certain discoveries in the rapidly developing science of nuclear physics, founded when Rutherford and Chadwick 'split the atom' in 1919." [1] Nevertheless, when equipped with the data of science the inventor has been in a much better situation to create his new inventions. Hence science has been to a considerable extent, and is increasingly the foster mother of invention.

It is to be assumed that invention was at the outset a hit-or-miss affair. It is doubtful if new inventions can be attributed to non-human animals. The earliest human animals were little if any in advance of their non-human relatives. The first inventions doubtless were stumbled on, so to speak, by accident and without intention by the earliest inventors. Seeds gathered for food which dropped on the ground and sprouted into new plants probably caused the invention of agriculture. Some time must have passed before the earliest intended inventions took place. This probably arose from the recognition of a need which resulted in the conscious search for a means of satisfying it.

What the original sequence of inventions may have been we can only conjecture. Were the original inventions of tools or of consump-

[1] H. Stafford Hatfield, *The Inventor and His World*, New York, 1948, p. 111.

tion goods? Of the latter, the invention of foods and of ways of preparing them such as cooking, of clothing and of the textile art, of shelter and of the art of construction, were taking place during the long paleolithic periods. At the same time, not only tools but improvements in tools were being invented. During the later paleolithic and neolithic periods were being invented agriculture, the domestication of animals, the ceramic art, the various industrial arts, mining and metallurgy, and various styles in the fine arts.

The technique of invention can be readily surmised from the contemporary practice of it. The first step beyond the hit-or-miss stage could not come until a gradual comprehension of nature began slowly to arise and to create a conscious desire for some measure of control over it. Later this comprehension was greatly expanded by science. There has been much difference of opinion as to the relative importance of the individual and the social factor in invention. According to some writers, inventions are due largely to inspirations on the part of creative minds.[2] While inspiration is a common human experience, probably due to the emergence into the conscious mind of elements from the unconscious substratum, and while some persons are more creative than most individuals, the history of every invention of which we have a record demonstrates conclusively that invention is largely, if not predominantly, a social process. No invention has sprung majestically from the forehead of Jove. Each invention of any importance has been due to the slow accretion of minor changes and combinations into new forms which finally became a major invention. The contention of some writers that certain races have been hereditarily more inventive than other races has had no support in the available data. Such differences between the numbers of inventors produced have been due to environmental differences or to the course which the history of a given race or nation has taken.

As for consciously planned invention, that has been a very modern development due on the one hand to the rapid rise of science and technology, and on the other hand to the needs of capitalism at most times and of governments in time of war. However, institutionally planned invention has not completely supplanted the planning of the independent inventor who, like the Wright brothers and their airplane heavier than air, may make a valuable contribution in any field of invention.

Many cultural changes have been due more or less directly and almost entirely to inventions. The great increase in the available

[2] For example Dixon asserted that inventions and discoveries are "essentially one-man affairs." (R. B. Dixon, *The Building or Cultures*, New York, 1928, p. 59.) Dixon also alleged that most of the great cultures were due to gifted peoples so located as to become numerous, and favorably placed to receive the benefits of diffusion, but also where nature was not too kind.

supply of food caused by the invention of agriculture and of many agricultural methods gave rise to large urban aggregations of population. The invention of various transportation methods rendered possible an extensive commerce. The invention of the steam engine gave rise to large-scale industry. In fact, some writers have asserted that all human and social progress has been due to inventive or creative minds. While there is some truth in this assertion, it ignores the large part played by the social factors in the process of invention which has rendered possible this human and social progress.

Invention is hindered as well as stimulated by social forces. These forces may be forms of economic organization threatened by certain kinds of invention. They may be religious and magical beliefs hostile to the changes which would be brought about by certain inventions. The social classes whose interests would be injured by the changes which would be caused by some of these inventions, frustrate the forces for these inventions. In fact, generally speaking, the more conservative elements in a population are more likely to oppose inventions because of the changes which they would bring about.

Many illustrations can be given of the ways in which inventions are frustrated. The priests of religion always favor the traditional and the archaic because their deities are alleged to speak in absolutes, otherwise these mythical divine beings cannot be depended upon as sure and unfailing guides to conduct. In the early days of the industrial revolution the workers often rioted against the newly invented machines, because they knew that these machines would deprive many of them of their jobs and livelihod. They saw no prospect in the society in which they were forced to live of new jobs being provided for them. The capitalists have made some use of science and invention. But as we have already had occasion to note, capitalism is ambivalent in its attitude toward science and invention. Capitalism has also suppressed many inventions for financial reasons. It has not wanted the expense of replacing its obsolescent machinery with the newly invented more efficient machines even when these new machines are labor-saving. The decisive consideration for the capitalist is as to whether he will save and profit more by replacing the old with the new machinery or by continuing with cheap labor.

Invention often accentuates the capitalist crisis by increasing production in proportion to labor. Under such conditions sufficient purchasing power is not widely distributed to absorb many of the goods produced. Surplus inventories accumulate, and sooner or later precipitate a business crisis with which commences a period of depression.

As has been repeatedly pointed out in this treatise, capitalism is a scarcity economy, and as such is threatened by an economy of abun-

1198

dance. Science, the inventions which it fosters, and the technology which results from both of these parents, can readily bring into being an economy of abundance. The capitalists have some realization of this situation. From time to time there arises the cry that there should be a holiday of science, invention, and technology, so that the markets of the world shall not be glutted with a surplus of goods which capitalism is incapable of distributing to needy consumers. Monopoly capitalism is selective in its choice of potential or existent inventions in order that these inventions will aid its profit making, and not push capitalism nearer to its demise. Thousands of patents are purchased but not used by corporations because their use might result in flooding the markets with goods which would lower prices to such a degree as to diminish greatly or wipe out completely the profits from their sale.

Warfare has usually stimulated a good many inventions. These have been destined primarily for belligerent and destructive purposes. During the war of 1939-45 the German, British and American armies were responsible for the invention of the atomic power-plant, the atomic bomb, radio-isotopes, rockets and super-rockets, guided and homing missiles and torpedoes, radar, jet and turbine propelled and supersonic planes, the proximity fuse, magnetic and acoustical mines, magnetic submarine detection from the air, and many other inventions. During wartime the role of government in stimulating inventions for war purposes has usually greatly increased.

Some of these wartime inventions have been useful for peacetime as well. Firearms have been used for hunting. Explosives have been used in industrial processes. During the first half of the 20th century the first great development of aviation was made primarily for warlike purposes. Whether or not the peacetime uses of warlike inventions have more than counterbalanced the destructive effects of their warlike use is very difficult if not impossible to measure. The decisive question is as to whether these inventions would have been invented if there had been no war. On this question a number of pertinent comments may be made.

In wartime, capitalism is inconsistent in that it becomes somewhat collectivist because it turns to government not only to foster inventions for warlike purposes but also to finance the manufacture of munitions and of other objects for warlike uses. Some useful inventions are incidental results of this passing phase for war collectivism. As soon as capitalism returns to its peacetime routine, it ceases to stimulate inventions except insofar as it has reason to believe that they will augment its profits. And here we encounter a fundamental distinction between capitalism and collectivism. The latter is interested at all times in peace as well as in war, in inventing tools, machines and commodities of all sorts which will be useful to mankind, and not merely to give rise to private profits. Here is unquestionably the solution of the dilemma of wartime inventions under capitalism. Under collectivism war is not the necessary stimulus to bring into being these inventions.

During the nineteenth century invention became to a large extent an organized business. It has been described as follows:

> Invention is an act, based like other acts on instinct, habit, a little emotion for a drive, and preeminently based on reason, as a rational effort to satisfy needs of society and oneself, needs perceived by the inventor and usually today by non-inventive men who hire him. For invention is no longer chiefly the work of craftsmen nor manufacturers who seek to improve their own methods. It has become for the most part a specialized profession (if indeed not further specialized), either of free-lance inventors, whom the patent system enables to sell their product, or more often of employees or officers of governments or corporations, employed wholly or partly to improve the methods or products of the government, usually in its military department, or of corporations usually relying partly on the patent system to keep their product or method ahead of their competitors', or to exact royalties from them.[3]

In Chapter XXIV and Chapter XXXI of this treatise, we have seen that a good deal, perhaps the larger part of science, has had a pragmatic origin. In other words, human beings have been confronted with certain problems and someone has endeavored to ascertain the causes of the phenomena which give rise to the problem with a view to solving it. This scientist, or someone making use of his data, has in some of these cases invented a tool or a machine or a method of doing something or a commodity or a device of some sort destined to solve the problem.

Some science has been pure in its origin in the sense that it has been due to an intellectual curiosity on the part of the scientist as to the nature and causes of certain phenomena. However, such science also has often eventually had great practical value. Both kinds of science have been somewhat influenced by the effect of the dominant social system on the scientists concerned. This system has not so often affected such science as physics, chemistry, astronomy and mathematics, as it has the sciences in which the human element is much more

---

[3] S. C. Gilfillan, "The Lag Between Invention and Application with Emphasis on Prediction of Technical Change," 1951, unpublished, p. 8.

prominent. It has given rise to considerable bias in the social sciences. For example, the so-called science of economics taught in American universities is almost entirely biased in favor of capitalism. This bias has in turn affected materially the sort of problems studied by psychological and social scientists, and thereby determined in considerable part what sort of inventions it was attempted to attain. Under capitalism the phenomena of the price and monetary system attract an enormous amount of attention, and many are the devices invented or at least faintly sketched to solve these ever present problems of capitalism.

The collateral or parallel aspect of invention is diffusion. In surveying the cultures of the past, especially of the prehistoric period but also of the historical present, it is often difficult or impossible to determine whether a cultural phenomenon originated where it has been observed or has been introduced from elsewhere. The cultural anthropologists have devoted much study to this question. By acculturation is usually meant the transmission of cultural elements. This is a more technical term for diffusion of culture. Some anthropologists are inclined to limit the number of the centers of cultural origin and to extend and emphasize the range of cultural diffusion. Among these anthropologists have been G. Elliot Smith, his disciple W. J. Perry, the German anthropologists F. Graebner and Leo Frobenius, and the American anthropologists Franz Boas, Alfred L. Kroeber and Robert H. Lowie. The extreme form of this diffusionist theory was attained by the Englishman Smith who traced practically all aboriginal American culture to Egypt.

There is no intrinsic reason for restricting the frequency of invention. We have reason to believe that such inventions as poetry, agriculture, certain kinds of tools, and many other devices or commodities have been invented more than once. To assume that most of the important inventions had been invented only once would be to assume either that certain peoples had an unusual inherited inventive faculty, or that certain environments were peculiarly adapted for inventive achievements. There is no evidence for the first assumption and a limited amount of evidence for the second assumption. Where a plentiful supply of a metallic ore exists is a suitable region for inventions in the metallurgical art. On the other hand, the many regions where arable soil makes agriculture feasible, or where there are plentiful supplies of clay for the ceramic art, render it almost certain that these arts have been invented over and over again. Invention and diffusion are parallel or complementary processes, or both of these processes at the same time or successively.

The contact of peoples causes diffusion and may also give rise to cultural variations and innovations which constitute inventions.

1201

Specific diffusion factors have been described at many points in this treatise. Among them are such factors as migration of peoples and the establishment of colonies, conquest, commerce, revolution which has repercussions outside its own region, religious proselytizing to a minor degree, and infiltration of customs and ideas through many types of communication.

In addition to the duplicate inventions already mentioned are the equivalent inventions where two different methods of meeting the same problem have been invented at different places or times. These equivalent inventions are to be found in many fields of activity such as cultivation of the soil, transportation, mining, and clothing. They furnish an alternative possibility to duplicate invention or diffusion.

Certain other cultural processes which are significant with respect to invention and diffusion may be mentioned. Convergence takes place when societies isolated from each other arrive along separate lines of evolution at the same or a similar cultural situation with respect to one or more aspects of their whole culture. In this connection also may be mentioned the principle, or what may more correctly be called the condition, of limited possibilities. This situation exists when a culture may develop along only one or two or a limited number of paths primarily because of the limitations placed upon it by its earlier development. Another cultural situation is that of cultural focus, namely, where there is concentration on certain cultural features resulting in the overshadowing of other features of the cultural situation. There have been concrete illustrations of all of these cultural processes in the course of this treatise.

Perhaps the most striking feature of the cultures of the world is their diversity. On the one hand is the more or less established fact of the essential and fundamental likeness of the various human races and varieties. While there is a good deal of variation between individuals in any racial group, there is no conclusive proof of marked differences in the instinctive, emotional and intellectual traits of the several races of mankind. Insofar as inheritance is concerned it might be expected that the cultures evolved by the different races, even when not in contact and communication with each other, would be substantially the same. Nevertheless, we have to note these wide cultural differences.

The first and most obvious cause for cultural diversity is the vast range of geographical and topographical environment within which or over which mankind lives. These environmental differences are so obvious and so well known that they need no description here. What is often difficult to explain is why a given environment has produced or at least has been the site of a given culture. The reason for this difficulty is that any culture is not due solely to its immediate geographical environment. With the exception of a few extremely isolated human groups, such as the Eskimo in the Arctic north, or the Patagonians near the Antarctic south, nearly every human group has been somewhat subjected to the diffusion of cultural influences from other human groups.

Another factor contributing to the oft recurring difficulty of explaining the diversity of culture is that a culture may acquire a trend or a tendency or a set in a certain direction due to events in its earlier history which at their occurrence did not seem to have decisive importance. This statement may appear to justify what may be called the explanation of history or of cultural development by accident. In another work I have described how the Marxists have disproved this fallacious explanation of history, though the historical explanations which they have offered may or may not be acceptable on other grounds.

> The principal and peculiar merit of Marx and his ablest disciples is that they have eliminated not only supernaturalism but also "chance" and "accident" as causes of historical events and of social phenomena more completely than any other school of thinkers. This is strikingly manifested in connection with the so-called "superior" race, the "great" man, and the "accidental" concatenation of events, each of which has often been used as the supposititious cause or explanation of a set of circumstances or train of events. These mystifying and obscurantist explanations are not characteristic of Marxist writings. On the contrary, the Marxists usually endeavor to dig down to the roots of the economic processes which are the principal if not the sole causal factors in history and social evolution.[4]

As has been pointed out in this treatise, patents were introduced several centuries ago partly in order to encourage inventors by assuring them a reward from the proceeds of their inventions. This purpose has somewhat decreased as inventing has been institutionalized to a considerable extent by big business. For example, in the United States in 1938 corporations of over $50,000,000 capital apiece were issued 17 percent of the patents, smaller corporations received 35 percent, foreign corporations 5 percent, and individuals 43 percent even though they had received as high as 72 percent as recently as 1921.[5]

[4] Maurice Parmelee, *Bolshevism, Fascism and the Liberal-Democratic State,* New York, 1934, p. 49.

[5] "In the modern corporation the technician becomes little more than a proletarian: the tools, funds, and ends for invention are controlled by the managers." (A. B. Stafford, "Is the Rate of Invention Declining?" *Am. Jour. of Sociology,* May 1952, p. 542.)

By 1950 the corporations owned more than 60 percent of the patents acquired in part by purchase.

However, there is reason to believe that even before the corporations owned so large a proportion of the patents, they were profiting heavily from their proceeds to the detriment of the inventors who owned the patents. In 1915 Taussig revealed these facts about inventors who often are not skilled financiers. Furthermore, they are usually without the funds necessary to commence the manufacture of the commodities which they have invented. The latter fact puts them more or less at the mercy of capitalists and corporations, which are able either to buy their patents for a relatively small sum, or to make contracts with the inventors which pay the inventors a very small amount of the profits derived from the inventions while the capitalists and corporations retain the bulk of these profits.[6]

Even assuming that patents are no longer playing as large a role in stimulating inventions, the question may be raised as to whether the progressive rise in the educational standard of mankind and especially the spread of scientific knowledge will not stimulate the inventive talents of many individuals even more than patents have done in the past. In this connection it has been suggested and even prophesied that technical progress is not endless. This hypothesis has been stated by an English writer on invention as follows:

> One of the characteristic fallacies of present-day popular philosophising is the belief that technical progress is bound to continue without end. It is supposed that the human mind will never be content to leave invention alone, but that no sooner is one problem solved than another will be attacked. This view overlooks the fact that human invention in the widest sense has never been, until quite recently, mainly utilitarian in its aim, but has expended a great deal of its creative effort in endeavours to hitch wagons to stars. The dismay excited by the consequences of hitching them to coal, oil, and atoms may result in a reversion to the old attitude which put marvels of technical skill and invention, as well as artistic creation, into temples and cathedrals, while the wealthiest were content with a standard of domestic comfort which would drive our miners to riot.[7]

A more important reason why there may be a slowing down of technical progress in the future is if and when an era of abundance is reached for all of mankind. In that case the populace would sooner

[6] F. W. Taussig, *Inventors and Money Makers*, New York, 1915.

[7] H. Stafford Hatfield, *The Inventor and His World*, New York, 1948, pp. 104-105.

or later have to decide whether it wished to continue increasing the flood of goods or would rather diminish its labor and increase its leisure time and avocational activities. In the latter case there would be less stimulation for invention.

A still more fundamental question is as to whether invention is the prime cause of social change, and perhaps for what is euphemistically and optimistically called social progress. The engineers and technicians are inclined to exalt the role of invention. While there is much justification for their contention, they do not give sufficient weight to the influence of certain psychological and social factors. These factors are illustrated in the rise and evolution of institutions discussed elsewhere in the present treatise, such as in Chapter XIV, and in the following chapter.

Chapter LXXI

Institutional Selection and Survival

IN Chapter XII an institution has been defined by me as a complex of beliefs, ideas, or activities shared by many persons who are not necessarily living together or within specific territorial limits, and who may or may not be organized. A somewhat looser definition reads as follows "Institution is a verbal symbol which for want of a better describes a cluster of social usages. It connotes a way of thought or action of some prevalence and permanence, which is embedded in the habits of a group or the customs of a people. In ordinary speech it is another word for procedure, convention or arrangement; in the language of books it is the singular of which the mores or the folkways are the plural." [1]

Institutional selection and survival is a social process like invention, diffusion, division of labor, growth of science, social control, technological change, conservation, revolution, and the other social processes. In fact, the term social process has been applied to so many social phenomena as to give it a certain vagueness of meaning. As one social scientist has said: "At the core of social process theory is thus the notion of movement, change, flux—of society as a continual becoming." Another sociologist has said of it: "Society exists only as a time-sequence. It is a becoming, not a being; a process, not a product." [2]

Many examples of institutions may be mentioned, some of which existed from an early stage in cultural evolution. Among them are language, magic, religion, marriage, the various fine arts, science, ethics, law, education, barter, burial, worship, theology, agriculture, democracy, politics, economics, money, capitalism, feudalism, monarchism, collectivism, property, market, nationalism, citizenship, suffrage, sovereignty, authoritarianism, libertarianism, and many others.

[1] *Encyclopedia of the Social Sciences,* Volume VIII, 1932, p. 84. in the article entitled "Institution" by Walton H. Hamilton.

[2] *Encyclopedia of the Social Sciences,* Volume XIV, 1934, article entitled "Social Process" by Max Lerner.

An institution often corresponds to or is a corollary of a form or forms of social organization. This is a more concrete and therefore more definite expression of an institution than the vague term social process. It comes into being when a considerable number of individuals who adhere to the institution either in their activities or in their beliefs are joined together by some unifying bond. An American anthropologist has characterized some of these bonds as follows: "Kinship, sex, age, coresidence, matrimonial status, community of religious or social interests are among the unifying agencies; and in stratified societies members of the same level form a definite class." [3]

Some of the examples of social organization are horde, clan, tribe, oligarchy, thearchy, aristocracy, kingdom, republic, fief, state, nation, church, and political party. Certain traits of a social organization are illustrated by some or all of these examples. Among them are consciousness on the part of the members that they belong to this organization, loyalty to the organization, residence in and ownership of the same territory, and more or less compulsory observation of the same practices and acceptance of the same beliefs.

There are no institutions among animals. This is partly or entirely because no non-human animal has developed language. Without language it is impossible to communicate and to share the beliefs and ideas which constitute an institution. Congeners of the same species share many activities and some emotions. If these activities and emotions are not inspired or at least accompanied by certain beliefs and ideas, it would be misleading and meaningless to call them institutions. As a matter of fact, most of these activities and emotions are due to inherited instincts and innate tendencies. These animals learn a good deal and acquire habits in the course of their lifetimes. Since many of them learn the same things and acquire the same or similar habits, they may appear to be acting in a similar fashion because of a common institutional bond. However, in the case of no animal except man is it possible to assume communication by language, and the growth of traditions and complexes of beliefs and ideas such as we witness in the case of such institutions as religion or magic, science or ethics, democracy or capitalism.

Coming now to the specific subject of this chapter, the question arises as to whether institutional selection and survival are similar to biological selection and survival. In both cases we find a multiplicity of phenomena some of which survive for a greater or shorter length of time while other phenomena perish. In the biological process of natural selection, this is necessary to the survival of a species. Biological evolution has taken place largely because this process of selection

[3] *Encyclopedia of the Social Sciences*, Volume XIV, 1934, article entitled "Social Organization" by Robert H. Lowie.

has selected out for extinction certain types of individuals and of species and has, so to speak, chosen other types for survival.

An analogous if not similar process takes place in institutional selection and survival. There are, to be sure, no biological factors involved. There are, however, institutional phenomena which if they persist long enough would destroy or transform the type of society and of culture in which they exist. On the other hand, there are institutions which tend to the survival of the societies and cultures which they characterize. Since there is much diversity of culture, as we have already had occasion to note, and since many of these cultural traits are contradictory, in other words could not co-exist permanently in the same culture, the process of selection and survival has, so to speak, a large choice.

While we have ruled out the biological factors as operative, or at least decisive, in the social process of institutional selection and survival, there remain many ecological factors. Among these factors are such features of the natural environment as climate, which includes temperature and the precipitation of rain; topography including the relief of the land; the quality of the soil; the distribution of land and water; the availability of navigable water; and the supply and distribution of such natural resources as the useful minerals, and the sources of power such as oil and water power, and now the unlimited supply of atomic energy.

Arising out of and determined by these factors of the natural environment are the factors of the secondary artificial environment created by man. Among these factors of the secondary environment are cultivated arable land, exploited mines, towns and cities, harbors and artificial waterways, and the other numerous artificial factors of its environment which mankind has created. This artificial environment has changed somewhat the conditions under which the process of institutional selection and survival operates. An institution which may have had some utility for survival at an earlier stage of social and cultural evolution may become a mortal danger at a later stage. In fact, many of the difficulties harassing recent and present-day mankind are due to survivals of certain institutions.[4] In the case of some of them, forms of social organizations which correspond to or arise out of

---

[4] "War in our own civilization is as good an illustration as one can take of the destructive lengths to which the development of a culturally selected trait may go. If we justify war, it is because all peoples always justify the traits of which they find themselves possessed, not because war will bear an objective examination of its merits. . . . Now for the first time the comparative study of religions is free to pursue any point at issue. It is not yet possible to discuss capitalism in the same way, and during wartime, warfare and the problems of international relations are similarly tabu." (Ruth Benedict, *Patterns of Culture,* New York, 1934, second edition, 1947, pp. 29, 230.)

these institutions have survived until they have become dangerous to mankind even though they may have had some utility or at least have been relatively harmless at earlier stages of social and cultural evolution. In fact, there have been and still are many institutions which have never been useful in the sense of promoting the welfare and happiness of human beings, or which have long survived their usefulness. An interesting and important question arises out of this situation. Is it possible to detect any methods or principles by which the selection for survival or extinction of these institutions take place? This is one of the most difficult problems involved in the analysis of the origin, evolution, and devolution of cultural phenomena.

In Chapter XXXVI Machiavelli (born 1469) has been cited: "The cause of every man's success in life is owing to the temperature of his mind in conformity to the times in which he lives." This adage applies to institutions as well as to individuals. Ideas, habits and customs which arise in a horseback or horse-and-buggy age are often quite unsuitable for an automobile or airplane age. The chaotic condition which often exists between contradictory institutions may arise from the mingling of more or less different cultures through conquest or migration, or it may be due to more or less extensive changes in the artificial environment created by man which necessitate corresponding changes in ideas, habits and customs. These changes have to come because an agricultural society is becoming industrialized, because large cities are arising and substituting urban for rural habits and customs, because transportation is becoming much more rapid, and because of the other extensive cultural changes which have taken place since paleolithic time.

Let us look at a few of the pairs of contradictory institutions now present, one of which must be destined for extinction. Nationalism and world federation are in the main incompatible with each other. If world federation materializes, it will drive nationalism, or at least its more extreme forms, from the world. Even more emphatic is the contradiction between war and humanitarianism. As I have pointed out in Chapter XLIV, this contradiction may seem to arise out of contradictory elements in human nature. In another work I have said: "The co-existence in human nature of the traits which are ordinarily called humanity and cruelty appears to be a strange anomaly. This anomaly manifests itself in many different forms in individual cases and at different times and places. . . . The peoples of modern civilized nations are displaying much concern over the welfare of the poor, and yet with the utmost readiness rush into wars with each other which cause untold suffering and loss of life."[5]

[5] Maurice Parmelee, *Poverty and Social Progress,* New York, 1916, Chapter XVII entitled "The Modern Humanitarian Movement," p. 233.

In that book I have explained that war is not due to these aggressive elements in human nature but to certain social factors. The contradiction mentioned is not insoluble as many writers have alleged. On the contrary, certain social changes may result in eliminating either war or humanitarianism.

Another contradiction similar to the above is that between racialism and what may be called humanism in order to distinguish it from humanitarianism. In this case also, while these somewhat contradictory elements in human nature are involved, the contradiction is greatly exacerbated by social factors which are very mutable.

The contradiction between not only institutions but also forms of social organization of most critical importance today is that between capitalism and collectivism. Not so obvious as this contradiction is the contradiction between capitalism and science and technology. While capitalism has made a good deal of use of science and is to a large extent based upon technology, it is nevertheless true that capitalism does not use science and even goes so far as to check technology when its fundamental purpose of making private profits is endangered. I have furnished ample evidence of the ambivalent attitude of capitalism toward both science and technology in an earlier book[6] and in Chapters XXXVI through XL of this treatise.

A contradiction of institutions in another field of human life and activity is that between what may be termed sacramental as contrasted with companionate or free contractual marriage. The first alleges that marriage is an institution ordained by God, or at least by the State, which has a significance for society far surpassing its significance for the individuals immediately concerned. Back of this conception of marriage lie not only influential religious and ecclesiastical interests but certain powerful economic forces. The inhertance of private property which is fundamental to capitalism would be gravely endangered if the legitimacy of birth was not upheld and safeguarded. In order to do so it is essential to make of marriage an almost sacred institution. It is one of the seven sacraments of the Roman Catholic religion.[7]

The partial disregard of the individual interests of the parties to a marriage in the alleged interest of society has, however, brought about its reaction. It has encouraged the view that marriage is primarily the private affair of the parties concerned. Unless the interests of third parties become involved, such as the offspring of a marriage, it is

---

[6] Maurice Parmelee, *Farewell to Poverty*, New York, 1935; Chap. VI, "The Profit Motive *versus* Technical Efficiency," Chap. XXII, "The Development of Social Technology."

[7] Baptism, confirmation, the Eucharist, penance, holy orders, matrimony, and extreme unction are these seven sacraments.

recognized that interference in the marriage by society is not justified. This opposing concept of marriage which has sometimes been termed companionate marriage is slowly gaining ground in some of the more advanced countries of the world through the broadening of the divorce laws. This renders it comparatively easy for a marriage to be terminated, thereby approximating the conditions which would exist if companionate marriage was recognized by law. This change in public attitude toward the relations between the sexes is due partly to the spread of recognition of what I have termed the play function of sex as described in Chapter XLVIII, the legal recognition of which I have proposed in Chapter LII, under the title of "Free Contractual Marriage." The complete recognition of this function of sex, and the legal realization of a form of marriage in harmony with it, depend in part upon the abolition of the inheritance of private property. This is an illustration of how changes in institutions, and also of forms of social organization in one field of human life and activity, may be seriously affected by and largely depend upon changes in entirely different fields of human life and activity. The contradictions involved in past and current institutions concerning sex are discussed in the following chapter.

History shows clearly that institutions have a crucial point of self-destruction at which they must disappear. This has often been true of the practice of magic in the past. Certain magical practices have failed so completely to attain the ends toward which they were directed, and have often been so destructive, that they have destroyed themselves, sometimes even before science and the technology based upon it have supplanted magic. Religion has so far only partially reached this point, as will be shown in a later chapter.

Another illustration is that of slavery. This institution has attained economic ends of production at certain times and places in the past. However, new methods of production have been so much more efficient, and therefore productive, than the methods using slave labor that slavery has destroyed itself, so to speak, through its own relative inefficiency. A notable recent example was that of slavery in the southern part of the United States. While the immediate cause for its formal disappearance was its legal abolition during the Civil War of 1861-65, slavery was already on its way out, because the plantation method of cultivating the soil was far less productive than the method of cultivation by free labor. Furthermore, the industrialization which has spread from the north to the south in the United States is incompatible with slavery.

Another instance of the waste of natural resources and of other forms of wealth due to one phase of an extensive institution and form of social organization is furnished by the United States of the present day. The flood waters of the rivers cause an enormous loss of fertile soil as well as destroying a good deal of human handiwork. These losses could be prevented in large part by dams which would impound the surplus water and render it available for irrigation purposes and also furnish power. The United States Government has already accomplished these ends in the Tennessee River valley. But the private utility interests vigorously oppose the Government's flood control plans for other river valleys because they foresee a decrease in their private profits. How long this conflict of institutions can continue remains to be seen.

As we have seen, many institutions are crystallized, so to speak, in forms of social organization. By becoming organized some of these institutions are strengthened and in most of these cases their lives are prolonged thereby. For example, capitalism as an institution has been strengthened and perpetuated because it has been bolstered by the law and the various agencies of the state, so that it has in effect become a form of social organization.

On the other hand, it has often been alleged of religion that when organized in a church its spirit is deadened if not killed. Whether or not this is true of religion, it is true of a few other institutions which can be readily injured by organized forms of a bureaucratic nature. For example, this is notably true of science, and perhaps as true of invention insofar as we can regard invention as an institution. The case of science we will presently investigate.

The same is perhaps equally true of the fine arts. In this field of human activity it is extremely important that the individual artist finds scope for the free expression of his individual personality. Any form of organization is likely to curb, deaden, and sometimes extinguish this free expression which is the only possible source of originality in art.

Before proceeding with a more detailed discussion of the effects of organization on science, art, and religion, we may note that vestiges of usages often survive disappearing institutions, sometimes for a long time. The British monarchy is an instructive illustration. It has become a wholly useless and futile institution. And yet it survives as a hollow form and symbol partly through social inertia and partly because of traditional sentiments pertaining to it which have been handed down from the past. Its absurdity is emphasized by the fact that monarchism has been abolished or has never existed in the vast majority of the nations of the world.

Vestiges of colonialism also persist in certain nations of the world. This is true in such self-governing commonwealths as Canada and Australia which are to all intents and purposes independent of Great Britain and yet cherish an outworn sentiment of the past.

1212

Games both for children and adults often are pale vestiges of institutions and forms of social organization of the past. Many of the games of today simulate forms of warfare which are not yet of the past. Some of these games simulate hunting which is already of the past for the great majority of human beings.

Diplomacy also is a vestige of the monarchical institution and form of social organization which is now almost entirely of the past. The diplomat was the personal representative of his sovereign. He still goes through many of the same forms, though he should now be representing the people to which he belongs, and not a ghostly monarch. Owing largely to his effete status, he has little contact with the largest and most important portions of the population of the country to which he is accredited. He associates almost exclusively with the small upper class which is engaged principally in exploiting the much more numerous lower classes.

While these vestiges of usages of extinct or moribund institutions and forms of social organization may not constitute a mortal danger, nevertheless they hinder in varying degrees the effective functioning of institutions and forms of social organization which are more suitable for the present and future.

The apparent ambivalence in the application of science suggests that here again we have an instance of a sharp contradiction between science and certain other institutions. Science and its offspring technology are the principal factors in constructing the material structure of culture and of civilization. Science has also already had a marked effect upon man's outlook upon the universe, and is likely to affect that outlook even more in the future.

On the other hand, science and technology have often been used to destroy human lives and the wealth which has been produced by human labor. As these lines are being written, there is taking place on a desert in western United States a terrific atomic blast capable of slaughtering millions of human beings and destroying billions of dollars worth of wealth. This blast is the result of scientific investigation and skillful technology. And yet there is nothing inherently destructive in science or in technology. Both are neutral insofar as the use to which they are put is concerned.

The age-old rivals of science have been magic and religion. Magic has been largely defeated by science in the more literate portions of the world. The chief reason for this defeat is the fact that magic has not responded to the pragmatic test as well as science. Magic has usually failed to attain the ends sought whereas science has more often succeeded, partly because it is more subject to test and control as to whether it works than is either magic or religion. Religion has not as yet yielded because it is not subject to the pragmatic test as rigorously

1213

as magic. Whereas magic attempts to coerce the forces of nature and fails, religion attempts to cajole the mythical deities, and it is alleged that these deities may or may not feel inclined to respond favorably. Prayer is a form of supplication which may and often does fail to attain its end.

The apparent ambivalence of applied science is more directly and immediately due to the fact that it is utilized by economic and political factors which are sometimes directed toward constructive and at other times toward destructive ends. War is the most striking illustration of the use of both science and technology for destructive ends. The cult of violence instigated by patriotism and chauvinism and hero worship of warriors, often leads to a justification if not glorification of war, which leads in turn to the contradiction between war and humanitarianism described above.

Capitalism often illustrates how economic factors may use science and technology for constructive ends, or may render them temporarily nonproductive if not destructive. In Chapter XXXVI, I have described how capitalism as an economic system often fails to master its internal contradictions and rigidities. At its core is its fundamental contradiction between competition and monopoly. While it has used science a good deal and technology a great deal during its more expansive stages, it ceases to use science almost entirely and diminishes greatly its use of invention and technology during its contractive stages. Generally speaking, private enterprise for profit encourages applied science but not so much abstract and theoretical science. The reason is obvious because such enterprise is interested only in making profits as soon as possible. It may, however, not be logical from its own point of view because applied science and the technology which results from it are possible on the basis of abstract scientific theory. In any case, capitalism has proved to be a vacillating and unreliable sponsor of science and to a smaller degree of invention and technology.

Capitalism also hampers science in other respects. In capitalist countries like the United States the universities and scientific institutions are under a very strict financial control. This can be illustrated by one or two concrete examples from American universities. One of the most liberal of these institutions (Yale University) was accused in a book of promoting irreligion among its students and teaching communism through its courses. The university authorities responded by alleging that religion was never more widespread among its students, in spite of the fact that this is a subjective and intangible phenomenon which cannot be quantitatively measured; that it has no communists in its faculty, though there is no evidence that communists are less competent to teach many if not all subjects as non-communists, and that the courses in economics are not communistically but impartially

1214

taught, in spite of the fact that it is well known that the courses on economics in this university as in all American universities are biased at least 99 percent in favor of capitalism. The financial group in control of another American university (Columbia University) chose as its president the leading militarist and war-hero in the world, who has no competence either as a scholar or as a teacher to be the head of a scientific and educational institution. An official of this university informed the writer that this was done in order to secure millions of dollars of endowment for this university. It was also in order to groom him successfully for the presidency of the United States. So long as universities and other scientific institutions are under such financial control, they cannot be primarily centers for scientific research and instruction.

In succeeding chapters will be discussed institutional selection and survival with respect to sex and religion and the fundamental contradiction between capitalism and collectivism. At this point may be mentioned the contradiction involved in the form of collective bargaining as organized and practiced in the labor movement of today. While more or less vigorous at present, this movement is implicated and compounded with its class enemy the employing capitalist class. The purpose of each of these enemies in this more or less armed truce is to secure as large a portion as possible in the partition of the wealth now being produced. Neither party in this conflict is concerned primarily or at all with the purpose of increasing as much as possible the amount of wealth produced, as well as with the purpose of securing the distribution of wealth on the basis of justice and not of class warfare. Labor strife as it now exists often injures the interests of consumers by raising the rates of wages and injures the interests of wage-earners by raising prices, and usually fails to strive for and often opposes the only ultimate solution for this strife in some form of collectivism.

A similar contradiction is between status and class on the one hand as opposed to occupational groups on the other hand. Inherited status has disappeared in a good deal of the world. Class distinctions which are not inherited in name but are transmitted from generation to generation, mainly through the inheritance of private property, are still predominant in all capitalist countries. American sociologists have gathered data which indicate that American society is changing from an open to a closed class system.

The strata are becoming more rigid; the holes in the sieves are becoming smaller. Status is crystallizing. There is both a tendency toward restriction of access to the means of personal and family advancement, and an apparent reduction in the vertical mobility drive and psyche and ethos. Needless to say, in this

1215

rigidifying and "closing" of our class structure, and in this reduction of vertical mobility, we may be depriving our society of many potential contributions that might emanate from the lower ranks. The situation limits the use of intrinsic merit; much merit remains undiscovered.[8]

Both status and class are opposed to the most effective occupational grouping which can result only from thoroughgoing application of the principle of the division of labor. As we have already seen in Chapter LXIX, the division of labor requires a grouping of individuals according to inborn capacity and acquired skill. This principle cannot be applied to a large extent when artificial class distinctions exist which are bolstered up and supported by inherited wealth. The solution of this contradiction is bound up with the fundamental contradiction between collectivism and capitalism to be discussed in a later chapter.

One of the obstacles in the way of discussing the numerous contradictions mentioned above, and the process of selection and survival which is going on all the time among them, is the apparent permanence of the contemporary existent. For example, with an imposing ecclesiastical edifice on nearly every city corner, it is difficult for the average man to believe that science by its very nature may some day drive religion from the beliefs and practices of mankind. It requires historical perspective to discern the process of change which is so gradual as to require many generations to become evident and to constitute a major cultural transformation.

Among the pairs of contradictory institutions which have been described are nationalism and world federation, war and humanitarianism, racialism and humanism, capitalism and collectivism, private profits *versus* technology, slavery and industrialization, sacramental and free contractual marriage, animism (including magic and religion) *versus* science.

---

[8] J. O. Hertzler, "Some Tendencies Toward a Closed Class System in the United States,' *Social Forces*, March 1952, pp. 313-323.

Hertzler cited many of these American investigations, among them being F. W. Taussig and C. S. Joslyn, *American Business Leaders*, New York, 1932; Elbridge Sibley, "Some Demographic Clues to Stratification," *American Sociological Review*, June, 1942; J. O. Hertzler, *Social Institutions*, Lincoln, 1946; G. Myrdal, *An American Dilemma: The Negro Problem and Modern Democracy*, New York, 1948, 2 vols.; W. L. Warner, M. Meeker and K. Eells, *Social Class in America*, Chicago, 1949; Carson McGuire, "Social Stratification and Mobility Patterns," *American Sociological Review*, April 1950; David Riesman, *The Lonely Crowd: A Study of the Changing American Character*, New Haven, 1950; C. Wright Mills, *White Collar: The American Middle Classes*, New York, 1951.

Chapter LXXII

Sex and Ethics

IT is a singular fact that sex has been mainly ignored as a cultural factor by social scientists. Anthropologists making field studies have often recorded some of the institutions as forms of social organization with regard to sex of preliterate people largely because they varied considerably or greatly from the corresponding institutions of civilized peoples. These have usually been the forms of marriage. Not only the institutions directly related to sex but also the part played in the lives of nearly all individuals by sex itself has been overlooked by most of these social scientists.

On the other hand, it is a curious if not a contradictory fact that prepossessions with respect to sex have to a large extent flooded and almost submerged ethical ideas and beliefs in Occidental culture. This is peculiarly true with regard to ethical rules applied to women. Female virtue and purity have been identified to a large extent with sex. Virginity has often been exalted as if it constituted a superior type of female virtue and purity.

The same has not been equally true with respect to men. It has been more or less tacitly recognized that male violations of sex taboos are not so serious provided they do not become publicly known. In other words, a certain amount of covert male license has been regarded as permissible provided the conjugal and familial virtues are openly respected.

The inevitable consequence of this situation with regard to both sexes has been that many ethical traits that are as important as or even more important than the ethical traits related to sex have been regarded more lightly or even largely ignored. A woman who causes much trouble in her social circle by her malicious tongue is little reprehended publicly provided she maintains her reputation for a virtuous life with respect to sex. In Anglo-American society a spiteful woman who is sexually frigid can hold her head high, though she may cause much misery. A man who publicly recognizes the conjugal and

1217

familial virtues may nevertheless do much damage by means of his business practices, and yet get away with it.

It has been alleged by some social scientists that a high degree of sex regulation is necessary in order to maintain an effective social control. A notable example was the English anthropologist and historian J. G. Frazer who published about the beginning of the 20th century a book under the obscure title of *Psyche's Task,* later published under the more accurate title of *The Devil's Advocate.* In this book Frazer alleged that superstition, by which he meant magical and religious beliefs, has among certain races and at certain times strengthened respect for (1) government, especially monarchical government; (2) private property and the security of its enjoyment; (3) marriage and stricter observance of sexual morality; and (4) human life and its security. However, he recognized that superstition has in other ways done much harm in the world.

Another English anthropologist was even more insistent that social order is due to sex regulation: "The sense of ownership has been the seed-plot of jealousy. To it we are indebted for the first germ of sexual regulations. To it in the last resort, reinforced by growing physiological knowledge and sanctioned by religion, is due the social order enjoyed by the foremost nations of Europe and America." [1]

By placing excessive emphasis upon sex regulation, many kinds of invasive conduct are likely to be ignored or at least to be ineffectively restrained. On the other hand, a good deal of non-invasive sexual conduct has been restrained, by unwarranted prohibition. Even when such conduct was invasive it has often been brutally repressed. At the same time the far more invasive conduct involved in predation, exploitation, and warfare has not been restrained and has received the commendation of the dominant classes.

Unlike other social scientists, I have devoted six chapters (XLVIII through LIII) of this treatise to the subject of the social and cultural significance of sex. Conventional moral ideas serve in the first instance as obstacles to the free and unprejudiced study and frank discussion of sex as a social and cultural factor. Of much more far-reaching importance is the effect of these ideas in creating social conflicts and contradictions. In this chapter I shall summarize briefly what has been discussed at length in the above-mentioned six chapters.

Certain magical and religious beliefs have influenced greatly the treatment of sex not only among primitive peoples but even down to the present day among civilized peoples. One of these beliefs was that sex is unclean, especially in woman, because of the various sexual issues from her. This belief has encouraged asceticism and celibacy,

---

[1] E. S. Hartland, *Primitive Paternity,* London, 1910, Volume II, pp. 102-103.

especially in Christianity which is the dominant religion of the Occident.

Among most civilized peoples monogamy only is regarded as the pure, chaste and continent form of sex relations, however contradictory the use of those terms may be, because marriage is always unchaste and often incontinent. Marriage is sacramental and legitimate or at least the latter. As a sacrament it is supposed to have a divine sanction. As a legal institution it is supposed to guarantee the legitimacy of offspring. This is important wherever the inheritance of private property is in force.

Another phase of current sex mores is the so-called double standard of "morality" which is in reality a double standard of freedom for the two sexes. That there is a biological basis for this double standard is obvious. In sex relations the woman runs the risk of pregnancy and procreating which the man escapes. But here again the importance of legitimacy under an economic system based upon inheritance of private property buttresses this double standard of sex freedom which discriminates against women.

There have been other economic factors limiting women mainly to the home and certain kinds of agricultural activity which have resulted in both political and economic discriminations against woman. The modern industrial revolution has broken down these discriminations and barriers to a considerable extent. In many countries women have already secured the suffrage. What is more important, they have been admitted to a large number of occupations not because of any notion that this was their right but because modern industry with its highly developed and detailed division of labor has required the services of the female sex for carrying on its operations. This has been true not only in the factory and machine shop but even more in the office and counting house where women have become many or most of the typists, stenographers, clerks, bookkeepers, and other clerical workers. However, there is as yet no decisive indication that women will attain an equality with men in directing industry. From this position she may be excluded not so much by economic as by biological factors because of her reproductive function.

The male gallantry which is a sort of sop to woman in lieu of her deprivation is derived largely from the medieval chivalry which characterized the men of the upper and dominant class under feudalism. This chivalry included not only a romantic and sentimental attitude toward the relations between the sexes, but also the martial traits of the warrior and the pious traits of the Christian devotee. It was directed toward the relatively few women of the upper and dominant class and included no sympathy whatsoever for the far more numerous women of the lower and exploited classes. Male affection

and genuine sympathy for women as a sex arise out of sexual feelings and attraction, and out of certain profound human traits which
underlie altruism and humanitarianism and which have no causal relation with chivalry and gallantry. These traits not only toward wom-
en but toward mankind in general can expand and attain their full
scope only as warfare, class conflict and the exploitation of class by
class and of individual by individual are checked and gradually
eliminated.

Procreation has been regarded as a duty of women for a variety
of reasons, all of which are more or less anti-social. The generals,
military leaders, and conquerors have wanted more human beings
to slaughter as cannon fodder. The employers and exploiters of labor
have wanted a reserve of unemployed labor which would keep the
labor cost low, and thereby furnish them cheap labor. The nation-
alists and chauvinists have wished to exalt their nations by increasing their populations to the highest possible degree. Many of the
religionists have alleged that the deity has commanded mankind to
multiply. No one of these alleged reasons for reproducing the human
species gives due consideration or any consideration to the decisive
questions as to the relation between the human population and the
available supply of food and other commodities to support it, and
also to the equally important question as to the desired standard of
living for this human population.

Under a socialized organization of society there would be no
ethical or social reason for procreation. If this socialized system was
world-wide, warfare would be eliminated from the world. There would
be no exploiter desirous of cheap labor. Nationalism would be eliminated or at least so weakened that patriotic demands for increase of
population would cease. The alleged commands to procreate from a
mythical deity would lose all weight. Reproduction would then become not a matter of duty but of choice and of pleasure on the
part of individuals to whom it appeals as a source of satisfaction.
Under such a socialized system the demographic problems which now
plague mankind would largely if not entirely disappear.

Elsewhere I have proposed the creation of a new social institution
which I have called the amatorium.[2] This would be the first and,
so far as I know, the only public recognition of sex for its own sake.
The function of sex, which I have named the play function, is already
a powerful dynamic factor in the life of society and is capable of
considerable expansion under favorable conditions. Such an institution is hardly possible so long as the present mores, institutions, and
forms of social organization related to sex continue to dominate. With

[2] See my *The Play Function of Sex*, 1960, Chapter III, entitled "The Amatorium as a Public Institution."

1220

the gradual breakdown of these obstacles, such an institution as the amatorium can begin to operate and to perform the functions to be described presently.

The chapters dealing with sex as a social and cultural factor in this treatise have shown that in our society there is no adequate sex education for children and adolescents and no appropriate means to introduce and initiate young adults in sexual practices. In these respects civilized peoples understand even less than some primitive peoples the important part played by sex in the life of mankind. An American anthropologist commenting on this contrast between literate and nonliterate peoples said of the young adults of the latter peoples: "The pre-marital experimentation that many nonliterate cultures sanction has a very definite role in inculcating skill and finesse in sex behavior. Those who enter on marriage are thus not exposed to the psychological hazards, manifest in the frequency of frigidity in women and impotence in men found by modern psychopathology in our own society, where matters of sex must be spoken of secretively, are often considered as partially evil, and for which the young person is prepared in a haphazard manner." [3]

Among some of these primitive peoples, the initiation of the young adult is often performed by an older adult of the opposite sex. Among others of these primitive peoples, the initiation comes about more informally among the young people themselves. These primitive folk did not have the sort of religious beliefs and economic institutions which have placed inhibitions and restrictions upon the natural expression of the sex instinct. Owing to these inhibitions and restrictions, among many civilized peoples, the young adults, especially the young women, blunder and stumble blindly and unprepared into marriage and their sex life. The sexual maladjustment due to ignorance and lack of preparation is often the cause of frigidity in women, due to dread or disgust, and psychic impotence in men, caused by frustration and disappointment.

Some of the anthropological field studies which furnish data with regard to the premarital sex relations of the young are instructive with regard to the contrast with the sex mores of the civilized Occident. A few of these cases will illustrate this point.

The Muria are an agricultural tribe of the Bastar State in the Central Provinces, India. The ghotul is the common dormitory of the unmarried girls and boys. Children are sent to the ghotul usually before puberty so as not to embarrass parents when having sexual intercourse, and to accustom the young to take sexual life easily. The children are betrothed at an early age for marriage at a later date by

[3] Melville J. Herskovits, *Man and His Works, The Science of Cultural Anthropology*, New York, 1948, p. 321.

their parents according to clan and economic status, usually to cross-cousins. Their first sex relations are in the ghotul which decides how they are to be paired and for how long. Sometimes the "ghotul marriage" lasts for five or six years during which ghotul partners are expected to be faithful to each other. Then the boy and the girl marry their betrothed with whom they have had no previous sexual or familiar relations.

In the modern ghotul the partners change every three or four days. This is supposed to lessen the danger of pregnancy and to discourage emotional attachments which may be hard to break when the time of the permanent formal marriage comes. The Muria consider sexual relations good if observed according to their rules which determine formal permanent marriage relations largely by kinship.[4] This may not be a satisfactory form of marriage owing to the lack of personal choice, but the young have at least been sexually prepared for marital life.

The Nuba hillmen of Kordofan are about 300,000 Negro tribesmen leading a primitive life in the Nuba Mountains about 300 miles southwest of Khartoum in the Anglo-Egyptian Sudan. A British official who lived among them for several years has characterized them as follows. "I never knew a Nuba who was really mean. They were honest, frank, generous and good-natured. . . . They had few inhibitions about domestic bliss. Marriage was very simple. The partners indicated their admiration for each other, lived together, and stopped living together when tired of it. But they were not promiscuous, and there was much respect and affection shown. Small dowries were exchanged."[5]

Margaret Mead has studied the sex relations among the young of several peoples in the South Pacific region. These customs among the Samoans she has compared with the contrasting customs in the civilized Occident. After considering the confusion and conflicting views as to sex presented to the children and adolescents of the Occident, she said of the Samoan young: "The Samoan child faces no such dilemma. Sex is a natural, pleasurable thing; the freedom with which it may be indulged in is limited by just one consideration, social status." Of the consequences of this confused and conflicting attitude upon the adolescents and the adults of the Occident, she said: "To attain what we consider a more dignified standard of personal relations we are willing to pay the penalty of frigidity in marriage and a huge toll of barren, unmarried women who move in unsatisfied procession across the American and English stage." Of the sex knowl-

[4] Verrier Elwin, *The Muria and Their Ghotul*, Bombay, 1948.

[5] Robin Strachan, "With the Nuba Hillmen of Kordofan," *National Geographic Magazine*, February 1951, pp. 249-278.

edge of the Samoan children she said: "Samoan children have complete knowledge of the human body and its functions, owing to the custom of little children going unclothed, the scant clothing of adults, the habit of bathing in the sea, the use of the beach as a latrine and the lack of privacy in sexual life. They also have a vivid understanding of the nature of sex." She compared the Samoan with the Occidental attitude toward sex as follows: "Romantic love as it occurs in our civilization, inextricably bound up with ideas of monogamy, exclusiveness, jealousy and undeviating fidelity does not occur in Samoa. Our attitude is a compound, the final result of many converging lines of development in western civilization, of the institution of monogamy, of the ideas of the age of chivalry, of the ethics of Christianity." [6]

Miss Mead also studied the sex mores of several more or less primitive tribes in New Guinea which display certain contrasts. Of the Manus tribe she said: "The whole picture is one of a puritan society, rigidly subduing its sex life to meet supernaturally enforced demands which are closely tied up with its property standards. To interfere with marriage arrangements for which thousands of dogs' teeth have been paid, is blasphemy." Of the mountain dwelling Arapesh, a gentle cooperative tribe without warfare and head hunting she said: "The Arapesh do not conceive of sex outside the marriage bond. The casual encounter, the liaison, a sudden stirring of desire that must be satisfied quickly—these mean nothing to them. Their ideal is essentially a domestic one, not a romantic one." Of the river dwelling Mundugumor who are cannibals and head hunters, she said: "We have seen how the Mundugumor ideal of character is identical for the two sexes; how both men and women are expected to be violent, competitive, aggressively sexed, jealous and ready to see and avenge insult, delighting in display, in action, in fighting." Of the lake dwelling Tchambuli she said: "Yet the course of true love runs no smoother here where women dominate than it does in societies dominated by men."

Miss Mead summed up her studies of the last three primitive peoples as follows:

> We have now considered in detail the approved personalities of each sex among three primitive peoples. We found the Arapesh —both men and women—displaying a personality that, out of our historically limited preoccupations, we would call maternal in its parental aspects, and feminine in its sexual aspects. We found men, as well as women, trained to be cooperative, unaggres-

[6] Margaret Mead, *Coming of Age in Samoa*, New York, 1928. Second edition 1949, pp. 134, 139-40, 94-5, 74.

sive, responsive to the needs and demands of others. . . . In marked contrast to these attitudes, we found among the Mundugumor that both men and women develop as ruthless, aggressive, positively sexed individuals, with the maternal cherishing aspects of personality at a minimum. . . . In the third tribe, the Tschambuli, we found a genuine reversal of the sex-attitudes of our own culture, with the woman the dominant, impersonal, managing partner, the man the less responsible and the emotionally dependent person.[7]

Mrs. Benedict has furnished another illustration of sex mores in contrast to Occidental conventions. The Dobuans are a Melanesian people on Dobu Island off the coast of New Guinea. They have been described by Malinowski and Fortune.[8] Mrs. Benedict has described the prudery as well as license of the Dobuans as follows:

The deep-seated prudery of Dobu is familiar enough to us in our cultural background, and the dourness of Dobuan character that is associated with it accompanied also the prudery of the Puritans. But there are differences. We are accustomed to associate this complex with a denial of passion and a lesser emphasis upon sex. The association is not inevitable. In Dobu dourness and prudery go along with prenuptial promiscuity and with a high estimation of sex passion and techniques. Men and women alike rate sex satisfaction high and make achievement of it a matter of great concern. . . . The stock sex teaching with which women enter marriage is that the way to hold their husbands is to keep them as exhausted as possible. There is no belittling of the physical aspects of sex.[9]

Mrs. Benedict also cited the case of the attitude toward sex of the Zuni Indians of the pueblo region of southwestern United States in contrast to the puritanical attitude.

The Puritan attitude toward sex flows from its identification as sin, and the Zuni have no sense of sin. Sin is unfamiliar to them, not only in sex but in any experience. They do not suffer

[7] Margaret Mead, *From the South Seas, Studies of Adolescence and Sex in Primitive Societies*, New York, 1939, pp. 173, 99, 225, 259, 279.

[8] B. Malinowski, *The Sexual Life of Savages*, London, 1929; *Sex and Repression in Savage Society*, London, 1927; *Argonauts of the Western Pacific*, London, 1922; and R. F. Fortune, *The Sorcerers of Dobu*, New York, 1932.

[9] Ruth Benedict, *Patterns of Culture*, New York, 1934; second edition, 1947, p. 155.

from guilt complexes, and they do not consider sex as a series of temptations to be resisted with painful efforts of the will. Chastity as a way of life is regarded with great disfavor, and no one in their folk tales is criticized more harshly than the proud girls who resist marriage in their youth.[10]

An American sociologist has summed up the data with respect to sex regulation the world over as follows:

> From available evidence, however, it seems unlikely that a general prohibition of sex relations outside of marriage occurs in as many as five percent of the peoples of the earth. The bias of our own highly aberrant traditional sex mores has not only distorted the analysis of sexual restrictions but has led generations of writers to postulate for early man or for primitive peoples the antithesis of our own type of regulation, namely, a generalized sexual permissiveness variously called "hetairism, primitive promiscuity," or "sexual communism." The factual support for this assumption is as insubstantial as for its opposite.[11]

An American anthropologist has arrived at a similar conclusion:

> Euroamerican culture, however, has no monopoly on puritanical attitudes toward sex. There are nonliterate groups where the conspiracy of silence is as strong where matters of sex are involved as was ever the case in Europe or America in mid-Victorian times. Yet these are in the minority. Most peoples, in numbering the facts of life, do not draw the line this side of the problems of reproduction. Training in sexual habits can be formalized, or informally given, or both methods may be utilized even in the same culture. Much of the formal schooling given nonliterate boys and girls in the various "initiation" rites they undergo at puberty is concerned with preparation for marriage.[12]

Ford and Beach have made an extensive survey of "behavior involving the stimulation and excitation of the sexual organs." They

---

10 Ruth Benedict, *op. cit.* p. 115.

"Without the clue that in our civilization at large man's paramount aim is to amass private possessions and multiply occasions of display, the modern position of the wife and the modern emotions of jealousy are alike unintelligible. Our attitudes toward our children are equally evidences of this same cultural goal." (P. 226.)

11 George P. Murdock, *Social Structure*, New York, 1949, p. 264. Murdock has surveyed this subject in Chapter IX entitled "The Regulation of Sex."

12 M. J. Herskovits, *op. cit.*, p. 321.

described 190 human societies, the American being the only so-called "civilized" one. In addition they described many animal species mostly primate. They correctly pointed out that cultural biases have led Occidental social scientists to ignore sex in the main and their results corroborate the conclusions of Murdock and Herskovits cited above.[13]

The eminent American sociologist Lester F. Ward at the beginning of the 20th century pointed out the significance of sex apart from and in addition to reproduction. "Sex has fundamentally nothing whatever to do with reproduction. . . . *Sex is a device for keeping up a difference of potential.* . . . The object of sex is not reproduction at all but variation. It is organic differentiation, higher life, progress, evolution."[14] This statement by Ward adumbrates in part my conception of the play function of sex first expounded by me 13 years after Ward, but without knowing what he had written. However, his conception of sex was much more teleological than mine.

A similar concept of sex has been expressed by the French judge René Guyon who has published a series of books on sex. An English writer has summarized Guyon's views as follows:

> It is important to realize the truth that René Guyon has so often emphasized, namely, that sexual activity is one thing and reproduction another. The sexual sense, can, does, and ought to function in many cases for its own sake alone. This view logically necessitates a revision of the standards by which normalcy is judged. Any type of sexual activity would be accepted as normal which was not anti-social when judged by rational standards; when it inflicts no injury to structure or function; when it is spontaneously adopted by both partners and when it gives a full and satisfactory release from tension.[15]

An American psychiatrist has asserted that there is nothing normal in the biological and psychological meanings of the word about a social code which declares man's deepest biological drives to be obscene. As he expressed it: "There is something wretchedly obscene in the whole ideal of chastity; it is something of an incubus on human life." Dr. Myerson described the profound contradiction and conflict between human nature and social convention as follows: "The lip homage to chastity and continence has been offset by droll stories,

[13] C. S. Ford and F. A. Beach, *Patterns of Sexual Behavior*, New York, 1951.
[14] Lester F. Ward, *Pure Sociology*, New York, 1903, pp. 232, 234.
[15] R. Wood, "Psychology and Sexual Behavior," *The Journal of Sex Education*, London, April-May 1951, Volume III, No. 5, p. 198.

bawdy songs, and a complete though hidden defiance of the sexual code." [16]

An American psychologist has graphically described how the average American is torn between the social conventions which have been impressed upon him and the profound biological and psychological traits which drive him in the opposite direction. As. Dr. Ellis expressed it: "The true picture of the proverbially average American should be that of an individual whose sex attitudes are woefully addled, straddled, and twaddled." He characterized the American attitude toward sex as follows: "American attitudes toward human sex behavior as expressed in our most popular types of mass media are amazingly diverse, conflicting, ambivalent, and confused." Ellis described the contradictory nature of American ethical and legal standards as follows: "In the face of the unofficial and extralegal mixed-up sex views of millions of our citizens our official, legal and traditional views on sex are, to a large extent, unworkable, illogical, and obviously not born for this world." [17]

How this situation should be met and this problem solved by civilized peoples it would be premature to predict in detail. But this is one of the situations which should be handled by the amatorium, a public social institution which should be supported by the State.

In addition to furnishing sex education and training for the young, now inadequately provided in home and school, the amatorium should also furnish facilities for sex expression for adults which they lack in their own homes and lives. It should serve as a meeting place for adults of both sexes who know each other or who are strangers seeking a temporary or permanent mate. It should be a comfortable and attractive place for consummating sex relations equipped with devices for contraception and cleanliness. This would furnish the opportunity for the expansion of the play function of sex mentioned above. This expansion will be of great cultural value for mankind. All forms of sex expression should be permitted including as many persons as is desired, provided that no non-participants are inconvenienced.

The amatorium should also prove to be of great social value in a negative sense. It should be a preventive of and a substitute for prostitution. As we have seen, prostitution is not caused primarily by the perversity of men and the lack of virtue in women, but is due to the lack of opportunity for gratification of the natural and normal sexual impulse on the part of many men and some women. Indeed, in some of the earlier cultures the temples furnished the opportunity

[16] Abraham Myerson, *Speaking of Man,* New York, 1950, pp. 88, 92. See Chapter VI entitled "Social Ambivalence."

[17] Albert Ellis, *The Folk Lore of Sex* , New York, 1951, pp. 246, 261, 264.

for sexual gratification by means of prostitutes. The amatorium would furnish a suitable place for securing this gratification without the unhealthy, dangerous, sordid, and often vicious accompaniments of prostitution. Hence it should serve as a healthy substitute for most of this unsatisfactory institution called prostitution created by society itself to gratify the normal sex craving.

The contradiction and conflict between human nature and social convention concerning sex is one of the most acute that mankind has created. It ranks alongside of the contradiction between reason and religion, the conflict between humanitarianism and homicidal warfare, and the opposition between a genuine social economy, such as collectivism, and a predatory capitalism. It gives rise to a vast amount of hypocrisy and of furtive behavior. It is causing an enormous amount of neurosis and other psychiatric disorders by the wholesale suppression of normal sexual impulses and desires. It is inflicting severe punishment upon the men and women who have the courage and intelligence to repudiate this unwholesome social code. It will continue to create vast injury until conventional ethics, now dominated by prudery and persecuting puritanism, becomes more in conformity with human nature.

Artificial modesty has extended sex unduly to all or a large part of the human body, especially in women. Orthodox Hinduism and Islam, and some other religions cults, have compelled women to cover the whole body, even the face, in public. It is alleged on both sexual and religious grounds that all of the female body and part of the male body is indecent, and therefore not to be exposed in public. In this instance also, as in the cases already cited, ethics is extended to sex where it does not belong. The total concealment of the woman is partly or mainly due to economic considerations, because it demonstrates that she belongs to her male possessor who alone has the right to view her as she really is in body.

Some of the satirists have recognized the contradiction inherent in artificial modesty as contrasted with the genuine modesty which arise out of a just estimation and appreciation of one's self. In his satire *Gulliver's Travels*, which exposes many human contradictions, prejudices, foibles and follies, Swift described how the noble-minded Houyhnhnm could not understand the justification alleged by his human visitor for concealing his body, a practice which seemed to him unnatural. "I therefore told my master that in the country whence I came those of my kind always covered their bodies with the hairs of certain animals prepared by art, as well for decency as to avoid the inclemencies of air, both hot and cold; of which, as to my own person, I would give him immediate conviction, if he pleased to command me; only desiring his excuse, if I did not expose those parts that

1228

nature taught us to conceal. He said my discourse was all very strange, but especially the last part; for he could not understand why nature should teach us to conceal what nature had given. That neither himself nor family were ashamed of any parts of their bodies; but however I might do as I pleased." [18] Though two and a half centuries have passed since Swift penned these lines, artificial modesty is almost as strong as ever. This illustrates how persistent are some of these contradictions between human nature and social convention, however unnatural and injurious to mankind they may be.

In another book I have discussed at length the origin, characteristics and harmful effects of artificial modesty, and the beneficent effects of what I have termed the "new gymnosophy." [19] To at least a slight extent the whole body is sensitized by sex, but there are erogenic zones which are highly sensitive. If artificial modesty was consistent it would decree the concealment of the whole body, like the Moslem and Hindu women, or at least and above all of the erogenic zones. And yet there is no taboo upon showing the lips and tongue though they are erogenic zones. The nipples of the breasts are such zones, and yet there is no taboo upon showing them for men everywhere and for women in many parts of the world.

Exhibitionism is a universal and harmless human trait in its normal form. And yet it is punished severely in all parts of the so-called "civilized" world, and even among some primitive peoples. What could be more natural than the desire of each sex to expose and display itself to the other sex in all of its beauty and strength, or lack of them. The person who violates this taboo is usually driven to it by lack of opportunity for sex expression or by the conventional suppression of other natural impulses. Furthermore, there is a great deal of mental exhibitionism which is innocuous and useful or harmful according to its degree and the direction it takes. Thus the exhibitionism of the dictator does vast injury to mankind. [20]

Artificial modesty degrades the human body by asserting that certain parts of it are indecent or even sinful. And yet his own body

[18] Jonathan Swift, *Gulliver's Travels*, London, 1726, "A Voyage to the Country of the Houyhnhnms," Chapter III.

[19] Maurice Parmelee, *The New Gymnosophy, The Philosophy of Nudity as Applied in Modern Life*, New York, 1927. Later editions published under the title of *Nudism in Modern Life*, fifth revised edition with "Historical Foreword" added, 1952.

[20] Among the exhibitionists have been the christs, messiahs, saviors and pretenders to divine rank, and such megalomaniacs as Jesus (Yeshua) the Jew, (33? A.D.) who claimed to be the "Son of God"; Alexander the Macedonian (B.C. 323); Julius Caesar the Roman (B.C. 44); Attila the Hun (453 A.D.); Genghis Khan the Mongol (1227 A.D.); Ivan the Terrible of Russia (1534); Napoleon Bonaparte the Corsican (1821); Porfirio Diaz the Mexican (1915); Benito Mussolini the Italian (1943); and Adolph Hitler the Austrian (1945).

is the closest and the most important object in the universe for every human being. Many religions have done untold injury by preaching this false doctrine. They have alleged that the body as a whole is immeasurably inferior to a mythical immortal soul. Christianity has been exceptionally guilty in this regard. Nationalism, imperialism and the other causes of warfare have added to this degradation by teaching that the human body is less important than one or another of such fallacious and often brutal ends as patriotism, national aggrandizement, colonization, dynastic glorification, imperial conquest, capitalist "free" enterprise to exploit the masses, etc. In fact, warlike homicide and genocide constitute the supreme affront and outrage against the human body.

Artificial modesty materially hampers child rearing and education. It prevents the child from acquiring an accurate knowledge of the appearance not only of other children but also of adults of both sexes. It is almost certain to arouse a furtive desire to acquire this knowledge which is likely to lead to erroneous information. The conflict between the natural and normal search for this knowledge and the social inhibition which renders it furtive causes many mental complexes which harass the child throughout his or her adult life.

Artificial modesty detracts from the most natural and normal sex relations between adults. Sexual selection is based largely upon the exposed portions of the body, especially the face. And yet such choice should be based upon a knowledge of the whole body and will be more satisfactory both for temporary and for permanent mating. Furthermore, it will have greater eugenic value when it leads to reproduction. Too often parenthood and motherhood in particular is determined by a beautiful face superimposed upon an ugly and unhealthy body. The most beautiful as well as the healthiest mankind can be procreated only under gymnosophic conditions.

Last but not least is the injurious effect of clothing upon the health of mankind. While needed all or most of the time in cold climates, and some of the time in certain occupations, it is superfluous a good deal of the time in the temperate zones and all of the time in the tropical and equatorial zones, where insect pests can be readily eliminated. It keeps away from the body the health-giving sunlight and to a certain extent the air. Furthermore, it places an artificial barrier between mankind and nature which detracts from the feeling of the unity of man with nature which would help to remove some of the contradictions and cultural survivals such as religion and war. Clothing, the use of which is largely due to artificial modesty, is one of the more important and the most visible example of a largely unnecessary and often harmful burden which man has imposed thoughtlessly and almost wilfully upon his own body. Its effects, both useful and harmful, are fully described in Chapter LXIV of this treatise. Artificial modesty is another of the many institutions which injure human health and happiness by setting up a convention which violates human nature and creates a physical condition injurious to the welfare of mankind.[21]

<hr />

[21] The Kinsey report entitled *Sexual Behavior in the Human Male,* (1948), and *Sexual Behavior in the Human Female* (1953), demonstrated how sex practices in the United States often conflict with conventional ethical ideas. The study of 5940 female cases revealed that 50 percent were non-virgins before marriage, 26 percent of the married were adulterous before age 40, only 5 percent had the most rudimentary sex education, and that sex problems had deranged two out of every three marriages and influenced three out of every four divorces. An important discovery is that sexual desire awakens later in the female than in the male, so that "the male may be the most desirous of sexual contact in his early years, while the responses of the female are still underdeveloped and while she is still struggling to free herself from the acquired inhibitions which prevent her from participating freely in the marital activity."

Chapter LXXIII

The Repudiation of the Supernatural

THE most striking example of the failure of institutional selection to eliminate the less useful, or the more archaic, or the more harmful, of the phases of culture is the survival of animism. Other phases of culture have advanced far ahead, especially within the last few centuries. Among them are science, technology, economic organization, commerce, industry, music, art, and literature.

Of the two main forms of expression of animistic belief, magic has fallen far behind because it palpably does not work. In an earlier book I have said:

> With the evolution of civilization magical ideas have lost their power, because of the failure of magical attempts to coerce and control natural processes, and because effective scientific methods have superseded the ineffective magical methods. Religion also has lost much of its power, and has been superseded by science to a large extent, because of the apparent failure of religious attempts to propitiate the alleged spiritual beings which are reputed to control the processes of nature. However, religion has one great advantage for survival over magic. When religious attempts fail, it is always possible to fall back upon the hypothesis that the gods have been unwilling to grant the requests of men. Inasmuch as mankind can never hope to attain absolute knowledge by means of the most effective human method of acquiring knowledge, namely, the method of science, it will never be possible to disprove categorically the existence of these hypothetical spiritual beings, however far fetched and improbable these hypotheses may be, nor the traits attributed to them by religious devotees.[1]

[1] Maurice Parmelee, *Criminology*, New York, 1918, pp. 106-107.

Religion still remains widely accepted in spite of the profound contradiction between it and science. This contradiction is even more extreme than the numerous contrasts and contradictions between institutions which we have described, or at least noted, in the course of this treatise.

Science disproves conclusively for all human purposes everything that religion professes and alleges. The universe can be conceived of only as limitless in space and eternal in time, because otherwise the questions arise as to what is beyond space and what is before and after time. It is inconceivable that there is any being or force outside of the universe which is controlling it. Hence it is the height of folly, as well as abysmal ignorance, to permit religious delusions to influence the life and activities of mankind.

The concept of a creator of the universe is unthinkable bcause it immediately raises the question as to who or what created the creator.[2] Since it is logically unthinkable that there was nothing before the universe existed, and that space and time have not always existed, the whole concept of creation of something out of nothing becomes utterly preposterous. In fact, the belief in an absolute beginning of space, time, energy, and matter, is denied by all that mankind has been able to learn about the universe which demonstrates a fundamental unity and not a duality in nature and in the universe. Everything that mankind has been able to learn about man himself denies the anthropomorphism and anthropocentrism which characterize all animistic beliefs including religion. These facts demonstrate the fallacy of the belief in human dualism, namely, an absolute distinction between body and soul or mind which has almost always been a part of animism including all religions. As I have said in an earlier book:

> Many writers in the past and a few still in the present have regarded consciousness as something spiritual and mystical in its character which resides in certain animals or in all living beings. Usually these writers have regarded it as a distinct entity or category which enters the body at the beginning of life and leaves it at death. Such theories are closely related to the religious doctrine of the soul and regard consciousness as something entirely distinct from matter. No such theory of consciousness can

[2] A Burmese authority on Buddhism has said: "Buddhism is not a religion at all, in the sense in which the word is commonly understood. . . . It is meaningless to inquire for a First Cause. A First Cause is inconceivable; rather, cause and effect are cyclical. . . . The origin of the universe, like that of every individual or thing in it, is dependent on the chain of previous causes." (Bhikku U Thittila, " The Meaning of Buddhism, Fundamental Principles of the Theravada Doctrine," Atlantic Monthly, February, 1958, pp. 12-5.

be regarded as scientific because there can be no inductive evidence of the existence of any spiritual entity. Furthermore, it denies the fundamental postulate of science that all things must be reduced as far as possible to the same terms, and assumes an ultimate dualism in the universe.[3]

Another reason why the survival of religion is surprising is the fact that the origin of animism has been satisfactorily and rationally explained by social science. While there can be no historical record of the origin and evolution of animistic beliefs, there is conclusive evidence of their existence at least as far back as the Mousterian period in middle paleolithic time. The archeological data prove that the Mousterians buried their dead, in their cave drawings and designs indicated a belief in life after death, and had other practices which could have arisen only out of animistic beliefs. Field studies of numerous nonliterate peoples furnish a fairly complete picture of the nature of these animistic beliefs, and indicate how they have developed into the current animistic beliefs in the form of religion among literate and civilized peoples. It is, therefore, no more reasonable to assume that the truth of these animistic beliefs is demonstrated by their antiquity, than it would be reasonable to assume that the world is flat simply because mankind as a whole has believed it to be true down to very recent times, and many still believe it.

In view of the fact that science and religion are diametrically opposed to each other, it might be reasonably expected that no scientist would be religious. In Chapter XXIV I have quoted statements from three scientists, all of them Nobel Prize winners, namely, the late Albert Einstein, the late Robert A. Millikan, and Arthur H. Compton, which indicate that they hold or held religious beliefs. However, there is reason to believe that these scientists are atypical in this regard. An American psychologist sent a questionnaire with respect to their beliefs concerning religion to 1,000 American scientists chosen by chance from the biographical publication *American Men of Science*. He found that only 41.8 percent of these scientists believed in a personal god, and that 58.2 percent were disbelievers. After dividing the thousand into two groups of 600 less eminent scientists and 400 more eminent scientists, he found that 48.2 percent of the less eminent believed in a personal god, while only 31.6 percent of the more eminent believed in a personal god. In similar fashion he ascertained the beliefs of these thousand men of science with respect to their belief in personal immortality. He found that 50.6 percent of the total number believed in personal immortality, and that 49.4 percent were disbelievers. Of

[3] Maurice Parmelee, *The Science of Human Behavior, Biological and Psychological Foundations*, New York, 1913, p. 282.

1234

the 600 less eminent, 59.3 percent believed in personal immortality while of the 400 more eminent, only 36.9 percent held this belief. This psychologist also made a similar investigation of the religious beliefs of several college classes which seemed to indicate that the religious beliefs of these students decreased with the degree of advancement of their studies.[4]

This investigation furnished evidence that religion declines with increase of knowledge and ability, both of which are essential factors for the progress of civilization. There is every reason to believe that since this investigation was made early in the 20th century. the spread of secularization as well as of scientific knowledge has increased the amount of religious disbelief not only among scientists, but also among the people at large. It may therefore be said that disbelief rather than belief in religion is typical of scientists.

Many of them, to be sure, do not give public expression to their disbelief, and may even seem outwardly to conform with the dominant religion for prudential reasons. In many parts of the world, religious disbelief results almost certainly in loss of means of livelihood, and sometimes in even more serious consequences. Like all other human beings, scientists have reason to fear these material consequences from revealing their religious disbelief. Another group of scientists, though not believing in religion, may think that religion has a certain social utility, and should therefore be perpetuated. This may have been true of the two English anthropologists whom I quoted in an earlier chapter, namely, Frazer and Hartland. These men apparently thought that religion not only supports what they regarded as sexual morality, but also government and the social order in general.

Another English writer, who catered exclusively to the prejudices of the upper class and to religious sentiments, alleged that altruism and humanitarianism are due to the "ultra-rational" sanction of religion. He implied that human society itself could not exist without this sanction. He conceived of religion largely erroneously as a social, integrating factor which he contrasted with reason which he described as an individualistic, disintegrating force. While recognizing that religion is non-rational and irrational, he displayed complete ignorance of modern psychology.[5] Like some of the older psychologists he conceived of man as a rational being always impelled from within to act by purely egoistic motives, who must therefore be coerced from without to be altruistic. The chapters on human psychology early in this treatise have demonstrated that humanitarianism is due in part to the sexual and parental instincts and the sympathetic emotions, and

[4] J. H. Leuba, *The Belief in God and Immortality*, Chicago, 1921, 2nd edition.
[5] Benjamin Kidd, *Social Evolution*, London, 1894.

therefore partially determined from within.[6] To these internal forces must be added not the "ultra-rational" sanction of a more or less anti-social religion, but the external institutional factors of a cooperative and collectivist society.

The scope of religion is being narrowed all the time. As has already been stated, much that was regarded as sacred has come to be recognized as secular. There is a rising belief in the unity of man and nature. Both of these effects are due in large part to the rapid advance in modern times of science. As an American historian has said: "Never before has man been able so fully to order events sequentially, to explain their interrelationships, or to control his physical-material environment." [7]

Nevertheless religion, and in particular organized religion in ecclesiastical bodies, continues to play an influential part in the life of mankind. For this archaic and contradictory phenomenon may be cited on the one hand forces external to the individuals sharing the religious beliefs. On the other hand, may be cited factors psychological in their character within the individuals sharing these beliefs. They are not, however, inborn religious traits as is often alleged, but are stimulated by the circumstances and conditions under which these individuals are compelled to live.

Religion has almost invariably been used by rulers for purposes of social control. In the earlier days this was often accomplished by the crude but direct method of attributing divinity to the person of the ruler. The ancient kings of Egypt, Alexander the Macedonian (356-323 B.C.), the Roman emperors beginning with Augustus (63 B.C.-A.D. 14), and most of the ancient emperors, monarchs and potentates, assumed divinity or had it bestowed upon them by the ecclesiarchs and theocrats. By this means their authority was greatly strengthened because most humans even down to the present day would obey more readily a god than a mere man. Kings have usually claimed a "divine" right to rule.

Religion has been used to attain social control or at least control by a monocrat or an oligarchy, by depicting the deity as vindictive toward the individuals who disobeyed the ruler who was supposed to have derived his authority from the deity. Until recently the minatory role of religion has been one of the most effective not only in buttressing the authority of rulers, but also in perpetuating religion itself, because many individuals would not risk the denial of a religion which they feared might bring upon them the threatened punishment.

[6] I have described humanitarianism at length in my *Poverty and Social Progress,* Chap. XVII, New York, 1916; and in my "The Rise of Modern Humanitarianism," in *The Am. Jour, of Sociology,* Nov., 1915, Vol. XXI, No. 3, pp. 345-349.

[7] S. B. Clough, *The Rise and Fall of Civilization,* New York, 1951, p. 221.

Religion has been used to attain social control, or at least control propagandizing the alleged words of the deity to the effect that the master class had received its authority from the deity, the lower and subject class could be made more servile and amenable to the will and orders of their masters. Another way in which religion has been used by the master class to exploit the lower classes has been by means of holding forth the prospect and promise of an after life of happiness which would be a reward for the miseries of the present life. A good deal of the exploitation and predation up to the present time has been rendered possible by means of this fraud and delusion imposed upon the lower classes.

It is often alleged by the professional representatives of religion that there are certain innate religious traits such as religious instincts or emotions or both which characterize all humans. There is not the slightest shred of evidence in support of these allegations. Human instincts and emotions have probably changed very little since early man. Insofar as religion is concerned, they are much the same as the psychological traits of the higher animals such as the primates and mammals most closely related to man. As mankind came to realize the insecurity of its existence, it was to be expected that it would seek the desired security in some way or other. It was therefore not surprising that mankind began to beseech such security from the gods which mythology had led them to believe existed. It is perhaps safe to say that it is the fear inspired by insecurity, and no innate religious trait which is still the most powerful factor for religion.

The fear of the vindictiveness and penalties attributed to the deity also constitute an important internal factor for religion. This fear arouses in its turn the fear of death which leads to the divine penalties. The cumulative effect of all these fears is to coerce the individual human to accept the religion or religions of his society, and to obey the behests of his religion. In a Chinese funeral, priests of Confucianism, Taoism, Buddhism, and sometimes even of Islam and and of Christianity, are represented, because it is safer in the after life to recognize the deities of all these religions. In similar fashion, in China and some other Oriental countries are found the temples of all the gods, in which are placed the images of all those gods, so that by worshiping them the present mundane life may be made safer and more agreeable.

Until 1917 no country had freed itself entirely officially from some form of religion. Even the United States which in the first amendment of its constitution, adopted on December 15, 1791, declared that "Congress shall make no law respecting an establishment of religion, or prohibiting the free exercise thereof;" had nevertheless repeatedly recognized the Christian religion by all three branches of its govern-

1237

ment.[8] One of the first results of the Russian Revolution was the complete secularization of the government of Russia. It was a most notable event in the annals of mankind that the official ideology adopted for the Soviet Union was and is science and not religion, theology, ethics, metaphysics, or any other more or less mystical ideology. Over the entrance to the Red Square in Moscow is inscribed this quotation from Karl Marx: "Religion is the opiate of the people."

While the secularization of the Russian people has gone on apace since the Russian Revolution, there are still a good many Russians who go to church and display other signs of religious belief. This is not an indication, as is often alleged, that humans are innately religious or that no country can be governed and survive without religion. It is due to the fact that like their fellow men in other countries the Russians still have reason to feel a high degree of insecurity, especially due to the capitalist conspiracy led by the United States against communism. Until peace can be assured throughout the world, and safety from hunger and the other miseries which afflict mankind, it is to be expected that men and women in all parts of the world will turn to the futile and hopeless desire for relief and comfort from a mythical deity.

The upshot of the above discussion is that mankind is not likely to abandon religion so long as it is cursed by war, poverty, disease, and the other afflictions which are man-made, or which at least could be prevented by man. The so-called "acts of god," such as earthquakes, tidal waves, and volcanic eruptions, cannot be prevented by man, and will presumably persist until the end of human existence upon this planet. Whether they will be sufficient to perpetuate at least a modicum of religion remains to be seen. It is significant that during and for a time after each war there is a recrudescence of religious belief. Human beings are literally scared into superstitious belief by the menace not only of war but also of other dangers.

The foregoing is a conclusion not only of practical but also of theoretical significance. It has a bearing not only upon the future of culture but also upon the theories of cultural evolution to be discussed in the penultimate chapter of the present treatise. It raises the question whether the fideism expressed in its most extreme form in the dictum *"credo quia absurdum* (or *impossible) est"* will always persist.[9] This dictum asserts that religious belief is based upon faith rather than reason and may be absurd or even impossible according to any rational standard. It has been accepted in varying degrees by every religion at all times. This is because every religion alleges that it

---

[8] See Maurice Parmelee, *Criminology*, New York, 1918, pp. 470-479.
[9] "I believe because it is absurd (or impossible) ."

teaches and preaches absolute truth which cannot be attained through reason.

More than a century ago, Arthur Schopenhauer (1788-1860 A.D.), the German pessimist philosopher, said that he could not believe in a good god or in an evil god and therefore believed in a god with a sense of humor.[10] He was doubtless spoofing religion because he realized the folly of a belief in a deity. Many of the more enlightened men and women have recognized this folly. But so long as the miseries, many of them preventable, which afflict mankind persist, religion will continue to serve as a brake upon human and social progress.

Until mankind ceases to hope that a mythical deity is going to solve its problems, a hope as foolish and futile as the slang saying "Let George do it," it cannot expect to have these problems solved. Mankind must recognize sooner or later that it is on its own on this tiny planet of a minor solar system and in the universe at large, and that it cannot expect any help from any other part of this universe. Whether or not mankind will ever succeed in solving all of its problems is debatable, but at least an important step toward such a solution is to recognize that it must do it itself.[11]

---

[10] A. Schopenhauer, *Complete Essays.*

In his essay on religion Schopenhauer characterizes Christianity, Islam, and Judaism as follows: "It is only in monotheism that intolerance is essential; an only god is by his nature a jealous god, who can allow no other god to exist. Polytheistic gods, on the other hand, are naturally tolerant; they live and let live."

[11] The Roman Catholic theology illustrates the casuistry and sophistry which characterize all attempts to justify religion. Among the Catholic "proofs" of "God" are that he (or it) is the—

1. Unmoved Mover in an unstable universe;
2. Efficient Cause as distinguished from secondary causes;
3. Necessary Being as implied by contingent beings;
4. Absolute Perfection among graduated perfections;
5. Order and Design in the universe.

The alleged "proofs" are refuted by the facts that (1) the whole universe is mobile; (2) all energy is efficient according to its extent; (3) all being is necessary because it exist; (4) perfection is subjective; (5) order and design are teleological concepts imposed by man.

1239

Chapter LXXIV

Collectivism versus Capitalism

IN the 20th century the conflict and contradiction between collectivism and capitalism has become the most acute and crucial of the many contradictions described in this treatise. To a considerable extent it underlies most of the other contradictions. It was an unforeseen consequence of the European war of 1914-18. When this war started it was to all appearances another struggle for the balance of power in Europe. The Russian Revolution of 1917 was at first regarded as an incidental and not very important consequence of this war.

The World War of 1939-45 was also primarily a struggle for the balance of power in Europe, but with a somewhat incidental aspect of being a war against the excesses of fascism. This was alleged to be its moral justification by the Anglo-French allies. It was foreseen by few persons that this war would result in the Chinese Revolution of 1949.[1] With these two nations, Russia the largest in area and China the largest in population, and their so-called satellite nations on the side of collectivism, the struggle between these two economic and political systems and their ideologies became global in its scope.

In Chapters XXXVI through XLIII of this treatise I have described at length the characteristic traits of capitalism with some comparisons with collectivism. In two earlier books I have described in greater detail the traits of capitalism.[2] This chapter will be a brief recapitulation with some additional details with regard to collectivism.

Perhaps the most spectacular feature of capitalism is the accumulation of large fortunes not by producing wealth, but by profiting

[1] Fifteen years earlier in 1934, I wrote: "Soviet China has probably 100,000,000 inhabitants and is more than twice as large in area and larger in population than any capitalistic country of Europe. . . . China may become communist before its capitalism develops to a high degree, thus following the example of Soviet Russia." (Maurice Parmelee, *Bolshevism Fascism, and the Liberal-Democratic State*, New York, 1934, pp. 145-6.)

[2] Maurice Parmelee, *Poverty and Social Progress*, New York, 1916; *Farewell to Poverty*, New York, 1935,

from increases in market (not intrinsic) value, from monopolistic advantages, and by exploiting natural resources. This has been the case especially in so-called "new" countries, such as the United States, where there is an abundance of natural wealth. "In every decade a considerable number of able, venturesome, and/or lucky persons experience substantial additions to their private fortunes not by receiving, saving, and investing ordinary income but through increases in the market value of investments they have made in real estate, business enterprises, or other property. Such gains are known as 'capital gains' or 'capital profits.' . . . For many persons capital gains have supplied prodigious short-cuts to tremendous riches. . . . In fact, capital gains have played such an outstanding role in the creation of large fortunes as to suggest that they have been their main source." [3]

Nor have these capital profits come only from the private ownership of land, though some of the largest family fortunes have arisen from the increase of market land values, "unearned" so far as the private owners were concerned. They have come also from speculation in the securities markets; from exploitation of the mineral resources, such as coal and iron mines, gold, silver, copper, lead, uranium, and other ores, oil and natural gas; from taking advantage of the monopolistic features of privately owned so-called "public" utilities; and by profiting from similar features of the large industrial, mercantile, and transportation enterprises which are able to crush competition. In fact, the large fortunes of scores and hundreds of millions of dollars could not have been accumulated by saving and investment from even the largest salaries. They have arisen in the main from luck, business cunning, and in many cases from chicanery, fraud, and downright larceny.

Capitalism consists primarily of the private ownership of the land, of the productive equipment, and of the raw materials; of wage labor sold in the market; and of private profits to the owners and manipulators of the means of production. Collectivism, on the other hand, consists primarily of the public and social ownership of the means of production, including the land, tools, and raw materials.

The capitalist state is predominantly an agency of power. The power consists of the class control of the great majority by the small minority of the master class or of the dominant classes. The collectivist state is primarily and in theory at least entirely a cooperative social economy. The Marxist theory of the "withering away" of the state asserts that it will disappear as an agency of power under collectivism. In Chapters XXXV and XLIII I have criticized this theory on the ground that even the collectivist state must always retain at least a minimum of coercive power. However, it is certain that the collectiv-

[3] L. H. Seltzer, *The Nature and Tax Treatment of Capital Gains and Losses,* New York, 1951, pp. 1, 5, 6. (National Bureau of Economic Research, Inc.)

ist state is primarily an agency of economic administraticn and not of coercive action. In the collectivist state may become possible a genuine social, that is to say, cooperative and collective control. As I have pointed out in Chapters XVIII and XIX of this treatise, so-called social control up to the present has been wholly or mainly spurious because it has in fact been class control.

Various consequences have arisen from the above-mentioned conditions. Liberal democracy is mainly a fraudulent device of the capitalists to retain control in a population which has become alphabetically but not politically literate, because of the education which has been introduced partly by capitalism itself in order to qualify the workers to perform certain tasks for the capitalists. This situation underlies and causes in part the incompetence of capitalist parliaments to perform even the limited amount of economic and social functions which have so far been entrusted to them.

In Chapter LXIX I have pointed out that capitalism limits the scope and range of competition between individuals as producers because of the inequality of opportunity under this economic system. This limitation also limits the scope and efficiency of the division of labor, because this should be based and determined according to acquired skill and inherited aptitude. Collectivism, on the contrary, should and probably will eliminate all forms of discrimination, and thereby render possible the most efficient form of the division of labor.

In similar fashion, capitalism restricts invention in certain respects, whereas collectivism should place no restraints whatsoever upon it. As we have seen in Chapter LXX, under capitalism the privileged classes are more likely to get possession or control of many of the inventions and derive the profits therefrom, some of which should go to the impecunious inventor. Furthermore, capitalism sometimes attempts to restrain the process of invention itself. This is principally because it fears that an abundance of goods will destroy the scarcity which is for capitalism the goose that lays the golden egg. The chief aim of collectivism, on the other hand, is to produce a great abundance of goods, and therefore it has every incentive to encourage productive inventions.

Perhaps the most striking contradiction within capitalism is between competition and monopoly. While the protagonists of capitalism boast of its alleged competitive character, and capitalists and entrepreneurs may start as rivals, the temptation to reap the rich harvest of a monopoly often results in the capitalist rivals uniting to form a monopoly and sharing their booty. Under collectivism both competition and monopoly of a sort exist, but very different from what exists under capitalism. The competition consists in a rivalry of skills between individuals. The monopoly consists of the cooperation of

1242

all elements in society to promote the social welfare, and not to procure private profits.

As we have noted repeatedly in the course of this treatise, the attitude of capitalism toward science and technology is ambivalent. When capitalism can utilize science and its disciple technology to create or secure profits for itself, it gladly and willingly uses them. If, however, they threaten these profits by making commodities so plentiful as to destroy the profits arising from scarcity, capitalism becomes the enemy of both science and technology.

Capitalism has created a fairly efficient technology of production in the form of mechanized large-scale industry. While recognizing its limitations mentioned above, nevertheless its achievements in this field are great. It has also created a technology of distribution characteristic of itself. This consists of the price and market system which, when it is successful, is destined to bring the largest profits to the most skillful or shrewdest merchants and salesmen. In the course of this process there is a good deal of wasteful moving goods around not to give them place and time value, but to secure the highest price in the best market. Here again, since collectivism is not in search of private profits, it is not so likely to commit these wastes. It endeavors at all times to convey goods, wealth, or value of any sort to the human beings most in need of them.

Under capitalism there takes place an accumulation of surplus capital, some of which is exported and furnishes the basis for economic imperialism. There takes place also an accumulation of debt, which sometimes becomes so burdensome as to seriously hamper the wheels of industry. There arise finance, corporate, and monopoly capitalism, which are far removed from the early primitive capitalism characterized by the alleged virtue of competition. The fate of competition under these latter stages of capitalism has already been noted. Perhaps the most anomalous trait of capitalism is the business cycle in which in the course of only ten or a dozen years, there takes place this wide variation in the amount produced. That production should fall to half, as happened from 1930 to 1933, and then recover gradually, is wholly inconsistent with the concept of a stable economy which produces an adequacy if not an abundance of goods at all times for all of the population it is serving.

In an earlier book I have characterized the nearest approach to collectivism which so far exists in the world: "It is often asserted that state capitalism now prevails in Soviet Russia. This widespread notion is due in large part to the fact that many of the forms and much of the terminology of capitalism still persist there. Among them are wages, prices, rent, money, a banking system, so-called state trusts for the administration of industry, labor unions, etc. . . . The fact that state socialism and not state capitalism is now dominant in Russia is of more than theoretical or terminological significance. Without a recognition of this important fact it is difficult to appreciate the extent of the changes which have already taken place, the true nature of the present system, the principles upon which it is based, and the ends toward which it is working." [4]

In 1949 China joined Russia by adopting state socialism. Both of these great countries, together with their so-called "satellites," in varying degrees have abolished economic capitalism. But they have retained for the time being the state as an agency of power. This is due partly if not largely to the fact that they are menaced by hostile, belligerent forces from outside. It may also be due in part because they contemplate using armed force as one of the means of spreading collectivism, though they recognize that the two principal factors for attaining this end are the positive force of effective propaganda and the negative force of the breakdown of the capitalist system. Whatever the reasons may be, for the present these nations are not communist in the full sense of the word. This fact also probably explains in part why many of the forms of capitalism have been retained even though its essence has fled.

In Soviet Russia all economic activities are carried on in accordance with the state plan. Production is organized in the form of enterprises called "trests" derived from the English word trusts. These enterprises are state-controlled and mostly state-owned. Some of them are organized as cooperatives though these enterprises also are under state control. All of these enterprises maintain records of their assets and liabilities, and keep account of their profits and losses. There is no sale of land except for a relatively few private homes. There is no sale of securities except government bonds. An enterprise is required to complete the production planned for it under the state plan. It secures credit and other financial assistance through the state banking system.

Money is still used in Soviet Russia as a convenient method of exchange. The State Bank (Gosbank) established in 1921 was made a bank of issue in 1922 and authorized to issue bank notes against a precious metal reserve of at least 25 percent. This bank issues much of the currency based on its reserve assets which are now gold and foreign exchange. Its other assets are the government debt when there is any, the short-term advances to cover delays in the settlement of accounts between enterprises, and longer term loans to enterprises up to 12 months. Its liabilities consist of the bank notes it has issued, the deposits of enterprises, and of the commissariat of finance. The Gov-

[4] Maurice Parmelee, *Bolshevism, Fascism and the Liberal-Democratic State*, New York, 1934, pp. 111-112.

ernment Treasury issues notes without a reserve backing, in other words, fiat money.

The State Bank controls its note circulation by a plan to balance the outflow of currency in wages, salaries, and social services with the inflow of currency from retail trade, tax payments, and subscriptions to government bonds. "The economic planning mechanism of the Soviet Union imposes a wide variety of controls over production and distribution, many of which are administered by the banking system." [5]

Capital formation in the Soviet Union is of exceptional importance because of the rapid expansion of the productive mechanism in an insufficiently industrialized country. The procuring of this capital is planned and organized by the finance commissariat which collects the taxes. A somewhat anomalous feature of the Soviet fiscal scheme is taxation. It raises the question whether a calculated amount of labor and capital cannot be set aside in the state economic plan to furnish capital formation for new capital equipment. This would be more consistent with collectivism than taxing producers and consumers, like the power state of capitalism, and the police state of fascism.

The banks furnish a considerable amount of credit to the expanding productive system. While all commercial credit has been abolished, the planning of long-term credit is a part of the state economic plan. The banking system includes not only the State Bank with about 5,500 branches throughout Russia, but also several other large banks, primarily for giving loans for long-term capital investment, such as the Bank for Foreign Trade, the Industrial Bank (Prombank), Agricultural Bank (Selkhosbank), Trade Bank (Torgbank), and Municipal Bank (Tsekombank), as well as many savings banks. [6]

Most individuals in the Soviet Union receive their money incomes in the form of wages or salaries from state or state-owned enterprises. Their transactions are largely in cash as, indeed, is also the case in capitalist countries. They can save some of their incomes if they so desire by purchasing government bonds or by depositing in savings banks. These savings go toward building up the surplus funds to be devoted to capital formation.

The state and state-owned enterprises use the banks to settle their accounts with each other, and with the government. In other words, there is little transfer of cash among them. Their debits and credits with each other are settled by transfer on the books of the bank recording their deposits as, indeed, is the case also in capitalist countries.

[5] Edward Ames, "Banking in the Soviet Union," *Federal Reserve Bulletin,* April 1952, pp. 351-358.

[6] *Cf.* Harry Schwartz, *Russia's Soviet Economy,* New York, 1950.

There is perhaps sufficient justification for retaining some of the forms and financial mechanisms of capitalism during the period of transition to a fully developed collectivism.

The crucial question with respect to the Soviet Union is as to whether collectivism works there as efficiently as capitalism in such countries as the United States, Canada, England, France, and Germany. However, no conclusive test has as yet been possible. Throughout the first four decades of Soviet rule, the Soviet Union has been subjected to the menace of attack. During at least five years it suffered from the ravages and destruction of the worst war in history. Under such conditions there could be no accurate measurement of the productive capacity of a collectivist economic system.

A frequent capitalist criticism of collectivism is that it does not furnish as many incentives for production and achievement as capitalism. Needless to say, it does not furnish the incentives for the acquisition of private profits, the accumulation of wealth, and its transmission to designated individual heirs. The important comparison, however, is as to whether it furnishes as much incentive for the production of wealth for society and not for individual possession. While no direct comparison has as yet been possible, some of the incentives which inspire workers under collectivism as contrasted with capitalism have been described. Among them are improvement of material conditions for the worker himself and his fellow workmen; payment by results, namely, piecework; stimulating group pride by socialist accumulation; social instead of private ownership of factories and other means of production; social approval and disapproval; the socialist attitude toward work; creative purpose; such antagonisms as against bureaucratism, religion, and nationalism; socialist competition; workers' rationalization of productive processes; participation in the government; etc.[7]

We have already seen that democracy is possible only in a very limited political sense under capitalism. A genuine thoroughgoing democracy will probably be possible only under a fully developed collectivist system. That it does not exist in Russia, China, and the other pioneer countries of collectivism is obvious. In any case, democracy is never possible under war conditions. These pioneer collectivist countries have been under conditions of cold if not hot war since their inception. Whether or not these pioneer collectivist countries have been and are more authoritarian than their conditions require is a matter for discussion.

A few more points of comparison may be touched upon. The

[7] Harry F. Ward, *In Place of Profit, Social Incentives in the Soviet Union*, New York, 1933.

[8] Werner Sombart, *Krieg und Kapitalismus*, Munich, 1913.

1246

leading German historian of capitalism asserted that war has stimulated capitalism.[8] It is true that armies and navies require extensive mercantile as well as productive operations. Modern warfare can be carried on only if correlated with large-scale industrial enterprises, which are necessary to produce not only the munitions and armaments, but also the food and clothing and other equipment needed by armies and navies. To that extent it probably is true that war has stimulated capitalism.

Science also may be stimulated to a certain extent in wartime, owing to the intensive search for more deadly weapons and methods of warfare. Science is therefore likely to become destructive in time of war, not because it is destructive in itself, but because it can be misused for destructive purposes. In a world-wide collectivist society warfare would perforce disappear, and science could and would be used only for productive purposes.

Under capitalism there is comparatively little and very ineffective correlation between the political and the economic organization of society. Under liberal-democratic capitalism the distinction between the executive, judicial, and legislative functions of government is largely for the purpose of checking and neutralizing whatever democratic tendencies a parliamentary government may have. The extent to which executive and judicial functions curb the legislative functions is abundantly illustrated in the United States. Since the choice of the legislators has already been largely influenced by the plutocratic groups through the reactionary Republican-Democratic party organizations and nominating conventions, not much in the way of democracy can be expected from any one of the three branches of government. In a collectivist and classless society this distinction between the executive, legislative, and judicial functions of government would largely disappear because there would no longer be a need even in theory for checks upon the different branches of the government, all of which would be subject to popular control. There would, indeed, be a better correlation of political and economic organization and activities under collectivism than has been the case under capitalism. Partly for this reason, it is probably true that the construction of a collectivist organization of society would be easier than the reconstruction of capitalism in such a fashion as to render it capable of attaining the social objectives for which it professes to be striving.

In summing up this chapter, it may be said that the basic contradiction between capitalism and collectivism can be solved only if mankind attains the following ends: a productive system planned to furnish an abundance of goods for all human beings, an effective distribution of this abundance to all human beings, work so organized as to be efficient, and at the same time to furnish ample leisure to the workers, and consumption so rationalized as to furnish the most satisfaction from the commodities produced. A society so organized should be under a democratic state control which would be the political correlative of economic planning. The outcome of these economic and political measures would be a functional organization of society which has so far not existed in the annals of mankind. The immediate outlook, deduced from the data presented in this treatise, is that these ends are more likely to be attained under collectivism than under capitalism.

Chapter LXXV

The Emergence of World Society

A current saying is "One world or none," expressed otherwise as "Unity or chaos." Perhaps the most characteristic feature of the immediate past is the tremendous expansion of warfare. During the first half of the 20th century took place the two greatest wars of history, the second being much more extensive and intensive than the first. A brief survey of the typical features of modern warfare will give some indication as to the causes for this enormous expansion of belligerent activity.

Wars are now fought mainly by citizen soldiers instead of by professional soldiers and mercenaries as in the past. This is due partly to the French Revolution which gave rise to a revolutionary army of citizen soldiery destined to carry the purposes of the revolution to the rest of the world. This army was soon diverted from these purposes to accomplish the megalomaniac ambitions of the Corsican adventurer, Napoleon Bonaparte. But the custom of maintaining armies made up of citizen soldiers has persisted down to the present day. Many of these soldiers are conscripted from civilian life to serve for a stated period in the armed forces. In time of war many of these citizens volunteer of their own accord to serve in the armed forces, even though such service is dangerous to life and limb in time of war. What induces these citizens to take this deadly risk?

In Chapter XXX of this treatise has been described the rise of modern nationalism since the medieval period. In the Occident this nationalism has made patriotism, and the loyalty to one's nation arising out of patriotism, the supreme virtue. This transcends all other virtues even to the extent of requiring the supreme sacrifice of one's own life. This may be contrasted with the places where and the times when the supreme virtue has been loyalty to one's family, or to one's sovereign, or to one's feudal lord, or to one's church and religion. On the other hand, treason has been and is the supreme crime surpassing in its heinousness murder, rape, and the other felonies of the first degree. Spying has become one of the gravest forms of treason.

Another factor which has inspired some of these citizens to serve voluntarily in the armed forces, or to reconcile themselves to such service, has been the desire for adventure and change from the dull monotony and economic perils of civilian life. For example, in time of economic depression, no civilian can be sure that he will not become unemployed, and thereby thrust into the pauper class. Military or naval service at least assures the civilian a subsistence for a given period of time and may also furnish a welcome change in his everyday life. These factors reveal themselves in the advertisements of the armed forces to induce enlistments in which appear appeals to greed, love of travel and adventure, occupational training, and, to a certain extent, desire for prestige.

In modern times in many countries there have been large standing armies and navies even in time of peace. The officers of these armed forces form a powerful pressure group whose personal and professional interest it is to stimulate at least the fear of war if not war itself. This officer caste has doubtless been one of the factors in causing modern wars, second only to the "merchants of death," who manufacture and traffic in munitions of war.[1]

The most appalling aspect of the recent expansion of warfare has been the widespread slaughter of civilians, including women and children, as well as armed combatants. Along with this slaughter has gone the wholesale destruction of industry much of which was not producing munitions of war. These drastic changes in the nature of warfare have arisen principally from the enormous increase in the destructive power of arms and munitions. These have been made effective principally by the development of aviation during and after the two great wars of the 20th century. Aviation has made every large city and every industrial concentration vulnerable to attack. In fact, it is probably true that at present the offensive forces for attack are stronger than the forces for defense. Aviation has also made distance and natural barriers disappear as defensive factors. Flying fortresses can now fly almost any distance over oceans and mountains. The sum total of these recent developments may appropriately be called total warfare.

 Needless to say, a genuine world society is hardly possible while war on a large scale exists. The moderate amount of world culture which already exists barely adumbrates a world society. The first essential step toward it would be the creation of a world state. A world federation which would abolish national sovereignty and would solve

---

[1] See H. C. Engelbrecht and F. C. Hanighen, *Merchants of Death*, New York, 1934; George Seldes, *Iron, Blood and Profits*, New York, 1934.

the global economic and political problems, would also obviate war. History has already shown that war cannot be prevented by treaties of disarmament, or any other forms of agreement between national states which can be violated in the name of national interest. War can be prevented only by eliminating the economic and political causes of war which we have described repeatedly in this treatise, especially in Chapter XLIV. If and when a world federation of geo-economic regions is created, as described in Chapters XLV to XLVII inclusive, then and only then can we begin to hope for the emergence of the world society.

Assuming that a world federation has come into being and has solved more or less successfully global economic and political problems, there will remain cultural problems of disharmony, some of which may prevent a world society. However, their solution does not necessitate global cultural identity in every respect.

There is nothing inherent in human nature against a world society. The diversity of cultures has been caused by ecological and social environmental factors. The ecological factors such as climate and topography will not change materially within a foreseeable time. The artificial man-made environmental factors can and will change greatly. Already a striking illustration presents itself in the extent to which the Orient is adopting some of the physical and material equipment of the Occident. This is notably visible in the outline and structure of the great cities arising in the East, its means of transportation, its manufacturing establishments, and even in its archaic agricultural methods and equipment.[2]

Three serious obstacles stand in the way of the emergence of the world society. These are racial prejudice, religion, and nationalism which has survived the world federation. The only one of these three due to or, better expressed, occasioned by a relatively immutable factor is racial prejudice. It is not to be expected that the races will ever become completely assimilated with each other, at any rate not for a very long time. There is, however, no evidence of any innate repugnance between the races. Insofar as such repugnance exists, it is artificial and man-made in the sense that derogatory opinions concerning certain races have been circulated and often propagandized by individuals and groups which think that it is to their interest to do so. Usually there is an exploitative and predatory motive back of such propaganda. The problem here therefore is to make such exploitation and predation completely impossible by the political and economic organization of society, so that there will no longer be any in-

[2] After 60 years, this was very evident to me during my travels in the Orient from 1952 to 1954.

ducement to these individuals and groups to carry on such anti-racial propaganda.

Religion is an obstacle to the emergence of the world society because it is based on the belief that there is a deity or are deities which are omniscient and omnipotent. Since each religious cult claims to have such a deity or such deities, these cults must necessarily conflict because not all of these rival deities can be omniscient or to say the least omnipotent. Both the Moslem Allah and the Christian God cannot be omnipotent, and it is doubtful if omniscience also can be shared. Hence each religious cult must perforce claim not only superiority but a monopoly of belief and of power, mundane as well as celestial, as against every other religious cult. This is why religion has been one of the most divisive factors in the history of mankind. This problem will be solved in the long run by the gradual substitution of scientific knowledge for religious superstitions. However, it would be regrettable if the emergence of the world state is postponed until that rather late date. In the meantime, it may be possible to give sufficient publicity to the idea that religion is a personal matter of individual belief and not to be institutionalized in the form of churches and ecclesiastical organizations. This will lessen considerably religion's power for mischief.

A genuine world federation should and will remove the economic and political discriminations between nations which have been among the principal causes of war. It will, however, not abolish the nations themselves which will continue to carry on most of the functions which they have heretofore performed. Some nationalism will, therefore, survive the creation of the world state, and will hamper the emergence of the world society. This is a problem which can probably not be solved by measures immediately directed at it. These nationalistic biases and prejudices, while they may no longer cause wars, will nevertheless stand in the way of the most fruitful cultural intercourse between the peoples of the world.

The outstanding question with regard to the emergence of the world society is as to whether Oriental and Occidental culture can merge with each other. Up to the present, the Occident has probably hindered this merging of cultures more than the Orient. In another book I have said: "Europeans and Americans usually assume that their culture is superior to that of the Orient. Whether or not this assumption is correct, it renders the West more or less immune to Eastern influence. The great majority of Westerners who have resided in the East have carried their own manners and customs with them to such a degree that they have learned little of the life and culture of the Orient. Even those who have written books about the East have usually

1252

displayed little genuine knowledge and no appreciation of Oriental culture." [3]

Insofar as Occidental contempt for Oriental culture arises out of racial prejudice, I have already discussed how this prejudice may gradually be eliminated. It is likely to affect even more seriously the relations between the white people of the Occident and the Negro inhabitants of Africa. Here the contrast, at least in color, is more visible than any contrast between the physical traits of the Asiatics as compared with Europeans and Americans. Here again, the gradual diminution and eventual elimination of racial prejudice will presumably be along the lines suggested above.

It has often been asserted that means of communication which render possible the exchange of knowledge about each other among the peoples of the world is the most effective factor for the emergence of the world society. Among the mass communication media which have been invented in modern times and their approximate dates are printing, 15th century; the post office for private communications in general, 17th century; the telegraph and telephone, 19th century; and the wireless, radio, motion picture and television, 20th century. The earlier of these media, namely, the printing press and the post office, probably helped nationalism at first more than a world society. This was because they helped to bring in touch with each other the small feudalities which dominated Europe to a large extent at the end of the Middle Ages. The nationalism so created was so strong that it has not yet yielded to the mass communication media invented in recent times. Instead of creating a world consciousness, these media up to the present have not even been able to prevent the most destructive wars of all time. However, when the world federation has solved more or less successfully the economic and political problems which have heretofore led to war, these mass communication media will aid materially in spreading knowledge about each other which will help to create cultural harmony if not unity among the peoples of the world.

While it is not possible to predict in detail the traits of the world society, it may not be amiss to make a few conjectures as to its nature. Probably the first requisite is a universal acceptance of the identity of mankind as one animal species. This fact is proved conclusively by the universal biological fertility among all the branches of the human species. While this fact is generally known, owing to the amount of miscegenation which exists, its significance for amity among the peoples of the world has as yet been little comprehended. It signifies that human beings are literally biological blood brothers bodily and mentally under the skin. A widespread if not universal comprehen-

[3] Maurice Parmelee, *Oriental and Occidental Culture, An Interpretation*, New York, 1928, p. 361.

sion and acceptance of this fact should be a powerful force for the disappearance of racial prejudice.

It is probably true that the second requisite for the emergence of the world society is a widespread if not universal sense of mutual interdependence between all the peoples and nations of the world. The fallacious notion that nations can and should be economically as well as politically independent of each other has been one of the divisive forces in the world. It has been aggravated by the ever present danger of war which might, by means of blockading operations, cut off a belligerent nation from its sources of food and other essential commodities. Hence the urgent desire to make itself self-sufficient in time of war. Assuming that the world federation has made war impossible forever, this need for self-sufficiency can and should completely disappear.

The third requisite for the emergence of a world society has already been mentioned above. It is the elimination of religion, at least in its institutionalized form. Ample evidence of the necessity for this disappearance is furnished by the many violent conflicts between religious cults which have taken place in the past, such as the recent conflict between Hinduism and Islam in India, and the numerous attempts of ecclesiastical organizations to greatly influence if not control the culture of the countries in which they have numerous adherents. This is strikingly illustrated in the current attempts of the Roman Catholic church to control marriage, education, and other important aspects of culture in the countries in which they have many adherents, even in the United States where they are in a minority. While religion cannot be abolished by fiat, its organized forms can be greatly restricted if not entirely prohibited by national, regional, and global authorities. Such prohibition would be justified as much as and even more than the prohibition of other types of attempts to overthrow and supplant the organized forms of government. This would not mean the prohibition of religious beliefs insofar as the individual is concerned. Such a prohibition could not in any case be carried out. People will go on believing what they think is true regardless of such prohibitions. The main hope for the eventual disappearance of religious beliefs in the minds of individuals is the spread of scientific ideas which will supplant these religious beliefs.

This problem of the prohibition of organized religion, because of its menace to secular government, raises the whole question of democracy in its relation to the world society. Modern capitalism has confused the meaning of the term by alleging that "free" private enterprise contributes to or even constitutes democracy. I have discussed this situation at length in another book in which I said: "The failure of liberal democracy to provide a decent standard of living for the

1254

vast majority has also resulted in destroying in large part the civil liberties. The capitalists in power have been chiseling away these rights and thus preparing the way intentionally or unconsciously for the coming of the authoritarian state under capitalism. With the proletarian and lower middle classes much weakened there can be little opposition to the rule of the capitalists. This is a class dictatorship which contemplates no termination because the capitalist class can never include the whole of mankind." [4]

Religion violates the civil liberties in many ways. For example, in the United States the testimony in court of an avowed atheist is highly suspect. It is popularly believed that a person who does not think that a mythical deity exists cannot or is not likely to tell the truth. A section of the Federal code of procedure provides that witness must state his religious beliefs or lack of them because this is supposed to have an important bearing upon his credibility.

The prohibition of organized religion would not mean a violation or restriction of democracy, but would be the elimination of one of its most dangerous foes. It would not mean that freedom of assembly and for the expression of opinions, however heretical and however contrary to public opinion, would not continue to exist. These are essential features of democracy and should exist the world over along with equality of opportunity, its most essential requisite. They will come slowly in some parts of the world, especially where not even the slight measure of political freedom permitted by liberal democracy has as yet existed. If then we are to regard democracy as the fourth requisite for the world society, it is obvious that the emergence of this society on a world-wide scale would be somewhat delayed. The world may nevertheless be gradually approaching it. In the meantime, we may discuss the question as to what extent there should be identity of the main cultural features the world over, or how high a degree of cultural similarity is desirable, or to what extent agreement as to differences of culture is possible.

The physical aspects of culture such as food, housing, clothing, etc., are dependent largely on the natural environment. Climatic and topographical differences cause inevitable differences in these physical cultural traits. Divergences in many minor cultural features are also possible without standing in the way of the emergence of the world society. Among such minor features may be mentioned formal courtesy, slang, games, humor, sport, food habits, dress, etc. The serious problem is as to the extent to which the main cultural features should be identical or similar the world over.

Earlier in this treatise (Chapters XLV to XLVII inclusive) I have

[4] Maurice Parmelee, *Bolshevism, Fascism and the Liberal-Democratic State,* New York, 1934. p. 362.

1255

suggested the possibility of creating a world federation even though the present widespread divergence between capitalism and collectivism continued to exist. There would also be widespread divergences in other phases of culture due to the repercussions of the economic system upon sex relations, ethical ideas, and the fine arts. For example, we have already noted the differences in the significance of the family, of marriage, and of so-called legitimacy of birth, between capitalism, where these three institutions are essential features or accompaniments of the economic system, and under collectivism. Under the latter, legitimacy of birth is of no importance whatsoever. Many of the functions of the family are taken over by the collectivist state. Marriage should become a more flexible and therefore freer institution, though there is little indication of such a change as yet in the comparatively new collectivism in the world of today. The question is therefore as to whether it will be possible to have what might be accurately described as a world society when the world is divided into two camps, at present highly militarized. In one of them a predatory class is dominant, whereas in the other this class has disappeared. In one of them industry is operated by private enterprises employing wage slaves. In the other industry is operated by the collectivist state sharing the proceeds of industry with the laborers who keep it going. In one of them agriculture is carried on mainly by a peasant small land-holding class. In the other agriculture is organized in large collectivized farms which are highly mechanized and which produce far more per agricultural laborer than under capitalism.

In view of the above considerations, it seems likely that the world society can be only faintly adumbrated so long as these radical and, to a large extent, hostile divergences of economic system continue to co-exist upon this planet. These economic divergences have extensive repercussions upon other cultural phases such as not only sex and ethics, which have already been mentioned, but also the fine arts such as literature, music, sculpture, and painting. Even to a certain extent science is affected, not because there are any differences between the facts of science under different economic systems, but because of the differences in the selection of what scientific subjects are to be studied and investigated, and because of the differences in the application made of scientific knowledge. In view of these considerations, the most that can be said now is that the emergence of the world society will be postponed. This situation will persist until there is a worldwide identity between the fundamental economic institutions and forms of organization which goes beyond mere tolerance and restraints upon warfare.

Another essential feature of the world society is world citizenship, which would supplant the subjection of the individual to the nation state, even to the point of requiring from him the supreme sacrifice of his life in wartime. As I have said in another book: "All inhabitants of the world would become citizens of the World Federation. They may continue to be designated and enumerated for census purposes as residents of a region and of a nation or of a local area. World citizenship would prevent national governments from depriving individuals and groups of the rights of citizenship for racial, religious, and other irrelevant reasons, and from driving them into exile." [5]

[5] *Geo-Economic Regionalism and World Federation,* New York, 1949, p. 53.

Chapter LXXVI

The Eventual Extinction of Mankind

FOR most of his career on this planet man has believed that his mundane abode is the center of the universe. This illusion was due to the fact that the heavens with their celestial inhabitants seem to go around the earth every 24 hours. It persisted until after the Polish astronomer Copernicus (1473-1543 A.D.) demonstrated that the sun is the center of the solar system, and that the earth goes around the sun, and the German astronomer Kepler (1571-1630 A.D.) formulated laws governing the motions of the planets. In other words, it is only three to four centuries since a small part of mankind began to realize that it occupies only an infinitesimally minute part of the universe.

While the anthropocentric conception of the universe was understandable and excusable in the past owing to ignorance, it has persisted psychologically until after the astronomers and the physicists have located the earth's position and relative insignificance in the universe. The human arrogance due to anthropocentrism has been perpetuated by religion which is archaic in this as in most respects. Mankind must have observed very early that the body dies and disintegrates. But there arose the myth that a more or less immaterial form of the body or occupant of it survives it. This myth may have been due to dreams or hallucinations of one sort or another. In any case, it developed into the religious doctrine of the immortal soul. This superstition has bolstered up and strengthened the arrogance originally due to the anthropocentric conception of the universe, and has helped to perpetuate the delusion that mankind is the most significant and important thing in the universe.

In contrast to the anthropocentric myth, science has demon-

1258

strated that the earth is a mere flyspeck in an infinite and eternal universe. It is a medium-sized planet in the solar system of a small star in a galaxy, popularly called the Milky Way, estimated to contain about forty billions of stars, and this galaxy is one of innumerable galaxies in the universe. Each nebula is presumably a galaxy or even a constellation of galaxies. There are about 100,000,000 of these stellar islands within the space of 500,000,000 light years observable through a 100-inch diameter lens of a telescope.[1]

In the first chapter of this treatise, I have cited a few of the facts which illustrate and demonstrate the immeasurable vastness of the universe contrasted with the relative minuteness of the planet earth and of its solar system.

The velocity of light is 186,284 miles per second of time. Light travels in one year about 5,878,713,000,000 or nearly 6 trillions of miles. This is about 63,200 times the mean distance of the earth from the sun. The nearest star, Alpha Centauri, is 4.3 light years or 25,370,000,000,000 miles away. This distance is about 273,000 times as great as the distance of the earth from the sun. Another near star is Sirius which is eight light years or 47,200,000,000 miles away. Even this distance is insignificant compared with most of the sidereal distances which have been measured.

The Milky Way is estimated to be at least 100,000 light years in diameter and 10,000 light years in thickness. The nearest spiral nebula is estimated to be about 680,000 light years away. How much greater distances exist in the universe depends upon whether space is finite or infinite or is relative in extent in the sense that space is curved, as is now being studied by physicists and astronomers.

The significance of these facts for mankind is that the earth will sooner or later in geological time grow old, and will lose its atmosphere and perhaps its water, so that all organic life including mankind will be destroyed, and this planet will forever after be uninhabitable. While these future events are still a long way off in human terms, some millions of years at least, the knowledge of them should have certain psychological effects upon mankind. It should, to say the least, give rise to a more becoming modesty in human beings. They should realize their utter insignificance in the universe and no longer be inflated with pride. They should realize that the career of mankind is not eternal, and that therefore they are not preparing for eternity.

[1] See George Gamow, *The Birth and Death of the Sun*, New York, 1945, for some of these astronomical facts.

The 200-inch diameter reflector telescope installed on Mount Palomar in California doubled the distance at which stars can be observed.

In spite of the scientific facts which have been cited, there has arisen in the Orient, but also in the Occident, a philosophy and extreme form of subjective idealism which in a sense evades or goes around these facts. It is known as solipsism, a word derived from the Latin words *solus* (alone) and *ipse* (self), and is discussed in Chapter IV. This philosophy alleges that the universe is unreal and exists only in the consciousness of the individual. Knowledge of the universe can reach human beings only through the senses. They can never know things-in-themselves. There is no guarantee that the senses represent the universe as it really is. This knowledge may be wholly illusory. It may be that there is no universe outside of the conscious individual. Its representation may be no more than a fantasmagoria of the imagination, or it may be one phase of the life or consciousness of this self which comprehends the universe. Such a belief professes to solve these ultimate problems, or at any rate renders them of negligible importance. In any case it is very gratifying to the ego. What could be more egocentric than solipsism? In its less extreme forms it postulates a universal consciousness or soul into which are merged individual souls. In this mystical conception of the universe, time, space, matter, and energy cease to have meaning and perturb its devotees no longer. These mystics bury themselves in their self-aggrandizement and in their alleged omniscience which is a negation of knowledge.

A solipsistic conception of the universe cannot suffice for science. It must assume an objective reality even though our knowledge of it is subjective. That the impressions of many individuals as well as the impressions of the same individual at different times coincide in the main is *a priori* evidence of its existence. As I have said in another book: "All our knowledge comes to us through our senses in the form of sensations, and we cannot be absolutely certain that these sensations represent to us truly the nature of the world which is exterior to us. For scientific purposes, however, we need to practice what is sometimes called 'naive realism' and assume that things in the exterior world are actually as our senses represent them to be." [2]

While the geocentric and anthropocentric conception of the universe has been effectually disproved, and there is, to say the least, widespread skepticism among the better educated people with regard to the superstition of immortality, and while solipsism is a somewhat esoteric belief even in the Orient where it is somewhat prevalent, new occasions for nurturing human vanity continue to arise. Recently this vanity has been fed by the dream of the so-called "con-

[2] Maurice Parmelee, *The Science of Human Behavior*, New York, 1913, p. 4.

1260

quest of space." [3] The discovery of methods of utilizing the expansive force of gases produced by the explosion of gasoline or some other combustible has made possible not only the motor vehicle on land and the motor vessel on the sea, but also the rocket which can be projected into the air. If a sufficient amount of energy is furnished, it is conceivable that such a rocket can be projected beyond the stratosphere of air and of heat which envelops the earth, and beyond the force of gravitation of the earth, into space where it can travel indefinitely unless deflected from its course by celestial bodies exercising a force of gravitation. These discoveries have given rise to the plans for constructing space ships capable of carrying human beings not only to the nearest celestial body, namely the moon, but also to some of the neighboring planets such as Mars and Venus.

It requires a speed of seven miles a second to enable any object to escape from the force of gravity of the earth This "velocity of escape" was first attained in 1959.[4] Many fuels, both solid and liquid as well as gaseous, have been tried. The cheapest and most reliable may be alcohol and oxygen. The gravitational field of the earth can be escaped by means of a step rocket. This consists of a series of rockets ejected together each of which drops off when its fuel is exhausted, until the speed is accelerated to the point when the rocket can escape from the earth.

Assuming that a space ship maintained its initial "velocity of escape," it would travel 420 miles in one minute, 25,200 miles in one hour, and 604,800 miles in one day. At this rate it would reach the moon in nearly ten hours, Venus when nearest the earth in about 43 days, and Mars when nearest the earth in about 79 days.

These ideas have already been seized upon by military minds. It has been proposed to establish a satellite craft or so-called "working platform" between the earth and the moon from which it might be possible to construct a lunar base on the moon itself. From this base it has been suggested that military operations might be carried on against a human foe on the earth. Who will construct this lunar base and who the foe is to be are still questions for the future to decide.[5]

However fantastic these plans may sound, they will at least feed the human vanity hitherto nurtured by geocentrism, anthropocentrism, solipsism, and the superstition of human immortality. Beyond the journey to the moon is the vague prospect of traveling to some

[3] This grandiose delusion is encouraged by the discovery of potential atomic energy.

[4] Soviet Russia sent a satellite around the moon.

[5] See Willy Ley, *Rockets, Missiles, and Space Travel*, New York, 1951.

1261

of the nearer planets. Even if this is accomplished, it will still be within the narrow limits of our insignificant solar system. To travel to a celestial body outside of the solar system would require a period of time far exceeding human life. As indicated above, the velocity of light is 186,284 miles per second of time, or nearly 6 trillions of miles in one year. It is inconceivable that mankind can ever concentrate enough potential energy in a rocket to project it beyond the stratosphere traveling at the rate of as much as 1,000 miles per second. Even at this incredible speed it would require 800 years to reach the nearest star, Alpha Centauri. At the rate of the "velocity of escape," (or 7 miles per second), it would be 115,000 years. The rocket could not project beyond the stratosphere the enormous amount of food and oxygen required for so long a journey. Furthermore, the space ship and its human inhabitants would be destroyed by the heat of the star before it was reached.

The investigation of some of these problems of space travel and interplanetary flight has some scientific value. It is regrettable that these investigations have been degraded and brutalized by being utilized and exploited by military interests. The most serious consequence, however, is in its possible and probable effect in inflating the human vanity which contemplates mankind as the supreme thing in the universe. The lesson, if any, to be learned from the above-mentioned considerations is that mankind should recognize its narrow limitations in space and in time and not be misled into foolish and dangerous ventures through a delusion of grandeur.

The discovery of atomic fission and fusion has so far been applied almost exclusively to destructive and warlike purposes. Its continued application to these ends, instead of using nuclear energy for the production of social wealth and the enhancement of human health and welfare, may result in a global disaster which will extinguish not only the human species but also all of organic life. The United States has disgraced not only itself but the whole of mankind by taking the lead in inventing not only the atomic bomb but also the even more frightful hydrogen bomb.[6] The outcome from such a disaster will be of no cosmic importance whatsoever. An incidental and insignificant consequence will be to render wholly meaningless and futile the attempt of this treatise, and of any similar treatise, to plot the mundane course of cultural evolution. This planet will

[6] A member of the U.S. Atomic Energy Commission (Thomas E. Murray) has predicted that within a few years super-super bombs will be developed which can "reduce our present civilization to ashes." He said that H-bombs already stored in the U.S.A. threaten a "hydrogen holocaust" of mankind. (*Miami Herald*, May 9, 1955.) Thus the United States may greatly hasten the extinction of mankind.

then continue the remainder of its career as a solar satellite free from the human miseries, hopes and aspirations toward which the universe is coldly and supremely indifferent.[7]

[7] Bertrand Russell has pointed out that not only interstellar, but also interplanetary human visitation and habitation, are impossible, because the Moon has no atmosphere, and no food (edible material) ; Mars has very little atmosphere; Venus has an atmosphere of poisonous gases; Mercury is too hot; and the outer planets are too cold. ("Can Scientific Man Survive?", *Saturday Review of Literature* December, 21, 1957.)

A Soviet Russian book on space travel discusses the escape velocity from the earth; gaseous, liquids and solid propellants, and atomic energy, for launching and landing space ships; compensation of weightlessness (zero g); space island in orbit to build space ships; helio-electricity for heat and light; conservation of air and water; manufacture of food in space from oxygen, carbon, etc. (M. Vassilie, *Sputnik into Space,* New York, 1958, Trans. from the Russian.)

Chapter LXXVII

Theories of Cultural Evolution

THEORIES of cultural evolution, or, at any rate, theories as to how cultural phenomena may take place are possible. There are several types of these theories. The *unilinear* theory is that there are uniform human tendencies to develop culture spontaneously along more or less similar lines. The theory assumes that there have been many independent duplicate inventions due to these uniform human tendencies. It is presumed that cultural evolution is progressive when it is toward a greater degree of variety and complexity. It is not assumed that these more or less independent lines of evolution have been entirely cut off from each other. It is recognized that some contact, diffusion, and assimilation has taken place. Among the advocates of this theory have been Herbert Spencer (1820-1903), Lewis H. Morgan (1818-1881), Edward B. Tylor (1832-1917), and, on a somewhat lower intellectual plane, James G. Frazer (1854-1941).[1]

At the other extreme from the unilinear theory is the *diffusionist* theory. In its most exaggerated form it alleges that all culture originated in one spot and was diffused therefrom over the whole world. The writers who have expounded this extreme diffusionist theory have been the Englishmen G. Elliot Smith and W. J. Perry. They have propounded the very dubious hypothesis that most of culture originated in ancient Egypt and was diffused from there, even across the oceans to the Western Hemisphere.

A more moderate diffusionist theory is that of the *culture strata*.

---

[1] See H. Spencer, *Synthetic Philosophy*; L. H. Morgan, *Ancient Society*; E. B. Tylor, *Primitive Culture*; J. G. Frazer, *The Golden Bough*...

Morgan terminated his book with this animistic and teleological ejaculation: "Their [our ancestors'] labors, their trials and their successes were a part of the plan of the Supreme Intelligence to develop a barbarian out of a savage, and a civilized man out of this barbarian." (P. 563.) This quotation demonstrates that it is difficult even for a would-be social scientist to free himself from the errors and fallacies described in the following chapter.

It asserts that there have been a few centers from which the forms of culture invented have been disseminated over most of the earth. The diffusion has taken place largely by means of migrations and of invasions which also caused an overlapping of these cultural strata with each other. The anthropologists who have propounded this theory have not furnished a map which shows all of these centers of invention. Among the principal protagonists for this theory have been the German anthropologists Franz Graebner and Leo Frobenius.

The last mentioned theory is expressed, or at least illustrated in nearly every description of cultural development. Until modern times among the important centers of invention have been Egypt, Mesopotamia, Asia Minor, Crete, the Indus Valley, the Valley of the Hoang-ho, the Hellenic Peninsula, the Italian Peninsula, the lowland of Yucatan, the highland of Mexico, and the table land of Peru.

The *cyclical* theory of cultural evolution has been encouraged by the apparent rise and fall of peoples and of states assumed to be rhythmic. In Chapter XIV, I have amply illustrated this theory by the writings of the Italian V. Pareto, the German O. Spengler, the Englishman A. Toynbee, and the Russian-American P. Sorokin. While there are similarities with the past, there is no complete recurrence, and history does not repeat itself in any literal sense. The cyclical theories are usually more or less teleological in their character, partly because if events are to be repeated in the future, it will be possible to foresee them in the same fashion as if they had been willed and compelled by a superior power. The chief defect of the cyclical theory is that it largely ignores technological inventions and economic factors transforming the material conditions of human existence, thereby augmenting greatly population and wealth. It does not explain adequately the vast cultural changes, such as mutations in social organization and institutions, ideas (science), ideals (ethics), etc, which have actually taken place in the past, whatever may happen in the future. It has almost completely overlooked ecological factors, such as climatic and topographical variations.

Strictly speaking, there can be no cyclical cultural evolution. Cultural change is going on all the time. Cultural systems and patterns are imperceptibly or perceptibly being transformed. They are going forward or backward according to whatever normative standard relating to or establishing a norm or criterion the observer chooses to apply. They are not going around in a circle. No great rhythm of the universe such as expansion alternating with contraction, is reflected in the course of cultural evolution which is infinitesimal in comparison with cosmic time and space. Even if a universal rhythm exists, human senses are too limited in their scope to discern it.

The *configurationist* theory is that culture develops in patterns which acquire a certain unity of their own which persists for a time, even though subjected to outside influences and forces. The American anthropologist Kroeber has attempted to confirm this theory by gathering profuse data on philosophy, science, philology, sculpture, painting, drama, literature, music, and the growth of nations, but not economic organizations, technology, class exploitation, and sex relations. Of this attempt he said: "The problem I have set myself in this book is an investigation of one of the forms which culture takes. This form is the frequent habit of societies to develop their cultures to their highest levels spasmodically: especially in their intellectual and esthetic aspects, but also in more material and practical aspects. The cultures grow, prosper, and decline, in the opinion of the world." His book ends with this vague and rather confused conclusion: "The endless events of history are lifted out of their level of near-uniformity into organized relief, by an attitude which consciously recognizes pattern-growth configurations in their space-time relations as well as in their value relations." [2]

The configurationist theory has sometimes been misused as if it furnished proof of the group fallacy that the whole is greater than the sum of its parts. Mrs. Benedict has said: "The whole, as modern science is insisting in many fields, is not merely the sum of all its parts, but the result of a unique arrangement and interrelation of the parts that has brought about a new entity. . . . Cultures, likewise, are more than the sum of their traits." [3]

That patterns of culture exist, that they have some internal consistency, for otherwise they would not survive at all, and that they have a certain amount of persistence, should be recognized. The configurationists overemphasize these traits and regard these patterns as more consistent and thoroughly integrated than they really are. In the preceding chapters, especially Chapter LXXI I have cited many instances of inconsistencies and contradictions in the cultures of the past and present. To the extent that such inconsistencies and contradictions exist, they disturb and detract from the smooth pattern of the configurationist theory. They signify that the configuration has never been perfect, and that internal disturbing forces are at work which will eventually break up the pattern.

We come now to a type of theory which for want of a better name may be designated as the *particularist* theory. It emphasizes one or a very few of the forces which have created or molded culture at the expense of all the other forces. Among these theories is that of Ellsworth

[2] A. L. Kroeber, *Configurations of Culture Growth,* University of California Press, Berkeley, 1944, pp. 5, 846.

[3] Ruth Benedict, *Patterns of Culture,* New York, 1934, pp. 42-43.

Huntington[4] who at first gave almost exclusive emphasis to climate, but later admitted also the force of heredity. In the last analysis, biological inheritance and physical environment include all of the forces which have influenced history and cultural evolution. Huntington, and the writers who have been influenced by him, use the terms in a narrower sense and largely exclude the effects of historical and cultural products such as economic and political organization, many kinds of institutions, and other more or less typical cultural factors.

Another example of a particularist theory is that of Kropotkin that mutual aid has been the predominant if not the almost exclusive factor in social and cultural evolution. The rather limited extent to which social phenomena characterize the organic world indicates that he exaggerated the role of mutual aid when he said: "In the practice of mutual aid, which we can retrace to the earliest beginnings of evolution, we thus find the positive and undoubted origin of our ethical conceptions; and we can affirm that in the ethical progress of man, mutual support—not mutual struggle—has had the leading part. In its wide extension, even at the present time, we also see the best guarantee of a still loftier evolution of our race." [5]

An extreme example of a particularist theory is that of Dixon that cultural differences are due almost entirely to racial differences, and that the evolution of culture has been caused mainly by the races which he tendentiously characterizes as superior.[6] I have dealt fully with this theory in Chapter XIV. Suffice it to say that cultural are much greater than racial differences. It is still more significant that great cultural differences exist even among peoples of the same race. These facts alone are sufficient to demonstrate that it is not possible to attach cultural patterns exclusively to racial types, or to assume that cultural levels are correlated with racial levels presumably of the same degree of evolution.

In an earlier work I have shown that particularism has been more or less prevalent in the psychological theories of social and cultural origin and evolution. In other words, various writers have attributed the origin and evolution of culture largely if not entirely to instinctive or to emotional or to intellectual factors. All of these factors have been prerequisites for cultural evolution. But as I said in that work: "This discussion has shown that each of these theories has been based upon only one of the groups of forces which have been at work in social evolution, and have therefore been inadequate. . . . All of the writers whose theories have been mentioned have made important contribu-

[4] Ellsworth Huntington, *Mainspring of Civilization*, New York, 1945.
[5] P. Kropotkin, *Mutual Aid, A Factor of Evolution*, New York, 1903, p. 300.
[6] R. B. Dixon, *The Building of Cultures*, New York, 1928.

tions to the analysis of social evolution, but their theories are too uni-lateral and do not include all the factors in social evolution." [7] Some of these writers have given an excessive emphasis to the influence of more complex psychological factors, such as imitation or communication. Tarde almost made imitation a universal phenomenon instead of recognizing that it is narrowly limited to only a small part of the organic world.[8] Analogies between cosmic events and organic phe-nomena and epiphenomena should be regarded with the utmost cau-tion and subjected to the severest tests. Indeed, the contrast in time and space between the cosmic and the organic is so vast that such analogies become meaningless.

We come at last to what may be called the *eclectic* theories which are in reality not genuine theories. They consist of an enumeration of factors without analysis and integration of the causal relations with cultural phenomena. A typical example is the American sociologist Ogburn who said: "What then are the factors that explain cultural evolution? They are four: invention, accumulation, diffusion, and adjustment." [9] Not only does such a theory omit many of the factors which have been described in the present treatise. It also fails to ex-plain cultural evolution even in the terms of the factors mentioned, a not easy task at best, but which cannot be avoided in any genuine theory.

I have enumerated at least seven types of theory of cultural evolu-tion: (1) Unilinear (2) Diffusionist, (3) Culture strata, (4) Cyclical, (5) Configurationist (pattern), (6) Particularist (7) Eclectic.

In the first chapter of this treatise I have defined culture as in-cluding everything made or changed by man. Among these forms or articles of culture are buildings, tools, clothing, cultivated soil, felled trees, boats, and domesticated animals. Culture also includes intangi-ble products of the mind such as institutions, forms of social organiza-tion, religion, art, and science. Though all-inclusive this definition of culture is clear and unmistakable.

The same is not true of the word civilization. This term implies a higher stage of culture. The dictionary defines it normatively as "a con-dition of organization, enlightenment, and progress." Immediately the question arises as to when civilization begins and what distinguishes it from a lower stage usually called barbarism. Like all normative terms, such as ethical terms, civilization is hard to define precisely. The nearest we can come to defining it is to say that it implies a certain

[7] Maurice Parmelee, *The Science of Human Behavior, Biological and Psycho-logical Foundations,* New York, 1913, pp. 417, 421.

[8] Gabriel Tarde, *Les lois de l'imitation,* Paris, 1900.

[9] W. F. Ogburn, *Social Change With Respect to Culture and Original Nature.* New York, 1922, revised 1950, p. 477.

The natural physical environment and human nature itself have often conflicted with the artificial creations of man himself. This conflict is strikingly illustrated by the clothing which mankind often wears when it is only useless but even harmful. It is illustrated by the indigestible foods and the noxious beverages which a large part of mankind ingests and imbibes. It is illustrated most of all by the violent clash between prudish puritanism and the natural sexual appetites of mankind. This is also a conflict between contradictory products, namely, the theological and ethical aberrations which constitute puritanism, against the elaboration and refinement of the sexual practices and the sentiments arising out of and associated with them which constitute the human love relationship.[12] This clash is reflected in the distinction between sacramental and free contractual marriage, described in Chapter LII.

Some of the contradictions mentioned above are due to the primitive animistic ideas perpetuated in religious beliefs. Religion itself is in drastic opposition to science. Animistic ideas intrude in many fields of human thinking and activity. Some of these contradictions are to be attributed to the ambivalent traits in human nature which drive mankind on the one hand to altruism and humanitarianism, and on the other hand to brutality and oppression. This is illustrated in the persecution due to racial prejudices and xenophobia. The supreme expression of this ambivalence is in the cruelty of war, and in the destitution and enslavement caused by the wage system, as contrasted with the healing activities of medicine and the welfare activities of many public and private organizations.

The contradiction now most extensive in its scope is between nationalism and world federation. However, even this contradiction is not so acute and perhaps not even so fundamental as the conflict between capitalism and collectivism, which is complacently ignored by many social scientists.

One of the two principal causes for these cultural inconsistencies and contradictions has been repeatedly mentioned in the course of of this treatise. It is the ambivalence of certain of the traits in human

[12] "The sexual life forms an organic part of the wider processes of society in which it occurs. Progress towards a more rational attitude is much easier during a peaceful and stable period than in one of anxiety and disorder in which loss of nerve, with its accompaniments of unreason and guilt, lead men to embrace reactionary and authoritarian political and moral theories." (*The Journal of Sex Education,* London, April-May, 1952, p. 193.)

"The book by Maurice Parmelee [*Personality and Conduct*] written [published] in 1918, considers in detail the needed revision of our sex laws, and not a line of it needs to be changed because of the Kinsey Report; perhaps now at last some attention will be pair to its proposals." (G. R. Weaver, "Sex in the World of Tomorrow," *The Journal of Sex Education,* London, August-September, 1949, p. 18.)

nature. The other cause is what is sometimes called cultural lag. Like every other phenomenon, culture is changing all the time. Sometimes changes take place more rapidly in one part of a culture than in other parts. In course of time this discrepancy in the rate of change leads to inconsistencies which may eventually be of a destructive and disruptive character. In fact, it is not unreasonable to assume that some of the extinct cultures have disappeared or have been transformed because of such internal inconsistencies and contradictions. At least a few such cases can be discerned in the historical record. There have doubtless been other cases of which we have no historical record.

A few of the writers on cultural evolution have recognized more or less adequately the role of the economic factors. They have discerned that an economic surplus is necessary to render possible non-economic achievements such as science, technology, and the fine arts. They have also recognized the civilizing influence of cities, and that cities are not possible until there is an economic surplus of food and other necessities which enable the agricultural and mining population to support the urban population which is devoted in part to the creation of the non-economic achievements.

Apart from the collectivist writers, however, not one of the cultural historians has recognized adequately the role of predatory exploitation which has permeated history to the present day. Some of them have ignored it completely. This grave ommision and the failure to recognize the social and cultural role of sex have materially abbreviated in value and distorted in form the writings of the cultural historians. They have been too deeply immersed in and committed to their own culture to take an objective and comprehensive view of cultural phenomena in time and space.

The economic factors can be classified under at least five heads. First are the natural resources including the land which existed before mankind appeared upon this mundane scene. Second is the human labor which utilizes these natural resources. It is an economic factor which has up to the present been coerced and controlled and often wasted by some of the predominant economic institutions, such as chattel slavery, serfdom, wage slavery and private ownership of the means of production. Third is the capital which is the product of labor and natural resources and which includes the tools of production or capital goods which mankind has invented and produced. These capital goods are often subject to the property rights of their owners who have not usually produced them, and which are not necessarily used in the most productive fashion, and sometimes are not used at all. Fourth are technology and the techniques of production, whose application and utilization depend very largely upon the dominant economic institutions.

1272

The fifth economic factor consists of the institutions which determine to a large extent how the preceding four groups of factors are to be utilized. If the dominant economic institution and form of economic organization is an economy of exploitation, production will not be primarily for use but for profits for the exploiters. In order to secure these profits, it is often necessary for the exploiters to prolong, or create, or stimulate scarcity. This means restricting the productive economic factors from producing enough to provide mankind with a plentiful supply of consumers' goods.

An economy of exploitation also often creates even more scarcity than was intended by the exploiters because of its inadequate technique of distribution. In any exchange economy in which money is used to facilitate the distribution and exchange of goods, an economy of exploitation cannot usually distribute enough of the purchasing power represented by money to distribute all of the consumers' goods which might otherwise be produced by the available factors of production.

What then are we to say as to the future? Prophecy is always risky. Only to the extent that forces now in existence can be projected or extrapolated into the future is there any basis for scientific prevision. For the first time in history the conflict between capitalism as a scarcity economy of exploitation, and collectivism as an economy of production for use, is acute on a world-wide scale. This conflict will continue for some time to come, probably until one or the other of these incompatible economic systems becomes predominant. The outcome of this conflict will have an important bearing in deciding another question of the future. Will mankind attain a global culture, or will it continue to have several regional cultures? This in turn involves the question as to whether the Oriental and the Occidental cultures are to survive side by side, or are to become more or less assimilated with each other. One aspect of the latter question is as to whether the familism which is more characteristic of the Orient is to survive, or is to be largely supplanted by the individualism which has developed mainly in the Occident.

More questions like the latter might be raised. However, they are sufficient to indicate that while a theory of cultural evolution as a generalization of what has occurred in the past may have some utility, a theory which professes to foresee what is to happen in the future must be regarded with the utmost caution. Most of the theories so far formulated have been characterized by grave defects either of a logical or deductive character, or due to a lack of factual information which was not available or was not utilized. Theory sometimes performs a pioneering function in science. It formulates hypothetical laws or principles which can be more readily tested and confirmed or dis-

1273

proved as the case may be. This pioneering function of theory exists also in the social sciences. It is applicable with more difficulty than in the so-called physical sciences. This is due to the intangible character of social and cultural phenomena, to the difficulty if not impossibility of setting experiments with human beings and groups to test hypotheses, and to the long period of time during which social and cultural phenomena develop and assume more or less definite forms.

The most and the best that the cultural historian can hope to accomplish is to give a fairly accurate description of the development of culture up to the present without ignoring such important aspects as exploitation, class division and conflict, and the social and cultural role of sex. No less important are the recognition of the animistic and anthropomorphic character of religion, the economic and technological factors, and the realization that science is the safest guide for mankind in an inattentive and impersonal universe. Science arises, not out of a mythical absolute truth which is alleged to be intuited or divinely revealed, but out of hypotheses from which are deduced conclusions which are tested against observation or experiment.

Chapter LXXVIII

Fallacies Concerning Culture

THE present treatise was conceived and planned in 1907. In 1909 I began writing an introductory chapter or two, giving its organic background. This introduction grew into a book of 443 pages published in 1913 under the title of *The Science of Human Behavior, Biological and Psychological Foundations*. In the Preface I said: "This book is the first of a series of works in which I propose to deal with the evolution of human culture and of human nature on the basis furnished by this book."

During the more than half century which has elapsed since its inception, I have written and published many books which contribute to it. The substance of some of these books is incorporated in this treatise. The question now arises as to whether a theory of cultural evolution has emerged or can be deduced from it. If not, it demonstrates the difficulty of formulating such a theory. It may also prove the incapacity of the present author, or of any one, to formulate it. Before attempting to answer this question, we should consider what contributions this treatise has made to the study of cultural evolution.

There are at least seven respects in which this treatise may be superior to similar comprehensive works.

1. The economic factors, determining the production and distribution of wealth, and indirectly the population, have been more adequately described than in most treatises of this nature. Seventeen chapters, constituting nearly one-fourth of the book, have been devoted exclusively to these economic factors with frequent references to them in other chapters. Many theories of cultural evolution have ignored these factors largely or entirely. They have concentrated attention upon less important phases, such as the fine arts or religion. The economic interpretation of history has been presented most effectively by the collectivist (socialist and communist) writers.

2. The role of technological change including inventions, trans-

forming the material conditions of human existence, has been discussed more adequately than is usually the case.

3. The exploitation of the masses by the upper classes has been described in connection with many historical occasions and situations. This is a subject largely ignored by philosophers of history and cultural historians, because they have been dominated by an upper class ideology. This predatory exploitation has permeated history down to the present day, conditioning social organization and institutions.

4. I have tried to give adequate recognition to the function of sex in cultural history as well as in the lives of all individuals, a subject which has been almost completely ignored by other writers owing usually to the customary taboo on sex. Nine chapters have been devoted exclusively to this subject, constituting one-ninth of the treatise with frequent reference elsewhere. As an important factor in cultural evolution, the play function, which is its role apart from and in addition to reproduction, cannot be neglected.

5. I have described religion not only more adequately but also more accurately because I have not been influenced by the customary biases in favor of religion, and am familiar with its animistic and anthropocentric origin and nature, which are ignored wittingly or unwittingly by most social scientists. They do so usually because they fear to criticize and attack a sacred cow, or because they think that religion has a moral influence in restraining some of the anti-social human tendencies, mainly through intimidation.

6. I have described the emergence and evolution of science, its gradual substitution for magic and religion, its far-reaching effect upon the ideas of mankind, and its role in rendering possible almost the whole of modern technology.

7. Much of my treatise deals with Oriental culture, of which Occidental historians are largely ignorant, whereas I have spent many years of research in the Orient. Ten chapters, constituting one-eighth of this treatise, are devoted exclusively to Oriental culture with many references to it elsewhere. Included are the ecological factors, such as climate and topography. Occidental culture is mainly of Mediterranean origin, and therefore, predominantly unitary; whereas the Orient includes two dominant cultures of independent origin, namely, the Hindu and Chinese cultures.

Most writers ignore the factors and subjects listed above partly, if not largely, because they fear for their own safety and welfare from the vested interests which profit from some of these conditions. These interests include the capitalist class, the church and clergy, the caste systems such as the monarchy and the hereditary nobility, and other predatory groups which profit by war, nationalism, imperialism, exploitation, religion, and the suppression of the spontaneous expression of human nature. The capitalist economic interests are now and have usually been the most powerful of the vested interests. While no cultural historian can master all of history and cover fully every phase of culture, there is no valid excuse for disregard and/or distortion of important factors due to religious, moral, class, national, and racial biases, and other sacred cows.

In this treatise, the main course of cultural evolution is traced insofar as feasible, thus eliminating the non-essential, instead of trying to cover all phases of history or every form of culture, many of which are insignificant and unimportant. The point of view expressed and methods used are strictly scientific. No ethical, magical, religious, political, economic, racial, national, patriotic, or esthetic considerations distort the treatment of the data, insofar as I have been able to avoid such bias. Human and cultural evolution is studied and analyzed like other natural phenomena, in order to determine as far as possible where and when the decisive steps in this evolution have taken place, and how they have been disseminated.

This treatise also includes a cautious look, within the limits of scientific prevision, at future factors for change which are already explicit or at least implicit in the existing culture, with a glance at the inevitable eventual extinction of mankind, but with no messianic or utopian prophecies. To predict outside of these limits is at best superfluous and at worst misleading and mischievous. Such scientific prevision may aid in formulating a theory of cultural evolution, or may demonstrate that such a theory is not feasible because of the limitations upon scientific prevision.

Before proceeding to a consideration of theories of cultural evolution which have been proposed, some of the major errors committed by authors of theories of cultural evolution should be considered. The most frequent fallacies are due to the desire for certainty which leads many writers into wishful thinking. They leap from the insecure basis of inference to the ostensible security of alleged certainty. To have discovered the "eternal verities" is indeed gratifying to such writers. Usually they arrive at these purported verities through some form of religious belief, because religion always claims a knowledge of absolute truth. Otherwise it could not maintain its hold upon a credulous mankind yearning for certitude and safety in a perplexing and often terrifying world.

When a difficult problem in science arises, often due to an insufficient number of data, *fideism* may arise, namely, faith in something or somebody, such as a mythical deity, in the place of knowledge and reason. The last stage usually reached by the searcher for certainty is some form of mysticism which, for present purposes, may

1277

be defined as the supposititious mergence with or in the universal soul. The mystic arrogates to himself absolute knowledge acquired at its original source independent of intellectual processes, such as thought and reason. To have learned the truth at first hand, as well as to have found eternal repose in the bosom of the Almighty, is indeed gratifying to the mystic ego.

When unable to explain a cultural phenomenon by means of a series of causes, some writers call in the role of *"accident."* Thereby they deny that every event is causally determined and does not merely happen. The notion that chance, namely, an unaccountable force, plays a part in history is a survival of animistic belief. As such, it is an evocation of the supernatural in human affairs. Equally misleading is the notion of a fate or destiny which is animistic and anthropomorphic, because it is alleged that this fate is directed toward a predetermined end.

A similar error is to put exceptional or even exclusive emphasis upon one particular factor in attempting to explain an event, or a train of events, or a phase of culture. Thus an "exceptional" person is said to be responsible for such a phenomenon or series of phenomena. For example, the beginning of the Roman Empire is called the Augustan Age (31 B.C.-A.D. 14), as if Augustus Caesar was responsible for it instead of the breakdown of the oligarchy which had ruled the preceding Roman Republic. Still more preposterous are the Elizabethan Age (1558-1603), and the Victorian Age (1837-1901) in England. Eponymous heroes and epic poems have often obscured the more sober and orderly narrative of history. A similar fallacy is when a culture is attributed to a race, usually characterized as "superior," which is alleged to be the reason why the culture attained a high level. Many a primitive or barbarous people has more naively and frankly called itself "mankind," thereby excluding the remainder of the species from the human fold.

A somewhat more plausible form of *particularism* is when cultural phenomena are attributed to climate, or topography, or heredity, which emphasizes a specific trait in a racial group. While the many features of the physical environment, and the inheritance of all of the mental traits, account for the whole of cultural evolution, to select any one or a few of these factors and attribute an overweening importance to them is an attempt to escape from the arduous task of recognizing and weighing all of the many factors involved.

A common error of cultural historians is the *group fallacy,* which I have refuted in Chapter XI. This is to the effect that the group is greater than or superior to the sum of its members. In a more generalized form, it is the fallacy that the whole is greater than the aggregate of its parts. This fallacy has manifested itself in the writings on so-called emergent evolution. According to this theory, a combination of elements results not only in something that is different from the individual elements but also greater than their aggregate. This is as if a pound of iron is added to a pound of lead and the combination becomes not two but three pounds. This theory is sometimes called creative synthesis, which reveals the animistic concept of creation included or at least implied in it.

In psychology the group fallacy has manifested itself in so-called *Gestalt* or configurationist psychology. The most exaggerated form of the group fallacy is in the pseudo-philosophic holism. This so-called philosophy extends the group fallacy to the whole universe. It alleges that a creative process of greater wholes arising from lesser parts is going on forever in the universe. This philosophy is usually given an anthropocentric and ethical turn, and is teleological in the sense that the universe is assumed to be striving for some unknown end.

In making a combination of elements, energy is expended. This energy is one of the factors in the new situation. The elements or parts are juxtaposed to each other in a somewhat different fashion than in their former positions. These two considerations alone are sufficient to explain why a whole made up of certain diverse parts may seem to be not only different from but even greater than its integral parts. In fact, it may actually be greater to the extent that energy has been added, or because combining the integral elements has made them more effective. Nuclear fission of the atom has revealed that energy is continually being released, or rather transmuted, from matter, which may form new combinations.

The group fallacy that the whole is not only greater than, but also superior to, its parts, has often been misused by giving it an ethical application. It has sometimes been alleged that the welfare of a class, which professed to include all of a society, was superior to the sum total of the welfare of its members. An exploiting class has often identified itself with a nation, and then has alleged that work for the class was equivalent to service for the nation. This has invariably happened in time of war, when citizens are urged and commanded, and often compelled to sacrifice themselves for their nation when they are rendering a service to their exploitative and predatory master class which is reaping a rich harvest from the murderous war. As I have pointed out in Chapter LXXI, in the United States, the last stronghold of capitalism, the master class tries to give currency to the notion that capital and labor form one class, whereas the evidence demonstrates that class division is becoming deeper, and the class struggle and conflict more acute.

One of the commonest errors into which the social scientist falls, along with most of his congeners, is the *teleological* interpretation or explanation of social and cultural processes and events. This usually takes the form of implying, if not explicitly asserting, that function exists before structure and, as it were, calls the latter into being in order to fulfil itself. The persons who commit this egregious error have not realized that there are no perceptible designs or ends in the universe. They have not grasped the significance of the adaptation of means to ends. They have not understood that this adaptation is due to a process of natural selection, and is not the outcome of a preconceived design. The social scientist is prone to fall into this error especially when he finds social and cultural phenomena too complicated to be able to explain it in terms of causation. A Polish-English anthropologist in expounding a theory of culture defined it as follows: "Culture is essentially an instrumental apparatus by which man is put in a position the better to cope with the concrete specific problems that face him in his environment in the course of the satisfaction of his needs." [1] This definition implying that culture is a designed aid to man is a part of a so-called functional theory of culture.

The persistence with which animistic modes of thought intrude even in scientific thinking is manifested by the dualism and subjectivism which often appear in both psychological and social science. I have already commented upon the intrusion of animism into psychology in connection with the fallacies of psycho-physical parallelism and of interactionism. [2] Both of these fallacies assume a duality of mind and matter or of soul and body for which there is not the slightest evidence. In behaviorism we find a satisfactory explanation of the fundamental identity of mind and matter or energy. These subjects have been fully discussed in Chapters IV to VI inclusive.

Corresponding to the above psychological fallacies is the *super-organic* fallacy in social science which I have already refuted in Chapter VII. Not unlike the group fallacy, it is animistic and assumes a fundamental duality in the universe. The disproof of the super-organic fallacy demonstrates that identity of or even a close analogy between, cultural and organic processes is not justified by the facts. However, that cultural phenomena are based upon and arise out of organic phenomena is so obvious as to need no demonstration.

At this point may be raised the question as to whether there is or can be a cultural evolution which corresponds in any way to

---

[1] B. Malinowski, *A Scientific Theory of Culture*, Chapel Hill, 1944, p. 150.

[2] I have said of psycho-physical parallelism and of interactionism that "both of these theories regard mind as a distinct entity of a superphenomenal if not supernatural sort. . . . Science cannot recognize anything of which it can have no tangible evidence." (*Science of Human Behavior*, New York, 1913, p. 322.)

organic evolution. In the course of the latter have come into being organisms which are perpetuated by inheritance, and which are modified from time to time through the process of natural selection. Culture is a relatively unimportant epiphenomenon of organic evolution. It is not inherited, and is transmitted from generation to generation only by tradition. Cultural phenomena are secondary by-products and accompaniments of organic phenomena, and are their effects only in a derivative sense. They form the outcome or end product of some of human behavior.

Cultural phenomena came into being long after organic evolution had commenced, and will vanish before organic evolution, in the shape of some of the more hardy of the protozoa and metazoa terminates on the surface of this planet. Only in this sense can culture be accurately oriented in its relation to organic evolution. By this means the teleological and ethical biases often attached to social and cultural phenomena can be avoided. It is customary to stigmatize certain social and cultural phenomena as being abnormal or pathological. Such phenomena can be abnormal only in relation to a given type of society or culture. Whether such a society or culture is good or bad is an ethical question, which is irrelevant so far as describing the type of society or culture and establishing its relationship to other types, is concerned.

At least six major fallacies concerning culture have been described. These are (1) *fideism* or faith in place of knowledge and reason, usually arising from a craving for certainty, which often leads to mysticism; (2) *accident* which may be called "happenstance," or chance, which sometimes leads illogically to fate or destiny, which is presumed to be pre-ordained, and therefore could not be due to chance; (3) *particularism* or excessive emphasis on one or a few factors; (4) *group fallacy,* which sometimes leads to emergent evolution or creative synthesis; (5) *teleology,* foreshadowed by fate and destiny, which usually assumes that function exists before structure; and (6) *super-organicism,* which assumes a fundamental duality in the universe.

Five of these six fallacies, namely, fideism, accident or chance, group fallacy, super-organicism, and teleology, invariably and inevitably involve animistic and anthropomorphic beliefs. Particularism does not necessarily involve religion. Most of the fallacies concerning culture, both minor as well as major, include or result in ethical biases because they assume normative criteria or standards of merit and of value. All of those fallacies are illustrated in one or another of the theories of cultural evolution described in the preceding chapter.

The seven theories which have been described are the (1) *Unilinear*; (2) *Diffusionist*; (3) *Culture strata*; (4) *Cyclical*; (5) *Configurationist*; (6) *Particularist*; and (7) *Eclectic*.

In so far as my treatise has resulted in a theory of cultural evolution, it combines the unilinear and diffusionist theories, including whatever is scientific in any of the other theories, without being eclectic. All fallacies and errors concerning culture I have sedulously avoided, in so far as is humanly feasible.

Inorganic evolution is inconceivable as the creation of something out of nothing. Mankind has witnessed only a brief passage of events out of eternity and infinitude.

The organic evolution of plants and animals upon this planet has been demonstrated through the natural selection of the fittest for survival during some hundreds of millions of years.

Cultural and social evolution can be apprehended as analogous to organic evolution, but not as identical with it, as has been indicated in the super-organic fallacy. It will last only during the few millions of years that mankind will survive on this planet.

INDEX

A

Acton, W., 895, 900
Adloff, 24
Adonis, 219, 229
Africa, 21, 30, 85, 89, 96, 100, 102, 111, 136, 223, 228, 302
Agriculture, 103, 105, 107, 109, 113, 168, 170, 173-7, 189, 195, 294, 298, 301, 333-5, 694-5
Ahriman, 383
Ahura Mazda, 383, 443
de Albuquerque, Alfonso, 319, 547, 1043
Alexander the Macedonian, 112, 309, 318, 341, 375, 455, 457, 496, 543, 546, 1043, 1229, 1236
Alexander, S., 147
Allee, W. C., 11, 14
Allport, F. H., 76, 122, 125, 149
Alphabet, the, 142-143, 374, 376
Amaterasu-omikami, 208, 223, 493
Amatorium, the, 857, 915, 924, 1220, 1227-8
Amenhotep (Ikhnaton or Akhetaton), 423
America, 24, 103, 112-116, 136-137, 187, 189-190, 302, 307, 388, 433-7, 582
Ames, E., 1245
Ammon, 208
Amos, S., 900
Anau, 104, 109, 163, 302, 304, 336
Ancestor worship, 223-4
Anderson, J. G., 304
Angell, J. R., 73, 762

Animals, domestication of, 103-104, 174-180, 334
Animatism, 211
Animism, 147, 150, 151, 171, 209-231, 274-5, 366, 399-400, 516, 1232-9, 1271, 1274, 1278, 1281
Anthropocentrism, 6, 7, 152, 386-7, 1258-9, 1260, 1261
Anthropomorphism, 225, 516, 1274, 1281
Aphrodite, 208
Aristarchus, 379
Aristotle, 375, 379-380, 422, 455-6, 495-6
Artaxerxes, 443
Aryans, 307, 311
Asceticism, 1010-11
Ashoka, 248, 309, 544, 954, 1036
Asia, 24, 89, 98, 100, 103, 111, 132, 160, 208, 247, 302
Assyrians, 111, 208, 303, 339-340, 543
Astarte, 208
Aston, W. G., 1009, 1023
Astrology, 367-9
Astronomy, 379, 380
Athens, 454, 458
Atkinson, J. J., 233, 846
Attila, 1229
Attis, 219, 229, 383
Augagneur, V., 900
Aurignacian period, 30, 89, 94-5, 101, 164, 170, 209, 215
Australia, 22, 23, 167
Autran, C., 132
Aztecs, 434

B

Babylonia, 208, 245, 302-3, 306, 339-340, 344, 367-9, 415
Bacher, R., 721
Bacon, Alice M., 1123
Baker, O. E., 812
Ball, C. J., 140
Banking, 643-5
Barnes, H. E., 93, 140, 206, 450, 458, 903
Barnett, L., 336
Beach, F. A., 1226
Beauty, concept of, 380, 1108-1126
Beer, M., 380
Behaviorism, 58, 126, 151, 276-7, 1166-7, 1174, 1177-8
Bell, S., 719
Bender, H. H., 134
Benedict, R., 165, 215, 268, 273, 1208, 1224-5, 1266
Berle, A. A. Jr., 654
Berman, H., 293
Bernal, J. D., 682, 699
Bernard, L. L., 75, 76, 296, 766
Betelgeuse, 4
Bhandakar, D. R., 248
Bhikku U Thittila, 1233
Bierstedt, R., 205
Bjerre, J., 275
Blanshard, P., 499
Blasphemy, 217, 284, 498
Blockade, 596, 767-8, 780
Bloomfield, L., 138, 139
Boas, F., 166
Bolshevism, 606-7, 619, 746-7
Bonbright, J. C., 655
Bonger, W., 887
Bonn, M., 660
Boule, M., 29
Bowen, E., 928
Bowley, A. L., 678
Bowman, I., 814
Bradley, F. H., 35
Brady, R. A., 689
Brain, the, 42-44, 152
Brandes, G., 449
Breasted, J. H., 475

Breuil, H., 161, 162
Breysig, K., 327
Briffault, R., 159, 239, 253, 1013
Brinkmann, 414
Bronze Age, 110-112, 347
Brunton, G., 105
Bryan, C. P., 371
Buddhism, 143, 225, 249, 261, 444, 553, 953-961, 1057, 1233
Budge, E. A. W., 943
Buecher, K., 1160
Bukharin, N., 617, 618
Bureaucratism, 622
Burma, 249, 261
Business cycle, 669-676
Butler, N. M., 650
Byzantium, 365, 382, 406

C

Caesar, Julius, 357, 406, 431, 1229
Caesar, Octavian (Augustus), 357, 406, 431, 1278
Calendar, the, 367-8, 714-23, 754-5
Calhoun, D., 212
Cannibalism, 228
Cannon, W. B., 71, 72, 1171-2
Capitalism, 157, 295-6, 354-7, 362-3, 385-6, 392, 427-8, 505, 507-8, 525-7, 575-6, 621, 626-642, 1184-5, 1193, 1214-15, 1240-8
Carlyle, T., 1132
Carter, T. F., 143, 979
Carthage, 353
Cartwright, E., 107
Casson, S., 181, 184
Caste, 257-264, 393, 410, 466, 707-8
Caton-Thompson, G., 105
Centaurus Constellation, 3
Chamberlin, B. H., 960
Chamberlin, R. T., 11
Chamberlin, T. C., 27
Charles, Enid, 932
Charles, P., 1270
Cherry, R. R., 291
Chieftainship, 301
Childe, V. G., 134
China, 20, 96, 129, 138, 139, 140,

Galton, F., 450
da Gama, Vasco, 319, 547, 574, 1043
Gamow, G., 3, 1259
Gautama, 261, 309, 449, 955, 972, 1004
Geddes, D. P., 864
Gelb, I. J., 338, 373
Gellhorn, W., 602
Genghis Khan, 1229
van Gennep, A., 219, 236, 850
Gentility, the, 460
Geo-Economic Regionalism, 784-800, 1189
Gerontocracy, 268, 282, 397
Gibbon, E., 475, 557
Giles, H. A., 1017
Gilfillan, S. C., 107, 201, 540, 546, 1141-3, 1200
Gillen, F. J., 234, 847
Ginnell, L., 292
Ginsberg, M., 551
Gladwin, H. S., 115
Glotz, G., 141, 372
Goetze, A., 373
Goltz, F., 74
Goncourt, E. and J., 1009
Graebner, F., 188, 203, 1265
Grammar, 138-139
Grant, M., 450
Grant, U. S., 614
Greece, 134, 141, 142, 208, 219, 231, 294, 311, 375-384, 451-8
Greek Catholic (Orthodox) Church, 365
Gregory, W. K., 33
Groos, K., 764
Griswold, A. W., 584
Grosse, E., 1150
Grotius, H., 331-2, 594-5
Gsovski, V., 716
Guerard, A. L., 1085
Gutenberg, B., 192
Guthrie, E. P., 205
Guyon, R., 1226
Guyot, Y., 900
Gymnosophy, 1107, 1125-6, 1127-38, 1154-6, 1229

H

Habit, 50, 68, 278
Haddon, A. C., 1151-2
Haire, N., 1091
Hall, H. F., 249, 1088
Hamburger, M., 422
Hamilton, W. H., 1206
Hammurabi, 303, 347, 371-2, 402, 415
Hanighen, F. C., 502, 586, 782, 1250
Hansen, G., 896
Hart, H. H., 320
Hartland, E. S., 234, 235, 237, 847, 849, 850, 873, 1218, 1235
Haskell, H. J., 430
Hatfield, H. S., 1189, 1196, 1204
Hay, D. R., 1109
Head, H., 71
Hegel, G. W. F., 581
Heidelbergensis, 21, 23, 29, 90, 118
Hellenism, 375-387, 496
Heraclitus, 377
Herodotus, 376
Herskovitz, M. J., 541, 925, 1191, 1221, 1225
Hertzler, J. O., 1216
Hesiod, 453-4
Hinduism, 224, 248, 260, 262, 444, 951-3, 1056-7, 1228
Hirn, Y., 1149, 1153
Hitler, A., 450, 1229
Hittites, 111, 130, 132, 141, 183, 187, 303, 339, 373, 432-3
Hobgoblinism, 346, 362, 400
Hobhouse, L. T., 290
Hobson, J. A., 322, 549, 553, 563, 566, 585, 663, 711, 1049
Holmes, G., 71
Hooton, E. A., 26, 33, 119
Horde, the, 167-8, 252, 272
Horse, the, 442-3
Howitt, A. W., 234, 847
Hoyle, F., 517
Hudson, W. H., 1100, 1105, 1146, 1161
Hume, R. E., 558, 1060

Proselytizing, 228
Prostitution, 171-2, 881-7, 889-907
Protestantism, 220-2
Pumpelly, R., 104
Punic Wars, 359

R

Rabutaux, A. P. E., 883
Race, 201-3, 450, 550-1, 1122, 1133-5, 1251, 1267, 1270
Randall, J. H., 205
Rank, O., 1148
Rautenstrauch, W., 720
Read, C., 210
Reflex Action, 36, 37, 45, 68, 77-8, 1169-70
Regnault, F., 883, 900
Reincarnation of Souls, (see Metempsychosis)
Reinach, S., 215
von Reitzenstein, F., 1094, 1115, 1121
Relativity, Theory of, 3
Religion, 145, 158, 167, 168, 208-231, 275, 279, 498, 517-18, 776, 1233-9, redemptive (intercessionary), 449, 962-3
Renaud, E.-B., 115
Reproduction, 235
Republic, 351-7, 412-13
Revolution, 295, 327, 346, 414, 503, 1178-1186, 1193-4
Rhodesiensis, 21, 22, 23, 30, 32
Rickard, T. A., 184
Riesman, D., 1216
Rigel, 4
Ritual, 217-220
Rivet, P., 137
Robertson, J. M., 449, 728, 730
Robinson, L., 118
Rodin, A., 1155
Roman Catholicism, 219-20, 365, 388, 499, 553, 925, 961, 1147
Rome, 208, 231, 245, 294, 311, 316, 350-362, 375-6, 382, 400, 405-6, 413, 458

Romer, A. S., 27, 33, 118
Roosevelt, T., 583
Rosebery, A. P. P., 322, 552, 1049
Ross, E. A., 1151
Rostovtzeff, M. I., 361, 497, 525, 526
Russell, B., 231, 1088, 1263
Russia, 134

S

Sabine, G. H., 299
Sacrilege, 284
Salisbury, R. D., 27
Salz, A., 171
Sanger, W. W., 900
Santayana, G., 1110, 1159
Sapir, E., 124, 128
Sargon, 163, 337, 410, 543
Sarkar, B. K., 1007, 1090
Sastri, R. S., 259
Schapera, I., 301
Schapiro, J. S., 505, 512
Schmidt, R., 1091
Schmidt, W., 254
Schopenhauer, A., 1122, 1239
Schroeder, T., 415
Schuchert, C., 27
Schultz, F., 442
Schultz-Naumburg, P., 1090, 1115
Schwartz, H., 1245
Science, 6, 7, 8, 146, 154, 157, 210-212, 226, 366-390, 516-532, 687, 689-90, 755, 975-984, 1233-5
Scott, K., 432
Sea Power, 329-332, 583, 590-600
Seclusion of women, 244, 994-9, 1032
Seebohm, F., 288, 290
Seebohm, H. E., 288
Selden, J., 329, 591
Seldes, G., 502
Seltzer, L. H., 1241
Sex, nature of, 232, 1000-14, 1124-5, 1217; play function of, 872-7, 1014, 1147, 1220; regulation of, 285-6, 861-8; uncleanness of, 850

1292